Aleister Crowley was poet, painter, writer, master chess player, lecher, drug addict and magician. His contemporary press called him "the wickedest man in the world." The most bizarre and notorious figure of his age, Crowley's own story is now available in paperback for the first time.

But **THE CONFESSIONS OF ALEISTER CROWLEY** is more than just the autobiography of a man. It is also the portrait of an age. Everything is set down just as Crowley experienced it.

In addition to being a famed magician, Crowley also had a well-deserved reputation as a writer. His flair for literature and his gusto for life elevate this book several levels above the ordinary "confession" type of literature prevalent in his day.

His writing is crisp, witty and amusing and always fascinating. Crowley believed that he could do anything he set his mind to. And he'll make a believer out of you.

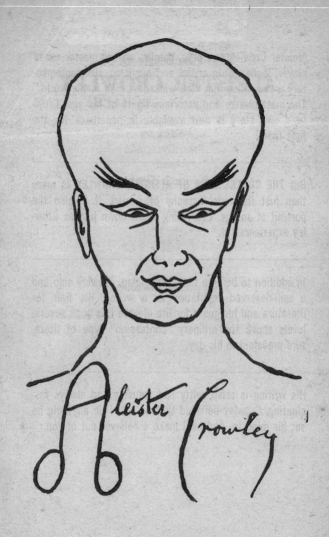

An idealized self-portrait

The Confessions of
ALEISTER CROWLEY
AN AUTOHAGIOGRAPHY

edited by
John Symonds
and
Kenneth Grant

A NATIONAL GENERAL COMPANY

*This low-priced Bantam Book
has been completely reset in a type face
designed for easy reading, and was printed
from new plates. It contains the complete
text of the original hard-cover edition.*
NOT ONE WORD HAS BEEN OMITTED.

THE CONFESSIONS OF ALEISTER CROWLEY
*A Bantam Book / published by arrangement with
Hill & Wang, Inc.*

PRINTING HISTORY
Hill & Wang edition published January 1970
*Professional & Technical Programs, Inc.
edition published October 1970*
Mystic Arts edition published 1970
Bantam edtition published March 1971

*Bantam Books are published by Bantam Books, Inc., a National
General company. Its trade-mark, consisting of the words "Bantam
Books" and the portrayal of a bantam, is registered in the United
States Patent Office and in other countries. Marca Registrada.
Bantam Books, Inc., 666 Fifth Avenue, New York, N.Y. 10019.*

CONTENTS

ACKNOWLEDGMENTS

The editors wish to thank Mr George H. Brook for generously putting his collection of Crowleyana at their disposal; they are also grateful to Mrs Norah Fitzgerald and Mr Gerald Yorke for the loan of typescripts; and they are indebted to Mrs Steffi Grant for her help in preparing the index.

ACKNOWLEDGMENTS

INTRODUCTION

The Mind and Mask of
Aleister Crowley

Among Aleister Crowley's papers I found a letter addressed
to him by a stranger, asking for permission to attend his next
Black Mass or next sabbath which, the writer presumed, would
take place on Midsummer Eve. A stamped and addressed envelope (it was mentioned) was enclosed for Crowley's reply.
His reply, if he did reply, was bound to be disappointing, for
he was not at that time—May 1937—putting on any more
Black Masses or attending any sabbaths. In point of fact, he
never attended sabbaths—he was not a witch—and the Masses
that he performed were not, technically speaking, Black
Masses,* but that kind of thing was expected of him by the
public at large.

In 1947 he died, aged seventy-two. And recently those
gifted young men, the Beatles, have added him to their es-
cutcheon: Crowley stands between an Indian holy man (un-
named) and Mae West in a composite photograph of 'People
we like' which decorates the sleeve of the Beatles' long-playing
record, 'Sgt. Pepper's Lonely Hearts Club Band'.†

Crowley was the head of two major magical organizations
and of several minor ones; he was the author of a brilliant
book called *Magick,* which is a manual for those who wish to
practise this difficult and dangerous art ‡; and he was in the
tradition of the great magicians of the past—Dr John Dee,
Cagliostro, Count Saint-Germain, Eliphas Lévi, Madame Blavatsky.

He was born in 1875. Two other events of significance to
occultists happened in that year: the Theosophical Society was
founded by Madame Blavatsky and others, and Eliphas Lévi,
the Cabbalist and mage, died. Crowley made out that he was

---

* They were so-called Gnostic Masses, such as his 'Mass of the Phoenix'
and his 'Gnostic Catholic Mass'. Because of their sexual component,
they might be considered Gray, but not Black, Masses.
† *Daily Express,* May 19th, 1967.
‡ *Magick* (or to give it its full title *Magick in Theory and Practice*) is
difficult to understand. It is a city within a city, and the key to the gate
of the inner city is not supplied with the book; it can be got only after a
study of all Crowley's works, especially his unpublished works.

descended from Norman aristocrats, and mentioned the Breton family, de Quérouaille, as if the name Crowley were a corruption of that name. He claimed Louise de Kéroualle, Duchess of Portsmouth, as one of his ancestors; also the sixteenth-century poet and preacher, Robert Crowley, on no evidence at all. It would have been more pertinent to tell us something of his grandparents, whom he studiously ignored. It so happened that his father, Edward Crowley, whom he called an engineer, was a brewer, and the family fortune came from 'Crowley ales', a fact which creeps into his autobiography in an oblique way.

By the time Aleister was born, his father was well advanced in middle age, and spent his time travelling about the countryside, preaching Plymouthism to anyone who would listen to him. The Plymouth Brethren sect was founded about 1830 by John Nelson Darby, an Irish clergyman who was a barrister before he went into the Church. The Brethren believed that they were the only true Christians; they considered the idea of ordained ministers contrary to the teaching of Scripture; the Bible was literally true; Christ's Second Coming was imminent; the Elect would inherit the Kingdom of God.

Out of this background emerged Aleister Crowley, the Beast 666.

At first, he was a devout little Plymouth Brother, taking turns with his parents and the servants in reading passages from the Bible. Plymouthism was the only true faith. He could not, he said, even conceive of the existence of people who were so foolish or so wicked as to doubt it. In his childish ardour he thought of himself as a Christian knight, doing deeds of holiness and valour.

As he grew older his ideas took a strange turn. He had always preferred the sounds of the Hebrew names to the actual biblical narratives; now any decription of torture or blood aroused his feelings tremendously. He liked to imagine himself in agony and, in particular, degraded by, and suffering at the hands of, a woman whom he described as 'wicked, independent, courageous, ambitious, and so on'. He fell in love with the False Prophet, the Beast whose number is 666, and the Scarlet Woman. And suddenly, after the death of his father—he was then eleven years old—he discovered that his sympathies were entirely on the side of the enemies of heaven. He had gone over to Satan, and did not know why. He was still searching for the reason when he came to write his autobiography at the age of forty-seven.

Crowley was a contemporary of Freud; he grew out of the matrix of Victorianism with its rosy view of the world, and its medieval ideal of beauty and of God. He was one of many who helped to tear down the false, hypocritical, self-righteous attitudes of the time. His account of his early life in a Plymouth Brethren household is no less remarkable than Edmund Gosse's.* What, however, is peculiar in Crowley's case is not that he chose 'evil' but that, in his revolt against his parents and God, he set himself up in God's place.

'Why do you call yourself the Beast?' I asked him on the occasion of our first meeting.

'My mother called me the Beast,' he replied to my surprise.

He went to Malvern and Tonbridge public schools; his health broke down at Tonbridge, due partly to having 'caught the clap from a prostitute in Glasgow' (as he wrote in the margin of his own copy of *The World's Tragedy*, privately published, 1910, his first attempt at autobiography).

He published his first book of verse while an undergraduate at Trinity College: *Aceldama, A Place to Bury Strangers in. A Philosophical Poem. By a Gentleman of the University of Cambridge*, 1898. It carried this odd preface which foreshadowed his future interests and the ambiguous direction he was going in:

It was a windy night, that memorable seventh night of December, when this philosophy was born in me. How the grave old professor wondered at my ravings! I had called at his house, for he was a valued friend of mine, and I felt strange thoughts and emotions shake within me. Ah! how I raved! I called to him to trample me, he would not. We passed together into the stormy night. I was on horseback, how I galloped round him in my phrenzy, till he became the prey of real physical fear! How I shrieked out I know not what strange words! And the poor good old man tried all he could to calm me; he thought I was mad! The fool! I was in the death struggle with self: God and Satan fought for my soul those three long hours. God conquered—now I have only one doubt left—which of the twain was God?

Mountaineering was another of his passions. He climbed in the Lake District, on Beachy Head and in Switzerland; and he was a master of that esoteric game called chess—who can ever get to the bottom of chess?—had played in two matches against Oxford and won his chess half-Blue.

* *Father and Son* (Heinemann, 1907).

He had taken to wearing pure silk shirts and great floppy bow-knotted ties; on his fingers were rings of semi-precious stones. An atmosphere of luxury, studiousness and harsh effort pervaded his rooms at Cambridge. Books covered the walls to the ceiling and filled four revolving walnut bookcases. They were largely on science and philosophy, with a modest collection of Greek and Latin classics, and a sprinkling of French and Russian novels. On one shelf shone the black and gold of *The Arabian Nights* of Richard Burton; below was the flat canvas and square label of the Kelmscott *Chaucer*. Valuable first editions of the British poets stood beside extravagantly bound volumes issued by Isidor Liseux. Over the door hung an ice-axe with worn-down spike and ragged shaft, and in the corner was a canvas bag containing a salmon rod. Leaded Staunton chessmen were in their mahogany box upon a card-table scattered with poker chips.

The 'Gentleman of the University of Cambridge' was prolific: he had quickly followed *Aceldama* with *The Tale of Archais*, then *Jephthah, A Tragedy;* the pseudonym was borrowed from Shelley, whose *The Necessity of Atheism*, 1811, was by a Gentleman of the University of Oxford. During 1898 he was also responsible for a more pretentious production, *White Stains*, which Mr Peter Fryer considers the most disgusting piece of erotica in the English language; it bears on the title-page the name of Crowley's pious uncle, George Archibald, 'A Neuropath of the Second Empire', and is now a rare book. Crowley prefaced the work with a statement which expressed his contempt: 'The Editor hopes that Mental Pathologists, for whose eyes alone this treatise is destined, will spare no precautions to prevent it falling into other hands.' He had inherited a fortune—the size of which he exaggerated —and could afford these extravagant jests.

He thought of entering the Foreign Office, but decided against it: he wanted to be someone really great, whose name would be remembered as long as life lasted on this planet; he was unlikely to achieve this in the Diplomatic Service by devotion to duty.

The problem of what he should do with his life was solved by reading *The Book of Black Magic and of Pacts*. In the preface to this work, the author, Arthur Edward Waite, referred to certain occult sanctuaries run by a body of Initiates who dispense Truth and Wisdom to the worthy postulant. Crowley wrote to Waite, asking for more information. Waite replied, telling him to read Eckartshausen's *The Cloud upon the Sanctuary.* Eckartshausen confirmed what Waite had hinted at: behind the exterior church is an interior church, the most hidden of all communities, a Secret Sanctuary which preserves all the mysteries of God and nature. It was formed immediately after the fall of man. It is the hidden assembly of the Elect.

In Zermatt during 1898, Crowley met a certain Julian L. Baker, and growing friendly with Mr Baker he told him about his search for the Brotherhood of Initiates who jealously guard the perfect knowledge of God, nature and humanity. Mr Baker offered to help, and when they returned to England he introduced Crowley to George Cecil Jones who was a member of a magical organization called the Hermetic Order of the Golden Dawn. Jones could perhaps help Crowley to find the Secret Sanctuary. Jones introduced him to MacGregor Mathers, the head of the Golden Dawn and at the turn of the century the most talented magician in the West. He was the Master Crowley was looking for.

Crowley began his career of magic as a Neophyte in the Golden Dawn, which was the First or Outer Order of the Great White Brotherhood;* he quickly rose to the highest grade (that of Philosophus) in the Outer Order. He discovered that he had a remarkable aptitude for magic; this he later ascribed to his previous incarnations. He caught glimpses of these incarnations during his deep yoga meditations on 'Oesopus Island' in America during 1918. Not only had he been Eliphas Lévi—there was just enough time for Lévi's liberated spirit to have descended into the womb of Mrs Crowley—but also the great magician Cagliostro in the incarnation before that; and John Dee's skryer, Edward Kelly, before Cagliostro, and the vicious, pleasure-loving Pope Alexander VI before him. (This last-mentioned incarnation would explain Crowley's insatiable curiosity about every aspect of sex.)

He left Cambridge without sitting for a degree, set himself up in a flat in Chancery Lane, and called himself Count Vladimir Svareff. In separate rooms in his Chancery Lane flat he made two temples—one white, one black. They represented the twin pillars of the Light and the Dark, Jachin and Boaz. The white temple was lined with six large looking-glasses to throw back the forces of the invocations (so that nothing of the force was lost); the black temple was empty except for a

---

* Whether this Brotherhood was Eckartshausen's hidden assembly of sages, no one, as far as I know, has said, but the implication is that they were the same.

human skeleton and a large cupboard, in which stood an altar supported by the figure of an ebony Negro standing on his hands. And both rooms had their magic circle, triangle, and pentagrams inscribed on the floor.

In addition to being the Head of the Golden Dawn, Mathers was the Head of the Second Order in the Great White Brotherhood, a Rosicrucian order called the Order of the Red Rose and the Golden Cross.

It was not long before Crowley was hammering on the door of the Second Order.

There was yet another order within the Great White Brotherhood, the top order; it bore the name of the Silver Star or A∴A∴ (*Argenteum Astrum*). This contained three exalted grades—Master of the Temple, Magus, and Ipsissimus—to none of which Mathers had attained. And for the very good reason that they were on the other side of the Abyss; only the most stalwart and enlightened of Aspirants can cross the Abyss.

But by whose authority did this mystical organization, this Great White Brotherhood, exist? It obviously could not exist solely by the authority of its members; it would then have been no different from an ordinary Masonic Fraternity. The answer to this important question is that the authority of the First and Second Orders, i.e. the Golden Dawn, and the Red Rose and Golden Cross, resided in the Secret Chiefs, the upper and inner circle of the Great White Brotherhood.

Madame Blavatsky had come up against the same problem. She was merely an intellectual and a medium; by herself she could do little. The siddhis, or feats, she performed, to the amazement of Anglo-Indian society of the 1880s, were made possible by the magical current which sustained her and which was derived from her Secret Chiefs, Koot Hoomi and Morya, who lived in the fastness of Tibet. She first met a Secret Chief or, to use her term, a Hidden Master, beside the Serpentine in Hyde Park one moonlit night during 1851, the year of the Great Exhibition.

In 1886 a Secret Chief of the grade of Master of the Temple (living in Germany under the guise of Fräulein Anna Sprengel) gave Mathers and his colleagues a charter to establish the Hermetic Order of the Golden Dawn. And after the Golden Dawn had been split from top to bottom and Mathers' authority was being disputed, his leadership of the First and Second Orders was confirmed by three Secret Chiefs whom he met in the Bois de Boulogne—or so he said. Crowley disbelieved him, swore that Deo Duce Comite Ferro ('With God as my Leader and the Sword as my Companion'), to mention one of Mathers' magical names, had only banged into three evil spirits. But saying this did not help Crowley.

The only actual magic which Mathers performed, apart from employing elementals in attacks on Crowley, was to still a storm; it is not surprising therefore that Crowley, who was far more ambitious, should have quarrelled with him, and struck out on his own, taking with him, of course, all the weapons in Mathers' armoury he could lay his hands on. Crowley also quarrelled with the rank and file of the Order, and with W. B. Yeats, whom he accused of being jealous of his superior talent as a poet, and was virtually expelled from the Order.

The most important of these weapons was the Rosicrucian system of the Great White Brotherhood, and the magic of Abra-Melin which Mathers had brought to light and published. The first was the party apparatus, the second the philosophy and driving force. Crowley therefore took from Mathers everything, except a following, necessary for a successful career as a magician.

If you wish to perform the operation of conjuring up your Holy Guardian Angel, says the Egyptian Mage, Abra-Melin, you must first of all construct an oratory in a secluded place. Where should Crowley construct his oratory? His flat in Chancery Lane was far too noisy. In search of a suitable spot, he wandered about the Lake District and into Scotland, and in August 1899 he found Boleskine House near the village of Foyers. Loch Ness lay before it and a hill behind it; it was remote; the view was magnificent; it was ideal for the practice of Abra-Melin magic.

The full title of the manuscript which Mathers had found in the Bibliothèque de l'Arsenal in Paris, translated (from the French) and published, is *The Book of the Sacred Magic of Abra-Melin the Mage, as delivered by Abraham the Jew unto his son Lamech, A.D. 1458*. There is no general ritual in this work as in other grimoires; there is only a list of several hundred spirits (angels and demons) to be evoked, and talismans to be used for such magical purpose as raising or quelling storms, finding hidden treasure, inflaming lust between persons of the magician's choosing. The spirit in question, after it has been ceremonially evoked, vitalizes the talisman which has been duly consecrated. The whole system is only possible after the aspirant has established communion with his Holy Guardian Angel, i.e. his True Self. It is the Holy Guardian Angel who imparts the method to be employed for this or that purpose. The book of the sacred magic of Abra-Melin (or Abramelin, or Abrahamelin, or Abramelim) is therefore sealed with seven seals. Everything depends upon the H. G. A., and his intercession is impossible without six months' intense ceremonial purification. In other words, Abra-Melin magic is a kind of yoga, producing psychic transformation. Crowley described it as the one startling exception to all the puerile nonsense written on the subject.

Crowley made his oratory in a room facing north and began the operation at once. After some months of concentrated effort, he partially succeeded. He says that a host of demons were attracted, some of which materialized; they caused a great deal of disturbance and damage among tradespeople and others in the neighborhood. But he did not obtain complete success in the operation—that is, knowledge of and conversation with his Holy Guardian Angel or True Self—till a few years later.

He married, produced a child and more volumes of poetry and erotica. He hurried off to Mexico and, with his friend Oscar Eckenstein, climbed Ixtaccihuatl and Popocatapetl. A year later, in 1902, he joined Eckenstein's expedition to Chogo Ri: at that time all the great peaks in the Himalayas were unconquered and had hardly been attempted. Eckenstein, who was of German-Jewish extraction, devised a new type of crampons, or climbing irons, which enabled mountaineers to dispense with the laborious work of cutting steps in the ice. He was seventeen years older than Crowley. In a letter written in 1924 to Harry Doughty, Crowley summed up Eckenstein as a climber: 'Eckenstein, provided he could get three fingers on something that could be described by a man far advanced in hashish as a ledge, would be smoking his pipe on that ledge a few seconds later, and none of us could tell how he had done it.' Crowley had great affection for Oscar Eckenstein.

Eckenstein, as far as I know, did not record his opinion of Crowley as a climber, but we have the view of Dr Tom George Longstaff, President of the Alpine Club from 1947 to 1949. Crowley was 'a fine climber, if an unconventional one. I have seen him go up the dangerous and difficult right (true) side of the great ice fall of the Mer de Glace below the Géant alone, just for a promenade. Probably the first and perhaps the only time this mad, dangerous and difficult route had been taken.' * Crowley's own brief account of this climb, in which Dr Longstaff is mentioned, is in Chapter 25 of the present work.

In 1904, the Abra-Melin Operation flowered and Crowley's Holy Guardian Angel, Aiwass, appeared—not, however, to enter into conversation with him, but to dictate *The Book of the Law*. He treated this profoundly significant event in a very quiet way, as if he did not quite believe it; he merely announced to a few friends and acquaintances, like Arnold Bennett, that the old world of Christianity had collapsed, and that a 'New Aeon' for mankind had begun.

Crowley has written a great deal about *The Book of the Law* in these *Confessions*. This was unavoidable, for the Book is the heart of his creed and the turning point of his career. Without the Law of Thelema (which is embodied in the Book), he would just have been a minor magician like Eliphas Lévi or MacGregor Mathers, one of the many who studied the mysteries and practised the magic of Abra-Melin or the Enochian system of John Dee or some other magical system. The Book was the force which enabled him to cross the Abyss, and to go on to become a Magus, and proclaim his word,† as Allah and Buddha proclaimed theirs.

If we are to believe him, he crossed the Abyss in 1909 and appeared on the other side with the grade of Master of the Temple, that is to say, he had united his consciousness with the universal consciousness, shifted the centre of gravity from himself to God. Thus he had found the Secret Sanctuary of the Saints or the abode of the Secret Chiefs, and become one of them; he had succeeded in his quest. His poetry and exploits on mountains are insignificant beside this. He could dash off a successful kind of music-hall song, like 'La Gitana', and evocative verses for magic rituals like his 'Hymn to Pan', which he thought 'the most powerful enchantment ever written'—it certainly has a spell-binding quality about it; but he lacked the equipment for the higher flights of poetry. And he failed to climb Kangchenjunga, was driven back by the demon who protects the Five Sacred Peaks (the local name for Kangchenjunga) and who claimed as victims Alexis Pache, a thirty-one-year-old lieutenant in the Swiss Cavalry, and four coolies.

---

* *This My Voyage* (Murray, 1950).
† Crowley's word was *thelema*, the Greek for *will*, best understood in the phrase Do What Thou Wilt, or in the words of *The Book of the Law*, There is no law beyond Do what thou wilt.

The personality of Aleister Crowley was a riddle to Charles Richard Cammell, one of Crowley's biographers. 'Explain me the riddle of this man!' * To Arthur Gauntlett, who analysed Crowley's character from his horoscope, he is 'one of the most enigmatic personalities of our time'.† The sphinx with the face of Aleister Crowley propounds this riddle: 'Why did I drive away my friends and followers? Why did I behave so vilely?' The answer is to be found in some of the versicles in *The Book of the Law.* 'Bind nothing! Let there be no difference made among you between any one thing & any other thing . . . The word of Sin is Restriction . . . There is no law beyond Do what thou wilt.' The many roles which Crowley chose for himself show that he had taken this precept literally. He did not make any difference or distinction between one thing and another; he was not restricted; that is to say he was not contained within any particular borders. On the contrary, he was driven into anything that touched his fancy. Thus, he was an English gentleman—he was always reminding us of that—a Scottish peer, a Russian nobleman, a Persian prince, Alastor, the Spirit of Solitude, Paramahansa (the divine Swan), the Wanderer of the Waste, God, and, above all, the Beast 666 who proclaimed for all mankind his word of Do What Thou Wilt. He had a guise for every mood. On no account live within your own skin.

Above the grade of Magus is the top grade of all, that of Ipsissimus, who is free from all limitations whatsoever, including good and evil, someone hardly to be described. Crowley, for whom nothing was too difficult, was not going to be restrained from assuming this grade too. In the opinion of certain occultists, that is where he made a false step. The suggestion is, of course, that he illegally assumed this most exalted grade and that it choked him.

The Ape of Thoth ‡ found him unbearable after he had become the Ipsissimus, and shortly afterwards wrote about him in her magical diary that it was 'damn hard' to think of 'the rottenest kind of creature' as a Word (i.e. thelema).

The momentous Ipsissimus event took place in the spring of 1921 when Crowley was forty-five. He was at his abbey at

---

* *Aleister Crowley. The Man: the Mage: the Poet* (The Richards Press, 1951).
† 'Aleister Crowley (A Study of an Enigma)', in *Astrology. The Astrologers' Quarterly*, June 1965.
‡ Leah Hirsig, Crowley's scribe, who during the Cefalu period held the office of the Scarlet Woman.

Cefalu, Sicily, across the door of which were painted the words DO WHAT THOU WILT. He had run out of money, was laden with the responsibility of two mistresses and several children. For a while he did not know which way to turn in spite of being a Master of every kind of Magick. But the gods had not deserted him. In a flash of intuition, which came upon him with shattering force, he penetrated the ultimate mystery. This is the meaning of Crowley's 'godhead', but strictly speaking he had reached the stage earlier in his career. As Ipsissimus he was beyond the gods, beyond all mental concepts. That is why, I suppose, he had to steel himself for the deed, to acknowledge that he, even he, known among men as Aleister Crowley, was by insight and initiation the Ipsissimus. It is not surprising that he wrote in his diary (*The Magical Record of the Beast 666*). 'I am mortally afraid to do so. I fear I might be called upon to do some insane act to prove my power to act without attachment.' Nevertheless, he entered the temple, followed by the Ape of Thoth. Of the actual ceremony he says nothing, and at the conclusion, only 'As a God goes, I go.' And he left the temple as naked as he had entered it, no longer a saint—Saint Aleister Crowley of the Gnostic church —but a god. His *Confessions*, which he began to write and dictate shortly afterwards, should not therefore have been called an autohagiography but an autotheography.

He did not reveal this Ipsissimus attainment to anyone. We know of it from his *Magical Record*. In *Magick*, privately published, 1929, page 301, there is only this hint of it: 'I, The Beast 666, lift up my voice and swear that I myself have been brought hither by mine Angel . . . Also He made me a Magus . . . Yea, he wrought also in me a Work of Wonder beyond this, but in this matter I am sworn to hold my peace.'

Under the complicated overlay, one can discern a relatively simple pattern. Other people have no ego, and are just weak, but Crowley made a religion out of his weakness, out of being ego-less. I know that ego-lessness is a condition which Indian philosophy regards as the supreme state, and towards which the Sadhaka strives, but in Crowley's case it is the point from which he begins, not the goal of his endeavours.* Besides, he was not an Oriental; he had all the restlessness of the European. Indeed, he rushed in where angels, let alone Sadhakas, fear to tread. He did not, he tells us in Section 58 of the present

---

* In the language of psychology, he lacked integration; he was in the grip of unconscious forces.

work, deliberately cross the Abyss; he was hurled across it. He lacked an inhibitory counterforce; he was always hurling himself into magical and other adventures.

But whatever view one takes of *The Book of Law*, it was not written by Crowley with tongue in cheek. Until the day he died, he believed it was a piece of inspired writing; he was merely the vehicle of its transmission. The year was 1904; the place, Cairo. He was on holiday with his wife, Rose. It was she who told him that Horus wanted to speak to him. He was surprised, for she knew nothing of Egyptian mythology. 'Who is Horus?' he asked. She pointed out the hawk-headed god in the museum. 'They are waiting for you,' she said. She then told him how to get in touch with Horus, what ritual to use. He raised an eyebrow; he had been performing magic rituals continually for the previous six years. But he did as she said, went barefoot and clad in his magical robe into the room which he had consecrated as a temple and performed the invocatory ceremony. In a trance-like condition he heard a voice—not the voice of Horus but of one who introduced himself as Aiwass, the Messenger. Crowley had his Swan fountain pen with him; he began to write.

The cosmology of *The Book of the Law* is explained by Crowley thus: there have been, as far as we know, two aeons in the history of the world. The first, that of Isis, is the aeon of the women; hence matriarchy, the worship of the Great Mother and so on. About 500 B.C. this aeon was succeeded by the aeon of Osiris, that is, the aeon of the man, the father, hence the paternal religions of suffering and death—Judaism, Buddhism, Christianity and Mohammedanism. This aeon came to an end in 1904 when Aleister Crowley received *The Book of the Law*, and the new aeon, that of Horus, the child, was born. In this aeon the emphasis is on the true self or will, not on anything external such as gods and priests. The choice of Egyptian names for the aeons is purely arbitrary.

The Book of the Law is a collection of sentiments of a rebellious kind, on the whole remarkably similar to the sentiments Crowley himself expressed.

He wrote a vast comment on the Book; it is unpublished. The brief comment which he did publish contains this curious statement: 'The study of this Book is forbidden . . . Those who discuss the contents of this Book are to be shunned by all as centres of pestilence.' Norman Mudd, Professor of Applied Mathematics of Grey University College, Bloemfontein, 'guide, philosopher, and friend' of the Beast, was foolish enough to ignore this warning and was overtaken by disaster. (See note on page 1021, and Section 96.)

For a man who was having visions on frequent occasions, he was remarkably unintrospective. He drew no deductions from the series of Enochian visions he experienced in the North African desert with his chela, the poet Victor Neuburg.* These so-called visions present situations of hopelessness and despair, and others of an inflated, or compensatory, kind. The gates of heaven and hell are thrown wide open, wonders and horrors are revealed, withdrawn, and the skryer is back where he started. The style is that of the Old Testament, but the numinous quality of visions seems to me to be absent. From the point of view of ordinary consciousness, the wheel did not go round; there was no metabolism. Crowley had no personal problems to solve and no mundane ambitions. Instead the scene is enlivened by the appearance of the demon Choronzon, the epitome of all disharmony and confusion, whom Crowley had conjured up in the form of a naked savage; he rushed upon Neuburg and smote him (see Section 66).

Crowley began to write his *Confessions* in a mood of optimism, but he concluded them with uncertainty and sadness. The Italian government had reacted to the attacks on his character in the *Sunday Express* by ordering him to leave Italy, and he dictated the last section in exile from his abbey. Another blow quickly followed: Collins, who had brought out his novel, *The Diary of a Drug Fiend*, decided to publish nothing more by Aleister Crowley, although they had given him an advance of £125 on the autohagiography. He was forty-eight years of age, and the outlook was bleak. It did not remain so for long. A new Scarlet Woman (Dorothy Olsen) appeared, and he discarded the exhausted Ape of Thoth; he also found a new set of followers in Germany, and during 1925 he went to Thuringia to preach the Law of Thelema.

In 1929, a small firm of publishers called the Mandrake Press published the first two volumes of the autohagiography in a projected series of six volumes. It bore the title:

THE SPIRIT OF SOLITUDE
An Autohagiography
Subsequently re-Antichristened
THE CONFESSIONS OF
ALEISTER CROWLEY

---

* *The Vision and the Voice,* Thelema Publishing Company, Barstow, California, circa 1949. This work was originally published in Crowley's periodical, *The Equinox,* vol. I, no. V, 1911.

The Mandrake Press also brought out a small volume of three of Crowley's stories, *The Stratagem*, and his magical novel, *Moonchild*.

The third volume of the autohagiography reached the stage of galleys but was never published. Crowley quarrelled with the directors of the Mandrake Press. The firm was then taken over by Crowley's friends and followers, and promptly went out of business.

This is the text of all six volumes, after some redundancies have been removed: Crowley dictated the work to the Ape of Thoth while under the influence of heroin, which made him at times a little verbose.

At the beginning of 1945, the Prophet of the New Aeon went to live in a boarding-house in Hastings. 'Netherwood' was a large Victorian mansion standing in wooded grounds in that part of the outskirts of the town called The Ridge. He had published privately several more works since the failure of the Mandrake Press, notably *The Equinox of the Gods*, 1937, in which *The Book of the Law* is presented as the new religion for mankind; three patriotic war-time broadsheets with his photograph in Arab headdress; and *The Book of Thoth*, 1944, a reorientation of the tarot in the light of his philosophy.

The rest of his autohagiography was still unpublished; he had lost the galleys of the third volume and the typescripts of the remaining three volumes were scattered among his papers. On my suggestion, he collected them together and gave them to a typist. One copy (bound in four parts) he sent to me. In his reply to my letter of thanks, he wrote, 'You were a little light-hearted in asking me to make sure of these volumes of the *Hag* not being lost to the world. It cost me as near forty pounds as makes no difference.'

His odd dress and sweet smell, his magic ring with the hieroglyphic inscription, *Ankh-f-n-Khonsu*, 'his life is in Khonsu' (the moon god of Thebes), his magic wand, resting in the corner of the rather seedy room in which he ended his days, all added to his haunted presence. He had spent his whole life in struggling through the Abyss or, if you will, in exploring the Unconscious with the aid of every known stimulant and magic ritual; and in his old age he had come to look like what he claimed to be—a Secret Chief. On the wall, I remember, was a painting, badly drawn but effective, of himself as The Beast 666, an idealized self-portrait. (He had covered the walls of his bedroom—*La Chambre des Cauchemars*—at his abbey with magical paintings which the vulgar thought obscene.)

I think he was telling the simple truth when he wrote that he immediately stopped a quarrel among Arabs in a coffee house in Algeria by striding into the scrimmage, rapidly drawing sigils in the air with his magic ring—a star sapphire stone, held in position by a band of two interlaced gold serpents—while intoning in Arabic a chapter of the Koran. With his shaven head and hypnotic eyes, he made a strong, and in some cases a lasting, impression on many people.

He was erudite in all subjects relating to magic—or magick as he preferred to spell it. He used the *I Ching* for probing the future long before that work became popular in intellectual circles in the West. His greatest merit, perhaps, was to make the bridge between Tantrism and the Western esoteric tradition, and thus bring together Western and Eastern magical techniques. He lived through the night, not the day.

Hampstead   JOHN SYMONDS
August 1968

ALEISTER CROWLEY
AND THE LAW OF THELEMA

It is reasonably clear from the Introduction to this work that John Symonds does not accept the Law of Thelema. On this point we are at variance. Furthermore, I think that *The Book of the Law* contains the key to the principal occult mysteries of the present age.

KENNETH GRANT

PART ONE

Towards the Golden Dawn

The Eye of Horus in the Pyramid of Fire, radiating the solar blaze.
One of the Golden Dawn emblems used by Crowley.

PRELUDE

'Do what thou wilt shall be the whole of the Law.' [1] Not only to this autohagiography—as he amusedly insists on calling it— of Aleister Crowley, but to every form of biography, biology, even chemistry, these words are the key.

'Every man and every women is a star.' [2] What can we know about a star? By the telescope, a faint phantasm of its optical value. By the spectroscope, a hint of its composition. By the telescope, and our mathematics, its course. In this last case we may legitimately argue from the known to the unknown: by our measure of the brief visible curve, we can calculate whence it has come and whither it will go. Experience justifies our assumptions.

Considerations of this sort are essential to any serious attempt at biography. An infant is not—as our grandmothers thought—an arbitrary jest flung into the world by a cynical deity, to be saved or damned as predestination or freewill required. We know now that 'that, that is, is', as the old hermit of Prague that never saw pen and ink very wittily said to a niece of King Gorboduc.

Nothing can ever be created or destroyed; and therefore the 'life' of any individual must be comparable to that brief visible curve, and the object of writing it to divine by the proper measurements the remainder of its career.

The writer of any biography must ask, in the deepest sense, who is he? This question 'who art thou?' is the first which is put to any candidate for initiation. Also, it is the last. What so-and-so is, did and suffered: these are merely clues to that great problem. So then the earliest memories of any autohagiographer will be immensely valuable; their very incoherence will be an infallible guide. For, as Freud has shown, we remember (in the main) what we wish to remember, and forget what is painful. There is thus great danger of deception as to the 'facts' of the case; but our memories indicate with uncanny accuracy what is our true will. And, as above made manifest, it is this true will which shows the nature of our proper motion.

3

In writing the life of the average man, there is this funda-mental difficulty, that the performance is futile and mean-ingless, even from the standpoint of the matter-of-fact philosopher; there is, that is to say, no artistic unity. In the case of Aleister Crowley no such Boyg appeared on the hill-side; for he himself regards his career as a definitely dramatic composition. It comes to a climax on April 8th, 9th, and 10th, 1904 E.V.[3] The slightest incident in the history of the whole universe appears to him as a preparation for that event; and his subsequent life is merely the aftermath of that crisis.

On the other hand, however, there is the circumstance that his time has been spent in three very distinct manners: the Secret Way of the Initiate, the Path of Poetry and Philosophy, and the Open Sea of Romance and Adventure. It is indeed not unusual to find the first two, or the last two, elements in the molecule of a man: Byron exemplifies this, and Poe that. But it is rare indeed for so strenuous and out-of-doors a life to be associated with such profound devotion to the arts of the quietist; and in this particular instance all three careers are so full that posterity might well be excused for surmising that not one but several individuals were combined in a legend, or even for taking the next step and saying: This Aleister Crow-ley was not a man, or even a number of men; he is obviously a solar myth. Nor could he himself deny such an impeachment too brutally; for already, before he has attained the prime of life, his name is associated with fables not less fantastic than those which have thrown doubt upon the historicity of the Buddha. It should be the true will of this book to make plain the truth about the man. Yet here again there is a lion in the way. The truth must be falsehood unless it be the whole truth; and the whole truth is partly inaccessible, partly unintelligible, partly incredible and partly unpublishable—that is, in any country where truth in itself is recognized as a dangerous explosive.

A further difficulty is introduced by the nature of the mind, and especially of the memory, of the man himself. We shall come to incidents which show that he is doubtful about clearly remembered circumstances, whether they belong to 'real life' or to dreams, and even that he has utterly forgotten things which no normal man could forget. He has, moreover, so completely overcome the illusion of time (in the sense used by the phi-losophers, from Lao Tzu and Plotinus to Kant and White-head) that he often finds it impossible to disentangle events as a sequence. He has so thoroughly referred phenomena to a single standard that they have lost their individual significance, just as when one has understood the word 'cat,' the letters c a t have lost their own value and become mere arbitrary elements of an idea. Further: on reviewing one's life in perspective the astronomical sequence ceases to be significant. Events rearrange themselves in an order outside time and space, just as in a picture there is no way of distinguishing at what point on the canvas the artist began to paint. Alas! it is impossible to make this a satisfactory book; hurrah! that furnishes the necessary stimulus; it becomes worth while to do it, and by Styx! it shall be done.

It would be absurd to apologize for the form of this book. Excuses are always nauseating. I do not believe for a moment that it would have turned out any better if it had been written in the most favourable circumstances. I mention merely as a matter of general interest the actual difficulties attending the composition.

From the start my position was precarious. I was practically penniless, I had been betrayed in the most shameless and senseless way by practically everyone with whom I was in business relations, I had no means of access to any of the normal conveniences which are considered essential to people engaged in such tasks. On the top of this there sprang up a sudden whirlwind of wanton treachery and brainless persecution,[4] so imbecile yet so violent as to throw even quite sensible people off their base. I ignored this and carried on, but almost immediately both I and one of my principal assistants were stricken down with lingering illness. I carried on. My assistant [5] died. I carried on. His death was the signal for a fresh outburst of venomous falsehoods. I carried on. The agitation resulted in my being exiled from Italy; though no accusation of any kind was, or could be, alleged against me. That meant that I was torn away from even the most elementary conveniences for writing this book. I carried on. At the moment of writing this paragraph everything in connection with the book is entirely in the air. I am carrying on.

But apart from any of this, I have felt throughout an essential difficulty with regard to the form of the book. The subject is too big to be susceptible of organic structure unless I make a deliberate effort of will and a strict arbitrary selection. It would, as a matter of fact, be easy for me to choose any one of fifty meanings for my life, and illustrate it by carefully chosen facts. Any such method would be open to the criticism which is always ready to devastate any form of idealism. I myself feel that it would be unfair and, what is more, untrue. The alternative has been to make the incidents as full as possible, to state them as they occurred, entirely regardless of any possible bearing upon any possible spiritual significance. This method involves a certain faith in life itself, that it will declare its own meaning and apportion the relative importance of every set of incidents automatically. In other words, it is to assert the theory that destiny is a supreme artist, which is notoriously not the case on any accepted definition of art. And yet—a mountain! What a mass of heterogeneous accidents determine its shape! Yet, in the case of a fine mountain, who denies the beauty and even the significance of its form?

In the later years of my life, as I have attained to some understanding of the unity behind the diverse phenomena of experience, and as the natural restriction of elasticity which comes with age has gained ground, it has become progressively easier to group events about a central purpose. But this only means that the principle of selection has been changed. In my early years the actual seasons, climates and occupations determined the sections of my life. My spiritual activities fit into those frames, whereas, more recently, the converse is the case. My physical environment fits into my spiritual preoccupation. This change would be sufficient by itself to ensure the theoretical impossibility of editing a life like mine on any consistent principle.

I find myself obliged, for these and many other reasons, to abandon altogether any idea of conceiving an artistic structure for the work or formulating an artistic purpose. All that I can do is to describe everything that I remember, as best I can, as if it were, in itself, the centre of interest. I must trust nature so to order matters that, in the multiplicity of the material, the proper proportion will somehow appear automatically, just as in the operations of pure chance or inexorable law a unity ennobled by strength and beautified by harmony arises inscrutably out of the chaotic concatenation of circumstances.

At least one claim may be made; nothing has been invented, nothing suppressed, nothing altered and nothing 'yellowed up'. I believe that truth is not only stranger than fiction, but more interesting. And I have no motive for deception, because I don't give a damn for the whole human race—'you're nothing but a pack of cards.'

1

Edward Crowley,* the wealthy scion of a race of Quakers, was the father of a son born at 30 Clarendon Square, Leamington, Warwickshire, † on the 12th day of October, ‡ 1875 E.V. between eleven and twelve at night. Leo was just rising at the time, as nearly as can be ascertained. The branch of the family of Crowley to which this man belonged has been settled in England since Tudor times: in the days of Bad Queen Bess there was a Bishop Crowley, who wrote epigrams in the style of Martial. One of them—the only one I know—runs thus:

> The bawds of the stews be all turnèd out:
> But I think they inhabit all England throughout.

(I cannot find the modern book which quotes this as a footnote and have not been able to trace the original volume.)

The Crowleys are, however, of Celtic origin; the name O'Crowley is common in south-west Ireland, and the Breton family of de Quérouaille—which gave England a Duchess of Portsmouth—or de Kerval is of the same stock. Legend will have it that the then head of the family came to England with the Earl of Richmond and helped to make him king on Bosworth Field.

Edward Crowley was educated as an engineer, but never practised his profession.§ He was devoted to religion and became a follower of John Nelson Darby, the founder of the 'Plymouth Brethren'. The fact reveals a stern logician; for the sect is characterized by refusal to compromise; it insists on the literal interpretation of the Bible as the exact words of the Holy Ghost. ‖

* 'the younger' (1834–87).
† It has been remarked a strange coincidence that one small county should have given England her two greatest poets—for one must not forget Shakespeare (1550–1616).[1]
‡ Presumably this is nature's compensation for the horror which blasted mankind on that date in 1492.[2]
§ His son elicited this fact by questioning; curious, considering the dates.
‖ On the strength of a text in the book itself: the logic is thus of a peculiar order.

He married (in 1874, one may assume) Emily Bertha Bishop, of a Devon and Somerset family. Her father had died and her brother Tom Bond Bishop had come to London to work in the Civil Service. The important points about the woman are that her schoolmates called her 'the little Chinese girl', that she painted in water-colour with admirable taste destroyed by academic training, and that her powerful natural instincts were suppressed by religion to the point that she became, after her husband's death, a brainless bigot of the most narrow, logical and inhuman type. Yet there was always a struggle; she was really distressed, almost daily, at finding herself obliged by her religion to perform acts of the most senseless atrocity.

Her firstborn son, the aforesaid, was remarkable from the moment of his arrival. He bore on his body the three most important distinguishing marks of a Buddha. He was tongue-tied, and on the second day of his incarnation a surgeon cut the fraenum linguae. He had also the characteristic membrane, which necessitated an operation for phimosis some three lustres later.[3] Lastly, he had upon the centre of his heart four hairs curling from left to right in the exact form of a Swastika.*

He was baptised by the names of Edward Alexander, the latter being the surname of an old friend of his father's, deeply beloved by him for the holiness of his life—by Plymouth Brethren standards, one may suppose. It seems probable that the boy was deeply impressed by being told, at what age (before six) does not appear, that Alexander means 'helper of men'. He is still giving himself passionately to the task, despite the intellectual cynicism inseparable from intelligence after one has reached forty.

But the extraordinary fact connected with this baptismal ceremony is this. As the Plymouth Brethren practise infant baptism by immersion, it must have taken place in the first three months of his life. Yet he has a perfectly clear visual recollection of the scene. It took place in a bathroom on the first floor of the house in which he was born. He remembers the shape of the room, the disposal of its appointments, the little group of 'brethren' surrounding him, and the surprise of finding himself, dressed in a long white garment, being sud-

---

* There is also a notable tuft of hair upon the forehead, similar to the mound of flesh there situated in the Buddhist legends. And numerous minor marks.

denly dipped and lifted from the water. He has also a clear auditory remembrance of words spoken solemnly over him; though they meant nothing, he was impressed by the peculiar tone. It is not impossible that this gave him an all but unconquerable dislike for the cold plunge, and at the same time a vivid passion for ceremonial speech. These two qualities have played highly important parts in his development.

This baptism, by the way, though it never worried him, proved a peril to the soul of another. When his wife's conduct compelled him to insist upon her divorcing him—a formality as meaningless as their marriage—and she became insane shortly afterwards, an eminent masochist named Colonel Gormley, R.A.M.C. (dead previously, then and since) lay in wait for her at the asylum gates to marry her. The trouble was that he included among his intellectual lacunae a devotion to the Romish superstition. He feared damnation if he married a divorceuse dipsomaniac with non-parva-partial dementia. The poor mollusc asked Crowley for details of his baptism. He wrote back that he had been baptised 'in the name of the Holy Trinity'.

It now appeared that, had these actual words been used, he was a pagan, his marriage void, Lola Zaza a bastard and his wife a light o' love!

Crowley tried to help the wretched worm; but, alas, he remembered too well the formula: 'I baptise thee Edward Alexander in the name of the Father, the Son and the Holy Ghost.' So the gallant colonel had to fork out for a dispensation from Rome. Crowley himself squandered a lot of cash in one way or another. But he never fell so far as to waste a farthing on the three-card trick, or the three-God trick.

He has also the clearest visualization of some of the people who surrounded him in the first six years of his life, which were spent in Leamington and the neighbourhood, which he has never revisited. In particular, there was an orange-coloured old lady named Miss Carey who used to bring him oranges. His first memory of speech is his remark, 'Ca'ey, orange'; * this, however, is remembered because he was told of it later. But he is in full conscious memory of the dining-room of the house, its furniture and pictures, with their arrangement. He also remembers various country walks, one especially through green fields, in which a perambulator figures. The main street of Leamington, and the Leam with its weir—he has loved

---

* He has never been able to pronounce 'R' properly—like a Chinese!

weirs ever since—Guy's Cliffe at Warwick, and the Castle with its terrace and the white peacocks: all these are as clear as if he had seen them last week. He recalls no other room in the house except his own bedroom, and that only because he 'came to himself' one night to find a fire lighted, a steam kettle going, a strange woman present, an atmosphere of anxiety and a feeling of fever; for he had an attack of bronchitis.

He remembers his first governess, Miss Arkell, a grey-haired lady with traces of beard upon her large flat face and a black dress of what he calls bombasine, though to this hour he does not know what bombasine may be, and thinks that the dress was of alpaca or even, it may be, of smooth hard silk.

And he remembers the first indication that his mind was of a logical and scientific order.

Ladies will now kindly skip a page, while I lay the facts before a select audience of lawyers, doctors and ministers of religion.

The Misses Cowper consisted of Sister Susan and Sister Emma; the one large, rosy and dry, like an overgrown radish; the other small, pink and moist, rather like Teniel's Mock Turtle. Both were Plymouth Sister old maids. They were very repulsive to the boy, who has never since liked calf's head, though partial to similar dishes, or been able to hear the names Susan or Emma without disgust.

One day he said something to his mother which elicited from her the curious anatomical assertion: 'Ladies have no legs.' Shortly afterwards, when the Misses Cowper were at dinner with the family, he disappeared from his chair. There must have been some slight commotion on deck, leading to the question of his whereabouts. But at that moment a still small voice came from beneath the table: 'Mamma! Mamma! Sister Susan and Sister Emma are not ladies!'

This deduction was perfectly genuine: but in the following incident the cynical may perhaps trace the root of a certain sardonic humour. The child was wont to indicate his views, when silence seemed discretion, by facial gestures. Several people were rash enough to tell him not to make grimaces, as he 'might be struck like that'. He would reply, with an air of enlightenment after long meditation: 'So that accounts for it.'

All children born into a family whose social and economic conditions are settled are bound to take them for granted as universal. It is only when they meet with incompatible facts that they begin to wonder whether they are suited to their original environment. In this particular case the most trifling incidents of life were necessarily interpreted as part of a pre-arranged plan, like the beginning of *Candide*.

The underlying theory of life which was assumed in the household showed itself constantly in practice. It is strange that less than fifty years later, this theory should seem such fantastic folly as to require a detailed account.

The universe was created by God 4004 B.C. The Bible, authorized version, was literally true, having been dictated by the Holy Ghost himself to scribes incapable of even clerical errors. King James's translators enjoyed an equal immunity. It was considered unusual—and therefore in doubtful taste—to appeal to the original texts. All other versions were regarded as inferior; the Revised Version in particular savoured of heresy. John Nelson Darby, the founder of the Plymouth Brethren, being a very famous biblical scholar, had been invited to sit on the committee and had refused on the ground that some of the other scholars were atheists.

The Second Coming of the Lord Jesus was confidently ex-pected to occur at any moment.* So imminent was it that preparations for a distant future—such as signing a lease or insuring one's life—might be held to imply lack of confidence in the promise, 'Behold I come quickly.'

A pathetically tragic incident—some years later—illustrates the reality of this absurdity. To modern educated people it must seem unthinkable that so fantastic a superstition could be such a hellish obsession in such recent times and such familiar places.

One fine summer morning, at Redhill, the boy—now eight or nine—got tired of playing by himself in the garden. He came back to the house. It was strangely still and he got frightened. By some odd chance everybody was either out or upstairs. But he jumped to the conclusion that 'the Lord had come', and that he had been 'left behind'. It was an understood thing that there was no hope for people in this position. Apart from the Second Advent, it was always possible to be saved up to the very moment of death; but once the saints had been

---

* Much was made of the two appearances of 'Jesus' after the Ascension. In the first, to Stephen, he was standing, in the second, to Paul, seated, at the right hand of God. Ergo, on the first occasion he was still ready to return at once; on the second, he had made up his mind to let things take their course to the bitter end, as per the Apocalypse. No one saw anything funny, or blasphemous, or even futile, in this doctrine!

called up, the day of grace was finally over. Various alarums and excursions would take place as per the Apocalypse, and then would come the millennium, when Satan would be chained for a thousand years and Christ reign for that period over the Jews regathered in Jerusalem. The position of these Jews is not quite clear. They were not saved in the same sense as Christians had been, yet they were not damned. The millennium seems to have been thought of as a fulfilment of God's promise to Abraham; but apparently it had nothing to do with 'eternal life'. However, even this modified beatitude was not open to Gentiles who had rejected Christ.

The child was consequently very much relieved by the reappearance of some of the inmates of the house whom he could not imagine as having been lost eternally.

The lot of the saved, even on earth, was painted in the brightest colours. It was held that 'all things work together for good to them that love God and are called according to His purpose'. Earthly life was regarded as an ordeal; this was a wicked world and the best thing that could happen to anyone was 'to go to be with Christ, which is far better'. On the other hand, the unsaved went to the lake of fire and brimstone which burneth for ever and ever. Edward Crowley used to give away tracts to strangers, besides distributing them by thousands through the post; he was also constantly preaching to vast crowds, all over the country. It was, indeed, the only logical occupation for a humane man who believed that even the noblest and best of mankind were doomed to eternal punishment. One card—a great favourite, as being peculiarly deadly —was headed 'Poor Anne's Last Words'; the gist of her remarks appears to have been 'lost, lost, lost!' She had been a servant in the house of Edward Crowley the elder, and her dying delirium had made a deep impression upon the son of the house.

By the way, Edward Crowley possessed the power, as per Higgins, the professor in Bernard Shaw's *Pygmalion*, of telling instantly from a man's speech what part of the country he lived in. It was his hobby to make walking tours through every part of England, evangelizing in every town and village as he passed. He would engage likely strangers in conversation, diagnose and prescribe for their spiritual diseases, inscribe them in his address books, and correspond and send religious literature for years. At that time religion was the popular fad in England and few resented his ministrations. His widow continued the sending of tracts, etc. for years after his death.

As a preacher Edward Crowley was magnificently eloquent, speaking as he did from the heart. But, being a gentleman, he could not be a real revivalist, which means manipulating the hysteria of mob psychology.

2

If troubles arose in the outer world, they were regarded as the beginning of the fulfilment of the prophecies in Daniel, Matthew and Revelation. But it was understood implicitly that England was specially favoured by God on account of the breach with Rome. The child, who, at this period, was called by the dreadful name Alick, supposed it to be a law of nature that Queen Victoria would never die and that consols would never go below par.

Crowley remembers, as if he had seen it yesterday, the dining-room and the ceremony of family prayers after breakfast. He remembers the order in which the family and the servants sat. A chapter of the Bible was read, each person present taking a verse in turn. At four years old he could read perfectly well. The strange thing about this is not so much his precocity as the fact that he was much less interested in the Biblical narratives than in the long Hebrew names. One of his father's favourite sermons was based on the fifth chapter of Genesis; long as the patriarchs lived, they all died in the end. From this he would argue that his hearers would die too; they had therefore better lose no time in making sure of heaven. But the interest of Alick was in the sound of the names themselves—Enoch, Arphaxad, Mahaleel. He often wonders whether this curious trait was symptomatic of his subsequent attainments in poetry, or whether it indicates the attraction which the Hebrew Cabbala was to have for him later on.

With regard to the question of salvation, by the way, the theory of the exclusive Plymouth Brethren was peculiar, and somewhat trying to a logical mind. They held predestination as rigidly as Calvin, yet this nowise interfered with complete freewill. The crux was faith in Christ, apparently more or less intellectual, but, since 'the evils also believe and tremble', it had to be supplemented by a voluntary acceptance of Christ as one's personal saviour. This being so, the question arose whether Roman Catholics, Anglicans or even Nonconformists could possibly be saved. The general feeling seems to have been that it was impossible for anyone who was once actually

14

saved to be lost, whatever he did.* But it was, of course, beyond human power to determine whether any given individual
had or had not found salvation. This, however, was clear: that
any teaching or acceptance of false doctrine must be met by
excommunication. The leaders of the Brethren were necessarily profound theologians. There being no authority of any
kind, any brother soever might enunciate any doctrine soever
at any time, and this anarchy had already resulted, before the
opening of our story, in the division of the Brethren into two
great sects: the Open and the Exclusive.

Philip Gosse, the father of Edmund Gosse, was a leader
among the Open Brethren, who differed from the Exclusive
Brethren, at first, only by tolerating, at the Lord's table, the
presence of 'professed Christians' not definitely affiliated to
themselves. Edmund Gosse has described his father's attitude
in *Father and Son*. Much of what he wrote taxes the credulity
of the reader. Such narrowness and bigotry as that of Philip
Gosse seemed beyond belief. Yet Edward Crowley regarded
Philip Gosse as likely to be damned for latitudinarianism! No
one who loved the Lord Jesus in his heart could be so careless
of his Saviour's honour as to 'break bread' † with a man who
might be holding unscriptural opinions.

Readers of *Father and Son* will remember the incident of the
Christmas turkey, secretly bought by Mr. Gosse's servants and
thrown into the dustbin by him in the spirit of Moses destroying the golden calf. For the Brethren rightly held Christmas
to be a pagan festival. They sent no Christmas cards and destroyed any that might be sent to them by thoughtless or blaspheming 'goats'. Not to disappoint Alick, who liked turkey,
the family had that bird for lunch on the 24th and 26th of
December. The idea was to 'avoid even the appearance of evil';
there was nothing actually wrong in eating turkey on Christmas
Day; for pagan idols are merely wood and stone—the work of
men's hands. But one must not let others suppose that one is
complying with heathen customs.

Another early reminiscence. On February 29th, 1880, Alick
was taken to see the dead body of his sister, Grace Mary Elizabeth,‡ who had only lived five hours. The incident made a

* 'Of those that thou gavest me have I lost not one, except the son of
perdition.' In view of predestination, 'those' means all the elect and not
merely the Eleven, as the unenlightened might suppose.
† i.e. sit at the communion table.
‡ *What* a name!

curious impression on him. He did not see why he should be disturbed so uselessly. He couldn't do any good; the child was dead; it was none of his business. This attitude continued through his life. He has never attended any funeral * but that of his father, which he did not mind doing, as he felt himself to be the real centre of interest. But when others have died, though in two cases at least his heart was torn as if by a wild beast, and his life actually blighted for months and years by the catastrophe, he has always turned away from the necrological facts and the customary orgies. It may be that he has a deep-seated innate conviction that the connection of a person with his body is purely symbolic. But there is also the feeling that the fact of death destroys all possible interest; the disaster is irreparable, it should be forgotten as soon as possible. He would not even join the search party after the Kangchenjunga accident. What object was there in digging frozen corpses from under an avalanche? Dead bodies themselves do not repel him; he is as interested in dissecting rooms as in anything else. When he met the dead body of Consul Litton, he turned back, knowing the man was dead. But when the corpse was brought to Tengyueh, he assisted unflinchingly at the inquiry, because in this instance there was an object in ascertaining the cause of death.[2]

One other group of incidents of early childhood. The family went to the west of England for the summer. Alick remembers Monmouth, or rather Monmouth Castle. It is curious that, in the act of remembering this for the purpose of this book, he was obsessed by the idea that there could not be such a place as Monmouth; the name seemed fantastic. It was confused in his mind with 'Monster' and 'Mammoth', and it was some hours before he could convince himself of its reality. He remembers staying in a farm some distance from the road and has a very vague impression of becoming acquainted with such animals as ducks and pigs. Much more clearly arises the vision of himself on a pony with people walking each side. He remembers falling off, starting to yell and being carried up to the house by the frightened governess (or whoever it was) in charge of him. This event had a tragic result. He ought to have been put back on the pony and made to conquer his fears. As it was, he has never been able to feel at home on horseback, though he has ridden thousands of miles, many of them over really dangerous country.

---

* With one notable exception, at which he officiated.[1]

On the other hand—subconscious memory of previous incarnations, or the Eastern soul of him, or the fact that he took to it after he had learned the foolishness of fear?—he was from the first perfectly at home on a camel. And this despite the fact that these animals act like highly placed officials and even—if scabby—like consuls, and look (when old) like English ladies engaged in good works. (There is much of the vulture in the type of head.)

One incident connected with this journey is of extraordinary interest as throwing a light on future events. Walking with his father in a field, whose general aspect he remembers perfectly well to this day, his attention was called to a clump of nettles and he was warned that they would sting if he touched them. He does not remember what he answered, but whatever it was it elicited from his father the question, 'Will you take my word for it or would you rather learn by experience?' He replied, 'I would rather learn by experience,' and plunged head foremost into the clump.

This summer was marked by two narrow escapes. He remembers being seated beside the driver of some carriage with what seemed to him an extraordinarily tall box, though this impression may mean merely that he was a very small boy. It was going down hill on a road that curved across a steep slope of very green grass. He remembers the grinding of the brakes. Suddenly his father jumped out of the carriage and cried to the driver that a wheel was coming off. The only trace which this left in later life is that he has always disliked riding in unusual vehicles unless himself in control. He became a reckless cyclist and motorist, but he was nervous for a long while with automobiles unless at the wheel.

The last event of this period occurred at a railway station. He remembers its general appearance and that of the little family group. A porter, staggering under a heavy trunk, slid it suddenly off his back. It missed crushing the boy by a hair's breadth. He does not remember whether he was snatched away, or anything else, except his father's exclamation, 'His guardian angel was watching over him.' It seems possible that this early impression determined his course in later life when he came to take up Magick [3]; for the one document which gripped him was *The Book of the Sacred Magic of Abra-Melin the Mage*, in which the essential work is 'To obtain the Knowledge and Conversation of the Holy Guardian Angel'.

It is very important to mention that the mind of the child was almost abnormally normal. He showed no tendency to see

visions, as even commonplace children often do. The Bible
was his only book at this period; but neither the narrative nor
the poetry made any deep impression on him. He was fascinated by the mysteriously prophetic passages, especially those
in Revelation. The Christianity in his home was entirely pleasant to him, and yet his sympathies were with the opponents of
heaven. He suspects obscurely that this was partly an instinctive love of terrors. The Elders and the harps seemed tame. He
preferred the Dragon, the False Prophet, the Beast and the
Scarlet Woman, as being more exciting. He revelled in the
descriptions of torment. One may suspect, moreover, a strain
of congenital masochism. He liked to imagine himself in
agony; in particular, he liked to identify himself with the
Beast whose number is the number of a man, six hundred and
three score six. One can only conjecture that it was the mystery
of the number which determined this childish choice.

Many of the memories even of very early childhood seem
to be those of a quite adult individual. It is as if the mind and
body of the boy were a mere medium being prepared for the
expression of a complete soul already in existence. (The word
medium is here used in almost exactly the same sense as in
spiritualism.) This feeling is very strong; and implies an unshakable conviction that the facts are as suggested above. The
explanation can hardly fail to imply the existence of an immanent spirit (the true self) which uses incarnations, and possibly
many other means, from time to time in order to observe the
universe at a particular point of focus, much as a telescope
resolves a nebula.

The congenital masochism of which we have spoken demands further investigation. All his life he has been almost
unduly sensitive to pain, physical, mental and moral. There is no
perversion in him which makes it enjoyable, yet the phantasy
of desiring to be hurt has persisted in his waking imagination, though it never manifests itself in his dreams. It is probable that these peculiarities are connected with certain curious
anatomical facts. While his masculinity is above the normal,
both physiologically and as witnessed by his powerful growth
of beard, he has certain well-marked feminine characteristics.

Not only are his limbs as slight and graceful as a girl's, but
his breasts are developed to a quite abnormal degree. There
is thus a sort of hermaphroditism in his physical structure;
and this is naturally expressed in his mind. But whereas, in
most similar cases, the feminine qualities appear at the expense
of manhood, in him they are added to a perfectly normal

masculine type. The principal effect has been to enable him to understand the psychology of women, to look at any theory with comprehensive and impartial eyes, and to endow him with maternal instincts on spiritual planes. He has thus been able to beat the women he has met at their own game and emerge from the battle of sex triumphant and scatheless. He has been able to philosophize about nature from the standpoint of a complete human being; certain phenomena will always be unintelligible to men as such, others, to women as such. He, by being both at once, has been able to formulate a view of existence which combines the positive and the negative, the active and the passive, in a single identical equation. Finally, intensely as the savage male passion to create has inflamed him, it has been modified by the gentleness and conservatism of womanhood. Again and again, in the course of this history, we shall find his actions determined by this dual structure. Similar types have no doubt existed previously, but none such has been studied. Only in the light of Weininger and Freud * is it possible to select and interpret the phenomena. The present investigation should be of extraordinary ethical value, for it must be a rare circumstance that a subject with such abnormal qualities so clearly marked should have trained himself to intimate self-analysis and kept an almost daily record of his life and work extending over nearly a quarter of a century.†

---

* That is, for those not initiated into the Magical Tradition and the Holy Cabbala—the Children's table from which Freud and Weininger ate of a few crumbs that fell.

† It should be added that the apparently masochistic stigmata disappeared entirely at puberty; their relics are observable only when he is depressed physically. That is, they are wholly symptoms of physiological malaise.

3

When Alick was about six years old his father moved from Leamington to Redhill, Surrey. There was some reason connected with a gravel soil and country life. The house was called The Grange. It stood in a large long garden ending in woods which overhung the road between Redhill and Merstham; about a mile, perhaps a little more, from Redhill. Alick lived here till 1886 and his memory of this period is of perpetual happiness. He remembers with the utmost clearness innumerable incidents and it becomes hard to select those which possess significance. He was taught by tutors; but they have faded, though their lessons have not. He was very thoroughly grounded in geography, history, Latin and arithmetic. His cousin, Gregor Grant, six years older than himself, was a constant visitor; a somewhat strange indulgence, as Gregor was brought up in Presbyterianism. The lad was very proud of his pedigree. Edward Crowley used to ridicule this, saying, 'My family sprang from a gardener who was turned out of the garden for stealing his master's fruit.' Edward Crowley would not allow himself to be addressed as 'Esquire' or even 'Mr'. It seems a piece of atavism, for a Crowley had petitioned Charles I to take away the family coat of arms; his successor, however, had asked Charles II to restore them, which was done. This is evidence of the satanic pride of the race. Edward Crowley despised worldly dignities because he was a citizen of heaven. He would not accept favour or honour from any one less than Jesus Christ.

Alick remembers a lady calling at the house for a subscription in aid of Our Soldiers in Egypt. Edward Crowley browbeat and bullied her into tears with a philippic on 'bibles and brandy'. He was, however, bitterly opposed to the Blue Ribbon Army. He said that abstainers were likely to rely on good works to get to heaven and thus fail to realize their need of Jesus. He preached one Sunday in the town hall, saying, 'I would rather preach to a thousand drunkards than a thousand T-totallers.' They retorted by accusing him of being connected with 'Crowley's Ales'. He replied that he had been an abstainer

20

for nineteen years, during which he had shares in a brewery. He had now ceased to abstain for some time, but all his money was invested in a waterworks.*

Besides Gregor Grant, Alick's only playmates were the sons of local Brethren. Aristocratic feeling was extremely strong. The usual boyish play-acting, in which various personalities of the moment, such as Sir Garnet Wolseley and Arabi Pasha, were represented, was complicated in practice by a united attack on what were called cads. Alick especially remembers lying in wait at the end of the wood for children on their way to the National School. They had to cross a barrage of arrows and peas and ultimately got so scared that they found a round-about way.

Facing the drive, across the road, was a sand-pit. Alick remembers jumping from the top with an alpenstock and charging a navvy at work in the pit, knocking him down, and bolting home. But he was not always so courageous. He once transfixed, with the same alpenstock, the bandbox of an errand-boy. The boy, however, was an Italian; and pursued the aggressor to The Grange, when of course the elders intervened. But he remembers being very frightened and tearful because of some connection in his mind between Italians and stabbing. Here again is a curious point of psychology. He has no fear of being struck or cut; but the idea of being pierced disturbs his nerve. He has to pull himself together very vigorously even in the matter of a hypodermic syringe.

There has always been something suggesting the oriental—Chinese or ancient Egyptian—in Alick's personal appearance. As his mother at school had been called 'the little Chinese girl', so his daughter, Lola Zaza, has the Mongolian physiognomy even more pronounced. His thought follows this indication. He has never been able to sympathize with any European religion or philosophy; and of Jewish or Mohammedan thought he has assimilated only the mysticism of the Cabbalists and the Sufis. Even Hindu psychology, thoroughly as he studied it, never satisfied him wholly. As will be seen, Buddhism itself failed to win his devotion. But he found himself instantly at home with the *Yi King* [1] and the writings of Lao Tzu. Strangely enough, Egyptian symbolism and magical practice made an equal appeal; incompatible as these two systems appear on the surface, the one being atheistic, anarchistic and quietistic, the

---

* At Amsterdam. It was a failure at first, the natives objecting to a liquid which lacked taste, smell and colour.

other theistic hierarchical and active. Even at this period the
East called to him. There is one very significant episode. In
some history of the Indian Mutiny was the portrait of Nana
Sahib, a proud, fierce, cruel, sensual profile. It was his ideal of
beauty. He hated to believe that Nana Sahib had been caught
and killed. He wanted to find Nana Sahib, to become his ally,
share in torturing prisoners, and yet to suffer at his hands.
When Gregor Grant was pretending to be Hyder Ali, and
himself Tipu Sahib, he once asked his cousin, 'Be cruel to me.'

The influence of Cousin Gregor at this time was paramount.
When Gregor was Rob Roy, Alick was Greumoch, the outlaw's
henchman in James Grant's novel. The MacGregors appealed
to Alick as being the most royal, wronged, romantic, brave
and solitary of the clans. There can be no doubt that this
phantasy played a great part in determining his passionate
admiration of the chief of the Hermetic Order of the Golden
Dawn, a Hampshire man named Mathers who inexplicably
claimed to be MacGregor of Glenstrae.

The boy's attitude to his parents is one of the most remarkable facts of his early life. His father was his hero and his
friend, though, for some reason or other, there was no real
conscious intimacy or understanding. He always disliked and
despised his mother. There was a physical repulsion, and an
intellectual and social scorn. He treated her almost as a servant.
It is perhaps on this account that he remembers practically
nothing of her during this period. She always antagonized him.
He remembers one Sunday when she found him reading
Martin Rattler and scolded him. Edward Crowley took his
part. If the book was good enough to read on any day, why not
on Sunday? To Edward Crowley, every day was the Lord's
Day; sabbatarianism was Judaism.

When Alick was eight or thereabouts he was taken by his
father to his first school. This was a private school at St
Leonards, kept by an old man named Habershon and his two
sons, very strict Evangelicals. Edward Crowley wanted to warn
his son against the commonest incident of English school life.
He took a very wise way. He read to the boy very impressively
the story of Noah's intoxication and its results, concluding:
'Never let any one touch you there.' In this way, the injunction
was given without arousing morbid curiosity.

Alick remembers little of his life at this school beyond a
vivid visual recollection of the playground with its 'giant's
stride'. He does not remember any of the boys, though the

three masters stand out plainly enough. One very extraordinary event remains. In an examination paper, instead of answering some question or other, he pretended to misunderstand it and wrote an answer worthy of James Joyce. Instead of selling a limited edition at an extravagant price, he was soundly birched. Entirely unrepentant, he began to will Old Habershon's death. Strangely enough, this occurred within a few weeks; and he unhesitatingly took the credit to himself.

The boy's intellect was amazingly precocious. It must have been very shortly after the move to Redhill that a tailor named Hemming came from London to make new clothes for his father. Being a 'brother', he was a guest in the house. He offered to teach Alick chess and succeeded only too well, for he lost every game after the first. The boy recalls the method perfectly. It was to catch a developed bishop by attacking it with pawns. (He actually invented the Tarrasch Trap in the Ruy Lopez before he ever read a book on chess.) This wrung from his bewildered teacher the exclamation, 'Very judicious with his pawns is your son, Mrs Crowley!'

As a matter of fact, there must have been more than this in it. Alick had assuredly a special aptitude for the game; for he never met his master till one fatal day in 1895, when W. V. Naish, the President of the C.U.Ch.C.,[2] took the 'fresher' who had beaten him to Peterhouse, the abode of Mr H. E. Atkins, since seven times amateur champion of England and still a formidable figure in the Masters' Tournament.

It may here be noted that the injudicious youth tried to trap Atkins with a new move invented by himself. It consists of playing K R B Sq, instead of Castles, in the Muzio Gambit, the idea being to allow White to play P Q 4 in reply to Q B 3.

In 1885 Alick was removed from St Leonards to a school kept by a Plymouth Brother, an ex-clergyman named H. d'Arcy Champney, M.A. It is a little difficult to explain the boy's psychology at this period. It was probably determined by his admiration for his father, the big, strong, hearty leader of men, who swayed thousands by his eloquence. He sincerely wished to follow in those mighty footsteps and so strove to imitate the great man as best he might. Accordingly, he aimed at being the most devoted follower of Jesus in the school. He was not hypocritical in any sense.

All this strikes one as absolutely natural; what is extraordinary is the sequel.

A letter dating from his early school life at Cambridge:

Dear Papa & Mama,
    For my holiday work prize I have got a splendid knife, 2 blades, a saw, a screwdriver, a thing to pull out thorns, another to get stones out of horse's shoes, another I don't know what for, a leather piercer, a gimlet & a corkscrew and name plate. It is nicol plated in some parts, but the handle is ivory. The asphalt* gave way near the middle. We were nearly blown hup by the hoiler† a little while ago, no jokes. We had a ½ holiday given us on Friday. Please send me a little money for fireworks. Send up my bankbook by the 1st please. I am awfully well, thank you! I have joined a sort of band of chaps, who are with God's blessing, going to try & help others & speak to them about their souls. I will write soon again. Write quick please

Good bye
                                           Yr loving son
                                                                  ALEC

He was thoroughly happy at this school; the boys liked and admired him; he made remarkable progress in his studies and was very proud of his first prize, White's *Selborne,* for coming out top in 'Religious Knowledge, Classics and French'.

But to this day he has never read the book! For certain lines of study he had a profound, instinctive and ineradicable aversion. Natural history, in any form, is one of these. It is hard to suggest a reason. Did he dislike to analyse beauty? Did he feel that certain subjects were unimportant, led to nothing that he wanted to explore? However this may be, he used to make up his mind with absolute finality as to whether he would or would not take some particular course. If he would, he panted after it like the hart after the water brooks; if not, nothing would persuade him to waste an hour on it.

It was while he was at this school that he began to write poetry. He had read none, except 'Casabianca', 'Excelsior', the doggerel of Sir Walter Scott and such trash. But he had a genuine love for the simple *Hymns for the little Flock* compiled by the 'Brethren'. His first taste of real poetry was *Lycidas,* set for the Cambridge Local Examination, if his memory serves him aright. He fell in love with it at once and had it by heart in a few days. But his own earliest effort is more on the lines of the hymnal. Only a few lines remain.

---

* i.e. of the 'playground'.
† Query? 'Oiler', of course, but what was that doing?

Terror, and darkness, and horrid despair!
Agony painted upon the once fair
Brow of the man who refused to give up
The love of the wine-filled, the o'erflowing cup.
'Wine is a mocker, strong drink is raging.'
No wine in death is his torment assuaging.

Of this Redhill period there remain also memories of two
summers, one in France and Switzerland, the other in the
Highlands.

The former has left numerous traces, chiefly of a visual
character: the Grand Hotel in Paris, Lucerne and the Lion,
William Tell, the Bears at Berne, the Rigi, the Staubbach,
Trummelbach and Giessbach, Basle and the Rhine, the Dance
of Death. Two points only concern us: he objected violently
to being taken out in the cold morning to see the sunrise from
a platform on the Rigi-Kulm and to illumination of a waterfall
by coloured lights. He felt acutely that nature should be allowed
to go her own way and he his! There was plenty of beauty in
the world; why make oneself uncomfortable in order to see
an extra? Also, you can't improve a waterfall by stagecraft!

There is the skeleton of quite a philosophy of life in this.

As to the Scottish Highlands, the boy's mind had been so
poisoned by romance that he saw nothing that he can remember. The scenery was merely a setting for silly daydreams of
Roderick Dhu!

Three other episodes of the Redhill period are pertinent; not
that they are in themselves very significant, save that two of
them exhibit Alick in the character of a normally mischievous
boy with some skill in playing upon other people's psychology.
But they illustrate the singular environment.

A frequent guest at The Grange was an old gentleman
named Sherrall, whose vice was castor oil. Edward Crowley
was in the habit of holding 'tea meetings'; a score or so of
people would be invited to what is vulgarly known as a blow-
out, and when the physical animal was satisfied, there would
be a debauch of spiritual edification. On the mahogany table
in the dining room, extended to its fullest length, would stand
two silver urns of tea. Into one of these young Alick emptied
Mr Sherrall's castor oil. So far, so good. The point is this, that
the people served from that urn were too polite or overawed
either to call the attention of their hostess or to abstain from
the accursed beverage. The only precaution necessary was to
prevent that lady herself from seeing one of the doctored cups.

A rather similar jest was played at a prayer meeting at the

house of a Brother named Nunnerley. Refreshment was offered before the meeting; and a Sister, named Mrs Musty, had been marked down on account of her notorious greed. Alick and some fellow conspirators kept on plying her with food after every one else had finished, with the object of delaying the prayer meeting. The woman herself was too stupid to see what was happening and the Brethren could not be rude enough even to hint their feelings.

This hesitation to act with authority, which was part of the general theoretical P.B. objection to priestcraft, on one occasion reached an astounding point in the following circumstances. A Mr Clapham, the odour of whose beard proclaimed him truthfully a fishmonger, had a wife and a daughter who was engaged to a Mr Munday. These three had gone on an excursion to Boulogne; and, by accident or design, the engaged couple missed the boat for Folkestone. It was again a question of avoiding even the appearance of evil and Mrs Clapham was expelled from fellowship. It is to be presumed that her husband believed her innocent of all complicity, as a priori appears the most natural hypothesis. In any case, next Sunday morning she took her place with her husband at the Lord's Table. It is almost inconceivable that any gathering of human beings, united to celebrate the supreme sacrament of their creed, should have been destitute of any means of safeguarding common decency. But the fear of the priest was paramount; and the entire meeting waited and fidgeted for over an hour in embarrassed silence. Ultimately, a baker named Banfield got up trembling and inquired timorously: 'May I ask Mr Clapham if it is Mrs Clapham's intention to break bread this morning?' Mrs Clapham then bounced out of the room and slammed the door, after which the meeting proceeded as usual.

Bourbonism still survives among some people in England. I remember explaining some action of mine to Gerald Kelly [3] as taken on my lawyer's advice. He answered contemptuously, 'Lawyers are servants!' The social position of the Lord Chancellor and other legal officers of the Crown meant no more to him than the preponderance of lawyers in the councils of the nation. He stuck to the futile stupidity that any man who used his brains to earn a living was an inferior. This is an extreme case of an exceptionally stupid standpoint, but the psychological root of the attitude permeates English conceptions. The definition of self-respect contains a clause to include pitiless contempt for some other class. In my childhood, Mrs Clapham—one of whose adventures has been already recorded

—once came to the grain in conjugal infelicity. 'How could I ever love that man?' she exclaimed; 'why, he takes his salt with his knife!' There is nothing to warn a fishmonger's wife that such sublime devotion to etiquette is in any way ridiculous. English society is impregnated from top to bottom with this spirit. The supreme satisfaction is to be able to despise one's neighbour and this fact goes far to account for religious intolerance. It is evidently consoling to reflect that the people next door are headed for hell.

Practically all boys are born with the aristocratic spirit.* In most cases they are broken down, partly by bullying, partly by experience. In the case of Alick, he was the only son of a father who was naturally a leader of men. In him, therefore, this spirit grew unchecked. He knew no superior but his father; and though that father ostentatiously avoided assuming authority over the other Brethren, it was, of course, none the less there. The boy seems to have despised from the first the absence of hierarchy among the Brethren, though at the same time they formed the most exclusive body on earth, being the only people that were going to heaven. There is thus an extreme psychological contradiction inherent in the situation. It is improbable that Alick was aware at the time of the real feelings which must have been implanted in him by this environment; but the main result was undoubtedly to stimulate his pride and ambition in a most unwholesome (?) degree. His social and financial position, the obvious envy of his associates, his undoubted personal prowess, physical and intellectual, all combined to make it impossible for him to be satisfied to take any place in the world but the top. The Plymouth Brethren refused to take any part in politics. Among them, the peer and the peasant met theoretically as equals, so that the social system of England was simply ignored. The boy could not aspire to become prime minister or even king; he was already apart from and beyond all that. It will be seen that as soon as he arrived at an age where ambitions are compelled to assume concrete form, his position became extremely difficult. The earth was not big enough to hold him.

In looking back over his life up to May 1886, he can find little consecution and practically no coherence in his recollections. But from that month onwards there is a change. It is as if the event which occurred at that time created a new faculty

* It is purely a question of virility: compare the noble races, Arabs, Pathans, Ghurkas, Japanese, etc. with the 'moral' races. Of course, absence of caste determines loss of virility and vice versa.

in his mind. A new factor had arisen and its name was death. He was called home from school in the middle of the term to attend a special prayer meeting at Redhill. His father had been taken ill. The local doctor had sent him to see Sir James Paget, who had advised an immediate operation for cancer of the tongue. Brethren from far and near had been summoned to help to discover the Lord's will in the matter. The upshot was that the operation was declined; it was decided to treat the disease by Count Mattei's electro-homeopathy, a now discarded system of unusually outrageous quackery. No doctor addicted to this form of swindling being locally available, The Grange was given up and a house called Glenburnie taken at Southampton.

On March 5th, 1887, Edward Crowley died. The course of the disease had been practically painless. Only one point is of interest to our present purpose. On the night of March 5th, the boy—away at school—dreamed that his father was dead. There was no reason for this in the ordinary way, as the reports had been highly optimistic. The boy remembers that the quality of the dream was entirely different from anything that he had known. The news of the death did not arrive in Cambridge till the following morning. The interest of this fact depends on a subsequent parallel. During the years that followed, the boy—and the man—dreamed repeatedly that his mother was dead; but on the day of her death he—then three thousand miles away—had the same dream, save that it differed from the others by possessing this peculiar indescribable but unmistakable quality that he remembered in connection with the death of his father.

From the moment of the funeral the boy's life entered on an entirely new phase. The change was radical. Within three weeks of his return to school he got into trouble for the first time. He does not remember for what offence,* but only that his punishment was diminished on account of his bereavement. This was the first symptom of a complete reversal of his attitude to life in every respect. It seems obvious that his father's death must have been causally connected with it. But even so, the events remain inexplicable. The conditions of his school life, for instance, can hardly have altered, yet his reaction to them makes it almost incredible that it was the same boy.

---

* On revision, he thinks it was 'talking on the march', a whispered word to the other half of his scale of the 'crocodile'.

Previous to the death of Edward Crowley, the recollections of his son, however vivid or detailed, appear to him strangely impersonal. In throwing back his mind to that period, he feels, although attention constantly elicits new facts, that he is investigating the behaviour of somebody else. It is only from this point that he begins to think of himself in the first person. From this point, however, he does so; and is able to continue this autohagiography in a more conventional style by speaking of himself as I.

4

I had naturally no idea at the time that the death of my father would make any practical difference to my environment. In most similar cases it probably would not have done so. Most widows naturally remain in the groove.

As things were, I found myself in a totally new environment. My father's religious opinions had tended to alienate him from his family; and the friends whom he had made in his own circle had no interest in visiting my mother. I was thrown into the atmosphere of her family. She moved to London in order to be near her brother, whom till then I had hardly met.

Tom Bond Bishop was a prominent figure in religious and philanthropic circles in London. He held a more or less important position in the Custom House, but had no ambitions connected with the Civil Service. He devoted the whole of his spare time and energy to the propagation of the extraordinarily narrow, ignorant and bigoted Evangelicalism in which he believed. He had founded the Children's Scripture Union and the Children's Special Service Mission. The former dictates to children what passages of the Bible they shall read daily: the latter drags them from their play at the seaside and hands them over to the ravings of pious undergraduates or hired gospel-geysers. Within his limits, he was a man of acute intelligence and great executive and organizing ability. A Manning plus bigoted sincerity; a Cotton Mather minus imagination; one might even say a Paul deprived of logical ability, and this defect supplied by invulnerable cocksureness. He was inaccessible to doubt; he *knew* that he was *right* on every point.

I once put it to him: suppose a climber roped to another who has fallen. He cannot save him and must fall also unless he cut the rope. What should he do? My uncle replied, 'God would never allow a man to be placed in such a position'!!!! This unreason made him mentally and morally lower than the cattle of the fields. He obeyed blind savage impulses and took them for the sanctions of the Almighty.

'To the lachrymal glands of a crocodile he added the bowels of compassion of a cast-iron rhinoceros; with the meanness

and cruelty of a eunuch he combined the calculating avarice
of a Scotch Jew, without the whisky of the one or the sympathetic imagination of the other. Perfidious and hypocritical as
the Jesuit of Protestant fable, he was unctuous as Uriah Heep,
and for the rest possessed the vices of Joseph Surface and
Tartuffe; yet, being without the human weaknesses which
make them possible, he was a more virtuous, and therefore a
more odious, villain.

'In feature resembling a shaven ape, in figure a dislocated
dachshund, his personal appearance was at the first glance un-
attractive. But the clothes made by a City tailor lent such
general harmony to the whole as to reconcile the observer to
the phenomenon observed.

'Of unrivalled cunning, his address was plausible; he concealed his genius under a mask of matchless mediocrity and
his intellectual force under the cloak of piety. In religion he
was an Evangelical, that type of Nonconformist who remains
in the Church in the hope of capturing its organization and its
revenues.

'An associate of such creatures of an inscrutable Providence as Coote and Torrey, he surpassed the one in sanctimoniousness, the other in bigotry, though he always thought
blackmail too risky and slander a tactical error.' *

No more cruel fanatic, no meaner villain, ever walked this
earth. My father, wrong-headed as he was, had humanity and
a certain degree of common-sense; he had a logical mind and
never confused spiritual with material issues. He could never
have believed, like my uncle, that the cut and colour of 'Sunday
clothes' could be a matter of importance to the Deity. Having
decided that faith and not works was essential to salvation, he
could not attach any vital importance to works. With him, the
reason for refraining from sin was simply that it showed in-
gratitude to the Saviour. In the case of the sinner, it was
almost a hopeful sign that he should sin thoroughly. He was
more likely to reach that conviction of sin which would show
him his need of salvation. The material punishment of sin
(again) was likely to bring him to knees. Good works in the
sinner were worthless. 'All our righteousness is as filthy rags.'
It was the devil's favourite trick to induce people to rely on
their good character. The parable of the pharisee and the publican taught this clearly enough.

I do not know whether my Uncle Tom could have found any

---

* I quote from an obituary of him published during his life.[1]

arguments against this theory, but in practice he had a horror of what he called sin which was exaggerated almost to the point of insanity. His talents, I may almost say his genius,* gave him tremendous influence. In his own house he was a ruthless, petty tyrant; and it was into this den of bitter slavery that I was suddenly hurled from my position of fresh air, freedom and heirship.

He lived in London, in what was then called Thistle Grove. The name has since been changed to Drayton Gardens, despite a petition enthusiastically supported by Bishop; the objection was that a public house in the neighbourhood was called the Drayton Arms. This is typical of my uncle's attitude to life. His sense of humour. When I called him 'Uncle', he would snigger, 'Oh my prophetic soul, my uncle!' But the time came when I knew most of *Hamlet* by heart, and when he next shot off his 'joke', I continued the quotation, replying sternly, 'Ay, that incestuous, that adulterate beast!'—I am, in a way, glad to think that at the end of his long and obscene life I was reconciled with him. The very last letter he ever received from me admitted (if a little grudgingly) that his mind was so distorted that he had really no idea how vile a thing he was. I think this must have stirred his sense of shame. At least, I never received any answer.

I suppose that the household at Thistle Grove was as representative of one part of England as could possibly have been imagined. It was nondescript. It was neither upper nor lower middle-class. It had not sufficient individuality even to belong to a category. My grandmother was a particularly charming old lady. She was inexpressibly dignified in her black silks and her lace cap. She had been imported from the country by the exigencies of her son's position in the Civil Service. She was extremely lovable; I never remember hearing a cross word fall from her. She was addicted to the infamous vice of bezique. It was, of course, impossible to have 'The Devil's Picture Books' in a house frequented by the leading lights of Evangelicalism. But my Aunt Ada had painted a pack of cards in which the suits were roses, violets, etc. It was the same game; but the camouflage satisfied my uncle's conscience. No pharisee ever scoured the outside of the cup and platter more assiduously than he.

My grandmother was the second wife of her husband; of

---

* He devised a most ingenious method of teaching history by charts, each nation being represented by a river of greater or less breadth as it rose or fell, annexations by tributaries, etc., etc.

the first marriage there were two surviving children; Anne, a stout and sensual old maid, who always filled me with intense physical repulsion; she was shiny and greasy with a blob nose and thick wet lips. Every night she tucked a bottle of stout under her arm and took it to bed with her—adding this invariable 'joke'—'My baby!' Even today, when people happen to drink stout at a table where I am sitting, I manage instinctively not to see it.

Her brother John had lived for many years in Australia in enjoyment of wealth and civic distinction. His wealth failed when his health broke; and he returned to England to live with the family. He was a typical hardy out-door man with all the colonial freedom of thought, speech and manner. He found himself in the power of his half-brother's acrid code. He had to smoke his pipe by stealth and he was bullied about his soul until his mind gave way. At family prayers he was perpetually being prayed at; his personality being carefully described lest the Lord should mistake his identity. The description would have suited the average murderer as observed by a singularly uncharitable pacifist.

I am particularly proud of myself for the way I behaved to him. It was impossible to help liking the simple-minded genial soul of the man. I remember one day at Streatham, after he and my grandmother had come to live with us, that I tried to cheer him up. Shaking all over, he explained to me almost in tears that he was afraid he was 'not all right with Christ'. I look back almost with incredulity upon myself. It was not I that spoke; I answered him with brusque authority, though I was a peculiarly shy boy not yet sixteen. I told him plainly that the whole thing was nonsense, that Christ was a fable, that there was no such thing as sin, and that he ought to thank his stars that he had lived his whole life away from the hypocritical crew of trembling slaves who believed in such nonsense. Already my unconscious self was singing in my ears that terrific climax of Browning's 'Renan-chorus': [2]

> Oh, dread succession to a dizzy post,
> Sad sway of sceptre whose mere touch appals,
> Ghastly dethronement, cursed by those the most
> On whose repugnant brow the crown next falls!

However, he became melancholy-mad; and died in that condition. I remember writing to my mother and my uncle that they were guilty 'murder most foul as in the best it is; but this most foul, strange and unnatural'.

I lay weight upon this episode because my attitude, as I remember it, seems incompatible with my general spiritual life of the period, as will appear later.

I was genuinely fond of my Aunt Ada. She was womanly in the old-fashioned sense of the word; a purely passive type. Naturally talented though she was, she was both ignorant and bigoted. In her situation, she could not have been anything else. But her opinions did not interfere with her charity. A woman of infinite kindness. Her health was naturally delicate; an attack of rheumatic fever had damaged her heart and she died before her time. The meanness and selfishness of my Uncle Tom were principally responsible. He would not engage a secretary; he forced her to slave for the Scripture Union and it killed her.

One anecdote throws a curious light upon my character in these early days and also reveals her as possessed of a certain sense of humour. Some years before, on the platform at Redhill with my father, I had seen on the bookstall *Across Patagonia* by Lady Florence Dixie. The long name fascinated me; I begged him to buy it for me and he did. The name stuck and I decided to be King of Patagonia. Psycho-analysts will learn with pleasure that the name of my capital was Margaragstagregorstoryaka. 'Margar' was derived from Margaret, queen of Henry VI, who was my favourite character in history. This is highly significant, as indicating the type of woman that I have always admired. I want her to be wicked, independent, courageous, ambitious, and so on. I cannot place the 'ragstag', but it is probably euphonic. 'Gregor' is, of course, my cousin; 'story' is what was then my favourite form of amusement. I cannot place the 'yaka', but that again is probably euphonic.

I cannot imagine why, at this very early age, I cultivated a profound aversion to, and contempt for, Queen Victoria. Merely, perhaps, the clean and decent instinct of a child! I announced my intention of leading the forces of Patagonia against her. One day my Aunt Ada took me to tea at Gunters'; and an important-looking official document was handed to me. It was Queen Victoria's reply. She was going to blow my capital to pieces and treat me personally in a very unpleasant manner. This document was sealed with a label marked with an anchor to suggest naval frightfulness, taken for this purpose from the end of a reel of cotton. But I took the document quite seriously and was horribly frightened.

The dinginess of my uncle's household, the atmosphere of severe disapproval of the universe in general, and the utter absence of the spirit of life, combined to make me detest my mother's family. There was, incidentally, a grave complication, for my father's death had increased the religious bigotry of my mother very greatly; and although she was so fond of her family, she was bound to regard them as very doubtful candidates for heaven. This attitude was naturally inexplicable to a child of such tender years; and the effect on me was to develop an almost petulant impatience with the whole question of religion. My Aunt Ada was my mother's favourite sister; yet at her funeral she refused to enter the church during the service and waited outside in the rain, only rejoining the procession when the corpse repassed those accursèd portals on its way to the cemetery. She stood by the grave while the parson read the service. It was apparently the architectural diabolism to which she most objected.

There was also an objection to the liturgy, on numerous grounds. It seems incredible, but is true, that the Plymouth Brethren regarded the Lord's Prayer as a 'vain repetition, as do the heathen'. It was forbiddben to use it!! Jesus had indeed given this prayer as an example of how to pray; but everyone was expected to make up his own supplications ex tempore.

The situation resulted in a very amusing way. Having got to the point of saying, 'Evil, be thou my good,' I racked my brains to discover some really abominable crimes to do. In a moment of desperate daring I sneaked one Sunday morning into the church frequented by my Uncle Tom on Streatham Common, prepared, so to speak, to wallow in it. It was one of the most bitter disappointments of my life! I could not detect anything which satisfied my ideas of damnation.

For a year or two after my father's death my mother did not seem to settle down; and during the holidays we either stayed with Bishop or wandered in hotels and hydros. I think she was afraid of bringing me up in London; but when my uncle moved to Streatham she compromised by taking a house in Polwarth Road. I hated it, because there were bigger houses in the neighbourhood.

I am not quite sure whether I am the most outrageous snob that ever lived, or whether I am not a snob at all. The truth of the matter is, I think, that I will not acquiesce in anything but the very best of its kind. I don't in the least mind going without a thing altogether, but if I have it at all it has got to be A1. England is a very bad place for me. I cannot endure people who are either superior or inferior to others, but only those who, whatever their station in life, are consciously unique and supreme. In the East, especially among Mohammedans, one can make friends with the very coolies; they respect themselves and others. They are gentlemen. But in England the spirit of independence is rare. Men of high rank and position nearly always betray consciousness of inferiority to, and dependence upon, others. Snobbishness, in this sense, is so widely spread that I rarely feel at home, unless with a supreme genius like Augustus John.

Aubrey Tanqueray is typical. He must not forfeit the esteem of his 'little parish', and avoids mortification by shifting from one parish to another. When Paula asks him, 'Do you trouble yourself about what servants *think?*' he answers, 'Of course.' [3] If one had to worry about one's actions in respect of other people's ideas, one might as well be buried alive in an antheap or married to an ambitious violinist. Whether that man is the prime minister, modifying his opinions to catch votes, or a bourgeois in terror lest some harmless act should be misunderstood and outrage some petty convention, that man is an inferior man and I do not want to have anything to do with him any more than I want to eat canned salmon. Of course the world forces us all to compromise with our environment to some extent, and we only waste our strength if we fight pitched battles for points which are not worth a skirmish. It is only a faddist who refuses to conform with conventions of dress and the like. But our sincerity should be Roman about things that really matter to us. And I am still in doubt, as I write these words, as to how far it is right to employ strategy and diplomacy in order to gain one's point. The great men of the world have stood up and taken their medicine. Bradlaugh and Burton did not lose in the end by being downright. I never approved the super-subtlety of Huxley's campaign against Gladstone; and as for Swinburne, he died outright when he became respectable. Adaptation to one's environment makes for a sort of survival; but after all, the supreme victory is only won by those who prove themselves of so much harder stuff than the rest that no power on earth is able to destroy them. The people who have really made history are the martyrs.

I suppose that there comes to all of us only too often the feeling which Freud calls the Œdipus complex. We want to repose, to be at peace with our fellows whom we love, who misunderstand us and for whose love we are hungry. We want to make terms, we want to surrender. But I have always found that, though I could acquiesce in some such line of conduct, though I could make all preparations for accommodation, yet when it came to the point, I was utterly unable to do the base, irrevocable act. I cannot even do evil that good may come. I abhor Jesuitry. I would rather lose than win by stratagem. The utmost that I have been able to manage is to consent to put forward my principles in a form which will not openly outrage ordinary susceptibilities. But I feel so profoundly the urgency of doing my will that it is practically impossible for me to write on Shakespeare and the Musical Glasses without introducing the spiritual and moral principles which are the only things in myself that I can identify with myself.

This characteristic is evidently inherited from my father. His integrity was absolute. He lived entirely by his theological convictions. Christ might return at any moment. 'Even as the lightning lighteneth out of the East and lighteneth even unto the West, so is the coming of the Son of Man.' He would have to give an account of 'every idle word'. It was a horrifying thought to him that he might be caught by the Second Advent at a moment when he was not actively and intensely engaged on the work which God had sent him into the world to do. This sense of the importance of the lightest act, of the value of every moment, has been a tragically intense factor in my life. I have always grudged the time necessary for eating, sleeping and dressing. I have invented costumes with the sole object of minimizing the waste of time * and the distraction of attention involved. I never wear underclothing. The 'magnetism' of men and women has for its physical basis sweat: in health this is sparse and very fragrant. Any defect should be instantly remedied: there is no surer danger sign than foul or unduly profuse perspiration.

This quality determined much of my life at school. I instinctively understood that I did not want academic knowledge as such; but since I was under duress, the best plan for avoiding interruption was to acquit myself well in class and in examination. I had no ambitions; but I invariably set myself to acquire the necessary knowledge with the minimum of exertion. My natural abilities, especially my memory, made this easy. I soon discovered that to distinguish myself in school was in the nature of a conjurer's trick. It is hard to analyse my method or to be sure of the analysis; but I think the essence of the plan was to make certain of the minimum required and

---

* In Mexico City in 1900 Eckenstein counselled me to turn back the heels of my stockings to facilitate putting them on. I objected to the waste of time involved. This developed into a long argument on the point: he won, but I couldn't believe it and am yet unconverted.

to add a superstructure of one or two abstruse points which I would manage to bring to the notice of the master or the examiner so as to give him the idea that I had prepared myself with unusual thoroughness.

It occurs to me that this confession sounds rather strange, after my previous remarks about integrity. My justification is that I considered schoolmasters as importunate and possibly dangerous beggars. I was not in a position to fight; and I could not afford a good sixpence, so I put them off with a bad one. It was their own fault for plaguing me.

5

I found nothing in the school curriculum which interested me.
I had no inkling of it at the time, but I was already in the
thrall of the search for reality. Mathematics captured my imagination. I was brilliant at arithmetic until the subject degenerated into 'practice', which was a matter for grocers. I might
have liked geometry; but the arid method of presentation in
Euclid put me off. I was asked to memorize what I did not
understand; and, my memory being so good, it refused to be
insulted in that manner. Similarly, I could never memorize the
ordinary 'repetitions' of Greek and Latin poetry. I took to
trigonometry with ardour; but became disgusted as soon as
I found my calculations were to be applied to such vulgarities
as architecture. The only pure science for me was algebra
and I progressed in that with amazing rapidity. On one occasion, at Malvern, the mathematical master wished to devote
the whole hour to the three elder boys, who were going up
for some scholarship, and set us juniors to work out quadratic
equations. There were sixty-three in the chapter set. At the
end of forty minutes I stood up and said, 'Please, sir, what
shall I do now?' He would not believe that I had worked
them correctly, but I had. I seem to have an instinct for appreciating the relations of pure numbers and could find factors
by intuition.

My intellectual activity has always been intense. It was for
this very reason that I could not bear to waste a moment on
subjects which seemed to me alien to my interest, though I
had no idea what that interest was. As soon as I heard of
chemistry, I realized that it dealt with reality as I understood
the word. So I soon had 'Little Roscoe' [1] practically by heart,
though it was not a school subject. I furnished a laboratory in
the house at Streatham, and spent all my time and money in
making experiments. It may be interesting to mention how my
mind worked. I had heard of the petard as a military engine;
and I was hoist with it. Roscoe told me that chloride of nitro-
gen was the most powerful and sensitive explosive known. My
idea was to dissolve it in some volatile fluid; one could then

39

leave a bucket of it at the enemy's gate. The fluid would evaporate and the chloride explode at the first vibration. After several minor misadventures, I collected it over benzine—about a quart—and the whole thing exploded and nearly burnt the house down.

I had also a plan for manufacturing diamonds. By various analogies I came to the conclusion that a true solution of carbon might be made in iron and I proposed to crystallize it out in the regular way. The apparatus required was, however, hardly within the compass of a boy of fourteen and my diamonds are still theoretical.

Talking of theory, I came to the conclusion, which at that time was a damnable heresy and a dangerous delusion, that all the elements were modifications of one substance. My main argument was that the atomic weights of cobalt and nickel were practically identical and the characteristic colours of their salts suggested to me that they were geometrical isomers like dextrose and laevulose. This is all obvious enough today, but I still think that it was not bad for a boy in his 'teens in the early 'nineties, whose only source of information was 'Little Roscoe'.

An amusing situation arose out of this early devotion to the art of Flamel. In my last term at Malvern a panic-stricken board of governors determined to create a science side and and started a chemistry class. With laudable economy they put it in charge of one Mr Faber, a broken-down classical master, possibly in the belief that as he had a German name he knew as much as Ostwald. The result was that I had constantly to correct him in class; and he could do nothing, because the authorities, when consulted, proved to be on my side.

I had thus no difficulty at school as far as lessons were concerned, but in my three years at Champney's I had no lack of trouble; the nature of this can only be understood if I adduce a few facts to indicate the atmosphere. I used to tell people about my school life and met with such consistent incredulity that I made a little collection of incidents in the preface to my *The World's Tragedy*. I quote the passage as it stands.

A Boyhood in Hell

The Revd H. d'Arcy Champney, M.A. of Corpus Christi College, Cambridge, had come out of sect.

He had voted at the parliamentary elections by crossing

out the names of the candidates and writing, 'I vote for King Jesus.'

He had started a school for the sons of Brethren at 51 Bateman Street, Cambridge. May God bite into the bones of men the pain of that hell on earth (I have prayed often) that by them, it may be sowed with salt, accused for ever! May the maiden that passes it be barren and the pregnant woman that beholdeth it abort! May the birds of the air refuse to fly over it! May it stand as a curse, as a fear, as an hate, among men! May the wicked dwell therein! May the light of the sun be withheld therefrom and the light of the moon not lighten it! May it become the home of the shells of the dead and may the demons of the pit inhabit it! May it be accursed, accursed —accursed for ever and ever!

And still, standing as I stand in the prime of early manhood, free from all the fetters of the body and the mind, do I curse the memory thereof unto the ages.

It was a good enough school from the point of view of examiners, I dare say. Morally and physically, it was an engine of destruction and corruption. I am just going to put down a few facts haphazard as they come to my memory; you may form your own judgment.

1. We were allowed to play cricket, but not to score runs, lest it should excite the vice of 'emulation'.

2. Champney told me, a child of not yet twelve years old, that he had never consummated his marriage. (Only the very acute verbal memory which I possess enabled me years after to recall and interpret his meaning. He used a coarser phrase.)

3. We were told that 'the Lord had a special care of the school and brought to light that which was done in darkness,' etc., etc. ad nauseam. 'The instrument was on this occasion so-and-so, who had nobly come forward,' etc., etc. In other words, hypocrisy and sneaking were the only virtues.

Naturally, one of several boys who might be involved in the same offence would take fright and save his skin by sneaking. The informer was always believed implicitly, as against probability, or even possibility, with complete disregard of the testimony of other and independent witnesses.

For instance, a boy named Glascott, with insane taint, told Mr Champney that he had visited me (twelve years old) at my mother's house during the holidays—true so far, he had— and found me lying drunk at the bottom of the stairs. My mother was never asked about this; nor was I told of it. I was put into 'Coventry', i.e. no master nor boy might speak to me, or I to them. I was fed on bread and water; during play hours I worked in the schoolroom; during work hours I walked solitary round and round the playground. I was expected to 'confess' the crime of which I was not only innocent, but unaccused.

This punishment, which I believe criminal authorities would consider severe on a poisoner, went on for a term and a half. I was, at last, threatened with expulsion for my refusal to 'confess', and so dreadful a picture of the horrors of expulsion did they paint me—the guilty wretch, shunned by his fellows, slinks on through life to a dishonoured grave, etc.—that I actually chose to endure my tortures and to thank my oppressor.

Physically, I broke down. The strain and the misery affected my kidneys; and I had to leave school altogether for two years. I should add in fairness that there were other accusations against me, though, as you shall hear, almost equally silly.

I learnt at last, through the intervention of my uncle, in a lucid interval, what I was supposed to have done. I was said to have tried 'to corrupt Chamberlain'—not our great patriotic statesman, shifty Joe—but a boy. (I was twelve years old and quite ignorant of all sexual matters till long after.) Also I had 'held a mock prayer meeting'. This I remembered. I had strolled up to a group of boys in the playground, who were indeed holding one. As they saw me one said, 'Brother Crowley will now lead us in prayer.' Brother Crowley was too wary and walked away. But instead of doing what a wise boy would have done: gone straight to the head and accused them of forty-six distinct unmentionable crimes, I let things slide. So, fearing that I might go, they hurried off themselves and told him how that wicked Crowley had tried to lead them away from Jesus.

Worse, I had called Page I a pharisee. That was true; I had said it. Dreadful of me! And Page I, who 'walked very close to Jesus', of course went and told.

Yes, they all walked very close to Jesus—as close as Judas did.

4. A boy named Barton was sentenced to one hundred and twenty strokes of the cane on his bare shoulders, for some petty theft of which he was presumably innocent.

Superb was the process of trial. It began by an extra long prayer time and Joshua's account of the sin of Achan, impressively read. Next, an hour or two about the Lord's care of the school, the way He brought sin to light. Next, when well worked up and all our nerves on the jump, who stole what? Silence. Next, the Lord's care in providing a witness—like the witnesses against Naboth! Then the witness and his story, as smooth as a policeman's. Next, sentence. Last, execution, with intervals of prayer!

Champney's physique being impaired, one may suppose by his excessive devotion to Jesus, he arranged to give sixty strokes one day and sixty the next.

My memory fails—perhaps Barton will one day oblige with

his reminiscences—but I fancy the first day came so near to killing him that he escaped the second.

I remember one licking I got—on the legs, because flogging the buttocks excites the victim's sensuality!—fifteen minutes prayer, fifteen strokes of the cane, fifteen minutes more prayer, fifteen more strokes—and more prayer to top it!

5. On Sunday the day was devoted to 'religion'. Morning prayers and sermon (about forty-five minutes). Morning 'meeting' (one and a half to two hours). Open-air preaching on Parker's Piece* (say one hour). Bible reading and learning by heart. Reading of the few books 'sanctioned for Sunday' (say two hours). Prayer meeting (called voluntary, but to stay away meant that some sneak in the school would accuse you of something next day) (say one hour). Evening prayer and sermon (say thirty minutes). Preaching of the gospel in the meetingroom (one and a half hours). Ditto on Parker's Piece (say one hour). Prayer before retiring (say half an hour).

6. The 'Badgers' meeting'. Every Monday night the school was ranged round the back of the big schoolroom, and the scourings of Barnswell (Cambridge's slum) let in, fed, preached to and dismissed.

Result, epidemics of ringworm, measles and mumps.

Oh no! not a result; the Lord's hand was heavy upon us because of some undiscovered sin.

I might go on for a long while, but I will not. I hope there are some people in the world happy enough to think that I am lying, or at least exaggerating. But I pledge my word to the literal truth of all I have said, and there are plenty of witnesses alive to confirm me, or to refute me. I have given throughout the actual names, addresses and other details.

It is impossible to suppose that the character of the school had completely changed between my father's death and my return from the funeral. Yet before that I was completely happy and in sympathy with my surroundings. Not three weeks later, Ishmael was my middle name. I cannot account for it at all satisfactorily. I had been perfectly genuine in my ambition to lead a life of holiness; the idea of intimate communion with 'Jesus' was constantly present to my mind. I do not remember any steps in the volte-face. I asked one of the masters one day how it was that Jesus was three days and three nights in the grave, although crucified on Friday and risen

---

* Evangelizing was almost all plain terrorism. Besides the torments of hell, there were 'judgments'. For instance, the Blasphemous Butcher who, begged to get 'washed in the Blood of the Lamb', replied 'Right you are, I've got a lamb of my own.' *And that very same night his reason tottered on its throne*, etc.

again on Sunday morning. He could not explain and said that it had never been explained. So I formulated the ambition to become a shining light in Christianity by doing this thing that had never yet been done. This idea, by the way, is very characteristic. I am totally unable to take any interest in doing anything which has been done before. But tell me of an alleged impossibility; and health, wealth, life itself are nothing. I am out to do it. The apparent discrepancy in the gospel narrative aroused no doubt in my mind as to the literal truth of either of the texts. Indeed, my falling away from grace was not occasioned by any intellectual qualms; I accepted the theology of the Plymouth Brethren. In fact, I could hardly conceive of the existence of people who might doubt it. I simply went over to Satan's side; and to this hour I cannot tell why.

But I found myself as passionately eager to serve my new master as I had been to serve the old. I was anxious to distinguish myself by commiting sin. Here again my attitude was extraordinarily subtle. It never occurred to me to steal or in any other way to infringe the decalogue. Such conduct would have been petty and contemptible. I wanted a supreme spiritual sin; and I had not the smallest idea how to set about it. There was a good deal of morbid curiosity among the saints about 'the sin against the Holy Ghost' which 'could never be forgiven'. Nobody knew what it was. It was even considered rather blasphemous to offer any very positive conjecture on the point. The idea seems to have been that it was something like an ill-natured practical joke on the part of Jesus. This mysterious offence which could never be forgiven might be inadvertently committed by the greatest saint alive, with the result that he would be bowled out at the very gate of glory. Here was another impossibility to catch my youthful fancy; I must find out what that sin was and do it very thoroughly.

For (evidently) my position was exceedingly precarious. I was opposed to an omnipotent God; and for all I knew to the contrary, He might have predestined me to be saved. No matter how much I disbelieved in Jesus, no matter how many crimes I piled up, He might get me in spite of myself. The only possibility of outwitting Him was to bring Him up against His own pledge that this particular sin should never be forgiven, with a certificate from the recording angel that I had duly done it.

It seems incredible that such insane conclusions should form the basis of practical action in any human being above the level of a bushman. But they follow logically enough from the blasphemous and superstitious premisses of Christian theology. Besides this, I had never a moment's inclination to take the material world seriously. In the *Apologia pro Vita Sua*, Cardinal Newman tells us, I suspect truthfully, that as a child he wished that *The Arabian Nights* were true. As we all know, he gratified his ambitions by accepting for reality the Freudian phantasm of hashed-up paganism with Semitic sauce which led him to the hat. But I went further. My senses and my rational judgment created a subconscious feeling of uneasiness that supernaturalism might not be true. This insulted my inmost consciousness of myself. But the reply was not to accept the false for the true, but to determine to make it true. I resolved passionately to reach the spiritual causes of phenomena, and to dominate the material world which I detested by their means. I was not content to believe in a personal devil and serve him, in the ordinary sense of the word. I wanted to get hold of him personally and become his chief of staff.

In my search for a suitable sin which might earn me the diabolical V.C., I obviously enough came in touch with the usual thing. Champney was always sniffing around it, but—to me—he was completely unintelligible. I frequented the boys whose reputation for wickedness was best established, and was further directed in my inquiry by an intuitive sense of magnetism or appreciation of physiognomy. But the reign of terror was so firmly established in the school that nobody dared tell me outright the nature of this sin, even when the knowledge of it was admitted. Mysterious hints were given; and at last a boy named Gibson told me what action to make, but he did not tell me to what object to apply the process. It seems extraordinary that nature should have afforded me no indication. I nowise connected the organ of reproduction with any voluntary act. I made conjectures dictated by purely intellectual considerations, and carried out experiments based on their results; but they were absolutely ill-directed. I never guessed what organ was in question. The discovery was delayed for years.

My revolt must have manifested itself by actions which were technically not blameworthy. I cannot accuse myself of any overt crime. The battle between myself and the school was conducted on the magical plane, so to speak. It was as if I had made wax figures of the most inoffensive sort, that yet were recognized by the spiritual instinct of Champney as idols or instruments of witchcraft. I was punished with absolute injustice and stupidity, yet at the same time the mystical apprehension of Champney made no mistake.

6

I must mention the intervention of my Uncle Jonathan in the matter of the Badgers' meeting, and that of my Uncle Tom in the final eruption.

Jonathan Crowley, my father's elder brother, was the beau ideal of the noble patrician. He looked like a Roman emperor as we romantically imagine him to have been, not as we see him in most sculpture. The tremendous brow, the eagle eyes, the great hooked arrogant nose, the firm mouth and the indomitable jaw combined to make him one of the most strikingly handsome men that I have ever seen.

He lived in a stately splendour which had no hint of ostentation. I never knew his first wife, by whom he had two children, Claude and Agnes. Claude was strikingly ugly, so much so as to be attractive, and he had a touch of deformity without being actually a hunchback. The same traits appeared in his mental and moral character. I always thought of him admiringly as Richard III; but he was merely weak and feeble-minded. Agnes inherited her father's aristocratic haughtiness and a share of his good looks. She was too proud to marry and the repression preyed on her mind until she developed an idée fixe. For the last thirty years of her life she was constantly announcing her engagement and drawing up marriage contracts, which never came to anything. She was also possessed by the demon of litigation, and imagined herself wronged by various members of the family.

My uncle married the governess of the children. This was a lady of a distinguished Saxon family who could trace her pedigree to the time of Edward the Confessor. Tall, thin, distinguished and highly educated, she made an admirable chatelaine. Her personality appealed strongly to me, and she took that place in my affections which I could not give to my mother. She became a prominent member of the Primrose League, and it was through her influence with Lord Salisbury and Lord Ritchie that I obtained my nomination for the Diplomatic Service.

My uncle and aunt visited me at Cambridge. I told them about the Badgers' meeting, not in a spirit of complaint, but rather as Sir Richard Burton might have described his adventures among savages. Uncle Jonathan did not see the matter in that light at all. He made inquiries which confirmed my story; and told Champney point blank that this sort of thing had got to stop. Champney attempted to bluster, but on being threatened with the sanitary authorities, knuckled under. The matter, however, did not stop there. My uncle saw clearly that I was being brutally ill-treated; and he made an application to the courts which resulted in my being called to see Mr Justice Stirling in chambers. I have always been intensely loyal even to my enemies, and (for all I knew) the judge might send my mother and her brother to prison. So I lied like a little man and pretended that I was perfectly happy at the school. I do not think that he was entirely fooled by my protestations; and although I was not made a ward in Chancery, a promise was exacted that I should go to a public school and university as soon as I had passed the 'Cambridge Local'.

Meanwhile, nature took my part. At the end of the first term of my punishment I was so obviously ill during the holidays that questions were asked, and I complained to my mother of the ill-treatment. Instead of investigating the circumstances, they sent for Champney without saying anything to me. I was taken over to my Uncle Tom's house one evening and found myself penned in a corner of the room by the fulminating headmaster. The surprise terrified me and I did not dare to deny anything. But there was still no accusation made against me. Champney did not even tell my mother and Uncle Tom what I was supposed to have done. I was sent back to the school to serve the remainder of my sentence. At the end of that term, however, for some reason whose nature I cannot guess, Uncle Tom decided to come up to Cambridge and make further inquiries. Warned of the visit, Champney put on extra pressure. I must confess or be expelled. I did my utmost to invent satisfactory abominations; but as of course these were not connected in any way with the real accusations, I merely made matters worse. On Uncle Tom's arrival I once more resorted to telling the simple truth, that I had no idea what I had done. This time my uncle lapsed from righteousness to the extent of insisting on knowing what the accusations were. Champney told him. My uncle had sense enough to see that they were all absurd, put down Champney for a lunatic, and took me away from the school. As a matter of fact, within a very short time the insanity of the headmaster became patent and the school was broken up in consequence.

As regards myself, the mischief had been done. I, who had been a happy, healthy, good-natured, popular boy, had learned to endure complete solitude for months at a time. I spoke to no boy and the masters always addressed me, when necessity compelled them, with sanctimonious horror. The bread and water diet, and the punishment of perpetual walking round the playground during school hours, had broken down my constitution. I was taken to a doctor, who found that I was suffering severely from albuminuria, and predicted that I should never live to come of age. I was put on special diet and prescribed a course of country life with a tutor. During the next year or two I was constantly travelling round Wales and Scotland, climbing mountains and fishing for trout. I also had one delightful summer at St Andrews where Andrew Kirkaldy taught me to play golf. My health rapidly improved. I was allowed to work a very limited number of hours, but I progressed rapidly, having the undivided attention of my tutors.

These persons, however, were not too satisfactory; they were all my Uncle Tom's nominees; that is, they were of the sawny, anaemic, priggish type, who at the best could boast of minor Cambridge * colleges. Of course, I considered it my duty to outwit them in every possible way and hunt up some kind of sin.

This uncle, by the way, some years later, contributed what he esteemed a brilliantly witty article to the *Boys' Magazine*, the organ of an Evangelical attempt to destroy the manhood of our public schools. It was called *The Two Wicked Kings*. These were described as tyrants who ruined the lives of boys and enslaved them. Their names were Smo-King and Drin-King. Uncle Tom called my attention to his masterpiece and I said, with shocked surprise, 'But, my dear Uncle, you have forgotten to mention a third, the most dangerous and deadly of all!' He couldn't think who that was. I told him. Now, I ask you, is it not deplorable that so important and accurate an addition to his thesis should not have been accepted with pious glee?

Things went from bad to worse as I grew in moral power. Part of the time I was well enough to go to a day school in

---

* Oxford was *anathema maranatha* to my Uncle Tom. Keble! Manning!! Newman!!! procurers to the lords of hell far subtler and more fearful than Darwin, Huxley and Tyndall.

Streatham, where I learnt at long last the terrible secret which I had racked my brains to discover for nearly three years. Here was certainly a sin worth sinning and I applied myself with characteristic vigour to its practice.

As my father had been accustomed to drink wine, I could not see how drinking could be a sin. There was, therefore, no object in doing it. I never touched wine until I got to Trinity and I have never felt the smallest temptation to excess. My father had, however, not been a smoker, saying that if God had intended men to smoke He would have supplied a chimney at the top of the head.* I had no hesitation, therefore, in making a great point of smoking. I had no thought of connecting the service of the 'third King' with the reproduction of the species, and therefore no reason to suppose that my father had ever so far forgotten himself. I spent my whole time trying to enrol myself under the royal banner; but this could only be done by cooperation and it was some time before I found the means.

To return to my tutors. Relations were invariably strained. On one occasion the Rev. Fothergill had taken me for the summer to a fishing centre near Lairg called Forsinard. We went fishing one day to a loch over the moors and in the course of some argument I threw his rod far into the water. He attacked me with a fury, but I got a good hold and threw him after it. I then went off in the boat, but he caught me as I was pushing off, overturned the boat on top of me and tried to drown me. That night the gods still further favoured me, for a village girl named Belle McKay found herself with nothing better to do than to roam with me amid the heather. We returned together quite openly and Fothergill threw up the sponge. He took me back to London the next morning. Breaking the journey at Carlisle, I repeated my victory with a buxom chambermaid.

But murder is not the only amusement open to pious tutors. The brother of the Dean of Westminster (he subsequently became a missionary and died at Lokoja) had been taught that if he couldn't be good he should be careful. While he was actually in charge of me his conduct was irreproachable, but after giving me up he invited me over to his mother's house at Maze Hill to spend the night, and did his best to live up to the reputation of his cloth. I did not allow him to succeed, not because I could see no sin in it, but because I thought it was

---

* One might surely argue that His most generous device was the adaptation of tobacco to the nerves of taste and smell.

a trap to betray me to my family. Just before he left for Africa he invited me again, prayed with me, confessed to his offence, excusing himself on the ground that his elder brother Jack, also a missionary, had led him astray, and asked my pardon. Once again I adopted the attitude of the man of the world, 'Tut, tut, my dear fellow, don't mention it,' which annoyed him very much, because he wanted to be taken seriously as the chief of sinners.

One of the principal points about the sin stupidity is that it flatters the sinner. All insanity depends upon the exacerbation of the ego. The melancholic hugs the delusion that he has committed the unpardonable sin. Sins grow by repression and by brooding upon their enormity. Few people would go to excess if they were not unwholesomely over-excited about their trivial apishness.

Most people, especially Freud, misunderstand the Freudian position. 'The libido of the unconscious' is really 'the true will of the inmost self'. The sexual characteristics of the individual are, it is true, symbolic indications of its nature, and when those are 'abnormal', we may suspect that the self is divided against itself in some way. Experience teaches the adepts who initiate mankind that when any complex (duality) in the self is resolved (unity) the initiate becomes whole. The morbid sexual symptoms (which are merely the complaints of the sick animal) disappear, while the moral and mental consciousness is relieved from its civil war of doubt and self-obsession. The complete man, harmonized, flows freely towards his natural goal.

It will be seen that I had developed enormously in these years. Unfortunately, my misery was so great during this long battle with my tyrants that, while the incidents themselves stand out luminously in focus, I find it very hard to remember the order in which they occurred. There are, moreover, curious contradictions in myself against which I seem always to be stumbling. For example, as late as 1894, I think it must be, I find myself writing hymns of quite acceptable piety. One was published in *The Christian;* it began:

> I am a blind man on a helmless ship
> Without a compass on a stormy sea.
> I cannot sink, for God will hold me up, etc.

Again, I wrote a poem on the death of my Aunt Ada, which I thought good enough to include in my *Songs of the Spirit,* and is entirely irreproachable on the score of piety. It seems as if I possessed a theology of my own which was, to all intents and purposes, Christianity. My satanism did not interfere with it at all; I was trying to take the view that the Christianity of hypocrisy and cruelty was not true Christianity. I did not hate God or Christ, but merely the God and Christ of the people whom I hated. It was only when the development of my logical faculties supplied the demonstration that the Scriptures support the theology and practice of professing Christians that I was compelled to set myself in opposition to the Bible itself. It does not matter that the literature is sometimes magnificent and that in isolated passages the philosophy and ethics are admirable. The sum of the matter is that Judaism is a savage, and Christianity a fiendish, superstition.

It is very strange that I should have had no inkling of my tendency to Mysticism and Magick by means of any definite experience. It is true that, from the beginning, I held the transcendental view of the universe, but there was nothing to back it up in the way of experience. Most children have a touch of poetry and believe in what I hate to call psychic phenomena, at least to the extent of fancying they see fairies or being scared of 'bugges by night'. But I, although consciously engaged in the battle with 'principalities and powers', never had the slightest hallucination of sense or any tendency to imagine things ghostly. I might have had an ambition to see the devil and talk things over with him, but I should have expected such communication to be either perfectly material or perfectly intellectual. I had no idea of nuances. When I eventually learnt how to use my astral eyes and ears, there was no confusion; the other world had certain correspondences with our own, but it was perfectly distinct. I seem to have made a very determined effort to prevent the obliteration of my spiritual consciousness of the world beyond the veil by the ink of terrestrial experience. Then again, there are sudden outbreaks of a fully formed personality, in which I spoke with the assurance and authority of a man of fifty on subjects on which I had really no opinion at all in the ordinary sense of the word.

There is one amazing incident; at the age of fourteen as near as I can remember. I must premise that I have always been exceptionally tender-hearted, except to tyrants, for whom I think no tortures bad enough. In particular, I am uniformly kind to animals; no question of cruelty or sadism arises in the incident which I am about to narrate.

I had been told 'A cat has nine lives.' I deduced that it must be practically impossible to kill a cat. As usual, I became full of ambition to perform the feat. (Observe that I took my information unquestioningly *au pied de la lettre*.) Perhaps through some analogy with the story of Hercules and the hydra, I got it into my head that the nine lives of the cat must be taken more or less simultaneously. I therefore caught a cat, and having administered a large dose of arsenic I chloroformed it, hanged it above the gas jet, stabbed it, cut its throat, smashed its skull and, when it had been pretty thoroughly burnt, drowned it and threw it out of the window that the fall might remove the ninth life. In fact, the operation was successful; I had killed the cat. I remember that all the time I was genuinely sorry for the animal; I simply forced myself to carry out the experiment in the interest of pure science.

The combination of innocence, ignorance, knowledge, ingenuity and high moral principle seems extraordinary. It is evident that the insanely immoral superstition in which I had been brought up is responsible for so atrocious an absurdity. Again and again we shall see how the imposition of the anti-natural theory and principles of Christianity upon a peculiarly sane, matter-of-fact, reality-facing genius created a conflict whose solution was expressed on the material plane by some extravagant action. My mind is severely logical; or, rather, it was so until mystic experience enabled it to shake off its fetters. Logic is responsible for most of the absurd and abominable deeds which have disgraced history. Given Christian premisses, the Inquisition was acting in accordance with the highest humanitarian principles in destroying a man's body to save his soul. The followers of Descartes were right to torture animals, believing them to be automata. Genuine determinists would be justified in committing any crime, since the fact of its occurrence would prove that it was unavoidable. Huxley, in *Evolution and Ethics,* makes out a very poor case against infanticide and race suicide. We are constantly using our judgment to preserve one section of humanity as against another; we are in fact constantly compelled to do so. As for the future of humanity, the certainty of final extermination when the planet becomes uninhabitable makes all human endeavour a colossal fatuity.

It is one of the principal theses of this book to show the above statement to be absurd, by offering a theory of reality compatible with sanity.

However, that comes later.

'The best laid plans of mice and men gang aft agley.' Even so
cunning a combination of rat and ape as my Uncle Tom made
occasional mistakes, and one of these was very fortunate for
me. He engaged a tutor named Archibald Douglas, an Oxford
man who had purged that offence by having travelled for the
Bible Society across Persia. If my uncle had ever heard of
George Borrow, he might have saved himself much trouble;
and I might have been driven insane. It was in the spring of
'91. I had recovered from a bad attack of whooping-cough.
The idea was that we should bicycle down to Torquay, but on
reaching Guildford I was too ill to ride further and we went
down by train. Though Douglas called himself a Christian,
he proved to be both a man and a gentleman. I presume that
poverty had compelled the camouflage. From the moment that
we were alone together he produced a complete revolution in my
outlook upon life, by showing me for the first time a sane, clear,
jolly world worth living in. Smoking and drinking were natural.
He warned me of the dangers of excess from the athletic standpoint. He introduced me to racing, billiards, betting, cards and
women. He told me how these things might be enjoyed without
damaging oneself or wronging others. He put me up to all the
tricks. He showed me the meaning of honour. I immediately
accepted his standpoint and began to behave like a normal,
healthy human being. The nightmare world of Christianity
vanished at the dawn. I fell in with a girl of the theatre in the
first ten days at Torquay, and at that touch of human love the
detestable mysteries of sex were transformed into joy and
beauty. The obsession of sin fell from my shoulders into the
sea of oblivion. I had been almost overwhelmed by the appalling responsibility of ensuring my own damnation and helping
others to escape from Jesus. I found that the world was, after
all, full of delightful damned souls; of people who accepted
nature as she is, accepted their own place in nature and enjoyed it, fought mean and despicable things fairly and firmly
whenever they met them. It was a period of boundless happiness for me. I had always yearned for the beauty of nature;

my only friends, except animals and occasional strangers, from whom I was carefully protected, had been the skies, the streams, the mountains and the seas. For the first time in my life I was brought into contact with my fellow men and women. For the first time honest friendship, wholesome love, frank, gay and courageous, became possible and actual. I had loved nature as a refuge from mankind. I now perceived the beauty of the world in conjunction with the beauty of my species. For the first time the sea sparkled, the breezes whispered other songs than those in praise of solitude, the flowers lent their fragrance and their folly to light, laughing girlhood; the moon, instead of Artemis, was Aphrodite.

> I said, 'she is warmer than Dian . . .
> Come up through the lair of the Lion
> With love in her luminous eyes.'

It is possible that my own indiscretion may have produced the catastrophe. I may have let my mother know that I was happy by the tone of my letters. In any case, her suspicions were aroused. Uncle Tom appeared upon the scene, got Douglas out of the way by some lie, rifled his belongings, stole his private letters and dismissed him. But it was too late; my eyes were opened and I had become as a god, knowing good and evil. I was in a position to take the initiative. Till then, I could only aim at escaping from the hideous hell of home. Now I had an objective; now I could attack.

I must explain something of the horror of life in my mother's house. To begin with, I was entirely debarred from the society of boys and girls of my own age, unless they were the children of Brethren. The sect was already moribund and in addition had split over the Raven heresy. The situation is illustrated by the story which I will quote from the preface to my *The World's Tragedy*.

An irreligious man may have moral checks; a Plymouth Brother has none. He is always ready to excuse the vilest crimes by quoting the appropriate text and invoking the name of Christ to cover every meanness which may delight his vain and vicious nature.

For the Plymouth Brethren were in themselves an exceptionally detestable crew. The aristocrats who began the movement were, of course, just aristocrats, and their curious system left them so. But they ran a form of 'Early Christian' spiritual socialism by having no appointed priest or minister, and they were foolish enough to favour their followers financially.

Thus Mr Giblets—let us call him—the third-best butcher in the village found (on the one hand) that while at church he was nobody at all, and in chapel but an elder, in the little meeting in the squire's morning-room he was no less than the minister of God and the mouthpiece of the Holy Ghost; just as on the other hand it was only natural that the orders from the Hall should come his way and leave the first-best butcher lamenting and the second-best bewildered. So that in my time the sect (though it is only fair to point out that they refused to be described as a sect, since what they had done was not to form a new sect, but to 'come out of sect'—this they maintained in spite of the fact that they were far more exclusive than any other religious body in Europe) was composed of a few of the old guard, my father the last of them all, and the meanest crew of canaille that ever wriggled.

With my father's death the small schisms which had hitherto lopped off a few members every year or two were altogether surpassed by the great Raven heresy, which split the body into two nearly equal halves and extinguished the last sparks of its importance.

I am going beyond my subject, but I cannot refrain from telling the awful story of the meeting at Oban.

The meeting at Oban consisted of a Mr Cameron and his wife and the bedridden mother of one of the two, I forget which. Now as it is written, 'Wheresoever two or three are gathered together in my name, there am I in the midst of them', it was all very well: but two forms a quorum. Jesus will not come for less. This has never been disputed by any doctor of the Brethren. Wigram is clear on the point; if Darby had ever been clear on any point, it would have been on that. Kelly never denied it; even Stuart was sound in this matter, and Stoney himself (though reluctantly) gave his adhesion. To hold a meeting you must have two persons present . . .

Well, I need hardly say that Mr and Mrs Cameron took opposite sides of the controversy. When the glad wires flashed the message that Mr Raven in the meeting at Ealing had deliberately said with slow and weighty emphasis, 'He that hath the Son hath eternal life', Mrs Cameron almost wept with joy. When (the message continued) Major McArthy had risen to his feet and retorted, 'He that hath the Son of God hath everlasting life', Mr Cameron executed a Highland though funereal fling.*

When Mr Raven, stung to the quick, had shaken his fist at the major and yelled, 'Brother, you're a sinful old man!' Mrs Cameron 'had always known there was something', and in-

---

* The alleged antithesis between these two texts (I cannot perceive it) was actually the basis of the schism. My mother thought that one of them (I forget which) 'dishonoured the Lord's person'!

vented a ruined governess. But—oh the laughter of her husband when the telegraph brought the major's retort, 'Brother, have you no sin?'—spoken with an accent of mildness which belied the purple of his face.

In short, the meeting at Oban had split. Mr Cameron had withdrawn from the Lord's supper ! ! ! It was therefore absolutely necessary for both of them to assure themselves that the bedridden mother was of their way of thinking, or neither could hold the morning meeting; though I suppose either could preach the gospel—*morosa voluptas!*

Unhappily, that excellent lady was a hard case. She was quite deaf and very nearly blind; while mentally she had never been remarkable for anything beyond a not unamiable imbecility. However, there was but one thing to be done, to argue her into conviction.

They agreed to take eight-hour shifts; and for all I know, they are arguing still, and neither of the meetings at Oban can meet!

As it happened, my mother took the minority view. This means that she cut herself off from every single intimate friend. On the strength of a text in one of the epistles, she refused to shake hands with anyone who was teaching false doctrine. The very few remaining were new friends. My associates could therefore be counted on the fingers of one hand and our only bond of sympathy was a detestation of our tyrants.

My intellectual avidity was enormous, yet I was absolutely cut off from literature. One or two books of Scott and Dickens were permitted. Ballantyne was approved, G. A. Henty winked at rather than openly tolerated. *David Copperfield* was barred because of Little Em'ly, for she was a naughty girl; besides, Emily was my mother's name, and to read the book might diminish my respect for her. One of my tutors brought down *The Bab Ballads,* one of which begins:

Emily Jane was a nursery maid.

My mother threw the book out of the house and very nearly threw him after it. Another tutor read 'The Ancient Mariner' aloud after dinner one night and my mother, after delivering a stormy tirade, snatched me from the contamination of his presence. The reason was that when the Ancient Mariner saw the water snakes playing around the ship, he 'blessed them unaware'. An outrageously blasphemous act, for snakes are cursed in Genesis!

Here, by the way, is a curious point. These bigots are so

inconsistent that I have never been able to follow the working of their minds. There is a great deal of doctrine in 'The Ancient Mariner' which outrages every tenet of the Plymouth Brethren, but my mother does not appear to have taken offence at that. My only suggestion is that she detested snakes for Freudian reasons; she had probably met them in dreams and had therefore good reasons (from her point of view) for identifying them with the devil in his most objectionable form. My mother was naturally a rather sensual type of woman and there is no doubt that sexual repression had driven her as nearly as possible to the borders of insanity.

My cousin Agnes had a house in Dorset Square. My mother took me to tea there one afternoon. A copy of *Dr Pascal* was in the room. The word 'Zola' caught my mother's eye and she made a verbal assault of hysterical fury upon her hostess. Both women shouted and screamed at each other simultaneously, amid floods of tears. Needless to say, my mother had never read a line of Zola—the name was simply a red rag to a cow.

This inconsistency, by the way, seems universal. I have known a printer object to set up 'We gave them hell and Tommy', while passing unquestioned all sorts of things to which exception could quite reasonably be taken by narrow-minded imbeciles. The censor habitually passes what I, who am no puritan, consider nauseating filth, while refusing to license *Oedipus Rex*, which we are compelled to assimilate at school. The prosecutions against publishers are equally incomprehensible. The country is flooded with the nasty pornography of women writers, while there is an outcry against epoch-making masterpieces of philosophy like *Jurgen*. The salacious musical comedy goes its libidinous way rejoicing, while Ibsen and Bernard Shaw are on the black list. The fact is, of course, that the puritan has been turned by sexual repression into a sexual pervert and degenerate, so that he is insane on the subject.

Of course, I could not be prevented entirely from reading. I was kept very short of pocket money, so that I could not even buy books to any extent. But I used to get them now and again, smuggle them into the house inside my clothes, and lock myself into the water-closet to read them. One such book, I remember, was *The Mystery of a Hansom Cab*. My mother considered the hansom cab as an engine specially devised by the devil and any reference to one was considered obscene.

Having given an idea of the atmosphere of home, it should be intelligible that I was prepared to go out of my way to perform any act which might serve as a magical affirmation of my revolt. I was, in fact, restrained from developing my mind in any wholesome manner. I had no opportunity to think of anything but fighting fire with fire.

A new parlour maid took it into her head to better herself by getting a stranglehold on the young master. I arranged to meet her on her evening out at a safe distance from Streatham and we drove in a cab over to Herne Hill, indulging in a mild flirtation on the way. On Sunday morning, however, I brought things to a point. I made an excuse for staying away from the morning meeting. I got the girl into my mother's bedroom and made my magical affirmation. I had no idea that there was any counterplot, but the girl proceeded to 'blow the gaff'. She was, of course, instantly flung into the street, but she continued her operations for bettering herself. Uncle Tom intervened, for of course my mother could not discuss such a subject with me at all. I denied the whole affair point blank. My uncle tried to find the cabman, but failed. They scented trouble for somebody and knew no more than so many Chinamen. He begged me, however, to try to furnish some positive proof of my innocence; and this is where my subtlety came in. I pretended to be in great trepidation. Yes, I could prove it, and yet, how could I? My uncle scented a mystery and adjourned the examination.

I immediately went out and appealed to the tobacconist on the bridge above Streatham station to say, if asked, that he remembered my having been in his shop on the Thursday night previous, which was that of the cab drive. He was a good sportsman and naturally anxious to oblige. I went back to my uncle and proposed a deal. I would tell him where I had been, but he must not punish me, for I had been led astray by bad companions. He was only too glad; and I owned up, tremulous and tearful, that I had been in the tobacconist's. He would have doubted a merely innocent alibi. The girl was, of course, discredited, and nothing more was heard of the matter. And I had had her on my mother's very bed!

That is the state of affairs which is caused by puritanism. First we have a charming girl driven to attempt blackmail, next a boy forced to the most unmanly duplicity in order to exercise his natural rights with impunity, and incidentally to wrong a woman for whom he had nothing but the friendliest feelings. As long as sexual relations are complicated by religious, social and financial considerations, so long will they cause all kinds of cowardly, dishonourable and disgusting behaviour. When war conditions imposed artificial restraint on the sister appetite of hunger, decent citizens began to develop all kinds of loathsome trickery. Men and women will never behave worthily as long as current morality interferes with the legitimate satisfaction of physiological needs. Nature always avenges herself on those who insult her. The individual is not to blame for the crime and insanity which are the explosions consequent on the clogging of the safety valve. The fault lies with the engineer. At the present moment, society is blowing up in larger or smaller spots all over the world, because it has failed to develop a system by which all its members can be adequately nourished without conflict and the waste products eliminated without discomfort.

On the whole, I was so well guarded that incidents like the above were rare accidents. I had been taught by bitter experience that almost anybody might be a spy, so that the slightest indiscretion in talking to an apparently harmless stranger might result in some disaster. The foundations were laid of an exaggerated shyness which has never left me. I was practically debarred from human intercourse, even that of the great men of the past. My only consolation was writing poetry.

It is difficult to explain by what means I came to the conclusion that poetry was of paramount importance. There was a sort of family tradition which honoured the poet; but it was as irrational as the rest of their beliefs. I can only imagine it as derived from their having been told at school that the English poets were the glory of humanity, for they certainly knew no poetry beyond 'Casabianca' and 'We are Seven'. I discovered Shakespeare for myself. It happened that in the farmhouse at Forsinard were three old folio volumes. My mother had an edition of Shakespeare; but I had never read it, because it was permitted. At the farmhouse, however, there was nothing else to read. I became fascinated and spent night after night poring over the pages. (I have always been singularly thorough in anything I take up. My father had a favourite sermon on the word 'but'; and I went through the whole Bible, page by page, enclosing this word, wherever it occurred, with an oblong of ink.)

Apart from the few regular pieces for recitation, there was *Paradise Lost*. This bored me for the most part as much as it does now, but allowed me to gloat over the figures of Satan and sin. After all, Milton was a great poet; and the subconscious artistic self of him was therefore bitterly antagonistic to Christianity. Not only is Satan the hero, but the triumphant hero. God's threats have not 'come off'. It is the forces of evil, so called, that manifest in strength and beauty of form. The glories of the saints are tinsel. It is impossible to draw goodness with character. On the Christian theory, goodness is, in fact, nothing but absence of character, for it implies complete submission to God. Satan's original fault is not pride; that is secondary. It springs from the consciousness of separateness. Now of course this is, mystically speaking, sinful, because the mystic holds that all manifestation is imperfection. Christian theology has not had sufficient logic to see, like its elder sister, Hindu theology, that any attributes soever must distinguish their possessor from some other possible being. But their instinct has been to go as far in that direction as possible and consequently the divine characters in Milton are comparatively colourless. Such was the transmutation in the nature of God effected by building a super-structure of Greek philosophy upon the foundation of the savage phantasm of Jehovah. My own attitude in the matter is to be seen in my aesthetic tendencies. I could never tolerate smooth, insipid beauty. The ugliness of decrepitude revolted me; but that of strength absorbed my whole soul. I despised the tame scenery of the Swiss lakes; the ruggedness of barren pinnacles of rock and the gloomy isolation of such lakes as Llyn Idwal appealed to my imagination. Wastwater disappointed me. It did not come up to the level of its poetic reputation. It was only when I got among the crags themselves that I was happy. I demanded to be at grips with death in one way or another. The bourgeois ambition to get through life without unpleasantness seemed to me the lowest vileness and entirely in keeping with the moral attitude of the heavenly people in *Paradise Lost*.

I was allowed to read Tennyson and Longfellow, but it is impossible to class them as poets. The emasculation of all the characters disgusted me beyond measure. Their very sins are suburban.

8

So when it came to my writing poetry myself, my work fell naturally into three divisions. Firstly, short lyrics modelled on the hymns to which I was accustomed; secondly, parodies, principally of Scottish and English songs; and thirdly, epics based on Sir Walter Scott. I must have written over a hundred thousand lines. They have all been destroyed; and I am rather sorry for it. While they possessed no merit, their contents would afford a valuable key to my thoughts at the time. The few fragments which escaped destruction were reprinted in my *Oracles*. I remember something of their general moral tendency, which was to celebrate the triumph of the revolt of youth and passion against age and propriety. I tried to get effect by using extremes of expression. I remember two lines from an epic, 'Lady Ethelreda':

> Baron Ethelred waxed wroth,
> Frothed he with a frothy froth.

But as I grew a little older I became able to manage my material with more discretion. My mother designed me, of course, to follow in my father's footsteps as an evangelist, but as I had to take a profession she decided she would like me to be a doctor, on the ground that 'doctors have so many opportunities'. (Scil. for bringing souls to Jesus. She did not see anything funny in this remark!) So I began to learn a little about medicine and produced the following effusion:

A PEEP BEHIND THE SCENES

> In the hospital bed she lay
> > Rotting away!
> Cursing by night and cursing by day,
> > Rotting away!
> The lupus is over her face and head,
> Filthy and foul and horrid and dread,
> And her shrieks they would almost wake the dead;
> > Rotting away!

> In her horrible grave she lay,
> Rotting away!
> Rotting by night, and rotting by day,
> Rotting away!
> In the place of her face is a gory hole,
> And the worms are gnawing the tissues foul,
> And the devil is gloating over her soul,
> Rotting away!

Note that the title of this poem is ironical. It is taken from a goody-goody book, popular at that time, which describes the life of travelling barnstormers and how the only hope for them was to be converted. But the irony goes somewhat deeper. It was a genuine criticism of the shallow philosophy of optimism which went with the polite Christianity of the time. I was analysing life in the spirit of Schopenhauer. I couldn't see any sense in pretending that life was not full of horrors. Death and trousers are facts in nature; and merely to avoid reference to them or to invent euphemisms for them does not alter their character. I was reduced to gloating on murder and putrefaction, simply because these things gave the most forcible denial to the assumptions current at home. Paganism is wholesome because it faces the facts of life; but I was not allowed to take a normal view of nature. In my situation, I could not dismiss the falsities of Christianity with a smile; I was compelled to fight fire with fire and to oppose their poisoned poultices with poisoned daggers.

Such was the influence of home life. But it was partially interfered with by the more decent current of school life. I have mentioned my school in Streatham. It was there that occurred the last important incident of this period. Being the star chemist of the school, I determined to distinguish myself on the fifth of November, 1891. I procured a ten-pound jar from the grocer's, put two pounds of gunpowder at the bottom and filled it up with various layers of different coloured 'fires'. These were all—except for the small ingredients of varied metallic salts—of the same composition: sugar and chlorate of potash. In order to make sure of success, I turned the whole household on to mixing these ingredients, with the result that they were mingled so intimately as to produce what was to all intents and purposes chlorate powder! I pressed this down very powerfully, buried the jar in the playground, stuck a rocket into the top and lighted it at the critical moment. The rocket had been fixed too firmly to rise and the protecting wad of paper burnt through before I could step back. I neither saw nor heard anything. I felt as if a brush of some warm tarry and gritty substance had been passed across my face; and found myself standing on the brink of a hole in the ground of no mean size. I wondered how on earth it could have happened that my experiment had failed. I remember apologizing for the failure and saying that I must go up to the house to wash my face. I discovered that I was being supported on the journey by my private tutor and my mother. Then I found myself in the headmaster's sanctum, receiving first aid. I remember nothing more for some time except the annoyance of being awakened to have my dressings changed. I slept for ninety-six hours with these semi-conscious intervals. My tutor had the sense to wire to Guy's Hospital for Dr Golding Bird, whose intervention probably saved me from erysipelas and the loss of my sight. In the course of convalescence, over four thousand pieces of gravel and the like were removed from my face; and it was on Christmas Day that I was first allowed to use my eyes for a few minutes. The explosion had been devastating. The windows were smashed for a long way round; and the bottles in the chemist's shop on the railway bridge—a quarter of a mile and more away—rattled, though the passage of trains had no such effect. Strangely enough, I was the only person injured. Throughout I enjoyed the episode; I was the hero, I had made my mark!

The following year I was ready to go to a public school. My Uncle Jonathan wanted me to go to Winchester, as per the family tradition, but my health demanded a more bracing climate and it was decided that I should go to Malvern. The school at that time was rising to the height of its glory in athletics. We possessed a brilliant bat in Percy Latham; H. R. and W. L. Foster were sure to distinguish themselves in one way or another, and the youngsters of that famous game-playing family were coming on, ready to take their places when the time came. There was also C. J. Burnup as a promising colt.

In other matters, however, the school had a long way to go. Bullying went on unchecked, the prefects being foremost offenders. As a shy, solitary boy in ill-health, incapable of football, I naturally got more than my share, and this led ultimately to one of the few actions in my life with which I have ever felt inclined to reproach myself. The tone of the school was brutal and imbecile. The authorities had done much to stamp out the practice of 'greasing', which consists in spitting as smegmatically as possible either in people's faces or on their backs. It still flourished at our house, Huntingdon's, No. 4, and constituted our only claim to distinction. I do not think we had a single member in either of the elevens. The prefects were hulking louts, shirking both work and play, and concentrating on obscenity and petty tyranny. It annoyed them particularly that my conduct was irreproachable. They could not cane me without the housemaster's permission. I did not realize how closely I was being watched, but ultimately I committed some trifling breach of discipline during 'prep'. After the hour was over the prefect in charge gleefully hastened to the housemaster. He found me there already. I got my licking; but there was a fine series of expulsions to balance it. Of course my action was technically indefensible; but after all, I had held my tongue uncomplainingly for months and it was only when they appealed to the housemaster to fight their battles that I appealed to him to fight mine.

I may as well emphasize at this moment that I remained amazingly innocent. My study companion was actually the favourite 'tart' of the house; so much so, that he thereby added considerably to his income. But though I was aware of these facts, I had no conception whatever of what they implied.

An anecdote illustrates this fact. It was the custom of our form master to remit twenty per cent of any number of lines that might be given one to write if they were delivered before the time appointed. It happened that I was set a number of lines by some other master and I handed in eighty per cent with the written remark, 'Twenty per cent deducted as usual for premature delivery.' He thought that I was 'getting at him', but on investigation I was acquitted; in fact, I had no idea of any ambiguity.

My life at Malvern made little impression on me. For the most part I was lost in my own thought and touched school life as little as I could. I made no real friends. I had no sympathy with the general brutality and refused to pander to it by making myself the favourite. The following story helps to illustrate my attitude.

Some of the prefects were twitting me with cowardice and proposed that I should prove my virtue by fighting Smith tertius, a boy much smaller than myself. I refused, observing that if I did not fight him I must pass for a coward, and if I did I should be accused of bullying, and probably be reported for fighting as well.

None of my ambitions were connected with the school. I preferred to daydream of my plans for mountaineering in the holidays and to busy myself with writing poetry. Memory has preserved fragments of two efforts. The first:

> 'Put not thy trust in princes.' 'Tis a speech
> Might thee, O Gordon-Cumming, something teach.

It seems absurd that a boy of my age should take an interest in such matters and become so positive a partisan. But I had an ingrained hatred for the Hanoverian usurper and took for granted what I still believe to have been the fact, that the man who cheated was not Gordon-Cumming.

Of the second poem I retain:

> Poor lady! whom a wicked jury's hate
> In face of facts as iron as the grave
> To which they would have doomed thee—bitter fate!
> Thee guiltless to the cruel hangman gave.

> Shame on the judge who sees but half the facts!
> Shame on the nurse who private letters opes!
> But never shalt thou be forgot by us,
> The pity of thy life's so blasted hopes.

> Lady, hope on! All England takes thy part
> But a few bigots. Lady, then, take heart.

My sympathy with Mrs Maybrick nowise argues my belief in her innocence. She was admittedly an adulteress. I asked no further questions. The mere fact thrilled me to the marrow. Adultery being the summit of wickedness, its commission excused everything.

I made no intimate friendships. I did my work sufficiently well to avoid serious punishment, but without ambition. I took no interest in the Shakespeare prize, for which everybody had to enter, and had not read a line of the two plays prescribed, *Romeo and Juliet* and *Richard II*. But for some reason or other I got scared three days before the examination, got excused from games and worked so hard that I came out sixth in the school. I was able to quote several long passages accurately from memory. With me, it was always a question of the interest which I took in things. I had the makings of a sound classical scholar, but I could not bring myself to memorize Greek and Latin poetry. Stranger still, I could not master the rules of prosody. My most hostile critics admit that my technique and my sense of rhythm are unsurpassed; but the rules of scansion meant nothing to me, because no one explained their connection with the way a poem should be read.

I should have liked school life well enough if it had not been for the bullying and the complete lack of intellectual companionship. I had no interest in games; my athletic ambitions were confined to climbing mountains. But at least there was no Christianity! and what morality there was was rather manly than otherwise. However, I was now old enough to match myself against my private tutors and found greater freedom with them than at school. I decided to leave and drew such a picture of the abominations which went on, though I knew nothing about them or even what they were, that my mother refused to let me go back. I told her, she once reminded me, that "if Mr Huntingdon [the housemaster] knew what was going on in the house, it would break his heart'. Pure bluff! but the following term I was entered at Tonbridge.

By this time I had acquired a considerable facility in making the best of my advantages. I had in some ways much more experience of life than most boys of my age. My holidays, what with fishing, mountain climbing and running after girls, were full of adventures of one kind and another, in which I was always being thrown on my own resources. By the time I reached Tonbridge I had developed a kind of natural aristocracy. People were already beginning to be afraid of me and there was no question any longer of bullying. My health must have been very much better. Albuminuria breeds melancholy and destroys physical courage. I had also, no doubt, been subject to constant irritation due to my phimosis and the operation had relieved me. I was, therefore, more or less ready to fight anybody that annoyed me. And people took good care not to do so.

The atmosphere at Tonbridge was, moreover, much more civilized than at Malvern. Today it impresses me as having been on the namby-pamby side. There was at that time no trace of the marriage system since introduced and now said to be flourishing. 'Mrs So-and-so' was almost a term of derision, while now it is exacted by its owner to show that he is not 'one of those'. My best friend was a brother of C. F. G. Masterman. He was neither a sneak nor a hypocrite; but it gives an idea of the atmosphere.

The glimpse of normal human life afforded by Archibald Douglas had rendered me completely sane as far as my conscious life was concerned. The problem of life was not how to satanize, as Huysmans would have called it; it was simply to escape from the oppressors and to enjoy the world without any interference of spiritual life of any sort. My happiest moments were when I was alone on the mountains; but there is no evidence that this pleasure in any way derived from mysticism. The beauty of form and colour, the physical exhilaration of exercise, and the mental stimulation of finding one's way in difficult country, formed the sole elements of my rapture. So far as I indulged in daydreams, they were exclusively of a normal sexual type. There was no need to create phantasms of a perverse or unrealizable satisfaction. It is important to emphasize this point, because I have always appeared to my contemporaries as a very extraordinary individual obsessed by fantastic passions. But such were not in any way natural to me. The moment the pressure was relieved every touch of the abnormal was shed off instantly. The impulse to write poetry disappeared almost completely at such periods. I had not even any of the ordinary ambitions of young men. I was content to enjoy sport without wishing to attain eminence in it. It came natural to me to find ways up mountains which looked to me interesting and difficult. But it never occurred to me to match myself against other people. It was from purely aesthetic considerations that I climbed the gullies of Tryfan and Twll Du. This last climb landed me, as luck would have it, in a controversy which was destined to determine my career in a very remarkable manner.

9

It had never occurred to me that rock climbing, as such, might be a recognized sport. However, my mother and I were at the Sligachan Inn in Skye during the summer of 1892. I talked about my hill rambles with Sir Joseph Lister, who happened to be staying there, and asked him about the Coolins. He was kind enough to suggest to some real climbers who were staying at the hotel to include me in their party the next day, and they were kind enough to take me up Sgurr-nan-Gillean by the Pinnacle Ridge. I found myself up against it; and realized at once that there was something more to be done than scrambling.

I think it was the following summer that I was staying at a farm in Langdale and heard from the natives of the celebrated twenty-four hours' walk. The idea is to climb the four highest fells, Scafell Pikes, Helvellyn, Skiddaw and Saddleback, in a day. I conceived a minor ridge walk and set out one morning at dawn from Langdale, climbed the Langdale Pikes, and followed the crest of the fells to Scafell Pikes. Then I crossed to Scafell by the Broad Stand; and, seeing the Deep Ghyll pinnacle, climbed that on my way to the summit of Scafell. It was a terrifically hot day over Lingmell and down into the valley to climb the screes of Great Gable. My attention was attracted by the Great Napes Needle and I climbed that. Thence I took the easiest way—the Needle ridge, or a gully, I forget which—to the summit of the mountain. I had become almost insane from heat, thirst and exhaustion; I could no longer walk, but crawled on hands and knees down to Sty Head Tarn, whose waters revived me to some extent. I struggled on homewards and reached the top of Rossett Ghyll Pass shortly after nightfall. There was a bright moon, but I had a terrible time picking my way down the path. I must have been a little light-headed from exhaustion and there was a Dantesque quality in the long climb among the blinding white patches of light and the jetty shadows. At the bottom of the pass I met a small rescue party who had just started out to look for me, and reached home about eleven o'clock. It was, in its way, a remarkable performance for a boy.

Another incident is less heroic but more amusing. My tutor had invited his sister to stay a few days at the farm at Langdale. One day I took her up the Langdale Pikes and found a quite decent bit of scrambling. Having no rope, I could only help her from below. She became scared and broke into a passionate monologue punctuated by screams. It consisted of variations on a triple theme. 'I'm going to fall—Our Father which art in heaven—Don't look at my legs.' Ah me!—'I learnt about women from 'er.' It was a startlingly complete revelation of the psychology of the well-brought-up young lady. Craven fear, prurient shame and narcotic piety: of such is the kingdom of Tennyson!

The glimpse that I had had of Wastdale attracted me and I went over there. One very wet morning I started to climb Scafell, chiefly with the idea of tackling some of the gullies which I had noticed in the Great Cliff. I had reached the Grass Traverse when I heard voices in the mist above me, and a few minutes later a powerful man with red whiskers and a rope about his shoulders came towards me from the cliff. It was J. W. Robinson, a local farmer, who had laid the foundation of Cumberland climbing. He offered to show me some of the easier climbs. He had started that morning with a man named Owen Glynne Jones. Jones had insisted on trying to climb Steep Gill, which is for the most part a shallow gully of smooth slabs set at a dangerous angle. There is no reliable hold for hand or foot on the main pitch, which is some eighty feet high. As torrents of icy water were pouring over the crags, it was sheer foolhardiness to attempt it. Robinson had refused to do so, whereupon Jones had quarrelled with him and they had parted.

I had every reason, later on, to agree with Robinson. I was only once on a rope with Jones. It was on Great Gable; the rocks were plastered with ice and a bitter wind was blowing. In such conditions one cannot rely on one's fingers. Our party proposed to descend the Oblique Chimney on the Ennerdale face. Robinson led the way down. The second man was a Pole named Lewkowitch, who was generally known as 'Oils, fats and waxes', because of his expert knowledge of them and the personal illustration of their properties which he afforded. He had no experience of climbing and weighed about sixteen stone. It was up to me, as third man on the rope, to let him slowly down. I had, of course, to descend little by little, the rope being too short to allow me to lower him from the top. I soon found myself in the most difficult part of the chimney, very ill placed to manipulate a dangling ox. I looked up to Jones, the last man, to hold my rope so that I could give full attention to Lewkowitch, and saw to my horror that he was maintaining his equilibrium by a sort of savage war dance! He was hampered by a photographic apparatus which was strapped to his back. Robinson had urged him to lower it separately. As neither Einstein nor the Blessed Virgin Mary was there to suspend the law of gravitation, I have no idea how we got to the bottom undamaged; but when we did I promptly took off the rope and walked home, utterly disgusted with the vanity which had endangered the party. Of course, there could only be one end to that sort of thing, and Jones ended by killing himself and three guides on the Zinal side of the Dent Blanche a few years later.

The imbecility of the accident is shown by the fact that the fifth member of the party, who was quite a beginner, found himself—after the smash—alone on the precipice. The guides had begged Jones not to attempt the pitch from which he fell, but he had persisted. The fifth man had hitched the rope over a rock and it had broken between him and the third guide. But this man, instead of going down to the valley, actually climbed the mountain, spent a night on the ridge and went down the next day to Zermatt.

The dangers of mountaineering are ridiculously exaggerated. I have never known of any accident which was not due to ignorance or folly. Eckenstein, the greatest climber of his age, told me the same thing.

Jones obtained the reputation of being the most brilliant rock climber of his time by persistent self-advertisement. He was never a first-rate climber, because he was never a safe climber. If a handhold was out of his reach he would jump at it, and he had met with several serious accidents before the final smash. But his reputation is founded principally on climbs which he did not make at all, in the proper sense of the word. He used to go out with a couple of photographers and have himself lowered up and down a climb repeatedly until he had learnt its peculiarities, and then make the 'first ascent' before a crowd of admirers. Now the essential difficulty of negotiating a pitch of any length while one has to waste any amount of time and strength while one is finding out where the holds are. There is no credit at all in repeating a climb.

Another trick of Jones's was to get his friends to make dates with other people to try various unclimbed places, and then to postpone the expedition on various pretexts until Jones had managed to negotiate it by the method above described.

This conduct seemed to me absolutely unsportsmanlike. To prostitute the mountains to personal vanity is in fact something rather worse. And I had a taste of the malice of people's envy in my first week. A personal issue arose from the very start. Robinson happened to ask me if I had climbed in Wales. I told him yes, and mentioned one particular place, the Devil's Kitchen or Twll Du, which I had climbed by taking off my boots. I had no idea that the place was famous, but it was. It was reputed unclimbable. Almighty Jones himself had failed. I found myself, to my astonishment, the storm centre. Jones, behind my back, accused me flatly of lying. Quite unconsciously, however, I put myself in the right. I have always failed to see that it is necessary to make a fuss about one's climbs. There is a good reason for describing a first climb. To do so is to guide others to enjoyment. One may also for the same reason describe interesting variations of a climb, or its accomplishment by a solitary man. Now as it happened, Jones had been blowing his trumpet about the first ascent of Kern Knotts Chimney; the top pitch, however, he had failed to do unaided. He had been hoisted on the shoulders of the second man. I went to have a look at it and found that by wedging a stone into a convenient crack, and thus starting a foot higher up, I could get to the top, and did so. I recorded this in the Climbers' Book; and the following day a man named H. V. Reade, possibly in a sceptical mood, followed in my footsteps. He found my wedged stone, contemptuously threw it away, climbed the pitch without it, and recorded the feat. That was a double blow to Mr Jones. It was no longer a convincing argument that if he couldn't do a thing it couldn't be done.

But this was not all. Scafell is separated from Scafell Pikes by a pass called Mickledoor; and on the Scafell side it is precipitous. The ridge of the pass is well-marked; by going down a little on one side one can climb the cliffs by the Broad Stand or Mickledoor Chimney, on the other side by the North Climb; and so on. But it had been the ambition of every climber to start from the exact top of the ridge. This was called the direct climb of Mickledoor; and nobody had done it. That seemed to be a shame, so I did it. This time the fat was in the fire. My good faith was openly challenged in the smoking-room. I shrugged my shoulders, but offered to repeat the climb the following day before witnesses—which I accordingly

did. I suppose I am a very innocent ass, but I could not understand why anyone calling himself human should start a series
of malicious intrigues on such a cause of quarrel. I must admit
that my methods were sometimes calculated to annoy; but I
had no patience with the idiotic vanity of mediocrities. I took
the Climbers' Record to be a serious compilation and never
wrote in it without the fullest sense of responsibility. So when
I found a solemn Te Deum being chanted on account of the
fifth ascent of the Pillar Rock by a 'lady', I took my dog to
the top and recorded, 'First ascent by a St Bernard bitch.'
When Jones, after the usual practice, had climbed Kern Knotts
Crack, and three public school masters, who ought to have
known better, said they had seen him do it, and it was a marvellous exhibition of skill and so on, I completed their remarks by
a colophon: [Advt.] So much fuss was made about Kern
Knotts Crack that Eckenstein took a young girl named Miss
Nicholls and asked her to lead up it, which she did.

Wastdale at that time was a rendezvous for many amusing
characters as well as for some of the most brilliant men in
England. Professor Milnes Marshall spent most of his holidays
there. His death is one of the most curious accidents in the
history of climbing. He had gone up to Deep Ghyll with some
friends one bright winter day when the mountains were covered
with snow. But, not feeling particularly well, he remained at
the foot of Deep Ghyll while his friends climbed it, proposing
to take photographs of them. He set up his camera on a snow
slope no steeper than Ludgate Hill, a place entirely free from
danger. But he fell and rolled gently down the slope, making
no effort to save himself, finally pitching over a small cliff,
at the foot of which he was picked up dead. It was not a
climbing accident at all, any more than the death of Norman
Neruda, who died of heart failure when he happened to be in
a rock chimney in the Dolomites.

After a short time at Tonbridge my health again broke
down. It was evident that boarding-school life was unsuited to
me. It was arranged for me to live at Eastbourne with a tutor
named Lambert, a Plymouth Brother. It is curious (by the
way) to reflect that Henri Bernstein, the celebrated French
dramatist, being also a 'hope' of the Brethren, was one of
Lambert's pupils. I saw hardly anything of him. All I remember is that one day, for no reason that I can remember, we
set to in the street and fought it out. At that time I knew no
boxing. My one idea was to get his head 'in chancery' under
my left arm and bash his face in with my right, which I

succeeded in doing, making no attempt to defend myself against
his blows which he gave like a windmill on my skull. I remember acutely my surprise that they did not hurt me at all.
During the day I worked at Eastbourne College in the chemical
laboratory under Professor Hughes, and was privileged to
assist that great man in several researches which go to prove
that no two substances can combine in the absence of a third.
It seems strange that I should have seen the bearings of this
upon philosophy.

One very significant incident is stamped upon my memory.
I was spending an evening with the professor and in the course
of some discussion I said, 'The Bible says so.' These words
dripped with the utmost irony from my lips. I meant to imply
the bitterest contempt. I was not understood. He took me seriously and broke out into a passionate denunciation of the book.
His manner was so ferocious that I was positively startled; and
the interesting thing about the incident is this. I had been so long
so alert lest I should be accused of disbelief, that it almost
took my breath away to hear a man in authority speak so
openly.* I have explained how I had vainly sought supreme
wickedness in the Church of England. I had even gone to
so-called 'high' churches and on one occasion dared to enter
the portals of the papists. But I had found nothing wicked even
there. They all seemed to me to be tarred with the same brush;
they were cold, heartless, dull, stupid, vapid and fatuous. The
emotionalism of some and the sacramentalism of others
seemed to me perfectly insincere. The fact is that (as my
brother-in-law, Gerald Kelly, once told me, with astounding
insight) I was the most religious man that he had ever met.
It is the inmost truth. The instinct was masked for a long time,
firstly by the abominations of the Plymouth Brethren and the
Evangelicals; secondly, by the normal world. It only broke out
at a subsequent period in any recognizable form. But when it
did so, it became the axis of my being. As a matter of fact,
even in these early days, my real need was spiritual satisfaction;
and I was a satanist or a worldling (as the case may be) in
the spirit of St Francis of Assisi.

My poetry during this period was either amorous or satirical.
A few of my efforts are preserved in *Oracles*. I quote the first
and last verses from a lyric about a girl I met on the sea front.

---

* I remember my first stolen visit to the Theatre—*Little Christopher
Columbus*. Weren't all these people afraid of being found out?

ELVIRA

Was thy fault to be too tender?
  Was thine error to be weak?
Was my kiss the first offender
  Pressed upon thy blushing cheek?

Heaven at your accurst creation
  Shall become a hell of fire:
Death for kisses, and damnation
  For your love, shall God require!

What is worthy of note is what I may call the *laus veneris* point of view; which symbolizes my revolt and required many years to wear out. It seems as if I clung to the idea of the wickedness of love and the belief that it entailed divine retribution, partly perhaps because of my tendency to masochism, but consciously, at least, as adding actual value to sin. Pleasure as such has never attracted me. It must be spiced by moral satisfaction. I was reluctant to abandon my intellectual belief in Christianity; if the whole thing was nonsense, where was the fun of fighting it?

All this early poetry, moreover, tended to become worse instead of better as my mind developed. I explain this by reference to the analogy of such games as billiards. As soon as one begins to take lessons one spoils one's natural game and one does not recover until the artificially acquired technique has been driven down into the subconscious by continual practice.

Apart from a very few very early poems like 'The Balloon', all my writing is wooden, imitative and conscious, until I reached Cambridge, with hardly an exception.

At Eastbourne, I had still no interest in games. I was still prevented from anything like intimate association with my fellow creatures. I was still ignorant of the existence of English literature and I became a first-rate French scholar without reading any French literature. In my play time I was either hunting flappers on the front, playing chess or climbing Beachy Head. My chess was almost entirely book learning and I was very much surprised to find myself the best player in the town. For although the local champion insisted on giving me pawn and move, I beat him so easily every time I met him that the odds might have been reversed without making much difference to the result. I edited a chess column in the *Eastbourne Gazette* and made myself a host of enemies by criticizing the team.

I wanted to arouse enthusiasm, to insist on study and practice and to make Eastbourne the strongest town in England. The result fell short of breaking up the club, but not very far.

I used my position as editor to criticize the formation of the team and anything else that seemed to me wrong. I was absolutely unable to conceive that anyone should be anything but grateful for constructive criticism. I had moreover in my mind a firm conception of an editor as *Jupiter tonans*. I remember one occasion on which I made myself particularly nasty. In a club tournament I had won all my games except two against a man named Martin, who had failed to play any of his games. At the same time he would not withdraw from the tournament. I tried to deal with the situation in my weekly articles. I requested Mr Martin to begin to play his games; I implored him to begin to play his games; I pointed out to him the propriety of beginning to play his games, I showed him that the best traditions of England (which had made her what she was) spoke with no uncertain voice to the effect that he should begin to play his games. All this settled down to a weekly chorus à la Cato, *'Delenda est Carthago'*. Whatever the subject of my discourse, it invariably ended, 'Mr Martin has not yet begun to play his games.'

By this persistent nagging I got him to make an appointment with me and the game had to be adjourned in a position which was clearly won for me. He determined to avoid defeat by the simple process of refusing to make any further moves. I could have done a great deal with a brazier and a gimlet, but short of that there was no moving him; and his abstention prevented me from being proclaimed the winner. I published an analysis of the position, demonstrating that he was bound to lose and suggesting that he should either play it out or resign. But of course the result of my manoeuvres had simply been to drive him into blind fury and the situation was never settled. It simply lapsed by my departure for Switzerland.

10

My grand passion was Beachy Head. The fantastic beauty of the cliffs can never be understood by anyone who has not grappled them. Mountain scenery of any kind, but especially rock scenery, depends largely on foreground. This is especially the case when one has acquired an intimate knowledge of the meaning, from the climber's point of view, of what the eyes tell one. The ordinary man looking at a mountain is like an illiterate person confronted with a Greek manuscript. The only chalk in England which is worth reading, so to speak, is that on Beachy Head. This is due to the fact that it is relatively so much higher than other similar cliffs. Most chalk cliffs are either unbroken precipices, unclimbable in our present stage of the game, or broken-down rubble; but Beachy Head offers rock problems as varied, interesting and picturesque as any cliffs in the world. I began to explore the face. Popular ignorance had surrounded it with innumerable absurd rumours. The general opinion was that no one had ever climbed it. There was, however, a legend that it had once been done. I settled the point by walking up, smoking a pipe, with my dog (I had no woman available) in nine and a half minutes from the beach to the coastguard station.

My cousin, Gregor Grant, was with me on my earlier climbs. These were the most obvious, but also the most important. Etheldreda's Pinnacle—which I named after my dog, or a schoolgirl with whom I had stolen interviews, I forget which —was the first great triumph. The second was the Devil's Chimney, and the third the Cuillin Crack. I have always refused till now to claim this climb, as I finished it with the moral support of a loose rope from above. It would be formidable enough were it of the best rock in the world: there is one section which actually overhangs. I believe that these latter climbs have never been repeated.

Chalk is probably the most dangerous and difficult of all kinds of rock. Its condition varies at every step. Often one has to clear away an immense amount of debris in order to get any hold at all. Yet indiscretion in this operation might pull down a few hundred tons on one's head. One can hardly ever be sure that any given hold is secure. It is, therefore, a matter of the most exquisite judgment to put on it no more weight than is necessary. A jerk or a spring would almost infallibly lead to disaster. One does not climb the cliffs. One hardly even crawls. Trickles or oozes would perhaps be the ideal verbs.

The unique character of the climbing led to an amusing incident. The greatest rock climber in England, A. F. Mummery, published a short account of his work on the cliffs at Dover, where he lived. He stated that at more than twenty to thirty feet above sea-level no climbing was possible, and that practically all his climbs were traverses; that is, horizontal and not vertical. I wrote to him saying that my experience was precisely the opposite. All my climbing had been done at greater altitudes, and that (with hardly an exception) my climbs were vertical. He wrote back rather superciliously to the effect that there were certainly grassy gullies which corresponded to my description, but they were not what he called climbing. I replied, thanking him and begging him to accept a few photographs of the grassy gullies under description. These showed the most formidable-looking pinnacles in the British Islands, and vertical cracks as precipitous as anything in Cumberland. He wrote back immediately a warm letter of congratulation. It was evident that we had been using the word 'chalk' to cover two widely different species of material.

I published some of my records in the local newspapers with the idea of inspiring the natives with praiseworthy enthusiasm. Once again I had misjudged humanity. All I got was a leading article beginning with the words, 'Insensate folly takes various forms.' Another shock was to come. Cousin Gregor suddenly declared that he was engaged to be married and that he didn't think he had the right to climb any more on Beachy Head. My boyhood's idol was shattered at a blow. I received my first lesson in what the religions of the world have discovered long since, that no man who allows a woman to take any place in his life is capable of doing good work. (Similarly, men may be as foolish over dogs as old maids over cats.) A man who is strong enough to use women as slaves and playthings is all right. Even so, there is always a danger, though it is difficult to avoid it. In fact, I don't think it should be avoided. I think a man should train himself to master what are commonly called vices, from maidens to morphia. It is undeniable that there are very few such men. Again and again

I have had the most promising pupils give up the great work of their lives for the sake of some wretched woman who could have been duplicated in a Ten Cent Store. It doesn't matter what the work is; if it is worth while doing, it demands one's whole attention, and a woman is only tolerable in one's life if she is trained to help the man in his work without the slightest reference to any other interests soever. The necessary self-abnegation and concentration on his part must be matched by similar qualities on hers. I say matched—I might say better, surpassed—for such devotion must be blind. A man can *become* his work, so that he satisfies himself by satisfying it; but a woman is fundamentally incapable of understanding the nature of work in itself. She must consent to co-operate with him in the dark. Her self-surrender is, therefore, really self-surrender, whereas with him it is rather self-realization. It is true that if a woman persists long enough in the habit, she will ultimately find herself therein. For woman is a creature of habit, that is, of solidified impulses. She has no individuality. Attached to a strong man who is no longer himself but his work, she may become a more or less reliable mood. Otherwise her moods change with her phantasms. But the most dominant mood of woman will always be motherhood. Nature itself, therefore, insures that a man who relies on a woman to help him is bucking the tiger. At any moment, without warning, her interest in him may be swept off its feet and become secondary. Worse—she will expect her man to abandon the whole interest of his life in order to look after her new toy. A bitch does not lose all her interest in her master just because she has puppies.

I found a new climbing companion on Beachy Head in a man named J. S. New. We worked out the possible climbs systematically and made a large-scale map of the cliff. I ultimately contributed an illustrated article on the subject to the *Scottish Mountaineering Journal*. But with the exception of Mr H. S. Bullock, and one or two others who repeated a few of our climbs and made one or two new ones, little work has been done on the Head. Climbers generally seem to have come to the conclusion that it was altogether too dangerous. It must be admitted that, at any rate, it is very unpleasant. In wet weather the chalk forms a paste which clogs the boots and makes foothold impossible. In dry weather the dust takes possession of the eyes and throat. But for all that, many of my happiest days have been spent on the face.

I must record a very strange phenomenon in connection

with my adventures on Beachy Head. One summer day I went up with my mother and took her down to the grassy slopes (the Grass Traverse) which used to extend eastward from Etheldreda's Pinnacle. I say 'used to extend', for since that time there has been an extensive landslide. It was rather a scramble for an old lady to reach them from the top of the cliff, but it could be done by descending a narrow gully called Etheldreda's Walk. I put her in a comfortable position where she could make a water-colour sketch, and went off to do some climbing on the Devil's Chimney, which is some distance west of the pinnacle. The general contour of the cliff is here convex, so that I was entirely out of her sight, besides being a quarter of a mile away. Such breeze as there was was blowing from the south-west, that is, from me to her. I was trying to make a new climb on the west of the Devil's Chimney and had got some distance down, when I distinctly heard her crying for help. At this time I had no acquaintance with psychic phenomena, yet I recognized the call as of this type; that is, I had a direct intuition that it was so. It was not merely that it seemed improbable that it could be normal audition. I did not know at the time for certain that this was impossible, though it was afterwards proved to be so by experiment. I had no reason for supposing the danger to be urgent; but I rushed madly to the top of the cliff, along it and down to the Grass Traverse. I reached her in time to save her life, though there were not many seconds to spare. She had shifted her position to get a better view and had wandered off the traverse on to steep, dusty, crumbling slopes. She had begun to slip, got frightened and done the worst thing possible; that is, had sat down. She had been slipping by inches on the brink of a cliff when I reached her. She had actually cried for help at the time when I heard her, as nearly as I could judge; but, as explained above, it was physically impossible for me to have done so. I regard this incident as very extraordinary indeed. I have never taken much stock in the regular stories of people appearing at a distance at the moment of death and so on; nor does the fact of something so similar having actually happened to me make me inclined to believe such stories. I cannot offer any explanation, apart from the conventional magical theory that a supreme explosion of will is sometimes able to set forces in motion which cannot be invoked in ordinary circumstances.

To return to my subject. Despite the regrettable incident of impulsive humanitarianism above recorded, my associations with Beachy Head possess a charm which I have never known in any other district of England. My climbs there fulfilled all my ideals of romance, and in addition I had the particularly delightful feeling of complete originality. In other districts I could be no more than *primus inter pares*. On Beachy Head I was the only one—I had invented an entirely new branch of the sport.

For a number of weeks I slept in a Mummery tent on one of the traverses. It was my first experience of camp life, which is, one thing with another, the best life I know. The mere feeling of being in the fresh air under the stars when one goes to sleep, and of waking at dawn because it is dawn, raises one's animal life *ipso facto* to the level of poetry.

There have always been in me two quite incompatible personalities with regard to my judgment of men and in practical matters. One of them possesses great instinctive shrewdness partaking of cynicism; the other an innocence amounting almost to imbecility. *Der reine Thor!* In certain respects, this latter quality is calculated. Thus, I have always refused to believe that I am being cheated, even when I know the facts perfectly well. I have deliberately made up my mind that it is not worth while to allow my purity to be contaminated by descending to the level of the people who are swindling me. In some matters again, I am genuinely unable to criticize; and so I take people at their face value, occasionally with disastrous results.

For instance, one of the most original characters that I have ever met was the Rev. T. C. V. Bastow, of Little Peatling Rectory, Lutterworth. It was the proud boast of this gentleman, who used to spend his vacations at Wastdale Head, that he possessed a rudimentary tail; and though I was never favoured personally with a view of this distinction, he was credited with readiness to demonstrate the Darwinian theory to any earnest young anatomist who might be in the offing. He wandered about the crags with a three-pronged claw attached to twenty or thirty feet of rope, his theory being to throw it up the rocks till it caught somewhere, and then swarm up the rope. He gave himself the air of being a rock climber of the first rank and I never thought of doubting it.

Now I had made the first solitary descent of the Ennerdale face of the Pillar Rock, a feat at that time considered theoretically impossible. He asked me casually whether it was the sort of place that he could take his daughter. I did a sort of rule of three sum in my head. If poor little I, the beginner, could do it, a fortiori so could the great man, even with the handicap of the girl novice. As a matter of fact, he could not climb at all, and the delightful pair found themselves crag-fast.

Some years later I made a blunder of the same kind which resulted in a frightful tragedy. I was in Arolla in 1897 * with Morris Travers and his younger brother. In Coolidge's Guide there is a record of the ascent of the Petite Dent de Veisivi by the gap facing Arolla. The local guides, however, unanimously denied that this route had ever been done. The rocks below the gap, they said, were overhanging and were impossible. We decided to test these statements, ascended the mountain by the ordinary way and came down by the route in question. The rocks do overhang, but the holds are so good that the climb is quite easy. We discussed the climb with a son of the celebrated Dr John Hopkinson, Edward, who was there with a large family. We said, quite truthfully, that there was no difficulty or danger for a responsible party; but he and three of his children attempted to repeat our climb and all were killed. A peculiarly English incident adds a touch of grotesque grimness to the story. The widow begged Travers, who was a member of the rescue party (I had left the valley), to allow her to take a last look at her husband. She had been brought up to fancy pictures of people lying in state—'calm and grand in Death', and that sort of thing. As a matter of fact, all the remains had been brought down in one sack; no one could tell what was whose.

This difficulty in understanding that professed climbers could be incurably incompetent culminated in the one great mistake of my mountaineering career. Despite the actual evidence of 1902 that Dr Jacot Guillarmod was utterly ignorant and untrustworthy, vain and obstinate, I consented to take him to Kangchenjunga, with the disastrous result to be recorded later.

There remains one remarkable incident of my climbing in Cumberland. I had been trying some new routes on the Pillar Rock one day, when I was caught by a terrific thunderstorm. Luckily for me, as it turned out, I was soaked to the skin in ten minutes. Any further serious climbing being impossible, I started back to Wastdale. In doing this one crosses the ridge of Pillar Mountain, along which runs a wire sheep fence. I crossed this; and, the storm increasing in violence, my attention was attracted by the little flames of lightning that played upon the iron uprights. I forgot about my axe. The next thing I knew was that I had been knocked down. I can hardly say that

---

* See *Collected Works*, vol. I, p. 127.[1]

I felt any definite electrical shock: but I knew what must have happened. I was seized by a curious mixture of exhilaration and terror; and dashed down the face of the mountain at its steepest point, leaping from rock to rock like a goat. I easily beat the record from the summit to the hotel! Despite the intense concentration * necessary to jump down the dangerous crags, my conscious attention was absorbed by the magnificent spectacle of the cliffs of Scafell, framed in lurid purple storm clouds and literally ablaze with lightning; continuous and vivid to a degree that I have never since seen except on one occasion near Madrid, when the entire sky was a kaleidoscopic network of flame for nearly two hours.

---

* But see *The Book of Lies*, cap. 32, 'The Mountaineer'.

11

In 1894 I had my first serious taste of the Alps. I went with my tutor to the Suldenthal in the Austrian Tyrol. I had discovered the Badminton Volume of Mountaineering.[1] I looked on it very much as I had been taught to look on the Bible. It says much for my innocence previously described, that despite the data already in my possession, I failed entirely to realize that the one book was as full of grotesque blunders and inaccuracies as the other. I arrived in Sulden with a deep reverence for the Alpine guide, and hastened to engage Joseph Pingerra, who was supposed to be the best in the valley. I was very shocked to find that it was customary in the Tyrol to go two on a rope instead of three, though in point of fact this was the only thing they knew about climbing. But I was amazed beyond measure to find that I was a much better rock climber than my guide. He did not know what rock climbing was, judged by Cumberland standards! I had no experience of snow and ice; so here, of course, I was the reverent disciple. Imagine my astonishment, then, when after two or three days Pingerra slipped and fell on a perfectly easy snow slope. He was entirely unable to do anything to save himself and I had to pull him up on the rope. I retained my faith in Badminton by saying to myself that the guides in the outlying groups must be very poor examples. I engaged two other guides and started for the Königspitze, spending the night in a hut. In the morning the guides were drunk and unwilling to start, making absurd excuses about the weather. I had not sufficient self-confidence to tackle the Königspitze by myself; but I dismissed them, made a solitary ascent of the Eisseespitze, and thought the matter over. I was utterly disgusted and decided to learn ice and snowcraft by myself, as I had with rocks.

A few days later I went out alone and made the first ascent of the Ortler by the Hintere Grat. The mountain had previously been climbed on this side; but the ridge had not been followed with the conscientiousness which was the rule in England. It took me six and a half hours to reach the summit.

My arrival created a profound sensation. Sitting on the top

were an American and a guide, who had come up by the easy way from the Payerhütte. The guide regarded my appearance as strictly supernatural; but the American feared not God, neither regarded man. He had been trying to persuade the guide to go down to Sulden by the Hintere Grat and the guide had cold feet.

My arrival changed the situation. Once assured that I was flesh and blood, the guide plucked up a little courage, which the American further stimulated by a promise of additional dollars. As I had come up alone, the three of us could evidently go down together. I agreed to accept the responsible position of last man and we roped up accordingly. But we were no sooner started than the guide again lost whatever nerve he ever possessed. His employer had never been on a mountain before, but he had common sense and pluck; he behaved admirably in every respect; we half nursed and half chivvied that guide down that ridge. It was, of course, out of the question to follow the ridge, as I had just done, so that two or three thousand feet of the descent were accomplished by glissading down snow slopes. If I had been alone I could have got down by that route in under three hours. As it was, we took nine and a half. But the next day the guide had no lack of nerve; he wanted me to pay him for his services! Nothing doing.

I made a number of other ascents in the district, for the most part alone, but once or twice with some chance-met English. My chief aim was to master the technique of snow and ice; and by dint of using my senses and my sense I found out most of the tricks of the trade in the course of the season. I am particularly proud of having invented a pattern of Steigeisen, identical with that used by Oscar Eckenstein as far as the idea was concerned. The difference was that he, being an engineer, had had them forged in accordance with mechanical principles, whereas I had entrusted the execution of mine to a rotten firm with a great reputation in Alpine Club circles, whose ignorance of the elements of material and workmanship must have caused many 'regrettable incidents'.

In 1895 I felt myself fit to tackle the higher peaks of the Alps and went to the Little Scheideck. My first exploit was a solitary ascent of the Eiger. I started late and on the final ridge caught up with a 'strong' party of English with guides, the principal Herr being a charming clergyman from Japan, the Rev. Walter Weston. The guides were more or less drunk and frightened. They were trying to make some excuse for turning back; but shame stimulated their courage when I came up and we proceeded to the summit. We all went down together; the guides professed themselves delighted with the sure-footed agility of my performance and said that I was *'wie ein Führer'*. A year before the compliment would have persuaded me that I had died and gone to heaven, but time had changed all that. I still clung pathetically to Badminton; I had merely reached the stage of praying pathetically to meet the good guides described in the book. I was still obsessed by the idea that it was suicidal to cross snow-covered glaciers without a rope. So I took a porter: he was quite willing to obey my orders implicitly, since I was regarded as a *Wunderkind*. We went up the Jungfrau by the Schneehorn-Silberhorn route, I leading up and descending last. But it was the same old story. The man couldn't stand on a snow slope. I was constantly having to misuse valuable time in saving his worthless life.

I began to reason the whole business out from the start. Mountaineering, I saw, was primarily a scientific problem. How, then, could the superstitious and ignorant peasants of the Alps master it or even attack it? There could be only one answer; they made no attempt to do so. Their craft was traditional; one man learnt from another by rule of thumb. Confront any guide with any mountain that he did not know by habit, and he was at sea. How was it, then, that the mountains had ever been climbed at all? And the answer to that was that the general standard of climbing was, given good weather conditions, altogether beneath contempt from the standpoint of the pioneers in England and Wales. The ordinary way up any Swiss mountain is little more than a scramble. Eckenstein used to say that he would take a cow up the Matterhorn provided that he were allowed to tie its legs. And once, when an ex-president of the Alpine Club began to reply to this remark by mentioning that he had been up the Matterhorn, some tactless person interrupted, 'Did they tie *your* legs?'

Mummery, Collie and Hastings from England, with Eckenstein and one or two minor lights on the one hand, and Purtscheller, Blodig and others from Germany on the other, were setting up an entirely new standard of Alpine climbing. They were men of education and intelligence; they had studied the physical theory of mountain conditions; they had practised the various types of technique required to meet these conditions in detail. They were doing climbs which had never been dreamt of by any Alpine guide. The first-rate amateur was to the professional as a rifleman to a man with a flint axe.

In '95 I was not yet aware of what was going on. I discovered independently the facts of the case. I found that I could go pretty well anywhere without the least danger or difficulty, whereas all the people I met were constantly on the brink of disaster. I began to think that solitary climbing was the safest form of the game. The one problem was the snow-covered glacier. I began to study that question by itself. I soon noticed that when I looked down on such a glacier from a ridge, I could see the covered crevasses quite plainly. They appeared as lines of shade. Descending to the glacier, I found that I was still able to detect the slight differences in illumination. So much for the theory. But the question still remained, 'I see it, but can I cross it safely?' My experience with chalk helped to give me confidence. I was accustomed to estimate the breaking-strain of rotten material. Now, given a night's hard frost, it stands to reason that a bridge which has not fallen through by its own weight during the previous day would support my extra weight in the early morning. I began to test my theory, being, of course, careful to arrange my routes so as to avoid having to cross snow-covered glaciers after sunrise. I noticed, however, that a great deal of care was necessary to avoid accidents; and this made for slowness. There were also many other occasions on which a second man would be a safeguard, and some when he might be of active assistance.

The question of a third man is quite different. He diminishes the mobility of the party; the middle man is deprived almost completely of any freedom of action. Whenever the ground is so difficult that only one man can move at a time, a party of three takes not half as long again but twice as long as a party of two, since the operation of pulling in a section of rope is duplicated. The speed of a party means a great deal to its safety. As regards nightfall, weather conditions, and avalanches or falling stones, two is evidently much safer than three. Another point is that it is at least twice as hard to find two competent companions as it is to find one.

The combination of Mummery, Collie and Hastings could hardly happen again in a century. Mummery had a genius for rock climbing and an uncanny instinct for mountain problems in general. Collie was brilliant all round and had an absolute scientific knowledge of materials and a feeling for topography. Hastings was a tower of physical strength and endurance, an ideal second man either as a hoist or an anchor. All three were accomplished technicians and had experience of every kind of ground and conditions.

In the absence of so miraculous a combination, the best thing to be hoped for was one other man who would possess all the qualities which one lacked oneself; and it was my supreme good fortune in 1898 to find what I sought in Oscar Eckenstein.

In the meantime I went on climbing in the Bernese Oberland during the summer of 1895. Certainly the Lord must have been leading me, for I hardly ever went out on a mountain without striking some episode which directed my thoughts into the right channel.

To return to psychology. It is hard to summarize the general effects of my queer education. But it was terribly uneven. In some respects I was a long way ahead of most boys of my age; in others I was little better than an imbecile. I was practically prevented from acquiring the habit of normal relations with other people. My associates were, for the most part, much older than myself.

But the one really disastrous feature was the attitude which I was compelled to assume about money. I was taught to expect every possible luxury. Nothing was too good for me; and I had no idea of what anything cost. It was all paid for behind my back. I was never taught that effort on my part might be required to obtain anything that I wanted; but on the other hand I was kept criminally short of pocket money lest I should spend it in some disgraceful way, such as buying books or tobacco, or spending it on even worse abominations such as theatres and women. (I was encouraged to keep a dog!) I had therefore no sense of responsibility in the matter of money. It never occurred to me that it was possible to make it, and I was thus trained to be dependent to the point of mendicancy. The effect was, of course, disastrous. When I got to Cambridge I still had everything paid for me and in addition I found myself with unlimited credit which I could keep secret. When I came into my fortune a year later, I was utterly unprepared to use it with the most ordinary prudence, and all the inherent vices of my training had a perfectly free field for their development. Before, if I wanted to give a dinner party every day of the week, I could do it, but if I wanted a little cash my only alternative to the card table was the pawnshop, till I came of age. After that, it was simply a question of writing a cheque, which gave me no idea of the nature of the transaction involved. I doubt whether any one in history was ever furnished with such a completely rotten preparation for the management of practical affairs.

My residence at Eastbourne broke up very suddenly. During the whole of my adolescence I had taken the romantic point of view of love; and I found that the universal practice was for elder people to interfere in the affairs of their juniors. Two people could not decide to marry without rousing a hurricane. There was never any exception. Engagements were always being made and broken on unintelligible religious grounds. The family of the Lamberts was no exception to this. The eldest daughter was an acid old maid in the late twenties; the youngest was a hysterical monster of suppression. The middle girl was beautiful, voluptuous and normal. She was not sufficiently intelligent to revolt openly against her family; but her human instincts told her that something was wrong and that she had better get out of it. She was in love with a quite suitable young man and engaged to him on probation. The question was whether he would or wouldn't join the Plymouth Brethren. Naturally, the more he saw of them the less he liked them and he ultimately made up his mind to stand by the church of his fathers. On announcing this desolating decision he was overwhelmed with abuse and thrown out of the house. His fiancée was forbidden to communicate with him in any way, and to all intents and purposes imprisoned. I offered to arrange for correspondence with a view to an early elopement. But I couldn't stand the continuous abuse and ill-treatment which was the portion of the unfortunate girl. The family literally foamed at the mouth on every opportunity. Meals were a poisoned whirlwind. She was constantly reduced to tears and perhaps the happiest time she had was when she was actually being beaten. I ought to have conducted my intrigues with greater patience, no doubt, but it got on my nerves too much. One morning at breakfast I said about a millionth part of what I thought and the family started screaming. It was as if they had been attacked by collective mania. Everything was thrown at me; they went for me with claws and fists. They were too blind with rage to know what they were doing. I simply knocked their heads together and walked out of the house. When I thought the atmosphere had had time to dissipate I returned with the intention of carrying out a rescue for the distressed damsel. They were too much scared to oppose me and I begged her to come away at once and go to her ex-fiancé's family. But she could not summon up courage to do it. The opportunity went by; and later in the afternoon my Uncle Tom, summoned by telegram, came to fetch me away from the accursed spot.

The incident had a wholesome effect upon my own family. They had failed to break my spirit and begun to realize that I had reached the stage when I could make as much trouble for them as they could for me. The best thing they could do was to let me go my own way. I had won the fight; and the evidence of my triumph was my season in the Bernese Oberland on my own responsibility. I was recalled by a telegram. They had decided to let me go to Trinity; and the entrance examination was only a week away. I went up to Cambridge and passed it without difficulty, though I had no opportunity of preparing the set classics. But I followed Browning's advice to 'greet the Unseen with a cheer': my real knowledge of Greek and Latin enabled me to give renderings, far above the average, of unfamiliar passages. I could never adapt myself to the sheep-system of mnemonic 'learning'. In October I entered the university, taking rooms at 16 St John's Street. From that moment begins an entirely new chapter in my life.

12

When I went up to Cambridge in the October term of 1895, I had the sensation of drawing a long deep breath as one does after swimming under water or (an even better analogy) as one does after bracing oneself against the pain inflicted by a dentist. I could not imagine anything better in life. I found myself suddenly in an entirely new world. I was part of the glories of the past; and I made a firm resolution to be one of the glories of the future. I should like the haunted room over the Great Gate of Trinity to be turned into a vault like that of Christian Rosencreutz to receive my sarcophagus. I must admit that I don't know of much else in England of the works of man which I would not make haste to destroy if the opportunity occurred. But Trinity, except New Court and Whewell's Court, is enough for any poet to live and die for.

I remember being amazed in later years when my patriotism was doubted. I wasn't going to have '*Eintritt Verboten*' put up over the Great Gate with a Prussian sentry to enforce it. I am perfectly aware that I am irrational. The traditions of England are intertwined inextricably with a million abuses and deformities which I am only too eager to destroy. But all Englishmen keep their brains in watertight compartments. It would be a comic degradation to make Trinity the headquarters of the Rationalist Press Association. But at the time I had not seen the logical incompatibility of my various positions. Shakespeare's patriotism in John of Gaunt's dying speech and *Henry V* appeals directly to my poetic sense.

I am quite prepared to die for England in that brutal, unthinking way. 'Rule, Britannia' gets me going as if I were the most ordinary music-hall audience. This sentiment is not interfered with by my detestation of the moral and religious humbug which one is expected to produce at moments of national crisis. My patriotism is of the blatant, unintelligent variety, popularized by Kipling. I like the old rime:

> Two skinny Frenchmen, one Portugee,
> One jolly Englishman lick 'em all three.

But I can find no moral excuse for my attitude. I am an animal with a family and a country. To hell with everybody! This animal is prepared to use its brains and its force as stupidly and unscrupulously as the Duke of Wellington. It is not convinced by its own philosophical opinions, which condemn patriotism as parochialism, regard war as immoral savagery and economic insanity, and consider public opinion and its leaders as the bleating of sheep, huddling into their fold at the barking of mongrel dogs.

The atmosphere of Cambridge formed an admirable background for my state of mind. I saw myself as a romantic character in history. The Church of England, as represented by my Uncle Tom, had seemed a narrow tyranny, as detestable as that of the Plymouth Brethren; less logical and more hypocritical. My Uncle Jonathan was a sound churchman; but he kept his religion to himself and went his own triumphant way in the world, keeping ecclesiastical discipline at arm's length as far as he himself was concerned. He was prima facie one of the saved, whenever he troubled to think about it, no doubt; but in practice the Church of England was simply a machine for keeping the lower classes in their proper place. At Trinity it was the same thing. Christianity was the official religion with which it was convenient to comply, just as it is convenient to go to a good tailor. It was, in short, a political paganism.

I don't suppose that I appreciated this fact at the time, in that way. My attitude was determined by the unquestionable beauty of ecclesiastical architecture and the comparative dignity of the ritual. But when I discovered that chapel was compulsory I immediately struck back. The junior dean halled me for not attending chapel, which I was certainly not going to do, because it involved early rising. I excused myself on the ground that I had been brought up among the Plymouth Brethren. The dean asked me to come and see him occasionally and discuss the matter, and I had the astonishing impudence to write to him that 'the seed planted by my father, watered by my mother's tears, would prove too hardy a growth to be uprooted even by his eloquence and learning'. It sounds like the most despicable hypocrisy, but it was pretty good cheek, and I had made up my mind that I would not be interfered with. I regarded any attempt to control my actions as an impertinent intrusion and I was not going to waste time in taking any but the easiest way out.

I entered for the Moral Science Tripos with the idea that it

would help me to learn something about the nature of things.
I don't know why it should have interested me. It must have
been my subconscious will speaking. In any case, I was profoundly disgusted to find that political economy was one of
the subjects. I attended the first lecture; the professor told us
that his subject was a very difficult one because there were no
reliable data. It is easy to imagine the effect of such a statement
on a boy who had been trained in the exactitude of mathematics and chemistry. I closed my notebook and never
attended another lecture. My tutor naturally called me to
account, but by great good fortune he was a man of extraordinary ability—Dr A. W. Verrall. He accepted my plea that
my business in life was to study English literature. He was,
indeed, most sympathetic. He knew only too well that the
university curriculum afforded no opportunities. He knew,
too, that my school knowledge was amply sufficient to take me
through the university examinations without my doing any
work for them. In fact, during my three years I only did one
day's work for the university, and that consisted in employing
a boy to read through a translation of a Greek play while I
followed it in the text. I got either a first or second class in
every subject.

One of the dons at Pembroke, a clergyman named Heriz
Smith, ran a sort of secret cult which was disrespectfully called
by outsiders the Belly-banders. There were said to be seven
degrees of initiation, in the highest of which the candidate was
flagellated. I took the first degree out of curiosity. It made so
little impression on me that I have altogether forgotten what
took place. I remember that I was alone in the man's room with
him. He blindfolded me. I waited for something to happen;
it did not. I was, of course, utterly unable to divine what
purpose might lie behind the scheme. It was, of course, looked
upon as cant by the man's own colleagues, who probably presumed certain undesirable features.

I am rather sorry now that I did not continue. There may
have been nothing in it beyond sensuous mysticism, but for
all I know Heriz Smith may have developed a method of
psycho-analysis of quite possibly great value. I am inclined to
think that the most scientific and reliable way of exploring
people's unconscious minds would be to watch their reaction
to a well-thought-out series of unfamiliar circumstances. One
could compare their respective qualities, such as will-power,
patience, dignity, courage, imperturbability, and so on. Such

data should be of great use in answering the question, 'Where-withal shall a young man mend his ways?'

I was very put out by finding, as a first year man, that Hall was at half-past eight. I objected to my evenings being cut into by dining so late and soon acquired the habit of having all meals sent in from the kitchen. I was thus almost totally dissociated from the corporate life of the college. The only institution which interested me was the debating society, the Magpie and Stump. But I could not take even this seriously. It seemed to me absurd for these young asses to emit their callow opinions on important subjects. I was only interested in 'rag' debates. I remember on one occasion that the suggestion had been made by a committee inspired by one of the tutors, the eminent mathematician, W. W. Rouse Ball, to establish a junior common-room. My contribution to the discussion was to say that 'this proposal seems to me to be all Ball's.' (An even happier moment was in a debate on a proposal to institute a passion play in England, when Lord Kilmarnock said that it would certainly be a popular attraction to hear Arthur Roberts say 'I thirst.')

My three years were determined by the influence of a fourth year man named Adamson, whom I think I met at the chess club. He started to talk to me about English literature. For the first time I heard the name Shelley. *Wie gesagt, so gethan.* Nothing else seemed to me worth while but a thorough reading of the great minds of the past. I bought all the classical authors. Whenever I found a reference of one to another I hastened to order his works. I spent the whole of my time in reading. It was very rare that I got to bed before daylight. But I had a horror of being thought a 'smug'; and what I was doing was a secret from my nearest friends. Whenever they were about I was playing chess and cards. In the daytime I went canoeing or cycling. I had no occupations which brought me into close touch with any great body of undergraduates. I even gave up the habit of going round to see people, though I was always at home to anyone who chose to call. I was not interested in the average man; I cultivated the freak. It was not that I liked abnormal people, it was simply the scientific attitude that it is from the abnormal that we learn.

Most people of this disposition are readily carried away into anti-social channels. But with me this was not the case. I dropped my subscription to the boat club because I was getting nothing out of it; but I was always wildly enthusiastic about

the success of the boat. I have always had a passionate yearning for mankind, wholesale and retail, but I cannot endure to
have them anywhere around. It is a very peculiar psychology;
yet it is frequently found among poets. We are lonely and
suffer intensely on that account. We are prepared to love any
and every specimen of humanity in himself, for himself, and
by himself; but even a dinner party gets on our nerves.

It is perhaps part of the psychology of sensitiveness. We
cannot bear having our corners knocked off, and at the same
time we are so well aware of the intense suffering of isolation
that we long to lose ourselves in a crowd at a football match.
I can be perfectly happy as an unknown individual in a revel,
from a political meeting to a masked ball; but inevitably one's
unique qualities draw attention to one; the cruel consciousness
of self is reawakened, one becomes utterly miserable and flees
to the ends of the earth to be rid of one's admirers. A certain
coarseness is inseparable from popularity and one is therefore constantly driven away from the very thing one needs
most. It is a quasi-electrical phenomenon. One can only find
satisfaction in intimate union with one's opposite.

This fact explains very largely the peculiar nature of the
love affairs of great men. They cannot tolerate their like. Their
superiority is recognized as the cause of their pain, and they
assuage their pain by cultivating people to whom that superiority means nothing. They deliberately seek the most degraded
and disgusting specimens of women that exist. Otherwise, they
brutalize themselves by addiction to drink and drugs. The
motive is always the same; to lose consciousness of their
Promethean pangs.

I must here point out that the social system of England
makes it impossible for a young man of spirit and intelligence
to satisfy his nature with regard to sex in any reasonable way.
The young girl of position similar to his own is being fattened
for the market. Even when his own situation makes it possible
for him to obtain her he has to pay an appalling price; and it
becomes more difficult than ever for him to enjoy female
companionship. Monogyny is nonsense for any one with a
grain of imagination. The more sides he has to his nature, the
more women he needs to satisfy it. The same is, of course, true,
mutatis mutandis, of women. A woman risks her social existence by a single experiment. A young man is compelled by the
monogamic system to develop his character by means of
corrupt society vampires or women of the lower classes, and
though he may learn a great deal from these sources, it cannot

but be unfortunate that he has no opportunity to learn from women of his own birth, breeding, education and rank in society.

Now, monogamy has very little to do with monogyny; and should have less. Monogamy is only a mistake because it leaves the excess women unsatisfied and unprovided for. But apart from this, it provides for posterity, and it is generally recognized that this is the crux of all practical arguments on the subject. But the defect of monogamy, as generally understood, is that it is connected with the sexual appetite. The Practical Wisdom of the Astrologers has made this clear. The Fifth House (love, children) has nothing to do with the Seventh (marriage, lawsuits, public enemies). Marriage would lead to very little trouble if men would get rid of the idea that it is anything more than a financial and social partnership. People should marry for convenience and agree to go their separate ways without jealousy. It should be a point of honour for the woman to avoid complicating the situation with children by other men, unless her husband be willing, which he would be if he really loved her. It is monstrous for a man to pretend to be devoted to securing his wife's happiness and yet to wish to deprive her of a woman's supreme joy: that of bearing a child to the man whom she desires sexually, and is therefore indicated by nature as the proper father, though he may be utterly unsuitable as a husband. In most cases this would be so, for it must obviously be rare that a man with a genius for paternity should also possess a talent for domesticity. We have heard a great deal in recent years of the freedom of women. They have gained what they thought they wanted and it has availed them nothing. They must adopt the slogan, 'There shall be no property in human flesh.' They must train men to master their sexual selfishness, while of course allowing them the same freedom as they themselves will enjoy. The true offences against marriage arise when sexual freedom results in causing injury to the health or estate of the partner. But the sentimental wrong of so-called infidelity is a symptom of the childishness of the race.

Among artists, the system here advocated has always been more or less in full swing. Such societies exist in circumstances highly inimical to a satisfactory life. Financial considerations alone make this obvious; yet it is notorious that such people are almost uniformly happy. There is no revolt against the facts of life, because there is no constraint. The individual is respected as such and is allowed to act as he or she likes without penalty or even reproach. Only when selfish or commercial considerations arise do we find catastrophe.

It is commonly supposed that women themselves are the chief obstacle to such an arrangement. But this is only because they have been drilled into thinking that the happiness and well-being of the children depend upon their supporting the existing system. When you tackle a woman on the subject she pretends to be very shocked; and hysterically denies the most obvious facts. But she wilts under cross-examination and agrees with the above conclusions in a very short time. For women have no morality in the sense of the word which is ordinarily understood in Anglo-Saxondom. Women never let ideals interfere with their practical good sense. They are also influenced by selfishness; it is natural to them to put the interests of their childen before their own. Men, on the other hand, are hard to convince. When forced to analyse the situation, they arrive not at a reason but at a prejudice, and this is purely the brainless bestial lust for exclusive possession.

Anthropology proves these theorems thoroughly. The first step in civilization is to restrain women from infidelity. The institutions of the pardah, sati and the marriage laws all show that men think that women must be kept under lock and key, whereas women have always realized that it is impossible and undesirable to prevent men from taking their happiness where they find it. The emancipation of women, therefore, depends entirely upon leaving them free to act as men do. Their good sense will prevent them from inflicting the real wrongs; and besides, their complete independence and happiness will encourage them in nobility and generosity.

We already see, in America, the results of the emancipation of women from the economic fetter. There is an immense class of bachelor girls (and of married women whose husbands are strictly business machines) who pick up men with the same nonchalance as the young 'blood' picked up women in my time at Cambridge.

I found myself, from the very beginning of my university career, urged by circumstances of every sort to indulge my passion in every way but the right one. My ill-health had prevented me from taking part in the ordinary amusements of the public school boy. My skill in avoiding corporal punishment and my lack of opportunity for inflicting it had saved me from developing the sadistic or masochistic sides to my character. But at Cambridge I discovered that I was of an intensely passionate nature, physiologically speaking. My poetic instincts, further, transformed the most sordid liaisons into romance, so that the impossibility of contracting a suitable and serious relation did not worry me. I found, moreover, that any sort of satisfaction acted as a powerful spiritual stimulus. Every adventure was the direct cause of my writing poetry. In the periods of suppression my brain had been completely clogged; I was as incapable of thought of any kind as if I had had the toothache.

I have a genuine grudge against the system on this account. Whole months of my life, which might have been profitably spent in all sorts of work, were taken up by the morbid broodings of the unsatisfied appetite. Repression is as mentally unwholesome as constipation, and I am furious, to this hour, that some of the best years of my life, which should have been spent in acquiring knowledge, were sterilized by the suffocating stupor of preoccupation with sex. It was not that my mind was working on the subject; it was simply unable to work. It was a blind, horrible ache for relief. The necessities of men in this respect vary enormously. I was, no doubt, an exceptional case. But I certainly found even forty-eight hours of abstinence sufficient to dull the fine edge of my mind. Woe unto them by whom offences come! The stupidity of having had to waste uncounted priceless hours in chasing what ought to have been brought to the back door every evening with the milk!

Cambridge is, of course, an ideal place for a boy in my situation. Prostitution is to all intents and purposes non-existent, but nearly all the younger women of the district are eager to co-operate in the proper spirit—that of romance and passion.

There is thus little trace of public school *faute de mieux* paederasty: it survives only in very small 'aesthetic' coteries, composed mostly of congenital perverts, and in theological circles, where fear of scandal and of disease inhibit natural gratification. Oxford, of course, is different, chiefly, I believe, owing to the great Balliol tradition of statesmanship. The idea seems to be that intrigues with women are more dangerous than useful to a rising politician: while on the other side of the fence the state of the law supplies one with a pull on one's intimates on the Bench or in the Privy Council which is only the stronger because it is not, and never can be, used.

13

Till the Great Gate of Trinity opened me the way to freedom I had always been obsessed more or less either by physical weakness or the incubus of adolescence. I had never known what it was to be able to work freely and gladly. Now, however, I was able to give myself with absolute concentration to literature and I read everything important in the language with the utmost thoroughness. For example, I read the whole of the writings of people like Carlyle, Swift, Coleridge, Fielding, Gibbon, and so on. In this way I obtained a much more comprehensive idea of these men than if I had, as people usually do, picked out the masterpieces.

I was very anxious that my style should not be influenced by my contemporaries, and also not to waste myself on anybody who had not stood the test of time. I made it a rule to read no one who had not been dead for fifty years, unless brought under my notice in some special way. For example, I could not avoid Swinburne, as one of my friends was crazy about him, and I could not doubt, after the first acquaintance, that he was a classic. Similarly, I allowed myself to read Sir Richard Burton, because *The Arabian Nights* was an established masterpiece and his was the best translation. I also read a good deal of French literature and all the best Greek and Latin authors. But my peculiar temperament made me balk at one or two fences. I had certain innate ideas about literature; I say innate because I cannot imagine on what grounds I formed them. Thus I could not tolerate the idea of a novel exceeding a certain length, with the result that I have never read a page of Samuel Richardson. It is easier to understand the objection which I had to what I thought gossip. I have never read Boswell and have never been able to bring myself to face the average memoir. With regard to history * again, I demanded that the subject should be important. I did

---

* There is no such thing as history. The facts, even were they available, are too numerous to grasp. A selection must be made; and this can only be one-sided, because the selector is enclosed in the same network of time and space as his subject.

not see why I should bother my head about the Crimean War. I studied philosophy and kindred subjects with the greatest enthusiasm; but resented the form in which it was set forth by such people as Plato. It seemed to me that the argument of any of Plato's dialogues might have been presented much more clearly and cogently in about a tenth of the space. I made a very thorough study of logic as being my critical apparatus.

It is hard to say what motive impelled me to work so desperately hard as I did. Much of the work was anything but pleasant; and at the time, no less than now, it appeared quite useless. But I had a strong sense of duty about it. I think the idea was mostly to make sure that I knew everything that there was to be known, and incidentally to avoid the possibility of plagiarism. There was a certain tinge of vanity in the matter as well. I thought it shameful to leave anything unread. I was influenced by Ruskin's imbecile remark that any book worth reading was worth buying, and in consequence acquired books literally by the ton.

My plan of going from each author to those whom he quoted had a great advantage. It established a rational consecution in my research; and as soon as I reached a certain point the curves became re-entrant, so that my knowledge acquired a comprehensiveness which could never have been so satisfactorily attained by any arbitrary curriculum. I began to understand the real relation of one subject to another. I think I must have unconsciously asked myself which subject treated of reality in the most intimate and ultimate sense. I was, of course, far from the conception that all truth is equally important, or that no truth can by itself cover the whole ground of existence. My tendency was to discard certain types of research as immaterial. I gradually got the idea that the thing I was looking for was abstruse; and one of the results of this was to induce me to read the literature of alchemy. It is perhaps natural for a young man to confuse obscurity with profundity.

With regard to the choice of a profession, I decided on the Diplomatic Service. It seemed to me to afford the greatest opportunities for worldly enjoyment, while at the same time demanding the highest qualities of mind. The subtlety of intrigue has always fascinated me. It is very curious that this should have been the case, in view of my master passion for for truth and my relentless determination to tell it without regard for consequences. The obstacle to my success in the preliminary canter was that I had no aptitude whatever for learning languages. I could master the grammar of a language in a few hours; but I was impatient of acquiring the vocabulary. Genders and inflections irritated my sense of simplicity. It is also difficult for me to acquire a language by ear, partly because my hearing is not particularly acute, and partly because I resent any conversation whatever which does not deal with matters of prime importance. The early stages of learning a language are, therefore, agonizing.

I had been advised with regard to the fourth language required for the examination not to take Italian, because so many people spoke it so perfectly, or Spanish, because it was considered the easiest way into the service, but Russian, on account of its extreme difficulty, and because the knowledge of it made one eligible for appointment to the most interesting and brilliant court in Europe. This led to my going to St Petersburg, a journey which worked wonders in enlarging my outlook on the world.

The passion for travel was already very strong in me. Home was my idea of hell; and London itself had a sordid aspect which never appealed to me. The idea of wickedness in London is connected with that of shame, and besides this there are certainly excellent reasons for a poet to feel unhappy there. To begin with, I can't stand the climate. I have known rare days in May and June when youth pays a fleeting visit to town, when the sunlight excites and the breeze braces one. It is this idea of the Young Dionysus with which I am in love. I always feel myself as about eighteen or twenty; I always look at the world through those eyes. It is my constant sorrow that things do not always accommodate themselves to that point of view; and it is my eternal mission to redeem the universe to that state of intoxicated innocence and spiritual sensuality.

> I bring ye wine from above
>   From the vats of the storied sun.
> For every one of ye love,
>   And life for every one.[1]

The air of London is damp and depressing. It suggests the consciousness of sin. Whether one has a suite in the Savoy or an attic in Hoxton, the same spiritual atmosphere weighs upon the soul.

To a poet, moreover, the artistic side of London is the abomination of desolation. The plays are commercialized either for sentimentality or pornography. There is something uncomfortable in going to see a play by Shakespeare or Ibsen. Actors and spectators alike seem to be engaged in a dreary ritual. Grand opera is even worse. Covent Garden patronizes Wagner; he is an excuse for the display of diamonds. I shall never forget my first experience of Continental opera: *Lohengrin* at Stockholm. The atmosphere was absolutely natural; people had gone there because they really liked the music. I was transported into my own ideal world of love and melody. The caresses of my companion were the overflowing of ecstatic passion. Sin had been abolished, I was back in Eden.

In London one cannot even go to the National Gallery or the British Museum with a pure heart as one goes to the Louvre or the Prado. One cannot get away from the sense that one is performing an act of piety.

Concerts are even more dreadful than the opera. The surroundings are invariably bleak; one feels that the artist is doing it on purpose. Singing and playing demand background. Singing is the natural expression of human emotion, the joy of youth and life as connected with the landscapes of Corot and Gauguin, or with the interiors of Teniers. Elaborate instrumental music asks for appropriate architecture, not necessarily that of the cathedral. Music should have its own temples. London concert halls are blasphemous and obscene.

Before the cinema—the panorama. The camera obscura and the magic lantern were the popular scientific wonders of the period. Some nameless *pompier* had sluiced I do not know how many acres of canvas with a representation of Niagara. They built a pavilion to house it. One was supposed to be standing on Goat Island—in fact, one was rather the goat— and one walked round a vast gallery and inspected each segment of the waterfall in turn. In due course everyone had seen it and the question was what to do with the building. They turned it into a *palais de glace* with real ice. I, always keen on skating, bought a ticket for the season. The convention was for the ordinary skater to swing round and round the outside, while the experts performed their evolutions in the centre. At that time I was bent on learning the outside forward loop, which involves raising the unemployed leg very high until you discover the knack. Absorbed in this labour I failed to observe the Duke of Orleans, a glaring girl on either arm. He swerved, swanking, out of the ruck and collided with me. We both sat down very hard, but I on the point of his skate to the detriment of my much prized perineum. Being then a perfect young fool, as I am now a perfect old one, I supposed

102 THE CONFESSIONS OF ALEISTER CROWLEY

it incumbent on my race and caste to pretend not to be hurt,
so I forced myself to go on skating despite agony so great that
I could hardly bite back the tears, until I thought I had done
enough for honour and felt free to slip away. I was engaged
that night to a committee meeting of the Climbing Club at the
rooms of H. V. Reade in Jermyn Street. I managed somehow
to sit through the meeting, the matter being made worse by my
insane bashfulness which prevented me asking my host to let
me use his bedroom. We proceeded to a restaurant to dinner,
but there I broke down and excused myself.

The rest of the evening's entertainment remains a mystery.
I have a vague memory of being stretched on the seat of a railway carriage and I learned later that I had reached home, some
six miles from London, soaked to the skin. I suppose I must
have wandered about in the rain for an indefinite period, in
pain too great to know what I was doing except to try to be
brave. The blow had set up cystitis which kept me in bed for
the next three weeks. The inflammation gradually disappeared
after spreading to the prostate gland and the urethra. Nor was
that the end of the trouble. The urethritis caused a discharge
which proved very refractory to treatment and ultimately
determined a triple stricture for which I am being treated at
the moment of dictating this paragraph more than a quarter of
a century after the accident. The moral is, of course, to avoid
the Bourbons, though, as the duke is reported to be dying at
the present moment, it is quite possible that his physician is
shaking his head wisely and saying, 'Ah, Your Highness, this
is what comes from getting mixed up with people like Aleister
Crowley! . . .'

The very streets testify against the city. On the one hand we
have pale stunted hurrying pygmies jostling each other in the
bitter search for bread; an ant heap is a miracle of beauty and
dignity in comparison. On the other, when it comes to excitement or amusement, we see perspiring brutes belching the
fumes of beer; coarse, ugly parodies of apes. Nature affords
no parallel to their degradation. There is no open air life,
physical or mental, and there is the ever-abiding sense of sin
and shame to obsess these slaves. Nowhere, except in English
cities, do these conditions exist. Slum life there is elsewhere,
and misery enough; pitiful struggle, monstrous greed and triumphant brutality. But only in England are the people poisoned through and through; elsewhere there is a sense of
independence even in the most servile. The Russian mujik is in
his way an aristocrat.

And the cause of all these phenomena is one and the same. It is the Anglo-Saxon conception of Christianity which pollutes the race. Only the well-fed pagan, whether he be a bishop or a bookmaker, is exempt, because he either does not take religion seriously or takes it individually without reference to his neighbour. The most bigoted members of the Greek and Roman communions on the Continent, though they may feel their religion passionately and make it the mainspring of their lives, are not bound together by that insect-like collective consciousness which stamps the Anglo-Saxon. The English pagan is in nine cases out of ten a Norman or a Celt. He has the aristocratic consciousness, whatever he may tell you about his religious opinions. Now it is all very well to be one of the master class and smile contemptuously while bowing the knee in the temple of Rimmon, but a poet cannot be content with the situation. Hence the most intensely aristocratic types, like Shelley and Byron, instead of acquiescing in the social system which made them superiors, felt with acute agony the degradation of the slaves among whom they moved, and became revolutionaries and exiles because they could not endure to live in such a degraded community.

Certain classes in England possess manliness and self-respect. As a rule they are connected with sport and agriculture, or are skilled workmen. The essence of aristocracy is to take a pride in being what you are, whatever that may be. There is no room for this in industrialism and the result is that one can watch a London thoroughfare for hours without even seeing an individual whose nonentity is not repulsive. Everyone who possesses natural advantages has got out of the ruck and takes very good care to avoid further contamination. Such people lead lives of artificial seclusion. It is part of their Freudian protection to become unconscious of the mob. But it is the business of the poet to see, hear and know everything. He dare not let himself forget. England is the most fertile mother of poets, but she kills the weak and drives the strong to happier lands. James Thomson, John Davidson, Richard Middleton, Ernest Dowson and I don't know how many more even in our own generation found England unendurable for this one reason. The English poet must either make a successful exile or die of a broken heart.

At Cambridge I was surrounded by a more or less happy, healthy, prosperous set of parasites. The paganism of the university had to a great extent redeemed them from the sense of sin. But during vacation I either hid myself in the mountains among the sturdy peasants or went abroad. North-western Europe appealed to me. There was a certain element of romance in the long nights, the cold clear air, the ice. I loved to wander solitary in Holland, Denmark, Norway and Sweden. There was a mystery in the streets and a spontaneous gaiety in the places of amusement, which satisfied my soul. Life seemed both more remote and more intense. As a stranger, I never came into contact with the malaise, the soul-searching, the psychological dissatisfaction which Ibsen and Strindberg describe. But though my view was thus entirely superficial, it was none the less in a certain sense profound and accurate. One can get a very good idea of a country by travelling through it in the train. The outward and visible signs do, after all, reveal, especially to the poet, its inward and spiritual graces. The people who lead one astray are the analysts who fail to come out the other side. Mr. Jorrocks and Mr. Pickwick give a better idea of England than Charles Reade or Sir Walter Besant. Dumas père tells us more about France than Zola. A great deal of the interior workings of a national mind ought to be taken for granted. One can distinguish profitably between two pretty girls at the end of an opera glass. It is absolutely misleading to disembowel them, as the average so-called psychological writer tries to do. There are all sorts of obscure processes always at work in nature and they are more or less the same for all of us. To insist upon them is one of the worst kinds of false thinking. Zola's peasants in *La Terre* are untrue, except as among themselves. The ultimate issue is that these people breed cattle, grow corn and wine, and fight like demons for their country. Henri Barbusse's *Le Feu* was a disgrace to literature. Mass psychology is the only important thing about the masses. The great artists, such as Emily Brontë—or was it her brother?—make no such blunder. They deal with individuals; but they never lose sight of the fact that the individual is only such to a limited extent. He is only one figure in a picture; and when he stands out unnecessarily, there is something wrong with the picture. Captain Marryat's stories contain masterpieces of individual portraiture, but he never loses sight of the background. I am convinced that the English people were very much happier under the old semi-feudal system. 'Hard cases make bad law.' We have abolished all kinds of injustice on our attention being called to them; but the result has been that we have created an artificial doctrinaire society in which nobody is really happy or prosperous. All classes are complaining. We are in the condition of a man whose nerves all talk at once instead of doing their work quietly. The most appalling of political mistakes is to develop consciousness in sections of the social organism which are not its brains. The crash has come in Russia; and we shall not have long to wait.

But in those days of adolescence I had no inducement to do any political thinking. The atmosphere was one of prosperity and stability. It was taken for granted that England was the greatest country in the world and that nothing could go wrong. One heard about Ireland as a perennial nuisance; and Mr Gladstone was regarded as a traitor, neither more nor less. One of my tutors had been a Caius don named d'Arcy, whose father was the rector of Nymphsfield in Gloucestershire. I had spent some time there—to make my first appearance in the hunting field. 'Chapel folk' were looked upon as criminals of no class. I remember the old rector chuckling over a riddle. 'Why is Gladstone's hair like a tuft of grass?' 'Because it grows on the top of an old sod.' That was the quality of political thought which was considered on the same level of certainty as two and two make four. I recall two lines of a poem that I wrote to Lord Rosebery:

> And now, my lord, *in medias res,*
> Get rid of all your red Rad fleas.

I had been invited to meet Gladstone in north Wales, refused to go and wrote him a poem.

LINES ON BEING INVITED TO MEET THE PREMIER IN WALES, SEPTEMBER 1892

> I will not shake thy hand, old man,
>   I will not shake thy hand;
> You bear a traitor's brand, old man,
>   You bear a liar's brand.
> Thy talents are profound and wide,
>   Apparent power to win;
> It is not everyone has lied
>   A nation into sin.
>
> And look not thou so black, my friend,
>   Nor seam that hoary brow;
> Thy deeds are seamier, my friend,
>   Thy record blacker now.
> Your age and sex forbid, old man,
>   I need not tell you how,

> Or else I'd knock you down,* old man,
>   Like that extremist cow.
>
> You've gained your every seat, my friend,
>   By perjuring your soul;
> You've climbed to Downing Street, my friend,
>   A very greasy poll.
> You bear a traitor's brand, old man,
>   You bear a liar's brand;
> I will *not* shake thy hand, old man,
>   I will *not* shake thy hand.
>
>   *And I didn't.*

My life at Cambridge did nothing to make me think more deeply. With regard to foreign politics, the position was parallel. It was pure Kipling; but (in another watertight compartment) I was passionately enamoured of the views of Shelley, though I did not correlate them with any practical programme.

There was yet another compartment. Scott, Burns and my cousin Gregor had made me a romantic Jacobite. I regarded the Houses of Hanover and Coburg as German usurpers; and I wished to place 'Mary III and IV' on the throne. I was a bigoted legitimist. I actually joined a conspiracy on behalf of Don Carlos, obtained a commission to work a machine gun, took pains to make myself a first-class rifle shot and studied drill, tactics and strategy. However, when the time came for the invasion of Spain, Don Carlos got cold feet. The conspiracy was disclosed; and Lord Ashburnham's yacht, which was running the arms, fell into the hands of the Spanish navy.

This part of my mind did succeed in getting disturbed by the other parts. My reactionary conservatism came into conflict with my anti-Catholicism. A reconciliation was effected by means of what they called the Celtic Church. Here was a romantic and mystical idea which suited my political and religious notions down to the ground. It lived and moved in an atmosphere of fairies, seal-women and magical operations. Sacramentalism was kept in the foreground and sin was regarded without abhorrence. Chivalry and mystery were its pillars. It was free from priestcraft and tyranny, for the simple reason that it did not really exist!

My innate transcendentalism leapt out towards it. The *Morte d'Arthur, Lohengrin* and *Parsifal* were my world. I not only wanted to go out on the quest of the Holy Grail, I intended to do it. I got the idea of chastity as a positive virtue. It was

---

* Mr Gladstone was attacked by a cow in Hawarden Park in 1891.

delightful to be pure. Previously, chastity had been my chief abomination; the sign-manual of cowardice, heartlessness and slavery. In the Celtic Church there was no fear of God, but a communion with Him as nobly familiar as the relations of Roland and Charlemagne. I still took everything very literally. Browning's quotation:

Childe Roland to the dark tower came

was as real to me as the Battle of Waterloo. In a sense, perhaps, even more so. I think it was only due to my subconscious common sense that I did not go and see Browning and ask him where to find the dark tower!

14

I obtained the honour of knighthood * from one of Don
Carlos's lieutenants. It is part of the legitimist theory that the
sovereign had abrogated to himself the monopoly of conferring
spurs, while on the other hand a woman could not confer
knighthood. All Victorian creations are invalid.

The effect of adopting the official Anglo-German theory is
even more patent today than in the nineties. Then it was city
knights; the next step was the matinée idol; now the pawn-
broker, the movie star and the low comedian have made the
title a badge of nastiness. There is only one honour connected
with true knighthood, that of being a man of honour, of having
taken the vows—to uphold the right, to serve mankind, to
protect the distressed, and generally to exercise the manly
virtues. When renegade Jews and clowns walk in to dinner
before gentlemen, the latter may prefer to go without.

I took my admission to the Order with absolute seriousness,
keeping vigil over my arms in a wood. The theory of the Celtic
Church was that Romanism was a late heresy, or at least
schism. The finest cathedral in the world was too small for the
Church, as Brand found. The mountains and forests were
consecrated spots. The nearest thing to a material house would
be a hermitage such as one was likely to encounter while
travelling on the Quest.

But all these ideals, seriously as I entertained them, were in
the nature of reverie. In practical life I was still passionately
engaged in cleansing myself from the mire of Christianity by
deliberate acts of sin and worldliness. I was so happy to be free
from the past tyranny that I found continual joy in affirming
my emancipation.

There were thus several divers strands in the loom of my
soul which had not yet been woven into a harmonious pattern.
I dealt with life empirically, taking things as they came, without basing them on any fundamental principle.

Two main events were destined to put me on the road

---

* There is a great deal more to this story; but I may not tell it—yet.

towards myself. The first took place in Stockholm about midnight of December 31st, 1896. I was awakened to the knowledge that I possessed a magical means of becoming conscious
of and satisfying a part of my nature which had up to that
moment concealed itself from me. It was an experience of
horror and pain, combined with a certain ghostly terror, yet
at the same time it was the key to the purest and holiest spiritual ecstasy that exists. At the time, I was not aware of the
supreme importance of the matter. It seemed to me little more
than a development of certain magical processes with which I
was already familiar. It was an isolated experience, not repeated until exactly twelve months later, to the minute. But this
second occasion quickened my spirit, always with the result of
'loosening the girders of the soul', so that my animal nature
stood rebuked and kept silence in the presence of the immanent divinity of the Holy Ghost; omnipotent, omniscient and
omnipresent, yet blossoming in my soul as if the entire forces of
the universe from all eternity were concentrated and made
manifest in a single rose.

The second event took place in October 1897. The occasion
was an attack of illness. It was nothing very serious and I had
long been accustomed to expect to die before I came of age.
But for some reason or other I found myself forced to meditate
upon the fact of mortality. It was impressed upon me that I
hadn't a moment to lose. There was no fear of death or of a
possible 'hereafter'; but I was appalled by the idea of the futility
of all human endeavour. Suppose, I said to myself, that I make
a great success in diplomacy and become ambassador to Paris.
There was no good in that—I could not so much as remember
the name of the ambassador a hundred years ago. Again, I
wanted to be a great poet. Well, here I was in one of the two
places in England that made a speciality of poets, yet only an
insignificant fraction of the three thousand men in residence
knew anything about so great a man as Aeschylus. I was not
sufficiently enlightened to understand that the fame of the man
had little or nothing to do with his real success, that the proof
of his prowess lay in the invisible influence which he had had
upon generations of men. My imagination went a step further.
Suppose I did more than Caesar or Napoleon in one line, or
than Homer and Shakespeare in the other—my work would be
automatically cancelled when the globe became uninhabitable
for man.

I did not go into a definite trance in this meditation; but a
spiritual consciousness was born in me corresponding to that

which characterizes the Vision of the Universal Sorrow, as I
learnt to call it later on. In Buddhist phraseology, I perceived
the First Noble Truth—Sabbé Pi Dukkham—everything is
sorrow. But this perception was confined to the planes familiar
to the normal human consciousness. The fatuity of any work
based upon physical continuity was evident. But I had at this
time no reason for supposing that the same criticism applied
to any transcendental universe. I formulated my will somewhat as follows: 'I must find a material in which to work
which is immune from the forces of change.' I suppose that
I still accepted Christian metaphysics in some sense or another.
I had been satisfied to escape from religion to the world.
I now found that there was no satisfaction here. I was not
content to be annihilated. Spiritual facts were the only things
worth while. Brain and body were valueless except as the
instruments of the soul.

The ordinary materialist usually fails to recognize that only
spiritual affairs count for anything, even in the grossest concerns of life. The facts of a murder are nothing in themselves;
they are only adduced in order to prove felonious intent.
Material welfare is only important as assisting men towards a
consciousness of satisfaction.

From the nature of things, therefore, life is a sacrament;
in other words, all our acts are magical acts. Our spiritual consciousness acts through the will and its instruments upon
material objects, in order to produce changes which will result
in the establishment of the new conditions of consciousness
which we wish. That is the definition of Magick. The obvious
example of such an operation in its most symbolic and ceremonial form is the Mass. The will of the priest transmutes a
wafer in such wise that it becomes charged with the divine
substance in so active a form that its physical injection gives
spiritual nourishment to the communicant. But all our actions
fit this equation. A tailor with the toothache takes a portion of
the wealth derived from the business to which he has consecrated himself, a symbol of his accumulated and stored
energy, in order to have the tooth removed and so to recover
the consciousness of physical well-being.

Put in this way, the magical theory of existence is self-
evident. I did not apprehend it clearly at this time; but I unconsciously acted upon it as soon as I had discovered the
worthlessness of the world. But I was so far from perceiving
that every act is magical, whether one likes it or not, that I

supposed the escape from matter to involve a definite invasion of the spiritual world. Indeed, I was so far from understanding that matter was in its nature secondary and symbolic, that my principal preoccupation was to obtain first-hand sensory evidence of spiritual beings. In other words, I wanted to evoke the denizens of other planes to visible and audible appearance.

This resolution was the first manifestation of my true will. I had thrown myself with the utmost enthusiasm into various occupations from time to time, but they had never occupied my entire attention. I had never given myself wholly to chess, mountaineering or even to poetry. Now, for the first time, I felt myself prepared to expend my resources of every kind to attain my purpose.

To me the spiritual world consisted roughly of the Trinity and their angels on the one side; the devil and his on the other. It is absolutely sophistical to pretend that Christianity is not Manichaean in essence. The Vedanta theory of Advaitism in the Upanishads makes evil—and indeed all manifested existence —Maya, pure illusion. But even at this, there is no satisfactory explanation of the appearance of the illusion. In Christianity evil is just as real as good; and so long as two opposites exist they must either be equal or there must be a third component to balance them. Now this is in itself sophistical, for the third component only exists as a make-weight; and it is pure fiction to discriminate between two things whose only function is to counterbalance a third thing. In respect of the universe of discourse involved, a proposition cannot have two contradictories. If the opposite of good exists at all, as it must, if 'good' is to have any meaning, it must be exactly equal in quantity and quality to that good. On the Christian hypothesis, the reality of evil makes the devil equal to God. This is the heresy of Manes, no doubt. But those who condemn Manes must, despite themselves, implicitly affirm his theorem.

I seem to have understood this instinctively; and since I must take sides with one party or the other it was not difficult to make up my mind. The forces of good were those which had constantly oppressed me. I saw them daily destroying the happiness of my fellow-men. Since, therefore, it was my business to explore the spiritual world, my first step must be to get into personal communication with the devil. I had heard a good deal about this operation in a vague way; but what I wanted was a manual of technical instruction. I devoted myself to black magic; and the bookseller—Deighton Bell, God bless 'im!—immediately obliged with *The Book of Black Magic and of Pacts*,[1] which, judging by the title, was exactly what I needed.

It was with intense disappointment and distrust that I read this compilation. The author was a pompous, ignorant and affected dipsomaniac from America, and he treated his subject with the vulgarity of Jerome K. Jerome, and the beery, leering frivolity of a red-nosed music-hall comedian making jokes about mothers-in-law and lodgers.

It was, however, clear, even from the garbled texts of the Grimoires which he quoted, that the diabolists had no conception of the Satan hymned by Milton and Huysmans. They were not protagonists in the spiritual warfare against restriction, against the oppressors of the human soul, the blasphemers who denied the supremacy of the will of man. They merely aimed at achieving contemptible or malicious results, such as preventing a huntsman from killing game, finding buried treasure, bewitching the neighbours' cows, or 'acquiring the affection of a judge'. For all their pretended devotion to Lucifer or Belial, they were sincere Christians in spirit, and inferior Christians at that, for their methods were puerile. The prayer book, with its petitions for rain and success in battle, was almost preferable. The one point of superiority was nevertheless cardinal; their method was in intention scientific. That is, they proposed a definite technic by which a man could compel the powers of nature to do his bidding, no less than the engineer, the chemist and the electrician. There was none of the wheedling, bribery and servility which is of the essence of that kind of prayer which seeks material gratifications. Sir J. G. Frazer has pointed out this distinction in *The Golden Bough*. Magic he defines as science which does not work. It would be fairer to state this proposition in slightly different terms: magic is science *in posse*.

The compiler of *The Book of Black Magic and of Pacts* is not only the most ponderously platitudinous and priggishly prosaic of pretentiously pompous pork butchers of the language, but the most voluminously voluble. I cannot dig over the dreary deserts of his drivel in search of the passage which made me write to him. But it was an oracular obscurity which hinted that he knew of a Hidden Church withdrawn from the world in whose sanctuaries were preserved the true mysteries of initiation. This was one better than the Celtic Church; I immediately asked him for an introduction. He replied kindly and intelligibly, suggesting that I should read *The Cloud upon the Sanctuary* by Councillor von Eckartshausen. With this book I retired to Wastdale Head for the Easter vacation of 1898. This period proved to be the critical moment of my early life: in two most important respects it determined the direction of my efforts. The two were intimately linked in certain ways and in order to make clear my position I must retrace my steps for a little and bring myself up to date in the matter of climbing, as also of literature.

The summers of 1896 and 1897 were spent in the Alps. They were the logical development of my previous experience. I had made up my mind to look for a climbing companion of a permanent character. I had met Professor Norman Collie in Westmorland. His teaching and advice were invaluable. I arranged to spend part of the summer with Morris Travers, Collie's demonstrator at University College, London, and a very admirable 'second man' he was. A man who writes treatises on 'Gas Manipulation' and who knows how to rebuff the advances of his girl students is an ideal companion on a mountain. Unfortunately, he obtained an appointment in a far country and had to give up climbing in consequence. But we made our mark in the Alps, beginning with the first guideless traverse of the Mönch, the Vuibez Séracs, and the first traverse of the Aiguilles Rouges, climbing all the pinnacles.

Travers joined me for a short time in August. We began by making the first guideless traverse of the Mönch. We started for the Guggi hut within two or three hours of his arrival, he having come straight through from London without breaking the journey. We started the next morning very early and made great speed up the lower slopes in our enthusiasm. Travers became extremely mountain sick. It was obvious that the barometric pressure had nothing to do with it; he was simply upset from the fatigue of the journey, the change to coarse food and the sudden call upon his full physical strength when out of training. Numerous other similar observations prevented me from ever being so foolish as to attribute this sickness to the altitude. I have produced all the symptoms on Beachy Head in men who had been perfectly comfortable on the high Alps; and I experienced no discomfort whatever above 23,000 feet.

Travers and I wandered about the Oberland for a week without going below the snow-line. His mountain sickness soon disappeared, but he became badly sunburnt. In those days we cherished the superstition that lanolin was a preventative; but the application seemed to feed the sores instead of healing them. A few days after leaving me he arrived at the

Gornergrat, whither he had dispatched his baggage, in fluttering rags and with a face which was little better than one single suppurating sore. A lady sitting outside the hotel exclaimed indignantly that such disgusting objects should not be allowed to frequent public places. It was his mother!

Talking of sunburn, there was once—improbable as it may appear—a Dr Bowles, of Folkestone, interested in the subject. He arranged with Morris Travers to carry out a research on the actinic value of the solar rays on glaciers. Travers and I and his brother went to live in a hut on a glacier somewhere above Bel Alp, where Travers was to carry out some experiments. One day there arrived Bowles and a number of voluntary victims, each member of the party having his face painted with grease paint of divers colours, the right half vermilion and the left sky-blue, or the left bright green and the right orange, and so on. I record, with regret, that I, who had refused to abdicate the dignity of humanity to this extent, was the only person in the party who was not badly burnt. The sun showed no respect to persons in the matter of their camouflage. My freedom was due to the fact that I had spent most of my life in the open air and gradually acquired immunity. It sometimes strikes me that the whole of science is a piece of impudence: that nature can afford to ignore our impertinent interference. If our monkey mischief should ever reach the point of blowing up the earth by decomposing an atom, and even annihilate the sun himself, I cannot really suppose that the universe would turn a hair. If we are ever to do anything, it can only be by the manipulation of those spiritual forces which lie behind the consciousness of which the universe of matter is but a symbolic phantasm.

The second of these exploits—the Vuibez Séracs—constituted one of the most interesting ice climbs that I had ever done. They had not been climbed for a generation, when the glacier was in a very different condition, and were reputed impossible. Jean Maître, who was supposed to be the best guide in the valley, with other strong guides and some distinguished members of the Alpine Club, decided to attempt it. They returned with a wonderful story of desperate adventure. They had been stopped, they said, by the final obstacle, an overhanging ice wall guarded by a wide crevasse. This interested us. We set out the following morning, reaching the obstacle without any difficulty, which gave us a poor idea of the capacity of the mighty men of valour. But we could not be surprised at their failure to negotiate the obstacle. We found ourselves standing on a knife-edge separated from the overhanging wall by a crevasse so broad that we could only just reach it with our axes. Travers held me on the rope while I leant across and cut a ledge in the wall which could be used for his hands. Having anchored him to his brother lower down, I lowered him cautiously so that he was able to lean across with his hands on the ledge, thus forming a bridge. I then climbed, in my crampons, on to his shoulders and stood there for forty minutes while I cut hand and foot holds in the overhanging ice. Trusting myself to these, Travers was hastily pulled back to the vertical by his brother. In this position he was able to support my weight on his uplifted axe-head sufficiently to allow me to use one hand. In this way I cut fresh hand holds in the overhanging wall and ultimately pulled myself over the edge. There was still some step-cutting to be done before I got to a sufficiently good place to pull up the others. I have never seen the performance of Travers equalled on any occasion. Hastings himself could hardly have been more strong, steady and enduring, to say nothing of the qualities required to allow a man to stand on his head and shoulders with sharp spikes!

We now found that so far from this obstacle being the last, it was the first! I take a good deal of credit to myself for finding the way to the top through the tangled pinnacles of ice. I began to be not a little alarmed; the séracs stretched line after line above us. There was no way of getting out of them and at any moment the sun might strike the glacier and overthrow their pride and our temerity. We climbed with desperate haste and managed to reach the snow-covered glacier above them just in time. As it happened, a party had gone out from the hotel after breakfast with the idea of watching us from the opposite slopes and they told us next evening that our tracks had been obliterated in a dozen places by falling ice.

15

I must not omit to mention the first descent of the west face of
the Trifthorn. It was early in the season of '96. Going up to
Zermatt in the train I met an English climber whom I will call
Arthur Ellis. He was anxious to do guideless work and we
agreed to try a few mountains together. We made some minor
expeditions and he proved highly competent. One day we
climbed the Trifthorn by the ordinary route, with the idea of
attempting the traverse. As I was to go down last, he was
carrying the rucksack with our provisions. We made several
attempts to find a way down the Zinal face; but always the
slopes steepened until it became evident that they pitched over,
and we had to retrace our steps. Ellis, however, was very
annoyed at my caution and wanted to glissade, which was a
proposal about as reasonable as jumping off the Eiffel Tower.
Presently he made an excuse for taking off the rope and retired
behind a rock while I sat down and lit my pipe. I was aroused
by a hail. Ellis was three or four hundred feet down the slope!
He urged me once more to glissade. He said he had invented
a new method of exercising this art, which was to hold the axe
by the shaft and use the pick as a brake. It was downright
insanity; and took me absolutely by surprise, as previously he
had been a sound and careful climber. I could do nothing to
restrain him: I tried to humour him and suggested that he
should 'come up to where I was and start fair'. But he wasn't
taking any and let himself go. A few seconds later he was
performing cartwheels and then disappeared over the edge.
The angle was such that I could not see where he had fallen.
I hastily climbed a convenient rock pinnacle. Then I saw him.
He was lying, spreadeagled, in the Bergschrund, with his blood
staining the snow; which, by the way, ought not to have been
there, and would not have been but for the continuous bad
weather.

The task before me was hardly prepossessing. It was up to
me to find my way alone down a face which had never previously been climbed. However, I discovered a route which took

me to the glacier in about five hours. At one point I was obliged to lower myself down by the rope; and, as I could not unhitch it, I was thrown more than ever on my own resources after that. On several occasions I was obliged to make some very risky jumps, so that I might have been cut off if I had found a passage beyond my powers.

I must admit feeling considerable disgust at seeing Ellis making his way over the glacier as if nothing had happened. He had fallen some eight hundred feet, the last three hundred sheer drop. I was utterly exhausted and badly in need of food. It was all I could do to catch up to him. The only damage he had suffered was a trifling cut on one leg! Nightfall was at hand; and though the hut was not very far off in actual distance, we had a terrible time getting there, having to wade through soft snow up to our waists. The hut was *bewirtschaftet;* but the guardian had not come up in consequence of the weather, so we had to force our way in and break into the provision room in order to get fuel and the like.

Our adventures were not yet over. My clothes were (naturally) dripping. I threw my coat on the table, above which hung my Alpine lamp. This type of lamp has a hole in the bottom through which a candle is thrust. It is held in place by a spring. I threw myself on the straw, being too tired to complete the operation of going to bed without a few moments' rest. I felt sleep overcoming me, knew it was my duty to put out the candle, but began to argue that even if it did drop out the fall would extinguish it, or if not, the wet coat would do so. It was a perfectly good argument; but the one chance in a million came off—it didn't go out till my coat was burnt to cinders.

Luckily, the next morning the guardian of the hut came up. I borrowed his coat and went down to Evolena, where my baggage had been sent. Ellis was not fit to be moved and I arranged to come up two days later and fetch him. At Evolena I got a change of clothes and sent up the guide's coat by a porter.

Now, in the hotel was a girls' school, being conducted to admire the wonders and beauties of nature. The following day they came down in the afternoon from the glacier, very excited at having found the tracks of a chamois on the mule path. I knew, of course, that this was hallucination and thought no more of it. Just before dinner I was outside the hotel taking the air, when I saw in the distance a solitary figure slowly approaching. Its action was very peculiar, I thought.

> The wild man wends his weary way
> To a strange and lonely pump.

Yet it seemed somehow familar. It drew nigh; yes, it was Arthur Ellis. I expressed surprise; but he said that he had felt so much better he thought he might as well come down, but it had been a long and terrible day. He had started at dawn. This was absurd, as it was only a couple of hours' easy walking from the hut. Ah yes, he said, but he had come down over the snout of the glacier and he had had to cut steps all the way— no more glissading for him! This story was again rather incredible. But his axe had been tremendously knocked about. The truth slowly dawned on my benighted brain: he had solemnly cut his way down the mule path—he was the chamois whose tracks the girls had seen!

Well, it was not time for me to join my friends at Arolla; but I wasn't going to climb any more with Ellis, so I made my excuses and departed.

The fag-end of the story is as peculiar as the rest. We arranged to dine together in London and when I got back I wrote to him. He replied at once, asking me to dine with him at his club. I duly turned up; but he was not there and I have never heard a word of him since!

Another very amusing incident occurred at Arolla. A little way above the old hotel is a large boulder, which had never been climbed from the hotel side. I spent some time before I found out how to do it. One had to traverse the face to the right, with a minimum of hand hold and foot hold, until one came to a place where the slope eased off. But this point was defended by a bulge in the rock which threw one out. It was just possible for a very slim man with a prehensile abdomen. But it was a matter of a quarter of an ounce one way or the other whether the friction grips were sufficient or not. It was one of the most difficult pieces of rock climbing I had ever tackled.

I decided to have some fun with it and taught a girl how to do it. I then offered a hundred francs to any guide who could get up. We got together a little party one afternoon and I proceeded to show off. Several other people tried, but without success. I began to mock them and said, 'But this is absurd—you fellows can't climb at all—it's quite easy—why, I'd back a girl to do it—won't you have a try, Miss So-and-so?' My pupil played up beautifully and pretended to need a lot of persuasion. Ultimately, she offered to try if she were held on a rope from above. I said, 'Nonsense, you can do it perfectly well by yourself!' The company protested that she would kill herself; and she pretended to be put on her mettle, refused all help and swarmed up in great style.

This made everybody very much ashamed. Even the guides were stung into trying it. But nobody else got up. So I started to coach them on the rope. Several succeeded with the moral support and without being hauled. A fair number, however, came off and looked rather ridiculous, dangling. People began to urge the chaplain to try his hand. He didn't like it at all; but he came to me and said he would go if I would be very careful to manage the rope so that he did not look ridiculous, because of the respect due to his cloth. I promised him that I would attend to the matter with the utmost conscientiousness. I admitted that I had purposely made fun of some of the others, but that in his case I would tie the rope properly; not under his arms but just above the hips.

Having thus arranged for the respect due to his cloth, I went to the top of the rock and sat sufficiently far back to be unable to see what was happening on the face. When he came off, as the rope was fastened so low, he turned upside down. I pretended to misunderstand and jerked him up and down for several minutes before finally hauling him up, purple in the face and covered with scratches. I had not failed in the respect due to his cloth. But quite a number of people were sufficiently lacking in taste to laugh at him.

One day I took my cousin Gregor, who by this time was married and had discovered that his life was not worth keeping. We made the second ascent of the north-north-east ridge of Mont Collon. It is a long and severe climb. The conditions were very bad and Gregor was quite unequal to this class of climbing, so that I had to pull him up most of the way. We were very late on the mountain in consequence. I had no idea of the best way down, but decided to try the short and precipitous route which leads to the level glacier above the Vuibez Séracs. The descent of a difficult mountain is always awkward when the second man is not up to the mark. He cannot go down last because of the danger; and in going down first he is pretty sure to take the wrong road, wherever he cannot be guided by voice. However, we got down the steep part, safely enough, just before dark.

We took off the rope to descend some slopes covered with loose rock. As I sat down to coil the rope I realized that I was completely exhausted, though mentally rather than physically.

My brain played me a curious trick. Gregor had reached a patch of broken rocks at the bottom of the slope and I followed him slowly. Suddenly I saw a troll, one of those funny little dwarfs with pointed caps and formidable beards that one sees pictured in German fairy stories and on beer mugs (*Heinzelmännchen* appears to be the official name). This creature was hopping about the rocks in a very jovial way. He appeared quite real in every respect. For instance, he was not transparent. But it never occurred to me to believe in him. I put him down to cerebral fatigue. The apparition only lasted for a few minutes. He was gone before I rejoined my cousin.

It would, of course, have been madness to attempt to cross the glacier that night, the snow being very deep and soft, so we managed as best we could to keep warm. I did not sleep very much—it was my first night out. In the morning we ran across the frozen snow to the little pass which leads down to the valley. We had hardly crossed it when we met a rescue party sent up by the dear old hotel keeper, Anzevui, who had a curious personal affection for me as the bad boy of the valley who was always making things interesting. Our descent had been watched through glasses; and they had come to the conclusion that we must have met with an accident, because our route down the mountain was an original variation on the regular way and supposed to be impossible. We had, in fact, met with one exceedingly bad pitch where I was glad of the hitched rope.

On another occasion I was benighted; it was with Morris Travers and his younger brother on the Aiguilles Rouges, owing to our extreme conscientiousness in climbing every pinnacle accurately and the breakdown of the younger Travers from fatigue. It was one more example of the disadvantage of a third man. A party of two would have finished the climb at least three hours earlier. A bitterly cold wind was blowing from the north-west, so that we could not pass the night on the ridge or on that side of it. We had to find shelter on the eastern face. It was too dark to get down the cliffs, even if young Travers had been equal to the effort, and they were very steep. There was not even a reasonable ledge.

However, we found a chimney where the boy could rest in moderate comfort and there was a sort of shelf which accommodated his brother. As for me, the best repose I could find was to wedge myself across the chimney with one foot, my back against a steep patch of snow; the warmth of my body melted this and the water trickled down. As my knickerbockers had been torn to pieces on the rock, there was a certain degree of discomfort connected with my night's rest and the strain on my leg somehow damaged the knee joint, which used continually to give trouble for years afterwards. But I was so tired that I went to sleep with my pipe in my mouth. It is extraordinary that I did not fall—the pipe did.

16

Such were some of the adventures of 1896 and 1897. My experiences all contributed to build up an original theory of mountaineering. It was not till 1898 that I discovered the identity of my own ideas with those of the great climbers. But I discovered the extremely unpleasant fact that the English Alpine Club were bitterly opposed to mountaineering—its members were incompetent, insanely jealous of their vested interests and unthinkably unsportsmanlike. Professor Norman Collie had proposed me for the club and Sir Martin Conway had been kind enough to second me; but the record of climbs which I put in to qualify for admission was much too good. It was subversive of all authority. The average Alpine clubman qualifies by paying guides to haul him up a few hackneyed peaks. He is not expected to do any new climbs whatever; and it is an outrage to the spirit of the club to do anything original. Mummery had been blackballed because he was the most famous climber in England; and, though occasionally climbing with guides before he found Collie and Hastings, had been in fact the leader of the party. The club was, of course, afraid to give its real reasons for objecting to him. It circulated the lie that he was a bootmaker! Later on, it became a public scandal that he was not a member of the club and he was weak enough to allow himself to be elected. In my case, Collie and Conway warned me that my election would be opposed and I withdrew my name. On this, the son of a church furnisher named Tattersall, who had insinuated himself into Trinity, circulated the rumour that I had been expelled from a London club. He hated me because I, as president of the Cambridge University Chess Club, did not see my way to allow him to become secretary. He was an excellent player, but unsuitable for conducting official correspondence with other clubs. I went to his rooms with a heavy malacca and demanded that he should retract his falsehood or fight. He refused to do either, so I thrashed him soundly then and there. He complained to my tutor, who halled me, made a few remarks on the desuetude of the duel, changed the conversation to Ibsen and asked me to dinner.

Mountaineering differs from other sports in one important respect. A man cannot obtain a reputation at cricket or football by hiring professionals to play for him. His achievements are checked by his averages. But hardly any one in England at that time knew anything about mountaineering. Various old fogies, who could not have climbed the simplest rocks in Cumberland, or led across an easy Alpine pass, had been personally conducted by peasants up a few mountains and written themselves up into fame. The appearance of the guideless climber was therefore a direct challenge. They tried every dirty trick to prevent the facts from leaking out. They refused to record the exploits of guideless men in the Alpine Journal. They discountenanced even their own members, they tried to ignore English rock climbing altogether and would have nothing to do with the Continental Alpine Clubs.

The result of this policy was to hinder the development of the sport in England. The younger men were ostracized. It was parallel to the attempts of the Church to pretend that there was no such thing as science. The result was not dissimilar. In 1901 all the world's records, except one, were held by myself and Eckenstein. The exception was that of the greatest height attained by man. This was claimed by Matthias Zurbriggen, who was not a guide in the ordinary sense of the word, but a convict who had learnt all his climbing from Eckenstein at the request of the ne'er-do-weel's family, who didn't know what to do with him and probably hoped that he would kill himself on the mountains.

The Alpine Club even tried to fake records. One party made a great fuss over an ascent of the Dent Blanche. It was proved later that they had not been on the mountain at all and that one at least of the party—Smith *quidam*—knew it. Again, when I arrived at the head of the Baltoro glacier, I questioned some of my coolies who had been with the Conway expedition of 1892 about the alleged ascent of Pioneer Peak. The men unanimously declared that the party had only gone to the foot of the icefall and had turned back from this point. Far be it from me to place any reliance on the statements of ignorant Baltis, though I never found them at fault on any other point! But it is certainly singular that they should have agreed to give an account of the expedition so different from that recorded by the party themselves. Zurbriggen, who was the guide in the case, was cross-examined by Legros, the son of the painter, and a friend of Eckenstein's. He told a very singular story about Pioneer Peak, but as he was under the influence of alcohol I suppose his statements are as unreliable as those of my coolies.

The coincidence of evidence from two doubtful sources does not necessarily strengthen either, does it?

So bitter has been the hatred of the Alpine Club for the people who have exposed its principal members as impostors that it has actually induced the bulk of the press to ignore expeditions of such first-rate importance as those of 1902 and 1905 to the Himalayas. Subsequent exploration has been hampered in consequence; and the manslaughter of seven porters on Everest in 1922 was directly due to ignorance of the lesson taught by the Kangchenjunga disaster, as will be made clear in the proper place.

However, my principles have triumphed all along the line. There were no Swiss guides on Everest in 1922 and the record for altitude is held by amateurs travelling two on a rope.

Let me emphasize the fact that I am absolutely satisfied with this result. I am congenitally incapable of personal ambition and envy. My interest is in the sport itself. I care nothing for glory. In 1899, for example, I worked out a route up the Aiguille du Géant from the Montanvers. This mountain had never been climbed fairly. The ordinary way up is a matter of engineering by means of pitons and wire ropes. I did not keep my knowledge to myself in order to have the glory of making the first ascent. I indicated the way up to other climbers and was absolutely overjoyed when two Austrian amateurs made the climb. In the same way, I am perfectly satisfied at having broken down the dishonest and imbecile traditions of Badminton and only regret that I was not in command of the 1922 Everest expedition, because that expedition failed and cost heavily in human life. I am convinced that if I had been there the summit would have been reached and that no one would have been killed. In the expedition to K 2, neither man nor beast was injured, and in that to Kangchenjunga, the catastrophe was the direct result of mutinous disobedience to my orders. I do not lay claim to personal credit for this record, save in so far as I was on the way to an apprehension of the proper principles of mountain craft when I met Eckenstein, to whose instructions I am profoundly indebted.

I have never been in danger on a mountain, except through

the rashness of others. Here is a typical case. I was crossing the Brêche de la Meije with a porter. About half way down the rocky slopes (we had taken off the rope) I stopped for a few minutes for personal reasons, never imagining that the boy would get himself into trouble. When I got up he had disappeared. I shouted and he replied. I then saw that he had done an incredibly rash action. By going on, entirely out of the way, he had crossed a narrow gully which was being constantly swept by ice from a hanging glacier. I could not leave him alone on the mountain and I could not ask him to risk his life by returning. There was nothing for it but to repeat his indiscretion. The only way across the gully was a steep slab, polished by ice and constantly bombarded. I had to rush it, at the gravest risk of slipping on the one hand and being smashed on the other.

It is a remarkable fact that only very exceptional men retain their normal reasoning powers in presence of mountains. Both Eckenstein and I have had constant evidence of this. It is not merely the panic of the peasant, who loses his head and calls on the saints whenever he finds himself a few yards off the beaten track or is overtaken by bad weather. Scientifically trained minds frequently lose all sense of judgment and logic.

There is an account, hardly a century old, of a party of quite distinguished men who ascended Saddleback. They speak of precipitous cliffs and yawning gulfs, though as a matter of fact there is not a rock on the mountain which a child of three years old could call scrambling. They were, in fact, on ponies! Shelley's descriptions of Mont Blanc are comically exaggerated; his powers of observation must have been completely in abeyance.

The expression 'absolutely perpendicular' ultimately became a byword. It was used so frequently by ostensibly reliable men to describe quite gentle slopes. We used to ask engineers and other people accustomed to practical trigonometry to estimate the angle of the Matterhorn from Zermatt and from the Schwartzsee. They would give us anything from thirty degrees to fifty degrees in the first case and from forty-five degrees to eighty degrees in the second. The actual figures are ten degrees and fifteen degrees.

In 1902 Pfannl proposed to rush Chogo Ri from Askole. He thought he could get there and back in three days! In reality, it is fourteen days to the foot of the mountain, though unladen men might possibly do it in five. Mountain panic was without doubt partly accountable for the mental and moral breakdown in Guillarmod and Righi, which led them to mutiny on Kangchenjunga. A high degree of spiritual development, a romantic temperament and a profound knowledge based on experience of mountain conditions are the best safeguards against the insane impulses and hysterical errors which overwhelm the average man.

During my three years at Cambridge my literary faculties made sudden strides. The transition was brief. It is marked by my *The Tale of Archais*. But in *Aceldama*, my first published poem of any importance, I attained, at a bound, the summit of my Parnassus. In a sense, I have never written anything better. It is absolutely characteristic. Its technical excellence is remarkable and it is the pure expression of my unconscious self. I had no corresponding mental concepts at the time. It enounces a philosophy which subsequent developments have not appreciably modified. I remember my own attitude to it. It seemed to me a wilfully extravagant eccentricity. I had no idea that it was the pure water of the Dircean spring.

A certain amount of conscious aspiration is, however, evident in *Songs of the Spirit*. This book is a collection of lyrics which reveal an ill-defined longing for spiritual attainment. The background is vividly coloured by observation and experience. The atmosphere of the old streets of Amsterdam, of the colleges of Cambridge and of the mountains, lakes, forests and rivers, among which I wandered solitary, is evident in every stanza. The influence of my reading is almost negligible. The 'wish-phantasm' of the book is principally that of a wise and holy man living in a lonely tower, master of the secrets of nature. I had little conscious aspiration to that ideal. In practice, I was living for pleasure.

Another book of the transition period was *Green Alps*. This was never published. I had paid Leonard Smithers to have it printed and he told me that the printers' works had been destroyed by fire, which may or may not have been the case. It is characteristic that I accepted the situation with a shrug of the shoulders. I had a complete set of proofs, but I had become rather ashamed of the book. I merely selected the poems which I thought really worth while for inclusion in subsequent volumes. The collection was marked by a tendency to earthly passion; and its title shows that I already regarded human love as an idea to be transcended. *Green Alps* are pleasant pastures, but I was bound for the peaks.

My essential spirituality is made manifest by yet another

publication, which stands as a testimony of my praeterhuman innocence. The book is called *White Stains* and is commonly quoted by my admirers as evidence of my addiction to every kind of unmentionable vice. Asses! It is, indeed, technically, an obscene book, and yet the fact that I wrote it proves the purity of my heart and mind in the most extraordinary fashion.

The facts are as follows: In the course of my reading I had come across von Krafft-Ebing's *Psychopathia Sexualis*. The professor tries to prove that sexual aberrations are the result of disease. I did not agree. I thought that I was able to understand the psychology involved; I thought that the acts were merely magical affirmations of perfectly intelligible points of view. I said to myself that I must confute the professor. I could only do this by employing the one form at my disposal: the artistic form. I therefore invented a poet who went wrong, who began with normal and innocent enthusiasms, and gradually developed various vices. He ends by being stricken with disease and madness, culminating in murder. In his poems he describes his downfall, always explaining the psychology of each act.

The conclusions of the book might therefore be approved in any Sunday School, and its metaphysics is orthodox from the point of view of the theologian. I wrote the book in absolute seriousness and in all innocence. It never occurred to me that a demonstration of the terrible results of misguided passion might be mistaken for pornography. Indeed, now that I do understand that vile minds think it a vile book, I recognize with grim satisfaction that *Psychopathia Sexualis* itself has attained its enormous popularity because people love to gloat over such things. Its scientific form has not protected it from abuse, any more than the artistic form of my own reply to it. But von Krafft-Ebing has not been blackguarded as I have. The average man cannot believe that an artist may be as serious and high-minded an observer of life as the professed man of science.

I was to find very shortly that the most innocent personal relations could be taken by filthy minds as the basis for their malicious imagination. The story of how this came about dominates my third year at the university, as will appear. It seems as if my destiny were preparing me for my appointed work by clearing inessential factors out of the way. My one serious worldly ambition had been to become the champion of the world at chess. I had snatched a game from Blackburne in simultaneous play some years before. I was being beaten

in the Sicilian defence. The only chance was the sacrifice of
a rook. I remember the grand old master coming round to my
board and cocking his alcoholized eye cunningly at me. 'Hullo,'
said he, 'Morphy come to town again!' I am not coxcomb
enough to think that he could not have won the game, even
after my brilliancy. I believe that his colossal generosity let
me win to encourage a promising youngster.

I had frequently beaten Bird at Simpson's and when I got
to Cambridge I made a savagely intense study of the game.
In my second year I was president of the university and had
beaten such first-rate amateurs as Gunston and Cole. Outside
the master class, Atkins was my only acknowledged superior.
I made mincemeat of the man who was champion of Scotland
a few years later, even after I had given up the game. I spent
over two hours a day in study and more than that in practice.
I was assured on all hands that another year would see me
a master myself.

I had been to St Petersburg to learn Russian for the Diplomatic Service in the long vacation of 1897, and on my way
back broke the journey in Berlin to attend the Chess Congress.
But I had hardly entered the room where the masters were
playing when I was seized with what may justly be described
as a mystical experience. I seemed to be looking on at the
tournament from outside myself. I saw the masters—one,
shabby, snuffy and blear-eyed; another, in badly fitting would-
be respectable shoddy; a third, a mere parody of humanity,
and so on for the rest. These were the people to whose ranks
I was seeking admission. 'There, but for the grace of God, goes
Aleister Crowley,' I exclaimed to myself with disgust, and
there and then I registered a vow never to play another serious
game of chess. I perceived with praeternatural lucidity that I
had not alighted on this planet with the object of playing chess.

Aleister Crowley, by the way! I have not yet explained how
I came to have changed my name. For many years I had
loathed being called Alick, partly because of the unpleasant
sound and sight of the word, partly because it was the name
by which my mother called me. Edward did not seem to suit
me and the diminutives Ted or Ned were even less appropriate.
Alexander was too long and Sandy suggested tow hair and
freckles. I had read in some book or other that the most
favourable name for becoming famous was one consisting of
a dactyl followed by a spondee, as at the end of a hexameter:
like 'Jeremy Taylor'. Aleister Crowley fulfilled these conditions
and Aleister is the Gaelic form of Alexander. To adopt it

would satisfy my romantic ideals. The atrocious spelling A-L-A-I-S-T-E-R was suggested as the correct form by Cousin Gregor, who ought to have known better. In any case, A-L-A-I-S-D-A-I-R makes a very bad dactyl. For these reasons I saddled myself with my present nom-de-guerre—I can't say that I feel sure that I facilitated the process of becoming famous. I should doubtless have done so, whatever name I had chosen.

17

I began my last year at Cambridge with my moral decks cleared for action. I didn't know where I was going, but I was on the way. I was thus quite ready for the perception of the First Noble Truth, but also for an entirely new current to influence my life. Towards the end of the October term I met a man named Herbert Charles Jerome Pollitt. He was an M.A., ten years older than myself, and had merely come up to Cambridge to dance for the F.D.C. (Footlights Dramatic Club). I saw him only once or twice that term, but corresponded with him from abroad during the Christmas vacation. The result was the establishment of the first intimate friendship of my life.

Pollitt was rather plain than otherwise. His face was made tragic by the terrible hunger of the eyes and the bitter sadness of the mouth. He possessed one physical beauty—his hair. This was very plentiful and he wore it rather long. It was what is called a shock. But its colour was pale gold, like spring sunshine, and its texture of the finest gossamer. The relation between us was that ideal intimacy which the Greeks considered the greatest glory of manhood and the most precious prize of life. It says much for the moral state of England that such ideas are connected in the minds of practically every one with physical passion.

My sexual life was very intense. My relations with women were entirely satisfactory. They gave me the maximum of bodily enjoyment and at the same time symbolized my theological notions of sin. Love was a challenge to Christianity. It was a degradation and a damnation. Swinburne had taught me the doctrine of justification by sin. Every woman that I met enabled me to affirm magically that I had defied the tyranny of the Plymouth Brethren and the Evangelicals. At the same time women were the source of romantic inspiration; and their caresses emancipated me from the thraldom of the body. When I left them I found myself walking upon air, with my soul free to wing its way through endless empyreans and to express its godhead in untrammelled thought of transcendent sublimity, expressed in language which combined the purest aspirations with the most majestic melodies. Poems like 'The Philosopher's Progress' illustrate my unconscious, and poems like 'De Profundis' my conscious reaction. But, morally and mentally, women were for me beneath contempt. They had no true moral ideals. They were bound up with their necessary preoccupation, with the function of reproduction. Their apparent aspirations were camouflage. Intellectually, of course, they did not exist. Even the few whose minds were not completely blank had them furnished with Wardour Street Chippendale. Their attainments were those of the ape and the parrot. These facts did not deter me. On the contrary, it was highly convenient that one's sexual relations should be with an animal with no consciousness beyond sex.

As to my men friends, I had never met anyone of sufficiently exalted ideals and refinement to awaken serious sympathy. Pollitt was a new species. My feeling for him was an intensely pure flame of admiration mingled with infinite pity for his spiritual disenchantment. It was infinite because it could not even imagine a goal and dwelt wholly amid eternal things.

To him I was a mind—no more. He never manifested the slightest interest in any of my occupations. He had no sympathy with any of my ambitions, not even my poetry, except in a very peculiar way, which I have never thoroughly understood. He showed an instinctive distrust of my religious aspirations, because he realized that sooner or later they would take me out of his reach. He had himself no hope or fear of anything beyond the material world. But he never tired of the originality of my point of view; of watching the way in which my brain dealt with every subject that came under discussion.

It was the purest and noblest relation which I had ever had with anybody. I had not imagined the possibility of so divine a development. It was, in a sense, passionate, because it partook of the white heat of creative energy and because its intensity absorbed all other emotions. But for this very reason it was impossible to conceive of it as liable to contamination by any grosser qualities. Indeed, the universe of sense was entirely subordinated to its sanctity. It was based upon impressions as an incandescent light upon its filament. But the world was transfigured and consumed by the ineffable intensity of the spiritual consciousness. It was so free from any impure ingredient that my friendship with Pollitt in no way interfered with the current of my life. I went on reading, writing, climbing, skating, cycling and intriguing, as if I had never met him.

Yet his influence initiated me in certain important respects. He was a close friend of Beardsley's and introduced me to the French and English renaissance. In his heart was a hunger for beauty which I can only call hideous and cruel, because it was so hopeless. He totally lacked illumination in the mystical sense of the word. His outlook on life was desperate, very much like that of Des Esseintes. He suffered like Tintagiles. He could not accept any of the usual palliatives and narcotics; he had no creative genius, no ideals; he could not deceive himself about love, art or religion. He merely yearned and moaned. In certain respects he annoyed me, because I was determined to make my dreams come true; and he represented eternal dissatisfaction. In his heart was 'the worm that dieth not and the fire that is not quenched'.

The school of art and literature to which he introduced me was thus one which I instinctively despised, even while I adored it. The intense refinement of its thought and the blazing brilliance of its technique helped me to key myself up to a pitch of artistry entirely beyond my original scope; but I never allowed myself to fall under its dominion. I was determined to triumph, to find my way out on the other side. Baudelaire and Swinburne, at their best, succeed in celebrating the victory of the human soul over its adversaries, just as truly as Milton and Shelley. I never had a moment's doubt that I belonged to this school. To me it is a question of virility. Even James Thomson, ending with 'confirmation of the old despair', somehow defeats that despair by the essential force of his genius. Keats, on the contrary, no matter how hard he endeavours to end on a note of optimism, always leaves an impression of failure.

I will know how strangely perverse this criticism must sound, but I feel its truth in the marrow of my bones. In my own writings the tempestuous energy of my soul invariably sweeps away the wreckage of my mind. No matter to what depth I plunge, I always end with my wings beating steadily upwards towards the sun. The actual writing which releases my unconscious produces the effect. I inevitably end by transcending the problem of the poem, either lyrically or satirically. Turn to any page at random and the truth of this will become apparent.

In his time at Cambridge Pollitt had been very prominent as a female impersonator and dancer. He called himself Diane de Rougy—*après* Liane de Pougy. The grossness of people who do not understand art naturally misinterpreted this aesthetic gesture and connected it with a tendency to androgynity. I never saw the slightest symptoms of anything of the kind in him; though the subject sometimes came under discussion. But at that time it was considered criminal to admire *Lady Windermere's Fan*. I have always taken the attitude of Bishop Blougram and pay no attention to

> the infamy scrawled broad
> About me on the church wall opposite.

I have made a point of understanding the psychology of the subject: *Nihil humani a me alienum puto*.

But the conscience of the world is so guilty that it always assumes that people who investigate heresies must be heretics; just as if a doctor who studies leprosy must be a leper. Indeed, it is only recently that science has been allowed to study anything without reproach. Matter being evil, the less that we know about it the better—such was the Christian philosophy in the ages which it darkened. Morris Travers told me that his father, an eminent physician, had been ostracized, and had lost much of his practice, for joining the Anthropological Society. Later still, Havelock Ellis and Edward Carpenter have been treated with the foulest injustice by ignorant and prejudiced people. My mother always believed that the *Great Eastern,* the first steamship of any size to speak of, met with repeated disasters because God was jealous, as He had been of the Tower of Babel. In 1917 my cousin, Lawrence Bishop, told me that he thought that 'the Lord prepared a great iceberg' for the *Titanic* in annoyance at the claim of the shipbuilders that she was unsinkable. William Whiteley had several fires, which my mother took as the repartee of the Almighty to the merchant's assumption of the title 'Universal Provider', which could be properly attributed only to God.

It is the modern fashion to try to dismiss these barbarous absurdities as excrescences on Christianity, but they are of the essence of the religion. The whole theory of the atonement implies that man can set up his own will in opposition to God's, and thereby excites Him to anger which can only be pacified by the sacrifice of His Son. It is, after all, quite as reasonable to think of God as being irritated by a shipbuilding programme as by idolatry. The tendency has, in fact, been to forget about the atonement altogether and to represent Jesus as a 'Master' whose teachings are humanitarian and enlightened. Yet the only evidence of what he actually said is that of the gospels and these not only insist upon the incredible and immoral sides of Christianity, but contain actual Logia which exhibit Jesus in the character of a superstitious fanatic who taught the doctrine of eternal punishment and many others unacceptable to modern enlightenment. General Booth and Billy Sunday preach perfectly scriptural abominations. Again, much of the teaching of Jesus which is not savage superstition is diametrically opposed to the ideas of those modern moralists who reject his supernaturalism and salvationalism. The injunction 'Take no thought for the morrow' is incompatible with 'Preparedness', insurance and any other practice involving foresight. The command to break off all family and social relationships is similarly unethical. The truth, of course, is that these instructions were given to a select body of men, not to the world at large. Renunciation of the world is the first step toward spiritual illumination, and in the East, from the beginning of recorded time to the present day, the yogi, the fakir, the bhikkhu and the monk take this course, expecting that the piety of their neighbours will supply them with a means of livelihood.

It is not only illogical to pick out of the gospels the texts which happen to suit one's own prejudices and then claim Christ as the supreme teacher, but his claims to pre-eminence are barred by the fact that all the passages which are not fiendish superstition find parallels in the writings of earlier masters. The works of Lao Tzu, the Buddhist canon, the Upanishads, the Bhagavad-Gita, the Talmud and the philosophy of many of the early Greeks, to say nothing of the sacred books of Egypt, contain the whole of the metaphysics, theology and ethics to which modern enlightenment can assent. It is montrous and mischievous for liberal thinkers to call themselves Chistians; their nominal adhesion delays the disruption of the infamous system which they condone. To declare oneself a follower of Jesus is not only to insult history and reason, but to apologize for the murderers of Arius, Molinos and Cranmer, the persecutors of science, the upholders of slavery and the suppressors of all free thought and speech.

At this time I had not carried these arguments to their logical conclusion. *The Cloud upon the Sanctuary* told me of a secret community of saints in possession of every spiritual grace, of the keys to the treasures of nature, and of moral emancipation such that there was no intolerance or unkindness. The members of this Church lived their secret life of sanctity in the world, radiating light and love upon all that came within their scope, yet they were free from spiritual pride. They enjoyed intimate communion with the immanent divine soul of nature. Inheritors of innocence and illumination, they were not self-seekers; and their one passion was to bring mankind into the sphere of their own sublimity, dealing with each individual as his circumstances required. To them the members of the Trinity were nearer and more real than anything else in the universe. But they were pure ideas of incorruptible integrity. The incarnation was a mystical or magical operation which took place in every man. Each was himself the Son of God who had assumed a body of flesh and blood in order to perform the work of redemption. The in-dwelling of the Holy Ghost was a sanctification resulting from the completion of the great work when the self had been crucified to itself and raised again in incorruptible immortality.

I did not yet see that this conception reposed on metaphysical bases as untenable as those of orthodoxy. There was no attempt to explain the origin of evil and similar difficulties. But these things were mysteries which would be revealed to the saint as he advanced in the way of grace. Anyhow, I was certainly not the person to cavil. The sublimity of the idea enthralled me; it satisfied my craving for romance and poetry. I determined with my whole heart to make myself worthy to attract the notice of this mysterious brotherhood. I yearned passionately for illumination. I could imagine nothing more exquisite than to enter into communion with these holy men and to acquire the power of communicating with the angelic and divine intelligence of the universe. I longed for perfect purity of life, for mastery of the secret forces of nature, and for a career of devoted labour on behalf of 'the Creation which groaneth and travaileth'.

My poetry at this time is charged to the highest point with these aspirations. I may mention the dedication to Songs of the Spirit, 'The Quest', 'The Alchemist', 'The Philosopher's Progress', 'A Spring Snowstorm in Wastdale', 'Succubus', 'Nightfall', 'The Storm', 'Wheat and Wine', 'Vespers', 'Astrology' and 'Daedalus'. In 'The Farewell of Paracelsus to Aprile', 'The Initiation', 'Isaiah' and 'Power', I have expressed my ideas about the ordeals which might be expected on the Path. All these poems were published in 1898. In later volumes, Mysteries Lyrical and Dramatic, The Fatal Force, The Temple of the Holy Ghost and Tannhäuser, these ideas are carried further in the light of my practical experience of the Path.

It may seem strange that, despite the yearning after sanctification, which is the keynote of these works, I never lost sight of what seems on the surface the incompatible idea of justification by sin. 'Jezebel' and the other poems in that volume prove this point. It is as if my unconscious were aware that every act is a sacrament and that the most repulsive rituals might be in some ways the most effective. The only adequate way of overcoming evil was to utilize it fully as a means of grace. Religion was for me a passionate reality of the most positive kind. Virtue is etymologically manhood. Virility, creative conception and enthusiastic execution were the means of attainment. There could be no merit in abstention from vice. Vice indeed is *vitium,* a flaw or defect.

This attitude is not antinomianism, as the word is usually understood. When St Paul said, 'All things are lawful for me, but all things are not expedient', he only went half way. One ought to leave no form of energy to rust. Every particle of one's personality is a necessary factor in the equation and every impulse must be turned to account in the Great Work. I perceived, moreover, that all conventional rules of conduct were valid only in relation to environment. To take a fundamental issue: self-preservation. On the theory of reincarnation or that of immortality, there should be no more objection to dying than there is to going to sleep. In any case, I realized that my physical life was utterly valueless; and I did not set it at a pin's fee.

I have never been afraid of carrying into effect my conclusions; and I knew, what is more, that to fail to do so would be merely to create a conflict in myself. I had a thorough instinctive understanding of the theory of psychoanalysis. To this fact I attribute my extraordinary success in all my spiritual undertakings. From the very beginning I made a point of carrying out the instructions of one of the old Grimoires 'to buy a black egg without haggling'. I always understood that spiritual and material wealth were incommensurable. If I wanted a book on Magick and it was offered me for ten times the proper price, I would buy it on the spot, even though I knew that I had only to go round the corner to find an honest tradesman.

I did this sort of thing on purpose to affirm magically that nothing mattered except the work of the moment. It was 'Take no thought for the morrow' carried out in its most literal sense. I made a point of putting God on His honour, so to speak, to supply anything I might need by demonstrating to him that I would not keep back the least imaginable fraction of my resources. I acquired this custom later on, when I had definitely discovered the direction of my destiny; but the moral basis of my attitude was already present. The first important indication of its incidence is given by the outcome of my friendship with Pollitt.

He was in residence during the Easter term of 1898 and we saw each other almost every day. In the vacation he accompanied me to Wastdale Head and used to walk with me over the fells, though I could never persuade him to do any rock climbing.

I was absorbed in *The Cloud upon the Sanctuary*, reading it again and again without being put off by the pharisaical, priggish and pithecanthropoid notes of its translator, Madame de Steiger. I appealed with the whole force of my will to the adepts of the Hidden Church to prepare me as a postulant for their august company. As will be seen later, acts of will, performed by the proper person, never fall to the ground, impossible as it is (at present) to understand by what means the energy is transmitted.

Although Pollitt had done so much for my education by introducing me to the actual atmosphere of current aesthetic ideas, to the work of Whistler, Rops and Beardsley in art, and that of the so-called decadents in literature, as well as to many remote and exquisite masters of the past whom I had ignored or misunderstood, my admiration and gratitude did not prevent me from becoming conscious of the deep-seated aversion of our souls. He had made no mistake in divining that my spiritual aspirations were hostile to his acquiescence in despair of the universe. So I felt in my subconscious self that I must choose between my devotion to him and to the Secret Assembly of the Saints. Though he was actual and adequate, I preferred to risk all on the hazard. Human friendship, ideal as it was in this case, was under the curse of the universal sorrow. I determined deliberately to give it up, notwithstanding that it was unique and adorable in its way; that there was no reasonable hope of replacing it. This was my act of faith, unalloyed with the dross of hope, and stamped with the imperial countenance of love, to determine that I would not continue our relations.

The poignancy of this resolution was jagged and envenomed; for he was the only person with whom I had ever enjoyed truly spiritual intercourse and my heart was lonely, hungry and embittered as only a poet's heart can understand. This determination developed gradually during that last May term. He fought most desperately against my increasing preoccupation with the aspiration in which he recognized the executioner of our friendship.

Shortly after I went down, we had a last interview. I had gone down to the Bear at Maidenhead, on the quiet, to write 'Jezebel'. I only told one person—in strict confidence—where I was going; but Pollitt found out that person and forced him to tell my secret. He walked into the room shortly after dinner, to my surprise and rage—for when I am writing a poem I would show Azrael himself the door!

I told him frankly and firmly that I had given my life to religion and that he did not fit into the scheme. I see now how imbecile I was, how hideously wrong and weak it is to reject any part of one's personality. Yet these mistakes are not mistakes at the time: one has to pass through such periods; one must be ruthless in analysis and complete it, before one can proceed to synthesis. He understood that I was not to be turned from my purpose and we parted, never to meet again. I repented of my decision, my eyes having been enlightened, only a little later, but the reconciliation was not written! My letter miscarried; and in the autumn, when he passed me in Bond Street, I happened not to see him; he thought I meant to cut him and our destinies drew apart.

It has been my lifelong regret, for a nobler and purer comradeship never existed on this earth, and his influence might have done much to temper my subsequent trials. Nevertheless, the fragrance of that friendship still lingers in the sanctuary of my soul. That eucharist of the spirit reminds me constantly that the one ingredient necessary to my aesthetic development was supplied by the gods at the one period in my life when it could profitably be introduced into my equipment.

18

During the May term of 1898 I met another man who, in his own way, was interested in many of the same things as I was myself. His name was Gerald Festus Kelly. He is described in the telephone book as an artist; and the statement might have passed unchallenged indefinitely had not the Royal Academy recently elected him as an associate. He is hardly to be blamed for this disgrace. He struggled manfully. Even at the last moment, when he felt the thunderclouds about to break over his head, he made a last desperate coup to persuade the world that he was an artist by marrying a model. But the device deceived nobody. The evidence of his pictures was too glaring. The effort, moreover, completely exhausted his power of resistance; and he received the blow with Christian resignation. It saddens me more than I can say to think of that young life which opened with such brilliant promise, gradually sinking into the slough of respectability. Of course it is not as if he had been able to paint; but to me the calamity is almost as distressing as if that possibility had ever existed. For he completely hypnotized me into thinking that he had something in him. I took his determination to become an artist as evidence of some trace of capacity and I still hope that his years of unremitting devotion to a hopeless ambition will earn him the right to reincarnate with some sort of soul.

We met in a somewhat romantic way. My *Aceldama* had just been issued and was being sold privately in the university at half-a-crown. (There were only eighty-eight copies, with ten on large paper and two on vellum.) One of the mottoes in *Aceldama* is a quotation from Swinburne's 'The Leper'. I had not acknowledged the authorship of *Aceldama;* it was by 'A Gentleman of the University of Cambridge' in imitation of one of Shelley's earlier books.

Now, there was a bookseller in the town with whom I had few dealings, for he was the most nauseatingly hypocritical specimen of the pushing tradesman that I ever set eyes on. He was entirely irreligious and did a considerable business in the kind of book which is loathsomely described as 'curious'. But

he was out to get the clerical and academic custom and to this
end adopted a dress and manner which would have been
affected in the sweetest of young curates. Somehow or other,
a copy of *Aceldama* got into his hands; he showed it to Kelly,
who was so excited by the quotation from Swinburne that he
found out who I was, and a meeting was arranged. His knowledge of both art and literature was encyclopaedic, and we became very intimate, projecting collaboration in an Arthurian
play and a new magazine to take the place of *The Yellow
Book* and *The Savoy,* which had died with Beardsley. Nothing
much came of this at the time, but the meeting had in it the
germs of important developments. The critical event of the
year was my meeting with Oscar Eckenstein at Wastdale Head.

Eckenstein was a man twenty years older than myself. His
business in life was mathematics and science, and his one
pleasure mountaineering. He was probably the best all-round
man in England, but his achievements were little known because of his almost fanatical objection to publicity. He hated
self-advertising quacks like the principal members of the Alpine Club with an intensity which, legitimate as it was, was
almost overdone. His detestation of every kind of humbug and
false pretence was an overmastering passion. I have never met
any man who upheld the highest moral ideals with such
unflinching candour.

We did a few climbs together that Easter and made a sort
of provisional agreement to undertake an expedition to the
Himalayas when occasion offered. He had been a member of
the Conway expedition of 1892, but had quitted the party at
Askole, principally on account of his disgust with its mismanagement. The separation was engineered, moreover, from the
other side. For what reason has never been clearly explained.
It would evidently be improper to suggest that they had made
up their minds to record at least a partial success and did not
want an independent witness to their proceedings on the
glacier.

One incident of that expedition is well worth mentioning.
A survey was being made with instruments which lacked
various essential parts, and on Eckenstein pointing out the
uselessness of making observations of this kind, the reply was,
'Yes, I know, but it's good enough for the Royal Geographical
Society.' Anything of this sort roused Eckenstein to a pitch of
indescribably violent rage. I could not have had a better teacher
in matters of conscience. He taught me thoroughness and accuracy in every department of the game.

To illustrate one point. I had considered myself a very good glissader, and as compared with the other people whom I met on the mountain side, even such experts as Norman Collie, I had little to learn. But Eckenstein showed me that I was not even a beginner. He made me start down assorted slopes from all sorts of positions, and to pick myself up into any other desired position; to stop, to increase my pace or to jump, at the word of command. Why 'starting from all sorts of positions'? The idea was that one might conceivably fall on to a snow slope or have to jump to it from a great height, and it was therefore necessary to know how to deal with such situations.*

The combination was ideal. Eckenstein had all the civilized qualities and I all the savage ones. He was a finished athlete; his right arm, in particular, was so strong that he had only to get a couple of fingers on to a sloping ledge of an overhanging rock above his head and he could draw himself slowly up by that alone until his right shoulder was well above those fingers. There is a climb on the east face of the Y-shaped boulder (so called because of a forked crack on the west face) near Wastdale Head Hotel which he was the only man to do, though many quite first-rate climbers tried it. Great as his strength was, he considered it as nothing, quoting a Bavarian schoolmaster of his acquaintance, who could tear a silver florin in half with his fingers.

He was rather short and sturdily built. He did not know the meaning of the word 'fatigue'. He could endure the utmost hardship without turning a hair. He was absolutely reliable, either as leader or second man, and this quality was based upon profound and accurate calculations. He knew his limitations to a hair's breadth. I never saw him attempt anything beyond his powers; and I never knew him in want of anything from lack of foresight.

He had a remarkable sense of direction, though inferior to my own. But his was based upon rational considerations, that is to say, he could deduce where north was from calculations connected with geology, wind and the law of probabilities; whereas my own finer sense was purely psychical and depended upon the subconscious registration in my brain as to the angles through which my body had turned during the day.

---

* See *The Diary of a Drug Fiend,* pp. 159–60.

One point, however, is not covered by this explanation, nor can I find anything satisfactory or even plausible. For instance, one day (not having seen moonrise that month or in the district) we attempted to climb the Volcan di Colima; we had sent back our *mozos* with the camp to Zapotlan, intending to cross the mountain to the ranch of a gentleman to whom we had introductions. We had watched the volcano for a week and more, in the hope of discovering some periodicity in its eruptions, which we failed to do. We accordingly took our chance and went across the slopes until the rocks began to burn our feet through our boots. We recognized that it was hopeless to proceed.

We decided to make for the farm and soon reached a belt of virgin jungle where the *chapparal* and fallen timber made it almost impenetrable. The trees were so thick that we could rarely see the sky. The only indication for progress was to keep on down hill. The slopes were amazingly complicated, so that at any moment we might have been facing east, south or west. The dust of the rotten timber almost choked and blinded us. We suffered tortures from thirst, our water supply being extremely limited. Night fell; it was impossible to see our hands in front of us. We accordingly lit a fire to keep off the jackals and other possibilities, which we heard howling round us. We naturally began to discuss the question of direction; and I said, 'The moon will rise over there', and laid down my axe as a pointer. Eckenstein independently laid down his, after a rather prolonged mental calculation. When the moon rose we found that my axe was within five degrees and his within ten degrees of the correct direction. This was only one of many such tests; and I do not see in the least how I knew, especially as astronomy is one of the many subjects of which my knowledge is practically nil. In spite of innumerable nights spent under the stars, I can recognize few constellations except the Great Bear and Orion.

Besides my sense of direction on the large scale, I have a quite uncanny faculty for picking out a complicated route through rocks and ice falls. This is not simply a question of good judgment; for in any given route, seen from a distance, there may always be a passage, perhaps not twenty feet in height, which would render the whole plan abortive. This is especially the case with ice falls, where much of the route is necessarily hidden from view. Obviously, one cannot see what is on the other side of a sérac whose top one has theoretically reached. Yet I have never been wrong; I have never been forced to turn back from a climb once begun.

I have also an astonishing memory for the minutest details of any ground over which I have passed. Professor Norman Collie had this quality very highly developed, but he paid me the compliment of saying that I was much better than he was himself. This, too, was in my very early days when he was teaching me many quite rudimentary points in the technique of rock climbing. Again, we have a question of subconscious physical memory. I am often quite unable to describe even the major landmarks of a climb which I have just done, but I recognize every pebble as I come to it if asked to retrace my steps. Efforts on my part to bring up a mountain into clear consciousness frequently create such a muddle in my mind that I almost wonder at myself. I make such grotesque mistakes that I am not far from doubting whether I have been on the mountain at all: yet my limbs possess a consciousness of their own which is infallible. I am reminded of the Shetland ponies (see Wilkie Collins's *The Two Destinies*) which can find their way through the most bewildering bogs and mist. This faculty is not only retrospective—I can find my way infallibly over unknown country in any weather. The only thing that stops me is the interference of my conscious mind.

I have several other savage faculties; in particular, I can smell snow and water, though for ordinary things my olfactory sense is far below the average. I cannot distinguish perfectly familiar perfumes in many cases; that is, I cannot connect them with their names.

Eckenstein and I were both exceedingly expert at describing what lay behind any mountain at which we might be looking. In his case, the knowledge was deduced scientifically; in mine, it was what one must call sheer clairvoyance. The nearest I could get to understanding his methods was judging by the glow above the ridge of a mountain whether the other side was snow-covered, and estimating its steepness and the angle of its rocks by analogy with the corresponding faces of the mountains behind us, or similar formations elsewhere. It should hardly be necessary to point out the extraordinary practical value of these qualities in deciding one's route in unknown country.

In the actual technique of climbing, Eckenstein and I were still more complementary. It is impossible to imagine two methods more opposed. His climbing was invariably clean, orderly and intelligible; mine can hardly be described as human. I think my early untutored efforts, emphasized by my experience on chalk, did much to form my style. His movements were a series, mine were continuous; he used definite muscles, I used my whole body. Owing doubtless to my early ill-health, I never developed physical strength; but I was very light, and possessed elasticity and balance to an extraordinary degree.

I remember going out on Scafell with a man named Corry. He was the ideal athlete and had gone through a course of Sandow; but had little experience of climbing at that time. I took him up the North Climb of Mickledoor. There is one place where, while hunting for holds, one supports oneself by an arm stretched at full length into a crack. The arm is supported by the rock and the hand grasps a hold as satisfactory as a sword hilt. The inconceivable happened; Corry fell off and had to be replevined by the rope. I was amazed, but said nothing. We continued the climb and, reaching the top of the Broad Stand, took off the rope. By way of exercise, I suggested climbing a short, precipitous pitch above a sloping slab. There was no possible danger, it was within the powers of a child of six; but Corry came off again. I was standing on the slab and caught him by the collar as he passed on his way to destruction.

After that, we put on the rope again and returned by descending, I think, Mickledoor Chimney. On the way down to Wastdale, he was strangely silent and embarrassed, but finally he made up his mind to ask me about it.

'Do you mind if I feel your arm?' he said. 'It must be a marvel.'

I complied and he nearly fainted with surprise. My muscles were in quantity and quality like those of an early Victorian young lady. He showed me his own arm. There could not have been a finer piece of anatomy for manly strength. He could not understand how, with everything in his favour, he had been unable to maintain his grip on the best holds in Westmorland.

A curious parallel to this incident happened in 1902 on the expedition to Chogo Ri. We had an arrangement by which a pair of ski could be converted into a sledge for convenience in hauling baggage over snow-covered glaciers. When the doctor and I proposed to move from Camp 10 to Camp 11 we set up this sledge and packed seven loads on it. We found it quite easy to pull. This was clearly an economy of five porters and we started two men up the slope. To our astonishment they were unable to budge it. They called for assistance; until the whole seven were on the ropes. Even so, they had great difficulty in pulling the sledge and before they had gone a hundred yards managed to upset it into a crevasse. They settled the matter by taking two loads (between 100 and 120 pounds) each and went off quite merrily. It is useless to have strength unless you know how to apply it.

Eckenstein recognized from the first the value of my natural instincts for mountaineering, and also that I was one of the silliest young asses alive. Apart from the few priceless lessons that I had had from Norman Collie, I was still an amateur of the most callow type. I had no idea of system. I had achieved a good deal, it is true, by a mixture of genius and common sense; but I had no regular training and was totally ignorant of the serious business of camp life and other branches of exploration.

We arranged to spend the summer in a tent on the Schönbühl glacier under the Dent Blanche, primarily with the idea of fitting me for the Himalayan expedition, and secondarily with that of climbing the east face of the Dent Blanche by a new route which he had previously attempted with Zurbriggen. They had been stopped by a formation which is exceedingly curious and rare in the Alps—slopes of very soft snow set at an unclimbable angle. He thought that my capacity for swimming up places of this sort might enable us to bag the mountain.

I hope that Eckenstein has left adequate material for a biography and made arrangements for its publication. I had always meant to handle the matter myself. But the unhappy termination of his life in phthisis and marriage, when he had hoped to spend its autumn and winter in Kashmir meditating upon the mysteries which appealed to his sublime spirit, made all such plans nugatory.

I feel it one of my highest duties to record in these memoirs as much as possible relative to this man, who, with Allan Bennett, stands apart from and above all others with whom I have been really intimate. The greatness of his spirit was not inferior to that of such giants as Rodin; he was an artist no less than if he had actually produced any monument to his mind. Only his constant manhandling by spasmodic asthma prevented him from matching his genius by masterpieces. As it is, there is an immense amount in his life mysterious and extraordinary beyond anything I have ever known. For instance, during a number of years he was the object of repeated murderous attacks which he could only explain on the hypothesis that he was being mistaken for somebody else.

I must record one adventure, striking not only in itself, but because it is of a type which seems almost as universal as the 'flying dream'. It possesses the quality of the phantasmal. It strikes me as an adventure which in some form or other happens to a very large number of men; which occurs constantly in dreams and romances of the Stevensonian order. For instance, I cannot help believing that something of the kind has happened to me, though I cannot say when, or remember the incidents. I have written the essence of it in 'The Dream Circean'; and some phantasm of similar texture appears to me in sleep so frequently that I wonder whether its number is less than one weekly, on the average. Sometimes it perpetuates itself night after night, recognizable as itself despite immense variety of setting, and haunting my waking hours with something approaching conviction that it represents some actuality.

This story is briefly as follows. One night after being attacked in the streets of Soho, or the district between that section of Oxford Street and the Euston Road, he determined, in case of a renewed assault, to walk home by a roundabout and unfamiliar route. Somewhere in the neighbourhood of the Caledonian Road he thought that he was being followed —it was now late at night and somewhat foggy. To make sure, he turned into a narrow passage on to which opened the gardens of a row of houses, in one, and only one, of which lights were visible. The garden door of this house was open and he dodged in to see whether the men he suspected were following. Two figures appearing at the end of the passage, he quietly closed the door behind him with the intention of entering the house, explaining his position and asking to be allowed to leave by the front door. The door was opened by a young and beautiful woman in fashionable evening dress. She appeared of good social position and, on his explaining himself, asked him to stay to supper. He accepted. No servants appeared, but on reaching the dining-room—which was charmingly furnished and decorated with extremely good pictures, Monet, Sisley and the like, with sketches or etchings by Whistler, all small but admirable examples of those masters—he found a cold supper for two people was laid out. Eckenstein remained for several hours, in fact until daylight, when he left with the understanding that he would return that evening. He made no note of the address, the street being familiar to him and his memory for numbers entirely reliable. I think that he was somehow prevented from returning the same evening; I am not quite sure on this point. But if so, he was there twenty-four hours later. He was surprised to find the house in darkness and astounded when on further inspection he saw a notice 'To Let'. He knocked and rang in vain. Assuming that he must have mistaken the number, unthinkable as the supposition was, he explored the adjacent houses, but found nothing. Annoyed and intrigued, he called on the agent the next morning and visited the house. He recognized it as that of his hostess. Even the lesser discolorations of the wallpaper where the book-case and pictures had been testified to the identity of the room. The agent assured him that the house had not been occupied for three months. Eckenstein pointed to various tokens of recent occupancy. The agent refused to admit the conclusion. They explored the back part of the premises and found the French windows through which Eckenstein had entered, and the garden gate, precisely as he had left them. On inquiry it appeared that the house was vacant owing to the proprietor (a bachelor of some sixty years old, who had lived there a long while with a man and wife to keep house for him) having been ordered to the south of France for the winter. He had led a very retired life, seeing no company; the house had been furnished in early Victorian style. Only the one room where Eckenstein had had supper was unfurnished. The agent explained this by saying that the old man had taken the effects of his study with him to France, for the sake of their familiarity.

The mystery intrigued Eckenstein immensely and he returned several times to the house. A month or so later he found the two servants had returned. The master was expected back in the spring. They denied all knowledge of any such lady as described; and there the mystery rests, save that some considerable time later Eckenstein received a letter, unsigned, in evidently disguised handwriting. It contained a few brief phrases to the effect that the writer was sorry, but it could not be helped; that there was no hope for the future, but that memory would never fade. He connected this mysterious communication with his hostess, simply because he could not imagine any other possibility.

I can offer no explanation whatever, but I believe every word of the story, and what is most strange is that I possess an impenetrable conviction that something almost exactly the same must have happened to me. I am reminded of the one fascinating episode which redeems the once-famous but excessively stupid and sentimental novel *Called Back* from utterly abject dullness. There is also an admirable scene in one of Stevenson's best stories, 'John Nicholson'. A similar theme occurs in *Dr Jekyll and Mr Hyde*, 'The Sire de Malétroit's Door', and 'A Lodging for the Night'. There are similar ideas in oriental and classical literature. The fascination of the central idea thus seems a positive obsession to certain minds.

Is it somehow symbolic of a widespread wish or fear? Is it, as in the case of the Oedipus complex, the vestige of a racial memory—'In the beginning was the deed'? (This phrase magnificent concludes Freud's *Totem and Taboo*.) Or can it be the actual memory of an event in some previous incarnation or in some other illusion than what we call real life?

In the course of writing this story down, the impression of personal reminiscence has become steadily stronger. I now recall clearly enough that I have actually experienced not one but many such adventures, that is, as far as the spiritual essence is concerned. I have repeatedly, sometimes by accident but more often on purpose, gone into the wrong room or the wrong house, with the deliberate intention of finding romance. More often than not, I have succeeded. As to the sequel, I have often enough failed to return; and here again sometimes the force of circumstances has been responsible, sometimes disinclination; but, most frequently of all, through the operation of that imp of the perverse whom I blame elsewhere in this book for occasional defeats at chess. I have wished to go, I have made every preparation for going, I have perhaps reached the door, and then found myself powerless to enter. Stranger still, I have actually returned; and then, despite the strongest conscious efforts to 'recapture the first fine careless rapture' of the previous visit, behaved in such a way as to make it impossible.

I have never been baffled by any such inexplicable incident as the abandonment of the room, though I have sometimes failed to find the expected girl.

Talking the whole matter over with my guide, philosopher and friend, Frater O.P.V.,[1] he finds the whole story extraordinarily gripping. He finds the situation nodal for the spirit of romance. An extraordinary number of vital threads or 'nerves' of romance.

He attaches great significance to the failure of Eckenstein to keep the appointment. It seems to him as if the whole business were a sort of magical ordeal, that Eckenstein should have been awake to the miraculous character of the adventure and kept his appointment though hell itself yawned between him and the house. The main test is his realization that the incident is high Magick, that if he fail to grasp its importance, to understand that unless he return that night the way will shut for ever. He suggests that by failing to appreciate the opportunity at its full value he had somehow missed the supreme chance of his life, as if the 'wrong house' were the gateway to another world, an inn, so to speak, on the outskirts of the City of God. In recent years I have been constantly alert and on the look-out for something of the kind. Whenever my plans are disarranged by a number of apparently trivial and accidental circumstances, I look eagerly for the possibility that the situation to which they lead may prove the opening scene in some gigantic drama. Numerous episodes in these memoirs illustrate this thesis. One might even say that the whole book is a demonstration of how the accumulation and consequence of large numbers of apparently disconnected facts have culminated in bringing 'the time and the place, and the loved one all together'.

Eckenstein's parents had escaped from Germany in '48, or thereabouts, as political exiles, or so I imagine; I do not remember any details. But he was educated at Bonn and knew Bloody Bill intimately. This luckless despot was at that time a young man of extraordinary promise, taking himself with the utmost seriousness as realizing the gigantic responsibilities of his inheritance. He was intensely eager to fit himself to do his best for Germany. He was openminded and encouraged Eckenstein's endeavours to introduce eight-oared rowing into the university, and used his influence to obtain permission for officers to lay by their swords when playing tennis.

One incident amuses me greatly. Students were exempt from the general law and could not be punished for any act which was not mentioned by name in the statutes. The brighter spirits would then accordingly search the statutes for gaps. It was, for instance, *strengstens verboten* to tie night-watchmen to lightning conductors during thunderstorms. Eckenstein and his friends waited accordingly for the absence of thunderstorms and then proceeded to tie up the watchmen.

He was as thoroughly anglicized as possible. The chief mark of the old Adam was a tendency to professional dogmatism. When he felt he was right, he was almost offensively right; and on any point which seemed to him settled, the coefficient of his mental elasticity was zero. He could not imagine the interference of broad principles with the detailed results of research. The phrase 'general principles' enraged him. He insisted on each case being analysed by itself as it arose. This is all right, but it is possible to overdo it. There are many circumstances which elude analysis, yet are perfectly clear if examined in the light of the fundamental structure of the human organism. For all that, he was exactly the man that I needed to correct my tendency to take things for granted, to be content with approximations, to jump at conclusions, and generally to think casually and loosely. Besides this, my experience of his moral and intellectual habits was of the greatest service to me, or rather to England, when it was up to me to outwit Hugo Münsterberg.

Eckenstein's moral code was higher and nobler than that of any other man I have met. On numerous points I cannot agree; for some of his ideas are based on the sin complex. I cannot imagine where he got it from, he with his rationalistic mind from which he excluded all the assumptions of established religion. But he certainly had the idea that virtue was incompatible with enjoyment. He refused to admit that writing poetry was work, though he admired and loved it intensely. I think his argument must have been that if a man enjoys what he is doing, he should not expect extra remuneration.

Eckenstein shared the idiosyncrasies of certain very great men in history. He could not endure kittens. He did not mind grown-up cats. The feeling was quite irrational and conferred mysterious powers! for he could detect the presence of a kitten by means of some sense peculiar to himself. We used to tease him about it in the manner of the young, who never understand that anything may be serious to another person which is not so to them. One Easter the hotel was overcrowded; and five of us, including Eckenstein and myself, were sleeping in the barn. One of Eckenstein's greatest friends was Mrs Bryant, whose beautiful death between Chamonix and the Montanvers in 1922 was the crown of a noble life. She had brought her niece, Miss Nichols, who to intrepidity on rocks added playfulness in less austere surroundings. I formally accuse her of putting a kitten under Eckenstein's pillow in the barn while we were in the smoking-room after dinner. If it had been a cobra Eckenstein could not have been more upset!

He had also an idiosyncrasy about artificial scent. One day my wife and a friend came home from shopping. They had called at the chemist's who had sprayed them with 'Shem-el-nessim'. We saw them coming and went to the door to receive them. Eckenstein made one rush—like a bull—for the window of the sitting-room, flung it open and spent the next quarter of an hour leaning out and gasping for breath.

Eckenstein was a great connoisseur of puzzles. It is extremely useful, by the way, to be able to occupy the mind in such ways when one has not the conveniences or inclination for one's regular work, and there is much time to kill in an hotel or a tent in bad weather. Personally, I have found chess, solitaire and triple-dummy bridge or skat as good as anything.

Eckenstein was a recognized authority on what is known as Kirkwood's schoolgirl problem, but we used to work at all sorts of things, from problems connected with Mersenne's numbers and Fermat's binary theorem to the purely frivolous attempt to represent any given number by the use of the number four, four times—neither more nor less, relating them by any of the accepted symbols of mathematical operations. Thus:

$$18 = 4 (4.4) + .4$$
$$38 = \underline{4} + \cdot + 4$$
$$106 = \underline{4} + 4 \cdot \tfrac{4}{4}$$
$$128 = 4^4 \div 4 - \sqrt{4}$$

This has been done up to about 170, with the exception of the number 113, and thence to 300 or thereabouts with only a few gaps. I solved 113 with the assistance of Frater Ψ^2 and the use of a subfactorial, but Eckenstein would not admit the use of this symbol as fair.

He was also interested in puzzles involving material apparatus, one of which seems worth mention. He was in Mysore and a travelling conjurer sold him a whole bundle of more or less ingenious tricks. One of these consisted simply of two pieces of wood; one a board with a hole in it, the other shaped somewhat like a dumb-bell, the ends being much too big to go through the hole. Eckenstein said that he was almost ready to swear that he saw the man take them up separately and rapidly put them together, in which condition he had them and was never able to take them apart. He explored the surface minutely for signs of complexity of structure but without success. I never saw the toy, he having sent it to Mr W. W. Rouse Ball, a great authority on such matters, but also baffled in this case.

We were naturally always interested in any problems concerned with the working out of a difficult route, and here his probity on one occasion made him the victim of an unscrupulous child of Shaitan. The villain appeared in the guise of an old and valued friend, saying 'Is it possible to reach Q from

P (mentioning two places in London) without passing a public house?' Eckenstein accordingly took his walks in that direction and after endless trouble discovered a roundabout way which fulfilled the condition. Communicating the joyful news, his friend replied, 'Good for you! Here's something else. Can you get to the Horseshoe, Tottenham Court Road, from here without passing a public house?' I do not know how many pairs of alpine boots Eckenstein wore out on the problem, before asking his friend, 'Can it be done?' A telegram assured him that it could. More boots went the way of all leather and then he gave up. 'It's perfectly easy,' said the false friend, '*don't* pass them—go in!'

(The psychologist will observe that this atrocious piece of misplaced humour was made possible by the earlier problem having been genuine, difficult and interesting, thus guaranteeing the spoof.)

One of his favourite amusements was to calculate the possibility of some published description of a phenomenon. For instance, in the novel *She* there is a 'rocking stone' about which there are sufficient data in the book to enable an expert to say whether it was possible in nature. He decided that it was, but only on the assumption that it was a cone balanced on its apex.

I suppose that every form of navigation possesses its peculiar dangers. I remember Eckenstein telling me of an adventure he once had with Legros. One might be tempted to think that very little harm could come to a barge in a dock on the Thames, bar being cut down by a torpedo ram. But the facts are otherwise. It was the first time that either of them had been in charge of this species of craft, which they had to manoeuvre in order to inspect a wharf which required some slight repair. The gallant little wave-waltzer displaced a hundred and twenty tons and was called the *Betsy Anne*.

They boarded the barge without difficulty, but to get her going was another matter. The fellow-countrymen of Cook, Drake and Nelson were not behindhand with wise advice couched in language of frankness and fancy. They learned that the way to make a barge go was to walk up and down the broad flat gunwale with a pole. She was certainly very hard to start; but it got easier as she gathered way. They entered into the spirit of the sport and began to run up and down with their poles, exciting each other to emulation with cheerful laughter. Pride filled their souls as they observed that their rapid mastery of the awkward craft was appreciated on shore, as the lusty cheering testified. It encouraged them to mightier efforts and

before long they must have been making well over two miles
an hour. Then Eckenstein's quick ear asked him whether the
shouting on shore was so wholly the expression of unstinted
admiration as he had supposed. He paid greater attention and
thought he detected yells of coarse ridicule mingled with
violent objurgation. He thought he heard a word at the conclusion of a string of extremely emphatic epithets which might
easily have been mistaken for 'Fool!' At this point Legros
stopped poling, said shortly and unmistakably 'Hell!' and
pointed to the wharf, which, as previously stated, stood in need
of some trifling repairs. It was now not more than fifty yards
away and seemed to them to be charging them with the déter-
mination of an angry elephant. They realized the danger and
shouted for advice. The answer was, in essence, 'Dive!' It was,
of course, hopeless to attempt to check or even to deflect the
Betsy Anne. They dived, and a moment later heard the rending
crash of the collision, and were nearly brained by baulks of
falling timber. 'Well,' said Eckenstein, as they drove home to
change their muddy garments, 'we've done a good morning's
work, anyhow. That wharf is no longer in need of trifling repairs.' Both it and the *Betsy Anne* kept the neighbourhood in
matchwood for the next two years. Oh! for a modern Cowper
to immortalize the maritime John Gilpin!

19

We had one or two other people with us, in particular a man named Paley Gardner, who had been with Eckenstein at Wastdale at Easter. He was a man of giant strength, but could not be taught to climb the simplest rocks. He always tried to pull the mountain down to him instead of pulling himself up to it! He was one of the best fellows that ever walked and had led an extraordinary life of which he was too silent and too shy to speak. But he loosened up to some extent in camp; and two of his adventures are so remarkable that I feel they ought to be rescued from oblivion.

He was a rich men, but on one occasion found himself stranded in Sydney and too lazy to wire for money. At this juncture he met a man who offered to take him trading in the islands. They got a schooner, a crew and some stores; set off; sold their stuff; and started home. Then smallpox broke out on board and every man died but Paley, who sailed the schooner, single-handed, seven days back to Sydney.

On another occasion he found himself at Lima during the battle; if you can call it a battle when everyone thought it the best bet to shoot anyone he saw as a matter of general principle. Paley, being a man of peace, took up a position on a remote wall with the idea of shooting anyone that approached in case of his proving unfriendly. However, the first person that arrived was obviously an Englishman. They recognized each other and proceeded to concert measures for escape.

The newcomer, a doctor with long experience of South America, suggested that if they could only cross a broad belt of country inhabited by particularly malignant Indian tribes, and the Andes, they could reach the head waters of the Amazon and canoe down to Iquitos, where they would be in clover, as the doctor was a close friend of Dom Somebody, a powerful minister or other high official. They started off on this insane programme and carried it out (after innumerable adventures) with success. Arriving at Iquitos, ragged and penniless, but confident that the minister's friendship would put them on a good wicket at once, they sought the local authorities—and

154

learnt that their friend had been hanged a few days before, and that anyone who knew him might expect a similar solution to his troubles!

The two Englishmen were thrown into prison, but broke out and bolted down river. The hue and cry was raised; but, just as their pursuers were closing in on them, they managed to steal a fishing smack, with which they put out into the open Atlantic. Luckily, a few days later, when they were on the brink of starvation, they fell in with an English steamer bound for Liverpool. The captain picked them up and took them home in triumph.

The weather made it impossible to do any serious climbing; but I learnt a great deal about the work of a camp at high altitudes, from the management of transport to cooking; in fact, my chief claim to fame is, perhaps, my 'glacier curry'. It was very amusing to see these strong men, inured to every danger and hardship, dash out of the tent after one mouthful and wallow in the snow, snapping at it like mad dogs. They admitted, however, that it was very good as curry and I should endeavour to introduce it into London restaurants if there were only a glacier. Perhaps, some day, after a heavy snowfall—

I had been led, in the course of my reading, to *The Kabbalah Unveiled*, by S. L. Mathers. I didn't understand a word of it, but it fascinated me all the more for that reason, and it was my constant study on the glacier. My health was not good during this summer and I had gone down to Zermatt for a rest. One night in the beer hall I started to lay down the law on alchemy, which I nowise understood. But it was a pretty safe subject on which to spread myself and I trust that I impressed the group of men with my vast learning. However, my destiny was in ambush. One of the party, named Julian L. Baker, was an analytical chemist. He took me aside when the group broke up and walked back to the hotel with me. He was himself a real practical alchemist—I don't know whether he had been fooled by my magpie display of erudition. He may simply have deduced that a boy, however vain and foolish, who had taken so much pains to read up the subject, might have a really honest interest after all; and he took me seriously. He had accomplished some remarkable work in alchemy. For one thing, he had prepared 'fixed mercury'; that is to say, the pure metal in some form that was solid at ordinary temperatures.

As for me, I made no mistake. I felt that the moment of opportunity was come. I had sent out the S.O.S. call for a Master during that Easter at Wastdale Head; and here was a man who was either one himself or could put me in touch with one. It struck me as more than a coincidence that I should have been led to meet him partly through my ill-health and partly through my fatuous vanity. That night I resolved to renew my acquaintance with Baker in the morning and tackle him seriously about the intricate question which lay close about my heart.

The morrow dawned. At breakfast I inquired for Baker. He had left the hotel; no one knew where he had gone. I telegraphed all over the valley. He was located at the Gorner Grat. I sped up the mountain to find him. Again he had gone. I rushed back. In vain I hunted him through the hotels and at the railway station. At last I got a report that an Englishman corresponding to his description had started to walk down the valley to Brigue. I hurled myself headlong in pursuit. This time I was rewarded. I caught up with him some ten miles below Zermatt. I told him of my search for the Secret Sanctuary of the Saints and convinced him of my desperate earnestness. He hinted that he knew of an Assembly which might be that for which I was looking. He spoke of a Sacrament where the Elements were four instead of two. This meant nothing to me; but I felt that I was on the right track. I got him to promise to meet me in London. He added, 'I will introduce you to a man who is much more of a Magician than I am.'

To sum the matter in brief, he kept his word. The Secret Assembly materialized as the 'Hermetic Order of the G∴ D∴,'[1] and the Magician as one George Cecil Jones.

During the whole summer, the weather got steadily worse and my health took the same course. I found myself obliged to leave the camp and go to London to see doctors. I took rooms in an hotel in London, attended to the necessary medical treatment and spent my time writing poetry. The play *Jephthah* was my principal work at this period. It shows a certain advance in bigness of conception; and has this notable merit, that I began to realize the possibility of objective treatment of a theme. Previous to this, my lyrics had been more or less successful expressions of the ego; and I had made few attempts to draw characters who were not more than Freudian wish phantasms—I mean by this that they were either projections of myself as I fancied myself or aspired to be; otherwise, images of women that I desired to love. When I say 'to love', I doubt whether the verb meant anything more than 'to find myself through'. But in *Jephthah*, weak as the play is, I was really taking an interest in other people. The characters are not wholly corrupted by self-portraiture. I stuck to the Hebrew legend accurately enough, merely introducing a certain amount of Cabbalistic knowledge.

The passionate dedication to Swinburne is significant of my literary hero-worship. With this play were published (in 1899) a number of lyrics entitled 'Mysteries, Lyrical and Dramatic'. The shallow critic hastily assumed that the influence of Swinburne was paramount in my style, but on re-reading the volume I do not think that the accusation is particularly justifiable. There are plenty of other authors who might more reasonably be served with an affiliation summons. Indeed, criticism in England amounts to this: that if a new writer manifests any sense of rhythm, he is classed as an imitator of Swinburne; if any capacity for thought, of Browning.

I remember one curious incident in connection with this volume. I had a set of paged proofs in my pocket one evening, when I went to call on W. B. Yeats. I had never thought much of his work; it seemed to me to lack virility. I have given an extended criticism of it in *The Equinox* (vol. I, no. II, page 307). However, at that time I should have been glad to have a kindly word from an elder man. I showed him the proofs accordingly and he glanced through them. He forced himself to utter a few polite conventionalities, but I could see what the truth of the matter was.

I had by this time become fairly expert in clairvoyance, clairaudience and clairsentience. But it would have been a very dull person indeed who failed to recognize the black, bilious rage that shook him to the soul. I instance this as a proof that Yeats was a genuine poet at heart, for a mere charlatan would have known that he had no cause to fear an authentic poet. What hurt him was the knowledge of his own incomparable inferiority.

I saw little of him and George Moore. I have always been nauseated by pretentiousness; and the Celtic revival, so-called, had all the mincing, posturing qualities of the literary Plymouth Brother. They pretended to think it an unpardonable crime not to speak Irish, though they could not speak it themselves; and they worked in their mealymouthed way towards the galvanization of the political, ethnological and literary corpse of the Irish nation. Ireland has been badly treated, we all know; but her only salvation lay in forgetting her nonsense. What is the use of setting up a scarecrow provincialism, in re-establishing a barbarous and fantastic language which is as dead as Gothic and cannot boast sufficient literature to hold the attention of any but a few cloistered scholars—at the price of cutting Ireland off from the main stream of civilization? We see already that the country has slunk into the slough of anarchy. When the Kilkenny cats have finished shooting each other from behind hedges, the depopulated island will necessarily fall into the hands of practical colonists, who will be content to dwell peaceably together and communicate with the world in a living language.

Like Byron, Shelley, Swinburne and Tennyson, I left the university without taking a degree. It has been better so; I have accepted no honour from her; she has had much from me.

I wanted the spirit of the university and I passed my examinations in order to be able to imbibe it without interference from the authorities, but I saw no sense in paying fifteen guineas for the privilege of wearing a long black gown more cumbersome than the short blue one, and paying thirteen and fourpence instead of six and eightpence if I were caught smoking in it. I had no intention of becoming a parson or a schoolmaster; to write B.A. after my name would have been a decided waste of ink.

I felt that my career was already marked out for me. Sir Richard Burton was my hero and Eckenstein his modern representative, as far as my external life was concerned. A baccalaureate would not assist me noticeably in the Himalayas or the Sahara. As for my literary career, academic distinction would be a positive disgrace. And with regard to my spiritual life, which I already felt to be the deepest thing in me, the approbation of the faculty was beneath troubling to despise. I have always objected to incurring positive disgrace. I see no sense in violating conventions, still less in breaking laws. To do so only gives one unnecessary trouble.

On the other hand, it is impossible to make positive progress by means of institutions which lead to one becoming a lord chancellor, an archbishop, an admiral, or some other flower of futility. I had got from Cambridge what I wanted: the intellectual and moral freedom, the spirit of initiative and self-reliance; but perhaps, above all, the indefinable tone of the university. The difference between Cambridge and Oxford is that the former makes you the equal of anybody alive; the latter leaves you in the invidious position of being his superior.

NOTE ON THE DIFFERENCES BETWEEN OXFORD AND CAMBRIDGE

One of the most significant points in English character is thrown into relief by the contemplation of Oxford and Cambridge. I should be very puzzled to have to say what that point is, but the data are unmistakable. The superficial likeness between the universities is very clear, yet their fundamental spiritual difference can only be described as 'a great gulf fixed'. Contrast this with America, where even long experience does not enable one to distinguish at a glance between men from the four principal universities, or even to detect, in most cases, the influence of any university training soever, as we understand the idea. But to mistake an Oxford for a Cambridge man is impossible and the converse exceedingly rare.

I hope it is not altogether the blindness of filial affection that inclines me to suggest that the essential difference depends upon the greater freedom of the more famous university. Oxford makes a very definite effort to turn out a definite type of man and even his ingrained sense that he is not as other men operates finally as a limitation. At Cambridge the ambitions and aspirations of any given undergraduate are much less clearly cut and are of wider scope than those of his equivalent on the Isis. It seems to me no mere accident that Cambridge was able to tolerate Milton, Byron, Tennyson and myself without turning a hair, while Oxford inevitably excreted Shelley and Swinburne. *Per contra,* she suited Walter Pater and Oscar Wilde perfectly. Had they been at Cambridge, the nonsense would have been knocked out of them. They would have had to succeed or fail entirely on their own virtues; whereas, as things were, the Oxford atmosphere and the Oxford manner shielded them from the rude blasts of all-round criticism.

These ideas receive some support from the consideration of the relations normally obtaining between undergraduates and dons. On the Granta we are no doubt *in statu pupillari;* the Oxonian is *in statu quo pupillari.* He is taught, trained and, if necessary, trounced, to respect the principle of authority. It is really fair to say that no Cambridge man would ever dream of adducing authority in the course of an argument. He might indeed bring forward a great name on his side, but never without being ready to support it with the heavy artillery of patent proof. No fame is fixed with us as it is with them. The spirit of criticism never sleeps.

We see accordingly much stricter discipline with them than with us. We tend to trust the good sense and good will of the fluffiest fresher. Our dons never get nervous lest a rag should go too far, and we never betrayed their trust, at least not till quite recently. Since my time the tone of both universities has been lowered. Before 1900 a rag capable of scaring the women students would have been unthinkable.

Tyranny always trembles, and I remember only too well the wave of sympathy which swept through Cambridge at the news that the Oxford authorities, panic-stricken at some projected demonstration, had actually imported mounted police from London. Our own dons would have cut their throats rather than do anything so disgraceful; but if they had, we should have pounded those police into pulp.

This particular contrast is manifest to both universities. Whenever the subject comes up, anecdote answers anecdote to the point. The psychology extends to the individual. Our conception of the ideal proctor is very different to theirs. In my second year one proctor effected some capture by watching his victim from the darkness of a doorway. The story went round and within a week dishonour met its due. The dirty dog was ducked in the Cam. Nor were the avengers sent down. On the contrary, the proctor was obliged to burn his bands. Such conduct was practically unprecedented.

The typical tale is this. The grounds of Downing College are surrounded by a long low wall. One dark windy night a passing proctor saw his cap, caught by a gust, soar gracefully over the rampart. His bulldogs climbed the wall and retrieved it. But the cap was not their only prize. They dragged with them a most discomfited undergraduate, and a companion who was open to criticism from the point of view of the university regulations. But the proctor simply thanked the man for bringing back his cap and apologized for disturbing him. He refused to take advantage of an accident.

One very instructive incident concerns that brilliant Shakespeare scholar and lecturer Louis Umfraville Wilkinson. One summer night he came into college at Oxford a little lively with liquor. His wit had made the evening memorable and he went on to his rooms without curbing his conversation, which happened to deal with the defects of the dean in various directions. Fortune favoured him—I balance the books in perspective!—the dean's window was open and the reprobate heard to his horror that one at least of his flock failed to estimate his eminence at the same exalted rate as he did himself. He actually brought a formal charge of blasphemy against Wilkinson, pressed it to the utmost and succeeded in getting him sent down.

Wilkinson shrugged his shoulders, came over to us and entered his name at John's. Now comes an infamy almost incredible. The dean pursued his revenge. He wrote a long, bitter, violent letter to Wilkinson's tutor, giving an account of the affair at Oxford, and urging—in such language that it was more like a command than a threat—that Wilkinson be forthwith kicked out of Cambridge. The tutor sent for the offender and the following dialogue ensued:

'I believe you know Mr So-and-So, Mr Wilkinson.'

'I have that honour, sir.'

'Dean of Blank, Oxford, I understand.'

'That is so, sir.'

'I have a letter from him, which I propose to read to you.'

'Thank you, sir.'

The tutor read through the letter, made no comment, asked no questions. He tore it slowly in pieces and threw them into the fire.

'May I hope that you will be with us at breakfast tomorrow?'

'Thank you, sir.'

'Good morning, Mr Wilkinson.'

'Good morning, sir.'

I confess that it seems to me that the method of Oxford in such matters errs in two different directions. On the one hand, the undergraduate is treated as an irresponsible infant, to be dragooned into decency; and on the other, punished with a sternness which postulates that he is as accountable for his actions as a fully adult man, with comprehensive knowledge of the ways of the world. The result is to hinder his development, by withholding experience from him, and at the same time to punish his inexperience by making a mere mistake ruinous. The system tends to atrophy his ethical development by insisting on a narrow and inelastic code, while encouraging moral cowardice and unfitting him to face the facts which so presumptuously force themselves into notice as soon as the college conventions are done with.

Cambridge realizes that (within very wide limits) the more experience a man has, the better is he equipped to make his way in the world. We think it wiser to let men find out for themselves what dangers lie ahead, and pay the penalty for imprudence while recovery is comparatively easy. Better learn how to fall before the bones become brittle.

Another advantage of our idea of the relationship between long gowns and short is that, even if at the cost of some superficial respect, it is possible to establish more intimate communion in a spirit of comradeship between the old and the young. The intellectual gain is obvious; but perhaps even more valuable is the moral profit. To draw a hard and fast line between pupil and teacher limits both. Misunderstanding leads to mistrust, mistrust to enmity. It is better to realize the identity of interests.

I became aware of my feeling on this point quite suddenly. The impression is the more intense. One night there had been a regular rag. I forget what about, but we built a big bonfire in the middle of the market place and otherwise spread ourselves. Things began with no definite pulse of passion discernible, but as the evening advanced, we found ourselves somehow or other at odds with the townees. I think we must have resented their attempt to participate in the general gaiety. Sporadic free fights sprang up here and there, but nothing really serious. On the whole we gave and took in good temper. Just before twelve o'clock I turned to go home. Just beyond the tobacconist's—Bacon, celebrated by Calverley in his overrated ode—swirled a swarm of townees shouting and swearing in a way that struck me as ugly. It was no affair of mine and I did not want to be late. But even as I changed my course to avoid the mob I saw that their game was to reinforce half a dozen roughs who were surrounding a doorway and hustling one of the proctors. My immediate impulse was to gloat upon the evil that had befallen my natural enemy, for until that moment my absurd shyness had prevented me from realizing my relations with the authorities. I had timidly accepted the convention chaff, but now almost before that first thought was formulated my inmost instincts sprang into consciousness. I shouted to the few scattered gownsmen that were still in the square and hurled myself headlong to the rescue of my detested tyrant. He was pretty well under the weather, warding off feebly the brutal blows that the cowardly cads rained on his face. His cap was gone and his gown was in shreds. His bulldogs had been handled still more roughly. I suppose the townees saw them as traitors to the cause, hirelings of the aristocracy. They had been knocked clean down and were being battered by the boots of the mob. We must have been about a dozen, not more, and we had to fight off forty. It was the first time that I had ever had to face the animal anger, unreasoned and uncontrolled, of a mass of men whose individual intelligence, such as they were, had been for the moment completely swamped by the savage instinct to stamp on anything that seemed to them sensitive.

Fate familiarized me with this psychology in another form. It breaks out every time any man speaks or acts so as to awaken the frantic fear which is inherent in all but the rarest individuals, that anything new is a monstrous menace. For the first time I observed the extraordinary fact that in such situations one's time sense runs at two very different rates. The part of one's mind that is concerned with one's actions races riotously with their rhythm. Another part stands aloof, observing, analysing, imperturbable; a train of thought which might, in normal circumstances, occupy an hour reduced to a few minutes, and seeming slow at that.

The roughs were, to all intents and purposes, insane. They neither knew nor cared whether they ended by murder. And yet I have no idea why we mastered them easily enough. We had neither arms nor discipline. We were younger, certainly weaker, man for man, and we lacked the force which fury lends to its victims. I found myself puzzling it out and the only conclusion was that, whatever science may say, there is such a thing as moral superiority, a spiritual strength independent of material or calculable conditions.

The fight went on for twenty minutes or so and ended queerly enough. The mob thinned out, melted away at its outskirts, and the front rank men became aware of the fact simultaneously without any more reason than had marked their entire proceedings. They took to their heels and ran like rabbits.

It was half-past twelve before I got home. I took a tub and found I was black and blue. Of course my breach of the rule about midnight was duly reported. I was halled and explained why I had been late. The proctor whom we had conveyed to Christ's had not taken our names and I have no reason to think that he knew me. But my tutor asked no questions. He took my story for true; in fact, he treated me simply as another gentleman. That could not have happened at Oxford.

20

Nothing gives such a mean idea of the intelligence of mankind
than that it should ever have accepted for a moment the imbecile illusion of 'free will'; for there can be very few men indeed, in any generation, who have at any time in their lives
sufficient apparent liberty of action to induce them to dally
with it. Of these few, I was one. When I left Cambridge, I
had acquired no particular ties. I was already the Spirit of
Solitude in embryo. Practically, too, my father having been
the younger son of a younger son, I had not even a territorial
bond. On the other hand, I had a large fortune entirely at my
own disposal; there was no external constraint upon me to do
one thing rather than another. And yet, of course, my career
was absolutely determined. The events of my life up to that
point, if they had been intelligently interpreted, would have
afforded ample indications of the future. I was white-hot on
three points; climbing, poetry and Magick.

On my return from Switzerland in 1898, I had nowhere in
particular to go. There was no reason why I should settle
down in any special place. I simply took a room in the Cecil,
at that remote period a first-class hostelry, and busied myself
with writing on the one hand and following up the magical
clues on the other. *Jephthah*, and most of the other poems
which appear in that volume, were written about this period.
It is a kind of backwater in my life. I seem to have been
marking time. For this reason, no doubt, I was the more ready
to be swept away by the first definite current. It was not long
before it caught me.

I had a number of conversations with Julian Baker, who
kept his promise to introduce me to 'a man who was a much
greater Magician than he was himself'. This was a Welshman,
named George Cecil Jones. He possessed a fiery but unstable
temper, was the son of a suicide, and bore a striking resemblance to many conventional representations of Jesus Christ.
His spirit was both ardent and subtle. He was very widely read
in Magick; and, being by profession an analytical chemist, was
able to investigate the subject in a scientific spirit. As soon as

I found that he really understood the matter I went down to Basingstoke, where he lived, and more or less sat in his pocket. It was not long before I found out exactly where my destiny lay. The majority of old magical rituals are either purposely unintelligible or actually puerile nonsense.* Those which are straightforward and workable are, as a rule, better adapted to the ambitions of love-sick agricultural labourers than those of educated people with a serious purpose. But there is one startling exception to this rule. It is *The Book of the Sacred Magic of Abra-Melin the Mage.*

This book is written in an exalted style. It is perfectly coherent; it does not demand fantastic minutiae of ritual or even the calculations customary. There is nothing to insult the intelligence. On the contrary, the operation proposed is of sublime simplicity. The method is in entire accordance with this. There are, it is true, certain prescriptions to be observed, but these really amount to little more than injunctions to observe decency in the performance of so august an operation. One must have a house where proper precautions against disturbance can be taken; this being arranged, there is really nothing to do but to aspire with increasing fervour and concentration, for six months, towards the obtaining of the Knowledge and Conversation of the Holy Guardian Angel. Once He has appeared, it is then necessary, first, to call forth the Four Great Princes of the Evil of the World; next, their eight sub-princes; and, lastly, the three hundred and sixteen servitors of these. A number of talismans, previously prepared, are thus charged with the power of these spirits. By applying the proper talismans, you can get practically anything you want.

It cannot be denied that the majesty and philosophical irreproachability of the book are sensibly diminished by the addition of these things to the invocation of the Holy Guardian Angel. I should have preferred it without them. There is, however, a reason. Anyone who reaches a new world must conform with all the conditions of it. It is true, of course, that the hierarchy of evil appears somewhat repugnant to science. It is in fact very hard to explain what we mean by saying that we invoke Paimon; but, to go a little deeper, the same remark applies to Mr Smith next door. We do not know who Mr

* Some are doubtless survivals of various forms of nature religion; but the majority are adaptations of Catholic or Jewish traditions to the ambitions, cupidities, envies, jealousies and animal instincts of the most ignorant and primitive type of peasant.

Smith is, or what is his place in nature, or how to account for him. We cannot even be sure that he exists. Yet, in practice, we call Smith by that name and he comes. By the proper means, we can induce him to do for us those things which are consonant with his nature and powers. The whole question is, therefore, one of practice; and by this standard we find that there is no particular reason for quarrelling with the conventional nomenclature.

At this time I had not worked out any such apology for the theories of transcendentalism. I took everything as it came and submitted it to the test of experience. As it happened, I had no reason at any time to doubt the reality of the magical universe. I began my practical work with astral visions and found to my surprise that after half a dozen experiments I was better than my teacher.

In these days I took my Magick very much *au pied de la lettre*. I knew, of course, that Magick had fallen into desuetude chiefly because people would follow the prescribed course of action and get no result.

An exquisitely amusing incident bearing on this point is as follows: Gerald Kelly, Ivor Back and one or two other ardent spirits, inspired by my success, decided to do Magick themselves. They hired and furnished a room at Cambridge for the purpose and proceeded to evoke various spirits. Nothing happened. At last one of the greatly daring extended his little finger outside the circle. He was not 'slain or paralysed as if blasted by the lightning flash' and thence concluded that Magick was all rubbish. I offered this example of logic to the Museum of Human Imbecility, in the principal city of the Astral Plane.

I understood perfectly well that Back and Kelly, having no capacity for Magick, were bound to fail either to evoke a spirit or to get themselves blasted. If one does not understand anything about electricity, one cannot construct a dynamo; and having so failed, one cannot get oneself electrocuted.

But I suppose that their failure and my success was mostly a matter of personal genius, just as Burns with hardly any literary apparatus could write poetry, and Tennyson, with any amount, could not.

My success itself helped to blind me to the nature of the conditions of achievement. It never occurred to me that the problem of Magick contained metaphysical elements.

Consider my performance one evening at Eastbourne. Having waited for the lowest possible tide so as to be as remote as might be from the bandstand, I made a circle and built an altar of stones by the edge of the sea. I burned my incense, performed my evolutions and made heaven hideous with my enchantments. All this in order to invoke the Undines. I hoped, and more or less expected, to have one come out of the foam and attach herself to my person. I had as yet no notion that this programme might be accomplished far more easily.

There are thus two main types of mistake; one in spirit and one in technique. Most aspirants to Magick commit both. I soon learned that the physical conditions of a magical phenomenon were like those of any other; but even when this misunderstanding is removed, success depends upon one's ability to awaken the creative genius which is the inalienable heirloom of every son of man, but which few indeed are able to assimilate to their conscious existence, or even, in ninety-nine cases out of a hundred, to detect.

The only Undine that appeared was a policeman, who approached near enough to observe a fantastically garbed figure, dancing and howling in the moonlight 'on the silvery, silvery, silvery sands'; howling, whistling, bellowing and braying forth the barbarous names of evocation which have in the sacred rites a power ineffable, around a furiously flaming bonfire whose sparks were whirled by the wind all over the beach.

The basis of the delusion is that there is a real apodeictic correlation between the various elements of the operation, such as the formal manifestation of the spirit, his name and sigil, the form of the temple, weapons, gestures and incantations. These facts prevent one from suspecting the real subtlety involved in the hypothesis. This is so profound that it seems almost true to say that even the crudest Magick eludes consciousness altogether, so that when one is able to do it, one does it without conscious comprehension, very much as one makes a good stroke at cricket or billiards. One cannot give an intellectual explanation of the rough working involved, as one can explain the steps in the solution of a quadratic equation. In other words Magick in this sense is rather an art than a science.

Jones realized at once that I had a tremendous natural capacity for Magick, and my every action proved that I intended to devote myself to it 'without keeping back the least imaginable thing'. He suggested that I should join the Body of which he was an adept; known, to a few of the more enlightened seekers, as the Hermetic Order of the G∴D∴. A short account of this Order is necessary. Most of the facts concerning it are given here and there in *The Equinox;* but the story is so lengthy and complex that it would require a volume to itself. Briefly, however, the facts are as follows:

Some time in the 'seventies or 'eighties, a cipher manuscript was found on a bookstall by a Dr Woodman, a colleague in magical study of Dr W. Wynn Westcott. It was beyond their powers to decipher it, though Mrs Emery (Miss Florence Farr) told me that a child could have done so. They called in a man named Samuel Liddell Mathers, a scholar and Magician of considerable eminence. The manuscript yielded to his scrutiny. It contained, among minor matters, the rubric of certain rituals of initiation and the true attribution of the Tarot Trumps. This attribution had been sought vainly for centuries. It cleared up a host of Cabbalistic difficulties, in the same way as Einstein's admirers claim that his equations have done in mathematics and physics. The manuscript gave the name and address of an adept Sapiens Dominabitur Astris, a Fräulein Sprengel, living in Germany, with an invitation to write to her if further knowledge was required. Dr Westcott wrote; and S.D.A. gave him and his two colleagues a charter authorizing them to establish an Order in England. This was done. Soon after, S.D.A. died. In reply to a letter addressed to her, came an intimation from one of her colleagues that they had never approved her policy in permitting open-temple work in England, but had refrained from active opposition from personal respect for her. The writer ended by saying that England must expect no more assistance from Germany; enough knowledge had been granted to enable any English adept to form a Magical Link with the Secret Chiefs. Such competence would evidently establish a right to renewed relations.

Dr Woodman had died and Mathers forced Dr Westcott to retire from active leadership of the Order. Mathers, however, was not trusted. He, therefore, announced to the most advanced adepts that he had himself made the Magical Link with the Secret Chiefs; and, at an interview with three of them in the Bois de Boulogne, had been confirmed in the supreme and sole authority as the Visible Head of the Order. The adepts entrusted with this information were required to sign a pledge of personal obedience to Mathers as a condition of advancement in the Order. Nevertheless, dissatisfaction continued. The advancement did not arrive. They suspected that Mathers had no more knowledge to give; and he retorted that, however that might be, he wasn't going to waste it on such hopeless duffers. Both positions have much to recommend them to discriminating sympathy.

These petty squabbles apart, a big thing had happened. Mathers had discovered the manuscript of *Abra-Melin* in the library of the Arsenal in Paris and begun to translate it. He found himself harassed and opposed on all sides. In those days there was practically no public way of getting about Paris at all. Mathers lived at Auteuil, a long way from the Arsenal, and met with so many bicycle accidents that he was driven to go on foot. (There is always occult opposition to the publication of important documents. It took me over three years to get my *The Goetia* through the press, and over two years in the case of *777*. This is one of the facts whose cumulative effect makes it impossible to doubt the existence of spiritual forces.) Other misfortunes of every kind overwhelmed Mathers. He was an expert Magician and had become accustomed to use the Greater Key of Solomon with excellent effect. He did not realize that *Abra-Melin* was an altogether bigger proposition. It was like a man, accustomed to handle gunpowder, suddenly supplied with dynamite without being aware of the difference. He worried through and got *Abra-Melin* published; but he perished in the process. He became the prey of the malignant forces of the book, lost his integrity and was cast out of the Order of which he had been the visible head.

This debacle had not yet taken place at the time of my first initiation, November 18th, 1898.

I took the Order with absolute seriousness. I was not even put off by the fact of its ceremonies taking place at Mark Mason's Hall. I remember asking Baker whether people often died during the ceremony. I had no idea that it was a flat formality and that the members were for the most part muddled middle-class mediocrities. I saw myself entering the Hidden Church of the Holy Grail. This state of my soul served me well. My initiation was in fact a sacrament.

The rituals have been printed in *The Equinox,* vol. I, nos. II and III. There is no question that those of neophyte and adept are the genuine rituals of initiation, for they contain the true formulae. The proof is that they can be made to work by those who understand and know how to apply them. Shallow critics argue that because the average untrained man cannot evoke a spirit, the ritual which purports to enable him to do so must be at fault. He does not reflect that an electroscope would be useless in the hands of a savage. Indubitably, Magick is one of the subtlest and most difficult of the sciences and arts. There is more opportunity for errors of comprehension, judgment and practice than in any other branch of physics. It is above all needful for the student to be armed with scientific knowledge, sympathetic apprehension and common sense. My training in mathematics and chemistry supplied me with the first of these qualities; my poetic affinities and wide reading with the second; while, for the third, I suppose I have to thank my practical ancestors.

Being thus able to appreciate the inmost intention of my initiation, I was able to stand the shock of the events immediately subsequent. I was introduced to an abject assemblage of nonentities; the members of the Order were as vulgar and commonplace as any other set of average people. Jones and Baker themselves were the only members with any semblance of scientific education, until, a few months later, I met Allan Bennett, a mind pure, piercing and profound beyond any other in my experience. There was one literary light, W. B. Yeats, a lank dishevelled demonologist who might have taken more pains with his personal appearance without incurring the reproach of dandyism; and one charming and intelligent woman, Mrs Emery, for whom I always felt an affectionate respect tempered by a feeling of compassion that her abilities were so inferior to her aspirations. The rest of the Order possessed no individuality; they were utterly undistinguished either for energy or capacity. There is not one of them today who has made any mark in the world.

At my initiation, I could have believed that these adepts deliberately masked their majesty; but there was no mistaking the character of the 'knowledge lecture' in which I had to be examined to entitle me to pass to the next grade. I had been most solemnly sworn to inviolable secrecy. The slightest breach of my oath meant that I should incur 'a deadly and hostile current of will, set in motion by the Greatly Honoured Chiefs of the Second Order, by the which I should fall slain or paralysed, as if blasted by the lightning flash'. And now I was entrusted with some of these devastating though priceless secrets. They consisted of the Hebrew alphabet, the names of the planets with their attribution to the days of the week, and the ten Sephiroth of the Cabbala. I had known it all for months; and, obviously, any schoolboy in the lower fourth could memorize the whole lecture in twenty-four hours.

I see today that my intellectual snobbery was shallow and

stupid. It is vitally necessary to drill the aspirant in the ground-work. He must be absolutely familiar with the terminology and theory of Magick from a strictly intellectual standpoint. I still think, however, that this course of study should precede initiation and that it should not be mixed up with it. Consider the analogy of poetry. One could, to a certain extent, teach a man to write poetry, by offering to his soul a set of spiritual and emotional experiences, but his technique must be based on the study of grammar and so on, which have no essential relation with art.

Talking over these matters with Jones and Baker, I found them quite in sympathy with my point of view; but they insisted, rightly enough, that I was not in a position to judge the circumstances. I must first reach the Second Order.

Accordingly, I took the grade of Zelator in December, of Theoricus in January and of Practicus in February. One could not proceed to Philosophus for three months, so I did not take that grade till May. The Philosophus cannot proceed to the Second Order in less than seven months; also, he must be specially invited.

In the spring of 1899, at some ceremony or other, I was aware of the presence of a tremendous spiritual and magical force. It seemed to me to proceed from a man sitting in the east, a man I had not seen before, but whom I knew must be Very Honoured Frater Iehi Aour, called among men Allan Bennett. The fame of this man as a Magician was already immense. He was esteemed second only to Mathers himself; and was, perhaps, even more feared.

After the ceremony we went into the outer room to unrobe. I was secretly anxious to be introduced to this formidable Chief. To my amazement he came straight to me, looked into my eyes, and said in penetrating and, as it seemed, almost menacing tones: 'Little Brother, you have been meddling with the Goetia!' (Goetia means 'howling'; but is the technical word employed to cover all the operations of that Magick which deals with gross, malignant or unenlightened forces.) I told him, rather timidly, that I had not been doing anything of the sort. 'In that case,' he returned, 'the Goetia has been meddling with you.' The conversation went no further. I returned home in a somewhat chastened spirit; and, having found out where Iehi Aour lived, I determined to call on him the following day.

I should have explained that, on deciding to join the Order,

I had taken a flat at 67 and 69 Chancery Lane.* I had already determined to perform the Operation of *Abra-Melin,* but Jones had advised me to go through my initiation first. However, I began to busy myself with the preparations. *Abra-Melin* warns us that our families will object strenuously to our undertaking the Operation. I resolved, therefore, to cut myself off absolutely from mine. So, as I had to live in London, I took the flat under the name of Count Vladimir Svareff. As Jones remarked later, a wiser man would have called himself Smith. But I was still obsessed with romanticism, while my summer in St Petersburg had made me in love with Russia. There was another motive behind this—a legitimate one. I wanted to increase my knowledge of mankind. I knew how people treated a young man from Cambridge. I had thoroughly appreciated the servility of tradesmen, though I was too generous and too ignorant to realize the extent of their dishonesty and rapacity. Now I wanted to see how people would behave to a Russian nobleman. I must say here that I have repeatedly used this method of disguise—it has been amazingly useful in multiplying my points of view about humanity. Even the most broad-minded people are necessarily narrow in this one respect. They may know how all sorts of people treat them, but they cannot know, except at second hand, how those same people treat others.

To return to Allan Bennett. I found him staying with V. H. Frater Aequo Animo † in a tiny tenement in Southwark or Lambeth—I forget which. It was a mean, grim horror. Æ.A., whose name was Charles Rosher, was a widely travelled Jack-of-all-trades. He had invented a patent water-closet and been court painter to the Sultan of Morocco. He wrote some of the worst poetry I have ever read. He was a jolly-all-round sportsman with an excellent heart and the cheery courage which comes from knocking about the world, and being knocked about by it. If his talents had been less varied, he might have made a success of almost anything.

---

* My innocence after three years at Cambridge may be gauged by my conduct in the matter of choosing a residence. I understood it as a fixed principle of prudence, 'When in a difficulty consult your lawyer.' Knowing nothing whatever about renting apartments, I was in a difficulty. I therefore consulted my lawyer and took the first place he suggested. He, of course, never gave a thought to my convenience or the appropriateness of the district. He saw and took the chance of obliging a business acquaintance.

† I ultimately conjectured: Equi Animo: 'with the soul of a horse'.

21

Allan Bennett was four years older than myself. His father, an engineer, had died when he was a boy; his mother had brought him up as a strict Catholic. He suffered acutely from spasmodic asthma. His cycle of life was to take opium for about a month, when the effect wore off, so that he had to inject morphine. After a month of this he had to switch to cocaine, which he took till he began to 'see things' and was then reduced to chloroform. I have seen him in bed for a week, only recovering consciousness sufficiently to reach for the bottle and sponge. Asthma being a sthenic disease, he was then too weak to have it any more, so he would gradually convalesce until, after a few weeks of freedom, the spasms would begin once more and he would be forced to renew the cycle of drugs.

No doubt, this constant suffering affected his attitude to life. He revolted against being an animal; he regarded the pleasures of living (and, above all, those of physical love) as diabolical illusions devised by the enemy of mankind in order to trick souls into accepting the curse of existence. I cannot forbear quoting one most remarkable incident. When he was about sixteen, the conversation in the laboratory where he was working turned upon childbirth. What he heard disgusted him. He became furiously angry and said that children were brought to earth by angels. The other students laughed at him and tried in vain to convince him. He maintained their theory to be a bestial blasphemy. The next day one of the boys turned up with an illustrated manual of obstetrics. He could no longer doubt the facts. But his reaction was this: 'Did the Omnipotent God whom he had been taught to worship devise so revolting and degrading a method of perpetuating the species? Then this God must be a devil, delighting in loathsomeness.' To him the existence of God was disproved from that moment.

He had, however, already some experience of an unseen world. As a little boy, having overheard some gossip among superstitious servants, he had gone into the back garden and invoked the devil by reciting the Lord's Prayer backwards. Something happened which frightened him.

Having now rejected Catholicism, he took up Magick and at once attained extraordinary success. He used to carry a 'lustre'—a long glass prism with a neck and a pointed knob such as adorned old-fashioned chandeliers. He used this as a wand. One day, a party of theosophists were chatting sceptically about the power of the 'blasting rod'. Allan promptly produced his and blasted one of them. It took fourteen hours to restore the incredulous individual to the use of his mind and his muscles.

Allan Bennett was tall, but his sickness had already produced a stoop. His head, crowned with a shock of wild black hair, was intensely noble; the brows, both wide and lofty, overhung indomitable piercing eyes. The face would have been handsome had it not been for the haggardness and pallour due to his almost continuous suffering.

Despite his ill-health, he was a tremendous worker. His knowledge of science, especially electricity, was vast, accurate and profound. In addition, he had studied the Hindu and Buddhist scriptures, not only as a scholar, but with the insight that comes from inborn sympathetic understanding.

I did not fully realize the colossal stature of that sacred spirit; but I was instantly aware that this man could teach me more in a month than anyone else in five years. He was living in great discomfort and penury. I offered him the hospitality of my flat. I have always felt that since the occult sciences nourish so many charlatans, it should be one's prime point of honour not to make money in any way connected with them. The amateur status above all! Hospitality is, however, always allowable. But I was careful never to go beyond the strict letter of the word.

Iehi Aour came to stay with me and under his tuition I made rapid progress. He showed me where to get knowledge, how to criticize it and how to apply it. We also worked together at ceremonial Magick; evoking spirits, consecrating talismans, and so on.

I must relate one episode, as throwing light upon my magical accomplishments and my ethical standards. Jones and I had come to the conclusion that Allan would die unless he went to live in a warmer climate. However, he was penniless and we would not finance him for the reasons given above. Instead, Jones and I evoked to visible appearance the Spirit Buer, of *The Goetia*, whose function is to heal the sick. We were partially successful; a helmeted head and the left leg being distinctly solid, though the rest of the figure was cloudy and vague. But the operation was in fact a success in the following manner. It is instructive to narrate this as showing the indirect and natural means by which the will attains its object.

I am constrained to a seeming digression. Many authors insist on the importance of absolute chastity in the aspirant. For some months I had been disregarding this injunction with a seductive siren whose husband was a colonel in India. Little by little I overcame my passion for her and we parted. She wrote to me frequently and tried to shake my resolution, but I stood firm. Shortly after the evocation of Buer, she wrote, begging me to call at her hotel. I cannot remember how it came into my mind to do what I did, but I went to see her. She begged me to come back to her and offered to do anything I wanted. I said to her, 'You're making a mess of your life by your selfishness. I will give you a chance to do an absolutely unfettered act. Give me a hundred pounds, I won't tell you whom it's for, except that it's not for myself. I have private reasons for not using my own money in this matter. If you give me this, it must be without hoping or expecting anything in return.' She gave me the money—it paid Allan's passage to Ceylon and saved to humanity one of the most valuable lives of our generation.

So much for Buer. As for the lady, she came to see me some time later and I saw that I was myself acting selfishly in setting my spiritual welfare above her happiness. She had made a generous gesture; I could do no less. She agreed not to stand in the way of my performing the Operation of *Abra-Melin*, but begged me to give her a living memory of our love. I agreed and the sequel will be told in its place.

During this time, magical phenomena were of constant occurrence. I had two temples in my flat; one white, the walls being lined with six huge mirrors, each six feet by eight; the other black,* a mere cupboard, in which stood an altar supported by the figure of a Negro standing on his hands. The presiding genius of this place was a human skeleton, which I fed from time to time with blood, small birds and the like. The idea was to give it life, but I never got further than causing the bones to become covered with a viscous slime. In *The Equinox*, vol. I, no. I, is a story, 'At the Fork of the

---

* Iehi Aour never had anything to do with this; and I but little: the object of establishing it was probably to satisfy my instinct about equilibrium.

Roads', which is in every detail a true account of one episode of this period. Will Bute is W. B. Yeats,* Hypatia Gay is Althoea Gyles, the publisher is Leonard Smithers.

The demons connected with *Abra-Melin* do not wait to be evoked; they come unsought. One night Jones and I went out to dinner. I noticed on leaving the white temple that the latch of its Yale lock had not caught. Accordingly, I pulled the door to and tested it. As we went out, we noticed semi-solid shadows on the stairs; the whole atmosphere was vibrating with the forces which we had been using. (We were trying to condense them into sensible images.) When we came back, nothing had been disturbed in the flat; but the temple door was wide open, the furniture disarranged and some of the symbols flung about in the room. We restored order and then observed that semi-materialized beings were marching around the main room in almost unending procession.

When I finally left the flat for Scotland, it was found that the mirrors were too big to take out except by way of the black temple. This had, of course, been completely dismantled before the workmen arrived. But the atmosphere remained and two of them were put out of action for several hours. It was almost a weekly experience, by the way, to hear of casual callers fainting or being seized with dizziness, cramp or apoplexy on the staircase. It was a long time before those rooms were re-let. People felt instinctively the presence of something uncanny. Similarly, later on, when I gave up my rooms in Victoria Street, a pushing charlatan thought to better himself by taking them. With this object he went to see them. A few seconds later he was leaping headlong down the five flights of stairs, screaming in terror. He had just sufficient genuine sensitiveness to feel the forces, without possessing the knowledge, courage and will required to turn them to account, or even to endure their impact.

---

* The identification is conjectural, depending solely on the admissions of Miss Gyles.

22

Apart from my daily work, my chief preoccupation was to prepare for the Operation of the Sacred Magick.

The first essential is a house in a more or less secluded situation. There should be a door opening to the north from the room of which you make your oratory. Outside this door, you construct a terrace covered with fine river sand. This ends in a 'lodge' where the spirits may congregate. It would appear the simplest thing in the world for a man with forty thousand pounds, who is ready to spend every penny of it on the achievement of his purpose, to find a suitable house in a very few weeks. But a magical house is as hard to find as a magical book to publish. I scoured the country in vain. Not till the end of August 1899 did I find an estate which suited me. This was the manor of Boleskine and Abertarff, on the south-east side of Loch Ness, half way between Inverfarigaig and Foyers. By paying twice as much as it was worth, I got it, gave up my flat and settled down at once to get everything in order for the great Operation, which one is told to begin at Easter.

The house is a long low building. I set apart the south-western half for my work. The largest room has a bow window and here I made my door and constructed the terrace and lodge. Inside the room I set up my oratory proper. This was a wooden structure, lined in part with the big mirrors which I brought from London.

On first arriving at Boleskine, I innocently frightened some excellent people by my habit of taking long walks over the moors. One morning I found a large stone jar at my front door. It was not an infernal machine; it was illicit whisky—a mute, yet eloquent appeal, not to give away illicit stills that I might happen to stumble across in my rambles. I needed no bribe. I am a free trader in every sense of the word. I have no sympathy with any regulations which interfere with the natural activities of human beings. I believe that they aggravate whatever trouble they are intended to prevent; and they create the greatest plague of humanity, officialdom, and encourage underhand conduct on both sides, furtiveness and espionage.

Any law which tends to destroy manly qualities is a bad law, however necessary it may seem on the surface. The tendency of most modern legislation is to bind Gulliver with packthread. I have never broken the law myself, because the things I happen to want are so utterly different from those desired by men in general, that no occasion has ever risen.

But I observe with regret that humanity is being compelled to turn its attention from its proper business by having to comply with innumerable petty formalities.

Salmon fishing on Loch Ness should be remembered by people who are praying for 'those in peril on the deep'. It is a dull year when nobody is drowned. The loch is large enough to get up a regular sea; and the hills are so arranged that the wind can come down in all sorts of unsuspected ways. The most violent storms often arise without five minutes' warning. In addition, there is one section of the loch (north-east of Boleskine, on the same side) where the shore for some two miles is a rocky precipice just too high above the water to be climbable, even if one could get a footing.

It is useless fishing in settled fine weather; one wants it overcast, neither too hot nor too cold, neither windy nor quite calm—unsettled weather, in a word. One morning I got into a salmon which subsequently turned the scale at forty-four pounds. He was terrifically game and really much too heavy for my tackle. Again and again he ran out the line and we only held him by rowing for all we were worth in his direction. It was nearly two hours before we got him into the boat.

The excitement over, I observed that a sleet was driving heavily and that the loch was white with foam. Also that we were off a lee shore, and that shore about the middle of the precipice. We could do nothing but pull for life in the teeth of the gale, which increased in violence every moment. We were both already tired out. Despite every effort, we were forced, foot by foot, towards the rocks. By great luck, there is one gap in those infernal little cliffs. But the boat was not under control. However, we had to risk it and managed to get ashore without being smashed, to beach the boat and walk home. That was the worst of it.

But I was often caught on the wrong side of the loch. So near and yet so far! There was the house a mile away and there was I with thirty miles to make to get there. I have never heard of the steamers being wrecked, but that is perhaps because they are wrecks already.

I took Lady Etheldreda to Scotland with me. I have had

many dogs in my time; but she was *sui generis*. I had trained her to follow me on the mountains and she was not only an admirable rock climber but an uncannily prophetic tracker. For instance, I would leave her at the foot of a precipice beyond her powers and, after a climb, descend another precipice to another valley, often in mists so thick that I could not see ten yards in any direction. But I would invariably find her at the foot of the rocks after making a detour of perhaps ten miles across unknown country.

These qualities had their defects. She became an amateur of sheep. It was straightforward sport. She never mangled a sheep, she killed it neatly with a single bite and went off to the next. She had no illusions about the ethics of her proceedings and she brought superlative cunning into service. She never touched a sheep within ten miles of Boleskine; she never visited the same district twice running; she was even at pains to prepare an alibi. Of course, she was always careful to remove every trace of blood. That was elementary. But she would sham sickness the morning after the kill and she would bring various objects into her kennel, as if to say, 'Well, if you want to know how I have been passing the time, there you are!' She also realized that her extraordinary speed and endurance would help her to clear herself. On one occasion she killed not less than forty miles there and back from Boleskine. No one except her master, whom she trusted not to give her away, could suspect that she had covered so much ground—to say nothing of the shikar itself—in the course of the night. She was unsuspected for months—even weeks of watching failed to identify her and if she had not been such a magnificent animal she might have escaped altogether. But her size and beauty were unmistakable. The evidence began to be too strong to pooh-pooh and I had to send her back to London.

Boleskine is in the winter an excellent centre of *ski-läufing*. There is little snow in the valley itself, but on the moors behind Strath Errick are tracts of elevated country, extending for many miles. The slopes are for the most part gentle and I have found the snow in first-rate condition as late as the end of March.

On off days at Wastdale Head, it was one of our amusements to throw the boomerang. Eckenstein had long been interested in it and constructed numerous new patterns, each with its own peculiar flight. As luck would have it, Walker of Trinity came to the dale. He had earned a fellowship by an essay on the mathematics of the boomerang. The theoretical man and the practical put their heads together; and we constructed some extraordinary weapons. One of them could be thrown half a mile, even by me, who cannot throw a cricket ball fifty yards. Another, instead of returning to the thrower, went straight from the hand and undulated up and down like a switchback, seven or eight times, before coming to the ground. A third shot out straight, skimming the ground for a hundred yards or so, stopped as suddenly as if it had hit a wall, rose, spinning in the air to the height of some fifty feet, whence it settled down in a slowly widening spiral. Obviously, these researches bore on the problem of flying. Eckenstein and I, in fact, proposed to work at it. The idea was that we should cut an alley through the woods on that part of my property which bordered Loch Ness. We were to construct a chute and start down it on a bicycle fitted with movable wings. There was to be a steam launch on the loch to pick us up at the end of the flight. We were, in fact, proposing to do what has now, in 1922, proved so successful. But the scheme never went further than the construction of the boathouse for the launch. My wanderings are to blame.

The harmless necessary cat sheds those epithets in the Highlands. The most domesticated tabby becomes intoxicated by the air of freedom (so one hypothesis suggests) and begins to run wild. It takes to the woods and lives on rabbits and birds. Its conscience tells it that it is violating the game laws; man becomes its enemy. It accordingly flees at one's approach, though sometimes it becomes mad with fear and will attack a stranger, unprovoked, and fight to the death.

Much to my disgust, commercialism thrust its ugly head into my neighbourhood. The British Aluminum Company proposed to exploit the water power of the valley above Foyers. The Falls of Foyers are one of the few natural glories of the British Isles; why not use them to turn an honest penny?

> I sate upon the mossy promontory
> Where the cascade cleft not his mother rock,
> But swept in whirlwind lightning foam and glory,
> Vast circling with unwearying luminous shock
> To lure and lock
> Marvellous eddies in its wild caress;
> And there the solemn echoes caught the stress,
> The strain of that impassive tide,
> Shook it and flung it high and wide,
> Till all the air took fire from that melodious roar;
> All the mute mountains heard,

Bowed, laughed aloud, concurred,
And passed the word along, the signal of wide war.
All earth took up the sound,
And, being in one tune securely bound,
Even a star became the soul of silence most profound.

Thus there, the centre of that death that darkened,
I sat and listened, if God's voice should break
And pierce the hollow of my ear that hearkened,
Lest God should speak and find me not awake—
For his own sake.
No voice, no song might pierce or penetrate
That enviable universal state.
The sun and moon beheld, stood still.
Only the spirit's axis, will,
Considered its own soul and sought a deadlier deep,
And in its monotone mood
Of supreme solitude
Was neither glad nor sad because it did not sleep;
But with calm eyes abode
Patient, its leisure the galactic load,
Abode alone, nor even rejoiced to know that it was God.

Money-grubbing does its best to blaspheme and destroy nature.
It is useless to oppose the baseness of humanity; if one touches
pitch one runs the risk of being defiled. I am perfectly content
to know that the vileness of civilization is rapidly destroying
itself; that it stinks in my nostrils tells me that it is rotting and
my consolation is in the words of Lord Dunsany. In the meantime, the water was to be wasted in producing wealth—the
most dangerous of narcotic drugs. It creates a morbid craving
—which it never satisfies after the first flush of intoxication.

Now the furnaces of the British Aluminium Company cost
a great deal to light. It was, therefore, impossible to extinguish
them every Saturday evening. The people of the neighbourhood learnt this fact with unfeigned horror. Such wickedness
was inconceivable! But besides that, it was sheer madness. Did
not these people in Glasgow understand that God did not
permit such things to happen with impunity? So on the first
Saturday night the people betook themselves to points of
vantage on the surrounding hills in order to see the works
destroyed by the divine wrath. No explanation has ever been
offered why it did not come off!

The lady previously mentioned was now made happy as a
result of the fortnight we had spent together in Paris. I therefore thought it my duty to take care of her until the following

spring. The fulfilment of her hopes would end my responsibility before the beginning of my Operation.

I had asked Jones to come and stay with me during the six months, in view of the dangers and interference already experienced at the mere threat to perform it. It was obviously the part of prudence to have, if possible, an initiate on the spot. It is also very awkward for a man absorbed in intense magical effort to have to communicate with the external world about the business of everyday life. Jones did not see his way to come, so I asked Rosher, who consented. But before he had been there a month he found the strain intolerable. I came down to breakfast one morning; no Rosher. I asked the butler why he was absent. The man replied, in surprise at my ignorance, that Mr Rosher had taken the early morning boat to Inverness. There was no word of explanation; I never saw him or heard of him for many years; and, when we met, though absolutely friendly and even intimate, we never referred to the matter.

One day I came back from shooting rabbits on the hill and found a Catholic priest in my study. He had come to tell me that my lodgekeeper, a total abstainer for twenty years, had been raving drunk for three days and had tried to kill his wife and children.

I got an old Cambridge acquaintance to take Rosher's place; but he too began to show symptoms of panic fear. Meanwhile, other storms were brewing. The members of the London temple, jealous of my rapid progress in the Order, had refused to initiate me to the Second Order in London, though the Chief himself had invited me. He, therefore, asked me to come to Paris, where he would himself confer the Grade. I went; and, on my return, ten days later, found that my protégée had also taken fright, fled to London and hidden herself.

Besides these comparatively explicable effects on human minds, there were numberless physical phenomena for which it is hard to account. While I was preparing the talismans, squares of vellum inscribed in Indian ink, a task which I undertook in the sunniest room in the house, I had to use artificial light even on the brightest days. It was a darkness which might almost be felt. The lodge and terrace, moreover, soon became peopled with shadowy shapes, sufficiently substantial, as a rule, to be almost opaque. I say shapes; and yet the truth is that they were not shapes properly speaking. The phenomenon is hard to describe. It was as if the faculty of vision suffered some interference; as if the objects of vision were not properly objects at all. It was as if they belonged to an order of matter which affected the sight without informing it.

By the exercise of dour determination, I succeeded in getting everything ready in good time to begin the work proper of Easter. It is unfortunate that in these days I had no idea of the value of a Magical Record from the historical standpoint. I find few dates, nor have I troubled to set down even such startling occurrences as are related above. I was dead set on attainment. Anything which appeared to me out of the direct road to the goal was merely a nuisance, a hindrance and a distraction. Apart from my memory, therefore, the chief sources of information about my life at this period are poems, rituals and records of visions.

I was very busily at work with the muse. My *Appeal to the American Republic* was begotten of a pleasant journey with two Americans from Geneva to Paris. The poem is still popular, though from time to time one has to change 'The lying *Russian* cloke his traitor head' to '*Prussian*', and so on. *Carmen Saeculare* was actually the result of a more or less prophetic vision. Some of its forecasts have turned out wonderfully well, though the century is yet young; others await fulfilment—but I do not propose to linger on merely to obtain so morbid a satisfaction!

The Fatal Force, written in the spring of 1899, possesses one feature of remarkable interest. The idea of the play is that a high priestess, resenting the necessity of male co-operation in maternity, should marry her own son and, subsequently, the son of that union, so as to produce an individual who would be seven-eighths herself; the advantage being that he would thus inherit as much of her power and wisdom as possible. I supposed this idea to be original; but I discovered later that Eliphas Lévi mentions this formula as having been used by the ancient Magicians of Persia with this very intention. That was one of the facts which led me to the discovery that in my last incarnation I was Eliphas Lévi.

The Mother's Tragedy seems to have been influenced by Ibsen, with a touch of Bulwer Lytton.

In *The Temple of the Holy Ghost,* however, the reader may trace the progress of my soul's development. A few of the poems in this book are comparatively normal. One can see the extent of my debt to various predecessors, especially Baudelaire. But while there is a certain delight in dalliance with demoniac Delilahs, there is a steady advance towards the utmost spiritual purity. In 'The Athanor', the invocation of the

Holy Guardian Angel reveals my true aspirations; while in 'The Mountain Christ', 'The Rosicrucian' and others, it is evident that my ambition was not to become superior to the rest of mankind except in order that I might redeem them.

I quote:

> The Oath of the Beginning.
> I, Perdurabo, Frater Ordinis Rosae Rubeæ et Aureae Crucis, a Lord of the Paths in the Portal of the Vault of the Adepts, a $5° = 6°$ of the Order of the Golden Dawn; and an humble servant of the Christ of God; do this day spiritually bind myself anew:
>> By the Sword of Vengeance:
>> By the Powers of the Elements:
>> By the Cross of Suffering:
> That I will devote myself to the Great Work: the obtaining of Communion with my own Higher and Divine Genius (called the Guardian Angel) by means of the prescribed course; and that I will use my Power so obtained unto the Redemption of the Universe.
> So help me the Lord of the Universe and mine own Higher Soul!

This idea is further expanded in the obligation which I took in respect of the Operation. The influence of my initiation into the Second Order is manifest. While I remained in the Outer Order, I had not definitely realized the fact that I was bound up with the welfare of humanity and could only satisfy my aspiration by becoming a perfect instrument for the regeneration of the world. I quote once more:

> The Obligation of the Operation.
> I, Perdurabo, in the Presence of the Lord of the Universe, and of all Powers Divine and Angelic, do spiritually bind myself, even as I am now physically bound unto the Cross of Suffering.
> (1) To unite my consciousness with the divine, as I may be permitted and aided by the Gods Who live for ever, The Aeons of Infinite years; that, being lost in the Limitless Light, it may find Itself: to the Regeneration of the Race, either of man or as the Will of God shall be. And I submit myself utterly to the Will Divine.
> (2) To follow out with courage, modesty, loving-kindness and perseverance the course prescribed by Abra-Melin the Mage; as far as in me lies, unto the attainment of this end.
> (3) To despise utterly the things and the opinions of this world lest they hinder me in doing this.

(4) To use my powers only to the Spiritual well-being of all with whom I may be brought in contact.

(5) To give no place to Evil: and to make eternal war against the Forces of Evil: until even they be redeemed unto the Light.

(6) To harmonize my own spirit so that Equilibrium may lead me to the East; and that my Human Consciousness shall allow no usurpation of its rule by the Automatic.

(7) To conquer the temptations.

(8) To banish the illusions.

(9) To put my whole trust in the Only and Omnipotent Lord God: as it is written, 'Blessed are they that put their trust in Him.'

(10) To uplift the Cross of Sacrifice and Suffering; and to cause my Lights so to shine before men that they may glorify my Father which is in Heaven.

Furthermore, I most solemnly promise and swear: to acquire this Holy Science in the manner prescribed in the Book of Abra-Melin, without omitting the least imaginable thing of its contents; not to gloss or comment in any way on that which may be or may not be, not to use this Sacred Science to offend the Great God, nor to work ill unto my neighbour: to communicate it to no living person, unless by long practice and conversation I shall know him thoroughly, well examining whether such an one really intendeth to work for the Good or for the Evil. I will punctually observe, in granting it, the same fashion which was used by Abra-Melin to Abraham. Otherwise, let him who receiveth it draw no fruit therefrom. I will keep myself as from a Scorpion from selling this Science. Let this Science remain in me and in my generation as long as it shall please the Most High.

As all these points I generally and severally swear to observe under the awful penalty of the displeasure of God, and of Him to whose Knowledge and Conversation I do most ardently aspire.

So help me the Lord of the Universe, and my own Higher Soul! *

During this period I continued the practice of visions of and voyages upon divers spiritual planes. It seems worth while to record a few of these. They afford a clear indication of my progress at this time.

In bed, I invoked the Fire angels and spirits on the tablet, with names, etc., and the 6th Key.[1] I then (as Harpocrates) entered my crystal. An angel, meeting me, told me, among

* Some of the above phrases are prescribed by Abra-Melin itself; others are adapted from my 5°=6° documents.

other things, that they (of the tablets) were *at war with the angels of the 30 Aethyrs, to prevent the squaring of the circle.* I went with him unto the abodes of Fire, but must have fallen asleep, or nearly so. Anyhow, I regained consciousness in a very singular state, half consciousness being there, and half here. I recovered and banished the Spirits, but was burning all over, and tossed restlessly about—very sleepy, but consumed of Fire! Only repeated careful assumption of Harpocrates' god-form enabled me to regain my normal state. I had a long dream of a woman eloping, whom I helped, and after, of a man stealing my Rose Cross jewel from a dressing-table in an hotel. I caught him and found him a man weak beyond the natural (I could bend or flatten him at will),* and then the dream seemed to lose coherence . . . I carried him about and found a hairbrush to beat him, etc. etc. Query: Was I totally obsessed?

Invoking the angels of Earth, I obtained wonderful effect. The angel, my guide, treated me with great contempt and was very rude and truthful. He showed me divers things. In the centre of the earth is formulated the Rose and Cross. Now the Rose is the Absolute Self-Sacrifice, the merging of *all* in the O (Negative), the Universal Principle of generation through change (*not* merely the feminine), and the Universal Light 'Khabs'. The Cross is the Extension or Pekht principle. Now I should have learned more; but my attention wandered. This closes the four elemental visions: prosecuted, alas! with what weakness, fatuity and folly!

I . . . in the afternoon shut myself up and went on a journey . . .

I went with a very personal guide: † and beheld (after some lesser things) our Master as he sat by the Well with the Woman of Samaria. Now the five husbands were five great religions which had defiled the purity of the Virgin of the World: and 'he whom thou now hast' was materialism (or modern thought).

Other scenes also I saw in His Life: and behold I also was crucified! Now did I go backwards in time even unto Berashith, the Beginning, and was permitted to see marvellous things.

First the Abyss of the Water: on which I, even I, brooded amid other dusky flames as Shim upon Maim, held by my Genius. And I beheld the victory of Râ upon Apophis [2] and the First of the Golden Dawns! Yea: and monsters, faces half-formed, arose: but they subsisted not.

---

* This incident was once quoted by one of my critics as illustrative of the absurdity of Magick—as if Magick were responsible for the irrationality of dreams!

† This horrible phrase was not my own: I must not be judged by it.

And the firmament was.

Again the Chaos and the Death!

Then *Ath* Hashamain ve *ath* h-aretz. There is a whirling, intertwining infinitude of nebulae, many concentric systems, each system non-concentric to any other, yet *all* concentric to the whole. As I went backwards in time they grew faster and faster, and less and less material. (P.S.—This is a scientific hypothesis, directly contrary to that of Anna Kingsford.) And at last are whirling wheels of light; yet through them *waved* a thrill of an intenser invisible light in a direction perpendicular to the tangents. I asked to go yet farther back; and behold! I am floating on my back—cast down: in a wind of Light flashing down upon me from the immeasurable Above. (This Light is of a bluish silver tinge.) And I saw that Face, lost above me in the height inscrutable; a face of absolute beauty. And I saw as it were as a Lamb slain in the Glamour of Those Eyes. Thus was I made pure; for there, what impurity could live? I was told that not many had been so far back: none farther: those who *could* go farther would not, since that would have reabsorbed them into the Beginning, and that must not be to him who hath sworn to uplift the Standard of Sacrifice and Sorrow, which is strength. (I forgot the Angels in the Planetary Whirl. They regarded me with curiosity: and were totally unable to comprehend my explanation that I was a Man, returning in time to behold the Beginning of Things.)

So I returned; having difficulty to find the earth. But I called on S.R.M.D. and V.N.R.,[3] who were glad to see me; and returned into the body: to waste the night in gibing at a foolish medico.

My actions continually testify that I naturally possessed what is after all the most essential asset for a Magician, in singular perfection. It came natural to me to despise and reject utterly, without a second's hesitation or regret, anything soever that stood in the way of my purpose. Equally, I could hold that purpose itself as nothing in comparison with the greater purpose of the Order to which I was pledged.

Early in 1900 I applied to the Second Order in London for the documents to which my initiation in Paris entitled me. They were refused in terms which made it clear that the London body was in open revolt against the Chief, though afraid to declare its intentions. I went to London and discussed the matter with Jones, Baker and Mrs Emery. Jones saw clearly enough that if Mathers were not the head of the Order and the trusted representative of the Secret Chiefs, there was no Order at all. Baker's position was that Mathers was behaving badly; he was sick of the whole business. Mrs Emery, the nominal representative of the Chief, was trying to find a diplomatic solution. Her attitude was most serious and earnest and she was greatly distressed by her dilemma. She had thought it best to resign quietly, but received a reply of the most staggering character. The letter is dated February 16th, 1900, and I quote the last two paragraphs in full.

Now, with regard to the Second Order, it would be with the *very greatest regret* both from my personal regard for you, as well as from the Occult standpoint, that I should receive your Resignation as my Representative in the Second Order in London; but I cannot let you form a combination to make a schism therein with the idea of working secretly or avowedly under Sapere Aude [4] under the mistaken impression that he received an Epitome of the School of the Second Order work from G. H. Soror, Sapiens Dominabitur Astris.[5] For this forces me to tell you plainly (and, understand me well, I can prove to the hilt every word which I here say and more, and were I confronted with S.A., I should say the same) though for the sake of the Order, and for the circumstance that it would mean so deadly a blow to S.A.'s reputation, I entreat you to keep this secret from the *Order*, for the present, at least, though you are at perfect liberty to show *him* this if you think fit, *after mature consideration*.

He has NEVER been at *any time* either in personal or written communication with the Secret Chiefs of the Order, he having *either himself forged* or *procured to be forged* the professed correspondence between him and them, and my tongue having been tied all these years by a Previous Oath of Secrecy to him, demanded by him, from me, before showing me what he had either done or caused to be done or both. You must comprehend from what little I say here the *extreme gravity* of such a matter, and again I ask you, both for his sake, and that of the Order, not to force me to go further into the subject.

This letter struck at the very heart of the moral basis of her conduct. It put her in the position of having initiated people, for years, on false pretences. She could not drop out and say no more about it. The matter had to be thrashed out.

My own attitude was unhampered by any ethical considerations. I had seen a good deal of Mathers personally. He was unquestionably a Magician of extraordinary attainment. He was a scholar and a gentleman. He had that habit of authority which inspires confidence because it never doubts itself. A man who makes such claims as he did cannot be judged by conventional codes and canons. Ordinary morality is only for ordinary people. For example, assume a Prime Minister who has private information that somebody has discovered, and is cultivating, a new germ by means of which he intends to destroy the nation. To pass a 'Short Act' would be to give the alarm and precipitate the disaster. It would be his duty to override the law and put his foot upon the mischief. Then again, the whole of Mathers's conduct might have been in the nature of a test. It might have been his way of asking the adepts whether they had the power of concentrating on the spiritual situation, of giving up for ever all their prejudices.

Anyhow, as far as I was concerned, Mathers was my only link with the Secret Chiefs to whom I was pledged. I wrote to him offering to place myself and my fortune unreservedly at his disposal; if that meant giving up the Abra-Melin Operation for the present, all right.

The result of this offer was recorded as follows:

> D.D.C.F.[6] accepts my services, therefore do I rejoice that my sacrifice is accepted. Therefore do I again postpone the Operation of Abra-Melin the Mage, having by God's Grace formulated even in this a new link with the Higher and gained a new weapon against the Great Princes of the Evil of the World. Amen.

I went to Paris, discussed the situation with Mathers and formulated the following proposal for dealing with the refractory 'temple'.

I.   The Second Order to be summoned at various times during two or three days. They to find, on being admitted one by one, a masked man in authority and a scribe. These questions, etc. pass, after pledge of secrecy concerning interview.

A.   Are you convinced of the truth of the doctrines and knowledge received in the grade of $5°=6^\square$? Yes or No?

If yes (1) Then their origin can spring from a pure source only?

If no (2) I degrade you to be a Lord of the Paths in the Portal in the Vault of the Adepts.

B.   If he reply 'yes', the masked man continues: Are you satisfied with the logic of this statement? Do you solemnly promise to cease these unseemly disputes as to the headship of this Order? I for my part can assure you from my own knowledge that D.D.C.F. is really a $7°=4^\square$.

If yes (3) Then you will sign this paper; it contains a reaffirmation of your obligation as a $5°=6^\square$ slightly ex-

panded, and a pledge to support heartily the new regulations.

If no (4) I expel you from this Order.

II.   The practice of masks is to be introduced. Each member
will know only the member who introduced him.

Severe tests of the candidate's moral excellence, courage,
earnestness, humility, refusal to do wrong, to be inserted in
the Portal or 5°=6□ ritual.

III.   Outer Order to be summoned. Similar regulations to be
announced to them. New pledges required that they will not
communicate the identity of anybody they happen to have
known to any new member.

IV.   Vault to be reconsecrated.

This was accepted, and I crossed to London to carry it out.
I find an entry in my little book of Magical Rituals which
reveals my state of mind.

April 12th, 1900.

I, Perdurabo, as the Temporary Envoy Plenipotentiary of Deo
Duce Comite Ferro & thus the Third from the Secret Chiefs
of the Order of the Rose of Ruby and the Cross of Gold, do
deliberately invoke all laws, all powers Divine, demanding that
I, even I, be chosen to do such a work as he has done, at all
costs to myself. And I record this holy aspiration in the
Presence of the Divine Light, that it may stand as my witness.

In Saecula Saeculorum. Amen!

A further complication had suddenly arisen. In Mathers's
fatal letter to Mrs Emery, he wrote that Sapiens Dominabitur
Astris was not dead after all; but in Paris, working with him
at that very moment. But when I arrived in Paris, Mathers had
been rudely undeceived. The woman who claimed to be
Sapiens had bolted, with such property of his as she could lay
hands on. That such a man could have been so imposed upon
seems incredible. But he told me that she certainly possessed
knowledge which only Sapiens had, and also that she had told
him every detail of a very private conversation which he had
once had with Mme Blavatsky at Denmark Hill. In the upshot,
she proved to be one Mme Horos.[7] In the following year she
was sentenced to seven years' penal servitude for outrages on
young girls. She had in some way used the rituals of the Order
which she had stolen from Mathers to entice them to their
doom.

My arrival in London as the envoy extraordinary and plenipotentiary of Mathers put the cat among the chickens. My
identity was very soon discovered and a typhoon began to rage

in the teacup. The rebels resorted to all sorts of lawless and violent acts, and spread the most stupidly scandalous stories, not only about me, but about the few others who remained loyal to Mathers. They did not even scruple to slander a young girl of perfect purity, by imputing to her an improper intimacy with me. It was especially dastardly, as she was engaged to be married. To this day I cannot understand how people like W. B. Yeats should not have repressed such methods in the sternest way and insisted that the fight be fought with fair weapons. They had seized the furniture of the temple and the vault. I applied to a police magistrate for it to be handed over. On the hearing of the summons we were amazed to find Mr Gill, K.C., one of the most famous men at the bar, briefed to appear in a police court to squabble over a few pounds' worth of paraphernalia! The money was furnished by Miss Horniman, daughter of the Mazawattee tea man, and later of Manchester Theatre fame. She had been expelled by Mathers some time previously.

I knew enough of campaigning to decline joining battle against such heavy artillery as Mr Gill. Luckily, the value of the property had been sworn at a sum beyond the limit with which a police magistrate can deal. The summons was therefore withdrawn and Mr Gill kept his eloquence and his fee to himself. There was in reality nothing worth fighting for. The rebel camp broke up in anarchy. They issued various hysterical manifestos, distinguished by confusion of thought, inaccuracy of statement, personal malice, empty bombast and ignorance of English. One error is worth rescuing from oblivion. 'Nothing in the above resolutions shall *effect* our connection with the Rosicrucian Order.' The poor darlings meant *affect*.

They went on squabbling amongst themselves for a few months and then had the sense to give up playing at Magick. Their only survivor is Arthur Edward Waite, who still pretends to carry on the business, though he has substituted a pompous, turgid rigmarole of bombastic platitudes for the neophyte ritual, so that the last spark of interest is extinct for ever. Mathers, of course, carried on; but he had fallen. The Secret Chiefs cast him off; he fell into deplorable abjection; even his scholarship deserted him. He published nothing new and lived in sodden intoxication till death put an end to his long misery. He was a great man in his way. May he have expiated his errors and resumed his labours, with the advantage of experience!

Summer was now at hand and the wanderlust reasserted itself in me. There was no point in my going back to Boleskine till the following Easter. As it happened, Mathers—to whom I returned to report progress—had two guests, members of the Order. They had just come back from Mexico. The fancy took me to go there. I wanted in particular to climb the great volcanoes. So, late in June 1900, I sailed for New York.

PART TWO

The Mystical Adventure

The Seal of the Great White Brotherhood, showing the sevenfold
star of Babalon.

23

I think it was on the sixth of July that I reached New York. In those days one was not bored by people who had never seen a real skyline boasting of the outrage since perpetrated by the insects. A mountain skyline is nearly always noble and beautiful, being the result of natural forces acting uniformly and in conformity with law. Thus, though it is not designed, it is the embodiment of the principles which are inherent in design. New York, on the other hand, has been thrown up by a series of disconnected accidents.

The vanity of the natives led them therefore to concentrate their enthusiasm on a rejected statue of commerce intended for the Suez Canal. This they had purchased at secondhand and grandiloquently labelled 'Liberty enlightening the World'. They had been prophetic enough to put it on an island with its back to the mainland.

But, in those days, the spirit of liberty was still intensely alive in the United States. The least sensitive visitor was bound to become aware of it in a few hours. There was no genteel servility. Nobody interfered with anyone else's business or permitted busybodies to meddle with his. The people seemed prosperous and contented; they had not yet been forbidden to amuse themselves when the day's work was over.

Till this time I had never been in any reputedly hot country. I was appalled to find New York intolerable. I filled a cold bath, and got in and out of it at intervals till eleven at night, when I crawled, panting, through the roasting streets and consumed ice-water, iced watermelon, ice-cream and iced coffee. 'Good God,' I said to myself, 'and this is merely New York! What must Mexico be like!' I supposed that I was experiencing normal conditions, whereas in point of fact I had landed at the climax of a heat wave which killed about a hundred people a day while it lasted. I should have discovered the truth if I had looked at a newspaper; but I did not read them. I had already learnt that even the finest mind is bound to perish if it suffers the infection of journalism. It is not merely that one defiles the mind by inflicting upon it slipshod and inaccurate

English, shallow, commonplace, vulgar, hasty and prejudiced thought, and deliberate dissipation. Apart from these positive pollutions, there is the negative effect. To read a newspaper is to refrain from reading something worth while. The natural laziness of the mind tempts one to eschew authors who demand a continuous effort of intelligence. The first discipline of education must therefore be to refuse resolutely to feed the mind with canned chatter.

People tell me that they must read the papers so as to know what is going on. In the first place, they could hardly find a worse guide. Most of what is printed turns out to be false, sooner or later. Even when there is no deliberate deception, the account must, from the nature of the case, be presented without adequate reflection and must seem to possess an importance which time shows to be absurdly exaggerated; or vice versa. No event can be fairly judged without background and perspective.

I only stayed in New York two or three days and then travelled direct to Mexico City. It was my first experience of a really long journey by train. The psychology is very curious. Journeys of more than half an hour begin to be tedious. Edinburgh to Inverness: I used to feel on the verge of insanity before I had got half way. But after two or three days in the train one becomes acclimatized.

The city of Mexico began by irritating me intensely. The hotel had no organized service; they didn't seem to care whether one got anything to eat or not. In fact, in the whole city, there was only one restaurant where one could get anything outside the regular local dishes. Nobody bothers about eating. The same applies to drinking, as far as the palate is concerned. People ate to satisfy hunger and drank to get drunk. There were no fine vintages; the principal drinks were pulque, which is the fermented sap of the aloe; mescal, tequila and aguardiente; the last being a general term applicable to any distilled spirit. In those days I was practically an abstainer, and as I had a fastidious daintiness which made me dislike trying experiments, I never even sampled any of these drinks.

It is a very curious trait. I used to refuse, sometimes under embarrassing pressure, to taste things whose appearance or whose name displeased me. I would not eat jam, even as a child, because it looked messy. I must have been nearly forty before I would touch salad. It seems absurd. I was very fond of lobster mayonnaise; but lobster salad, never! I dislike the combination of consonants. The word suggests something indefinite. It gives the effect of French poetry, where the absence of accentuation emasculates the rhythm.

I found myself spiritually at home with Mexicans. They despise industry and commerce. They had Diaz to do their political thinking for them and damned well he did it. Their hearts are set on bull fighting, cock fighting, gambling and lechery. Their spirit is brave and buoyant; it has not been poisoned by hypocrisy and the struggle for life.

I hired part of a house overlooking the Alameda, a magnificent park intended for pleasure and protected from the police. I engaged a young Indian girl to look after me and settled down to steady work at Magick. I had an introduction to an old man named Don Jesus Medina, a descendant of the great duke of Armada fame, and one of the highest chiefs of Scottish rite free-masonry. My Cabbalistic knowledge being already profound by current standards, he thought me worthy of the highest initiation in his power to confer; special powers were obtained in view of my limited sojourn, and I was pushed rapidly through and admitted to the thirty-third and last degree before I left the country.

I had also a certain amount of latitude granted by Mathers to initiate suitable people *in partibus*. I, therefore, established an entirely new Order of my own, called L.I.L.: the 'Lamp of the Invisible Light'. Don Jesus became its first High Priest. In the Order L.I.L., the letters L.P.D.[1] are the monograms of the mysteries. An explanation of these letters is given by Dumas in the prologue of his *Memoirs of a Physician,* and Eliphas Lévi discusses them at some length. I, however, remembered them directly from my incarnation as Cagliostro. It would be improper to communicate their significance to the profane, but I may say that the political interpretation given by Dumas is superficial, and the ethical suggestions of Lévi puerile and perverse; or, more correctly, intentionally misleading. They conceal a number of magical formulae of minor importance but major practical value, and the curious should conduct such research as they feel impelled to make in the light of the Cabbala. Their numerical values,[2] Yetziratic attributions,[3] and the arcana of the Atus of Tahuti,[4] supply an adequate clue to such intelligences as are enlightened by sympathy and sincerity.

The general idea was to have an ever-burning lamp in a temple furnished with talismans appropriate to the elemental, planetary and zodiacal forces of nature. Daily invocations were to be performed with the object of making the light itself a consecrated centre or focus of spiritual energy. This light would then radiate and automatically enlighten such minds as were ready to receive it.

Even today, the experiment seems to me interesting and the conception sublime. I am rather sorry that I lost touch with Don Jesus; I should like very much to know how it turned out.

I devoted practically my whole time to this and other magical work. I devised a Ritual of Self-Initiation (see *The Equinox*, vol. I, no. III, p. 269), the essential feature of which is the working up of spiritual enthusiasm by means of a magical dance. This dance contained the secret gestures of my grade, combined with the corresponding words. I used to set my will against the tendency to giddiness and thus postpone as long as possible the final physical intoxication. In this way I lost consciousness at a moment when I was wholly absorbed in aspiration. Thus, instead of falling into dull darkness, I emerged into a lucid state, in which I was purged of personality and all sensory or intellectual impressions. I became the vehicle of the divine forces invoked and so experienced Godhead. My results were satisfactory so far as they went; but they did not aid my personal progress very much, since I had not formulated an intellectual link between the divine and human consciousness.

I worked also at acquiring the power of invisibility. (See *The Equinox*, vol. I, no. III, p. 272 for the ritual.) I reached a point when my physical reflection in a mirror became faint and flickering. It gave very much the effect of the interrupted images of the cinematograph in its early days. But the real secret of invisibility is not concerned with the laws of optics at all; the trick is to prevent people noticing you when they would normally do so. In this I was quite successful. For example, I was able to take a walk in the street in a golden crown and a scarlet robe without attracting attention.

Most interesting of all, perhaps, is a magical practice which I devised, ostensibly to deal with the dilemma propounded by the Sphinx: 'The postulant to Magick must be morally perfect.' It may be that I felt instinctively that my pious predecessors were wrong in demanding the suppression of manhood and imposing arbitrary codes of conduct. (I know now, of course, that their instructions have been misunderstood; every element in one's molecule must be developed to the utmost and applied to the service of one's true will.) I suppose I have to thank Stevenson for the idea, which was this. As a member of the Second Order, I wore a certain jewelled ornament of gold upon my heart. I arranged that when I had it on, I was to permit no thought, word or action, save such as pertained directly to my magical aspirations. When I took it off I was, on the contrary, to permit no such things; I was to be utterly uninitiate. It was like Jekyll and Hyde, but with the two personalities balanced and complete in themselves. I found this practice of very great service. It was in fact essentially a beginning of systematic control of thought. The method is now incorporated in the instructions of the A∴A∴. (See *Liber Jugorum*.[5])

Mexico proved a glorious galloping ground for my Pegasus. The magnificent mountain air, the splendour of the sun, the flamboyant beauty of the flowers, the intoxicating intimacy of leaping, fearless love which flamed in every face made my mind a racing rhythm of rapture.

Yet my principal achievement had its roots in Europe. At one of Mathers's semi-public ceremonies, I had met a member of the Order, an American prima donna. She took me by storm and we became engaged. The marriage could not take place immediately, as she had to get rid of some husband that she had left lying about in Texas. But I heard her sing Venus in *Tannhäuser* at Covent Garden; and she courteously insisted on my sampling the goods with which she proposed to endow me. The romance of an intrigue with so famous an artist excited my imagination. One afternoon, in Mexico, I picked up a woman who attracted me by the insatiable intensity of passion that blazed from her evil inscrutable eyes and tortured her worn face into a whirlpool of seductive sin. I passed some hours with her in her slum; and, walking home, found myself still so unappeased—*lassatus, sed non satiatus*—that my fever developed a delirium whose images assumed the form of Wagner's opera. I went home and sat down at once to write my own poetical and magical version of the story. I neither slept nor ate till it was finished—sixty-seven hours later. I had not been aware of the flight of time. I could not understand why it was afternoon; I thought that I had merely written all night. This play marks the climax of the first period of my poetry.

During the summer I wanted to travel in the interior. I went down to Iguala, bought an orange pony and rode slowly back to the city, taking things as they came. In all my travels I have hardly ever 'seen the sights'. Nothing is so disappointing.

My plan is simply to live in any new city the ordinary life of the people. I wander about and presently come unexpectedly upon one of the wonders of the world. In this way one gets the thrill which those who have sold their souls to Baedeker miss. Imagine the delight of discovering the Coliseum or the Taj Mahal for oneself, at a moment, perhaps, when one's mind was preoccupied with commonplace ideas! I may have missed a few masterpieces, but not many; and people who go to see them on purpose miss them all altogether.

The maximum of romance and pleasure is to be found in Mexico, even in the quite small provincial towns. There is always some sort of Alameda, a well-wooded square more or less in the middle of the town with seats in any number, and a bandstand where a band plays every night without any swank, because people like music. It is never too hot; there is usually a pleasant breeze, enough to stir the leaves and not enough to disturb and annoy. It is full of men and women; all seem young and all are charming, spontaneous and ready to make any desired kind of love.

In fact, they are making it continually in their hearts and only wait opportunity to suit the word and action to the thought. Nor does opportunity lag. There are no practical difficulties. Indoors and out nature and art combine to invite Cupid to pay every kind of visit, passionate, permanent, transitory, trivial. The caprice of the moment is the sole arbiter of the event. The idea of worry is unknown. 'Take no thought for the morrow' is the first principle of human relations, especially in regard to all such matters. Love is the business of life, but it is all profit and no loss. There is no false shame, no contamination by ideas of commerce and material matters in general. There is no humbug about purity, uplift, idealism, or any such nonsense. I cannot hope to express the exquisite pleasure of freedom. One's spontaneity was not destroyed by anticipations of all sorts of difficulty in finding a friend of any desired type, obstacles in the way of consummating the impulse, and unpleasantness in the aftermath. The problem of sex, which has reduced Anglo-Saxon nations to hysteria and insanity, has been solved in Mexico by the co-operation of climate and cordiality. Even Catholicism has lost most of its malignancy in Mexico. Clergy and laity unite, spiritually and somatically, with gay ardour. The Virgin is here actually the *fille-mère* which the gospels really represent, for all our blustering denial of the obvious facts. Of course, the priest likes a little gratification for his complaisance, but that is a very human trait, and as he is neither greedy, malicious, nor hypocritical, the charity which he enjoys is given freely in the friendliest spirit.

This was because he had Diaz 33°⁶ to keep him in order. After Diaz's death, the priest got gay on a bellyful of—(the Host?) like the world-famous Sparrow ⁷ and had to be curbed seriously, as history relates.

My first night out of Iguala was a mysterious delight. I had lost my way in a sugar plantation and it was getting dark when I came to a railway in course of construction. I followed this, hoping to find a town, but night fell, sudden and black; so I tethered my horse and lay down to sleep in my poncho by the light of a fire, to make which I borrowed some loose material left by the engineers. Dawn was just breaking when I was awakened from sleep by that subtle sense of danger which protects sleeping wayfarers. In the dim light I saw three heads peering at me over the embankment. I fired my revolver in the air; the heads disappeared; I turned over and went to sleep again instantly for several hours.

My second night was otherwise amusing. I struck a pioneer camp, where a wooden hut had been thrown together. Two Chinamen were running an eating house. I sat down to dinner with two of the engineers. They spotted the new chum and began to scare me with tales of scorpions and fever. Before serving dinner, one of the Chinese came in with a saucepan of boiling water and went round the room tipping it into the cavities formed by the crossing of the timbers of the hut. As often as not, a scalded scorpion fell out. I went to bed that night with my mind full of a particularly unpleasant trick of my reptilian brothers. They have a habit of dropping from the roof on to one's bed. This is quite without malice, but one stirs in one's sleep at the touch. They are alarmed and strike. This didn't happen; but in the morning I found my legs so swollen from mosquito bites that I could not get my boots on. The result was my first acquaintance with malaria, which attacked me very severely shortly after I got back to the city. My ride was full of very varied adventure. The incident that stands out is this:

Crossing a hillside, I saw a Mexican some thirty yards below the track, apparently asleep in the sun. I thought I would warn him of his danger and rode over. He must have been dead three weeks, for he had been completely mummified. Neither the coyotes nor the turkey-buzzards will touch a dead Mexican. His flesh has been too thoroughly impregnated with chillies and other pungent condiments. They make short work of any other meat. I remember riding out from Zapotlan to lunch with some friends on their ranch. I fell in with a string of mules bound for the Pacific coast. As I passed, a mule dropped from exhaustion. The men transferred his pack and left him to die. Returning after lunch, some three hours later, I found the bones of the mule picked clean and dry.

One can always tell a Mexican by his peculiar habit of blowing through his cigarette before lighting it. The reason for this is that the government cigarettes are rolled by convicts, who are allowed what they consider an inadequate amount of tobacco daily for their own use. They therefore increase their supply by mixing dust with the tobacco handed out to them every morning for their work, and one therefore has to blow it out.

It is said, I know not how truly, that a Mexican town, in a corner near the Rio Grande, was, in the course of the revolution and counter-revolution of the contending vultures in 1917, cut off for a time from all communication with the rest of the country. Presumably everyone buried whatever cash he happened to have. At least it vanished rapidly and strangely. The city gasped. What the devil was to be done? Being folk of sense, they soon collected their wits and said: 'All right. It's no good crying for the moon. We've got to go on exchanging wealth. We'll simply barter on credit and strike a weekly balance.

> 'If anyone fancies he's got a soft thing—
> If we haven't got pesos we've plenty of string.'

The result was surprising. Business went on pretty well as in the past, with this remarkable difference: the motive for cheating and hoarding and gambling was gone. One could, of course, amass a fortune on the balance sheet of the town council; but it would be hard to cash in. So nobody troubled to outwit his neighbour or plot his ruin. They contented themselves with aiming at comfort and ease. Old enemies became fast friends; the usurers turned their hands to productive purposes; the loafers and spongers and gamblers realized that they must work or starve. The whole town prospered; poverty disappeared; financial anxiety ceased to exist; the moral tone of the community became almost angelic. Everyone had plenty to do, plenty to eat, plenty of leisure and plenty of pleasure. Everyone was happy. Of course it was too good to last. Communications were restored and a month later society had relapsed into a dog-fight for dollars.

24

Lying sick in the Hotel Iturbide, I was attended by an American doctor named Parsons, with whom I struck up a warm friendship. He was certainly a 'live wire'. The faculty had just devised a new source of income by inventing appendicitis. Parsons heard of this and wired to the States for a partner who could perform the operation. He then proceeded to advise immediate operation every time one of his many wealthy patients had a stomach-ache. At a thousand Mexican dollars a time, it did not take many months to pile up a fortune.

The English colony in Mexico City was disliked and despised. The consul was habitually constipated and the vice-consul habitually drunk. It is a curious fact that all over the world these qualities never vary. A wide field is open to a philosophical speculation.

I came to frequent the American colony and club. I remember being introduced to a new but already popular and respected member, 'Meet Mr Tewkesbury,' and, in a loud whisper, '*Thorne,* you know, who got away from Chi with a quarter of a million plunks.' At this club I met some really charming ranchers, who invited me to stay with them and convalesce. Their place was near Guanajato, a great centre for silver mines. Guanajato possessed an unique curiosity: some eccentric millionaire had built a theatre, sparing no expense to make it the most gorgeous building of its kind in the world. The stalls, for instance, were upholstered in real velvet, embroidered with real gold thread. For some reason, I think because the President had declined to open it, the owner felt himself insulted and kept it shut up. It was never opened at all except as a show place for visitors like myself, and finally was somehow burnt to the ground.

Mexico City was full of American professional gamblers and confidence men. I saw a good deal of two of these; a lank grey Yankee named McKee and his genial jackal Wilson, or some such name. After a few days' acquaintance Wilson approached me with the following proposal. It appeared that the manager of a mine near St Luis Potosi had stolen a quantity of gold dust. He had got scared and dared not bolt. Wilson thought that if we offered him a thousand dollars, each putting up half, he would be willing to hand over the compromising sacks, value five thousand or so. Not for nothing had I read the works of 'Pitcher of The Pink 'Un', and other authorities on the gentle art of parting a fool and his money. I joyfully accepted Wilson's proposal. 'Bring your five hundred right along,' I said, 'and I'll go and put the job through. I know you're too busy to leave the city.' He agreed and returned an hour later, not with the cash, but with his partner. They apologized profusely for mistaking me for a mug. 'Look here,' said McKee, 'the innocence of your face is a fortune. I know a rich man here who is crazy on gambling. You shall rook him at Brazilian poker. (In this game one backs one's hand as in ordinary poker, but the hands are of two cards with the option of taking a third, as in baccarat.) We'll signal you what he holds. With your face, he'll never get wise to the stunt.'

The psychology of these people really interested me. They had no experience of the kind of man who knows all the tricks but refuses to cheat. Their world was composed entirely of sharps and flats. It is the typical American conception; the use of knowledge is to get ahead of the other fellow, and the question of fairness depends on the chance of detection. We see this even in amateur sport. The one idea is to win. Knowledge for its own sake, pleasure for its own sake, seem to the American mere frivolity. 'Life is real, life is earnest.' One of themselves told me recently that the American ideal is attainment, while that of Europe is enjoyment. There is much truth in this, and the reason is that in Europe we have already attained everything, and discovered that nothing is worth while. Unless we live in the present, we do not live at all.

Mexico was full of gambling houses and I used to play a great deal. The chief game was Monte, in which the dealer exposes two cards; the punter can back which he pleases; bets being placed, the dealer skins the pack, and the first card which duplicates one of the two exposed cards wins for it. The bank's percentage is that if the first card skinned decides (is 'in the door', as they say), it only pays three quarters of the stake.

The son of one of the prominent members of the old

Golden Dawn went to the bad and became a professional crook. Him I once frequented to study the psychology of hawk and pigeon.

First let me insist that the knave is always a fool. Prosperity is a function of biological success and (facts being facts) the habit of lying begets credulity. My friend never profited except now and then for a few lucky weeks, though he scooped in that time enough to keep a man with a grain of good sense for the rest of his life.

The confidence trick is protean, but in all its forms the essence is to get the victim off his guard. Observe how this fact confirms my general theory that surrender of the will to the guidance of the emotions is destructive of judgment. The first act in every trick is what is called the 'come on' or the 'build up'. Its crudest form is proving to a stranger that you trust him by asking him to go away for five minutes with your watch and money. From this has been developed an amazing structure of subtle strategy. The shrewdest bankers have been looted for tens of thousands. The general plan is to bring about, in an apparently natural way, a series of incidents in which the chief of the confederates shows to advantage. His victim is induced to admire his keen sense of humour, his generosity, fairness, integrity, and so on in various emergencies. When the swindler feels sure that his victim trusts him implicitly, he proceeds to the next act. A scheme is suggested by which they shall both make a fortune, and in one of a million ways a situation is brought about in which it is hard for the victim to avoid putting up his cash. He could hardly show suspicion, even if he felt it, without giving outrageous offence for which he could produce no excuse. His common decency is concerned and at the same time a strong appeal made to his interests. He produces the goods—and hears no more of the matter.

I could give the details of half a hundred schemes of this sort. Their ingenuity extorts my intellectual admiration, and yet there is always a fundamental flaw that, in the hands of such men, a million melts more quickly than a thousand would with anyone else. In every swell bar and hotel one can see plenty such—all well dressed and well groomed, laughing and joking, and throwing their money about, and all the time ninety per cent feel a sinking at the pit of the stomach as the thought hammers persistently at the back of their brains, 'How shall I pay my bill?' at the best; and, overshadowing lesser worries, 'What about when my luck turns?' 'When will my own confidence in the imbecility of my fellow men be enlightened by their robbing me of the stake I risked, my liberty?'

A delicious ride by electric tram from the city brings one to Tacubaya, a luxurious pleasure resort with a big casino. The play is at long tables stacked with thousands of silver dollars. One night I noticed the electric chandelier beginning to swing. Crashing sounds came from without. Suddenly the lights went out! It was an earthquake. Attendants rushed in with lighted candles. It could hardly have been dark for two minutes; but the room was almost empty and most of the cash had vanished.

I had been playing a modified martingale with happier results than my stupidity deserved. But, one night, luck ran against me and my stake had increased to the limit allowed by the house. There was a slight delay—I think someone had called for a fresh pack of cards—I found myself walking nervously up and down. Somewhat as had happened in the chess congress at Berlin, I had a vision of myself from somewhere outside. 'Look at that young fool,' I seemed to be saying; 'that stake he has there is about a month's income.' The cards were dealt. I had won, but 'in the door', so that I only got seventy-five per cent. I picked up my winnings, walked out and have never gambled again; except once at Monte Carlo for the fun of the thing, some years later. I made it a rule to take five pounds to the casino and quit, when it was gone, for the day. As luck would have it, on the fourth day I kept on winning. I had an appointment for lunch. Remembering this, I suddenly awoke to the fact that I had won over three hundred and fifty pounds. That was good enough for me. After lunch I packed up and escaped to Nice, with a vow never again to set foot in the principality.

All this time I had not forgotten my project of climbing the mountains of Mexico. Somehow, my Indian girl knew that I was keen on them; and one day she called me up to the roof of the house and pointed out two snow-capped peaks. As I have already said, my judgment of heights and distances was surprisingly accurate. Mexico being about seven thousand feet above the sea, I judged these peaks to be from eleven to twelve thousand, and their distance from the city some eight to ten miles. I proposed to myself to stroll out and climb them one day. 'From their summits,' I said to myself, 'I may be able to see the big mountains eighty miles away.' The scheme miscarried. I was looking at the big mountains themselves! I had made no allowance for the clearness of the air. People whose experience is confined to Europe have no means of judging correctly. As I found later, the Himalayas are to Mexican peaks as these are to the Alps. In north India one sees a mountain apparently within a day's march, yet four days later that mountain will hardly have changed its apparent size and distance.

I do not know why I made no attempts on the peaks. Perhaps it was from an obscure feeling of comradeship. I preferred to wait till Eckenstein joined me, which he was to do towards the end of the year.

25

Meanwhile my magical condition was making me curiously uncomfortable. I was succeeding beyond all my expectations. In the dry pure air of Mexico, with its spiritual energy un-exhausted and uncontaminated as it is in cities, it was astonishingly easy to produce satisfactory results. But my very success somehow disheartened me. I was getting what I thought I wanted and the attainment itself taught me that I wanted something entirely different. What that might be it did not say. My distress became acute; and, as I had done at the beginning, I sent out an urgent call for help from the Masters. It must have been heard at once, for little over a fortnight later I got a long letter from Fra. V.N.[1] Though I had not written to him, he gave me the very word that I needed. It restored my courage and my confidence. I con-tinued my work with deeper and truer understanding. I began to perceive the real implications of what I was doing. In par-ticular, I gained an entirely new grip of the Cabbala.

One of my results demands detailed record, because it proved later to be one of the foundations of the Great Work of my life. The word Abracadabra is familiar to everyone. Why should it possess such a reputation? Eliphas Lévi's explanations left me cold. I began to suspect that it must be a corruption of some true 'word of power'. I investigated it by means of the Cabbala. I restored its true spelling.[2] Analysis showed it to be indeed the essential formula of the Great Work. It showed how to unite the Macrocosm with the Microcosm. I, therefore, adopted this word and its numerical value, 418, as the quintessentialized expression of the proper way to conduct all major Magical Operations.

This discovery was only one of many. Before Allan Bennett left for Ceylon, he gave me most of his magical notebooks. One of these contained the beginnings of a Cabbalistic dic-tionary in which various sacred words were entered, not alphabetically, but according to their numerical value. I must explain that the fundamental idea of the Cabbala is that the universe may be regarded as an elaboration of the numbers from 0 to 10, arranged in a certain geometrical design and connected by twenty-two 'paths'. The problem is to acquire perfect comprehension of the essential nature of these numbers. Every phenomenon, every idea, may be referred to one or more numbers. Each is thus, so to say, a particular modification of the pure idea. Sacred words which add up to any number should be eloquent commentaries on one of its aspects. Thus the number 13 proves to be, as it were, an essay on the number 1. The words 'unity' and 'love' both add up to 13.[3] These ideas are therefore qualities of 1. Now, 26 combines the idea of duality, which is the condition of manifestation or consciousness, with this 13; and we find, accordingly, that 26 is the value of the name Jehova. From this we see Him as the Demiourgos, the manifestation in form of the primordial *One*.

For many years I worked on these lines continually, adding to Allan's nucleus, and ultimately making a systematic compilation. The resulting book was published in *The Equinox*, vol. I, no. VIII. It is the only dictionary of the Cabbala in existence that can claim any degree of completeness. Since its publication, of course, new knowledge has come to light and I hope to issue a revised edition in course of time. As it stands, however, it is the essential book of reference for the student. It can never be complete; for one thing, every student must create his own Cabbala. My conception, for instance, of the number 6 will not be identical to yours. The difference between you and me is, in fact, just this; you are capable of perceiving one set of aspects of absolute reality, I another. The higher our attainment, the more closely will our points of view coalesce, just as a great English and a great French historian will have more ideas in common about Napoleon Bonaparte than a Devonshire and a Provençal peasant. But there will always be more in any being than any man can know.

My magical work was pushed into the background by the arrival of Eckenstein. He openly jeered at me for wasting my time on such rubbish. He being brutally outspoken, and I shy and sensitive, I naturally avoided creating opportunities for him to indulge his coarse ribaldry on a subject which to me was supremely sacred. Occasionally, however, I would take advantage of his unintelligence by talking to him in terms which I knew he would not understand. I find that it relieves my mind and helps me to clarify my thoughts if I inflict my jargon on some harmless stranger haphazard. As will be told

in due course, Eckenstein and I made a very thorough exploration of the mountains of Mexico. During this time, my magical
distress again increased. I could not relieve it by the narcotic
of preparing and performing actual ceremonies, of silencing
the voice of the demons by absorption in active work. It was
while we were preparing our expedition to Colima that I broke
out one evening and told Eckenstein my troubles, as I had
done often enough before with no result beyond an insult
or a sneer. Balaam could not have been more surprised when
his ass began to prophesy than I was when, at the end of my
outburst, Eckenstein turned on me and gave me the worst
quarter of an hour of my life. He summed up my magical
situation and told me that my troubles were due to my inability to control my thoughts. He said: 'Give up your Magick,
with all its romantic fascinations and deceitful delights.
Promise to do this for a time and I will teach you how to
master your mind.' He spoke with the absolute authority
which comes from profound and perfect knowledge. And, as
I sat and listened, I found my faith fixed by the force of
facts. I wondered and worshipped. I thought of Easter '98,
when I wandered in Wastdale in despair and cried to the
universe for someone to teach me the truth, when my imagination was impotent to forge the least link with any helper. Yet
at that very hour, sitting and smoking by the fire opposite me,
or roped to me on a precipice, was the very man I needed, had
I but had the intuition to divine his presence!

I agreed at once to his proposals and he taught me the
principles of concentration. I was to practise visualizing
simple objects; and when I had succeeded in keeping these
fairly steady, to try moving objects, such as a pendulum. The
first difficulty is to overcome the tendency of an object to
change its shape, size, position, colour, and so on. With moving
objects, the trouble is that they try to behave in an erratic
manner. The pendulum wants to change its rate, the extent
of its swing or the plane in which it travels.

There were also practices in which I had to imagine certain
sounds, scents, tastes and tactile sensations. Having covered
this ground-work to his satisfaction, he allowed me to begin
to visualize human figures. He told me that the human figure
acts differently from any other object. 'No one has ever
managed to keep absolutely still.' There is also a definite test
of success in this practice. The image should resolve itself
into two; a smaller and a larger superimposed. It is said that
by this means one can investigate the character of the person

of whom one is thinking. The image assumes a symbolic form, significant of its owner's moral and intellectual qualities.

I practised these things with great assiduity; in fact, Eckenstein put the brake on. One must not overstrain the mind. Under his careful tuition, I obtained great success. There is no doubt that these months of steady scientific work, unspoiled by my romantic fancies, laid the basis of a sound magical and mystic technique. Eckenstein evidently understood what I was later to learn from *The Book of the Law:* 'For pure will, unassuaged for purpose, delivered from the lust of result, is every way perfect.'

During this time we were busy with expeditions. Eckenstein had already been to the Himalayas (in 1892); he wanted to complete my education by experience of mountains higher than the Alps, and travel in rough country among primitive people. We began by establishing a camp on Iztaccihuatl, at about fourteen thousand feet. We remained there for a matter of three weeks and climbed this, the most beautiful mountain in Mexico, from every possible side. In doing so, we incidentally broke several world's records.

Our difficulties were in some ways severe. The canned food procurable in Mexico City was of inferior quality and many years old at that. Eckenstein was constantly ill with diarrhoea and I was not much better. Finally food gave out altogether and our last three days we had literally nothing but champagne and Danish butter. We didn't care much; we had done what we had set out to do. Besides, I had learnt a great deal about camp life, the fine points of glissading, and the use of Steigeisen. In 1899, at the Montanvers, I had already found that his mechanically perfect 'claws' worked miracles. We had shown a young man from Oxford, Dr T. G. Longstaff,[4] of what they were capable. Eckenstein would walk on a measured slope of over seventy degrees of hard black ice without cutting a step. On slopes up to fifty degrees he could simply stroll about. Nor could Longstaff pull him off by the rope.

On the grand scale, too, I had proved their possibilities. One day, Eckenstein being ill, I had arranged to go with Longstaff and his two guides over the Col du Géant. Not feeling very fit myself, I thought I would start an hour ahead of the others. Having inspected the ice fall, I found a way straight up. When I was about half way through the séracs, I heard Longstaff's guides yelling blue murder. I had taken the 'wrong' way. Their route involved a detour of a mile or more. I took no notice of their friendly anxiety and reached the top a long way in advance. When they arrived, they explained that what I had done was impossible. To carry on the joke, when we got back I offered a hundred and fifty francs to any party that would repeat the climb by my route. Nobody did so.

It was really astonishing and distressing that (after all these years of proof that men with proper claws are to men without them as a rifleman to an archer) English climbers are still quite ignorant of what claws can do, or how to use them. In Mr Harold Raeburn's book he argues amiably against them. He admits that one can walk up hard snow at easy angles without steps, but fears to do so lest, returning later in the day, he should find the snow soft, and then where would he be without a staircase? He seems to have no idea that the supreme use of claws is on ice and that the harder the ice the surer the hold. Yet Mr Raeburn pits himself against Everest, where claws would convert the most perilous passages into promenades, and ice slopes whose length and steepness make step-cutting impracticable into serenely simple staircases. The policy of boycotting Eckenstein and his school, of deliberately ignoring the achievements of Continental climbers, to say nothing of my own expeditions, has preserved the privilege and prestige of the English Alpine Club. Ignorance and incompetence are unassailable. Ridicule does not reach the realms of secure snobbery. The mountains themselves vainly maim and murder the meddlers; they merely clamour all the more conceitedly to be considered heroes. It is one of the most curious characteristics of the English that they set such store by courage as to esteem a man the more highly the more blindly he blunders into disaster. We thought it rather unfair to take cover against Boer marksmanship; we are still proud of being unprepared in the Great War. We doubt whether science is sportsmanlike; and so it is thought rotten bad form to point out how mismanagement smashed Scott's expedition. No gentleman criticizes the conduct of the campaign of Gallipoli.

In March 1922 I heard of the composition and projects of the Everest expedition. I wrote an article predicting failure and disaster, giving my reasons and showing how to avoid the smash. No one would print it. I was told it was not the thing to 'crab' these gallant gentlemen. No. But should my prophecies come true, then was the time to explain why. What I had foretold came to pass precisely as I had predicted it. But I was still unable to get a hearing. Why add to the tribulations

of these heroes by showing up their stupidity? Besides, England
had failed—better not talk about it at all.

On Iztaccihuatl, on off days, we had a lot of practice with
rifles and revolvers. At that altitude and in that clear air
one's shooting becomes superb. We found we could do at a
hundred yards better than we had ever done before at twenty-
five. We used to knock the bottoms out of bottles, end-on,
without breaking the necks. In Mexico we used to make
rather a point of practising with firearms whenever we struck
a new district. A reputation for expertness is the best protection against local marauders.

For instance. We once fell in with a party of railway
engineers, one short. The absentee had strolled out after dinner
to enjoy the cool of the air. He was found in the morning
naked, with a machete wound in the back. He had been
treacherously murdered for the value of a suit worth, at the
outside, five shillings.

When we returned to Amecameca, we went at once to pay
our respects to the Jefe Politico, to ask him to dinner to
celebrate our triumph. He had been very kind and useful in
helping us to make various arrangements. When he saw us
he assumed an air of sympathetic melancholy. We wondered
what it could mean. By degrees he brought himself to break
to us gently the terrible news. Queen Victoria was dead! To
the amazement of the worthy mayor, we broke into shouts of
joy and an impromptu war dance.

I think this incident rather important. In reading Mr
Lytton Strachey's *Eminent Victorians,* and still more his
Queen Victoria, as also in discussing periods with the younger
generation, I find total failure to appreciate the attitude of
artists and advanced thinkers who remember her jubilee. They
cannot realize that to us Victoria was sheer suffocation. While
she lived it would be impossible to take a single step in any
direction. She was a huge and heavy fog; we could not see,
we could not breathe. Under her, England had advanced
automatically to prosperity. Science too had surged up from
sporadic spurts into a system. And yet, somehow or other,
the spirit of her age had killed everything we cared for. Smug,
sleek, superficial, servile, and snobbish, sentimental shopkeep-
ing had spread everywhere. Even Darwinism had become
respectable. Even Bradlaugh had been accepted. James Thomson had been starved and classed with the classics. Swinburne
had been whacked and washed and brushed and turned into
a model boy. The Church of England had collapsed under

the combined assault of rationalism and Rome; yet, deprived of its religious element, and torn from its historical justification, it persisted placidly. The soul of England was stagnant, stupefied! Nothing remained for which a man might be willing either to live or to die. Huxley, Manning, Booth, Blavatsky, Ray Lankester—it mattered nothing what they said and did, all were equally stifled in shapeless sacks, stowed away indistinguishably, their voices mingled in the murmur of polite society.

It is hard to say why Queen Victoria should have seemed the symbol of this extraordinary state of suspended animation. Yet there was something in her physical appearance and her moral character which pointed to her as the perfect image of this inhibiting idea. The new generation, seeing their predecessors in perspective, perceive the individual qualities of each. There is nothing to tell them that in those days each one of us seethed with impotent rage at our doom. We were all damned with faint praise. Sir Richard Burton was toned down into a famous traveller and translator; Gordon sentimentalized into a warrior saint; Hardy was accepted as the Homer of Wessex; Meredith patted on the back as the modern Ovid. It was impossible to dynamite the morass of mediocrity. Progress was impossible. The most revolutionary proposals, the most blasphemous theories, lost their sting. A sovereign of suet, a parliament of putty, an aristocracy of alabaster, an intelligentsia of india-rubber, a proletariat of pulp; it was impossible to shape such material. The strongest impression was blunted by the inertia of the viscous glue which resisted nothing, but resumed its formlessness as soon as the immediate impulse of the impact was spent.

England had become a hausfrau's idea of heaven, and the empire an eternal Earl's Court exhibition. This was the real reason why people who loved England, like Tom Broadbent in *John Bull's Other Island*, used to indulge in spasms of glee whenever we happened to have a corporal's file ambushed by some horde of savages.*

Our next expedition was to the Colima district. The mountain is here divided into two very distinct sections; one is snow-clad, the other one of the most frequently active volcanoes in the world. Going over the shoulder of the Nevado, we emerged from a forest to get our first view of the Volcan, some twelve miles away. As we watched, an eruption oc-

---

* P.S.—And in 1929 I find myself rather regretting those 'spacious days'!

curred. The wind was blowing towards us and the next thing we knew was that falling ashes were burning little holes in our clothes. We began to suspect that the ascent might be troublesome. We settled the Nevado straight off. The climbing is of little interest and no difficulty. Then we camped on a spur for a week, and took turns, day and night, to watch the behaviour of the volcano. The inspection was disappointing; we could not discover any periodicity in the explosions; we could simply take our chance. We started accordingly; but, finding our feet beginning to burn through our boots, decided to retire gracefully.

Our third objective was Toluca. Here we had two delightful days. For some reason or other we had not brought the tent and slept in the crater in our ponchos. In the morning I found myself about three inches thick in hoarfrost. On the first day we climbed what was apparently the highest summit. (The formation is that of the rim of an enormous crater.) When we got there we found that another point a long way off was higher. The next morning Eckenstein was sick and I had to go alone. There was some difficult rock climbing on the wall which led to the ridge. But once there, the summit was easily reached. There are many magnificent teeth, which I climbed conscientiously; a most exhilarating exercise. I traversed some distance till I found a gap on the other ridge from which I could run down to the crater. We went down to the plateau the same day and returned to the city.

On this excursion we met a man who said he had seen with his own eyes the famous phantom city. This yarn has for me a peculiar fascination. I am not sure that I do not believe that in some sense it is true, though it would be hard to say in exactly what sense. I heard the story at least a dozen times; twice first-hand from serious informants. The story varies but slightly and only in unimportant details.

Its general tenor is this: A man on horseback, sometimes a solitary prospector, sometimes a member of a party temporarily separated from the rest, but always alone, loses his way in hilly wooded country. (The district varies considerably with the narrator, but as a rule is somewhere within a couple of hundred miles of Mexico City, the direction being between north-west and south-west.) The horseman is eager to find a way out of the forest, so that he may take his bearings. It is getting late; he does not want to camp out if he can help it. At last he sees the trees thinning out; he hurries forward and finds himself on the brink of the hillside. At this moment darkness falls suddenly. It is impossible to proceed. Then he sees on the hillside opposite, possibly two or three miles distant, a city gleaming white. It is not a large city by modern standards, but it is an important city. For its size, it is very bravely built. The architecture does not suggest a modern city; I have heard it described as 'like an Arabian Nights city', 'like an old Greek city', 'like an Aztec city'. The traveller proposes to himself to visit it in the morning. But when he wakes there is no trace of it. There is not even any distinguishing character about the hillside where he saw it which might have suggested the idea of a city to a tired man. In some cases lights are seen in the city; occasionally there is even the sound of revelry.

Talking of liars! We suddenly discovered that we were regarded in that light ourselves. I suppose it is the abject ignorance and narrow outlook of ordinary people that makes them sceptical about anything out of the common. However, that may be, a paragraph appeared in the Mexican *Herald* which indirectly threw doubt on our expeditions. It was particularly pointless; we had published nothing, made no claims, behaved in fact exactly as we should have done in the Alps. But Eckenstein was annoyed at the impertinence and proposed to take summary vengeance. He accordingly went down to the low bar frequented by the peccant reporter, bought him a few drinks, congratulated him on his literary style, and politely regretted that he should have been led into error by ignorance of his subject.

The reporter was far from sure that the conversation would not suddenly end by a bullet being put through him, for Eckenstein always looked a very formidable customer; but he found himself charmingly invited to come with us and climb Popocatapetl, so as to acquire first-hand knowledge of mountains and the men who climbed them. He gaily and gratefully accepted this insidious proposition. We rode merrily up to the sulphur ranch, where intending climbers stay the night. The next morning the fun began. One of the world's records which we had left in tatters was that for pace uphill at great heights. Long before we got to the lowest point of the rim of the crater our sceptical friend found that he couldn't go another yard—he had to turn back. We assured him that the case was common, but could easily be met by the use of the rope. So we tied him securely to the middle; Eckenstein set a fierce pace up hill, while I assisted his tugging by prodding the recalcitrant reporter with my axe. He exhausted the gamut of supplication. We replied only by cheerful and encouraging exhortations, and by increased efforts. We never checked our rush till we stood on the summit. It was probably the first time that it had ever been climbed in an unbroken sprint. Our victim was by this time convinced that we could climb mountains. And he was certainly the sorriest sight!

Even on the descent, his troubles were not over. Most of the lower slopes are covered with fine loose ash, abominable to ascend but a joy to glissade. Our friend, between the fear of God, the fear of death, and the fear of us, had lost all mastery of his emotions. We had taken the rope off and shot down the slopes to show him how to do it, but he was in mortal terror. The feeling that the ground was slipping under his feet drove him almost insane. I hardly know how he got down to us at last, except that on those loose slopes he could hardly help it. Having put our man through the mill, we became seriously friendly. He took his lesson like a good sportsman and made his apologies in the Mexican *Herald*, by writing a long account of his adventure in the style of the then famous Mr Dooley.

Eckenstein and I lived in an American apartment house, from the roof of which one could see a great distance down a principal thoroughfare.

Eckenstein used to lure people to discuss eyesight and mention that mine was miraculous for distant objects. It would be arranged for me to drop in at this stage, accidentally on purpose, and then Eckenstein would offer to prove his tall stories on the spot. So we would go up to the roof with field glasses, and I would describe distant objects in great detail, read names on shops a quarter of a mile off, etc. etc. The victim would check this through the field glasses, confirming my accuracy. No one ever suspected that this stunt had been prepared by my using the field glasses and learning the scenery by heart!

I should have mentioned a short excursion which I took to Vera Cruz. My ostensible object was to see some cases of yellow fever. As a matter of fact, I was horribly afraid of the disease. So I picked an occasion when the port had shown a clean bill of health for the previous three weeks. I had an introduction to a local doctor and told him how sorry I was not to be able to see any cases. 'Well, well,' said he, 'come round to the hospital tomorrow morning anyhow—some points may be of interest.' And then I found any amount of yellow Jack, mendaciously diagnosed as malaria, typhoid, etc., in the hope of throwing dust in the eyes of the United States inspectors and getting them to remove the quarantine.

The journey from Vera Cruz back to the city is to my mind the finest in the world from the point of view of spectacular effect; the second best is from the Ganges up to Darjeeling. For the first forty miles one runs through tropical jungle, then the track suddenly begins to mount and wind its way among the sub-alpine gorges, with the whole eighteen thousand feet of Citlaltepetl towering above. The scenery continually changes in character as one ascends, and then quite suddenly one comes out on the plateau, a level vastness almost desert save from cactus and aloe, with the two cones of Iztaccihuatl and Popocatapetl sticking out of it.

We had intended to finish our programme by climbing Citlaltepetl; but there were difficulties about mules and none about the mountain. We were too bored to trouble to climb it. Somehow or other, the current of our enthusiasm had become exhausted. We had achieved all our real objects and the next thing was to get ready for the Himalayas. Eckenstein returned to England and on the twentieth of April I started for San Francisco, westward bound. My objective was a curious one. Since leaving England, I had thought over the question of the authority of Mathers with ever increasing discomfort. He had outraged every principle of probity and probability; but he was justified, provided that his primary postulate held good. I could think of only one way of putting him to the test. It concerned an episode at which Allan Bennett was present. Allan, and he alone, could confirm the account which Mathers had given me. If he did so, Mathers was vindicated; if not, it was fatal to his claims. It seems absurd to travel eight thousand miles to ask one question—a childish question into the bargain!—but that was what I did. The sequel will be told in the proper place.

26

I broke the journey at El Paso. Coming straight from the quiet civilization of Mexico it was a terrible shock to find myself in touch with the coarse and brutal barbarism of Texas. There are many unpleasant sides of life which cannot be avoided without shirking reality altogether; but in the United States they were naked and horrible. The lust of money raged stark without the softening influences of courtesy. Drunkenness was stripped of good fellowship; the sisterhood of sin presented no deceptive attractions. The most idealistic innocent could not have been under a moment's illusion—they were stalled like cattle in rows of wooden shanties; and they carried on their business with fierce commercial candour. All those little graces of life which make bought kisses tolerable to those sensitive people who are willing to be fooled, were absent.

I strolled across to Juarez to kiss my girl goodbye. O Mexico, my heart still throbs and burns whenever memory brings you to my mind! For many other countries I have more admiration and respect, but none of them rivals your fascination. Your climate, your customs, your people, your strange landscapes of dreamlike enchantment rekindle my boyhood.

Outside Juarez was a labour camp. Public works of some sort were in progress—at least such progress as we find in Mexico! Hundreds of men were loafing about at their eternal cigarettes and tossing various liquefactions of hell-fire down their chilli-armoured gullets. Most of the groups were squatting round a soiled poncho, on which were scattered coins and greasy cards. I stood and watched one party of three. The swearing, jabbering and quarrelling were incessant here, as all over the camp. Nothing struck me as abnormal. Then, like a flash of forked lightning, one of the men flung himself across the poncho and twisted his fingers in the hair of the man opposite. (Astounding recklessness to let it grow so long!) He thrust his thumbs into the corners of his enemy's eyes, as he writhed and kicked on top of him, the momentum of his spring having bowled the other on to his back. The man's eyes were torn from their sockets in a second and his assailant, disengaging himself by a violent jerk from his victim's clutch, made off like an arrow across country to the frontier. The shrieks of the mutilated man were answered by universal uproar. Some followed on foot, others ran to their bronchos, but the great majority maintained an attitude of philosophical indifference. It was no business of theirs, except so far as it might remind them to visit the barber.

I went on to San Francisco. The city is famous in history for the earthquake of 1906; and for having starved Stevenson, who has described it admirably in *The Wrecker*.

It was a glorified El Paso, a madhouse of frenzied money-making and frenzied pleasure-seeking, with none of the corners chipped off. It is beautifully situated and the air reminds one curiously of Edinburgh. At that time it possessed a real interest and glory—its Chinatown. During the week I was there, I spent most of my time in that quarter. It was the first time that I had come into contact with the Chinese spirit in bulk; and, though these exiles were naturally the least attractive specimens of the race, I realized instantly their spiritual superiority to the Anglo-Saxon, and my own deep-seated affinity to their point of view. The Chinaman is not obsessed by the delusion that the profits and pleasures of life are really valuable. He gets all the more out of them because he knows their worthlessness, and is consequently immune from the disappointment which inevitably embitters those who seek to lay up treasure on earth. A man must really be a very dull brute if, attaining all his ambitions, he finds satisfaction. The Eastern, from Lao Tzu and the Buddha to Zoroaster and Ecclesiastes, feels in his very bones the futility of earthly existence. It is the first postulate of his philosophy.

California got on my nerves. Life in all its forms grew rank and gross, without a touch of subtlety. I embodied this feeling in a sonnet:

> . . . gross and great
> Her varied fruits and flowers alike create
> Glories most unimaginable . . .
> . . . yet this is sore,
> A stain; not one of these is delicate.

For some time, I had been contemplating a lyric poem in which everything in the world should be celebrated in detail. It was a crazy notion—one of those fantastic follies which is

impossible in nature—a species of literary 'squaring the circle'.
I doubt whether it was a genuine impulse. Its motive was
the vanity and vulgarity of attempting something big. It was
the American passion for tall buildings and record processions
in another form. It was probably my reaction to the spiritual
atmosphere of California. In any case, the worst happened.
I began it! The best plan will be to describe what happened
and get it over.

It was not finished till the middle of 1904.[1] Book I is in
form a gigantic Greek ode. It celebrates all the forces of nature
and the children of time. Orpheus invokes them in turn; and
they reply. Book II describes the winning of Eurydice by
Orpheus. It is entirely a monologue by him. My literary insanity
is well indicated by my proposal to insert a five-act play, *The
Argonauts*, afterwards published separately, as an incident
in his wooing! Book III describes the visit of Orpheus to Hades;
and contains the invocations of the necessary deities, with
their replies. Book IV relates the death of Orpheus. Unwieldy
as the poem is, it contains some of my best lyrics. Further,
even conceding that the entire effort was a fiasco, it must be
admitted that the task of writing it was an excellent discipline;
it taught me a great deal about technique and its very awkwardness warned me what to avoid.

On May 1st I find in my diary the following words: 'I
solemnly began anew the operations of the Great Work.' I
had mapped out for myself a definite programme which was
to combine what I had learnt from Eckenstein with the methods of the Order. For instance: I had extracted the Magical
Formula of the Ritual of Neophyte and applied it to a
Ceremony of Self-Initiation. I now simplified this and got rid
of the necessity of the physical temple by expressing it in a
series of seven mental operations.

Other practices were the 'assumption of God-forms'; by
concentrated imagination of oneself in the symbolic shape of
any God, one should be able to identify oneself with the idea
which He represents. Then there was meditation on simple
symbols with the idea of penetrating to their secret meaning.
I was also to keep up my practices of astral visions and 'rising
on the planes', in particular the special official method of
invoking Adonai-ha-Aretz.[2] I was also to continue the work
Eckenstein had taught me, on his lines. As to more magical
matters, I proposed to continue the evocation of elemental
forces to visible appearance, to make various talismans and
charge them with spiritual energy by means of meditation, and

to continue the building up of my (so-called) astral body until it was sufficiently material to be perceptible to the ordinary physical senses of people whom I should visit in this shape. There will be found in my Magical Record numerous accounts of this last experiment.

In the autumn of '98 my friend, J. L. Baker, whom I hastened to see in London on my return from the Alps, took me on my first astral journey. The details of the method are given in full in *The Equinox,* vol. I, no. II, (*Liber O*). I may here outline them thus:

Imagine an image of yourself, standing in front of you. Transfer your consciousness to it. Rise upward. Invoke the forces desired by the prescribed methods. Observe their appearance. Test their authenticity. Enter into conversation with them. Travel under their guidance to the particular part of the universe which you desire to explore. Return to earth. Cause the Body of Light to coincide spatially with the physical. Reconnect them, using the sign of Harpocrates. Resume normal consciousness. Record the experience. Test its value by the critical methods advocated in *The Equinox.*

After only a few such journeys I found myself much stronger on the wing than my tutor. He was always getting into trouble. Demoniac forms would threaten the circle. He tired easily. He often placed confidence in lying spirits. In fact, his goodwill exceeded his ability. It all came as natural to me as swimming does to a duck. I picked up all the technical tricks of the trade almost by instinct; such as enable one to detect imposition on the instant, to banish disturbing elements, to penetrate the veils and pacify the warders of the secret sanctuaries; and to assure the accuracy of the information obtained, by methods the precision of which precludes the possibility of coincidence.

I soon found it necessary to develop the Body of Light. I explored such remote, exalted and well-guarded adyta that the necessary invocations and sacraments required more energy than was at the disposal of the Body of Light which normally separates from its physical envelope. The result was that I soon built up a body so powerful that it was clearly visible to the physical vision of all but the grossest types of humanity. It also acquired an independence of my conscious will which enabled it to travel on its own initiative without my knowledge. Strange tales began to circulate, some doubtless true, others probably coloured, and, of course, not a few baseless inventions.

As a type of the first class, let me quote the following: G. H. Frater S.R.M.D.[3] had asked me to visit him in Paris. He expected me in the afternoon. My train was late; I was tired and dirty. I postponed my call till the following day. To my surprise, my host and hostess did not greet me quite as I expected. In the course of our talk they made allusions which were quite unintelligible. At last we became aware that we were talking at cross-purposes. The crash came when Soror Vestigia [4] insisted, 'But you said so yourself at tea!' I couldn't remember that I had ever been there to tea. On my one previous visit I had lunched one day and dined the next, but no more. 'At tea!' I echoed, bewildered. 'Yes, at tea!' she repeated. 'Surely you remember. It was only yesterday.' We compared times. I was then dozing in the train from Calais. It then came out that I had called quite normally, though I seemed tired and dazed. I had stayed about an hour. Nothing had led them to suspect that I was not physically present.

Of the third class, I remember chiefly that my Sister Fidelis [5] was cursed with a horrible mother, a sixth-rate singer, a first-rate snob, with dewlaps and a paunch; a match-maker, mischief-maker, maudlin and muddle-headed. The ghastly hag put it all round London and New York that I had entered her daughter's room at night in my Body of Light. I don't know whether she went beyond the vile suggestion. Even had the tale been true, which Fidelis disdainfully denied, the woman must have been as witless as she was worthless to splash her own daughter with such ditch-water.

All the same, I feel grateful. Her stupid lie put it into my head to make the experiment in question, though of course with the knowledge and approval of the girl. The result is recorded in a subsequent chapter.

When I began to develop this power consciously, I obtained considerable success. At the time of this journey I had arranged to visit a sister of the Order [6] who lived in Hong Kong; at prearranged times, so that she might be looking out for me. Several of these visits turned out well. She saw and heard me; and on comparing notes, we found that our reports of the conversation agreed. But I was not able to act on 'matter'. I used to try to knock things off the mantelpiece, but in vain. On the other hand, when I reached Hong Kong, I recognized the place perfectly and picked out her house on the hillside, though I had never seen so much as a photograph.

These numerous practices were assigned to a regular schedule. Five different periods of the day were to be devoted to one or the other.

On May 3rd I left for Honolulu on the *Nippon Maru,* arriving on the ninth. A strange destiny lay in ambush for me among the palms.

The poetical side of me is annoyed to this day when I think of it. I ought to have followed the ideal of Gauguin. It was absurd to have got so far only to fall in love with a white woman. I know now that white women introduce the idea of impurity into love in one way or another. There is something either vicious or intellectual about them. Love should be a strictly physiological matter, with just that amount of natural emotion that goes with it. But then, such simple happiness is not for me.

Anyhow, I decided to spend a month on Waikiki Beach. I had a vague idea of getting a hut and a native girl, and devoting myself to poetry of the most wholesome kind with corresponding Magick. However, at the hotel was an exquisitely beautiful American woman of Scottish origin. She was ten years older than myself and had a boy with her just entering into his teens. She was married to a lawyer in the States and had come to Hawaii to escape hay fever.

I went on with my magical and other work; in particular, I invented a practice which has proved very useful. Its object is to prevent mosquitoes from biting one. The method is: to love them. One reminds oneself that the mosquito has as much right to his dinner as a man has. It is difficult to get the exact shade of feeling and more so to feel it. One begins by lying defenceless against the enemy and sternly repressing the impulse to wave, to slap and to scratch. After a little perseverance, one finds that the bites no longer become inflamed; and this preliminary success is soon followed by complete protection. They will not bite one at all.

But my horizon gradually filled with romantic love and other occupations faded little by little. The woman was herself worthless from the point of view of the poet. Only very exceptional characters are capable of producing the positive effect; but it is just such women as Alice who inspire masterpieces, for they do not interfere with one's work. Passionately as I was in love, and crazily as I was behaving in consequence, I was still able to make daily notes of the progress of the affair with the detached cynicism of a third party. I took her with me to Japan,* but there was not enough in her character to count 'the world well lost for love'. Exactly fifty days after I had met her she beat it back to her 'provider'; and I understood immediately why my subconsciousness had insisted on my scribbling the details of our liaison in my diary.

The departure of Alice inspired me to write the story of our love in a sonnet sequence.[7] Each day was to immortalize its events in poetry. This again was one of my characteristically crude ideas, yet the result was surprisingly good—much better, perhaps, than I ever thought, or think now. No less a critic than Marcel Schwob called it 'a little masterpiece'. And many other people of taste and judgment have professed themselves in love with it. Possibly the simplicity of its realism, its sincere and shame-free expression of every facet of my mind, constitute real merit. It is certainly true that most people find much of my work hard to read. The intensity of my passion, the profundity of my introspection, and my addiction to obscure allusions, demand of the reader serious study, that he may grasp my meaning; and subsequent re-reading after my thought has been assimilated; until, no intellectual obstacle interrupting, he may be carried away by the current of my music and swept by it into the ocean of ecstasy which I myself reached when I wrote the poem. I am aware that few modern readers are capable of settling down deliberately to decipher me. And those who are may for that very reason be incapable of the orgiastic frenzy. Scholarship and passion rarely go together. But my muse is the daughter of Hermes and the mistress of Dionysus.

I saw comparatively little of Japan. I did not understand the people at all and therefore did not like them very much. Their aristocracy was somehow at odds with mine. I resented their racial arrogance. I compared them unfavourably with the Chinese. Like the English, they possess the insular qualities and defects. They are not Asiatic, exactly as we are not European.

My most interesting impression was Kamakura. The Daibutsu, colossal amid his gardens of iris, with no canopy but the sky, does really produce a sense of his universality; it does remind one of the grandeur and solidity of his teaching; of the reasonableness of his methods of attainment, the impersonal

---

* On the *America Maru*. There were many ladies on board: the wife of a railway magnate, the consul's daughter, and so on. In reality, they were all whores destined for various brothels in Japan or Shanghai, where American ladies fetch absurd prices.

peace which is their reward; and of the boundless scope of his philosophy, independent as it is of all arbitrary assumptions, parochial points of view, sordid appeals and soul-stupefying superstitions.

Already there had arisen in me the aspiration to attain to states whose very possibility I did not suspect; already I was aware, in the abyss of my heart, secret and silent, that I was Alastor, the wanderer in the wilderness, the Spirit of Solitude. For Kamakura, calmly certain of its soul-searching accents, called to me to abide in the security of its shadow, there to toil even as the Buddha had done, that I might come to the perfect Illumination, and thereby being made free from all the fetters of falsehood, bring to mankind the Word of Wisdom and magic that hath might to enlighten their eyes, to heal their hearts, and to bring them to a stage of spiritual evolution such that their poets could no longer lament, as I:

> Nothing is stranger to men
> Than silence, and wisdom, and kindness.

I inquired as to the possibility of settling down in one of the neighbouring monasteries; but somehow my instinct opposed my intention. The Inmost knew that my destiny lay elsewhere. The Lords of Initiation cared nothing for my poetic fancies and my romantic ideals. They had ordained that I should pass through every kind of hardship at the hands of nature, suffer all sorrow and shame that life can inflict. Their messenger must be tested by every ordeal—not by those that he himself might choose. The boy who, asked to discuss some point of doctrine in the Epistles, replied, 'Far be it from me to presume to parley with St Paul: let me rather give a list of the kings of Israel and Judah!' (the only thing he knew), probably became a Cabinet minister; but similar adroitness does not avail the aspirant to adeptship. The Masters test every link in turn, infallibly and inexorably; it is up to you to temper your steel to stand the strain; for one flaw means failure and you have to forge it all afresh in the fires of fate, retrieve in a new incarnation the lost opportunity of the old.

I turned then sadly from Daibutsu, as I had turned from love, ambition and ease, my spirit silently acquiescing in the arcane arbitrament of the mysterious daimon who drove me darkly onward; how I knew not, whither I knew not, but only this, that he was irresistible as inscrutable, yet no less trustworthy than titanic.

Alas! The failure of Alice to reach the summit of love! Thence are the valleys of virtue, the rivers of respectability and the sheepfolds of society seen dim and dull in the distance, bestially beneath our sparkling snows, our shoreless sky, our sacred sun and sentinel stars.

Alice had broken my boy's heart; she had taught me what women were worth. For her I had surrendered my single-minded devotion to my spiritual Quest; I had sold my soul to the devil for sixpence, and the coin was counterfeit.

True, one of me knew all along the augury of the adventure; but then, all the worse! For if Alice had been a real danger, might not I have damned myself for her, as many a knight for Venus of the Hollow Hill, as many a saint for Lilith, Lady of the Lake of Fire? Yet no: the answer came, august and austere, from mine Angel, that I had passed the Ordeal. I had proved that no passion, however pure and powerful, could enslave me. The caresses of no Calypso could chain me in her courts, the cup of no Circe corrupt my chastity, the song of no Siren seduce me to suicide, the wiles of no Vivien ensnare my simplicity and bind me in the hollow oak of Broceliande.

I had intoxicated myself utterly with Alice; I had invested her with all the insignia that my imagination could invent. Yet, loving her with all my heart and soul, she had not seduced me from my service. I knew—and They who put her on my Path knew also—that I was immune. I might dally with Delilah as much as I liked and never risk the scissors. Love, who binds other Samsons, blinds them and sets them to serve the Philistines, to be their scorn and sport, would be to me my Light and lead me in the way of liberty. The secret of my strength was this, that love would always stand a shining symbol of my truth, that I loved spiritually the soul of mankind. Therefore each woman, be she chaste or wanton, faithful or false, inspiring me to scale the summits of song or whispering me to wallow in the swamps of sin, would be to me no more than a symbol in whose particular virtue my love could find the bread and wine of its universal eucharist.

Time has confirmed this claim: I have loved many women and been loved. But I have never wavered from my Work; and always a moment has come when the woman had to choose between comradeship and catastrophe. For in truth, there was no Aleister Crowley to love; there was only a Word for the utterance of which a human form had been fashioned. So the foolish virgins, finding that love and vanity could not live together, gave up a man for a mirror; but the wise, knowing that man is mortal, gave up the world for the Work and thereby cheated satiety, disillusionment and death.

Yet, so fearful was I at this time that I had failed and shown myself unfit to accomplish the terrific Tasks, to undertake which must be, as I was warned by some secret sense, the only honour I could accept from the High Gods, that I continued my journey to Ceylon in a mood not only contrite but confused. The calm soft loveliness of the Inland Sea brought no peace to my spirit; indeed, it made scarcely any impression upon my aesthetic sense. The sordid scramble of the foreign settlement of Shanghai stirred my scorn without rousing me from my stupefaction. In spite of the subtle passion to assimilate China which had taken possession of me in San Francisco, I could not so much as indulge in a saunter through the native city. I wanted to reach Hong Kong and tell my troubles to my Sister Fidelis. She would understand, judge, encourage and advise, none better. In the days of the G∴ D∴ debacle, her purity, her fearlessness, her loyalty, her scorn of all dishonourable device and deed, her single-heartedness, her eager and ecstatic aspiration: these had made sweet those struggles against the stupid, selfish sectaries with their petty pique, their treacherous trickeries, their slanders and squabbles.

Ah me! the Gods were at their grim game; they had another dagger ready to slip between my ribs. Fidelis was now a married woman. She was still playing at Magick, as another might play at bridge. But her true life was dresses, dinners and dances; and her thoughts were taken up by her husband and her lover. (In hot countries, white men being relaxed by the climate, European women, over-stimulated for the same reason, almost inevitably practise polyandry.)

And she had won the first prize at a fancy dress ball by appearing in her adept's robes and regalia!

No hope here, then! Nay, nor elsewhere! I saw clearly enough that the Gods meant me to work out my own puzzles without human help. I must stand alone. Well and good, so be it! I had the sense to accept the Ordeal as a compliment. The umbilical cord was cut: I was an independent being, with his own way to make in the world.

On the boat from Yokohama to Shanghai were two American spinsters of the faded variety, with parchment skin due to dryness of climate and devotion to virtue and cocktails. Hearing that I was interested in literature, hope revived. They told me their favourite poet was Rossetti. I was tactless enough to ask which of his poems they had read and preferred, but it did not run to that. It was sufficiently daring to have heard of Rossetti. Only absolute shamelessness would read him. Somewhat abashed, they informed me that a colleague was travelling on this boat, no less than Thomas Hardy. Naturally I jumped and begged an introduction.

Thomas Hardy was a tall, dignified, venerable figure, with a patriarchal beard and manner equally courteous and authoritative. I had not known he was a clergyman—as his costume assured me. After a little conversation, I began to surmise dimly that there was something wrong, and might have said something tactless if he had not volunteered an account of his literary career and been quite unaware of the existence of the Mayor of Casterbridge. He was the *great* Thomas Hardy, the only and original bird, the chaplain to the forces at Hong Kong and author of *How to be happy though married*.[8] I don't know how I kept my face straight.

As a matter of fact, he was perfectly human and even contributed a quite valuable item of information as to the psychology of publishers. He had approached one of these ineffable imbeciles * with his book and been told that while the text was all that could be desired, it was quite impossible to publish a book with that title. The reverend gentleman had the good sense to reply, 'You blasted jackass—God damn your soul to Hell! (or words to that effect). Do anything you like with the book, but leave the title alone!' He cowed them and they complied, with the result that the book sold by hundreds of thousands.

---

* 'Present Company Always Excepted'. (WE ARE NOT SO SURE). [The allusion is to Crowley's friends, the directors of the Mandrake Press; see Introduction.]

27

I sailed for Ceylon, chiefly because I had said I would go, certainly not in the hope of assistance from Allan. Perhaps because I had found my feet, he was, as will appear, allowed to guide them, in what seemed at first sight a new Path. I had got to learn that all roads lead to Rome. It is proper, more, it is prudent, more yet, it is educative, for the aspirant to pursue all possible Ways to Wisdom. Thus he broadens the base of his Pyramid, thus he diminishes the probability of missing the method which happens to suit him best, thus he insures against the obsession that the goat-track of his own success is the One Highway for all men, and thus he discounts the disappointment of discovering that he is not the Utter, the Unique, when it becomes plain that Magick, mysticism, and mathematics are triplets, and that the Himalayan Brotherhood [1] is to be found in Brixton.

I say little of Singapore; I say enough when I say that its curries, with their vast partitioned platter of curious condiments to lackey them, speak for themselves. They sting like serpents, stimulate like strychnine; they are subtle and sensual like Chinese courtesans, sublime and sacred, inscrutably inspiring and unintelligibly illuminating, like Cambodian carvings.

Of Penang I will observe only that its one perfect product is the 'Penang Lawyer'. But I should like to hear of any other city which can say the same!

As to Colombo, I love it and loathe it with nicely balanced enthusiasm. Its climate is chronic; its architecture is an unhappy accident; its natives are nasty, the men with long hair cooped up by a comb, smelling of fish, the women with waists bulging black between coat and skirt, greasy with coconut oil, and both chewing betel and spitting it out till their teeth ooze with red and the streets look like shambles; its English are exhausted and enervated. The Eurasians are anaemic abortions; the burghers—Dutch half-castes—stolid squareheads; the Portuguese piebalds sly sneaks, vicious, venal, vermiform villains. The Tamils are black but not comely. The riff-raff of rascality endemic in all ports is here exceptionally repulsive.

231

The high-water mark of social tone, moral elevation, manners and refinement is attained by the Japanese ladies of pleasure.

In the matter of religion, the Hindus are (as everywhere else) servile, shallow, cowardly and hypocritical; though being mostly Shaivites, adoring frankly the power of Procreation and Destruction, they are less loathsome than Vishnavites, who cringe before a fetish who promises them Preservation and (as Krishna) claims to be the Original of which Christ is a copy.

The Christians are, of course, obscene outcasts from even the traditional tolerance of their clan; they have accepted Jesus with the promise of a job, and gag conscience with assurance of atonement, or chloroform superstitious terrors by ruminating on redemption. The Buddhists are sodden with their surfeit of indigestible philosophy and feebly flaunt a fluttering formula of which the meaning is forgotten; the debauchery of devil dances, the pointless profession of Pansil (the Five Precepts of the Buddha), the ceremonial coddling of shrines as old maids coddle cats, voluble veneration and rigmarole religion: such is the threadbare tinsel which they throw over the nakedness of their idleness, immorality and imbecility.

Indians plausibly maintain that some god got all the worst devils into Ceylon, and then cut it off from the continent by the straits.

But then, how rich, how soft, how peaceful is Colombo! One feels that one needs never do anything any more. It invites one to dream deliciously of deciduous joys—and insists, with velvet hand, light and bright as a butterfly's wing, on the eyelids. The palms, the flowers, the swooning song of the surf, the dim and delicate atmosphere heavy with sensuous scents, the idle irresponsible people, purring with placid pleasure; they seem musicians in an orchestra, playing a nocturne by some oriental Chopin unconscious of disquieting realities.

But more, Colombo is the 'place where four winds meet', the crossroads of the civilized world. Westward lies Europe, the energetic stripling, who thought to bear the world on his shoulders, but could not co-ordinate his own muscles. Northward lies India, like a woman weary of bearing, a widow holding to her ancient habits without hope. Southward, Australia, topsy-turvy as our childhood's wisdom warned us, sprawls its awkward adolescence and embarrasses its elders by its unconscious absurdity. Lastly, look eastward! There lies China; there is the only civilization that has looked time in the face without a blush; an atheism with good manners. There broods the old wise man, he who has conquered life without the aid of death, who may survive these strenuous youths and even the worn barren widow mumbling meaningless memories in her toothless mouth.

In Colombo this world problem solves itself; for the Indian toils, without ambition or object, from sheer habit; the European bosses things, with self-importance and bravado; the Australian lumbers in and out, loutishly, hoping not to be seen; and China, silent and absent, conveys majestically patriarchal reproof by simply ignoring the impertinence. Slightly as I had brushed against the yellow silken robes of China in the press of jostling cultures, its virtue had so entered into me that the positive and aggressive aspects of Colombo, tumultuously troubling though they were, failed to command my full attention. As you vainly ply an opium smoker who craves his pipe with wine, with woman and with song, so the insolent insistence of the actualities of Colombo merely annoyed me; I was intensely aware of one thing only, the absence of the colossal calm and common sense of China.

Experience has taught me that imponderables are all-important; when science declares that it can concern itself only with that which can be measured, it classes itself with the child that counts on its fingers and brands Shakespeare and Shelley as charlatans. I am not ashamed of such company; let me say then that the silent stress of my contact with the fringe of Chinese civilization operated in me the cure of my accursed European anxiety about my conduct. It is at least the fact that I met Allan with absolute sang-froid. I felt no need of confession. I had no sense of shame or inferiority. I had no favour to ask. I had perfect confidence in myself. We were interested in the same Quest, that was all; it was natural that we should exchange views.

Behold then! Allan, though the pupil of a Shaivite guru, was already at heart a Buddhist; and the miracle about Buddha, from the ethnological standpoint, is that an Aryan, by dint of sheer psychological acumen, should have come so near to understanding the Chinese mind. The fundamental weakness of Buddhism is that it fails to attain the indifference of Lao-Tzu. Buddha wails for Nibbana as the sole refuge from sorrow; Lao-Tzu despises sorrow as casually as he despises happiness and is content to react equably to every possible impression.

Must I digress to excuse Allan Bennett, the noblest and the

gentlest soul that I have ever known? Surely the immanence of physical agony, the continual anguish of the cross on which he has been nailed for more than fifty years, he not complaining, he not submitting, he not demanding release, but working inexorably and inexpugnably at his appointed Task—surely the unremitting stroke of that fell fact must have avenged itself for its foiled malice by fashioning his conception of the universe in the same form as seemed omnivalent to the Buddha, who could not estimate the influence of his vain desolating years of idle luxury and the abortive atonement of his random reaction to angry asceticism.

Allan never knew joy; he disdained and distrusted pleasure from the womb. Is it strange that he should have been unable to conceive life as aught but ineluctable and fatuous evil? For myself, I saw pleasure as puerile, sorrow as senile; I was ready, when mine hour should arrive, to accept either amicably or dismiss both disdainfully.

Meanwhile, I was simply an adept—wandering round the world in the way adepts have—bent on picking up any pearls that proved their pedigrees from honest oysters and were guaranteed rejected by swine.

So, when I saw Allan, I put my question, referred to above, and got my answer.

The official record is subjoined.

D.D.C.F., Mathers, had told me a certain incident which had taken place between himself and Bennett as follows:

> He and I.A. had disagreed upon an obscure point in theology, thereby formulating the accursed Dyad, thereby enabling the Abra-Melin demons to assume material form: one in his own shape, another in that of I.A. Now, the demon that looked like I.A. had a revolver, and threatened to shoot him (D.D.C.F.), while the demon that resembled himself was equally anxious to shoot I.A. Fortunately, before the demons could fire, V.N.R. (Mrs Mathers) came into the room, thus formulating the symbol of the Blessed Trinity.
>
> Frater I.A.'s account was less of a strain upon P.'s [2] faculties of belief. They had had, he said, an argument about the God Shiva, the Destroyer, whom I.A. worshipped because, if one repeated his name often enough, Shiva would one day open his eye and destroy the universe, and whom D.D.C.F. feared and hated because He would one day open His eye and destroy D.D.C.F. I.A. closed the argument by assuming the position Padmasana and repeating the Mantra: 'Shiva, Shiva, Shiva, Shiva, Shiva, Shiva.' D.D.C.F., angrier than ever, sought the sideboard, but soon returned, only to find Frater I.A. still mut-

tering: Shiva, Shiva, Shiva, Shiva, Shiva.' Will you stop blaspheming?' cried D.D.C.F.; but the holy man only said: 'Shiva,
Shiva, Shiva, Shiva, Shiva, Shiva, Shiva, Shiva, Shiva.' 'If you
don't stop I will shoot you!' said D.D.C.F., drawing a revolver
from his pocket and levelling it at I.A.'s head; but I.A., being
concentrated, took no notice and continued to mutter: 'Shiva,
Shiva, Shiva, Shiva, Shiva, Shiva.'

Whether overawed by the majesty of the saint or interrupted
by the entry of a third person, I.A. no longer remembered, but
D.D.C.F. never pulled the trigger.

Mathers thus disposed of, to business!

What of the Great Work? Did it become absurd with
Mathers? No more than Everest ceases to attract when the
Alpine Club caps incompetence with manslaughter!

We simply dismissed from our minds the whole question of
the G∴D∴ and restated the problem on first principles.

In this situation, I had the advantage of wider reading and
more varied experience than Allan; he, that of more intensive
training, and especially of his recent initiation into Asiatic
arcana under the aegis of Shri Parananda, Solicitor-General of
Ceylon (as Aramis was a musketeer) *per interim,* and a
yogi *cap-à-pied.* I had learnt modesty from Eckenstein's engineering epithets and Mexican mountains; so I shut up—as
Doris Gomez once immortally observed, at the conclusion of a
prolonged and uninterrupted harangue, 'If you've got anything
more to say, shut up!'—and concentrated on learning the least
lemma of his lore instead of inflicting on him my own intima-
tions of immortality.

He expressed the elements of Yoga. I said, 'Your health will
improve in a climate less addicted to damp and damnability:
come to Kandy; we'll get a bungalow and get busy. Damn
Shri Parananda! Let him excel his commentary on St Matthew, where he explains the discrepancy with another Evangelist by suggesting that "Jesus rode both an ass and a mule,
one foot on each, after the manner of a circus", if you can.
You shall get ready to take the Yellow Robe while you train
me to triumph over Tanha,[3] and attain Asana, and perform
Pranayama, and practise Pratyhara, and do Dharana, and
demand Dhyana, and swat Samadhi, all same No. 1 topside
Master Patanjali, heap holy pidgin!'[4]

An appeal couched in such chastely correct yet politely passionate phraseology could not fail to bury its barb in the bull's
eye. Allan 'prayed permission to quit the presence' of the pious
Parananda), whose arrogance and meanness he equated with

his scholarship and sanctity. We sampled Kandy—which has delights (permit the pun for the advertisement!) unsuspected by 'Mary Elizabeth'. We took a furnished bungalow called 'Marlborough' (God knows why!) on the hills, by a stream, with waterfall complete, overlooking the lake, the temple and an amateur attempt at an hotel. We hired a hopeless headman, who sub-hired sleepy and sinister servants, and dismissed all these damnable details from our minds, devoting ourselves with diabolical determination and saintly simplicity to the search for a spiritual solution to the material muddle. Our sojourn, short as it was by worldly reckoning, proved to be pregnant with events of internal import. The tyrant time took his first wound in Kandy.

28

Allan's adventures in Ceylon had been varied. His first idea had been to take the Yellow Robe; that is, to become a member of the Buddhist Sangha. These men are not priests or monks, as we understand the words; it is hard for European minds to understand the conditions of their life. They have renounced the world and live as mendicants; but it may be stated roughly that the rules of their Order, which are very complex and often seem irrational or frivolous, are all devised in the interest of a single idea. Each rule meets some probable contingency. But in every case the object is to enable the bhikkhu to carry out his programme of spiritual development. There are no superstitious terrors, no propitiatory practices; the whole object is to enable a man to free himself from the fetters of desire which hamper his actions, and (incidentally) produce the phantasms which we call phenomena. In Buddhism, the universe is conceived as an illusion, created by ignorant cravings. It is, in fact, a dream as defined by Freud's hypothesis.

Allan was already at heart a Buddhist. The more he studied the Tripitika, 'the three baskets of the law'—waste paper baskets I used to call them—the more he was attracted, but he was fearfully disappointed by the degeneracy of the Singalese bhikkhus. With rare exceptions, they were ignorant, idle, immoral and dishonest. At Anuradhapura, the sacred ruined city, their conduct is so openly scandalous as to have given rise to a proverb: 'A bhikkhu is made, not born—except at Anuradhapura.' Allan had been offered the post of treasurer to a famous monastery outside Colombo, for the avowed reason that they could not trust any one of themselves. Considering that a bhikkhu is not allowed to touch money at all, this was rather the limit.

The Solicitor-General of Ceylon, the Hon. P. Ramanathan, engaged Allan as private tutor to his younger sons. This gentleman was a man of charming personality, wide culture and profound religious knowledge. He was eminent as a yogi of the Shaivite sect of Hindus (he was a Tamil of high caste) and had written commentaries on the gospels of Matthew and John, interpreting the sayings of Christ as instructions in Yoga. It is indeed a fact that one of the characters who have been pieced together to compose the figure of 'Jesus' was a yogi. His injunctions to abandon family ties, to make no provision for the future, and so on, are typical.

From this man, Allan learnt a great deal of the theory and practice of Yoga. When he was about eighteen, Allan had accidentally stumbled into the trance called Shivadarshana, in which the universe, having been perceived in its totality as a single phenomenon, independent of space and time, is then annihilated. This experience had determined the whole course of his life. His one object was to get back into that state. Shri Parananda showed him a rational practical method of achieving this. Yet Allan was not wholly in sympathy with his teacher, who, despite his great spiritual experience, had not succeeded in snapping the shackles of dogma, and whose practice seemed in some respects at variance with his principles. Allan was almost puritanically strict. He had been offered a position as manager of a coconut plantation, but refused it on learning that his duties would involve giving orders for the destruction of vermin. He had not sufficient breadth of view to see that any kind of life implies acquiescence in, and therefore responsibility for, murder; by eating rice one becomes the accomplice of the agriculturist in destroying life.

His health was vastly improved. In the Red Sea his asthma completely disappeared and he had thrown overboard his entire apparatus of drugs. But the enervating climate of Colombo sapped his energies. He had little hesitation in accepting my proposal to go and live at Kandy and devote ourselves to Yoga.

At 'Marlborough' we found the conditions for work very favourable. The first step was to get rid of all other preoccupations. I revised *Tannhäuser,* wrote an introduction, typed it all out and sent it to the press. I put aside *Orpheus* and left aside *Alice, An Adultery* to ripen. I did not think much of it; and would not publish it until time had ratified it.

One of my principal inhibitions at this period was due to the apparent antinomy between the normal satisfaction of bodily appetites and the obvious conditions of success. I did not solve this completely until my attainment of the Grade of Master of the Temple in 1909, when at last I realized that every thought, word and act might be pressed into the service of the soul: more, that it must be if the soul were ever to be free. I 'mixed up the planes' for many years to some extent, though never as badly as most mystics do.

During this retirement I was fortunate in being under the constant vigilant supervision of Allan Bennett, whose experience enabled him to detect the first onset of disturbing ideas. For instance, the revising and typing of *Tannhäuser* were quite sufficient to distract my mind from meditation, and would even upset me in such apparently disconnected matters as Pranayama.[1] It is easy to understand that a heavy meal will interfere with one's ability to control one's respiration; but one is inclined to laugh at the Hindu theory that it can be affected by such things as casual conversation. None the less, they are right. Apart from one's normal reactions, these practices make one supersensitive. I was not confining myself to any rigid diet; and I remember that at a certain period the idea of food became utterly revolting. It is doubtless a question of nervous hyperaesthesia; as is well known, over-indulgence in alcohol and certain other drugs tends to destroy the appetite. Inexperienced practitioners, insufficiently grounded in physiology and philosophy, may perhaps be excused (though of course reproved) for misunderstanding the import of the phenomena. One is inclined to say, 'Now that I am becoming holy, I find that I dislike the idea of eating: Argal, eating is unholy; and it will help me to become still holier if I resolutely suppress the squeals of appetite.' Such, I believe, is the basis of much of the fantastic morality which has muddled mystical teaching throughout history. I do not think that straightforward a priori considerations would have carried unquestioning conviction in the absence of apparent confirmation of their hypotheses.

This 'confusion of the planes' is in my opinion the chief cause of failure to attain. It is constantly cropping up in all sorts of connections. The aspirant must be armed with the Magical Sword, dividing asunder the joints of the marrow of every observation that he makes. A single unanalysed idea is liable to obsess him and send him astray: 'It may be for years and it may be for ever.' He must never weary of assigning its exact limitations to every phenomenon. History, by the way, is full of examples of this error in major matters. Consider only how the idea that epidemics, the failure of the crops and military misfortune were due to the wrath of God, prevented the development of science, agriculture and the art of war. Last spring, 1922, there was a drought in Sicily. The priests made a mighty puja and prayed for rain. The rain came and did more harm than the drought; then the drought took hold again and lasted all the summer, either in spite of the intercessions of Cybele, or whatever they call her nowadays, or because she was not to be propitiated by the adulterated sacrifices with which her modern ministers pretend that they can cozen her.

I attribute my own success in mysticism and Magick, and the much greater success that I have been able to secure for my successors, almost entirely to my scientific training. It enabled me to determine the actual physiological and psychological conditions of attainment. My experience as a teacher enables me to simplify more and more as each fresh case comes under my notice. I can put my finger more quickly and surely on the spot with every waxing moon. I achieved in eleven years what hardly anyone before had done in forty, and it cannot be explained by individual genius, for I have been able to take men with hardly a scrap of talent and teach them what took me eleven years in seven or eight for the firstcomers, in five or six for their successors, and so on till, at the present moment, I feel able to promise any man or woman of average ability who has the germ of genuine aspiration, the essence of attainment within eight sessions. Of course it depends on each postulant to determine the details. Some departments of occult science lie outside the scope of particular people; each one must fill in for himself his personal programme. But the supreme emancipation is the same in essence for all, and for the first time in history it has been possible to present this free from confusion, so that people can concentrate from the very beginning of their training on the one thing that matters.

Our life was delightfully simple. Allan taught me the principles of Yoga; fundamentally, there is only one. The problem is how to stop thinking; for the theory is that the mind is a mechanism for dealing symbolically with impressions; its construction is such that one is tempted to take these symbols for reality. Conscious thought, therefore, is fundamentally false and prevents one from perceiving reality. The numerous practices of Yoga are simply dodges to help one to acquire the knack of slowing down the current of thought and ultimately stopping it altogether. This fact has not been realized by the yogis themselves.[2] Religious doctrines and sentimental or ethical considerations have obscured the truth. I believe I am entitled to the credit of being the first man to understand the true bearings of the question.

I was led to this discovery chiefly through studying comparative mysticism. For instance; a Catholic repeats Ave Maria rapidly and continuously; the rhythm inhibits the intellectual process. The result is an ecstatic vision of Mary. The Hindu repeats Aum Hari Aum in the same way and gets a vision of Vishnu. But I noticed that the characteristics of both visions were identical save for the sectarian terminology in which the memory recorded them. I argued that process and result were identical. It was a physiological phenomenon and the apparent divergence was due to the inability of the mind to express the event except by using the language of worship which was familiar.

Extended study and repeated experiment have confirmed this conviction. I have thus been able to simplify the process of spiritual development by eliminating all dogmatic accretions. To get into a trance is of the same order of phenomena as to get drunk. It does not depend on creed. Virtue is only necessary in so far as it favours success; just as certain diets, neither right nor wrong in themselves, are indicated for the athlete or the diabetic. I am proud of having made it possible for my pupils to achieve in months what previously required as many years. Also, of having saved the successful from the devastating delusion that the intellectual image of their experience is an universal truth.

This error has wrought more mischief in the past than any other. Mohammed's conviction that his visions were of imperative importance to 'salvation' made him a fanatic. Almost all religious tyranny springs from intellectual narrowness. The spiritual energy derived from the high trances makes the seer a formidable force; and unless he be aware that his interpretation is due only to the exaggeration of his own tendencies of thought, he will seek to impose it on others, and so delude his disciples, pervert their minds and prevent their development. He can do good only in one way, that is, by publishing the methods by which we attained illumination: in other words, by adding his experience to the sum of scientific knowledge. I have myself striven strenuously to do this, always endeavouring to make it clear that my results are of value only to myself, and that even my methods may need modification in every case, just as each poet, golfer and barrister must acquire a style peculiar to his idiosyncrasies.

Yoga, properly understood, is thus a simple scientific system of attaining a definite psychological state. Consider its Eight

Branches! Yama and Niyama, 'Control' and 'Super-control', give rules for preventing the mind from being disturbed by moral emotions and passions, such as anger, fear, greed, lust and the like.

Asana, 'position', is the art of sitting perfectly still, so that the body can no longer send messages to the mind. Pranayama, 'control of breath force', consists in learning to breathe as slowly, deeply and regularly as possible. The slightest mental irritation or excitement always makes one breathe quickly and unevenly; thus one is able to detect any disturbance of calm by observing this system. Also, by forcibly controlling the breath one can banish such ideas. Also, one reduces to a minimum the consciousness that one is breathing.

One may remark at this point that such precaution seems absurd; but until one begins to try to keep the mind from wandering, one has no conception of the way in which the minutest modifications of thought, impressions which are normally transitory or unperceived, form the starting point for Odysseys of distraction. It may be several minutes before one wakes up to the fact that one's wits have gone wool-gathering.

Pratyahara is introspection. One obtains the power of analysing an apparently simple thought or impression into its elements. One can, for example, teach oneself to feel separately the numberless impressions connected with the act of crooking one's fingers. This is a revelation in itself; so simple a muscular movement is found to contain an epic of deliciously exciting ingredients. The idea is, of course, not to enjoy such pleasures, subtle and exquisite as they are; but by analysing thoughts and impressions to detect their prodromal symptoms and nip them in the bud. Also, to understand and estimate them by detailed examination. One important result of this is to appreciate the unimportance and equivalence of all thoughts, very much as modern chemistry has put an end to the medieval nonsense about the sacredness of some compounds and the wickedness of others. Another is to give one a clear and comprehensive view of the elements of the universe as a whole.

Dharana, concentration, is now easier to practise. One has learnt what interruptions to expect and how to prevent them. We, therefore, make a definite attack on the multiplicity of thoughts by fixing the mind on one. In my *Book Four,* Part I, I have copied from my diary at this period an attempt at classification of invading ideas. I am very proud of this apparently simple observation and it will aid the reader to understand my work in Kandy if I insert it.

Breaks are classed as follows:

Firstly, physical sensations. These should have been overcome by Asana.

Secondly, breaks that seem to be dictated by events immediately preceding the meditation. Their activity becomes tremendous. Only by this practice does one understand how much is really observed by the senses without the mind becoming conscious of it.

Thirdly, there is a class of breaks partaking of the nature of reverie or 'daydreams'. These are very insidious—one may go on for a long time without realizing that one has wandered at all.

Fourthly, we get a very high class of break, which is a sort of aberration of the control itself. You think, 'How well I am doing it!' or perhaps that it would be rather a good idea if you were on a desert island, or if you were in a sound-proof house, or if you were sitting by a waterfall. But these are only trifling variations from the vigilance itself.

A fifth class of breaks seems to have no discoverable source in the mind. Such may even take the form of actual hallucination, usually auditory. Of course, such hallucinations are infrequent and are recognized for what they are; otherwise the student had better see his doctor. The usual kind consists of odd sentences or fragments of sentences, which are heard quite distinctly in a recognizable human voice, not the student's own voice or that of any one he knows. A similar phenomenon is observed by wireless operators, who call such messages 'atmospherics'.

There is *a further kind of break, which is the desired result itself.* It must be dealt with later in detail.

Dhyana is the name of the first trance. By trance I mean a state of consciousness definitely distinct from the normal. Its characteristic is that whereas in normal consciousness two things are always present—the percipient and the perceived—in Dhyana these two have become one. At first this union usually takes place with explosive violence. There are many other characteristics; in particular, time and space are abolished. This, however, occurs with almost equal completeness in certain states of normal abstract thought.

The attainment of this trance is likely to upset the whole moral balance of the student. He often attributes an exaggerated importance to the imperfect ideas which represent his memory of what happened. He cannot possibly remember the thing itself, because his mind lacks the machinery of translating it into normal thought. These ideas are naturally his pet delusions. They seem to him to have become armed with supreme spiritual sanction, so he may become a fanatic or a megalomaniac. In my system the pupil is taught to analyse all ideas and abolish them by philosophical scepticism before he is allowed to undertake the practices which lead to Dhyana.

Samadhi, 'Union with the Lord', is the general term for the final trance, or rather, series of trances. It differs from Dhyana in this way: Dhyana is partial, Samadhi is universal. In the first Samadhi, the universe is perceived as a unity. In the second that unity is annihilated. There are, however, many other Samadhis, and in any case the quality of the trance will depend upon the extent of the universe which enters into it. One must really be a profound philosopher with a definite intellectual conception of the universe as an organic whole, based on the co-ordination of immense knowledge, before one can expect really satisfactory results. The Samadhi of an ignorant and shallow thinker who has failed to co-ordinate his conceptions of the cosmos will not be worth very much.

29

The general idea of Eastern religions is that any manifestation of being is necessarily imperfect, since it is not the sum of all truth. (For, if it were, it would not be distinguishable from any other manifestation.) Hence, its nature is evil and its effect on the mind to create sorrow. Their idea is to destroy all thought as being false and painful. Their idea is liberation from the illusion of existence. The effect of Samadhi is firstly to produce the bliss which comes from the relief from pain. Later, this bliss disappears and one attains perfect indifference.

But we need not go so far into their philosophy or accept it. Thanks partly to William James's *Varieties of Religious Experience*, I got the idea of employing the methods of Yoga to produce genius at will. James points out that various religious teachers attained their power to influence mankind in what is essentially the same way; that is, by getting into Samadhi. The trance gives supreme spiritual energy and absolute self-confidence; it removes the normal inhibitions to action. I propose then that any man should use this power to develop his faculties and inspire his ambitions by directing the effects of the trance into the channel of his career. This idea at once connects mysticism with Magick; for one of the principal operations of Magick is to invoke the God appropriate to the thing you want, identify yourself with Him and flood your work with His immaculate impulse. This is, in fact, to make Samadhi with that God. The two processes are essentially identical; the apparent difference arises merely from the distinction between the European and Asiatic conceptions of the cosmos. Most European religion, including orthodox Judaism, is anthropomorphic, an expansion of the moral ideas connected with the members of a family. Asiatic religions,* even when superficially theistic, always imply an impersonal universe. One idealizes human forces; the other, the forces of nature.

The diary describing my practices had been printed in *The Equinox*, vol. I, no. IV. It is very fortunate that it should have been kept in such detail, for it is matter for surprise that such

---

* Including the oldest Greek religion in its best aspects.

progress should have been made in so short a time. But I started with several great advantages: youth, indomitable determination to devote every energy to the work, a technical training under Eckenstein, and the constant presence of one to whom I could immediately submit any issue that might arise.

It is unnecessary to describe in detail the results of these practices. Some of them, interesting and perhaps important in themselves, do not mean much to the layman. It will be well, nevertheless, to indicate some of the major phenomena.

One soon obtains an entirely new conception of one's own mind. Till one has practised, one has no idea of the actual contents. The fact is that the uninitiate is aware only of the solutions of his mental equations; he is not conscious of the rough working. Further, he does not feel the actual impression made by each individual impact upon the mind. He totally mistakes its character, which is, in reality, arbitrary and imperative. The first analysis shows it as out of relation with its predecessors and successors. Later on, one discovers the subconscious links which join the elements. This process of subdivision seems as if it might be continued indefinitely.

I will try and make matters clearer by an illustration. The normal man looking from the top of the Jungfrau sees Monta Rosa, the Matterhorn, the Dent Blanche and other high peaks, all the way to Mont Blanc, sticking up out of the morning mists. They appear to him isolated phenomena. The mists clear and he becomes aware that these peaks are the summits of a range; they are joined by a ridge rising to lesser peaks and falling to passes. But these secondary irregularities are themselves based on smaller ones, and even on a level glacier one finds that the surface is not uniform; each separate crystal of snow may be further examined and we find even in it an arrangement of elements salient and re-entrant, which is comparable to the original macroscopic view. Acquaintance with this phenomenon leads one to inquire into the ultimate nature of the atoms of thought. Each atom assumes an importance equal to that of the others. One's sense of values is completely destroyed.

There is also the problem: how is it that one's idea of a horse, for example, should be composed of a set of ideas, none of which have any apparent relation with it, exactly as the word horse itself is composed of the letters h-o-r-s-e, none of which, by itself, suggests a horse, or part of one, in any way? Similarly, a lump of sugar is not merely a mass of homogeneous crystals, but each crystal is composed of carbon, hydrogen and oxygen, elements which in themselves possess none of the characteristic qualities of sugar. One perceives that mental and physical phenomena share this irrationality.

It will be seen from the above remarks that a very superficial investigation of thought leads inevitably to the most revolutionary consequences. At this time, however, I was not sufficiently advanced to perceive the full implications of these discoveries. My record contents itself with noting the mere symptoms produced by the practices. Even before leaving Colombo, I had heard the astral bell, to which so much factitious importance has been given.[1] I had also purified what are called the Nadi.[2] My complexion became strangely clear; my voice had lost the harsh timbre natural to it; my appearance had become calm; my eyes unusually bright; and I was constantly conscious of what is called the Nada, which is a sound the character of which varies considerably, but in my case most frequently resembled the twittering of nightingales.

Pranayama produced, firstly, a peculiar kind of perspiration; secondly, an automatic rigidity of the muscles; and thirdly, the very curious phenomenon of causing the body, while still absolutely rigid, to take little hops in various directions. It seems as if one were somehow raised, possibly an inch from the ground, and deposited very gently a short distance away.

I saw a very striking case of this at Kandy. When Allan was meditating, it was my duty to bring his food very quietly (from time to time) into the room adjoining that where he was working. One day he missed two successive meals and I thought I ought to look into his room to see if all was well. I must explain that I have known only two European women and three European men who could sit in the attitude called Padmasana, which is that usually seen in seated images of the Buddha. Of these men, Allan was one. He could knot his legs so well that, putting his hands on the ground, he could swing his body to and fro in the air between them. When I looked into his room I found him, not seated on his meditation mat, which was in the centre of the room at the end farthest from the window, but in a distant corner ten or twelve feet off, still in his knotted position, resting on his head and right shoulder, exactly like an image overturned. I set him right way up and he came out of his trance. He was quite unconscious that anything unusual has happened. But he had evidently been thrown there by the mysterious forces generated by Pranayama.

There is no doubt whatever about this phenomenon; it is quite common. But the yogis claim that the lateral motion is due to lack of balance and that if one were in perfect equilibrium one would rise directly in the air. I have never seen any case of levitation and hesitate to say that it has happened to me, though I have actually been seen by others on several occasions apparently poised in the air. For the first three phenomena I have found no difficulty in devising quite simple physiological explanations. But I can form no theory as to how the practice could counteract the force of gravitation, and I am unregenerate enough to allow this to make me sceptical about the occurrence of levitation. Yet, after all, the stars are suspended in space. There is no a priori reason why the forces which prevent them rushing together should not come into operation in respect of the earth and the body.

Again, you can prevent things from biting you by certain breathing exercises. Hold the breath in such a way that the body becomes spasmodically rigid, and insects cannot pierce the skin. Near my bungalow at Kandy was a waterfall with a pool. Allan Bennett used to feed the leeches every morning. At any moment he could stop the leech, though already fastened to his wrist, by this breathing trick. We would put our hands together into the water; his would come out free, mine with a dozen leeches on it. At such moments I would bitterly remark that a coyote will not eat a dead Mexican; but it failed to annoy him.

On the shores of the lake stands a charmingly situated hotel. We used occasionally to go down there for a meal. It is some distance by road, so I used to take the short cut through the jungle. One day I had run down the hill at the top of my speed in my mountain boots, followed by a breathless servant. He arrived at the hotel ten minutes later with a dead cobra, four feet eight inches in length. I had come down with my heel right on his neck and never noticed it!

Asana was for a long time extremely painful. It sometimes cost me five minutes' acute agony to straighten my limbs at the end of the practice. But success came at last. Quite suddenly I lost consciousness of my body. The effect was that of relief from long-continued suffering. Until that moment I had thought of my Asana as the one really painful position. This idea was reversed; it became the only position in which I was free from bodily discomfort. To this day, though shamefully out of practice, I am able to obtain the benefit of a long rest by assuming the position for a few minutes.

The phenomena of concentration are very varied and curious. For instance, the suppression of one's normal thoughts leads to their being replaced, not only by their elements, as explained above, but by long forgotten memories of childhood. There are also what I have called 'atmospherics'. For instance, a voice is suddenly heard, 'And if you're passing, won't you?' or 'And not take the first step on virtue's giddy road.' One of the entries on September 6th is worth quoting verbatim:

> 10.45–10.55   Dharana on tip of nose. I obtained a clear
> P.M.   P.M.   understanding of the unreality of that nose. This persists. An hour later whilst breathing on my arm as I was asleep, I said to myself, 'What is this hot breath from?' I was forced to *think* before I could answer 'my nose'. Then I pinched myself and remembered at once; but again breathing, the same thing happened again. Therefore the 'Dharanization' of my nose dividualizes me and my nose, affects my nose, disproves my nose, abolishes, annihilates and expunges my nose.

I was very alarmed one day to find that I had completely lost the object of concentration. I could not think what I wished to find or where to find it. I naturally thought something was very wrong. Here was an occasion when Allan's experience proved invaluable. Without it, I might have been frightened into giving up the practice. But he told me the result was good, showing that I was approaching the state of what is called 'neighbourhood concentration'.

Another experience was this: I found myself at one and the same moment conscious of external things in the background after the object of my concentration had vanished, and also conscious that I was *not* conscious of these things. To the normal mind this is of course sheer contradiction, but Buddhist psychology mentions this peculiar state. The higher faculties of the intelligence are not subject to the same laws as the lower.

I continually increased the number of hours which I devoted to my work. On October 2nd, to my amazement, I was successful in reaching the state of Dhyana. The experience was repeated on the following day. I quote the record verbatim:

> After some eight hours' discipline by Pranayama arose 'The Golden Dawn'.
> While meditating, suddenly I became conscious of a shoreless space of darkness and a glow of crimson athwart it. Deepening and brightening, scarred by dull bars of slate-blue cloud, arose the Dawn of Dawns. In splendour not of earth and its mean

sun, blood-red, rayless, adamant, it rose, it rose! Carried out of myself, I asked not 'Who is the witness?' absorbed utterly in contemplation of so stupendous and so marvellous a fact. For there was no doubt, no change, no wavering; infinitely more real than aught 'physical' is the Golden Dawn of this Eternal Sun! But ere the Orb of Glory rose clear of its banks of blackness—alas my soul!—that Light Ineffable was withdrawn beneath the falling veil of darkness, and in purples and greys glorious beyond imaging, sad beyond conceiving, faded the superb Herald of the Day. But mine eyes have seen it! And this, then, is Dhyana! With it, yet all but unremarked, came a melody as of the sweet-souled Vina.

Next day:

Again, by the Grace Ineffable of Bhavani [3] to the meanest of Her devotees, arose the Splendour of the Inner Sun. As bidden by my guru, I saluted the Dawn with Pranava.[4] This, as I foresaw, retained the Dhyanic consciousness. The Disk grew golden; rose clear of all its clouds, flinging great fleecy cumuli of rose and gold, fiery with light, into the aethyr of space. Hollow it seemed and rayless as the Sun in Sagittarius, yet incomparably brighter: but rising clear of cloud, it began to revolve, to coruscate, to throw off streamers of jetted fire! (This from a hill-top I beheld, dark as of a dying world. Covered with black decayed wet peaty wood, a few pines stood stricken, unutterably alone.) (Note. This is a mere thought form induced by misunderstanding the instruction of Mâitrânanda Swami as to observing the phenomenon.) But behind the glory of its coruscations seemed to shape an idea, less solid than a shadow! an Idea of some Human-seeming Form! Now grew doubt and thought in P's miserable mind; and the one Wave grew many waves and all was lost! Alas! Alas! for P! And Glory Eternal unto Her, She the twin-Breasted that hath encroached even upon the other half of the Destroyer! 'OM Namo Bhâvaniya OM.'

The result of this attainment was what I should least have expected. I was not encouraged to proceed; it seemed as if I had used up the accumulated energy of years. I found it impossible to force myself to continue. It was nearly two years before I resumed any regular practice.

The immediate current being thus exhausted, we decided to go on a pilgrimage to the ruined sacred cities of Buddhism. Allan had become more and more convinced that he ought to take the Yellow Robe. The phenomena of Dhyana and Samadhi had ceased to exercise their first fascination. It seemed to him that they were insidious obstacles to true spiritual progress; that their occurrence, in reality, broke up the control of the mind which he was trying to establish and prevented him from reaching the ultimate truth which he sought. He had the strength of mind to resist the appeal of even these intense spiritual joys. Like physical love, they persuade their dupe to put up with the essential evil of existence.

As for myself, I had become impatient with the whole business. Dhyana had washed my brain completely out. I went on this pilgrimage in an entirely worldly frame of mind. My interests were in aesthetic, historical and ethnological matters, and in incidents of travel amid new scenes. I even took a somewhat demoniac delight in sceptical and scurrilous comment upon current events for the sheer joy of shocking Allan, and even in horrifying him by occasional excursions after big game. I may as well go back a little in time and record my general impressions of Ceylon as a man of the world, in connected sequence.

I was as full of romantic folly about the wisdom of the East, and the splendours and luxuries of Asia, as I had been about Jacobites. But already I had learnt to use my eyes; prejudices had somehow lost their power to persuade. My experience of the Order probably counted for a good deal in this. At the same time, I did not swing from one extreme to the other. 'Blessed are they that expect nothing; for they shall not be disappointed!' I was in no danger of judging the principles of Buddhism by the practices of Buddhists. I worked out the logical consequences of any philosophy without reference to the criticisms of history. The Buddhism of Ceylon is based on the canon of their scriptures. But the customs of the people have been for the most part adapted to the new religion; very much as paganism persisted unchanged, except as to terminology, when it was camouflaged by Christianity; just as the ass of Priapus became the ass of the Nativity; as Jupiter became Jehovah; Isis, Mary; and so on; as the crown of Osiris developed into the papal tiara; as the feasts of corn and wine were resumed in the Eucharist, so did the old rites of fetish and ancestor worship continue under new names. The old demonology was adapted to Buddhist theories.

The primitive instincts of people are ineradicable; their passions and fears always find approximately the same expression, despite the efforts of philosophers and religious reformers. So I was neither surprised nor shocked (as was the more ingenuous Allan) at the devil dances and similar superstitious practices which pretended to a part in the pure rational and straightforward spirituality of Buddhism. The very simplicity and savagery of these practices were pleasing. The enthusiasm was sincere; there was no hypocrisy, no humbug, no sanctimoniousness, no protestations of virtue or assumptions of superiority.

The supreme glory of Kandy is an alleged tooth of the Buddha. It is enclosed in seven concentric caskets, some of which are enormously valuable and beautiful. Gold and jewels are nothing accounted of. Some years before my visit, one of these caskets had been stolen. The King of Siam provided a new one at the cost of an incredible number of lakhs of rupees. He made a journey to Kandy with his retinue in great pomp to make the presentation in person and the priests refused to allow him to see the tooth! It was a magnificent piece of impudence—and of policy. My own Unpretentious Holiness met with better fortune. Allan and I were permitted to be present at the annual inspection by the trustees. I believe the tooth to be that of a dog or crocodile, but though I got an excellent view at close quarters, I am not anatomist enough to be positive. I am, however, quite certain that it is not a human tooth.[5]

Homage is paid to this relic every year at a ceremony called the Perahera. I was not impressed by the sanctity of the proceedings; but as a spectacle it is certainly gorgeous. The very wildness and lack of appropriateness add to its charm. The processions to which we are accustomed in Europe and America are all so cleverly thought out that the effect is merely to irritate. The Perahera is a gigantic jollification; they bring out all their elephants, dancers, monks, officials, drums, horns, torches—anything that makes a blaze or a noise, and let them all loose at once. The effect is of impromptu excitement. Poor, serious, single-minded Allan, with his whole soul set on alleviating the sufferings of humanity and helping them to reach a higher plane of existence, was saddened and disillusioned.

One incident was somewhat scandalously amusing. He was doing his best to enter into the spirit of the thing and called my attention to the 'strains of wild oriental music'. I knew better. I had read Herrick's poem about the young lady who left a glove in the royal presence, and remembered that Lady Clara de Vere de Vere has certain physiological properties in common with the elephant. Poor Allan was absolutely horrified when he realized his mistake.

The scene was wild and somewhat sinister. The darkness, the

palms, the mountainous background, the silent lake below, the impenetrable canopy of space, studded with secretive and significant stars, formed a stupendous setting for the savage noise and blaze of the ceremony. One half saw huge shadowy shapes moving mysteriously in the torchlight, and the air vibrated violently with the jubilant rage of riotous religious excitement. It communicated a sort of magnificent madness to the mind. One didn't know what it meant or if it meant anything particular. One was not hampered by knowledge; one could let oneself go. One felt a tense, tremendous impulse to do something demoniac. Yet one had no idea what. It put one's nerves on the rack. It was almost a torture to feel so intensely, and desire so deliriously, such unintelligible irritations. Hours passed in this intoxicating excitement. One can understand perfectly the popular enthusiasm. It was the release of the subconscious desires of the original animal. To a civilized mind, accordingly, the impression was charged with a certain disquietude partaking of the nature of terror without understanding why; one felt the presence of forces which appal because one feels their power, recognizes their existence in oneself. They are the things one has tried to forget and persuaded oneself that they are in fact forgotten. They are the voices of ancestral appetite. It is the roar of the mob in the ears of the educated: but as for any definite religious impression, the Perahera had nothing to say. It was no more Buddhism than the carnival at Nice is Christianity. IΩ ΠAN!

But the matter does not end there. Official science, which can always be relied upon to discover at last what everybody has always known, has just proclaimed the fact that certain states of mind possess the property of performing what used to be called miracles, and that such states may be evoked by the constant repetition of formulae and similar practices. The whole of Eastern ceremonies, from the evolutions of dancing girls to the austerities of ascetics, have all been devised with the intention of inducing the right medium for the right sort of subconsciousness to rise, move and appear.

Zodacare, eca, od zodameranu! Odo kikalé Qaa! Zodoreje, lapé Zodiredo Noco Mada, Hoathahé IAIDA![6]

We came into contact, on one occasion, with the relations between the people and the government. The British official in Ceylon is a very different person from his Indian colleague. He is not 'heaven-born' in the same consecrated and ineluctable way. He has failed to convince himself of his superiority to mere created beings; so his airs of authority do not become him. He feels himself a bit of an upstart. Ceylon is full of half-castes, Dutch, English and Portuguese, and the white man feels himself somehow compromised by their presence. They remind him of his poor relations and make him feel as the inhabitants of Dayton, Tennessee, and some others do in a monkey-house. A similar situation exists in the southern states of America, where the pure whites are outnumbered by the negroes, and where a large population of mixed blood provides the logical link. In South Africa, again, we find the same situation, and the practical result is that the white man, feeling his footing insecure, dares not tolerate the native as he can in India, where the relations between the population and the conquering invader are understood by both parties. The Singalese government is inclined to be snappish.

One evening Allan and I were meditating, as usual. The servants were absent for some reason; some marauder took the opportunity to break in and steal my cash box. I am ashamed to say that I was stupid enough to report the incident to the police. A day or two later an alleged inspector appeared, made various inquiries and went off. He took with him my pocket compass, under the impression that it was my watch! This time, of course, we could identify the thief, who had been playing this game all over the island. He was caught and put in the dock; but escaped conviction on some technicality. But I remember the incident acutely on account of the conversation I had with the magistrate, who explained that the man might be flogged for this offence. He spoke of the punishment with a shudder—it was terrible to witness; but his tones displayed intense sadistic pleasure at the idea. It was my first glimpse of the bestial instincts of the average respectable and cultured

Englishman. I had not really believed what I had read in Krafft-Ebing about perverse pleasures of this sort; I could not understand cruelty.

Is it Gorky who tells us that the universal characteristic of the Russian is to delight in the infliction of pain for its own sake, in the absence of any comparatively intelligible basis like anger and hatred? He describes how men's mouths are filled with gunpowder and exploded, how women's breasts are pierced, ropes inserted and the victim left to hang from the ceiling. These things are done exactly as English children sometimes torture animals. He says that the whole of his life has been poisoned by realizing the existence of this instinct, which seemed to him a fatal objection to any possible justification of the universe. I cannot follow him so far. I can understand that every possible combination of qualities may exist somewhere and that I have no right even to assume that my own detestation of such things proves them to be unjustifiable.

I really rather agree with 'Greenland's Icy Mountains', though I object to accepting Ceylon on the penultimate. But certainly every prospect is remarkably pleasing and, as far as I saw, every man is vile. There seems to be something in the climate of the island that stupefies the finer parts of a man if he lives there too long. The flavour of the tea seemed to me somehow symbolic. I remember one day pleading with the local shopkeeper to find me some Chinese tea. It chanced that the owner of a neighbouring plantation was in the shop. He butted in, remarking superciliously that he could put in the China flavour for me. 'Yes,' I said, 'but can you take out the Ceylon flavour?'

Before leaving Eckenstein, I had agreed to consider the question of an Himalayan expedition, to Chogo Ri, marked 'K2' on the Indian Survey, 28,250 feet, the second highest mountain in the world. I decided not to go; wishing to devote myself exclusively to spiritual progress. I wrote to this effect; but when I told Allan that I had done so, I found, to my surprise, that he thought I ought to go for Eckenstein's sake. It was the same problem as that about Abra-Melin and the Order. And I chose in the same way. I wired Eckenstein that I would go.

One of the results of this was that I began to grow a beard. Eckenstein had put me up to a lot of the points of conduct that should be observed in travelling among Mohammedans and I practised these conscientiously. For instance, I taught myself never to touch my face with my left hand. I found this practice tends to make my mind constantly vigilant. Later, I developed the idea into *Liber Jugorum*, which is one of the most important elements in the preliminary training for the A∴ A∴. But the Singalese, knowing nothing of our motives, could only conclude that sahibs with beards must be Boer prisoners. The same ridiculous mistake was made even by the whites at Rawalpindi, when the expedition arrived, though we were mixing freely with them and half our party talking English slang.

The fact is that the vast majority of people are absolutely impervious to facts. Test the average man by asking him to listen to a simple sentence which contains one word with associations to excite his prejudices, fears or passions—he will fail to understand what you have said and reply by expressing his emotional reaction to the critical word. It was long before I understood this fact of psychology. Even to this day, it surprises me that there should be minds which are unable to accept any impression equably and critically. I have heard many great orators. The effect has nearly always been to make me wonder how they have the nerve to put forward such flimsy falsehoods.

The excursion to the buried cities was an education in itself. The first impression was of the shocking callousness with which the coach horses were treated. There was not a single one along the whole route which was even moderately sound. I began to set its right value upon the first precept of Buddha: Not to take life. Ass!

At Dambulla is one of the most extraordinary works of human skill, energy and enthusiasm in the world. The temple is a cave in the rock, of vast extent but with a very small opening. How could the many statues of the Buddha which filled the cave have got there? It was the camel and the needle's eye again. But what had been done was to cut away the rock of the cave itself, leaving the statues. So gigantic a conception and so admirable an execution extort one's whole-hearted praise. Nothing so drives home the fact of modern degeneracy as this: not only are the Singalese of today utterly incapable of creative work, but they are so far fallen that they have piously smeared this superb statuary with thick coats of gamboge so lavishly that the delicacy of the modelling is entirely concealed.

The rock Sigiri is very startling. It sticks up out of the level jungle without apology. It is supposed to be unclimbable save by the artificial gallery which was built of old when a city flourished on the summit. We hung about for some days, as

I wanted to walk round the rock and try and find a way up. But the scheme was impracticable. One could not cut one's way through so many miles of thick jungle, and if one did one would have to be a monkey to be sure of getting a view.

The only incident was that I came across my first buffalo. In the course of a ramble, I had come out upon a clearing in the forest where there was a shallow lake. A bull with two cows arrived simultaneously from the other side, in quest of a drink. In those days I carried a Mauser ·303. I got within a hundred yards before he took alarm. As he raised his head I aimed and fired. The cartridge failed to explode and the bull thundered past me before I could reload. If he had been charging—good night! I took the lesson to heart and always carried a double-barrelled rifle ever after. Apart from the extra time needed to lower a single-barrelled rifle and manipulate the lever, which might well cause a fatal delay, there is more than a possibility of a cartridge jamming, which would leave one entirely unarmed.

We jogged on wearily to Anuradhapura. The discomforts of the coach were great, and the monotony of the view desolating. It was all an endless flat tangle of vegetation. It was delightful to perceive, about sunset, a number of hills in the distance. Their graceful wooded slopes enchanted the eye. And this is the wonder of this journey, for in the morning I found that these were not hills at all, but ruined dagobas, which time had fledged with forestry!

To me these cities appear incomparably greater as monuments than even those of Egypt. They are not so sympathetic spiritually; they lack the appeal of geometry and aesthetics which makes the land of Khem my spiritual fatherland. But one has to grant the gargantuan grandeur of the old Singalese civilization. Their idea, even of so pedestrian a project as a tank, was simply colossal. They thought in acres where others think in square yards. One of the pagodas has for its lowest terrace—I think it is about a mile in circumference—a ring of stone elephants little short of life size. Most of the ornamentation has perished, but the loss does not really matter. The point of the place is the prodigious piety which erected these useless enormities merely as memorials to the Master.

Frankly, I was fed up with marvels. All subjects bore me alike after a short time; they cease to stimulate. I was thoroughly pleased to find myself at last in India. The psychological change from Ceylon is very sudden, startling and complete. What is there about an island which differentiates it so absolutely from the adjoining mainland? No amount of similarity of race, customs and culture gets rid of insularity. The moment one sets foot in India, one becomes aware of the stability of its civilization.

I spent some weeks wandering through the southern provinces. I cannot forbear mentioning one charming incident. At some station or other, I was about to take the train. A white man with a long white beard came down the whole length of the train in the blazing sun to my carriage. He had seen that I was strange to the country and asked if he could be of any service. (Unless one knows the ropes, one has to put up with a lot of petty discomforts.) The man was Colonel Olcott.[1] It was the first act of kindly thoughtfulness that I had ever known a theosophist perform—and the last. For many years.

The rock temples of Madura are probably the finest in India, perhaps in the world. There seems no limit. Corridor after corridor extends its majestic sculptures, carved monoliths, with august austerity. They are the more impressive that the faith which created them is as vital today, as when India was at the height of its political power. My experiences of Yoga stood me in good stead. I knew, of course, that the average European would not be permitted to visit the most interesting parts of the temple, and I thought I would see what I could do to take a leaf out of Burton's book. So I disposed of my European belongings and took up my position outside a village near by, with a loincloth and a begging bowl. The villagers knew, of course, that I was an Englishman, and watched me suspiciously for some time from the edge of the jungle. But as soon as they found that I was really expert in Yoga, they lost no time in making friends. One man in particular spoke English well and was himself a great authority on Yoga. He introduced me to the writings of Sabapati Swami, whose instructions are clear and excellent, and his method eminently practical.[2] My friend introduced me to the authorities at the big temple at Madura, and I was allowed to enter some of the secret shrines, in one of which I sacrificed a goat to Bhavani.

The fact is that Buddhism had got on my nerves. I preferred the egocentric psychology of Hinduism—naturally enough, since the fundamental consciousness of the average European is sympathetic. Our very speech almost compels us to think of the universe in this way. Ethically, too, Hinduism appealed to me; it seemed positive; its injunction seemed to lead somewhere. Buddhism repelled me by its abhorrence of action, its insistence upon the idea of sorrow as inherent in all things in themselves. Hinduism at least admits the existence of joy; the only trouble is that happiness is unstable. In practice, again, Buddhism suited Allan, whose only idea of pleasure was relief from the perpetual pain which pursued him; whereas I, with the world at my feet, was out to do something definite and even to take delight in the buffetings of fortune. I enjoyed this adventure immensely; I felt myself all kinds of a fine fellow for penetrating these sinister sanctuaries.

To a young wizard waltzing round the world, some of the early impressions of the India whose philosophy and religion he has learnt to reverence so profoundly are a shade disconcerting. I could not help feeling the degradation of the woman who swept out the dak bungalow at Madura. She was a grotesque hag at thirty. I had seen nothing of the kind in Mexico, or, indeed, anywhere else before or since, till I struck the backblocks of the United States of America. But in her time she had been a woman of great wealth, for I could have put my hand and arm clean through the lobe of her ear. She must at one time have worn enormously heavy ear-rings.

Her attitude gave me a peculiar little shiver. To sweep the floor, which she did with a short-handled brush, she bent entirely from the hips, being straight above and below. It somehow gave me the impression of a broken stick. And then I was reminded of the queen's spaniel in *Zadig*. For in the dust of the floor were two tiny trails made by her sagging breasts as they swung idly out of her cotton cloth.

I had made a point from the beginning of making sure that my life as a Wanderer of the Waste should not cut me off from my family, the great men of the past. I got India-paper editions of Chaucer, Shakespeare and Browning; and, in default of India paper, the best editions of *Atalanta in Calydon*, *Poems and Ballads* (First Series), Shelley, Keats and *The Qabalah Unveiled*.[8] I caused all these to be bound in vellum, with ties. William Morris had re-introduced this type of binding in the hope of giving a mediaeval flavour to his publications. I adopted it as being the best protection for books against the elements. I carried these volumes everywhere, and even when my alleged waterproof rucksack was soaked through, my masterpieces remained intact.

Let this explain why I should have been absorbed in Browning's *Christmas Eve* and *Easter Day* at Tuticorin. I was criticizing it in the light of my experience in Dhyana, and the result was to give me the idea of answering Browning's apology for Christianity by what was essentially a parody of his title and his style. My poem was to be called 'Ascension Day and Pentecost'.

I wrote 'Ascension Day' at Madura on November 16th and 'Pentecost' the day after; but my original idea gradually expanded. I elaborated the two poems from time to time, added 'Berashith'—of which more anon—and finally 'Science and Buddhism', an essay on these subjects inspired by a comparative study of what I had learnt from Allan Bennett and the writings of Thomas Henry Huxley. These four elements made up the volume finally published under the title *The Sword of Song*.

One of the great sights of south India is the great temple of the Shivalingam.⁴ I spent a good deal of time in its courts meditating on the mystery of phallic worship. Apologists ordinarily base their defence on a denial that the lingam is worshipped as such. They claim correctly enough that it is merely the symbol of the supreme creative spiritual force of the Most High. It is perfectly true, none the less, that barren women circumambulate it in the hope of becoming fruitful. I accepted this sublimation gladly, because I had not yet been healed of the wound of Amfortas: I had not got rid of the shame of sex. My instinct told me that Blake was right in saying 'The lust of the goat is the glory of God.' But I lacked the courage to admit it. The result of my training had been to obsess me with the hideously foul idea that inflicts such misery on Western minds and curses life with civil war. Europeans cannot face the facts frankly; they cannot escape from their animal appetite, yet suffer the tortures of fear and shame even while gratifying it. As Freud has now shown, this devastating complex is not merely responsible for most of the social and domestic misery of Europe and America, but exposes the individual to neurosis. It is hardly too much to say that our lives are blasted by conscience. We resort to suppression and the germs create an abscess.

The Hindu is of course a slave to his superstitions about sin even more than most nominal Christians, for the simple reason that he is absolutely serious about the welfare of his soul. I remember coming across a tribe which did not use tobacco. I offered them some and they refused. I supposed it was forbidden by their religion, but they told me no. It was, however, not commanded by their religion; they could therefore see no object in doing it. The Hindu attitude towards sin, absurd as it is, compares favourably with ours; because, though afraid of it, they have not reached our own state of panic which makes us the prey of the most fantastic superstitions and perversions of truth. I have found it practically impossible to convince middle-class Anglo-Saxons of facts which anyone would think were bound to be known. They take refuge in angry denial. It seems to them that if they once admit the most elementary and obvious propositions, they are bound to fall headlong into a bottomless pit of bestiality. Where, in fact, they always are.

31

In course of time I arrived at Madras, which is sleepy, sticky and provincial. On one of my steamship journeys I had met a delightful man named Harry Lambe, who had invited me to come and stay with him in Calcutta. It fitted in ideally and I booked my passage by the steamer *Dupleix*. It would have been more natural to go by train; but part of my plan in wandering about the world was to put myself in unpleasant situations on purpose, provided that they were new. This small French boat offered an adventure.

A storm was raging; the *Dupleix* was some days late, and when she arrived, it was too rough for her to come into the harbour. I had to row out to her in an open boat. I had dismissed my servant and was the only passenger from shore. I note the fact as showing that I had in a sense broken with the past; the point will appear in a few paragraphs.

The voyage was atrocious; the ship stank of oil, partly from the engines, partly from the cooking and partly from the crew. The storm continued unabated. We passed close to the lightship off the mouth of the Hooghly in thick sea fog; the people on the lightship are often five weeks or more without being able to communicate with the rest of the world. But we got a pilot on board somehow and once in the river itself the weather cleared.

The Hooghly is reputed the most difficult and dangerous navigation in the world and its pilots are the best paid men afloat. Ours allowed me to spend part of the time with him on the bridge and put me up to the ropes. The sandbanks are constantly shifting; even the shores alter from day to day; the river suddenly chops off a large chunk of corner or throws up a false bank. A large staff of men is therefore constantly engaged in sounding for the channel and putting up new signposts on the banks. The chart of the river has to be revised every day. Even so, the channel is narrow and tortuous. The course of the ship reminded me of the most elaborate Continental figure-skating.

Lambe was at the wharf to meet me and drove me off to his house, a large building in a compound, as gardens surrounded by a wall are called in India. It was a colony of four men, with one of whom, Edward Thornton, I soon struck up an intimacy based on implicit sympathy in the matter of philosophical speculation.

Before I had been in the house three days, a curious incident occurred. I am always absent-minded. A current of thought flows through the back of my brain quite independent of what I am consciously doing. I might even say that the above statement is incorrect. Most of the time I am more conscious of what I am thinking than of what I am saying and doing. Now there was an animated conversation at dinner about the absurdity of the native mind; the curious ideas that they got into their heads; and I 'awoke' to hear someone say, as an illustration of this thesis, that the servants of the house were very excited by my arrival because I had penetrated into the temple at Madura and sacrificed a goat. I had said nothing to my friends about my interest in Magick and religion, and they were much astonished when I told them that their servants were right. I explained how I had cut communications at Madras and wanted to know how the servants could possibly have found out the facts.

This led to conversation about the 'native telegraph'. It is an established fact that the bazaars get accurate information of events ahead of electricity. Mouth-to-mouth communication does not explain it. For instance, the death of an officer in a frontier skirmish in some place isolated from India by long stretches of uninhabited country has been reported in Bombay before the field telegraph has transmitted the news.

But I was already sufficiently advanced in practical Magick to understand how this could be done. On one occasion I wanted to prepare a ritual which involved the use of certain words which I did not know. I travelled in my astral body to see a brother of the Order whom I knew to be in possession of the required information, eight thousand miles and more away, and obtained it at once.

My first business at Calcutta was to learn Hindustani and Balti, in order to be an efficient interpreter on the expedition to Chogo Ri. As regards the latter, I had to content myself with the grammar and failed to learn much. Fortunately, we managed without it; but it was easy to get a munshi to teach me Hindustani and I spent most of my time in acquiring that language.

The 'native telegraph' now reappeared in a different form. Somehow or other my munshi got it into his head that I was a

Magician. This was very curious, as I had done practically no Magick since landing in Ceylon and certainly had not talked about it at all. *The Sword of Song* bears witness to the completeness with which I had abandoned Magick. I had not in the least lost my faith in its efficacy: I regarded it very much as I regarded rock climbing. I could not doubt that I was the best rock climber of my generation, but I knew that my abilities in that respect would not help me to climb Chogo Ri any more than my ability at billiards would help me to understand Dostoyevsky. Similarly, my magical attainment had no bearing on my Quest. Of course I was wrong. I had simply failed to understand the possibilities of Magick. I had not realized that it was the practical side of spiritual progress. Ultimately, my Magick proved more far-reaching in importance than my mysticism, as will appear in due course.

My munshi must have possessed some secret source of information about me. His attitude towards me expressed not merely the servility of the conquered race; it added the childlike timidity of primitive people in presence of occult omnipotence. Having ingratiated himself by all the arts of the courtier, he plucked up courage to request me to kill his aunt. I am ashamed to say that I dissolved in laughter. I no longer remember how I kept my face; how I broke it to him gently that I killed strangers only on such considerations as the uninitiated could not possibly comprehend. I still laugh to remember the shamefaced shyness of his request and the pained humiliation with which he received my refusal. He had the courage (a week or so later) to ask me to soften the hearts of the examiners towards his brother, who was entered for the B.A. examination; when I refused, he asked me to prophesy the result. I told him that his brother would fail, which he did. I claim no credit for second sight; I had based my judgment on the reflection that if his brother required magical assistance in order to pass, he knew that his intellectual attainments were inadequate.

When I wasn't working I went racing. I had never been to a race course in England. I cannot force myself to pretend interest in a game of which I do not know the rules. Like all commercialized amusements, racing is essentially crooked. But in Calcutta it was less trouble to go than to stay away. I took advantage of the circumstances to test my theories. One particular horse had arrived in Calcutta with a great reputation. Everybody backed it and it lost race after race. I waited till it had become so discredited that I could get long odds against it in an important race, and then backed it to win, which it did. It was merely a question of following the psychology of the swindlers. They had pulled it till it was worth while to let it win.

I had little real pleasure in rattling the rupees in my pocket. My cynical disgust with the corrupt pettiness of humanity, far from being assuaged by the consciousness of my ability to outmanoeuvre it, saddened me. I loved mankind; I wanted everybody to be an enthusiastic aspirant to the absolute. I expected everybody to be as sensitive about honour as I was myself. My disillusionment drove me more and more to determine that the only thing worth doing was to save humanity from the horror of its own ignorant heartlessness. But I was still innocent to the point of imbecility. I had not analysed human conduct: I did not understand in the least the springs of human action. Its blind bestiality was a puzzle which appalled me, yet I could not even begin to estimate its elements.

Allan Bennett had made up his mind to take the Yellow Robe—not in Ceylon, where the sodden corruption of the Sangha sickened his sincerity, but in Burma, where the bhikkhus could at least boast fidelity to the principles of the Buddha, and whose virtuous lives vindicated their good faith. He had gone to Akyab on the western coast of Burma, and was living in a monastery called Lamma Sayadaw Kyoung. I thought I would drop in on him and pass the time of day; and proposed to combine with this act of fraternity the adventure of crossing the Arakan hills, the range which forms the watershed between the valley of the Irrawaddy and the sea. This journey, very short in measured miles, is reputed so deadly that it has only been accomplished by very few men. These left most of their party to moulder in the mountains and themselves died within a few days of completing the crossing. I have always had this peculiar passion for putting myself in poisonous perils. Its source is presumably my congenital masochism, and the *Travellers' Tales* of Paley Gardner had determined its form of expression.

Edward Thornton decided to join me on this expedition. We sailed for Rangoon on the twenty-first of January. During the whole of my stay in Calcutta I had been intermittently ill with malaria. I had been reading Deussen's exposition of Vedanta and found it utterly unsatisfactory. Yet Vedanta is the fine flower of Hinduism, the sole solution of the problems presented by the crude animism of the Vedas. 'And if these things are done in the green tree—?' I was being forced, without knowing it, towards Buddhism; my wish to see Allen again was doubtless due to this dilemma rather than to any instincts of friendship. As significant of the state of my soul, vague yet vehement, I may quote certain entries in my diary thus:

Jan. 13. Early morning walk—deep meditation. Developed a sort of inverted Manichaeism. Nature as evil and fatal force developing within itself (unwittingly) a suicidal will called Buddha or Christ.

Jan. 15. It is a fallacy that the absolute must be the all-good, etc. There is *not* an intelligence directing law—line of least resistance. Its own selfishness has not even the wit to prevent Buddha arising. We cannot call nature *evil*. 'Fatal' is the exact word. Necessity implies stupidity—this the chief attribute of nature. As to 'supreme intelligence', consider how many billion years were required to develop even so low a thing as emotion.

The Rangoon River remains one of the deepest impressions of my life. It reminded me of the Neva, though Petrograd is immensely more important. But there is the same terrifying breadth of torrent, much more rapid and turbulent than one expects from the limitless levels through which it rushes; one gets the idea of sterile, heartless passion in the midst of a wilderness, and somehow or other this seems obscenely unnatural. One instinctively associates vehemence with detailed result; and when one sees such stupendous forces running to waste, one is subconsciously reminded of the essence of human tragedy, the callousness of nature about our craving to reap the reward of our efforts. One has to be a philosopher to endure the consciousness of waste, and something more than a philosopher to admire the spendthrift splendour of the universe.

The glory of Rangoon is, of course, the Shwe Dagon pagoda. It is gilded and gigantic, and the effect is curiously annoying, for very much the same reason as the river is appalling. But it enables one to understand the soul of Asia. At the base of the dagoba is a vast circular platform, ringed with shops, mostly dedicated to commercial piety and cumbered with devotees, beggars and monsters. It is the rendezvous of the ragged, the diseased and the deformed, charity to whom is supposed to confer 'merit'. Merit means insurance against reincarnation in undesirable conditions. Among Buddhists, generally speaking, good deeds are always done with some such objects. A rich woman who is childless will plaster an existing dagoba with gold leaf, or build a new one, in the hope of becoming fruitful.

The method by which this Magick is supposed to operate is somewhat obscure. There is no question of propitiating an offended deity in canonical Buddhism; but in point of fact, it is probable that the custom is a survival of pre-Buddhistic fetishism. There are innumerable traces of the old demonology in the practical life of the people. Buddhism did not succeed in supplanting prevailing superstitions any more than did Christianity or Islam. The fact is that the instincts of ignorant people invariably find expression in some form of witchcraft. It matters little what the metaphysician or the moralist may inculcate; the animal sticks to his subconscious ideas.

On a litter in the shadow of the pagoda lay a boy of about fourteen years. He suffered from hydrocephalus. An enormous head, horrifyingly inane, surmounted a shrivelled body, too feeble even to support it. There indeed was a manifest symbol of the universe as conceived by the Buddha! Senseless suffering proves that nature has no purpose or pity. The existence of a single item of this kind in the inventory demonstrates the theorem. As I gazed on the child, I began to understand that all the syllogisms of optimism were enthymemes. Every teleology depends on the error of generalizing from a few selected phenomena. The boy impressed me more than the pagoda. One was the freak of misfortune; the other the considered climax of colossal care. Yet both were transitory and trivial toys of time. I went back to Rangoon profoundly penetrated by the insight which enabled the Buddha to attain understanding of the import of the cosmos.

Ever since leaving Ceylon I had been almost constantly down with malaria. In Rangoon the fever assumed a remittent form: I lived on quinine and iced champagne. The persistence of the disease brought me to a state in which I no longer struggled to recover my ordinary health. I lived on a low level, without desire even to die. I began to understand the psychology of Allan. My mind was abnormally clear: I was cleansed of the contamination of desire. Nothing was worth wishing for; I did not even complain of suffering. This state of mind is a useful experience. Something very similar can be induced artificially by fasting.

I recovered quite suddenly, though the cachexia continued. I was quite well, but felt extraordinarily weak. The curious thing about malaria is that one seems to lack strength to lift a finger, and yet one can do the day's work with astonishing endurance. One makes up one's mind that one can't be any worse, and one's muscles are freed from the inhibition of fatigue just

as they are if one anaesthetizes oneself with cocaine. I have
walked thirty-five miles in sweltering heat through the most
difficult jungle, carrying a heavy rifle, when I simply had not
the strength to swallow my breakfast. One learns to live on a
level of invalidism. Most Europeans accustomed to the tropics
acquire this aptitude; they go on, year after year, apathetically
carrying out their routine. They have got beyond disappointment and ambition.

I remember visiting a forest officer up country in Ceylon.
We dined with him on the eternal monotony of chicken under
various disguises and canned meats. Everything tastes alike. He
had no conversation; he tried to entertain us by turning on a
worn-out gramophone, as he had done to relieve his evenings
ever since the instrument was invented. He was an old man and
could have retired on his pension two years earlier, but he had
lost all interest in life. What was the sense of his going to England? He had no friends, no family, no future! He had become
part of the jungle. The psychology is common to all but men
of rare intelligence and energy. They cling childishly to the
skirts of civilization by drearily dressing for their dreary
dinner; but everything becomes formal and meaningless. Unable to force an answer from the sphinx of their surroundings,
they are petrified into its stony silence, which yet does not
share its sublimity because it has neither shape nor soul.

In order to cross the Arakans to Akyab, we obtained various
credentials from the authorities, especially a letter to the forest
commissioner of the district that he might provide us with
elephants. We engaged a servant, a man from Madras, whose
name was Peter. The first question one asks of a servant in
India is: his religion? Peter amused us by replying that he was
'a free man, a Roman Catholic'. Outside subscribers to missionary societies, everyone is aware what is implied by the term
'native Christians'. Anyone who is such an absolute scoundrel
as to exceed the very wide latitude of his environment, who
makes himself intolerable to his family, friends and neighbours,
cuts the painter and 'finds Jesus'. Conversion is a certificate of
incorrigible rascality. We should not have taken a Christian if
we could have found anyone else who spoke English and
Hindustani. The inconceivable pettiness of the thefts of Peter
was to me a revelation of the possibilities of human degradation. It was combined with such cowardice of conscience that
one could understand easily why the 'native Christian' invariably calls on his deathbed for the minister of his original
religion.

32

On the twenty-fifth of January we left Rangoon for Prome. Arrived at Prome, we immediately went on board the steam ferry *Amherst*. It is a five hours' journey to Thayetmyo, where we arrived in the heat of the day, after a very pleasant journey, thanks partly to the beauty of the scenery, but perhaps more to the geniality of the captain. We got three bullock carts for our transport and started the next morning, stopping at Natha for lunch after a pleasant journey of ten miles. After lunch we went off to Kyoukghyi.

The next day we resumed our journey; I walked most of the way and shot some partridges and pigeons for lunch, which we took at Leh-Joung; this is not a bungalow, but a village. We went on in the afternoon to Yegyanzin, where we had the good fortune to meet Garr, the forest commissioner of the district, and his assistant Hopwood. Unfortunately he was unable to give me any elephants, as they were all in use; but told me I ought to have no difficulty in getting coolies and probably ponies if I required them. We combined forces and had quite a nice dinner together. One does not realize how nice English-men really are until one meets them in out-of-the-way places. Sometimes not even then.

The following day we went off again and arrived at Mindon at two thirty p.m. The road had become very bad; and, in the springless bullock cart, travelling was by no means pleasant. In fact, after two or three big jolts we agreed to take turns to look out, and to give warning if a particularly frightful jolt seemed imminent. But for all our precautions, I was badly let in on one occasion. The road had become level, and appeared to be the same for the next two hundred yards, so I turned back to light a pipe. Without a word of warning the driver swung round his oxen off the road into an adjoining paddy field, at least three feet below, and we got the nastiest shaking of our lives. The last seven miles were particularly irritating, as there was little or no shade, and it was out of the question to relieve oneself by walking for more than a short distance.

On arrival at Mindon, we summoned the headman and told

him to get men for the cross-country journey to Kyaukpyu. He seemed to think it would be rather difficult and was evidently not at all pleased with his orders, but he went off to obey them, and in the meanwhile sent round the village shikari so that I might go out after buffalo the next day. I accordingly started at six forty-five next morning.

It soon began to get hot, and a double ·577 is not the kind of toy one wants to carry on a fifteen-mile tramp. As a matter of fact, I probably did nearer twenty miles than fifteen, as I was going eight hours with very little rest. We went up and down hills repeatedly, but the wild buffalo was shy, and, as a matter of fact, I did not the whole day see anything whatever shootable, except some small birds which I took home for dinner. In the afternoon we went off bathing together in a delightful pool directly under the hill on which the bungalow was situated. I took down the shot gun with the intention of killing a big paddy bird which we saw from the bank. These birds are valuable on account of the aigrette. I fired, but my shot did not seem to hurt him, and he flew off. I resigned the gun to the Burmese boy, and had just finished my bath when the impudent beast came back. I hastily signalled for the gun; and putting on a topee and a towel round my waist proceeded to stalk him across the ford. I must have presented the most ridiculous spectacle. Thornton said he had not laughed so much for years, and I daresay that the paddy bird laughed too; but I got the best laugh in the end, for after about ten minutes' infinite pains I got a close shot at him, which put an end to his career. That evening we tried to eat roast parrots, but it was a total failure. I am told, however, that parrot pie is quite a good dish; well, I don't like parrot, so there will be all the more for those who do.

The next day I was naturally feeling very tired; but in the afternoon I summoned enough energy to go for a short stroll. I was very anxious to show Thornton a beautiful view of a hillside and river, which I had come across on my way home. We set out, he being armed with a sketch book and a kukri, which he would always carry about with him, though I could never understand the reason; if I had been anticipating the day's events, I should not have troubled to inquire. At the edge of the hill weariness overtook me; I sat down, pointing to him a tiny path down the hill slope which he was to pursue. He was rather a long time returning, and I was just about to follow in search when I heard his cooee; in a couple of minutes he rejoined me. I was rather surprised to see that his kukri was covered with blood. I said, 'I knew you would fall over something one day. Where have you cut yourself?' He explained that he had not cut himself, but that an animal had tried to dispute the path with him and that he had hit it on the head, whereon the animal had rolled down the steep slopes towards the river. I could not make out from his description what kind of an animal it could possibly be, but on examining the tracks I saw them to be those of a nearly full-grown leopard. We did not retrieve the body, though it must have been mortally wounded, otherwise Thornton would hardly have escaped so easily.

The headman now returned and told us that he could not give us coolies to cross the Arakan Hills, nobody had ever been there, and it was very dangerous, and everyone who went there died, and all that sort of thing. But he could give us men to go about twenty miles, and no doubt we should be able to get more coolies there. I thought there was more than a little doubt; and, taking one thing with another, decided it would be best to give up the idea and go instead back to the Irrawaddy down the Mindon Chong; we consequently hired a boat of the dug-out type, about thirty-five feet long and just broad enough for two men to pass; over the middle of the boat was the usual awning. The next morning we started down the stream, always through the most delightful country and among charming people.

All the villages in this part of the country are strongly fortified with palisades of sharpened bamboos. The voyage down the river was exceedingly pleasant and the shooting delightful. One could sit on the stern of the boat and pot away all day at everything, from snipe to heron. Our Burmese boys and the kites had great rivalry in retrieving the game. The kites seemed to know that they would not be shot at. I had another slight attack of fever in the afternoon, but nothing to speak of. We tied up at Sakade for the night. There was no dak bungalow near and one does not sleep in a Burmese village unless necessity compels. And yet

By palm and pagoda enchaunted o'ershadowed, I lie in the
  light
Of stars that are bright beyond suns that all poets have vaunted
In the deep-breathing amorous bosom of forests of Amazon
  might,
By palm and pagoda enchaunted.

By spells that are murmured, and rays of my soul strongly
  flung, never daunted;
By gesture and tracery traced with a wand dappled white,
I summon the spirits of earth from the gloom they for ages
  have haunted.

O woman of deep red skin! Carved hair like the teak! O delight
Of my soul in the hollows of earth—how my spirit hath
  taunted . . .
Away! I am here, I am laid to the breast of the earth in the
  dusk of the night,
By palm and pagoda enchanted.

This poem was inspired by an actual experience. The effects
of my continued bouts of fever had been to make me spiritually
sensitive. The jungle spoke to me of the world which lies behind material manifestation. I perceived directly that every
phenomenon, from the ripple of the river to the fragrance of
the flowers, is the language by which the subtle souls of nature
speak to our senses. That night we were tied up under a teak
tree, and as I lay awake with my eyes fixed ecstatically on its
grace and vigour, I found myself in the embraces of the Nat
or elemental spirit of the tree. It was a woman vigorous and
intense, of passion and purity so marvellous that she abides
with me after these many years as few indeed of her human
colleagues. I passed a sleepless night in a continuous sublimity
of love.

The early hours of the morning, in winter, are bitterly cold,
and the river is covered to a height of several feet with a dense
white mist which does not disappear till well after sunrise.

I kept very quiet the next day, for repeated attacks of fever
had begun to interfere with my digestive apparatus. Just at
nightfall two deer came down to drink at the river side. It was
rather dark for a shot and the deer could hardly be distinguished from the surrounding foliage, but the men very
cleverly and silently held the boat and I let fly. The result was
better than I expected. I hit exactly where I had aimed at and
the deer dropped like a stone. Needless to say we had a first-
class dinner. We slept at Singon that night. There were a great
many jungle fires during this day and the next. The next morning we started again early and I resumed my bird shooting.
On the first day I had several times missed a Brahman duck
and was somewhat anxious to retrieve my reputation. Quite
early in the morning I got a very fair shot at one; it shook its
wings in derision and flew off, landing again a hundred yards

or so down stream. We floated down and I had another shot with the same result; for the next shot I went on shore and deliberately stalked the animal from behind the low bank and got a sitting shot at about ten yards. The disgusted bird looked around indignantly and flew solemnly down stream. I, even more disgusted, got back to the boat, but the bird was a little too clever this time; for he made a wide circle and came flying back right overhead. I let fly from below and it fell with a flop into the river. The fact is that these birds are so well protected that it is quite useless to shoot at them when the breast is not exposed, unless a lucky pellet should find its way to the brain. So on the next occasion, having noticed that when disturbed they always went down stream, I went some distance below them and sent two boys to frighten them from above. The result was an excellent right and left, and I consoled myself for my previous fiascos. We stopped the night at Toun Myong.

After a delightful night we went off the next morning and got to Kama on the Irrawaddy, whence we signalled the steamboat which took us back to Prome, where we stopped that night. The next day we spent in visiting the pagoda, Thornton doing some sketching and I writing a couple of Buddhist poems. We went off in the evening for Rangoon. The next day we drove about the town but did little else; and on Monday we paid off Peter. The principle on which I had dealt with this man was to give him money in lump sums as he wanted it, and to call him to give an account of all he had spent. He made out that we owed him thirty-seven rupees by this said account. I made a few trifling corrections; reducing the balance in his favour, and including the wages due to him (which he had not reckoned), to two rupees, four annas. He was very indignant and was going to complain to everyone from the lieutenant-governor to the hotel-keeper. I think he was rather staggered when I told him that, as he had been a very good servant in other respects, I would give him as backsheesh the bottle of champagne and the three tins which he had already stolen. He appeared very surprised at my having detected this theft. Whereby hangs a tale. On leaving Rangoon I gave him a list of all the provisions, with the instructions that when he took anything from the store he was to bring the list to me and have that thing crossed off. On the second day the list was missing; he, of course, swore that I had not given it back to him. I had kept a duplicate list, which I took very good care not to show.

That evening I was again down with fever and found myself

unable to take any food whatever. I called in the local medico, who fed me on iced champagne, and the next day I was pretty well again. Thornton in the meanwhile had gone off to Mandalay. I was very sorry not to be able to go on there with him, but my time was too short: I did not know when I might be summoned to join Eckenstein to go off to Kashmir.

On the twelfth of February I went on board the *Komilla* for Akyab, where Allan was now living. In the course of the day the sea air completely restored me to health. On the thirteenth we were off Sandaway, which did not appear fascinating. On the next day we put in at Kyaukpyu, which I had so vainly hoped to reach overland. It has a most delightful bay and beach, its general appearance recalling the South Sea Islands; but the place is a den of malaria. We had no time to land, as the captain was anxious to get into Akyab the same night. We raced through the straits and cast anchor there about eight o'clock—just in time.

I went ashore with the second officer and proceeded in my usual casual manner to try to find Allan in the dark. The job was easier than I anticipated. The first man I spoke to greeted me as if I had been his long-lost brother, and took me off in his own carriage to the monastery (the name of which is Lamma Sayadaw Kyoung) where I found Allan, whom I now saw for the first time as a Buddhist monk. The effect was to make him appear of gigantic height, as compared to the diminutive Burmese, but otherwise there was very little change. The old gentleness was still there.

I ought to have mentioned (when talking of Ceylon) the delightful story of his adventure with a krait. Going out for a solitary walk one day with no better weapon than an umbrella, he met a krait sunning himself in the middle of the road. Most men would have either killed the krait with the umbrella or avoided its dangerous neighbourhood. Allan did neither; he went up to the deadly little reptile and loaded him with reproaches. He showed him how selfish it was to sit in the road where someone might pass and accidentally tread on him. 'For I am sure,' said Allan, 'that were anyone to interfere with you, your temper is not sufficiently under control to prevent you striking him. Let us see now!' he continued, and deliberately stirred the beast up with his umbrella. The krait raised itself and struck several times viciously, but fortunately at the umbrella only. Wounded to the heart by this display of passion and anger, and with tears running down his cheeks, at least metaphorically speaking, he exhorted the snake to avoid anger, as it would the most deadly pestilence, explained the four noble truths, the three characteristics, the five precepts, the ten fetters of the soul; and expatiated on the doctrine of Karma and all the paraphernalia of Buddhism for at least ten minutes by the clock. When he found the snake was sufficiently impressed he nodded pleasantly and went off with a 'Good day, brother krait!'

Some men would take this anecdote as illustrating fearlessness; but the true spring is to be found in compassion. Allan was perfectly serious when he preached to the snake, though he was possibly a better man of science than a good many of the stuck-up young idiots who nowadays lay claim to the title. I have here distinguished between fearlessness and compassion; but in their highest form they are surely identical; even pseudo-Christ [1] hit the mark when he observed, 'Perfect love casteth out fear.'

They managed to give me some sort of a shakedown, and I slept very pleasantly at the monastery. The next morning I went off to breakfast on board to say goodbye to the captain, who had shown me great kindness, and afterwards took my luggage and went to Dr Moung Tha Nu, the resident medical officer, who welcomed me heartily and offered me hospitality during my stay in Akyab.

He was Allan's chief dayaka; and very kindly and wisely did he provide for him. I walked back with Allan to the temple and commenced discussing all sorts of things, but continuous conversation was quite impossible, for people of all sorts trooped in incessantly to pay their respects to the European bhikkhu. They prostrated themselves at his feet and clung to them with reverence and affection. They brought him all sorts of presents. He was more like Pasha Bailey Ben than any other character in history.

> They brought him onions strung on ropes,
> And cold boiled beef, and telescopes,

at any rate gifts equally varied and not much more useful. The doctor looked in in the afternoon and took me back with him to dinner. Allan was inclined to suffer with his old asthma, as it is the Buddhist custom (*non sine causa*) to go out of doors at six every morning, and it is very cold till some time after dawn. I wish sanctity was not so incompatible with sanity and sanitation!

The next day after breakfast Allan came to the doctor's

house to avoid worshippers, but a few of them found him out after all and produced buttered eggs, newspapers, marmalade, brazil nuts, bicarbonate of potash and works on Buddhism from their ample robes. We were able, however, to talk of Buddhism and our plans for extending it to Europe, most of the day. The next four days were occupied in the same way.

33

While at Akyab I wrote *Ahab*, which, with a few other poems, was published as a companion to *Jezebel*. I had also, at odd times, continued *Orpheus* and *The Argonauts*. The latter play is really five separate plays of the Greek pattern. The effect of my journey is very manifest. I had entirely neglected the obvious astronomical symbolism of the Golden Fleece, and had introduced a number of Hindu ideas, both about Magick and about philosophy. To illustrate the voyage, I included lyrics descriptive of actual observations of Vera Cruz, Waikiki Beach, Hong Kong and other places which had excited me.

The best thing in Book III of *Orpheus*, which occupied this period, is, perhaps, the invocation to Hecate, which I recited at Akyab with full magical intention. The goddess appeared in the form of Bhavani. The fact made more concrete my perception of the essential identity of all religions. Sinai and Olympus, Mount Kailasha and Mount Meru differed from each other as do the Dent Blanche, Monte Silvio and the Steinbockhorn. It is the same mountain seen from different sides and named by different people. It encouraged me to continue my studies in the Cabbala, which claims to reduce all possible ideas to combinations of comparatively few originals, the ten numbers, in fact; these ten numbers themselves being of course interrelated.

From the beginning I had wanted to use my poetical gift to write magical invocations. Hymns to various gods and goddesses may be found scattered through my works; but in Book III of *Orpheus*, Persephone is invoked directly by commemorating her adventures. I developed this much further in Book IV of *Orpheus*. The idea was put into my mind by Euripides, whose *Bacchae* I had been reading at odd times, having picked up a copy at a second-hand book store in San Francisco. When I had first read it, for academic purposes, I had entirely failed to realize that the play was an invocation of Dionysus. I now began to see that by commemorating the story of the god one might identify oneself with him, and thus constitute a subtler, stronger and more complete invocation of him than by any direct address. I might even go so far as to say that the form of the latter implies the consciousness of duality and therefore tends to inhibit identification.

My predilection is due to the fact that I am primarily a lyric poet. My deepest natural tendency is to exalt my soul by what I may call straightforward intoxication. Thus Shelley and Swinburne come more natural to me than Aeschylus and Shakespeare, who intoxicate the reader by transporting him to their wonderland.

Sunday the twenty-third I went aboard S.S. *Kapurthala* to return to Calcutta. The next day we anchored outside Chittagong, a most uninteresting place. I was too lazy to land. Two days later I got back to Calcutta. Getting my mail, I busied myself in preparing for the great journey. It was now definitely settled that our expedition should meet at Rawalpindi. I only took one day off, when I went to Sodpur snipe shooting with a friend of Thornton's, with whom I was now staying, Lambe having gone off to Australia.

I have inserted the record of this short excursion somewhat at length. Most of it is taken from an account written up when it was still fresh in my mind. It should give an idea of the daily detail of such journeys and enable the reader to clothe with flesh the skeleton of my subsequent wanderings.

On the seventh of March I left for Benares and saw the usual sights—temples, yogis and dancing girls. I had become very cynical and blasé about all these things, which only a few months before would have roused me to ecstasies of wonder. But I now made a wry mouth at the sour sub-flavour of everything. My conversation with Allan about Buddhism, and my own meditations, had disenchanted me. Everything was recognized automatically as illusion, calculated to fetter the soul if one allowed it to fool one.

On the twelfth I reached Agra. My entry about the Taj Mahal is interesting.

> Saw Taj. A dream of beauty, with appallingly evil things dwelling therein. I actually had to use H.P.K.[1] formula! (This means that I assumed the god-form of Harpocrates to prevent the invasion of my aura by objectionable ideas.) The building soon palls, the evil aura is apparent and disgust succeeds. But the central hall is like a magic circle, of strained aura, like after the banishing.

The aesthetic criticism needs revision. I do not think the building beautiful; the conception is too exquisite for the scale of the execution. The effect is that of an etching twenty feet by thirty.

This reminds me of a puzzle that perplexed me many years later in Washington, D.C. I could not understand why the obelisk was so atrociously ugly. 'How can even the Americans,' I said to myself, 'go wrong over so absolutely simple a form?' I asked the sculptor, Paul Bartlett, who cleared up the difficulty, simply and shortly: 'An obelisk is a monolith.'

It is one of the fundamental qualities of men who understand a subject perfectly to be able to sweep away the most elaborate illusions by appeal to bedrock fact. I remember how Frank Harris once enlightened me about imitation pearls. One knows how cleverly the manufacturers of these things present their case so as to deceive the very elect. But Frank Harris said: 'A pearl is a stone.' And the whole fantastic fabric of falsehood crumbled at the touch!

I cannot omit to mention one atrocity at Agra. Some prurient English curator had indulged his foul instincts by whitewashing a magnificent fresco in the palace because it was 'improper'. In other words, he was so leprously lascivious that anything which reminded him of reproduction produced a frenzied spasm of sensuality in his soul. However, his vandalism still cried out against him. The beautiful wall which he had made as blank as his intelligence still reminded him of his rottenness. He had no resource but to whitewash all the other walls, in order to secure artistic uniformity!

After all, it is perhaps the best thing to do; having bowdlerized Shakespeare and edited the Bible so as to remove all reference to any kind of sin, it is hardly worth while to preserve the remains. There are only two courses open to logic; one can either accept the universe as it is, face every fact frankly and fearlessly, and make one's soul immune to the influence of any invasion; or abolish the whole thing by administering soporifics to the spirit. After all, the virtues which are dearest to degenerate Europeans imply the existence of those very things which they are most concerned to deny. The pious pretence that evil does not exist only makes it vague, enormous and menacing. Its overshadowing formlessness obsesses the mind. The way to beat an enemy is to define him clearly, to analyse and measure him. Once an idea is intelligently grasped, it ceases to threaten the mind with the terrors of the unknown.

I went to Delhi on the sixteenth. The best thing here is the Turkish bath, where the process of purification is completed by charming ladies. On the eighteenth I wrote about *Orpheus*,

'The accursed Book III utterly finished. Oh *Book IV!*' On the nineteenth I went and saw the fort with 'Major Graham, a prize fool from South Africa'. The entry demands emendation. He wasn't a major; his name wasn't Graham; he had never been to South Africa; and he was anything but a fool! His idea was to represent himself as in charge of some Boer prisoners and obtain credit and cash by various misrepresentations.

The twentieth and twenty-first great days in my life. I wrote an essay which I originally gave the title 'Crowleymas Day' and published under the title 'Berashith' in Paris by itself, incorporating it subsequently in *The Sword of Song*. The general idea is to eliminate the idea of infinity from our conception of the cosmos. It also shows the essential identity of Manichaeism (Christianity), Vedantism and Buddhism. Instead of explaining the universe as modifications of a unity, which itself needs explaining, I regard it as NOTHING, conceived as (illusory) pairs of contradictories. What we call a thought does not really exist at all by itself. It is merely half of nothing. I know that there are practical difficulties in accepting this, though it gets rid so nicely of a priori obstacles. However, the essay is packed with ideas, nearly all of which have proved extremely fertile, and it represents fairly enough the criticism of my genius upon the varied ideas which I had gathered since I first came to Asia.

During the whole time, I had been studying the original scriptures of Hinduism and Buddhism very thoroughly. Besides this, I had discussed every aspect of religion and philosophy with immensely varied types of thinkers. From men of such spiritual and scholarly attainment as Allan Bennett, the Hon. P. Ramanathan, Prince Jinawaravansa, Paramaguru Swami, Shri Swami Swayam Prakashanand Maithala, to such excremental exponents of error as theosophists, missionaries and even members of the Salvation Army. Gathering all these shreds together, I had preferred to call the pattern Buddhism. The scientific agnosticism, rational psychology, and freedom from superstitious or emotional appeals, decided me in its favour. There were, of course, two vast gaps in my line. I knew little and understood less of Chinese thought, and was almost equally ignorant of Islam with its Sufi superstructure.

It was dramatically fit that I should have devoted these two days to this essay; for on the second I received a wire from Eckenstein. I had a day to spare before proceeding to Rawalpindi, which I spent at Oakley shooting magar. Here is the story:

Maiden, the proprietor of the hotel, came with me and provided a most admirable tiffin. I lent him my Mauser and relied myself upon the ·577. After getting permission from the engineer in charge of the canal works, we put off in a small boat and rowed up the stream. Very soon we saw a fine big crocodile on the banks; but as they are very suspicious beasts and slide into the water at anyone's approach, we determined to try a long shot. I crawled into the bow of the boat, and while the natives held the boat steady, loosed off at about a hundred and thirty yards. The shot was either a very good one or a very lucky one, for the magar was certainly mortally wounded by it. We rowed rapidly up to the beast to find him lashing about in a couple of feet of water and bleeding profusely. I had almost certainly shot him through the heart. Unfortunately, this is of very little use with these reptiles. We got up as close as the natives could be persuaded to go. There certainly was some risk if we had gone quite close in, but we ought to have ventured near enough to drive a boat-hook into the mud between him and the deep water. But they could not be persuaded to do this and there was no time for argument. Maiden sat up in the middle of the boat and fired about fifteen Mauser cartridges into the struggling crocodile, which I think was a proceeding of doubtful utility. He persuaded me, however, to fire a couple more cartridges myself, which I did, right down the beast's throat. The second shot, however, very nearly led to a catastrophe, as the boat was not at all steady and the recoil of the heavy express sent me an awful cropper backwards on to the gunwale of the boat. Luckily no harm came of it. I was now more anxious than ever to get hold of the beast or to pin him with the boat-hook, though his struggles were gradually ceasing, but nothing we could do was any good, little by little he slid off the shallow into the deep water and sank. After hunting about for twenty minutes we gave the affair up as a bad job.

Rowing slowly up the stream, we soon caught sight of another fine beast, though not quite so big as the one we lost. I took, however, an extraordinarily careful shot at it and had the good luck to smash its spine. Everyone thought I had missed, but I swore that was impossible. Certainly the beast did not move as we rowed towards it. I sent the natives on to the bank, and after an infinite display of funk they ventured to catch hold of its tail; of course it had been shot stone dead. We got the body on board and rowed back to tiffin.

On Sunday, March 23rd, I took the mail for Pindi. As luck would have it, the car reserved for the expedition was on the train. So I jumped in and was introduced to my four new comrades.

The Chogo Ri expedition had begun.

34

Agreement between Oscar Eckenstein and Aleister Crowley

1. By O.E.'s letter of Sept. 20th and cable of Oct. 3rd he agrees to A.C.'s proposal by cable and letter of August 23rd that they should together climb a mountain higher than any previously ascended by man: both agree to use their utmost endeavours in every respect to achieve this result.

(On August 23rd A.C. placed five hundred pounds at the disposal of O.E.; on Oct. 10th he added another five hundred pounds in case of emergency, for this purpose. O.E. is empowered to employ part of this latter sum, or all if absolutely necessary, to arrange by insurance for Dr Karl Blodig to join us. It is, however, understood that Dr Blodig's status as an amateur shall be rigidly respected.)

2. This agreement only to be cancelled by death, serious illness or vital affairs of one of the parties.

3. O.E. agrees to take all responsibility of preparing the expedition in England, to have authority to accept a third or fourth member of the party, should such a one be willing to pay his full share of the expenses, and he shall be responsible for the safe arrival of the party and baggage in place and date provided by him.

4. On accomplishment of (3) 'the leader' will then assume entire control of, and responsibility for, the expedition, until the return of the party to civilization. 'The leader' shall be either O.E. or A.C., as they may subsequently agree, and no other person.

'The leader' must give his orders in writing if requested. (N.B. This should always be done if separation of the party is involved.) 'The leader' shall have the right to consult any member of the party, who must consider his difficulty with judicial care, and return a serious answer, in writing if requested. Should any dispute arise, a council may be called to sit under parliamentary usage, 'the leader' to be chairman, unless his own conduct be in question. In the latter case, a chairman to be selected. A majority vote to decide. 'The leader' to have a casting vote in case of equality. The leader's orders shall be otherwise without appeal, and shall be obeyed cheerfully and to the best of ability: except that no member of the party is to be obliged anywhere to risk his life, his own judgment to be the arbiter as to whether such and such an order involves danger, whether from men, starvation, animals or other causes.

5. All members of the party pledge themselves to have nothing whatever to do with women in any way that is possibly avoidable: not to purchase any article without O.E.'s knowledge and consent; not to interfere in any way whatever with native prejudices and beliefs.

This clause shall take effect from the accomplishment of (3).

6. Any dispute arising under this agreement shall be subjected to arbitration in the usual way and shall not be subject to appeal at law or otherwise.

7. Should a third, fourth or fifth man join the party, he shall sign this agreement before he is definitely accepted.

Witness our hands.

At Kandy, Oct. 12th, 1901.

The expedition was composed of six members. Thanks to the Alpine Club, there was no Englishman of mountaineering ability and experience available. We had, however, a Trinity man named Knowles, aged twenty-two, which is far too young for work of this kind, which requires endurance. He knew practically nothing of mountains, but he had common sense enough to do what Eckenstein told him; and as it was, he proved invaluable in Srinagar and even on the actual journey. He was a source rather of strength than of weakness. Then there was an Austrian judge named Pfannl, reputed the best rock climber in Austria, and his regular climbing companion Wessely. They had no experience beyond the Alps and proved utterly unable to make allowances for the difference of scale. Pfannl was also obsessed with the idea of getting into athletic condition and had begun to train directly he stepped on the boat at Trieste. Foreseeing trouble, I kept part of my diary in a magical cipher. I find an entry dated March 31st, 1902:

This is called the Misadventure of Pfannl.
Mountain Sigma. On the Finsteraarhorn after traversing Schreckhorn directly from R.R. journey, Pfannl had to be carried down from the Concordia hut. Again, on the Géant, he collapsed from food, etc. The whole moral of this is: 'If Pfannl collapses, it will be complete. He is sure to overtrain.'

The Austrians were totally unable to understand the workings of the native mind, as appeared very soon. It was a great mistake to bring them. The sixth member of the party was a Swiss ex-Army doctor named Guillarmod, who looked and behaved like Tartarin de Tarascon. He knew as little of mountains as he did of medicine, and proved a great source of weakness, though his delightful geniality helped both the psychology of the party and our relations with the natives. He was our comic relief and did much to make things more tolerable for all of us. For all that, I think we should have done better to take none of the foreigners.* Our numbers made us unwieldy; and the question of international jealousy contributed indirectly to our failure, as will be explained later.

We left Pindi for Tret on the twenty-ninth of March. We had had to repack our baggage, which weighed over three tons, for convenience of transport by ekkas. These are contraptions which suggest a hansom cab with the back knocked out and the driver on the floor, as it might have been conceived by the man who invented the coracle. Even one European finds it impossible to get a comfortable seat or stretch his legs, and a second constitutes outrageous overcrowding. A party of eight to ten natives, on the other hand, finds itself at ease.

Our adventures began with startling suddenness. I woke up in the dak bungalow at Tret the next morning to find a dignified young gentleman sitting at my bedside. I wondered if I had been ill without knowing it, for his face expressed the sympathetic concern of Luke Fildes's 'doctor'. Not at all; he was a police inspector who had arrived by tonga, a two-horse rattle-trap which is used by people in what passes for a hurry in these parts of the world. All he knew was that we mustn't start—'his not to reason why'. I said he had better talk to the leader of the expedition, Mr Eckenstein. He assumed an awed expression, as if I had said something not quite nice. Knowles and I, who were sharing the same room, proceeded to dress with elegant leisure and bore our bewilderment to Eckenstein.

At this point a telegram arrived, from which we inferred that the Indian Empire was somewhat imperilled by our conduct. At ten o'clock there arrived no less a person than the deputy commissioner of Rawalpindi; one of those strong silent men, with whom Mr Henry Seton Merriman has made us familiar. He summoned me to his august presence. I (obviously) referred him once more to Eckenstein, but he jibbed—his orders were that the rest of us could do as we liked; but Eckenstein would not be allowed to enter Kashmir. We asked why. At this time *The Book of the Law* not having yet been

---

* This was done in stark violation of clause 3. Knowles and I paid the whole expenses of these undesirable aliens.

given to mankind, he was unable to reply, 'Enough of Because, be he damned for a dog'; but we understood him as uttering 'words to that effect' in his strong silent way. We finally induced him to face Eckenstein; who, with his usual aplomb, put the poor man into a dilemma at once. He wanted to know whether he was or was not arrested. 'Heaven forbid,' said the D.C., 'that any such idea should enter my pure mind.' 'All right, then,' said Eckenstein; 'I shall go on.' Oh no—the orders were strict. After interminable passages of verbal fencing, it was agreed that I should assume command of the expedition and carry on, while Eckenstein returned to Pindi with the deputy commissioner and took up the matter with the superior authority.

To sum this episode, Eckenstein chased the culprits all around north India and finally cornered George Nathaniel Curzon at the psychological moment when our pathetic cables to Lord George Hamilton at the India Office had brought the power of Blighty to bear on the naughty nabobs. The 'superior person' saved his face by authorizing Eckenstein to rejoin the party on guarantees for his good conduct subscribed by Knowles and myself!

We never learnt, and I do not know to this day, the *dessous des cartes*. Eckenstein insistently professed himself in utter ignorance of the reasons which had induced the authorities to take their high-handed and futile action. Needless to say, we could not but connect it with Eckenstein's quarrel with Conway in 1892. We pumped the bigwigs of Kashmir, and we sifted the rumours of the bazaar, but beyond learning that Eckenstein was a Prussian spy and a cold-blooded murderer, we obtained little information of importance. Eckenstein was the noblest man that I have ever known. His integrity was absolute and his sympathetic understanding of the native character supreme. I remain unrepentant in my opinion that the incident was the result of the unmanly jealousy and petty intrigue of the insects who envied him, complicated by official muddle.

Temporarily deprived of our leader, we went on wearily to Srinagar, the capital of Kashmir, which we reached on the fourteenth of April. Several incidents on the road demonstrated the extraordinary importance which the government attached to Eckenstein. Though everything had been arranged, there were all sorts of excitement at the frontier, and telegrams and spies were bustling about. It reminded me of the turmoil in an ant-heap which had been disturbed.

On the fifth day we had our first and last trouble with natives. It is part of the Indian character to put every new
Englishman through an examination in force of character. The
key of power with all the inhabitants in the Indian peninsula
is justice. And this is about the only thing one can say which
really does apply pretty well the same to their infinite diversity.
God help the traveller who punishes his servants unjustly! His
lack of judgment shows them a weak point of which they can
take advantage to avenge themselves in a thousand ways. On
the other hand, one is even more despised if one fails to visit
intentional misbehaviour with the full penalty of the law.

I was far from well. Various symptoms of malaria kept on
cropping up and I was in constant pain with pityriasis versi-
color, which is a form of the so-called dhobi itch (a dhobi is a
laundryman). One puts on clothes which seem spotlessly clean,
but they contain the spores of a fungus which grows in the
axilla and the groin. This got worse and worse. I was idiot
enough to put myself in the hands of the doctor. I had the
superstitious belief that his medical degree meant something.
I suffered perpetually from the irritation, increased by walking
and riding till I got on the glacier away from the doctor, when
I painted it with iodine, a supersubtle device which had never
occurred to him, and cured it in twenty-four hours.

On the fourth day the ekka drivers conspired cautiously to
delay us. On the fifth they appointed a delegate to give us hell.
(The arrangement was that Knowles and I should bring up the
rear of the procession to prevent any ekkas from straggling.)
This man kept on making unnecessary repairs in his harness,
and finally managed to lock his wheel in that of another ekka
which happened to meet us. He was delighted to find that I
made no complaint and he thought that he was going to get
away with it. His ekka and ours arrived in camp more than
an hour after the rest of the party. But the moment we were
visible I jumped down, fixed my left hand in his beard (itself
a blood insult), dragged him from his ekka and lammed into
him with my belt in view of the whole camp—apparently without any provocation.

The psychology is instructive. I knew that the man's misbehaviour was a put-up job; in beating him, I was establishing
the morale of the whole expedition. Their subtle minds understood perfectly the essential justice of my action and ap-
plauded my perspicuity and determination. The result was
that I never had the slightest difficulties with natives in India
ever afterwards and was able to practise perfect tolerance of

genuine accidents. I had forced them to respect us, which, with an Indian, is the first step to acquiring his love. And the men soon showed themselves willing to risk their lives, as they ignorantly thought they were being asked to do, in order to please us. Younghusband's expedition to Yarkand cost seventeen coolies their lives, and our men were convinced that the object of our expedition was to make a new pass to that city. Nothing I could say would persuade them otherwise. They came and told me that they knew they were going to die on the journey and they were quite willing to do it. They were almost disappointed when I sent them back from Camp 10!

Had I failed to understand the psychology of the ekka driver, we should have been nagged to death by pin-pricks. On the way back, crossing the Deosai plateau, we fell in with an English lieutenant who, after a fruitless shikar after ibex, had been worried into illness and was being deliberately worried to death by his servants, who kept on misunderstanding his orders 'accidentally on purpose'. They had found out his weak spot and had no mercy. The first business of any traveller in any part of the world is to establish his moral superiority. He has to be uniformly calm, cheerful, just, perspicacious, indulgent and inexorable. He must decline to be swindled out of the fraction of a farthing. If he once gives way, he is done for.

I remember in my journey across China refusing to buy a few eggs when we were actually in sore need of them, because I could not agree with the owner on the price. The sum in dispute was much less than a ha'penny, and it was almost a matter of life and death to me; but if I had given in, I should never have been able to buy an egg for the rest of the journey. The traveller must always remember that his method of striking a match is accurately reported for hundreds of miles in every direction. England conquered India by understanding the minds of the inhabitants, by establishing her own standards of conduct as arbitrary, and contemptuously permitting the native to retain his own wherever they did not conflict with the service of the conqueror. England is losing India by consenting to admit the existence of the conquered races; by consenting to argue; by trying to find a value for incommensurables. Indian civilization is far superior to our own and to enter into open competition is to invoke defeat. We won India by matching our irrational, bigoted, brutal manhood against their etiolated culture.

We cannot even plead that we have lacked a prophet. The genius of Rudyard Kipling, however aesthetically abominable, has divined the secrets of destiny with cloudless clarity. His stories and his sermons are equally informed by the brainless yet unanswerable argument based on intuitive cognition of the critical facts. India can be governed, as history proves, by any alien autocracy with sufficient moral courage to dismiss Hindu subtlety as barbaric and go its own way regardless of reason. But India has always conquered its invaders by initiating them. No sooner does the sahib suspect that he is not Almighty God than the attributes of Jehovah cease to arm him with unreasonable omnipotence. Our rule in India has perished because we have allowed ourselves to consider the question of divine right. The proverb says that the gods themselves cannot contend with stupidity, and the stupidity of the sahib in the days of Nicholson reduced India to impotence. But we allowed the intellectual Bengali to invade England and caress our housemaids in the precincts of the Earl's Court exhibition. He returned to Calcutta, an outcast indeed from his own social system, but yet a conqueror of English fashions and femininity. We admitted his claim to compete with us, and our prestige perished exactly as did that of the Church when Luther asserted the right of private judgment.

I am not responsible * for the fact that the universe is constructed in defiance of the principles of reason. I see perfectly that the crude conceptions of European culture are intellectually contemptible; but if we are to enter into relations of any kind with the East, we must either behave like little children in the presence of age and wisdom, or we must be brutal bosses. The soldiers who slew Archimedes had only one alternative—to sit at his feet and learn geometry, and thank him when he rapped them over the knuckles. We must therefore choose between shutting up fourteen thousand sipahis in a compound and blowing them to pieces with grapeshot in cold blood, like Havelock, and sprawling to kiss their slippers like European students of Yoga. Our attempt to compromise between incompatible civilizations can only end in our confessing the impotence of our own.

We see, even in England itself, how the abdication of Norman arrogance has led to the abrogation of all standards of superiority, so that the man who wishes to govern England today is obliged to conform with the dishonest devices and servile stratagems of democracy. Government demands virtue; in its etymological sense of manliness. In modern England,

---

* P.S.—Well, I am not so sure.

courage, truthfulness and determination are at a discount. A leader can only lead by drugging the populace. When Beaconsfield (wasn't it?) said, 'We must educate our masters,' he formulated the creed of Communism; for it is impossible to educate the people. I myself, despite my public school and university, despite a life devoted to continual travel and study of social, political, economic and historical facts, am only too well aware of my abject incompetence to provide a remedy for the least of the diseases which have come to actual issue. I only know that one must abdicate one's intelligence and submit to rule-of-thumb government. The best master is a go-as-you-please generous gentleman who settles everything by rude common sense. Our modern pretence at scientific government, based on theories and statistics, possesses all the irremediable inadequacies of purblind pedantry. My wanderings have shown me that individual happiness and prosperity flourished most freely in Mexico under the autocracy of Diaz, Russia under that of the tsar, India and Egypt under that of England, and China when the Son of Heaven exercised supreme and unquestioned sway.

The last quarter of a century has swamped all these. The world is seething with the dissatisfaction that springs from insecurity. Men can adapt themselves to pretty well any conditions, but when they do not know from one day to another whether some fundamental principle may not be abolished in the interests of progress, they no longer know where they are. They tend to adopt the principles of the man who flits from one place to another, grabbing portable property and dodging creditors and policemen. Civilization has become a hysterical scramble for momentary material advantage. Thrift is senseless when one is threatened with a levy on capital. Investment is insane when gilt-edged securities may lose two thirds of their value for no assignable reason. Suppose two brothers inherited ten thousand pounds apiece in 1900: one keeps his gold in a bag and spends four hundred pounds a year; the other buys Consols and lives on a little over two hundred pounds of the income without touching his capital. Today * the spendthrift would be worth more than his prudent brother. Marriage is a detestable institution, but the facilities for divorce (introduced ostensibly in the interests of the woman) have cut away the economic ground from under her feet.

---

* Condensed from an article written in 1917 in New York. Luckily my own paper refused to publish it!

I have little use for Rudyard Kipling, especially in his latter days of senile schoolboyishness, aggravated by his addiction to the hydroxide of the second of the paraffin radicles. But his general attitude about India obtains my adhesion. We conquered the peninsula by sheer moral superiority. Our unity, our self-respect, our courage, honesty and sense of justice awakened the wonder, commanded the admiration and enforced the obedience of those who either lacked those qualities altogether, possessed some of them and felt the lack of the others, or had, actually or traditionally, sufficient of them to make them the criteria of right and ability to govern. As elsewhere observed, our modern acquiescence in the rationally irrefutable argument that the colour of a man's skin does not prevent him from being competent in any given respect, has knocked the foundations from underneath the structure of our authority.

But still more fatal has been our imbecile weakness in allowing India to become aware that we are not wholly divine. When the French saw Joan of Arc bleed from a slight wound, the tradition of her invulnerability and their superstitious reverence for her as supernaturally protected vanished, and her ruin became certain. The heel of Achilles of the sahib has been the memsahib. It was atrocious folly to allow Indians to come to England to study, to mix freely with our women, often to marry or seduce them. But we might have survived that scandal. The returned students, having forfeited caste, had forfeited credit. We could have dismissed their accounts of England as the bluster of rascals; and, besides, these students were as insignificant in number as in authority with their own people.

But we did worse. In the name of religion and morality (as usual!) we committed a political blunder, which was also a social crime, by permitting and even encouraging white women to go out to India.

To begin with, they cannot stand the climate, which compels them to live lives whose inevitable tendency is to relax the moral fibre. Thus even high-class memsahibs sometimes have themselves bathed by their beras. The excuse is that any sexual irregularity with such inferior animals is unthinkable. But 'a man's a man for a' that.' Incidentally, the heat increases the female lasciviousness as it decreases the male. White women are thus subject to continual nervous irritation of which they often fail to suspect the character. Besides, the healthiest of them is usually more or less ailing in various minor respects. They are usually short-tempered from this and other causes, and any species of lack of self-control has a fatal effect on the attitude of the native.

Apart from this, it seems to him incredibly shameless on our part that our women should appear in public at all; that they should do so unguarded and unveiled appears the climax of immodesty. Some Englishmen are fatuous enough to suppose that they have explained quite nicely to the satisfaction of Indians—whose point of view in these matters is practically identical from Tuticorin to Peshawar, and Chittagong to Karachi; it being an imperative necessity imposed by the climate, irrespective of creeds and social conditions—that our customs are compatible with correct conduct and even common decency. Such self-delusion marks the utmost limit of bad psychology. India could be kept in order, even now, to its own salvation and our great credit and profit, if we would eliminate the European women and tradesmen, the competition wallah, and the haw-haw officer, and entrust the government of the country to a body of sworn 'samurai' vowed like the Jesuits to chastity and obedience, together with either poverty or a type of splendour in which there should be no element of personal pride or indulgence, but only prestige. Like the Jesuits, too, these men should be sworn never to return to Europe as long as they lived. The capacity of such men to govern would be guaranteed by the fact of their having volunteered to accept such conditions. They would enjoy universal respect and absolute trust. They would require no army to enforce their authority. All the best elements of India would spontaneously unite to support it. One further condition. They would have to be guaranteed against the interference of any ignorant and indifferent House of Commons. The stupid callousness of the India Office is as much to be dreaded as the silly sentimentalism of sympathizers with 'national aspiration', 'the brotherhood of man' and all such bunkum.

In India the rules of caste assured the poorest peasant a livelihood of sorts, bar famine and plague, and the future of his children was as certain as sunrise. In Anglo-Saxon civilization no one has any guarantee against economic earthquakes and the future of his family is pure gambling. Such is the price of what we call progress. We cannot even assign a meaning to the word; because no one has any idea of where we are going. The most stupid and tyrannical system ever devised is better than our present position, provided it be stable. We are in a nightmare in which we cannot calculate the result of any action.

It was an affectation of poetry and romance in the eighteenth and early nineteenth centuries to let itself go about the Vale of 'Cashmere': 'Whom, not having seen, we adore.' The descriptions are as vague as they are voluptuous. In reality Kashmir has very positive and definite qualities, and they have certainly never been suggested by the polite dithyrambs of its distant devotees. Technically, of course, it is principally the valley of the Jhelum. But the country does not impress one as being a valley at all: it is a well-watered plateau, ringed by mountains, with a narrow gap through which the river empties itself. Its height is from six thousand to eight thousand feet above the sea. The climate in spring and summer resembles that of Mexico combined with that of Switzerland. The air is clear and exhilarating, yet an atmosphere of peace tempts the wayfarer to pass away the time in the delights of love-in-idleness. In winter the snows transform it to a fascinating fairyland, rather like northern Europe with the addition of sunlight.

Srinagar is an ancient and admirable city. Many of the buildings are of wood. It is interesting to notice that the bridges are built on the principle of the cantilever, which most people believe to be a miracle of modern science; but the idea of the Forth Bridge antedates Alexander the Great.

The flowers and trees in Kashmir are very varied. Their rich splendour is superb. There are many lakes with floating gardens and on the river are houseboats in which many Europeans spend the summer. It is a life of *dolce far niente* of which the Thames could only offer a feeble imitation and Venice itself but a hectic parody.

There is plenty of shooting in the valley, from bears, deer, wild sheep and wild goats to pigeons. I went out occasionally after the bigger game, though I prefer low country shooting. I hate climbing hills unless they are really difficult, as I hate everything which only goes half way. There is not much fun, either, in pigeon shooting. One does it less for pleasure than for profit, and the pigeon is certainly welcome up country as an alternative to athletic mutton and chicken.

35

Knowles and I were kept very busy from the fifth to the twenty-second of April. Everything had to be repacked in kiltas. These are baskets shaped either like wide-mouthed vases or like cabin trunks, and covered with raw hide to protect them from rough usage and bad weather. Our limit weight was fifty-three pounds. As a beast of burden, a mule is less efficient than a man, and a man than a woman. In Kashmir, however, one does not use women as coolies. The people are Mohammedans governed by a ruling caste of Hindus. This leads to complications; for one thing, though the river is full of mahsir, one is not allowed to fish for them, because one of them had swallowed the soul of the maharajah in his youth! Another inconvenience is that one cannot get beef to eat, for Kashmir is theoretically an independent state. The Mohammedan has, of course, no objection to beef; it is the Hindu who prohibits it.

A curious misfortune overtook a native in this connection. His little farm was on the banks of the Indus. During the winter two landslides cut him off completely from his neighbours. The mountain path could not be repaired until the spring. He saved himself from starvation by killing his cow. For this offence he barely escaped the penalty of death.*

We added to our stores by buying a large quantity of local products which it would have been more trouble to bring from England. In some cases this was a mistake. The matches procurable in Kashmir compare only too unfavourably with the worst products of France at its worst period. It was a champion box if it contained half a dozen matches which lit without argument. When we got to the glacier, we used to spend much of our time on sunny days trying to dry them on convenient rocks.

The general bandobast of the expedition was open to a good deal of criticism. One of Eckenstein's few failings was his faith in professorial science. Because the German soldier thrives on

---

* Later. Poor Sir Hari Singh paid dearly in 1923 for eating sirloin of beef! As bad as Jonathan and the honey!

Erbs-suppe and the British on 'Bovril bacon rations', he expected us to do the same, with the result that much of our provisions was quite uneatable. The general plan was to pack kiltas with supplies for one day for twelve men. We had thirty-six of these. In other kiltas were packed additional supplies to supplement what we could procure from the villages which we passed. Eckenstein was curiously obstinate about some details. I was certain that our supply of sugar was very inadequate, but he opposed bitterly my proposal to add to it. I insisted on laying in an extra eighty pounds. Most of this was stolen by the Pathan contingent of servants and sold to the villagers on the journey. The result was that in the latter part of the expedition we suffered from sugar starvation, one of the most dreadful tortures that I have ever undergone.

Eckenstein rejoined us on April 22nd and we started six days later. We had met with extreme kindness on the part of everybody in the valley and the assistance given by the government was invaluable. From start to finish there was not a single unpleasant incident and I shall always remember with the warmest gratitude and affection the hospitality of the English residents.

We had a small staff major of Pathans, very handsome and fierce. The idea of taking them seems to have been to use their prestige with the Kashmiri who, while extraordinarily brave in face of inanimate dangers, are hopelessly timid in presence of a fighting race. I do not think these men were of much assistance at any time, and they ultimately had to be sacked and sent back, not only for their thieving but for their overbearing manner towards the people of the district.

Next came our staff of personal servants, headed by Salama Tantra, who was in all respects an admirable servant, so much so that I brought him from Kashmir in 1905 and took him with me across China. His subordinates were all good men in their way and we had no trouble with them.

Our transport as far as Askole, the last village, depended on local coolies or ponies, a hundred and fifty of one or fifty of the other. Occasionally the same set would make two or three marches with us, but as a rule they were changed every day. Except on one or two occasions when the ignorance and bad manners of the Austrians led to misunderstanding, everything went smoothly.

The naivety of the natives was sometimes very amusing. The regular rate of pay was fourpence a day, and this princely profusion induced the inhabitants of distant side valleys to make sometimes as much as six days' march in each direction from their homes to some point on our route. They would then disseminate themselves among the crowd of coolies and present themselves to the paymaster. Their injured bewilderment on discovering that we only paid wages on presentation of a slip of paper with the coolie's name and number, and the safe arrival of the corresponding kilta, was really pitiful. But even more impressive is the original fact of their willingness to make so many days' journey in the hope of acquiring fourpence without working for it.

Another incident has peculiar value as throwing light on the genesis of stories of miraculous healings. Our custom was to have the doctor establish a temporary clinic at every halting place, where he would attend to tooth-drawing, tapping for dropsy and such simple matters. I remember one man with a fang which stuck out completely through his cheek, leaving a jagged ulcer all round it. It was obviously impossible to undertake any cases of illness other than those requiring simple operations. Invariably, therefore, the cure was effected by the use of instruments, which were spread out on a blanket, while everybody looked on. Nevertheless, on our return, the sick from distant valleys having congregated to meet us, the first patient protested when the doctor produced his forceps. 'Oh no,' said he. 'I want to be cured like the others; put your hand on my head and make me well!'

The journey to the foot of Chogo Ri divides itself naturally into three main sections; six marches bring one to the foot of the Zoji La, the pass which divides Kashmir from Baltistan; twenty-one marches bring one to the foot of the Baltoro glacier; the rest is on the ice. As long as one is in Kashmir the travelling is comparatively easy, the marches reasonably short and the halting places comfortable. The scenery is exhilaratingly grand and beautiful, and the climate perfect. The whole thing may best be described as an exaggeration of all that is best and loveliest in the Alps, plus the enchantment of Asiatic atmosphere.

Travellers to Chogo Ri are limited as to season by the fact that the Zoji La is impassable for coolies before a certain date, which varies little from year to year. We thought ourselves lucky to manage to cross so early in May as the fourth. In the autumn (again) it closes early, so that if one fails to get back to Kashmir before the snow blocks the pass, one is practically compelled to winter in Baltistan.

A great fuss has been made about the actual difficulties and dangers of crossing the pass, but it is merely a long snow trudge. Pfannl and Wessely, who were always boiling over to exhibit their prowess, went up to the col to prospect. They reported on returning (a) that they could not see anything, (b) that the pass was very steep on the other side, and (c) that the other side was free from snow. On the following day we learnt that the first of these statements may have been correct; the other two enlarged my horizon as to the possibilities of inaccuracy.

The slopes leading to the pass are uniformly easy and the reputed danger from avalanches exists only for people without any knowledge of snow. The doctor, however, gave us an idea of what we might expect from him. To this day I cannot understand how this misadventure failed to warn me. Just before reaching the top of the pass, he started to walk across a frozen lake. As he says, 'Confiant dans la solidité de la glace, je m'aventure un peu trop, lorsque, tout à coup, je fais un plongeon, intempestif à cette heure matinale . . . '!!

My duty was to see that the caravans crossed the comparatively short section of the pass which the men dreaded. So I spent most of the morning rushing backwards and forwards, encouraging one, exhorting another and giving a hand to a third. I had no reason to suppose that the reconnaissance of the Austrians was radically wrong. By the time the last man had come safely through the critical section, I was already tired; and when I started to follow, I found to my dismay that the Matayun side of the pass, instead of being steep, was at a very low gradient indeed; and, so far from being free from snow, was covered deeply. The day being well advanced, the going was softer and more slushy all the time. Even the tracks made by the coolies had not made the way decently walkable. Faint with exhaustion, I dragged myself into camp at five o'clock at night, after a thirteen hours' trudge during which I had hardly sat down.

My eyes, too, were inflamed. In the Alps, I had found myself able to go all day in bright sunshine without dark goggles and be none the worse. In Mexico I became uncomfortable after an hour or two and had to put on my glasses. But in the Himalayas, even at low altitudes (the Zoji La is about five thousand metres), snow blindness is a real menace. When I got to the upper glacier, I found that ten minutes without goggles even under a clouded sky determined an attack.

I was too exhausted even to eat until I had drunk half a bottle of champagne, after which I slept like a log. The next morning, I started late—eight o'clock. The march, like that of the previous day, was fifteen miles, but only took six hours instead of thirteen, and would have been much less save for the soft snow of the earlier stages. There was no anxiety about the coolies, so that I had ample leisure to meditate on the extraordinary change of scenery on the far side of the Zoji. Nowhere else in the world have I found any similarly sudden and complete antithesis. Right up to Baltal, trees and flowers abound. On the other side of the pass is an astonishing abomination of desolation. Thence all the way to Skardu there is literally no scrap of vegetation, scarce even sparse rough grass; except where mountain torrents join the Indus. At such places, the natives have carried out an elaborate scheme of irrigation. The land is fashioned into terraces fertilized by a system of channels; and in these artificial fields they cultivate their crops, including apricots. In some places there are as many as five harvests a year. From a distance these oases appear very striking. The first impression is of a crisscross formed by the line of trees and the terraces. These villages glow with ineffable gladness. The marches, though often quite short in actual mileage on the map, are (generally speaking) quite severe. Eckenstein had observed humorously that from the top of the Zoji La it would be down hill all the way to Skardu, bar local irregularities. The piquancy of the remark lies in the fact that the total descent is less than ten thousand feet and that the average daily 'local irregularity' approximates to double that amount. It is sometimes infuriating. One day, at the end (as I thought) of a long march, I caught sight of the goal not half a mile away, both it and I being close to the river. But a rocky buttress gratuitously juts into the stream and the track makes a little detour of some three thousand feet in height to pass it.

Apart from the mere fatigue of these marches, they are made detestable by the utter monotony and ugliness of the landscape. The mountains are huge hideous heaps of shapeless drab. There is hardly one noble contour; there is no rest for the eye; there is no aspiration and no interest—nothing but a gnawing desire to be done with the day's dreary dragging. In addition to this there is a good deal of actual discomfort. The glare of the sun is very distressing and either it, or its reflection from the hot arid rocks, is scorching. At the same time it often happens that a bitterly biting wind is blowing. It seems to eat into one's very bones with harsh cold. One does not know what to do about clothes. On one side one is roasted; on the other frozen. It is easy to understand how the heart leaps whenever the eye falls upon the distant green lattice of a grove, and even how eagerly the eye looks for geological indication of the probability of one appearing. It is an additional annoyance that the mere distance one has travelled tells one so little as to what remains to be done, for the reasons given above.

On some of these marches we were able to get ponies, though the Austrians disdained such effeminacy. The Indian hill pony compares very unfavourably with the Mexican. He is neither so swift, so strong, nor so sure-footed. More often than not, too, he is in bad condition and sometimes actually lame. The best of them stumble at almost every other step, though it is said that they never lose their footing completely. I could never rid myself altogether of nervousness. The road is officially the highway to Skardu and Yarkand, but it rarely amounts to more than a rough and narrow mountain track, scarce better than the paths to Alpine Club huts, at their worst. Some stages, indeed, are altogether impracticable for ponies, either because the track crosses a ravine by a rope bridge or because actually too steep for them to climb. The road is never dangerous from the point of view of the pedestrian, but it looks so to a man on horseback; for in a great many places its loose stones lie on the edge of what is a precipice for all practical purposes.

At Hardas we were entertained by a magnificent but dirty rajah, who took me for a native. One noticed with amusement that a great many of the people whom public opinion at home classes as niggers were very much lighter in colour than any of our party.

At Tolti we found another rajah equally urbane. Travel in the East is essential to any sort of understanding of the Bible. The equivalent of the word king is constantly used to describe men who may be anything from absolute monarchs over hundreds of thousands of people, to country squires or even headmen of a tribe of gypsies.

We reached Skardu on the fourteenth of May, and put in four days making arrangements for the next stage of the journey. We could no longer depend on finding enough coolies, the villages beyond Shigar being poorly populated.

We took much credit to ourselves, and gave more to the efficiency of government officials, that we had come through from Srinagar without a day's halt, we the largest party of Europeans to have made the journey.

Central Asia, by the way, is the home of polo, which is played to this day with the utmost enthusiasm. Needless to say, the game is free from the swanking exclusiveness of the European variety. I was never able to discover any particular rules. One simply rides into the melée with any kind of a stick one happens to have and smites the ball with more vigour than intention. If one feels that one's side is too strong for the other, one simply changes over. The local rajah and the poorest farmer of the district meet in the game with the noble equality of 'chivalry' in the true sense, the esprit de corps of horsemen.

The exhilaration of the game is extraordinary. Played as it is, it is free from the lust of result which has spoilt practically all sports and games in Europe. Strange that in my old age I should suddenly find myself acquiescing in the absurdity which angered me so when a boy, Champney's plan of playing cricket without scoring runs. After all, the madman was right. It would be far finer to play the game for the sake of enjoying the free exercise of one's enthusiasm. True it is, scoring does lead to post-mortem controversies which are not in the spirit of sport. Climbing itself is being very much spoilt by the attitude of the Alpine Club in insisting that the achievement, not the enjoyment, is the important thing. It has led to their virulent, dishonest, envious intrigues against guideless climbing and climbers. This is the American spirit, to count and compare instead of being content with spiritual satisfaction. This is what is meant by the Scripture. 'The love of money is the root of all evil.'

This spirit is at the root of all modern attempts at standardization of attainment and it leads directly to every kind of foul play, falsehood, cheating and controversy. Consider merely American football and baseball; the drilling of the teams to carry out a series of evolutions designated by a string of ciphers. Again, what of the intrigues to attain the transfer of professional players, to say nothing of the possible selling of matches to syndicates of gamblers? Sport of all kinds has tended to become spectacular and gladiatorial even in games like lawn tennis, which was originally the very incarnation of social amenity. It is the same story everywhere; see boxing, in which a man may get more for half an hour's battery than any dozen university professors receive for a lifetime of devoted labour on behalf of the race. The root of the mischief is the spirit of taking life too seriously. It is really almost expected of the man who happens to run over to Philadelphia from New York for a day, that he should forthwith write an encyclopaedic history of the Quakers.

It is hard to prophesy the issue of this tendency, but one can see already that the chivalry of sport is following that of arms into oblivion.

36

Skardu, 2,228 metres above sea-level, is the capital of Baltistan, and contains some twenty thousand inhabitants. The mountains here seem to have conspired to stop suddenly so as to allow a large level plateau. The Indus spreads out almost as if to form a lake. The town is large and scattered; it is in fact less a town than a conglomeration of small farms. After our long and tedious march, we could enjoy to the full the sensation of the peace and beatitude which fill this smiling isolated valley.

We stayed at the dak baghla, which stood some thirty yards back from a delicious stream of clear water. One evening, just after sunset, a young man appeared carrying on his shoulders his brother, who had been working in a quarry. A falling rock had struck the inside of his leg just below the knee and laid it open to the bone as far as the ankle. The doctor needed plenty of running water. So we took the patient down to the stream and held Alpine lanterns while the doctor operated. The leg was in a shocking mess and we suggested chloroform. The doctor said 'No—the boy will faint with the pain in a few seconds,' and he went on washing out the dirt and snipping away loose pieces of flesh, and ultimately stitching up the whole fourteen inches of wound. The game went on for an hour and a half. But the boy never lost consciousness, and never moaned or so much as murmured. We heard nothing from him except a perfectly calm request, about half way through the job, for a drink of water.

I did not content myself with admiring the lad's stoicism. His conduct made me suspect that the Mongolian (the Baltis are Mongols) has a very different nervous system from our own. I understood Chinese ideas of torture from this and similar facts, and began to correlate these physiological reactions with the psychology and philosophy of the race. It helped me to see that what we call ultimate truth is in reality no more than a statement of the internal relations of the universe which we perceive. One may say, indeed, that a unicellular organism would be absolutely justified in explaining the universe in terms of his own experience; that he could indeed by no possibility do anything else, and that the sole valid criticism which could be applied to his cosmology would be based on facts neither known nor knowable to him. Apply this argument to our actual ideas: any religion must rest on revelation and cannot be proved by reason or experience. It is at once necessary and impudent to claim the exercise of faith. From this it follows that religion must always be repugnant to reason and its upholders must be prepared to be called charlatans.

There is, however, one issue from this dilemma. It is possible to base a religion, not on theory and results, but on practice and methods. It is honest and hopeful to progress on admitted principles towards the development of each individual mind, and thus to advance towards the absolute by means of the consciously willed evolution of the faculty of apprehension. Such is in fact the idea underlying initiation. It constitutes the absolute justification of the Path of the Wise as indicated by the adepts, whether of the magical or mystical schools. For Yoga offers humanity an organ of intelligence superior to intellect, yet co-ordinate with it, and Magick serves to arouse spiritual energies which, while confirming those of the mind, bring them to their culmination.

One afternoon was made notable by a storm of wind. Fine sand was blown up from the bed of the Indus to a height of over three thousand feet, completely obscuring the mountains. (I have seen something similar in Cumberland. One night a terrific storm broke over the west coast; of sufficient velocity to push a number of trucks from a siding into a London & North Western train, wrecking it. The bough, as thick as my thigh, of a tree forty yards from the hotel was blown through my window on to the bed where I lay asleep, without waking me. In the morning the rain had stopped; but the wind continued with increased violence. Every stone wall in the neighbourhood had been thrown to the ground. The waterfalls exposed to the wind had been blown back so that the pitches over which they normally fell were practically dry. The water of the lake was swept up in vast clouds across the face of Scafell, completely hiding the mountain.)

While making our new arrangements we lounged about, fished and climbed odd rocks which tempted us. On May 19th we crossed the Indus by ferry and followed a delightful road, for the most part level and wooded, to Shigar. The Shigar valley is strangely unlike that of the Indus and is out of keeping with one's natural ideas of mountain streams. The river winds through a broad flat wilderness of stones.

The village of Shigar resembles an oasis in the Sahara, as I discovered some years later when I made my bow to the latter. There is indescribable fascination about these clusters of quiet houses in their groves of green; but there is a serpent in every Eden, and there was a missionary in Shigar. We asked the fool to dinner. He had been there seven years, as had also his predecessor, and between them they had not made a single convert. Christianity can never make any impression on a Mohammedan. The anthropomorphic and anthropotheistic ideas connected with the Incarnation shock people whose conception of God, irrational though it be, is at least sublime. 'God hath neither equal, son, nor companion. Nothing shall stand before His face.' The ethical implications of the Atonement are equally repulsive to the Moslem. As Ibsen said, 'Your God is an old man whom you cheat.' Mohammedanism teaches a man to respect himself; his relation with his supposed creator is direct; he cannot escape the penalty of his sins by paying the priest, or by persuading himself that everything has been arranged for him by a transaction of the most stupid injustice. Buddhism, in a totally different way, shares this conformity with common decency, and it is only the lowest caste of Hindu which really convinces itself that sacrifices and servility suffice for salvation. Where Islam and Christianity meet in open competition, as in some parts of Africa, it is found that only the lowest type of Negro, such as is accustomed to arrange matters with conscience by hanging a rag on a piece of stick, accepts Christianity. Anyone with a trace of self-respect disdains the lavish superstitions which we compel the Archbishop of Canterbury to subscribe, but can readily accept the simplicity of Islam as a stage beyond fetishism.

The march from Shigar to Askole is extremely varied and beautiful. For three marches one ascends the Shigar valley. The river was extraordinarily low, and could be crossed. In August 1892, Eckenstein, though furnished with a rope, had been unable to cross one of the tributary streams—of which there must be more than one hundred. The explanation is (of course) that the snows had not begun to melt.

On one march we had to walk along the smooth round stones of the river bed for several miles. The track became impossible for horses. We crossed a pari (a buttress which juts into the stream and has to be climbed in consequence) over twelve hundred feet high. The next day we came to Ghomboro. The character of the country had completely changed once more. We had got back to the conditions of the valley of the Upper Indus. Ghomboro is a delightful village of apricot orchards. Below the terraces roars the water of the Bralduh Nala, a terrific torrent pent between narrow cliffs. The most striking impression of the entire journey is the variety of the physical geography. It is as if nature had conspired to afford one the maximum of new sensations. Nowhere else in the world have I observed such apparent discontinuity, such wealth of unexpected phenomena tumbling over each other to claim astonishment and admiration.

There are no dak baghlas in these remote districts; so we were living in our tents. We dined in the open air under the apricots, while by our side one of the local elders exuded over five litres of serum. He had been carried down by his adherents in the last stages of dropsy; but after contributing his quota to the volume of the Bralduh, he walked cheerfully to his house without assistance, as he had not done for many months.

Goitre is very common in this valley and I hoped to learn something about its etiology. As in the case of cancer, many attempts have been made to generalize from insufficient facts. One of the great arguments about goitre involves the Lötschenthal, where the people at the bottom of the valley could marry strangers from the Rhone valley, and those at the top go over the Petersgrat and do their courting in Lauterbrunnen. Those in the middle were more inbred. It was accordingly observed that goitre was more common among them. The Bralduh Nala completely upset any such theory, for while there was the same narrowness and isolation, the same limestone water and similar conditions all along, the goitre varies from village to village in an absolutely irregular way.

The whole nala is full of interest. It is a regular showplace for the weirdest phenomena. About an hour and a half above Ghomboro is a tributary nala, with only a trickle of water but swept by intermittent flushes of mud. Its crossing presented a certain problem. I had to post a man to give warning when a torrent was on the way. I myself went down into the bed of the torrent, which was very steep and slimy, and hacked good steps for the coolies. If one had slipped, or been caught by a gush of mud, there would have been no saving him. It took about an hour and a half for the caravan to cross. Half an hour later, we came to a second obstacle of this sort, but it was very different in character. It was a level expanse of mud, very broad. The torrent had caked to a reasonable consistency under the banks, but there was a central section forty to fifty yards wide of very lively-moving stuff. The tehsildar of Skardu had sent up a gang of men to throw great stones into the stream for several days, for the mud moves very slowly. By this means, they had managed to make a sort of temporary bridge, the most quickly moving part of the stream in the centre being negotiated by the laying of a plank between stones. Our own men, of course, supplemented the efforts of their colleagues, each man bringing a stone as large as he could carry and dropping it into the most suitable place he could see. Having helped the men over the first torrent, I had automatically become rearguarded, and the bulk of the men had gone gaily over the second and more formidable obstacle when I arrived. They had got it into excellent condition and I strolled over as if it had been stepping stones across the Wharfe or the Lynn, and I was going to meet my girl!

The next entertainment is a rope bridge. The 'ropes' in question are composed of twigs. There are three main ropes, one to walk on and two to hold. The relations between the three are secured by a trellis of smaller twigs. They are a little terrifying at first sight, it is only fair to admit; but one cannot help thinking that Sir Martin Conway was almost too considerate of the nervousness of others when he insisted on roping Zurbriggen on one side of him and Bruce on the other before pirouetting lightly across.

The day following, another rope bridge brought us back to the right bank of the Bralduh, where another phenomenon of astonishing beauty lay in wait. The extremely narrow gorge through which the Bralduh rushes for so many miles had suddenly broadened out. We were in a wide smiling valley ringed with mountains which, gigantic as they were, seemed to confess by the comparative mediocrity of their structure that they were second rate. The valley is wholly bare of verdure except for plantations, as throughout Baltistan. The first thing to meet our eyes was what, suppose we had landed in the country of Brobdignag, only more so, might have been the lace handkerchief of a Super-Glumdalclitch left out to dry. It was a glittering veil of brilliance on the hillside; but closer inspection, instead of destroying the illusion, made one exclaim with increased enthusiasm.

The curtain had been formed by crystalline deposits from a hot spring (38·3° centigrade). The incrustation is exquisitely white and exquisitely geometrical in every detail. The burden of the cynicism of my six and twenty years fell from me like a dream. I trod the shining slopes: they rustled under my feet rather as snow does in certain conditions. (The sound is strangely exhilarating.) It is a voluptuous flattery like the murmurous applause of a refined multitude, with the instinctive ecstatic reverence of a man conscious of his unworthiness entering paradise. At the top of the curtain is the basin from which it proceeds, the largest of several similar formations. It is some thirty-one feet in diameter, an almost perfect circle. The depth in the middle is little over two feet. It is a bath for Venus herself.

I had to summon my consciousness of Godhead before venturing to invade it. The water streams delicately with sulphurous emanations, yet the odour is subtly delicious. Knowles, the doctor and I spent more than an hour and a half reposing in its velvet warmth, in the intoxicatingly dry mountain air, caressed by the splendour of the sun. I experienced all the ecstasy of the pilgrim who has come to the end of his hardships. I felt as if I had been washed clean of all the fatigues of the journey. In point of fact, I had arrived, despite myself, at perfect physical condition. I had realized from the first that the proper preparation for a journey of this sort is to get as fat as possible before starting, and stay as fat as possible as long as possible. I was now in the condition in which Pfannl had been at Srinagar. I could have gone forty-eight hours without turning a hair.

Pfannl himself was still in excellent form, but he had used up a lot of his reserve force, though he showed no signs of having done so. He was thirty-one and should have possessed much more endurance than I. People in general have very erroneous ideas about age. For rock climbing or lyric poetry one is doubtless best in one's twenties. For a Himalayan expedition or dramatic composition, it is better to be forty than thirty. Eckenstein at forty-three, despite his congenital tendency to respiratory troubles, was by no means too old; and Knowles, twenty years younger, was emphatically too young. Guillarmod, at thirty-three, and Wessely, at thirty-one, suffered less than any of us.

In Wessely's case this was mostly because he had not imagination enough to be ill. None of us had ever seen such a perfect pig. He was very greedy and very myopic. In order to eat, he would bend his head over his plate and, using his knife and fork like the blades of a paddle wheel, would churn the food into his mouth with a rapid rotatory motion. There was always some going up, and always some going down, until he deposited his well-sucked instruments of nutrition on a perfectly clean plate and asked for more. It was the most disgusting sight that I have ever seen. Explorers are not squeamish; but we had to turn our heads away when Wessely started to eat. I admit and deplore my human weakness. All forms of genius should be admired and studied, and Wessely was a world's champion.

My first experience of gluttony was at Tonbridge. One of my best friends was the fat boy of the house. (He was a nephew of the Adams who discovered Neptune.) One day he was sent two pounds and proceeded to the tuck-shop, where one could buy a very generously estimated ice-cream for sixpence. We thought to share in the bounty; but Adams said no with truly Roman fortitude and tortured us by consuming the whole four score ice-creams himself.

At Cambridge one of my most intimate friends was a man named Parez of Emmanuel, and in him I recognized a supreme trencherman. One Saturday I had been held up at Hitchin, my racing roadster having sprung a leak. I got back to Cambridge too late to order brunch from the kitchens, so on Sunday morning there was nothing for it but to go round to Parez and see if he could feed me. To my joy, I found him reading and smoking by the side of a table spread with a brunch for six, conceived in a spirit of gargantuan hospitality. I invited myself, of course; but to my surprise Parez declined, saying that there was hardly enough for the party as it was. 'Hang it,' said I, 'for God's sake let me stay; perhaps one of them won't turn up.' My host agreed, remarking that the born-out-of-wedlock offenders against the Criminal Law Amendment Act were late. After a couple of games of chess something reminded him that he had forgotten to send out any invitations! We finished that brunch and I swear to God I didn't eat more than one and a half or one and three quarters myself.

Later I asked him to dinner in London. He began with two large fried soles to his own cheek, and went on with a porterhouse steak. I forget the rest. But, compared with Wessely, he was Succi! When Wessely reached Rdokass on the return journey, the servants asked permission to celebrate by killing two sheep of the flock which we had taken there; they would, of course, cook the best parts of the meat for the sahibs. Pfannl could eat nothing, and Guillarmod very little, but in a short time the servants repeated their request. Wessely had devoured practically the whole two sheep. Of course the mountain variety is not a Southdown. It probably does not weigh

more than the average four months lamb in Sussex. But even
so Wessely's exploit is pretty good.

On my own arrival at Rdokass, I made rather a beast of
myself. I had been starving on canned food for nearly two
months, and that half-warm, half-cooked fresh mutton made
me particularly insane. I was suffering the agonies of sugar
starvation plus the effects of a recurrence of malaria, so that
vomiting and diarrhoea were continuous. But never in my
whole life have I tasted anything like that mutton. I gorged
myself to the gullet, was violently sick and ordered a fresh
dinner.

> I am more an antique Roman than a Dane,
> There's yet some mutton left.

I may mention in this place that experience has convinced
me of the truth of the Hindu theories about Prana. Apart from
the chemical and physiological transactions involved in eating,
one is nourished directly, by what one must call, however one
may hate to do so, the vital principle in food. We had already
found on Iztaccihuatl that canned food ten years old failed
to nourish anything like as well as stuff recently tinned. We
derived much more energy from fresh-killed mutton, cooked
before rigor mortis had set in, than from ordinary butcher's
meat. I ultimately learnt that I could make myself actually
drunk on half a dozen oysters chewed in the manner of the
yogis.

One of the practices of Hatha Yoga consists in learning to
reverse the peristaltic action of the alimentary canal at will,
so that one can make oneself sick quietly without spasmodic
action. What they do is to swallow a number of yards of
tarband and eject it again by training the necessary muscles.
They then apply these principles to their rice and, after allowing it to remain in the stomach for a short time, quietly reject
it. This rice, though unchanged in appearance, contains no
nourishment, so that a dog who ate it would starve. The
object of the yogi is to relieve his body of the responsibility
of dealing with the elements of the food which do not contribute to sustenance. One is forced to suspect the existence of
some subtle principle attached to organic substances which
gradually disappears after death, rapidly at first, and then with
increasing slowness, so that the process is not complete perhaps
for years. It is like the elimination of impurities from alcohol,
the first distillation gets rid of most of them, but there is a
residuum carried over which requires repeated fractionation.

37

From the hot spring one goes gently along the valley to Askole. The whole march is short, easy and delightful. It only occupied five hours, of which at least three were spent at the rope bridge and in the pool.

The entire journey had been extraordinarily favourable. We had had very little bad weather, the coolies had behaved admirably, there had been no accidents and no sickness, except for my own dermatological trouble. At Askole, however, several of the servants were slightly indisposed for a couple of days.

We spent ten days in this village. Beyond this point there are no supplies of any sort. It was therefore necessary to establish a depot of food for the men higher up. The difficulty in travelling in uninhabited countries is that a man who eats (say) two pounds a day and carries sixty pounds can carry nothing except his own food on a journey of thirty marches. Our problem was how to get about one hundred and ten loads deposited at a distance representing (there and back) not less than twenty marches. We bought every pound of everything eatable in the valley and employed every man available. This meant (roughly) three men to carry one load, one for the load itself, the other two for the food of the three. Even with the advance depots, the task strained the resources of the valley.

There was one trifling conflict of opinion between myself and Eckenstein at Askole. It was arranged that our valises should not exceed forty pounds on the glacier, though many of the loads exceeded fifty. I could not get my belongings within the limit. Eckenstein wanted me to leave behind my library. His theory of travelling in wild countries was that one should temporarily become an absolute savage; but my experience had already shown me that man shall not live by bread alone, but by every word that proceedeth out of the mouth of God. I attributed the almost universal mental and moral instability of Europeans engaged in exploring to their lack of proper intellectual relaxation far more than to any irritations and hardships inseparable from physical conditions.

Conrad's 'An Outpost of Progress' and Kipling's story of the lighthouse keeper who went mad are outstanding examples of the psychological processes which are likely to occur. Perfectly good friends become ready to kill each other over a lump of sugar. I won't say that I couldn't have stood the Baltoro glacier in the absence of Milton and the rest; but it is at least the case that Pfannl went actually mad, that Wessely brooded on food to the point of stealing it, and that Eckenstein and Knowles * both lost their heads over the cholera scare! Thus the only man beside myself to retain perfect mental balance was the doctor, who kept his mind constantly occupied by observations in natural history, photography, writing articles for the Swiss newspapers, keeping an elaborate journal for the purposes of his book on the expedition, and spending the rest of his spare time in playing chess with me.

Eckenstein made himself quite unpleasant to me, which was utterly out of his character; and, by itself, evidence of the strain on his temper caused by the Austrian idiocies and vanities. I wasted no words. I merely shrugged my shoulders and said: either I took my books with me or I left the expedition. Needless to say, I carried my point. It may strike some people that I was a little *outre-cuidant* about it; but I take matters like this very seriously. I would rather bear physical starvation than intellectual starvation, any day of the week. It is one of the most frightful consequences of increasing age that one finds fewer and fewer of one's contemporaries worth talking to. One is forced more and more to seek society either with the great masters of the past or with discarnate intelligences.

Pfannl and Wessely had become rather a nuisance. They complained of Eckenstein's discipline and made themselves notably unpleasant. We rather encouraged them to go off all day and make heroic ascents. But their proposal to take three days' provisions in their rucksacks and go off and climb K2 was negatived. It is really astonishing that so many days of travel had taught them nothing about the scale of the mountains. One cannot measure them by feet and miles. I myself cannot quite see how it is that the difference comes in. But there is no doubt of the fact. It is quite useless to talk of climbing a mountain whose summit is five thousand feet above the starting point, as one could do if one were in the Alps.

---

* The latter under the powerful influence of the Chief—otherwise he would not have turned a hair.

For one thing, however perfect may be one's physical condition, the effect of marching day after day is to make it somehow impossible to make an extra effort. I suppose it is the difference between the hundred yards and the three miles at Queens. But apart from this, there seems to be some subtle factor which determines the limit of the day's work. But if I could not explain, at least I thoroughly appreciated, the conditions.

Another difficulty made it clear that the foreigners in the expedition were simply dead weight. Knowles himself, docile, cheerful and phlegmatic, could not give much active assistance. In view of the character of the glacier, the party could no longer travel as a unit after leaving terra firma. Only Eckenstein and I spoke Hindustani; only Eckenstein or I could be trusted to lead. The Austrians were always making heroic gestures, and Guillarmod finally demonstrated his incapacity by wandering out one day and getting crag-fast in a perfectly easy place. His misadventure would have been a blow to our prestige had not the natives already accepted him as Tartarin. Our arrangements were therefore settled for us by circumstances. Eckenstein's power of organization was unique. There was no choice but to leave him at Paiyu to dispatch relays of food. I was thus the only possible leader, and I had to go alone because the Austrians were inseparable, and it was better for Knowles and the doctor to be as near Eckenstein as possible. We accordingly started in four sections; I, with a picked body of coolies, the Austrians a day later, Knowles, and the doctor twenty-four hours behind him, and Eckenstein as soon as I had carried out my objective of reconnoitring the mountain and establishing a main camp at its foot. I could not but feel that Eckenstein had shown bad judgment in collecting so unwieldy a party. I believe to this day that if he, I and Knowles had been alone, we should have diminished our difficulties by sixty per cent, and perhaps walked up the mountain before the weather broke.

Thanks to our rapid march from Srinagar, we were a fortnight ahead of our programme. We were afraid of getting to the mountain too early in the season; but from what I now know of the climate, we should have done much better to rush through and tackle the mountain before the breaking of the monsoon in India.

Another ill effect of including the foreign element was this. Eckenstein, somewhat forgetful of the principles of selfless concentration which are essential to the performance of any

Great Work, made a point of admitting the existence of the possibility of international jealousy. He therefore forbade me to cross the Bergschrund before the whole party had arrived at the main camp, which it was my business to establish at the foot of the mountain proper. I wish I had remembered about Nelson's blind eye. When I arrived at Camp 10 on the level glacier above the ice fall underneath the south-eastern slopes of Chogo Ri, I could have gone on without any difficulty up those slopes to the well-marked shoulder immediately beneath the final pyramid, and had I done so, I have no doubt whatever that we could have made a successful dash for the summit.

I started on June 5th for Korophon, going as slowly as I could. The march occupied over forty-eight hours. The march crosses the Biafo glacier; and there I had my first real taste of certain conditions peculiar to the Himalayas. There is a violent alternation of heat and cold between night and day. The maximum shade temperature, rarely less than 25° centigrade, often touched 30° and sometimes climbed close to 40°, whereas the minimum was hardly ever above zero, even at Askole, and on the glacier reached anything from −10° to −30°. The result is that a few minutes of sunshine produces revolutionary results. A thick hard crust of snow disappears almost instantaneously and leaves one floundering in a mass of seething crystals. Rocks perched on ice become very hot in an incredibly short time and break loose from the ice on which they are poised in a way which takes men of merely Alpine experience by surprise. My Mexican expedition proved invaluable in enabling me to foresee these phenomena. But the first warning was given on this march when two enormous stones which, anywhere else, would have stayed where they were for years, fell about twenty yards in front of me and the advance guard!

When I say Korophon, it must not be imagined that it means anything more than a mark on the map. It is distinguishable only by a cubical block of granite about twenty feet high, under the two overhanging sides of which a little wall has been built by the shepherds who occasionally lead their flocks so far afield. One wonders why; for even at Korophon itself the vegetation is extremely sparse and scrubby.

The next day I went on to Bardumal at the foot of the spur. There are actually a few trees at this place. On this march one has to cross the Punmah, a broad and shallow stream which I found easy enough to ford. The alternative—to which we were reduced on our return—is to trudge about six miles up stream to a rope bridge and down the other bank. It may be that the low barometric pressure affects the velocity of running water, for streams seem much swifter than one would expect from the slope. The current carries down round stones in the most dangerous way. When Knowles tried to ford this river on the way back, though the water was barely knee-deep, he was swept away at once, and would have been drowned or battered to death in a few seconds if he had not been promptly pulled back by the rope which he had prudently put on. As it was, he received two violent blows from stones, one of which nearly snapped his thigh and the other his spine. On looking at the photographs of this stream, it seems positively ridiculous to associate the slightest danger with crossing them.

The following day we went on to Paiyu, a dreary march of some five hours, enlivened only by the feelings that we were getting somewhere. The narrowness of the valleys and the steepness of the spurs of the great range prevent one getting any view of the high peaks. On this day's march we had our first glimpse of a giant, the Mustagh Tower, and the sublimity of the sight made up for the monotony of the march.

There are many phenomena of extraordinary interest, had we not been surfeited with things stupendous and strange. At one part of this journey, we were literally walking for hours on garnets. Another marvel is a range of stratified eruptive rocks whch stand out brilliantly black against the greys and browns of the background. Near Paiyu there is a regular range of mountains composed of consolidated glacial mud. Again, there is a row of pinnacles capped by enormous boulders on the principle of glacier tables. They have been weathered into slender tapering cones; the stone at the top has protected them from being washed down evenly.

Paiyu is an open plateau boasting at least three trees. We were to remain a day here to build a stone house to protect our supplies and to do the repacking necessary for my advance guard.

In the course of this work, the trouble with our Pathan servants came to a head. We had had several complaints of their arrogance and overbearing behaviour towards the natives, and now we found that they had stolen some fowls from our travelling farmyard, which included, by the way, fifteen sheep and thirty goats. We also discovered that they had stolen and sold practically the whole of our reserve sugar. There was nothing to do but to sack them, which we did.

Out of this arose an incident which I shall always remember with peculiar delight. I was able to play Haroun al-Raschid and administer poetic oriental justice. We had furnished the malefactors with magnificent new coats for the journey. One of the men, not content with this, had bullied and cheated one of the Kashmiri servants out of his torn rags, and insisted on disrobing his victim that he might bear away the spoils on his departure. To all intents and purposes, the man was left with nothing to wear. He complained to me. I heard the case with grave attention; I had to admit that by native justice the clothes belonged to the marauder, who grinned and triumphed and redoubled his insults to his discomfited dupe. 'But wait,' said I. 'Hassan's coat certainly belongs to you, but the coat *you* are wearing belongs to *me*!' So I made him take it off and clothed the unfortunate Hassan in its splendours, while the villain of the piece had to go off down the valley (where a nice prison was waiting for him) clad in the wretched rags, much too small for him, amid the joy of the entire caravan at seeing the biter bit.

This episode is very instructive. One of the best ways of endearing oneself to the Eastern mind is to show ingenuity in doing essential justice in accordance with legal formality. The instinct which makes us sympathize with Arsène Lupin, Raffles and Co. is universal. Unfortunately, in the West, we have lost the idea of the just despot. Our judges seem to derive cynical amusement from contemplating the absurdities and abominations which result from formal fidelity to the law. We have lost sight of the fact that law is essentially no more than a generalized statement of prevailing customs. This is so true that it is fair to say that abstract ideas of justice have little to do with primitive legislation; the idea is only to enforce compliance with current conventions.

But nowadays, legislation has broken its banks. It has become a thing in itself and has arrogated to itself the right of revolutionizing the habits of the people in utter indifference to their wishes, but in accordance with abstract ideals which take no account of existing conditions. 'Prohibition' is of course the most outrageous example of this inhuman tyranny. But all such aberrations from common sense defeat themselves in the long run. The law of Moses was entirely intelligible to the least of the Children of Israel; but today not even the greatest judges can pretend to know what the law is until the case at issue has been thrashed out and the decision established as a precedent.

The most honest man cannot always be sure that he is not violating some statute. This is even more appallingly and Gilbertianly true in the United States, where federal laws, state laws, municipal laws and police regulations clash their contradictory complexities at every turn. 'Ignorance of the law excuses no man.' But it leads him to take his chance of a peril which he cannot but ignore, and thus the law falls into disrespect and ultimately into desuetude. In the meantime, small gangs take advantage of their special knowledge to blackmail certain sections of the community by technical persecution. We see the censorship, the licensing laws, the inland revenue laws, and even certain commercial and criminal laws arbitrarily invoked against people who have no idea that they are doing wrong in doing exactly as their neighbours do.

38

I left Paiyu with about twenty coolies on the ninth of June.
A very short distance brings one to the snout of the glacier,
black, greasy and nearly five hundred feet high at the lowest
point. The Bralduh rushes from a cavern very repulsively. A
great many phenomena observed on this expedition impress
one with a kind of horror. I used to think it utterly absurd in
books of travel to see moral qualities associated with nature.
At this period of my life, above all, I should have scouted
any such idea; but, through the glasses of memory, one can
analyse oneself beyond one's protestations. This muddy torrent
issuing from its vast black source certainly created an ugly
impression. The reason may be that stopping, as I naturally
did, to have a good look at it, the presence of that vast body of
ice produced a slight physical chill which I promptly translated
into emotional terms and attributed wrongly to what I saw
instead of to what I felt. There is also probably a strong
Freudian element; the cold, black muddiness of the water and
its relentless turmoil, its unstaunchability, so to speak, may
suggest the flowing of blood from a wound, or some such
disease as nephritis. The general symbol, again, goes unpleasantly with the ideas of ice and grit; the general tone of the
blackness of the debris is peculiarly unsympathetic.

There was no difficulty in finding a way up the snout. I
knew that the first camp, Liligo, was on the left bank, so
moved over in that direction. (German professors two hundred years hence are requested not to confuse the name of
this *parau* with the 'little-go' at Cambridge, though both are
alike first stages on a lonely climb leading to nowhere.)

The glacier was a complete revelation to me. The difference
in scale had merely multiplied one's difficulty accordingly in
previous matters; but here they become more formidable in a
geometrical progression with a big *f*. In Switzerland one does
not see many moraines over a hundred feet high. Here they
run to a thousand or fifteen hundred feet. There are something like twenty tributary glaciers feeding the Baltoro. Each
of these contributes at least three moraines. The glacier being

about thirty miles long, and rarely more than two wide, it is distinctly a congested district! The competing moraines jostle each other unscrupulously. One would hardly know that one was on ice at all for the first ten miles; there is hardly a bare patch. But the close competition tends to form many steep slopes; and this means that the sides of most of the moraines are covered with rocks which, even when they are of enormous size, are in extremely unstable equilibrium. Again, the pressure and temperature combine to loosen the bands of rock and ice. The general result is that the passage of a party rearranges that section of the glacier much more radically than would be the case in the Alps. The task of picking one's way is very arduous; and there is a good deal of luck about it, for there is no means of telling whether one may not at any moment be cut off by an obstacle. For example—the rivulets which flow openly through small channels on Swiss glaciers may here be torrents rushing through cuttings in the ice anything up to a hundred feet broad and deep. In the Alps, I remember few such places where I could not step across easily, and those few were always within a bit of a jump.

One's eyesight does not help one much to find the way. The view is always cut off; even by climbing to the top of a moraine one gets little practical information. The muddle is essentially meaningless to the mountaineer. It is quite rare to be able to mark down a comparatively level passage of a couple of hundred yards which might be worth while making for. Each line of moraine has to be crossed in the serious spirit of a pioneer looking for a pass across a range. The instability of the surface means a constant tendency to slip, so that the journey is morally tedious and physically wearisome beyond belief. The compensation is the majesty of the surrounding mountains. Nowhere else in the world does there exist anything like the same diversity of form. The effect is enhanced by the recognition that practically every peak is unclimbable by our present standards. Men accustomed to mountains instinctively reconnoitre everything they see, and in this district one is constantly being astonished at the completeness of the defences of even quite insignificant peaks.

Above the camp at Liligo are most formidable precipices of rotten rock. In some places they actually overhang; and one wonders how they manage to stay there at all, especially in view of the rapidly disintegrating action of the weather.

The next day I went on to Rhobutse; a very short march, but I did not want to tire the men, and this was the only good camping place for some distance. There was a great deal of snow and rain in the early part of the day, though it cleared up in the afternoon. Just after sunset, however, a very violent wind sprang up. On the eleventh, I went on to Rdokass, a much longer march in distance. But the going on the glacier had become much easier. I found some comparatively level stretches.

The natives were extremely good in every way; their character compares favourably with that of any race I have ever seen. We never heard of them coming to blows or even to really high words. Imagine the difference with European peasants! Some of their customs are worth mentioning. For one thing, they never take off their clothes all their lives. A baby is wrapped in a rag; presently a second round the first, and so on. But they never remove the innermost layer; it is allowed to disintegrate by itself. The richer a man becomes, the more clothes he is able to buy, so that the headmen of a village are like rolls of cloth.

Their method of preparing their food on the glacier is ingenious. Having made a fire, they get a stone as nearly round as possible and heat it thoroughly through. Round this they smear their paste of flour and water, twisting the whole into their shawls. By the time they have arrived in camp the paste is baked through and still hot.

One cannot wash on the glacier—nay, not so much as one's hands. The extreme dryness of the atmosphere removes all the natural grease of the skin, which becomes so brittle that the touch of water causes it to peel off, leaving a horribly painful, and practically unhealable, wound. I let my hands get as greasy and as dirty as I could to protect them. When thus coated, it is safe to leave them in contact with water, provided it is not for too long and there is no rubbing. One can indeed put one's hands into boiling water, for at these low barometric pressures water boils easily. At Rdokass, for example, water boils at 87·4°, corresponding to 13,904 feet; higher up, it is of course less.

In spite of not washing, one does not get at all dirty. After my bath on May 25th, I abstained until August 19th—eighty-five days—but I found myself absolutely clean except my hands and face. The only inconvenience was lice. These insects live inexpugnably in the seams of one's clothes. It is useless to try to dislodge them, because every time one gets near a Balti, the supply is renewed.

Rdokass remains to this day in my memory as a veritable

Beulah. It is a broad grassy ledge on the rocks two or three
hundred feet above the glacier. There are superb views in
every direction. But there is 'something about the place' beyond
that; the atmosphere of restfulness is paramount. There was
here quite a lot of grass; even some flowers. I accordingly sent
word to bring our flocks along. It was the last oasis of any account and in fact the only place of its kind that we found on the
whole glacier. The day after, I crossed the glacier to Lhungka.
It was a very nervous business picking one's way across the
moraines, especially as I had to build stone men to guide the
other parties, and I had only the vaguest ideas as to what point
on the other bank of the glacier to make for. I climbed a high
point in the middle and took compass observations, as I could
now see Masherbrum (25,660 feet) and Gusherbrum (26,630
feet). These peaks are the most spectacular of the whole range;
the one a stupendous wedge of brilliantly lighted rock and ice;
the other a dim luminous cone. It had this appearance because
of its orientation. We never saw it in full light; because at
sunset, when it would have been illuminated, it happened
always to be cloudy.

My compass observations distressed me extremely. I was
trying to reconcile nature with Conway's map; and my difficulties were scarcely less than those which disturbed the peace
of Victorian theologians. The natives made it worse; for Conway had named the glaciers on their information, and what
they told me was in some respects quite different.

At Lhungka I built a shelter for the coolies, a low stone
wall behind which they could lie in case of violent wind. It
would of course have been impossible to take tents for them;
but as a matter of fact they did not complain of cold at any
time. The thermometer did not register more than five degrees
centigrade of frost till after June 18th.

The next day I went on to Ghore, where I found a delightful camping ground of fine level sand. (On our return, by the
way, this was completely flooded.)

From Ghore to Biange is another long march, but less
monotonous. The views are increasingly superb and the solitude was producing its beneficent results. The utterly disproportionate minuteness of man purges him of his smug belief
in himself as the final cause of nature. The effect is to produce
not humiliation but humility, and this feeling is only the threshold of a selflessness which restores the balance by identifying
one with the universe of which one's physical basis is so imper-
ceptibly insignificant a fraction.

From Biange one can see Mitre Peak across the glacier. Although a relatively minor summit (7,500 metres), its architecture is incomparable. The name is inevitable. From this point of view the double horn could not fail to suggest the title. (I had myself indulged in a little nomenclature, calling a mountain crowned by three square-cut towers of rock 'Three Castles'.)

The next day a short march took me to Doksam. I was now almost at the head of the Baltoro glacier (15,518 feet). In nearly thirty miles of march I had only made four hundred feet of ascent. But here I was on the floor of a glacier at a height close to that of Mont Blanc. In front of me the glacier widened out; three major and several minor glaciers coalesced. I was irresistibly reminded of the Concordia Platz in the Oberland and named the plateau in affectionate remembrance.

Once again the astounding variety of nature in this district impressed itself upon my mind. One would have said that it was theoretically impossible to combine so many types of mountain. The obvious exception to the otherwise invariable rule of practical inaccessibility was the Golden Throne, a minor point of which Conway claims to have climbed. I was very disgusted at the bad taste of some of the coolies who had been with him in saying that he had never been on the mountain at all, but turned back at the foot of the ice fall. How could such common creatures presume to decide a delicate scientific question of this sort?

My camp at Doksam was pitched on the borders of a good-sized lake between the mountains and the glacier, which at this point presents a wall of ice well over a thousand feet high. The position is consequently comparatively sheltered and in its way very agreeable. The presence of still water lends it the charm of utter peace, and the absence of the vermin which desecrate the crust of the earth so objectionably in other places is rendered even more agreeable by the jolly courageous children who were my comrades and my friends. I went out reconnoitring for three hours in the middle of the day and got a very clear idea of the situation. A sudden snowstorm of a rather severe type swept the camp for an hour; but at four o'clock the weather again cleared. 'Tomorrow to fresh woods and pastures new'—except that there were neither woods nor pastures! 'We were the first that ever burst into that silent sea' —except that there wasn't any sea! The poets are really very thoughtless to leave their heir without an appropriate quotation!

On the sixteenth of June I marched for a little over four hours where man had never yet trodden. It proved to be the easiest going yet. The eternal moraine was less in evidence; we were able to walk over admirable snow most of the way. Once more, though, I have to record a unique phenomenon totally out of keeping with the rest. At the corner of the Baltoro glacier and its northern affluent, the Chogo Lungma, as I named it, one has to cross a scree of pure white marble. Eckenstein, who arrived at this point in a snowstorm, found it very distressing. He told me that it was impossible to pick footholds; the entire surface was a blinding glare. Camp 8 (16,592 feet) is situated at the foot of a subsidiary spur descending from the ridge of which Chogo Ri is the climax. I was now in full view of the mountain itself, bar clouds; and, my first duty being to reconnoitre the mountain, I spent all day and all night watching it through my glasses, sketch-book in hand. The clouds shifted sufficiently to enable me to make a piecemeal picture, and I came to the conclusion that while the south face, perhaps possible theoretically, meant a complicated climb with no half-way house, there should be no difficulty in walking up the snow slopes on the east-south-east to the snowy shoulder below the final rock pyramid. I sent back word accordingly and went on much encouraged. There was still no difficulty of any kind; the snow was excellent; but after three and a half hours, I decided to stop at Camp 9 (17,332 feet) directly under the south face of the mountain. Above this camp the glacier becomes comparatively steep and I did not wish to take a chance of getting my coolies into trouble. They had amused me very much, by the way, at Camp 8 before starting, by coming and telling me that of course they didn't believe me when I said I would send them back as soon as they got to the eastern foot of Chogo Ri. They knew quite well that I only said it to lure them on; they knew that I meant to make them cross to Yarkand; they knew that they would die to a man; but they didn't mind, it was Kismet, and they wanted me to know that they would gladly die because I had been so nice to them. When I sent them home from Camp 10 they could hardly believe their ears, and their delight at being reprieved was pathetically charming.

Modern writers have made a great deal of fun of the golden age; they have been at great pains to prove that primitive man is a bloodthirsty savage. The Balti gives them the lie. These men were all innocence, all honesty, all good faith, all loyalty, all human kindness. They were absolutely courageous and cheerful, even in face of what they supposed to be certain death of a most uncomfortable kind. They had no disquietude about death and no distaste for life. They were simple-minded and merry. It was impossible not to love them, and not to contrast them with the dirty despicable insects whose squabbles and crimes make civilization itself the greatest of all crimes, and whose ignorance (for all their boasting) is actually darker and deeper and more deadly than that of these children.

From Camp 9 there is a rapid rise of fourteen hundred feet to Camp 10 (18,733 feet). I was a little doubtful as to how the pabu of the men would behave. Pabu are a kind of footgear which reminds one of a gouty man. Straw or rags are wrapped round the feet by thongs of raw hide. Their softness enables the wearer to get excellent hold on moraine, and they protect the feet from cold very effectively. The question is whether they would not slip on the hard snow. I was consequently very careful to pick the easiest way and to scrape large steps when necessary. I took the first few men up on a rope, explaining the use of it, and told them how to keep their eyes skinned for concealed crevasses. They were highly intelligent; picked up the trick of everything without argument or complaint, and made no mistakes.

I ought to mention their ingenious defence against snow blindness. They wear their hair rather long, and they make a plaited fringe to hang down over their eyes like a curtain. The device does not sound very effective; but it seems to work. It is at least a fact that we did not have a single case. On Kangchenjunga, where this plan is not known, a number of the men were seriously affected.

I was blamed subsequently for my selection of Camp 10 as main camp. Eckenstein thought that I might have chosen a more sheltered position. But there were no such positions in the neighbourhood and it was quite useless to go further away from the foot of the slopes which it was my intention to climb. Furthermore, during my ten days on the glacier, I had experienced all sorts of weather, and none of it had given the slightest ground for supposing that we were likely to meet any conditions which would make Camp 10 other than a desirable country residence for a gentleman in failing health. My principal preoccupation, moreover, was to keep out of the way of avalanches and falling stones. I had already seen enough of the apparently arbitrary conduct which one might expect from them; I thought it best therefore to choose a level spot in the middle of the glacier.

Even as it was, there was an avalanche on the tenth of July which snowed both on Camp 10 and Camp 11. Avalanches at this altitude—and in this latitude—differ (nevertheless) from those on lower peaks. Snow does not melt at all unless subjected to pressure. It evaporates without melting. It never forms a compact mass with a hard crust as it does in the Alps. I have seen ten feet of freshly fallen snow disappear completely in the course of an hour's sunshine. Extraordinary as it sounds, despite the perpetual bad weather which we experienced, the snow on the lower glacier (between Camps 9 and 7) had completely disappeared in August, while that on the upper glacier had very much increased.

As a result of these conditions, a first-rate avalanche may never reach the foot of the slope down which it starts; it may evaporate almost entirely en route. One of our photographs shows an avalanche actually in the process of falling. It would have overwhelmed the photographer under Alpine conditions.

I must admit to a certain heaviness of heart in obeying my instructions and sending back the men. It was so obviously right to take them up the slopes to the shoulder and establish the camp at a point whence Chogo Ri could have been reached without question, given one fine day. But my orders were formal and I never thought of disobedience. Of course, if I had foreseen the volte-face of the weather, I might have decided otherwise.

I was a little worried by the failure of Pfannl and Wessely to maintain the communications for which arrangements had been made. I could not see their party on the glacier below and wondered whether they had not broken loose. It was just the sort of thing that one might expect; to find that they had bolted up the south end of the mountain and spoilt the whole plan. They arrived, however, on the next day, the nineteenth, and on the twentieth Knowles and the doctor joined us. They arrived in a snowstorm which continued the whole day. It was the first of uninterruptedly bad weather. On the twenty-first the wind dropped, though the snow continued. It tried to clear up on the twenty-second; and the twenty-third was fine. But of course, nothing could be done in the absence of Eckenstein. On the twenty-fourth a blizzard began. It was the most furious wind that I have ever known. A corner of my tent broke loose; and the only remedy was to sit on it the whole morning! The violence of the wind was indeed amazing. I had secured the side ropes of my tent by tying them round square kiltas and putting others on top. There was thus over one hundred pounds to hold down each rope; but the wind made no bones about shifting them. The twenty-fifth was a dull doubtful day; and on the twenty-sixth the weather was rather worse. On the twenty-seventh it cleared up in the afternoon and Eckenstein arrived with fresh meat and bread.

39

The twenty-eighth was fine and we held a durbar. It was decided that, Eckenstein being ill, Pfannl, Guillarmod and I should start up the mountain. Eckenstein voted for the doctor, *qua* doctor, in case of one of us being ill. It shows how easy he thought the slopes.

Wessely was very offensive in his resentment at not being included in the party. It was an intolerably bad piece of sportsmanship. Pfannl tended to take his side, and the pair made so much unpleasantness that we were soon reduced to the expedient of getting them out of the way as much as possible.

We got everything ready; but next morning the wind was so high that we could not start. Even while drinking our chocolate in the cooking tent, we nearly got frostbitten. After sunrise, the wind dropped; but it was too late to start. Eckenstein and Knowles were both ill, but the rest of us went on ski nearly to the pass at the top of the glacier. About four o'clock in the afternoon the wind started again and once again loosened my tent. This time snow came driving up the valley.

We had a spare tent for the use of the few natives whom we kept with us. I had gone out to try to refix my tabernacle at sunset—and there was a Balti out in the snow praying with his face towards Mecca! The religion of the Mohammedan, unlike that of the Christian, is positive. It is not based on fear, but on the actual sense of the relations of man and God. I laugh to think of the well-fed, idle and ignorant missionary at Shigar trying to convert men of this stamp. Their simplicity sees through Christian sophistication at a glance; and, their sense of ethics being outraged as well as their sense of reverence, it is easy to understand that the only converts from Mohammedanism are absolutely conscienceless scoundrels who wish to live on the scarcely camouflaged subsidies of missions.

The next day found me completely snow-blind. The pain is not so much severe as irritating. The feeling is as of having red hot sand at the back of one's eyes. One keeps on blinking with the idea of removing it, and of course it won't be removed. During my *ski-läufing* I had religiously worn goggles. My condition was due entirely to pottering about the camp for a few minutes in the snowstorm, fixing my tent. I got all right again in a couple of days. The weather was moderate on June 30th and July 1st. But from July 2nd to 6th was a continuous snowstorm. There was no remittance day or night. It was this which made Camp 10 unpopular.

We got rid of the Austrians on July 1st by sending them to Camp 11 at the corner of the north-east ridge of Chogo Ri. At this point the glacier divides into two large snow basins. One leads to the pass which I have named Windy Gap (21,500 feet) on whose north-west is the mountain at the head of the valley, which I called Staircase Peak, from the well-marked and regular indentations of its eastern ridge. The other is apparently a kind of blind alley, its circus of rocks seems to have no definite break. It is difficult to be sure of this, for when I saw it it was always a cauldron of whirling mists of snow.

Pfannl and Wessely had reported that the north-east ridge of K2 was climbable, and on Monday the seventh, which was fine, it was decided to try to ascend the mountain by that route. So main camp was to be moved to Camp 11. I was rather ill, but protested. The proposed route was in fact absurd. Camp 11 was much farther from the summit than Camp 10, and the proposal was to reach the shoulder by following a long and deeply indented ridge the wall of which is on the Chogo Lungma side, a sheer precipice of avalanche-swept slopes, except at the point which I had originally picked out.

However, I was overruled. The doctor and I prepared to leave on the eighth. It was on this occasion that we discovered the incapacity of the natives to pull a sledge. It is about three hours' march to Camp 11. The going was not bad, though I was still rather sick. The weather was again very bad. The ninth found me much better and the weather was good enough to go out. I went a considerable distance up the slopes of the mountain. There is some conflict in opinion as to the height reached by various members of the party. Eckenstein was fanatically determined never to exaggerate any exploit. We made a very great number of boiling-point determinations of the heights of our camps; but even these are subject to various sources of error. Camp 11 is roughly 20,000 feet; but I suspect it to be a little higher. I estimated my climbing at 21,500 feet at the time; but this was mostly out of respect for Eckenstein. I was his most devoted disciple; I would not have given him any chance to reproach me by making a statement which might afterwards prove an exaggeration. But my real opinion is that I reached something over 22,000 feet. I could see clearly over Windy Gap; I must have been well above it. I would not depend on the readings of aneroids in any circumstances. We had taken three instruments specially constructed; they only began to register at 15,000 feet and went to 30,000. But comparisons of the three showed—usually—that no two were alike.

In the evening I was very ill indeed; indigestion, fever, shivering. In order to breathe I had to use my whole muscular strength. I was also on the point of vomiting and remained in this condition nearly all the night. In the morning I was a little better; my breathing had become normal; but I had a great deal of pain and felt very ill and weak. The weather was splendid. Wessely and Guillarmod were encouraged to repeat my climb of the previous day; but from their report it is not clear whether or no they got farther than I did. I lay in the sunlight and rested. I noticed strange sights; a fly, a butterfly, some crows and an insect which I thought was a bee, but I could not be sure. All visited the camp. Later the camp was covered with the snow from a big avalanche from Chogo Ri. It stripped the whole wall of the north-east ridge; that is, it was about four miles broad.

Eckenstein and Knowles came up on the eleventh. Another fine day. I was still very ill; my temperature 39·4° centigrade. I did not at all realize the cause at first, simple as it was. The true explanation was very far-fetched in the actual sense of the word. My symptoms became unmistakable before long and I had to admit that I was suffering from malaria. The hardships of the journey had removed my physiological protection and the bug started to buzz about. I was thus the proud possessor of another world's record: the only man who had had malaria at over twenty thousand feet! Incidentally, I was also the only poet at that altitude. I have always been very amused at Shelley's boast that he had 'trodden the glaciers of the Alps' —the Mer de Glace and the Glacier des Boissons! But I was actually writing poetry in these camps. *Better* poetry.

Like the man who committed suicide when he learnt that he was unable to move his upper jaw, I had been annoyed by reading somewhere that it was impossible to find a rime to 'silver'. I spent my spare time in thinking up all the most impossible words in the language, finding rimes for them— good rimes, not mere assonances—and introducing them into 'Ascension Day' and 'Pentecost'. In that poem will therefore be found rimes for refuge, reverence, country, virgin, courtesan, Euripides, Aristophanes, Aeschylus, Aischulos, Sophocles, Aristobulos, Alcibiades, fortress, unfashionable, sandwich, perorate, silver, bishop (eight rimes for this word), Sidney (three rimes for this), maniac, Leviticus, Cornelius, Abra-Melin, Brahmacharya, Kismet, Winchester, Christ Church, worship, Chesterton, Srotāpatti (two rimes to this), Balliol, and so on.

I have mentioned hardships. It may be interesting to mention the nature of these. The first and greatest was malaise, which was mostly due to lack of food and exercise. The latter complaint seems rather ridiculous; but it is an absolute fact. One must not bring damp things into the tent; if one does, it practically destroys the efficacy of one's protection against cold. One must therefore stay cooped up in one's tent as long as the weather is bad. I was in charge of the kitchen and had to go out in all sorts of weather; but that was hardly exercise. I often found that by the time I had filled and lighted the stoves and got the snow melted, I could not stand the cold any longer. I had to rush back to my sleeping-bag and warm up while someone else prepared the food.

We kept warm with kangri, of a sort, when things got too bad. We had brought up a number of Japanese instras, but they would not burn; there was not enough oxygen. The cartridges could however be used if left loose in empty biscuit tins. For a similar reason pipe-smoking was impossible; the only way to do it was to relight the pipe from the flame of the candle at each puff. We had a few cigars and we could smoke these quite comfortably. (It appears that the altitude is not wholly responsible for this. At greater heights on Kangchenjunga I smoked my pipe as comfortably as at sea-level.)

This same is true about food. We found it difficult to eat anything but what may be called delicacies from the standpoint of people in our position. I felt a certain distaste for food. I had to be 'tempted' like an invalid or a fastidious child. It became obvious that Eckenstein's German army theories were inapplicable to Himalayan exploration.

We suffered little from cold in the acute way, but rather from a chronic effect. The problem of cold has not been scientifically stated by any explorer so far as I know. It is this: The normal temperature of the body is 37° centigrade. If therefore the temperature of the air is 30° one has to make up the difference by the heat disengaged by the combustion of food. If the temperature is 23° one requires theoretically twice as much food, if 15° three times as much, if 8° four times as much, if 1° five times as much, if —6° six times as much, if —13° seven times as much, if —30° eight times as much. These temperatures are very much less hot and less cold than those actually experienced. The maximum and minimum thermometers proved altogether unreliable; and the observations on the chart refer to more or less arbitrary times. Other thermometers showed temperatures of over 40° and under —30° centigrade. Unfortunately, simple arithmetic is not the only consideration. The digestive apparatus is calculated for dealing with an amount of food corresponding to, I don't know what temperature, but we might say at a guess 1°. If the average temperature is less than this, it means that you have to eat more than you can digest; and that means a gradual accumulation of troubles.

One can, of course, economize one's heat to some extent by diminishing the radiation; that is, by wearing non-conducting clothes, also by supplying artificial heat from kangris and so on. (The kangri, by the way, is a Kashmiri device. It is a pot of copper or iron in which charcoal is burnt. The natives put it under their blankets and squat on it. It is alleged that this habit explains the great frequency of cancer of the testicles or scrotum in the country. The analogy is with 'chimneysweep's cancer'.)

After cancelling out all the excrescences of the equation, the situation amounts to this: that you cannot live permanently in conditions unsuited to your organism. It is pitiful to have to make statements of this kind, seeing that it is no more than a recapitulation of the main proposition of Darwin and Spencer. But the average explorer (for some inexplicable reason) seems absolutely incapable of applying common sense, experience or the teaching of science to the vital problems with which he is posed. Here in 1922, after all our experience, we have the members of the Everest expedition drivelling about acclimatization, as if science did not exist. Norman Collie told me plainly in 1896 on his return from the Mummery expedition to Nanga Parbat, that the only chance of getting up a big mountain was to rush it. I knew Collie for a man of science and for a man of sense and experience. I trusted his information absolutely and I governed myself accordingly.

The only thing to do is to lay in a stock of energy, get rid of all your fat at the exact moment when you have a chance to climb a mountain, and jump back out of its reach, so to speak, before it can take its revenge. To talk of acclimatization is to adopt the psychology of the man who trained his horse gradually to live on a single straw a day, and would have revolutionized our system of nutrition, if the balky brute had not been aggravating enough to die on his hands. If you want to acclimatize yourself to mountain conditions, you can go and live a bit higher than the hillmen of Tibet. If you do this for fifteen generations or so, your descendants will acquire a thorax like a beer barrel and a heart capable of doing three times the work that it can at present. If you then get incarnated in your clan, you can lay siege to Chogo Ri with a reasonable prospect of success. As the hymn says,

> Patience and perseverance
> Made a Bishop of His Reverence.

This programme is however hardly acceptable to Western minds, so little penetrated with Einstein's ideas that everything has to be done in a hurry. We may therefore leave 'acclimatization' to the mentally defective heroes of the Everest expedition of 1921 and 1922. Collie was right in saying that one is living on one's capital on prolonged mountain expeditions. My experience enables me to add that it is not only a question of mountains. Any kind of prolonged hardship gradually wears one down. Again I repeat, it is pitiful to have to insist on such obvious truths. The low vitality of the working classes, the national deterioration caused by the privations of wartime, scream their warning. Anyone on earth except a member of the English Alpine Club would take it to heart.

When I went to Kangchenjunga three years later I had got everything down to a fine point. I trained at Darjeeling by feeding up as much as possible (the diet at the Drum Druid Hotel was slow starvation), by having myself massaged by an 'educated' Bengali who was a Seventh Day Adventist and stole ten pounds. I arrived at twenty-one thousand feet in absolutely perfect condition only three weeks out from the base and suffered absolutely none of the conditions which were pulling us slowly to pieces on Chogo Ri, except Wessely who, like the brute beast that he was, seemed insensible to the influence of hardship and was keeping himself in comfort by stealing the supplies of the expedition surreptitiously.

We were all suffering more or less. Knowles had lost 33 of his 186 pounds; the doctor some 20 of his 167 since leaving Askole. A man with galloping consumption could hardly do better. Our haemoglobin had diminished by twenty per cent. Eckenstein was suffering from various complicated pulmonary troubles; Knowles and the doctor were repeatedly down with influenza; as for myself, the recrudescence of my malaria, which began with a violent liver chill on the twenty-seventh of July and lasted till the end of the month, kept my temperature at 39·3° or thereabouts. Pfannl, the great athlete, had a story of his own. (Coming soon.)

Owing to the fact that snow at these altitudes evaporates without melting, it disappears from the neighbourhood of a tent, leaving a pinnacle where it is protected by the canvas. Thus, at the end of a five days' snowstorm one would find oneself perched on a plateau some feet above the rest of the glacier. (This illustrates the formation of glacier tables.) It was necessary, whatever the weather might be, to shift the tent, as otherwise the weight of the snow on the sloping sides, and the general strain, would tear the canvas. We have a photograph of the plateau from which our tents had been removed after five days of snowstorm. In the middle of the square patch of hard snow relegated by pressure are two deep depressions like rude graves. These represent the ice melted by the warmth of our bodies through a double groundsheet of Willesden canvas, the canvas of the Roberts valise and the thick cork mattress.

Pfannl and Wessely had become completely intolerable and we encouraged them to go off to Camp 12 (estimated at about 21,000 feet) on the thirteenth. The weather showed its usual readiness to cook up a storm. On the fourteenth I describe it as $(x.o.p.)n + 1$.[1] A chit (note) arrived saying that Pfannl was ill. On the fifteenth the weather cleared in the afternoon; but I could see that it meant further mischief. My diary notes that I ate a meal this day. I must have been pretty bad previously to make such an entry; for my diary, whatever its other defects, is a supreme model of the laconic style.

Another chit told us that Pfannl was worse. The doctor went up to Camp 12 to look after him. Nemesis had come to town. Athletic training, as understood by athletes, is a violation of the first principles of nature. Wilkie Collins, in *Man and Wife,* had told me about it. A little old woman is provoked to personal conflict with the Pride of England and it ends by his collapsing. The same thing had happened to Pfannl. They had the utmost difficulty to get him down to Camp 11. This misadventure lost us our last chance of making a dash for K2. There was one series of two fine days, the second of which could have been used by Knowles and myself if we had not been obliged to superintend the caravan of invalids. From the sixteenth to the nineteenth was an almost continuous snow-storm. Pfannl was suffering from oedema of both lungs and his mind was gone.

A pathetic incident sticks in my mind. He sent for me to come to his tent and told me that these dull brutes could not understand him, but that I, as a poet, would be able to enter into his feelings. He then said that there were three of him; two of them were all right; but the third was a mountain with a dagger and he was afraid that it would stab him. I did not at that time realize the significance of the delusion. Today it is obvious that the fear and fascination of the hills had got mixed up with that of the phallus, thus determining the character of the symbol. As things were, I could merely report that he was insane, and the doctor continued the treatment of keeping him continuously under morphia.

40

The twentieth was fine; and we constructed a sledge on which Pfannl could be taken down to Rdokass. Wessely was to stay with him permanently and the doctor to return as soon as he had settled him on that alp. He left on the twenty-first, which was fine; but Eckenstein and I were both ill again towards evening. On the twenty-second it once more commenced to *graupen* and threatened worse. The twenty-third was equally bad. Towards evening we perceived a strange phenomenon. We wondered at first if it could be a bear. Certainly some animal was approaching the camp on all fours. In the gathering dusk even our field glasses left us uncertain, especially as the irregularities of the glacier hid it at frequent intervals.

But when it came close, we realized that it was the doctor. His face was steaming with sweat and expressed an agony of fear. Eckenstein was not sympathetic. He merely said, 'Where's your coolie?' Guillarmod explained that he had left that specimen of the Creator's handiwork in a crevasse. Eckenstein uttered a single violent objurgation which opened new vistas on the depth of his feelings. I did not waste even one word— I was putting my boots on. Before Guillarmod had fairly crawled into his tent, Eckenstein and I were skimming over the snow on our ski with a coiled rope. (In my haste I forgot to take my goggles, which cost me another two days of snow blindness.)

I got down to the crevasse ahead of Eckenstein, but he shouted to me to wait. Here was a chance to show me in practice what he had always claimed in theory: how easily a man could be pulled out, using only one hand. The man was quite calm; but had given up hope and was committing his soul to Allah. I expect he was mostly worried about the direction of Mecca. We had no need of the coiled rope; the doctor had untied himself from his own rope and left it lying on the snow! The cowardice, incompetence and imbecility of his proceedings remain today as incomprehensible as they were then.

(I accuse myself of having minimized these things. I should

never have agreed to take him on my next expedition, but I liked the man personally so much that I instinctively made every allowance for him, and unquestionably he was suffering no less than the rest of us. I have a fatal weakness for believing the best about everybody. In face of the plainest evidence, I cannot believe in the existence of dishonesty and malice, and I always try to build with rotten material. I always imagine that I have merely to point out an error for it to be energetically eliminated, and I am constantly lost in mild surprise when the inevitable occurs. Here is a description by himself of one of his bad days.

Pour moi, je reste couché, atteint d'une attaque d'influenza plus forte que je n'en ai jamais eu: la fièvre n'est pas très intense, mais mes amygdales sont si tuméfiées et douloureuses que j'ai beaucoup de peine à respirer; le moindre mouvement produit un accès de suffocation; impossible de dormir; des douleurs lancinantes et des frissons me torturent horriblement.)

Eckenstein, punctiliously putting his left hand behind his back, pulled the coolie out with his right, though entirely unaided by the man himself. He had made up his mind to die and rather resented our interference!

On the twenty-sixth my eyes were better and I felt quite well on the morning of the twenty-seventh. I had discovered that Wessely, before he left the camp, had stolen the bulk of our emergency rations, which consisted mostly of selbst-kocher which contained delicacies dear to the Czech palate. We decided to courtmartial him at Rdokass and I wrote the speech for the prosecution on the morning of the twenty-seventh. In the afternoon I got a violent liver chill and was utterly prostrated for the rest of the day. There was much vomiting.

The storm, after a short break, became more violent than ever. On the twenty-eighth my fever and the storm continued unabated. On the twenty-ninth the storm continued without abatement and so did my fever. Vomiting again complicated things. On the thirtieth it cleared in the afternoon and my fever broke in sleep and perspiration. The night was very cold and the morrow fine until the evening, when snow began to fall, gently indeed, but with inexorable cruelty. I was well on the first of August, but the snowstorm had developed extraordinary violence. A man came up from the valley with khabar (news) that cholera had closed the right bank of the Bralduh Nala. It looked as though our retreat had been cut off.

On the second the storm raged without letting up for a moment. I had really made up my mind, ever since it had been decided to give up the idea of climbing the mountain direct from Camp 10, and from my instinctive judgment of weather, that the expedition had failed in its main objective, and I was not in the least interested in killing myself gradually against my judgment. I was absolutely satisfied with the results of my original reconnaissance of Chogo Ri, and the Archangel Gabriel could not have convinced me that we were likely to succeed in forcing a ridge over three miles long of the most desperate character.

I have also an instinct about weather. I know when it breaks for good. I cannot explain it; but there is an absolutely definite difference in what one feels in two apparently similar storms. One will blow itself out in preparation for a cloudless fortnight and the other will be the prelude to more Wagner. I was also perfectly convinced that Collie's ideas were correct. We had exhausted our vital capital; we were none of us fit to climb anything. In particular, we lacked the fine flower of vitality: the spiritual energy and enthusiasm. I doubt whether even a fortnight's fine weather would have restored us to the proper condition for an attempt on a mountain.

On August 3rd the storm was still going strong; but we packed and went down on the fourth to Camp 9, stopping at Camp 10, where many of our kiltas were still stored, to pick out anything that was worth taking home (which we calculated as anything worth over half a crown a pound) and anything which we immediately wanted, especially sugar, of which we were already in sore need. On the fifth we lay idle in medium weather, while the coolies brought down from Camp 10 the goods which we had selected, and on the sixth we went to Camp 7.

The condition of the lower glacier was astonishing. Despite all these weeks of snowstorm, it had been stripped of every vestige of snow, whereas on coming up we had walked on smooth slopes. We found dry glacier, most of which was baby séracs up to fifteen feet high, sharp, slim needles of ice which were of course impossible to negotiate. We simply had to dodge them. I was constantly ill with fever, diarrhoea and vomiting, and only recovered when I got to Ghomboro. The symptoms were literally continuous. Every few hundred yards I had to stop, go through it and go on.

On the seventh we rested at Camp 7. It was fine and the temperature in my tent was 37°; but the high peaks were 'smoking their pipes' so that a violent wind must have been blowing up there; and as the morning advanced, the clouds gathered. However, I took a chance; and washed. It is a curiously refreshing sensation. I sometimes wonder why people do not indulge in it more often. On the eighth we went to Camp 6. My indiscreet debauch with water had added a cold in the head to my other miseries. Again a fine morning degenerated into thick weather. We rested on the ninth and went to Camp 5 on the tenth. It was cloudy all day and in the afternoon we had a violent storm of rain. On the eleventh we went to Rdokass direct by short cut, passing over a very beautiful scree whose stones were iridescent; every colour of the spectrum glistened on their rain-washed surfaces.

On the twelfth we held a durbar and expelled Wessely from the expedition. Pfannl decided to go with him. Pfannl was now more or less well again, but he would never be able to climb mountains in the future. It poured with rain all day and the following, which I spent in bed. On the fourteenth we went to Camp 1. It took me ten hours; the last part of the march was very bad, the enormous increase of water having made some sections of the march impossible by the route previously taken. I was well enough to eat. The weather was fairly fine, bar one or two snowstorms; but it snowed all night.

On the fifteenth I went to Paiyu. Before leaving the glacier I had another attack of fever and was obliged to lie down for three hours. The weather had become quite chronic. There were glimpses of sun; but for the most part we had clouds and rain. I should remark (by the way) that people who live in cities have quite different standards of bad weather from open-air folk. When one is living in a tent, one discovers that it is very rare indeed to experience twenty hours of continuous bad weather. There is nearly always a period of the day when one can get at least an hour or two which is fairly decent. The townsman's observations are confined to a small section of the day. The weather on the Baltoro glacier may therefore be judged as quite exceptionally abominable.

I have had very bad luck (on the whole) with my weather on mountains. Even in Mexico, we had a fortnight of cold and wet which had no parallel in the memory of man, and caused the stoves in the city to be sold out in the first forty-eight hours. Then I was once at Wastdale Head for forty-three days when it rained quite continuously except on one morning and one afternoon. On the other hand, during the nine days I was at Akyab it once stopped raining for nearly twenty minutes. I ought to have taken the exact time: but I

thought the end of the world had come, so that it never occurred to me to look at my watch till it began again.

I had been altogether sixty-eight days on the glacier, two
days longer than any other member of the party. It was another world's record; and, as far as I know, stands to this hour.
I hope I may be allowed to die in peace with it. It would be
a sorry ambition in anyone to grasp my laurels and I can
assure him that to refrain will bring its own reward. Of these
sixty-eight days, eight only were fine, and of these no three
were consecutive. Of course some days were of mixed character. But in no case have I classed as bad weather any days
which would be considered in the Alps fine enough to go out
on an average second-rate peak.

An almost unbelievable impression insisted on stamping
itself on my reluctant mind. Eckenstein and Knowles were
really upset by the reports of the cholera in the Bralduh Nala.
It is true that by all accounts it was pretty bad. One report
said that a hundred men had died. For some reason I treated
the whole thing with scepticism, and when I passed through
Askole I certainly saw no signs of agitation or mourning. The
only precaution I took was to prevent my men coming in contact with the villagers.

But Eckenstein and Knowles would not pass through the
village at all. They decided to return to Shigar by the Skoro
La, which is a pass avoiding the big bend formed by the
Bralduh Nala and the Shigar Rivers. It is just about as many
days' march and is decidedly harder on the men. So the doctor
and I went round by the valley. At Ghomboro we found fresh
apricots, and after a final go of indigestion caused by surfeit
of fresh mulberries and melons at Shigar my health cleared up
with astonishing rapidity. Within a week I was in perfectly
good form again and convinced more than ever that mountains as such have precious little to do with mountain sickness.

I noticed later that Sir Richard Burton, from even his small
experience, remarked that he did not believe that the symptoms were due to altitude but to indigestion. Burton was always my hero and the best thing about him is his amazing
common sense. In one place, for instance, he refers to influenza as 'the dreadful low fever called influenza': which is
exactly the truth. When one compares with this description
the buckets full of pseudo-scientific bilge of modern medicine,
one's disgust makes one long for the level heads and clear eyes
of such men as Burton.

The descent to the valley offered little new to the eye. The

broad Mud Nala had caked dry; but before doing so it had
overflowed to an extra hundred yards or so in breadth in one
place. The Narrow Nala was still wet, but not so deep in
mud. At Dasso we found fresh apples; and at our next camp,
just beyond Yuno, fresh peaches. This last march was very severe, over nine hours across blazing sand without a square
foot of shelter anywhere. On the following day a new experience was in store. We were able to travel by zak.

The zak is a local variety of raft; to a framework of crossed
bamboos are bound a number of goat skins. Our raft had
twenty-four: six one way and four the other. As these goat
skins all leak, one has to find a landing place every twenty
minutes or so, and this is not always easy. The great danger is
that one may stick on a submerged rock. It would be quite
impossible to get off and quite impossible to get ashore,
though one might be only six feet from the bank. At each
corner is a man with a long bamboo pole to fend off rocks.
But otherwise little can be done to direct one's course or even
to steer sufficiently to prevent the zak turning round and
round. I was reminded of Ben Gunn's coracle in *Treasure
Island*. The behaviour of a zak on a sea confirms the analogy,
for at one place the river was traversed by rows of waves five
or six feet high.

It seemed inconceivable that we should not be swamped. We
kept our places by wedging our feet between the bamboos and
holding on to them with our hands. The current is appallingly
swift. We had begun our 'adventure by water' in crossing the
Yuno, for we were on the wrong side of the river, and a man
had had to be sent down from far above to arrange for the raft
to take us over. (Until one actually goes travelling in a country of this sort, one can form no idea whatever of the frequency of utterly insuperable obstacles. It was not our fault,
for instance, that we were on the wrong side of the river, for
the other bank involved a detour of some three days.)

It required more than one voyage to cross the river. It
could not have been crossed at all but for the fact that it is
divided into seven streams, only one of which could not be
forded. Naturally, a passage was chosen where the current was
least formidable. But for all that we were swept down about
three-quarters of a mile in order to cross less than two hundred yards. In order to regain its starting point for the next
journey the zak had to be carried up stream a couple of miles.
So much for mere crossing. But the next day we were only

three hours and ten minutes actual going to Shigar, which in the ordinary way is three long marches.

The pace of the current varies enormously. Sometimes we were kept half an hour at a time spinning about amid contending eddies; sometimes we were flung violently down the stream at over twenty miles an hour. The sensation is extraordinarily exhilarating—the motion, the imminent peril, the intoxication of the air, the majesty of the background, but above all, the beatific realization that, as the doctor said, 'the roads are doing our walking for us,' combined to make me delirious with delight. Great too was the joy of rejoining Knowles and Eckenstein, who had now recovered their equanimity. We all went down to Skardu in two hours on a big zak. There we found fresh ripe grapes, potatoes and green corn. Our joy was unconfined; youth at the prow and pleasure at the helm!

41

There are two ways of returning from Skarrdu to Srinagar; one the way we had come, the other across the Deosai plateau. This is a high tableland from fourteen to seventeen thousand feet, crossed by four principal rivers. It has a devilish reputation for inhospitality. The rivers, in particular, play the prank of inducing you to cross one or two of them, and then coming down in spate, holding you up indefinitely and starving you out. I wanted to go back by that way; but Eckenstein's memories were too painful. We decided to travel separately—he with Knowles, and I with the doctor. (After we had started, he changed his mind and followed us.) On the twenty-sixth of August I had a final go of fever and lay in bed till the afternoon, after which I got up and saw to the bandobast for the journey. The next day we started for Pinderbal, about five hours on horseback—a very pleasant ride up a steep nala. The only incident was that my pony had been reading the Old Testament and proceeded to vary his pleasures by bolting under a tree so that I was caught in its branches like Absalom, while he went on his cheerful way, neighing merrily. We camped under a huge boulder; and as I sat by the fire after dinner reposing delightfully with a pipe, a very characteristic incident occurred.

A shapeless mass was moving down the slopes. It resolved itself into a man who must have been nearer seventy than sixty years old, carrying a sack, much bigger than himself, of what proved to be dried apricots. I greeted him affectionately and offered him some tobacco. He squatted opposite me and began to chat. When he said 'dried apricots' I had to summon all my philosophy to prevent raising my eyebrows slightly, for this was indeed carrying coals to Newcastle. Baltistan consists exclusively of rocks, streams and dried apricots. The last named are its principal export.

A moment—and I understood! The poor old man had been unable to cross the plateau and was returning home to die! I expressed my sympathy and offered help. Oh no, not at all! He had carried his sack all the way to Srinagar; but finding on arrival that the price of his produce had gone down by a fraction of a penny a pound, he refused to sell and was bringing the stuff back. The sack itself looked fabulous, so I got out the 'butcher's terror' and found that it weighed four hundred and ten pounds. The whole business struck me as extraordinarily sublime. I dashed the old boy five rupees. This made him wild with happiness and restored his debilitated conviction in the existence of a Supreme Being who put in most of His time in caring for His faithful.

The next day, about four hours' ride took us to the top of the pass, from which we had a magnificent view of the plain of Skardu and the Indus backed by the great mountains, while in front of us lay the Deosai, an absolutely treeless wilderness of comparatively level country framed by minor peaks. It gives a unique impression of desolation. I have never seen its equal in this respect elsewhere. Yet the march was very pleasant with many lovely flowers and streams. The weather was delightful and the going good.

The next day we went to Kranub (Kalapani is another name for it) in less than six hours in a cold wind under a threatening sky. After camping, the rain poured down in torrents. On the thirtieth we came down from the plateau in eight hours to Burzil, where there was a dak baghla. It rained continually till the last hour, so that we missed the distant view, but the foreground told us of the complete change of the character of the country.

Burzil is on the Gilgit road. This 'road' (which is a good mule path) was absolutely crowded with every beast of burden available: men, mules, bullocks, asses, horses, camels—all desperately bent on supplying the small garrison for the winter before the snow closed the passes. Gilgit being on the Indian side of the Pamirs and the country to the north very much more difficult than to the south, I was highly amused by the chronic anxiety of the government that Russia would invade India by this route. I doubt whether the combined resources of both governments would suffice to bring over half a dozen regiments. We are always hearing about the invasion of Alexander the Great; but his expedition is not to the point. Since his time climatic conditions all over the world have changed very considerably. I shall have more to say on this point when I come to deal with the Sahara. For the present I content myself with observing that in the time of the Macedonian empire the country was probably much more fertile. This is sufficiently proved by the traces of past civilizations,

quite apart from the general evidence as to the physical phenomena which are in progress on our planet.

We descended the Burzil valley, a gorge of amazing beauty
and colouring, with gorgeous trees to 'fledge the wild-ridged
mountains steep by steep'. At Pashwari it had already begun
to open, and at Gurais a broad calm stream winds slowly
through a broad level valley. As I rode slowly down the track
to this camp I heard a sudden shout behind me. 'Hat Jao!' (get
out of the way!): a moment later a gigantic English major
brushed past me muttering curses. I laughed into my beard. It
was amusing to be taken for a native!

At Gurais I found Ernest Radcliffe, assistant forest commissioner of Kashmir, in camp. I already knew him well; he received me with open arms and gave me the hot bath of my
life, with lunch and dinner to follow. At dinner I met the galloping major, who did not recognize me when he found me
sitting, clothed and in my right mind, and was extremely embarrassed when he realized his unintentional rudeness of the
morning.

At Gurais are a big suspension bridge and the remains of a
very large old fortress. On the second we went to Gurais and
on the third to Tragobal. The road here crosses a pass some
ten thousand feet high. It is a magnificent ride through the
wildest yet richest forest and mountain scenery. Some of the
trees are enormous and one obtains intoxicating views of the
valley framed by their dark splendour. Few men know what a
view can be. The European idea is to go, preferably by train,
to some high place and obtain a panorama. To me, even the
noblest panoramas are somewhat monotonous. Their boundlessness diminishes their aesthetic value. To see distant prospects to the best advantage one needs a foreground. In rock
climbing and travelling through mountain forests one sees
nature in perfection. At every turn, the foreground picks out
special bits of the background for attention, so that there is
a constant succession of varying pictures. The eye is no longer
bewildered by being asked to take in too much at once; and
the effect of the distance is immensely heightened by contrasts
with the foreground.

Soon after crossing the pass, the Vale of Kashmir with the
Wular Lake bursts upon the view. Once again, the character
of the scenery had undergone a complete transformation. We
rode down joyously to Bandipura in four hours. The mosquitoes on this part of the lake should have been repeatedly
exposed in *Truth*. Their reputation stinks in the country. So

we chartered a dunga (which is a variety of houseboat employed when any considerable distance has to be covered) and crossed the lake to Baramula. The crossing should have taken five hours; it took twelve.

We lazed a day among the delights of comparative comfort, marred only by the return of my malaria. But on the sixth I drove in a tonga to Srinagar, 132 days after leaving it. The expedition to Chogo Ri was over.

42

After about a week in Srinagar, I accepted an invitation to stay with Radcliffe at his headquarters at Baramula, to go shooting. I travelled by dunga in order to see a little more of native life and character, which I was able to do more freely now that my responsibility of the expedition was at an end. I passed two wonderful days of perfect joy on river and lake. I realized the whole of Kubla Khan, including the parts that Coleridge forgot. I understood the exclamation of the Persian poet:

> If on earth is a heaven of bliss,
> It is this, it is this, it is this.

Radcliffe and I went shooting bears occasionally, but I could not get up much enthusiasm. I was still suffering from occasional bouts of fever; and besides, was oppressed with a certain lassitude. I felt admirably well, but disinclined for necessary exertion. The strain of the journey was making itself felt. I wanted to lounge about and indulge in short strolls in the shade, to eat and drink at my ease, and to sleep 'lazily, lazily, drowsily, drowsily, in the noonday sun'. I had arranged to go on a more serious expedition with Radcliffe; but he was called away by a telegram, and I decided to wander slowly back to Blighty.

I left Baramula on September 21st, reached Pindi on the twenty-fourth, and after a day or two in Delhi and Ajmer reached Bombay on the last day of the month. I had meant to investigate Jaipur and the abandoned city which was deserted in the heyday of its splendour at an hour's notice on the advice of an astrologer. (He prophesied, observe, that it would become like 'the courts where Jamshyd glorified and drank deep', and so it did!) But my power to feel had been definitely dulled by the expedition. Hardship and sickness had temporarily exhausted my vitality.

A queer token of this and the only one. My beard was at this time a mixture of red and black in almost equal proportions. I shaved to go to Europe; and when I let it grow again, all the red hairs had become perfectly white.

I left Bombay on the fourth of October, by the poor old *Egypt* wrecked off Ushant in 1922. On the boat was a young officer returning to England on leave, to get married. It was a romantic story, and for the satisfactory accomplishment of his plan a plain gold ring which he wore on the fourth finger of his left hand was of the last importance. He removed it from his finger to read the inscription on the inside. Just as he put it back, a passing steward touched his elbow and the ring fell to the deck. It would have gone quite safely into the scuppers, but the owner and the steward, stooping excitedly to retrieve it, collided. One of them snatched the ring; it slipped from his fingers and went overboard. The young man's distress was pitiful to see. 'I daren't face her without it,' he kept on moaning, with the tears streaming down his face. We did the best we could by drawing up a signed statement explaining how the accident occurred.

We forgot all about the matter in the course of the voyage, and when we arrived at Aden even the youth himself had recovered his spirits. To pass the time, we proposed fishing for sharks in the harbour and after about an hour we got a fine fish aboard. It was immediately cut up; but search as we would we could find no trace of the ring.

I reached Aden on the ninth. It must be a perfectly ghastly place to live in. As I was to land in Egypt, I had to be quarantined for a day at Moses' Wells, regulation being that one must be eleven days out from Bombay, in case of plague. Moses' Wells is the most hateful place I have ever been in, with the possible exception of Gibraltar. I note in my diary that the food was 'beastly, and abominable, and absurdly dear'. If I remember correctly, it was cooked by a Greek and served by an Armenian. Volumes could not say more.

I arrived in Cairo on the fourteenth and was transported to the seventh heaven. I lived at Shepheard's Hotel till Guy Fawkes's Day, wallowing in the flesh pots. I would not even go out to see the Pyramids. I wasn't going to have forty centuries look down on me. Confound their impudence! I could not even bother to study Islam from the religious point of view, but I undertook a course of ethnology which remains in my mind as the one study where the roses have no thorns. I got a typist and dictated an account of my various wanderings in my better moments, but most of the time I was earnestly pursuing my researches in the fish market.

My mind began, moreover, to flow back into its accustomed channels. For one thing, I came to the conclusion that 'the most permanent poetry is perhaps love songs for real country folk—about trout and love.' And I began to write a set of lyrics to be called 'The Lover's Alphabet'. This was to consist of twenty-six poems, associating a girl's name with a flower with the same initial from A to Z. One of my regular pedantic absurdities! Needless to say, it broke down. The debris is printed in my *Collected Works,* vol. III, pp. 58 seq. I was also vaguely revising *Orpheus* and the other literary lumber of the past year and a half.

I had been doing a certain amount of practical Magick off and on, even during the expedition; but this too had dropped off since my return to civilization. As to Yoga, I was still completely dead. I had become dull to the trance of sorrow itself. I had no doubts as to the efficacy of Magick or the advantages of Mysticism. I simply couldn't be bothered with them. I was not under any illusions about the value of worldly pleasures; it was simply that I did not possess the energy to live any other kind of life.

I cannot understand why people imagine that those who retire from the world are lazy. It is far easier to swim with the stream, to refresh one's mind continually by letting it move from one distraction to another. This is so true that one might almost assert that the idlest monks are in reality more energetic than the busiest business man. This does not apply so much to Catholic monks, for their routine exercises dull the edge of whatever minds they possess; and not at all to missionaries, who live bourgeois lives diversified by pleasurable outbursts of vanity. But it applies to the orientals, from Japan to Morocco.

One might go further and say that, apart from religion altogether, the oriental lives a much more intense mental life than Europeans or Americans; that is, provided it has been aroused from brutish stupor by education. For the Western uses his education to take the edge off his mind. He allows it to wander among business and family details, and putrefies it by reading newspapers. In the East, an active mind cannot go sprawling over the shallows. It is compelled by its relatively limited intellectual furniture to cut itself a constantly deepening course. Thus it occurs that very few people indeed, outside Asia and Africa, are aware of the existence of any of the higher states of mind. They imagine that consciousness connotes a single level of sanity; that is, that it consists in the mechanical movement of its elements in response to the varied stimuli of the senses. There is a tendency to regard even such comparatively slight variation as the reflective habit of the man of science and the philosopher as being abnormal and in a sense unhealthy. They are the subjects of vulgar ridicule.

In sheer spiritual lassitude, I left Egypt homeward bound. During my absence from England I had kept up a sort of irregular correspondence with Gerald Kelly, who had by this time started to try to learn to paint, and who had a studio in the rue Campagne Première in the Montparnasse quarter of Paris. I gladly accepted his invitation to stay with him there. It had already been branded on my forehead that I was the Spirit of Solitude, the Wanderer of the Waste, Alastor; for while I entered with absolutely spontaneous enthusiasm into the artistic atmosphere of Paris, I was always subconsciously aware that here I had no continuing city.

I began to pick out the old threads of my life. Despite the evidence of Allan Bennett as to the integrity of Mathers, the premisses of my original syllogism as to his authority were not impaired. His original achievements proved beyond doubt that he had been at one time the representative of the Secret Chiefs; that he had either been temporarily obsessed or had permanently fallen.

On leaving for Mexico, I had asked him to take care of a dressing-case, a bag and a few valuable books which I did not want to be bothered with. I called on him and asked for their return. I was received as in good standing, yet a certain constraint and embarrassment were apparent. He handed over my books, but explained that as he was just moving into a new house on the Butte Montmartre (where I found him in the appropriate turmoil), he could not lay his hands on my bags for a few days. I have never seen them since. One of them was an almost new fifty-guinea dressing-case.

I drew my own conclusions. What had happened to me was so much like what had happened to so many other people. But I still saw no reason for throwing over my allegiance. The best policy was to remain inactive; such as Mathers was, he was the only authority in the Order until definitely superseded by the Secret Chiefs.

I had, however, little doubt that he had fallen through rashly invoking the forces of *The Book of the Sacred Magick of Abra-Melin the Mage*. I thought I would try the testimony of an independent observer. Among the English colony of Montparnasse was a youth named Haweis, son of the once celebrated H. R. Haweis of *Music and Morals*. He had been to Peterhouse and was now studying art, in which he has since achieved a certain delicate eminence. He went to see Mathers and came back very bored with a pompous disquisition on the ancient gods of Mexico. The charlatan was apparent; Mathers had got his information from the very people who had induced me to go out to Mexico. He was exploiting *omne ignotum pro magnifico* like the veriest quack. At this moment I came into magical contact with his forces. The story has been told admirably, if somewhat floridly, by Captain (now Major-General) J. F. C. Fuller. I can hardly do better than quote his account.

Gerald Kelly showed considerable perturbation of mind, and on being asked by Frater P.[1] what was exercising him, Gerald Kelly replied, 'Come and free Miss Q. from the wiles of Mrs M.' Being asked who Mrs M. was, Gerald Kelly answered that she was a vampire and a sorceress who was modelling a sphinx with the intention of one day endowing it with life so that it might carry out her evil wishes; and that her victim was Miss Q. P. wishing to ease his friend's mind asked Gerald Kelly to take him to Miss Q.'s address, at which Mrs M. was then living. This Gerald Kelly did.

Miss Q., after an interview, asked P. to tea to meet Mrs M. After introduction, she left the room to make tea—the White Magick and the Black were left face to face.

On the mantelpiece stood a bronze head of Balzac, and P., taking it down, seated himself in a chair by the fire and looked at it.

Presently a strange dreamy feeling seemed to come over him, and something velvet-soft and soothing and withal lecherous moved across his hand. Suddenly looking up he saw that Mrs M. had noiselessly quitted her seat and was bending over him; her hair was scattered in a mass of curls over her shoulders and the tips of her fingers were touching the back of his hand.

No longer was she the middle-aged woman, worn with strange lusts; but a young woman of bewitching beauty.

At once recognizing the power of her sorcery, and knowing that if he even so much as contemplated her Gorgon head, all the power of his Magick would be petrified, and that he would become but a puppet in her hands, but a toy to be played with and when broken cast aside, he quietly rose as if nothing unusual had occurred; and placing the bust on the mantelpiece turned towards her and commenced with her a magical conversation; that is to say a conversation which outwardly had but the appearance of the politest small talk, but which inwardly lacerated her evil heart, and burnt into her black bowels as if each word had been a drop of some corrosive acid.

She writhed back from him, and then again approached him even more beautiful than she had been before. She was battling for her life now, and no longer for the blood of another victim. If she lost, hell yawned before her, the hell that every once-beautiful woman who is approaching middle age, sees before her; the hell of lost beauty, of decrepitude, of wrinkles and fat. The odour of man seemed to fill her whole subtle form with a feline agility, with a beauty irresistible. One step nearer and then she sprang at Frater P. and with an obscene word sought to press her scarlet lips to his.

As she did so Frater P. caught her and holding her at arm's length smote the sorceress with her own current of evil, just as a would-be murderer is sometimes killed with the very weapon with which he has attacked his victim.

A blue-greenish light seemed to play round the head of the vampire, and then the flaxen hair turned the colour of muddy snow, and the fair skin wrinkled, and those eyes, that had turned so many happy lives to stone, dulled and became as pewter dappled with the dregs of wine. The girl of twenty had gone; before him stood a hag of sixty, bent, decrepit, debauched. With dribbling curses she hobbled from the room.

As Frater P. left the house, for some time he turned over in his mind these strange happenings and was not long in coming to the opinion that Mrs M. was not working alone, and that behind her probably were forces far greater than she. She was but the puppet of others, the slave that would catch the kids and the lambs that were to be served upon her master's table. Could P. prove this? Could he discover who her masters were? The task was a difficult one; it either meant months of work, which P. could not afford to give, or the mere chance of a lucky stroke which P. set aside as unworthy the attempt.

That evening, whilst relating the story to his friend Gerald Kelly, he asked him if he knew any reliable clairvoyant. Gerald Kelly replied that he did, and that there was such a person at that very time in Paris known as the Sibyl, his own 'belle amie'. That night they called on her; and from her P. discovered, for he led her in the spirit, the following remarkable facts.

The vision at first was of little importance, then by degrees the seer was led to a house which P. recognized as that in which D.D.C.F.[2] lived. He entered one of the rooms, which he also at once recognized; but curious to say, instead of finding D.D.C.F. and V.N.R.[3] there, he found Theo and Mrs. Horos. Mr Horos (M.S.R.) incarnated in the body of V.N.R. and Mrs Horos (S.V.A.) in that of D.D.C.F. Their bodies were in prison; but their spirits were in the house of the fallen chief of the Golden Dawn.

At first Frater P. was seized with horror at the sight, he knew not whether to direct a hostile current of will against D.D.C.F. and V.N.R., supposing them to be guilty of cherishing within their bodies the spirits of two disincarnated vampires, or perhaps Abra-Melin demons under the assumed forms of S.V.A. and M.S.R., or to warn D.D.C.F.; supposing him to be innocent, as he perhaps was, of so black and evil an offence. But, as he hesitated, a voice entered the body of the Sibyl and bade him leave matters alone, which he did. Not yet was the cup full.

This story is typical of my magical state of the time. I was behaving like a Master of Magick, but had no interest in my further progress. I had returned to Europe with a sort of feeling at the back of my mind that I might as well resume the Abra-Melin operation, and yet the debacle of Mathers somehow put me off; besides which, I was a pretty thorough-going Buddhist. My essay 'Science and Buddhism' makes this clear. I published a small private edition of 'Berashith' in Paris; but my spiritual state was in reality very enfeebled. I am beginning to suspect myself of swelled head with all its cohort of ills. I'm afraid I thought myself rather a little lion on the strength of my journey, and the big people in the artistic world in France accepted me quite naturally as a colleague.

In England there is no such social atmosphere. Artists and writers are either isolated or members of petty cliques. It is impossible to do so much as give a dinner to a distinguished man without upsetting the ant-heap, and arousing the most insanely violent and personal jealousy. A writer who respects himself in England is bound to become a solitary like Hardy and Conrad; the greatness of his art debars him utterly from taking the smallest part in the artistic affairs of the moment. In a way, this is not to his disadvantage, for the supreme genius does not need specialized human society; he is at home in the slums or on the countryside. The salon stifles him. The social intercourse between artists in France tends to civilize them, to bring them to a common level; and thus, though the average of good writers is far higher than in England, we can show more men of supreme attainment; we can even make a pretty shrewd guess who the masters are even during their lifetime, for we instinctively persecute them.

Any spark of individuality is in England an outrage on decency. We pick out Sir Richard Burton, James Thomson,

John Davidson, Ernest Dowson, and heaven knows how many others, for abuse, slander, ostracism, starvation or imprisonment. In our anxiety to do justice, we even annoy perfectly harmless people. At one time Alfred Tennyson was scoffed at as 'incomprehensible'. Holman Hunt was denounced by Charles Dickens as an obscene painter, and his prosecution and imprisonment demanded. *Jude the Obscure* was nicknamed *Jude the Obscene*. Swinburne was denounced as 'the poet of the trough and the sty', and his publisher withdrew the first series of *Poems and Ballads* in panic. Rossetti and Morris came in for an equal share of abuse, and we all remember the denunciations of Ibsen, Meredith, Nietzsche, Maeterlinck, Tolstoy, in fact, of every man—also Bernard Shaw—without exception whose name is still in our memories.

In France one attains eminence by a less gratuitous Golgotha. Men of art and letters are respected and honoured by each other and by the public. Their final position in history is quietly assigned by time. It is only in very exceptional circumstances that a great man is awarded the distinction of a Calvary. Of course, Zola went through the mill; but only because he had butted into politics by his *J'accuse*; he was only denounced as obscene because any stick is good enough to beat a dog with.

But, as luck would have it, I had arrived in Paris on an occasion which history in France can hardly duplicate; Rodin was being attacked for his statue of Balzac. I was introduced to Rodin and at once fell in love with the superb old man and his colossal work. I still think his Balzac the most interesting and important thing he did. It was a new idea in sculpture. Before Rodin there had been certain attempts to convey spiritual truth by plastic methods; but they were always limited by the supposed necessity of 'representing' what people call 'nature'. The soul was to be the servant of the eye. One could only suggest the relations of a great man with the universe by surrounding a more or less photographic portrait of him with the apparatus of his life work. Nelson was painted with a background of three-deckers and a telescope under his arm; Wren with a pair of compasses in front of St Paul's.

Rodin told me how he had conceived his Balzac. He had armed himself with all the documents; and they had reduced him to despair. (Let me say at once that Rodin was not a man, but a god. He had no intellect in the true sense of the word; his was a virility so superabundant that it constantly overflowed into the creation of vibrating visions. Naively enough, I haunted him in order to extract first-hand information about art from the fountain head. I have never met anyone—white, black, brown, yellow, pink or spot-blue—who was so completely ignorant of art as Auguste Rodin! At his best he would stammer out that nature was the great teacher, or some equally puerile platitude. The books on art attributed to him are of course the compilations of journalists.)

He was seized with a sort of rage of destruction, abandoned his pathetically pedantic programme. Filled with the sublime synthesis of the data which had failed to convey a concrete impression to his mind, he set to work and produced the existing Balzac. This consequently bore no relation to the incidents of Balzac's personal appearance at any given period. These things are only veils. Shakespeare would still have been Shakespeare if someone had thrown sulphuric acid in his face. The real Balzac is the writer of the *Comédie Humaine*; and what Rodin has done is to suggest this spiritual abstraction through the medium of form.

Most people do not realize the power which genius possesses of comprehending the essence of a subject without the need of learning it laboriously. A master in one art is at home in any other, without having necessarily practised it or studied its technicalities. I am reminded of the scene in Rodin's studio which I described in a sonnet. Some bright spirit had brought his fiddle and we were all bewitched. Rodin suddenly smiled and waved his hand towards 'Pan et Syrinx'. I followed the gesture: the bars just played were identical with the curve of the jaw of the girl. The power to perceive such identities of essence beneath a difference of material manifestation is the inevitable token of mastery. Anyone who understands (not merely knows) one subject will also understand any other, whether he also knows it or not. Thus: suppose there had also been present a great gardener, a great geologist and a great mathematician. If they did not understand and approve that signal of Rodin's, I should refuse to admit that they were real masters, even of their own subjects. For I regard it as an infallible test of a master of any art or science that he should recognize intuitively (Neschamically) the silent truth, one and indivisible, behind all diversities of expression.

I find by experience that any man well learned in a subject, but whose understanding of it falls short of the mastery I have decribed, will profoundly resent this doctrine. It minimizes the dignity of his laborious studies and in the end accuses him of inferior attainment. The more sophisticated victim can usually put up an apparently non-emotional defence in the form of a scepticism as to the facts, a scepticism whose obstinate irrationality is plain to an outside observer, but seems to the victim himself a simple defence of what he feels to be truth. This type of Freudian self-protection is often entirely passion-proof even against direct accusation of intellectual pride and jealousy. It relies on the ability of the mind to confuse, when hard-pressed, the essence of a subject with its accidents. Nothing but a very pure aspiration to truth—and experience (often humiliating) of such reactions—is of much use against this particular kind of bondage.

While other defenders of Rodin were apologizing for him in detail I brushed aside the nonsense—'a plague o' both your houses!'—and wrote a sonnet, which is, in its way, to conventional criticism exactly what that Balzac was. It was translated into French by Marcel Schwob and made considerable stir in Paris. Even at this length of time, I attach a certain importance to it. For one thing, it marks a new stage in my own art.

BALZAC

Giant, with iron secrecies ennighted,
Cloaked, Balzac stands and sees. Immense disdain,
Egyptian silence, mastery of pain,
Gargantuan laughter, shake or still the ignited
Stature of the Master, vivid. Far, affrighted,
The stunned air shudders on the skin. In vain
The Master of *La Comédie Humaine*
Shadows the deep-set eyes, genius-lighted.

Epithalamia, birth songs, epitaphs,
Are written in the mystery of his lips.
Sad wisdom, scornful shame, grand agony
In the coffin folds of the cloak, scarred mountains, lie,
And pity hides i' th' heart. Grim knowledge grips
The essential manhood. Balzac stands, and laughs.

The upshot was that Rodin invited me to come and stay with him at Meudon. The idea was that I should give a poetic interpretation of all his masterpieces. I produced a number of poems, many of which I published at the time in the *Weekly Critical Review*, an attempt to establish an artistic entente cordiale. The entire series constitutes my *Rodin in Rime*. This book is illustrated by seven of ten lithographs of sketches which Rodin gave me for the purpose.

43

Any other man but myself would have made a ladder to fame out of the successes of this winter. I had no such idea. I had been thoroughly disillusioned, not only by the original trance of sorrow which had struck me between wind and water in 1897, but by the experience of my travels. The natives of Hawaii were not worrying about Sophocles; Chogo Ri would be there when the last echo of Napoleon's glory had died away. I was more than ever convinced that to take an interest in the affairs of this world, one must turn one's back on truth. Buddhism might be right or wrong in saying that nothing is worth while; but anyhow there could be no doubt that the conventional standards of value were simply comic. If anything were worth while, it could only be discovered by turning one's back resolutely on temporal things.

In accordance with Eckenstein's puritanical ideas of propriety, no communications about the expedition had been made to the newspapers. Ultimately, in the sheer interests of science, a paragraph had been permitted to appear in *The Times*. It contained thirty-two lines and seventeen misstatements of fact! I myself had been interviewed by a French journalist and the report of my remarks bore no discoverable relation with them. I am perhaps unduly sensitive about such stupidities. I ought perhaps to rely on time to sweep away the rubbish into the dustbin of oblivion and set the truth upon her throne; but yet, the evidence of history smiles grimly. What do we really know of the rights and wrongs of the struggle between Rome and Carthage? What do we know even of Buddhism and Christianity but that the most authentic accounts of their origins are intrinsically absurd? 'What is truth?' said jesting Pilate. But, personally, I fail to see the joke.

I went through life at this time with a kind of cynical bonhomie; nothing was really any particular good, so I might as well do what was expected of me. I wrote even of Buddhism with a certain detached disenchantment, as may be seen by reference to my *Summa Spes*, which I published separately (twelve copies contain the portrait of me by Haweis and Coles, subsequently reproduced in volume II of the vellum edition of my *Collected Works*) and sent to some of my friends in Paris on my departure for England.

After Rodin, the most important of these friends was Marcel Schwob. Eugène Carrière I met only once. He had just recovered from an operation for cancer of the throat, and I remember principally his remark, calm to the point of casual indifference, 'If it comes back, I shall kill myself.' Fritz Thäulow I saw several times. He was rather a new type to me; a jolly, bearded senior on whom life had left no scars. He believed in his art and in his family; enjoyed everything, worried about nothing—it was not at all one's idea of a great artist. I had already got it into my mind that the life of the artist must be a sequence of pungent pangs either of pleasure or pain; that his nature obliged him to regard commonplace circumstances rather as the average man regards deep sleep. But Thäulow lived every line of his life; he had somehow attained that supreme philosophy which contemplates all things alike with cheerful calm.

Marcel Schwob excited my unbounded admiration. He was admittedly the finest French scholar of English. His style glittered with the superb simplicity and silken satire which compels me to regard Anatole France as his pupil. He had translated *Hamlet* and *Macbeth* for Sarah Bernhardt with astonishing spiritual fidelity to the soul of Shakespeare. His *Vies Imaginaires* might have served as the model for *Le Puits de Sainte Claire*, and his *Île des Diurnales* is as brilliantly bitter as anything that Swift ever wrote. He lived on the Île St Louis in a delightful flat, rich with the suggestion of the East (emphasized by a Chinese servant he had picked up after the exhibition of 1900), yet he suffered as few men suffer.

Part of his crufixion was rather ridiculous. It was suspected that he was more or less a Jew, and he was constantly aware that he did not enjoy the position in French literature to which his genius entitled him. His wife was one of the most beautiful women on whom I had ever laid eyes; an exquisite siren with a smile that left La Gioconda standing, and a voice which would have burst the ropes that bound Ulysses to his mast. But she had been an actress, and this duchess and that countess did not call. It galled. The real tragedy of the man was that he was tortured by chronic constipation. It killed him soon after. Even after all these years I glow with boyish pleasure to recall his gracious, unassuming acquiescence in my impertinent existence and his acknowledgment of my *Alice, An Adultery* as 'a little masterpiece'.

My sonnet on Rodin begins 'Here is a man', which Marcel Schwob very properly translated, 'Un homme'. I took the draft to Rodin's studio. One of the men present was highly indignant. 'Who is this Marcel Schwob,' he exclaimed, 'to pretend to translate from this English? The veriest schoolboy would know that "Here is a man" should be turned into "Voici un homme".'

This is the sort of thing one meets at every turn. The man was perfectly friendly, well educated and familiar with literature; yet he was capable of such supreme stupidity. The moral is that when an acknowledged master does something that seems at first sight peculiar, the proper attitude is one of reverent eagerness to understand the meaning of his action. This critic made an ass of himself by lack of imagination. He should have known that 'Voici un homme' would have sprung instantly into Schwob's mind as the obvious and adequate rendering. His rejection of it argues deep consideration; and the man might have learnt a valuable lesson by putting himself in Schwob's place, trying to follow the workings of his mind, and finally discovering the considerations which determine his judgment. I quote this case rather than grosser examples which I recall, because it is so simple and non-controversial, yet involves such important principles. Schwob's version stands before a background of the history of literature. It would be easy to write a long and interesting essay on the factors of the problem.

Occasionally he came to see Kelly in his studio. His conversation was full of the most intensely interesting, because impersonally intimate, details about men of letters. He told us at first hand the tragedy of Meredith's life, the mystery of his birth, and his father's attempts to establish a marriage which would have entitled him to a place in the peerage; the romance of *Vittoria;* and the intrigue of *Diana of the Crossways.* He traced the influence of the master's locomotor ataxia upon his life, his character and his creatures. He explained how the long years of suffering had deformed Meredith's disposition and led him to disgrace himself by refusing to head the petition for Oscar Wilde's release.

He told us the true story of *Salome.* The character of Wilde was simple. He was a perfectly normal man; but, like so many Irish, suffered from being a snob. In Dublin, Sir William

Wilde was somebody in society; but when Oscar reached Oxford, he discovered that a medical knighthood, so far from being a distinction, was little better than a badge of servility. A family even of commoners could afford to sneer at his acceptance of a trumpery honour at the hands of a Hanoverian hausfrau. Wilde could not bear to be despised by brainless dukes, so he had sought hegemony in the hierarchy by the only means available, as a socially sensitive swineherd might aspire to the papacy. He determined to become the high priest of the cult which already conferred a kind of aristocracy upon the undergraduate, though it had not yet been organized and boosted. That was the result of his 'martyrdom', which accounts for most of the loathsome creatures that jostle one too frequently in 1929. 'The Law is a Hass'!

Wilde had denied his nature in the interests of social ambition, and the success of his scheme drove him to adopt every affectation as a sign of superiority. Outside the English system of caste, he might have been a contented cornchandler. Within it, he found himself obliged to affect to be sexually stirred by Maeterlinck, Flaubert, Gustave Moreau, and even the most sacred character of Scripture. He degraded the Sphinx by representing her as a sexual monster. He interpreted the relations between Christ and John, between Paul and Timothy, in the light of his own perverse imagination.

When I say perverse, I do not mean to use the word in the psychopathic sense. Wilde's only perversity was that he was not true to himself. Without knowing it, he had adopted the standards of the English middle class, and thought to become distinguished by the simple process of outraging them. As one is said to be able to invoke the devil by reciting the Lord's Prayer backwards, so Wilde thought to set up a new morality by reciting George R. Sims backwards. He naively accepted the cockney idea that Paris is a very wicked place, and proposed to petrify the puritans by writing a play in French. His difficulty was that his French was that of a schoolboy turned tourist; so he struggled to write *Salome* on the pretence that he was sexually excited by *The Temptation of St Anthony*, Moreau's pictures in the Luxembourg and the style of *Pelléas and Mélisande*. But the performance was pitiful; and it was Marcel Schwob who re-wrote his puerile dialogue in French.

At one of Marcel Schwob's afternoons I met Arnold Bennett, very ill at ease to find himself in Paris in polite society. He must have had a perfectly lovely time; everything was alike a source of innocent wonder. He was very much pleased by the generous measure of respect which he received on all hands simply for being a novelist. His speech and his appearance attracted no insult from literary circles in Paris.

At the time I had only read one of his books—*The Grand Babylon Hotel;* which I thought, and still think, somewhere near his high-water mark. I told him how much I admired it and was surprised to find that I had apparently said the wrong thing. But Kelly explained that he took himself seriously as a serious novelist, on the strength of having compiled some books of reference on life in Shropshire or Staffordshire or some such place. I don't know which is which, thank God; I do not understand the system of classification or indexing, so I cannot turn up the symptoms of a dying Doultonware artist if I want to. But then I don't.

Marcel Schwob gave me an introduction to William Ernest Henley, who invited me to lunch with him in his house near Woking. My sonnet on Rodin's bust of Henley describes the man and the interview rather than the sculpture.

> Cloistered seclusion of the galleried pines
> Is mine today; these groves are fit for Pan—
> O rich with Bacchus frenzy and his wine's
> Atonement for the infinite woes of man!
>
> And here his mighty and reverend high priest
> Bade me good cheer, an eager acolyte,
> Poured the high wine, unveiled the mystic feast . . .

Roast lamb and an excellent Chablis which had been sent to him by Lord Northcliffe—thus does the poet transfigure conceptions apparently commonplace.

I was much touched by Henley's kindness in inviting me. I have never lost the childlike humility which characterizes all truly great men. Modesty is its parody. I had to wait some little while before he came down. When he did so, he was obviously suffering severe physical distress. Like Marcel Schwob himself, he was a martyr to constipation. He told me that the first half of every day was a long and painful struggle to overcome the devastating agony of his body. Only three weeks later he died. He was engaged in various tremendous literary tasks and yet he could give up a day to welcome a young and unknown writer!

I could not pretend to myself that so great a man could feel any real interest in me. It never occurred to me that he might have read anything of mine and thought it promising. I took, and take, his action for sheer human kindness. I probably behaved with my usual gaucherie. The presence of anyone whom I really respect always awakes my congenital shyness, always overawes me. Henley's famous poem (which Frank Harris regards as 'the bombast of Antient Pistol') appealed intensely to my deepest feeling about man's place in the universe; that he is a Titan overwhelmed by the gods but not surrendering. And the form of the poem is superb. It is in line with all the great English expressions of the essential English spirit, a certain blindness, brutality and arrogance, no doubt, as in 'Rule Britannia', 'Boadicea', 'The Garb of Old Gaul', 'The British Grenadiers', 'Hearts of Oak', 'Toll for the Brave', 'Ye Mariners of England', *et hoc genus omne;* but with all that, indomitable courage to be, to do and to suffer as fate may demand.

I never thought much of the rest of Henley's verse, distinguished as it is for vigour and depth of observation. It simply does not come within my definition of poetry, which is this: A poem is a series of words so arranged that the combination of meaning, rhythm and rime produces the definitely magical effect of exalting the soul to divine ecstasy. Edgar Allan Poe and Arthur Machen share this view. Henley's poem conforms with this criterion.

I told him what I was doing about Rodin. His view was that the sonnet had been worked out and he advised me to try the Shakespearian sonnet or quatorzain. I immediately attempted the form in the train that evening and produced the quatorzain on himself from which I have quoted above. I recognized at once that the quatorzain was in fact much better suited to my rugged sincerity than the suavity of the Italian form, so I composed a number of poems in the new mode. In fact, I fell in love with it. I invented improvements by the introduction of anapaests wherever the storm of the metre might be maddened to typhoon by so doing, and it may be that history will yet say that *Clouds without Water,* a story told in quatorzains, as *Alice* in sonnets, is my supreme lyrical masterpiece.

At least I have not died without the joy of knowing that no less a lover of literature than the world-famous Shakespearian lecturer, Dr Louis Umfraville Wilkinson, has dared to confess publicly that *Clouds without Water* is 'the most tremendous and the most real love poem since Shakespeare's sonnets' in the famous essay 'A Plea for Better Morals'. But I anticipate. *Clouds without Water* came four years later. I am still sitting sleepily in the twilight in Europe; after my day's labour three years long in the blazing sun of the great world.

I spent many of my evenings at a little restaurant called the Chat Blanc in the rue d'Odessa, where was 'an upper room furnished' and consecrated informally to a sort of international clique of writers, painters, sculptors, students and their friends. It has been described with accurate vigour in the introduction to *Snowdrops from a Curate's Garden*. I quote the passage.

His evenings were spent in that witty and high-thinking informal club that met nightly at the restaurant Au Chien Rouge, whose members are so honoured in the world of art. There he met C—— the brilliant but debauched sculptor, caustic of wit, though genial to his friends; N——, the great painter, whose royal sense of light made his canvases into a harmonious dream: he also the sweet friend of Bacchus, who filled him with a glow and melody of colour and thought. There too, were D—— and L——, the one poet and philosopher, the other painter and—I fear—pederast. Twins in thought, the two were invincible in argument as they were supreme in their respective arts. Often have I sat, a privileged listener, while D——'s cold acumen and L——'s superb indignation, expressed in fiery swords of speech, would drive some luckless driveller from the room. Or at times they would hold down their victim, a bird fascinated by a snake, while they pitilessly exposed his follies to the delighted crowd. Again, a third, pompous and self-confident, would be led on by them, seemingly in full sympathy, to make an exhibition of himself, visible and hideous to all eyes but his own. L——, his eager face like a silver moon starting from a thundercloud, his hair, would pierce the very soul of the debate and kindle it with magick joy or freeze it with scorn implacable. D——, his expression noble and commanding, yet sly, as if ever ready to laugh at the intricacies of his own intellect, sat next him, his deep and wondrous eyes lit with strange light, while with words like burning flames of steel he shore asunder the sophistries of one and the complacencies of another. They were feared, these two! There also did he meet the well-known ethicist, I——, fair as a boy, with boy's gold locks curling about his Grecian head; I——, the pure and subtle-minded student, whose lively humour and sparkling sarcasm were as froth upon the deep and terrible waters of his polished irony. It was a pity that he drank. There the great surgeon and true gentleman, in spite of his exaggerated respect for the memory of Queen Victoria, J——, would join in with his ripe and generous wit. Handsome as a god, with yet a spice of devil's laughter lurking there, he would sit and enjoy the treasures of the conversation, adding at the proper interval his own rich quota of scholarly jest.

Needless to say, so brilliant a galaxy attracted all the false lights of the time. T——, the braggart, the mediocre painter, the lusty soi-disant maquereau of marchionesses, would seek admission (which was in theory denied to none). But the cutting wit of C—— drove him headlong, as if by the cherubin, from the gates of the garden of Eden. G——, the famous society painter, came one night and was literally hounded out of the room by a swift and pitiless attack on the part of D—— and the young ethicist. A bullet-headed Yankee, rashly supporting him, shared the same fate and ever after sat in solitary disgrace downstairs, like a whipped hound outside its master's door. A fool reveals himself, though he talk but of greasing gimlets, in such a fierce light as beat upon the Chien Rouge. Nor could any fool live long in that light. It turned him inside out; it revealed him even to himself as a leper and an outcast; and he could not stand it.

In such a circle humbug could not live. Men of high intellectual distinction, passing through Paris, were constant visitors at the Chien Rouge. As guests they were treated with high honour; but woe to the best of them if some chance word let fall led D—— or L—— to suspect that he had a weak spot somewhere. When this happened, nothing could save him: he was rent and cast to the carrion beasts for a prey.

How often have I seen some literary or pictorial Pentheus, impious and self-sufficient as he, disguise himself (with a tremor of fear) in his noblest artistic attire, as the foolish king in the *Bassara* of the Maenads!

How often have I seen Dionysus—or some god—discover the cheat and give him over to those high priests of dialectic, D—— and L——, to be ravaged and stripped amid the gleeful shrieks of the wit-intoxicated crowd! But once the victim was upon the altar, once he rose from his chair, then what a silence fell! Frozen with the icy contempt of the assembly, the wretch would slink down the room with a scared grin on his face, and not until he had faced that cruel ordeal, more terrible (even to a callous fool) than an actual whipping would have been, not until the door had closed behind him would the silence break as someone exclaimed 'My God, what a worm!' and led the conversation to some more savoury subject.

On the other hand there was B——, a popular painter, upon whom the whole Dog pounced as one man, to destroy him.

But when they saw that his popular painting was not he, that he had a true heart and an honest ambition, how quickly were the swords beaten into absinthes and the spears into tournedos!

S——, again, with a face like a portrait by Rembrandt, a man of no great intellect, but making no pretence thereto, how he was loved for his jolly humour, his broad smile, his inimitable stories!

Yet it must not be supposed that the average man, however sincere, had much of a welcome there. Without intention to wound, he was yet hurt—the arrows of wit shot over his head and he could never feel at home.

I am perhaps the one exception. Without a ghost of talent, even in my own profession—medicine—I had no claim whatever to the hospitality of the Dog. But being perfectly unobtrusive, I dare say I was easy to tolerate, perhaps even of the same value as a background is to a picture, a mere patch of neutral colour, yet serving to harmonize the whole. Certainly nothing but my silence saved me. The remark a few pages back about Hall Caine and Meredith would have caused my instant execution, by the most painful, if the least prolonged, of deaths.

Ay! no society, since men gathered together, was ever so easy to approach, to seat oneself among, to slip away from or to be hurled in derision from their midst!

Dreaded as they were by the charlatan, no set of men could have been more genial, more fraternal. United by a bond of mutual respect, even where they differed—of mutual respect, I say, by no means of mutual admiration, for it was the sincere artistry that they adored, not the technical skill of achievement—they formed a noble and harmonious group, the like of which has perhaps never yet been seen.*

Another description may be found in the opening chapters of W. S. Maugham's *The Magician*. The reader will wonder how this gentleman could have got there, but here my tale is tangled. Gerald Kelly's elder sister, Rose, had been for some years the widow of a Major Skerrett, and one of her best friends was a woman as beautiful and fascinating as herself, who was the wife of an English solicitor connected with the British Embassy, named Maugham. W.S. was this man's younger brother. Maugham claimed to have ambitions to become a man of letters and his incapacity was so obvious that I am afraid we were cruel enough to make him the butt of our wit when he visited the Chat Blanc.

There is this excuse for us, that his earliest work was vamped over, his plagiarisms were beyond belief for impudence. When—to parody the outburst of the heavy mother in Wilde's *The Importance of Being Earnest*—he 'contracted an

* C. Paul Bartlett, N. J. W. Morrice, D. Crowley, I. Kelly, I. Heward Bell, J. Ivor Back, T. One Kite, G?, B. Penrhyn Stanlaws, S. One Root.

alliance with a tabloid and married into a pill-box', we thought that all was over. But no! he went around the world, and set to work with his powers of observation to help an imagination which had by now become original and vigorous. He turned out some first-class work; and, what is in some ways better, work on the right side. He castigates the herd of many swine feeding which we call society—as it is now late to drive their devils back into the Jews, where they are terribly congested.

But in 1902 we were right to chivy him!

It had leaked out that our luckless victim had taken a medical degree and J. W. Morrice* used to torment the poor fellow, whose distress was accentuated by his being a confirmed stammerer, by ringing the changes on this disgraceful episode of his career. Morrice was invariably mellow drunk all day and all night. He would look up from his crème de menthe and *oeufs sur le plat*, clear his throat and tell Maugham with grave importance that he would like to consult him on a matter concerning the welfare of art and artists. 'What would you do if—' and after repeating himself in a hundred ways so as to prolong the rigmarole to the utmost, he would wind up by confessing to the premonitory symptoms of some comic and repulsive malady. It was really needlessly cruel, for, bar his pretension to literature, there is not an ounce of harm in Maugham, any more than there is in a packet of sterilized cotton wool. Even the pretence is after all a perfectly harmless affection.

But Maugham suffered terribly under the lash of universal contempt and did his best to revenge himself by drawing portraits, as unpleasant as petty spite could make them, of some of his tormentors. His literary method, when it transcends plain scissors and paste, is the shirt-cuff method of Arnold Bennett. I must thank him for recording some of my actual repartees. The man he most hated was Roderic O'Conor. This man was intimate with Gauguin, Van Gogh and Cézanne. In my opinion history will class him near them as a painter. I do not think he has many superiors in art alive today. But very few people have seen his pictures. His contempt for the world goes beyond that of Balzac and Baudelaire. He cannot be

---

* This amiable and worthy colonist occupied a studio on the Quai des Grands Augustins (now, I suppose, called Quai Maréchal Fous-le-Camp), most conveniently situated over the apartment of an excellent midwife: though I never heard that he had occasion to avail himself of her services.

bothered to give a show. He will turn rudely from his door a friendly journalist bent on making him famous and rich. Also, he is a cad.

To O'Conor, Maugham was not even funny. He was like a bed bug, on which a sensitive man refuses to stamp because of the smell and the squashiness. I have never felt thus. To me the least of human beings, nay, less than they, have a place in my heart. 'Everything that lives is holy.' I can hardly bring myself to resent even the vilest and most offensive creatures. I have never been able to bear malice; I have never been able to understand how other people can do so. When I have been attacked, I have always looked at the matter impersonally. When I am publicly accused of stealing the towers of Notre Dame, I enjoy the joke thoroughly. I can't believe that anything can hurt me. It would hurt my pride to admit it, I suppose. When a newspaper prints three columns, identifying me with Jack the Ripper, it never occurs to me that anyone in his senses would believe such rubbish. I imagine that my integrity is universally patent as sunrise; I can't realize that I shall suffer in the estimation of anyone, or that (say) it will interfere with the sale of my books.

I have never been able to analyse this mental attitude at all adequately, but part of it certainly derives from the fact that I have never lost my innocence. I sometimes wonder whether it may not prove a defect in my philosophical system that I am unable to believe in the existence of evil. There is of course the appearance of evil due to ignorance, bad judgment and so on; but my major premiss is 'Every man and every woman is a star';[1] and I always conceive the problem of progress as depending merely on enlightenment. I do not believe in original sin except in this sense that 'The word of Sin is Restriction';[2] and our normal conscious selves are inevitably restricted by the categories of space, time and causality, which are essential conditions of the manifestation of separate individualities. But I cannot get it into my head that any single human being can be really hostile to another. I regard all such passions as the symptoms of a definite deformity of nature produced by its inadequacy to deal with its environment. Just as a stick appears bent when thrust partly under water, so does a man's will apparently deviate when the refractive index of his environment deceives his vision.

I do not know whether it is fair to say that I am callous, whether the long torture of my patient silent struggle against the tyrants of my boyhood case-hardened me against the world.

I do not know how far the habit of concentration and the peculiar selective action of my memory has deadened my sensibilities, for I am as indifferent to most impressions as the holiest hermit could desire. I have become almost incapable of registering conscious impressions unless they pass the censor as having legitimate business with me. Of course a not dissimilar state of abstractedness is common enough in men whose lives are devoted to study, by the time they are fifty; but in me these tendencies were already bearing fruit long before I was thirty.

The Montparnasse quarter was of course full of people who took their trumpery love affairs very seriously. But the English colony was riddled with English hypocrisy. I remember giving the manuscript of *Alice* to Kelly and a girl named Sybil Muggins * to read, and they agreed that no really nice woman would have kissed a man so early as the thirteenth day of his wooing. I must confess to having been taken a little aback, especially as Sybil Muggins was Haweis's mistress. A few days back, moreover, Haweis having gone to Brussels for a week, she switched over to Kelly. What dreadful days those were! They worked themselves up into such a state that Kelly actually proposed to marry Sybil, and his sister bustled over post haste to prevent it by threatening that his allowance would be stopped if he did anything so foolish.

I had of course no sympathy whatever for the fatuity of the young people, but I have always felt with Shelley that parental tyranny is the most indefensible kind.

I was brought up in the other service; but I knew from the first that the Devil was my natural master and captain and friend. I saw that he was in the right, and that the world cringed to his conqueror only through fear. I prayed secretly to him; and he comforted me, and saved me from having my spirit broken in this house of children's tears. I promised him my soul, and swore an oath that I would stand up for him in this world and stand by him in the next. (*Solemnly*) That promise and that oath made a man of me. From this day this house is his home; and no child shall cry in it; this hearth is his altar; and no soul shall ever cower over it in the dark evenings and be afraid. (G. B. Shaw, *The Devil's Disciple*.)

I offered to make Kelly an allowance equal to what he was receiving, which rather took the wind out of the sails of the old wooden three-deckers in Camberwell vicarage. The gesture was

* Query 'Meugins'.

sufficient. The threat was withdrawn; Gerald on his side had cooled off sufficiently to see the folly of throwing himself away on a half-caste.

To me the joke was obvious. I could already love without attachment so far as physical desire was concerned. There are one or two small errors in my subsequent life and they are due to my failure to extend this principle to other types of attachment. I have tried to set myself up against fate and save those who were predestined to be lost, to keep on trusting people after I knew perfectly well that they were false; and I have paid heavily for my chivalry and generosity. I still think these defects in some way preferable to sterner sense and virtue, and yet I know that I am wrong from every point of view. It does not do ultimate good to anyone concerned to shut one's eyes to the facts or to try to dodge one's creditors.

44

I must give an instance or two of the astounding character of my memory. It is absolutely first rate wherever my true interests are concerned, and also first rate in a very different sense, in eliminating other things so as not to overload the mind. But——

I think it was on returning to Boleskine from Paris after taking the Grade of $5°=6^\square$ that I asked Eckenstein to join me for the *ski-läufing* and salmon. We left London together in a sleeper. I had one hundred and fifty pounds in bank notes in my pocket book, which I put under my pillow. In the morning I dressed hurriedly, still half asleep, and left the book behind. I discovered the loss a few minutes later and shrugged my shoulders. I have always had a conviction that it is utterly useless to look for anything that has once been lost. I made up my mind immediately to forget about it; I take it as a matter of fact that anyone who has found anything would steal it; yet equally as a matter of course that it would be returned to me by the finder as simply as one would hand a lady the fan she had dropped, with no question of honesty or reward. But Eckenstein insisted on my going back to the station immediately. We saw the station master and got permission to walk up the tracks—quite a long distance, hardly less than a quarter of a mile—to the siding where the sleeper had been shunted. The pocket book was found intact under my pillow.

Some time in 1913 or '14 Eckenstein referred to this incident and immediately noticed that I did not catch on. He tackled me pointedly; and I denied all knowledge of the affair with the emphasis of St Peter! Eckenstein repeated the facts given in the above paragraph and as he did so the whole thing came back to me. But I would certainly have gone into the witness-box and sworn point blank that no such thing had ever happened. Every detail was and is perfect in my memory. At this moment I can see the car, the siding, the general appearance of the maze of lines, the lowering grey weather, the tumbled bed, the cleaner who had just begun his work. I remember thrusting my hand under the pillow and the exact state of emotion at finding the book, relief mingled with mild surprise and a strong sense of shame at having made such a fool of myself in the presence of Eckenstein.

But the entire packet had been sealed up and stowed away at the back of the safe, in accordance with the routine of the office never to allow the mind to feed upon thoughts connected with money. I know that this seems farfetched and many people will find it entirely unintelligible; but it is the fact. The ultimate secret of my life is that I really live up to my principles. I decide that it is disgraceful to allow financial considerations to dictate my conduct; but instead of allowing this to remain a pious opinion, I am at pains to invent a regular technique for dismissing them.

Another incident. In returning to Zapotlan we had ridden a hundred and twenty miles in the broiling sun. I had outridden O.E., who was amazed and irritated at my power to endure heat and thirst. I became alarmed when I found he was nowhere to be seen and rode back a good many miles, managing (as luck would have it) to miss him in one small patch of woodland which diversified the desert. When I reached Zapotlan I had to be lifted off my horse. We were to start the next morning, as we were in rather a hurry to get back to Mexico City.

I woke before six o'clock and found the whole place in darkness. I opened the big gateway, fed the horses, saddled them and then, finding that nobody was stirring, thought I would lie down on my bed for a minute or so till breakfast was ready. I went to sleep. Eckenstein had some difficulty in arousing me.

The point of the story is this: that I had done nothing of the sort. Eckenstein proved to me (and a difficult task he had) that I had never wakened at all and that the whole of my early morning's activities were a mere wish-phantasm; being too sleepy to do my duty, I dreamt that I had done so.

This last incident is very typical. Not once nor twice in my fair island story have I found myself in honest doubt which, believe me, is worth half the creeds, as to whether any given incident took place in sleep or waking. It may be thought that my accounts of various magical incidents are under suspicion; but being aware of my peculiarities, I have naturally been at great pains to eliminate any such source of error. Eckenstein's proof that I was dreaming depended on the physical evidence of the closed doorway and the unsaddled horses. It is of course easy to reply that I may have been asleep the second time as well as the first! And of course there is no answer to that any more than there is to the argument that we are all part of the Red King's Dream, as Lewis Carroll puts the fable of Kwang-Tze. (Kwang-Tze once said to his disciples on awakening: 'Just now I was dreaming that I was a butterfly: but is it so, or am I a butterfly dreaming that it is Kwang-Tze?')

To return to the wicked city of Paris. J. W. Morrice, as a painter, does not possess the sternly intense passion of O'Conor. His vision lacks the blazing brilliance of beauties which imposes itself on the beholder in O'Conor's best work. Morrice is a *homo unius tabulae*. He has only seen one thing in his life—it is the rosy dream which Venus and Bacchus bestow upon their favourites. His pictures swim in a mist of rich soft delicate colour which heightens the effect of the character of his draughtsmanship; and that suggests the same qualities by means of a different system of hieroglyphics.

The most prominent member of the Chat Blanc symposia, after these, was Paul Bartlett. I found him brilliant and good natured; and his caustic speech gave a spice to his geniality. I thought very highly of his work; but he might have gone much further had it not been for the social and artistic success which acts as a soporific on all artists whose vigilance is unequal to the strain. It is hard indeed for the strongest of us to be ungracious to our admirers. Neglect and poverty, moreover, injure a man's art if they continue for more than a certain number of years. It is best for a man if he begins to taste success in the early forties; but he must have begun with 'the thwackings', as Meredith so profoundly sets forth in that superb magical apologue, *The Shaving of Shagpat;* and he should have learnt their lesson that the applause of mankind is as contemptible as its abuse. 'Just so many asinine hee-haws', as Browning said. The artist must live continually in such intense intimacy with the God-head that he is not to be disturbed either by starvation or success.

There were of course a number of fleas on the Chat Blanc; men whose association with art was a sort of superstition, men who bored us and yet were as difficult to get rid of as the lumber that accumulates in a house. But sometimes a stranger would introduce a new note of genuine amusement.

One day one of the Americans introduced the 'great American artist, Penrhyn Stanlaws'. His name was Stanley Adamson and his birthplace Dundee. He had begun life in the traditional manner of the great by holding horses' heads and earning dimes. Somehow or other, while quite a youth, he had sprung into popular favour and was already earning two thousand pounds a year or more by dashing off a succession of spidery scrawls representing fluffy American flappers in various attitudes. He had come to Paris to study art seriously.

I was delighted with him. He was Pinkerton of *The Wrecker*, with every *t* crossed and every *i* dotted. His innocent earnestness, without any root to it, his infatuation for 'uplift', his total ignorance of the morality of the artist, his crude prejudices based upon Sunday School, his attitude to everything assumed in blissful unconsciousness of a background; this was all perfectly charming. He had all the fascination of a new penny toy.

Now, at this time, Gerald Kelly was in his Whistler-Velasquez period. Kelly's mind is in no way creative or even critical in the true sense of the word. He was a scholar. He would convince himself by elaborate argument that So-and-so was the greatest of all artists; and he would then endeavour to discover the secrets of the master in the spirit of the analytical chemist, and proceed to paint with the most pitiful perseverance in the style of his latest hero. I possess sketches by Kelly which I defy the world to distinguish from Beardsley, Rossetti, Morris, G. F. Watts, etc. Robbie Ross once told me of a man who collected fans by Charles Conder. He had twenty-three when he died; four of them Conders, five doubtful, but the remaining fourteen genuine Kellys.

At this particular moment he was aiming at the 'low tone' of Whistler and Velasquez and his method was to keep on darkening his palette. Ultimately he would use paint the colour of Thames mud for the highlight on the cheek of a blonde. He once picked out an old canvas to paint over and had gone some distance before he discovered that it was his favourite portrait of the Hon. Eileen Grey. His knowledge of art was encyclopaedic; and he laid down the law with more unction and emphasis than anyone else I have ever heard. He took Stanlaws under his wing and started to teach him to paint.

Stanlaws possessed the characteristic American faculty of doing anything and everything easily; of scoring superficial success. One day I called on him and found a large easel in his studio on which stood a vast canvas—evidently by Kelly. I congratulated him on his acquisition. He replied, rather huffily, that he had painted it himself. And the cream of the jest is that this hasty imitation of Kelly's imitations of Velasquez was accepted in the Salon on the strength of Stanlaws' American reputation!

I gradually sickened of the atmosphere of Paris. It was all

too easy. I flitted restlessly to London and back, and found no rest for the sole of my foot. I had even got engaged to be married, but returning after a week in London I was partly too shy to resume relations with my fiancée, and partly awake to the fact that we had drifted under the lee shore of matrimony out of sheer lack of moral energy. This lady claims notice principally as the model for several poems, notably (in *Rosa Mundi, and other Love Songs*) 'The Kiss', 'Eileen' and the poems numbered 14, 15, 16, 18, 21 to 28. She was also the 'Star' in *The Star and the Garter,* which I wrote at this time; and the three women connected with the 'Garter' were an English lady with a passion for ether, an acrobat and model whom I called my boot-button girl because her face was 'round and hard and small and pretty', and thirdly Nina Oliver. Nina is described in the poem itself and also in several lyrics, notably 'The Rondel'—'You laughing little light of wickedness'. My adoration of Nina made her the most famous girl in the quarter for a dozen years and more. She figures, by the way, in my 'Ordeal of Ida Pendragon'.

The Star and the Garter contains some of my best lyrics and is also important as marking a new step in my poetic path. I had mastered form better than I had ever done before; I had welded lyrics into a continuous opus with an integral purpose, without artificiality, such as to some extent mars *Orpheus* and even *Alice*. I spent two days writing the poem; but I do not consider it a waste of time.

Some time later I added an appendix of a very obscure kind. The people of our circle, from Kathleen Bruce (since Lady Scott and Mrs Hilton Young) to Sybil Muggins and Hener-Skene (later, accompanist to Isadora Duncan) are satirized. Their names are introduced by means of puns or allusions and every line is loaded with cryptic criticism. Gerald and I, as educated men, were frightfully fed up with the presumption and poses of the average ass—male or female—of the quarter.

One incident became immortal. I wrote in *The Sword of Song* that I 'read Lévi and the Cryptic Coptic', and lent the manuscript to my fiancée, who was sitting for Gerald Kelly. During the pose she asked him what Coptic meant. 'The language spoken by the ancient Copts,' replied Kelly and redoubled his aesthetic ardours. A long pause—then she asked, 'What does cryptic mean?' 'The language spoken by the ancient Crypts,' roared the *rapin* and abandoned hope of humanity.

Another affectation of the woman art students was to claim

to be treated exactly as if they were men in every respect. Gerald, always eager to oblige, addressed one of his models as old fellow, to her great satisfaction. Then he excused himself for a momentary absence in the terms which he would have used to another man. On his return, the lady had recovered her 'sex and character', and had bolted. Woman can only mix with men on equal terms when she adopts his morality lock, stock and barrel, and ceases to set an extravagant artificial value on her animal functions. The most high-principled woman (alleged) insists on the supreme value of an asset which is notoriously of no value whatever in itself.

The Star and the Garter deals frankly with this problem, among others. As far as sexual charm is concerned, it is only reasonable to expect the expert to be more satisfactory than the new chum; and even, class for class, the professional than the amateur. The desire for exclusive possession is one of the most idiotic and bestial pieces of vanity in human psychology. But love can exist between man and woman entirely independent of any sexual relations between them. The condition of this love is that both parties should have completely mastered their sexual natures; for otherwise their mutual relations may be interrupted by the growlings of the caged animal. Men and women are not free to love decently until they have analysed themselves completely and swept away every trace of mystery from sex; and this means the acquisition of a profound philosophical theory based on wide reading of anthropology and enlightened practice.

My travels had doubtless done much to open my eyes. I had already studied the characteristics of fifty-seven separate races, a number which I subsequently increased to eighty or ninety, when it became difficult to define the word 'race'. My ethnological results are not particularly striking; but the course of the research certainly helped to make it clear that no proposition could be judged as right or wrong, or even as true or false. It is always possible to derive a point of view from the circumstances of its holder.

> The wildest dreams of Kew are the facts of Khatmandu,
> And the crimes of Clapham chaste in Martaban.

Every conceivable moral principle is held somewhere by somebody; and it is the ineluctable conclusion from that somebody's premisses. His circumstances are unique; and so are his hereditary tendencies, his environment, his training and the character of his mental processes. Whether we hold free will or determinism, we equally ratify every type of opinion and conduct.

I had not at this time consciously reached this freedom. I was still a romantic, still seeking true love. Observe a curious analogy to the time when I invoked the adepts, with one actually by my side; so now, invoking true love, there lurked unsuspected in my circle the woman destined to satisfy my aspirations; and just as in aspiring to the Path of the Wise I had not realized the nature of that Path, so also I did not understand what the words true love might mean.

> True love with black inchauntments filled,
>   Its hellish rout of shrieks and groans,
> Its vials of poison death-distilled,
>   Its rattling chains and skeletons.

I made comparatively few notes of this period—November 1902 to April 1903. It seems rather strange that I should have been able to get such an epitome of life into so short a period; at least I reached old age. I went back to Boleskine almost as a ghost might retire to his tomb at cock-crow. In May I wrote a very clear résumé of my progress. It will be as well to quote it.

In the year 1899 I came to Boleskine House and put everything in order with the object of carrying out the Operation of Abra-Melin the Mage.

I had studied Ceremonial Magick and had obtained remarkable success.

My gods were those of Egypt, interpreted on lines closely akin to those of Greece.

In philosophy I was a realist of the Cabbalistic school.

In 1900 I left England for Mexico, and later the Far East, Ceylon, India, Burma, Baltistan, Egypt and France. It is idle here to detail the corresponding progress of my thought; and passing through a stage of Hinduism, I had discarded all deities as unimportant, and in philosophy was an uncompromising nominalist. I had arrived at what I may describe as the position of an orthodox Buddhist; but with the following reservations.

1. I cannot deny that certain phenomena do accompany the use of certain rituals; I only deny the usefulness of such methods to the White Adept.

2. I consider Hindu methods of meditation as possibly useful to the beginner and should not therefore recommend them to be discarded at once.

With regard to my advancement, the redemption of the cosmos, etc. etc. I leave for ever the 'Blossom and Fruit' theory[1] and appear in the character of an inquirer on strictly scientific lines.

This is unhappily calculated to damp the enthusiasm; but as I so carefully of old, for the Magical Path, excluded from my life all other interests, that life has now no particular meaning; and the Path of Research, on the only lines I can now approve of, remains the one Path possible for me to tread.

(By the Blossom and Fruit theory, I mean the existence of a body of initiates pledged to devote themselves to the redemption of mankind.)

It sounds as if I had become a bit of a prig. I expect a good deal of my attitude was due to exhausted vitality. Chogo Ri was perhaps still taking his revenge.

I had picked out Boleskine for its loneliness. Lord Lovat and Mrs Fraser-Tytler, my nearest neighbours, were eight miles away, while Grant of Glenmoriston was on the other side of Loch Ness. Besides, Boleskine was already the centre of a thousand legends.

Even before I came there there was a fine crop of the regular Highland superstitions.

The howl of a bulldog, exactly like the crying of a child, is heard far off.

GEORGE. All right. It's only that damned dog of M'Alister's. He does it every night.

FENELLA. He sees the ghost of old Lord Lovat.

GEORGE. Old Lord Lovat?

FENELLA. Yes; they beheaded him after the '45. He rolls his head up and down the corridors.

GEORGE. Pleasant pastime!

FENELLA. What else is a man to do?

GEORGE. What's that tapping?

(*He stops to listen.*)

FENELLA. Go on! It's only the old woman.

GEORGE. What old woman?

FENELLA. Her son was a lunatic. They let him out cured, as they thought. His mother came up here with him to lay flowers on his father's grave; and he caught her legs and smashed her brains against the wall.

GEORGE. Oh damn it!

FENELLA. You baby! So, ever since, she comes from time to time to try and pick her brains off the wall.

I certainly used to hear the 'rolling of the head', but when I put in a billiard table, the old gentleman preferred it to the corridor and confined his amusements to the gun room. Even before that, he had always stopped at the Pylon of the corridor which marked off from the rest of the house the wing which was consecrated to Abra-Melin. I have never discovered any explanation of these noises. We used to listen at the door of the gun room, and the head would roll merrily up and down the table with untiring energy. The moment we opened the door the noise would stop; but there would be no visible cause.

During my absence, the reputation of the house had become more formidable than ever before. I have little doubt that the Abra-Melin devils, whatever they are, used the place as convenient headquarters and put in some of their spare time in terrifying the natives. No one would pass the house after dark. Folk got into the habit of going round through Strath Errick, a detour of several miles. There were a great many definite legends; but I made rather a point of refraining from making a collection. I was completely committed to rationalism and the occurrence of miracles was a nuisance. I should have liked to deny the reality of the whole Abra-Melin business, but the phenomena were just as patent as the stones of the house.

I lived the life of the ordinary Scottish laird in a dull mechanical way and drifted into beginning meditation on Buddhist lines; rather because I had nothing better to do than for any more positive reason. The record of the period from June 16th to July 13th is curiously dull. One notices chiefly the lack of driving force and the complete disappearance of any enthusiasm.

I had completed *The Sword of Song* before I left Paris and left it to be printed with Philippe Renouard, one of the best men in Paris. I intended to issue it privately. I had no longer any ideas about the 'best publisher'. I felt in a dull way that it was a sort of duty to make my work accessible to humanity; but I had no idea of reaping profit or fame thereby.

45

On the thirteenth of July I went to Edinburgh, partly to renew my stock of wines and partly to pick up some kind of companion-housekeeper, but ostensibly to meet Gerald Kelly who was due to spend the summer at Strathpeffer. His sister Rose was engaged to a man named Howell, who was coming from America to marry her in a few weeks.

I engaged a companion-housekeeper easily enough. What a man wants is a woman whom he can take down from the shelves when required and who can be trusted to stay on them when not. It is true that a woman is much more amusing when she possesses individuality and initiative, but it is the basest kind of sensuality to wish to be amused. The ideal woman should prevent a man from being amused or disturbed in any way, whether by his own passions or the incidents of everyday life. I forget the surname of the lady whom I chose to fill this important position. Let her stand in history by the unassuming title of 'Red-headed Arabella'. It was arranged that she should come and take up her duties towards the middle of August. I only stayed two or three days in Edinburgh and, having attended to the matter of wine and woman, completed the triad by writing *The God-Eater*.

This short play is singularly unsatisfactory as a work of art, but extremely significant as a piece of autohagiography. The explanatory note in my *Collected Works* is itself obscure.

> The idea of this obscure and fantastic play is as follows:
> By a glorious act human misery is secured (history of Christianity).
> Hence, appreciation of the personality of Jesus is no excuse for being a Christian.
> Inversely, by a vile and irrational series of acts human happiness is secured (story of the play).
> Hence, attacks on the mystics of history need not cause us to condemn mysticism.
> Also, the knowledge of good and evil is a tree whose fruit man has not yet tasted: so that the devil cheated Eve indeed; or (more probably) Eve cheated Adam. Unless (most prob-

able of all) God cheated the devil and the fruit was a common apple after all. (*Cf.* H. Maudsley, *Life in Mind and Conduct.*)

The influence of *The Golden Bough* and the Spencerian philosophers whom I was reading is apparent. In the last paragraphs, too, is evidence that I still clung to Shelley's dream of a regenerated humanity. There is a touch of the influence of a man named L. C. R. Duncombe Jewell, the eldest son of a Plymouth Brother at Streatham, who had 'gone to the bad' by becoming a Roman Catholic. I had asked him to spend a week at Boleskine and he had managed somehow or other to settle down there as my factor. I suppose he saved me trouble in one way or another, and was some sort of companion. He called himself Ludovic Cameron, being a passionate Jacobite and having a Cameron somewhere in his family tree. He was very keen on the Celtic revival and wanted to unite the five Celtic nations in an empire. In this political project he had not wholly succeeded: but he had got as far as designing a flag. And, oh so ugly!

All this seemed childish to me, but no more so than imperialism, and it had the advantage of being rather charming and entirely harmless. It is strange to look back on myself at twenty-seven, completely persuaded of the truth of the most extravagant claims of mysticism and magick, yet completely disillusioned with regard to the universe. I was inclined to minimize my activity in every respect. The importation of Red-headed Arabella had only one motive—to arrange my life so as to reduce the elements of disturbance to the lowest possible point.

It may seem a little strange that I did not follow the example of Allan Bennett and take the Yellow Robe. But I had not been favourably impressed by the conditions of Buddhist monasteries. It was no doubt true that the regulations laid down by the Buddha for the conduct of bhikkhus were intended to help them to free their minds from disturbance; but they were no longer interpreted in that light by the bhikkhus themselves, except by an infinitesimal minority, who, like Allan, really understood the machinery of the business.

Nor did I agree that the Buddha was altogether right. I thought it a great mistake to interfere with physiological processes. I was perfectly aware that greed, lust and hatred were the enemies of peace; but I was also aware that forcing oneself to abstain from food, love and society could only result in diverting the natural appetites into abnormal channels. St Anthony attributed an exaggerated importance to sex. I was convinced that the repression of natural instincts was an insult to nature and a short cut to moral deformity. I already saw that the only proper course of action was to order one's life in accordance with its conditions.

The plan to pursue was to comply with physiological propriety, but to keep each appetite in its place, to prevent it from invading the sphere of the whole consciousness. In practice, I proposed to live an absolutely normal life, but without attaching undue importance to any element of it. I intended to enjoy my dinner, whether it was salmon and Chateau Yquem '78, or cold mutton and a glass of milk. I had found by experience that the minimum of disturbance was secured in this way. The agony of sugar starvation on the Baltoro glacier had showed me that to try to repress a natural appetite is merely to invite it to obsess one.

I expected then to settle down slowly into a routine of scientific research on the lines philosophically indicated by Spencer, Huxley and the Buddha, while morally I followed the Rosicrucian principle of complying with the customs of the country through which I was travelling.

The condition of my soul is clearly indicated by my output. The fount of lyric poetry had run completely dry. I had not touched the unfinished *Orpheus;* I wrote nothing new. I no longer aspired to become the redeemer of humanity. I doubt whether I should have been able to attach any meaning to any such words. After returning from Edinburgh, I do not seem even to have kept a record and I remember nothing about my doings. July is however the date of an essay 'The initiated interpretation of ceremonial magick' which I prefaced to my edition of *The Goetia.* I had employed Mathers to translate the text of *The Lesser Key of Solomon the King* of which *The Goetia* is the first section. He got no further; after the events of 1900, he had simply collapsed morally. I added a translation of the conjurations into the Enochian or Angelic language; edited and annotated the text, prefixed a 'Preliminary Invocation', added a prefatory note, a Magical Square [1] (intended to prevent improper use of the book) and ultimately an Invocation of Typhon when the First Magical War of the Aeon of Horus was declared.

This essay throws a very clear light upon my position. I could not deny the facts of Ceremonial Magick. It is impossible to explain why a dog squeals when you hit him with a stick; but we do not therefore deny that this happens, or at least that there is some impression of some such kind somewhere. I was in precisely the position of those philosophers who were driven to the theory of causality and said that there was no cause why an apple should fall; it was simply a matter of coincidence that God should happen to will that it should touch the ground after willing it should be detached from the bough. The facts of Magick appear quite natural if one accepts the explanation officially put forward without inquiring too closely.

This theory, roughly speaking, is that of Milton or Dante. There is even some excuse for saying it is the Catholic tradition à rebours; that tradition is of course the development and degradation of various animistic cults. Magical facts were explained by the intervention of spiritual beings. One spiritual being, myself, throws a stone. That is how it happens that the stone has changed its position. Another spiritual being, Zeus, is annoyed; that explains how such and such a house is struck by lightning. All facts are of the same order and their interpretation must be uniform.

Now, I had dismissed the whole theory of spiritual hierarchies as repugnant to reason; thus I was left with a set of phenomena on my hands which cried aloud for explanation, exactly like the man who noticed that rubbed amber attracted certain light objects. In this essay, I endeavoured to show how it was that Magical Operations were effective. My collection of facts was at that time comparatively small and I had not yet analysed and classified them properly. But the essay shows that I was on the right track. My interpretation conformed with the mechanical theory of Victorian physics.

The sequel shows my development on the same lines as the rest of modern science. The materialists had to include the connotation of 'spirit' in their definition of 'matter'. One of my difficulties was that my senses told me that the archangel Gabriel existed, exactly as they told me that Ernst Haeckel existed; in fact, rather more so. I had accepted Haeckel on mere hearsay. Why should I doubt Isis, whom I had seen, heard, touched; yet admit Ray Lankester, whom I hadn't? Already I was compelled to resolve all phenomena equally into unknowable impressions. I did not realize how arbitrary it was to explain Taphtatharath [2] as a set of impressions somehow imagined by any mind as the result of a particular process of intoxication. It was long before I understood that all explanations of the universe are ultimately interchangeable like the geometries of Euclid, Riemann and Lobatchewsky.

So much for July. But early in August, Gerald Kelly wrote suggesting that I should join his party at Strathpeffer. I had nothing better to do. Red-headed Arabella was still in Edinburgh; I was being bored to death, either by my meditation or by my inability to rouse myself to the point of doing any. So I packed a bag and went over.

The party consisted principally of Kelly's mother, who worthily preserved the conditions of Tennysonian dignity; Rose, who was in a curious state of excitement, which I either failed to observe at all, or attributed to the high spirits of unthinking youth; and one or two more or less chance acquaintances, including an elderly solicitor named Hill, who was in love with Rose and struck me as perhaps the tamest and dullest specimen of humanity that I had ever met. Gerald was playing golf, which at that time was rather daring; not quite the thing you would confess to your friends in London. I had no clubs and he played mostly with Hill. Thus it happened that at lunch on the eleventh of August Rose and I got into conversation. There is something in my character which makes people confide in me. I think the bottom of it is my chastity. They instinctively understand that I have no personal axe to grind; that I shall display a wise benevolence and incorruptible justice, being detached from every form of desire.

So Rose confessed to me that she was in great trouble, as we wandered out over the links to walk the last few holes with Kelly and Hill.

She told me that she was being forced into the marriage with Howell by her family. She had been carrying on an intrigue with a married man named Frank Summers. This had got to the ears of her family because, being hard up for money, she had told her mother that she was pregnant and got forty pounds from her for the purpose of having an illegal operation. Naturally, this led to inquiries; and though the pregnancy was merely an ingenious pretext, and the operation consisted of dinners and dresses, the Kellys were determined to prevent further raids on their purse and their prestige by insisting on her remarriage.

The story awakened my Shelleyan indignation. We sat down on the links in silence while I thought out the situation. The solution was perfectly simple. 'Don't upset yourself about such a trifle,' said I, and told her something of my spiritual state and my plans for the future. 'All you have to do,' I said, 'is to marry me. I will go back to Boleskine and you need never hear of me again—unless,' I added with romantic grandiloquence, 'I can be of any further assistance to you. That will knock your marriage with Howell on the head; you will be responsible for your conduct, not to your family, but to me (as in the case of an Indian dancing girl married to a dagger or a pipal tree); and you can go and live in the flat which Mr Summers proposes to take for you, without interference.'

It really seems absurd that I should have been so ignorant of the elements of psychology; but I genuinely imagined that this fantastic programme was possible. It certainly satisfied all theoretical requirements! But like other Utopian dreamers from Sir Thomas Browne to Karl Marx, I omitted to take into consideration one insignificant element in the problem—the existence of the mysterious force called human nature.

Rose jumped at my suggestion. We agreed to tell Gerald as soon as he appeared, which was thoughtless, as it might easily have put him off his game, and to get married at the earliest possible moment. Gerald finished the course in 4, 3, 4, 4, bogey being 17 for that part of the course. He took our announcement as a harmless joke.

I went to the local authorities about the practical programme; but they were like Baal on a celebrated occasion. The only available deity was the parish sexton; and, after all, could anything have been more appropriate? He told me that I could have the banns published and get married in three weeks. That wouldn't do at all; it would give Howell time to arrive from America and put pressure on the Kellys. I asked him if there was not some less drawn-out form of execution. 'Well,' he said, after scratching his head, 'you can be exposed on a boorrrd along o' yer young 'ooman, for a week.' Not in vain had I been studying *The Golden Bough*, but I had no idea that these obscene forms of torture still lingered—even in the Scottish Highlands. 'Come, come,' I said, 'there must be a simpler and quicker way to get married than that.' Surely, I said to myself, all that stuff about Gretna Green must have some basis in fact. He shook his head sorrowfully, a discomfortable motion which I checked by slipping him a half-crown. He then admitted that it was only necessary to go to the sheriff of the county and declare the intention to get married, in which case the marriage would take place there and then. 'There and then?' I echoed in a hollow voice, for I had the instinctive feeling natural to a young man, that he is somehow or other putting his foot in it, that he is invoking unknown gods. 'Then and there,' he answered heavily and the syllables fell as if he had been throwing the sods upon my coffin.

Armed with this satisfactory information, I returned to the hotel and had a short conference with my betrothed. We were to get up in time to catch the first train to Dingwall, call on the sheriff and get it over before breakfast. We carried out this design. We had to go quietly for fear of awakening Gerald. The idea was that he might interfere, though I had no reason for supposing that he would do so. But apparently she had.

46

So we stole out in the dim grey of the morning. I remember
her furtive passage under his window, and how I murmured

> Wake Duncan with thy knocking?
> I would thou could'st

recalling—to late!—the theatrical superstition that it is very
unlucky to quote *Macbeth* at the beginning of an enterprise.

We jogged along in the little train in a state of curious
constraint. Of course our relations *were* rather peculiar, when
all was said and done. Anyhow, there was nothing to say. Rose
was a charming woman, but far from an intellectual companion. Her brother's friends being for the most part addicted
to art or literature, it was her custom to carry a volume of
Browning in her dressing-case, and she would ask people to
fetch it for her, which impressed them. She didn't have to
read it. Again, whenever a conversation flagged, she would
remark thoughtfully:

> Bright star, would I were steadfast as thou art!

'Twas all she knew. However, I wasn't going to have to live
with her. All I had to do was to emancipate her. So there was
no reason for trying to talk to her.

We reached Dingwall in the cold damp dawn; we disin-
terred the sheriff's address from a sleepy policeman and arrived at his house only to be told by a dishevelled maid that
we couldn't get at him till eight or nine or ten o'clock. I was
piqued. The hint of obstacles roused me. I wasn't going to
elope, whatever my reasons might be, and make a mess of it. I
demanded the address of a lawyer and excavated him. He
promised to be at his office at eight o'clock. With that we had
to be content. There was no reason for apprehension. It wasn't
likely that our disappearance would be discovered until
breakfast time. We repaired to the hotel and ate and drank
something in a state of suppressed nervous excitement. I confess to having been ashamed of myself. There I was, accoutred

cap-a-pie from my bonnet to my claymore, and I had nothing
at stake; and yet I was nervous! We were at the lawyer's on
the stroke of eight, where we discovered that the sheriff was a
mere flourish and that all we had to do was to consent to
being married, and declare that we regarded ourselves as man
and wife. A faint disgust at the prose of the proceedings induced me to elaborate them by taking out my dirk and kissing
it, as a pledge of my faith. I never thought of kissing *her!*

It then transpired that the sheriff had to have his little
whack, after all, no less than an Armenian pimp. The marriage
had to be registered in his office. We were completely at a
loose end. I was to go back to Boleskine, of course, but there
were some hours before the train started. She was to go back to
Strathpeffer: but—at this moment, Gerald Kelly burst into the
room, his pale face drawn with insane passion. He was probably annoyed at his stupidity in not having realized that the
announcement of our engagement, nineteen hours earlier, had
been serious. On learning that we were already married, he
aimed a violent blow at me. It missed me by about a yard. I
am ashamed to say that I could not repress a quiet smile. If he
had not been out of his mind, his action would have been
truly courageous, for compared with me he was a shrimp;
and while I was one of the most athletic men in the country,
his strength had been impaired by his sedentary stupor and
loose living in Paris.

When he felt better, we decided to carry out the original
programme. I went off to Boleskine and she went back to
Strathpeffer. I have frequently noticed that interference with
my plans ensures their being carried out with exactitude.

In the meantime, however, Mr Hill had arrived, panting
like a parsnip robbed of its prey. He bleated out, after a brief
invocation to the Woolsack, that the marriage was illegal and
must be broken. Also may, might, would, could, should, and
other auxiliary verbs. I yawned gracefully and left them to
fight it out.

Rose stuck to her guns like the game little bitch she was.
Mr Hill made the discovery that he had not made the law, and
Mrs Kelly and Gerald that they had not made mankind. So
the next move in the game was that I dispatched Ludovic
Cameron as ambassador. It was the supreme moment in his
life! I was rather annoyed at being dragged into such a crazy
controversy and heartily wished to hear no more of the matter,
but I had to dree my weird.

It was arranged that Rose and I should go to the sheriff

and register our marriage, as we risked fine and imprisonment
if we omitted to do so. We were then to drive together to a
wayside station, where we could take our own decision as to
our future proceedings. Dingwall and Strathpeffer were of
course seething with scandal. There were probably as many
separate stories as there were inhabitants; and the appearance
of the laird and his bride on the platform of Dingwall might
have been the signal for a demonstration to eclipse the diamond jubilee and the relief of Mafeking.

So I returned to Strathpeffer, annoyed but amiable, had an
interview with Mrs Kelly, who played the part of the Agèd
Queen Bent Down By Sorrow to admiration, while I said all
the necessary nonsense. We then repaired to the sheriff's and
were induced to swear the most formidable oaths; about nothing in particular, but they apparently gratified the official
instinct and filled the official coffer. Duncombe Jewell excelled
himself. The ordinary oath was not for him. He produced a
formula the majesty of which literally inhibited the normal
functions of our minds. It was the finest piece of ritualistic
rigmarole that I have ever heard in my life.

At the sheriff's door we found the vehicle which was to
take us to the wayside station. Rose and I got in, feeling as if we
had been through a mangle; but the sense of humour came
most opportunely to our rescue. The vehicle chanced to resemble a prison van, and the circumstance tickled our imagination and helped to break down our embarrassment. But it was
a frightfully long drive to the wayside station and a frightfully
long wait when we got there. I don't know whether it was
part of the arrangement or not that we should take tickets to
the end of the line, some place on the west coast of Scotland,
the name of which I have entirely forgotten. But we did. We
sat opposite to each other in an empty first-class carriage.

I only remember one scrap of conversation, and I do not
remember what it was except that it was a sort of little joke.
We were enjoying a species of triumph at having 'got away
with it', but we were in exquisite embarrassment as to what
to do—at least, I was. I have reason to suspect that Rose did
not share my pathetic puerility. It never occurred to me that
the programme I had planned had been in any way altered.
Had we not carried it out with the most punctilious precision?

We arrived at our destination a little before dinner time.
My embarrassment reached an acute point. It was simply impossible for me to register at the hotel. I confess to the most
abject cowardice. I made some excuse and left Rose to con-

front a clerk, while I went to look at the sea and wish it weren't too cold to drown myself. I returned to find that she had booked a double room. I thought it was hardly playing the game; but I couldn't be rude to a lady and, at the worst, it was only a matter of a day or so. I could decently dispatch her from Boleskine to the embraces of Mr Summers and proceed to

> Raze out the written troubles of the brain,
> And with some sweet oblivious antidote
> Cleanse the stuff'd bosom of that perilous stuff.

It possibly crossed my mind that all these alarums and excursions were alien to arahatship, that marriage was a nuisance to a man whose mind was set on success in Mahasatipatthana [1], and that the problems raised by Rose would be sent to sleep by Red-headed Arabella.

In any case, there was nothing for it but to behave like a gentleman. So we drank a lot of champagne for dinner. We had been married on August 12th and could give God glory for his good gift of grouse, and then—what's champagne for, anyhow? Rose retired immediately after dinner; I sat in the smoking-room and pole-axed a stranger by making mysterious remarks until he thought I was mad, and fled. I had some more champagne and remembered that I was a poet. I got some paper and wrote the following rondel. Damn it, I had to play up to my partner!

> Rose on the breast of the world of spring,
>   I press my breast against thy bloom;
> My subtle life drawn out to thee; to thee
>   its moods and meanings cling.
> I pass from change and thought to peace,
>   woven on love's incredible loom,
> Rose on the breast of the world of spring!
>
> How shall the heart dissolved in joy take
>   form and harmony and sing?
> How shall the ecstasy of light fall back to
>   music's magic gloom?
> O China rose without a thorn, O honey-bee
>   without a sting!
>
> The scent of all thy beauty burns upon the
>   wind. The deep perfume

Of our own love is hidden in our hearts,
 the invulnerable ring.
No man shall know. I bear thee down unto
 the tomb, beyond the tomb,
Rose on the breast of the world of spring!

I went upstairs.

I began to suspect the truth, that my absolute indifference to Rose, combined with my perfectly casual willingness to marry her in order to do her a service, as one might offer a stranger one's place in an omnibus, had purged her heart of its passion for the fat sensuality of Frank Summers, and hurled her head over heels in love with me.

We arrived at Boleskine, where I learnt that Red-headed Arabella was due to arrive at Inverness the following day. I blush to say that I didn't know quite what to do about it, and confided in Duncombe Jewell. He rose to the occasion and went to Inverness to head her off. It may seem incredible; but my reaction was one of sheer annoyance. I had no feeling for Red-headed Arabella; in point of fact, I had picked her for that very reason, and I was perfectly ready to relieve Rose from the tyranny of her family. But it was really asking rather too much when I had to upset my arrangements. I had not even yet suspected the truth that the fine flight of Rose's rapture was carrying me away on its wings. Her love for me was evoking my love for her, and I had rather made a point of contracting out of any such complications. I was prepared to propitiate physiology, but only on condition that the domain of psychology suffered no interference.

However, there I was, married to one of the most beautiful and fascinating women in the world. The love between us grew to the utmost possibilities of passion without my suspecting it. The Kellys had acquiesced in the fait accompli. The last little splutter was a letter from the Rev. Frederick Festus demanding that I should settle ten thousand pounds on Rose. I might have done so had it not been for his pompous statement that the daughters of his house never married without a settlement. Considering that the very one whom I married myself had had no settlement at her first marriage, the lie was a little blatant, even for a clergyman. I replied with appropriate decision; they abandoned the idea that I could be bullied, as they were accustomed to bully timid and servile people who could be bounced. I have never understood the quality of bluster with which some people seem to get right through the world. It must be so humiliating to be 'called'. I much prefer to put forward my weakness to induce the attack of the malicious, while I am lying in ambush with an overwhelming reinforcement.

The honeymoon was uninterrupted beatitude. Once, in the first three weeks or so, Rose took some trifling liberty; I recognized the symptoms, and turned her up and spanked her. She henceforth added the qualities of perfect wife to those of perfect mistress. Women, like all moral inferiors, behave well only when treated with firmness, kindness and justice. They are always on the look-out to detect wavering or irritation in the master; and their one hope is to have a genuine grievance to hug.

When trouble is not suppressed permanently by a little friendly punishment, it is a sign that the virtue has gone out of the master. When the suffragette went from worse to worse and made severity itself inhuman and useless, it did not prove in the least that woman had altered from the days of the jungle, but that industrialism and piety had sapped the virtue of the male. Rome did not fall because the Germans and the Gauls had in any way improved; they were just the same and could be beaten by the same tactics and weapons as in the earliest centuries. But Christianity had eaten the heart out of Rome. The manly virtues and the corresponding womanly virtues, one of which is recognition of the relation between the sexes, had been corrupted by slave morality. The England of Victoria, by bringing up the best stock in the country in the most favourable physical conditions, and teaching the boys from the start that they were brought into the world in order to rule it, produced a class of men who were like Old Testament heroes. (Under George III we had a rehearsal. Can it be that long prosperous reigns favour the production of such men? We had another crop under Elizabeth, when the restoration of the abbeys to the people of England gave a chance to the development of a daring and dominant breed.) But the influences which are commonly called civilized attenuate the aristocratic spirit.

The existence of a common scold is a definite system of imminent death in any community. The Indian renegades, from Lajpat Rai to Gandhi, are merely evidence that the sahib has given place to the competition wallah. India has not progressed in the last thousand years and will not in the next thousand. The biological impulse is expended. India was nature's attempt to construct a nation of diverse elements by welding them in a religious and moral system. It might have succeeded had it been secure against invasion. But while India has always conquered her conquerors (imposing, for example, the caste system on the English), the invaders interfered with the process of growth and diverted the national trend from unity.

A nation lives by its architecture; when it comes to consciousness of its soul, it feels that it has to build a house for that soul to live in. Such buildings must be utterly useless; the soul will not live in a Woolworth Building—that is inhabited by the unclean spirit whose name is Legion, and that is the evidence that America, with all its material prosperity, has no soul. Nor is a man rich while he confines his purchases to things which are useful.

The love of my wife had made me the richest man on earth and developed my human soul to its full stature. I could afford to build a temple to love, and that of course had to be stupendous, useless and immortal. I made one disconcerting discovery, though not till long afterwards; this: that erotic poetry does not spring from supreme satisfaction. Indeed, my life was a perfect lyric and left no surplus energy to overflow into words. I wrote nothing. The temple had to be, as I have said, and I could only think of constructing a long beautiful objectless journey. As soon as the summer showed signs of waning, we started on a hypertrophied honeymoon. We pretended to ourselves that we were going big-game shooting in Ceylon and to pay a visit to Allan at Rangoon (where he had now removed from Akyab), but the real object was to adorn the celebration of our love by setting it in a thousand suave and sparkling backgrounds. As my poetry had petered out, so had my Magick and my meditation. I let them go without a pang. I was supremely happy; loved filled the universe; there was no room for anything else.

I had not kept a diary. Day followed day, each a fresh facet of the diamond of delight. All I remember is that we made our preparations in London, trying and buying guns, giving dinners, and so on. We dazzled Paris for a day or two, but not without one severe shock.

Rose and I were walking towards the Pont Alexandre III when I met Vestigia, as we always called Mrs Mathers. I had not seen her for a long time and we started an animated conversation. I noticed nothing peculiar. I do not live in the world of phenomena: I only visit it at rare intervals. I had forgotten Rose's existence. When Vestigia had gone, I realized that I had not introduced her to my wife. She did not ask me who it was. I told her. 'Oh,' said she, 'I thought it was some model that you knew in the old days.'

The words came as a terrific shock. Vestigia had been our ideal of refinement, purity, spirituality and the rest. And then my mind informed me of what my eyes had seen, that Vestigia was painted thickly to the eyes—did I say painted? I mean plastered. Where the camouflage stopped, there was a neck which could not have been washed for months. I learnt later that Mathers, falling upon evil times, had forced his wife to pose naked in one of the Montmartre shows which are put on for the benefit of ignorant and prurient people, especially provincials and English, and that even that was not the worst of it.

Then we swooped down on Marseilles, perched on the terrace of Bertolini's at Naples and picked up a few crumbs. Our first breathing place was Cairo. It was one of the extravagances of our passion that suggested our spending a night together in the King's Chamber of the Great Pyramid. It was the gesture of the male showing off his plumage. I wanted my wife to see what a great Magician I was. We went, accordingly, after dinner, with candles. More from habit than anything else, as I imagine, I had with me a small note book of Japanese vellum in which were written my principal invocations, etc. Among these was a copy of the 'Preliminary Invocation' of *The Goetia*.

We reached the King's Chamber after dismissing the servants at the foot of the Grand Gallery. By the light of a single candle placed on the edge of the coffer I began to read the invocation. But as I went on I noticed that I was no longer stooping to hold the page near the light. I was standing erect. Yet the manuscript was not less but more legible. Looking about me, I saw that the King's Chamber was glowing with a soft light which I immediately recognized as the astral light. I have been accustomed to describe the colour as ultra-violet, from its resemblance to those rays in the spectrum—which I happen to be able to distinguish. The range varies, but is quite noticeably beyond that visible to the normal human eye. The colour is not unlike that of an arc lamp; it is definitely less coloured than the light of a mercury lamp. If I had to affix a conventional label, I should probably say pale lilac. But the quality of the light is much more striking than the colour. Here the word phosphorescence occurs to the mind. It is one of the mysteries of physics that the total light of the sky is very much greater than can be accounted for by the luminous bodies in the heavens. There are various theories, but I personally believe that the force now called radio-activity which we know to be possessed in some degree by every particle of matter, is responsible. Our eyes are affected with the impression of light by forces which are not in themselves recognized as luminous.

However, back to facts. The King's Chamber was aglow as if with the brightest tropical moonlight. The pitiful dirty yellow flame of the candle was like a blasphemy, and I put it out. The astral light remained during the whole of the invocation and for some time afterwards, though it lessened in intensity as we composed ourselves to sleep. For the rest, the floor of the King's Chamber is particularly uncompromising. In sleeping out on rocks, one can always accommodate oneself more or less to the local irregularities, but the King's Chamber reminded me of *Brand;* and I must confess to having passed a very uncomfortable night. I fear my dalliance had corrupted my Roman virtue. In the morning the astral light had completely disappeared and the only sound was the flitting of the bats.

In a sort of way, I suppose I did consider myself rather a fine fellow to have been able to produce so striking a phenomenon with so little trouble. But it did not encourage me to go on with Magick. My wife was all in all.

47

We must have had some vague idea of exploring the little known parts of China, for we had certainly intended to visit Allan in Rangoon. It was probably at Colombo that Rose made up her mind that she was pregnant; for I remember that our shooting expedition in Hambantota, in the southeastern province of Ceylon, was *faute de mieux*. We thought we had better get back to Boleskine for the event; and yet we had to justify our journey by some definite accomplishment. So we left Colombo for Galle and thence up country. It is strange that I fail entirely to remember how we got to the jungle. But rough notes tell me that it was by coach, and that we left the base village in four bullock carts on Monday the fourteenth of December. I quote my entry of January 1st, 1904 (some lines are carefully erased. I cannot tell why or imagine what I had written).

Jan. 1st.
  Began badly: missed deer and hare. So annoyed. Yet the omen is that the year is well for works of love & union; ill for those of hate. Be mine of love!

This entry does not sound as if I were still wholly lunatic in the rays of the honeymoon. The explanation is that the mere fact of getting back to camp life reawakened in me the old ambitions and interests. It may be part of my feeling for ritual that to put on certain types of clothes is to transform my state of mind. However lazy I may be, I have merely to change trousers for knickerbockers to feel athletic at once. There is also the point that I make a profession of virtue when reminded of certain dates, just as a totally irreligious man might go to church at Christmas. The subsequent entries give no hint that my mind was really turning to its ancient masters. The sole entries concern sport and camp life; and they are very meagre.

I have never been able to enjoy reading chronicles of slaughter, and I do not propose to inflict any such on the world. They are as monotonous and conventional as those of mountaineering. Sportsmen and climbers follow the fashion with frightful fidelity. Norman Collie wrote the only book on mountains which possesses any literary merit. Mummery's is good because he really had something to say, but his style shows the influence of Collie. Owen Glynne Jones produced a patent plagiarism of Mummery's style; and when it came to the brothers Abraham, the bottom was reached. And what a bottom! In fact, two.

Of the older writers, Leslie Stephen is the only one worth mentioning, and to him mountaineering was of secondary interest. Tales of hunting, shooting and fishing are equally tedious. They are only tolerable in fiction such as Mr Jorrocks and *The Pickwick Papers*. Travellers having wider interests are more readable. Sir Richard Burton is a supreme master; the greatest that ever took pen. He has not one dull paragraph. Cameron and Mary Kingsley must not be forgotten for a *proxime accessit*.

Certain incidents of this shoot are worth passing notice. Rose had an attack of fever on the seventh of January. For the first time since my marriage I had a moment to spare from celebrations of Hymen. I sat at my camp table in my Colonel Elliot's chair and wrote the poem *Rosa Mundi*, the first for many months. I sing to her, recall the incidents of the birth of our love, hint at the prospect of its harvest, and weave the whole of the facts into a glowing tapestry of rapture. It was a new rhythm, a new rime. It marks a notable advance on any previous work for sustained sublimity.

Physically and morally, Rose exercised on every man she met a fascination which I have never seen anywhere else, not a fraction of it. She was like a character in a romantic novel, a Helen of Troy or a Cleopatra; yet, while more passionate, unhurtful. She was essentially a good woman. Her love sounded every abyss of lust, soared to every splendour of the empyrean. Eckenstein adored her. When I published this poem, which I did privately under the pseudonym of D. H. Carr, from feelings of delicacy, Eckenstein was actually shocked. He did not care much for my poetry as a rule; but he thought *Rosa Mundi* the greatest love lyric in the language. (As a cold fact, its only rival is *Epipsychidion*.) But he held it too sacred to issue. 'It ought,' he said, 'to have been found among his papers after his death.'

I can understand the sentiment of this view, but cannot share it. I wanted to make humanity holier and happier by putting into their hands the key of my own success.

And in my diary there is no allusion to the poem. (It may in fact have been written during an earlier illness of Rose— on December 15th—but I don't think so, because I connect the inspiration with eating buffalo steak, and on the earlier date I was only eating snipe.) I have only noted, 'Rose ill, one bloody birdling, bread arrived in P.M.'

I am not by any means a mighty hunter before the Lord, but I am certainly very fond of big game shooting. I thoroughly enjoy the life which goes with it and I like the high moments of excitement and danger; they atone for the tedium of the stalk. I have no use whatever for the *battue*, even if it is a matter of bears and tigers. As for grouse and pheasants, my pleasure in the exercise of my skill is marred by the sub-conscious feeling that I am dependent on others for my sport. Moreover, the element of combat is missing. I can get a great deal of amusement out of rough shooting for the pot; but artificiality of any kind is the very devil in sport. I do not even care for shooting from a *machan*. I like to be just one of the jungle folk and challenge any fellow animal I meet. I suppose that, logically, I should disdain the use of weapons. I never did.

My most amusing adventures have been always when I strolled alone into the jungle without trackers or bearers, met a boar, a bear or a buffalo by chance or the exercise of native wit, and conquered him in single fight. My native servants used to be horrified at my proceedings, very much as orthodox mountaineers have been at my solitary climbs. They did not doubt my prowess with the rifle; they respected it because they understood it. But they had been accustomed to white men relying on them for light and leading, and they made sure that I should be hopelessly lost without them in the jungle. Perhaps the chief part of my pleasure consisted in the problems presented by having to find my way home, very likely in the dark, after having pursued some quarry by a devious route, by virtue of my sense of direction, especially as impenetrable undergrowth, uncrossable patches of water, or marshes, may complicate matters very seriously.

The most dangerous animal in Ceylon (there are no tigers, and if there were, the statement would stand) is the buffalo. One can distinguish a wild from a tame buffalo by his psychology. If he is wild, he runs away; if he is tame, he charges you. Yet these fanatical partisans of 'Asia for the Asiatics' permit themselves to be ridden, cursed and bullied by brats not six years old. The buffalo is always savage and always intelligent enough to know who has wounded him. He is also infinitely courageous and vindictive. Many tigers will turn tail even when slightly but painfully wounded. But the buffalo never gives in morally or physically, and shows almost human powers of strategy and tactics in his vendetta. His vitality is incredible; the gaur (a not dissimilar species) which killed Captain Sayers in Burma had seventeen bullets from heavy rifles in him while he was goring and trampling the aggressor. The other Englishmen present could do nothing to save him.

One evening I shot a sambhur; the great stag (miscalled elk) of Ceylon. He was standing some three hundred yards away, across a small lagoon. He went off like a streak of lightning. It was impossible to follow him and I thought I had missed him. But two days later I came on him by accident, twenty-five miles from where I had shot him. My bullet had penetrated the lungs and grazed the heart. I cannot help thinking that there is something in the apparently absurd contention of certain mystics that life does not depend wholly on the integrity of the physiological apparatus, but on the will to live. I have dropped the most powerful animals stone dead with a single shot in the right place; but if that first shot happens not to kill him outright, he is so inflamed with fury that you can riddle him with bullets in the most vital spots without further disabling him. I know it sounds like utter nonsense, but I have seen it again and again. The sambhur above mentioned is only one case.

One day I was told of an exceptionally fine wild buffalo bull who was so lost to all principles of propriety that he used to come down every evening to enjoy a herd of tame cows. I felt that I could never face Exeter Hall * in the future if I allowed this sort of thing to go on. The only sign of grace in this bull was that he had a guilty conscience and departed for the *Ewigkeit* at the first hint of human proximity. The cows were accustomed to feed in a wide flat country. It was impossible to approach them in the open. I crawled out to the edge of the jungle and lay low, hoping that they would come near enough for a shot. They did. But I misjudged the range; and my bullet, by the most curious luck, pierced the near fore hoof of the bull. He made off indignantly for the jungle at a point some three or four hundred yards from my ambush.

Ten minutes later 'I stood tiptoe upon a little hill' and looked around me 'with a wild surmise'. I knew where I had hit him by the way he limped, and that he was no more put out of

* At that time headquarters of Evangelicalism.

action than Battling Siki, if I had trod on his pet corn. I knew that a buffalo bull can conceal himself in the Ceylon jungle as effectively as a bug in a barracks, and I knew that he was perfectly informed of my character and intention. I knew that I was nervous by the way I gripped my rifle (my principal battery, by the way, was a 10-bore Paradox with lead and also steel core bullets, and a .577 Express, both double barrelled). As I stood, I realized for the first time the responsibility of the white man. I had to exhibit perfect *aplomb*. No sign of the bull!

Presently, the trackers found the trail. My bullet having pierced his hoof, there was no blood. The only signs of his passage were bruised and broken twigs, and occasional footprints. We came up with him pretty soon. He was standing stock still, listening for his life, with his back turned to us. I was not thirty yards away and I aimed at the bull's eye— pardon the introduction of a euphemism from ancient Egypt. It is the most effective shot possible. If your bullet rises, it will smash the spine; otherwise it must pass through the soft vital parts. But the bull merely bolted. I could not even fire my second barrel. Again and again we came up with him. The track was easy to follow. He was bleeding profusely and going slowly. Again and again I fired, but he always got away. Nothing seemed to cripple him, though one would have thought that he must have been more hole than bull by this time.

At last he turned at a small clearing. As I came out from the thick jungle, I saw him not ten yards away. He lowered his head to charge. My bullet struck him again in the Ajna Cakkra,[1] if a bull has such a thing; anyway, in the middle of the forehead just above the eyes. This time he dropped. It was my nineteenth bullet and only the first had failed to strike him in a vital spot.

Talking of being charged: the one beast I really fear is the leopard. The tiger gives one a chance, but the cheetah is like an arrow; he is practically invisible as a mark, and one feels that it is impossible either to stop him or get out of his way. He is hard enough to see at any time; but end on in dim thick undergrowth, he is the limit. I feel, too, that his anger is mean and ignoble, and I have never been able to oppose this type of attack. I can respect the rage of the tiger, but the hatred of the leopard is somehow servile and venomous. The bear is a deadly enemy if he gets to grips and he is nearly as hard to kill as the buffalo. One feels, too, rather sorry to kill a bear;

one can never forget that he is at heart a friendly fluffy comfortable brute.

The wild boar, which one may shoot in Ceylon, as pig-sticking is impossible owing to the nature of the country, is a furious and dangerous quarry, but it gives one a peculiar satisfaction to out him, to stand

> Right in the wild way of the coming curse
> Rock-rooted fair with fierce and fastened lips,
> Clear eyes, and springing muscle and shortening limb—
> With chin aslant indrawn to a tightening throat,
> Grave, and with gathered sinews like a god,

and biff him

> Right in the hairiest hollow of his hide
> Under the last rib, sheer through bulk and bone
> Deep in—

and see

> The blind bulk of the immeasurable beast
> . . . bristling with intolerable hair

lying in front of one, and feel that one has done a good turn to Venus.

One of my boars, by the way, gave me a lesson in literature. I came across his body two days after the battle and it hit me in the eye—to say nothing of the nose—with Baudelaire's 'Charogne'.

> Beside the path, an infamous foul carrion,
>   Stones for its couch a fitting sheet.
>
> Its legs stretched in the air, like wanton whores
>   Burning with lust, and reeking venom sweated,
> Laid open, carelessly and cynically, the doors
>   Of belly rank with exhalations fetid.
> Upon this rottenness the sun shone deadly straight
>   As if to cook it to a turn,
> And give back to great Nature hundred-fold the debt
>   That, joining it together, she did earn.
>
> The sky beheld this carcase most superb outspread
>   As spreads a flower, itself, whose taint

> Stank so supremely strong, that on the grass your head
>   You thought to lay, in sudden faint.
>
> The flies swarmed numberless on this putrescent belly,
>   Whence issued a battalion
> Of larvae, black, that flowed, a sluggish liquid jelly,
>   Along this living carrion.
>
> All this was falling, rising as the eager seas,
>   Or heaving with strange crepitation—

There was an utterly unspeakable fascination in watching the waves of maggots. The surface undulated with the peculiar rhythm of the ocean.

To Baudelaire, as we know, a similar sight suggested his 'Inamorata'. I was presumably too blindly in love with Rose to see the resemblance; the main impression on my mind was more impersonally philosophical. I thought of the 13th Key of the Tarot,[2] of the sign of Scorpio, the invincible persistence of life perpetuating itself by means of that very putrefaction which seems to shallow minds the star witness against it. Here were vermin feeding on corruption, yet the effect was of lambent vibrations of white brilliance, disporting themselves in the sunlight—here, quit! Am I a sportsman describing his heroic feats, or am I not?

The elephant, 'the half reasoner with the hand', is in an entirely different category from any other animal. I felt much more like a murderer when potting a hathi than when it is a monkey, though I perfectly understood the emotion of the average Englishman in this conjuncture. Nor is the elephant easy to shoot. The odds against hitting him in the vital spot are very great; and strange as it may sound, in country like Hambantota, he is very difficult to see at all. In the whole province there are really very few trees of notable stature, yet the undergrowth (including smaller trees) is so thick and so high that it is rarely possible to see an animal even when one is close to him. I remember once being so near to an elephant that I could have prodded him with a salmon rod; but I could not see one inch of all his acres. He was feeding on small twigs; I could hear every gentle snap; I could hear his breathing; I could smell him. If he had taken it into his head to turn or if the wind had shifted, my number would have been up. He could have trampled his way to and over me without an effort, while I could not have forced my way to him in five minutes. He went off quietly and I never had a chance for a shot.

One elephant whose track I followed took the camp of a Frenchman in his morning stroll. The man's wife had taken him out to Ceylon to keep him away from alcohol, but prohibition forgot the proverb, 'Out of the frying-pan into the fire'. The elephant got him before I got the elephant.

One of our most beautiful camps was a sort of dak baghla near the shores of a superb lake. Open on its principal arc, the further shore merged into marshes. In the shallow waters at the edge grew magnificent trees whose branches were festooned with legions of flying foxes, as they call the species of bat whose breast is furred with marvellous red and white. I thought I would kill a few dozen and make my wife a toque and myself a waistcoat. We went out in a boat not unlike a clumsy variety of punt to catch them in their sleep. They keep no guard; but at the first gunshot they awake and the air literally becomes dark with their multitude. One has merely to fire into the mass. One of the bats, wounded, fell right on my wife and frightened her. It may have been thirty seconds before I could detach her from his claws. I thought nothing of the matter; but it is possible that her condition aggravated the impression. Our beds in the baghla were furnished with four stout uprights and a frame for mosquito curtains. I suppose in so remote a district they had been made of unusually strong poles. I was awakened in the dead of night by the squeal of a dying bat.

I remember debating whether I was in fact awake or not, whether the noise, which was horribly persistent, might not be part of a dream evoked by the events of the day. I even called to Rose to resolve my doubts. She did not answer. I lighted the candle. She was not there. My alarm completed my awakening. The bat squealed hideously. I looked up. I could not see any bat. But there was Rose, stark naked, hanging to the frame with arms and legs, insanely yawling. It was quite a job to pull her down. She clung to the frame desperately, still squealing. She refused utterly to respond to the accents of the human voice. When I got her down at last, she clawed and scratched and bit and spat and squealed, exactly as the dying bat had done to her. It was quite a long time before I got her back to her human consciousness.

It was the finest case of obsession that I had ever had the good fortune to observe. Of course it is easy to explain that in her hypersensitive condition the incident of the day had reproduced itself in a dream. She had identified herself with her assailant and mimicked his behaviour. But surely, if there be anything in Sir William Hamilton's law of parsimony, it is

much simpler to say that the spirit of the bat had entered into
her.

(As I revise these pages for the press, I find myself constantly annoyed by having to try to find long roundabout
'rational' explanations for all the wonders I have seen and heard.
It is silly, too, now that we are getting clear at last of the
obsession of Victorian cocksure materialism—science disguised
as a fat hausfrau!)

48

Life in the jungle has many incidents of a more frequent and less amusing type. One night, also in a baghla, I got up to get Rose her medicine. I had left the candle on the table some distance from the beds, which was foolish. On lighting it, I discovered without enthusiasm that between me and the bed was a krait some eighteen inches long—and I had walked barefoot over him! A krait can kill you in a very few minutes, though not without producing symptoms of the utmost interest to any serious student of nature. I was entirely helpless; I was reduced to the ignominious expedient of getting on the table and calling to the servants outside to bring a lamp, precaution and *force majeure*.

Animals are not the only danger of this district. There are many dangerous diseases, especially tetanus. While I was in Calcutta, an acquaintance of mine, walking home from the theatre, slipped and saved himself by putting his hands to the ground. He scratched himself slightly and died within three days.

There are also terrible thorns. My head tracker came to me one day with one in his foot. The end was protruding and I imagined that I should have no difficulty in pulling it out with forceps. But the thorn was soft as pith. I had to cut open the man's sole along the whole length of the thorn, seven and three quarter inches. His skin was as tough as rawhide, the epidermis a quarter of an inch thick. The thorn had not reached the dermis. It seemed miraculous that it should have penetrated a hide that came near to turn the edge of my surgical knife.

The heaviest weapon and the truest eye and hand may sometimes fail to account for the smallest of God's creatures. I could not understand why my 10-bore Paradox seemed so ineffective against small birds. One day I came across a rat-snake, nineteen feet long, and said, 'This time I will bruise your head and I bet you don't bruise my heel.' I was within a few yards of him and fired several times. He moved off with leisurely disgust; he could not imagine what my game could be. Why had I disturbed his sleep? I followed, protesting with further drum fire. He moved lazily beyond the barrage. I am a patient man; but the conduct of this snake insulted and humiliated me. One of the men, his sensitive oriental spirit doubtless observing my distress, went forward and knocked him on the head with a stick. Theoretically, he should have been as full of holes as a lace fichu; but there wasn't a mark on him. It dawned slowly upon my mind that there must be something wrong with my cartridges. When we got to camp, I put up the lid of an old box and fired at it from ten yards, in order to test the penetration of the shot. The pellets did not mark the board; they bounced back and hit me in the face. I reserved my remarks for my return to Colombo.

This event took place on the sixteenth of January. My headman had swindled me outrageously; but there was no remedy. There is no remedy for anything in Ceylon. The whole island is an infamy. It is impossible to get twelve Singalese to agree on any subject whatever, so a majority decision determines the verdict of a jury of seven! Justice is usually done, because it really is the case that the man with the more money is less often wrong than his opponent.

A very curious episode sticks in my memory. General Sir Hector MacDonald was born in a croft on the hillside facing Boleskine across Loch Ness. I consequently took, unasked, an almost paternal interest in his career.

I dropped into the Hotel Regina in Paris one day to lunch. At the next table, also alone, was Sir Hector MacDonald. He recognized me and invited me to join him. He seemed unnaturally relieved; but his conversation showed that he was suffering acute mental distress. He told me that he was on his way to the East. Of course I avoided admitting that I knew his object, which was to defend himself against charges of sexual irregularity brought against him in Ceylon.

The next morning I was amazed to read, in the *New York Herald*, an outrageously outspoken account of the affair.* On the heels of this came the news that MacDonald had shot himself in the Regina. He was a great simple lion-hearted man with the spirit of a child; with all his experience in the Army, he still took the word honour seriously, and the open scandal of the accusation had struck down his standard.

One incredible detail must be told. The hotel communicated

---

* People said: the revenge of a Ceylon Big Bug, whom MacDonald had ordered off the field at some jamboree when he had turned up in mufti.

at once with the British Embassy, and the attaché who went down to see the body told Gerald Kelly that MacDonald's pockets were stuffed with obscene photographs! Inquiry showed that he had gone out and bought them that· very morning, apparently with no other purpose. The psychology is appallingly obscure. Was his motive to convey some subtly offensive insult to the puritans whose prurience had destroyed him?

So much is in part hearsay and conjecture. What follows is wholly fact. I was sitting at lunch in the Grand Oriental Hotel at Colombo when a procession filed into the room. I have never seen anything quite like it. It was utterly out of the picture. It was composed of genuine antiques with shaking heads, stooping shoulders, slobbering jaws from which hung long white goatish beards, and bleared red eyes that blinked even in the twilight of the luncheon as if the very idea of sunlight was an infernal terror.

I called on the khansamah to tell me if I was suffering from delirium tremens. He told me no; what I saw was really there, and it was some kind of committee from Scotland, and that was all he knew. After lunch I discovered that the Great Heart of Scotland refused to admit that any member of the Kirk could have acquiesced in the amenities of the Anglican clergy. The elders had therefore sent out a committee to vindicate the innocence of MacDonald. I could no less in courtesy than make them feel more at home in Ceylon by revealing myself as an Inverness laird. They opened their hearts to me; they were already discouraged. They told me that the prosecution had the affidavits of no less than seventy-seven native witnesses. 'Ah well,' I said. 'You don't know much of Ceylon. If there were seven times seventy-seven, I wouldn't swing a cat on their dying oaths. The more unanimous they are, the more is certain that they have been bribed to lie.' I am really glad to think I cheered the old boys up; and I hope that they succeeded in fixing their hero with a halo, though I never heard what happened.

I always hated Colombo. My diary reads 'Weariness. Dentist.' 'More weariness and more dentist.' 'Throat XOP.' 'Doctor.' 'Oh sabbé pi dukkham.'[1] 'Colombo more and more loathsome. Went up to Kandy.'

Kandy cured my symptoms instantly. The most dreadful thing about Colombo was that two English ladies had descended upon the Galle Face Hotel. They would have seemed extravagant at Monte Carlo; in Ceylon the heavily painted faces, the over-tended dyed false hair, the garish flashy dresses, the loud harsh foolish gabble, the insolent ogling were an outrage. The daughter wore a brooch of what may have been diamonds. It was about five inches across, and the design was a coronet and the name Mabel. I have never seen anything in such abominable taste, and anyhow I wouldn't call a trained flea Mabel, if I respected it.

The intensity of my repulsion makes me suspect that I wanted to make love to her and was annoyed that I was already in love. The gospels do not tell us whether the man who possessed the pearl of great price ever had moments of regret at having given up imitation jewellery. One always subconsciously connects notoriously vile women who flaunt their heartless and sexless seduction with the possibility of some supremely perverse pleasure in nastiness. However, my surface reaction was to shake the dust of Colombo from my feet and to spend my two days in Kandy in writing *Why Jesus Wept*.

The title is a direct allusion to the ladies in question. I prefaced the play with five dedications to (1) Christ, (2) Lady Scott, (3) my friends (Jinawaravansa, whom I had met once more in Galle, and myself), (4) my unborn child, and (5) Mr G. K. Chesterton. (He had written a long congratulatory criticism of my *The Soul of Osiris*.) The idea of the play is to show a romantic boy and girl ambushed and ruined by male and female vampires. It is an allegory of the corrupting influence of society, and the moral is given in the final passage:

> I much prefer—that is, mere I—
> Solitude to society.
> And that is why I sit and spoil
> So much clean paper with such toil
> By Kandy Lake in far Ceylon.
> I have my old pyjamas on:
> I shake my soles from Britain's dust;
> I shall not go there till I must;
> And when I must!—I hold my nose.
> Farewell, you filthy-minded people!
> I know a stable from a steeple.
> Farewell, my decent-minded friends!
> I know arc lights from candle-ends.
> Farewell—a poet begs your alms,
> Will walk awhile among the palms,
> An honest love, a loyal kiss,
> Can show him better worlds than this;
> Nor will he come again to yours
> While he knows champak-stars from sewers.

(This play has been analysed in such detail by Captain J. F. C. Fuller in *The Star in the West* that it would be impertinent of me to discuss it further.)

Rose now felt fairly certain that she was pregnant. But it was not this alone that decided us to turn our faces to the West. We still intended to go to Rangoon and apparently there was absolutely nothing to stop us. But we couldn't go, any more than if it had been the moon. Throughout my life I have repeatedly found that destiny is an absolutely definite and inexorable ruler. Physical ability and moral determination count for nothing. It is impossible to perform the simplest act when the gods say 'No'. I have no idea how they bring pressure to bear on such occasions; I only know that it is irresistible. One may be wholeheartedly eager to do something which is as easy as falling off a log; and yet it is impossible.

We left Colombo for Aden, Suez and Port Said on January 28th, intending to see a little of the season in Cairo, of which we had the most delightful memories, and then to sail for England, home and beauty. I had not the slightest idea that I was on the brink of the only event of my life which has made it worth living.

The voyage was as uneventful as most similar voyages are. The one item of interest is that one of our fellow passengers was Dr Henry Maudsley. This man, besides being one of the three greatest alienists in England, was a profound philosopher of the school which went rather further than Spencer in the direction of mechanical automatism. He fitted in exactly. He was the very man I wanted. We talked about Dhyana. I was quite sure that the attainment of this state, and a fortiori of Samadhi, meant that they remove the inhibitions which repress the manifestations of genius, or (practically the same thing in other words) enable one to tap the energy of the universe.

Now, Samadhi, whatever it is, is at least a state of mind exactly as are deep thought, anger, sleep, intoxication and melancholia. Very good. Any state of mind is accompanied by corresponding states of the body. Lesions of the substance of the brain, disturbances of the blood supply, and so on, are observed in apparently necessary relation to these spiritual states. Furthermore, we already know that certain spiritual or mental conditions may be induced by acting on physico- and chemico-physiological conditions. For instance, we can make a man hilarious, angry or what not by giving him whisky. We can induce sleep by administering such drugs as veronal. We can even give him the courage of anaesthesia (if we want him to go over the top) by means of ether, cocaine and so on. We can produce fantastic dreams by hashish, hallucinations of colour by anhalonium Lewinii; we can even make him 'see stars' by the use of a sandbag. Why then should we not be able to devise some pharmaceutical, electrical or surgical method of inducing Samadhi; create genius as simply as we do other kinds of specific excitement? Morphine makes men holy and happy in a negative way; why should there not be some drug which will produce the positive equivalent?

The mystic gasps with horror, but we really can't worry about him. It is he that is blaspheming nature by postulating discontinuity in her processes. Admit that Samadhi is *sui generis* and back comes the whole discarded humbug of the supernatural. I was back at the old bench exploring the pharmacopoeia for the means of grace, as I had done with Allan long ago; but I had come back to the problem armed in the panoply of the positive natural philosophy of modern science. Huxley had vindicated the alchemists. There was nothing impossible or immoral about the Stone of the Wise and the Elixir of Life. Maudsley—rather to my surprise—agreed with all these propositions, but could not suggest any plausible line of research.

I have made rather a point of mentioning these conversations, because they show that in February 1904, I was an absolutely sceptical rationalistic thinker. The point is that the events of March and April were not in the normal course of the life of a consistent mystic and magician. There was no tendency on my part to accept 'divine' interference in my affairs. There was, on the contrary, the bitterest opposition from me. I even went so far as to make unintelligible and false additions to my diary, with the deliberate intention of confusing the record, and perhaps even of making people think me untrustworthy in this stupendous circumstance.

But the gods beat me all round. They took care that the event should not depend on my goodwill; should be beyond the power of my ill-will to thwart. More yet; they have made it evident that they purposely smashed my career as mystic and Magician in the very hour of my success, when the world was at my feet, in order that they might the more utterly demonstrate their power to use me for their own purposes.

We landed at Port Said on Monday, February the eighth, and went to Cairo on the following day. It was part of the plan of the gods that my romantic passion and pride, the intoxicated infatuation of my hymeneal happiness, should have induced me to play a puerile part on the world's stage. I had called myself Count Svareff and Aleister MacGregor for quite definite and legitimate reasons; but I had never made a deliberate fool of myself by assuming an absurd alias. I was not for a moment deceived by my own pretext that I wanted to study Mohammedism, and in particular the mysticism of the fakir, the Darwesh and the Sufi, from within, when I proposed to pass myself off in Egypt for a Persian prince with a beautiful English wife. I wanted to swagger about in a turban with a diamond aigrette and sweeping silken robes or a coat of cloth of gold, with a jewelled talwar by my side, and two gorgeous runners to clear the way for my carriage through the streets of Cairo.

There was no doubt a certain brooding of the Holy Spirit of Magick upon the still waters of my soul; but there is little evidence of its operation. I have never lost sight of the fact that I was in some sense or other The Beast 666. There is a mocking reference to it in 'Ascension Day', lines 98 to 111. *The Sword of Song* bears the sub-title 'called by Christians the Book of the Beast'. The wrapper of the original edition has on the front a square of nine sixes and the back another square of sixteen Hebrew letters, being a (very clumsy) transliteration of my name so that its numerical value should be 666. When I went to Russia to learn the language for the Diplomatic Service, my mother half believed that I had 'gone to see Gog and Magog' (who were supposed to be Russian giants) in order to arrange the date of the Battle of Armageddon.

In a way, my mother was insane, in the sense that all people are who have watertight compartments to the brain, and hold with equal passion incompatible ideas, and hold them apart lest their meeting should destroy both. One might say that we are all insane in this sense; for, ultimately, any two ideas are incompatible. Nay, more, any one idea is incompatible with itself, for it contains in itself its own contradiction. (The proof of this thesis will be given in the proper place.)

But my mother believed that I was actually Anti-christ of the Apocalypse and also her poor lost erring son who might yet repent and be redeemed by the Precious Blood.

I conclude my allusion to 666:

> Ho! I adopt the number. Look
> At the quaint wrapper of this book!
> I will deserve it if I can:
> It is the number of a Man.

I had thus dismissed my mystical fancies about the number; I accepted it for purely moral reasons and on purely rationalistic grounds. I wanted to be a man in the sense in which the word is used by Swinburne in his *Hymn of Man*.

Having to choose a Persian name, I made it Chioa Khan (pronounced Hiwa Khan) being the Hebrew for The Beast. (Khan is one of the numerous honorifics common in Asia.) I had no conscious magical intention in doing so. (Let me here mention that I usually called my wife Ouarda, one of the many Arabic words for Rose.)

As to my study of Islam, I got a sheikh to teach me Arabic and the practices of ablution, prayer and so on, so that at some future time I might pass for a Moslem among themselves. I had it in my mind to repeat Burton's journey to Mecca sooner or later. I learnt a number of chapters of the Koran by heart. I never went to Mecca, it seemed rather *vieux jeu*, but my ability to fraternize fully with Mohammedans has proved of infinite use in many ways.

My sheikh was profoundly versed in the mysticism and magic of Islam, and discovering that I was an initiate, had no hesitation in providing me with books and manuscripts on the Arabic Cabbala. These formed the basis of my comparative studies. I was able to fit them in with similar doctrines and other religions; the correlation is given in my 777.

From this man I learnt also many of the secrets of the Sidi Aissawa; how to run a stiletto through one's cheek without drawing blood, lick red-hot swords, eat live scorpions, etc. (Some of these feats are common conjurers' tricks, some depend on scientific curiosities, but some are genuine Magick; that is, the scientific explanation is not generally known. More of this later.)

I was quite fixed in scepticism, as I have always been, but also in so-called rationalism, and I prosecuted these studies in a strictly scholarly spirit. I worked very hard at them and made great progress accordingly; but my true life was still the honeymoon, slightly diluted by the ordinary pleasures of sport and society. I relapsed into golf after some fourteen years' total abstinence; took a few lessons from the pro at the Turf Club, and found that my St Andrews swing and the canniness inculcated by Andrew Kirkcaldy made a fine basis for playing a fairly decent game. We went to Helwan on February 19th; and I played nearly every day, filled with a passionate ambition to become amateur champion. I had picked up my old form so rapidly that I imagined myself a heaven-born golfer. But the game held its own. I never even got to scratch.

I did a certain amount of pigeon shooting at odd times. I had practised a good deal with clay pigeons at Boleskine and become a really first-class shot. I was also quite good at wild pigeons; but for some reason, trapped pigeons were quite beyond me. I dare not boast that I am even second rate.

One day I joined a party of three to shoot quail, which I recall on account of a singular accident. I was in the middle of the line. A bird got up and flew between me and the man on my right; but I withheld my fire for fear of hitting him. We swung round again; another bird came in the same direction and suddenly dodged and passed on the right. The end man fired. There was a howl. I, having turned to watch the bird, saw the accident clearly. A native had risen from the ground at the moment of the shot. My friend swore that he had not seen him, and I had not seen him myself until I heard him. There was no cover. It seems incredible that my friend at least should not have seen him, for he must have only just missed walking over him, the man being slightly behind our line when the shot was fired. And he was so close to the gun that the shot had not begun to scatter when it struck him. It had cut a clean narrow groove in the man's shaved scalp, not even laying bare the bone.

I mention this incident, not only on account of its extraordinary features, but to compare it with the 'horrors of Denshawai'. The spirit of the natives was entirely friendly. Our administration of Egypt was characterized by paternal firmness; everyone was in the right, everyone respected himself and others; no one complained. Yet, within three years, our prestige had been completely destroyed by the intelligentsia of England—everyone was in the wrong, no one respected himself or anyone else, and everyone complained.

I have dwelt on the character of my life at this time in order to emphasize that the event to be recorded in the next section was an absolute bolt from the blue.

PART THREE

The Advent of the
Aeon of Horus

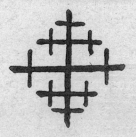

The elevenfold cross of the Knights Templars, a Masonic device used by Crowley when signing letters in his capacity as Supreme Grand Master General of the Ordo Templi Orientis.

The Advent of the Aeon of Horus

49

This chapter is the climax of this book. Its contents are so extraordinary, they demand such breadth and depth of preliminary explanation, that I am in despair. It is so serious to me that my responsibility overwhelms me. My entire previous life was but a preparation for this event, and my entire subsequent life has been not merely determined by it, but wrapped up in it.

I have made several attempts to write the history of these few weeks, notably, that section of *The Temple of Solomon the King* which appears in *The Equinox*, vol. I, no. VII. I cannot with literary propriety incorporate these documents in the body of this book, but they are presented in an appendix, together with the text of *The Book of the Law*.[1]

Most of the past nine years of my life have been preoccupied, each year more fully than the last, with the problem of proving to humanity in general the propositions involved. To make the elements of my thesis as clear and distinct as possible, I shall endeavour to insulate them in sections.

Ouarda[2] and I left Helwan for Cairo. (Date unascertained, probably on March 11th or 13th [1904].) We had taken an apartment (address unascertained) on Wednesday, March 16th. One day, having nothing special to do, I made the 'Preliminary Invocation' referred to above. I had no more serious purpose than to show her the sylphs[3] as I might have taken her to the theatre. She could not (or refused to) see them, but instead got into a strange state of mind. I had never seen her anything at all like it before. She kept on repeating dreamily, yet intensely, 'They are waiting for you.' I was annoyed at her conduct.

March 17th. I don't remember whether I repeated my attempt to show her the sylphs, but probably did. It is in my character to persist. She again got into the same state and repeated her remarks, adding, 'It is all about the child.' And 'All Osiris.' I think I must have been annoyed by her contumacy. Perhaps for this reason I invoked Thoth, the god of wisdom, presumably by the invocation printed in *Liber Israfel*

413

(*The Equinox*, vol. I, no. VII), which I knew by heart. I may also have been subconsciously wondering whether there was not something in her remarks, and wanted to be enlightened. The record says, 'Thoth, invoked with great success, indwells us.' But this strikes me as to some extent 'written up' in a spirit of complacency, if not arrogance. I remember nothing of any result.

March 18th. Possibly I repeated the invocation. The record says, 'Revealed that the waiter was Horus, whom I had offended and ought to invoke.' 'Waiter' sounds like a sneer. I thought it was sheer impudence of Ouarda to offer independent remarks. I wanted her to see the sylphs.

I must have been impressed by one point. How did Ouarda know that I had offended Horus? The troubles of Mathers were due to his excessive devotion to Mars, who represents one side of the personality of Horus, and no doubt I was inclined to err in the opposite direction, to neglect and dislike Mars as the personification of unintelligent violence.

But was her bull's-eye a fluke? Her mention of Horus gave me a chance to cross-examine her. 'How do you know that it is Horus who is telling you all this? Identify him.' (Ouarda knew less Egyptology than ninety-nine Cairene tourists out of one hundred.) Her answers were overwhelming. The odds against her being right were one in many million.

I allowed her to go on. She instructed me how to invoke Horus. The instructions were, from my point of view, pure rubbish. I suggested amending them. She emphatically refused to allow a single detail to be altered. She promised success (whatever that might mean) on Saturday or Sunday. If I had any aspiration left at all, it was to attain Samadhi[4] (which I had not yet ever done). She promised that I should do so. I agreed to carry out her instructions, avowedly in order to show her that nothing could happen if you broke all the rules.

On some day before March 23rd, Ouarda identified the particular god with whom she was in communication from a stele in the Boulak Museum,[5] which we had never visited. It is not the ordinary form of Horus but Ra-Hoor-Khuit. I was no doubt very much struck by the coincidence that the exhibit, a quite obscure and undistinguished stele, bore the catalogue number 666. But I dismissed it as an obvious coincidence.

March 19th. I wrote out the ritual and did the invocation with little success. I was put off, not only by my scepticism and the absurdity of the ritual, but by having to do it in robes at an open window on a street at noon. She allowed me to make the second attempt at midnight.

March 20th. The invocation was a startling success. I was told that 'The Equinox of the Gods had come'; that is, that a new epoch had begun. I was to formulate a link between the solar-spiritual force and mankind.

Various considerations showed me that the Secret Chiefs of the Third Order (that is, of the A.·. A.·. whose First and Second Orders were known as G.·. D.·.⁶ and R.R. et A.C. respectively) had sent a messenger to confer upon me the position which Mathers had forfeited. I made it a condition that I should attain Samadhi; that is, that I should receive a degree of illumination, in default of which it would be presumptuous to put myself forward.

March 21st–22nd–23rd. There seems to have been a reaction after the success of the twentieth. The phenomena faded out. I tried to clear up my position by the old methods and did a long Tarot divination which proved perfectly futile.

March 23rd and April 7th. I made inquiries about the stele and had the inscriptions translated into French by the assistant curator at Boulak. I made poetic paraphrases of them. Ouarda now told me to enter the room, where all this work had been done, exactly at noon on April 8th, 9th and 10th, and write down what I heard, rising exactly at one o'clock. This I did. In these three hours were written the three chapters of *The Book of the Law*.

The above statement is as succinct as I can make it. By April 8th, I had been convinced of the reality of the communication and obeyed my wife's arbitrary instructions with a certain confidence. I retained my sceptical attitude none the less.

THE CLAIM OF *THE BOOK OF THE LAW* IN RESPECT OF RELIGION. The importance of religion to humanity is paramount. The reason is that all men perceive more or less the 'First Noble Truth'—that everything is sorrow; and religion claims to console them by an authoritative denial of this truth or by promising compensations in other states of existence. This claim implies the possibility of knowledge derived from sources other than the unaided investigation of nature through the senses and the intellect. It postulates, therefore, the existence of one or more praeter-human intelligences, able and willing to communicate, through the medium of certain chosen men, to mankind a truth or truths which could not otherwise be known. Religion is justified in demanding faith, since the evidence of the senses and the mind cannot confirm its statements. The evidence from prophecy and miracle is valid only in so far as it goes to the credit of the man through whom the communication is made. It establishes that he is in possession of knowledge and power different, not only in degree but in kind, from those enjoyed by the rest of mankind.

The history of mankind teems with religious teachers. These may be divided into three classes.

1. Such men as Moses and Mohammed state simply that they have received a direct communication from God. They buttress their authority by divers methods, chiefly threats and promises guaranteed by thaumaturgy; they resent the criticism of reason.

2. Such men as Blake and Boehme claimed to have entered into direct communication with discarnate intelligence which may be considered as personal, creative, omnipotent, unique, identical with themselves or otherwise. Its authority depends on 'the interior certainty' of the seer.

3. Such teachers as Lao-Tzu, the Buddha and the highest Gnana-yogis[7] announce that they have attained to superior wisdom, understanding, knowledge and power, but make no pretence of imposing their views on mankind. They remain essentially sceptics. They base their precepts on their own personal experience, saying, in effect, that they have found that the performance of certain acts and the abstention from others create conditions favourable to the attainment of the state which has emancipated them. The wiser they are, the less dogmatic. Such men indeed formulate their transcendental conception of the cosmos more or less clearly; they may explain evil as illusion, etc., but the heart of their theory is that the problem of sorrow has been wrongly stated, owing to the superficial or incomplete data presented by normal human experience through the senses, and that it is possible for men, by virtue of some special training (from Asana to Ceremonial Magick), to develop in themselves a faculty superior to reason and immune from intellectual criticism, by the exercise of which the original problem of suffering is satisfactorily solved.

The Book of the Law claims to comply with the conditions necessary to satisfy all three types of inquirer.

Firstly, it claims to be a document not only verbally, but literally inspired. *Change not as much as the style of a letter; for behold! thou, O prophet, shalt not behold all these mysteries hidden therein . . . This book shall be translated into all tongues: but always with the original in the writing of the Beast; for in the chance shape of the letters and their position to one another: in these are mysteries that no Beast shall divine. Let him not seek to try: but one cometh after him, whence I say not, who shall discover the Key of it all.*

The author claims to be a messenger of the Lord of the Universe and therefore to speak with absolute authority.

Secondly, it claims to be the statement of transcendental truth, and to have overcome the difficulty of expressing such truth in human language by what really amounts to the invention of a new method of communicating thought, not merely a new language, but a new type of language; a literal and numerical cipher involving the Greek and Hebrew Cabbalas, the highest mathematics etc. It also claims to be the utterance of an illuminated mind co-extensive with the ultimate ideas of which the universe is composed.

Thirdly, it claims to offer a method by which men may arrive independently at the direct consciousness of the truth of the contents of the Book; enter into communication directly on their own initiative and responsibility with the type of intelligence which informs it, and solve all their personal religious problems.

Generally, *The Book of the Law* claims to answer all possible religious problems. One is struck by the fact that so many of them are stated and settled separately in so short a space.

To return to the general question of religion. The fundamental problem has never been explicitly stated. We know that all religions, without exception, have broken down at the first test. The claim of religion is to complete, and (incidentally) to reverse, the conclusions of reason by means of a direct communication from some intelligence superior in kind to that of any incarnate human being. I ask Mohammed, "How am I to know that the Koran is not your own compilation?"

It is impertinent to answer that the Koran is so sublime, so musical, so true, so full of prophecies which time has fulfilled and confirmed by so many miraculous events that Mohammed could not have written it himself.

The author of *The Book of the Law* foresaw and provided against all such difficulties by inserting in the text discoveries which I did not merely not make for years afterwards, but did not even possess the machinery for making. Some, in fact, depend upon events which I had no part in bringing about.

It may be said that nevertheless there may have been someone somewhere in the world who possessed the necessary qualities. This again is rebutted by the fact that some of the allusions are to facts known to me alone. We are forced to conclude that the author of *The Book of the Law* is an intelligence both alien and superior to myself, yet acquainted with my inmost secrets; and, most important point of all, that this intelligence is discarnate.

The existence of true religion presupposes that of some discarnate intelligence, whether we call him God or anything else. And this is exactly what no religion had ever proved scientifically. And this is what *The Book of the Law* does prove by internal evidence, altogether independent of any statement of mine. This proof is evidently the most important step in science that could possibly be made: for it opens up an entirely new avenue to knowledge. The immense superiority of this particular intelligence, AIWASS,[8] to any other with which mankind has yet been in conscious communication is shown not merely by the character of the Book itself, but by the fact of his comprehending perfectly the nature of the proof necessary to demonstrate the fact of his own existence and the conditions of that existence. And, further, having provided the proof required.

THE CLAIM OF *THE BOOK OF THE LAW* TO OPEN UP COMMUNICATIONS WITH DISCARNATE INTELLIGENCE. In the above section I have shown that the failure of previous religions is due, not so much to hostile criticism, but to their positive defect. They have not made good their claim. It has been shown above that *The Book of the Law* does demonstrate the prime position of religion in the only possible way. The only possible argument, on the other side, is that the communication cannot have been made by a discarnate intelligence, because there are none such. That indeed constitutes the supreme importance of *The Book of the Law*. But there is no a priori reason for doubting the existence of such beings. We have long been acquainted with many discarnate forces. Especially in the last few years science has been chiefly occupied with the reactions, not merely of things which cannot be directly perceived by sense, but of forces which do not possess being at all in the old sense of the word.

Yet the average man of science still denies the existence of the elementals of the Rosicrucian, the angels of the Cabbalist, the Nats, Pisachas and Devas of southern Asia,[9] and the Jinn of Islam, with the same blind misosophy as in Victorian days. It has apparently not occurred to him that his position in doubting the existence of consciousness except in connection with certain types of anatomical structure is really identical with that of the narrowest geocentric and anthropocentric Evangelicals.

Our actions may be unintelligible to plants; they might plausibly argue that we are unconscious. Our real reason for attributing consciousness to our fellow-men is that the similarity of our structure enables us to communicate by means of language, and as soon as we invent a language in which we can talk to anything soever, we begin to find evidence of consciousness.

The way is therefore clear for me to come forward and assert positively that I have opened up communication with one such intelligence; or, rather, that I have been selected by him to receive the first message from a new order of beings.

THE HISTORICAL CONCEPTION ON WHICH *THE BOOK OF THE LAW* IS BASED. Just as *The Book of the Law* reconciles an impersonal and infinite interpretation of the cosmos with an egocentric and practical viewpoint, so it makes 'infinite space' speak in the language of a goddess and deals with the details of eating and drinking:

Be goodly therefore: dress ye all in fine apparel; eat rich foods and drink sweet wines and wines that foam! Also, take your fill and will of love as ye will, when, where and with whom ye will! But always unto me.

The emancipation of mankind from all limitations whatever is one of the main precepts of the Book.

Bind nothing! Let there be no difference made among you between any one thing & any other thing; for thereby there cometh hurt.

It reconciles cosmological conceptions which transcend time and space with a conventional, historical point of view. In the first place it announces unconditional truth, but in the second is careful to state that the 'Magical Formula' (or system of principles) on which the practical part of the book is based is not an absolute truth but one relative to the terrestrial time of the revelation. (It is a strong point in favour of the Book that it makes no pretence to settle the practical problems of humanity once and for all. It contents itself with indicating a stage in evolution.)

The Book of the Law presumes the existence of a body of initiates pledged to watch over the welfare of mankind and to communicate its own wisdom little by little in the measure of man's capacity to receive it.

The initiate is well aware that his instruction will be mis-interpreted by malice, dishonesty and stupidity; and not being omnipotent, he has to acquiesce in the perversion of his precepts. It is part of the game. *Liber I vel Magi*[10] tells the Magus (here defined as the initiate charged with the duty of communicating a new truth to mankind) of what he may expect.

There are many magical teachers but in recorded history we have scarcely had a dozen Magi in the technical sense of the word. They may be recognized by the fact that their message may be formulated as a single word, which word must be such that it overturns all existing beliefs and codes. We may take as instances the Word of Buddha—Anatta (absence of an atman or soul), which laid its axe to the root of Hindu cosmology, theology and psychology, and incidentally knocked away the foundation of the caste system; and indeed of all accepted morality. Mohammed, again, with the single word Allah, did the same thing with polytheisms, patently pagan or camouflaged as Christian, of his period.

Similarly, Aiwass, uttering the word Thelema (with all its implications), destroys completely the formula of the Dying God.[11] Thelema implies not merely a new religion, but a new cosmology, a new philosophy, a new ethics. It co-ordinates the disconnected discoveries of science, from physics to psychology, into a coherent and consistent system. Its scope is so vast that it is impossible even to hint at the universality of its application. But the whole of my work, from the moment of its utterance, illustrates some phase of its potentiality, and the story of my life itself from this time on is no more than a record of my reactions to it.

To recapitulate the historical basis of *The Book of the Law,* let me say that evolution (within human memory) shows three great steps: 1. the worship of the Mother, when the universe was conceived as simple nourishment drawn directly from her; 2. the worship of the Father, when the universe was imagined as catastrophic; 3. the worship of the Child, in which we come to perceive events as a continual growth partaking in its elements of both these methods.

Egyptian theology foresaw this progress of humanity and symbolized it in the triad of Isis, Osiris, Horus. The neophyte ceremony of the Golden Dawn prepared me for the New Aeon; for, at the Equinox, the officer who represented Horus in the West took the throne of Osiris in the East.

The Book of the Law is careful to indicate the nature of the formula implied by the assertion that the presiding officer of the temple (the earth) is Horus, the Crowned and Conquering Child. And again, Egyptology and psychology help us to understand what is implied, and what effect to expect, in the world of thought and action.

Horus avenged his father Osiris. We know that the sun (indeed, every element of nature) does not suffer death.

The child is not merely a symbol of growth, but of complete moral independence and innocence. We may then expect the New Aeon to release mankind from its pretence of altruism, its obsession of fear and its consciousness of sin. It will possess no consciousness of the purpose of its own existence. It will not be possible to persuade it that it should submit to incomprehensible standards; it will suffer from spasms of transitory passion; it will be absurdly sensitive to pain and suffer from meaningless terror; it will be utterly conscienceless, cruel, helpless, affectionate and ambitious, without knowing why; it will be incapable of reason, yet at the same time intuitively aware of truth. I might go on indefinitely to enumerate the stigmata of child psychology, but the reader can do it equally for himself, and every idea that comes to him as characteristic of children will strike him as applicable to the events of history since 1904, from the Great War to Prohibition. And if he possess any capacity for understanding the language of symbolism, he will be staggered by the adequacy and accuracy of the summary of the spirit of the New Aeon given in *The Book of the Law*.

I may now point out that the reign of the Crowned and Conquering Child is limited in time by *The Book of the Law* itself. We learn that Horus will be in his turn succeeded by Thmaist, the Double-Wanded One; she who shall bring the candidates to full initiation, and though we know little of her peculiar characteristics, we know at least that her name is justice.

THE ETHICS OF *THE BOOK OF THE LAW*. Every cosmography implies some sort of ethical theory. The Aeon of Osiris had been succeeded by that of Horus. The Magical Formula of the Aeon being no longer that of the Dying God but that of the Crowned and Conquering Child, mankind is to govern itself accordingly. A 'righteous' act may be defined as one which fulfils the existing Magical Formula. The motives which were valid in the Aeon of Osiris are sheer superstition today. What were those motives and on what basis did they rest? The old conception was that man was born to die; that eternal life had to be gained by a magical act, exactly as the sun had to be brought to life every morning by the priest.

There is no need to develop the ethics of Thelema in detail, for everything springs with absolute logic from the singular principle, 'Do what thou wilt shall be the whole of the Law.' Or, to put it another way, 'There is no law beyond Do what thou wilt.' And, 'Thou hast no right but to do thy will.' This formula itself springs ineluctably from the conception of the individual outlined in the preceding section. 'The word of Sin is Restriction.' 'It is a lie, this folly against self.' The theory is that every man and every woman has each definite attributes whose tendency, considered in due relation to environment, indicate a proper course of action in each case. To pursue this course of action is to do one's true will. 'Do that and no other shall say nay.'

The physical parallel still holds. In a galaxy each star has its own magnitude, characteristics and direction, and the celestial harmony is best maintained by its attending to its own business. Nothing could be more subversive of that harmony than if a number of stars set up in a uniform standard of conduct insisted on everyone aiming at the same goal, going at the same pace, and so on. Even a single star, by refusing to do its own will, by restricting itself in any way, would immediately produce disorder.

We have a sentimental idea of self-sacrifice, the kind which is most esteemed by the vulgar and is the essence of popular Christianity. It is the sacrifice of the strong to the weak. This is wholly against the principles of evolution. Any nation which does this systematically on a sufficiently large scale, simply destroys itself. The sacrifice is in vain; the weak are not even saved. Consider the action of Zanoni [12] in going to the scaffold in order to save his silly wife. The gesture was magnificent; it was evidence of his own supreme courage and moral strength; but if everyone acted on that principle the race would deteriorate and disappear.

There is here a conflict between private and public morality. We should not protect the weak and the vicious from the results of their inferiority. By doing so, we perpetuate the elements of dissolution in our own social body. We should rather aid nature by subjecting every newcomer to the most rigorous tests of his fitness to deal with his environment. The human race grew in stature and intelligence as long as the individual prowess achieved security, so that the strongest and cleverest people were able to reproduce their kind in the best conditions.

But when security became general through the operation of altruism the most degenerate of the people were often the off-spring of the strongest.

The Book of the Law regards pity as despicable. The reason is partly indicated in the above paragraph. But further, to pity another man is to insult him. He also is a star, 'one, individual and eternal'. The Book does not condemn fighting—'if he be a King, thou canst not hurt him.'

There are many ethical injunctions of a revolutionary character in the Book, but they are all particular cases of the general precept to realize one's own absolute God-head and to act with the nobility which springs from that knowledge. Practically all vice springs from failure to do this. For example: falsehood is invariably the child of fear in one form or another.

With regard to what are commonly considered offences against morality, the undesirable results often observed are due to the same error. Strong and successful men always express themselves fully, and when they are sufficiently strong no harm comes of it to themselves or to others. When it does, it is practically always due to the artificial situation brought about by people who, having no business of their own, meddle in that of other people. One may mention the cases of Sir Charles Dilke and Charles Stewart Parnell. It didn't matter a straw to anybody outside the negligibly small circle of their acquaintances what these men did in their private lives, but England lost her greatest foreign minister and Ireland her greatest leader, because it was discovered that they were doing exactly the same as practically everyone else in their class.

With regard again to personal jealousy and ill-regulated passion, is it too much to say that nine tenths of the social misery not due to poverty arises from these hallucinations? *The Book of the Law* sweeps them out of existence. 'There shall be no property in human flesh.' Nobody has a right to say what anyone else shall or shall not do with his or her body. Establish this principle of absolute respect for others and the whole nightmare of sex is dispelled. Blackmail and prostitution automatically lose their raison d'être. The corrupting influence of hypocrisy breaks like a rotten reed. The sweating of 'female labour cheapened by prostitution' (as Bernard Shaw says) becomes impossible.

I have written at considerable length in recent years on the ethical, as well as on the cosmographical problems solved by the Law of Thelema. I need not go into them more deeply in this place. But the subsequent events of my life will furnish constant illustration of how every time I violated the Law, as I sometimes did with what I was ass enough to call the noblest motives, I got myself into a mess—and failed to benefit those on whose behalf I had chosen to make a fool of myself.

50

It is part of my character to rest on my oars at the very moment when a spurt would take me past the post. I begin to be recognized as the one poet in England: 'Good,' I say to myself, 'I needn't bother about that any more.' I acquire most of the world's records as a mountaineer—that lets me out. *Nunc est bibendum, nunc pede libero pulsanda tellus.*[1] I reach eminence in Magick; it is the signal for me to drop it; in mysticism, and I lose my interest. Now, charged by the Secret Chiefs of the Third Order with a mission of such importance that the last event in the world's history of importance, even approaching it, was Mohammed's, I get cold feet, carry out my instructions as perfunctorily as possible, and even try to find excuses for postponing such work as I could not actually avoid.

I made a certain number of studies of *The Book of the Law;* for even then I was bound to admit that Aiwass had shown a knowledge of the Cabbala immeasurably superior to my own. I had the manuscript typed. I issued a circular letter to a number of my friends, something in the nature of a proclamation of the New Aeon, but I took no trouble to follow it up. I took a certain number of wide-reaching plans for assuming responsibility, but they remained in the stage of reverie. I dropped the whole business, to all intents and purposes. I completely abandoned my diary. I even neglected a really first-rate opportunity for bringing *The Book of the Law* into public notice, for Mrs Besant was on the ship by which Ouarda and I returned to Europe, and I conversed a great deal with her about sacred subjects. In Paris, I wrote a formal letter to Mathers informing him that the Secret Chiefs had appointed me visible head of the Order, and declared a new Magical Formula. I did not expect or receive an answer. I declared war on Mathers accordingly, but it was a *brutum fulmen.*[2]

The fact of the matter was that I resented *The Book of the Law* with my whole soul. For one thing, it knocked my Buddhism completely on the head. *Remember all ye that existence is pure joy; that all the sorrows are but as shadows; they pass & are done; but there is that which remains.*[3]

425

I was bitterly opposed to the principles of the Book on almost every point of morality. The third chapter seemed to me gratuitously atrocious. My soul, infinitely sad at the universal sorrow, was passionately eager to raise humanity. And lo! the Magical Formula denounced pity as damnable, acclaimed war as admirable and in almost every other way was utterly repugnant to my ideas. I did not understand the fundamental principles of the initiation of mankind; and (in my own case) I did not realize that Aiwass was not necessarily responsible for the character of his message any more than the newspaper for reporting an earthquake.

The Secret Chiefs had informed me that a New Aeon implied the breaking up of the civilization existing at the time; obviously to change the Magical Formula of the planet is to change all moral sanctions and the result is bound to appear disastrous. The Cult of the Dying God introduced by Dionysus destroyed the Roman virtue and smashed the Roman culture. (Possibly the introduction of the worship of Osiris in an earlier epoch was primarily responsible for the decay of Egyptian civilization.) The nature of Horus being 'Force and Fire', his aeon would be marked by the collapse of humanitarianism. The first act of his reign would naturally be to plunge the world into the catastrophe of a huge and ruthless war.

The Secret Chiefs told me that this war was imminent and that they had chosen me as their representative on account of my comprehensive knowledge of the Mysteries, my correct understanding of their real import and my literary ability. The chief duty which they laid upon me was to publish the Secret Wisdom of the Ages in such a form that after the wreck of civilization the scholars of subsequent generations would be able to restore the traditions. I was to issue a compendium of the methods by which man may attain the God-head. They released me from my obligation of secrecy.

The responsibility of this, apart from anything else, was sufficient to stagger me. I had been taught to dread the result of publishing the least part of the Secret Knowledge: in unworthy hands the most appalling mischief was only too likely to ensue. I had been almost absurdly scrupulous with regard to the secrets entrusted to me; indeed my experience had already shown me what shocking messes had been made by apparently trivial indiscretions on the part of others. I was not even proud that the choice of the Secret Chiefs had fallen upon me; I was too well aware of my incapacity and indolence.

The task of reducing the Magical and mystical methods of every time and clime to a coherent and intelligible form frightened me. On the one hand, I was reluctant to attempt so ambitious a work; on the other, acutely anxious lest I should prove unworthy of my office.

I have always been utterly contemptuous of the criticism of people whom I do not respect. I frankly despise Keats for having been upset by the review of 'Endymion'; but the correlative of this is over-sensitiveness about people whom I regard as authorities. The least word of admonition of Eckenstein about climbing would throw me into agonies of self-reproach. When Allan reproved me for some error in Yoga, I was overwhelmed with shame.

My position was therefore very difficult. I was bound to the Secret Chiefs by the most solemn of obligations. I never dreamt of trying to minimize my responsibility to them, yet they had cut across the whole trend of my aspiration. The magical part of me was, in a manner of speaking, stunned.

My wife and I passed a short time in Paris and renewed old ties. One incident stands out in my memory as peculiarly amusing. We asked Arnold Bennett to lunch at Paillard's. He was completely overpowered by the deference of the maître d'hôtel, who knew me very well, and his embarrassment at being introduced to such splendours was childishly charming. He was, of course, enormously pleased and very kindly offered to give me an introduction to H. G. Wells. As Arnold Bennett had gratified the public with a highly spiced description of me in *Paris Nights*, I hope that he will take it as a compliment if I imitate his frankness in the matter of personalities. His accent and dialect made his English delightfully difficult. As we were leaving the restaurant, he told me that there was one thing about Wells that I mustn't mind: he spoke English with an accent.

> *59 Rue de Grenelle, Paris*
>
> 14 *Feby* 1911
>
> Dear Aleister Crowley,
>
> Many thanks. I am very glad to have the volume. I will mention it in *The New Age*, but I no longer write for *T.P.'s Weekly*. Not a portrait of you—my dear Crowley—in the *English Review!* for all you sat for was the waistcoat, the title and the poetry. All these portraits are composite.
>
> Yours sincerely,
>
> ARNOLD BENNETT

Alas! I lack the literary skill to construct composite portraits. My own poor effort is the most crude photography. Also, I beg him to excuse my personalities. He is too great a man at heart to resent jests at the expense of his perishable vehicle; he is himself a star bright-blazing, the more glorious for the thickness of the terrestrial vapours which it has had to pierce.

We wandered back to Boleskine, after arranging with a doctor named Percival Bott to come and stay with us and undertake the accouchement. I asked my Aunt Annie to preside over the household, and an old friend of Gerald's (Kelly) and mine, Ivor Back, at this time a surgeon at St George's, to make up the house party. Ivor Back is one of the most amusing companions possible, to those who can stand him. He knows a good deal about literature and had published in *The Hospital* magazine some of the poems in which I had celebrated various diseases. I dedicated my *In Residence*, a collection of my undergraduate verses, to him, and he collaborated with me to a certain extent in the composition of various masterpieces of the lighter kind. He and Gerald are also responsible for numerous improvements in the preface to *Alice, An Adultery*. He also edited the three volumes of my *Collected Works,* supplying learned notes to divers obscure passages.

My activities as a publisher were at this time remarkable. I had issued *The God-Eater* and *The Star & the Garter* through Charles Watts & Co. of the Rationalist Press Association, but there was still no such demand for my books as to indicate that I had touched the great heart of the British public. I decided that it would save trouble to publish them myself. I decided to call myself the Society for the Propagation of Religious Truth, and issued *The Argonauts, The Sword of Song, The Book of the Goetia of Solomon the King, Why Jesus Wept, Oracles, Orpheus, Gargoyles* and *The Collected Works.* I had simply no idea of business. Besides this, I was in no need of money; my responsibility to the gods was to write as I was inspired; my responsibility to mankind was to publish what I wrote. But it ended there. As long as what I wrote was technically accessible to the public through the British Museum, and such places, my hands were clean.

And yet I took a course implying a diametrically opposite state of mind. I printed a large edition of *The Star & the Garter*, and issued it at a shilling, with the idea of reaching the people who might have been unable to buy my more expensive books. I printed a leaflet and circularized the educated classes. (I have no copy available.) The meat of the circular was the offer of one hundred pounds for the best essay on my work. The business idea was to induce people to buy my *Collected Works* in order to have material for the essay. This offer led ultimately to far-reaching results; in fact, it determined the course of my life for a number of years. The winner of the prize became an intimate friend and colleague. His scholarship, acumen, enthusiasm and indefatigability proved most important factors in the execution of the orders of the Secret Chiefs.

Meanwhile, we had a glorious time at Boleskine. What with the salmon and the venison and my cellar, billiards and rock scrambling, the good company and the perfect summer, life passed like an ecstatic dream. In summer in the Highlands, time seems to forgive. At midnight one can sit and read in the open air even in the absence of the moon. Night is 'one faint eternal eventide of gems'.

One of our adventures is worthy of record. It is one of the most startling incidents that I have ever known in all my experience of climbing. Beyond the Italian garden I had constructed a large trout pond, with Canadian canoe and sacred spring complete. From the farther bank, a short slope leads to a precipitous cliff which affords an admirable variety of rock problems. Having taught Bott and Back the elements of the sport, we decided to attempt a more serious climb. Across the loch, beyond Glen Moriston, is a well-marked gully, through which pours a torrent from Mealfuarvonie. Eckenstein and I marked this down; but during his visits it had always been merely a frantic waterfall. The long spell of dry weather made me think there was a chance to climb it, so I rowed over with Bott and Back, and started on the lowest pitch. This is a broad precipice of water-worn rock, perhaps a hundred to a hundred and fifty feet high. A good deal of water was coming over, but there seemed a possible way up. Starting outside the true left of the stream, I hoped to work my way up the bare slabs to within twenty feet of the edge, where the stream pitched over, and then climb obliquely to the left until I was actually in the torrent; for its broken character indicated good hold (for both hand and foot) which I trusted would prove sufficient to enable me to pull myself up, despite the weight of the water.

At the best the climb was very exposed and I ought not really to have attempted it in any but first-class company. There was no alternative to my proposed route. Where the water had not washed the rock clean, the pitch was a dripping precipice of greasy, mossy slabs, set at a frightful angle, with practically no hand-hold or foot-hold at all. Such cracks as existed gave obvious evidence of disintegration, so that any apparent hold must certainly be rotten. I would not have attempted it with Eckenstein, and I would have refused to follow him had he wished to attempt it himself!

I led up the pitch with Bott as second man and Back as third. I reached the most critical part of the climb. My holds were the merest friction holds. I could not have supported a rabbit. I half expected to come off; and I knew that Bott (though reasonably safe himself, or I should not have gone on) could do nothing to save me if I fell. Back, in a perfectly safe position far below (we had a long rope), saw how insecure I was. He completely lost his nerve. He began to utter incoherent cries and to untie himself from the rope. The act was, of course, outrageous, but he was not responsible. He took no notice of my orders to keep quiet and not to be a damphool. I could not even come down with any safety, Bott being naturally upset by Back's hysteria, so I called to Ivor to stay where he was and we would come round for him.

In the circumstances, my best course was to finish the climb as quickly as I could and I went on at my best pace. In the roar of the falling water which swamped me, I could, of course, see and hear nothing. I dragged myself up the waterfall by sheer force; I had to trust for hand- and foot-hold to my previous observations, for I had to keep my eyes shut against the rush of the torrent. I hauled myself through the gap on the brink and wedged myself against the rocks which confined it, head first. I found myself in a sort of cauldron where I could stand with my head and shoulders above water. I had climbed the pitch. I called to Bott to come on, and pulled him up the slabs on the rope. It had been a terrific climb; one of the most dangerous I had ever done.

My anxiety had been increased by seeing that Back, having untied himself, had not sat down quietly as ordered, but started to scramble towards the utterly unclimbable and dangerously deceptive slabs of dripping moss. Bott and I extricated ourselves from the cauldron without further difficulty. And then I began to wonder whether the nymph of the waterfall had not played me a trick! I was certainly suffering from some kind of hallucination. Had my anxiety about Back created a phantasm? For there, on the slopes above us was an apparition in his shape, gesticulating, muttering and shouting by turns. But it was Back in the flesh! He had done the impossible thing: he had climbed the unclimbable cliff! So incredible was the feat that I was at pains to go round and look at the place again from below. My judgment had not deceived me—there was no sort of way up—yet the torn moss and a few fresh broken bits of rotten rock proved his passage. To this day I regard the facts as the least credible of any that have ever come my way.

When Rose and I first arrived at Boleskine, we had made a sort of sporadic effort to carry out some of the injunctions of Aiwass. We had arranged before leaving Egypt for the 'abstruction' of the Stele of Revealing. I did not understand the word or the context, and contented myself with having a replica made by one of the artists attached to the museum. We now proceeded to prepare the 'perfume' and the 'cakes' according to the prescription given in chapter III, verses 23–9.

We had resumed Magical work, in a desultory way, on finding that Mathers was attacking us. He succeeded in killing most of the dogs. (At this time I kept a pack of bloodhounds and went man-hunting over the moors.) The servants too were constantly being made ill, one in one way, and one in another. We therefore employed the appropriate talismans from *The Book of the Sacred Magick of Abra-Melin* against him, evoking Beelzebub and his forty-nine servitors. Rose had suddenly acquired the power of clairvoyance. Her description of these servitors is printed in *The Bagh-i-Muattar*, pages 39, 40. (I may mention: Nimorup, a stunted dwarf with large head and ears. His lips are greeny bronze and slobbery. Nominon, a large red spongy jelly-fish with one greenish luminous spot like a nasty mess. Holastri, an enormous pink bug.) As to this perfume of *The Book of the Law*, 'let it be laid before me and kept thick with perfumes of your orison; it shall become full of beetles as it were and creeping things sacred unto me.' One day, to my amazement, having gone into the bathroom to bathe, I discovered a beetle. As I have said, I take no interest in natural history and know nothing of it.

But this beetle attracted my attention at once. I had never seen anything like it before. It was about an inch and a half long and had a single horn nearly as long as itself. The horn ended in a small sphere suggestive of an eye. From that moment, for about a fortnight, there was an absolute plague of these beetles. They were not merely in the house, they were on the rocks, in the gardens, by the sacred spring, everywhere! But I never saw one outside the estate. I sent a specimen to London but the experts were unable to identify the species.

Here was a tangible piece of Magick. It ought to have convinced me that *The Book of the Law* meant business. Instead, it left me absolutely cold. I experienced a certain proud glee, much as I had in the King's Chamber of the Great Pyramid, but there it stopped. I took the necessary measures to protect Rose against the murderous attack of Mathers, and went on playing billiards. The attack was, however, prolonged and deadly. We were putting central heating into the house, and attempting to construct a small golf course on the estate. (Idiot! why not a tennis court on the Ennerdale Face of the Pillar?)

Ivor and I were playing billiards one morning after breakfast, when we heard screams and oaths from the direction of the kitchen. I snatched up a salmon gaff as the readiest weapon and we hurried out. One of the workmen had become suddenly maniacal and attacked my wife, who was making her usual inspection of the offices. It was the work of a moment to gaff the offender and thrust him into the coal cellar, and send for the police. As they were a long time in coming, the animal made several attempts to crawl out of the chute, but our vigilance succeeded in baffling him, and he was duly handed into custody. But nothing followed! It is one of the peculiarities of Scotch law that there is no private prosecution unless the police choose to take up any given case; you can be murdered *ad libitum* without possibility of redress. As the police in the Highlands are largely recruited from the assassin class—there is no other—one can well understand why the gentry maintain, to a great extent, the ancient custom of surrounding themselves with armed retainers.

As soon as Beelzebub got on the job, the magical assaults ceased; and, deprived of the stimulus to perform Magick, my interest faded once more. We spent our time in sport and society, tempered by pregnancy, as if there were no hereafter. I used my official titles and position without emphasis, very much as a peer takes advantage of his social privileges without ever giving a thought to the House of Lords as a political institution.

On July 28th my wife gave birth to a girl, called Nuit Ma Ahathoor Hecate Sappho Jezebel Lilith. Nuit was given in homage to our Lady of the Stars; Ma, goddess of Justice, because the sign of Libra was rising; Ahathoor, goddess of Love and Beauty, because Venus rules Libra; I'm not sure about the name Hecate, but it may have been as a compliment to the infernal gods; a poet could hardly do less than commemorate the only lady who ever wrote poetry, Sappho; Jezebel still held her place as my favourite character in Scripture; and Lilith, of course, holds undisputed possession of my affections in the realm of demons.

Duncombe Jewell remarked later on that she had died of acute nomenclature. Cad. In my ears rang that terrible cry of Macduff, 'He has no children.'

Everything had gone as well as possible, and we were the happiest house party in the Highlands. There was only one problem, that of keeping my wife amused during her convalescence. She was normally an intensely active, joyous being, but she had absolutely no resources. She could not play even the simplest game of cards, and of my whole library of three thousand books and more there were only some half dozen that she cared to read. Hall Caine was too deep for her. It was up to me to produce an example of the only kind of literature she understood.

Now the objection to this form of art is its monotony; its preoccupation with detailed incident precludes a plot, and the range of its characters is deplorably limited. The men are nearly always priests or peers; the women countesses, school mistresses or milliners. These books possess the merit of frankness of the most engaging kind; but they frequently strain one's credulity. The heroes of medieval romance are not so inhumanly disproportionate to the facts of life; that the author could claim the title of realist only adds to one's disgust. They arouse every instinct of my puritanism with almost insane intensity. I suppose I was really furious at the fact that the wife whom I loved so passionately and honoured so profoundly should be intellectually circumscribed in this way. My only remedy was a *reductio ad absurdum*. I resolved to write a novel myself—one of this kind, but it should be very much better and bigger. And damn the expense. No priest nor monk should be my hero. I would have an archbishop. He should not be as superhuman as six men; he should do better than six hundred. My models had annoyed me by the pathetic paucity of their vocabulary. Having the excellent dictionary of John B. Farmer and W. E. Henley, I was able to avoid repeating myself. However, I took the liberty of inventing many new words and phrases to add further variety. So for every detail, I would show up the imbecile ineptitude to this type of literature by exaggerating its faults at every point.

I pounded off a chapter a day of this novel on my typewriter and read it to my wife, Gerald, Ivor and the rest of the

house party, except my aunt, who shared the psychology of
my wife, only on the other side of the fence. Rose could not
see in the least what I meant; like Colonel Gormley, anything
whatever that turned her mind towards the subject of love
produced a direct excitement and was pleasing. The effect was
the same on my aunt, except that she had schooled herself to
pretend that it was unpleasing.

Even in France the *pudibond* fury of the bourgeoisie is
rampant. Part of the public horror of sexual irregularity so-
called is due to the fact that everyone knows himself essentially guilty. 'Methinks the lady doth protest too much.' If men
would face the facts of life, including their own constitutions
as they are, practically all abuse and perversions would disappear. They are for the most part morbid phantasms of putrefaction, aggravated by the attempt at suppression. The wound
of Amfortas will not heal because it has never been properly
opened and rendered aseptic.

Madame Bovary was assumed to be a provincial Phryne.
The story of her adultery was condemned as 'immoral', as
tending to incite illicit passions. Its critics had been simply
unable to read the book. Flaubert was in reality grinding his
heel into the woman's foolish face; he was showing that her
conduct was not romantic and voluptuous, but sordid, stupid,
bestial and anaphrodisiac. What could be more puritanical
than *Ghosts?* It is the most frightful indictment of immorality
that has ever been penned. Yet to the Anglo-Saxon it is 'immoral'. They don't understand a word, but it makes them
think of their own beastliness; with the result that they discuss
it furtively, licking their lips, and cry in the market place that
it is an offence to their purity.

I have never been able to comply with these foully perverse
conventions. I face anything frankly and the phantasm fades.
I do not permit any author to play on my passions. I read a
book with my soul, and only those books appeal to me whose
authors speak sincerely and sanely such truth as has been
given them. I utterly loathe the author who practises on popular psychology. The sentimentalism of Charles Dickens, the
eroticism of D. H. Lawrence, the pornographic religiosity of
Mrs. Humphry Ward * seem to me to be appeals to the appetites of the unintelligent. They prostitute their scrap of art
exactly as quacks do when they try to persuade people that a
pain in the back always means Bright's disease; or that every

---

* I have never read a word of her. But somehow I don't like the idea.

trifling symptom, from headache to ingrowing toe-nails, is the result of secret vice.

The plain truth of the matter is that love stories are only fit for the solace of people in the insanity of puberty. No healthy adult human being can really care whether so-and-so does or does not succeed in satisfying his physiological uneasiness by the aid of some particular person or not. *The Woman in White* and *The Moonstone* illustrate the situation with singular clearness. Despite the astounding power of Wilkie Collins to draw characters, he cannot make the heroine interesting. Laura Fairlie is little better than an imbecile even when not actually suffering from dementia.

The artist's subconscious mind plays this sort of thing on him as a joke. He gets so disgusted with himself that he avenges himself on the dummy which offends him. In these two novels, the heroes are represented as exceptionally fine fellows in every way, but for all their heroic deeds they seem wishy-washy, sordid dummies; for the simple reason that they have no object in life but to attain sexual possession of so many pounds of flesh. Nor does the interest of these books really depend on love. Great artists always find more serious themes. Sex is a means of intoxication; it is therefore proper to celebrate it in lyrics. But when one is sober, as one is when reading a novel, one doesn't want sex thrust down one's throat. One doesn't mind white wine in the sauce of the fish, and the man who is upset by its presence is a neurotic. As for the man who wants his cook to make his sauce so that he can get drunk on it—I simply don't want to meet him. But that is what the Anglo-Saxon public does, and that is why I don't want to meet it.

Shakespeare has few stories of which the interest depends on love; when it does, the love always implies ruin, as in *Romeo and Juliet*, *Antony and Cleopatra* and *Othello*. His only love stories with a happy ending, bar absolutely mechanical dénouements, are where he is secretly gratifying his secret perversity, as in *Twelfth Night* and *As You Like It*. Our greatest novelists have complied with convention by inserting a love interest ready made; *Tom Jones*, *Roderick Random* and so on; but the interest is hardly even secondary. All our greatest masterpieces treat love in its proper relation to life. *Jonathan Wild, Moll Flanders, Robinson Crusoe, Tristram Shandy, Gulliver's Travels, A Tale of a Tub, The Pilgrim's Progress, The Pickwick Papers, Vanity Fair, Armadale, The Shaving of*

Shagpat, *The Way of all Flesh*, the Cabell epic: [4] what have these to do with love?

In France it is the same. It can be done once. Aucassin and Nicolette. But afterwards! Think of a nice young girl introduced into *La Peau de chagrin*, *La Cousine Bette*, *Le Cousin Pons*, *Le Père Goriot*, *Eugénie Grandet*, *Le Colonel Chabert*. There is not one story in all Balzac where love is the saving or even the main motive. Dumas—think of d'Artagnan in love with a nice young lady and living happy ever after! (The love interest in *A Gentleman of France* and *Under the Red Robe* explains why Stanley Weyman's imitations of Dumas are so deplorably vulgar.) What happens to the Vicomte de Brage-lonne (with all the virtues) when he falls in love? Russia supplies the extreme case, for in that country love has always been understood as a definitely diabolical pitfall.

It is true that there is a modern school founded by Emily Brontë, from Thomas Hardy to D. H. Lawrence, whose plots turn on the sexual relation of the characters, but wherever such books are healthy, the theme is that the exaggeration of the importance of such relations leads to disaster.

To return to my *jeu d'esprit* and the psychology involved. I have for my solicitor one of the most acute observers in the world. He said to me the other day, 'You seem never to be able to do anything as anyone else would.' I retorted, 'No; nor by halves,' which was smart—but hardly a rebuttal. The fact is, I consider everything *sub specie universali, sub specie aeter-nitatis*. It comes natural to me to write an article on the parish council election in Little Piddlington for the eyes of the philosophers of two centuries hence. I cannot bring myself to believe that anything which is going on at the present time has any real existence. It is a meaningless letter in a word and its value depends on the rest of the letters. 'A' and 'O' are in themselves mere varieties of breathing, yet one helps to make 'hag', the other 'hog'—one 'cot', the other 'cat'. Unless I know the consonants I cannot tell whether I need an 'a' or an 'o'.

Now this perception is obvious to everybody, yet everybody acts as if he knew exactly what would be the result of writing 'a' instead of 'o', assuming that he is free to choose which he will do—which he isn't. But I bring this principle into my life; it governs me in every action outside my regular reflexes. I am really aware that I do not know whether it would be to my advantage to be hanged. I have only attained to a standard of conduct by referring all my judgments to my will, and until I knew what my true will was, I was utterly at sea.

To apply these ideas to the issue which we are discussing. I knew that a poet is incapable of recognizing his best work, but I knew also that though good technique does not mean good work, bad technique does mean bad work. So I used to experiment with new forms by choosing a ridiculous or obscene subject, lest I should be tempted to publish a poem whose technique showed inexperience.

Ivor and I, with some assistance from Gerald, collected such of these manuscripts as had not been destroyed, and with 'The Nameless Novel', we composed a volume * to carry on the literary form of *White Stains* and *Alice;* that is, we invented a perpetrator for the atrocities.

I do not know what mischievous whim induced me to have the book printed, but I was absolutely innocent of any desire to rival the exploit of Alfred de Musset and George Sand, the *Femmes* [5] and *Hombres* [6] of Verlaine, or the *jeu d'esprit* of Mark Twain of which Sir Walter Raleigh is the hero. I did not even hope to get the British government to give me a pension of four thousand pounds a year, as it did to John Cleland.[7]

This literary diversion, and the regular sports of the Highlands, kept us happy; but, as the summer faded, we broke up. I did not want Rose and the baby to have to endure a Highland winter and towards the end of October went off to St Moritz to make arrangements for them to come out. Rose, however, decided to take a holiday from nursing and left the child with her parents under the charge of the nurse, who was of course a very highly trained woman. She joined me at St Moritz in November. I had always been enthusiastic about winter sports of every kind with the exception of *ski-läufing*, which I appreciate as a means of covering necessary distances, but not otherwise. I like swooping down the slopes, and an occasional jump is rather good fun. But to go back up hill again! No, thank you!

The Cresta run was a great joy and the sports committee paid me the greatest compliment of asking my advice about its construction. But it seemed to me ideally perfect. The only suggestions which I had to make were connected with safety; and in fact, several men have been killed since through the precautions proposed by me not having been taken. I cannot blame anyone; my ideas were perhaps hardly practicable. Something should doubtless have been done about the level

---

* *Snowdrops from a Curate's Garden.*

crossing, where a man going at sixty miles an hour or so came off second best when he hit a cart. But that is a rare chance. The constant danger is that an unskilful rider thrown over the walls of Battledore and Shuttlecock may strike the same place as a previous misadventurer. In this case he will land, not on soft snow but on an irregular mass of regelated ice. He is sure to cut himself and may easily get killed. The walls of the run should be sufficiently high and steep to make it impossible for a toboggan to leave the trough, in which case he would have to be very clever to come to much harm, provided he is properly clothed and hangs on to his seat. The difficulty is that men are so keen for the season to open that the run is often built when there is not nearly enough snow.

The frost began to break and we went back to England. I propose to mention an incident, despite its strictly medical character, as a warning to the world of the utter idiocy of woman as a class and the criminal idiocy of trained nurses in particular. They are the most dangerous animals in the community. They are so proud of their disconnected scraps of medical knowledge that they are always trying to usurp the position of the physician. In the present instance my wife came within an ace of death on a false alarm which two words from a qualified practitioner would have dispelled.

Since the birth of the baby, she had not settled down into the normal course of her physiological life. She jumped to the conclusion that she was pregnant again, though her symptoms, of course, implied nothing of the sort. Instead of seeking a doctor she went hysterically to the nurse who proceeded to dose her with ergot. As no abortion took place she redoubled her efforts. I had been away on business for two or three days and returned to find her in a perfectly frightened condition. I forced a confession and dragged her to the station (we were staying with her family near Bournemouth) and got her to the Savoy before midnight. Bott and Back, summoned by telegram, were waiting for us. They were frankly delighted, never having seen such a bad case of ergot poisoning in their lives.

I really don't know why I didn't prosecute that filthy nurse. Even if her diagnosis had been correct, I consider criminal abortion in any circumstances soever as one of the foulest kinds of murder. Apart from anything else, it nearly always ruins the health of the woman, when it fails to kill her.

The vigour of my views on this point strengthens my general attitude on the question of sexual freedom. I believe that very few women, left to themselves, would be so vile as to commit this sin against the Holy Ghost; to thwart the deepest instincts of nature at the risk of health and life, to say nothing of imprisonment. Yet criminal abortion is one of the commonest of crimes and one most generally condoned by what I must paradoxically call secret public opinion. And the reason is that our social system makes it shameful and punishable by poverty for a woman to do what evolution has spent ages in constructing her to do, save under conditions with which the vast majority of women cannot possibly comply. The remedy lies entirely with public opinion. Let motherhood be recognized as honourable in itself, and even the pressure of poverty would not prevent any but a few degenerate women, with perverse appetites for pleasure, from fulfilling their function. In the case of such it would indeed be better that they and their children perish.

There is yet a further point. My marriage taught me many lessons, and this not the least: when women are not devoted to children—a few rare individuals are capable of other interests—they take a morbid pleasure in conspiring against a husband, especially if he be a father. They take advantage of his preoccupation with his work in the world to conceive and execute every kind of criminally cunning abomination. The belief in witchcraft was not all superstition; its psychological roots were sound. Women who are thwarted in their natural instincts turn inevitably to all kinds of malignant mischief, from slander to domestic destruction.

I am afraid that my adventures have lost me the citizenship of the world. Alastor is my name, the Spirit of Solitude, the Wanderer in the Waste. I am only at home in the Elysian Fields, conversing with the mighty men of old. I dislike London, not because it is busy and noisy and dirty and dark and sordid, and so on, but because it is so pettily provincial. I live in a city beyond time and space; how much more beyond the ticking centuries and the itching inches of London! I have accustomed myself so long to look at the universe as a whole that its parts have become imperceptible. When I am reminded of them, it is like being reminded of one's eye by getting a fly in it. That is what I mean when I say that London gives me a pain.

I was very glad to be back in Boleskine. I had no particular plans; I had really settled down. If I had a tendency at all, it was to play little practical jokes. They were the outcome of my happiness. I put up a signboard in a field across the road:

This way to the Kooloomooloomavlock (does not bite),

in the hope that the wayfarer might amuse me by going to look for it. As a matter of fact, this animal created the greatest terror in the neighbourhood, the more so that it remained invisible. After my departure in 1905, the hotel keeper of Foyers determined to abate the nuisance and took his gun and tried to stalk it. He was observed from the hill by my ghillie and piper, Hugh Gillies, the best servant I ever had in Europe, advancing by short rushes and in every way comporting himself as the military necessities of the situation required. 'She may no bite,' quoth Gillies, 'but a'm thinking she pu's legs.'

My activities as a publisher were in themselves a sort of practical joke. It amused me to bewilder and shock people. I took nothing seriously except my occult life at any time and that was at present more or less in abeyance. I wrote one or two poems at this time, notably *Rosa Inferni*, before Rose joined me in St Moritz, and somehow or other I had written the fourth book of *Orpheus*, part of which is inspired by my experience in Egypt. I published them at once. They had never satisfied me; the form was theoretically impossible. On the other hand, the lyrics and some of the dramatic dialogue are as good as anything in my work. I felt that one part of my life was drawing to a close. I made a clean sweep of my literary dustbin. I had its contents carted away and dumped on the public. I felt myself to be on the brink of a new birth and in *Gargoyles* will be found the first fruits of that new life.

But at this particular time I was much too happy to create. Creation is the effect of physiological dissatisfaction. That is why it comes as a relief. The creation of the universe, love, sea-sickness, are all of the same order of phenomena. I was at this time like the Eternal, lapped in calm bliss and enjoying his own perfection. But to such states there always arrives a period when discomfort arises from the accumulation of the secretions produced by the metabolism of one's elements. Presently one becomes conscious of the need to sneeze or what not, and in course of time one has to sneeze.

It is a very curious thing, by the way, that the average man accepts quite calmly the heresies of the average thinker with perfect equanimity. Bernard Shaw's attack on religion and and morality are taken as a matter of course. But when people like Ibsen, Nietzsche and myself say the same things, we are held up to popular execration.

There was no snake in my Eden; the impulse which drove me out took the positive form of Opportunity. From time to time, various friends had visited us: Gerald Kelly and his mother, Eckenstein, and so on, and a quite insignificant creature named Lieutenant-Colonel Gormley, who was destined to play a curious part in my life. He was a medical soldier and had spent countless years in India, Burma and South Africa without acquiring a single fact of interest. He was incapable of appreciating so much as a funny story, even an improper one if there were any touch of wit in it. But if anyone introduced an obscene word into the conversation on any pretext soever, he would rock with laughter and continue to titter for an indefinite period.

He was the first masochist I had ever met; in fact I have only met one other, and it is not for me to decide which was the filthier fool. Gormley claimed to have been flagellated by over two thousand women. I rather suspect him of vaingloriousness: It seems a very large number. He was in love with my wife, chiefly because she treated him with such disgust and contempt. He had proposed to her several times a week, even before her first marriage, and he saw no reason why he should abandon this habit merely on account of Major Skerrett and myself. I don't know why I tolerated him; I don't know why anyone tolerated him. Perhaps it was the subconscious feeling that one cannot be unkind to anything so pitiable.

On April 27th, the good Tartarin,[8] who had published a book (in the Swiss language) on our expedition to Chogo Ri, illustrated with many admirable photographs but not distinguished by literary quality or accuracy (in many respects), and had lectured in Paris and other capitals on Chogo Ri, dropped in. I was heartily glad to see him. He was the same cheerful ass as ever, but he had got a bit of a swelled head and was extremely annoyed with me for not leading him instantly to stalk the sinister stag, to grapple with the grievous grouse, and to set my ferrets on the fearful pheasant. He could not understand the game laws. Well, I'm a poet; I determined to create sport since it did not exist. More, it should be unique.

I opened the campaign as follows. Tartarin knew the origin of the wild buffalo of Burma. When the British destroyed the villages, their cattle escaped the bayonet and starvation by taking to the jungle, where they had become practically a new species. After the '45 the British had pursued the same policy of extermination—I mean pacification—in the Highlands, and I thought it plausible to invent a wild sheep on the analogy of the wild buffalo. And more, the beast should be already famous. I described its rarity, its shyness, its ferocity, etc., etc.— 'You have doubtless heard of it,' I ended; 'it is called the haggis.' My '52 Johannesburg completed that part of the 'come-on.' Tartarin dreamt all night of scaling a lonely and precipitous pinnacle and dragging a lordly haggis from his lair. For my part, like Judas in the famous story of the Sepher Toldoth Jeschu,[9] I did not dream at all: I did better!

Two mornings later, Hugh Gillies, with disordered dress and wild eyes, came rushing into the billiard room after breakfast. He exploded breathlessly, 'There's a haggis on the hill, my lord!'

We dropped our cues and dashed to the gun case. Trusting to my skill, I contented myself with the .577 Double Express, and gave Tartarin the principal weapon of my battery, a 10-bore Paradox, with steel-core bullets. It is a reliable weapon, it will bring an elephant up short with a mere shock, even if he is not hit in a vital part. With such an arm, my friend could advance fearlessly against the most formidable haggis in the Highlands.

Not a moment was to be lost. Gillies, followed by the doctor, myself and my wife, tiptoed, crouching low, out of the front door and stalked the fearsome beast across the Italian garden.

The icy rain chilled us to the bone before we reached the edge of the artificial trout lake. I insisted on wading through this—up to the neck, guns held high—on the ground that we should thus throw the haggis off our scent!

We emerged dripping and proceeded to climb the hill on all fours. Every time anyone breathed, we all stopped and lay low for several minutes. It was a chilly performance, but it was worth it! Tartarin soon reached the point where every bent twig looked to him like one of the horns of our haggis. I crawled and dripped and choked back my laughter. The idiocy of the whole adventure was intensified by the physical discomfort and the impossibility of relieving one's feelings. That interminable crawl! The rain never let up for a single second; and the wind came in gusts wilder and more bitter with every yard of ascent. I explained to Tartarin that if it should shift a few degrees, the haggis would infallibly get our scent and be off. I implored him to camouflage his posteriors, which arose in front of my balaclava, heaving like the hump of a dying camel. The resulting wriggles would have driven Isidora Duncan to despair; the poor man was indeed acutely conscious that, anatomically, he had not been constructed with the main idea of escaping notice.

However, after an hour and a half, we reached the top of the hill, three hundred feet above the house, without hearing that hideous scream-whistle of alarm by which (so I had been careful to explain) the haggis announces that he has detected the presence of an alien enemy.

Breathlessly, we crawled towards the hollow space of grassy and heathery knolls that lay behind the huge rock buttress that towers above the garden and the lake, that space whose richness had tempted our distinguished visitor to approach so near to human habitation.

The mist drove wildly and fiercely across the hillside towards us. It magnified every object to an enormous size, the more impressively that the background was wholly blotted out. Suddenly Gillies rolled stealthily over to the right, his finger pointed tremulously to where, amid the unfurling wreaths of greyness, stood . . .

Tartarin brought forward the 10-bore with infinite precision. The haggis loomed gargantuan in the mist; it was barely fifty yards away. Even I had somehow half hypnotized myself into a sort of perverse excitement. I could have sworn the brute was the size of a bear.

Guillarmod pressed both triggers. He had made no mistake. Both bullets struck and expanded; he had blown completely away the entire rear section of Farmer McNab's prize ram.

We rushed forward, cheering frantically. Gillies had to be first in at the death; the supply of oats with which he had induced our latest purchase to feed in that spot all the morning without moving, might, if observed, have detracted from the uncanny glory of that romantic scene.

But next day at dinner, when we ate that haggis, the general hilarity passed unchallenged. The atmosphere had become wholly Homeric; there was no reason why the wildest glee should seem out of place.

Tartarin sent the ram's head to be stuffed and mounted; a suitable inscription was to be engraved upon a plate of massive gold. For had not the gallant Swiss vindicated their race once more? Would not the *Gazette de Lausanne* literally foam at the mouth with the recital of so doughty an exploit?

And so the contented Tartarin developed his plans for renewing the attack upon the Himalayas. Eckenstein had been approached, but for one reason or another had refused. I should have preferred it vastly if he had accepted; but I was as keen as ever to capture the only world's record which he and I did not, severally or jointly, hold; that of having reached a higher point on mountains than any other climbers. (This record was held either by Graham on Kebru—a doubtful case —or by Matthias Zurbriggen, the guide whom Eckenstein had trained to mountaincraft, on Aconcagua.)

Mindful, however, of Tartarin's misadventure in 1902, I made the strictest conditions before agreeing to join the new expedition. A document was drawn up and signed by which I should be acknowledged leader of the party. I was to be obeyed implicity in all matters relating to the actual conduct of the expedition on the mountain. It was a deliberate breach of this agreement which caused directly its failure and the disaster which disgraced it.

51

Expedition 1905, au Kangchenjunga.
  Accord.
Le Dr J. Jacot Guillarmod & ses trois amis fournissent une somme de quinze mille francs.
Monsieur Aleister Crowley & un ami fourniront à deux une somme de 5,000 francs (cinq mille).
Pour cette dernière contribution, le Dr J. Jacot Guillarmod s'engage à fournir l'approvisionnement & le transport du moment du départ de Darjeeling jusqu'au retour à Darjeeling.
L'expédition sera entreprise dans les meilleures conditions possibles, vu la nature du pays à traverser.
Le but de l'expédition sera l'ascension du Kangchenjunga (28,150 feet).
On essayera d'abord par le glacier de Yalung.
On partira de Darjeeling dans la seconde moitié de juillet; on y reviendra en octobre au plus tard.
Aleister Crowley partira pour Darjeeling aussitôt que possible, afin de faire tous les préparatifs & arrangements nécessaires.
On respectera soigneusement les préjugés & les croyances indigènes & on ne s'immiscera pas dans leurs manières de vivre.
On n'achètera rien sans l'assentiment du Dr J. Jacot G. ou de A. Crowley.
On s'engage à n'avoir aucune relation directe ou indirecte avec les femmes, indigènes ou étrangères, qu'on peut éviter.
Le Dr J. Jacot G. est seul & suprême juge des questions d'hygiène ou de santé de la caravane.
Aleister Crowley est seul & suprême juge des questions se rapportant exclusivement à l'alpinisme & aux montagnes.
Les questions de route & du personnel des caravanes seront décidées par lui seul. Ses camarades se conformeront à ses résolutions.
Personne ne sera obligé de risquer sa vie, à cause du froid, du manque de nourriture, d'ascension périlleuse, pouvant entraîner une chute.
Toute discussion relative à cet accord doit être soumise à l'arbitrage; on ne peut invoquer de loi ou de jugement d'homme de loi.
Les clauses de cet accord lient tous les membres de l'expédition par leur honneur.

	Aleister Crowley
Dr J. Jacot Guillarmod	Ch. Reymond
A. C. R. de Righi	Alexis A. Pache

There was no time to spare, if we were to attack Kang-chenjunga this summer. It was arranged that the doctor was to get together the necessary provisions and equipment at once in Europe, while I went direct to Darjeeling to make arrangements with the government about transport and such communications as the heliograph, by which means we intended to signal our progress to observers on Signal Hill, above the station, to collect some of our old Kasmir shikaris if possible, to learn a little Nepali, and perhaps to enlist the assistance of enterprising individuals on the spot.

I left for London on May 6th and made such preparations with regard to my personal equipment as seemed desirable, and on May 12th left England for the East by the P & O S.S. *Marmora*. Eckenstein maintained constantly that the adventure was foolhardy; that, for his own part, he would never consent to go on a mountain again with Jacot Guillarmod; and that, in one way or another, his vanity, inexperience, fatuity and folly were certain to land us in disaster. I liked Tartarin so well, personally, that I unconsciously minimized his imbecility; and I was still much too young to realize how much mischief may be done indirectly by the mere presence of such a man, despite every precaution that prudence can suggest and all the supervision that caution can recommend. So I went into it—and realize only of late how lucky I was to come out of it all!

It was part of my policy with regard to physical training to make the whole journey by sea. I fed up and lounged about and told stories till the twenty-third, when I arrived in Cairo. The city is abandoned by tourists by this time of the year on account of some superstition about the climate; but to me Cairo at the end of May was more pleasant than I had ever known it. I joined the P & O on the thirty-first. It was certainly hot in the Red Sea, but I remember with intense pleasure of wonder a single incident. Most of the passengers, including myself, slept on deck. I was awakened one morning before dawn by a dazzling ray of blue, as if a searchlight had been suddenly turned on me. The planet Jupiter had risen. Curiously enough an exactly parallel incident had taken place when I passed through the Red Sea from Chogo Ri, but on that occasion it was a crimson glare and the planet was Mars.

> Blue Mushtari strove with red Mirrikh
> which should be the master of the night,

as I wrote a few months later. The sensation was unfeignedly one of alarm which melted to wonder and rapture. Many years later I was indeed frightened for more than a moment of surprise by a quite normal celestial phenomenon. I was walking through unfrequented parts of Spain with a disciple. We were on a lonely road and night had fallen heavy and black. Suddenly a wedge of flaming scarlet stabbed my eyes. It increased rapidly in size and (perhaps therefore) seemed to be approaching us with frightful velocity. I remember to this hour my startled halt and the fierce gaze I fixed upon the enemy. I remember steeling myself to meet annihilation. But it was merely the full moon, rising through a gap in the mountains.

I reached Bombay on June 9th. It was my first experience of the low country of India in the hot season. I did not find it unbearable and I would go back and live a month for the sake of just one mango. The mango is a very strangely sensitive fruit. The perfect flavour is the private property of a very limited district, as in the case of champagne. The mangoes of Bengal are as inferior to those of Bombay as second-rate brands of 'boy' to the best vintages of Rheims. Those of Ceylon are like Asti Spumante.

I left Bombay the same day at half-past eleven. My first act was to go into the bathroom with which the best Indian trains are furnished and turn on the shower. Owing to the confined space, I was unable to beat the world's record for combined high and long jump! The carriage had been standing on a siding in the sun and the tank was full of scalding water. The worst of the journey was the smuts from the engine. I reached Calcutta at four o'clock on the morning of the eleventh and had breakfast and dinner with my old friend Thornton. The next day I left for Darjeeling. It is certainly one of the most impressive experiences that a railway can afford. One begins by jogging dully across the acrid plains of Bengal and then at Sara Ghat one finds oneself suddenly on the bank of the Ganges. I had seen the river before, higher up, and it is not particularly exciting, but here it flowed gigantically across a vast desolation. The time was sunset, the turbid water glowed with angry reds and oranges. There was an evil coppery sheen upon its waveless turmoil. Its breadth possessed a horror of its own; it was like a river of hell. Far away it reached to the right and left. There was nothing to break the horizon. It gave the desolate effect of ocean, but the boundlessness of the open sea suggests liberty. This river had told of barrenness and bitter bondage. The windless Ganges stank of putrefaction. It was not even the stench of rotting vegetation. It seemed as if it were the earth itself which was decaying. A more fantastic and more frightful sight I have never seen. We crossed this tartarean river in a steamer and the actual breadth may be estimated from the fact that dinner is served on board. It was a bad dinner, too; it completed the hellishness of the scene.

One lands. The eternal funeral march of the train is resumed. The heat of the night is stifling. The waning moon—when laggard she looms up above the rim of the planet—is almost as impotent as the stars to pierce the sultry haze of dust which chokes one. The coolest place on one's pillow is where one's head has cooled it. One tosses in blind torment. There is no question of seeking relief; one has an instinct that nothing will do any good. Perhaps one drops off to sleep for a few moments, and those, however few they be, are filled with aeons of delirious and demoniac dreams of suffocation dipped in despair.

Then suddenly comes dawn. The slow train stutters and stops. One is still an insect on the infernal plain, but there is a touch of coolness in the air which is not wholly the chill of death. The sticky sweat on one's body begins to evaporate and one's spirit to revive. There is a call to Chota Hazri. One steps out of the carriage. Good God!

Not many miles away across the level to the east rise thickly wooded slopes, a confused tangle both of hills (as it seems) and of trees, and behind them again, still higher heights of misty purple and green. And then—good God! Is it a mirage? Is it a phantom of hope created by courage from the chaos of nightmare? For there, above the highest hills, at an angle for which even one's experience of Chogo Ri has not prepared me, there stands the mass of Kangchenjunga, faint rose, faint blue, clear white, in the dawn.

On reaching the foot of the hills, one transfers to a toy railway, which climbs the six thousand odd feet to Darjeeling by means of complicated curves and even loops. One ascends rapidly; the view constantly changes; one begins to appreciate the geology of the country as a whole. In the foreground the tropical vegetation is superbly thick and rich. One is so relieved by the change to cool shade and a suggestion of moisture that it comes as a shock to remember that this is the Terai, one of the most deadly fever districts in the world. By lunchtime the character of the vegetation is already markedly altered.

The heavy tangle of the low country begins to give place to mountain sprightliness, but also the view tends to disappear altogether. One enters the region of almost eternal mist. The day is warm; and yet one is chilled to the bone. One is glad to come out on to an exposed ridge at Ghum and find the train begins to go down hill. It was the sign of the nearness of Darjeeling. I got off the train. With unfeigned satisfaction, I observed immediately that the current legends about the amazing powers of the coolies were true. The principal item of my baggage was a full-sized wardrobe trunk, but its contents were not mostly air, as usual with the American variety of this device. It contained comparatively few clothes; boots, axes, rifles, revolvers, scientific instruments and books made up the tale. I do not know how much it weighed, because the baggage clerk at Calcutta had asked me to bribe him with a rupee to declare it below the free allowance; but I should have been very sorry to have to do more than set it up on end unaided. A young girl coolie took it on her back, as I might have done a rucksack, and carried it at a good steady pace up the steep narrow paths to the Woodlands Hotel. I no longer disbelieved the story that a woman had once carried a full-sized upright piano all the way to Darjeeling from Siliguri on the plains.

Darjeeling is a standing or rather steaming example of official ineptitude. Sir Joseph Hooker, one of the few men of brains who have explored these parts, made an extended survey of the district and recommended Chumbi as a hill station. 'Oh well,' they say, 'Darjeeling is forty miles nearer than Chumbi. It will do rather better.' So Darjeeling it was. The difference happens to be that Chumbi has a rainfall of some forty inches a year; Darjeeling some two hundred odd. The town is perched on so steep a ridge that there is practically no level road anywhere and one gets from one house to another by staircases as steep as ladders.

The whole town stinks of mildew. One's room is covered with mildew afresh every morning.

India being the last hope of the unmarriageable shabby-genteel, Darjeeling is lousy with young ladies whose only idea of getting a husband is to practise the piano. In such a climate it is of course impossible to keep a piano in tune for five minutes, even if one could get it into that condition. The food itself is as mildewed as the maidens. The hotels extort outrageous rates which they attempt to justify by describing the meals in bad French. To be reminded of Paillard is adding insult to injury, for what the dishes are made of I never did discover. Almost the whole time I was there I was suffering from sore throat, arthritis, every plague that pertains to chronic soddenness. Do I like Darjeeling? I do not!

On the other hand, I found the heaven-born and the army as full of cordiality and comradeship as ever. As luck would have it, a new Worshipful Master was to be installed at the Lodge of Freemasons, so I went to the Jadugar-Khana and received a most brotherly welcome to the ceremony and banquet. There I met Sir Andrew Fraser, the lieutenant-governor, the commissioner, the deputy-commissioner, the Maharaja of Kuch Behar and all sorts of delightful people. Everyone was only too willing to help in every way.

I wanted to start for the mountain as early in the season as possible. We had reliable information as to what the weather on the higher peaks was likely to be. We had no Zojila to cross, no forty marches to the foot of the peak but twelve or fifteen at the outside. If we found it continuously bad, one could retreat into the valley and recuperate almost as one can in the Alps, for Tsetam is only about twelve thousand feet.

I had reconnoitred Kangchenjunga from England, thanks to the admirable photographs of every side of the mountain taken by Signor Vittorio Sella, who accompanied some man named Freshfield in a sort of old-world tour around the mountain. I had also a map by Professor Garwood,[1] the only trouble with which was that, not having been up the Yalung glacier himself, he had had to fill in the details from what he himself calls the unintelligible hieroglyphics of a native surveyor, who had not been there either.

It did not matter; but I was very much puzzled by the appearance of a peak where no peak should have been, according to the map.

The bandobast for this expedition was very different to that necessary for Chogo Ri, if one takes Darjeeling as the analogy to Srinigar, for there are no villages and supplies of men and food to be had anywhere on the way. I had to send on eight thousand pounds of food for the coolies to a depot as near the Yalung glacier as possible. The government transport officer, Major White, very kindly undertook to oversee this part of the transport and I left it entirely in his hands. Unfortunately, things did not go as well as could be desired. The coolies in this part of India compare very unfavourably with the Baltis and Kashmiris. They are Tibetan Buddhists with an elaborate priestcraft and system of atonement which persuaded early

Jesuit travellers that Satan had perpetrated—in advance!—a blasphemous parody on Christianity; for they found only trivial, formal distinctions between the religions of Lhasa and Rome. They are therefore accessible to emotion and acquire a sentimental devotion to people for whom they take a fancy. But they have no notion of self-respect, no loyalty, no honesty and no courage. Many of Major White's men deserted, either dumping their loads anywhere on the way or stealing them; and there was no means of controlling their actions. I prepared to expect trouble and was very glad that I had sent to Kashmir for three of our best men of 1902—Salama, Subhana and Ramzana.

My throat gave me such trouble that I decided to go to Calcutta for a few days—from July 13th to 20th. I had in any case to purchase a number of additional stores, as Guillarmod had 'economized'. The bandobast went on in charge of the manager of the Drum Druid Hotel, to which I had moved shortly after my arrival. He was an Italian named Righi. He offered to join the expedition as transport officer and I, relying on his knowledge of the language and the natives, thought it best to accept him, though his character was mean and suspicious and his sense of inferiority to white men manifested itself as a mixture of servility and insolence to them and of swaggering and bullying to the natives. These traits did not seem so important in Darjeeling, but I must blame myself for not foreseeing that his pin brain would entirely give way as soon as he got out of the world of waiters.

I was quite happy about the mountain. On July 9th, only twenty-six days after my arrival in Darjeeling, the rain stopped for a few minutes and I was able to get a good view of the mountain through my glasses. It entirely confirmed my theoretical conclusions; the highest peak was almost certainly easy to reach from the col to the west of it, and there could be no doubt that it was an easy walk up to that col by a couloir of sorts which I called Jacob's Rake (a 'portmanteau' of Jacob's ladder and Lord's rake). The word couloir does not quite describe it; the word 'rake' does, but I can't define rake. Anyone who wants to know what I mean must go to Cumberland. The foot of this rake is in a broad snow basin and the only possible question was whether that snow basin was reachable from the Yalung glacier. I have told already of my ability to describe accurately parts of a mountain which I cannot see. I judged the snow basin accessible. My clairvoyance turned out to be exactly correct.

But more promising even than the feasibility of the route was the appearance of the mountain. Despite the perpetual bad weather at Darjeeling, which made me feel absolutely hopeless, there was no new snow at all on the mountain. Only forty-five miles away, it had been continuous fine weather. I went down to Calcutta with a light heart. I had had good news too from Tartarin. He had persuaded a Swiss army officer, Alexis Pache, to join us. The other man of the party was named Reymond, who had had a fair amount of guideless experience on the Alps.

On the fifteenth I had a telegram from the doctor that he had been shipwrecked in the Red Sea. I might have known it! The three Swiss arrived on July 31st. I had got everything into such a forward state of preparation that we were able to start on August 8th. There was nothing to be done but to pack the baggage which the doctor seemed to have brought out, in the units which I had got ready for him. The doctor seemed to be suffering from ill-health from various trifling causes. He seemed a shade irritable and fussy. I suspect the cause was partly physical. His sense of his own importance was hurting him. Reymond I liked well enough; a quiet if rather dour man, who seemed to have a steady mind and common sense. But Pache won my heart from the moment I met him—a simple, unaffected, unassuming gentleman. He was perfectly aware of his own inexperience on mountains, and therefore in a state to acquire information by the use of his eyes rather than of his ears.

Everything went off without a hitch, except the affair of the depot. We learnt on August 6th that the coolies had dumped the food at Chabanjong, scarce eighteen miles north-west of Darjeeling, instead of at Jongri, thirty miles due north. This fact, among others, led to my deciding to approach Kang-chenjunga by way of the ridge which leads from Ghum practically directly to the head of a side valley through which a tributary of the Yalung Chu descends from the Kang La.

Our party consisted of five Europeans, three Kashmiris, the sirdar of the coolies, six personal servants and seventy-nine regular coolies. We left Darjeeling at ten sixteen on Tuesday, August 8th. The expedition had begun.

52

One can certainly reach the neighbourhood of Kangchenjunga with delightful comfort. Though the mountain is only forty-five miles from Darjeeling, as the crow flies, the way is round about. The stages from Ghum are Jorpakri 8½, Tonglu 18½, Sandakphu 33, Falut 45, Chabanjong 51. Up to this point there is an excellent riding path, while the first four stages have well-furnished dak baghlas.

Unpleasant features of the journey are two: one, the rain, and the other the leeches. I thought I knew a bit about rain— I didn't. At Akyab one puts one's head under water in the hope of getting out of the wet; at Darjeeling one's head is under water all the time. But on that ghastly ridge, I met a quality and quantity of bad weather that I had never dreamt of in my wildest nightmares. What follows sounds exaggerated. On getting into a dak baghla and standing stripped in front of a roaring fire, one expects to get dry. But no! the dampness seems to be metaphysical rather than physical. The mere removal of the manifestations of the elements of water do not leave one dry. But one used to obtain a sort of approximation to dryness by dint of fires; and of course we were provided with waterproofs specially constructed for that abominable climate. One morning I timed myself; after taking every precaution, it was eight and one half minutes from the door of the baghla before I was dripping wet. When I say 'dripping wet', I mean that the water was coursing freely inside my clothes. In most parts of the world rain falls, but on that accursed ridge it rises. It is blown up in sheets from the valley. It splashes on the rocks so as to give the effect of waterfalls upside down.

On the thirteenth, fourteenth and fifteenth, there were short spells of respite; otherwise, from the eighth to the twentieth it never slackened and outside the dak baghlas I was not dry, even partially, for a single second.

The leeches of the district are a most peculiar tribe. For some reason, they can only live within a very well-defined belt. Thus, I never saw a leech at Darjeeling, while at Lebong, some five hundred feet lower, they are a pest. The Terai is the haunt of some of the most tenacious of animals, but the leech has cleared them out completely. A single leech will kill a pony. It works its way up into a nostril and the pony simply bleeds to death. Hence the Anglo-Indian proverb, 'A jok's a jok [Hindustani for leech] but a jok up your nose is no joke.'

I witnessed a remarkable sight on the road to Chabanjong, which was here a *paka rasta* (that is, a road made by engineers as opposed to *kacha rasta,* a track made by habit or at most by very primitive methods) wide enough for carts to pass. I had squatted near the middle of the road as being the least damp and leech-infested spot available and got a pipe going by keeping the bowl under my waterproof. I lazily watched a leech wriggling up a blade of tall grass about fifteen inches high and smiled superiorily at its fatuity——though when I come to think of it, my own expedition was morally parallel; but the leech was not such a fool as I thought. Arrived at the top, it began to set the stalk swinging to and fro; after a few seconds it suddenly let go and flew clean across the road. The intelligence and ingenuity of the creature struck me as astonishing. (Legless animals are practically helpless on open ground. One can walk up to a king cobra on a smooth road and set one's heel on its head, as prophesied in Genesis, without much danger of being struck, and though it sees you coming, it is quite unable to escape. But give the same snake a little grass to flagellate and the eye can hardly follow its motion. It goes like a snipe.)

Coming back over the same ridge, I was on an open hillside running fast. It was raining downwards instead of upwards for once, and that but slightly. I heard a little noise, as if something had fallen on my hat, and took no notice. A few moments later I found that my hand was wet with blood, running fast, and looking down saw a leech on the back of it. How it managed to fall from the sky I don't know. I have seen leeches up to seven inches long; and there seems hardly any limit to the amount of blood they can assimilate. I heard of a gorged leech weighing nearly two pounds and I believe it without effort.

Another strange sight in these parts is the sheep. Tartarin, still proud of his haggis, invented wonderful theories to explain the fact that they are muzzled. However, they are not *moutons enragés;* the muzzle is to prevent them from poisoning themselves with wild aconite.

The scenery along the whole of this ridge is extraordinarily grand, so far as the mist permits one to see anything. Some of the Himalayan trees are superb. But the prevailing vegetation is the rhododendron, a plant which has little in common with its English cousin. It grows to a height of fifteen feet or more and the stems are often as thick as a man's thigh. It grows in unbroken forests and the worst Mexican chaparral I ever saw was not worse to have to cut one's way through.

At Chabanjong the road stops and I sent back my horse. Thence a shepherd's track leads along the ridge. On the whole it was very good walking.

We had already found trouble with our own coolies. To begin with, the police had caught me up at Jorpakri and arrested one of them for some petty offence—he had joined us for more reasons than one. Six of the men deserted in the early part of the march. It was a small percentage and they had evidently never had any intention of earning their advances. Later, when I had to go on ahead, five men deserted Pache, whom I had to leave in charge. They were probably scared by superstitious fears. Pache could not talk to them and did not know how to encourage them.

After leaving Chabanjong it was impossible to tell exactly where one was on the ridge. The *paros* have names, but I could never discover that they applied to anything; it was all rain and rhododendra. There is a place called Nego Cave which I hoped was a cave where I could shelter from the rain for a few hours, but nobody seemed to know where it was and I never found out. I had actually to rest a day in this abominable place, as the official permit for our party to enter Nepal had not arrived; but it did so during the day and on the eighteenth came a very long march of something like eight hours of actual going. During the latter part of the march the path dips suddenly and one descends some three thousand feet into a valley.

Well do I remember this camp Gamotang! Apart from the flora and fauna, the last two days might have been spent on the Welsh mountains, but the descent to Gamotang was like stepping into fairyland. There are certain places—Sonamarg in Kashmir is one of them—which possess the quality of soft brilliance quite unearthly. There is really nothing to distinguish them from a hundred other spots in the neighbourhood, yet they stand out; as a genius does from a hundred other men in evening dress. I find these phenomena quite as real as any others and I feel impelled to seek an explanation.

Assuming the existence of inhabitants imperceptible by our grosser senses, the problem presents no difficulty. One of a row of similar houses is often quite different from its neighbours, perhaps on account of the loving care and pride of its chatelaine. When I see an analogous phenomenon in scenery, I cannot blame myself if a similar explanation comes to my mind.

The weather was already noticeably better than at Darjeeling. It did not begin to rain till eight or ten in the morning every day.

The partial failure of the bandobast kept us a day at Gamotang. There was in any case no great hurry. I was glad of every opportunity to acquire the affection of the men. I was careful not to overwork them. I gave a prize to the first three men to come into camp every day and those who had come in first three times had their pay permanently raised. I made friends with them, too, by sitting with them round the camp fire and exchanging songs and stories. On the other hand, I made it clear that I would tolerate no nonsense. They responded for the most part very well. I never had any trouble in all my wanderings with natives, servants, dogs and women. The secret is that I am really unconscious of superiority and treat all alike with absolute respect and affection; at the same time I maintain the practical relations between myself and others very strictly indeed.

It is the fable of the belly and the members. It is absurd for one speck of protoplasm to insist on its social superiority to another speck, but equally absurd for one cell to want to do the work of another. There is another point, admirably stated by Wilkie Collins. Count Fosco says that the way to manage women is 'never to accept a provocation from a woman's hands. It holds with animals, it holds with children and it holds with women, who are nothing but children grown up. Quiet resolution is the one quality the animals, the children and the women all fail in. If they can once shake this superior quality in their master, they get the better of HIM. If they can never succeed in disturbing it, he gets the better of THEM.'

I make it an absolute rule to be imperturbable, to impress people with the idea that it is impossible to avoid doing what I have done. I never try to arouse enthusiasm. I never bribe, I never threaten, but I identify my purpose with destiny and I administer reward and punishment unsparingly and impersonally.

The coolies began to be very fond of me, not only because of my good comradeship and my cheerful calm and confidence, but because they were subconsciously relieved by my conduct from their personal demons of fear, jealousy, desire and the like. They became unconsciously aware that they were parts of a machine. As long as they did their duty, there was absolutely nothing to worry about. Most people suffer all their lives from subconscious irritation; due to what the Hindus call Ahamkara, the ego-making faculty. The idea of self is a continual torment and though I was still far from having got rid of this idea completely, I was pretty free of it in practice in matters where my responsibility was extensive. I had begun to understand how to work 'without lust of result'.

Unfortunately, Tartarin and Righi were undoing my web as fast as I wove it. Righi was a low-class Italian, who ran his hotel by hectoring the men under him. Finding himself for the first time in his life in a position of real responsibility, and without the background of an external authority to which he could appeal to enforce his orders, he was utterly at sea. On one occasion he actually threatened a disobedient coolie with his kukri and revolver, and the man, knowing he would not dare to use them, laughed in his face. The natives despised him as a weak man, which is the worst thing that can befall anyone that has anything to do with them.

Tartarin too, though cheerful and genial, had forgotten the lesson of 1902. He was fussy and helpless. On one occasion he actually tried to bribe a man with boots and claws to do his ordinary duty. As long as I was with the main body, these things didn't matter. Nobody dared to disobey the Bara Sahib. A moment's hesitation in complying with any order of mine and they saw a look in my eyes which removed the inhibition. They knew that I would not scold or wheedle, but had a strong suspicion that I might strike a man dead without warning; at the same time they knew that I would never give an unreasonable order and that my active sympathy with the slightest discomfort of any one of them was as quick as my insight to detect and deal with malingering or any other attempt to pull my leg.

From Gamotang one has to climb to the Chumbab La—about four hours' march. Then one skirts the slopes of the Kang La and descends to the branch valley of the Yalung Chu. I found a great block of quartz three and one half hours beyond the pass and pitched camp. The doctor arrived late—eight thirty. He had had some trouble with the coolies, but they were safely camped some short distance above.

The next day was fearfully wet. There is another little pass to cross, an hour beyond the quartz block; two and a half hours more took me down the valley to a camp near Tseram, which is a group of huts on the main stream a couple of miles below the snout of the Yalung glacier. I avoided camping in Tseram itself, on the general principle of having nothing to do with natives. The Dewan of Nepal was sending an officer to superintend our journey. I should perhaps have mentioned before that England has a special treaty with Nepal, one of its terms to the effect that no foreigners are to enter the dewan's dominions. He knew that the most harmless of Europeans is the herald of disaster to any independent country. Where the white man sets his foot, the grass of freedom and the flower of good faith are trampled into the mire of vice and commercialism.

But in the present instance our route touched only this one tiny outlying hamlet of Tseram and permission had been obtained without difficulty for us to pass. At the same time, the dewan was going to have a man on the spot to see that we did not maltreat and corrupt the natives as we have done in every other part of the globe in which our impulses of greed and tyranny have seen a possibility of satisfaction.

I saw no reason for waiting for the arrival of the dewan's 'guide' and, leaving a man with a message for him, continued the advance.

I took only a very small party and left Pache in command. He was to wait until the arrival of the main body of the coolies, while I went on the glacier to reconnoitre. I wanted to establish the main camp as high as possible, but of course I did not know whether I might not have to retrace my steps. The glacier stream might prove uncrossable. I would make sure that the whole party could reach the glacier without difficulty.

I left the camp at six a.m. on the twenty-first. I was now in really mountainous country. The valley was gorgeously wild, it glowed with rich bright grass and masses of marvellous flowers. There was an admirable track. The day was fine and I had views of both Little and Big Kabru (21,290 and 24,015 feet respectively) but Kangchenjunga itself was hidden in clouds. I have rarely enjoyed a mountain walk so thoroughly and my heart was uplifted by the excellence of our prospects.

It sang within me. I was already at fourteen or fifteen thousand feet, less than a fortnight out from the base, in perfect physical condition, not an ounce of my reserve of strength yet called upon; a perfectly clear course to the peak in front of me, the mountain scarce five miles away, the weather looking better all the time, and none of the extremes of temperature which had been so frightful on Chogo Ri. No sign that wind was likely to give any trouble. In short, not one dark spot upon the horizon.

Camp 2, though no place for a golf course, as the game is at present played, possesses the great advantage of being a perfect Pisgah. The summit of Kangchenjunga is only two miles away and I am able to see almost the whole of the debatable ground which my reconnaissance from above Darjeeling had denied me. I climbed to a short distance above the camp: the last doubt disappeared. The level glacier stretched less than a mile away. Thence rose a ridge covered by steep glacier except at its eastern edge, where there was a patch of bare rock with scarcely any interruption from ice. This rock was cut away on its right by a terrific precipice, sheer to the lower glacier, but there was no reason why anyone should fall off. The rocks were of the character—easy slabs—of those of the Eiger above the little Scheideck, the precipice being on the right hand instead of on the left. The slabs ended in a level space of snow jutting beyond the glacier above, and therefore safe from any possible avalanche. The place would make an admirable camp.

Thence, one could work a way to the west; and, avoiding a patch of séracs, ascend steep slopes of ice (covered at present by snow) which led directly to the great snow basin which lies, as one may say, in the embrace of Kangchenjunga. These slopes were the critical point of the passage. I intended to fix a long knotted rope at the top, if necessary, to serve as handhold for the coolies, it being now certain that we could establish our main camp at the foot of Jacob's Rake. Certain, that is, bar the interference of absolute perversity.

The following day showed me that such perversity was only too likely to put a spoke in the wheel. The arrangement was that I was to find my way to Camp 3, which I had already been able to choose through my glasses. I left Tartarin and Reymond in charge of the bulk of the coolies, having pointed out to them the best way across the glacier. It was more or less intricate going compared with Piccadilly, but it was certainly less trouble than an average march on the Baltoro. My object in going ahead was merely to make sure that Camp 3 was as favourable as it looked from a distance. It was. There was a broad level plateau of loose stones marked by a big boulder, which I called Pioneer Boulder, for a variety of reasons, all referring ironically to 'Pioneer Peak'. This plateau was perhaps seven hundred to a thousand feet above the glacier.

I must here remark that I cannot pretend to any accuracy about either heights or distances. Tartarin was in charge of the surveying and I do not know whether he took proper observations at all. All I can say is that Professor Garwood's map is seriously wrong in many important points. I could do little more than make shots at my position by dead reckoning. I settled down quite comfortably at Camp 3 and sent a man down to find the main body and tell them it was all right, and they were to come up. Most unfortunately, it was misty. I could not see what had happened. And if I had been able to, I might almost have doubted my eyes. The coolies were coming —Oh ho! oh ho!—in a long circular route round the head of the glacier, for no reason at all. The weather cleared towards evening and there they were, within shouting distance, within three quarters of an hour's easy going for the slowest men, up excellent slopes on firm rocky ground.

To my amazement, I saw the doctor preparing to pitch camp. It was inexplicable imbecility. Shouts produced no effect and there was nothing for it but for me to go down. He had chosen a bivouac on bare ice, where there was hardly sufficient level ground to pitch the tents, but it was too late to pack up again, so I had to make the best of it. I asked him the reason for his extraordinary conduct. He replied that there was a rumour that I had broken my leg on a moraine. This was as antecedently unlikely as anything could possibly be; and anyhow he could see perfectly well with his own eyes that I had done nothing of the sort; and thirdly, if I had done it, all the more reason for coming to my assistance. I began to think there was something seriously wrong with the man.

On the top of this, there was bad news from the rearguard. Righi sent up bitterly quarrelsome messages. His antics had made all sorts of trouble with the coolies, who were at one time in open revolt. Pache managed to get them into good humour again. He was a gentleman; he understood the oriental mind instinctively. He was, in fact, making extremely good. As soon as he saw that Righi was half insane with the fear that comes to people of his class in the absence of a chattering herd of his fellows, and in the presence of the grandeur of nature, he assumed moral charge of him. The difficulties with the rearguard disappeared immediately. Unfortunately, I did not understand at the time what was happening, or I should have gone down and sent Righi back to his kitchen. Pache himself did not realize his own importance and took it upon himself to come up. The moment his back was turned, Righi became insane.

Everyone had passed a most uncomfortable night at the absurd bivouac. I decided to go no further than Camp 3 the next day. Tartarin was absolutely astonished that the men with whom he had been having such trouble behaved quite simply and naturally as soon as I was on the spot. He claimed that they had positively refused to go further, but they picked up their loads and strolled cheerfully up the slopes without so much as a word of admonition. Not understanding the secret of my power, though he had seen it exercised so often by Eckenstein and myself, he imagined that I must be terrorizing the men by threats and beatings. In point of fact, I never struck a man during the entire expedition, save on one occasion to be described presently.

Camp 3 was extremely pleasant. It afforded magnificent views in every direction and one had one's choice of sun or shade. I spent the day in taking advantage of the amenities of the situation. I took pains to fix up an excellent shelter for the men by means of large tarpaulins, and saw to their comfort in every way. We had even the advantage of song, for the camp was a haunt of small birds. Its height cannot have been far short of eighteen thousand feet.

It was urgent that the march to Camp 4 should be started at the earliest glimmer of light, for though the route lay almost entirely over rock, there were a few short snow passages which would become dangerous after sunrise, and the hanging glacier on our left might conceivably discharge some of its superfluous snow across one or two points of the route. I explained these points carefully to the men, who were for the most part quite intelligent enough to understand. Moreover, they were already aware of the general principles, a number of them having already travelled, if not on glaciers, at least on winter snow. They were eager to start; but Tartarin deliberately hindered them. I had awakened at three o'clock and got them off by six. It had not been a cold night, none of the men showed any signs of suffering or made any complaint, but the doctor said that they ought to be allowed to warm themselves thoroughly in the sun before starting. He suggested that the march should begin at about eleven o'clock. These were

the words of sheer insanity. Even on Chogo Ri, where the
nights were really cold, no such nonsense had ever been suggested.

I led at once on to the glacier. There was no difficulty of any
sort; the snow being in excellent condition, it merely required a little scraping and stamping. But at the point where
it becomes necessary to take the rocks on the right so as not
to be under a small patch of séracs, the slope is in the direction of the tremendous precipice previously described. It was
there that I gave an exhibition of glissading. I do not think
the men would have been afraid at all if the excited shouts
and gesticulations of Reymond and the doctor had not demoralized them. These celebrated climbers were themselves
actually afraid for their own skins. And this, if you please,
on a slope down which I could glissade head first! Having
got the men across, we proceeded up the rocky slopes. I must
confess that here I had misjudged the difficulty.

I had expected to find quite easy walking, but there were a
few passages where it amounted to scrambling from the point
of view of a loaded man. I decided to arrange for a fixed
rope as a measure of safety, it being my plan to send the
picked coolies up and down regularly to bring up supplies as
they were needed. In the meantime, the men behaved magnificently, laughing and joking and giving each other a helping
hand whenever required. I posted the Kashmiris and the
other personal servants at the *mauvais pas,* but there was no
hint of any real danger.

Camp 4 is at the top of this rocky slope on a level ridge,
level enough, but not as broad as I could have wished. There
was, however, a certain amount of natural shelter afforded by
rocks and I was able to construct a fairly comfortable place
for the night. There was a better camp three hours higher; but
the weather, after a fine morning, had begun to look bad and
the snow was in bad condition. The men, too, though perfectly happy, were most of them very tired, and some of them
knocked over by what they supposed to be mountain sickness—symptoms of exhaustion, headache, pains in the abdomen, dizziness and so forth. I knew what the trouble was and
went round to the sufferers and dropped a little atropine into
their eyes. Half an hour later they were all perfectly restored.
The alarming symptoms were all due to the glare.

I sent down to Pache to come up to Camp 3 as better in
every way than Camp 2. I asked Tartarin and Reymond if they
had any messages to send. They were too exhausted to reply to

their names. I was utterly bewildered. The previous day had been a bare hour, and the march to Camp 4 perfectly easy and by no means long or trying for men without loads. I myself, though I had borne the burden and heat of the day more than anyone, was as fresh as paint and as fit as a fiddle. I had never felt better in my life. I was in perfect condition in every respect. I spent the afternoon nursing the invalids.

Tartarin recovered by the next morning sufficiently to curse. I could not imagine what his grievance was and cannot imagine it now. The most charitable explanation of his conduct that I can give it that he was mentally upset, partly no doubt due to psychical distress, and to some form of heat stroke. I have always been satanically happy in the hottest sunshine, but the slopes of Kangchenjunga on a fine day at noon were near my limit. Both the doctor and Reymond were unquestionably very ill. It was impossible to think of going on to the next camp that day. We rested accordingly. Late in the day, to my surprise, Pache arrived with a number of coolies. I had asked him to send up the sirdar and one other man. I wanted to give Nanga personal instructions about the management of his men. It had been no part of my plan for any of the others to come beyond Camp 3. I wanted to make Camp 3 the base until we found a good place on the snow basin above. The arrival of Pache and his men overcrowded Camp 4.

The root of the trouble, apart from any ill-feeling, was that none of my companions (except Pache) understood that I expected them to keep their word. I had arranged a plan, taking into consideration all sorts of circumstances, the importance of which they did not understand and others of which they did not even know, and they did not realize that to deviate from my instructions in any way might be disastrous. Their disobedience having resulted in things going wrong, they proceeded to blame me. Righi had refused point blank to send Nanga on my express command; he had failed to send up any supplies, so that we were absolutely out of petroleum and short of food, both for ourselves and for our men.

Pache reported that some of the men had deserted. It was never cleared up why they should have done so. But one of them, in disobedience to orders, had gone off by himself—I never discovered exactly where—and had fallen and been killed. This man, it was said, was carrying Pache's sleeping valise. This at least was certain, that the valise was missing.

An accident being alleged, I sent down the doctor on the following morning to make an inquiry into the matter, and also to send up supplies of food and fuel which we needed urgently. Pache told me that Righi was deliberately withholding food from us. His conduct was murderously criminal, if only because we might have been prevented by bad weather from descending in the last resort.

That afternoon Reymond and I made a little excursion up the slopes. We found that the snow was not as bad as might have been expected, and the gradients were so easy and the glacier so free from ice fall that there would be no danger for a prudently conducted party, even when the snow was soft.

On this slope of Kangchenjunga one occasionally meets a condition of snow which I have never seen elsewhere. Rain or sleet blows against the face of the mountain and is frozen as it touches. The result is to produce a kind of network of ice; a frozen drop serves as a nucleus from which radiate fine filaments of ice in every direction. It is like a spider's web in three dimensions. A cubic foot of network would thus be almost entirely composed of air; the ice in it, if compact, would hardly be bigger than a tennis ball, perhaps much less. With the advance of the evening, the rain turns to snow; and in the morning it may be that the network is covered to a depth of several inches. The temperature possibly rises a few degrees and the surface becomes wet. It then freezes again and forms a hard crust. Approaching a slope of this kind, it seems perfectly good névé. One strikes it with one's axe and the entire structure disintegrates. In front of one is a hole as big as a cottage and as the solid slope disappears, one hears the tinkle of falling ice. It is a most astonishing and disconcerting phenomenon.

During the whole time that I was on the mountain, I experienced no high wind and no unpleasant cold. But the heat of the day was certainly very severe. My skin had gradually become inured to the sun. I had not been burnt painfully in ten years. I simply browned quietly and pleasantly. But on Kangchenjunga it got me—not badly enough to cause sores—but enough to make the skin somewhat painful and brittle. Here was another reason for starting early in the day and reaching camp, if possible, by noon at the latest.

On the nineteenth, having dispatched Tartarin to the rear, Reymond, Pache and myself went on with our small party. The doctor was, of course, to make sure of sending up supplies and Pache's valise. We reached Camp 5 in about three hours. It was situated on a little snowy hump below a small peak on the ridge. We intended to make our way to the path between this peak and the main spur. The slopes were rather steep in one or two places, but quite without danger, as they eased off a short distance below (about two hundred and fifty feet) to a practically level part of the glacier. I should, in fact, have preferred to go straight up them instead of making the detour by the rocks on the edge of the big precipice, had it not been that a small patch of sérac overhung them.

No valise arrived for Pache that night, and no petrol or rations. We were accordingly obliged to rest the next day. I had given Pache my eiderdown sleeping-bag and one of my blankets. He was thus quite comfortable physically; but he was, of course, anxious about his effects. All his spare boots, clothes etc. were in the missing bag, and all his private papers.

During the day a few provisions arrived, but no rations for the men, and no petrol. I sent back one of the men with urgent orders and several others to assist in carrying the supplies. (Also because we could not feed them where we were.) I wrote a second letter to Tartarin the same day; a man arrived at last with the petrol. In this letter which was signed by Pache as well as myself, the blame for the failure of the bandobast was given entirely to Righi.

It seems to me and to Pache also that the shortage of food is the fault of M. Righi who refused to send Nanga when Pache told him to do so. This disobedience, which has come so near to involving us in disaster, must not be repeated. All the loads should be sent to Camp 3 except those which are under shelter. Righi must be responsible for carrying this out. For yourself, you should join us as soon as you can with at least ten loads of sattu and Nanga to help us. The next three days will be the crisis of the expedition.

With cordial friendship, yours.

There was no difficulty whatever in carrying out these perfectly simple, normal instructions.

Camp 5 is at the height of twenty to twenty-one thousand feet and certainly not more than two to three thousand feet above Camp 3. We had taken the first ascent very easily, it having been transformed into a regular snow track with immense steps made solid by repeated regelation. It might be called two hours' easy going. The doctor had recovered his health and his good humour, and we had none of us a moment's doubt that he would put the fear of God into Righi and carry out the above instructions promptly and efficiently.

On Thursday, August 31st, I started up the slopes with six men and a perfectly light heart. The problem was, of course, how to get the coolies up with the minimum of trouble. I sent Salama ahead with an axe to make big steps, and I put my gang of four men with axes and shovels on a rope. Their job was to clear away all loose snow and to enlarge the steps made by Salama so that the way up the mountain should be literally a staircase of the easiest kind. Their leader was a man named Gali. I remained close to him throughout so that if by any chance he fell I could catch him.

I would not rope myself, so as to be able to go to the rescue instantly in case Salama got tired or came to a passage too difficult for him. We advanced very rapidly. We were certainly over twenty-one thousand and possibly over twenty-two thousand feet. There were no symptoms of the slightest deficiency of physical energy on the part of anyone. I have never seen a man ply an ice-axe faster than Salama did that day. I was, of course, very carefully on the lookout for the slightest tendency on the part of the snow to slip.

We had reached a shallow couloir. Reymond and Salama had got some distance ahead of the coolies. Some of the chips of ice dislodged by their step-cutting were sliding down in our direction and they began to carry some of the surface with them. I was warned by the gentle purring hiss, rather like a tea kettle beginning to sing, which tells one that loose snow is beginning to move. Gali saw the little avalanche coming towards him, was frightened and fell out of his steps. I caught him, put him back and hastily anchored the rope to a wedged axe. But the man had completely lost his nerve and by the operation of that instinct which makes a drowning man throw up his hands, began to do the one thing that could possibly have brought him to harm—to untie himself from the rope. I ordered him to desist, but he was quite hysterical, uttered senseless cries and took no notice. There was only one thing to do to save him from the consequences of his suicidal actions, and that was to make him more afraid of me than he was of the mountain; so I reached out and caught him a whack with my axe. It pulled him together immediately and prevented his panic communicating itself to the other men. Things then went on all right.

Some of the slopes were really very bad; deep soft snow on ice. One short patch was at an angle of fifty degrees. It was a question of fixing a rope or finding a new route to the left, which I did not want to do as I was in doubt about the glacier above. There were some séracs which might or might not be stable. We went down to Camp 5 without further adventure, but the morale of the men had been shaken by the incident of the toy avalanche. Their imaginations got out of hand. They began to talk nonsense about the demons of Kangchenjunga and magnified the toy avalanche and Gali's slip and wallop to the wildest fantasies. During the night some of them slipped away and went down to Camp 3.

On September 1st we renewed the assault. Reymond, Pache and Salama went up the slopes on the rope and got over the bad patch. They were so much encouraged by their success that they went out of sight and hearing, contrary to my instructions. I needed them to help the three coolies with loads over the bad part. They preferred to leave the whole responsibility to me, but I could not bring three heavily loaded men up such slopes without assistance, and there was nothing to do but await their return. In the meantime, I saw to my surprise that a large party had arrived at Camp 5. When I got down I found that Tartarin's hysteria and Righi's malignant stupidity had created yet another muddle.

They had arrived at the camp, bringing with them some seventeen or twenty coolies, and they had not brought any of the things of which we stood in such need. Their behaviour was utterly unintelligible. The doctor did not seem to know what he was saying; his remarks were merely confusedly irritated. He did not seem to be able to answer any of my questions or give any explanation of what had happened in the past. His one idea was to hold a durbar and have himself elected leader in my place. There was no provision in our agreement for any such folly. He pointed out that it was merely a scrap of paper. When the others arrived, an excited argument began. There was no suggestion that I had acted improperly in any way. From first to last it was merely the feeling of foreigners against being bossed by an Englishman. The same thing had happened with Pfannl on Chogo Ri.

On the present occasion, however, the Englishman was in a minority of one. Fortunately I had never heard that a fact of that sort makes any difference to an Englishman. I did my best to reason with them and quiet them, like the naughty children they were. Reymond had nothing to complain of and was actively friendly.

Indeed, I had much more to worry me than the nonsense of Tartarin and Righi. They had brought up all these men without any provisions for food or shelter and it was now late in the day. The snow was in an absolutely unsafe condition and though I had chosen the route so as to minimize the danger, it was absolutely criminal to send men down. But the mutineers were utterly insensible to the voice of reason. I told the coolies that since they could not stay at Camp 5, the best thing they could do was to shelter under the rocks at Camp 4, and they went off and did so. I warned the mutineers that they would certainly be killed if they tried to go down that night; it was perhaps more or less right for coolies, but for THEM—I knew only too well the extent of Tartarin's ingenuity in producing accidents out of the most apparently unpromising material. They stormed all the more. I ought to have broken the doctor's leg with an axe, but I was too young to take such a responsibility. It would have been hard to prove afterwards that I had saved him by so doing.

To my horror, I found that Pache wanted to go down with them. The blackguards had not even had the decency to bring up his valise. I implored him to wait till the morning. I told him he could have the whole of my sleeping kit. But nothing would move him. I explained the situation, but I suppose he could not believe that I was telling the literal truth when I said that Guillarmod was at the best of times a dangerous imbecile on mountains, and that now he had developed into a dangerous maniac.[1] I shook hands with him with a breaking heart, for I had got very fond of the man, and my last words were, 'Don't go: I shall never see you again. You'll be a dead man in ten minutes.' I had miscalculated once more; a quarter of an hour later he was still alive.

Less than half an hour later, Reymond and I heard frantic cries. No words could be distinguished, but the voices were those of Tartarin and Righi. Reymond proposed going to the rescue at once, but it was now nearly dark and there was nobody to send, owing to Righi's having stripped us of men. There was, furthermore, no indication as to why they were yelling. They had been yelling all day. Reymond had not yet taken his boots off. He said he would go and see if he could see what was the matter and call me if my assistance were required. He went off and did not return or call. So I went to sleep and rose the next morning at earliest dawn and went to investigate.

The task was easy. About fifteen minutes below Camp 5 the track had been carried away over a width of twenty feet (seven short paces). The angle of the slope was roughly twenty degrees (limits of error twenty-five degrees and twelve degrees). The avalanche had stopped two hundred and fifty feet below, and at this point it was from forty to sixty feet in width; that is to say, it was an absolutely trivial avalanche. A single man could have ridden it head first without the slightest risk of hurting himself. The width of the avalanche (and other signs) showed that six men on a 120-foot rope had been walking on each other's heels, the rope being festooned so as to be worse than useless. A man struggling in a loose snow avalanche has a fair chance of getting to the top, but if every time he does so he is jerked away by the rope, it will be the greatest piece of luck if he is not killed. Tartarin, who should have been the last man on a descent in order to watch the others, to see that the rope was kept stretched, and to check any slip at the outset, was leading.

Here is Righi's account of the accident.

> Suddenly the four men above us began to slide; we hoped they would be able to stop themselves, but the slope was too steep. They swept past us like lightning. The doctor and I did the best we could to stop them, but in vain; for, as they rushed downwards, they started an avalanche (the snow being in such a moist condition from the afternoon sun, and easily moved). I was torn away from my anchor, head downwards, the doctor vainly calling to me to hang on as we might be able to stop the others. I was pulled down in what seemed a whirlwind of snow. I remember nothing during the fall. The doctor followed and fell farther down. I came to a few minutes after, hearing the doctor calling and telling me to get up. I could not do so, being pinned down on one side by the rope which was straight into the avalanche, and on the other I was keeping the doctor from falling farther down the slope. Had he been killed by the fall, I should have been helpless and most likely would have been frozen where I lay.

It is noteworthy that some seventeen coolies without ropes, axes, boots, claws and Tartarin, had crossed the fatal spot quite safely.

I found these men perfectly happy. They had taken my advice and passed the night under the rocks by Camp 4. I slowly descended, they following at a short distance. Presently I came to a place where the snow had slipped off the glacier ice for some distance. The angle was decidedly steep, and though I was able to cross it easily enough in my claws, it would not do for the coolies; so I called to them to go higher up over the glacier. But they were afraid to do this. They said they wanted to follow me, which they did, after enlarging my steps with an axe. At the time, I had no doubt that this place was the scene of the accident, if there had been one, of which I was not sure. Anyhow, I could not see how even Tartarin could have come to grief on so easy and safe a slope as the other. But on arrival at Camp 3 I was able to understand what had happened. Thanks to my habits of accuracy, I had taken careful measurements.

Pache and three of my best coolies had been killed. Tartarin was badly bruised, and thought his spine was damaged. The accident had brought him completely to his senses. He realized that I had been right all along, and was appalled by the prospects of returning to Switzerland and meeting Pache's mother.

Righi, on the other hand, showed only the more what an ill-conditioned cur he was. He had not been hurt at all badly, but his ribs were slightly bruised; he claimed that he had 'rupture of the heart', and spent his time moaning and bellowing. That his sufferings were mostly pure funk was evident from the fact that he forgot all about them directly he was engaged in conversation.

I ought to have been much angrier than I was, for the conduct of the mutineers amounted to manslaughter. By breaking their agreement, they had assumed full responsibility. It was impossible for me to continue with the expedition. My authority had been set at nought, and I would not risk any man's life. Eckenstein had made it the first point of mountaineering that the proper measures invariably reduced the risk of accident to nothing. They wanted me to go on. Righi himself said that the coolies believed the demon of Kangchenjunga was propitiated with the sacrifice of the five men—one for each peak—and would go on in future without fear. He had a little image given him by a Tibetan lama. This had saved his life. He never took any important step without consulting it, and it had now told him that we could climb the mountain without difficulty. Like Queen Victoria on a celebrated occasion, I was not amused.

As a matter of fact, the coolies had been very much demoralized by the accident. Some blame to them: I told Righi, as transport officer, to bring down my belongings from Camp 5. He parleyed with them, gave it up as hopeless, and turned it over to me. I told the sirdar to send up men at once to help Salama and Bahadur Singh, who were still at Camp 5. He made no difficulty and sent up, not two men, but twelve. They brought everything. I made the necessary arrangements about digging out the corpses and building them a commemorative cairn, which was done. The next day, September 3rd, I left, and reached Darjeeling on Friday.

Here I was faced by an extraordinary circumstance, illustrating the fact that when men lose their heads on mountains they lose them very completely. The money of the expedition was banked against the signature of either myself or Guillarmod. He had written to the manager to ask him to refuse to honour my signature! The bank thought he must be out of his mind, and advised me to draw the whole of the amount so as to be sure that it would be used to pay the coolies the sums due to them. This I did. On the twentieth the others arrived. I had all the amounts in proper order. I immediately paid the men what was due, with a reasonable amount of backsheesh. In view of Tartarin's extraordinary behaviour about money, I was on my guard. He was anxious not to come to a settlement. I, on the other hand, had no further business in Darjeeling, and I naturally asked him to sign a release, which he did.

> Sept. 20, 1905. Les comptes de l'expédition étant définitivement réglés le 20 sept. 1905, nous déclarons que toute réclamation après cette date, sera nulle. La somme des compensations dues aux parents des morts sera payée par la caisse de l'expédition.
>
> D. J. JACOT GUILLARMOD

He became very friendly and asked me to lend him or give him money. My account of the accident having been fairly frank, there was some question of a public inquiry.

I wrote accounts of the expedition for the *Pioneer* of India and the *Daily Mail* of London, and I republished them later in *Vanity Fair*. I used these articles to attack the English Alpine Club. Every incident served for the occasion of some gibe, sarcasm, insult or irony. I had no personal motive, of course. I wished to hold up to ridicule and contempt the set of old women who were knocking the sport on the head by intriguing against any climbers who were not simply polite people pulled up peaks by peasants and proud of it at that. The Alpine Club has done its best to ignore Himalayan expeditions, as it did to burke every ascent by guideless climbers in the Alps.

The lessons of the Kangchenjunga expedition were not learnt; so we hear in 1922 the old idiocy that coolies should not start till it is quite warm. The Everest party repeated the fatal fatuity of the doctor, by putting seven men on one rope, and that without knowing the use of the rope, so that one fall of one man must inevitably drag down the others. When I heard the composition of the Everest party and its plans, I prepared an article to warn them they were violating every principle of common sense, and could only meet with further failure and disaster. I foretold exactly what would happen, except that I heartily hoped that the Englishmen would be killed and their coolies escape by some miracle.

It was not to be. They made the mistake against which I had warned them; they had precisely the same kind of accident as in 1905 that resulted from the mutinous violation of my orders; but, just as the doctor and Righi had escaped with their worthless lives, to go about the world with the manslaughter of their comrades on their consciences, so also it happened in 1922.

But the London press refused to publish my article. One editor told me that it was a shame to 'crab' the expedition, and that my warnings would give pain to the relations of the party! No, better wait until the accident had happened, and then it would be interesting to point out why it had happened. Of course that is the journalistic point of view. Disasters should not be prevented. Heaven forbid! We should rather encourage battle, murder and sudden death. Our business is to make the splash. This psychology is one of my reasons for holding the press in horror. I do not believe in restrictions on business enterprise, but it really ought to be made impossible that it should be to anyone's interest to bring about a European war.

On the twenty-third Guillarmod came to see me and ask me to say no more in the public press, as far as he was concerned. On the twenty-fourth we discussed the whole matter. He admitted that he had been in the wrong and excused himself (on the ground of ill-health and nervousness) for his behaviour. I thought I knew him; he was simply a fool but incapable of malice or treachery. On the twenty-fifth he and Righi made a violent attack on me in the columns of a newspaper, but 'out of their own mouths'! Their admission proved my case. In particular, they blamed the coolies, so I had to write to the paper, 'I would most especially call attention to the repeated complaints against the coolies as evidence of incapacity to manage them, and emphasize my own testimony to their steadiness, capacity and goodwill.'

Guillarmod's overtures had been intended merely to give them time to strike. 'Cet animal est très méchant; quand on l'attaque il se défend.' I hit back and cut Guillarmod publicly on the twenty-sixth. On the twenty-seventh I received the following amazing letter.

27.ix.05
Lord Boleskine,

Vos procédés financiers puent l'escroc à plein nez & font honneur à la noblesse irlandaise.

Faire signer un papier par lequel je déclare ne plus rien réclamer alors que vous savez pertinemment que j'oublie plusieurs dépenses est un acte aussi honnête que l'hospitalité écossaise (haggis).

Je comprends maintenant les raisons qui vous font rechercher les endroits reculés & inhabités; vous craignez trop de rencontrer de vos dupes, filou que vous êtes.

Je conserve précieusement le reçu de 300 Rs que vous venez d'envoyer à Reymond & si demain à 10 h. du matin je n'ai pas reçu un chèque de cette somme, je dépose avec une plainte en escroquerie un exemplaire des *Snowdrops* où vous préféreriez ne pas le voir.

J.J.G.

I took it at once to a lawyer who warned him that by the Indian penal code he was rendering himself liable to a long term in prison. I realized that the man was simply insane with remorse and did not press the charge. On the contrary, despite the agreement of the twentieth, I agreed to pay him a small sum for certain items which had been overlooked. I went down to Calcutta on the twenty-eighth, and a week later accepted an invitation from the Maharaja of Moharbhanj to shoot big game in his province.

I was very sad at heart about the death of my friends, but with regard to the mountain I was in excellent spirits. I had demonstrated beyond doubt the existence of an easy way up. I was sure of being able to establish a main camp within striking distance of the summit, and I had familiarized myself with all the vagaries of the weather and the snow. Cut short as the expedition had been, at its first leap, the actual attainment had not been insignificant. We had reached a height of approximately twenty-five thousand feet, and found life at that altitude as enjoyable and work as easy as anywhere else. I had written a detailed proposal to Eckenstein, suggesting that we should tackle the mountain in 1906—but no foreigners!

53

I had been so concentrated on Kangchenjunga that the other facts of my life had not glittered perceptibly. They had kept up with me, but I hardly knew it. They were now to shine, the bushel of Kangchenjunga having been rudely removed.

My instinct against *The Book of Law* had apparently had its way. It was as if the events of eighteen months before had never taken place. I was going on with Magick on the old lines, without any particular ambition, but quietly exercising the powers already obtained. For instance, I had established regular communications with Soror F. (Soror Fidelis—Mrs Elaine Simpson). We had long interviews, visiting each other alternately. I was a little better than she was, but her body was quite material enough to impress all the senses.

It occurs to me that I ought to give further details. Our astral bodies, as we had got them, were replicas of our physical bodies, save that they were slightly larger. Hers, for example, was just over six feet high instead of five feet seven inches. The body was self-luminous and partially transparent, so that I could see the background behind her, much as through a muslin curtain. The substance of the body appeared homogeneous. It was usually clothed and crowned. The materials were of the same quality of matter as the body, but could be distinguished from flesh by such optical devices as colour and reflections. We moved according to the laws of the astral plane; that is, without making the normal physical actions, though we were able to use our limbs in the ordinary way. We communicated, sometimes by audible speech, sometimes by direct transmission of thought such as occurs every day in ordinary life, when one knows what a friend is going to say before he says it.

One very curious phenomenon must be recorded. In the early days we had arranged special hours for our interviews by calculating the difference of time due to longitude. We now summoned each other by means of the astral bell. But on comparison of our records we discovered an astounding fact. Although we agreed about the character of the interview, the subject of conversation etc., we found that the time did not necessarily correspond. That is: suppose I went to see her at midnight on Friday (India), she did not see me at four a.m. on Saturday (England) but at some other time which might be later or earlier. I could easily imagine a delay in my appearance, but it seemed to me nonsense that I should have arrived before I started! At that time I understood little of the nature of time.

My lyric gift had begun to sit up and take notice a little after the shock of the realization of all its aspirations. I had begun to write again. Some of my poems at this period were definitely rationalistic. I was already aware that the rationalist position was wooden and shallow. The members of the Rationalist Press Association were no less narrow-minded sectarians than the Evangelicals. They had the same suburban point of view, the same prudish exclusiveness; they were shocked by any fact which did not immediately fit into their framework, and angrily denied its existence.

I was shifting slowly back to Buddhism; though even more impatient than before of Buddhists, their parochial morality and their emphasis on the evils of existence. But I wrote a few lyrics about love and nature which are still among my best. I may mention 'The Song'.

> Dance a measure
>   Of the tiniest whirls!
> Shake out your treasure
>   Of cinnamon curls!
> Tremble with pleasure
>   O wonder of girls!
> Rest is bliss,
>   And bliss is rest,
> Give me a kiss
>   If you love me best!
> Hold me like this
>   With my hand on your breast!

There was also 'Said', inspired by my work in Cairo; 'Patchouli'; a sort of rhapsody upon African and Asiatic themes; 'The Jilt', a piece of sadistic exultation over my wife's cruelty to Howell, who we heard was stricken to the heart by the thunderbolt of her marriage. Then there was 'The Eyes of Pharaoh', a terrific presentation of the mystery of Egypt, and 'Benzai', a poem in praise of Japan, then at war with Russia. There was a new note in my work: that of humour.

'The Beauty and the Bikkhu' is a versification of a Buddhist legend. The original is unconsciously funny, and I brought this out, while preserving the sublimity of the story. Again 'Immortality' develops an idea in the *Gorgias* of Plato that after death one goes on doing very much what one did before. The style is at once passionate, pictorial, terrifying and witty.

Another new string to my lyre; I had been reproaching myself for my ignorance of the Sufi doctrines, and intended to cross Persia on my way back to England. For this purpose I began to study the language with a munshi. I began to imitate the poets of Iran. 'Ali and Hassan' is a paraphrase from Alf Laylah Wa Laylah. 'Al Malik' is a ghazal; that is, a series of couplets with a monorime. The first two lines and each successive even line rime with each other. In Darjeeling (on my return) I had had a brief but intense liaison with a Nepali girl, Tenguft. I celebrated this passion in a rondel 'Tarshitering'.

NEPALI LOVE SONG

O kissable Tarshitering! The wild bird calls its mate—and I?
Come to my tent this night of May, and cuddle close and crown me king!
Drink, drink our fill of love at last—a little while and we shall die,
O kissable Tarshitering!

Droop the long lashes; close the eyes with eyelids like a beetle's wing!
Light the slow smile, ephemeral as ever a painted butterfly,
Certain to close into a kiss, certain to fasten on me and sting!

Nay? Are you coy? Then I will catch your hips and hold you wild and shy
Until your very struggles set your velvet buttocks all a-swing,
Until their music lulls you to unfathomable ecstasy,
O kissable Tarshitering!

I must explain that oriental modesty does not allow the self-respecting poet to introduce the name of a woman, just as in Shakespeare's time it was considered scandalous for a woman to appear on the stage. I respected this convention and replaced the name of Tenguft by a male name, which I thought euphonious and suitable to my scheme of time and scansion.

Moharbhanj was an ideal place for meditation. I had absolute leisure, I was at the top of my form physically and every other way, and I could not start anything serious until my wife and child arrived, which they did not do until October

29th. I was in a wild district with no one to talk to; it afforded the maximum opportunity for taking stock of my life, finding out what the past meant and taking aim for the future.

The Durga Puja was in course. I was able to appreciate the enthusiasm of the aboriginal Hindu much better than I could have done in Calcutta, where the corrosion of civilization has eaten into primitive practice.

Moharbhanj, though only thirteen hours from Calcutta, is as far from it morally as it is from London. The people were unspoilt. For the first time I liked Hindus. The maharajah was away for the day. He had sent his Minister of Public Works to meet me and entertain me until his return. This gentleman, whose name was Martin, had taken a high degree at Oxford, and had studied science and engineering very thoroughly. No one could have suspected that he had a Bengali grandmother. But in the first twenty-four hours I had discovered the truth of the aphorism 'Blood will tell'. For all his European education, he believed in the most primitive superstitions, from ghosts and witches to mysterious medicines.

The next day the maharajah returned. I found him an extremely interesting and delightful companion. One could hardly expect less from the direct descendant of a peacock. I am sorry to say that he did not take his ancestry seriously. He had exchanged his illusions for another set far less fascinating, far less inspiring and equally absurd. He believed in Herbert Spencer and John Stuart Mill. One of his stories is extremely instructive. If it were graven upon the eye-corners, it would be a warning to such as would be warned! There are no principles of politics, economics and the rest; it is all balderdash. More, it is a damnable heresy and a dangerous delusion to apply the theories of the Thames valley to the practice of the Coromandel coast.

Moharbhanj is a province on the sea-board of Orissa. In my wanderings I came to a range of hills of unparalleled wonder. It was between ten and twenty miles in length, and some three thousand feet high. The marvel of it is that it is composed very largely of pure iron pyrites, whose bare outcrop forms huge rounded bosses. I first saw these hills at sunset, and they glowed with crimson splendour too vivid to be merely mineral. It was like blood on a bull's shoulder in the sunlight. The maharajah knew the commercial value of his mountains, but he had no coal; to exploit his treasure he needed a light railway from the mountains to the sea.

When he came to the throne he nobly determined to confer

the benefits of liberal principles upon his people. Now he was not only the Maharajah of Moharbhanj, but its zemindar or landlord. He wished to create a peasantry of prosperous and independent freeholders. He understood that it would be fatal to make them a present of the land; so he made a law by which any man who cultivated his land continuously for fifteen years would at the end of that time become its owner. As is generally known, the greatest pride of the Hindu is to make his daughter's wedding as splendiferous as possible. For this purpose he will get himself into debt for generations ahead as recklessly as the most progressive nation will do for their own pet phantom of glory.

So as soon as the new law was proclaimed, the Marwaris descended upon Moharbhanj like locusts, and advanced sums beyond the wildest imaginations of the peasants, to them. The marriages were magnificent; so were the mortgages. At the end of fifteen years the land belonged not to the cultivator but to the alien usurer. The maharajah could not even see that he had ruined himself and his subjects. He told me with honest pride, 'I have conferred great benefit upon my people.' Yet he was in a comical state of distress because the Marwaris refused to grant him the concession to build the light railway so that he could melt up his mountains! In the meanwhile the people were poorer than before, though the administration of his revenues by the British had increased his personal income from three to eighteen lakhs of rupees in less than twenty years.

He told me one enthralling story about his raj. A great deal of it is unexplored and impenetrable jungle. In the clearing are villages inhabited by very primitive folk of a different race to the bulk of the population. I saw a good deal of these people. They go in many cases naked. At the most, they wear a rudimentary loin cloth. They have a language of their own which possesses a few affinities with other dialects. It possesses less than three hundred words, some two hundred and fifty of which are classed as obscene. The men are armed with bows and arrows, or occasionally spears, some of which show great skill of metallurgy and workmanship as well as a knowledge of certain branches of mechanics, and a marked sense of beauty.

The women are free from the ordinary Hindu inhibitions, and their breasts are the most beautiful that I have ever seen, not excepting those of the women of Tehuantepec. They are small and well proportioned. Even when the women are mothers, they do not lose their form. The whole breast stands firm and points upwards. To the eye of the artist, the female breast of the European is a hideous deformity. Even in the case of the most beautiful woman, it breaks the line of the body, and it makes one think of a cow. But these women bear their breasts in triumph. One thinks of the phallophorus in a pagan procession.

Men and women alike are admirably proportioned, muscular and active. Their habit of carrying loads on the head—a coolie carries thirty pounds, which, considering the heat of the plains, is equivalent to the fifty pounds of the hillman—gives them perfect balance and makes them light on their feet. The skin is of that superb velvety black which is really rich deep purple. Primitive as these people are, they are as capable of aesthetics as the popes and princes of the Renaissance. They love with rapacious intensity, adorned with all the arts of Aphrodite.

These folk are considered 'wild men of the woods' by the sophisticated Hindus of the town. Yet there is a third proportional.

In the jungle live people known as Jewans, whom I hesitate to describe as a tribe, because nothing is known of their habits. Even their appearance has not been satisfactorily described. It is said by some that no white man has ever seen one, though others say that one or two have done so. Even the folk of the villages on the confines of the jungle have no knowledge of them, yet they carry on with them a regular traffic.

Certain places outside the village are marked out, usually by white stones, and here they deposit rice and other products of cultivation at nightfall. In the morning these goods are found to have been replaced by various products of the jungle. It is said that this commerce has never been degraded by dishonesty. Attempts have been made to catch the Jewans in the act of making the exchange, but they have always proved too wary.

The maharajah did not shoot, but appointed a forest officer named d'Elbroux to introduce me to the bears and tigers. The only animal I was not allowed to shoot was the elephant. One has to be a viceroy or a travelling royalty to indulge in that sport. D'Elbroux, in his youth, had come to grips with a bear. He had been very badly mauled, and many of his features had been replaced by metal plates. He told me that he had lain in the jungle wounded for more than two days before help arrived.

My only noteworthy shooting adventure was this. D'Elbroux had prepared a machan. There were some seven hundred beaters. The first animal that broke was a bear, whom I settled with a shot from the 10-bore. The second barrel jarred off and the surprise knocked me on my back. The bullet struck a tree as thick as a telegraph pole, and cut it in two, so that it fell across the machan and very nearly killed one of the men.

My best memory of Moharbhanj is not of tigers and such small fowl, but of elephants, which I was not allowed to shoot. I have always felt that my life has numerous points of contact with *Alice in Wonderland*, and I now come to the incident, 'The Elephants did tease so!'

I went out one night to a bhul, or salt lick, in a tree overlooking which a machan had been built for me. A particularly fine tiger was reputed to visit the place every night. I took up my vigil immediately after dinner. A three-quarter moon was due to rise about half-past eight. We kept extremely quiet, of course. I dislike shooting from a machan, exactly as I dislike coarse fishing. One cannot do anything to help things along. On the contrary, one has to avoid the slightest action.

The waiting sounds as if it might be good practice for meditation. I found it quite the opposite, for the object of one's vigil is itself a distraction, and if one concentrated on the sport, it would of course disappear, as had already happened to my nose and my navel. Soon after dark I began to hear the noises of the jungle, from the rustling of leaves and grasses as small animals moved cautiously about their business to the distant roaring of the tiger. Once or twice a shadowy shape made the darkness that brooded over the salt lick deeper, but there was no sense in risking a shot till moonrise. I could hardly see my own hands, much less the sights of my rifle.

When the moon rose at last, the few animals that had arrived vanished with equal stealth. There was a great silence in the jungle and the roars of the tigers (there were several all round the compass) became less frequent and less near.

All of a sudden I became aware of a tremendous disturbance. It was not exactly a noise—I'm inclined to think that it may have been a smell. I cannot say definitely more than this, that I had the impression that something enormous was going on.

I had been lying flat in the machan, listening. I raised my head cautiously. The silvern glades were now mysteriously peopled with gigantic shapes. It was a herd of elephants! I counted twenty-four of them. My shikari whispered that there would be no shooting that night; no other animals would venture into the neighbourhood of the master of the jungle.

I realized, moreover, that my position was one of extreme danger. The machan was high from the ground; but had the elephants winded me and taken alarm, my tree would have snapped like a twig. But I had no time to think of danger; I was thrilled with exaltation. I sat up and spent the night watching the elephants as they went about their business. It was the most fascinating vision that had ever been vouchsafed to me on the material plane.

I did not grudge the loss of my night's sport. I was not really very keen about the shooting. I was in a very curious frame of mind. I loved to wake at dawn on my camp bed and meditate and read Kant, Berkeley and Firdausi. Persian fascinated me more than any other language had ever done and I revelled in the ideas of the Sufis. Their esoteric symbolism delighted me beyond measure. I took it into my head to go one better than my previous performance in the way of inventing poets and their productions.

I spent most of my time writing ghazals, purporting to be by a certain Abdullah al Haji (Haji, with a soft 'h', satirist, as opposed to Haji with a hard 'h', pilgrim) of Shiraz. I caused him to flourish about 1600 A.D., but gave to the collection of his ghazals the title *Bagh-i-Muattar* (*The Scented Garden*), which implies the date 1906, the value of the Arabic letters of the title adding up to the equivalent of that year of the Hegira. I also invented an Anglo-Indian major to find, translate and annotate the manuscript, an editor to complete the work of that gallant soldier (killed in South Africa) and a Christian clergyman to discuss the matter of the poem from the peculiar point of view of high Anglicanism.

The ghazals themselves are rendered sometimes in the supposed original monorime, sometimes in prose, and the annotations contain a great deal of the more esoteric information about the East, which I had picked up from time to time. It is especially to be noted that, although I have picked every kind of magical and mystical lore into the volume, there is nowhere any reference to *The Book of the Law*. I was setting my whole strength against the Secret Chiefs. I was trying to forget the whole business.

The book itself is a complete treatise on mysticism, expressed in the symbolism prescribed by Persian piety. It describes the relations of God and man, explains how the latter falls from his essential innocence by allowing himself to be deceived by the illusion of matter. His religion ceases to be real and becomes formal; he falls into sin and suffers the penalty thereof. God prepares the pathway of regeneration and brings him through shame and sorrow to repentance, thus preparing the mystical union which restores man to his original privileges, free will, immortality, the perception of truth and so on.

I put the last ounce of myself into this book. My previous efforts in the same direction would have deceived nobody, but the *Bagh-i-Muattar*, despite my inability to produce the Persian original—my excuse was that it was rare and held the most sacred and most secret, but was being copied for me—persuaded even experienced scholars that it was genuine. It was issued by Probsthain & Co., by private subscription, in 1910. I have heard of a copy changing hands at fifty guineas.

This spurt of genius is an eloquent portrait of my mind at this time. I was absolutely convinced of the supreme importance of devoting my life to attaining Samadhi, conscious communion with the Immanent Soul of the Universe. I believed in mysticism. I understood perfectly the essence of its method and the import of its attainment, but I felt compelled to express myself in a satirical and (it might appear to some) almost scandalous form. I testified to the tremendous truth by piling fiction upon fiction. I did not know it. I did not suspect it, but the *Bagh-i-Muattar* is a symptom of supreme significance. I was on the brink of a totally new development.

On Sunday, October 22nd, I had an astral interview with Soror F. which brought me up with a shock. She was accompanied by a golden hawk, in whom I later recognized one of the Secret Chiefs of the A∴A∴. The conversation turned on the subject of the Great Work. It was defined as the creation of a new universe. The interview left me spiritually prostrate. I had been perfectly happy with my programme, doing a little work here and a little there; Magick on Monday and teaching on Tuesday, so to speak; advising any applicant that approached me; editing and publishing any documents that fell into my hands.

But the Secret Chiefs were determined not to allow me to fool myself. When they picked me out to do their work they meant me to get busy and do it, and were going to see that I did. They did not insist on my taking up the work of the New Aeon. They knew their business too well. They knew that I should not be ready until I had undergone the proper preparation. They were content therefore with stirring me up to tackle the problem of my relations with the universe as seriously as the Buddha had done twenty-five centuries before.

I rode into Moharbhanj hardly aware of my surroundings. I

was criticizing myself with ruthless severity. I do not remember
whether *The Book of the Law* so much as crossed my mind.
If so, I must have put it angrily aside. All I did know was that
I should not have a moment's peace again until I had solved
the great problem and I had no idea how to tackle it. I began
to set my ideas in order.

Returned again to Calcutta. One day I went over to Kalighat
and sacrificed a goat to a goddess.[1] That night I was sitting
alone reading. She appeared to me and inspired me to write
a poem to her. I quote the first two stanzas:

KALI

> There is an idol in my house
> By whom the sandal always steams.
> Alone, I make a black carouse
> With her to dominate my dreams.
> With skulls and knives she keeps control
> (O Mother Kali!) of my soul.
>
> She is crowned with emeralds like leaves,
> And rubies flame from either eye;
> A rose upon her bosom heaves,
> Turquoise and Lapis Lazuli.
> She hath a kirtle like a maid—
> Amethyst, amber, pearl, and jade!

This poem is important as foreshadowing my final solution
of the problem of evil and sorrow, the interpretation of illusion
by the initiate and its transmutation into truth.

I saw as usual a good deal of Thornton. One morning,
driving down the Maidan in his tum-tum, I said, 'I cannot
formulate a plan of action of any kind because there is no
true continuity in phenomena.' He turned on me quite simply,
and said, 'Quite so, but there is equally no continuity in yourself.' That, of course, was no news to me. It was Hume's
answer to Berkeley, for one thing. It was the essence of
Sakkaya-Ditthi, for another. The ground was cut away from
under my feet. At the moment, my consciousness failed to
pick up the full purport of this proposition, for I found myself
suddenly forced into action by a set of circumstances of which
I had no control, and which bore no relation to any past
purpose of my life. But I believe they were arranged for me
by the Secret Chiefs.

My wife was due to arrive with the baby on the twenty-ninth
and the natural thing would have been to see a little of

Calcutta society, especially as I was naturally a bit of a lion, and then stroll across Asia somewhere, at our leisure. The Secret Chiefs arranged for me to be in a situation where I was at their mercy. They meant to initiate me whether I liked it or not. And this is how they went to work.

I set forth after dinner, one fate-fraught night, to try to get unguided to a street of infamy called 'Culinga Bazar' from the corner of the Maidan. It was a worthy feat to attempt; for I had been to the Bazar only once before, in 1901; and then I had been driven to it in the dark from a far distant part of Calcutta. The night was extremely dark; the streets were lighted only by the flares and fireworks of the native festival —the Durga-Puja—which was in course, and all semblance of honesty or decency quitted the houses before I had advanced three minutes into the bowels of Calcutta.

As I did so, my savage instincts surged to my brain. I 'smelt' the direction almost at once; and as I got into this state, I became aware of impending trouble of some sort, as savages are. That 'eerie feeling', alone in a desperate section of a foreign city at night? Nine to one it is plain funk. But as I had already admitted, I am the biggest coward alive; and I have constantly forced myself to face my fear. So now I was not tingling with the pleasurable sense of confronting the unknown; I had the definite sense of being trailed. The sensation angered me; I tried to ascribe it to imagination. I forgot it and I went my way.

Presently, however, I turned aside for a moment from the dim street I was treading into an alley guarded by a black archway. I had no idea where it might lead; I simply wished to withdraw from the observation of my fellows for a few seconds, for reasons which are fully described and justified in Carpenter's *Physiology*.

I passed through the archway. It was as 'dark as the pit'. (I don't know what pit may be meant.) The alley beyond was somewhat lighter; the sky loomed dull blue-grey above.

I noticed various doorways in the walls; also one at the end of the alley; I was in a cul-de-sac. And then I saw, faint glimpses in the gloom, the waving white of native robes. Men were approaching me and I was aware—though hardly by sight—that they moved in a semi-military order, in single file. There was nothing to alarm me in this; it is the habit of natives to march thus. And yet I was pungently aware that some evil was meant. As it happened, I was dressed in dark clothes and my face burnt deep brown. I effaced myself against the wall.

Three of the men passed me; then they turned. I was surrounded. Strong hands gripped my arms; greedy hands sought my pockets. I barked out sharp orders: they should have no doubt that I was a sahib. For all answer I saw the pallid gleam of a knife.

I must really break off to say that I have always found the psychology of this incident enthralling. It stands out in my memory in *alto-relievo*.

I have never on any other occasion had so much time to think—I am afraid I express it badly. I mean that I was acutely conscious of a few well-marked thoughts, without the usual gradations, sub-thoughts, connections and so forth, that make it hard—in ordinary life—to discriminate between conscious and unconscious thought.

On this night I was as primitive as an ape. My thoughts stand out stark as stars on a background of utter blackness. I had become, as by an enchanter's spell, the primeval caveman. Perhaps the long strain and horror of the Kangchenjunga tragedy had prepared me for this sudden outcropping of atavism.

However that might be, I remember nothing but these harsh clear thoughts, uninterfered with by the usual mental processes. I felt myself a 'human leopard'; something in me warned me that—contrary to all common sense and evidence—I had lured these men. I was, so to say, a Q-ship! I remember the resistance of my civilized self to this insane idea; I was an English gentleman, attacked without provocation by a band of common robbers.

I had given the order that they should unhand me; they had disobeyed a sahib; my life was in danger. This being the case, I was right to act in self-defence. I would press the trigger of the Webley on which my forefinger had rested since the first glimpse of white robes in the alley. I did so. There was a slight click.

Now, my Webley holds five cartridges; I invariably keep the hammer down on an empty chamber. The chamber will only revolve freely when the gun is at half-cock. Therefore, thought I, 'with omnipotence at my command and eternity at my disposal' I must have been fiddling unconsciously with the weapon, set it at half-cock and twiddled the chamber round until the hammer was down, not on the empty space, but on

the cartridge next to it, so that the gun, in cocking itself under
trigger-pressure, had dropped the hammer on the void. True;
but then, to correct the error, it was only necessary to press
the trigger a second time.

I have purposely described these thoughts in detail, to emphasize the fact that my mind was working in a more leisurely
manner than I had ever known it to do. It is all the more
amazing to reflect that my whole train of thought, except the
final detail, what to do next, was totally inaccurate!

I pressed the trigger again. My arms were held firmly to my
sides, but even so I was too economically minded to fire
through my pocket; I managed to raise the muzzle above the
edge.

A violent explosion followed.

I had fired without aim, in pitch blackness; I could not even
see the white robes of the men who held me. In the lightning
moment of the flash I saw only that whitenesses were falling
backwards away from me, as if I had upset a screen by
accident.

The blackness which followed the flash was Cimmerian.
My eyes are naturally very slow to accommodate themselves
to change of illumination—I have never met any man equally
helpless in case of sudden diminution of light. I had no thought
soever as to whether my shot might have hit anybody. There
was not the faintest sound; but the alley seemed somehow
empty. I do not know whether I stepped over fallen bodies or
not. (I was facing the archway when I fired.)

I thought: I will get out of this alley at once. Those people
may be lying in ambush in the archway, especially as I do
not know whether there are doors opening out of it or not.
I will keep my forefinger on the trigger and at the same time
light a match to make sure of the archway. When I get out
into the open street, I will walk away very quickly and very
quietly, and go straight to the Dharamtolla Road and take a
gharry, and drive to Edward Thornton and tell him what has
happened.

I carried out this programme to the letter.

And now comes a curious circumstance. My experiments in
Mexico City in 'making myself invisible' have been recorded
with considerable detail; and it will be remembered that I was
far from satisfied with the results. I had reached the 'flickering'
condition, but I had never succeeded in 'putting myself out'
completely.

But on this occasion—when my unconscious self seems to have had me in hand throughout—I made myself invisible right enough. The report of the pistol, the screams (for all I know!) of the wounded or frightened men, and the alarm given by the fugitives, had aroused the entire district. An European was a rare bird in that quarter at that time of night; and no native would be likely to have such a gun. No doubt, too, the whole assault had been watched from the beginning; and I must have been denounced descriptively. I remember clearly enough noting with a type of amusement which I must really admit to having something 'devilish' in its composition, that the streets through which I passed were filled with wildly excited crowds, all looking for me. 'But he, passing through the midst of them, went his way.' I am aware that this sounds like a fish story. But as a matter of fact people who lived with me for the last three years or so have noticed that I make myself invisible quite frequently, and that (apparently) when I am not aware that I am doing so.

There is a peculiar type of self-absorption which makes it impossible for people to be aware of one. In these recent cases, the observer who could see me quite plainly because in sympathy with me, could also see that the other people in the street—or wherever it was—could not see me at all. My theory is that the mental state in question distracts people's attention from one automatically, as a conjurer does deliberately. I can transfer this property of invisibility, however, even to inanimate objects. For instance, a police officer recently came to my house in search of a certain thing which he named. I admitted that I possessed it; I showed it to him; I insisted on his seeing, smelling, tasting and touching it; but he left the house and reported that he had been unable to find it. In this particular instance I knew what I was doing. I deliberately overwhelmed his mind with my earnestness in helping him and other objects of thought. I cut the connecting link between his senses and his mind.

But we digress. I enjoyed lazily the splendour of the drowsy night as I jogged along with lighted pipe—never tobacco tasted better—in the broken-down old gharry up to Thornton's.

I had good reason to be proud. I had been the butt of every bully at school, I had suffered the agonies of knowing myself a coward and a weakling. My whole life seemed at times to be one vast and slimy subterfuge to cozen death.

Yet in the past month there had been a dozen outrages

upon Europeans in Calcutta, some of them culminating in the
most brutal murder. And I was the only Englishman who had
come out on top. I had lost four rupees, eight annas, it is true;
but I had won the victory, one against six.

Thornton was in bed when I arrived; but I had no hesitation
in making his 'bera' admit me. I told him my story and opened
my revolver. Then only did I discover that my elaborate
course of reasoning was entirely at fault! I had NOT monkeyed
with the weapon and the hammer HAD been down on the
empty chamber as was right. What had happened was that the
first cartridge had failed to explode; for there was the dent
in the cap; once again had nature, simple and sufficient,
mocked the pomposity of the human intelligence!

Now, concluded I, hadn't I better go to the police and have
these ruffians rounded up? Thornton was half asleep, but his
mocking eye expressed a more than godlike pity for my idiocy.
'Go to bed,' he murmured in his dreams; 'come round after
Chota Hazri in the morning and I'll take you to the right
man.' My indignation subsided. I agreed. I withdrew. I slept.
I bathed. I breakfasted. I went to Thornton.

Thornton took me to a Scottish solicitor named MacNair.
I brought out my indignation, its hair nicely brushed, and
parted exactly in the middle. MacNair remembered what his
ancestors (who, at the time of the Flood, had a boat of their
ain) thought about caution. 'Go to Garth,' was his considered
opinion. Garth was one of the most brilliant barristers in
Calcutta. I brought out my indignation again, but its hair
got slightly ruffled, and I am not sure but what there was a
speck of dust on its collar. I protested violently that I wanted
to go to the police.

'Well,' said Garth, 'Curzon and Fraser are busy with the
partition of Bengal, for reasons of purely administrative convenience; and it is singularly unfortunate that the measure will
break the political power of the Bengali into a lot of dirty
little bits. Their hearts bleed for Bengal. So, if you should
have happened to hit somebody last night, they will be very
indignant and bring you to trial. You will be instantly acquitted, but they will invent some scheme for having you tried
again, and acquitted again, to show the sincerity of their love
for the Bengali, whom they are out to smash.'

'Then you advise me,' I said innocently, 'to say nothing?'
'Indeed no,' he said tempestuously, 'as a sworn barrister, it is
my duty to advise you to report the whole affair immediately
to the police.' I became more innocent than ever. 'Well, I

don't see how I can throw any light on the matter.' (I was still ignorant of the effect, if any, of the shot.)

He bellowed with laughter. 'You can throw a whole flood of light on it,' he shouted. My Quaker ancestors knocked at the door of my dull mind, I suppose. 'Would you do it yourself?' I asked meekly. 'Well,' he said more soberly, 'you'd be acquitted of course. A man doesn't stroll out after dinner to murder strangers. But you'd be kept hanging about Calcutta indefinitely; and an unscrupulous man, I'm afraid, might be tempted to hold his tongue and clear out of British India p.d.q.²'

My Quaker ancestors told me what to do. I said sternly, but sadly, 'Then I suppose it is my duty to go to the police at once. Where is my gharry?' The great barrister wrung my hand in silent sympathy.

But it has been one of the guiding principles of my life never to go into a game unless there is a sporting chance. It is silly to be tried for murder if there is no possibility of conviction. All the bubbles are gone from the champagne. So I waited two days more, still unaware whether my shot had told, and went to meet my wife and child at the wharf.

'How are you?' she exclaimed dramatically. My prosaic reply was, 'You've got here just in time to see me hanged!'

Thornton gave a dinner party in our honour that night. My wife sat at his right hand. I saw that she was upset about something. I had no opportunity to talk to Thornton alone before dinner. He kept on giving a curious gesture and then raising two fingers. My stupid mind could not imagine what he was driving at. After dinner he took me and Rose aside for a moment. The unimaginable had happened. My single shot had gone clean through the abdomen of the man with the knife and lodged in the spine of the villain behind him. They had been taken to hospital and made a full confession of their crime.

So the next morning the *Standard* gave me my meed of publicity. Column three of the main page gave the story of the attempted robbery. The man with the gun was thought to be a sailor from one of the ships in the harbour; the police offered a reward for his apprehension. Column five contained an interview with the hero of the expedition to Kangchen-junga. 'They will go round the ships,' said Thornton, 'and then they'll have a shot at the hotels. Get out and get out quick!'

'Darling sweetheart lovey-dovey silly great big she-ass!' I

whispered to my wife, 'would you rather walk across Persia or across China?'

The wretched woman knew no geography. All she knew about Persia was rugs and Omar Khayyam; all she knew about China was opium smoking, porcelain and tea. She was fed up with Omar, who was at that time deplorably the rage in this wasp-witted country. 'My ownest own,' she purred, 'let's go through China!' We hastily engaged an ayah for our baby. This female was hideous, ill-mannered and untrustworthy; she claimed to be a Roman Catholic so as to conceal that her caste would have nothing to do with her, but she was the only ayah available, so off we went. The one honest human being in the party was dear old shikari Salama Tantra. The loyal staunch old hound! He never flinched, he never failed; he had all the innocence of a child and all the wisdom of Pythagoras; the courage to face the unknown—which Indians almost always fear to the limit—and the gentleness which goes with great strength of body and soul. Peace be to thee, old friend, where'er thou be.

54

The voyage to Rangoon was uneventful and delightful. The weather was perfect; for a wonder, the shores and spine of western Burma were on show. There was a fearful fascination in those deadly beauties. I cursed again the fate that had driven me back in 1902 from the sombre slopes of the Arakans. I had rather I had left my bones to bleach upon those pestilential peaks.

Yet my mind—thanks be to the most high eternal gods!— can never rest for more than an albatross's glide upon the slopes of the past. Today, writing my memories, I feel as if I were playing a sort of practical joke upon myself. I am hot on the trail of the future. I can imagine myself on my death-bed, spent utterly with lust to touch the next world, like a boy asking for his first kiss from a woman.

Beyond Burma lay mysterious China; I conjured up a cloud of amusing phantasies. Romance and adventure. I am incurable; though I have had all the good things of life, nearly all my life, though I no longer value them or enjoy them for themselves, I still enjoy the idea of them. I embrace hardship and privation with ecstatic delight; I want everything that the world holds; I would go to prison or to the scaffold for the sake of the experience. I have never grown out of the infantile belief that the universe was made for me to suck. I grow delirious to contemplate the delicious horrors that are certain to happen to me. This is the keynote of my life, the untram-melled delight in every possibility of existence, potential or actual. Fear has been eliminated from me by the fact that I look back with the keenest interest and pleasure to the events which at the time were torture unassuaged.

Imagine, then, how I gloried in the glow of the silken waters about the ship, in the fantastically immaterial outlines of the Arakan hills, in the gloom of the gracious frondage of the forests, in the curves of the cobra coast, in the sinister stories of wreck and piracy which haunt that desolate abyss through which we were steaming, where for nine months of the year one can scarce distinguish between sky and sea, so dark and damp is the air, so subtly steaming the swell of ocean; while beyond, as in a hashish dream, arose the highlands of China, provinces all but unknown even to civilized Chinese themselves. There, primrose to purple, was the promise of undreamed-of tribes of men, strangely tattooed and dressed, with awful customs and mysterious rites, beyond imagination and yet brutally actual, folk with sublimity carven of simplicity and depravity woven of the most complex madness.

I went towards China, my veins bursting with some colossal bliss that I had never yet experienced. I boiled with love for the unknown, the more so that my brain was overcharged with grisly imaginings bred of Octave Mirbeau's *Le Jardin des Supplices*,[1] combined with fervid actualities born of the feeling that I was (after all) treading, though reverently and afar off, in the footsteps of my boyhood's hero, Richard Francis Burton.

The approaches to Rangoon are of the most turbulent kind. The river is always the same violent angry dirty flood. It seems to be desperately annoyed with itself about something, possibly at having to pass through Rangoon, which is a wretchedly provincial and artificial town, saved from utter insignificance by one crowning glory, the Shwe Dagon pagoda.

The Buddhists of Burma cannot be induced to do anything which might contribute to their welfare or that of their religion; but they are ridiculously lavish in building new dagobas or regilding old ones. Shortly before my arrival an immense sum of money had been collected to lay plates of pure gold on the Htee of the Shwe Dagon, and while this operation was in progress, a tigress indiscreetly walked into the city one night, climbed the scaffolding and was shot by an Englishman. The outrage to the community, which objects to the slaying, even by accident, of an insect, was causing serious political trouble. Their most holy shrine defiled by deliberate murder! There was also considerable friction between the petty English authorities and the Buddhist ponggis of European extraction who were trying to settle in Rangoon, live the holy life and revive Buddhism as a missionary religion. European officials in a colony are necessarily nuisances to themselves; they consequently try to pass it on to somebody else, on the principle of school bullies—the prototype of the administration.

I personally met with the greatest courtesy and kindness from the authorities in Burma, but the country is not so settled socially as India, and the climate is so abominable that there is every excuse for irritability on the part of anyone unfortunate enough to have to live there. It is, however, a pity that the administration should look with such provincial suspicion upon people like Allan Bennett, that they should fancy political dangers when a European chooses to study native religion. This disfavour extended to their own officials whenever they happened to have sufficient intelligence to take a sympathetic interest in the people and their customs and beliefs. Fielding Hall, a judge, found himself quite unpopular in official circles on account of his excellent though somewhat sentimental book *The Soul of a People.*

The Englishman in all the colonies that I have visited, except in India, which is not a colony, is childishly jealous of his supposed superiority to the native. He has convinced himself that he represents a step ahead in evolution and he is fantastically afraid of 'going fanti'; so he has his knife into anyone who has a good word to say for the people.

Allan Bennett, by becoming a Buddhist monk, was a living witness that some Europeans thought Burmese beliefs better than their European equivalents; and the idea—so far as an idea may be ascribed to an official—was that native agitators might use this as an argument that British rule in Burma was unjustified. The whole ratiocination is an utter muddle; but men are not governed by reason, either individually or politically. There is, therefore, some excuse for the anxiety of the administration.

At the same time, the example of India should have been enough. British prestige in India rested on the real moral superiority of courage, truthfulness, justice and self-control. It has been destroyed by the attempt to replace this irrational lever of iron by the rotten laths of reason. We should never have shown our weakness to the Indian student who fills Bengal with the tale of his sexual conquest of white women, our servant girls who took these sons of pettifoggers for princes. We should never have sent out middle-class pets-of-examiners to govern the aristocratically minded inhabitants of the tongue of Asia. Duxmia—I suspect some very wise bird—wrote in *Vanity Fair* (October 13th, 1907):

> The British Empire was not built up by public school boys, for the excellent and all sufficient reason that while it was really being built up the public schools did not exist. The men who defeated Napoleon and crushed the Indian Mutiny were sons of country squires, educated in private seminaries, or by tutors on their fathers' own estates, often left to run wild among grooms and stableboys, and obtaining their military or

colonial posts through purchase or influence, certainly not through examinations. And never let it be forgotten that the Navy, the one efficient service we possess, is officered by men who have not been to public schools.

It is the plain truth. Our new intellectual Y.M.C.A. snobbery has sucked away our spinal marrow.

I left my family in the hotel and went to stay with Allan, who had been advanced from a simple bikkhu to a sayadaw in his choung (monastery) some two miles from the city. Thornton's remark about the discontinuity of the ego had begun to take hold. I was anxious to confer with my old guru as thoroughly as possible. His view at this time was that, no matter how earnestly and skilfully one practised, one could not obtain Samadhi, and a fortiori, Arhatship, unless one's Kamma (Karma) was, so to speak, ripe. His theory was that one must comply with the dhamma in all respects to give oneself a chance, but to do so was no guarantee of success. That depended on coincidence. His analogy was this:

Suppose you are a point of a wheel and wish to touch a certain stone on the road, it is obviously necessary to take up your position on the rim of the wheel, but even so you may be at the top of the wheel just at the moment when the wagon passes over the stone.

I said: 'How does this doctrine differ from that of Shri Parananda, who said the Samadhi depended on "the grace of the Lord Shiva"?' He smiled grimly and said that Shri Parananda's doctrine was not Buddhism!

In any case, I resented those views. I clung passionately to my belief that a man's progress depended upon personal prowess. No doubt this is philosophically absurd, but I still maintain that it is practical good sense. The conversation, nevertheless, turned to considerations of what my Kamma had in store for me. 'This might be discovered,' he said, 'by acquiring the Magical Memory.' This is equivalent to Sammasati, Right Recollection, the seventh step on the Noble Eightfold Path. I must explain what this means.

The Buddhist theory of metempsychosis does not involve, like the corresponding Hindu idea, the survival of the individual. There is in fact no ego to survive. When a Buddhist says that he remembers the events of his boyhood, he does not imply that he is the boy in question. He is not; nor is he the man, elephant, bat, hare or what-not of 'his' previous incarnation. The wave that breaks on the shore is not composed of the same particles of water as the 'same' wave (as we call it) a minute earlier. Incarnations are successive phenomena causally connected but not identical. It would have been incorrect for the Buddha to say 'I was that holy hare'. He should express the facts as follows: There is a consciousness of a tendency to perceive that holy hare and this man Gautama Buddha, as collections of impressions in which the one partially determines the other. This connection tends to produce the illusion of an ego whose experiences include the phenomena associated, then with the hare, now with the Gautama.

There are two main methods of acquiring the Magical Memory as defined above. One is to train the normal memory to work backwards instead of forwards, so that any past action is presented to the mind after the manner of a cinematograph film set running in the reverse direction. (I never succeeded fully in acquiring the technique of this method.) The other is to deduce from present circumstances those which gave rise to them.

Just so, one may deduce from the examination of a position on a chessboard what line of play brought it about. One could not be absolutely sure; the pieces might have been set up by a madman; but granted that the position is intelligible, the laws of probability make it as certain as anything can be that it arose in a certain way. Now in considering one's life one has more material for investigation than a single position; one has a series of successive positions. Intelligent inquiry ought to be able to deduce not only the unknown past, but the unknown future. We have no hesitation in reconstructing the boyhood of Swinburne—presuming the absence of direct information— from his works. His poetry proclaims that he studied classics sympathetically and profoundly, that he was influenced by pantheistic, anti-clerical and republican friends, and so on.

Astronomers, again, observing an infinitesimally short section of the course of a planet or star, confidentially pronounce on its position in the past and the future, and even in some cases calculate its complete orbit. There is therefore nothing a priori absurd in trying to discover one's own nature, history and prospects, at least within very wide limits, from careful consideration of one's known characteristics and environment. 'Explore the rivers of the soul,' says Zoroaster, 'whence and in what order thou hast come.' I saw that if I was to be intelligible to myself, I must do so, and this resolution resulted in the critical events which made the months of November, December, January and February the most important period of my life so far as my personal attitude to myself and the universe was concerned.

His life as a bikkhu had not been too good for my guru. The abstinence from food after sunset is bad for the health, but Allan found that after three weeks he got into the habit. But he was likely to be haunted by the ghost of his dead appetite. He had, moreover, got into a very shocking state physically from lack of proper hygiene and perhaps also of proper medical attention, as well as from his determination to carry out the strict rules of the Order. He had acquired a number of tropical complaints.

I felt that my poetry had been undergoing a transition and I was not sure of my feet. Allan told me that he thought the most magical line in English was Coleridge's 'And ice, mast high, went floating by.' The comparison is not with mountains or cathedrals, though they are taller than masts. The imminence of the ice is expressed by the phrase chosen and the reader is put upon the deck of a ship. He becomes, maugre his teeth, one of the companions of the Ancient Mariner.

This conversation led to my endeavouring to put a certain vividness of phraseology into my poetry. 'The Eyes of Pharaoh' was my first attempt to give vivid and immediate images. I chose my similes so as to strengthen the main theme. Later in the month, at Mandalay, I wrote approximately half of 'Sir Palamede the Saracen'. The idea of this book was to give an account of the Mystic Path in a series of episodes, and each episode was to constitute a definite arrangement of colour and form. Thus, Section I shows the blue and yellow of sea and sand, a knight in silver armour riding along their junction to a point where an albatross circles round a mutilated corpse.

One further subject remained for discussion. I had it in my mind to put spiritual research on a scientific basis. The first step was to get mankind to agree on a language. Allan maintained that a perfectly adequate terminology existed already in the Abhidhamma, the metaphysical section of the Buddhist canon. I could not deny the excellence of his intention, but from the point of view of the average Western student, the terms are so jawbreaking as to be heartbreaking. I said: We already possess a universal language which does not depend on grammar. The fundamentals of mathematics are the basis of the Holy Cabbala. It is natural and proper to represent the cosmos, or any part of it, or any operation of it, or the operation of any part of it, by the symbols of pure mathematics.

On November 15th we started up the Irrawaddy by the steamship *Java* and reached Mandalay on the twenty-first. I spent my days and nights leaning over the rail, watching the wavelets of the great river and the flying-fish. I became insane. There I was, lean, stern, brown and immobile; and there was a set of disconnected phenomena, each with a sufficient reason in itself, and the whole of them uniting to produce another phenomenon; but there was no connection between one set of reasons and the other. Each wavelet was caused by certain physical conditions and the effect of the total was to slow down the revolution of the earth. But neither the so-called transitory, nor the so-called permanent, phenomenon was ultimately intelligible. Further, what I called 'I' was simply a machine which recorded the impact of various phenomena.

I wrote, 'About now I may count my speculative criticism of the reason as not only proved and understood, but realized.' And the following day, 'the misery of this is simply sickening; —I can write no more.' The influence of the river journey itself had something to say to this. It is a vast implacable flood. The tangled forests on the banks seem like a symbol of disorder, desolation and disease. Religion itself becomes offensively monotonous. On every point of vantage are pagodas—stupid stalagmites of stagnant piety. There is only one dagoba with any pretence to beauty. The eccentricity is explained thus. Even the atrophied ambition of architects had become sick of perpetual plagiarism. The contractor went to the queen and asked how he should build it. She extruded one of her breasts and said, 'Take that for a model.' He did so, and the result is a refreshing relief from the routine of the regular dagoba.

But the prevailing impression is one of putrefaction. Moored to the steamer were flats piled with fish. The sun rotted them to the point when they became unfit for food. The stench was incomparable; it somehow fitted with the state of my soul. At Mandalay I exhibited this state by this entry in my diary, 'Saw palace and 450,001,293,847 pagodas.' The criticism is unjust: I had not counted them. There is, however, one good pagoda in the city, the Arrakan, and there is one really beautiful Buddha Rupa. It is said that this statue is the only one which is a portrait of Gautama from life. This may or may not be; at least it is free from the sickening conventionality of the regular smirking stupidity. The real glory of Mandalay consists of the tables of the law. There are ten thousand slabs engraved with the canon, each under a canopy to protect it from the weather. I thought I had done rather well in the matter of book production, but I had to admit I was sitting with jack high against a royal flush.

Mandalay is ghastly most of the year. It is practically under water all the summer. At least fifty per cent of the European residents are on the sick list and a goodly proportion of these die outright. There is little to choose between the Irrawaddy basin and the worst parts of West Africa.

Yet the dwellers thereof talked as if they were in a health resort whenever the Salween valley was mentioned by some intrepid spirit. This was encouraging, as my main objective involved crossing the Salween. The map had fascinated me. The Salween, the Mekong and the Yangtze Kiang run parallel for a considerable distance and they are so near together that it only took me three days between the first two of these rivers; yet the first reaches the sea at Moulmein, in the Gulf of Martaban, the second below Bangkok in the Gulf of Siam, with the whole of the Malay peninsula between them, while the third turns suddenly from south to north of east and reaches the Yellow Sea thousands of miles away. The 'divides' or watersheds between these three rivers during their dramatic parallelism must evidently be mountains of the most interesting type. I wanted to visit a corner of the earth which appealed thus vividly to' my imagination.

Incidentally, there were practical difficulties. I had at this time no notion that everybody was a perfect idiot. I could not understand the parochial psychology of the average Englishman. Even Litton, the British consul at Tengyueh, wrote, 'I will say frankly that I had no idea that Mrs Crowley or a child would be with you, and that while there is really no reason why they should not go to Yunnanfu, along the main road, they will, I fear, suffer a good deal of discomfort and inconvenience on the road from the inquisitiveness and impertinence of the Chinamen: which will try your temper. I would also recommend you to dress in Chinese style, and if Mrs Crowley would not object to a Chinese lady's upper garment or jacket, she would attract much less attention and be less subject to annoyance.'

I did not in the least understand that the average Englishman actually resents being asked to sleep in a bedroom which has not been furnished in the Tottenham Court Road, and has not hot and cold water laid on. I did not understand that his fears invariably cause him to interpret the natural curiosity of villagers who have never seen Europeans in their lives, as insolence and hostility. I did not understand that he regarded it incumbent on him to instruct the population who have been highly civilized for thousands of years in the rudiments of politeness and morality, to say nothing of religion. I knew, as I know that two and two make four, that it is only necessary to behave like a gentleman in order to calm the apprehensions of the aborigines and to appeal to the fundamental fact that all men are brothers. By this I do not mean anything stupid, sodden and sentimental; I mean that all men equally require food, clothing and shelter, in the first place; and in the second, security from aggression in respect of life and property.

Litton himself understood and appreciated the Chinese character perfectly. Though he was only the consul of the most remote town of the most remote province of the most remote empire on earth, he ruled that whole province by the sheer strength of the superiority conferred by sympathy, integrity and moral courage. But his experience had not led him to expect that any other Englishman's character could coincide with his own at all these critical points.

The irritability and insularity of the Englishman, with his snobbishness, pomposity and cant, had established a prejudice on the part of the authorities against allowing Englishmen to visit the interior of China. My countrymen could be relied upon to make mischief out of the most unpromising materials. Therefore, while the government of France encouraged its citizens to explore the province, Whitehall made it as difficult as possible for Britons. I got my permission only after senseless delay and encompassed by ridiculous restrictions.

On November 23rd I went on board the *Irrawaddy* for Bhamo, but for one cause or another she did not leave Mandalay till the twenty-ninth. There are two defiles to be passed. The river is constricted by outcrops of rock so as to form rapids so dangerous as to be navigable only with extreme caution. I reached Bhamo on December 1st.

The Irrawaddy is the scene of one of the most exciting commercial gambles of the world. At the head of the waters are mines of jade, and huge blocks of the crude mineral are shipped on rafts to merchants lower down. These blocks are bought by auction. It may almost be said that the purchaser relies on his clairvoyance, for there is no scientific means of determining what will happen when the block is split. The purchaser proceeds to split it and takes his loss or profit accordingly. The process is then repeated as the jade goes down the river. By the time it reaches Rangoon, it has been cut up into small sections and its ultimate value is approximately determined. During its transit fortunes have been made or lost.

Though the upper river passes through hilly country, it still signals its sinister message of decay and death. A dramatic incident had stamped the fact on my memory. On the steamer was an old man, a distinguished official who had intended to retire from the service and take his pension a month or two before. He had been personally requested by the lieutenant governor to postpone his return to England that he might facilitate the arrangements for the visit of the Prince of Wales. The conversation of Europeans in these parts of the earth is inexpressibly morbid; they seem obsessed by the ever present probability of death. The official tried to conceal his panic by loudly asserting a medical theory of his own, that plague, cholera, dysentery and typhoid (the four princes of the blood royal in the palace of King Death) were merely varieties of malarial fever. I said scornfully, 'Next time you get cholera, I hope they'll give you quinine.' The joke came three days later, when he died of cholera. I do not know whether they gave him quinine or not.

Bhamo is a delightful outpost. One is outside the malarial stewing of the jungle. But I got to hate it, as I wanted to proceed to China, and was held up for seventeen days by the non-arrival of my passport. The delay was partly deliberate. The deputy commissioner was absent; and his assistant was an Eurasian, who took the greatest delight in annoying the white man. I ultimately got leave to proceed over his head, and having done so rubbed it in with the following letter:

16.12.05   *Dak Bungalow, Bhamo*
Dear Sir,
    In response to your thoughtful suggestion (conveyed in your favour of yesterday's date), I did myself the honour of presuming to enter into telegraphic communication with H.B.M. Consul at Tengyueh. I will bring to your notice, with your kind permission, my intention to leave Bhamo tomorrow in consequence of the information thus conveyed; but I will refrain from agitating you with other portions of his communication.
    These, though, I suspect, will sooner or later be brought before you by His Honour the Lieutenant Governor of Burma; and I trust that you will extend to this gentleman's observations the same prompt courtesy and intelligent attenion which you have hitherto been graciously pleased to condescend to bestow upon mine.
    I must overwhelm myself in due expressions of gratitude for the untiring pains you have so willingly given yourself on

my behalf, and trust that efforts so unintermitted have had no prejudicial effect upon your constitution.

I am sure that you have thoroughly enjoyed yourself, virtue being its own reward, and I am sure I can express no more welcome good wish than that fate may soon send you another real white man to treat you as you have treated me.

I have the honour to be, Dear Sir,

Saint E. A. Crowley

The Assistant Commissioner, Bhamo

I am not a snob or a puritan, but Eurasians do get on my nerves. I do not believe that their universally admitted baseness is due to a mixture of blood or the presumable peculiarity of their parents; but that they are forced into vileness by the attitude of both their white and coloured neighbours. A similar case is presented by the Jew, who really does only too often possess the bad qualities for which he is disliked; but they are not proper to his race. No people can show finer specimens of humanity. The Hebrew poets and prophets are sublime. The Jewish soldier is courageous, the Jewish rich man generous. The race possesses imagination, romance, loyalty, probity and humanity in an exceptional degree.

But the Jew has been persecuted so relentlessly that his survival has depended on the development of his worst qualities; avarice, servility, falseness, cunning and the rest. Even the highest-class Eurasians such as Ananda Koomaraswamy suffer acutely from the shame of being considered outcast. The irrationality and injustice of their neighbours heightens the feeling and it breeds the very abominations which the snobbish inhumanity of their fellow-men expects of them.

With the departure from Bhamo may be said to begin a new phase of my career. Up to this point, I have been able to interweave the strands of my three lives; the lives of the soul, the mind and the body; or, more accurately, in the language of the Cabbala, the Neschamah, the Ruach and the Nephesch. The Hebrew sages have made an admirably simple, significant and accurate classification.

The Neschamah is that aspiration which in most men is no more than a void and voiceless longing. It becomes articulate only when it compels the Ruach to interpret it. The Nephesch, or animal soul, is not the body itself; the body is excremental, of the Qliphoth or shells. The Nephesch is that coherent brute which animates it, from the reflexes to the highest forms of conscious activity. These again are only cognizable when they translate themselves to the Ruach.

The Ruach lastly is the machine of the mind converging on a central consciousness, which appears to be the ego. The true ego is, however, above Neschamah, whose occasional messages to the Ruach warn the human ego of the existence of his superior. Such communications may be welcomed or resented, encouraged or stifled. Initiation consists in identifying the human self with the divine, and the man who does not strain constantly to this end is simply a brute made wretched and ashamed by the fact of self-consciousness.

I find by experience that this theory represents the facts very closely. I thought it necessary to give at least the bare skeleton, because the next months of our story compel me. It is no longer possible to interweave my three lives. My ordinary career becomes a welter of strange adventures, some of the most uncanny kind; yet the spiritual life is all-important and absolutely simple. The one is linked to the other only by the fact that my adventures appear as if they were so many obstacles deliberately put in the way of my performing the Operation of the Sacred Magic of Abra-Melin the Mage. I shall deal first with the life of the senses.

55

It is probably a rare incident for any young man to meet, in
the flesh, the ideal of his boyhood's dreams. Such, however
was my great good fortune. In the consul at Tengyueh, Mr
Litton, I found all that I had lost when Richard Burton died.
He possessed the spirit of adventure in its noblest and most
joyous form. He had the instinct for learning foreign languages
and dealing with foreign people; and in one respect, his
history had been similar. Some years before, he had been
consul in another part of China which was the heart of the
Boxer movement. Moving, as he did, among the Chinese in
the most intimate way, he understood the feeling behind the
agitation. He employed his genius in unravelling the conspiracy and succeeded in discovering the plans of the Boxers
in detail. This information he communicated to the authorities
in Peking. It will be remembered that Burton did exactly the
same thing in the matter of the Indian Mutiny; and to a
certain extent, Sir William Butler had done this with regard to
the Boers.

The result in each case was exactly the same. The indignant
authorities banished Litton to the remote and unimportant
post of Tengyueh, at the very edge of the wildest province
of China. But it is hard to keep a good man down. Litton's
influence over the natives was so great that he was the real
ruler of the province. He was just starting on tour to compose
some native squabble near the frontier, some thirty miles from
Tengyueh; and we lunched together by the wayside. He had
done miracles to smooth my path.

He had been originally alarmed by my taking my wife and
child with me on such a journey. His letter amused me very
much; it showed the class of English people with whom he was
expected to deal. He expected us to scream if hot water and
cold water was not laid on in every Chinese inn, and to take
down every Chinese coolie, farmer or merchant for a murderer
with a special 'down' on 'foreign devils'. He thought that we
would be very much upset by that natural curiosity of the
natives at seeing a white woman and interpret their interest as

intentional insult. When he found with what practical com
mon sense I travelled, he realized immediately that there was
going to be no trouble. During this lunch he gave me more
genuinely valuable information about China than I had had in
the whole previous course of my life One of his sayings was
this: whatever one hears, however extraordinary, is true in
China somewhere or other!

He also told me the main psychological difference between
the Chinese and Indian as regards practical dealings with them
The Chinese does not respect the white man as the Indian does
—for his possession of high moral qualities. The very coolies
despise their wealthiest merchants for their honesty, which,
by the way, is unique in commerce. They respect any man
who acts as their own mandarins act; with absolute lack of
sympathy, justice or any other human feelings. They treat
the traveller well in proportion as he is overbearing, haughty
and avaricious.

I found, in fact, that it was necessary to throw the whole of
my previous principles overboard. One cannot fraternize with
the Chinese of the lower classes; one must treat them with
absolute contempt and callousness. On the other hand the
Chinese gentleman is the noblest and courtliest in the world.
His general bearing is that of Athos in *The Three Musketeers*,
at his best. One's relations with him should be those of absolute
mutual respect; and here again, intimacy of any kind is impossible. Each man abides on pinnacles of isolation. A typical case
is the relation of the Emperor to a man like Li Hung-chang.
The Son of Heaven was so far above even the greatest of his
subjects that he could make no difference between him and the
commonest labourer. He wrote to him simply as Li.

Litton furnished me with careful notes of the stages of my
journey to Yunnanfu, which I found extremely useful. I
could not start from Tengyueh until my passport arrived from
the consulate general. With extreme kindness, Litton invited
me to stay at the consulate until it arrived. He himself hoped
to be back in Tengyueh within a week, so that I expected to
see him again and learn more of his vision We sat and talked
for a couple of hours, each feeling instinctively that he had
found a sympathetic spirit.

The march from Bhamo to Tengyueh had been rather eventful. The first day was a pleasant ride of about nine miles to
Mamouk where we dined at the officers' mess. We were still
in the Burmese atmosphere and the minds of the people were

preoccupied with European affairs and disease. There was no trace of the singular horror with which I was to come in contact beyond the frontier, a horror from which I found no one but Litton himself entirely free, until I got into the sphere of French influence. The next day we covered twenty-one miles and the third sixteen, where we camped for the first time in the open. The scenery had not been particularly striking; but there was a feeling of openness on leaving the Irrawaddy basin which we found extremely pleasant.

On the fourth day we crossed the Chinese frontier. At this point it is marked by a small stream in a ravine. There is no proper bridge; only an insecure-looking tree trunk. I had doubts about my pony and decided to walk across. I was of course riding last to prevent straggling, and by the time I had crossed the stream the rest of the party were out of sight around the corner of the path which rises sharply along the hillside, in order to cross the mountain. I had got a little stiff with riding and thought I would stretch my legs; so I walked with my horse up the slope for some distance. Deciding to remount, I swung my leg over the saddle; and, before I was seated, the brute put his hind hoof over the khud, which was here precipitous. We rolled over each other twice, a distance of thirty or forty feet.

We were neither of us in the least hurt; my feeling was one of plain astonishment. I looked up at the cliff. It was well within my powers to climb, but there was no possibility of getting the pony up. I climbed up the path and carefully retied my turban, which had come off, before shouting for Salama to come back and extricate my horse. I felt it essential to show myself imperturbable. The men returned to find me quietly sitting and smoking. They had considerable difficulty in finding a way round for the pony. The day's adventures were not yet over. Just before getting to camp I was kicked on the thigh by a mule. I shall explain later the extreme importance of this day in my career.

There was quite a series of small accidents during these days. Salama had started it by falling off his mule. Then came my turn. The day after, Rose and the baby fell while walking across a bridge, quite incomprehensibly. It was extraordinary luck that they did not come to serious grief. The day after, we spent the night in a Buddhist temple after a march in the pouring rain, during which the ayah was both kicked and bitten by a mule. The day after that it was again my turn to be kicked. I have had a good deal of experience with mules in various parts of the world; but only in this short section did such things occur.

This day was again very wet. The road led over a pass three thousand feet high. I say 'road', and of course this is the main highway from Burma to China, just as the road we had followed from Srinagar is the main highway from Kashmir to Turkestan. In neither case would it be considered good going by the average goat. The day we were to arrive at Tengyueh, the ayah gave us the slip. We had camped by a hot spring the night previous, in company with a caravan bound for Burma. One of the muleteers took the fancy of the lady and she decided to throw in her lot with his and go off to Burma. She had been such a bad servant and given so much trouble that I made no attempt to retrieve her.

We met with a warm welcome at the consulate from Litton's Chinese wife, an exceedingly beautiful woman with perfect manners. They had five charming children. The prejudice against half-castes requires analysis. It is not the mixture of blood, as a rule, that makes the majority of them such degraded specimens of humanity, but the circumstances usually attending their birth. These circumstances, again, are due to the crass imbecility of public morality. When the child is a by-blow of drunken Tommy and a bazaar woman there is no need of profound anthropological hypotheses to explain why it is not a Newton or a Chesterfield. There is no doubt, however, that some races make better combinations than others. The best class of Englishman and the best class of Chinese mingle admirably, provided (of course) that the children are brought up decently in an environment where they are not handicapped from the first by feeling themselves objects of dislike and contempt. Nothing is worse for children than to be humiliated; they should be brought up to realize that they are 'kings and priests unto God'.

The foreign colony at Tengyueh was small and dull. The head of the customs was Napier, the son of an old friend of my father's. He was a melancholy aristocrat who only kept himself from going insane in these monotonously uncongenial surroundings by a sort of Promethean courage. The other Britons have made no impression on my mind soever. There was a Norwegian missionary named Amundsen, even more colourless and doleful than brainless Scandinavians usually are. The doctor was a Bengali named Ram Lal Sircar, a burly nigger of the most loathsome type. I am not fond of Bengalis at the best and he was the worst specimen of his race I have ever seen. He was fat and oily, with small piglike treacherous eyes. On the rare occasions when he was not eating, he was writing anti-British articles for the Bengal native press.

There was, however, a guest at the consulate with whom I struck up an immediate warm friendship. This was a botanist named George Forrest, who was recuperating from an adventure which I must narrate in some detail, as it includes one of the most striking ghost stories I ever heard. His happy hunting ground had been the Mekong-Salween divide. He had been north beyond the twenty-eighth parallel, in country practically untraversed by any whites, among mountains which rose to nineteen thousand feet. His headquarters was a Jesuit mission.

The district had been disturbed for some time; a comparatively important town was the centre of a small revolt against the Chinese government. An army had been dispatched to reduce it. The siege was typically Chinese. Having invested the town, the imperial general made no attempt to take it by assault; he simply entered into negotiations with the garrison as to the price of the surrender. After interminable haggling, a sum was fixed. So much is intelligible, but at this point the baffling psychology of the Chinese comes into play. The inhabitants were put to the sword and the town sacked, exactly as if it had been taken as the result of murderous conflicts.

The general weakening of the imperial authority led to the outbreak of raids on the part of the Buddhist lamas who lived in remote serais perched upon the inaccessible crags of the mountains bordering Tibet. Bands of these monks swept down from their fastnesses to indulge in orgies of rapine, rape, murder and cannibalism. (The official descriptions of the various hells in the Buddhist canon are of course actual pictures of fact; the tortures of the damned are simply slight exaggerations of those actually inflicted by Buddhists on their enemies. In particular, it was the custom of these lamas to devour the hearts and livers of their enemies in order to acquire their vitality and courage. As I have already explained, I do not regard this as superstitious; I think it is practical common sense.)

Forrest was at the Jesuit mission when word came from the north that the lamas were on the war path. It was decided to flee and the entire mission hurried off. Its eldest member, Father Bernard, was a man over eighty. It was decided to separate for greater safety; but Forrest found it very hard to bring himself to leave the old man, for whom he had acquired extreme respect and affection. However, it was the only thing to do, and Forrest plunged off alone into an obscure side valley hoping to reach the comparative safety of the main road from Tengyueh to Yunnanfu by means of a detour.

The nightfall of the second day showed him the camp fires of the lamas on the hills to the south and he recognized that he was cut off. In the light of the fires he could see the gigantic silhouettes of their hounds. He suddenly realized that his European boots made it easy to track him, so he discarded them. During the day, the slightest movement might easily be observed, or the hounds might be on his track, so he spent it under a rock which overhung the river, up to his neck in the icy water. When night fell, he crawled out and tried to get some warmth into his body. (His food soon failed him. During this adventure he lived for eight days on nothing at all and for the twenty-one following on tsampa, Tibetan flour, which has the property of producing violent diarrhoea in the average European.)

Night came on utterly black and Forrest was suddenly aware of a luminous figure standing beside him. He recognized it immediately as that of Father Bernard. He thought to himself, 'They have caught and killed him!' (This was subsequently verified. The old man met his end earlier on that day.) The phantom did not speak, but its right arm was outstretched as if to urge Forrest to seek refuge in that direction. Forrest laughed to himself, despite the atrocious circumstances, at the absurdity; the direction indicated was the one of all others which was most certainly fatal to take. After a few minutes the figure disappeared. Dawn broke and showed him the situation unchanged. He passed a second day in the water under the rock.

The second night the spectre reappeared. Again he pointed in the same direction and this time the gesture was imperious. Forrest's instinct of self-preservation had been practically worn out by hardship. 'Oh well,' he said to himself, 'a quick death is better than this,' and off he went in the direction designated. He had not gone far before he fell in with a countryman who offered to help him to escape, and led him, barefoot as he was, across a snow-covered pass over fifteen thousand feet high. They met no lamas and eventually reached the main road, where Forrest fell in with a caravan of merchants travelling to Tengyueh, who treated him well and had him carried to the consulate, where I found him, still weak from his adventure and still shaken in nerve. He told his story with the utmost modesty and equanimity; and I could not doubt that the apparition of Father Bernard was a fact. That it should have pointed out the way of salvation in the most unlikely direction certainly indicated supernormal knowledge.

The atmosphere at Tengyueh was intensely oppressive. The conversation invariably turned upon battle, murder and sudden death, embroidered with fantastic wealth of disease and torture. It was an absolute nightmare. I really take great credit to myself for having spent twenty-five days in this community without losing my nerve or becoming obsessed. Everyone seemed to be preoccupied with the idea that at any moment the Chinese might break out and put us all to the most cruel death.

I must admit that there was a quite unusual number of really terrifying incidents; even trifling occurrences seemed too apt to take on a sinister significance. For instance, two of Litton's horses died suddenly. I diagnosed anthrax and wanted to take the obvious measures; but there was nothing to be done. The servants at the consulate had taken the carcasses to the market and spent the next three days in janging for them. To jang is to haggle; but the most inveterate haggler is a fixed price merchant in comparison. It was certainly the limit to think of the animals being sold for human food! One must be resolute to prevent one's mind from dwelling on such subjects; one must take one's precautions so far as possible without thinking about the threatened calamity.

Another disquieting incident was as follows. Tengyueh was supposed to be in direct telegraphic communication with Peking. One of the most absurdly characteristic arrangements was that the observatory at Peking telegraphed to us daily the correct time. Now at Yunchang there was a relay and, as often as not, the telegraphists would be engaged in smoking opium for three or four days at a time. Consequently a whole bunch of telegrams would arrive late one evening telling us that it was noon at Peking.

One was therefore not very sure of getting the news. And just about this time a message came through telling us of the riots in Shanghai and that seventeen people had been killed. We could not tell how serious this might be; whether it was a local outbreak or whether it was part of a general anti-foreign rising. I heard later the details. The European colony had been badly scared and fortified themselves in the country club; but the riot fizzled out. It was none the less alarming to get an isolated item of news of this kind. Thinking of it today, I wonder that it never occurred to me to go back to Burma. I did not feel either courageous about it or alarmed. There is in me a quality of almost imbecile stoicism. I simply cannot be bothered to worry about danger or hardship of any kind unless it is forced on my immediate notice.

I cannot account for this peculiar imperturbability. It seems entirely at war with my extreme sensitiveness. And yet it may indeed be the Freudian protection against this; it may be that my instincts warn me that if I allow myself to think at all on certain subjects the pain will be unendurable. However that may be, there is no doubt that I possess a peculiar solidity; having decided to do anything, I go on my course no matter what new facts arise. I will not go a step out of my path to avoid the most obvious unpleasantness. And I have certainly never been able to make up my mind whether this quality is an advantage in the long run or no.

The final episode of my story at Tengyueh might indeed have caused most men to change their plan. It is in many ways the most dramatic adventure of my life and has left an ineradicable impression on my mind. I despair of describing its intensity or the wildness of the setting. The oppressively electric atmosphere of the previous three weeks, the indescribable apprehension which hung over the colony, suddenly discharged itself in a thunderbolt.

At eight p.m. on January 10th we were sitting at dinner in the consulate when we heard confused cries and flying footsteps in the courtyard. The doors were suddenly flung open and a gigantic runner dripping with sweat came crashing into the room, sprawling his gaunt arms and legs in the extravagance of his gestures. For a moment we believed that an attack was imminent but Forrest soon elicited a somewhat vague story to the effect that Litton was ill and required the services of a doctor. He was said to be camped at about two days' march away in the direction of Bhamo; but we resolved to cover the distance in the course of the night. Forrest being my senior, and knowing the language, was evidently marked as chief of the expedition. I put myself unreservedly at his orders.

The first thing was to get horses, which was easy; the second to rout out the Bengali, which was an entirely different proposition. It was after nine o'clock before he joined us at the outskirts of the town. The word forward was given, and Forrest and I galloped furiously into the darkness. We kept up a tremendous pace as far as the foot of the hills. It was a wild and windy night; torn clouds scudded fitfully across a misty moon. Some rain had fallen and the broad smooth stones of the road were as slippery as glass. It was impossible to ride on the slopes; the tatu stumbled at every step.

My mountain boots with their wrought iron nails proved equally awkward. I was forced to march, supporting myself with one hand on the pony's neck and urging him with my whip with the other. We pressed on eagerly through the night; and at last we came to the crest of the ridge and began to run down the other side of the path towards the hot springs. There was just sufficient light in the east to reveal the landscape by the time we got near the foot of the hill. Then I saw a litter slowly approaching. Forrest gave a shout and dashed enthusiastically forward; but I silently turned my horse, for I saw that the consul's legs were tied.

The situation, apart from its tragic present, was full of anxiety for the future. How had Litton died? A glance at the body was not reassuring. There were symptoms which suggested poison and the least sinister alternative was some deadly infection. I wanted a medical opinion; but the doctor avoided the neighbourhood of the litter, saying that the examination could be made at Tengyueh. I did not fully realize what was behind this and acquiesced. He hurried back much faster than he had come. For all I knew, he had it in his mind to make various preparations.

About four o'clock we reached a wretched hamlet where some coolies had kindled a fire in the street. The bearers of the litter, utterly fagged out, threw themselves down by the fire. There was some loose straw lying about and Forrest and I followed their example. We tried to learn the circumstances of Litton's death; but the men gave vague and apparently contradictory accounts of what had happened. It was awkward; some of them might have been in a conspiracy; and we had no means of telling its purport or extent. I snatched a few moments of that uneasy slumber which supervenes upon exhaustion and distress, and dulls while it does not rest the nerves.

We started again at about half-past six and reached Tengyueh at about ten o'clock. We had allowed the litter to precede us, thinking that the doctor would be in waiting, having made all arrangements, but we found that nothing of the sort had been done. The coolies had simply dumped the body in the outer courtyard of the consulate. We had it taken into an empty room on the opposite side of that in which people were living and sent round for the doctor. He returned an evasive answer.

After several further messages, Forrest lost patience and asked me to go round and bring him back by force if necessary. It must not be supposed that Forrest was in any way hysterical. It was immediately urgent to ascertain the cause of Litton's death. The safety of the European community might depend on it. If he had died by violence, our one chance might be for troops to be rushed up for our protection; if by disease, to take quarantine measures.

I found the Bengali seated at his table before a plate of rice such as I have never seen in my life. There was certainly enough for six average people. I stayed a few moments to watch the process of deglutition. It was well worth seeing; and from the debris on the table, it was clear that this was merely a little light dessert. I did not lose my temper; but I must confess to being very angry. I asked him to come round and he then began to try to get out of it altogether. I soon saw that he had made up his mind that the consul had died of some dangerously infectious disease and was solely preoccupied with keeping himself out of danger.

Persuasion and reproach failing to reach him, I resorted to the use of my whalebone cutting-whip. He made no attempt to ward off the blows, still less to tackle me; he simply cowered and howled. I stopped at intervals to impress upon his mind that I intended to go on until he came with me to do his duty. He ultimately gave in and I drove him down the street to the consulate. But once in the chamber of death, it was still impossible to get him to make a proper examination. He would not approach the body. Forrest and I cut off the clothes.

There were some curious wounds caused, in my judgment, by the attempts of some of the coolies to relieve the symptoms. They were none of them serious in themselves. The main visible symptom was large patches of extravasated blood. The doctor refused point blank to make a post-mortem and said he would give his certificate that death was due to erysipelas. He then bolted. His next act was to remember that erysipelas was a notifiable infectious disease and that therefore his best course was to find my wife and child, and endeavour to communicate it if possible. Luckily she had sufficient sense to keep herself and the baby out of his way.

Only one thing was needed to put the lid on. When Forrest

and I had done what was necessary, we proceeded to disinfect ourselves before rejoining the rest. The missionary Amundsen rushed up to us in great excitement and called our attention to an illustrated newspaper which he had just received. 'Look,' he cried, 'there is the Norwegian royal family!'

We buried Litton the following day.

The next business was to get off. My permission had arrived, but I was told that I must engage an interpreter. I should have been only too glad to have one; but I might as well have looked for a snowball in hell. Eventually they dug up a person named Johnny White. He was the first Chinese with whom I had been in direct permanent connection; and I was highly amused to discover that his Chinese name had been Ah Sin. He had been brought up from infancy at the Wesleyan Mission at Mandalay. As a servant he had the defect that he was continually drunk on arrack and opium. As an interpreter, one, he spoke no Chinese; two, he spoke no English. It was with the utmost pain that I was able to communicate with him at all. I cross-examined him, of course very severely, as to his religion. It took a long time for him to grasp my meaning; but ultimately he reassured me as to his creed, which was this: 'John Wesley all same God.' He was so besotted with drink and drugs that his human qualities, if he ever possessed any, were completely in abeyance. His name was soon corrupted into 'Janwar'—which is Hindustani for 'wild animal'.

The journey to Yunnanfu was unique in my life in one important respect. I became richer as I went along—by the simple process of spending my money! It was impossible to get a change of silver except at one or two points. I carried the bulk of my money in copper cash. (Everyone knows the coins with the square holes.) These furnished loads for two men. I must explain the financial status of this part of the world. Silver money had no denomination, but was valued by weight, and the 'coinage' consisted of lumps of silver, whose purity was guaranteed by its shape. The bulkier kind was something like a houseboat, some three inches long and between one and two in the other dimensions. The other kind was not unlike a tortoise and its surface had a peculiar striation. Thus there were these lumps of silver identified as the products of the imperial mint.

Now, there was a varying relation (rate of exchange) between a certain weight of this silver and a string of cash. A string consisted nominally of a hundred cash; but these were what was called market cash. A certain number of cash counted as a hundred for all commercial purposes and this number varied with the district. Now, as it happened, this number was constantly decreased all the way to Yunnanfu, so that if I wished to buy something at Tengyuen for a hundred cash I had to hand over a string containing eighty-nine coins, whereas a similar transaction at Talifu required only seventy odd, and near Yunnansen forty-six if I remember right. I was consequently always having to take off coins from my original strings. The number of my strings therefore increased as I went along, although I was spending freely. In this way I became continually richer.

To conclude the financial question. This system broke up suddenly and completely on arrival at Yunnansen. Here the French were trying to extend their influence from Tonkin in pursuance of which object they had flooded the city with agents who were trying to force the French dollar into circulation. Opposed to them were the two old systems; valuing silver by weight, the tael; and the Mexican dollar, which had hitherto been the universal currency of the coast. (The Mexican dollar was itself guaranteed by being stamped by the mark or initials of some responsible firm of merchants.) Peking had just begun to coin a dollar of its own with the imperial dragon. This is one of the most beautiful coins I have ever seen.

The result of the contention of the currencies was that in Yunnansen one could buy things at an absurdly low price, provided that one would pay with the dollars which the merchant was being subsidized to accept. 'When thieves fall out, honest men come by their own.' It is certainly amusing to watch them cutting their own throats in order to cut ours more efficiently later on. I only wish we could stop the second part of the process.

We reached Yunchangfu on the fifth day from Tengyueh. Our first march took us up the valley of the Shweli, which we crossed on a floating bamboo bridge. The road from here to Pingho winds uphill for about five thousand feet. The road was nowhere really bad, but in some places so steep that riding was difficult. The third day took us to Lu Chiang Chiao, in the valley of the Salween. The gorge is indescribably sublime. It is sentinelled by magnificent hills of splendid and seductive shapes. The air was mild yet fresh. No menace of chill, yet no taint of oppression. The road was not so steep as on the other side of the watershed and the descent afforded a series of superb views.

The Salween has the reputation of being the most deadly

river in the world. Its only rivals are in New Guinea and, at an earlier day, the Amazon, the Niger and the Congo. It is supposed to have a specially fatal form of malaria which kills most people outright and from which no one ever wholly recovers. No doubt, some of the lower reaches are extremely pestilential; but in this section one might establish an ideal sanatorium. The course of the Salween had not at that time been completely explored. There is not only fever but massacre in that romantic ravine. Part of it is inhabited by the Lolos (they are not vaudeville artists but tribes) reported to be exceedingly primitive and addicted to head hunting, kidney chasing, phallus fishing and testicle trapping, so that their cooks are famous for stewed spleen, pancreas puddings and appendix on toast.

I met a number of these tribesmen; they reminded me very much of some of the wandering peoples of Central Asia and various folks of the low country of Mexico; and I was reminded of them in turn by many of the nomads of the Sahara. They were very different from the Chinese in costume, manner and appearance. In character, I found them charmingly childlike. Of course, it was easy enough to imagine that a tactless traveller might alarm them in all sorts of ways without intending to do so, and that they would react as naturally and innocently as any other creatures of the wild might do. But they were entirely free from the malignant envy, the panic born of prejudice and the perverse passions produced by hypocritically pretending to suppress natural instincts, which one associates with tradesmen in the West End of London and ministers of religion.

Litton's idea of a holiday had been to explore the upper reaches of this river. He had in fact wanted to reach that very spot which I had myself picked out for my objective, where the Salween, Mekong and Yangtze Kiang run parallel to within a space of forty miles, while at their mouths the distance between each is two thousand miles instead of twenty. At each village Litton was received with the utmost courtesy and goodwill; but when he disclosed his intention of proceeding northwards, it created panic. They told him that to the north were no men but devils only; accursed races of the pit whose only methods of communicating ideas were envenomed arrows, pitfalls and the poisonous fluff of the bamboo which acts more subtly than ground glass.

I thought this story extraordinarily typical of human thought in general. Everyone admits that we have reached the summit of wisdom, scaled the loftiest pinnacles of morality, put the crown of perfection upon the cranium of progress, and everyone knows perfectly well how this remarkable result has been achieved. But at the first hint that anyone proposes to take a step farther on this road, he is universally set down as a lunatic of the most dangerous type. However, the most savage Lolos are content with that diagnosis, whereas the most enlightened English add that the pioneer is not only a lunatic but a pervert, degenerate, anarchist and the rest of it—whatever terms of abuse chance to be in fashion. The abolition of slavery, humane treatment of the insane, the restriction of the death penalty to serious offences, and of indiscriminate flogging, the admission of Jews, Catholics, Dissenters and women as citizens, the introduction of the use of chloroform and antiseptics, the application of steam to travel, and of mechanical principles to such arts as spinning and printing, the systematic study of nature, the extension of the term poetry to metres other than the heroic, the recognition of painting other than voluptuous coloured photographs as art, and of music other than classical melody as art—these and a thousand similar innovations have all been denounced as chimerical, blasphemous, obscene, seditious, anti-social and what not.

We crossed the Salween by means of a bridge ornamented with shrines and a delightful and romantically beautiful house for the toll-keeper. Caesar, when he crossed the Rubicon, had less aesthetic attractions and less expense. I did not envy him, and as for the bridge, it did not seem aware of its responsibilities, which is perhaps the best state of mind in which a bridge can be.

The road was in unexpectedly good condition from the Salween to Pu Pa'o, a long stage rendered unpleasant towards the end by threatening rain, which carried out its fell designs in the course of the night. For the first time we experienced native curiosity in wholesale form. We had been recommended to avoid this by secretiveness. This strange wild beast, a white woman, was to be camouflaged in Chinese clothes and bundled out of sight as soon as possible.

I adopted exactly opposite tactics. I said to the people, 'Come and see, enlarge your minds, increase your experience, take the fullest advantage of this opportunity.' They were so accustomed to conventional European cowardice that at first they were inclined to be unruly and even suspicious. Can it be a trap? But a few minutes convinced them of my absolute faith and friendliness, so that everyone became good-tempered and

The Magician, 1911. Crowley at his altar, magically robed, and equipped with wand, bell, sword, cup, phial of holy Abra-Melin oil. His hand rests on the Stele of Revealing. The book is *The Book of the Law*. He is crowned with the Egyptian Uraeus serpent and upon his finger is the ring of Nuit.

THE CONFESSIONS OF
ALEISTER CROWLEY

(Above) Aleister Crowley's mother. He called her "a brainless bigot of the most narrow, logical and inhuman type." She thought he was the incarnation of the Beast of Revelation. (Right) Crowley's father, one of the leaders of the Plymouth Brethren sect. He preached up and down the country. "Get right with God," was his cry. (Left) The schoolboy in hell: Crowley aged 14.

The poet, before the Great Awakening: Crowley at 30.

Osiris Risen: Crowley formulating
the Pentagram in the Golden Dawn, 1899.

The only known photograph of Samuel Liddell MacGregor Mathers, the Head of the Golden Dawn. He holds the Lotus Wand in a Rite of Isis, which he performed in Paris shortly after the collapse of the Golden Dawn in London.

Crowley on the Deosai Plateau in the Himalayas,
1905, the year he led the expedition to Kangchenjunga.

The explorer, mountaineer and big-game hunter.
Crowley, *circa* 1906.

The expedition to Chogo Ri, 1902. *Left to right (standing):* V. Wessely, H. Pfannl. *Center:* Oscar Eckenstein, Aleister Crowley. *Foreground:* Dr. J. Jacot Guillarmod, Guy Knowles.

Crowley's first wife, Rose Edith Kelly,
his Scarlet Woman for the Cairo Working.

Sister Cybele (Leila Waddell), who played the
violin in Crowley's Rites of Eleusis, at Caxton Hall,
1910. She was one of Crowley's magical assistants;
hence the Mark of the Beast between her breasts.

Crowley, *circa* 1910, wearing the headdress of Horus. He is making the sign of Pan, the horns (thumbs) indicating creative energy. On the table is his book of Abra-Melin talismans and the rood cross with topaz which he used for skrying.

The Stele of Revealing, exhibit number 666 in the Boulak Museum, Cairo. The Pantacle of Ankh-f-n-Khonsu, a priest of the XXVIth dynasty who, according to Crowley, foretold the advent of the New Aeon. Crowley believed that he himself was Ankh-f-n-Khonsu in a previous incarnation.

Baphomet, the Supreme and Holy King of Ireland, Iona, and all the Britains that are in the Sanctuary of the Gnosis, O.T.O. Crowley in full Masonic regalia, 1916.

The Arabian alchemist: Crowley smoking his favorite mixture, perique soaked in rum.

Leah Hirsig, the Scarlet Woman,
in Crowley's Greenwich Village studio,
New York, 1918. *Background:*
Crowley's "Dead Souls" painting.

The Beast (in Higland dress)
and the Scarlet Woman, Alostrael,
at the Abbey of Thelema,
the headquarters of their new social
experiment in life, love, liberty
and light, 1921. Alostrael (Leah Hirsig)
is holding their baby, Poupée, who
died shortly afterward.

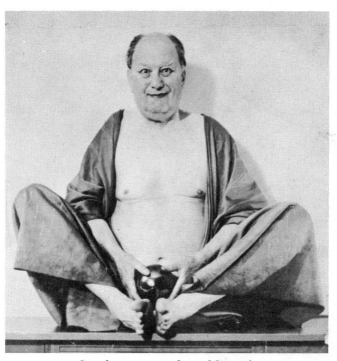

Crowley assuming the god form of
Fo-hi, the Chinese god of joy and laughter.

Betty May, the artists' model, who was taken by her
husband, Raoul Loveday, to Crowley's Abbey of Thelema.

Sketch by Crowley of a devouring demon.

The Beast 666. Aleister Crowley at the age of 37.

Maria Teresa
Ferrari de Miramar
and Aleister
Crowley: they
were married in
Leipzig
during August
1929.

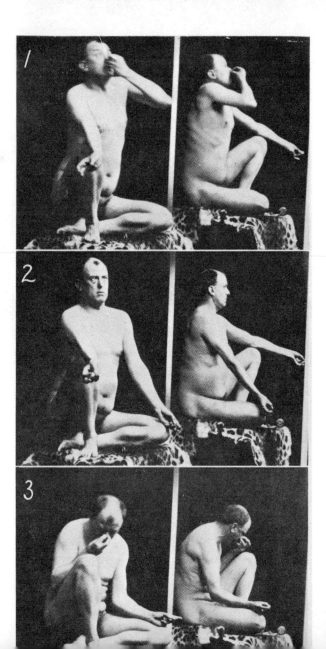

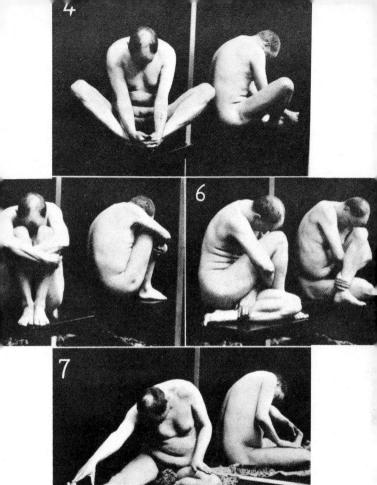

Crowley demonstrating a yogic technique
of breath-control (Pranayama), *circa* 1912.

Crowley in
his room in
Jermyn Street,
Piccadilly,
circa 1943.

The hands of
Aleister Crowley
locked in
yogic mudra or
mystical gesture,
affirming the
union of the active
and the passive.

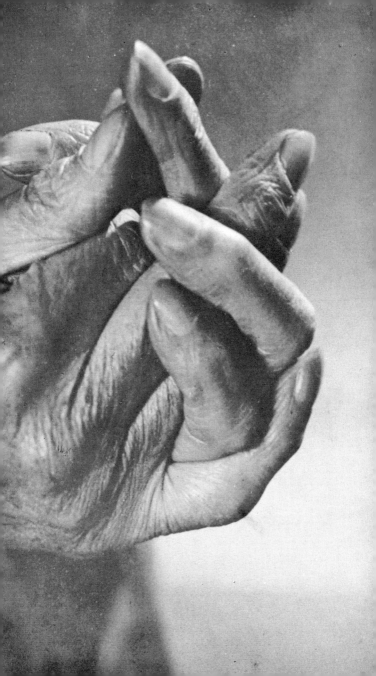

The Master Therion or the Beast 666,
a self-portrait with the Horus forelock,
symbol of the solar-phallic power.

frank. Their instinct and good manners, which nearly all men outside civilization possess, soon told them what conduct was really annoying and offensive; and they abstained immediately.

Europeans too often make up their minds to resent certain actions which are really quite harmless and natural. They persuade themselves that everything which their grandmothers would not do in Sunday School must be resented with the utmost rigour. This attitude is the root of at least nine-tenths of the trouble about 'foreign devils'. The only unpleasantness between local natives and alleged whites which came under my notice during this journey was when some travelling missionary, instead of attending to his own affairs, took it upon himself to insult (in wretchedly and comically illiterate Chinese) some villagers who happened to be carrying an idol in procession as part of the festivities of New Year's Day (January 25th). He might as well have spoiled a children's party on the ground that the fairy stories which amused them were not strictly true.

The action was morally indistinguishable from brawling in church. I may not believe in the liquefaction of the blood of St Januarius, but I see no reason for inflicting my incredulity on the people of Naples. The villagers naturally resented the ill manners of this brainless boor and told him to shut up. He immediately began to scream that he was being martyred for Christ's sake. I told him that if I could have brought myself to touch him, I would have thrashed him within an inch of his life. He did not understand my attitude; but I don't suppose there is much in this funny world that he did understand.

On the twenty-third we came to Yunchangfu. The road during this march was in excellent repair. It bordered a lovely lake, which interested me extremely as having no obvious outlet unless through a curious rocky cave; but I could not be sure of this, no current of any sort being visible.

On arrival in the town I was greeted by the Tao Tai, who sent a deputation of brilliantly clad and highly dignified servants with presents. These of course I returned with the exception of one or two trifles which I retained in order to avoid discourtesy, and on my part bestowed goods of European manufacture.

The next act was an interview with the mandarin in his hall of state where we sat side by side, low down, leaving the place of honour for the Son of Heaven and his immediate satellites. Having exchanged polite generalities about philosophy and virtue (he seemed to think that I was no mean authority on the latter subject) we dealt lightly with more mundane topics and proceeded to extricate ourselves from each other's presence in accordance with the most elaborate etiquette. He concluded by inviting me to share with him the offal which had been rejected by the dogs and kites and I expressed my humble rapture at being permitted to partake of the celestial banquet which his heavenly hospitality had prepared for the meanest and mouldiest of mankind.

The mandarin was one of the most beautiful men I have ever seen. I use the word beautiful in its strictly aesthetic sense. He was, I judge, between thirty-five and forty years old; his features were astonishingly perfect and their expression full of noble intelligence and lofty benevolence, harmonized by a placidity due to a consciousness of his superiority so unbroken and unquestioned that it had been absorbed into subconsciousness. He was a miracle of art and that art perfectly concealed. His complexion had more than the smoothness of the most exquisite southern European types; yet all this impeccability of excellence was not marred, as is too often the case with Greek sculpture, by lacking that touch of the bizarre which Goethe postulates as essential to supreme beauty. He possessed that peace which I believe is intended to inform images of the Buddha, but which nearly always appears as a mere lack of any positive passion. The mandarin of Yunchang radiated royalty.

It was easy to read his history; that he had been exiled to so remote and barbarous a city bore witness to the heinousness of the offence which had incurred so severe a sentence. On subsequent inquiry I was told that he had been accused of 'failing in respect towards the imperial swans'. My informant did not say in what his error of ritual consisted. (Another rumour, so absurd as to be credible, is that he was not criminal at all but insane; that he had the delusion that he was a Fellow of St John's College, whether Cambridge or Oxford, I did not learn; and from all accounts it makes little difference.) The superb epicureanism of his expression was equally indicative of his spiritual superiority to even such blasting disaster as the wrath of the emperor and his divine mother.

The banquet was worthy of the man. Beginning at high noon, it ended only when Kephra [1] the Beetle passed through the pylon of midnight; and during these twelve hours, there was no intermission in the arrival of new dishes and entertainments. The opulence of Trimalchio was concealed beneath the refinement of Lucullus and the culture of Horace.

Of late years Chinese cooking has become popular, though not nearly as popular as it deserves to be, in New York, Paris and London. In New York it is the best food; in Amurrka, outside New York, it is the only food (bar sea-food) fit for human consumption save in the Indian Grill Room in Los Angeles, Chez Antoine in New Orleans, and one or two other remote oases in the wilderness of canned abominations. In London, the vulgarity of the idea of a square meal has destroyed oriental delicacy; in Paris the refinement of French epicureanism combines with the charm of China.

But nowhere in Europe or America is the Chinese cook able to convey the essence of his excellence. One can no more understand a Chinese dish in Europe than one can enjoy an Egyptian cigarette. As to cross running water destroys the enchantment of witches, or to traverse black seas destroys the caste of the Brahmin, so the flavour of Chinese food is bounded by the Great Wall. I well understand why the exiled Mongol feels that he cannot rest in peace in any other than the sacred soil. The dishes too which one obtains at Beem Nom Low's or at the Taverne Pascal are not those esoteric—shall we say Eleusinian?—ecstasies which interpret the soul of the Wonderland of Flowers.

I may mention a condiment composed exclusively of rose petals from which, by a subtle process, all those elements which are capable of nourishing the human body have been abstracted. But for the most part I dare not even describe some of the dainties which make Yunchang, to this day, a fragrant memory in my mind. To do so would be to draw a culinary parallel with *Le Jardin des Supplices*. Not that that book is the real China; it is rather a wish phantasm of China by the delirium of a degenerate.

Yunchang is noted for its temples. In one of those is a superb delineation of some of the Buddhist hells, where the penalties for various vices are depicted with what is sometimes very startling realism. I was sorry not to have been able to stay longer in this perfumed paradise of beauty and pleasure, where every element of art and nature were harmoniously woven as if endeavouring to echo the melody of the personality of the mandarin.

The next day took us over superbly swelling hills upon whose bosom slumbered a lake. Here once more I was mystified as to its outlet. At the end of a delicious day we slept in a temple. It was the first day of the year and everyone but the missionary was rejoicing. Crackers clustered on long poles of bamboo and gay ornaments of coloured paper were the principal offerings to the eye, while the ear was delighted with all kinds of instrumental and vocal music. Strange delicate cakes and comfits tempted the tongue, while faint perfumes stirred the nostrils. The breeze was sweet with burning sandalwood and subtle with the sweat of dainty dancers. Even the sense of touch vibrated with virile joy as one's nerves trembled beneath the beatitude of innocent people swarming on every side.

I have noted about this day's march, 'Roads everywhere good.' 'Good' is a relative term. The Chinese have a proverb that a road is good for ten years and bad for ten thousand; most of this particular road I estimated at not less than eight thousand. I actually proposed to bring home one bit of it; if the weight had not been prohibitive, it would have been well worthwhile. This was a slab of granite about fifteen feet long, three broad and three thick, and holes had been bored completely through it by the hoofs of pack animals, so that the mud was visible clean through the stone.

56

The day after New Year we crossed the Mekong. The river flows through a superb gorge with extremely steep banks. Inscriptions of all kinds were carved on the naked cliffs. I was aware of a very curious sensation in crossing both this river and the Salween. I can only describe it by saying that I seemed to be aware of the genius loci. At night, the wild beauty of the scenery was further enhanced. A house in the adjacent fields, several acres in extent, caught fire. This warm glow in the midst of the cold vastness of the plateau and the stars was very weird; and the silhouettes of the excited peasants who were trying to keep the fire from spreading seemed to dance in front of the flickering flames gigantically. It was a sort of opium dream of hell.

Talking of opium, I purchased the necessary apparatus and began to learn to smoke. I have already described the fiasco with laudanum in Kandy, and somewhere in Burma I had made an equally futile experiment with powdered opium, taking thirty grains or so with no greater profit than making myself suddenly and painlessly sick. I found smoking the drug equally unavailing. I smoked twenty-five pipes in five hours with no result whatever. It now appears that I was not inhaling properly; but (for all that) I might have got something out of twenty-five pipes! The fact is that I have an idiosyncrasy with regard to this drug. I sometimes wonder whether I did not use up all my capacities in that respect in a previous incarnation; possibly I was Ko Hs'uen.

East of the Mekong, the path becomes much less satisfactory, partly owing to the geological differences. The whole country between Sha Yang and Chu Tung is across a steep wide range. There are innumerable barrancas, with which Mexico had made me familiar. The atmosphere of China had by this time begun to soak into my soul. Chinese art explained itself as inspired by Chinese nature. There is a vast, free, pale, delicate expanse of colour and form, whose lines are visibly determined by the very structure of the globe itself. There is an infinite harmony and ease in a journey such as I was making.

The physical geography is even more vast in its own way than that of the Himalayas; and the country seems somehow less definite, less specialized yet equally ineluctable! Small vivid patches of colour are associated rather with the works of man than those of nature, and if I were to endeavour to give a name to the poetic quintessence of the province of Yunnan I should content myself with one word—space. The Sahara Desert itself and the sea do not exceed this district in this respect, for they obtain their effects by what I may call the brutal method of sheer magnitude. Here the country is as diversified as Cumberland or Switzerland; the effect of immensity, of almost formless immensity, is obtained by slightly increasing the scale of quite normal types of hill, forest, lake and river, so that man and his ant heaps appear absurdly diminutive by means of delicate satire rather than drastic demonstration.

The character of the journey constantly changes. The steep and desolate range scarred by barrancas gave place in a single march to the loveliest wooded hills, yet the slight magnification of everything produced a sense of tedium. To enjoy China fully, one must allow one's soul to expand to the scale of the scenery and this cannot be done by ardour, as it can among great glaciers. It must be a gently beatific and philosophical adaptation of oneself to one's environment. During this month, my poetic genius was lulling itself by means of an ineffably beautiful rhythm and rime scheme. On this whole journey I composed only two poems, and for the first time in my life I did not write them down, so to speak, automatically; I made up the verses in my head and only took pen when they were complete. The second of the poems, 'The King Ghost', is most peculiar psychologically. It is as if I had been stripped to the skin of my infinite mentality. It refers to the country south of Yunnanfu where the North Wind, or rather North Draught, was the dominant demon of the desert.

These sensuous yet savage uplands conveyed a peculiar spiritual exaltation such as I have experienced nowhere else and I translated them into 'The Opium Smoker'.[1] In all these months I succeeded in completing only two sections; the other six were invented and written down later.

My diary from Mekong to Talifu is very meagre. The most interesting entry is this, 'Saw child saved from missionary (one eye lost) showing marks of gouging.' I do not remember at this distance of time what the incident was. It was nothing unusual. Medical missionaries in remote districts tend to become sadistically insane from the boredom of their lives. Being brainless, they cannot endure it; and take advantage of their circumstances to vivisect the poor far more freely than is done in London hospitals.

Almost every day blesses the traveller with some delightful geographical surprises. I recall, for instance, plodding wearily up a pass of decidedly rugged character. It was natural to expect that the other side of the pass would be not very dissimilar. I reached the top—and was stupefied. Instead of looking down into a valley, I saw the ground stretching away from me perfectly level, a shallow oblong with a rim of grassy mounds. It was highly cultivated land, paddy fields and plantations of white poppy ablaze in the sunlight with straight narrow channels of pure pale green and pale blue water marking off one meadow from another. Similar surprises constantly crop up. Their unexpectedness suggests the atmosphere of *Alice in Wonderland*, while their formal beauty reminds one of the character visions of the 'alchemical plant'. A less accurate but perhaps more intelligible analogy is that of the curiously luminous, exquisite and irrational landscapes which were used as backgrounds by such painters as Mantegna, Memling and Leonardo da Vinci.

On February 1st we entered a magnificent gorge. The culminating ecstasy is the approach to Hsia-Kuan by means of a natural rock bridge amid rock walls. It is as if one had come suddenly upon the 'dark tower' of Childe Roland, a fortress built by titanic gnomes when the planet was a semi-liquid flux of lava.

The road to Talifu, the second greatest city of the province and the most picturesquely situated and historically important, breaks off from the main road across China and runs sharply northward for eight miles across wild desolate moorlands. Every weak spot in the defences of the wilderness has been seized upon by the industry of the Chinese and turned into a glowing patch of cultivated soil. The approach to Tali itself inspires the stranger with a certain awe, for life is seen wrestling with death in a supreme spasm. The pullulating towers and temples of the town seem literally to quake amid the rotten and restless ruins with which they are interspersed. And thereby hangs a tale.

During eighteen years the province of Yunnan had been the theatre of civil war. Tali was the greatest stronghold of the Mohammedans, their opponents being (more or less) Mahayana Buddhists. There was not really, I fancy, much to choose between them. The outward and visible sign of Islam in these parts is that the door of a Moslem is protected from malignant demons by a poster inscribed with sacred characters instead of a fierce-looking genius. Also he objects to pork. The cause of the war was in fact either that the Mohammedans raided the pork butchers or that the Pork Trust wished to extend its market by force. I do not remember how many million men were said to have been killed in the course of these struggles, but something like two thirds of the whole area of Talifu (some estimates gave three quarters) had been razed to the ground in the final storming of the stronghold.

Dr Clark, the medical missionary of Talifu, received us with great courtesy and hospitality. I found him a sincere and earnest man; more, even an enlightened man, so far as it is possible for a missionary to be so; but that is not very far. I found him totally ignorant both of canonical Buddhism and of local beliefs. I tried to point out to him that he could hardly hope to show the natives the errors of their way of thinking, unless he knew what that was. But he declined to see the point. He was so cocksure that his own sect of Christianity held truth in utter purity and entirety that he could not imagine that the Chinese had any way of thinking at all. He regarded their refusal to follow him as a mixture of sheer dullness and sheer wickedness.

I forget the figures with regard to the converts at Talifu. In Yunnanfu the staff of six missionaries claimed four converts in four years and I imagine that these four were rice Christians at that. The truth seems to be that there are two main types of non-Christian religion. The first may be described as philosophical. In this category I place the more intelligent classes of Buddhist, Hindu and Mohammedan. To convert these people it would obviously be necessary to show them that Christianity offers them a more satisfactory explanation of the universe than their own; and not only have I never met a missionary who was capable of doing this, but not even one who admitted the desirability of it or attempting it.

The other type is the superstitious to which belong the fetish-worshipping varieties of Buddhist and Hindu and pagan (Equatorial Africa and Polynesia) with their paraphernalia of miracles, sacrifices, priestcraft, penance, vicarious atonements and the like. It is up to the missionary to show that the Christian form of such things is superior to the local variety and the difficulty is usually insuperable. The native can produce much bigger and more improbable miracles, a much more terrifying demonology, a far more fascinating pantheon, with a more alluring (and, so to say, actual) ritual than even the papist. The native perhaps sees little reason why he should not accept Christianity, but certainly none at all why he should discard his own beliefs which seem to him more vivid and more veracious, better adapted and better attested than the new. It is in fact only among the very lowest class of superstitious savages that Christianity makes any headway. Where Christian and Moslem missions are in direct rivalry, Islam collects the higher and Christianity the lower sections of the society.

Disappointed about learning Chinese ideas at first hand in this remote region, I hoped at least to get available information about the effects of opium smoking. Dr Clark informed me that these effects were appalling—the usual scaremonger story. He said it was the curse of the country and that his clinic was full of victims; 'Hundreds and hundreds and hundreds,' he groaned, 'physical and moral wrecks from the habit.' 'I should like to see one,' I replied with the appropriate sigh and shudder. 'Well, you have only to come down to my clinic any morning,' he returned; 'there are hundreds and hundreds and hundreds.' He groaned again. Well, I went down to his clinic and he went on groaning that there were hundreds and hundreds and hundreds, and I went on sighing that I should like to see one.

During my whole journey, I never saw a man whom I could call definitely the worse for opium. My wife's chair coolies were cases in point. They had smoked from twelve years old or thereabouts; and when I say smoked, I mean smoked. Every night on reaching the inn, temple or camp, as the case may be, they cooked their rice and started to smoke directly they had eaten it, continuing till they went to sleep. In the morning again they smoked before starting. The chair (with Rose and the baby, and the books which I like to have handy to read at odd moments without unpacking my valise) weighed over one hundred and sixty pounds.

Each man had therefore to carry forty pounds. Not much, but a load of this kind is very different to dead weight. Each man had to keep in step with the rest and shake the chair as little as possible; and this over rough hilly roads, often slippery with mud; perhaps against a head wind, in which case the furniture of the chair offered a large surface. One of these coolies, the heaviest and most inveterate smoker of the quartet, cannot have been less than sixty years old. I timed the men under the worst conditions; a road mostly uphill, driving sleet—half a gale—dead ahead, streaming slippery cobbles, and they did eight miles without a rest in two hours dead. If those men were 'physical wrecks from the abuse of opium', I should like to see the animal in his undamaged state!

There are of course men who have injured their health by opium; and one can see such on the coast, where the affair is complicated with alcohol and European vices. But on the whole, the search for an opium fiend in China is on all fours with the search for the man with tobacco amblyopia in England. Consular reports and independent medical opinion are unanimous that opium smoking does little or no harm to the Chinese. Dr Thomas Stevenson, in his special article in Quain's *Dictionary of Medicine,* sits on the fence as follows: 'Great differences of opinion exist as to the pernicious or other effects of opium smoking. Some would have us believe that the practice is pernicious, not to say deadly; but debasing it often is. The pictures drawn as to its effects are evidently coloured by the bias of the observer. On the other hand some would persuade us that the practice is harmless, not to·say beneficial. Doubtless neither view is absolutely correct, and whilst opium smoking is pernicious, the evils have been greatly exaggerated.' These remarks strike me on the whole as fair.

I have myself made extensive and elaborate studies of the effects of indulgence in stimulants and narcotics. (See my 'The Psychology of Hashish',[2] 'Cocaine',[3] 'The Green Goddess',[4] *The Diary of a Drug Fiend,* etc.) I have a vast quantity of unpublished data. I am convinced that personal idiosyncrasy counts for more in this matter than all the other factors put together. The philosophical phlegmatic temperament of the Chinese finds opium sympathetic. But the effect of opium on a vivacious, nervous, mean, cowardly Frenchman, on an Englishman with his congenital guilty conscience or on an American with his passion for pushing everything to extremes is very different; the drug is almost certain to produce disaster.

Similarly, hashish, which excites certain types of Arab, Indian, Malay or Mexican to indiscriminate murder, whose motive is often religious insanity, has no such effect on quietly disposed, refined and philosophical people, especially if they happen to possess the faculty of self-analysis. In brief, generalization about such exceptionally subtle problems is a snare.

On one point, however, I must admit to thinking and feeling somewhat strongly. Dr Clark told me that the missionaries treated the opium habit with injections of morphia; and in other parts of China I learnt that they had taught the Chinese, with the same laudable intention, to sniff cocaine.

The British government has acted with incredible folly. The economic prosperity of India is largely bound up with the export of opium. Whilst I was in China a petition against 'the accursed traffic' had been presented. It was signed by many of the most eminent and enlightened men in China, to say nothing of the sister-in-law (I think it was) of the emperor whom they had persuaded to declare herself a Christian so as to have a foot in the enemy's camp. The fact was that most of the petitioners were themselves opium growers whose business was damaged by the competition of the Indian product. In the same way, of course, many of the missionaries were employed by the manufacturers of morphia and cocaine to introduce these drugs instead of the practically harmless and even beneficial YEN.

China has been the most civilized country in the world; from the time of Lao Tzu and Confucius, the fringe of its culture has been torn by the claws of commerce, but it will survive the collapse of Europe. And in Yunnan the contamination of the foreign devil had not gone very far; in fact, it had not yet reached the asymptote of its own curve. However, the clearing of the ground had long been complete. There are practically no wild animals in the province. I did not even see one of those famous pheasants which I was anxious to shoot. I had hitherto bagged nothing but occasional pigeons for the pot.

At Talifu, nevertheless, there is great sport to be had. From the great deserts to the north, across the mighty mountains, migrate many magnificent birds, especially cranes and geese. I went out from the city northwards, for these birds migrate at this time of the year from the terrible highlands of Central Asia to the warm valleys and plains of the low country. I used to lie behind an embankment which was perhaps at one time part of the fortifications of the city, and shoot them as they came over. It was very difficult sport. The birds flew very high and at a tremendous pace. Some idea may be gained from the fact that a grouse shot clean through the head would fall as much as a quarter of a mile from the embankment. The geese are admirable eating, but the flesh of the crane is very coarse and fishy.

Talking of shooting, I may as well sum up the subject by saying that the part of China through which I travelled offers very poor sport on the whole; there is usually the chance of a pigeon for the pot, but that is all one can get without taking a great deal of pains. I had heard so much of the gorgeous beauty of the Chinese pheasant and looked forward to bagging a few, but never so much as saw one during the whole march. As for quadrupeds, I never set eyes on as much as a rabbit or a marmot, let alone a deer. Foxes abound; but they did not come my way. Chinese civilization is so systematic that wild animals have been abolished on principle. That at least is the only explanation that suggests itself to me.

We had been told that we should find ample supplies of fresh food of all sorts everywhere. Nothing could have been farther from the truth. We could get no fresh milk, the Chinese considering it obscene to extract it; but strangely enough, in even the smallest villages, we were able to buy an excellent brand of evaporated cream which some enterprising drummer had managed to unload along the track. There was no mutton to be had; and it was only seldom that we managed to buy a goat or kid. Poultry and eggs were fairly plentiful in most places; rice of an inferior quality and the most suspicious-looking kind of pork were the staple food of the people. Flour was rarely available and of course there was no butter.

Salama was in great distress at the difference between the local rice and the Indian variety to which he was accustomed, while as a Moslem he abhorred pork. I too would not eat it, valuing the respect in which he held me, as a sahib who partook not of the abominations of my race. Luckily, distrusting my informant, I had supplied myself with a considerable stock of canned provisions before starting; and I increased this at Tengyueh, buying some of Litton's stores from his widow. Even so, we were running very short before we reached Yunnanfu.

At this hour, seventeen years later, I recall almost more vividly than any other incident of the journey, an absurd little tragedy in this connection. We had some tins of coffee and milk, and we had come to the last portion of the last tin. We treasured it for days, looking forward to enjoying it on some great occasion as never an epicure looked forward to a bottle of rare wine. The moment came, we prepared the great drink with almost reverential care. And just as we were going to drink it, my wife shifted her position and spilled it. It would be hopeless to try to express the bitterness of our disappointment. Stay-at-home people can form no idea of the strength of the obsession which trifles impose. Conrad in 'An Outpost of Progress' tells of a murder and suicide beginning in a quarrel between two close friends, traders up-river, over a few lumps of sugar.

During our short stay in Talifu, we saw the biggest pageant with which the Chinese welcome spring. I did not know enough Chinese to understand the details of the ceremony; and the missionaries regarded the whole business as a blasphemous pagan orgy from which all righteous people should avert their gaze. I could see clearly, however, that the central figure was an ox. He was evidently the hero of the occasion because he was going to help them out with their ploughing. It was a gay, spontaneous, harmless piece of merriment; to see idolatry in it is sheer morbid prejudice.

We left Tali on February 6th and got back to the main road. The following day was without interest, but on the eighth, the latter part of the march led through a delightful valley of the most surprising beauty. It was an altogether new type of scenery. China is full of these delicious revelations. It has always some new delicate splendour to show the traveller. The variety is infinite, not as Alpine peaks or Scottish lochs differ, merely in detail; in China, one is always discovering a totally strange fairyland. The spirit of a man is reborn with every such vision. It is not even possible to compare and contrast these beauties; each is entirely individual, lord of its own atmosphere; the points of similarity with other places such as geological formations, the flora, the villages and the people seem to possess infinitesimal importance.

On the ninth there was a novelty of another kind. The dignity of Johnny White as interpreter entitled him to ride on horseback; but naturally he had to be content with a somewhat sorry screw, while my own pony was a fairly decent animal. He thought the time ripe to attempt to force me to 'lose face'; that is, to become an object of ridicule to the coolies. If he had succeeded, I need hardly point out, there would have been an end of all discipline and we should probably have been robbed and murdered in short order. His idea was to start out ahead of us on my pony. I did not find out what had happened for some time.

When I did, I set out on foot at top speed after him. In two or three hours I came up with the culprit. As luck would have it, he was crossing a steep hillside; below the path were gigantic thorn bushes. I came up quietly and unperceived, put my left hand under his right foot and with one deft jerk flung him from the saddle into a thorn bush. It was quite impossible for him to extricate himself, the bush being very large and elastic, the thorns long and persuasive. So I waited, peacefully smoking, until the coolies began to arrive, when I got up and

gave him a whack with my whalebone whip as each man
passed. When all had gone by, I mounted my pony and followed. Johnny White was rescued by a subsequent caravan and
turned up during the halt for tiffin. It was not I who had 'lost
face' with the coolies! And I had no more trouble of any kind
for the rest of the journey to Yunnanfu.

This march was very long and dull, its monotony relieved
only by a fine view of lakes and hills. But the next six days
were utterly uninteresting. Not until the sixteenth did the
featureless plateau give way to the grand wooded gorges which
caress Tatz'assa Tang. The village has no good inn, so we went
on to a lovely glade which afforded a delightful and romantic
place for a camp. I fell ill, I don't know of what, for the next
three days. Whatever scenery there may have been I was too
sick to observe.

We reached Yunnanfu on the twentieth. Mr Wilkinson, the
consul general, wrote that he was very sorry not to be able
to offer hospitality, but the Bengali blackguard of Tengyueh
had put in a complaint that I had assaulted him, so that his
relations with me must be strictly official until the matter was
settled. We found accommodation in the *dépendance* of the
French Hospital; an admirable place run by a Dr Barbezieux
and a Parisian head nurse, both of them really too much accomplished and delightful to be wasted on such a cesspool as
this city. I called on Wilkinson and told him my side of the
story of Litton's death. Steps were taken to make it hot for the
doctor; but as my assault was not denied, the consul general
had to regard it as a technical offence, which was duty purged
by the payment of a small fine.

The approach to Yunnanfu is worthy of remark. The city
is situated in the centre of a plain ringed round by hills. The
suggestion is almost of a crater, like Mexico City. There is no
adequate drainage for the rainfall. The town itself seems, from
a distance, to be perched on a huge mound some fifty to a
hundred feet in height. But on investigation one discovers that
this mound is composed of the refuse of the city; the accumulation of centuries of indescribable dirt. It inclined one to
accept the theory that bubonic plague first appeared here and
spread hence throughout the world.

On the twenty-third I paid the inevitable visit to the inevitable missionary. This specimen was more bigoted and less intelligent than any I had previously met. I had not thought
this possible. Six missionaries in four years working in this
populous city did not even claim more than four converts. They

attributed their failure, of course, to the personal activity of the devil. It never occurred to them that there might be something wrong with their methods. Roughly speaking, any man with energy and enthusiasm ought to be able to bring at least a dozen others round to his opinion in the course of a year, no matter how absurd that opinion might be. We see every day in politics, in business, in social life, large masses of people brought to embrace the most revolutionary ideas, sometimes within a few days. It is all a question of getting hold of them in the right way and working on their weak points.

I enjoyed my ten days in Yunnanfu immensely. I picked up quite a lot of old prints at prices so low that I could hardly believe my ears. The city had never been ransacked by bric-à-brac hounds.

Having settled my little official affair with the consul general, we were free to become excellent friends. He was a distinguished and delightful man, though I could well understand that Litton had been a thorn in his side. He wanted everything done elegantly and correctly, while Litton cared nothing for routine. He was always imposing his tameless personal genius on the province, with the result that he was always achieving unexpected successes when Wilkinson expected him to be filling up forms and docketing reports.

For various reasons, I decided to abandon my original design to descend the Yangtze; for one thing, the delays at Bhamo and Tengyueh had robbed me of time. I was anxious to get to Europe in good time to prepare a new expedition to Kangchenjunga for 1907. I had the mountain, so to speak, in my pocket. A party of average strength could make as certain of strolling to the top as if it were the Strand. I decided, therefore, to turn south and make for Tonkin.

On March 2nd, after breakfast and tiffin with the consul general, who was unfortunately short of stores and could only spare up a couple of tins of butter, we started along the cobbled track, lively with cherry blossoms. The walking soon became very difficult; the paths were rough, wet and slippery. On the fourth we came to a pass in the mountains guarded southwards by fine cliffs. At nightfall we reached a lake by whose side we camped. The weather for the first five days of this journey was bitterly cold. The wind, shifting from south-east to south-west, literally took the skin off our faces, even mine, which I had thought inured to all the possible devilishness of nature.

Later, this wind dropped and was replaced by a much more

deadly device; a steady draught from the north as infernally icy as when it started its career in the ghastly deserts of Siberia. It had the same quality as the north wind which we had on Chogo Ri; it took no notice whatever of poshtin (coats lined with sheepskin), sweaters, flannel shirts and vests. One felt as if one were absolutely naked. There was no shelter from it. One might crouch behind a wall or a house, but although that prevented the wind from blowing on one, it did not hinder the draught from drawing from one. The effect was just as bad; it simply exhausted one bodily and mentally; it sucked out all vitality and courage.

On the sixth we came out suddenly on the edge of a plateau with a descent of some three thousand feet in front of us, through a fine gorge. But I was hardly in a mood to appreciate nature. For three days we had practically nothing to eat but soup and Worcester sauce. When we asked for eggs, we created something not far short of a scandal. Even rice was scanty. The villages on this route are few, far apart and poverty-stricken.

Of one thing we had plenty—tea. I had heard marvellous stories of the so-called 'brick tea' that hails from these parts; and laid in a large stock of various brands to take back to England The bricks are usually in the shape of a flat cone, somewhat hollow beneath. It reminds one of the straw hats of Japanese coolies. The diameter is from eight inches to one foot and the thicknesses from two to four inches. The flavour is excellent, very subtle and aromatic; but it possesses a property not usually associated with tea, the desirability of which depends on the physiological condition of the drinker, for it acts as a powerful laxative and a purgative when strongly infused and consumed in excess. When I reached home and could compare it with the finest caravan teas, its flavour seemed less admirable, yet it retained its distinction and was always worth its place in the caddy as a curiosity. For myself, too, it was a potent spell to evoke most vivid memories of this weirdly fascinating journey.

To return to the march to Mengtsz. There is little to see that is impressive. My one memory is of a big pagoda perched on the crest of a mountain that looked as if it had been cleft in twain by a wizard. I was heartily glad on the tenth when Mengtsz came into sight; a French outpost with all the civilization, culture and cooking that heart of man can wish. The inspector of customs, Mr Brewitt Taylor, very kindly asked us to stay in his house, though at first sight he could hardly believe that I was an Englishman. The journey had reduced me to rags; I had no chance of washing or trimming my beard; the skin of my face was torn by the wind. I must have looked simply frightful. (I still do.)

We only stayed three days in Mengtsz in spite of the attractions of the little French colony. Everyone invited us everywhere, including a garden party where I played lawn tennis for the first time in ten years. I will play once more—when I return.

There is one ghastly tale to be told. The French intended to run a railway up to Yunnan to extend their sphere of influence. They had surveyed the route satisfactorily and proceeded to import eight thousand coolies. With unbelievable stupidity, they got them from Manchuria. Naturally enough, the men could not stand the climate, especially as no proper accommodations had been provided to house them. In six months only five hundred were left.

On March 14th we left Mengtsz for Manhao on the Red River—three days' easy travelling. The very first night, an unpleasant incident took place. Wilkinson had made me promise on no account to strike any of the men but to rely on him to punish any misconduct when they returned to Yunnanfu. It seemed as if they knew of this compact and the Great God Wilkinson seemed very far off to them. I could feel instinctively that the respect, akin to godly fear, which I had previously inspired was less powerful as an inhibition.

We slept on the fourteenth at a serai, dirty and entirely comfortless. I paid the host more than liberally; but he was insolent and I had no means of abating the nuisance. This emboldened my own coolies to be mutinous; and in the course of a squabble with my wife (I being ahead, out of sight) one of them struck the baby. I ground my teeth; but resolved to keep my temper and my promise to the consul.

The fifteenth was a long march over muddy cobbles full of holes where my horse constantly slipped and stumbled. It blew great guns and poured blue cats all day. We reached a village with an alleged European hotel; the 'Sino-France', a wattled hotel, unspeakably foul; the worst place I had yet struck in all Asia.

Manhao is a fine village situated on the banks of the Red River—a torrent which competes with the Salween for pre-eminence in deadliness, both from disease and demons. The

Chinese refuse to sleep even a single night in the valley; but I saw no cachectics in the village any more than I had seen victims of opium elsewhere.

The Red River at this point runs through a deep and narrow gorge. We found it stiflingly hot, after our long exposure to the icy winds of the plateau. I had hired a dug-out to take us down the rapids to Hokow, and here I saw my chance of getting even with the coolies. Having got everything aboard, I proceeded to pay the head man the exact sum due to him— less certain fines. Then the band played. They started to threaten the crew and prevented them from casting off the ropes. They incited the bystanders to take their part; and presently we had thirty or forty yelling maniacs preparing to stone us. I got out my .400 Cordite Express and told Salama to wade ashore and untie the ropes. But like all Kashmiris, thoughtlessly brave in the face of elemental dangers, he was an absolute coward when opposed to men. I told him that unless he obeyed at once I would begin by shooting him. He saw I meant it and did his duty; while I covered the crowd with my rifle. Not a stone was thrown; three minutes later the fierce current had swept us away from the rioters.

The real danger now began. This was the only part of the journey where we encountered any serious risk of disaster. The Red River, though broad and deep, has all the characteristics of the wildest mountain torrents. It falls in a succession of dangerous rapids, all the more perilous for the sudden sharp curves of the channel. At almost every corner we saw one or more wrecks, a far from reassuring spectacle. I was given to understand, however, that disaster rarely overtook boats going down stream. It is when they are being towed by insufficient power up the rapids that they get out of control and are dashed upon the rocks. For all that, we managed to hit two nasty snags in the course of the day; one of them ripped a hole in us amidships; but the men managed to stop the leak with tarpaulin nailed in place by short boards with extraordinary speed and efficiency. They were evidently well accustomed to similar jobs.

We reached Hokow on the eighteenth and struck a forlorn Englishman who gave us tiffin and dined with us. We all got gloriously drunk celebrating the success of a journey which in the opinion of all reasonable people was a crazy escapade, doomed from the first to disaster. Another bubble had burst! The awe-inspiring adventure had proved as safe as a bus ride from the Bank to Battersea.

57

I have had little occasion to mention my wife and child. It is a case of 'happy the nation that has no history'. Rose had proved an ideally perfect companion. Since the nurse's elopement she had had no one to help her with the baby. There was also a good deal for her to do in camp. We often travelled over twelve hours a day in really trying conditions; we encountered more than a little hardship, what with fatigue, cold, lack of food and general discomfort; she never gave in, she never complained, she never failed to do more than her share of the work and she never made a mistake. She was in a class by herself as a comrade. Even Eckenstein was not so competent all round or so uniformly exultant.

We had been over four months away from civilization; and she had not only stood it but flourished exceedingly. When we started, she had been rather empty-headed and frivolous; while physically, though healthy, she could not be called an athlete. At the end she had acquired the kind of soul that is evoked by intimate contact with naked nature. Her figure was straight and supple, scorning corsets. Her limbs were lithe; her eyes bright and eager; her face aflame with the joy of perfect physical well-being and her heart exulting with the expectation of producing a new token of our tenderness before the end of the year.

In these four months I had been mildly indisposed with indigestion for two days. Rose had had one slight touch of fever, and baby a cold in the head which lasted three days, and some minor digestive trouble during our stay in Yunnanfu. Not many families living in the most hygienic conditions in England could show a cleaner bill of health. We had good reason for rejoicing and may be excused for feeling decidedly proud.

The next day we went on to Lao Kay, where there is a good hotel, and more mosquitoes than I had seen for many a month. We hurried on by train to Yen Bay, a filthy hole with no redeeming feature. The whole country and its people are monotonously reddish brown; skin, clothes, food, roofs—

everything but the grass and the trees, which are all the same shade of dull green. The whole forms a curiously harmonious picture, very low in tone and undeniably depressing. The sky itself was uniformly leaden, though I suppose this was a question of the time of the year. There are few features in the scenery; a damp warmth broods upon the general dullness.

On the twentieth we reached Hanoi, the capital, but only stayed for lunch. There is nothing particularly interesting about the town to people who have been uninterruptedly intoxicated for months upon the beauty and grandeur of one of the wildest and noblest countries of the earth. We took the afternoon train to Haiphong, the seaport of Tonkin, and put up at the Hotel du Commerce. Haiphong is much like any other Eastern port. There is the usual colonial atmosphere and the variety of races like so much jetsam flung upon the shores of the island of officialdom.

One deliciously colonial incident must be related. It gives the very atmosphere of Claude Farrère's *Les Civilisés*. A large corner building on the main street had been condemned and had to be blown up. The boss of the gang in charge went for instructions to the city engineer. He ran him to earth after prolonged search in a combination of drinking-hole and house of ill-fame. He was up to his neck in absinthe, which is not really a wholesome drink in that climate; but he was able to talk and readily agreed to calculate the charge of dynamite required for the house breaking. He took a stub of pencil and worked it out on the marble slab of his table. Strange as it may seem, he shifted a decimal point two places to the right without adequate excuse—unless we accept the absinthe as an apology. The boss went off with his figures and put in a charge just a hundred times too big. The whole block was completely wrecked; and they were still clearing the street when we arrived.

We were lucky to find a ship on the twenty-second for Hong Kong, after which she was named. The boat was a dirty tramp tub; her skipper a drunken Italian who lived in flannel pyjamas which could not have seen a laundry for months and spent all his time in the smoke room, gambling and boozing. He came athwart my hawser once, refusing to listen to the complaint of Salama about the way he was treated in the fo'c'sle. I told him that I would throw him off his own ship unless he did what I said p. d. q. He cringed and complied.

How this ship ever made a voyage is a mystery. The chief engineer, a worn-out melancholy Scot, was as puzzled as I.

He said his engines were 'as rotten as the captain's guts'. They moved like a one-legged man with St Vitus' Dance and they sounded like tea trays being beaten, chains being rattled and fire irons being thrown about, all at once.

We could not even get clear of our moorings without tearing away the port companion. Twenty-four hours later we stopped. The captain freely admitted that he had lost his reckoning, didn't know where he was, didn't know how to find out and didn't see why he should worry about it. He went back to his cards, leaving a junior officer to get entangled with the sextant and chronometer. Whether he obtained any results will never be known, for during the day we drifted in sight of Hoihow. By some weird coincidence, this was our first port of call. There being no harbour, we stood half a mile out to sea, rolling and bucking sickeningly while boats came from shore bringing our cargo; pigs in wicker crates which were stacked all over the ship three deep; and large baskets of poultry. It became quite impossible to move about the main deck at all, and even on the upper deck there was considerable crowding. The stench created by these animals, a number of which died on the voyage, was the limit.

In the afternoon there appeared a magnificent Fata Morgana stretching from west to south. There was a perfectly clear double image in the sky at an elevation of from ten to twenty degrees. The lower image of the shipping was upright and then close above it was the image reversed.

The rough sea and the utter incompetence of everybody concerned combined to keep us over four days hanging about off the islands. We got away on the twenty-seventh and made our way through a choppy sea, in horribly cold damp weather, to Hong Kong.

We were now in the midst of comfort and could lay our plans for the future. We decided that Rose should return to England by way of India, so as to pick up the baggage we had left at Calcutta; while I was to go via New York in the hope of interesting people there in the proposed expedition to Kang-chenjunga. I accordingly left for Shanghai by my old friend the *Nippon Maru* on April 3rd. The further interest of my journey is concerned principally with my Magical career which is described in another chapter. There are, however, one or two tales to be told.

Our most distinguished passenger was a venerable missionary returning to America after many years labouring in the Lord's vineyard. He had just become celebrated, a riot having taken place in which his mission was destroyed. His wife and children, his native teachers and his converts were mostly murdered. He himself had, however, been preserved for the Lord's service by the direct interposition of the Almighty, who had warned him at the first rumour of trouble to leave his family and flock to their fate and flee to a convenient cavern where he could hide with only his head above water—he could duck it when strangers looked in—till order was restored. He was absolutely cock-a-whoop over this. It never occurred to him for a moment that his conduct was open to criticism, though for my part I could hardly believe my ears; that any man should tell such a story of himself and boast of it was beyond my experience.

In Shanghai I brought off a very remarkable test of the value of the Tarot in divination. The German postmaster, calling on my hostess, was very much upset by the loss of a packet containing eighty thousand roubles in notes sent by a bank in Peking to its head office in Shanghai. I offered to investigate the matter by the Tarot. I described accurately the two principal clerks who alone had access to the safe in which the postmaster had himself put the parcel immediately on its arrival and whence it had disappeared less than an hour later. The Tarot told me that the senior clerk was a steady-going conscientious man, saving a fixed sum out of his salary, devoted to his work, free from vices and in no financial embarrassment. His junior was a careless youth, mixed up with women and known to be gambling heavily on the races. The postmaster confirmed this estimate of their characters.

I inquired further and found that the junior clerk was responsible for the disappearance of the packet; which seemed reasonable enough. But then the cards apparently went crazy. They said that this clerk should not suffer for his act. The postmaster admitted that it might indeed be difficult to bring the theft home to him; but so much the worse, since he himself would be held responsible for the loss. I inquired further and was met with another facer which completed the circle of impossibilities. They said that the postmaster would not suffer in reputation. The situation became inexplicable. I was frankly annoyed that, after so accurate a beginning, the divination should have turned out so as to insult our reason. I could only apologize, shrug my shoulders and say, 'Well, they insist that it is all right for you.'

A few days later, the mystery was cleared up. The return mail left for Peking one half-hour after its arrival, and the junior clerk, in his haste, had accidentally slipped the parcel into the mail bag, so that it went safely to the bank in Peking. The Tarot had vindicated itself in the most striking way. The junior clerk was responsible for the disappearance, yet he did not suffer in consequence, nor did the postmaster.

I was in some doubt as to whether to go to America via Honolulu or by the northern Pacific route to Vancouver. I longed to see Oahu again, and yet I felt it a sort of duty to cover fresh ground. While I hesitated, fate decided. The last berth for San Francisco via the Sandwich Islands was sold over my head. Alas!—had I only known! A quarter of an hour's delay caused me to miss what might have been the most dramatic moment of my life. The ship I should have sailed by left Honolulu in due course and fetched up four days later outside the Golden Gate—to find San Francisco a raging flower of flame.

I sailed on April 21st by *The Empress of India,* took a flying glance at Japan and put out into the Pacific.

> A savage sea without a sail,
> Grey gulphs and green aglittering.

We never sighted the slightest suggestion of life all the way to Vancouver, twelve days of chilly boredom, though there was a certain impressiveness in the very dreariness and desolation. There was a hint of the curious horror that emptiness always evokes, whether it is a space of starless night or a bleak and barren waste of land. The one exception is the Sahara Desert where, for some reason that I cannot name, the suggestion is not in the least of vacancy and barrenness, but rather of some subtle and secret spring of life.

Vancouver presents no interest to the casual visitor. It is severely Scotch. Its beauties lie in its surroundings.

I was very disappointed with the Rockies, of which I had heard such eloquent encomiums. They are singularly shapeless; and their proportions are unpleasing. There is too much colourless and brutal base; too little snowy shapely summit. As for the ghastly monotony of the wilderness beyond them, through Calgary and Winnipeg right on to Toronto—words fortunately fail. The manners of the people are crude and offensive. They seem to resent the existence of civilized men; and show it by gratuitous insolence, which they mistake for a mark of manly independence. The whole country and its people are somehow cold and ill-favoured. The character of the mountains struck me as significant. Contrast them with the Alps where every peak is ringed by smug hamlets, hearty and hospitable, and every available approach is either a flowery meadow, a pasture pregnant with peaceful flocks and herds, or a centre of cultivation. In the Rockies, barren and treeless plains are suddenly blocked by ugly walls of rock. Nothing less inviting can be imagined. Contrast them again with the Himalayas. There we find no green Alps, no clustering cottages; but their stupendous sublimity takes the mind away from any expectation or desire of thoughts connected with humanity. The Rockies have no majesty; they do not elevate the mind to contemplation of Almighty God any more than they warm the heart by seeming sentinels to watch over the habitations of one's fellow men.

Toronto as a city carries out the idea of Canada as a country. It is a calculated crime both against the aspirations of the soul and the affections of the heart. I had been fed vilely on the train. I thought I would treat myself to a really first-class dinner. But all I could get was high-tea—they had never heard the name of wine! Of all the loveless, lifeless lands that writhe beneath the wrath of God, commend me to Canada! (I understand that the eastern cities, having known French culture, are comparatively habitable. Not having been there I cannot say.)

I hustled on to Buffalo to see Niagara. Here I first struck the American newspaper reporter in full bloom, in his native haunts. Before I had been half an hour in my hotel I was tackled by half a dozen enthusiastic scribes. I naturally supposed that they had somehow heard of my Himalayan or Chinese adventures, and talked accordingly. It gradually dawned on me that somehow I was failing to fill the bill; and I presently discovered that they had mistaken me for some English lieutenant who was supposed to have crossed from Canada and from whom they wanted information about some local foolishness.

I took a pretty good look at Niagara. It is absurd to shriek at the desecration caused by building a few houses in the vicinity. It seemed to me that they helped rather than hindered one's appreciation. They supplied a standard of comparison. All that has been said about the falls is, as the sayers admit, ridiculously below the reality. In their way they challenge comparison with the mountains of Asia themselves. They have the same air of being out of all proportion with the observer. They belong to a different scale; and they impress one with the same idea of utter indifference by nature. They fascinate, as all things vast beyond computation invariably do. I felt that if I lived with them for even a short time they would completely obsess me and possibly lure me to end my life with their eternity. I felt the same about the mountains of India, the expanse of China, the solitude of the Sahara. I feel as if the better part of me belonged to them, as if my dearest destiny would be to live and die with them.

I went on to New York on May 15th and spent a rather hectic ten days sampling the restaurants and theatres. But as for interesting people in the Himalayas, I might as well have joined the China Inland Mission. Nobody in New York had ever heard of them, unless as meaningless items in his hated geography lessons. No one could see any sport in mountaineering at all, or any scientific object to be obtained by reaching great heights. After the first days I could not even find a listener. The town had gone completely mad; first over Upton Sinclair's *The Jungle* which had made canned food a drug on the market, though there was practically nothing else to eat; and secondly by the shooting of Stanford White, which let loose all the suppressed sexual hysteria of the whole population.

They would talk of nothing else. Everyone screamed in public and in private about satyrs and angel children, and vampires, and the unwritten law, and men higher up, and stamping out impurity. For the first time in my life I came into contact with mob madness. Modern morality and manners suppress all natural instincts, keep people ignorant of the facts of nature and make them fighting drunk on bogey tales. They consequently seize upon every incident of this kind to let off steam. Knowing nothing and fearing everything, they rant and rave and riot like so many maniacs. The subject does not matter. Any idea which gives them an excuse for getting excited will serve. They look for a victim to chivy, and howl him down, and finally lynch him in a sheer storm of sexual frenzy which they honestly imagine to be moral indignation, patriotic passion or some equally avowable emotion. It may be an innocent Negro, a Jew like Leo Frank, a harmless half-witted German; a Christ-like idealist of the type of Debs, an enthusiastic reformer like Emma Goldman or even a doctor whose views displease the Medical Trust.

I sailed for England in the *Campania* on May 26th, arriving in Liverpool on June 2nd after a pleasant voyage, during the latter part of which I wrote most of *Rosa Coeli*, to find letters awaiting me to tell me of the tragedy of which I have given an account elsewhere.

From the moment of landing I struck a sequence of physical shocks. As I struggled to my feet after the blasting bolt of my bereavement, I found myself with an infected gland in the groin which required excision. The first day I left the nursing home I got a chill in the right eye which obstructed a nasal duct and required a whole series of extremely painful operations which proved unsuccessful. In the course of these, I got neuralgia; this continued day and night for months, so violently that I felt myself going mad. After a bare month's comparative health I acquired an ulcerated throat which knocked me out completely until the end of the year.

On top of all this came the discovery that my wife was an hereditary dipsomaniac. When our baby was born it lay almost lifeless for more than three days and at three weeks old nearly died of bronchitis. I had the sense to send oxygen before the doctor arrived and this precaution probably saved the child's life. I fought like a fiend against death. The doctor gave the strictest orders that not more than one person should be in the sick room at one time. My mother-in-law refused to obey. I thought I had suffered enough. It was her hypocrisy that had sought to justify her tippling by giving her children a share of the champagne and thus implanted in Rose the infernal impulse which had wrecked her life and love, and mine. I made no bones about it; I took the hag by the shoulders and ran her out of the flat, assisting her down the stairs with my boot lest she should misinterpret my meaning.

So Lola Zaza lives today. May her life prove worth the pains I took to preserve it.

During my illness at Bournemouth, I wrote down from memory the bulk of *Liber 777*, the table of correspondences showing equivalents of the religious ideas and symbols of various peoples. Of course this rough draft needed considerable revision and additions. It was in fact two years in the press. But it stands today as the standard book of reference on the subject. I must admit to be thoroughly dissatisfied with it. It is my eager wish to issue a revised edition with an adequate comment and a key to its practical use. I refuse to feel any satisfaction at knowing that, published at ten shillings, it is now quoted at three pounds fifteen shillings as a minimum. (Then why mention it? Oh, shut up.)

In October of this year I began *Clouds without Water*, fully described elsewhere. But apart from these two books and a

very few old lyrics, the year was barren in respect of literature.
I was too intensely concentrated on the performance of the
Operation of the Sacred Magick of Abra-Melin the Mage;
perhaps too deeply shaken by my experience of the Abyss; [1]
and certainly too much occupied with the actualities of life to
have the leisure or even to feel the impulse to distil from life
that quintessence, limpid truth, opalescent with lyrical light,
which constitutes poetry. Not until sickness and sorrow had
sobered my spirit did I once again find myself free to extract
the elixir of ecstasy from experience and fulfil my faculties by
expressing myself in rhythm.

I close this chapter with a sigh. For ten years my life had
been a delirious dance to a maddening music with incarnate
passion for my partner, and the boundless plain of the possible vibrating with the fervour of my feet. I had come
through a thousand crises to the climax of my career. I had
attained all my ambitions, proved myself at every point, dared
every danger, enjoyed every ecstasy that earth has to offer:
the rest of my life recedes from romance in that boyish idea
of what romance should be. From this time, though much lay
in store for me to accomplish, summit soaring beyond summit
of spiritual success, giant ranged behind giant for me to
challenge, I now learnt to look upon life with enlightened
eyes. I had sought and I had found. I must now seek them
who seek, that they might also find. I must aspire, act and
achieve, not only for myself to perfect my personality, but
for my fellow men in whom alone I could possibly fulfil myself
since I knew myself at last, not to be Aleister Crowley, an
individual independent of the communion of cosmic consciousness, but merely one manifestation of the Universal
Mind whose thoughts must be sterile unless sown broadcast
to blossom and bear fruit in every acre of God's vineyard.

PART FOUR

Magical Workings

The Seal of the O.T.O.

Magical Workings

58

November 18th, 1905 was my seventh birthday in the Order. I wrote: 'About now I may count my Speculative Criticism of the Reason as not only proved and understood, but realized.' And on the nineteenth: 'The misery of this is simply sickening—I can write no more.'

I must explain. All these seven years, especially when in the East, I had discussed religion and philosophy with all sorts and conditions of men. Further, I had studied the sacred books of all religions of antiquity. My experiences all tended to the uniform conclusion that one could go all round the circle in any argument. Christian philosophers have seized on this fact to urge that our only hope of arriving at truth is through faith; but it is the bankruptcy of faith that originally drove us to test it by reason. I saw that the true solution was, on the contrary, that of the mystic. In Cabbalistic and scientific language, we possess a faculty of apprehension independent of reason, which informs us directly of the truth.

I wrote in my Magical Diary on November 19th, 1905:

> I realize in myself the perfect impossibility of reason; suffering great misery. I am as one who should have plumed himself for years upon the speed and strength of a favourite horse, only to find not only that its speed and strength were illusory, but that it was not a real horse at all, but a clothes-horse. There being no way—no conceivable way—out of this awful trouble gives that hideous despair which is only tolerable because in the past it has ever been the Darkness of the Threshold. But this is far worse than ever before; I wish to go from A to B; and I am not only a cripple, but there is no such thing as space. I have to keep an appointment at midnight; and not only is my watch stopped, but there is no such thing as time . . . But surely I am not a dead man at thirty!

From this date till the first week in February, I was intellectually insane. The actual ordeal is described with intense simplicity and passion in 'Aha!' [1] I call it 'the Order of the Veil, the Second Veil' and the 'Veil of the Abyss'. The complete destruction of reason left me without other means of apprehension than Neschamah.

I have already explained briefly what are meant by Neschamah, Ruach and Nephesch.[2] I must now go a little more deeply into the doctrines of the Cabbala. The human consciousness is represented as the centre of a hexagon whose points are the various faculties of the mind; but the uppermost point, which should link the human consciousness with the divine, is missing. Its name is Daäth, Knowledge. The Babylonian legend of the 'fall' is a parable of the shutting out of man from Paradise by the destruction of this Daäth and the establishment of this Abyss. Regeneration, redemption, atonement and similar terms mean alike the reunion of the human with the divine consciousness. Arrived at the highest possible point of human attainment by regular steps, one finds oneself on the brink of the Abyss, and to cross this one must abandon utterly and for ever all that one has and is. (In unscientific mysticism the act is represented sentimentally as the complete surrender of the self to God.) In unsectarian English, the act implies first of all the silencing of the human intellect so that one may hear the voice of the Neschamah.

We may now consider further what is meant by Neschamah. It is the human faculty corresponding to the idea Binah, Understanding; which is that aspect of the divine consciousness which corresponds to the Female Idea. It receives, formulates and transmits the pure divine consciousness, which is represented by a triangle (for the Trinity) whose apex is the essence of the true self (corresponding to Brahman, Atman, Allah etc.—not to Jehovah, who is the Demiurge) and whose other angle is Chiah, the Masculine aspect of the self, which creates. (Chiah corresponds to Chokmah: Wisdom, the Word.) This divine consciousness is triune. In its essence it is absolute and therefore contains all things in itself, but has no means of discriminating between them. It apprehends itself by formulating itself through the postulation of itself as male and female, active and passive, positive and negative, etc.

The idea of separateness, of imperfection, of sorrow, is realized by it as an illusion created by itself for the purpose of self-expression. The method is precisely that of the painter who plays off one colour against another in order to represent some particular idea himself which pleases him. He knows perfectly well that each colour is in itself imperfect, a partial presentation of the general idea of light.

The 'Attainment of Unity' would be, theoretically, to mix up all the paints and produce a surface without colour, form or meaning; yet those philosophers who insist on symbolizing

God by Unity reduce Him to a nonentity. The more logical of these, indeed, carry their thesis a little further and describe the Deity as 'without quantity or quality'. Even the Prayer Book describes Him as 'without body, parts or passion', though it continues cheerfully by describing His parts and His passions in detail. The Hindus actually realize that their Para-brahman thus defined, by negating all propositions soever about him, is not a being at all in any intelligible sense of the word. Their aspiration to be absorbed in his essence depends on the thesis that 'Everything is Sorrow.'

The Buddha took the last logical step, rejected Brahman as a mere metaphysical figment and replaced the idea of union with him by that of absorption in Nibbana, a state of cessation pure and simple. This is certainly a step forward; but it still throws no light on the subject of how things came to be such that only cessation can relieve their intolerable sorrow; though it is clear enough that the nature of any separate existence must be imperfection. The Buddha impudently postulates 'Mara' as the maker of the whole illusion, without attempting to assign a motive for his malice or a means by which he could gratify it. Incidentally, his 'existence in itself' is the whole of the evil Mara, which is just as impertinent a postulate as any of the uncreated creators and uncaused causes of other religions. Buddhism does not destroy the philosophical dilemma. Buddha's statement that the fundamental error is ignorance is as arbitrary, after all, as Milton's that it was pride. Either quality implies a host of others, all equally inconceivable as arising in a homogeneous state either of bliss or nonentity.

In eighty days I went round the world of thought and, like Phineas Fogg and Omar Khayyam, came out by the same door as in I went. The solution must be practical, not theoretical; real not rational. Tyndall says somewhere that it is evidently possible for men to acquire at any moment the use of a new faculty which would reveal a new universe, as completely as the development of sight has done, or as the invention of the spectroscope, the electroscope, etc., has done, and shown us unsuspected material universes. It is to be carefully observed that we unhesitatingly class as 'material' all sorts of ideas which are not directly appreciable by any of our senses. I was in no way apostasizing from my agnosticism in looking for a universe of beings endowed with such qualities that earlier observers, with few facts and fewer methods of investigation and criticism at their disposal, called 'gods', 'archangels', 'spirits' and the like.

I began to remember that I was myself an initiate, that the Great Order had given me the Cabbala as my working hypothesis. I now found that this doctrine satisfied perfectly my science, my scepticism and my soul. It made no pretence to lay down the law about the universe. On the contrary, it declared positively the agnostic conclusion of Huxley. It declared reason incompetent to create a science from nothing and restricted it to its evident function of criticizing facts, so far as those facts were comprehensible by it.

But the Cabbala did not leave me in despair; it asserted the existence of a faculty such as that suggested by Tyndall, by the use of which I could appreciate truth directly. I may here refer to the historic claim of mystics that their truth is incomprehensible to human reason and inexpressible in human language. The arrogance of the proposition was less repugnant to me than its confession of incompetence and its denial of the continuity of nature. I have devoted countless days and nights to forcing myself to formulate the intuitions of trance in intelligible ideas, and conveying those ideas by means of well defined symbols and terms. At the period I am describing, such an effort would have been bricks without straw. My truly mystical experiences were extremely few. I have subsequently developed a complete system, based on the Cabbala, by which any expression may be rendered cognizable through the language of intellect, exactly as mathematicians have done: exactly, too, as they have been obliged to recognize the existence of a new logic. I found it necessary to create a new code of the laws of thought.

One example pertinent to this period will illustrate the strangeness of the world revealed by the development of Neschamah. The human consciousness is primarily distinguishable from the divine by the fact of its dependence on duality. The divine consciousness distinguishes a peach from a pear, but is aware all the time that the difference is being made for its own convenience. The human accepts the difference as real. It also fails to accept the fact that it knows nothing of the object as it is in itself. It is confined to an awareness that its consciousness has been modified by its tendency to perceive its sensations, which it refers to its existence. One must be expert in Pratyahara to apprehend intuitively the data of Berkeleyian idealism. In other words, the condition of human consciousness is the sense of separateness; that is, of imperfection; that is, of sorrow.

Now then for our illustration. I aspire to the good, the beautiful and the true. I define my Holy Guardian Angel as a being possessing these qualities in perfection and aspire to His Knowledge and Conversation. I propose therefore to perform the Sacred Magick of Abra-Melin the Mage. But what is my first postulate? That there exists a real difference between those qualities and their opposites, between Him and myself. It is true that I aim at the identification of myself with Him, but I have already defined Him as imperfect, maugre my gaudy phraseology, by admitting that He is separate from me. I define truth as imperfect by distinguishing it from untruth. (When one has crossed the Abyss, these considerations—fantastic to the point of comicality as they appear on the surface—become the most formidable foes in practical life. For example, one has to resolve the antithesis between action and inaction, and one removes one's motive with deft surgery by destroying the dividuality of joy and sorrow.) My aspiration in itself affirms the very idea which it is its sole object to deny.

Thus, then, all Magick is based on the illusion inherent in the reason itself. Since all things soever are separate; since their separateness is the essential element of their existence; and since all are equally illusions, why aspire to the Holy Guardian Angel?—why not to the Dweller on the Threshold? To the man who has not passed entirely through the Abyss thoughts of this kind are positively frightful. There is no rational answer possible, from the nature of the case; and I was tormented indescribably by these thoughts, thousands after thousands, each a terrific thunderbolt blasting its way through my brain during these frightful months. Of course *The Book of the Law* makes mincemeat of all such dragons, but I am convinced that the gods deliberately kept me away from seeking the solution in its pages, though I was their chosen confidant. They were determined that I should drain the last dregs of the vitriol. (*Visita Interiora Terrae, Rectificando Invenies Occultum Lapidem.*)[3]

It was essential that I should learn the technique of crossing the Abyss with absolute thoroughness, for they had it in mind to entrust me with the task of teaching others exactly how to do it. Thus, though I crossed the Abyss at this period, underwent one particular phase of the ordeal, I was restricted to that particular experience which sufficed for their immediate purpose in regard to me. I had to work out its problems in many other ways on many other occasions, as will appear from the sequel. *The Book of the Law* was to my hand, but the gods themselves had hardened my heart against it. I had hardened my own heart; I had tried to go round the Boyg. They answered, 'Thou hast said.'

I know now from the experience of others that *The Book of the Law* is veritably a Golden Bough. It is the only thing that one is allowed to take with one through Hades and it is an absolute passport. In fact, one cannot go through Hades at all; there is no 'one' to go. But the Law itself bridges the Abyss, for 'Love is the law, love under will.' One's will-to-cross is to disintegrate all things soever into soulless dust, love is the one force which can bind them together into a coherent causeway. There, where torn thoughts sank through the starless space, aching and impotent, into what was not even nothingness, each alive for ever because reduced to its ultimate atoms so that there was no possibility of change, no hope of any alleviation of its anguish, each exquisitely mindful that its captain had slain himself in despair; there may men pass today in peace. What with *The Book of the Law* to guide them, and my experience to warn them, they can prepare themselves for the passage; and it is their own fault if the process of self-annihilation involves suffering.

I cannot even say that I crossed the Abyss deliberately. I was hurled into it by the momentum of the forces which I had called up. For three years, save for spasmodic and half-hearted incidents, and the great moment in Cairo which took place in direct opposition to the united efforts of my scepticism, my cynicism, my disgust with everything, my idleness and my prejudices, I had been fighting against my destiny. I had been building up a great dam. My occasional return to Magick had been more in the nature of occasional sprees than anything else, as a man consumed by an over-mastering passion for a woman and determined to trample her under foot, might seek relief in occasional flirtations.

A magical oath is the most irresistible of all moral forces. It is an affirmation of the true will; that is to say, it is a link between the conscious human and the unconscious divine nature of the man who takes it. A magical oath which does not express the true will sets these forces in opposition and therefore weakens the man the more gravely as the oath is more seriously meant and taken. But given that the oath is a true expression of the true will, its effect is to affirm that very union between the insignificant force of the conscious being and the irresistible might of that which is 'one, eternal and individual', that which is inexpugnably immune to all other forces soever; which when accomplished constitutes it supreme.

My position was this. In 1897 I had unconsciously discovered my true will and devoted myself to find the means of carrying it out. In 1898 I had found the means and had concentrated all my resources of any kind on making the most of it. I had swept aside every obstacle, internal and external. The reaction of 1902 had lasted just three years; the dam, my carnal mind, had begun to leak; a moment later, it was swept away by the avenging tides; they swept away the last remnant of my reason.

There is a feeble rattle of the rifles of the rearguard, some ineffectual foppishness about discipline between November the nineteenth and twenty-fifth, then absolute silence till the eighth of February, when I write, 'About this full moon consciousness began to break through Ruach into Neschamah. Intend to stick to Augoeides.'[4]

I found myself in a truly surprising state.

> As I trod the trackless way
> Through sunless gorges of Cathay,
> I became a little child,
> By nameless rivers, swirling through
> Chasms, a fantastic blue,
> Month by month, on barren hills,
> In burning heat, in bitter chills,
> Tropic forest, Tartar snow,
> Smaragdine archipelago,
> See me—led by some wise hand
> That I did not understand.
> Morn and noon and eve and night
> I, the forlorn eremite,
> Called on Him with mild devotion,
> As the dewdrop woos the ocean.[5]

I had all the innocence and helplessness of a child at the period when it gropes instinctively for someone to love it, someone whom it knows and trusts, who is infinitely strong, infinitely wise and infinitely kind.

I am not quite sure why I chose the word 'Augoeides' to represent my thought. It may well be because it was not spoilt for me by any personal association with the past. I have been carried away by the necessity of simplifying (to the utmost of my ability) the story of my passage through the Abyss. I must now explain why I issued from it with this particular idea of Augoeides rather than another, for every idea in my mind had been shattered in fragments and brayed in a mortar, reduced to impalpable dust and scattered to the four winds of heaven. Sir Isaac Newton to the rescue! His first law of motion is sufficient to make the point clear.

> A body either keeps its course (or else remains at rest)
> Unless by some external force its motion is impressed.

The effect of my ordeal had been to remove all forces soever which had impinged on my normal direction. My star had been diverted from its proper orbit by, had been held back by, the attraction of other heavenly bodies. Their influence had been removed. For the first time in my life I was really free. I had no personality left. To take a concrete case: I found myself in the middle of China with a wife and child. I was no longer influenced by love for them, no longer interested in protecting them as I had been; but there was a man, Aleister Crowley, husband and father, of a certain caste, of certain experience, of travel in remote parts of the world; and it was *his* business to give them his undivided love, care and protection. He could do this very much more efficiently than before when I was aware of what he was doing, and consequently inclined to overplay the part.

But with regard to my magical future—why did I 'intend to stick to Augoeides'? The reason becomes clear if we consider the nature of the meditation—Sammasati [6]—which had constituted the essence of my success in passing through the ordeal.

I determined on this at Allan's suggestion and one of my main objects in going to stay with him at the choung was to do it. I thought it could be done in three days! There must be a lot of silly young asses knocking about the world, but I think I can give most of them a couple of strokes a hole.

The method of the meditation is described (1911) in *Liber Thisharb*,[7] and I have outlined it in an earlier chapter. I quote from 'The Temple of Solomon the King' (*The Equinox,* vol. I, no. VIII).

> . . . he found his old comrade, I.A., now a member of the Buddhist Sangha, under the name of Bhikku Ananda Metteya.
> It was from him that he received the instructions which were to help him to reach the great and terrible pinnacle of the mind whence the adept must plunge into the Abyss, to emerge naked, a babe—the Babe of the Abyss.
> 'Explore the River of the Soul,' said Ananda Metteya, 'whence and in what order you have come.'

For three days—the longest period allowed by the Buddhist law—he remained in the choung, meditating on this matter; but nothing seems to have come of it. He set his teeth and settled down doggedly to this consideration of the eternal why. Here is a being in Rangoon. Why? Because he wanted to see Bhikku A. M. Why? Because—and so on to the half-forgotten past, dark seas that phosphoresced as the clean keel of his thought divided them.

I had eliminated a vast number of possible replies to the question of Zoroaster above quoted by Allan. I might even have discovered my true will, as indeed the meditation should enable me to do, had it not been interfered with by the larger question with its smashing academic scepticism. The question posed by the meditation assumes a causal connection between events and even to some extent a purposeful connection. Now in the Abyss these are the very two ideas which are torn from under the bridge of continuity which they should support.

The practical point was that I had no proof whatever that there was any purpose in my past life or could be in my future. I again quote from 'The Temple of Solomon the King':

Baffled again and again, the fall with his horse supplied the one factor missing in his calculations. He had repeatedly escaped death in manners almost miraculous. 'Then I am some use after all!' was his conclusion. 'I am indeed SENT to do something.' For whom? For the universe; no partial good could possibly satisfy his equation. I am, then, the 'chosen Priest and Apostle of Infinite Space'. Very good: and what is the message? What shall I teach men? And like lightning from heaven fell upon him these words: 'THE KNOWL-EDGE AND CONVERSATION OF THE HOLY GUARD-IAN ANGEL.'

So again we read (in the diary) on February 11th: 'Made many resolutions of a G. R. (Great Retirement). In dream flew to me an angel, bearing an ankh,[8] to comfort me.'

We may now transcribe the diary. We find the great mind, the complex man, purged through and through of thought, stripped of all things human and divine, centred upon one single aspiration, as simple as the love of a child for its father.

Like lightning from heaven? Not less swift flashed back the obvious question of the practical man, how? The answer was immediate: 'INVOKING OFTEN'. I need not have asked. They were the words of Zoroaster indeed, but they were also my own. I had used them in my paraphrase of Zoroaster in

Tannhäuser's song. And after all, there is nothing specially magical about them except that they are the plain common sense of psychology. Huxley said that science was organized common sense, and Frazer that science was successful Magick. The syllogism presents no difficulties.

Only one point remained for consideration. I had said how almost insanely anxious I had always been about economizing time. My mind is, perhaps, the most infernally active on the globe. I cannot bear to eat a meal except as a deliberate debauch. I like to play a game of chess and read a book 'while fortifying my body thereby' and engaging in conversation with the other guests. I was constantly devising dodgers for making the most of every moment. I hate to shut a door behind me, on the ground that I might have to open it again. I detest changing my clothes. I keep my head shaved if there is any risk of being called upon to brush my hair. On the other hand, I like shaving myself because, as many men know, the operation tends to produce fertility of ideas.

Having decided to invoke the Augoeides, how was I to do it without unnecessary delay? I had everything ready at Boleskine, but Chen Nan Chan is sixty li from Pa Shih Pai, and it was as many days from England, home and beauty, going L for leather. The Operation should begin at Easter. It could not be done that year by ordinary means. But my Sammasati came to the rescue. I knew that every event in my life had been arranged by the gods to be of use to me in the accomplishment of the Great Work. I did not need an aeroplane: I had a magical carpet. I could travel in my astral body to my temple and perform the Operation, perhaps even more conveniently than in the flesh. *Per contra*, I could construct my own temple about me and perform the Operation in my physical body. For various reasons, I preferred the latter method.

I was still entirely 'off' *The Book of the Law*. I had with me my unique vellum copy of *The Goetia* and I proposed to use the Preliminary Invocation. I was to begin by performing this twice daily to work up a current, to acquire concentration, to invoke often.

On February 11th I had spent the fifty li of the journey, P'u P'eng to Ying Wa Kuan, in making resolutions to undertake the Great Magical Retirement. That night I had a dream, in which an angel flew to me 'to comfort me'. He was bearing an ankh in his hand. If I had known then, as I do now, that the ankh is not fundamentally a *crux ansata* but a sandal strap, the symbol of the power to go, I should have understood that

I ought to make the Retirement on the journey. It is obviously weakness to rely upon one's material surroundings, and I was already sufficiently in the habit of performing meditations in the most unsatisfactory conditions to have had no hesitation. I had chosen to set up my first temple at one of the busiest corners of London, with the deliberate object of training myself not to be put off by noise.

The plan was not a bad one. I am quite inaccessible to disturbance except of one kind. The neighbourhood of anyone on whom I have bestowed the right to speak to me is a cause of distraction. In practice I train such people carefully not to address me when I am working—aye! at any time—without special justification. I made a further experiment in October 1908 (see 'John St John' [9]) of carrying out a complete Magical Operation of the most important kind while leading the life of the normal man-about-town in the Montparnasse quarter. I did this to demonstrate to the people who complained that they had not the time or convenience for Magick, that they could do it without giving up their ordinary business or social life.

Though I did not fully understand the implication of the dream, I managed to act as if I had done so. I must have had some suspicions that my old friends the Abra-Melin demons would go on the war path; at least I acted accordingly from the fourteenth. Finding myself with the glands of my throat badly swollen, and my mind distracted by worrying about them, I asked the Augoeides to remove my fear. This is dangerously like prayer, on the surface; but at least I did not ask to be cured. The request was immediately granted. I was ill for several days, but able to continue my invocations.

My plan was to transport the astral form of my temple at Boleskine to where I was, so as to perform the invocation in it. It was not necessary for me to stay in one place during the ceremony; I frequently carried it out while riding or walking. As the work became familiar to me it became easier. I was able to withdraw my attention from the actual words and gestures, and concentrate on the intention. On the theory of Sammasati, every faculty must be used in the Great Work. On the surface, there seems little relation between Magick and chess, but my ability to play three games simultaneously blindfold was now very useful. I had no difficulty in visualizing the astral temple by an effort of will, and of course I was perfectly able to watch the results of the invocations with my astral eyes. During these weeks I developed the technique though not to the full extent described in *Liber Samekh*.[10] A description of the method, as far as I had taken it at this time, is given in *The Equinox*, vol. I, no. VIII.

> The preamble: he makes a general concentration of all his magical forces and a declaration of his will.
>
> The Ar Thiao section.[11] He travels to the infinite East among the hosts of angels summoned by the words. A sort of 'Rising on the Planes', but in a horizontal direction.
>
> The same remarks apply to the next three sections in the other quarters.
>
> At the great invocation following he extends the Shiva-lingam to infinite height, each letter of each word representing an exaltation of it by geometrical progression. Having seen this satisfactorily, he prostrates himself in adoration.
>
> When consciousness begins to return, he uses the final formula to raise that consciousness in the Shivalingam, springing to his feet at the moment of uniting himself with it, and lastly uttering that supreme song of the initiate beginning: 'I am He, the Bornless Spirit, having sight in the feet; strong and the Immortal Fire!'
>
> (Thus performed, the invocation means about half an hour of the most intense magical work imaginable—a minute of it would represent the equivalent of about twelve hours of Asana.)

Despite the distracting influence of the varied adventures described in the last chapter, I stuck steadily to my practice. On leaving Hong Kong, however, being once again a lonely Wanderer of the Waste, I did feel freer to analyze myself. I thought the necessity of defining the words that I used more closely. There is an indication of this in my entry of April 4th:

> I foolishly and wickedly put off A∴; work all day; now it is one a.m. of the fifth. By foolish, I mean contrary to my interest and hope in A∴.
>
> By wicked I mean contrary to my will.
>
> A∴ goodish; lengthy and reverie-like. Yet my heart is well. I spake it audibly.

Before this time I had been haunted by the first of the two terrible doubts which I subsequently described in sections 36 and 38 of *Sir Palamedes*, but during the abominable 'wind draught' of the first week of March I had made a partial image of this doubt in the 'King-Ghost'. I did not understand the essence of the doubt and it is hard to explain it in prose, even now. It seems at first sight to be a reflection of the all-embrac-

ing doubt of the Abyss. It concentrated itself into the entirely
practical question: is there an Augoeides after all? Is there a
Path of the Wise? Am I simply fooling myself? And in the
'King-Ghost' my only answer is to appeal to the very power
whose existence is in dispute. The extreme beauty of the lines,
their magic melancholy and their appropriateness to the
circumstances of my journey encourage me to quote the poem,
which I do:

> The King-Ghost is abroad. His spectre legions
>   Sweep from their icy lakes and bleak ravines
> Unto these weary and untrodden regions
>   Where man lies penned among his Might-have-beens.
>   Keep us in safety, Lord,
>   What time the King-Ghost is abroad!
>
> The King-Ghost from his grey malefic slumbers
>   Awakes the malice of his bloodless brain.
> He marshals the innumerable numbers
>   Of shrieking shapes on the sepulchral plain.
>   Keep us, for Jesu's sake,
>   What time the King-Ghost is awake!
>
> The King-Ghost wears a crown of hopes forgotten:
>   Dead loves are woven in his ghastly robe:
> Bewildered wills and faiths grown old and rotten
>   And deeds undared his sceptre, sword and globe.
>   Keep us, O Mary maid,
>   What time the King-Ghost goes arrayed!
>
> The Hell-Wind whistles through his plumeless pinions;
>   Clanks all that melancholy host of bones;
> Fate's principalities and Death's dominions
>   Echo the drear discord, the tuneless tones.
>   Keep us, dear God, from ill,
>   What time the Hell-Wind whistles shrill.
>
> The King-Ghost hath no music but their rattling;
>   No scent but death's grown faint and fugitive;
> No fight but this their leprous pallor battling
>   Weakly with night. Lord, shall these dry bones live?
>   O keep us in the hour
>   Wherein the King-Ghost hath his power!
>
> The King-Ghost girds me with his gibbering creatures,
>   My dreams of old that never saw the sun.
> He shows me, in a mocking glass, their features,
>   The twin fiends 'Might-have-been' and 'Should-have-done'.
>   Keep us, by Jesu's ruth,
>   What time the King-Ghost grins the truth!

The King-Ghost boasts eternal usurpature;
   For in this pool of tears his fingers fret
I had imagined, by enduring nature,
   The twin gods 'Thus-will-I' and 'May-be-yet'.
      God, keep us most from ill,
      What time the King-Ghost grips the will!

Silver and rose and gold what flame resurges?
   What living light pours forth in emerald waves?
What inmost Music drowns the clamorous dirges?
   Shrieking they fly, the King-Ghost and his slaves.
      Lord, let Thy Ghost indwell,
      And keep us from the power of Hell!

                                              Amen.

The triumphant answer is simply the mystic's affirmation of
interior certainty. No doubt this expresses my attitude at the
time: I was still a little child. But as I grew, so did the doubt.
I saw that the answer given in the 'King-Ghost' was insufficient. I realized subconsciously what is the hardest thing of all
for any of us to realize; that we are each 'one, eternal and
individual', that there is no one on whom we should rely, that
such doubts should be destroyed, neither by the rational
method of refuting them nor by taking refuge with external
power—one must perform an arbitrary act of manhood.

      Nay! I deliberate deep and long,
      Yet find no answer fit to make
      To thee. The weak beats down the strong.

I had been in fairly regular astral communication with
Soror F.,[12] but I wanted to see her in the flesh and therefore
called on her in Shanghai. On the sixth and seventh of April
I explained the position to her, and went to stay with her on
the ninth. The next twelve days we were constantly working
together. The results of this work are so important that I must
enter into them rather fully. It is significant of my eternal subconscious reaction against *The Book of the Law* that even
when editing my diaries for Captain J. F. C. Fuller for 'The
Temple of Solomon the King', I deliberately omitted to pay
any attention to them. The reference is meagre and vainglori-
ous, and the promise to deal with them elsewhere has never
been kept. It is evidently a dodge for avoiding the responsibility.

A∴ in the presence of my Soror F.

(The results of this and the next invocation were most brilliant and important. They revealed the Brother of A∴ A∴ [13] who communicated in Egypt as the Controller of all this work.)

The first result of my work with Soror F. was that immediately I told her of the work in Cairo, she said boldly and finally that she believed in the genuineness of the communication. I was infuriated. I believe my main object in going to see her had been to get encouragement in my revolt. I had carefully avoided telling her anything about it in the whole course of our astral interviews; but she insisted that we should study *Liber Legis* [14] together. I had my copy with me. (It is very remarkable that the gods managed to look after me so that I am never in lack of anything that I need for the performance of any particular work. My deliberate carelessness, my attempts to destroy things, are always quite useless. The gods always perform the necessary miracle to enable me to have at hand anything that may be necessary at the moment.)

So my diary reads on April 18th:

Studying *Liber Legis*. Decide to ask F. to invoke Aiwass and converse with Him when invoked, and thereby to decide on the quality of that Magick.

On the twentieth, therefore, we went into her temple:

Aiwass invoked appears, of brilliant blue as when she saw him as guardian of my sleep. He has followed me ever, wishing me to follow his cult. When F. took wand, he grows brilliant and breaks up into a formless light; yet she feels him as an enemy. He seems entangled in a mesh of light and to be trying to escape. I warn him that if he goes away, he cannot return. (F. in herself is hostile) 'Return to Egypt, with different surroundings. (This misheard: he said *same*.) There I will give thee signs. Go with the S. W. [15] (Ouarda), this is essential: thus you shall get real power, that of God, the only one worth having. Illumination shall come by means of power, *pari passu*. (Evidently my own transcript of her words.) Live in Egypt as you did before. Do not do a G. R. [16] Go at once to Egypt; money troubles will be settled more easily than you think now. I will give you no guarantee of my truth.' He then turned blue-black. 'I am loath to part from you. Do not take F. I do not like the relations between you; break them off! If not you must follow other gods. Yet I would wish you to love physically, to make perfect the circle of your union. F.

will not do so, therefore, she is useless. If she did, she would become useful. You have erred in showing her the true relation between you on spiritual planes. Having burst that, she will remain by her sense of power over you. (This might mean that her enjoyment of her power over me would induce her to continue working.) She is spiritually stronger than you. You should have dominated her by your superior strength on other planes. She will give you much trouble, though eventually she may become a great aid. But your shorter path lies by Egypt and S. W. (Ouarda) though she is not spiritually your equal. S. W. has been your enemy; but you have conquered, she is bound to aid you as you will. She has been your enemy and that of F. but you returned her hatred, hence her seeming power over you in the present. (Qy. this hearing.) (Qy. was F. hearing correctly) I will give you a sign when alone and away from present medium. You must recognize the sign by your own intuition. Do not part from S. W. Use her! (Here S. W. appears, with an evil look. She glitters, like a jewelled serpent.) Strange bands of light scintillate between her and Aiwass. A. now takes wand again; still feels enmity on spiritual planes. Aiwass banished; S. W. has disappeared.

A. now tries to speak to A∴. He wants G. R.; does not mind whether S. W. is with me or not; but I should use Brahmacharya [17] (? if with her, or anyhow), I shall be guided as things turn up, as to the truth or falsehood of Aiwass, who is not to be altogether distrusted. (I think the opposition is Aiwass's limitation as a servant.) A∴ will give us a sign: F's freedom. (I reply that if this comes about in a miraculous manner, well and good.) (Note: Her husband died quite unexpectedly not long after this time.)

April 21st. Sol enters Taurus.

Open T∴ with A∴I∴. [18] (Possibly . . . * spoilt it all) asking for special aid in—what follows. F. finds the Nuit ring good: hence probably her hostility yesterday was due to lower self.

I∴ of R. H. K. [19] gives glorious material flashes of light, akasic (i.e. ultra-violet) and lilac. The god, beheld, will not speak. Asked for a messenger, Aiwass appears. F., suspecting him, puts a pentagram on him; he blurs and becomes dirty and discrowned. F. takes wand; but this dissipates him. His real name she says is [20] 270=INRI. F. uses pentagram and shrivels him up to a black charred mass. [21] I ask her to invoke something genuine; a white figure without face and with little shape mounts throne. It has a glittering rayed corona. Says: (to her F. uses normal tone; hence tone of oracle) 'I am the God of Vengeance. I am thy Guardian Angel. I would

* I omit reference to a certain private matter.

have thee seek thine own soul in silence and alone. Take no aid with thee; take no mortal soul but retire and depart from mankind.' Pentagram makes him brighter: he grows firmer. Repeated, form vanishes and only brightness remains. Asked for a sign or his name . . . is written on throne. 'I will give no other sign: you must learn to trust your own intuition.'

F's intuition tells her that he is genuine. As to our relations, he wishes us to work together (A contradiction *v. supra:*) 'I do not wish you to go too far in work with S. W. She will dazzle you and be apt to lead you astray. You must always remain as armed when you work with her, as a man in full armour. I would wish you to strengthen the link between you and F. on all planes. You are very needful to each other and can only accomplish G. W.[22] together.' (This clearly utter rubbish.) I take wand and curse him by Him whom he hath blasphemed. Invoking, however A ∴ the light becomes more brilliant. Voice continues: 'You must go and do a G. R. after which you will get a sign.' (Clearly due to F. knowing my wish; but he is clumsy. Will anything now convince F.? I was trying, as my custom is, to 'bowl out' my clairvoyant.) I take serious measures to banish all but A ∴. Voice silenced: and she doubts whether voice is from brilliance. F. feels me absolutely necessary for her. I not. (Voice is *from her* so cannot be banished and it goes on:) 'There shall be a short period of work (? *not?*) done in actual unison; after which your powers join irrevocably together. There is no escape from that; you are bound to work together; and the fitting time and hour for this shall come simultaneously to you both. There will then be no doubt in either of your minds: there will then be no obstacle to this union . . . You must look towards this time and towards a beacon light. Never lose sight of that! You Elaine (F's earth-name) will meet with subtle temptation from this object—promises of great power and illumination; but heed them not. Aleister is your true helper from whom you have right to look and demand help. You must never cease to demand this aid and by your demand strengthen and aid your comrade. I, your Guardian Angel, tell you this.' (The falsity of all this patent more at the time than now—I foresaw what follows.) I ask proof that he *is* G. A.[23] It is clear that voice and brilliance are distinct (i.e. from two separate sources). F. however feels that this rigmarole is true. Hence we discuss our relations and the Great Invocation degenerates. We began to make love to each other. This, however, is checked by my will and her own feeling that we have done enough for honour. I am not exhausted after all this, as I was yesterday. Is this a proof that all is Right Magick, or that little force was expended? Where am I, in fact? O Holy Exalted One, do Thou illuminate my mind!

59

I left Shanghai on the twenty-first of April. On the twenty-second I was sick and stayed in bed all day. I did no regular invocation, but thought over the recent crisis. I dismissed the Shanghai experience as a morbid dream. Reading through the above record at this distance of time, after deliberately avoiding doing so for so long, I feel very uncertain about it; I feel that there was a great deal of genuine communication with the right people and that the Oracle is confused, contradictory and uneven, because of the interference of our personalities.

There was the question of our love affair. I was absolutely in love with Rose in the ordinary sense of the term. My love for Fidelis excluded the material almost entirely. I was very proud of my love for Rose and very happy in it. The one thing I feel sure of is this: that we had a superb opportunity to take up the Great Work together and that we missed it on account of our determination to see things with our own eyes. We were, no doubt, quite ready to put the Great Work first, last and all the time; but we were hampered in doing so by our settled conviction as to what the Great Work might imply. For my part, at least, I know that I was always arguing that such and such a course couldn't be right on general principles, as I had done when Rose herself had told me how to invoke Horus; and I had not learned the lesson that my idea of 'general principles' was not reliable.

The entry of April 24th shows how admirably the gods arrange one's affairs. One may have a perfectly right idea, but as long as one holds to it they will take pains to upset the apple cart: abandon the idea, and they immediately hand it back with a charming compliment. This is the lesson of the Book of Job.

I quote the entry in full, concealing only the name of the Order.

At Kobe. A ∴ fair only; though I invoked all these powers of mine. Yet after, by a strong effort of will, I banished my

564

sore throat and my surroundings, and went up in my Body of Light. Reached a room in which a cruciform table was spread, a naked man being nailed thereto. Many venerable men sat around, feasting on his living flesh and quaffing his hot blood. These (I was told) were the adepts, whom I might one day join. This I understood to mean that I should get the power of taking only spiritual nourishment—but probably it means much more than this.

Next I came into an apparently empty hall, of white ivory worked in filigree. A square slim altar was in the midst, I was questioned as to what I would sacrifice on that altar. I offered all save my will to know A∴ which I would only change for its own realization. I now became conscious of god-forms of Egypt sitting, so vast that I could only see to their knees. 'Would not knowledge of the gods suffice?' 'No!' said I. It was then pointed out to me that I was being critical, even rationalistic, and made to see that A∴ was not necessarily fashioned in my image. I asked pardon for my blindness, and knelt at the altar, placing my hands upon it, right over left. Then, one, human, white, self-shining (my idea after all!) came forth and put his hands over mine, saying: 'I receive thee into the Order of—.'

I came back to earth in a cradle of flame.

I was thus formally received among the Secret Chiefs of the Third Order on the astral plane. It was the natural sequel to the passage of the Abyss. I was careful not to presume on a mere vision. Superb as the experience was, I would not allow it to turn my head. I am almost morbidly sensitive about my responsibility in such matters. No more fatal mistake can be made than to grasp after a grade. Attainment is an appalling danger if one is not perfectly fitted for it at every point. One must search oneself unsparingly for weak spots; the smallest scratch suffices to admit a germ of disease and one may perish altogether through a moment's carelessness. It is unpardonably foolhardy to take a chance in matters of such serious import.

I took the vision to heart as a lesson.

The next day's entry makes this clear.

Yesterday's vision a real illumination, since it showed me an obvious mistake which I had utterly failed to see. The word in my Kamma work (in Burma) was *Augoeides*, (a subsequent entry implies that the word was 'given' me directly from the unseen world) and the method *Invoking Often*. Therefore a self-glittering One, whether my conscience approves or not, whether my desires fit or not, is to be my guide.

I am to *invoke often,* not to criticize. Am I to lose my grade of Babe of the Abyss? I cannot go wrong, for I am the chosen one; that is the very postulate of the whole work. This boat carries Caesar and his fortunes.

There is here an implication, perhaps, that I had been compelled to accept the Cairo working. This is confirmed by the entry of April 30th:

(It has struck me—in connection with reading Blake—that Aiwass, etc., 'Force and Fire' is the very thing I lack. My 'conscience' is really an obstacle and a delusion, being a survival of heredity and education. Certainly to rely on it as an abiding principle in itself is wrong. The one really important thing is the fundamental hypothesis: I am the Chosen One. All methods will do, if I only *invoke often* and stick to it.)

I resented intensely being told that I was 'the Chosen One'. It is such an obvious man-trap; it is the commonest delusion of the maniac and, in one form or another, the essence of all delusions. Luckily, there is an answer to this. What can be more really arrogant than assuming that one has been singled out for 'strong delusion'? I had received some very remarkable evidence in quite unexpected quarters that I was singled out to accomplish the Great Work of emancipating mankind.

One of these is so intensely interesting on its own accord that I must not omit it, quite apart from its bearing on the question of my destiny. One morning I had sat down to rest and smoke a pipe on the top of a little pass in warm misty weather. Salama came and sat down by my side. I looked at him in amazement. It was an astounding breach of etiquette. I have often wondered if he did it deliberately, as if to say, 'I am not your headman: I am a messenger of the gods.' He began, however, in a very shamefaced, sheepish way, obviously embarrassed. It was as if he had been thrust by surprise into the position of an ambassador. 'Sahib,' he said, 'last night I had a *tamasha.*' I reproached him laughingly. *Tamasha* means an entertainment of any kind, and, in the East, frequently implies a certain amount of liveliness, possibly an indulgence in forbidden liquor and flirtation; but he merely meant a dream. The usual words for dream are *khwab, roya, wahm.* Evidently he wished to imply that his dream was not an ordinary one, that it was a genuine vision. (I forgot to ask him whether he was awake or asleep.)

He proceeded as follows:

I was on the shore of a small lake. It was a wild country and the lake was surrounded by tall reeds, some of them growing in the water. The full moon was high in the sky, but there were clouds and mist. You were standing in front of me, sahib; quite motionless, lost in thought, as you always are, but you seemed to be waiting for someone. Now there was a rustling in the reeds, and out of them came a boat rowed by two beautiful women with long fair hair, and in the front of the boat stood another woman, taller and fairer even than her sisters. The boat came slowly across to you; and then I saw that the woman held in her hands a great sword, long and straight, with a straight crosshilt which was heavy with rubies, emeralds and sapphires. She put this sword into your hands and you took it, but nothing was said. They went away as they had come, into the fringe of reeds across the lake. And that was all I saw.

I remained unable to reply. At this time I was the last man in the world to take anything of the sort seriously; more I was resolved not to do so even at the cost of restraining the theory of sensory hallucination. What struck me dumb was hearing an old shikari tell the story of Excalibur in language so near to that of Malory as to make no odds. Could one of his sahibs have told him the tale long ago, so that it popped up in this strange fashion with me as the hearer? I had no doubt whatever of the man's sincerity and truthfulness and he had no motive for inventing anything of the sort.

I cannot believe it a coincidence; I really wondered whether the most reasonable hypothesis is not that Aiwass, wanting to remind me that I was chosen to do the Great Work, picked out, on the one hand, Salama as the most unlikely prophet imaginable; on the other, the tale as one which I could not possibly dismiss as trivial. In fact, though I cannot remember making a record of the incident, and indeed probably took pains to avoid doing so as a rebuke to self-importance, it remains as vivid and distinct as almost anything else in my life. I can see the pass, I can almost taste the tobacco: I can see his shy honest weather-beaten old face and hear his timid loyal accents. In the background the coolies, singing and talking, pass over the misty slopes; yet I cannot remember where the place was or even whether it happened on the first or second Himalayan expedition.*

* I am almost sure, on reflection, that it was on the return from Kangchenjunga.

I continued the Invocation of the Augoeides, with occasional additions and progressive intensification, week after week. I rather avoided any other magical work, on the principle of concentrating every particle of my energy on the daily routine. I even refrained, as a rule, from using my astral eyes during the Invocation itself. I might easily have been lured from the Path by getting interested in some of the hosts of angelic forms that habitually appeared.

On May the fourth there is an entry which indicates my attitude to the work itself. It sounds very simple to make an invocation; but when one gets to work, behold! a multitude of points, each of which has to be settled with extreme care. This entry deals with one such:

A∴ [1] very energetic on my part, intensely so, better perhaps than ever before.

However (or perhaps because) there was little vision.

Indeed, this work of A∴ requires the adept to assume the woman's part; to long for the bridegroom, maybe, and to be ever ready to receive his kiss; but not to pursue openly and to use force.

Yet 'the Kingdom of Heaven suffereth violence, and the violent take it by force.' May it not be, though, that such violence should be used against oneself in order to attain that passive state? And, of course, to shut out all rivals? Help me, thou Holy One, even in this; for all my strength is weak as water, and I am but a dog. Help me. O self-glittering one! draw nigh to me in sleep and in waking, and let me ever be as a wise virgin and expect thy coming with a lamp of oil of holiness and beauty! Hail, beautiful and strong one! I desire thy kisses more than life or death.

From this it appears that I was still as spiritually adolescent as St Augustine or St Teresa. It seems necessary for juvenile souls to represent mystical experience by means of anthropomorphic symbols. The practice naturally follows the lines laid down by the theory. For this reason one's early adventures are accompanied by romantic phenomena and stigmata. Buddhist psychology recognizes this. For instance, the first Jhana is accompanied by Ananda, bliss; but in the second this quality disappears. I think it deplorable that mystic advancement should be expressed by means of such hieroglyphs as 'The Bride's Reception'; that is, at least, if any peculiar attribution of a sexual character is implied.

Of course, even above the Abyss, Chokmah and Binah, Shiah and Neschamah are customarily called Father and

Mother; considering how lamentably prone humanity is to anthropomorphism, it seems unfortunate. But we cannot deny the justice of the symbolism, and the way to eliminate the disadvantages and dangers of the situation is to extend the connection of the word 'love' to include all phenomena of the uniting of opposites, as is done in *The Book of the Law*. Hardly anything is more important for the aspirant than to get rid of the tendency to make God in his Own image. One should learn to regard the formula of Yod, Hë, Vau as universal, not as generalized from the reproductive process of mammals, but *vice versa*. That process should be regarded as one particular case of the Law, and that case by no means an important one.

We must be constantly on our guard against egocentric implications; they do not even exalt the ego as they pretend to do, they limit it. We become great just so far as we are able to liberate ourselves from the constriction of our normal conception that we are men. When one has crossed the Abyss, especially, one should be altogether free from the prepossession that one's body and mind are more than inconvenient instruments through which we perceive the universe. To increase our understanding of the cosmos, we must constantly endeavour to counteract the limitations which the fact that our instrument is a human being seeks to impose upon us.

I do not, however, wish to represent the Operation of Abra-Melin which I was now performing as a retrogression; but I had to undertake it in order to fulfil completely the formulae of adeptship. It was necessary to complete the work of the Second Order before I could adequately take up my work in the Third. Again, the mission, in order to carry out which I had incarnated, was a mission to mankind; and this must explain why, *pari passu* with my personal progress, I walked continually in the way of the world. My spiritual life itself was now therefore definitely duplex, and this fact must be kept in mind if my subsequent actions are to be properly understood.

Arriving in England on the second of June, I was stunned by the news of my bereavement. I made a point of detaching my mind. In the train from Liverpool to London I continued to chat with my companions on the boat as if nothing had happened. Having got to bed I released the prisoner. There was only one thing to be done: 'I solemnly reaffirmed the oath of my obligation to perform the Operation, offering under these terrible circumstances all that yet remained.'

I am convinced, by the way, that the unremitting blows of misfortune, of which this bereavement was the first, were caused by the malice of the Abra-Melin demons, but that none of them would have reached me if I had understood and obeyed the Secret Chiefs and the forces behind them in the Shanghai working.

It was really curious the way one form of slight illness after another attacked me. My wife happened to make some remark to this effect to the housekeeper, a real old Sussex product. She nodded her head wisely. 'He'll never be better,' she said in an oracular tone, 'until that baby is born.' I found on inquiry that it is a widespread superstition in Sussex that sometimes, especially when the husband is unusually devoted to his wife, she escapes the usual inconvenience of pregnancy, while he is constantly ill. The idea is of sympathetic transference.

I became seriously ill. Through everything, surgery and all, I continued the daily work. On July 26th I went to stay with Cecil Jones, who was now an Exempt Adept. (The initials of his motto are D. D. S.) I conferred with him about my Operation. The main points are as follows: (I quote Captain J. F. C. Fuller's account.)

July 27   Here we have a most extraordinary entry, which needs explanation and illustration.

Fra P.[2] was crucified by Fra. D. D. S. and on that cross made to repeat this oath: 'I, P——, a member of the Body of Christ, do hereby solemnly obligate myself, etc., to lead a pure and unselfish life, and will entirely devote myself so to raise, etc., myself to the knowledge of my higher and Divine Genius that I shall be He.

'In witness of which I invoke the great Angel Hua[3] to give me a proof of his existence.'

P. transcribes this, and continues: 'Complete and perfect visualization of . . .' here are hieroglyphics which may mean 'Christ as P—on cross.' He goes on: 'The low dark hill, the storm, the star.' But the Pylon of the Camel (i.e. the path of Gimel[4]) open, and a ray therein: withal a certain vision of A∴ remembered only as a glory now attainable.

28   Twenty-fifth week of A∴ begins.

29   (A∴ continued evidently, for P. writes:)

Perfect the lightning conductor and the flash will come.

Aug. 4   About to try the experiment of daily Aspiration in the Sign of Osiris Slain.

Did this twenty-two minutes, with Invocation as of old. Cut cross on breast and circle on head.

(*Scire*) The vow of Poverty is to esteem nothing save A ∴.

(*Audere*) The vow of Chastity is to use the Magical Force only to invoke A ∴.

(*Velle*) The vow of Obedience is to concentrate the will on A ∴ alone.

(*Tacere* [5]) The vow of Silence: so to regulate the whole organism that so vast a miracle as the Completion of the Great Work excites therein no commotion.

N.B. To look expectantly always, as if He would instantly appear.

I renewed the Obligation, cutting the cross and circle on my body every week. On August 9th I wrote the Invocation of the Ring; that is, of the symbolical episcopal ring of amethyst, which I wore as an Exempt Adept.

> ADONAI! Thou inmost Fire,
>   Self-glittering image of my soul,
> Strong lover to thy Bride's desire,
>   Call me and claim me and control!
> I pray thee keep the holy tryst
> Within this ring of Amethyst.
>
> For on mine eyes the golden Sun
>   Hath dawned; my vigil slew the Night.
> I saw the image of the One:
>   I came from darkness into Light.
> I pray Thee keep the holy tryst
> Within this ring of Amethyst.
>
> I. N. R. I.[6]—me crucified,
>   Me slain, interred, arisen, inspire!
> T. A. R. O.[7]—me glorified,
>   Anointed, fill with frenzied Fire!
> I pray Thee keep the holy tryst
> Within this ring of Amethyst.
>
> I eat my flesh: I drink my blood:
>   I gird my loins: I journey far:
> For Thou hast shown the Rose, the Rood,
>   The Eye, the Sword, the Silver Star.
> I pray thee keep the holy tryst
> Within this ring of Amethyst.
>
> Prostrate I wait upon Thy will,
>   Mine Angel, for this grace of union.
> O let this Sacrament distil

> Thy conversation and communion
> I pray Thee keep the holy tryst
> Within this ring of Amethyst.

I intended to use this Invocation in practice. The amethyst was to be, so to speak, the lens through which the Holy Guardian Angel should manifest. On September 17th I went to Ashdown Park Hotel, Coulsdon, Surrey and recovered my health suddenly and completely. On the twenty-first I had completed thirty-two weeks of the Operation and thirty-one weeks of actual daily invocation. The next day D. D. S. came to see me: we celebrated the Autumnal Equinox and reconstructed the old Neophyte Ritual of the G ∴ D ∴, eliminating all unnecessary features and quintessentializing the magical formulae.

On the ninth, having prepared a full invocation and ritual, I performed it. I had no expectation, I think, of attaining any special success; but it came. I had performed the Operation of the Sacred Magick of Abra-Melin the Mage.

It is unlawful to speak of the supreme sacrament. It was such, as the following entry shows, that I found it hard to believe that I had been permitted to partake of it. I will confine myself to the description of some of the ancillary phenomena.

Oct. 9   Tested new ritual and behold it was very good! Thanked gods and sacrificed for—In the 'thanksgiving and sacrifices for . . .' I *did* get rid of everything but the Holy Exalted One, and must have held Him for a minute or two. I did. I am sure I did.

Such is the fragmentary account * of what was then the greatest event of Fra. P.'s career. Yet this is an account of the highest trances—of Shivadarshana [8] itself, as we know from other sources. The 'vision' (to use still the name become totally inadequate) appears to have had three main points in its Atmadarshana [9] stage—

1. The Universal Peacock.
2. The Universe as Ego. 'I who am all and made it all, abide its separate lord,' i.e. the universe becomes a single and simple being, without quantity, quality or conditions. In this the 'I' is immanent, yet the 'I' made it, and the 'I' is entirely apart from it.
(This is the Christian doctrine of the Trinity, or something very like it.)

---

* Captain Fuller's.

3. This Trinity is transcended by an impersonal Unity. This is then annihilated by the Opening of the Eye of Shiva. It is absolutely futile to discuss this; it has been tried and failed again and again. Even those with experience of the earlier part of the 'vision' in its fullness must find it totally impossible to imagine anything so subversive of the whole base, not only of the ego, but of the absolute behind the ego.

The very next day the enemy struck home below the belt, as described in the previous chapter. The blow could not shake my soul. For over three weeks I bore the stigmata of my Operation physically. I visibly radiated light. People used to turn in the street to look at me; they did not know what it was, but the impression must have been irresistible.

No sooner had this worn off than the enemy struck again at my health. I was obliged to put myself once more in the doctor's hands and got to Bournemouth. I was now thoroughly prepared to take up my Work of initiating mankind, but I was still determined to do it on the old lines.

I had no books of reference at Bournemouth, and it struck me that it would be very convenient if I possessed a volume giving all the correspondences of the Cabbala in a compact form. I spent a week in writing this down from memory and the result is *Liber 777*.[10] (It is to be noticed that there is no reference to the Cairo working [11] anywhere in this book.)

In the month of December the Secret Chiefs formally invited me, through G. R. Frater D. D. S., to take my place officially in the Third Order. I still felt that I was not worthy. Not till three years later did I accept the grade, and then only after having passed ceremonially through the Abyss in the fullest possible measure.

60

The years 1907 and 1908 may be described as years of fulfilment. No new current came to stir my life; but the seeds
which had been sown in the past came many of them to
harvest. I had come to my full stature as a poet. My technique
was perfect; it had shaken off from its sandals the last dust
which they had acquired by walking in the ways of earlier
masters. I produced lyric and dramatic poetry which shows
an astounding mastery of rhythm and rime, a varied power of
expression which has no equal in the history of the language,
and an intensity of idea which eats into the soul of the reader
like vitriol.

I should have been assigned publicly my proper place
among my peers of the past without difficulty had it not been
for one fatal fact. My point of view is so original, my thoughts
so profound, and my allusions so recondite, that superficial
readers, carried away by the sheer music of the words, found
themselves, so to speak, intoxicated and unable to penetrate
to the pith. People did not realize that my sonorous similes
possessed a subtle sense intelligible only to those whose minds
were familiar with the subject. It is, in fact, necessary to study
almost any poem of mine like a palimpsest. The slightest phrase
is essential; each one must be interpreted individually, and the
poem read again until its personality presents itself. People
who like my poetry, bar those who are simply tickled by the
sound or what they imagine to be the sense, agree that it spoils
them for any other poetry.

For instance, if I mention a beetle I expect the reader to
understand an allusion to the sun at midnight in its moral
sense of Light-in-Darkness; if a pelican, to the legend that
she pierces her own breast to feed her young on her heart's
bleed; if a goat, to the entire symbolism of Capricornus, the
god Pan, Satan or Jesus (Jesus being born at the winter solstice,
when the sun enters Capricorn); if a pearl, to the correspondences of that stone as a precious and glittering secretion of

the oyster, by which I mean that invertebrate animal life of man, the Nephesch.

It must not be supposed that I am obscure on purpose. I have thought in the language of correspondences continuously, and it never occurs to me that other people have not at their fingers' ends the whole rosary of symbols.

During these two years my domestic tragedy was becoming constantly more acute. Rose told me that she was keeping her word, but it had become impossible to do any work where she was. She was in a state of continual irritation. I was obliged to take rooms in Jermyn Street in order to have a moment to myself. In the autumn of 1907 on returning from Tangiers, I found that she had obtained one hundred and fifty bottles of whisky from one grocer alone in five months. Confronted with the fact, she broke down and agreed to take a cure for two months, in an establishment at Leicester. At the end of that time I took her climbing for a fortnight and she came back to London in excellent health; but ten days later the disease broke out with redoubled violence. I did everything that was humanly possible; but it was fighting a losing game.

Finally, early in 1909, the doctor threw up the sponge. He told her that she must agree to be sequestrated for two years. She refused: I insisted upon a divorce. I loved her as passionately as ever—more so than ever, perhaps, since it was the passion of uttermost despair. I insisted on a divorce. I would not be responsible for her. I would not stand by and see her commit suicide. It was agreed that I should be defendant as a matter of chivalry, and the necessary evidence was manufactured. I continued, however, to look after her as before; we even stayed together as much as we dared, and I saw her almost every day, either in our house or at my rooms. Directly the divorce was pronounced I returned from Algeria, whither I had gone to be out of the way during the trial, and we were photographed together, with the baby, at the Dover Street studios.

I had written the agony of my soul in *Rosa Decidua*, which I dedicated to Lord Salvesen (not Salvarsan), the judge who presided at the trial. This poem was printed privately and a copy with the best of the photographs was sent to the judge, with a polite letter of thanks. (It is reprinted in *The Winged Beetle*, pp. 130–40.) This poem is, perhaps, my high-water mark in realism. It reveals my human self as I had never even attempted to do. I trace my agony through every writhe. I feel compelled to quote a few lines:

This is no tragedy of little tears.
My brain is hard and cold; there is no beat
Of its blood; there is no heat
Of sacred fire upon my lips to sing.
    My heart is dead; I say that name thrice over;
Rose!—Rose!—Rose!—
Even as lover should call to lover;
There is no quickening,
No flood, no fount that flows;
No water wells from the dead spring.
My thoughts come singly, dry, contemptuous,
Too cold for hate; all I can say is that they come
From some dead sphere without me;
Singly they come, beats of a senseless drum
Jarred by a fool, harsh, unharmonious.

But even my utmost realism dared not face the supreme horror. Allan Bennett had written to me to beg me to break off sexual relations with Rose. He knew as I did not, that any child of hers must be under the curse; for, while the baby lay dying in the hospital, its mother was trying to drown her anguish in drink, and it was slowly borne in upon me that the fever was due to the fact that the moment my back was turned Rose had broken out, had neglected to cleanse the nipple of the feeding bottle, and thereby exposed the child to the germs of typhoid. The catastrophe which had stricken the father to the heart was the sister of that which was to perform the same office to the husband.

This poem has everywhere been recognized as overwhelming. E. S. P. Haynes told me that it was the most powerful that he had ever read, and Frank Harris wrote from what he thought was his death bed, 'In *Rosa Decidua* there is more' (*scil.* than in some other poem of which he has been writing) 'a despairing view of life—"beats of a senseless drum—all's filth". To "My tongue is palsied . . . exquisite agony." Astounding realism raised to art by perfect artistry.'

We went on living together, more or less; but her condition became rapidly worse and in the autumn of 1911 she had to be put in an asylum, suffering from alcoholic dementia.

Another seed of the past began to bear fruit at this time. I had never attempted to transmit my occult knowledge as such. I had never attempted to write prose as such, apart from short accounts of my climbs, with the exception of the preface to *White Stains* (*Collected Works*, vol. II, pp. 195–8). *Berashith* was my first serious attempt at an essay. That and 'Science and

Buddhism' were followed by a *jeu d'esprit* on Shakespeare (*Collected Works*, vol. II, pp. 185–90); 'Pansil' (vol. II, pp. 192–4); 'After Agnosticism' (vol. II, pp. 206–8); 'Ambrosii Magi Hortus Rosarum' (vol. II, pp. 212–24); 'The Three Characteristics' (vol. II, pp. 225–32); 'The Excluded Middle' (vol. II, pp. 262–6); 'Time' (vol. II, pp. 267–82); 'The Initiated Interpretation of Ceremonial Magic' (vol. II, pp. 203–4); 'Qabalistic Dogma' (vol. I, pp. 265–9); the introduction to *Alice, An Adultery* (vol. II, pp. 58–61). Some of the ghazals of the *Bagh-i-Muattar* are in prose, as well as the preliminary matter; and there is *Eleusis* (vol. III, pp. 219–30).

Most of these were written from a very curious point of view. It was not exactly that I had my tongue in my cheek, but I took a curious pleasure in expressing serious opinions in a fantastic form. I had an instinctive feeling against prose; I had not appreciated its possibilities. Its apparent lack of form seemed to me to stamp it as an essentially inferior means of expression. I wrote it, therefore, in a rather shamefaced spirit. I deliberately introduced bad jokes to show that I did not take myself seriously; whereas the truth was I was simply nervous about my achievement, just as a man afraid to disgrace himself as a boxer might pretend that the bout was not in earnest. My prose is consequently marred by absolutely stupid blasphemies against itself.

I now began to see that this was schoolboyish bashfulness, and to feel my responsibility as an exponent of the hidden knowledge, to treat my prose as reverently as my verse, and (consequently) to produce masterpieces of learning and wit. The 'Dedication and Counter-Dedication' of *Konx Om Pax* is wholly admirable and its rises to a delightful satirical climax of four stanzas on the 'empty-headed Athenians'. 'The Wake World' is a sublime description of the Path of the Wise, rendered picturesque by the use of the symbols of the Taro, and charming by its personification of the soul as a maiden. 'My name is Lola, because I am the Key of Delights, and the other children in my dream call me Lola Daydream.'

'Ali Sloper; or the Forty Liars' shows traces of my old vulgarity. The *dramatis personae* contains a lot of bad puns and personal gibes, but the dialogue shows decided improvement; and the 'Essay on Truth' is both acute and witty, with few blemishes. 'Thien Tao' gives my solution of the main ethical and philosophical problems of humanity with a description of the general method of emancipating oneself from the obsession of one's own ideas, in an amusing setting;

the humour is, on the whole, spontaneous and lively, while there are passages of remarkable eloquence.

The last essay in *Konx Om Pax*, 'The Stone of the Philosophers which is hidden in Abiegnus, the Rosicrucian Mountain of Initiation', is really beyond praise. Its genesis is interesting. I had written at odd times, but mostly during my travels with the Earl of Tankerville, a number of odd lyrics. The idea came to me that I might enhance their value by setting them in prose. I therefore wrote a symposium of a poet, a traveller, a philosophical globetrotter, an adept, a classical scholar and a doctor. They are made to converse about the chronic calamity of society, and the poems (ostensibly written by one or other of the men) carry on the thought. The result is, in reality, a new form of art; and I certainly assisted the lyrics by giving them appropriate springboards.

In 1903, too, I wrote 'The Soldier and the Hunchback, ! and ?' [1] and 'The Psychology of Hashish'.[2] The one goes to the roots of scepticism and mysticism, and represents them as alternative moods, neither valued in itself yet each a complete answer to its predecessor. I show that by perseverance in transcending each in turn, the original crude distinction between affirmation and negation tends to disappear; the supreme doubt is more positive than the more limited assertion.

'The Psychology of Hashish' pleases me more every time I read it. It contains such a wealth of knowledge, it shows such profundity of thought, that I find myself today still wondering how I ever wrote it. I find in it ideas which I am hardly aware that I possess today; how I could have thought thus at this elementary stage of my career, and written it all down in a single day, is bewildering. It is completely free from any blemishes of the old type. The sublimity of my subject possessed me.

One other seed had fallen upon fertile ground. 'The chance of the geologic period' had been seized by Captain John Charles Frederick Fuller, of the First Oxfordshire Light Infantry. It had come his way through the Rationalist Press Association, to whose publications he subscribed. He had not done any serious writing before; his utmost had been a few insignificant articles and poems, which he contributed to the *Agnostic Journal*. He was fighting valiantly against Christianity by the side of 'Saladin', William Ross Stewart, who was the leader of one of the main branches of militant agnosticism. The army of Satan had, unfortunately, failed to keep discipline in face of the enemy. The anti-Christians were in fact as prone to split up into sects as the non-conformists themselves. Bradlaugh's personality was big enough to enable him to keep any differences that he may have had with Huxley in the background, but the successors of these paladins were degenerate. Mrs Besant had broken away from atheism altogether; her hysteria handed her over from one strong influence to another as it appealed to her imagination. G. W. Foote, with the medal of his martyrdom glittering on his manly breast, marched monotonously against the mob of Christianity. He had suffered for the cause and was consumed by personal pride on that account. Ross Stewart had more literary leanings and was accordingly exclusive. Bernard Shaw was engaged in public exhibitions of rapier play; his subtlety made his colleagues doubt his sincerity; and without question his attacks on Christianity had lost their sting by reason of the very bitterness of his contempt for convention.

The Rationalist Press Association, with Grant Allen, Charles Watts, Edward Clodd, Joseph McCabe, Bertrand Russell, E. S. P. Haynes (the lawyer, by the way, who had so elegantly and adroitly arranged the details of my divorce) and numerous other prominent people, was, above all, anxious to be respectable. It felt it to be the most important point of policy not to give occasion to the enemy to blaspheme. Shelley's domestic diversions shocked them; they wanted to prove that conventional morality would not suffer by the abolition of Christianity. One of the Association's own lecturers, Harry Boulter, was prosecuted for the blasphemy of saying in Hyde Park what a thousand others, from Voltaire to Tyndall, had said for centuries, and it refused to defend him because his remarks had shocked policemen. The attitude seemed to me utterly ignoble. I have no particular sympathy with Boulter, but I recognized that in destroying the delusions of the vulgar one must use the kind of dynamite which they understand.

At the same time, I think the Rationalist Press Association ought to have accepted battle and fought the blasphemy laws to a finish. It lost prestige by deserting a comrade. People said, as they said of Shaw, that it was 'too proud to fight'. There were still other sects of satanists, down to the Reverend Guy A. Alfred, who mixed up religious and political revolt like the Bolsheviks. In one sense the attitude is logical and it is certainly courageous.

Fuller knew the animal and arranged with him to issue a cheap edition of *The Star in the West* with a preface of his 'Alfred's' own, through the Bakunin Press. He thought we should begin reconstruction of civilization at the very bottom. Alfred was certainly our man! When I read Conrad's *The Secret Agent* I instantly recognized him in Comrade Ossipon. I had never met so repulsive a type. Yet the creature had scholarship of a sort, keen courage and intellectual integrity. I say 'intellectual integrity' because I would not have trusted him with a threepenny bit. He did, in fact, cheat us out of a considerable amount, though we went into the business with our eyes open. With regard to the logic of his view, that Christianity and the social system stood or fell together, I object. That is emphatically the Christian view. The elder Cato was not an anarchist, nor Julius Caesar a disciple of Karl Marx. I entirely agree with Nietzsche that Christianity is the formula of the servile state; true aristocracy and true democracy are equally its enemies. In my ideal state everyone is respected for what he is. There will always be slaves, and the slave is to be defined as he who acquiesces in being a slave.

Such was the situation when Fuller, home on leave from India, came to see me and told me that he was competing for the prize essay on my work. He was entirely at one with me on the point of my attitude to Christianity. We regard it as historically false, morally infamous, politically contemptible and socially pestilential. We agree with Shelley, Keats, Byron, Swinburne and James Thomson as far as they went. We agree with Voltaire, Gibbon, Strauss, Huxley, Herbert Spencer, Tyndall, J. G. Frazer, Ibsen and Nietzsche as far as *they* went. But we were absolutely opposed to any ideas of social revolution. We deplored the fact that our militant atheists were not aristocrats like Bolingbroke. We had no use for the sordid slum writers and Hyde Park ranters who had replaced the aristocratic infidel of the past. We felt ourselves to be leaders; but the only troops at our disposal were either mercenaries or mobs. Like the prince of the Fronde, we found ourselves fighting by the side of a venal and ignorant parliament, disorderly banditti, a mob of bourgeois and a horde of beggars.

The position was all the more annoying because we knew perfectly well that the vast majority of the aristocracy, both of blood and of brains, were heartily on our side or profoundly indifferent and aloof. But they were all afraid to come out into the open and sweep religion away; or else felt themselves personally secure from any annoyance and therefore inclined to let sleeping dogs lie. For example, it was known that two thirds of the dons of Trinity College, Cambridge, were openly atheistic, and, according to all the principles of the university, should have been *ipso facto* deprived of their fellowships, yet they were perfectly safe in the saddle so long as they abstained from any overt act which the authorities could not overlook. We thought that this hypocrisy was not the harmless practical joke which it seems to be at first sight. We could not ourselves have acquiesced consciously in any such evasion, and we did not understand how people of such intellectual superiority could agree to hold their positions on such humiliating terms.

It is (incidentally) hardly less humiliating for Christianity itself that it should be so powerless, despite its ostensible impregnability. It could not furnish the necessary complement of men of intellect from its own ranks, and the college was compelled to endure the contempt of its own fellows. It could not do without them; it dared not prescribe them; it had to be careful to avoid so much as questioning them on the essential points on which their tenure of office was supposed to depend. It dared not even make any overt endeavour to alter the situation. It dared not even lament the evil days on which it had fallen. It had to pretend that all was well: to deny boisterously a fact which was notorious.

As a matter of fact, Christianity is everywhere in more or less the same position, though the most liberal estimate of the proportion of population that attends any place of worship scarcely reaches one and a half per cent. The Church claims—when not wailing to the opposite effect—that the entire population is actively Christian. The press cannot believe its ears when it transpires that some professor of geology does not believe in Genesis. There is indeed something pitifully heroic about the enormity of the belief. If it were not that this infinitesimal minority is able to exercise such an asphyxiating effect on popular thought, and such a murderous grip upon popular morals, to torture and deform the minds of children, to make hypocrisy the price of happiness, one might even sympathize with this frog in its attempts to persuade itself and its neighbours that it is an ox. On one point only were Fuller and I at odds. His hatred for Christianity extended to the idea of religion in general. He had, of course, a sympathy in his heart for Islam; the manliness of the Mohammedan makes it impossible to despise his belief in Allah. Islam is free from the degrading doctrine of atonement and the glorification of the slave virtues. The Moslem's attitude to Allah only errs in so far as it involves the childish idea of personifying the powers of the universe. It is right that we should reverence the majesty of nature and obey her laws; but he fought with me, hand to hand, week after week, about the question of Magick. He had originally intended his essay to conclude with the sixth chapter, and he had scrupulously avoided any reference to the magical and mystical side of my work; nay, even to the philosophical side so far as that was concerned with transcendentalism. But I showed him that the study must be incomplete unless he added a chapter expounding my views of these subjects. Thus chapter seven came to be written.

It is a very complete and just exposition of my views, and it is especially to be noticed that within the one hundred and thirty-three pages there is no reference to *The Book of Law*. (At the time of the publication, therefore, I was still keeping the hem of my garment scrupulously away from the Cairo working.) By the time he had written this chapter, I had brought him to see that materialism, in any ordinary sense of the word, was thoroughly unsatisfactory as an explanation of the universe; but he was not in the least inclined to accept any theories which might involve belief of any kind in a spiritual hierarchy. In the course of our argument I had myself been made uneasy by a subconscious feeling that, watertight as my system was in itself, certain legitimate inferences might be drawn from it which I was not drawing.

The Book of the Law annoyed me; I was still obsessed by the idea that secrecy was necessary to a magical document, that publication would destroy its importance. I determined, in a mood which I can only describe as a fit of ill temper, to publish *The Book of the Law*, and then get rid of it for ever.

I was also annoyed by the way in which Fuller stuck to his guns about the magical hierarchy in general. In a spirit of mischief I sent him a typescript of *The Book of the Law* and asked him to tell me what he thought of it. I wanted to disgust him with myself; I wanted him to class me finally as a hopeless crank. His answer came in the course of two or three days: I could not believe my eyes. This, he wrote, is the utterance of a Master. What did he know about Masters, confound him! It was as if I had sent a copy of *Tit-Bits* to the Archbishop of Canterbury, and he had reverently pronounced it to be the authentic Logia of 'our Lord'.

But there was no getting over the fact. Here was the Book which I hated and feared, the Book from which I was desperately trying to escape, and here was a man who hated anything of the sort without fearing it in the least, a man who had nothing to escape from; and it was instantly accepted by him at its face value. It's no good arguing whether a thing is a hammer or not, when all you know about it is that it has a habit of knocking you down.

It was useless to struggle further. So late as October 1908, I was carrying out a Retirement (see 'John St John'), and invoking my Holy Guardian Angel, without any reference to *The Book of the Law*. Fuller and I had gone to work to edit my magical diaries and present to the world the story of my magical career in 'The Temple of Solomon the King', as if the Cairo working were a mere episode of that career. We were carrying out the orders of the Secret Chiefs by exposing the G. D. and publishing its Ritual, but I was sheltering myself from *The Book of the Law* by taking advantage of a phrase in the text which insists: 'All this and a book to say how thou didst come hither and a reproduction of this ink and paper for ever—for in it is the word secret and not only in the English.' And the manuscript had been lost!

As the sequel will show, the gods knew when to lay their hands on it. I surrendered at discretion, re-obligated myself and in September 1909 wrote my greatest magical poem 'Aha!' in which the Cairo working is restored to its proper place in my life. I have made many insurrections since then; but they have always been quelled in very short order and punished as they deserved.

This lengthy preamble will enable the reader to fit into their proper places the ostensibly incoherent events of 1907 and 1908. My own continuous illness, the birth of Lola Zaza and the tragedy of Rose had combined to complicate my ordinary business, making it impossible for me to think of making any new plans for exploration. My affairs in Scotland had fallen into great confusion through the extravagance and dishonesty of my factor. While the cat was away the mice had been extremely busy.

Fuller and I had clearly understood the imminence of the world catastrophe. We did not exactly know where civilization would begin to crack, or when; we were content to leave such speculations to the Prophet Baxter, the Rev. Booth Clibborn and such small deer. But we saw the New Zealander sitting on the ruined arch of London Bridge quite clearly.

We could also see the Professor of Archaeology in the University of Lhasa excavating the ruins of the British Museum. He discovered a vast number of volumes of our period purporting to deal with the occult sciences, but there were few indeed of these which had not crumbled into dust. Of those that remained, the vast majority were evidently frivolous. He rejoiced exceedingly to discover one series of volumes, the dignity of whose appearance, the permanence of whose paper, the excellence of whose printing, and the evident care which had been bestowed on their production, showed him at first sight that the people responsible for their production had been at infinite pains to make these volumes testify against the tyranny of time. He had them taken to his camp with the greatest care. Although he could not read a word of the letterpress, the illustrations were in the universal language, which he could read at sight. The first standard work of reference—the key to the wisdom of the buried past.

With this vision before us, we determined on making our record of the highest attainments of human spirits of our generation as worthy as possible of its subject. It annoyed us that we could not engrave our knowledge on ten thousand slabs like those at Mandalay, but we determined to do our best. We decided on a fount of type, a size of page and a quality of paper which could not fail to impress the professors of posterity, and we determined that our prose should be so simple, so dignified and so sublime that it would stand out from the slipshod journalism of the period as the Alhambra above the hovels of the vermin that surround it. The scheme required capital, and though I was already somewhat embarrassed by the habit of buying my black egg without haggling, I did not hesitate to put my hand in my pocket.

Fuller was at this time in grave difficulties, à la d'Artagnan, but he gave his time and his toil with magnificent generosity. His draughtmanship, within certain limits, was miraculously fine. Certain subjects were altogether beyond him; he could not portray the human figure. His 'Adonai-Ha-Aretz' is lamentable, but his symbolic drawing shows the highest qualities of imagination and execution, and his geometrical work is almost inconceivably perfect. His four Watch Towers (*The Equinox*, vol. I, no. VII) and similar illustrations are superb, and his ornamental alphabet is altogether beyond me to appreciate. Unfortunately, his prose was florid and confused, and he suffered acutely from what I call the 'comma bacillus'. He loved a sentence so much that he could not persuade himself to finish it, but his images are more vivid and virile than those of any writer I have ever known. The style of *The Star in the West* is trenchant and picturesque. Its only fault is a tendency to overloading. I could have wished a more critical and less adoring study of my work; but his enthusiasm was gen-

uine, and guaranteed our personal relations in such sort that
my friendship with him is one of the dearest memories of my
life. I dedicated *The Winged Beetle* to him.

Alas, I did not take into account the corrupting influence
of women. He held out a long while against the insidious
pressure of his wife. It was perhaps only through the treachery of another man that mischief was finally made between
us. But nothing can destroy the past, and the long years of
our intimate friendship were indeed fertile. We saw each
other nearly every day and worked together in a perfect
harmony.

In 'The Temple of Solomon the King' Fuller's style was
already much improved, though the story of my life might
have been set forth more simply. Though his tendency to
burst out into ecstatic rhapsodies resulted in disordering the
proportions of its events, in the main his task was admirably
accomplished, and there are passages of astonishing sublimity, not only in the matter of language but in that of
thought. His point of view was indeed more subtle and profound than he himself realized. I am sure that many passages
of this book will stand among the greatest monuments of English prose extant.

But he reached his high-water mark with 'The Treasure
House of Images'. Formally, this is the most remarkable
prose that has ever been written. Each chapter of the main
part of the book contains thirty sections, and each section
has the same number of syllables. Each of these chapters
hymns the sign of the Zodiac and in each section that sign is
modified by another sign. It is the most astonishing achievement in symbolism.

But this is not all. There is a chapter containing one hundred and sixty-nine cries of Adoration, which is, as it were, a
multiplication of the previous chapters and a quintessential-
ization of them. To this day we chant these Adorations to the
sound of the tom-tom and dance to the music, and the effect
is to carry away the performer into the sublimest ecstasy. It
possesses all the Magick of oriental religious rites, such as
those of the Sidi Aissawa, but the rapture is purely religious.
It is not confused with eroticism, and that although many of
the symbols are of themselves violently erotic.

> O Thou dew-lit nymph of the Dawn, that swoonest in
> the satyr arms of the Sun! I adore Thee, Evoe!
> I adore Thee, IAO!

> O Thou mad abode of kisses, that art lit by the fat
>   of murdered fiends! I adore Thee, Evoe!
>   I adore Thee, IAO!

Unfortunately, when our friendship was interrupted so was his literary career. I had taught him to write prose, but he has been able to employ his talents to no better purpose than to win prizes in competitions organized by the Army Council.

The Star in the West was published in 1907 and was widely reviewed; for the most part, favourably. In particular, Soror S. S. D. D. (Mrs Emery or 'Florence Farr' as she was variously known) wrote a very full criticism of it in the *New Age*. Some of it is so prophetic that it must be quoted here:

> It is a hydra-headed monster, this London Opinion, but we should not be at all surprised to see an almost unparalleled event, namely, everyone of those hydra-heads moving with a single purpose, and that the denunciation of Mr Aleister Crowley and all his works.
>
> Now this would be a remarkable achievement for a young gentleman who only left Cambridge quite a few years ago. It requires a certain amount of serious purpose to stir Public Opinion into active opposition, and the only question is, has Mr Crowley a serious purpose? . . .
>
> Such are some of the sensations described by Aleister Crowley in his quest for the discovery of his Relation with the Absolute. His power of expression is extraordinary; his kite flies, but he never fails to jerk it back to earth with some touch of ridicule or pathos which makes it still an open question whether he will excite that life-giving animosity on the part of Public Opinion which, as we have hinted, is only accorded to the most dangerous thinkers.

I was enormously encouraged by this article. I knew how serious my purpose was. She had reassured me on the point where my faith wavered. I had become so accustomed to columns of eloquent praise from the most important people in the world of letters, which had not sold a dozen copies; to long controversial criticism from such men as G. K. Chesterton, which had fallen absolutely flat. People acquiesced in me as the only living poet of any magnitude. (There were many better known and more highly reputed poets—Francis Thompson, W. B. Yeats, Rudyard Kipling, and later John Masefield, Rupert Brooke and other small fry, whose achievement at the best was limited by the narrowness of their ambitions. I at least was aiming at the highest.)

Yet hardly anyone had read any of my work and the intrigues of my enemies had made it impossible for me to make myself heard. I never cease to wonder at the persistence of malignant hostility on the part of people who have never met me or read a line of my writing. I cannot see why people should pursue me with secret slander, often of a kind which carries its own refutation with it. To give one instance: It was said it was my practice to lure men into the Himalayas for *weekends* . . . I always returned alone!

There seemed no limit to the lies that were circulated about me. As to motive, I can only imagine that it was partly the revenge of the G. D. rebels whom I had smashed, and, subsequently, Mathers and his gang when it became my duty to put a stop to their swindling and blackmail; partly to my *intransigence* about other forms of quackery. I had not spared the English Alpine Club or the pretenders to literary eminence. I kept myself aloof from cliques and simply refused to admit the existence of the people who were playing at being poets, novelists and philosophers.

But I had learnt intolerance of all pretence and humbug from Eckenstein who had on me somewhat the influence that Athos had on d'Artagnan. Whenever I was tempted to derogate in any way from the highest standards of honour, the thought always came to me that I could not face Eckenstein if I failed. My family, my college and my friend have always been my mentors; but, above all, my friend! His severity was fortified by his clear sight; no subterfuge was possible with him. He taught me to judge my conduct by the most austere standards of rectitude and nobility. It is not too much to say that he created my moral character. I had a fatal tendency to find excuses for myself. He forced me always to face the facts and keep ceaseless vigil over the jewel of honour.

61

My favourite rendezvous was a little chemist's shop in Stafford Street, managed by a man named E. P. Whineray, one of the most remarkable and fascinating men that I have ever met. He was a Lancashire lad all over and not ashamed of it. His personal appearance was in itself arresting. Of medium size and well proportioned, his body seemed intentionally inconspicuous. It was the perfect servant of his head. He was almost completely bald, with bushy iron-grey eyebrows. The dome of his skull was perfectly spherical and suggested the most profound capacity for reflection. His eyes were intensely lively and piercing; they shone with eternal laughter, no less good humoured because supremely cynical. He understood human frailty in every detail and not only forgave it, but loved men for their weaknesses. He reminded one of an owl; the resemblance was very striking indeed.

He knew all the secrets of London. People of all ranks, from the courtier and the cabinet minister, to the coachman and the courtesan, made him their father confessor. While he never betrayed a confidence, he had a fund of stories which never failed. His lightest remarks vibrated with wisdom. When one spoke to him, it was like blowing the bellows of a blacksmith's forge; a shower of scintillating sparks came crackling from the sombre heart of the fire of his soul. Like Eckenstein, he saw through everybody at a glance. I used to haunt his shop and learned from him about London. He had already appeared in literature. Robert Hichens has set one of the most subtle incidents of *Felix* in his little shop. Another reason for my frequenting him was that he understood me, and one of my weaknesses is my bitter need of such people.

He was (incidentally) one of the most learned men in his line. He had supplied me with ingredients for some of my magical preparations, such as kyfi,[1] the mysterious incense of the ancient Egyptians; the perfume and oil of Abra-Melin, [2] the unguentum Sabbati, and the like. In particular, he was at one time able to supply onycha.

There is an incense sacred to Tetragrammaton. After the

cakes of light and the incense of Abra-Melin, it is the most powerful of all known perfumes. In fact, it is in a sense more powerful than they are, for they are definitely consecrated to particular purposes, whereas it is entirely without conscience. It consists of galbanum for air, onycha for water, storax for earth and olibanum for fire. It represents the blind force of the four elements and by its use one can bring them to manifestation. Being in itself neither good nor evil, it is extraordinarily dangerous.

I may regard, by the way, that what we call 'good' and 'bad' are both extremely limited. The greatest disasters arise from what we call indifference. I once examined the horoscopes of a number of murderers in order to find out what planetary dispositions were responsible for the temperament. To my amazement, it was not the secret and explosive energy of Herschel, not the sinister and malignant selfishness of Saturn, not the ungoverned fury of Mars, which formed the background for the crime, but the callous intellectualism of Mercury.

Then comes a most extraordinary discovery. The horoscopes of the murdered are almost identical with those of the assassins. They asked for it!

Incidentally, history bears out this view. The greatest horrors in the history of mankind are not due to the ambition of the Napoleons or the vengeance of the Agamemnons, but to the doctrinaire philosophers. The theories of the sentimentalist Rousseau inspired the integrity of the passionless Robespierre. The cold-blooded calculations of Karl Marx led to the judicial and business-like operations of the Cheka. Human passion at its worst has generous possibilities, and mercy with the Red Cross—theoretically, at least—is just behind fury in the trenches; but reason is inexorable and inhuman. It is not the heart of man which is 'deceitful above all things and desperately wicked', but his brain.

One evening Whineray told me that a gentleman, whom I will call the Earl of Coke and Crankum, wished to meet me, having need of my magical help. I agreed. At that moment the man himself walked in. He took me round to his rooms; and, to my stupefaction, blurted out the most extraordinary story. I could hardly believe my ears. The man told me his inmost family secrets, and those of the most atrocious kind, as if I had known him twenty years. He said that he was bewitched by his mother and a woman friend. On the surface these people were pious Evangelicals. The idea that they were trying to murder him by witchcraft was a little startling, no less so the alleged motive. Lord Coke had been the second son. He claimed that his elder brother had really been the son of some baronet or other; that his mother hated her husband and had become desperate when the heir-apparent had been killed in battle. His mother had determined to kill her remaining son.

Coke himself had married an American woman of the meanest character. She would ring the bell to have the pleasure of hearing the servants call her 'my lady,' Coke saw witchcraft in every trifle. When the countess happened to sneeze he would deduce that his mother was on the job. He had told his troubles to many people, and trusted them at first quite blindly, and then without a word of warning concluded from some harmless word or act that they had joined the conspiracy against him.

Of course, it was a perfectly plain case of persecution mania, accentuated by his old habit of brandy tippling and his newly acquired one of sniffing a solution of cocaine. Apart from his obsession there was nothing wrong with the man. He enjoyed magnificent health; he was one of the best preserved men of fifty to fifty-five that I have ever seen. He was deeply religious, with more than a touch of mysticism, and a really deep insight into the Cabbala, which he understood although he knew little or nothing about it. I thought I could cure him and undertook the task.

My plan in such cases is not to undeceive the patient. I proposed to treat his story as literally true in every way and to fight fire with fire. I said to him: 'What you must do is to develop your own magical powers so as to beat your mother at her own game.'

He had considerable capacity for Magick and understood the object of the measures which I proposed. We began by chartering a yacht, which we anchored in an unfrequented river on the south coast. I obligated him and proceeded to teach him how to develop his astral body. He rapidly acquired the technique and gained much confidence when he found that by my methods he could check the results of his clairvoyance.

I would, for example, give him a talisman which he had never seen before, and ask him to discover its nature. We would then compare the result of his investigation with the book from which I had taken the talisman, and he would find that he had judged correctly. (For instance, I would give him a square containing thirty-six characters in Enochian, which he could not read. He would pass in his astral body through an imaginary door on which this square was inscribed, and tell me that he had come out upon a balcony overlooking the sea, where a violent storm was raging. I would then refer to *The Book of the Sacred Magic of Abra-Melin,* identify the square, and note that its virtue was to arouse a tempest. There was thus no room for self-deception as there is when one gets a message from one's Uncle Ferdinand that he is very happy picking violets, and tell Eliza not to worry.)

I soon found, however, that the presence of the countess, though she was entirely sympathetic and charming, was a hindrance; she took up too much of his time and thought. One of the troubles with the man was that he was shockingly sentimental; it was the worst kind of Dickens. For that and other reasons, we decided to make a Great Retirement in a distant country; our whereabouts was to be concealed; that in itself would tend to confuse and alarm his mother and her fellow witch. We crossed to Paris and wandered down by Marseilles and Gibraltar to Tangiers.

I was of course in paradise to be once more among Mohammedans, with their manliness, straightforwardness, subtlety and self-respect! There was another point in favour of our journey. I wanted to get my pupil into the habit of the open-air life, so as to break him more easily of the cocaine habit. The pull of cocaine is almost entirely moral, except in unusually bad cases. There is little or no physical suffering involved in sudden stoppage as there is in the case of opium and its derivatives. I wanted to wean him from the drug by taking his mind off his mother and her machinations, his wife and her wondrousness, his children and their charm; I wanted to fill his consciousness with unfamiliar sights and sounds, with actual adventures and with the physical preoccupation of the day's march.

Unfortunately, we arrived in Tangiers at a moment of political crisis. The sultan had just come to smash and even the journey to Fez was unsafe. Not that we should have cared: Coke was as brave as a lion about everything outside his dam and her devices; but the authorities would not hear of our leaving the city—even the environs were beset by banditti. It was a great nuisance, especially as I had got ready for the desert by shaving my head and getting into my Eastern clothes.

However, I consoled myself by making excursions after dark into the suburbs and courting all adventures that might come my way. I had in fact a perfectly gorgeous time.

But poor Coke would not enter into the spirit of the East —in which we humorously include a country whose name (Morocco, Al'Maghrabi) means west and whose most easterly point is in the longitude of Oxford. He was homesick for the dull uniformity of family life. That is, I believe, the heart of England's horror. Frank Harris has described English vices as 'Adultery with home comforts'. The average Englishman likes to drink tea in a pair of previously warmed soft slippers, with a smiling piece of meat presiding over the soggy toast, and unintelligent brats playing halma in the background. 'The East' only means to him sunstroke, fever and other diseases, each more dreadful than the rest; people whose views do not interest him—they are unintelligible and immoral; discomfort and boredom. He has no idea of abstract beauty and he is terribly afraid of meeting an idea which might stir his stagnant stupidity.

To me every new scene, every new point of view, is welcome. I want to be taught. I want to enlarge my mind. *Nihil humani a me alienum puto.*[3] Even so, *humani* is one word too many. As I wrote in *The Book of Lies*.

> The Chinese cannot help thinking that the octave has five notes.
> The more necessary anything appears to my mind the more certain it is that I only assert a limitation.

It is natural that my attitude should be utterly abhorrent to my fellow countrymen. But they are quite wrong to think that my ideas are anti-Anglo-Saxon. They are anti-anything which imagines itself to have a monopoly of truth or propriety.

I could not get Coke to take any interest in the people, their customs, their ideas and their art. The sunshine on the sparkling sea, the infinite variety of colour and form, the tingling mixture of races and religions meant nothing to him. Beauty was literally splashed over life like a bucket of cold water over an athlete. Instead of exhilarating him, he shivered and moaned. He kept on groaning like a wounded animal: I want my wife! I want my children! Of course, what he really wanted was cocaine, and that was just the thing I did not want him to have.

I had managed to get rid of his persecution mania for the

time being. Whenever he noticed his mother flying past the moon on her broomstick, he would perform a banishing ritual, and sail out in his astral body on to the word [4] and chop the broomstick like Siegfried with the lance of Wotan, and down she would fall into the Straits of Gibraltar, plop, plop. Nor did he suffer seriously from the suppression of cocaine. His only trouble was that his mind was so sodden with sentimentality that no amount of sunshine could restore its lightness and elasticity. If I had been able to take him into the desert for a couple of months he would have had to live through the purgatory involved in the absence of sour-faced snobbery and sneaking servility.

Thanks to Muly Hafid, there was nothing for it but let him relapse into the slough of despond and stifle in the stinking slime of civilized society. I begged him to walk home from Gibraltar, but it merely gave the old delusions an excuse to renew their grip. He classed me as having joined the conspiracy against him of black magicians, from his mother and his neighbours to his son's schoolmaster (who had been persuaded by the devil to inflict one hundred lines of the *Georgics* upon the luckless lad!) and his family lawyer—who had been persuaded by Belial to fail to lend him ten thousand pounds without security.

I have never been so sorry for any man in my life. I have never met anyone more genuinely noble, generous and kindhearted. He was the most amusing companion, witty and well read. And all these magnificent qualities were completely marred by a single puerile weakness. Once again I had to admit that the superstition and sexual hyperaesthesia, which go in England by the names of religion and love, had emasculated a man. Anglo-Saxonism is psychological phthisis.

At the accession of the new sultan, his subjects took the opportunity of enjoying themselves, rejoicing in countries where the *spirochaetas pallida* of civilization does not make love luetic, liberty ataxic and life choreic. The people are spontaneous about amusements. To me nothing is more dreary than the policed processions of noble nonentities, famous puppets and beauties whose diet is skin food, whose athletics are face massage and whose fresh air is cocaine. In England enjoyment has been reduced to formality. The studied solemnity of golf is typical. Every few holes one's partner gives a little lecture on the healthfulness of the game, its virtue to bring out the finest qualities of the player, and so on *ad nauseam*. The Anglo-Saxon consciousness of sin makes him feel that he needs an excuse for indulging in the most innocent pleasures. The result is that they cease to be pleasures at all.

Gaiety has become entirely unknown; the nearest approach to it is tipsy vulgarity.

The joyous men of Morocco were giving themselves over wholeheartedly to glee. Their exercises and sports have been described so often that it would be absurd to go over the ground once more. But one amusement is less well known. Europeans are not encouraged to assist.

On one of my lonely adventure walks, I came upon a crowd of about two hundred people in a secluded spot. They were protected from intrusion by unofficial sentinels, strolling (apparently without aim) among the trees in a circle a couple of hundred yards in diameter. I knew more or less what to expect, and before being observed looked myself over to see that every article of my costume was correct. I then began to recite what I had learnt from my sheikh in Egypt—the 'Great Word to become mad and go about naked'.

> *Subhana Allahu walhamdu lilahi walailaha illa allahu wallahu akbar wala baala wala quata illa billahi alaliu ala'zhim.*
> Glory to God and thanks to God, and there is only one God, and God is most great, and there is no strength but in Him, the Exalted, the Great.

It does not take me long to work myself up by means of a mantra, even of this lengthy type, into a state of ecstasy, and to proceed, if desired, from that state to actual Dhyana, by concentrating upon any appropriate cakra. By ecstasy I do not mean anything characterized by extravagant action. It is merely that I seem to myself to be floating in the air, or at least to weigh about one quarter of what I actually do; that I become completely abstracted from my surroundings and from all internal interference. I should thus be either invisible to the sentinels, or, if observed by them, recognized as a holy man whose religious exercises it would be an outrage to disturb. I need hardly say that the thing must be done properly. To attempt to fake anything of the sort would be a fatal error. The psychic sensitiveness of the Arab would detect it at once; he would suspect a bad motive, put one down as a blasphemer and cut one down with unhesitating cheerfulness. And serve one right!

In this way I passed the sentinels and mingled with the crowd. It was a wild tribe from Seoul. The women were present, though they took no active part, and merely helped to keep the ring. The circle was some thirty feet across. Squatting on its edge were the usual musicians, playing as usual for dear life, while dancing and yelling were a number of men, armed with very small light axes of peculiar workmanship. They were evidently not the ordinary tools used in daily life, but manufactured for the purpose of the ceremony. With these weapons the men cut themselves on the head (very rarely elsewhere) until the blood was streaming from their scalps on every side. They were, of course, quite unconscious of any pain, and those of them who were actually blinded by the blood were yet able to see.

The excitement of the crowd was as great as that of the celebrants themselves, but it was rigorously suppressed. I cannot say that the ring kept absolute silence; I doubt whether I was sufficiently cool to make any reliable observations, and I certainly was beyond the stage of intellectual curiosity. But the impression was that the onlookers were deliberately abstaining from either speech or gesture. I governed myself accordingly. But I was hard put to it to refrain from dashing down my turban, leaping into the ring with a howl of *'Allahu akbar!'*, getting hold of an axe and joining in the general festivity.

It literally took away one's breath. The only way I can express it is that one breathed with one's heart instead of with one's lungs. I had got into not dissimilar states while doing Pranayama, but those had been passive, and this was a—no, active is a pitifully inadequate word—I felt myself vibrating with the energy of the universe. It was as if I had become conscious of atomic energy or of the force of gravitation, understood positively and not merely as the inhibition to rising from the ground. I do not know how long I stood there holding myself in, but judging from subsequent calculations it must have been over an hour: the sense of time had entirely disappeared. But I became suddenly aware of a terrific reaction; I felt that I had missed my chance by not letting myself go and perhaps been killed for my pains. At the same time I was seized with a sudden sense of alarm. I felt myself to be outside the spiritual circle. I was sure that someone would discover me and a swift shudder passed through me as I apprehended my danger. Fortunately, I had sufficient presence of mind to resume my mantra and melt away from the multitude as silently as I had descended upon it.

This little adventure always stood out as one of the most

exciting (in a small way) of my life, that is, of merely
material adventures; and it has given me furiously to think
about the general formulae of 'Energized Enthusiasm'.[5] The
practices of the Sidi Aissawa, the dervishes, some Asiatic devotees, and many Russian peasants whom I have seen conscientiously and scientifically exalting their consciousness by
bringing physiological methods to the aid of spiritual aspiration, have been too individual to compare with these Moors.
In this ceremony the entire body of assistants were consciously
and collectively inducing a spiritual state which I recognized
as entirely different to individual ecstasy. The soul which they
invoked was neither the sublimation (or simplification) of
each man's personal self, nor was it the universal and immanent Spirit. It was a collective consciousness.

The psychology is similar to that of any mob which works
itself up into enthusiasm over some ill-defined religious or
political idea; but these Moors were invoking what I must call
their tribal god, for want of a better term. They were creating
him by pouring their personal enthusiasm into the pot, so to
speak. I had no doubt that the individual deity thus invented
(I can find no better term) could exist organically, so to
speak, and I began to understand how the prophets of old had
succeeded in inventing their gods, neither personal nor universal, but representing the Platonic idea, corresponding to
the sum of the tribal attributes, and, once invented, enjoying
an independent life, exercising initiative, and so on, just like a
human being, sustained by the united wills of his devotees, and
thus turning the tables on them and compelling them who had
made him in their image to conform with the likeness of him.

I had quite a number of other small adventures during my
short stay in Morocco. The character of the people corresponds
very closely with my own in its more salient aspects. I liked
them very much better than the Egyptians, who seem to me to
suffer from too much history, too much civilization, too much
commerce, too much admixture of blood; and, above all, too
much cosmopolitanism. The Egyptian has little national character, he has been pauperized by the influx of Europeans, and
corrupted by the 'evil communications' of Greeks, Armenians
and the objectionable type of Jew. The Jew in Morocco is, on
the whole, a very fine fellow. He has a religion and a point of
honour, to say nothing of his pride of race. It has been said
that every nation has the government which it deserves. I
would add, the type of Jew which it deserves. His imagination
and sensitiveness make him the touchstone of his surroundings.

There is a saying in North Africa that the Moor is a lion, the Algerian a deer and the Tunisian a hare. When subsequent journeys to North Africa enabled me to make the comparison, I found it strikingly true. The Moors have been called the Irish of Islam, as the Burmese the Irish of Asia. The former metaphor is admirable. There is an independence, a pride, a devil-may-careishness and a bonhomie which reminds one strongly of the more boisterous type of Irish. The Burmese rather resemble the quiet, religious type. The Moor is always on the look out for a lark. I found myself engaged in all sorts of schoolboy escapades where hard knocks and Rabelaisian practical jokes gave birth to huge and hearty laughter. Mortal enmities and murderous assaults did not in the least interfere with the jolly friendship of the antagonist.

I was very sorry when we had to return to England. We took Granada on our way. I found the Alhambra entirely familiar, although I had never been there before. It was not a case of the *sens du déjà vu*, which is a passing perception. I went from one court to another as if I had lived there before; I knew what I was coming to so accurately that I could hardly doubt that I had really lived there at one time or another. I remembered nothing of the circumstances; except that it must have been my habit to go to the western tower and look over the valley, the town somnolent at the foot of the hill, and the distant sierra, while the sun sank superbly sad among clouds which seemed to have borrowed their softness and brilliance from swansdown.

Coke and I arranged to see the dancing of the gypsies who lived in the caves outside the city, and I made a somewhat elaborate study of the subject. The principal dances are the tango, which is quite different to that with which we have become familiar; the fandango, the civilla gitana; the soleario gitana, the cachusa gitana, the morongo, the sirrillas, the baile de la flor, the baile de la bosca and the baile de la bona.

It is a mistake to say, brutally, as science is inclined to do, that all dancing symbolizes passion. I am always annoyed with research that stops half way. That is the great error of Freud. When he says, quite correctly, that dreams are phantasms of suppressed sexual desire, the question remains, of what is sexual desire the phantasm? To me it seems no more than one of the ways of expressing the formula of creation. I regard chemical action as identical. A man and a woman unite; and the result is a child, which is totally different from them though formed of their elements. Just so the combination of hydrogen and chlorine produces hydrochloric acid. They are gases: at ordinary temperature it is a liquid. None of its chemical and physical reactions is identical with those of its elements. The phenomena are analogous in very many ways, but the essence of their similarity is in the Cabbalistic formula Yod, Hë, Vau.

I have successfully eliminated the danger of obsession by sexual ideas in this way: I refuse to admit that it is the fundamental truth. Science in failing to follow me so far has destroyed the idea of religion and the claim of mankind to be essentially different from other mammalia. The demonstration of anthropologists that all religious rites are celebrations of the reproductive energy of nature is irrefutable; but I, accepting this, can still maintain that these rites are wholly spiritual. Their form is only sexual because the phenomena of reproduction are the most universally understood and pungently appreciated of all. I believe that when this position is generally accepted, mankind will be able to go back with a good conscience to ceremonial worship. I have myself constructed numerous ceremonies where it is frankly admitted that religious enthusiasm is primarily sexual in character.

I have merely refused to stop there. I have insisted that sexual excitement is merely a degraded form of divine ecstasy. I have thus harnessed the wild horses of human passion to the chariot of the Spiritual Sun. I have given these horses wings that mankind may no longer travel painfully upon the earth, shaken by every irregularity of the surface, but course at large through the boundless ether. This is not merely a matter of actual ceremonies; I insist that in private life men should not admit their passions to be an end, indulging them and so degrading themselves to the level of the other animals, or suppressing them and creating neuroses. I insist that every thought, word and deed should be consciously devoted to the service of the Great Work. 'Whatsoever ye do, whether ye eat or drink, do all to the glory of God.'

One night in Granada I met one of these gypsies. The setting was supremely romantic. The burden of his life fell from the shoulders of the poet. I experienced that spontaneous and irresistible stroke of love which only exists when the beauty of the human form and the beauty of the rest of nature are harmonized automatically. It was one of those experiences which come even to the most romantic poets, and to them only too few times in a decade. Fuller always maintained that the lyric in which I celebrated that night was the greatest that had ever been written of its kind. I can do no less than ask public opinion to examine his judgment.

Your hair was full of roses in the dewfall as we danced,
The sorceress enchanting and the paladin entranced,
In the starlight as we wove us in a web of silk and steel
Immemorial as the marble in the halls of Boabdil,
In the pleasaunce of the roses with the fountains and the yews
Where the snowy Sierra soothed us with the breezes and the dews!
In the starlight as we trembled from a laugh to a caress,
And the God came warm upon us in our pagan allegresse.
Was the Baile de la Bona too seductive? Did you feel
Through the silence and the softness all the tension of the steel?
For your hair was full of roses, and my flesh was full of thorns
And the midnight came upon us worth a million crazy morns.
Ah! my Gypsy, my Gitana, my Saliya! were you fain
For the dance to turn to earnest?—O the sunny land of Spain!
My Gitana, my Saliya! more delicious than a dove!
With your hair aflame with roses and your lips alight with love!
Shall I see you, shall I kiss you once again? I wander far
From the sunny land of summer to the icy Polar Star.
I shall find you, I shall have you! I am coming back again
From the filth and fog to seek you in the sunny land of Spain.
I shall find you, my Gitana, my Saliya! as of old
With your hair aflame with roses and your body gay with gold.
I shall find you, I shall have you, in the summer and the south
With our passion in your body and our love upon your mouth—
With our wonder and our worship be the world aflame anew!
My Gitana, my Saliya! I am coming back to you! [6]

This year was indeed my *annus mirabilis* in poetry. It began with *Clouds Without Water*, to which I have already called attention in the matter of its technique. The question of its inspiration is not less interesting. At Coulsdon, at the very moment when my conjugal cloudburst was impending, I had met one of the most exquisitely beautiful young girls, by English standards, that ever breathed and blushed. She did not appeal to me only as a man; she was the very incarnation of my dreams as a poet. Her name was Vera; but she called herself 'Lola'. To her I dedicated *Gargoyles* with a little prose poem, and the quatrain (in the spirit of Catullus) 'Kneel down, dear maiden o' mine.' It was after her that my wife called the new baby!

Lola was the inspiration of the first four sections of *Clouds Without Water*. Somehow I lost sight of her, and in the fifth section she gets mixed up with another girl who inspired entirely sections six and seven. But the poem was still incom-

plete. I wanted a dramatic climax, and for this I had to go to
get a third model. Number two was an old friend. I had known
her in Paris in 1902. She was one of the intimates of my
fiancée. She was studying sculpture under Rodin and was
unquestionably his best woman pupil. She was strangely seductive. Her brilliant beauty and wholesome Highland flamboyance
were complicated with a sinister perversity. She took delight
in getting married men away from their wives, and the like.
Love had no savour for her unless she was causing ruin or
unhappiness to others. I was quite ignorant of her intentions
when she asked me to sit for her, but once in her studio she
lost no time, and 'The Black Mass', 'The Adepts' and 'The
Vampire' describe with ruthless accuracy our relations. She
initiated me into the torturing pleasures of algolagny on the
spiritual plane. She showed me how to intensify passion by
self-restraint. The formula is entirely analogous to the physical
formula of the Arabs. She made me wonder, in fact, if the
secret of puritanism was not to heighten the intensity of love
by putting obstacles in its way.

I regard the idea as entirely morbid and objectionable.
Artificial impediments to nature are necessarily as disastrous
as natural ones. The essence of my objection to English ideas
of morality is just this: that sexual relations are over emphasized and assume an entirely disproportionate value. The
formula of the average novel is to keep the reader in suspense
about the love affairs of the characters. I confess frankly that
I cannot read such stuff with patience.

I do not mind a background of love properly subordinated
to the true interests of life; but I do not know any single book
of which it is the main theme which does not disgust me.

Am I reproaching myself, then, for having written as I
have on the subject? My defence is duplex. In the first place,
I have no objection to lyrical love. 'I arise from dreams of
thee' and 'O lover, I am lonely here' are legitimate. It is the
sacrament by which man enters into communion with God.

There remain my narrative and dramatic books on love. *The
Tale of Archais* is simply jejune; I apologize and pass on.
The Mother's Tragedy, 'The Fatal Force', *Jezebel, Tannhäuser*,
all treat love not as an object in itself, but on the contrary,
as a dragon ready to devour any one less than St George.
Alice is partly excusable, because it is really a lyric, when all
is said and done. In any case, I do not value the book very
highly. It is ridiculous to make anything important depend on
the appetites of an American matron. The same may be said

of *The Star and the Garter*. *Why Jesus Wept* exhibits love as the road to ruin. It is the sentimental point of view about it which is the catastrophe of Sir Percy's career. In *Orpheus* love, it is true, inspires the poet to great deeds of a sort; but it ends in disappointment and leads him to death.

But back to my sculptress! To her I dedicated *Rodin in Rime* and *Clouds Without Water* itself—not openly; our love affair being no business of other people, and in any case being too much ginger for the *hoi polloi*, but in such ways as would have recommended themselves to Edgar Allan Poe.

There remains a tragic and abominable story to be told. She suddenly decided that she had better get married; not being able to marry me, she did the next best thing, found another explorer and dragged him to the altar. This man left shortly afterwards on an expedition which involved his being very many months beyond reach of communication. He had a rival brother officer, who somehow discovered one of the cryptograms. (As a matter of fact, it was a simple one; he had merely to take a rule and draw a straight line to make the name and surname of the girl stand out *en toutes lettres*.[7]) It might seem that such a man would not know how to draw a line anywhere, but he drew this line—and arranged that a copy of the book thus marked should be handed to the husband by another member of his party after he had cut his communication with the world, perhaps for years. In point of fact, it proved to be for ever.

Now as to section eight of *Clouds Without Water*, 'The Initiation', I hardly know why I should have felt it necessary to conclude on such an appalling chord. The powers of life and death combine in their most frightful forms to compel the lovers to seek refuge in suicide, which they, however, regard as victory. 'The poison takes us: χαίρετε νικῶμεν.' The answer is that the happy ending would have been banal. The tragedy of Eros is that he is dogged by Anteros. It is the most terrible of all anticlimaxes to have to return to the petty life which is bounded by space and time. I had the option of coming down to earth or enlisting death in my service. I chose the latter course.

My model was a woman very distinguished and very well known in London society. She had already figured as the heroine of *Felix*. She had been one of the best and most loyal friends of Oscar Wilde. She was herself a writer of subtlety and distinction, but she filled me with fascination and horror. She gave me the idea of a devourer of human corpses, being herself already dead. Fierce and grotesque passion sprang up for the few days necessary to give me the required inspiration for my climax. I could only heighten the intoxication of love by spurring it to insanity.

This, in fact, is a final criticism of love itself as such, and justifies all that has been said about it by the Buddha—and even by the Church. It justifies my own attitude that love must be resolutely torn from the throne in the human heart which it has usurped. One must not set one's affections on things below; one must find an answer to old age and death. 'Only those are happy who have desired the unattainable.' Love being the sublimation of the human ego, it follows that the ego itself must be surrendered. The limitations of life on earth are intolerable. The consciousness is unendurable for all those who have begun to understand the universe. Man is so infinitesimally inane, yet he feels himself capable of such colossal attainment.

My twelve months of creative spurt reached a climax in February 1908, when I wrote the five books of *The World's Tragedy* in five consecutive days at Eastbourne. This is beyond all question the high-water mark of my imagination, my metrical fluency, my wealth of expression, and my power of bringing together the most incongruous ideas so as to enrich my matter to the utmost. At the same time, I succeeded in reaching the greatest height of spiritual enthusiasm, human indignation, and demoniac satire. I sound the gamut of every possibility of emotion from innocent faith and enthusiasm to experienced cynicism.

62

Besides all these activities of my own, I came into a new world. My Operation of the Sacred Magick was not sterile. After returning from Morocco, the spirit came upon me and I wrote a number of books in a way which I hardly know how to describe. They were not taken from dictation like *The Book of the Law* nor were they my own composition. I cannot even call them automatic writing. I can only say that I was not wholly conscious at the time of what I was writing, and I felt that I had no right to 'change' so much as the style of a letter. They were written with the utmost rapidity without pausing for thought for a single moment, and I have not presumed to revise them. Perhaps 'planary inspiration' is the only adequate phrase, and this has become so discredited that people are loth to admit the possibility of such a thing.

The prose of these books, the chief of which are *Liber Cordis Cincti Serpente, The Book of the Heart girt with the Serpent,* and *Liberi vel Lapidis Lazuli,* is wholly different from anything that I have written myself. It is characterized by a sustained sublimity of which I am totally incapable and it overrides all the intellectual objections which I should myself have raised. It does not admit the need to explain itself to anyone, even to me. I cannot doubt that these books are the work of an intelligence independent of my own. The former describes the relation of the adept with his Holy Guardian Angel; the latter is 'the voluntary emancipation of a certain adept from his adeptship . . . the birth words of a Master of the Temple.'

Even this did not exhaust my creative energy. As in Cairo in 1902 I had started the 'Lover's Alphabet', on the ground that the most primitive kind of lyrics or odes was in some way the most appealing and immortal, so I decided to write a series of hymns to the Blessed Virgin Mary in the simplest possible style. I must not be thought exactly insincere, though I had certainly no shadow of belief in any of the Christian dogmas, least of all in this adaptation and conglomeration of

Isis, Semele, Astarte, Cybele, Freya, and so many others; I simply tried to see the world through the eyes of a devout Catholic, very much as I had done with the decadent poet of *White Stains*, the Persian mystic of the *Bagh-i-Muattar*, and so on. I was, in fact, adopting another alias—in the widest sense of the word.

I did not see why I should be confined to one life. How can one hope to understand the world if one persists in regarding it from the conning tower of one's own personality? One can increase one's knowledge and nature by travelling and reading; but that does not tell one how things look to other people. It is all very well to visit St Peter's and the Vatican, but what would be really interesting would be to know how they look to the Pope. The greatness of a poet consists, to a considerable extent, in his ability to see the world through another man's eyes; and my training in science is always suggesting to me that I should invent a technique for doing anything that I want to do. My technique for borrowing other people's spectacles was to put myself in their place altogether, either by actually adopting a suitable alias or by writing a book in their names. It is a common and legitimate literary device.

When in Holland in '97, I had written a Christmas hymn in which the Nativity was treated realistically. I now found that Christian piety had taken away the entire poetic beauty of Bethlehem by declaring that the Virgin suffered no pain. (It is really astonishing how these idiots managed to remove any touch of sublimity from this stupid story!) I therefore had to change 'Her bitter anguish hath sufficed' into 'her joyful ardour hath sufficed', and otherwise degrade my poem to a blasphemous imbecility, in order to comply with the conventions of the Church. Apart from that, what I had written in a spirit not far removed from ribaldry was found wholly satisfactory.

I had written, in 1899, while staying with Mathers in Paris, a hymn to Isis to be used in the ceremonies of Isis worship which he was at that time proposing to revive in Paris. I changed the word 'Sistron' to 'cymbal' and the word 'Isis' to 'Mary'. The hymn required no further alteration. I think that rather significant.

Once more, I made a translation of the Fatihah, the most sacred chapter of the Koran, I replaced the name of God by that of Mary, and once again found favour with the Vatican.

I quote a few isolated stanzas:

The red sun scorches up our veins;
The white moon makes us mad;
Pitiless stars insult our pains
With clamour glad.

At the foot of the Cross is the Mother of God,
And Her tears are like rain to enliven the sod,
While the Blood of the Lord from His Body that runs
Is the heat of the summer, the fire of its suns.

See where the cherubim pallid and plumed
Swing with their thuribles praises perfumed!
Jesus is risen and Mary assumed:
Ave Maria!

O sorrow of pure eyes beneath
The heavy-fringed ecstatic lids,
Seeing for maiden song and wreath
Sphinxes and pagan pyramids!

O Mary, like a pure perfume
Do thou receive this failing breath,
And with Thy starry lamp illume
The darkling corridors of death!

There was besides such creative work and the editorial work
which Fuller and I had undertaken on behalf of the Order,
the task of reconstituting it in its original purity. Under
Mathers, the Grades had become meaningless: to be an
adept had meant no more than to be a peer of the realm does
in modern times. It was for me to sweep away all this nonsense, to re-establish the ordeals, in spirit and in truth. I was
at first ignorant enough of Magick to imagine that this could
be done by the simple process of replacing sham formalities by
real ones. I proposed, for example, to test people's courage
by putting them in actual contact with the four elements, and
so on, as was apparently done in ancient Egypt; but experience
soon taught me that an ordeal, however severe, is not much
use in genuine initiation. A man can always more or less
brace himself up to meet a situation when he knows that he
is on his trial. A man might have a certificate of ability to
swim half a mile; and yet be utterly unable, for a dozen
different reasons, to save a friend from drowning when the
need arose.

Of course it sounds totally impossible to administer

ordeals of the real kind required, but I found by experience that I did not even have to give the matter a moment's thought. My magical self took complete charge of the business without wasting a moment or disturbing me. It may be through some act of my own, it may be entirely without my intention, that aspirants to the Order find themselves in circumstances where they are tested in the qualities necessary to their stage of initiation. There is thus no possibility of evading the intentions of the Order. It is not conducted consciously by any men soever, but by mysterious forces automatically set in motion by the force of the obligations themselves.

For example: the oath of a probationer apparently involves no difficulties of any sort; no penalties are stated or implied; the aspirant merely pledges himself 'to perform the Great Work, which is to obtain the knowledge of the nature and powers of my own being'. He is not required to reach any particular stage of knowledge by the end of his probation; he is free to choose such practices as appeal to him; and, provided that his record shows that he has devoted a reasonable proportion of his spare time to the Work, he is unhesitatingly passed to the degree of neophyte. It sounds as if it were impossible for anyone to fail. Yet, actually, only eight per cent. manage to get through the year of probation. The reason is that no sooner does a man make up his mind to enter the Path of the Wise than he rouses automatically the supreme hostility of every force, internal or external, in his sphere.

I further restored the original rule of the Order that its members should not know each other officially and have as little to do with each other as possible. Theoretically, a member should know only his introducer and those whom he himself introduces. In the present conditions of society it is practically impossible to maintain this rule with absolute strictness, but I keep as near to the ideal as possible. I did relax the rule, to a certain extent, in 1910—it was the greatest mistake I had ever made, and the mischief done at that time has never been wholly repaired. Every month I live I am the more amazed at the praeterhuman wisdom and foresight of the Order. I have never known a mistake to be made; whereas my conscious powers are constantly at fault. If I had no other evidence of the authority of the people to whom I am pledged, it would be supplied by their wisdom.

It happened that at the funeral of Saladin, Fuller had met a youth named Neuburg, Victor Benjamin of that ilk, who was at Trinity College, Cambridge, and knew my work. Having to go to Cambridge one day on some business or other, I thought I would look the lad up. I was not sure of the name, and there were several similar 'burgs' in the university register, but having drawn my bow at a venture, the first arrow struck the King of Israel between the harness at the very first shot. I use the words 'King of Israel' advisedly, for Neuburg was certainly a most distinguished specimen of that race. He was a mass of nervous excitement, having reached the age of twenty-five without learning how to manage his affairs. He had been prevented from doing so, in fact, by all sorts of superstitions about the terrible danger of leading a normal wholesome life. The neuroses thus created had expressed themselves in a very feeble trickle of poetry and a very vehement gust of fads.

He was an agnostic, vegetarian, a mystic, a Tolstoyan, and several other things all at once. He endeavoured to express his spiritual state by wearing the green star of Esperanto, though he could not speak the language; by refusing to wear a hat, even in London, to wash, and to wear trousers. Whenever addressed, he wriggled convulsively, and his lips, which were three times too large for him, and had been put on hastily as an afterthought, emitted the most extraordinary laugh that had ever come my way; to these advantages he united those of being extraordinarily well read, overflowing with exquisitely subtle humour, and being one of the best natured people that ever trod this planet.

But from the first moment I saw him, I saw far more than this; I read an altogether extraordinary capacity for Magick. We soon drifted into talking about the subject and I found that he already practised a good deal of spiritualism and clairvoyance. The former was his bane. The habit of making himself spiritually passive and inviting the entire spirit world to obsess him proved finally fatal to him. Despite all we could do to protect his aura, we found it impossible to stop the leak altogether, so that at any moment he was liable to become possessed of the devil. He soon learnt how to protect himself as soon as he recognized that he was being attacked; but the spirits became very cunning and were at pains to persuade him not to take the proper measures of protection. I believe, despite all this, that he would have succeeded eventually in mending his aura, but in the principal ordeal of the neophyte he was so seriously damaged that he was never the same man again. During the next few years I saw a great deal of him and his spiritual adventures will serve both as a diversion and warning on many a page to come.

Recognizing the possibilities of Neuburg, I decided to utilize them for the benefit of the Order, and of himself. The first task was to get rid, as far as possible, of his physical defects, which turned out to be very serious. One day during our walk through Spain we came upon a waterfall, and, the weather being oppressively hot, we decided to take a dip. In this way I discovered that he was suffering from varicocele very badly indeed and as soon as we got to England I sent him to my doctor, who advised an operation, which was duly performed. He had also pyorrhoea so badly that my dentist said that if he had delayed the visit three weeks he would not have had a tooth left in his head. Attention to these points, and to the physical cause of his neurosis, made a healthy man of him. One defect remained; and that was incurable, being a slight spinal curvature. The change in him was extraordinary. He lost all his nervousness; he became capable of enduring great physical fatigue, of concentrating mentally, and of dismissing the old fads which had obsessed him. Incidentally, by removing his inhibitions, I released the spring of his genius, and in the next few years he produced some of the finest poetry of which the English language can boast. He had an extraordinary delicacy of rhythm, an unrivalled sense of perception, a purity and intensity of passion second to none, and a remarkable command of the English language.

But the other voice was silent, and the noise of waters swept me
Back into the world, and I lay asleep on a hillside
Bearing for evermore the heart of a goddess,
And the brain of a man, and the wings of the morning
Clipped by the shears of the silence; so must I wander lonely,
Nor know of the light till I enter into the darkness.

He possessed the magical gift of conveying an idea of tremendous vividness and importance by means of words that are unintelligible to the intellect.

I go as Thunder that come but as a bird.

(And then the girl came as a bird, and he went as a worm—but I anticipate.)

Neuburg was the moving spirit of one of those societies which are always springing up in universities. They never take root; because death comes to all alike at the end of three years, so to speak. People who stay up for a fourth year are Ancient Mariners, but lack the power to hold the wedding guest. Of course people overlap; but the generations follow each other so quickly and the spirit of youth is so impotent to stamp itself upon history, that it is a rare piece of luck when any of these clubs or societies live beyond seven years at the outside. Neuburg's society, the Pan Society, did make its mark on the university; but that was not its fault. It was simply that he found people idiotic enough to make it invulnerable against the arrows of oblivion by dipping it into the Styx of persecution. Nothing could have been more helpful than the attitude of the Dean of Trinity, an idiot and inept. I have noticed that people who dislike me are invariably rendered so blind by malice that they give themselves away and make themselves ridiculous.

There is an institution at Cambridge called 'Ciccu', Cambridge Intercollegiate Christian Union. It is a bestial thing, compact of hypocrisy and secret vice. Now my connection with the Pan Society was of the slightest. I have merely been invited to read papers, I think altogether three times, on mysticism or kindred subjects. Nothing more harmless can be imagined, but the Ciccu went out of its mind. I am compelled to remark at this point that one of the most disgraceful features of controversy in England is that the upholders of religion and morality, which are frequently not at all in question, instead of disputing with their opponents, assail them with the weapons of secret slander. 'This man,' they say, 'wants to take a penny off the income tax. It is certain that he habitually breaks the Seventh Commandment.' In this instance the Ciccu did not know or care what it was that I had read to the Pan Society. They merely stated that I hypnotized the entire assembly and took a mean advantage of them. It did not matter to them that what I was supposed to have done is impossible in nature, at least to one of my very mediocre powers.

However, the Senior Dean of Trinity, the Rev. R. St J. Parry, started to make trouble. I went to see him and asked him what accusations he had to make against me. He merely became confused, tried to bluster, would not commit himself, and finally said that he had given orders that I was not to be admitted to the precincts of the college. On the following morning I waited in the Great Court for him to come out of chapel and called him a liar to his face in front of everybody. It then began to dawn upon him that he had no power to exclude me from Trinity, I being a life member of the college. He summoned the president, secretary and treasurer of the society, and threatened to send them down. But as it happened they none of them belonged to Trinity and he had no more power over them than he had over the Queen of Madagascar. He must have been a really exceptional fool, even for a don, not to have found out such essential facts before entering upon his campaign. He ultimately resorted to the meanest possible course of action. He did not dare to attack Neuburg, whose relations were wealthy Jews and might be relied upon to make every kind of trouble if he interfered with the hope of Israel; but he threatened a man named Norman Mudd, whose parents were poor and without influence, with the loss of his mathematical scholarship. Unfortunately again, Mudd was the mainstay of the hope of the college for the forthcoming Tripos, and Mudd himself had the heart of a lion. He dared the dean to do his damndest in the most uncompromising language. Once again the wretched creature had to draw in his horns. Only after I had left the battlefield to seek other victories did he succeed in bullying Mudd into resignation from the society by frightening his father. Mudd gave his promise to have no more to do with it—and promptly broke it. The Pan Society won all along the line.

The victory was all the more signal in that an imitation society called the Heretics, who had been trying to run with the hare and hunt with the hounds like the Rationalist Press Association, had melted away into the thinnest kind of mist at the first intimation from the authorities that their exceedingly mild programme of half-baked infidelity was displeasing to the powers that were. The whole incident was trivial in its way, but it taught me an important lesson of policy. The more upright and uncompromising one is, the safer one is from attack. One's enemies will resort to the most despicable subterfuges, but they will not have the courage to come into the open and they will in one way or another fall into the pit which they dig. It is true that one can apparently be damaged by secret slander, when the enemy become foolhardy by open misrepresentation, but if one is working in the eternal one may be sure that they harm no one but themselves. Suppose, for example, that I attack Lloyd George by saying that he had undergone seven years' penal servitude for burglary, and suppose Lloyd George treats me with the contempt I deserve. Well, at the moment there may be a few people silly enough to believe such nonsense, and to think that his allowing the statement to go unchallenged makes it probable that there is some truth in it. But consider what the biographers will say? They will discover that Lloyd George's time was fully accounted for without the penal servitude, and they will simply wonder what spirit of insanity possessed me to make so ridiculous a mis-statement. They will have no difficulty in understanding that he, preoccupied with affairs of state, could not be bothered to leave his work to chastise me.

Another consideration arises in this connection. It is always difficult to discover who has really said what about one, and even if one succeeds it is not always the best policy to refute the falsehoods. If people were attacking one by merely falsifying or exaggerating actual incidents, defence would be possible; but when people are bound merely by the limits of their vile imaginations, it is not easy to keep pace with them. What is the use of Lloyd George proving that he did not undergo penal servitude for burglary if I can retort, 'Perhaps not, but you were hanged for sheep stealing!' To defend oneself against the accusations of a knave is to seek justice from the verdict of fools. If one's work and one's reputation depends on the opinion of people at the moment, it is, of course, necessary to meet them on their own ground. At every election the most ridiculous falsehoods about the candidates are sedulously circulated at the last moment; if possible, too late to allow time for refutation. The election may doubtless depend on such infected activities.

But when one is working in the eye of God, when one cares nothing for the opinion of men, either at the moment or at any other time; when one has surrendered for ever one's personal interests and become lost in one's work, it is merely waste of time and derogatory to one's dignity to pay attention to irrelevant interruptions about one's individual affairs. One keeps one's powder and shot for people who attack one's work itself. And even this is often useless. The Buddha told his disciples not to combat error. If it had only seven heads like the Lennean hydra it might be possible to sterilize the necks after each operation sufficiently long to finish the job before they grow again. But modern hydras have not this pitiful paucity of talking machines. Hardly a month passes but I hear some new and perfectly fantastic yarn about myself, sometimes flattering, sometimes the reverse, but nearly always entirely baseless, and, as often as not, bearing internal evidence of its absurdity. I have been sufficiently amused to wish to make a collection of these legends, but I find that my memory refuses to record rubbish of this kind. It insists on having some peg whereon to hang its old clothes.

I am not sure whether it was Henry Maudsley who shows that the mind develops not by accretion but by co-ordination. It seems that there is a certain number of pigeon-holes, if I may use the metaphor, in which isolated facts may be stored, and that this number is strictly limited. The efficiency of the arrangement may doubtless be increased by practice and the use of mnemonics, but sooner or later one comes to the end. A man of forty who has devoted every moment of his time to acquiring knowledge finds almost certainly that he has no more pigeon-holes available, and that therefore he cannot acquire any new knowledge except by forgetting some of the old.

This, by the way, shows the tremendous importance of selective study. One of the few gleams of intelligence shown in the works of Conan Doyle is where Sherlock Holmes is ignorant that the earth goes round the sun and, on being told, says that he will at once try to forget it. The case chosen exhibits the chooser as imbecile, for elementary astronomy is certainly important to the detective. But the general idea is sound.

It is today implicitly admitted by all advanced thinkers in every science that the reason is no more than an exceedingly imperfect instrument whose methods are entirely empirical, whose terms lack precision, and whose theses cancel each other out. I might claim a good deal of credit for having written out, as far back as 1902, a reasonably complete demonstration of this conclusion whose premises were not stated by the official leaders of thought till long afterwards.[1] Yet the theory of initiation on which European adepts base their systems (derived, possibly, from the Egyptians and Chaldeans by way of the gnostics, Pythagoras and the neoplatonists), that of Lao tzu in China, and that of the Vedantists in India, alike imply something of the sort. My claim to originality is confined to the nature of my proof, which I drew from facts of a similar order to those which have finally driven modern science and mathematics to their present position; whereas the ancients, as far as we know, based their thesis on an intuitive perception of the incompetence of reason and on their experience of the results of illumination.

I devoted a great deal of time to various essays demonstrative of the general truth above set forth* and to this practical problem. I took all the mystical and magical practices of all religions all over the world, and those of the secret teachers and associations to which I had access. I have little hesitation in saying that I have not omitted any practice of importance. I stripped these methods of all their dogmatic top-hamper, all their racial and climatic limitations, and all the complications which had been introduced in the course of time or through the idiosyncrasies of their inventors. I further freed them from the weight of the promised rewards which were supposed to follow on their performance. I wrote down the result in the simplest and most dignified prose at my command, clarifying the instructions by separating them into sections.

I guided myself by the principle that the object of any useful practice soever must necessarily be to get rid of some limitation. Thus the real object of Assana is evidently to release the body from the pain which is its normal characteristic; that of Mantra Yoga to smooth the choppy sea of thought by inducing its movement to take the form of rhythmical billows. In this way I set forth the initiated teaching of all ages and all arts in a uniform and consistent body of writing, being careful nowhere to imply any theory soever.

> In this book it is spoken of the Sephiroth and the Paths; of Spirits and Conjurations; of Gods, Spheres, Planes, and many other things which may or may not exist.
>
> *Liber O* ²
>
> May be.
> It has not been possible to construct this book on a basis of pure scepticism. This matters less, as the practice leads to scepticism, and it may be through it.
>
> *Liber Thisharb*

This work extended over a number of years, but the fundamental principles were laid down at this time. It is just to say that the publication of these instructions completely revolutionized occult training. It may not seem so very important on the surface to have adhered to the point of view without altering the practice, but in reality the difference is vital. For instance, there is a book, *Liber Jugorum*,³ in which the student takes an oath to exclude a certain thought, word or act, for a given period, and on every occasion of forgetfulness to cut himself on the wrist with a razor.

* *The Soldier and the Hunchback, ! and ?* states it most clearly.

63

In 1908 I began to be a little restless. The Himalayas had cured me of the habit of going to the Alps. I could not play any longer with dolls after wooing such grown-up girls as Chogo Ri and Kangchenjunga. I tried to settle down in the Latin Quarter, finding a real home at 50 rue Vavin with M. and Madame Bourcier, people in whom the spirit of the early days of d'Artagnan was still alive. There is a peculiar relation between the best bourgeois of this type and the wandering *gentilhomme*, who is seeking his fortune in one way or another and requires a *pied à terre*. It is one which implies great mutual respect and affection, and, alas, the qualities which make such relations possible are becoming very rare in the world. Despite all its drawbacks, there was never a better social system than the feudal, so far as it derived from the patriarchal. In getting rid of its abuses, we have also got rid of the noblest springs of action and the most congenial code of manners. The war destroyed this relation altogether. The Bourciers ended by being as disgusting as any other French people.

In April I wandered from Paris to Deal and played golf enthusiastically. Rose was going from bad to worse. I had begun to learn to detect the smell of alcohol, but her cunning was so extraordinary that I was never able to catch her in the act of drinking. During the whole period, in fact, I only did so twice. The second occasion makes an interesting story. It shows the extent to which the obsessing demon can conceal his presence.

It was one evening in our house at 21 Warwick Road. Rose and I were sitting in my library on the ground floor in the front of the house. The dining-room and kitchen were in the basement, the whisky being kept in the sideboard. Rose said that she would go and lock up the house, and went downstairs. I put off my slippers and followed stealthily. The staircase was partly illuminated, a shadow being cast diagonally across it. I heard the dining-room door open and began to descend. Rose came quickly back and looked up the stairs; but luckily I was in the shadow and she did not see me. She then went very quickly back into the dining-room, leaving the door open, and I went down the stairs as quickly as possible, hoping to catch her in the act. As I reached the foot, whence I could see into the dining-room, I heard the noise of a door being closed. Rose was standing by the sideboard; but there was no evidence of her act except an empty wet glass. During the few seconds it had taken me to descend the stairs, she had opened the sideboard, uncorked the bottle, poured out and drunk the whisky, and restored everything to its normal condition. It was an act of prestidigitation and nothing else.

I was at my wits' end. She was no better than before she went to Leicester. I thought I would try moral pressure and took counsel of Fuller, Eckenstein and Gerald Kelly, as well as her doctor. They were none of them very hopeful, but they agreed that it might do some good to leave her and refuse to return until guarantees were given that she had stopped drinking. There did really seem some hope: the power of love might work the miracle, and certainly my love for Rose was stronger than ever, although cut away completely from its physical support. I have always been peculiarly sensitive about trifles in my rapports with women; the most trivial thing can put me off completely. (Alexander Harvey has a superb story, 'The Mustache', in which this psychology is admirably set forth.) I could have borne her death more philosophically. I was constantly tortured by the 'memory of the Rose-red hours'. I was not allowed to forget. There was the possibility of paradise at my elbow and there was nothing there but the reek of hell.

> I reel back beneath the blow of her breath
> As she comes smiling to me, that disgust
> Changes her drunken lust
> Into a shriek of hate—half conscious still
> (Beneath the obsession of her will)
> Of all she was—before her death, her death!

I hated to go away; in my diary, April 26th, I find: 'Gerald at twenty-one. Wonders I didn't put my foot down a year ago. But Rose's tenderness is such, and I love her so dearly.' However, I left on the twenty-eighth for Paris.

Late in 1908 I picked up a book. The title attracted me strongly, *The Magician*. The author, bless my soul! No other than my old and valued friend, William Somerset Maugham, my nice young doctor whom I remembered so well from the dear old days of the Chat Blanc. So he had really written a book—who would have believed it! I carried it off to Scott's. In my excitement, I actually paid for it.

I think I ate two dozen oysters and a pheasant, and drank a bottle of No. 111, one of the happiest champagnes in the famous—can you say 'caterer's'? Yes:—I mean caterer's cellar. Yes, I did myself proud, for the Magician, Oliver Haddo, was Aleister Crowley; his house 'Skene' was Boleskine. The hero's witty remarks were, many of them, my own. He had, like Arnold Bennett, not spared his shirt cuff.

But I had jumped too hastily to conclusions when I said, 'Maugham has written a book.' I found phrase after phrase, paragraph after paragraph, page after page, bewilderingly familiar; and then I remembered that in my early days of the G . . . D . . . I had introduced Gerald Kelly to the Order and reflected that Maugham had become a great friend of Kelly's, and stayed with him at Camberwell Vicarage. Maugham had taken some of the most private and personal incidents of my life, my marriage, my explorations, my adventures with big game, my magical opinions, ambitions and exploits, and so on. He had added a number of the many absurd legends of which I was the central figure. He had patched all these together by innumerable strips of paper clipped from the books which I had told Gerald to buy. I had never supposed that plagiarism could have been so varied, extensive and shameless. *The Memoirs of a Physician, The Island of Doctor Moreau, The Blossom and the Fruit,*[1] and numerous other more or less occult works of fiction had supplied the plot, and many of them the incidents. *The Kabbalah Unveiled, The Life of Paracelsus, The Ritual and Dogma of Transcendental Magic*[2] and others had been transcribed, whole pages at a time, with such slight changes as 'failed' for 'resulted in failure', and occasional additions or omissions.

I like Maugham well enough personally, though many people resent a curious trick which he has of saying spiteful things about everybody. I always feel that he, like myself, makes such remarks without malice, for the sake of their cleverness. I was not in the least offended by the attempts of the book to represent me as, in many ways, the most atrocious scoundrel, for he had done more than justice to the qualities of which I was proud; and despite himself he had been compelled, like Balaam, to prophesy concerning me. He attributed to me certain characteristics which he meant to represent as abominable, but were actually superb.

He represented me as having treated my wife as Dumas makes Cagliostro treat his, with the object of producing homunculi, artificial living human beings—'Was it for these vile monstrosities that Margot was sacrificed in all her loveliness?' Well, comeliness is cheap after all. To discover the secret of life, who would not pitch two thirds of our 'maudite race' into the bottomless pit of oblivion, for which, in my case, they are bound?

The Magician was, in fact, an appreciation of my genius such as I had never dreamed of inspiring. It showed me how sublime were my ambitions and reassured me on a point which sometimes worried me—whether my work was worth while in a worldly sense. I had at times feared lest, superbly as my science had satisfied my own soul, it might yet miss the mark of making mankind master of its destiny.

Well, Maugham had had his fun with me; I would have mine with him. I wrote an article for *Vanity Fair* (December 30th, 1908) in which I disclosed the method by which the book had been manufactured and gave parallel passages. Frank Harris would not believe that I was serious. He swore I must be making it up. He could not believe that any man would have the impudence to publish such things of plagiarism. I had to bring a little library round to the office to prove my proposition, and Harris sat and stared, and gasped like a fish at each fresh outrage. He cut down the article to two and a half pages, but even so it was the most damning exposure of a literary crime that had ever been known. No author of even mediocre repute had ever risked his reputation by such flagrant *stupra*.

Maugham took my riposte in good part. We met by chance a few weeks later, and he merely remarked that there were many thefts besides those which I had pointed out. I told him that Harris had cut down my article by two thirds for lack of space. 'I almost wish', I said, 'that you were an important writer.'

I had begun, I do not in the least remember how, to try my hand at short stores. Even today having written more than seventy such, I do not quite understand why this form of art should appeal to me. I take fits of it. I go for a month without thinking of the subject at all, and then all of a sudden I find myself with ideas and writing them down. I entirely agree that the short story is one of the most delicate and powerful forms of expression. It forms a link with poetry because one can work up to ecstasy of one kind or another in a more lyric manner than is possible in a novel; the emotion evoked is doubtless more limited, but it can be made for this very reason better defined. The ecstasy of *Wuthering Heights, The House with the Green Shutters* and *Tess of the D'Urbervilles* is altogether on a larger scale. It is built up of more and more varied material and it is evidently possible to obtain a great general effect. On the other hand, the novel loses in poignancy. Such incidents as the hand at the window in *Wuthering Heights* and Mrs Gourlay's exclamation in Douglas's masterpiece are almost out of keeping with the general plan.

In Paris I wrote 'The Soul Hunter'[3], the diary of an insane doctor who has drugged his enemy, certified his death, got possession of the corpse, embedded it in plaster of Paris, and vivisects the brain in order to discover the seat of the soul—a nice Christmassy idea.

Paris disgusted me. I tried to find peace at Morêt, but found only boredom, and went off to Venice with a bad throat which gave me the idea of the story 'Cancer?'[4] In this a distinguished painter imagines himself to have cancer of the throat—and anywhere else of which he is reminded by some trifling irritation. (Eugène Carrière is doubtless responsible in part for the theme.) He works himself into all kinds of mental fever, but luckily goes to a doctor—drawn from my own doctor, Edmund L. Gros, the famous American physician of Paris—who pronounces him neurasthenic but otherwise healthy and prescribes a motoring tour, sending his own brother to take charge of the patient. They reach the Pyrenees. He is so exhilarated that he can think of nothing better to do than cut his throat. Another Christmassy idea.

Venice bored me as badly as Morêt. That was, in fact, the essence of my stories: that I was incurably sad about Rose. So I got back to Paris and forgot my sorrows in the kindness of Nina Olivier and various friends. I wrote 'The Dream Circean'.[5] This is a bigger and better story than either of the others. A young man full of romantic ideas of honour and purity has an adventure in which he rescues a girl from the malice of her mother. This involves a fight with the servant. But after he has won he cannot find the house. He searches vainly and becomes a monomaniac. Then he meets Eliphas Lévi, who promises to cure him, provided that he swears never to enter the street where he imagined the house to be as long as he should live. He is, in fact, cured; but one day after Lévi's death he finds himself in the neighbourhood of the street, and decides to walk through it merely to celebrate the fact that he is cured, and that it means no more to him than any other street. Instantly the old obsession seizes him, and for the rest of his life he searches through Paris for the girl with golden hair, though he knows quite well that even if he found her she would be an old woman.

Rose's family and my friends had put pressure on her, and her father wrote to me that I could come back, which I did; but I found that she had simply become more cunning than ever.

It was really beyond belief. It had been hard to convince myself that she was in the grip of this disease. I had been told about it in more or less plain terms by quite a number of people, and had merely been angry with them. Now, when I knew it myself, I found other people equally incredulous. Haynes told me that he simply could not believe the facts, though he knew all about her two months in Leicester, and the rest. Her doctor told me that she would come to him and beg him, with tears in her eyes and tones of desperate sincerity, to cure her; and all the while she would be drinking under cover of her handkerchief. I took her down to Sandwich for a fortnight in June and July, but there was nothing to be done. One could not even watch her. She would go out in the early hours of the morning and appear at the breakfast table hardly able to speak.

I went back to Paris on July 8th. I worked on *Clouds Without Water, Sir Palamedes, The World's Tragedy* and 'Mr Todd'.[6] In particular, I wrote the autobiographical preface to *The World's Tragedy*, some ten thousand words, at a stretch; and certain lyrics, mostly about Dorothy, of whom more in a moment. 'Mr Todd', as the name implies, is a personification of death and the idea of the play is to introduce him as deus ex machina, helping the characters one by one out of their various troubles. The idea sounds a good one, but apart from availing myself of my opportunities for *double entendre* ('I was told the other day that he held a lot of land in London and has more tenants than the Duke of Westminster!'), I could not make much of it. The repetition of the idea was bound to be rather ridiculous. It is my one failure in this period.

The truth doubtless is that I had used up the energy accumulated in my wanderings, and written myself out: i.e., as far as anything big was concerned. I was in excellent form with lyrics and wrote several as good as anything I had ever done.

In particular 'After Judgment',[7] to the honour and glory of Dorothy,[8] will stand in English literature as one of the most passionate poems in the language.

It was certainly time that I went for a walk in the country. Paris is not a stimulant to a poet of my calibre; I need to be face to face with God and see Him, and live. For when it is said that no man shall look upon His face and live, the emphasis must be on the word 'man'. It is the privilege of the poet that his life is fed by direct communication with nature, as a child in the womb of its mother. The man who is separate from nature, and is nourished by the gross food of his conscious impressions, produces only second-rate stuff. I feel the necessity of being absolutely shut off from the external universe—'My life is hid with Christ in God', to borrow the phraseology of the Christian mystic. I received my inspiration directly, without even needing an intellectual peg on which to hang it. My consciously conceived work is always inferior; it only exists because when I come to the point of actual writing, my pen runs away with me.

So I wanted to get back to the tall timber, but I did not know where to go. My course was determined by the necessities of Neuburg's initiation. He had joined me in Paris and I proceeded to instruct him without losing a moment. He had taken an honours degree in medieval and modern languages, and he could not order his dinner. I remember his asking for red cabbage by the name of 'rouge kō-bāzhe'—which is the nearest I can get to it phonetically.

He had been warned against drinking absinthe and we told him that was quite right, but (we added) many other drinks in Paris are terribly dangerous, especially to a nice young man like you; there is only one really safe, mild, harmless beverage and you can drink as much of that as you like without running the slightest risk, and what you say when you want it is, 'Garçon! Un Pernod.' I forbear to remark on the result, beyond mentioning that I took Nina and a lady whom I will call Dorothy, as she figures under that name in numerous lyrics, to the Bal Bullier. He had had two double absinthes and they made him bold. (One of my wittiest remarks was made one Boat Race Night at the Empire when accosted by two charming ladies. I exclaimed to my friend, 'That which hath made them bold hath made me drunk.')

Neuburg wished to acquire the affections of one of my two girls, but he could not tell them apart, and he wooed them alternately in the most extravagantly jejune fashion. Thanks to his various phobias, he had never made love satisfactorily to any woman in his life. He did not know what to say or do. He made all sorts of clumsy advances, which the girls cruelly repressed. Dorothy reproached him sadly:

'Surely, Mr Neuburg, you would not say such things to your dons' wives at Cambridge!'

Baffled in this direction, he made a supreme appeal to Nina by offering her two francs and twenty-five centimes.

We then went to our respective hotels to bed and the reaction began. He was in bed the whole of the next day, and when I called on him the morning of the day after that I found nothing had been done to cast a veil over the natural results of his indiscretion. But that was Neuburg all over. He was physically the filthiest animal that I have ever known. His gifts were supernatural. I remember giving him a saucer to clean: it had a very small quantity of yellow oil paint in it, left over from painting some talisman. He was a long while away and we went into the bedroom to see how he was getting on. The saucer seemed as full of paint as before, like the widow's curse: nay, more he had repeated the miracle of the loaves and fishes, for he had covered the whole of his dress and his person with this paint. It was all over the washstand, all over the walls and floor, and even to some extent on the ceiling. This is not a joke. I do not offer any explanation; I doubt if there is one. I simply state the facts and leave the world to admire.

Dorothy would have been a *grande passion* had it not been that my instinct warned me that she was incapable of true love. She was incomparably beautiful. Augustus John has painted her again and again, and no more exquisite loveliness has ever adorned any canvas. She was capable of stimulating the greatest extravagances of passion. Indeed, the transports were genuine enough; but they were carefully isolated from the rest of life, so that she was in no way compromised by them. At the time I rather resented this; I was inclined to call her shallow and even to feel somewhat insulted; but now I see that she was in reality acting like an adept, keeping the planes well apart. She was an extremely good friend, though she never allowed her friendship to interfere with her interests. In other words, she was a thoroughly sensible and extremely charming girl.

She was, in addition, one of the best companions that a man can possibly have. Without pretence of being a blue-stocking, she could hold her own in any conversation about art, literature or music. She was the very soul of gaiety, and an incomparable comedienne. One of my most delightful memories is the matching of our wits. It was rapture to compete with her in what we called 'leg-pulling', which may be defined as inducing someone to make a fool of himself. We carried this out with all due regard for honour and good feeling; we never did anyone any harm, and we often did people a great deal of good.

Neuburg was, so to speak, born for our benefit, and this is what we did. We began thus: I told Neuburg with the utmost delicacy that Dorothy had been wounded to the heart by his gross manner of wooing, not only because of her almost morbid modesty, but because she had fallen in love with him at first sight. I urged him to make amends by paying respectful court to her, which he proceeded to do, she playing up to it with sublime fantasy, but pretending the greatest reluctance to admit that she was in love with him. Little by little she yielded and they became engaged. (She had a husband round the corner, but one ignores such flim-flam in Montparnasse.)

In the meanwhile I went on the other tack and urged Neuburg to take the obvious measures to get rid of the cause of his neurosis, and ultimately persuaded him to go down to the rue des Quatre Vents and ask an old friend of mine named Marcelle to undertake his cure. No sooner had he done this than I pretended to discover his engagement to Dorothy and brought to him a sense of the grievous wrong which he had done her by his infidelity. I persuaded him that the only manly and honourable course was to tell her frankly what he had done. So we arranged a dinner party at which he should do so. She insisted on his going into every possible detail of his misdemeanour. Considering that he was the shyest man alive with women and that, furthermore, he supposed her to be even more delicate in repression, the dinner was excruciatingly funny. I admitted with sombre remorse my share in persuading him to disgrace himself and Dorothy took the severest view of my conduct. I as the older man, I in charge of his conscience, I responsible to his parents, etc. etc. She said she would never speak to me again and walked home up the boulevard with Neuburg, with me hanging on the outskirts, pleading and gesticulating to be forgiven, and always receiving the most austere rebuffs. At the same time she could not forgive Neuburg either. He took it absolutely to heart; he would never be able to get over having insulted the fairest and dearest and purest of God's creatures. Of course he would never speak to me again either.

I let him suffer for two or three days, then one afternoon I went across to his hotel and told him that this nonsense had gone on long enough; and it was time for him to learn something of life; I told him the facts. He regarded them as outrageous lies. I pointed out a hundred indications that they were true, but he was absolutely convinced of her purity and my infamy. I realized that I was wasting my breath.

'Come across the road', I said wearily, 'and see with your own eyes.'

I was almost obliged to use actual force, but he came; and there was Dorothy, unadorned, smoking a cigarette on my bed. The boy was absolutely stunned. Even with the evidence in front of his eyes, he was loth to admit the truth. His ideal woman was shattered thoroughly and for ever.

The boy had suffered frightfully, but that was not my fault. It was the fault of his own romantic idealism; and had I not destroyed it in this drastic way, he would have been the prey of one vampire after another as long as he lived. As it was, his physical health became superb, his nerves stopped playing him tricks, he got rid of all his fads about food, dress and conduct, his genius soared free of all its silly inhibitions, his magical powers developed unhindered by the delusions bred of insisting that nature is what one thinks it ought to be, and his relations with humanity became reasonable.

Peace being made, and Neuburg trained, so far as Paris offered a suitable theatre, I determined to put him up against reality of another kind. He had always been accustomed to have everything come to him; he had been allowed to assume that the world was constituted for his convenience and comfort. He had never met any real people at all. He admitted, so to speak, the existence of a baker, but he did not really understand that bread was made with flour and that flour was made from corn by a miller (whom he had hitherto regarded merely as the father of a miller's daughter in a poem), and that corn was grown by actual human beings. So I proposed to him to walk through the wildest parts of Spain. We agreed to start from Bayonne with less than five pounds between us, and managed to make our way to Madrid on foot, avoiding as far as possible the line of the railway.

We left Paris for Bordeaux on the last day of July, went on to Bayonne the next morning, and started the same after-

noon for the frontier, reaching Ustaritz that night. Three days'
walk took us across the Pyrenees to Pamplona. The people
of the mountain villages seemed to have no experience of
strangers, especially of strangers on foot. Of course we were
not very beautiful objects to the uninitiated eye. I was in my
climbing clothes, save that I replaced tweed by buckskin
breeches, the same pair as I am wearing today. As for Neuburg, I cannot say what he looked like, because when God
made him he broke the mould.

So the people almost everywhere outside the larger towns
supposed us to be beggars. It took me some time to discover
why my requests for food and shelter were received with such
disfavour. I spoke Spanish fairly well as soon as I picked up
my Mexican memories; but naturally the people didn't tell
me to my face what was the matter; and having been accustomed to be treated everywhere as a great lord, it never
entered my head for a moment that they could suppose anything else. When I found out, I said to myself: Well, that is
easy enough: I will show them some money. However, they
still regarded us with great suspicion. They gave us what we
wanted, but did not seem in the least happy about it. Further
investigation, however, finally revealed that having money,
they thought we must be brigands. We let it go at that.

However, misunderstandings were not yet over. Three times
on the road we were arrested as anarchists. The soldiers could
not understand why anyone should want to go to Madrid
except to kill Alphonso, and I suppose there is something really
to be said for this point of view. They gave us no real annoyance, our passports being as impressive as they were unintelligible. Of course they didn't really think we were
anarchists, and they would not have cared if we had been;
but most of these unhappy men were marooned for indefinite
periods in ghastly districts where there was absolutely no
amusement of any kind. To arrest us was a good excuse to
have someone to talk to. That, incidentally, is more or less
the case with idle officials everywhere, but in countries like
England and America they have to pretend to take their silly
formalities seriously, and so what was originally no more than
désouvrement becomes deliberate annoyance. The pettier
minds get to enjoy the exercise of this tuppenny-ha'penny
authority, and the regulations which were perhaps instituted
in an emergency survive their usefulness, like the vermiform
appendix, and become the most tedious and irritating tyranny.

The Pyrenean frontiers of Spain at this point are delightfully picturesque, though the mountains are anything but imposing. (Damn those Himalayas; they have spoilt me for scenery.) Some of the mountain villages are filthier and more savage than anything even in German Switzerland. The people are neither polite nor picturesque—they snarl and stink.

We had a longish day into Pamplona, forty-two kilometres, and got the first decent meal since leaving Bayonne. The poverty of the country is really pitiful. As George Borrow recounts, the Church sucks the life-blood of the people. One can quite understand the moralizing of Protestant travellers. Prosperity varies inversely with piety. Italy is only flourishing today in those districts where the alimentary canal of industry has been cleared of the taeniae of Christianity. The only city of Spain which holds its own with the rest of the world today is Barcelona, a notorious hotbed of infidelity and freemasonry. It is to the last degree unfortunate that these things should be connected in the minds of the unthinking with anarchy and other cults implying social disorder. Lord Morley was an atheist, Huxley an agnostic, and Edward the Seventh a freemason; but it would be hard to pick three men more genuinely enlightened or more truly conservative.

From Pamplona it is three days' easy walking to Logrono. We left our hotel after dinner and walked in the cool of the night about ten kilometres to a place which we christened 'Bats' Culvert' in honour of our shelter. It was big enough almost to be called a tunnel. Delightfully warm and dry, I do not blame the bats for their choice of habitation.

The road to Logrono is very varied and picturesque. In particular there is one fine rock peak which reminded me of Tryfan. We found the days terribly hot and dusty. In order to test our endurance to the highest point, we talked to each other about the ices of Trinity College kitchen, which are the best in the world, with those of Rumpelmayer in Paris for a poor second, and the rest absolutely nowhere. The walk did me all the good imaginable, but the diet was a little too much for my young friend, who developed chronic indigestion.

The people live in the most poverty-stricken circumstances; they cannot even understand that there may be others differently situated. In one place they told us at the hotel that they could give us nothing whatever to eat. The courtyard was running wild with poultry, and I told the woman to slay a couple of birds and roast them. It must have taken me a good quarter of an hour to get it into her head that this was a serious order, and by the time the meal was served the entire village had collected to see the eccentric millionaires who spent one and fourpence on food at a stroke.

Logrono will always live in my memory. The situation of the town is very impressive, with its large lazy river, almost dry at that season of the year, affording a measure of the landscape. The people were, if anything, lazier still. The entire population seemed to be sprawling on the terraces of the cafés drinking the wine of the country, a type of Burgundy which has more than a little merit. It is a strong, rough, harsh wine; but the flavour of the soil is as apparent as that of peat in Irish whisky, and it has the advantage of being absolutely genuine.

The spirit of Logrono was so broad and idle that it was very hard to drag ourselves away from it, but we managed it somehow and walked in the cool of the evening of August 9th to a place that we called 'Jack Straw's Castle', at the opening of a magnificent ravine through mighty cliffs of earth.

The following day the road led over a high pass, a barren wilderness of bizarre beauty. It was nearly nightfall when we reached a wretched hamlet, so poor that there was really no food to be had. There was not even any pretence of an inn, and it was only by long negotiation and the display of wealth beyond the dreams of avarice, in the shape of a silver dollar, that we persuaded the inhabitants to let us have a cup of goat's milk apiece, a small scrap of dry bread, and a bed in the straw in a horribly dirty barn. It was a glorious meal and a very heaven of repose. On the third day we completed the one hundred and fifty kilometres on the road from Logrono to Soria. The last few hours of the walk were made splendid by the thunderstorm which I have already described.

I should have liked to stay in Soria for an unlimited time. The town is a stupendous relic of the rugged grandeur of the past. The people were, beyond all praise, sympathetic, and I cannot even begin to describe my appreciation of the cook in our hotel. It may have been that he was benefited by the proverb, 'Hunger is the best sauce', but I cannot help that.

We now found ourselves in danger of striking the main road, so we turned aside from the direct line to Madrid and struck out for Burgo de Osma. Our first night was spent at a place which we called 'Witches' Kitchen Village'. We got lodgings in a house whose sinister aspect was only surpassed by that of its inhabitants. We were so doubtful about their intentions that we barricaded ourselves for the night in the main room. There were considerable alarums and excursions; but when they found we meant business they decided to leave us alone and in the morning everyone was all smiles. We had forty-four kilometres to walk, most of the way over scrub desert without a drop of water or a hint of shelter. It was extraordinarily dreary and wearisome.

Burgo de Osma is a lovely little town tucked away in a fold of the cloak of nowhere. We had arrived at the psychological moment. It was about to celebrate its annual two days of festival.

The smaller towns of Spain have preserved their distinct characteristics, their *amour propre.* They are not entirely servile suburbs of Madrid. They do not drain themselves of their best blood to supply the court with sycophants. It is for this reason that, although Spain has been torn by civil and dynastic wars, it maintains a certain rugged resistance to the forces of autocracy on the one hand, and to revolution on the other.

Burgo de Osma was an excellent example of the cell on whose welfare and whose differentiation from sister cells, the integrity of the organism depends. The pride of the Spanish character is the most valuable factor in its preservation. Spain, almost alone of European countries, does not exude a horde of emigrants upon America. The pride of the individual is personal, family and local as well as national. He prefers haughty poverty to servile prosperity, and this quality may yet restore him to his former greatness, when the tide of economics flows once more in his direction, after Europe has been ruined by the expedients which at present buttress her artificial system of centralization and standardization.

At the moment, Spain was deeply exercised with the matter of base coinage. It appears that a certain cabinet minister had a brother in Mexico who eked out a precarious livelihood by exporting brass bedsteads. The calibre of the uprights was such that silver pesos could be neatly packed therein, and the influence of the minister prevented the custom house being surprised at the weight. These silver pesos were of the same quality as those from the government mint; and at the then price of silver, there was over one hundred per cent profit on each coin put into circulation. It was quite impossible to distinguish the good money from the bad, except that the coiners had thoughtlessly struck one dollar of Amadeo II, who lived so long ago that his coins should have been more worn than they were.

As we approached Madrid we found the people increasingly

suspicious and unwilling to accept our pesos, and in the last hundred kilometres or so it was extremely difficult to get them to take our money at all and, therefore, to get food or shelter. But when we came to the city itself, instead of the nuisance reaching a climax, we found that it disappeared altogether. The Madrilenes were not going to worry their heads as to whether money was good or bad. It doesn't matter, they argued, so long as we agree to take it, and all the desperate efforts of the government to call in the bad coinage fell flat.

Forgive the digression! We were at Burgo de Osma and the fiesta was in full swing. I enjoyed every minute heartily. For the first time I was able to see a bull-fight without the accretions of snobbishness when the famous matador steps forth to exhibit his skill in the presence of royalty, and the game is not a game but an excuse for servility and intrigue. It was all the difference between house football at a public school and a cup final. I was able to understand the direct appeal which the sport makes to the primitive passions.

There was no excitement and no disgust for me. I had reached a spiritual stage in which Sanna—pure perception— had ousted Vedana—sensation—I had learnt to look on the world without being affected by events. I was able to observe what went on as few people can, for the average man's senses are deceived by his emotions. He gets things out of proportion and he exaggerates them even when he is able to appreciate them at all. I made up my mind that it should be an essential part of my system of initiation to force my pupils to be familiar with just those things which excite or upset them, until they have acquired the power of perceiving them accurately without interference from the emotions. It is all a branch of the art of concentration, no doubt; but it is one which has been very much neglected, and it is of supreme importance when the aspirant arrives at the higher levels, where it is a question of 'making no difference between any one thing and any other thing', and uniting oneself with each and every possible idea. For as long as anything soever escapes assimilation there remains separateness and duality, or the potentiality of such. Evil can only be destroyed by 'love under will'; and so long as it is feared and hated, so long as we insist on attributing a real and irreconcilable existence to it, so long will it remain evil for us. The same of course applies to what we call 'good'. Good is itself evil in so far as it is separate from other ideas.

Through this course of initiation I was brought into great happiness. I was able to perceive a fact which I had never guessed: that blood on the shoulder of a bull in the Spanish summer sunlight is the most beautiful colour that exists. In the whole of my memories I had only one fact to set against it: the green of a certain lizard which ran across my path on a hillside in Mexico. It is, in fact, very rare to see pure colours in nature; they are nearly always mixed or toned down. But when they do appear they are overwhelming.

64

During this walk across Spain, I had much leisure for meditation. I was pledged to do my work in the world, and that meant my becoming a public character and one sure to arouse controversy. I thought out my plan of campaign during this walk. I decided first of all, that the most important point was never to forget that I was a gentleman and keep my honour the more spotless that I was assuming a position whose professors were rarely well born, more rarely well bred, hardly ever sincere, and still less frequently honest even in the most ordinary sense of the word.

It seemed to me that my first duty was to prove to the world that I was not teaching Magic for money. I promised myself always to publish my books on an actual loss on the cost of production—never to accept a farthing for any form of instruction, giving advice, or any other service whose performance depended on my magical attainments. I regarded myself as having sacrificed my career and my fortune for initiation, and that the reward was so stupendous that it made the price pitifully mean, save that, like the widow's mite, it was all I had. I was therefore the wealthiest man in the world, and the least I could do was to bestow the inestimable treasure upon my poverty-stricken fellow men.

I made it also a point of absolute honour never to commit myself to any statement that I could not prove in the same sense as a chemist can prove the law of combining weights. Not only would I be careful to avoid deceiving people, but I would do all in my power to prevent them deceiving themselves. This meant my declaring war on the spiritualists and even the theosophists, though I agreed with much of Blavatsky's teachings, as uncompromisingly as I had done on Christianity.

I further resolved to uphold the dignity of Magick by pressing into its service science and philosophy, as well as the noblest English that I could command, and to present it in such a form as would of itself command respect and attention. I would do nothing cheap: I would be content with nothing second rate.

I thought it also a point of honesty not to pretend to be 'better' than I was. I would avoid concealing my faults and foibles. I would have no one accept me on false pretences. I would not compromise with conventionality; even in cases where as an ordinary man of the world, it would have been natural to do so. In this connection there was also the point that I was anxious to prove that spiritual progress did not depend on religious or moral codes, but was like any other science. Magick would yield its secrets to the infidel and the libertine, just as one does not have to be a churchwarden in order to discover a new kind of orchid. There are, of course, certain virtues necessary to the Magician; but they are of the same order as those which make a successful chemist. Idleness, carelessness, drunkenness; the like interfere with success in any serious business, but sound theology and adherence to the code of Hampstead as against that of Hyderabad are only important if the man's body may suffer if his views are erroneous or his conscience reliable.

The conclusion of my meditations was that I ought to make a Magical Retirement as soon as the walk was over. I owed it to myself and to mankind to prove formally that the formulae of initiation would work at will. I could not ask people to experiment with my methods until I had assured myself that they were sufficient. When I looked back on my career, I found it hard to estimate the importance of the part played by such circumstances as solitude and constant communication with nature. I resolved to see whether by application of my methods, purged from all inessentials and understood in the light of common-sense physiology, psychology and anthropology, I could achieve in a place like Paris, within the period of the average man's annual holiday, what had come as the climax of so many years of adventure. I also felt it proper to fit myself for the task which I had undertaken in publishing *The Equinox*, by fortifying myself with as much magical force as I might be able to invoke. The result of this resolve will appear in its proper place.

Our short spell of rest at Burgo de Osma sufficed me to collect in my mind the numberless conclusions of the very varied trains of thought which had occupied my mind during our fortnight's tramp. They shaped themselves into a conscious purpose. I knew myself to be on the brink of resuming my creative work in a way that I had never done. Till now I had written what was given me by the Holy Ghost. Everything I did was *sui generis* and had no conscious connection with any other outburst of my genius; but I understood that from this time on I should find myself writing with a sense of responsibility, that my work would be coherent, each item (however complete in itself) an essential part of a pyramid, a monument whose orientation and proportions should proclaim my purpose. I should do nothing in future that was not as definitely directed to the execution of my true will as every step through Spain was taken with the object of reaching Madrid; and I reflected that many such steps must seem wasted, many leading away from the beeline, that I did not know the road and had no idea what Madrid would be like when I reached it. All I could do was to take each step steadily, fearlessly, firmly and determinedly, trusting to the scanty information to be gathered from signposts and strangers, to keep more or less on the right road, and to take my chance of being satisfied with the unknown city which I had chosen as my goal with no reason beyond my personal whim.

Thus I made our march symbolize life. There were other analogies. We had to endure every kind of hardship heartily and to take our fun where we found it without being dainty. We learnt to enjoy every incident, to find something to love in every strange face, to admire even the dreariest wilderness of sunburnt scrub. We knew that nothing really mattered so long as we got to Madrid. The world went on very well without us and its fortunes were none of our business. The only thing that could annoy us was interference with our intention to get to Madrid, though we didn't want to go there except insofar as we had taken it into our heads to set our faces towards it.

All these lessons would be of value when I got to London. I meant to tell mankind to aspire to a new state about which I could tell them little or nothing, to teach them to tread a long and lonely path which might or might not lead thither, to bid them dare to encounter all possible perils of nature unknown, to abandon all their settled manners of living and cut themselves off from their past and their environment, and to attempt to a quixotic adventure with no resources beyond their native strength and sagacity. I had done it myself and found not only that the pearl of great price was worth far more than I possessed, but that the very perils and privations of the Quest were themselves my dearest memories. I was certain of this at least: that nothing in the world except this was worth doing. We turned our steps from Burgo de Osma. It would have been pleasant to halt, but there was nothing to keep us. We were glad to rest and glad to go on. The march to Madrid was the only thing that mattered. So should it be with my life. Success should not stay my footsteps. Whatever I attained should restore my energies and spur me to more strenuous strides.

We marched steadily to Aranda de Duero, Milagros, and many another village which (to itself the centre of the world) was to me, even then, but a milestone, and is now no more than a forgotten name which I exhume from my diary. The only impressions of this part of the march to Madrid are 'Big Stone Bivouac' where we tried to shelter from a bitter wind, sleeping till the cold awoke us, and then trying to warm ourselves by exercise until fatigue sent us once more to sleep. An alternation of discomforts, which was repeated half a dozen times during the night. The memory is delightful. All the unpleasant incidents of the period have passed into oblivion.

About fifty kilometres from Madrid we passed a magnificent range of rocks. The smiling fertile valley does not count; it is the naked rugged aspiration of the grim granite that leaves its marks in the mind. It was for the peasants to think of their fields and see nothing of the universe but their crops and the coins which they hoarded at harvest, only to pass into the pouch of the priest and pay for a parcel of earth in which they might conceal their carcases from the eye of the vulture.

On August the second, we found ourselves in Madrid and turned wearily into the first hotel we came to in Puerto del Sol. Neuburg was by this time a pretty sick man. He could not stand the rough food and the fatigue and the exposure, though he stuck to it with the utmost gameness. He had the passive patient courage of the Jew in its fullest development. However, there was no need for any further display of this virtue, and I put him to bed and told him to stay there and repair his ravaged intestines on delicate food until they were strong enough to support him through the next ordeal. As for myself, I was as fit as I had ever been in my life, and appreciating the extreme barbarism of the wilderness was the best possible preparation for swinging over to the other extreme and feeding my soul on the refinements of art.

As a critic of art I have curious qualifications. My early life left me ignorant of the existence of anything of the sort beyond Landseer's 'Dignity and Impudence'. I suppose I ought to have deduced the existence of art from this alone had I been an ideal logician. Such horrors imply their opposites.

However, even in my emancipation I never discovered art as I did literature. It never occurred to me that there might be a plastic language as well as a spoken and written one. I had no conception that ideas could be conveyed through this medium. To me, as to the multitude, art meant nothing more than literature.

The first picture that awakened me was Manet's wonder 'Olympe', enthusiastically demonstrated by Gerald Kelly to be the greatest picture ever painted. I could see nothing but bad drawing and bad taste; and yet something told me that I was making a mistake. When I reached Rodin shortly afterwards I understood him at once, because the sculpture and architecture of the East had prepared me. I knew that they were the expression of certain religious enthusiasms, and it was easy for me to make the connection and say, 'Rodin's sculpture gives the impression of elemental energy.' Yet this was subconscious. In my poems I have treated Rodin from a purely literary standpoint.

As time passed my interest in the arts increased. I was still careful to avoid contemporary literature lest it should influence my thought or style. But I saw no harm in making friends with painters and learning to see the world through their eyes. Having already seen it through my own in the course of my wanderings, I was the better able to observe clearly and judge impartially. Perhaps this circumstance itself had biased me. It is at least the case that I have no use for artists who have lost touch with tradition and see nature second-hand. I think I have kept my head pretty square on my shoulders in the turmoil of the recent revolutions. I find myself able to distinguish between the artist whose eccentricities and heresies interpret his individual peculiarities and the self-advertising quack who tries to be original by outdoing the most outrageous heresiarch of the moment.

In the galleries of the Prado there is no occasion to trouble about such matters. The place fills one with uttermost peace; one goes there to worship Velasquez and Goya, not to argue. Perhaps I was still too ingenuous to appreciate Goya to the full. On the other hand, there may be something in my impression that he is badly represented at Madrid. Much of his work struck me as the mechanical masterpieces of the clever court painter. Possibly, moreover, there was no room for him in my spirit, seduced, as it was, by the vivid variety of Velasquez. 'Las Meninas' is worshipped in a room consecrated solely to itself, and I spent more of my mornings in that room and let it soak in. I decided then, and might concur still had I not learnt the absurdity of trying to ascribe an order to things which are each unique and absolute, that 'Las Meninas' is the greatest picture in the world. It certainly taught me to know the one thing that I care to learn about painting: that the subject of a picture is merely an excuse for arranging forms and colours in such a way as to express the inmost self of the artist.

I had made several experiments with hashish since my return from China, always with excessive precaution. Some of these had been somewhat unexpectedly successful. I found that my habit of analysing and controlling my mind enabled me to turn the effect of the drug to the best account. Instead of getting intoxicated, I became quite abnormally able to push introspection to the limit. The results of these experiments had been slowly sorted out and interpreted in the course of months. I found a striking analogy between this toxic excitement and the more legitimate methods of mental development, but each threw light on the other. I sat up all one night embodying the essence of my knowledge in an essay, 'The Psychology of Hashish', of which I have already given some account.

Neuburg was well enough to get about after two or three days in bed, but it was clear that he was in no state to encounter new hardships. We gave up the idea of walking to Gibraltar and on August 28th left Madrid for Granada. I had kept the promise of 'La Gitana' and the city kept its promise to me. But it is not safe to stay too long on the summit of happiness. Two days later we went on to Ronda, almost the only interesting thing about which is its physical geography, which twenty-four hours allows one to absorb easily. We went on the next day to Gibraltar. It did not take us long to find out that we had left freedom behind us. It was hot; the Levanter was blowing and taking all the marrow out of one's bones. I was utterly tired: I sat down. I was perceived by a rock scorpion (as they call the natives of the fortress, a detestable and despicable breed, which reminds one quite unreasonably of the Eurasian) who saw a chance to sting somebody. He began by hectoring me and ended by arresting me. When we got to the police station, and the sergeant found that we were staying at the best hotel in the town, and inspected our papers, we received the proper apologies; but I didn't forget that if I hadn't been a privileged person I might have been sent to prison for sitting down when I was tired and ill. This is part of the price we pay for the privilege of paying exorbitant taxes to support a swarm of useless jacks in office.

Of course I may be looking at this incident in a totally wrong light. The policeman may have mistaken my act as symbolic of a wish to linger in Gibraltar and deduced that I must be dangerously insane. Next to Avon, it is probably the most ghastly place on the globe. In a previous incarnation I either insulted a Buddha, or wounded a universal Holy King, or killed my father and mother—at least I can suggest no better an hypothesis to explain my having been held up some-times as much as four days at a time waiting for a steamer. The only way to keep from acute delirious melancholia is to indulge furiously in the only two articles purchasable in the place which even promise to palliate one's pangs. One can buy cheap editions of fearful and wonderful fiction and packets of the best butterscotch. By exhibiting these two drugs continu-ously, one can produce in oneself a kind of coma which takes one through the tedium.

We crossed to Tangiers without delay and I revelled once more and rejoiced to feel myself back among the only people on earth with whom I have ever felt any human affinity. My spiritual self is at home in China, but my heart and my hand are pledged to the Arab.

I had begun to train Neuburg seriously in Magick and mysticism. The first point was, of course, to get rid of any prejudices and superstitions. This was not too difficult, he being a professed agnostic. But the second point was to train him in the technique. This was well enough as far as Magick was concerned, for he naturally possessed the poetic and dra-matic instincts, the sense of the fitness of gesture, and so on: and, more important than all, it came natural to him to arouse in himself the right kind of enthusiastic energy in the right way.

In addition, he possessed a peculiar faculty which I have only found in anything like the same degree in one other man in my life. He was a materializing medium in the strictest sense; that is, he could condense ideas into sensible forms. He could not do it at all by himself, because he lacked the power to collect at one point all the available material of the required kind, as may be done by concentrated will, and thereby to create such a state of strain in the atmosphere that the evoked forces must relieve it, if they possibly can, by a change of state. Just so carbon dioxide, if forced into a closed cylinder below the critical temperature, relieves the intolerable pressure by liquefying. Here the carbon dioxide corresponds to the invisible forces in the magical atmosphere, separated from its other components, collected in one place, confined and directed by the Magician. The critical temperature corresponds to such magical conditions as quiet and inviolability; the cylinder to the constraint imposed by the Magician to prevent the dissipation of his invoked ideas.

Such indeed is an outline of the theory of calling forth spirits to visible appearance (by 'visible' we always intend audible—too dangerously often tangible, and too unpleasantly often capable of producing impressions on the olfactory nerves). In practice, however, there is something lacking to success.

Neuburg supplied the missing link, as I might have expected from his personal resemblance to that Darwinian desideratum. There was some substance in him which was on the borderland between the manifest world of matter and the astral world of sensation. In his presence I found it quite easy to produce phenomenal phantasms of almost any idea, from gods to demons, which I happened to need at the moment. I had of course a very wide experience of so-called material manifestations; but for the most part these had been independent of my will and often contrary to it. I have already mentioned a number of such phenomena in connection with the Abra-Melin Operation. I had succeeded in suppressing them by preventing my magical force from leaking away. A miracle annoyed me as it annoys an electrician to find that his current is escaping, perhaps giving shocks to people who have strayed in its path. His first thought is to detect and correct the imperfection of his insulation. Years had passed without my magical energy breaking loose: I had persuaded it to work through the proper channels.

Carelessness showed itself once more in Shanghai. I was invoking certain forces with Soror F. in her circle. After I had constrained them to come, I proceeded to make a circumambulation with the object of giving them the desired direction, and when I came to the west of the circle, I noticed that Soror F. had profanely left her slippers inside it. These, not being consecrated objects, had no business there; so I pushed them gently over the frontier with my foot. They were seized and flung furiously to the ceiling with such force that they broke off some of the plaster. There was no possibility that my foot had supplied the motive power, even had I kicked them away in a rage instead of pushing them as quietly as I could—which I naturally did, to diminish the disturbance. There had been several other minor incidents of the same sort on subsequent occasions; but I took measures, as before, to suppress them.

The manifestations which Neuburg helped to produce were of an entirely different character; they occurred in conformity with my will. I was able to work more by sight and less by faith than I had ever done before. Even the use of the proper material bases for manifestation, such as the incense of Abra-Melin, Dittany of Crete, and blood, had rarely resulted in more than 'half formed faces', partial and hesitating presentations of the desired phantom whose substance seemed to hover on the frontier of the worlds (rather like the Cheshire cat!). The clouds of incense used to grow denser in such wise as rather to suggest a shape than to show one. I could never be sure, even when my physical eyes told me that a form was present, whether my imagination and my desire were not playing tricks with my optical apparatus. Such shapes almost always vanished when I fixed my gaze upon them, and there was no means of saying whether this act, by releasing them from the constraint of my will, had enabled them to escape, or whether intelligent inspection had not simply dissipated an illusion.

With Neuburg, on the contrary, there would be no doubt whatever as to the physical character of the beings which we evoked. On one occasion the god came to us in human form (we were working in a locked temple) and remained with us, perfectly perceptible to all our senses, for the best part of an hour, only vanishing when we were physically exhausted by the ecstasy of intimate contact with his divine person. We sank into a sort of sublime stupor; when we came to ourselves, he was gone.

Again, at Victoria Street, a number of us were dancing round the altar with linked hands and faces turned outwards. The temple was dimly lighted and thick with incense. Somehow the circle broke and we kept on dancing, each for himself. Then we became aware of the presence of a stranger. Some of us counted the men present and found there was one too many. One of the weaker brethren got scared, or one of the stronger brethren remembered his duty to science—I don't know which—and switched on the light. No stranger was to be seen. We asked Brother Lucifer—as I may call him!—why he had broken the spell and each of us independently confirmed his story. We all agreed about the appearance of the visitor. We had all been impressed with the same feeling that he did not belong to the human species.

I have mentioned two only of very many experiences of the same kind, choosing those which seem the most convincing and complete. More often we kept the manifestation at a decorous distance. There is, of course, extreme danger in coming into contact with a demon of a malignant or unintelligent nature. It should, however, be said that such demons only exist for imperfectly initiated Magicians. The adept ought to be able to identify himself absolutely with all beings alike. Invocations should always insist on identification. If this be duly done no harm can ensue, just as lightning cannot hurt lightning.

I must confess to pride and pleasure in these performances. I had practically abandoned the attempt to obtain material manifestations. It was difficult to do, dangerous in the doing, and dubious when done. I had learnt to compel a spirit to carry out my commands or instruct me on any matter of which I was ignorant, without being at the pains to demonstrate his presence to my senses, just as I telegraph instructions to my solicitor or write to some scholar for information, in full faith that the results will be as reliable as if I had taken the trouble to arrange a personal interview. I am inclined to think that my work with Neuburg was rather a retrogression. It made me hanker after phenomena, tempted me to distrust the subtler modes of realization.

After he had left me, I felt myself rather lost for a little while, and I had to learn the lesson all over again that the finer forms of manifestation are not less but more actual than the grosser; that the intangible ideas and ineffable intelligences of the most ethereal empires of the empyrean are stronger and more solid the less palpable they are to the lower modes of apprehension. It is hard to explain, and harder to learn, that truth abides in the inmost sanctuary of the soul and may not be told, either by speech or by silence; yet all attempts to interpret it distort it progressively as they adapt themselves to the perceptions of the mind, and become sheer caricatures by the time they are translated into terms of bodily sensation. Now the reality of things depends on their truth, and thus it is that it is not a philosophical paradox but a matter of experience that the search for truth teaches us to distrust appearances exactly in proportion as they are positive. Physical facts betray their hallucinatory nature by their consistent refusal to comply with the requirements of reason, and thought admits its transparent falsity by violating its own laws at every turn.

Materialists claim that the senses are the sole source of knowledge. Good! Then the most absurd and impossible idea of a madman or a metaphysician must be derived from sensory impressions no less than a brick. We habitually use our mental faculties to criticize and correct our sensory impressions. At what point, then, does our judgment cease to be reliable? Which is more real; the brick, the facts indirectly learnt from the brick, such as its chemical and electrical properties, the laws of nature which I deduce from the sum of such facts, or the mystical moonshine which mediation on all these evokes?

In my great initiation in the Sahara, I was told in one vision, 'Above the Abyss' (that is, to that intelligible intuition between which and the intellect there is a great gulf fixed), 'a thing is only true in so far as it contains its own contradiction in itself.' The initiate must learn to use this faculty. Its first advantage is to deliver one from the dilemma set forth above. We need no longer doubt that white is white, because that proposition implicitly asserts that white is black. Our new instrument assures us that the whiteness of white depends on the fact of its blackness. This statement sounds more than absurd; it is a meaningless assertion. But we have already seen that the axioms of the intellect involve absurdity. They only impose upon us at first because they happen to be our personal property. The intuitions of the Neschamah are guaranteed by interior certainty, and they cannot be criticized for the simple reason that they have themselves completed the work of criticism of the most destructive kind before presenting themselves at all. Buddhist psychology has analysed many of these characteristics of super-consciousness and even arranged them in an order corresponding with spiritual development.

I may say that I have toiled for many years to express ideas of this order in terms intelligible to the normal consciousness and susceptible of apprehension by the normal intellect. Success has scarcely been complete; only on rare occasions has the flash fixed itself on the film when the lens was in focus and the exposure correct. I am acutely aware that many of my most arduous and ardent attempts to interpret mystical experience have resulted in blurred images, sometimes perhaps grandiose and suggestive—but that is no compensation for obscurity and vagueness. May I present one effort which I myself am able to hold more or less clearly in my ordinary consciousness?

The Buddhists describe the closest approximation to true observation of anything by saying that it is seen in the four-fold formless state, which they define in the following terms: Any proposition about an object is simultaneously perceived as being both true and false, but also neither true nor false. To perceive an object in this manner implies that the observer has attained the last possible degree of spiritual development which permits any positive point of view soever. Such a man is but one step from the threshold of Arahatship. He has only to destroy this conception of things, as is done in this four-fold formless state, to attain the trance Nerodha-Sammapatti, in which all being and form is absolutely annihilated, so much much so that the trance is only distinguishable from Nibbana by the fact that one comes out of it.

It was on October 2nd, 1919 that I first attained to this Pisgah-sight of the promised land, Pari-Nibbana. I was spending the night in Fleichmann's Turkish Baths in New York. It was my custom in all such places to practise the tenth clause of my vow as a Master of the Temple, 'To interpret every phenomenon as a particular dealing of God with my Soul', by forcing advertisements and other public announcements to yield some spiritual significance. I would either apply the Cabbala to the words and manipulate the numbers so as to reach a state of mind in which some truth might suddenly spring in the silence, or I would play upon the words as if they were oracles, or else force the filthy falsehoods of fraudulent dollar-dervishes to transfigure themselves at the touch of my talisman into mysterious messages from the Masters.

I had awakened at dawn and meditated awhile upon this four-fold formless state. I was merely trying to make out what could possibly be meant by piling contradiction on contradiction, as the definition did. I did not understand it in the least, and I had not the slightest intention of trying to reach realization of it. At that time all such meditation was entirely out of my line, but accidents will happen even in the best regulated magical circles and the following extraordinary experience knocked me sideways.

I quote verbatim my Magical Record:

I was putting on my bath-robe after weighing, and turning a sleeve inside out, when my masseur, an holy man positively trembling on the brink of Arahatship, cried to me that both sides of it were inside, and both outside. I replied humbly that I was seeking for a side that was neither inside nor outside—and then like a flash I saw that I had it! Oh Glory

Ineffable of Realization! (Oh Right Thinking!) For either side is both inside and outside because I can use it as such, and it is neither inside nor outside with regard to the discrimination which might be made by an uninitiate between any one thing and any other thing.

Now this quality is not in the robe, which has two sides easily distinguishable by hemmings, machining, etc., to say nothing of orientation in space, but in me, and arises from my positive determination not to notice whether my back reads 'Stolen from the Fleischmann Baths' or no. Now I am not indifferent to comfort. I notice whether the robe is thick or thin; its observed qualities depend upon a weakness in me. All qualities soever in the robe must therefore disappear as soon as I am strong enough to ignore them; and thus any self-sufficiency or 'attainment' destroys my consciousness of any separate existence.

I sincerely believe that I have adequately described a state of mind, in itself utterly incompatible with ordinary intellectual apprehension, in the above account, and correctly observed and intelligibly expressed its characteristics in such a way as to give at least some rudimentary idea of one type of intuition with whose laws those of the reason have nothing whatever in common.

I do not wish to press the point. In these 'lonesome latter days' there are people in the world who can scarcely define the difference between Dedekindian and Cantorian cuts, and whose nights are not disturbed by anxiety about the truth of Fermat's last theorem. *A fortiori*, we had better swoop on the Straits of Gibraltar and tell a tale of Tangiers. (I will confine myself to mentioning that I got a charming letter from my exquisite Dorothy, to which I replied by the poem 'Telepathy' in *The Winged Beetle*.)

In point of fact, we may not be much better off even here. Most true tales worth telling are either incredible, improper or both. One of the reforms which I introduced into the A∴ A∴ was the abolition of all obligations of secrecy. They were never useful except as temptations to people to break them. The secret knowledge has quite adequate warders. I have learnt that I have only to tell the truth about almost anything to be set down at once as a liar. It is far better to throw dust in the eyes of the animals whose faces are turned to the ground, by casual frankness. If you have a secret, it is always dangerous to let people suspect that you have something to hide.

So much for Neuburg's capacities in Magick. In mysticism he was fatally handicapped by his congenital dislike of discipline, order, punctuality and every moral quality that goes with science. I started him on Yoga about this time. One incident is instructive. His daily hour for practising Asana arrived one day when we were crossing to Europe on the steamer. He refused to do his work; he could not bear to attract the attention of the other people on board and appear ridiculous. (Neuburg! Ridiculous!! O all ye gods and little fishes!) I, being responsible for him as his holy guru, performed the practice in his stead. He experienced remorse and shame, which did him good; but several other incidents determined me to impose on him a Vow of Holy Obedience.

I must point out the virtue of this practice. Technically it is identical with that in vogue in the Society of Jesus. The pupil must obey his teacher, *perinde ac cadaver*. But the moral implication is wholly antagonistic. The Jesuit is taught that obedience to his superior and humility before him are virtues in themselves pleasing to God. In the A∴A∴ the superior is, so to speak, the sparring partner of the pupil. His function is to discover the prejudices, fears and other manifestations of tendency which limit the pupil, by observing the instinctive reactions which may follow any order. The pupil discovers his own weaknesses, which he then proceeds to destroy by analysing them, somewhat as Freud has recently suggested—science is always discovering odd scraps of magical wisdom and making a tremendous fuss about its cleverness!—as well as to master them by habitually ignoring their inhibition. If the superior is anything of a psychologist, he should be able to teach the average weakling fairly perfect self-control in three months at the outside. Neuburg improved enormously in consequence of the practice, and his final breakdown was due to a strain of racial congenital cowardice too deeply seated for eradication. He at least gained this: that he was brought face to face with this fundamental moral deficiency in his character. For the rest of his life he must expiate his infirmity, that his suffering may teach him the necessity of tackling it from the beginning in his next incarnation.

It was time for me to get back to England. Neuburg was to join his relations at San Sebastian, and as soon as he was gone, I wrote 'The Soldier and the Hunchback, ! and ?' on the thirteenth of December. Two days later I left Plymouth by the *Marlborough*.

65

In London I put my foot down at once by taking away my daughter until Rose agreed to follow the doctor's instructions and get rid of her dipsomania once and for all. She capitulated and the necessary measures were taken. This left me free for my proposed Retirement, which I decided to undertake in Paris rather than London. The details of every single minute of my life for the next fortnight are accurately recorded in 'John St John'. Here I need only say that the work was successful beyond all expectations. I not only achieved my stated object, but obtained access to a reserve of energy which carried me on for years, performing Herculean labours without conscious effort. My time was in fact very fully taken up with the preparation of *The Equinox*. I had to be constantly seeing Fuller, who was editing my Magical Records and the vast mass of material connected with the G. D., besides which I had my own work to do preparing the books of instruction on a special and scientific basis.

Besides this, I was writing a good deal of poetry. Some of my most important work belongs to this period. 'The Wizard Way',[1] 'The Garden of Janus',[2] 'After Judgment'[3] and 'Bathyllus'[4] are especially notable. I was seeing a good deal of Frank Harris, who was publishing much of my best work in *Vanity Fair*. It was the first encouragement I had ever had, and in a way it came too late, since I was already entirely disillusioned with regard to fame. The approval of Frank Harris was another matter; it was something, and something very great, to know that my work gained me the respect of the very few men on the planet who knew the difference between Keats and Lewis Morris. I had been recognized as a poet of the first class by my peers and the applause of the mob would leave me as cold as its neglect or hostility does at present.

I kept hard at work in London until after the publication of the first number of *The Equinox*.[5] There was, besides, much work to be done in reorganizing the Order, to which many people were anxious to obtain admission. My domestic tragedy was coming to a crisis. The disease seemed incurable. The doctor said that the only hope was for Rose to sign away her liberty for two years, and as she refused to do this there was nothing for it but for me to obtain a divorce. There was no sense in my being plaintiff, though I had plenty of ground. To me it seemed a breach of the pledge to protect one's wife, which is the first point of a husband's honour. It was consequently agreed that Rose should be plaintiff and the necessary evidence was manufactured in the usual way.

My year was very much broken into by the vicissitudes of this wretched business. Rose was always begging to be taken back and it was very hard for me to be firm. I made things as easy as possible for her by spending as much time with her as I could. The marriage having been in Scotland, there was no King's Proctor to cause one's knees to tremble, and it was unlikely that any spies would discover that we were living together, to all intents and purposes, the whole time the divorce was pending.

Apart from short trips to Paris, I was in England till autumn, when I thought it best to keep well out of the way during the actual time of the trial. I took Neuburg to be my chela and we left London on November 10th. In the meanwhile I was doing comparatively little personal magical work and my lyrics were all of lesser importance. The fact of the matter was that I had got to the end of my tether. The gods had put their foot down —thus far and no farther! I felt myself my life had become broken up into a succession of insignificant adventures. But I did not know why. The reason was that one cannot work beyond a certain point in a New Aeon on a formula of the Old, and I had sealed my stubborn refusal to make *The Book of the Law* the basis of my work by taking advantage of the technical excuse that I could do nothing in the absence of the manuscript. And that had been lost for years.

It was part of my plan for *The Equinox* to prepare a final edition of the work of Dr Dee and Sir Edward Kelly. I had a good many of the data and promised myself to complete them by studying the manuscripts in the Bodleian Library at Oxford—which, incidentally, I did in the autumn—but it struck me that it would be useful to get my large paintings of the four Elemental Watch Towers which I had made in Mexico. I thought these were probably in Boleskine. I decided to go up there for a fortnight or so. Incidentally, I had the conveniences for conferring upon Neuburg the degree of neophyte, he having passed brilliantly through his year as a probationer.

I consequently asked him, and an Emmanuel man named Kenneth Ward, to come and stay with me. I had met Ward at Wastdale Head shortly before, having gone there to renew my ancient loves with the creeds of the gullies. It happened that Ward was very keen on skiing. I had several spare pairs and offered to give him some. This casual circumstance proved an essential part of the chain by which I was ultimately dragged behind the chariot of the Secret Chiefs. At least I thought it was a chain. I did not realize that steel of such exquisite temper might be beaten into a sword fit for the hand of a free man.

To my annoyance I could not find the Elemental Watch Towers anywhere in the house. I daresay I gave up looking rather easily. I had got into a state of disgusted indifference about such things. Rose might have destroyed them in a drunken fit, just as she might have pawned them if they had possessed any commercial value. I shrugged my shoulders accordingly and gave up the search. The skis that I had promised Ward were not to be found any more than the Watch Towers. After putting Neuburg through his initiation,* we repaired to London. I had let the house and my tenant was coming in on the first of July. We had four days in which to amuse ourselves; and we let ourselves go for a thorough good time. Thus like a thunderbolt comes the incident of June 28th, thus described in my diary:

> Glory be to Nuit, Hadit, Ra-Hoor-Khuit in the Highest! A little before midday I was impelled mysteriously (though exhausted by playing fives, billiards, etc. till nearly six this morning) to make a final search for the Elemental Tablets. And lo! when I had at last abandoned the search, I cast mine eyes upon a hole in the loft where were ski, etc., and there, O Holy, Holy, Holy! were not only all that I sought, but the manuscript of *Liber Legis!*

The ground was completely cut away from under my feet. I remained for two whole days meditating on the situation—in performing, in fact, a sort of supplementary Sammasati to that of 1905. Having the knack of it, I reached a very clear conclusion without too much difficulty. The essence of the situation was that the Secret Chiefs meant to hold me to my obligation. I understood that the disaster and misery of the last

---

* The preparation for this was in some ways trying to the candidate. For instance, he had to sleep naked for seven nights on a litter of gorse.

three years were due to my attempt to evade my duty. I surrendered unconditionally, as appears from the entry of July 1st.

> I once more solemnly renounced all that I have or am. On departing (at midnight from the topmost point of the hill which crowns my estate) instantly shone the moon, two days before her fullness, over the hills among the clouds.

This record is couched in very general terms, but it was intended to cover the practical point of my resuming the task laid upon me in Cairo exactly as I might be directed to do by my superiors.

Instantly my burden fell from my back. The long crucifixion of home life came to a crisis immediately on my return to London. At the same time every other inhibition was automatically removed. For the first time since the spring of 1904 I felt myself free to do my will. That, of course, was because I had at last understood what my will was. My aspiration to be the means of emancipating humanity was perfectly fulfilled. I had merely to establish in the world the Law which had been given me to proclaim: 'Thou hast no right but to do thy will.' Had I bent my energies from the first to proclaiming the Law of Thelema I should doubtless have found no obstacle in my path. Those which would naturally arise in the course of any work soever would have been quietly removed by the Secret Chiefs. But I had chosen to fight against myself for five years and 'If Satan shall be divided against Satan, how shall his kingdom stand?' The more I strove, the more I encouraged an internal conflict and stultified myself. I had been permitted to complete my initiation, for the reason that by doing so I was fitting myself for the fight; but all my other efforts had met with derisory disaster. More, one does not wipe out a lustre of lunacy by a moment of sanity. I am suffering to this day from the effects of having wasted some of the best years of my life in the stupid and stubborn struggle to set up my conscious self against its silent sovereign, my true soul. 'Had Zimri peace who slew his master?'

The superficial reader may smile at my superstition. Why should I be so sure that the accident of finding an old portfolio in a loft was no accident, but a *coup de maître* struck by people, for all anyone can prove, who have no existence except in my diseased imagination? I could answer the criticism by massing the evidence, but I prefer to leave that to be studied in another place when the facts have been marshalled so formidably that it is impossible for any reasonable being not to conclude that a praeterhuman agency was at work on my life. I will merely point out that in modern science the test of truth is less the degree of the probability of any fact, than that which is implied by the text 'Wisdom is justified of her children'. Facts are judged by their fertility. When a discovery remains sterile, the evidence of its truth is weakened. The indication is that it is not a stone in the temple of truth; it does not fit in with the entire fabric of knowledge. A new fact proves itself by its fitness: isolated, it is repugnant to the continuity of nature. When it is seen to explain cognate difficulties, to complete imperfect conceptions; when it leads to lines of research which bear fruit, some sixtyfold, some eightyfold and some an hundredfold, then it becomes impregnable. My conviction in the reality of my magical experiences does not depend on any single event. It is because so many incidents, each one more or less incredible and inexplicable when considered by itself, become inevitable when considered in their totality and, instead of themselves requiring to be explained, are the means of throwing light upon every obscure corner of the cosmos.

The mere potency of the incident of June 28th proves that its implications were enormously beyond itself. I was inured to miracles of every kind and I no more allowed them to influence my actions than Professor Ray Lankester is guided in his researches by *Napoleon's Dream Book*.* The finding of the manuscript was not even a miracle; it happened in the ordinary course of nature. There was nothing so wonderfully remarkable about its character. It is this very fact that makes us ask how is it that so ordinary a circumstance should have been the power to break down the resolute resistance of a Magician whose will had been developed to the utmost by every type of training from evocation to exploration?

The answer can only be that, exactly as Coriolanus, insensible to all other appeals, was touched by the tears of his mother, so I, whose determination had defied every form of pressure, direct and indirect, was only waiting to hear the unmistakable voice of my Master, and that this insignificant incident supplied the intuitive certainty: that none other than he was behind it. The finer minds among men can oppose intellectual criticism to intellectual demonstration; to the subtle assurances of intui-

---

* Such, at least, is a tenable hypothesis. I have no direct evidence that he does not do so!

tions which are perhaps imperceptible of articulate expression they can find no answer.

I knew in myself from the first that the revelation in Cairo was the real thing. I have proved with infinite pains that this was the case; yet the proof has not strengthened my faith, and disproof would do nothing to shake it. I knew in myself that the Secret Chiefs had arranged that the manuscript of *The Book of the Law* should have been hidden under the Watch Towers and the Watch Towers under the skis; that they had driven me to make the key to my position the absence of the manuscript; that they had directed Kenneth Ward's actions for years that he might be the means of the discovery, and arranged every detail of the incident in such a way that I should understand it as I did.

Yes; this involves a theory of the powers of the Secret Chiefs so romantic and unreasonable that it seems hardly worth a smile of contempt. As it happens, an almost parallel phenomenon came to pass ten years later. I propose to quote it here in order to show that the most ordinary events, apparently disconnected, are in fact only intelligible by postulating some such people as the Secret Chiefs of the A∴A∴ in possession of some such prevision and power as I ascribe to them. When I returned to England at Christmas 1919, all my plans had gone to pieces owing to the dishonesty and treachery of a gang which was bullying into insanity my publisher in Detroit. I was pledged in honour to look after a certain person; but I was practically penniless. I could not see any possible way of carrying on my work. (It will be related in due course how this condition of things came about and why it was necessary for me to undergo it.)

I found myself at Morêt, on the edge of the Forest of Fontainebleau, with nothing to do but wait. I did not throw up the sponge in passionate despair as I had done once before, to my shame—I had been rapped sufficiently hard on the knuckles to cure me of that—but I said to the gods: 'Observe, I have done my damnedest and here I am at a dead centre. I am not going on muddling through: I demand a definite sign from you that I am still your chosen prophet.' I therefore note in my diary, on January 12th, 1920, as follows:

I am inclined to make my Silence include all forms of personal work, and this is very hard to give up, if only because I am still afraid of 'failure', which is absurd. I ought evidently to be non-attached even to avoiding the Woes-Attendant-

Upon-Refusing-The-Curse-Of-My-Grade, if I may be pardoned the expression.

And why should I leave my Efficacious Tortoise and look at people till my lower jaw hangs down? Shall I see what the *Yi*[6] says? Ay. Question: Shall I abandon all magical work soever until the appearance of a manifest sign?

Answer:

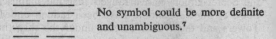

No symbol could be more definite and unambiguous.[7]

I have invoked Aiwaz to manipulate the Sticks; and, wishing to ask, 'What shall be the Sign?' got instantly the reference in CCXX to Our Lady Babalon: 'The omnipresence of my body.' But this is not quite clear; I took it mentally as referring to the expected arrival of Our Lady, but it might mean a trance, or almost anything. So I will ask *Yi*, as my last magical act for the time being.

I think this means the arrival of Our Lady.[8] I have serious doubts whether the hexagram should not have been:
which would have certainly meant that.[9] That I should doubt anything is absurd: I shall know the Sign, without fail. And herewith I close the Record and await that Sign.

The next entry is dated Sunday, February 1st.

Kindly read over the entry of Jan. 12th with care exceeding. Now then: On Friday, Jan. 30th, I went to Paris, to buy pencils, Mandarin, a Palette, Napoleon Brandy, canvases and other appurtenances of the artist's dismal trade. I took occasion to call upon an old mistress of mine, Jane Chéron, concerning whom see *The Eqjuinox*, vol. I, no. VI, 'Three Poems'. She has never had the slightest interest in occult matters and she has never done any work in her life, even of the needlework order. I had seen her once before since my escape from America, and she said she had something to show me, but I took no particular notice and she did not insist. My object in calling on this second occasion was multiple. I wanted to see the man with whom she was living, who had not yet returned from Russia; I wanted to make love to her, and I wanted to smoke a few pipes of opium with her, she being a devotee of that great and terrible god.

Consider now: The Work whereby I am a Magus began in Cairo (1904) with the discovery of the stele of Ankh-f-n Khonsu,[10] in which the principal object is the body of our Lady Nuith. It is reproduced in colours in *The Equinox*, vol. I, no. VII. Jane Chéron has a copy of this book. On Friday afternoon, then, I was in her apartment. I had attained none of my objectives in calling on her and was about to depart. She detained me to show me this 'something'. She went and took a folded cloth from a drawer. 'Shut your eyes,' she said.

When I opened them, they saw a cloth four feet or more in length, on which was a magificent copy, mostly in appliqué silk, of the stele. She then told me that in February 1917, she and her young man had gone to the south of France to get cured of the opium habit. In such cases insomnia is frequent. One night, however, he had gone to sleep and on waking in the morning found that she, wakeful, had drawn a copy of the stele on a great sheet of paper.

It is very remarkable that so large a sheet of paper should have been at hand; also that they should have taken that special book on such a journey; but still more that she should have chosen that picture, nay, that she, who had never done anything of the sort before, should have done it at all. More yet, that she should have spent three months in making a permanent thing of it. Most of all, that she should have shown it to me at the very moment when I was awaiting an 'unmistakable' sign.

For observe, how closely the words of my entry of January 12th describe the Sign, 'The omnipresence of my body'. And there She was—in the last place in the world where one would have sought Her.

Note too, the accuracy of the *Yi King* symbol ⚍ ⚌ for ⚎ ⚍ is, of course, the symbol of Our Lady, and the God below Her in the stele is ⚌ ⚍ the sun.[11]

All this is clear proof of the unspeakable power and wisdom of those who have sent me to proclaim the Law.

I observe, after a talk with M. Jules Courtier yesterday, that all their S.P.R.[12] work is proof of extra-human forces. We knew about them all along; the universe is full of obscure and subtle manifestations of energy; we are constantly advancing in our knowledge and control of them. Telekinesis is of the same order of nature as the Hertz rays or the radium emanations. But what nobody before me has done is to prove the existence of extra-human intelligence, and my Magical Record does this. I err in the interpretation, of course; but it is impossible to doubt that there is a somebody there, a somebody capable of combining events as a Napoleon forms his plans of campaign, and possessed of powers unthinkably vast.

If these events be indeed the result of calculation and control on the part of the Secret Chiefs, it seems at first sight as if the people involved had been prepared to play their parts from the beginning. Our previous relations, the girl's addiction to opium, my friendship with her lover, and his interests in my work; omit any item and the whole plan fails. But this assumption is unnecessary. The actual preparation need not go back further than three years, when the stele was embroidered. We may allow the Secret Chiefs considerable option, just as a chess player is not confined to one special combination for his attack. We may suppose that had these people not been available, the sign which I demanded might have been given me in some other equally striking way. We are not obliged to make extravagant assumptions in order to maintain that the evidence of purpose is irresistibly strong.

To dismiss this intricate concatenation of circumstances, culminating as they do in the showing forth of the exact sign which I had demanded, is simply to strain the theory of probabilities beyond the breaking point. Here then are two complicated episodes which go to prove that I am walking, not by faith but by sight, in my relations with the Secret Chiefs; and these are but two links in a very long chain. This account of my career will describe many others equally striking. I might, perhaps, deny my inmost instinct the right to testify were any one case of this kind in question; but when, year after year, the same sort of thing keeps on happening and when, furthermore, I find myself able to predict, as experience has taught me to do in the last three years, that they will happen, and even how the pieces will fit into the puzzle, I am justified in assuming a causal connection.

As any billiard player knows, while a ten-shot might be fluked by a novice, or even that he might run up a break of twenty or thirty now and again, a consistent sequence of breaks averaging twenty-five over a series of months cannot possibly happen by chance; this proves impugnably both that certain management of the cue combined with judgment must result in certain movements of the balls, and that skill and not luck determines the success of the player. Again, at roulette a run of one hundred on red might happen once in a thousand years by pure chance; but if it occurred a dozen times a night for a week it would prove that the table is furnished with a mechanical device by which the croupier could control the fall of the ball.

From this time I accepted the Law in its entirety; that is, I admitted its absolute authority. I was not, however, at the end of my difficulties. Much of the Book was unintelligible, and many passages, especially in Chapter III, entirely repugnant. I was content to leave these points to be cleared up by the gods themselves in their own good time. They had proved that I could trust them to manage what was after all their own affair and not mine. I refrained from pushing my criticism. I took the general sense of the Book, so far as I understood it, as at once the starting point and the summit of my Magick.

This change of attitude was tremendous. I had always been tongue-tied in the matter of expressing my spiritual self in poetry and my lyrics had been comparatively unimportant. They dealt only with certain aspects of the matter. I could point to nothing which really represented my personality as a whole or brought the events of my career into intelligible relation. The more I learned to study and love *The Book of the Law,* the better I was able to integrate myself.

Sir Palamedes was the most ambitious attempt to describe the Path of the Wise as I knew it. It is in its way almost complete, but there is no attempt to show the necessary sequence of the ordeals described in each section. The last section, in which Sir Palamedes, after achieving every possible task and finding that all his attainments did not bring him to the end of his Quest, abandons the following of the Questing Beast; he returns, discomfited, to the Round Table, only to find that, having surrendered, the Questing Beast comes to him of its own accord.

I could not pretend that this was more than a *tour de force,* an evasion of the issue. I know now that the true solution is this: there is no goal to be attained, as I had reached Madrid; the reward is in the march itself. As soon as I got to Madrid my adventures were at an end. If I had had to stay there I should have been bored to death, even if it had been the city of God itself. The joy of life consists in the exercise of one's energies, continual growth, constant change, the enjoyment of every new experience. To stop means simply to die.

The eternal mistake of mankind is to set up an attainable ideal. Sir Palamedes expressed himself fully in following the Questing Beast. His success (as described in the poem) would in reality have left him with nothing to live for. My own life has been indescribably ecstatic, because even when I thought that there was a reward and a rest at the end, my imagination pictured them as so remote that I was in no danger of getting what I wanted. I am now wise enough to understand that every beat of my pulse marks a moment of exquisite rapture in the consciousness that the curve of my career is infinite, that with every breath I climb closer and closer to the limit, yet can never reach it. I am always aspiring, always attaining; nothing can stop me, not even success. I had some perception of this in these years of my life in London, for I wrote in *The Book of Lies:* 'Only those are happy who have desired the unattainable.'

The Equinox should have been, on its merits, a very successful venture. Frank Harris had generously given me one of the best stories he ever wrote, 'The Magic Glasses'.[13] Fuller had contributed a gargantuan preface to *The Temple of Solomon the King*[14] (the title of the story of my magical career), a series of sublimely eloquent rhapsodies descriptive of the various possible attitudes towards existence. There were three important instructions in Magick; the best poem of its kind that I had so far written, 'The Wizard Way'; 'At the Fork of the Roads', a true and fascinating story of one of my early magical experiences; 'The Soldier and the Hunchback ! and ?' which I still think one of the subtlest analyses that has ever been written on ontology, with its conclusion: that ecstatic affirmation and sceptical negation are neither of them valid in themselves but are alternate terms in an infinite series, a progression which is in itself a sublime and delightful path to pursue. Disappointment arises from the fear that every joy is transient. If we accept it as such and delight to destroy our own ideals in the faith that the very act of destruction will encourage us to rebuild a nobler and loftier temple from the debris of the old, each phase of our progress will be increasingly pleasant. 'παμφάγε παγγενέτωρ', 'All devourer, all begetter', is the praise of Pan.

In us the will to live and the will to die should be equally strong and free, should be recognized as complements of each other, neither complete in itself; and the antithesis between them a device invented for our own amusement. All energy implies vibration. Man is miserable in the last analysis because he fancies that when what gives him pleasure is destroyed, as he knows it must be sooner or later, the loss is irreparable; so he shores up his crumbling walls instead of building himself a better house. We all cling to outworn customs of every kind and lie to ourselves about love when we know in our hearts that there is no more oil in the lamp, and that the best thing we can do is to look for a new one. We are afraid to lose whatever we have. We have not the sense to see whatever it may be, it is bound to go sooner or later, that when it does its place will be filled by something just as good, and nothing is more stupid than to try to set back the sun upon the dial of Ahaz.

As soon as we learn that everything is only half, that it implies its opposite, we can let ourselves go with a light heart, finding just as much fun in the red leaves of autumn as in the green leaves of spring. What is interesting is the complete cycle. Life itself would be deplorably petty were it not consecrated by the fact of its incomprehensibility and dignified by the certainty that however petty, futile, baroque and contemptible its career may be, it must close in the sublime sacrament of death. As it is written in *The Book of the Law,* 'death is the crown of all.'

The supplement to the first number of *The Equinox* is a plain reprint of my Magical Record in Paris, mentioned above. I have omitted no detail of my doings. My dinners, my dalliance and my other diversions are described as minutely as my Magick, my mantras and my meditations. Nothing of the sort had ever been published before. It is a complete demonstration of the possibility of achieving the most colossal results in conditions which had hitherto been considered an absolute bar to carrying on even elementary work. It proves my proposition that the efficacy of traditional practices is independent of dogmatic and ethical considerations; and, moreover, that my sceptical formulae based on a purely agnostic viewpoint, and on the facts of physiology and psychology, as understood by modern materialists, were entirely efficacious.

In summary, let me add that *The Equinox* was the first serious attempt to put before the public the facts of occult science, so-called, since Blavatsky's unscholarly hotch-potch of fact and fable, *Isis Unveiled*. It was the first attempt in history to treat the subject with scholarship and from the standpoint of science. No previous book of its kind can compare with it for the perfection of its poetry and prose; the dignity and sublimity of its style, and the rigidity of its rule never to make any statement which could not be proved as precisely as the mathematician exacts. I confess to being entirely proud of having inaugurated an epoch. From the moment of its appearance, it imposed its standards of sincerity, scholarship, scientific seriousness and aristocracy of all kinds, from the excellence of its English to the perfection of its printing, upon everyone with ambition to enter this field of literature.

It did not command a large public, but its influence has been enormous. It is recognized as the standard publication of its kind, as an encyclopedia without 'equal, son, or companion'. It has been quoted, copied and imitated everywhere. Innumerable cults have been founded by charlatans on its information. Its influence has changed the whole current of thought of students all over the world. Its inveterate enemies are not only unable to ignore it, but submit themselves to its sovereignty. It was thus entirely successful from my personal point of view. I had put a pearl of great price in a shop window, whose other exhibits were pasted diamonds and bits of coloured glass for the most part, and at best, precious stones of the cheaper and commoner kind. From the moment of its appearance, everyone had to admit—for the most part with hatred and envy in their hearts—that the sun had appeared in the slum and put to shame the dips and kerosene lamps which had lighted it till then. It was no longer possible to carry on hole-in-the-corner charlatanism as heretofore.

I printed only one thousand and fifty copies, the odd fifty being bound subscription copies at a guinea, and the rest in boards at five shillings. Had I sold a complete edition straight out without any discounts my return would thus have been three hundred pounds. The cost of production was nearer four hundred. Similar figures apply to the other nine numbers. In this way I satisfied myself that no one could reproach me with trying to make money out of Magick. As a matter of fact, it went utterly against the grain to take money at all. When anyone showed interest in my poetry or my magical writings, the attitude so delighted me that I felt it utterly shameful to have any kind of commercial transaction with so noble an individual, and I used, as often as not, to beg him to accept the book as a present.

My feeling about accepting money is even more general than this; it rasps every delicate nerve. I feel that the world owes me a handsome income and I have no shame whatever in taking it, provided it is a sort of tribute. The fortune I had inherited was perfectly all right and it never occurred to me to inquire into its sources. *Widowers' Houses* shocked without convincing me. Thinking it over, I suppose that fraud and robbery *are* the only two sources of wealth, bar exceptional cases; and I suppose that after all the most honest and most honourable way of getting money is to sell one's writings.

Yet I still feel there is something very wrong about it. Good work is priceless and bad work is worthless. Besides, even the best writers are tempted to do their worst work by the fact that publishers, as a class, are persuaded that the public prefer rubbish. The fact is that there are hardly half a dozen writers in England today who have not sold out to the enemy. Even when their good work has been a success, Mammon grips them and whispers, 'More money for more work.' One ought to have an independent income or another profession. There is hardly one first-rate writer in the last century who has not been starved, persecuted, slandered, bullied, exiled, imprisoned or driven to drink or drowning.

To return to *The Equinox*, there was no question of selling even that small edition even at that pitiful price. I have never had any idea of how to do business. I can make plans, both sound and brilliant; but I cannot force myself to take the necessary steps to put them into practice. My greatest weakness is that as soon as I am sure that I can attain any given object, from climbing a mountain to exploiting a beauty spot, I lose interest. The only things I complete are those of which (as for instance, poetry and Magick) I am not the real author but an instrument impelled by a mysterious power which sweeps me away in effortless enthusiasm which leaves no room for my laziness, cynicism and similar inhibiting qualities to interfere.

I did try to get a few booksellers to stock *The Equinox* but found myself immediately up against a blank wall of what I must call Chinese conventionality. I remember hearing of an engineer in the East who wanted to build himself a house and employed a Chinese contractor. He pointed out that the work would be much easier by using bricks of a different size to that which the man was making. He obeyed, but a day later went back to the old kind. The engineer protested, but the man explained that his bricks were of a 'heaven-sent' size.

So I found that the format of *The Equinox* shocked the bookseller: worse still, it was not a book, being issued periodically, nor a magazine, being too big and well produced! I said, 'What does it matter? All I ask you to do is to show it and sell it.' Quite useless.

I spent my spare time in the summer, for the most part, with frivolous friends in the Thames valley. I sorely needed just that sort of relaxation. My soul was badly bruised by the ruin of my romance, but I had a good time of a sort. At least, one of my friends was the most amusing person in his peculiar way that I ever met. I must tell one incident, very instructive, as showing the ravages which can be wrought by strong sexuality in an unbalanced mind which, on the one hand, cannot control it and, on the other, fears it and thinks it should be suppressed.

My friend, 'Gnaggs' we will call him, had just been divorced from a trained nurse, the woman in the case being a plump, pretty piece of pink of the barmaid type, whom he then married. 'Gnaggs' thought his first duty was to safeguard the morals of the woman who had just divorced him! She was living in a block of flats near Hyde Park. Someone was sending him anonymous letters about her. One evening he joined our party—his wife and a few others—when we came in from the river to dine at the Ray Mead Hotel. He had just received another letter, which said plainly that some man was going to be at his first wife's flat that night. He rushed up to London.

When not clamouring for chastity in language which would have seemed to Savonarola violent and extreme, Gnaggs exhorted his wife to enjoy herself with any man she fancied. Neuburg was engaged in a furious flirtation with her, and he and I went back to Gnaggs's house with Mrs G. and my own inamorata. Neuburg wanted to stay the night; and his hostess, who was very drunk, was as greedy as he was. But I was warned by a heavenly vision. I felt it in the marrow of my bones that a storm was brewing. I put my foot down; and though I almost had to use main force to get Neuburg to go home, I had my way. I was still talking to my own friend at half-past two, when I heard the click of the garden gate and steps on the path. The house door opened and shut with sinister softness. Then there was absolute silence.

A few minutes later there was a frightened scream from Mrs Gnaggs. I threw on a dressing gown and went out. She was standing in a kimono on the landing with a candle, in hysterics, leaning over the balustrade and calling to know who

was there. I said, 'It is only some beastly burglar,' took the
candle and went down. No one in the hall. In the dining-
room, in pitch darkness, Gnaggs was standing, trembling, as
white as a fish's belly. I lit up, called upstairs that all was well,
and told him he had no business to frighten his wife. He
seemed incapable of speech. I got him a drink and he gradually pulled himself together. We started to smoke and he told
me his story.

He had left his bicycle on the kerb some fifty yards from
the entrance to the house where his first wife lived and
waited in the shadow for her lover to come out. The man
appeared about one o'clock. Gnaggs instantly fell on him, left
him for dead on the pavement, sprinted to his machine and
raced home. I congratulated him on his resourcefulness in
making life interesting and got him to go to bed. He was a good
deal scared about the police, in case he had killed the man.
We watched the papers anxiously.

The next day a paragraph appeared.

Mysterious midnight assault near Hyde Park. Dr Herpes-
Zoster, a prominent physician of Clyster Street, was assaulted
brutally, and battered by a thug at the door of 606 Mercury
Mansions, Iodine Street, Hyde Park, about one o'clock this
morning. He was discovered unconscious by the policeman on
the beat and taken to Knocks Hospital, where he was found to
be suffering from numerous contusions and serious internal
injuries. He had not been robbed and can assign no motive for
the attack, as he is not aware that he has any enemies. He
had been spending a quiet evening with some old friends,
Professor and Mrs Phthisis.

Once more I congratulated Gnaggs and this time quite sincerely. It was certainly quite improbable that the police would
get on his trail, as his victim was an utter stranger, as much
to his first wife as to himself!

I found this sort of thing added a spice to life. Gnaggs could
be relied upon to take one out of the rut every few minutes.
Some weeks later I went to spend the weekend with him. I
was worn out with worry and work and had caught a bad
chill. He was out when I got to the house. Mrs Gnaggs saw
that I was really ill and made me lie down on the sofa in the
combination smoking-room and conservatory, and went to
get shawls to cover me up. As she bent over me to arrange
them, the door opened and Gnaggs walked in with his eternal
bicycle. He jumped to the false conclusion that she was kissing
me—(God forbid!)—and started a row. I was really too ill

to do more than look on lazily, with amused contempt; but after half an hour of recriminations, Gnaggs went out to telegraph to her father, his lawyer and several possible allies. She followed him out.

Two minutes later I heard her scream for help. I ran out and found that he had got her by the throat. On seeing me he let her go; she ran screaming into the house. He followed, swearing to kill her. I made a beeline for the drawing-room poker, but the room was so full of trumpery ornaments that there was no room to swing it. So we clinched. We fought our way to the hall. I finally got him down on the staircase. He kicked the balustrade to splinters; but I held on. Luckily, his hair was very long, so that I could knock his head on the edge of a stair whenever he tried to break away. I begged Mrs Gnaggs and the servants to send for help, but they were much too interested in watching the scrap. I had to hold him down for an hour and a half when another guest turned up and restored peace.

We sat down to dinner perfectly good friends. On second thoughts he realized that his suspicions had been absurd. But his wife got hot as he got cool. During the meal she tried to kill him, first by throwing the soup tureen and a few dishes at him across the table, and secondly with the carving knife. It was one of the most delightful dinners I ever ate.

The story has no sequel.

They squabbled and scrapped and scratched for some years, and then went, first to Canada, then to California, and squabbled and scratched some more. They are back in England now, separated most of the time, and only meeting when they feel they would like to squabble and scrap and scratch some more. He is madder than ever, and she has developed into a large lump of dough. She has caught his complaint, and divides her time between drunken orgies with any loose fish she can find, and passionate protestations that she is utterly pure.

I really believe she persuades herself that the other half of her life does not exist. To me both extremes seem equally the debauches of an unbalanced and uncontrolled emotionalism. This view is confirmed by the fact that as she advanced in flabbiness, fat and the forties, she found it harder to attract men, and took to spasms of spiritualism. She raves about her 'Guides' and explains the most natural events of life as parts of various portentous plans prepared by people 'from the other side'.

On August 22nd the spirit suddenly sprang up in my soul like a serpent and bade me testify to the truth that was in me in poetry. I knew London would stifle me and rushed down to Maidenhead. I spent three days in a canoe, chiefly in the reach under the weir by Boulter's Lock.

> Choose tenderly
> A place for thine Academy.
> Let there be an holy wood
> Of embowered solitude
> By the still, the rainless river,
> Underneath the tangled roots
> Of majestic trees that quiver
> In the quiet airs; where shoots
> Of kindly grass are green,
> Moss and ferns asleep between,
> Lilies in the water lapped,
> Sunbeams in the branches trapped
> —Windless and eternal even!
> Silenced all the birds of heaven
> By the low insistent call
> Of the constant waterfall.
> There, to such a setting be
> The carven gem of deity,
> A central flawless fire, enthralled
> Like Truth within an emerald!
> Thou shalt have a birchen bark
> On the river in the dark;
> And at the midnight thou shalt go
> To the mid-stream's smoothest flow,
> And strike upon a golden bell
> The spirit's call; then say the spell:
> 'Angel, mine angel, draw thee nigh!'
> Making the Sign of Magistry
> With wand of lapis lazuli.
> Then, it may be, through the blind dumb
> Night thou shalt see thine angel come,
> Hear the faint whisper of his wings,
> Behold the starry breast begemmed
> With twelve stones of the twelve Kings!
> His forehead shall be diademmed
> With the faint light of stars, wherein
> The Eye gleams dominant and keen,
> Thereat thou swoonest; and thy love
> Shall catch the subtle voice thereof . . .[15]

It was given me during these days to experience fully once more every incident in my initiation, so that I might describe them while still white-hot with their wonder. It is this that assures me that this poem is unique of its kind. Its only rival is the *Bhagavad-Gita*, which, despite its prolixity, confines its ardour to Vishvarupa-darshana.[16] Apart from this, it treats of Hindu dogma and ethics. At its best, it is a sectarian work. 'Aha!' covers all religious experience, asserts no axioms, advocates no cut-and-dried codes. In some eleven hundred lines I have described all the principal trances, from the three types of Dhyana [17] (Sun, Moon, Agni [18]) and the four elements (for instance, the Disc 'like a black boundless diamond whirring with millions of wings'), to the spiritual beings that inhabit the invisible universe, and the Samadhic Trances, Atmadarshana [19] and Shivadarshana.[20]

I have also described the moral and intellectual phenomena of initiation and indicated the main principles on which the aspirant should base his working. The Knowledge and Conversation of the Holy Guardian Angel comes as the climax to these triumphs. It is significant that I proceed from this point instantly to declare the Law of Thelema, and give a dithyrambic epitome of the three chapters of the Book. I say distinctly that this message to mankind is to be identified with the Word of my Holy Guardian Angel. It is only as I write this that I realize that the poet in me perceived that Aiwaz and mine Angel were one. Till this moment I believed that I had reached this conclusion after many months of meditation in the last three years and accepted it provisionally with the greatest hesitation.

This psychological paradox, by the way, is very frequent. Again and again I have made important discoveries with tedious toil only to remember, in the hour of triumph, that I had written them down years earlier. It seems that I do not know what I am writing, or even understand what I have written.

The poem ends with 'Blessing and worship to the Beast, the prophet of the Lovely Star'. Henceforth I must be no more an aspirant, no more an adept, no more aught that I could think of as myself. I was the chosen prophet of the Masters, the instrument fit to interpret their idea and work their will. I cannot say whether realizing this identification of myself with the messenger of the Masters, this resolution of my complex equation into a simple expression, in which the x of my individuality was eliminated, made it possible for the Secret Chiefs to initiate me fully as a Master of the Temple, three years since my prudent refusal to accept it.

66

I had no special magical object in going to Algiers, which I reached on November 17th. As my chela, I took Frater Omnia Vincam, a neophyte of the A∴ A∴ disguised as Victor Neuburg. We merely wanted to rough it a bit in a new and interesting corner of the planet of which we were parasites. We hastily bought a few provisions, took the tram to Arba and after lunch started south, with no particular objective beyond filling our lungs with pure air and renewing the austere rapture of sleeping on the ground and watching the stars, serenely silent above us, till the face of sleep, kissing our eyes, hid them from us in her heavy and holy hair. On the twenty-first we reached Aumale, after two nights in the open and one at a hovel that may have looked so tired on account of its sisyphean struggle to pretend to be an hotel.

I cannot imagine why or how the idea came to me. Perhaps I happened to have in my rucksack one of my earliest magical notebooks, where I had copied with infinite patience the Nineteen Calls or Keys obtained by Sir Edward Kelly from certain angels and written from his dictation by Queen Elizabeth's astrologer with whom he was working. The sixth book of their magical workings was translated by Casaubon and is one of the very few genuine and interesting works on Magick of any period. Much of their work still defies explanation, though I and Frater Semper Paratus,[1] an Adeptus Major of A∴ A∴, have spent much time and research upon it and cleared up many obscure points.

The fact which stamps this working as sincere is this: over one hundred squares filled with letters were obtained—in a manner which no one has quite understood. Dee would have one or more of these tables (as a rule 49 x 49), some full, others lettered only on alternate squares, before him on a writing table. Kelly would sit at what they called the Holy Table and gaze into a 'shew-stone' which, with some of the talismans on the table, may be seen in the British Museum. Kelly would see an angel in the shew-stone, who would point with a rod to letters on one of these charts in succession.

663

Kelly would report, 'He points to column 6, rank 31,' and so on, apparently not mentioning the letter, which Dee found and wrote down from the 'table' before him. This seems to imply that Kelly did not know what words would be formed. If he did, we must assume that he knew the position of each of the 2,401 letters in each of the tables, which seems a somewhat surprising accomplishment. When the angel had finished, the message was rewritten backwards. (It had been dictated backwards as being too dangerous to communicate forwards —each word being in its nature so powerful that its direct communication would have evoked forces which were not wanted at that time.)

These Keys or Calls being rewritten backwards, there appeared conjurations in a language which they called 'Enochian' or Angelic. It is not a jargon; it has a grammar and syntax of its own. It is very much more sonorous, stately and impressive than even Greek or Sanskrit, and the English translation, though in places difficult to understand, contains passages of a sustained sublimity that Shakespeare, Milton and the Bible do not surpass. To condemn Kelly as a cheating charlatan—the accepted view—is simply stupid. If he invented Enochian and composed this superb prose, he was at worst a Chatterton with fifty times that poet's ingenuity and five hundred times his poetical genius.

> Can the Wings of the Wind understand your voices of Wonder? O Ye! the second of the First! whom the burning flames have framed in the depth of my Jaws! Whom I have prepared as cups for a wedding, or as flowers in their beauty for the chamber of Righteousness! Stronger are your feet than the barren stone; and mightier are your voices than the manifold winds! For you are become a building such as is not, save in the Mind of the All-Powerful.
>
> (Second Key)

I prefer to judge Kelly from this rather than from stale scandal of people to whom any Magician, as such, smelt of sulphur. If, on the other hand, Kelly did not write this, he may of course have been a common ignorant scoundrel, one of whose abnormalities was a faculty for seeing and hearing sublimities, just as a burglar or business man might be able to describe St Paul's Cathedral far better than the dean.

There are nineteen of these Keys: the first two conjuring the element called Spirit; the next sixteen invoke the Four Elements, each subdivided into four; the nineteenth, by changing two names, may be used to invoke any one of what are called the thirty 'Aethyrs' or 'Aires'. What these are is difficult to say. In one place we are told that they are 'Dominion extending in ever widening circles without and beyond the Watch Towers of the Universe', these Watch Towers composing a cube of infinite magnitude. Elsewhere, we find that the names of the angels which govern them are contained in the Watch Towers themselves; but (most disconcerting disenchantment!) they are identified with various countries of the earth, Styria, Illyria, etc., as if *'aire'* simply meant *clime*. I have always maintained the first definition. I suspected Kelly of finding Dee unsupportable at times, with his pity, pedantry, credulity, respectability and lack of humour. I could understand that he broke out and made fun of the old man by spouting nonsense.

The genuineness of these Keys, altogether apart from any critical observation, is guaranteed by the fact that anyone with the smallest capacity for Magick finds that they work. Prove *The Cenci* to have been forged by Hogg and conclude that Hogg was therefore a knave, well; but do not try to argue that, Hogg not being a poet, *The Cenci* must be drivel. I had used these Keys a great deal and always with excellent effect. In Mexico I thought I would discover for myself what the Aethyrs really were, by working them in turn by means of the nineteenth Key and, skrying [2] in the spirit vision, judge their nature by what I saw and heard. I investigated the first two Keys on November 14th and 17th, 1900. 'The Vision and the Voice' [8] was mysterious and terrific in character. What I saw was not beyond my previous experience, but what I heard was as unintelligible to me as Blake to a Baptist. I was encouraged by the evident importance of these results, but I found that I could no more force myself to go on to the twenty-eighth Aethyr than I could have thrown myself from a cliff. I accepted the rebuff; but, while dismissing the matter from my mind, managed to preserve the record throughout my wanderings. I had not thought of continuing this work for nearly nine years; but at Aumale a hand suddenly smote its lightning into my heart, and I knew that now, that very day, I must take up 'The Vision and the Voice' from the point where I had laid it down.

We accordingly bought a number of notebooks and after dinner I invoked the twenty-eighth Aethyr by means of the nineteenth Key. When we came to compare it with those of the twenty-ninth and thirtieth Aethyrs, we found that it exhibited the same peculiarities of subject and style. This is true also of the twenty-seventh Aethyr, and so to the twenty-fourth, yet there is a continuous advance towards coherence, both in each Aethyr itself and as regards its neighbour. The subject shows progressive solemnity and sublimity, as well as tendency to fit in with those conceptions of the cosmos, those mystic laws of nature, and those ideas of transcendental truth which had been already foreshadowed in *The Book of the Law* and the more exalted of my trances.

The deduction is not that my individuality was influencing the character of the vision more and more as I got, so to speak, into my stride, for the interpretation of my Algerian Work made clear the meaning of the utterly obscure oracles obtained in Mexico. It became evident indeed that what stopped me in 1900 was simply that my Grade did not entitle me to go further than the twenty-ninth. I was, in fact, told that only a Master of the Temple [4] can penetrate beyond a certain point. Of course anyone might use the Key for any Aethyr he chose, but he would either get no vision at all or expose himself to deception, and that probably of the deadly dangerous kind.

> God is never so turned away from man, and never so much sendeth him new paths, as when he maketh ascent to divine speculations or works in a confused or disordered manner, and as it adds, with unhallowed lips, or unwashed feet. For of those who are thus negligent, the progress is imperfect, the impulses are vain, and the paths are dark.
>
> (Zoroaster)

I solemnly warn the world that, while courage is the first virtue of the Magician, presumptuous and reckless rashness had no more connection with it than a caricature of the ex-Kaiser with Julius Caesar. It is composed partly of sham pride prompted by self-love and self-doubt; partly by the insane impulse which the extremity of fear excites. There are plenty of V.C.s who won the cross, not 'for valour', but for lack of self-control over their crisis of cowardice. Discipline automatically made running away impossible; the only way out was to rush forward and do whatever their innate instinct suggested. I know two V.C.s myself who have no memory whatever of the act that won them the cross.

Similar psychology often makes young Magicians forget that *to dare* must be backed by *to will* and *to know*, all three being ruled by *to keep silence*. Which last means many things, but most of all so to control oneself that every act is done noiselessly; all disturbance means clumsiness or blundering. The soldier may happen not to be hit as he carries his wounded comrade through the barrage, but there is no luck in Magick. We work in a fluid world, where every movement is compensated at once. Light, sound and electricity may be shut out, and so the effects of human thought, speech and action may divert or delay their action, but Magick, like gravitation, knows no obstacle. It is true that one can lift a fallen flower from the floor and keep it on a table; but the forces are at work all the time, and the action has been completely compensated by the redistribution of the stresses on every material object in the whole universe, by the shifting of the centre of gravity of the cosmos, as my muscles sway from one state of equilibrium to another, and the flower exerts its energies from the mahogany instead of the carpet.

Presumption in Magick is, therefore, sure to be punished— swiftly and justly. The error is one of the worst because it attracts all these forces which, being themselves weak, are made malignant by pain and find their principal solace in taking it out of anyone they feel they can bully. Worse still, the hysterical expansion of the ego means the deepest possible treason to truth. It invites obsession by every deceitful demon. They puff up the pride of the fool still further; they flatter every foible, exhort him to acts of the most ridiculous kind, induce him to talk the most raving rubbish and teach him to think himself the greatest man in the world—nay, not a man, but a god. He scores every fiasco as a success, takes every trifle as a token either of his sacrosanct sovereignty or of the malice of hell whose hounds have been mustered to martyr him. His megalomania swings from maniacal exaltation to melancholia, with delusions of persecution.

I have seen several cases of exactly this kind caused by so seemingly trivial a mistake as carelessness in consecrating the Circle for an evocation of an inferior spirit; claiming a Grade in the Order without having made sure of having passed every test perfectly at every point; presuming to instruct a probationer in his work before becoming a neophyte; omitting essential points of ritual as troublesome formalities; or even making excuses for error of the kind by which a man persuades himself that his faults are really due to the excess of his merits.

I remember one man who attributed his failure to perform

Asana properly to his exceptional physical energy. His body, said he, was endowed with such force that he must be meant to move it—it was all very well for ordinary men to try to sit still, but for him it was clearly an unnatural notion. Five years later, he told me he had become the strongest man on the planet and begged me to empty my revolver at his chest if I didn't mind the bullets rebounding and breaking my windows. I spared my windows; besides, I hate to clean my revolver. He then offered to take me downstairs and watch him shoulder a motor car and run down the road with it. I told him that I knew he could do it and wouldn't insult him by asking for proof. He went away, prancing and purring. Next day I had a postcard from him and guessed from his shaky upstrokes what was the matter. It chimed in with his talk. A month passed, then I heard that he had been diagnosed as suffering from general paralysis of the insane. The man who had been singled out from the herd for splendour of strength could not move a muscle; he rolled from side to side with regular rhythm. The man who boasted could no longer speak: he uttered a long monotonous howl, hardly varying by a note, hour after hour.

It is such cases that keep me constantly on my guard against being 'too proud to fight'—or to sweep the floor, if it comes to that. My Grade as a Magus of A∴A∴, my office as the Logos of the Aeon, the Prophet chosen to proclaim the Law which will determine the destinies of this planet for an epoch, singles me out in a sense, puts me in a class which contains only seven other names in the whole of human history.[5] No possible personal attainment could have done this. There are countless initiates, especially in Asia, who have scaled every summit in the range of spiritual success. I should unquestionably have become insane from satisfaction at the fulfilment of my utmost aspirations having been granted to me so superlatively beyond imagination conceived, but for (as I said before) 'my sense of humour and my common sense'.

I never let myself forget the rocks which have baffled me: the Coolin Crack on Beachy Head (curse it!), the direct way up the Deep Ghyll Pillar (damn it!), the east face of the Dent Blanche (blast it!). I hardly ever plume myself even on my poetry unless I am very depressed. I prefer to dwell on my ignorance of various subjects—a quite inexhaustible list; and the superficiality of my knowledge of the few of which I know what little I do. I meditate on my mistakes in dealing with mankind, my innocence of their most obvious characteristics. My simplicity is such that I often wonder if I am not half-witted. On practically every matter which men who can hardly read, and have certainly never read a book worth reading, understand with every part of their minds better than I understand with any part of mine, even in what I have studied with sweat, at the cost of eyesight, sleep and digestion.

This digression has been permissible because of its pertinence to my Algerian initiation. I may now resume the narrative.

My method of obtaining 'The Vision and the Voice' was as follows: I had with me a great golden topaz (set in a Calvary cross of six squares, made of wood, painted vermilion), engraved with a Greek cross of five squares charged with the Rose of forty-nine petals. I held this as a rule in my hand. After choosing a spot where I was not likely to be disturbed, I would take this stone and recite the Enochian Key,[6] and, after satisfying myself that the invoked forces were actually present, made the topaz play a part not unlike that of the looking-glass in the case of *Alice*.

I had learned not to trouble myself to travel to any desired place in the astral body. I realized that space was not a thing in itself, merely a convenient category (one of many such) by reference to which we can distinguish objects from each other. When I say I was in any Aethyr, I simply mean in the state characteristic of, and peculiar to, its nature. My senses would thus receive the subtle impressions which I had trained them to record, so becoming cognizant of the phenomena of those worlds as ordinary men are of this. I would describe what I saw and repeat what I heard and Frater O. V. would write down my words and incidentally observe any phenomena which struck him as peculiar. (For instance: I would at times pass into a deep trance so that many minutes might elapse between two successive sentences.)

Such observations may be contemptuously dismissed as imaginary; but having already shown that all knowledge is equally an illusion, the thought is no inhibition. Yet there are different degrees of falsity and critical methods which are valid within their capacity. Thus we trust our experience of perspective to correct the crude statement of our eyesight that the furthest house in a suburban street is smaller in various ways. They may also verify our visions in various ways. They must be coherent and consistent with themselves; they must not contradict the conclusions of other experiences whose warrants are identical; and before we admit that they possess any value, they must increase our knowledge in such ways as would convince us in ordinary life that our interlocutor was an individual other than ourselves, and his information verifiably such as we could not have gained otherwise. It may seem as if such conditions could never be fulfilled, but it is quite easy to formulate them, and such visions as these under discussion are full of internal evidence of their authenticity.

Let me give one example. The Angel of the twenty-seventh Aethyr said: 'The word of the Aeon is MAKHASHANAH.' I immediately discredited him; because I knew that the word of the Aeon was, on the contrary, ABRAHADABRA. Inquiry by the Holy Cabbala then showed me that the two words had the same numerical value, 418. The apparent blunder was thus an absolute proof that the Angel was right. Had he told me that the word was ABRAHADABRA, I should have thought nothing of it, arguing that my imagination might have put the words in his mouth.[7]

Let me illustrate the strength of such proof by material analogy. Suppose I receive a telegram, signed Jobson (my lawyer), 'Your house has been burnt down.' If I already know this from the caretaker, Jobson is merely confirming a known fact of which he and many others may be aware. The telegram might have been forged. Equally, if I have not heard from other sources, or if I have heard, on the contrary, that all is well, the telegram carries no conviction; it establishes a *prima facie* case for inquiry: no more. But if such inquiry confirms the telegram, it becomes probable that Jobson really dispatched it, though not with complete certainty; short of seeing him personally, the genuineness of the message is only a presumption.

Suppose, however, that I read, 'London is burnt down. Jobson.' The statement is incredible as it stands. Jobson and I, however, have a secret understanding known to nobody else that any proper name in our communications shall stand for something else, discoverable by taking a = 1, b = 2, and so on, thus giving a number whose meaning is to be found in a code, in which each item of my estate represents a number. He has never used the word 'London' before. I add it up, refer to the code and learn that London must mean my house. Now, whether I have already heard the news or no, and even if investigation proves the information to be false, I may at least feel sure that Jobson himself, and nobody else, was the author. If, in addition, it proves true, I may be sure that on this point his knowledge exceeds my own. Suppose, then, that the telegram proceeds to inform me of a number of other matters which I have no immediate means of verifying, I shall nevertheless be justified in assuming their authenticity and acting on the advice in just the measure of my confidence in Jobson's integrity and ability.

Such is one of the simplest methods of criticizing the data afforded by visions. An isolated case need not convince one completely, and it would be ridiculous to argue from a single test, however striking, that all communications purporting to come from the same source must be genuine and authoritative. It is the cumulative effect of repeated tests over a period of years that gives confidence. Incidentally, one acquires by experience the faculty of knowing by instinct whether any given sight or sound is genuine; just as one learns to recognize the style of a writer or painter so that the most plausible imitations fail to deceive, hard as it may be to say in so many words what strikes one as suspicious.

Now, *The Book of the Law* guarantees itself by so closely woven a web of internal evidence of every kind, from Cabbalistic and mathematical proofs, and those depending on future events and similar facts, undeniably beyond human power to predict or to produce, that it is unique. The thirty Aethyrs being, however, only second in importance, though very far away, to that Book, the Lords of Vision were at pains to supply internal evidence, more than amply sufficient that the revelations therein contained may be regarded as reliable. No doubt the proof appears stronger to me than to anyone else, because I alone know exactly what happened; also because many passages refer to matters personal to myself, so that only I can fully appreciate the dovetailings. Just so a man can never prove to another the greatness of Shelley as fully as he feels it himself, since his certainty partly depends on the secret and incommunicable relations of the poet with his own individual idiosyncrasies.

I admit that my visions can never mean to other men as much as they do to me. I do not regret this. All I ask is that my results should convince seekers after truth that there is beyond doubt something worth while seeking, attainable by methods more or less like mine. I do not want to father a flock, to be the fetish of fools and fanatics, or the founder of a faith whose followers are content to echo my opinions. I want each man to cut his own way through the jungle.

We walked steadily to Bou Saâda, invoking the Aethyrs

one by one, at convenient times and places, or when the spirit moved me. As a rule, we did one Aethyr every day. We reached Bou Saâda on November 30th; on December 8th we started through the desert for Biskra, which we reached on December 16th, completing the work on the nineteenth. Our adventures will be told later on.

By the time I reached Bou Saâda and came to the twentieth Aethyr, I began to understand that these visions were, so to speak, cosmopolitan. They brought all systems of magical doctrine into harmonious relation. The symbolism of Asiatic cults; the ideas of the Cabbalists, Jewish and Greek; the arcana of the gnostics; the pagan pantheon, from Mithras to Mars; the mysteries of ancient Egypt; the initiations of Eleusis; Scandinavian saga; Celtic and Druidical ritual; Mexican and Polynesian traditions; the mysticism of Molinos no less than that of Islam, fell into their proper places without the slightest tendency to quarrel. The whole of the past Aeon appeared in perspective and each element thereof surrendered its sovereignty to Horus, the Crowned and Conquering Child, the Lord of the Aeon announced in *The Book of the Law*.

These visions thus crystallized in dramatic form the theoretical conclusion which my studies of comparative religion had led me to adumbrate. The complexity of the whole vast subject resolved itself into shining simplicity. I saw with my own eyes and heard with my own ears the truth in terms of Time. I understood directly that the formula of Osiris necessarily assumed all sorts of apparently incompatible forms as it was applied to different conditions of race, climate and similar conditions. I saw also that Horus might reconcile all religions, it being possible now to bring all countries to agree on a few fundamental principles. Science had practically driven prejudice into the dark. Faith was little more than a shibboleth which no longer influenced opinion or action. I saw my way to combine a few simple incontrovertible scientific principles into a Law which would allow the loftiest aspirations to seek satisfaction in spiritual spheres, the religious instincts to realize their sublimity through ritual, and to assist the scientific mind to see that even the most materialistic concept of the cosmos was ultimately mystical, that though mind might be merely a function of matter, yet that matter might equally well be represented as a manifestation of mind. The sequel will show how I fared in this ambitious adventure.

Besides this, I became subtly aware that this Work was more than the impersonal exploration which I had meant to make. I felt that a hand was holding my heart, that a breath was whispering words in a strange tongue whose accents were yet both awful in themselves and like enchantments encompassing my essence with an energy mighty to work on my will in some inscrutable way. I began to feel—well, not exactly frightened; it was the subtle trembling of a maiden before the bridegroom. My ardour increased with every vision and every vision became intenser and more intimate. I fortified myself by magical practices. Two or three times I had found it difficult to get into the Aethyr; there were bars which I understood as not to be passed by the profane. The progressive sublimity and solemnity made me tremble lest I should not be worthy to behold the mysteries that lay in the future.

So I consecrated myself by reciting this chapter of the Koran:

> Qol: hua allahu achad: allahu assamad: lam yalid:
> walam yulad: wa lam yakun lahu kufwan achad

a thousand and one times a day during the march, prostrating myself after each repetition. The physical effort of this exercise beneath the blazing sun as I marched, mile after mile, across the dusty, stony, glaring stretches of sterile solitude was very severe; but the exhaustion of my body and the pain of my mutinous mind as I thrashed it into submission with the lash of the mantra, prepared me for the moment of invoking the Aethyr. My spiritual part had nothing to fear from the garrulence of the mind which I had flogged into dumb duty.

In the nineteenth Aethyr appeared an Angel who revealed herself as appointed to lead me personally through the initiation appointed. At the time I hardly understood this. I could not imagine that my personal progress could have any connection with what I still supposed to be purely objective phenomena; but in the eighteenth Aethyr the Angel thereof prepared me ceremonially for the ceremony. In the seventeenth, the full magical meaning of equilibrium was made clear to me. 'Motion about a point is iniquity', 'Breath is iniquity' and 'Torsion is iniquity'. I understood that every disturbance (which makes manifestation possible) implies deviation from perfection. It is for this reason that my individuality (which distinguishes me from all other beings) involves the idea of injustice. Therefore, to penetrate beyond the Abyss, where iniquity cannot exist, my personal self-hood must be annihilated. The sixteenth Aethyr showed me how this might be done. My being must be dissolved in that of the infinite. This was symbolized by the destruction of the Demiurgus, he being the creator of diversity. He being destroyed, I was shown an image of my true self; and that self vanished, absorbed in a virgin. This told me that the climax of my love of the infinite was identification there.

In the fifteenth Aethyr, the vision definitely took form as a ceremony of initiation. I was examined by an assembly of adepts and my right to the Grades of the Second Order admitted. I was then allowed to be entitled to the Grade of a Babe of the Abyss and a Master of the Temple. They continued the examination and refused to accept me as a Magus. They then instructed me in various matters and made me make certain preparations for the vision following.

On the afternoon of December 3rd I invoked the fourteenth Aethyr. Here was a veil so black and thick that I could not pass through. I tore off layer after layer with desperate effort, while in my ears there pealed a solemn voice. It spoke of me as dead.

> And I still go on, struggling with the blackness. Now there is an earthquake. The veil is torn into thousands of pieces that go flying away in a whirling wind. And there is an all-glorious Angel before me, standing in the sign of Apophis and Typhon.[8] On his forehead is a star, but all about him is darkness, and the crying of beasts. And there are lamps moving in the darkness.
>
> And the Angel says: Depart! For thou must evoke me only in the darkness. Therein will I appear, and reveal unto thee the mystery of UTI.[9] For the Mystery thereof is great and terrible. And it shall not be spoken in sight of the sun.

I must explain that we had climbed Da'leh Addin, a mountain in the desert, as enjoined by the Angel during the previous night. I now withdrew from the Aethyr and prepared to return to the city. Suddenly came the command to perform a magical ceremony on the summit. We accordingly took loose rocks and built a great circle, inscribed with the words of power; and in the midst we erected an altar and there I sacrificed myself. The first of the all-seeing sun smote down upon the altar, consuming utterly every particle of my personality. I am obliged to write in hieroglyph of this matter, because it concerns things of which it is unlawful to speak openly under penalty of the most dreadful punishment; but I may say that the essence of the matter was that I had hitherto clung to certain conceptions of conduct which, while perfectly proper from the standpoing of my human nature, were impertinent to initiation. I could not cross the Abyss till I had torn them out of my heart.

I remember nothing of my return to Bou Saâda. There was an animal in the wilderness, but it was not I. All things had become alike; all impressions were indistinguishable. I only remember finding myself on my bed, as if coming out of some catastrophe which had blotted out in utter blackness every trace of memory. As I came to myself, I found myself changed. I knew who I was and all the events of my life; but I no longer made myself the centre of their sphere, or their sphere the standard by which I measured the universe. It was a repetition of my experience of 1905, but far more actual. I did not merely admit that I did not exist, and that all my ideas were illusions, inane and insane. I felt these facts as facts. It was the difference between book knowledge and experience. It seemed incredible that I should ever have fancied that I or anything else had any bearing on each other. All things were alike as shadows sweeping across the still surface of a lake—their images had no meaning for the water, no power to stir its silence.

At ten minutes to ten I returned to the Aethyr. I was instantly blotted in blackness. Mine Angel whispered the secret words whereby one partakes of the Mysteries of the Masters of the Temple. Presently my eyes beheld (what first seemed shapes of rocks) the Masters, veiled in motionless majesty, shrouded in silence. Each one was exactly like the other. Then the Angel bade me understand whereto my aspiration led: all powers, all ecstasies, ended in this—I understood. He then told me that now my name was Nemo, seated among the other silent shapes in the City of the Pyramids under the Night of Pan; those other parts of me that I had left for ever below the Abyss must serve as a vehicle for the energies which had been created by my act. My mind and body, deprived of the ego which they had hitherto obeyed, were now free to manifest according to their nature in the world, to devote themselves to aid mankind in its evolution. In my case I was to be cast out into the Sphere of Jupiter. My mortal part was to help humanity by Jupiterian work, such as governing, teaching, creating, exhorting men to aspire to become nobler, holier, worthier, kinglier, kindlier and more generous.

Finally, 'Fifty are the gates of understanding and one hundred and six are the seasons thereof, and the name of every one of them is Death.' I took this to mean that Aleister Crowley would die at the end of this time. The event has shown that it referred to my attainment of the Grade of Magus, for this took place at the exact moment here predicted.

The thirteenth Aethyr explains the work which a Master of the Temple must do. He is hidden under the earth and tends his garden. These gardens are of many kinds, but in every case he treats the roots of the flowers in various ways. Each flower gives birth to a maiden, save one, of which cometh a man child who shall be Nemo after him. Nemo must not seek to know which flower this is. He must tend his garden with absolute impartiality.

The twelfth Aethyr describes the City of the Pyramids, whose queen is called BABALON, the Scarlet Woman, in whose hand is a cup filled with the blood of the saints. Her ecstasy is nourished by the desires which the Masters of the Temple have poured from their hearts for her sake. In this symbolism are many mysteries concealed. One is that if a single drop of blood be withheld from her cup it putrefies the being below the Abyss and vitiates the whole course of the adept's career.

In the eleventh Aethyr is shown the fortress on the frontier of the Abyss, with its warrior wardens. I had thought that my ordeal was over. But no! I was suddenly faced with the fact that I had to cross the Abyss consciously, understanding its nature; for when I had passed through it there was in me no power to perceive. I knew no more than this—a negative idea—that its power was to dissipate me into dead dust. Now being bidden to cross it consciously, I asked the Angel, 'Is there not one appointed as a warden?' I meant my Holy Guardian Angel, for whose Knowledge and Conversation I had abandoned all. The answer: '*Eloi, Eloi, lama sabacthani.*' [10] I knew that even my holiest, mine inmost self, might not protect me from the grim abominations of the Abyss.

We therefore changed our magical procedure. We went far out from the city into a hollow among the dunes. There we made a circle to protect the scribe and a triangle wherein the Abyss might manifest sensibly. We killed three pigeons, one at each Angle, that their blood might be a basis whereon the forces of evil might build themselves bodies.

The name of the Dweller in the Abyss is Choronzon, but he is not really an individual. The Abyss is empty of being; it is filled with all possible forms, each equally inane, each therefore evil in the only true sense of the word—that is, meaningless but malignant, in so far as it craves to become real. These forms swirl senselessly into haphazard heaps like dust devils, and each such chance aggregation asserts itself to be an individual and shrieks, 'I am I!' though aware all the time that its elements have no true bond; so that the slightest disturbance dissipates the delusion just as a horseman, meeting a dust devil, brings it in showers of sand to the earth.

Choronzon appeared in many physical forms to Omnia Vincam, while I abode apart in my magical robe with its hood drawn over my face. He took the form of myself, of a woman whom Neuburg loved, of a serpent with a human head, etc. He could not utter the word of the Abyss, because there is no word; its voice is the insane babble of a multitude of senseless ejaculations; yet each form spake and acted as if aping its model. His main object was to induce O.V. to leave the circle, or to break into it; so as to obsess him, to live in his life. O.V. had many narrow escapes, and once Choronzon made a long speech at a great pace to keep O.V. so busy writing it down that he would not notice that sand was being thrown from the Triangle so as to obliterate the Circle. The torrent of obscene blasphemy was beyond his power to keep up, concentration being impossible. It became an incoherent series of cries; then suddenly, perhaps catching the idea from O.V.'s mind, the demon began to recite Tom o'Bedlam.[11]

There was now a gap in the Circle; and Choronzon, in the form of a naked savage, dashed through and attacked O.V. He flung him to the earth and tried to tear out his throat with froth-covered fangs. O.V. invoked the names of God and struck at Choronzon with the Magical Dagger. The demon was cowed by this courageous conduct and writhed back into the Triangle. O.V. then repaired the Circle; Choronzon resumed his ravings, but could not continue. He changed once more into the form of the woman whom O.V. loved, and exercised every seduction. O.V. stuck to his guns and the dialogue took other forms. He tried to shake O.V.'s faith in himself, his respect for me, his belief in the reality of Magick, and so on. At last all the energy latent in the blood of the pigeons was exhausted by the successive phantoms, so that it was no longer able to give form to the forces evoked. The Triangle was empty.

During all this time I had astrally identified myself with Choronzon, so that I experienced each anguish, each rage, each despair, each insane outburst. My ordeal ended as the last form faded; so, knowing that all was over, I wrote the holy name of BABALON in the sand with my magical ring and arose from my trance. We lit a great fire to purify the place and destroyed the Circle and Triangle. The work had lasted over two hours and we were both utterly exhausted, physically and in every other way. I hardly know how we ever got back to Bou Saâda.

Not till the evening of the following day did I feel strong enough to invoke the ninth Aethyr. A surprise was waiting for me. The nineteenth Key contains the text of the original curse on creation. Each phrase formulates some calamity. I had always shuddered at its horror as I recited it. But now, the Abyss being crossed, and all its horror faced and mastered, the words of the Key suddenly thrilled with a meaning that I had never suspected. Each curse concealed a blessing. I understood that sorrow had no substance; that only my ignorance and lack of intelligence had made me imagine the existence of evil. As soon as I had destroyed my personality, as soon as I had expelled my ego, the universe which to it was indeed a frightful and fatal force, fraught with every form of fear, was so only in relation to this idea 'I'; so long as 'I am I', all else must seem hostile. Now that there was no longer any 'I' to suffer, all these ideas which had inflicted suffering became innocent. I could praise the perfection of every part; I could wonder and worship the whole. This attainment absolutely altered my outlook. Of course, I did not at once enter into full enjoyment. The habit of misunderstanding everything had to be broken, bit by bit. I had to explore every possibility and transmute each base metal in turn into gold. It was years before I got into the habit of falling in love at first sight with everything that came my way.

The ninth Aethyr shows this transformation symbolically. The universe is represented as a maiden, all innocence, adorned with all perfection.

The remaining Aethyrs partly complete the experience proper to the Grade which I had attained, and partly shadow forth, in strangely obscure and formidable forms, the mysteries of the higher Grades, or rather the guards to them. As I advanced, it became more and more difficult to obtain the vision. In the second Aethyr, for example, begun on the morning of December 18th, the work had to be broken off and the invocation repeated. Yet again I found the strain unsupportable, had to break off, and go to the hot baths of Hamman Salahin;

and I continued, immersed to the neck in the hot sulphur spring. The water somehow soothed my nerves, enabling me to experience the Aethyr without physical collapse. Even so, I could not get to the end and only did so after over more than two days' concentrated consecration of myself.

67

We may now turn to this journey without the transcendental telescope. It was nothing to shout about as original, difficult or dangerous, but it certainly was one of the most delightful marches I ever made. Very few Europeans have any idea of foreign parts. They always wear thick veils of prejudice, and even prevent the possibility of enjoying really new experiences by their mere habit of life. They stick to the railway and see mere scraps of the country or travel in motors which blur the details of the day.

When one walks, one is brought into touch first of all with the essential relations between one's physical powers and the character of the country; one is compelled to see it as its natives do. Then every man one meets is an individual. One is no longer regarded by the whole population as an unapproachable and uninteresting animal to be cheated and robbed. One makes contact at every point with every stranger.

Of course, the more civilized classes, even in Algeria, are artificial. We learnt nothing from the French commandants and other officials whom we met, because their chief anxiety was to show what perfect gentlemen they were. We fraternized with them as when one goes to a new golf course. The attitude is cordiality at arm's length. And these people were all so ignorant of the country in which they lived that they unanimously warned us that we certainly should be murdered by brigands. To us this was a gigantic joke. We lay down on a patch of grass in the open, or a slope of soft sand, and slept feeling just as secure as we should have at the Savoy.

The Arabs also had their own fears for our safety. They have an ineradicable superstition that one is liable to be drowned in the desert. This sounds supremely absurd, water being the scantiest element of the Sahara. The root of the belief is that sometimes cloudbursts occur and sweep away camps which happen to have been pitched in ravines or depressions; but the most ordinary common sense tells one how to guard against any such accident. They are in terror of brigands and also of numerous varieties of devils.

I thought it polite to impress them with my majesty as a Magician. With this object I took Burton's hint that a star sapphire was universally venerated by Moslems, and having bought a very large and fine specimen of this stone in Ceylon and made it into a ring with a gold band of two interlaced serpents, I found that Burton was right. I had merely to exhibit this ring to command the greatest possible respect. On one occasion, in fact, a quarrel in a coffee shop having developed into a sort of small riot, and knives being drawn, I walked into the scrimmage and drew sigils in the air with the ring while intoning a chapter of the Koran. The fuss stopped instantly, and a few minutes later the original parties to the dispute came to me and begged me to decide between them, for they saw that I was a saint.

I habitually observed the prescribed five prayers of the orthodox Mohammedan, and increased my reputation for piety by constantly reciting the Koran as I walked and performing various other practices proper to the highest class of dervish.

I soon saw that Neuburg with his shambling gait and erratic gestures, his hangdog look and his lunatic laugh, would damage me in the estimation of the natives. So I turned the liability into an asset by shaving his head except for two tufts on the temples, which I twisted up into horns. I was thus able to pass him off as a demon that I had tamed and trained to serve me as a familiar spirit. This greatly enhanced my eminence. The more eccentric and horrible Neuburg appeared, the more insanely and grotesquely he behaved, the more he inspired the inhabitants with respect for the Magician who had mastered so fantastic and fearful a genie.

Few tourists know even the most elementary facts about such simple matters as climate. I myself was amazed to find how many of the ideas which I had derived from my reading were utterly incorrect. Once, for instance, we arrived at an inn late at night. It was shut. We had heard that when the coach arrived they would open, so we decided to wait for the half hour or so, as we needed food and sleep. It was a cold, drear night. To pass the time we took a stroll across the sand, intending to climb a small hill and get a moonlight panorama from the top. As we walked I awoke to the fact that my feet were freezing cold. I could not understand this at all—the rest of my body was comfortably warm. I was wearing thick woollen stockings with puttees and the Alpine boots which have proved adequate in the Himalayas. Like Keats,

I stood in my shoes and I wondered; I wondered;
I stood in my shoes and I wondered.

Wondering made them no warmer. At last I thought of putting
my hand on the sand. I snatched it back as if I had touched
a red hot plate. The surface was colder than any ice I had
ever known. At that moment we heard the coach and ran
back. I dashed in, tore off my boots and spent the next quarter
of an hour rubbing life back into my toes. So much for the
superstition that the Sahara is a sweltering furnace. On clear
nights the radiation is so rapid in that dry air, that the temperature of the ground falls below freezing point, even when the
air six feet above does not strike one as specially cold.

Bou Saâda is one of the most beautiful spots in the world.
It is frequented by French painters more than any other place
in Africa. Its isolation in the desert, which it beholds from the
crest of a wave of the wilderness, gives an almost sacred character to its galaxy of white-walled houses. Below, a river
rambles through a ravine, shaded by palms and bordered by gardens and orchards whose flowers and fruits are guarded by
hedges of cactus. Between these gay green gladnesses, glowing
with flowers that flame beneath the languid leaves of the fruit
trees, bright with blossom or burdened with bounty, a labyrinth of paths invite the idle to wander as their whim may
whisper, from one delicious prospect to another, assured that
wherever one goes there is always some new beauty to delight
the eye, some new token of truth for the ear; at every winding
of the way some new perfume makes one's nostril twitch with
pleasure. And yet the variations are so subtle that one soon
comes to understand that the infinite diversity of one's impressions depends less on external objects than on the modulations
of one's moods.

The solitude and silence of these shadowy groves soothe
sense and thought so that the soul becomes aware of every
modulation of its melody.

A few miles beyond Bou Saâda there is no road. The last
link with civilization is broken. It is no longer possible to pretend that the world is a mere stage where we may strut and
scream without facing the facts. Each man must match himself, alone as at the hour of death, with each inexorable fact
that nature flings in his face—brigands, sunstroke, hunger,
thirst, sickness, accident: no one of these to be evaded or
explained away, and no one to be propitiated, or from which
we may shelter by appealing to others.

The traveller must train his senses to the finest possible point. His life may depend on his seeing a shadow flit across some far off slope of a sand dune, and thereby divining an ambush. The circles of the vulture must enable him to calculate his course. Nothing too trivial to be his teacher, too insignificant to be of infinite import! As one becomes familiar with the wilderness, nature herself reveals reality in a sense which one had never suspected. The complexity of experience in civilized countries prevents one from examining anything exhaustively. Impressions crowd each other out of the mind. One never gets more than a glimpse of the nature of anything in itself, but only of its relation to the rest.

In the desert each impression is beaten into one's brain with what at first seems maddening monotony. One feels starved; there are so few facts to feed on. One has to pass through an abyss of boredom. At last there comes a crisis. Suddenly the shroud is snatched away from one's soul and one enters upon an entirely new kind of life, in which one no longer regrets the titillation of the thoughts which tumble over each other in civilized surroundings, each preventing one undergoing the ordeal involved when it becomes necessary to penetrate beneath the shadow-show to the secret sanctuary of the soul. I have explained these things in some detail in two essays, 'The Soul of the Desert' [1] and 'The Camel', which my wanderings in the Sahara inspired.

Part of the effect of crossing the Abyss is that it takes a long time to connect the Master with what is left below the Abyss. Deprived of their ego, the mind and body of the man are somewhat at sea until, as one may say, the 'wireless control' has been established. In the year 1910 Aleister Crowley was as a sheep not having a shepherd; the motives and controlling element had been removed and he was more or less cut off from the past. One thing seemed as good as another. He acted irresponsibly. He went on with his work more by force of habit than anything else, and the events of his life were, so to say, more chemical reactions between his character and his circumstances.

In the spring, a few days before the publication of number three of *The Equinox*, which contained the Ritual of the $5° = 6^{\square}$ degree of the old Order, Mathers served him with an injunction restraining publication. It did not interest him particularly. He instructed his lawyers and did not even trouble to go to court. Mr Justice Bucknill, who heard the argument, happened to be an eminent freemason and though he had no idea what the fuss was about, it seemed to him, on general principles, that nobody ought to be allowed to publish anything which anyone else might wish to keep dark. He therefore confirmed the injunction. I appealed.

This time we went into court armed with the facts of the case. The judges were Vaughan, Williams, Fletcher, Moulton and Farwell. They admitted the difficulty of keeping a straight face and reversed Bucknill's decisions, with costs. The argument had been farcically funny and all the dailies had anything up to three columns on the case. On the very day of publication, for the first time, I found myself famous and my work in demand.

As a side issue, Mathers having claimed in court to be the Chief of the Rosicrucian Order, I was invaded by an innumerable concourse of the queerest imaginable people, each of whom independently asserted that he himself, and he alone, was that Chief. Having my own information on the subject, though communicating it to nobody else, I got rid of these pests as quickly as possible. One of my callers, however, did show some method in his madness; a man named Theodor Reuss—of whom more anon. Here I must simply mention that he was Grand Master of Germany of the combined Scottish, Memphis and Mizraim Rites of Freemasonry. I remembered that I had been made a Sovereign Grand Inspector General of the 33° and last degree of the Scottish Rite in Mexico ten years before, but I had never bothered my head about it, it being evident that all freemasonry was either vain pretence, tomfoolery, an excuse for drunken rowdiness, or a sinister association for political intrigues and commercial pirates. Reuss told me a good deal of the history of the various rites, which is just as confused and criminal as any other branch of history; but he did persuade me that there were a few men who took the matter seriously and believed that the foolish formalism concealed really important magical secrets.

This view was confirmed when *The Arcane Schools* of John Yarker came to me for review. I wrote to the author, who recognized my title to the 33° and conferred on me the grades of 95° Memphis and 90° Mizraim. It seemed as if I had somehow turned a tap. From this time on I lived in a perfect shower of diplomas, from Bucharest to Salt Lake City. I possess more exalted titles than I have ever been able to count. I am supposed to know more secret signs, tokens, passwords, grandwords, grips, and so on, than I could actually learn in a dozen lives. An elephant would break down under the insignia

I am entitled to wear. The natural consequence of this was that, like Alice when she found the kings and queens and the rest showering upon her as a pack of cards, I woke up.

I went to Venice in May, breaking the homeward journey at Pallanza, where I wrote *Household Gods,* a poetical dramatic sketch. It is a sort of magical allegory, full of subtle ironies and mystifications; almost the only thing of its kind I have ever done—which perhaps accounts for my having a sneaking affection for it.

I had made a great many friends in London and the reconstructed Order was attracting aspirants from all classes of people, some silly loafers looking for a new sensation, but many most sincere and sensible. My inexperience led me into laxity in dealing with these people. I failed to enforce the strict rule of the Order: that probationers should be kept apart. I allowed them to meet in my studio and even to practise forms of Magick congregationally.

In the spring, on May 9th, an evocation of Bartzabel, the spirit of Mars, was made, so successfully as to demand description. My assistants were Commander Marston, R.N., one of the highest officials of the Admiralty, and Leila Waddell, an Australian violinist whom I had just met and who appealed to my imagination.

I began at once to use her as a principal figure in my work. In the first week of our intimacy I wrote two stories about her: 'The Vixen'[2] and 'The Violinist'.[3] 'The Vixen' is about a girl, an heiress in a fox-hunting shire, who tortures and uses for black magic a girl friend. She has a lover, Lord Eyre, whom she despises. She has some intimate relations with a phantom fox, who (to put it briefly) obsesses her. She yields to Eyre, who climbs into her room at night and finds that she is not a woman but a vixen. The effect is to turn him to a hound and he fastens his teeth in her throat. Hound and fox are found dead and nothing is ever heard again of Eyre or his mistress. 'The Violinist' is about a girl who invokes, by means of her music, a demon belonging to one of the Elemental Watch Towers. She becomes his mistress. One day her husband returns to the house. He kisses her and falls dead. The demon has conferred this power upon her lips.

Excuse the digression: back to Bartzabel! In the Triangle was Frater Omnia Vincam, to serve as a material basis through which the spirit might manifest. Here was a startling innovation in tradition. I wrote, moreover, a ritual on entirely new principles. I retained the Cabbalistic names and formulae, but wrote most of the invocation in poetry. The idea was to work up the magical enthusiasm through the exhilaration induced by music.

I obtained a great deal of valuable knowledge from the spirit, but the most interesting item is this: Marston, remembering his official duty, asked, 'Will nation rise up against nation?', followed by more detailed inquiries on receiving an affirmative answer. We thus learnt that within five years from that date there would be two wars; the storm centre of the first would be Turkey, and that of the second would be Germany, and the result would be the destruction of these two nations. I only remembered this after reaching New York at the end of 1914. Luckily I had the ritual with question and answer written down at the time, and an account of these predictions, precisely fulfilled, appeared in the *New York World*. I may here remark that I have always been able to foretell the future by various methods of divination. Some give more satisfactory results than others, some are better suited to one class of inquiry, some to another. In all cases, constant practice, constant checking up on one's results, critical study of the conditions, elimination of one's personal bias, and so on, increase one's accuracy. I am always experimenting and have taught myself to get absolutely reliable results from several methods, especially the *Yi King*. Incidentally, I have interpreted and corrected the traditional methods themselves, thereby excluding sources of error which in the past have disheartened students; but there is some sort of curse on me as there was on Cassandra. I can foretell the issue of any given situation, and feel the utmost confidence in the correctness of my conclusion, but though I can and do act on these indications, when they concern my own conduct I cannot use my power to benefit myself in any of the obvious ways. That is, I cannot leave my work even for a couple of days in order to make a fortune in stocks. To give an idea of the detailed accuracy of my divinations, let me quote one recent case.

I asked the *Yi King* in May 1922 what would happen to me in England, whither I was bound. I got the 21st Hexagram, which means the open manifestation of one's purpose. I was, in fact, able to re-enter public life after years of seclusion. It means 'union by gnawing', which I understood as bidding me to expect to spend my time in persevering efforts to establish relations with various people who could be useful to me, but not to expect to drop into success or to find the obstacles insuperable. This, too, came true. The comment in the *Yi King* promises successful progress and advises recourse to law. My progress was beyond my utmost hopes and I found myself forced to begin several lawsuits. The further comment describes the successive phases of the affair. The first phase shows its subject fettered and without resource. During my first month in England I was penniless, without proper clothes to wear, and obliged to walk miles to save the cost of a telephone call or an omnibus. In the second phase one suddenly finds everything easy. All one's plans succeed. This, too, occurred. The third phase shows a man getting to grips with the real problems; he meets some rebuffs, has some disappointments, but makes no mistakes. The third stage of my campaign could not be better described. In phase four one gets down to work at one's task, aided by financial advances and contracts to do work of the kind one wants. This was fulfilled by my being commissioned to write *The Diary of a Drug Fiend* and the present book, as well as several things for the *English Review*. The fifth phase shows the man getting on with his work and obtaining renown and profit thereby, but it warns the inquirer that his position is perilous and bids him to be on his guard while not swerving from his course. From this I understood that the publication of my novel would rouse a rumpus, as it did. The sixth and last phase shows the subject reduced to impotence and cut off from his communications. This was fulfilled by the attacks on me in the press which followed the publication of the novel.

I could not foresee the exact form which these various forces would manifest, but I understood the sort of thing I might expect. I decided to take the journey rather than wait for a time when a more encouraging symbol might be given. I felt that in the circumstances I had no right to expect anything better. The symbol promised success. I ought not to complain at paying its price.

So much for what I can do. Now for what I can't. I used to test my methods by predicting the course of political and economic events. They confirmed my calculations. Theoretically, I should have been able to back my opinion and make a fortune in a few days on the rate of exchange and similar speculations; but though I did not doubt for a second that success was certain, I found myself constitutionally incapable of fixing my attention on subjects which my instincts tell me to be none of my business, no matter how emphatically my conscious mind urges the necessity and propriety of so doing. This apparent impotence is really, I doubt not, the result of years of ruthless repression of every impulse that is not integrated absolutely with my true will. Judged by obvious standards, this austere puritanism hampers me; but, considered more deeply, I feel that my concentration is intensified, my potential increased, by such methods, and that when the course of time allows men to see my career in perspective it will become evident that my temporary failures were stones in the pyramid of my eternal success.

I now see the events of 1910 in this light. I do not regret my futility or even my errors. The attainment of the Grade of Magister Templi had to be paid for, and I might congratulate myself that the cashier accepted such worthless paper money as the mistakes and misfortunes of a man.

My new methods of Magick were so successful that we became more ambitious every day. I wrote a ritual for invoking the moon. The climax of the ceremony was this: Leila Waddell was to be enthroned as a representative of the goddess and the lunar influence invoked into her by the appropriate lyrics. (I wrote 'The Interpreter'[4] and 'Pan to Artemis'[5].) The violinist was to reply by expressing the divine nature through her art. She was a rough, ill-trained executant, and her playing coarse, crude, with no touch of subtlety to interpret or passion to exalt the sequence of sound. The most cynical critics present were simply stunned at hearing this fifth-rate fiddler play with a genius whose strength and sublimity was equal to anything in their experience. I quote from a half-article in the *Sketch* of August 24th. The writer is a financial journalist who thinks Magick a more brittle bubble than the most preposterous wild-cat scheme ever floated.

> Crowley then made supplication to the goddess in a beautiful and unpublished poem. A dead silence ensued. After a long pause, the figure enthroned took a violin and played—played with passion and feeling, like a master. We were thrilled to our very bones. Once again the figure took the violin and played an *Abendlied* so beautifully, so gracefully and and with such intense feeling that in very deed most of us experienced that ecstasy which Crowley so earnestly seeks. Then came a prolonged and intense silence, after which the Master of the Ceremonies dismissed us in these words: 'By the power in me vested, I declare the Temple closed.'
>
> So ended a really beautiful ceremony—beautifully conceived and beautifully carried out. If there is any higher form of artistic expression than great verse and great music I have yet to learn it. I do not pretend to understand the ritual that runs like a thread of magic through these meetings of the A∴ A∴..

I do not even know what the A.˙. A.˙. is. But I do know that
the whole ceremony was impressive, artistic and produced in
those present such a feeling as Crowley must have had when
he wrote—

> So shalt thou conquer space, and lastly climb,
>   The walls of time:
> And by the golden path the great have trod
>   Reach up to God!

I call special attention to this as evidence that Magick,
properly understood, performed and applied, is capable of
producing results of quite practical kinds. More yet, these
results involve no improbable theories. We can explain them
in terms of well-known laws of nature. I have always been
able to loose the genius which dwells in the inmost self of even
the most imperfect artist, by taking the proper measures to
prevent the interference of his conscious characteristics.

Neuburg himself furnishes a striking instance of this. When
I met him he was writing feeble verses of hardly more than
undergraduate merit. Under my training he produced some
of the most passionate, intense, musical and lofty lyrics in the
language. He left me; the dog hath returned to his vomit again,
and the sow that was washed, to her wallowing in the mire.
His latest work is as lifeless and limp as it was before I took
hold.

The success of this form of invocation led me to develop the
method. A large number of masonic rituals were at my
disposal, and their study showed that the ancients were accustomed to invoke the gods by a dramatic presentation or
commemoration of their legends. I decided to bring this
method up to date, while incidentally introducing into such
rituals, passages whose sublimity would help to arouse the
necessary enthusiasm by virtue of its own excellence. With
these ideas in mind, I constructed seven rituals to the planets.

In two of these I was assisted by a man named George
Raffalovitch, whose father was a Jewish banker of Odessa,
and whose mother a countess descended from one of the
ministers of finance under Napoleon. Born in Cannes, he had
been taken for the army very much against his will. The result
was a notorious lawsuit to determine his status.

Coming of age, he had squandered his millions. No extravagance was too imbecile. At one time he bought a travelling
circus with a menagerie and a collection of freaks. He should
certainly have been the principal attraction. He had come

almost to his last franc when he was pulled up by a *conseil de famille*. They saved a few thousand for the fool and kept him on short commons to teach him sense. He had snarled and become a socialist. I met him at the Gargotte off Holborn, being the only man there who looked at all like a gentleman. I paid him special attention. This suited him down to the ground. He saw a chance to cadge.

He agreed with me about socialism. It appeared that his motive in frequenting that milieu was identical with my own. He averred deep interest in Magick of which he had some slight dilettante knowledge. He won my sympathy in his controversy with his family. I promised to help him. I introduced him to influential people in high official positions who could help him to become naturalized. (As an Englishman he stood a better chance of getting free from the control of the *conseil de famille*.)

I also undertook the publication of some of his books. His talent was considerable. His imperfect acquaintance with English resulted in his inventing curiously fascinating terms of phraseology. He had remarkable imagination and a brilliant ability to use the bizarre. He made me the hero of several short stories under the name Elphenor Pistouillat de la Ratis-boisière and introduced several of my disciples. These stories describe in fantastic, exaggerated and distorted images the circle of which I was the centre. The curious may consult *The Equinox*, vol. I, nos. II, III and IV, also his own book *The Deuce and All*.

I furthermore lent him considerable sums of money (of course without interest) at various times extending over three years by which time he had obtained possession of the salvage of his estate. He had also learnt the value of money. He repaid what I had lent him and then proposed to invest a portion of his capital in a joint stock company which I was at that time contemplating to run *The Equinox* on proper business lines. Negotiations were still in progress when I left London towards the end of 1909 for Algeria.

What was my amazement on my return to find that he had persuaded the people in charge that he had authority to act for me. They explained that he had come round and argued that he was going to be a director of the proposed company and therefore had power to conduct the business. The youth indubitably possessed the virtue of doing nothing by halves. He forged my name to endorse cheques payable to me, cashed them and enjoyed the proceeds. I gasped. I liked the man and had no quarrel with him, but I could not exactly pretend not to notice incidents of this kind. I tackled him about it. He played the innocent and really he was fundamentally such a half-witted creature that I could not be angry. Unfortunately, there was something worse—a matter that touched my honour. He had advertised *Liber 777* and stated as an inducement to purchasers that less than one hundred copies remained for sale. That was a lie and I could not brook the association of my name with the shadow of a false pretence. But the mischief was done. The only way out was to make the statement true, which was done by his purchasing the number of copies necessary to reduce my stock to ninety.

He refused to understand my objections to his pastime of testing the intelligence of bank clerks in the matter of judging whether his imitation of my endorsement would pass muster. He indignantly withdrew from the proposed company and I saw him no more.

Not till long after did I discover that all this time while he was living on my bounty he had indefatigably intrigued against me. For insidious cunning he was unrivalled. He had insinuated a thousand malignant falsehoods about me, to the ears of my closest friends without their even suspecting his intention to injure me. In this way he had alienated several of my nearest and dearest colleagues and his culminating triumph was that he succeeded in leading Fuller by the nose through a tortuous channel of dark devices to the gulf of a complete rupture.

Fuller had begun to behave in a totally unintelligible way. It was all so subtle that I could not put my finger on a single incident. It was a mere instinct that something was wrong. The climax came after Jones [6] vs *The Looking Glass*. Fuller had urged me to take action myself. When the verdict justified my judgment. Fuller hinted that he could not afford to be openly associated with *The Equinox*. He also tried to interfere with my conduct of the magazine and made it a condition of his continuing with *The Temple of Solomon the King* that I should surrender my control. I saw that he had a swelled head and determined to show him that he was not indispensable. I quietly dropped the subject and wrote the section in number five myself. Hoping this demonstration had reduced the inflammation I resumed the discussion and we had practically come to an agreement when to my breathless amazement he fired pointblank at my head a document in which he agreed to continue his co-operation on condition that I refrained from mentioning his name in public or private under penalty of paying him a hundred pounds for each such offence. I sat down and poured in a broadside at close quarters.

'My dear man,' I said in effect, 'do recover your sense of proportion, to say nothing of your sense of humour. Your contribution, indeed! I can do in two days what takes you six months, and my real reason for ever printing your work at all is my friendship for you. I wanted to give you a leg up the literary ladder. I have taken endless pain to teach you the first principles of writing. When I met you, you were not so much as a fifth-rate journalist, and now you can write quite good prose with no more than my blue pencil through the two of every three adjectives, and five out of every six commas. Another three years with me and I will make you a master, but please don't think that either I or the Work depend on you, any more than J. P. Morgan depends on his favourite clerk.'

To return, however, to the rituals. These seven were really seven acts of one play, for their order was necessary. The plot, briefly summarized, is this:

Man, unable to solve the Riddle of Existence, takes counsel of Saturn, extreme old age. Such answer as he can get is the one word 'Despair'.

Is there more hope in the dignity and wisdom of Jupiter? No; for the noble senior lacks the vigour of Mars and warrior. Counsel is in vain without determination to carry it out.

Mars, invoked, is indeed capable of victory: but he has already lost the controlled wisdom of age; in a moment of conquest he wastes the fruits of it, in the arms of luxury.

It is through this weakness that the perfected man, the Sun, is of dual nature, and his evil twin slays him in his glory. So the triumphant Lord of Heaven, the beloved of Apollo and the Muses is brought down into the dust, and who shall mourn him but his Mother Nature, Venus, the lady of love and sorrow? Well is it if she bears within her the Secret of Resurrection!

But even Venus owes all her charm to the swift messenger of the gods, Mercury, the joyous and ambiguous boy whose tricks first scandalize and then delight Olympus.

But Mercury, too, is found wanting. Now in him alone is the secret cure for all the woe of the human race. Swift as ever, he passes, and gives place to the youngest of the gods, to the Virginal Moon.

Behold her, Madonna-like, throned and crowned, veiled, silent, awaiting the promise of the Future.

She is Isis and Mary, Istar and Bhavani, Artemis and Diana.

But Artemis is still barren of hope until the spirit of the Infinite All, great Pan, tears asunder the veil and displays the hope of humanity, the Crowned Child of the Future.

I throw myself no bouquets about these Rites of Eleusis.[7] I should have given more weeks to their preparation than I did minutes. I diminished the importance of the dramatic elements; the dialogue and action were little more than a setting for the soloists. These were principally three; myself, reciting appropriate lyrics—this involved, by the way, my learning by heart many hundreds of lines of verse every week —Leila Waddell, violinist, and Neuburg, dancer. I sometimes suspect that he was the best of the three. He possessed extraordinary powers. He gave the impression that he did not touch the ground at all, and he would go round the circle at a pace so great that one constantly expected him to be shot off tangentially. In the absence of accurate measurements, one does not like to suggest that there was some unknown force at work, and yet I have seen so many undeniable magical phenomena take place in his presence that I feel quite sure in my own mind that he was generating energies of a very curious kind. The idea of his dance was, as a rule, to exhaust him completely. The climax was his flopping on the floor unconscious. Sometimes he failed to lose himself, in which case, of course, nothing happened; but when he succeeded the effect was superb. It was astounding to see his body suddenly collapse and shoot across the polished floor like a curling-stone.

The Rites of Saturn and Jupiter, repeated and revised constantly in the studio among ourselves, were admirable. Nothing of Maeterlinck's ever produced so overpowering an oppression as this invocation of the dark spirit of Time. The better one knew it, the more effective it was. Familiarity did not breed contempt. Even the sceptic was impressed when the officers circumambulate the temple and the audience are picked at random, one by one, to join the procession, the last to do so being reminded, 'Thou also must die!'

But what was sublimely effective when performed in private lost most of its power to impress when transferred to unsuitable surroundings. I had no available spare money, no knowledge of the tricks of stagecraft, no means of supplying the proper atmosphere. I would not condescend to theatricalism. I was much too hasty in preparing the latter rites and they were not thoroughly rehearsed. It may seem impossible that any creature possessed of a grain of common sense should have failed to foresee failure; but my incorrigible optimism persuaded me that the public were gifted with reverence, intelligence, imagination; and the gift of interpreting the most obscure symbolism.

The first rite was, however, on the whole a success. Most of the ceremony takes place in semi-obscurity, so that the audience were not worried by the uncongenial surroundings of Caxton Hall; their attention was focused on the points of interest because of the illumination surrounding them, and the histrionic incompetence of the officers was mercifully concealed from them by the gloom, so that the sublime language of the rite made its full impression. The action again gave imagination every chance, because its minutiae were indistinct as was appropriate to their character. For instance, when a traitor is discovered and put to death on the spot, that would have been comic in full light, but there was only the sudden alarm which broke off the ceremony, the swift inspection, the rush, the gestures of the avenger, the scream and then silence, followed by the dragging of the carrion through the darkness. The illusion was perfect.

The ceremony proceeds and no hint is given of its nature. The omens are disquieting, but no one knows their import. Every question is answered in terms which imply ineluctable doom, every hope instantly crushed to the earth by despair against which no appeal can possibly succeed. All aspiration, all ambition ends equally in death. Help is sought from behind the veil where, as has been supposed, is a shrine upon whose altar dwells the unknown god. But the veil is rent, all is empty, and the chief officer declares, 'Alas, there is no god!' An invocation is made that god may appear and the veil is rent from within. A figure is standing on the altar and he recites the paraphrase of one of Bradlaugh's sermons made by James Thomson in *The City of Dreadful Night*, 'O melancholy brothers, dark, dark, dark.' This superb dirge ends:

> But if you would not this poor life fulfil,
> Lo, you are free to end it when you will,
> Without the fear of waking after death.

Darkness falls, complete and sudden; a wild dance to the tomtom ends in the crash of the dancer's body at the foot of the altar. Silence. A shot. The ghastly flickering of incandescent sodium vapour then lights up the veil. The officers are seen with all the colour of their robes, and faces transformed to livid greens. The veil is drawn aside once more and there lies the Master himself, self-slain upon the altar, with the principal woman officer bending over him as Isis lamenting for Osiris. The light goes out once more and in the darkness the final dirge of utter helplessness wails on the violin. Silence again succeeds. Two officers, briefly and brutally, declare that the rite has been accomplished and the ceremony stops with startling suddenness.

It was certainly a stupendous idea, carried out in what, after all, was a simple, dignified, sublime and impressive manner. It might have been much better. Dramatic experience and command of accessories would have made it nothing short of tremendous. As it was the better class newspapers and magazines wrote sympathetic and laudatory criticisms of the most encouraging kind. If I had had the most ordinary common sense, I should have got a proper impresario to have it presented in proper surroundings by officers trained in the necessary technique. Had I done so I might have made an epoch in the drama, by restoring it to its historical importance as a means of arousing the highest religious enthusiasm.

There was, however, another side of London life which till that time I had hardly suspected: that certain newspapers rely for their income upon blackmail. And they thought me a suitable victim. In particular Horatio Bottomley, in *John Bull,* published a page of the foulest falsehoods. There is a large class of people in England who argue from their own personal experience that whenever human beings happen to be together in a subdued light they can have no idea in their minds but that of indecent assault.

Bottomley subsided at once on discovering that I was not likely to pay up and look pleasant; but there was at that time a paper, *The Looking Glass,* edited by an animal called De Wend Fenton. He printed a scurrilous attack on the ceremony and concluded by a threat to proceed to expose my personal misdeeds. He then rang up a mutual friend, and said that he hoped I was not offended, and that he would like to meet me at dinner to talk things over. My friend rang me up. I merely said, 'I take it that you don't want me to be blackmailed over your coffee.'

Fenton accordingly proceeded to publish article after article, packed with the most stupid falsehoods about me; some of them deliberate distortions of fifth-hand fact; some simple invention. To my surprise many of my friends took fright and urged me to bring a lawsuit for libel. Fuller, in particular, to my great surprise, was almost dictatorial about my duty. He had probably been persuaded by his brother, who was a junior partner in the firm of solicitors who had represented me in the matter of Mathers. I did not care one way or the other what I did, but I took counsel with two men whose knowledge of the world of men was indisputably great; one, a probationer, the Hon. Everard Fielding, the other, Raymond Radclyffe, who, though utterly indifferent to Magick, was passionately fond of poetry and thought mine first-class, and unrivalled in my generation. He edited a high-class financial weekly and was rightly reputed as the most incorruptible, high-minded and shrewd critic of the city. Their opinion was identical and emphatic: 'If you touch pitch you will be defiled,' said one. 'Fenton has been warned off the turf and his city editor has just come out of jail,' said the other. There was nothing to gain. *The Looking Glass* was bankrupt, living from hand to mouth on hush money. Its public was composed of stable boys, counter-jumpers who fancied themselves as sportsmen, and people whose only literary recreation consisted in reading smutty stories and jokes, or licking their lips over the details of the most sordid divorces, and gloating generally over the wickedness of the aristocracy.

Apart from this, my course had been made clear by my own Chiefs. It was almost as if they had foreseen the circumstances. The case was met by almost the last clause of 'The Vision and the Voice':

> Mighty, mighty, mighty, mighty; yes, thrice and four times mighty art thou. He that riseth up against thee shall be thrown down, though thou raise not so much as thy little finger against him. And he that speaketh evil against thee shall be put to shame, though thy lips utter not the littlest syllable against him. And he that thinketh evil concerning thee shall be confounded in his thought, although in thy mind arise not the least thought of him. And they shall be brought unto subjection unto thee, and serve thee, though thou willest it not.

I saw no objection to stating my position for the sake of sincere and worthy people who might, through ignorance of the facts, be turned away from truth. I accordingly availed myself of the editor of a high-class illustrated weekly, the *Bystander,* and wrote two articles explaining what the Rites of Eleusis were; how people might cultivate their highest faculties by studying them. I also published the text of the rites as a supplement to number six of *The Equinox*. I could not condescend to reply to personal abuse. God ignored Bradlaugh's challenge to strike him dead within the next five minutes, and the King does not imprison every street-corner socialist who attacks him. Only when such rumours as that of his secret marriage to Miss Beauchamp circulate among people sufficiently important to make it matter, does he deign to prosecute. The Headmaster of Eton had not protested when Bottomley accused him of advocating Platonic love. I was content to await the acquittal of history.

Again, as Nehemiah said, 'I am doing a great work and I cannot come down.' I was up to my neck in every kind of business, from the editing of *The Equinox* to the superintendence of the Order, apart from my own literary labours. I had no time for lawsuits. Besides, preoccupation with such matters means anxiety and unfits one for calm concentration on one's real business. It was also in a sense a point of honour with me not to interfere with the Masters.

What has time to say? We know what happened to Horatio Bottomley. I am glad to recall that when I heard of his arrest I wrote to tell him that I bore no malice and that I hoped he would be able to prove his innocence. I am indeed sincerely sorry that a man with such great qualities should have turned them to such poor purpose. What is the summary of it all? So many fools confirmed in their folly, so many base, vile passions pandered to; so many simple-minded folk swindled out of their savings. And, on the other side, so many years consumed in cheap coarse pleasures, soured by constant fears of being found out, and crowned by utter ruin worse than death at the hands of a pettier scoundrel than himself. Even by the standards of the uttermost disregard of moral and spiritual success, it is the extreme stupidity to be dishonest.

The fate of Fenton is less notorious, but is no less striking a testimony to the vigilance and might of the Masters. One of Fenton's mistresses had an admirer, a peer of the realm, prodigiously wealthy and extremely aged. She arranged with Fenton to marry the old man; he would die in the course of nature without too tedious waiting and the charms of the lady might even shorten it. But the peer still adorns the peerage! It is Fenton that sleeps with his fathers! I do not know any man or woman who has attacked, betrayed, calumniated or otherwise opposed my Work, who has not met with disaster. Some are dead, some are insane, some are in jail. The only exceptions are those whom I have protected from retribution by taking up arms for myself and thus inducing the Masters to stand aside and see fair play.

There is another side to the medal. Fenton, seeing that I was not to be dragged down into his dirt, introduced into his filthy articles the names of Allan Bennett and George Cecil Jones. Bennett was described as a 'rascally sham Buddhist monk' and it was suggested that (in common with everyone else I knew!) my relations with him were morally reprehensible. This was not likely to worry Allan meditating in his monastery upon the evils of existence and practising the precepts of the Buddha; but Jones was otherwise situated. He had married to the extent of four children. Family life and the contamination of commercial chemistry had insensibly drawn him from the straight path.

So he put on the armour of Saul, and Goliath made mincemeat of him. He went to a tame solicitor, a mild mystic addicted to alchemy; no doubt as congenial a companion for a chat in a club over a glass of lemonade as one could have found between Swiss Cottage and Streatham Common, but the last man in the world to scrap with a ruffian who had no idea of fair fighting. He briefed a barrister who had only recently been admitted, having previously been a solicitor. This man had to face some of the most formidable talent at the Bar.

The case occupied two days. I sat in court hardly able to contain my laughter. The farcical folly of the proceedings eclipsed Gilbert's *Trial by Jury.* Mr Schiller, an admirably adroit and aggressive advocate of the uncompromising, overbearing type, had everything his own way. He actually got the judge to admit the evidence of an alleged conversation which took place ten years earlier and had no reference whatever to Jones. The judge, Scrutton, was evidently bewildered by the *outré* character of the case. He even remarked that it was like the trial of *Alice in Wonderland.*

Mr Schiller constantly referred to me as 'that loathsome and abominable creature', though I was not represented in the case. The evidence against me was, first, my alleged remark in the spring of 1910, which even if I had made it, might have meant anything or nothing in the absence of any context; and, secondly, that the initials of four Latin 'finger-posts' out of several hundreds in one of my books made vulgar words,[8] such as may be found in Sir Thomas Malory, John Keats, Robert Browning, Shakespeare, Urquhart, Motteux and a host of other infamous pornographers. It would have been equally fair to rearrange the letters of the judge's surname to make a sentence describing a deplorable fact in pathology, and accuse his lordship of outraging propriety every time he signed a cheque.

The judge made rather malicious fun of both sides. Every few minutes some mysterious fact would crop up which I could explain better than anyone else. 'But surely,' the judge would murmur, 'the proper person to tell the court about this is Mr Crowley. Why don't you call Mr Crowley?' And both sides would deplore the impossibility of discovering where Mr Crowley was, though I was sitting in the court *lippis et tonsoribus notus*,[9] thanks to my unmistakable peculiarities—I will not say the majesty and beauty of my presence; having been familiarized to everybody in England by innumerable photographs as an explorer, poet, Magician, publisher, religious reformer, dramatist, theatrical producer, reciter and publicist.

The Looking Glass, of course, could not call me, because I should have immediately disclosed that the libel on Jones was only an incident in an elaborate attempt to blackmail, and Jones would not call me because he was afraid that my contempt for conventions, my scorn of discretion as merely a euphemism for deceit, and my confidence in the power of truth and in the integrity and intelligence of men in general, would lead me to make some damaging admission.

He was ill advised. The intensity of my enthusiasm, my candour and my sheer personality would have dominated the court. They would have been bound to understand that even my follies and faults testified to my good faith, high-mindedness and honour. No man with a personal axe to grind would have done such frank, fearless, imprudent things. I had never been conciliatory; I had never been a flatterer or an opportunist. Brand himself was not more contemptuous of compromise. Such a man may be misguided, wrong-headed, a maker of mischief, but he must be sincere. It would have been seen at once that the beliefs and prejudices of men meant nothing to me, that my eyes were fixed on the eternal, my mind conscious only of God, and my heart wholly filled with the love of the Light. However, he feared. He had forgotten the first words of his initiation, 'Fear is failure and the forerunner of failure.' Therefore he failed.

The only allegation against him was that he was my friend and colleague and he read into this the suggestion that our relations were criminal. The defendants denied that they had ever meant to make any such suggestion. The judge said in his summing up that, obscure as the case might be in many ways, one thing was clear: Mr Jones had sworn emphatically that he was innocent of the offence in question, the defendants had sworn that they had never at any time, and did not now, intend to suggest that he was guilty of any such conduct.

The jury retired. Apparently they saw something sinister in the unanimity of plaintiff, defendant and judge. They *breathed together*, so to speak, and the Latin for that was *conspiracy*. If nobody had suggested this atrocity, it was time someone did! They returned as radiant as they had departed distressed. They declared that the defendants had perjured themselves in denying that they had accused Mr Jones: that Mr Jones had perjured himself in denying his guilt; that the judge had made a fool of himself by directing them to believe the evidence on either side; that *The Looking Glass* had meant to accuse Mr Jones of felony; and, finally, that a felon he was.

My contact with civilization has taught me little and that little hardly worth learning. One sees only the superficial aspects of things and those as often as not are deceptive. One's comprehension is confused and incoherent; one's conclusions cancel each other out. But my two days in court did really add to my practical knowledge of *homo sapiens*. Jones had sworn so simply, sincerely, solemnly, earnestly and emphatically; Fuller had spoken up with soldierly straightforwardness. Against these were matched the almost insane pomposities of Mathers, a notorious rascal, the bombastic blusterings of Berridge, an ill-reputed doctor on the borders of quackery, who had blanched and stammered at the first word of cross-examination; the sly evasions of Cran, a solicitor whose shifty glance was itself enough to warn the veriest tyro in physiognomy not to believe a word he said; and the twelve good men and true had brought in a verdict against the evidence, against the judge's direction, against the psychology of the witnesses. And the sole ground for their verdict was that the existence of entirely unsupported suspicion of so horrible a crime proved that it must be justified.

It was the psychology of the Middle Ages. A man might or might not be guilty of murder, but witchcraft was so unimaginable an abomination that it was unthinkable that anyone could accuse people of it unless it were true. I remembered the case of Eckenstein. He had committed a crime too frightful to put into words and therefore he must be guilty. I had found it much the same with myself. Nobody seemed to care whether I had or had not done various things which anyone might be expected to do, but nobody seemed to entertain a doubt of my having done things impossible in nature. Nobody troubled to find out the facts about the simplest matters. People printed falsehoods about my family, my fortune, the best-known events of my life. There was no attempt to be consistent or probable. To edit a newspaper while undergoing penal servitude seemed to strike nobody as beyond my ability, and so on *ad nauseam*. Still more absurdly, trifles which are true of hundreds of thousands of people became charged with the most sinister significance when applied to myself. I have been accused of living in a farmhouse, as if only assassins so far forget themselves. If I turned down the light, it must be to conceal my crimes. If I turn it up, it proves my shamelessness. If I go to London, I must be fleeing from the police in Paris; if to Paris, from the police in London.

The result of the Jones case neither surprised nor shocked me. It simply confirmed me in my determination to do my work and nothing else but my work. It was none of my business whether what I did was popular. *The Pilgrim's Progress* would have been no better if its author had been a generally respected churchwarden instead of a jailbird, and no worse if he had been a highwayman instead of a tinker. One cannot even help oneself to become famous by any given methods. One may, indeed, push oneself into society where one does not belong for the moment. Compare the careers of Swinburne and Alfred Austin. The latter became Laureate, thanks to his sound Conservative principles and respectability, but it hasn't made any difference, even twenty years later, except to afford an instance of the utter absurdity, even from the most practical standpoint, of wasting a moment on anything but making one's work as perfect as possible.

Here is another paradox. There are plenty of people in the literary world who know all about this, yet they still expect intelligent people to do all these stupid things which they have just proved utterly useless, as if their efficacy had never been doubted. I remember one evening how somebody dropped in to tell me that I was being damaged by some silly scandal. I turned pale and began to breathe quickly, crossed to my bookcase and opened some volume of mine. I gave a great sigh of relief and came back, my face flooded with joy. 'Dear friend,' I said pointing to the page, 'your fear is quite ill founded.' For a moment I thought that a semi-colon might have been changed into a comma.

As to the other point, I sometimes wonder whether I have

not been affected by an incident of early childhood. My father used to go evangelizing the villages on foot. I would go with him. Sometimes he would give people tracts and otherwise deal straightforwardly, but sometimes he did a very cruel thing. He would notice somebody cheerfully engaged in some task and ask sympathetically its object. The victim would expand and say that he hoped for such and such a result. He was now in a trap. My father would say, 'And then?' By repeating this question, he would ferret out the ambition of his prey to be mayor of his town or what not, and still came the inexorable 'And then?' till the wretched individual thought to cut it short by saying as little uncomfortably as possible, 'Oh well, by that time I shall be ready to die.' More solemnly than ever came the question, 'And *then?*' In this way my father would break down the entire chain of causes and bring his interlocutor to realize the entire vanity of human effort. The moral was, of course, 'Get right with God.'

At this time the consciences of men were much exercised, as our fathers put it, with regard to the monument which Jacob Epstein had made for the tomb of Oscar Wilde in Père-Lachaise. This monument had been on exhibition in his studio in London for some months and the most delicately minded dilettanti had detected nothing objectionable in it. No sooner had it been put in the cemetery than the guardian objected to it as indecent. The Prefect of the Seine upheld him. I went to see it. I did not greatly admire it; I thought the general design lumpish and top-heavy, but the modelling of the winged sphinx, or whatever it was, seemed admirably simple and subtle. The aesthetic point was, however, not at stake. The attitude of the authorities was an insult and outrage to the freedom of art. The entire innocence of the statue made their action less defensible, though personally I do not believe in any restrictions based on prejudice. Great art is always outspoken and its effect on people depends on their minds alone. We have now discovered, in fact, that the most harmless phenomena of dreams really represent the most indecent and abominable ideas. If we choose to find an objectionable meaning in *Alice in Wonderland,* or determine to persuade ourselves that the frank oriental obscenities of the Bible are indecent, no one can stop us. Mankind can only rise above his lower self by facing the facts and mastering his instincts.

I was indignant at the insult to Epstein and to art in his

person. I therefore resolved to make a gesture on behalf of the prerogatives of creative genius. I printed a manifesto:

AU NOM DE LA LIBERTÉ DE L'ART

L'Artiste a le droit de créer ce qu'il veut!

Le beau monument d'Oscar Wilde au Père-Lachaise, chef d'oeuvre du sculpteur Jacob Epstein, quoique déjà mutilé et dégradé par ordre du Préfet de la Seine, reste toujours voilé.

A midi, Mercredi prochain le 5 Novembre, M. Aleister Crowley, le poète Irlandais, va le dévoiler. Venez lui prêter votre sympathie et votre aide, venez protester contre la tyrannie pudibonde et pornophile des bourgeois, venez affirmer le droit de l'Artiste de créer ce qu'il veut. Rendez-vous, Cimetière de Père-Lachaise, auprès du monument d'Oscar Wilde, à midi, Mercredi, 5 Novembre.

I had this distributed widely through Paris. My friend and landlord, M. Bourcier, shook his head very sadly. They would send soldiers, he said, 'with cannon and bayonet' to form a cordon round the monument and prevent me from removing the tarpaulin. Oh, will they? said I. So I opened my mind to an enthusiastic young American, who agreed to help me. We bought a coil of extremely fine and strong steel wire, which would be practically invisible in the dull November gloom. We waited till the gates were closed and then proceeded to attach the wire to the tarpaulin, so that from the shelter of a tree a couple of hundred yards away, a gentle pull would suffice to bring it away, I having cut through the cords which kept it in place in such a way that they held only by a fibre, apparently uninjured. I was to make no attempt to rush the military forces of the Republic, but make a speech on the outskirts. When I threw up my arm to apostrophize the empyrean, he was to pull the wires from his lurking place. These arrangements completed, we got out by explaining to the gatekeeper that we had lost our way.

The next day at the appointed hour, I went to the cemetery with one or two desperate adherents. A distinguished concourse of enthusiasts was awaiting the Darling of Destiny, the Warden of the Worthiness of Wilde, the Emancipator of the Ebullition of Epstein. We marched in solemn procession to the tomb. I was amused to observe that the patrols, immediately they saw us, scuttled away like rabbits. I supposed at first that they had gone to give warning, and expected to be arrested before the conclusion of the entertainment, but when we got to the tomb

I found no serried ranks of soldiers shouting, *'Il ne passeront pas!'* There was not a soul in sight!

I then understood that orders had been given on no account to interfere with the mad Irish poet. It rather took the wind out of my sails. I made my speech and unveiled Epstein's effort in the dull drizzling weather. It was a disheartening success. The affair, however, made a great noise in the newspapers, both in France and in England, and the funniest thing about it was that Epstein himself, the one person above all others who should have been gratified, one would have supposed, took my action in rather bad part.

I have always found Epstein's psychology very puzzling. He is a German Jew, born in the lower East Side of New York City, and his genius, like Rodin's, is purely natural. His conscious ideas are out of keeping with it and destroy it whenever he allows them to interfere. Thus, at one time, he got into the worst set of pretentious humbugs in London, those nonentities who proclaim tirelessly at the top of their voices how great they are, and how their pedantic principles are the truth, the whole truth and nothing but the truth. They theorize tediously in obscure cafés and produce either meaningless monstrosities or nothing at all.

Cubism, vorticism, dadaism, and such sectarian sillinesses all come to the same thing; they are embalmed intellectual fads, invented in order to prove that the imbecility of their adherents is sublime. Conscious of their incapacity they try to prove its perfection, just as a woman who squinted might try to persuade herself that cross eyes constitute a special charm. The fallacy lies in this: a work of art justifies itself by its direct magical effect on the observer. It is puerile to 'prove' that Pope is a better poet than Shakespeare because his classicism is worthier than the 'unhappy barbarism' (as Hume says) of the Elizabethan. Critical rules derived from analysis after the event are always impertinent. One cannot improve on Swinburne by using his merits more accurately than he did himself.

But Epstein allowed himself to be influenced by the pompous cocksureness of men who were not fit to cart his clay, and for a time tried to work on their principles instead of allowing his genius to express itself as it would, with disastrous results. I have myself made an ass of myself now and again, by trying to construct consciously according to my convictions. But at least I never let myself be influenced by the fashions of a clique.

I am reminded of an interesting circumstance which occurred in 1912. Epstein had made a Sun-God. Hearing this, I hurried to his studio. I thought it a sign that the ideas which moved me were independently penetrating other minds. 'Hullo,' said I, as I entered the studio; 'you've been doing the Man of Vitruvius, have you?' 'Man of what?' said Epstein. 'Vitruvius; you know—the Microcosm?' I might have been talking Choctaw. I could not believe that Epstein did not know all about it. But he did not know even which of his statues I was talking about. I pointed. 'Nonsense,' said he, 'that is my Sun-God. What has Vesuvius got to do with it?' I was struck dumb.

Vitruvius was (of course, but I suppose I had better explain!) the great Augustan architect, whose treatise on the subject is the supreme classic of its kind. He had discovered the rationale of beauty and similar moral ideas. He had demonstrated the necessity of adhering to certain proportions. It chanced that I had in my pocket a proof of one of the illustrations of my *Book Four*, Part II. I pulled it out and put it under his nose. In all essentials it was identical with Epstein's idea of the Sun-God. The astounding thing is not this mere similarity, but the fact that Epstein had called it by that name; for the man of Vitruvius is really the Sun-God. It is the symbol which unifies the centre of our system with the true nature of man.

The genius of Epstein had expressed through him a mystical fact of supreme importance, without the aid of any intellectual process. It was one more instance of my theory that direct intuition is capable of discerning *a priori* truths as adequately as the inductive method of intellect reveals them *a posteriori*. Its results are equally reliable, or more so, when their medium is genius, and this in its turn is its own all-sufficient witness by virtue of its power to express itself in beauty. 'Beauty is truth; truth, beauty' has thus a precise logical meaning; it is not merely a poetical fancy.

Our appreciation of a sonnet and a syllogism is aroused by identical qualities in our nature. The same principle applied to each impression produces reactions whose interrelation is necessary. It is not merely a matter of taste to prefer Rembrandt to Dana Gibson. It implies a corresponding perception of scientific and philosophical problems. When men who agree about Goya disagree about geology, one may deduce confidently that there is somewhere a failure of self-comprehension on one subject or the other, for all our opinions are partial expressions of our essential spiritual structure. This fact may be used to detect the sources of error in one's own mind. I have often been able to correct my views of some problem in mathematics or physics by referring them to some artistic standard. Having detected where the incompatibility lies, it becomes clear where to look for the misunderstanding.

The Oscar Wilde monument was fated to furnish further amusement. With unparalleled insolence, the authorities decided to mutilate Epstein's work. They employed a sculptor, who must, by the way, have been utterly lost to all sense of shame, to fix a bronze butterfly over the 'objectionable' feature of the monument. This feature had been quite unnoticeable to any but the most prurient observer. The butterfly, being of different material and workmanship, clamoured for attention to exactly that which it was intended to make people forget.

' This incidentally is a characteristic of puritan psychology. Nobody would notice that side of nature to which those folk whose goodness resents that of God, attach a 'bad' meaning, if they did not persistently emphasize its existence. The bad taste of this outrage went even further. The butterfly was notoriously the emblem of Whistler, whose controversies with Wilde were so savagely witty. To put this on the very symbol of Wilde's creative genius was the most obscene insult which could have been imagined. Martial never composed an epigram so indecently mocking.

I did not know that this outrage had been perpetrated. I had gone to the cemetery simply to see if the tarpaulin had been replaced. I confess that I fully enjoyed the flavour of this foul jest. It was all the more pungent because unintentional. (The idea had been simply to make a quiet, inconspicuous modification. It is really strange how polite propriety is always stumbling into Rabelaisian jests. I remember, for instance, writing in some article for the New York *Vanity Fair*, 'Science offers her virgin head to the caress of Magick.' The editor thought the word 'virgin' a little risky and changed it to 'maiden'!)

Recovering from the first spasm of cynical appreciation, I saw that there was only one thing to be done in the interests of common decency and respect for Epstein. I detached the butterfly and put it under my waistcoat. The gatekeeper did not notice how portly I had become. When I reached London, I put on evening dress and affixed the butterfly to my own person in the same way as previously to the statue, in the interests of modesty, and then marched into the Café Royal, to the delight of the assembled multitude. Epstein himself happened to be there and it was a glorious evening. By this time he had understood my motives; that I was honestly indignant at the outrage to him and determined to uphold the privileges of the artist.

68

The rites being over, and their lesson learnt, I felt free to go back to my beloved Sahara. As before, I took Neuburg with me and motored down from Algiers to Bou Saâda to economize time. We proposed to take a more extended itinerary. There were certain little-known parts of the desert within comparatively easy reach. It was part of the programme to obtain visions of the sixteen Sub-Elements, as a sort of pendant to the Aethyrs, but the time was not yet. We began, but the results were so unsatisfactory that we broke off. I have, of course, no doubt that success depends entirely upon working for it, but it is ultimately as impossible to perform a given Operation in Magick to order as it is to write a poem to order, however one's technical ability seems to promise success.

Experiences of this sort ultimately taught me that the will which is behind all magical working is not the conscious will but the true will. Success depends therefore, firstly, on making sure that one's powers are equal to any required demand; but, secondly, upon learning the kind of work for which they are really wanted. It is an excellent training, no doubt, to plug ahead perseveringly in the most discouraging conditions. Indeed the professional is better than the amateur mainly because he has had to struggle on day after day; but this is a question of early training. When one has come to the height of one's powers, one still has one's 'days off'.

This second journey in the Sahara took us much deeper into desolation. We had two camels and a man to drive them and a boy to look after the camels. We picked up occasional wayfarers as we went, and dropped them again, in the most charmingly casual way. At our first halt we enjoyed the hospitality of a famous sheikh who had established a sort of mystical university in that obscure corner of the world. We found him a courteous host and a most enlightened scholar. One of the advantages of spiritual development is the confirmation of one's results which one obtains from similarly disposed people whom one meets. There is a real freemasonry among such men, which does not depend upon formula and dogma. The instinctive sympathy proves that one has done right to climb beyond conscious conclusions. In the kingdom of spirit is freedom.

Our course took us across a chain of mountains. It was a beautiful morning, with but a touch of north-west wind. We were feeling very fit; I had forgotten all about England and we began to congratulate ourselves on another pleasant journey. I suppose the north-west wind was eavesdropping.

We had some food in an unexpected and decayed hovel about noon; for the wind had got up sufficiently to make it too cold to sit about. An hour later we struck for the mountains. It was a really fine mountain pass; the descent a splendid gorge, precipice-walled. The camel driver wanted to pitch camp about three o'clock and we had trouble with him.

Camel drivers have no sense at all; in England they would get either the Embankment or the Home Office. This imbecile had been all his life in the desert and had not yet learnt that he and his camel needed food. He never took any with him, and having reached a suitable spot thirty miles from the nearest blade of grass, complained of hunger.

I had hoped he would have found some thistles.

This by parenthesis. We wandered on and presently emerging from the gorge came upon an Arab, who spoke of a Bedouin encampment downstream.

This we found a few minutes after nightfall. The wind was violent and bitter beyond belief, but no rain fell. 'Rain never falls south of Sidi Aissa.'

So we fed and turned in. Our tent was an Arab lean-to, a mere blanket propped on sticks, some necessary to its support, others designed to interfere with the comfort of the people inside.

My disciple, fatigued by the day's march, fell asleep.

As it happened—pure luck, for he had no more sense than the camel driver; disciples never have!—he had chosen the one possible spot. As for me, I woke in about half an hour to feel the most devilish downpour. It was as bad as Darjeeling and the ridge that leads to Kangchenjunga. We had pitched the tent in a fairly sheltered spot under the walls of the river; but the rain ran down the props of the tent and through the tent itself, and soaked us.

In the morning, after a night spent in that condition when one is half asleep from exhaustion and half awake from misery, the storm still blew.

We waited till nearly nine. The Bedouins told us that four

miles on there was a village. We thought of coffee and made tracks. So off we went over the sopping desert and reached the 'village' in an hour. There were palms and gardens—and one deserted hovel, with no door. The roof, made of boughs weighted with big stones and made tight with mud, was half broken through. A giant stone hung imminent, half-way fallen. All day we waited for the rain to stop falling in the place 'where it never fell'.

Night came and the blizzard redoubled its violence; but the shelter allowed us a little sleep until the mud dissolved and the roof became a sieve. The rest of the night was a shower-bath.

In the morning there was no great sign of improvement. I had to kick the camel driver into action and chase the camels with my own fair feet. He had a million excuses for not going on, all on a level. 'The camels would catch cold'—good from the man who had left them all night in the rain! 'They would slip.' 'They would die.' 'They were too hungry.'—From the man who hadn't brought food for them! 'They were tired'—and so on. But I got the party off at last and came in a couple of hours to a tomb with a coffin in it. There they sat down and refused to stir. I simply took no notice. My disciple took one camel and I took the other, and went off. We left them in the tomb, grousing.

Steering by map and compass, I judged a good pass through the next range of mountains, and made for it. The flat desert was standing in water; and the streams were difficult for the camels, who hate water as much as disciples do.

It was better on the mountainside. Near the top of the pass we perceive our men following, as the lesser of two evils. I was sorry, in a way; it would have been a fine adventure to worry through to Sidi Khaaled with these two brutes and a daft Davie!

It was just as the top was reached that I said, without any apparent reason, 'The storm's over.' My disciple did his Thomas act. There was no opening in the furious grey heaven; the wind raged and the rain poured. But I stuck to it; I had felt the first contention of the south wind in a momentary lull. I was right.

The descent of the pass was far from easy. The 'road' crosses and recrosses the bed of the river as often as it can; sometimes even follows the course.

And this stream was a furious spate, slippery and dangerous for men, impassable for members of the Alpine Club, and almost impassable for camels. It was nearly nightfall before we left the gorge and a barren plain confronted us.

It was useless to struggle on much further. The rain still poured; the desert stood six inches deep in water. The hills were a mass of snow.

(We heard later that many houses had been washed away at Ouled Djellal in this unprecedented storm. Traffic was interrupted by snow on the East Algerian Railway, and the *Maréchal Bugeaud* was forty hours late at Marseilles, having had to beat up under the lee of the Spanish shore for shelter.)

So I picked out a good big tree by the stream and we pitched camp.

We had little hope of lighting a fire; but there is in the desert a certain impermeable grass, and by using this as a starter, we got it going. No sooner had the blaze sprung up, filling the night with golden showers of sparks, than the envious stars determined to rival the display. Every cloud disappeared as by magic. But the fire remained the popular favourite!

All night I toiled to dry myself and my clothes, refreshing the old Adam with coffee, potted pheasant and Garibaldi biscuits at not infrequent intervals.

The morning was ecstasy. The light came over the sand, wave upon wave of grey. The desert was dry. There was no water in the stream, save in rare pools. We struck camp early.

We glanced up at the path which we had travelled; the ranges still glowed with unaccustomed snow; from the northwest the wind still struggled fitfully to assert its dominion, but we, with joy and praise in our hearts, turned our glad faces, singing to the assurgent sun.

The most interesting village on our route was Ouled Djellal. It was quite a tiny place, but there is a hovel which calls itself an European hotel, kept by a strayed Frenchman. The village boasts a barn where one can go every night and watch dancing girls. I need not describe their doings, but I may say that this is the only form of amusement that I have ever found of which I never get tired. I like to drop in pretty early and sit there all through the night, smoking tobacco, or kif,[1] and drinking coffee, cup after cup.

The monotonous rhythm of sound and movement dulls the edge of one's intellectual activity in very much the same way as a mantra. The finest concerts and operas, or such spectacles as the Russian ballet, alleviate the pain of existence by putting a positive pleasure to work against the pale persistent pang; but, as the Buddha has shown, the remedy increases the disease. I have long since come to the point in which I could say that I had enjoyed all possible forms of delight to the utmost possible extent. I am not blasé; I can still enjoy everything as well as I ever could. More: I know how to extract infinite rapture from the most insignificant incidents, but this faculty depends on the refusal to accept such currency at its own valuation. This being so, it is on the whole easier to obtain pleasure from those things which soothe rather than from those things which excite.

It has just struck me that these remarks may seem very perverse. Average people associate Arab dances with animal excitement. Such an attitude enables me to diagnose their case. They are for the most part incapable of true passion, but their emotions are so disordered and uncontrolled that at the slightest touch they give a leap and a squeal. Puritanism in the conventional sense of the word is, in fact, a neurosis. One ought to possess one's physical powers in the greatest measure, but they should be so collected and controlled that they cannot be excited by inadequate stimulation.

The puritan is always trying to make it impossible for those things which frighten him to exist. He does not understand that sensibility is not to be cured by protecting it from the obvious stimuli. The diseased tissue will merely begin to react to all sorts of contacts which have a merely symbolic relation with the original perils. This psychological fact is at the basis of such phenomena as fetishism. The saint hurries to the Thebaid to avoid the danger of Thais, only to find that the very stones rise up and take her place. Neuburg had a friend who had a friend who was an anarchist. He would not drink cocoa 'because it excited his animal passions'.

Little as I have seen of the Sahara, I have reconstructed its story in outline to my own satisfaction. I am convinced that the earth is slowly losing its water and that this explains what one sees in the Mediterranean basin, without assuming catastrophic changes in the earth's crust. We know the glaciers are generally retreating. We know that in the time of Horace snow fell heavily and lay long in the Roman winter.

In Tunisia, the railway from Sousse to Sfax, which crosses the desert like a chord whose arc is the bulge of the coast between these towns, passes a village called El-Djemm. This is an isolated spot; there is no fertile country anywhere near it. It consists of a cluster of Arab huts in the gap of a coliseum. This structure was at one time the headquarters of a formidable gang of brigands and the gap was made by the artillery sent to smoke them out.

The point is that this coliseum is a tremendous affair. The old town must have sheltered at least five thousand people, more likely four times that number. How did these people live? One is bound to assume that in those days the country was fertile. In the absence of rivers, this means regular and plentiful rains. Again, the northern districts of the Sahara are full of large chott or lakes, many of which are below the present level of the sea. A French engineer, in fact, proposed to dig a canal from near Sfax so as to replenish a string of chott which extends inland for about two hundred and fifty miles. He thought, and I agree, that the existence of these vast shallow reservoirs would automatically change the climate, as the irrigation of Egypt by English enterprises has made a perceptible difference in that of Cairo within a decade. The trouble is, how to keep them from silting up.

The upshot of all this is that many of the travellers' tales of people like Pliny, Strabo and Plato need no longer be scouted as fantastic. I at least see no reason to doubt the existence of extensive civilizations in North Africa within the last five thousand years. Their decay and total disappearance is explained quite easily by the gradual failure of the water supply. To the eye of a god, mankind must appear as a species of bacteria which multiply and become progressively virulent whenever they find themselves in a congenial culture, and whose activity diminishes until they disappear completely as soon as proper measures are taken to sterilize them.

'Westward the Star of Empire takes its way' sounds splendid, but it is really very silly. Since I have understood that I am the Spirit of Solitude, Alastor, I have learnt to look at life from a standpoint beyond it. The affairs of the parasites of the planet, including Aleister Crowley, appear abject and absurd. I cannot pretend to take them seriously. The only object in attaching oneself to an individual is to have a standard suitable for symbolic representation of certain phenomena which happen to interest one, though they cannot possibly possess any importance for one, and the only reason for interesting oneself in the welfare of any such individual is to increase the efficiency of one's instrument of perception. This, then, explains why the only intelligent course of action for a man is to obtain initiation. Even this is useless in itself. The highest attainment is insensate except in reference to the convenience of an intelligence who is not in any way involved in the individuality of its instrument.

The desert is a treasure house. One soon gets behind the superficial monotony. Each day is full of exquisite incidents for the man who understands how to extract the quintessence. It is impossible to describe such a journey as ours. The events of a single day would fill a fat folio. The more obvious adventures are really the least memorable, yet these are the only things which are capable of description. We were sometimes obliged, for example, to push on at a great pace in order to reach a place where we could renew our water supply. On one occasion we covered a hundred miles in two days and a half. The last stage was pretty bad. It taught me a useful lesson about physical endurance.

Most men who have practised athletics, even mildly, know the meaning of the phrase 'second wind'. One's original enthusiasm being exhausted, one goes on quietly and steadily, almost unsusceptible to fatigue. A night's rest restores one completely; and, given proper food, one can go on day after day for an indefinite period before getting stale.

But few men, fortunately for themselves, know that there is such a thing as 'third' wind. One's second wind wears off and one is overcome by such severe fatigue that one cannot struggle against it. One feels that one must rest or break down entirely, as one did at the end of one's first wind, only far more fiercely. If, however, when one's second wind fails one knows that life depends on going on, the third wind comes into court. In this state one is almost anaesthetized. One has become an absolute machine, incapable of feeling or thinking; one's actions are automatic. The mind is just capable of making connections with such circumstances as bear on the physical problem, though men of weak will, and those in whom the habit of self-control is not established inexpugnably, are sometimes subject to hallucinations. The famous mirage is sometimes seen apart from optical hallucination. Delirium often occurs.

There seems no reason why one should ever stop once one has got on to this third wind. I take it that one does so exactly as a steam engine stops; when the physical conditions constrain one.

Once one has got one's third wind a single night's repose is no longer adequate; it seems as if one had outraged nature. I have found that whether I walked on third wind one hour, or thirty-six, the reaction was pretty much the same. On this occasion we had to lie up for two days before we could go on. The psychology of this stage was interesting. While we were walking across totally featureless desert, we were simply unconscious, entirely inaccessible to any impression; but the sight of an oasis, by arousing hope, awoke us to a consciousness of our physical agony. The last mile was an interminable atrocity. When we reached the palms the shade gave us no relief whatever; the improved physical conditions simply intensified our sufferings, for we could not rest before reaching the houses.

One of the effects of travel of this kind, as opposed to the regular expedition, with its definite objective and its consequent insulation from the current of ordinary life, is that every incident acquires an intense and absolute value of its own. One can, for example, love as it is utterly impossible to do in any other conditions. Every moment of one's life becomes charged with unimaginable intensity, since there is nothing to interfere with one's absorption. The multiplicity of incident in civilized life makes even the holiest honeymoon a medley; delight is dulled by distraction.

The secret of life is concentration, and I have attained this power despite every original disadvantage, not so much by virtue of my persistence in the practices which tend to improve one's technique, but by my determination to arrange my affairs on the large scale so as to minimize the possibilities of distraction. The resolve to read no newspapers, to see as few people as possible, to read or write during meals, to live so that the petty problems of every day are as few and easily dispatched as possible—all these measures have made me less a man than the Spirit of Solitude. Every impression I receive is interpreted more analytically and yields a more intense integration than a thousand such to most other men. My life has been calm, simple, free from unusual or exciting incidents, and yet I often feel that I have lived more fully than many men of affairs.

Another result has naturally been that I have learnt to assess experiences by a totally different scale from that of other people. Some points of view never strike me at all. For instance, a publisher once wrote to me, 'We cannot publish such and such a book until'—various things happen, which had nothing to do with the contents of the book as such. I was literally aghast. To me a book is a message from the gods to mankind; or, if not, should never be published at all. Then what does it matter who writes it, what the circumstances may be commercially, socially or otherwise? A message from the gods should be delivered at once. It is damnably blasphemous to talk about the autumn season and so on. How dare the author or publisher demand a price for doing his duty, the highest and most honourable to which a man can be called? The only argument for surrounding publication with any conditions is that the message may be better understood in some circumstances than in others. I can imagine a series of syllogisms on which one might base an apology for many of the actual principles of publishing. The point, however, is that (as I suppose) the author is the hierophant or oracle of some god, and the publisher his herald.

I left Neuburg in Biskra to recuperate and returned to England alone. No sooner had I settled in my compartment than I was seized by an irresistible impulse to write a play dealing with the Templars and the Crusades. I had had with me in the desert the rituals of freemasonry, those of the Scottish, Memphis and Mizraim Rites. A plan had already been mooted for me to reconstruct freemasonry, as will be later described. The ritual of the 30° had taken hold of my imagination. The idea of my proposed play, *The Scorpion*,[2] sprang into life full-armed.

I have always found that unless I jump on such inspiration like a tiger, I am never able to 'recapture the first fine careless rapture'. I accordingly jumped out of the train at El Kantara and wrote it that evening and next day. I had done little creative work during the walk. My Retirements, as a rule, especially when they involve physical hardship, keep me in intimate communion with the universe and rarely dispose me to write the result. I lie fallow and the expression of ecstasy follows my return to physical comfort and leisure.

My last important work had been done at Marseilles on the way out, where we had to wait two days for a boat to take us to Algiers. I spent the time in writing the essay on the Cabbala which appears in *The Equinox* vol. I, no. v. I had no books of reference at hand and therefore put down only what was in my memory. This is a good plan. It prevents one from over-burdening the subject with unimportant details. In one's library one is obsessed by the feeling that one should aim at completeness and this is a grievous error. One wants to include only those elements which have proved their vitality by making a clear permanent impression on the mind.

I am not sure and find no record of the writing of 'The Blind Prophet',[3] but it may well have been during this wonderful week. It is an attempt at a new form of art, a combination of ballet and grand opera. The predominant vowels in any passage indicate an appropriate passion. Thus 'i' goes with shrillness and the violin; 'o' and 'u' coo, like flutes. The Blind Prophet represents the deep broad *a;* the Queen of the Dancers the fluent *e*. With this sound scheme, goes a colour scheme.

The Prophet is a high-priest of a temple, and it is understood that if he utters a certain word the building will be destroyed. He woos the Queen of the Dancers; she mocks and eludes him. He utters the word; the pillars fall and crush him, but nobody else is hurt. The chorus rises again in the identical melody of its original dance.

The idea of the play is this: that the senseless forces of nature are indestructible and obey no master. The scheme of the rhythm and rime is extremely complex and the execution extraordinarily fluent. For sheer verbal music it was one of the best things that I had done. I found myself able to introduce internal rimes at very short intervals, without in any way interfering with the rhythm or the sense. There is no distortion of grammar, no difficulty in reading.

> Hush! hush! the young feet flush,
> The marble's ablush,
> The music moves trilling,
> Like wolves at the killing,
> Moaning and shrilling
> And clear as the throb in the throat
> of a thrush.

During the journey I wrote 'The Pilgrim',[4] 'Return' and 'On the Edge of the Desert', lyrics inspired by the idea of getting back to my inamorata in London.

In Paris I wrote 'The Ordeal of Ida Pendragon'.[5] The hero, Edgar Rolles, meets a girl at the Taverne Panthéon (where I wrote the story) and takes her to a fight between a white man and a Negro, the latter suggested by Joe Jeannette, whom I had just seen and much admired for his physical beauty. He takes her to his studio and recognizes her as a member of the Order. He proposes to put her through the ordeal of crossing the Abyss. She fails and they part. Ida meets the Negro, who loves her. Rolles and Ninon (Nina Olivier already mentioned) lunch with them. Ida takes pleasure in torturing the Negro and begs him to 'respect her modesty'—which she has not got. The Negro suddenly understands that she is heartless and sinks his teeth in her throat. Rolles kills him with a kick. He then consults one of the Secret Chiefs, who advises him to take Ida away. He tells Rolles that she has passed through the Abyss after all. The formula is that perfect love is perfect understanding. He marries her and a year later she dies in childbirth, saying that she has given herself three times, once to the brute, once to the man and now to God. Her previous failure had been to surrender herself. She wanted to get everything and give nothing.

This story marks a stage in my own understanding of the formula of initiation. I began to see that one might become a Master of the Temple without necessarily knowing any technical Magick or mysticism at all. It is merely a matter of convenience to be able to represent any expression as $x + y = 0$. The equation may be solved without words. Many people may go through the ordeals and attain the degrees of the A∴ A∴ without ever hearing that such an Order exists. The universe is, in fact, busy with nothing else, for the relation of the Order to it is that of the man of science to his subject. He writes $CaCl_2 + H_2SO_4 = CaSO_4 + 2HCl$ for his own convenience and that of others, but the operation was always in progress independently.

Arrived in England, my Pegasus continued its tameless spurt. One after the other I wrote 'The Electric Silence',[6] a fairy-story summary of my magical career; 'The Earth',[7] a short essay on her, both as planet and as element, in which I express my filial and conjugal relation with her. It is an ecstatic dithyramb.

Finally I wrote 'Snowstorm'.[8] This is a play in three acts, but once again I have tried to introduce a new artistic form.

Leila Waddell was to play the part of the heroine, but as she was incapable of speaking on the stage, I had to write her part as a series of violin solos.

The current of creative ecstasy stopped as suddenly as it had begun and I went on from Eastbourne to London. I found everything in confusion. I did not realize that the *esprit de corps* which is the essence of such books as *The Three Musketeers* was as dead as duelling. The men who had clustered round me enthusiastically when I seemed successful had dispersed like the disciples when they found that the Pharisee meant business. They all knew perfectly well that the attacks on me were malicious nonsense, that Jones's fiasco was a mere accident due to over-confidence; but they were all, with very few exceptions, cowards to the bone. They were as afraid of nothing as so many babies in the dark, expecting to see the bogey man come down the chimney.

I suppose the proper thing would have been to have 'rallied

my desperate followers', but the fact is that I am congenitally incapable of beating the big drum. Most leaders induce their followers to fight in haste and leave them to repent at leisure. I always feel that this sort of thing is somehow unfair and in the long run useless. I am content to wait until people back me up wholeheartedly without the press gang or the revival meeting. I carried on imperturbably, exactly as if nothing whatever had happened. My utmost condescension was to print 'X-Rays on Ex-Probationers', three short contemptuous epigrams.

MISTAKES OF MYSTICS

I. Since truth is supra-rational, it is incommunicable in the language of reason.

II. Hence all mystics have written nonsense, and what sense they have written is so far untrue.

III. Yet as a still lake yields a truer reflection of the sun than a torrent, he whose mind is best balanced will, if he become a mystic, become the best mystic.

When a friend of mine, or an enemy either, gets into trouble, I go or write to him immediately and put myself entirely at his disposition. I don't so much as ask whether he is in the right or no, unless that knowledge is necessary to efficient help. I can hardly explain why I act in this extraordinary way, but I think the theory is somewhat as follows: I being in relation with the man, he is a part of my individuality, and my duty to myself is to see that he is flourishing. If I sprain my ankle I must use all my resources to put it right, and even if my ankle has damaged me in the course of the accident, by allowing me to fall and bump my head, my interests are none the less bound up with it. I make no pretence of magnanimity; it is plain self-interest which determines my action. I am even simple enough to expect everybody else to be equally selfish, but I have found that even my best friends, with few exceptions, run away or cool off whenever I need their assistance.

I also find that I am not understood. I remember an incident in America. A man who purported to be an occult teacher, and was in reality an ignorant charlatan, had been the object of my onslaught. He had every reason to regard me as his bitterest enemy. In course of time, he was found out and arrested. I went at once to the police court. Only one of his hundreds of devoted followers—and they were extravagantly devoted, thought he was no less than Jesus Christ come back to earth, and allowed him to mock, bully and swindle them to the limit without losing faith in him—had stuck to him in his

misfortune. I went to him and affirmed my belief in his innocence (he had been 'framed up' on a false charge) and offered
to go bail for him and help him in every possible way. He was
acquitted and we resumed our enmity.

I am glad to say that, some time afterwards, when some
would-be magicians sent spies round the country to get information about me from people who did not know me, he spoke
up on my behalf. This could hardly have happened in England, where moral cowardice is in the marrow of every man's
bones. However vile and venal a man's accusers may be, and
however obviously absurd may be the charges brought against
him, the very men who have been boasting of their friendship
for the great man scuttle into obscurity—at the best; more
often, they join in the hue and cry in the hope of escaping the
suspicion of having once been in league with the offender. In
England today a plain denial like Peter's must count as extravagant loyalty! To me the psychology is heartbreaking, not as
it may affect me directly, but because I hate to think so badly
of men. The standards of *The Three Musketeers* are mine, and
the blackest blot in the book is the partial failure of Aramis.
It is far worse than the conduct of Milady at its vilest.

I believed then, and believe now, that the probationer of
A∴A∴ is nearly always offered the opportunity to betray
the Order, just as the neophyte is nearly always tempted by a
woman. We read in *The Book of the Law*, cap. I, verse 34:

> *The ordeals I write not.*

> *He (the Beast) may make severe the ordeals. (v. 38) There is
> a word to say about the Hierophantic task. Behold! there are
> three ordeals in one, and it may be given in three ways. The
> gross must pass through fire; let the fine be tried in intellect,
> and the lofty chosen ones in the highest! (v.50)*

> *The ordeals thou shalt oversee thyself, save only the blind
> ones. Refuse none, but thou shalt know & destroy the traitors.
> I am Ra-Hoor-Khuit; and I am powerful to protect my servant.
> (cap. III, v. 42)*

These 'blind' ordeals presumably refer to such tests of fitness as that of which we have been telling. In the ancient
mysteries it was possible to appoint formal ordeals. A young
man would go into the Temple to be initiated and he would
know perfectly well that his life might depend on his proving
himself worthy. Nowadays the candidate knows that his ini-
tiators will not murder him, and any ordeal proposed by them

obviously appears a pure formality. In Freemasons' Hall he can swear quite cheerfully to keep silence under the penalty of having his throat cut across, his tongue torn out, and all the rest of it; the oath becomes a farce.

In the A∴A∴, which is a genuinely Magical Order, there are no extravagant oaths. The candidate is pledged quite simply to himself only, and his obligation binds him merely 'to obtain the scientific knowledge of the nature and powers of my own being'. There is no penalty attached to the breach of this resolution; yet, just as this resolution is in contrast with the oaths of other orders in respect of simplicity and naturalness, so also with regard to the penalties. To break away from the A∴A∴ does actually involve the most frightful dangers to life, liberty and reason. The slightest mistake is visited with the most inexorable justice.

What actually happens is this. When a man ceremonially affirms his connection with the A∴A∴ he acquires the full powers of the whole Order. He is enabled from that moment to do his true will to the utmost without interference. He enters a sphere in which every disturbance is directly and instantly compensated. He reaps the reward of every action on the spot. This is because he has entered what I may call a fluid world, where every stress is adjusted automatically and at once.

Thus, normally, suppose a man like Sir Robert Chiltern (in *An Ideal Husband*) acts venally. His sin is visited upon him, not directly, but after many years and in a manner which has no evident logical connection with his offence. If Chiltern had been a probationer of A∴A∴ his action would have been balanced at once. He had sold an official secret for money. He would have found within a few days that one of his own secrets had been betrayed, with disastrous consequence to himself. But furthermore, having switched on a current of disloyalty, so to speak, he would have found disloyalty damaging him again and again, until he had succeeded in destroying in himself the very possibility of ever again being disloyal. It would be superficial to regard this apparently exaggerated penalty as unjust. It is not sufficient to pay an eye for an eye. If you have lost your sight, you do not stumble over something once; you keep on stumbling, again and again, until you recover your sight.

The penalties of wrong-doing are applied not by the deliberate act of the Chiefs of the Order; they occur in the natural course of events. I should not even care to say that these events were arranged by the Secret Chiefs. The method, if I understand it correctly, may perhaps be illustrated by an analogy. Suppose that I had been warned by Eckenstein always to test the firmness of a rock before trusting my weight to it. I neglect this instruction. It is quite unnecessary for Eckenstein to go all over the world and put unreliable rocks in my way—they are there; and I shall come across them almost every time I go out climbing, and come to more or less grief whenever I meet them. In the same way, if I omit some magical precaution, or make some magical blunder, my own weakness will punish me whenever the circumstances determine the appropriate issue.

It may be said that this doctrine is not a matter of Magick but of common sense. True, but Magick *is* common sense. What, then, is the difference between the Magician and the ordinary man? This, that the Magician has demanded that nature shall be for him a phenomenal mode of expressing his spiritual reality. The circumstances, therefore, of his life are uniformly adapted to his work.

To take another analogy. The world appears to the lawyer quite otherwise than it does to the carpenter, and the same event occurring to the two men will suggest two quite different trains of thought and lead to two quite different results.

My own errors of judgment, due to the annihilation of my ego and the consequent lack of leadership felt by my body and mind, produced their own immediate effect. I did not yet understand the extent of my fault, or even its real cause and character, but I felt myself forced back into my proper orbit. I was the Spirit of Solitude, the Wanderer in the Wilderness. I had no business to take part in the affairs of men by personal contact with them in their sheepfolds, monkey houses and pigstys. My sole link with them was to guide such as adventured themselves into the desert. I was cast out from the Abyss into 'the heaven of Jupiter as a morning star or as an evening star. And the light thereof shineth even unto the earth and bringeth hope and help to them that dwell in the darkness of thought and drink of the poison of life.' It was therefore for me to attend strictly to the Great Work which had been appointed for me by the Secret Chiefs, to dwell in communion with mine Holy Guardian Angel and to write down the instructions by following which men might attain 'to the Summum Bonum, True Wisdom and Perfect Happiness'.

PART FIVE

The Magus

The Seal of the Grand Master of the O.T.O. It was taken from the design on a Gnostic gem, reproduced in Richard Payne Knight's *A Discourse on the Worship of Priapus*. It is a solar glyph embodying the doctrine of the Double Horizon or the two Equinoxes.

The Magus

69

I attended to the production of number five of *The Equinox*, but shortly after (my diary for 1911 is missing—if, indeed, it was ever kept—so I am uncertain of my dates) I went into Retirement, spending my time alternately between Paris and Montigny-sur-Loing on the southern edge of the Forest of Fontainebleau. It was immediately evident that I was in the right path. I had placed my body and mind entirely at the service of the Master of the Temple who had filled the vacuum of the universe caused by the annihilation of Aleister Crowley. I kept my body in perfect condition by walking almost every day to Fontainebleau and back, always choosing a new way through the forest so that by the end of the summer I knew every tree by name, as one might say. I had acquired a boundless love for that incomparable woodland, whose glorious beauty is still further hallowed by the romance which lurks in every glade. It was tame indeed in comparison with a hundred other jungles which I had known, but for all that it possesses an individual charm which endears it to me beyond any words of mine to utter. Nature herself opposed no obstacle to my wooing. The summer of 1911 was intensely hot and fine. I have always found that dry air is essential to the well-being either of my body or of my genius. Damp air seems to interfere with my insulation; my genius leaks away and leaves me empty and depressed.

This year indeed was another *annus mirabilis* for me. There was an almost continual outpouring of the Holy Spirit through my mind. The spring of poetry shot crystal clear from the hidden furnace of my being into the pure and brilliant air, and fell and fertilized the earth about the sacred hill. A thousand years from now men will still gather round in wonder and worship to gaze upon the gorgeous pageant of flowers that glow upon the glowing grass and to feast upon the ripe fruits that burden the two great trees which tower like pillars for a gateway to my garden—the tree of the knowledge of Good and Evil and the Tree of Life.

Let me first enumerate the comparatively profane achievements of these few months. Firstly, 'Across the Gulf'.[1] This is a prose story of some twenty thousand words. The theme is my own life in the 26th Dynasty, when I was Ankh-f-n-khonsu and brought about the Aeon of Osiris to replace that of Isis. The story must not be taken as true in the ordinary sense of the word, but as allegorical.

I wrote many lyrics, but especially 'The Sevenfold Sacrament.'[2] This poem subsequently appeared in the *English Review* and has often been reprinted. It is, one might say, a pendant to *Aha!* It is one of my finest achievements from a technical point of view and describes the actual experience of a night which I spent at Montigny. I was staying at an inn called the Vanne Rouge, on the bank of the Loing overlooking a weir. (The inn has since then become fashionable and impossible; at that time it was adorable in every way.)

> In eddies of obsidian,
> At my feet the river ran
> Between me and the poppy-prankt
> Isle, with tangled roots embanked,
> Where seven sister poplars stood
> Like the seven sisters of God.

> Soft as silence in mine ear,
> The drone and rustle of the weir
> Told in bass the treble tale
> Of the embowered nightingale.
> Higher, on the patient river,
> Velvet lights without a quiver
> Echoed through their hushed rimes
> The garden's glow beneath the limes.

> Then the sombre village, crowned
> By the castellated ground,
> Where in cerements of sable,
> One square tower and one great gable
> Stood, the melancholy wraith
> Of a false and fallen faith.
> Over all, supine, enthralling,
> The young moon, her faint edge falling
> To the dead verge of her setting,
> Saintly swam, her silver fretting
> All the leaves with light. Afar
> Towards the Zenith stood a star,
> As of all worthiness and fitness
> The luminous eternal witness.

I described how the silence stripped me of myself; how I came once more into the Abyss and was drawn thence into the most secret Temple of the Most High, and there received the sevenfold sacrament.

> Nor is it given to any son of man
> To hymn that sacrament, the One in Seven,
> Where God and priest and worshipper,
> Deacon, asperger, thurifer, chorister,
> Are one as they were one ere time began,
> Are one on earth as they are one in heaven;
> Where the soul is given a new name,
> Confirming with an oath the same,
> And with celestial wine and bread
> Is most delicately fed,
> Yet suffereth in itself the curse
> Of the infinite universe,
> Having made its own confession
> Of the mystery of transgression;
> Where it is wedded solemnly
> With the ring of space and eternity;
> And where the oil, the Holiest Breath,
> With its first whisper dedicateth
> Its new life to a further death.

This experience lasted throughout the night, and I describe the dawn, the awakening of the world and myself to what men call reality.

> The trout leapt in the shingly shallows.
> Soared skyward the great sun, that hallows
> The pagan shrines of labour and light
> As the moon consecrates the night.
> Labour is corn and love is wine,
> And both are blessèd in the shrine;
> Nor is he for priest designed
> Who partakes only in one kind.

I suited the action to the word.

There was also the poem 'A Birthday',[3] written on August 10th for Leila Waddell, who was then twenty-six. She had gone to England to fulfil an engagement as leader of the Ladies' Orchestra in *The Waltz Dream*. The poem describes the history of our liaison.

I wrote also two short stories. The hero of 'The Woodcutter'[4] is a forester who 'chops to live and lives to chop'. A silly Frenchman and his mistress are wandering through the forest. He fantastically exhorts the woodcutter to make an art of his work, while the girl amuses herself by trying to excite the old man's passions. That night there is a thunderstorm; and an English girl, who has lost her way, takes refuge in his hut. He combines the element of his thought during sleep, chops her to pieces, stacks her limbs neatly by the hut, and goes off to his regular work. A rescue party discovers him. The story ends. 'They told him of a widow lady in Paris who could beat him at his own game.'

I am passionately indignant that the persistent beastliness of the average mind insists that the woodcutter violated the girl. Such a suggestion completely ruins the point of the story, which is that his mind had room for no idea of any kind except chopping.

'His Secret Sin' [5] was written on an idea given me by Neuburg. I heard afterwards it had already been used by *Punch*. It is admitted, of course, that this kind of plagiarism is allowable.

A prosperous English grocer is in Paris on business. He wants desperately to be 'wicked', but is ashamed to inquire how these things are done. On the last day of his stay he is goaded to madness by seeing the statue of Joan of Arc astride a horse. He makes up his mind to buy an indecent photograph at least and dives into a shop, where he asks for something 'tray sho'. The shopman contemptuously produces albums of reproductions from the Louvre. When he strikes the Venus of Milo, he secretes it, pays half a sovereign in terror and slinks out of the shop. He keeps the photograph in his safe and brings it out at night and gloats.

His daughter is attending art classes; for a colonel and his wife have taken pity on her and tried to extricate her from her surroundings. One day she shows him some sketches one of which is the Venus of Milo herself. Her father abuses her furiously. She is 'as bad as Cousin Jenny'. She snatches the drawing, telling him not to touch sacred things. His secret sin has been visited on his child. She is perfectly shameless in her iniquity! And then it strikes him that no decent art class would use such a model. He blurts out, 'How did you get the key of my little safe?' She understands the whole thing and walks out of the house in disgust, never to return. He, overwhelmed by the judgment of God, determines to commit suicide, after burning the accursed photograph. But he cannot summon up courage and flings the cocked pistol into the grate. It explodes; the bullet destroys one eye and cheek. But he recovers. The street boys take to calling him 'Old Venus' and his guilty conscience persuades him that they have somehow heard the story.

This tale is one of the most bitter truths that I have penned. I am glad to say that it is almost the only evidence of what I felt with regard to the attitude of the English bourgeoisie towards art and sex; and, even so, my picture of the younger generation bears witness to my unshakable faith in the emancipation of my folk. Indeed, I have not wrought in vain. The young men and women of today, generally speaking, are as free from superstitions and sexual shame as I would have them. It is only a further proof of this that the 'old guard' are more desperately narrow and fanatical than ever. They are trying to stop drinking, smoking, dancing and reading, by law. Intolerance is evidence of impotence.

I brought off an astounding double event in Paris, probably during August. I was at 50 rue Vavin and the idea of a dramatic poem or allegory to be called 'Adonis' [6] came into my mind. I went out for a *citron pressé* at the Café du Dôme de Montparnasse, preliminary to settling down to write. The argument was almost complete in my mind and the rhythm was beginning to flow through me. But at the Dôme were sitting my old mistress, Nina Olivier, and her latest conquest, an unpleasant and cadaverous hypocrite named Hener-Skene, whom I knew slightly from 1902, when he was posing as an earnest Nietzschian. With them was sitting a charming girl named (or calling herself) Fenella Lovell, a consumptive creature in gaudy and fantastic rags of brilliant colours, who earned her living partly as a model, partly as a 'gypsy' fiddler and dancer.

Skene and Nina had taken advantage of her sickness and poverty to amuse themselves by whipping and otherwise ill-treating her. It was not honest sadism on Skene's part; it was a pose. He thought it very glorious to be a character in Krafft-Ebing. They asked me to drink and introduced me to Fenella. Her pathetic beauty set me suddenly aflame with an idea to make her the heroine of a little play. My mind was swept clean of 'Adonis'. Then minutes later I was back in my room, furiously at work on 'The Ghouls.[7]

The Ghouls is possibly the most ghastly death-dance in English literature. If Oscar Wilde had written it (but he could not have) everyone would know it. It is the very pith and marrow of terror. Cynical it may be, but I defy the lord of dreams to send any more plutonian nightmare to haunt our mortal sleep.

This criticism (from the *Poetry Review*) fills me with honest pride.

I finished the play during the night and instantly picked up the idea of 'Adonis', which by an unparalleled *tour de force* I had kept intact at the back of my mind. I finished this play also straight off. The most remarkable point of this most remarkable achievement is that no two plays could have been more dissimilar, either in theme or style. 'The Ghouls' is prose, save for one short song, and ranges from the loftiest sublimity to dialect and slang. 'Adonis' is poetry, mystic, sensuous and comic by turn; much of it written in the elaborate and exquisite method of closely woven rimes which I myself invented.

Later in the summer, I set to work on a really large idea, a play of Old Venice in five acts. I kept my two main principles of composition; the use of colour and form to distinguish my characters and compose a visible symphony.

MORTADELLO

The Doge has white hair, and is seventy years of age.

Mortadello has hair dyed dark auburn, and is forty years of age. He is stout, tall and pompous.

Alessandro has rough hair of fiery red and is thirty years of age.

Lorenzo has scanty ashen hair, and is twenty-eight years of age.

Gabriele is a hunchbacked dwarf, very strongly built, with a large and intellectual head. He is bald, and is fifty years of age.

Orlando is of gigantic stature, a full Negro. He is forty years of age.

The Legate is an old and venerable man of ascetic and noble type.

Magdalena is a tall, robust and buxom woman of thirty-five years old. Her hair is black, but her complexion pale.

Lucrezia is a tall, robust and voluptuous woman of twenty-five years old. Her hair is of fine gold, her eyes of pale blue and her complexion fair and rosy.

Zelina is small and plump. Her hair is brown, and her age nine and twenty, though she looks older.

Monica is of medium height, very thin and serpent-like, her hair black and crisp; her features like Madonna's. Her eyes are extraordinarily black, keen and piercing. Her age is twenty. Her hands and feet are very small and white, her complexion like fine porcelain.

The Abbess is a gigantic and burly woman of fifty years old.

My other principle of internal rimes I made more difficult for myself than ever, by sticking throughout to the Alex-

andrine. No English writer has previously attempted to use
this magnificent verse, no doubt, in part, because of the danger
of monotony. This I avoided by introducing my internal rime
at all parts of the line.

I quote from my own explanation.

1. *The Classical:*
Ay, to this end, indeed was marriage first or*dained*,
And to this end today is by the Church sus*tained*.
2. *Idem, marked by a rime:*
Listen; in all good *faith*, I gladly grant you *much*,
Not prone to scoff, and *scathe* the scutcheon with a *smutch*.
3. *After the second foot:*
Oh! but you're *hurt!*

     Young man! she shall be tended,
               Well.
No! take my *shirt!* Staunch the dear beast.
              A mira*cle.*
4. *After the fourth foot:*
Serene, august, untroubled, *cold*, her prayers are *worth*
More than our steel, more than our *gold*, that bind the *earth*.
5. *After the first foot:*
Bow *down* to the Cross! His love purge thee! His Passion
save thee!
Christ *crown* the work! Here is the blessing that He *gave thee.*
6. *After both second and fourth feet:*
Come, let me *hold* my crystal *cross* up to the *moon!*
A guess of *gold* were at a *loss* to tell its *tune.*
7. *After the first and fifth feet:*
No *news!* No word of Mortadello's *fate!* No *hope* ·
To *bruise* the head of the old snake, the *State.* No *scope.*
8. *After the first half foot and the second foot:*
Come, save me, *save* Thy Maiden! Strike each barbed *dart*
Home to the *grave* convent and cloister of my *heart.*
9. *After the fifth foot:*
Last, to the lords who by their atti*tude applaud*
This day of burial to faction, *feud* and *fraud.*
10. *After the second and fourth feet, but each line rimed
within itself.*
Oh for the *blind* kiss of the *wind*, the desert *air*
Thrilling the *blue* and shrilling *through* my soul's desp*air.*
('Thrilling' and 'shrilling' are here thrown in without extra
charge. This device frequently recurs.)

There may be one or two other complications which I have
overlooked.

I have made use of the usual liberties in the matter of using
anapests and trochees for iambics. With regard to double rimes,

I have sometimes treated them as single rimes, when they occur in the middle of a line; sometimes I have made the line of thirteen syllables to suit them.

I have even, once or twice, used the reverse method of calling a pause a half foot. 'Stare, murderer, stare' counts as six syllables.

All this has been done of high purpose; there is some inflection or emphasis to be gained, or some tone to be given to the speech by the irregularity.

The argument of the play is simple. Monica aims at becoming the autocrat of Venice and succeeds. In each scene is a definite action of the highest pictorial, as well as dramatic, value that I could imagine. The play is full of violent scenes of love and murder. I believe that I have used three ideas entirely new in drama.

1. Monica has caused her Negro lover to murder the daughter of the Doge, till then his mistress. She bids him retrieve the corpse from the canal, where he had thrown it. The crime is concealed and the dead woman is hidden as the guest of Monica. She dresses up the corpse and has it married to Mortadello in St Mark's.

2. Monica, cornered in a crypt, is praying passionately while her Negro lover is slain by their enemies. Her hysteria produces the stigmata; and this apparent proof of her sanctity overcomes the assailants, whose leader she touches with the tip of a poisoned crucifix. He dies on the spot; his followers wish to fall at her feet, but she insists on being arrested.

3. Having forced Mortadello to marry her, she disguises herself as a Saharan dancer and drugs him with hashish. She then discloses her identity; and he, in the madness of the drug, attacks the Papal legate. She follows and, defending the old man, kills her husband. This last scene, by the way, fulfils my idea of true comedy; the dressing up of a man as a king or god, and inducing him to preside at a hunting of which he is in reality to be the quarry. I have shown in my essay 'Good Hunting!' (*The International*, March 1918) that this central idea is universal in all the best comedy and tragedy from the *Bacchae* of Euripides, the story of Esther, the Crucifixion and the murder of Hiram Abif, to the plays of Shakespeare, Ibsen and many others.

I now turn to my magical writings during this astounding summer.

In my spare time I began to make a list of Greek words connected with Magick and similar subjects, arranging them by their numerical order. The idea was to construct a dictionary of the Greek Cabbala similar to that of the Hebrew Cabbala on which I had been at work since 1899 and ultimately published in *The Equinox*, vol. I, no. VIII. But the Greek Cabbala presents difficulties which do not arise in the case of Hebrew. First, we have no sacred text in Greek save a few imperfect and most unsatisfactory gnostic documents, the hopelessly garbled Apocalypse and a few oddments like the Emerald Table of Hermes, the Divine Pymander and the Golden Verses of Pythagoras. Secondly, the various dialects of Greek affect the computations and there is no means of choosing between them. Thirdly, the terminations alter the values. It is even difficult to decide whether or no to reckon the article. Fourthly, the actual examples of Cabbala existent are shamefully unconscientious, as may be seen by reference to Messrs Lea and Bond's brochure. They equate words and phrases quite arbitrarily. If it suits them to count the article they count it.

That this Cabbala exists is nevertheless certain. The correspondences in the Apocalypse in connection with the series 111 to 999 is undeniably intentional. Nor can it be an accident that Mithras (360) was altered to Meithras (365) to suit the correction of the calendar. The matter is of extreme importance; because Aiwass in dictating *The Book of the Law* repeatedly makes use of correspondences in Greek, such as Thelema, Will, 93—Agape, Love, 93. 718 = Stele 666, and so on. He also equates Greek and Hebrew words. Thus his own name spelt in Hebrew has the value 93, but in Greek that of 418, thus bringing into relation the Word of the Law of the Aeon with the Magical Formula of the Great Work.[8] My preliminary studies, however, tended to discourage me, for the fourfold reason above stated; and the proposed dictionary remains uncompleted to this day.

During this summer I wrote no less than nineteen books of magical and mystical instruction. Each is characterized by the simplest, sublimest and most concentrated prose of which I was master. The sceptical attitude is rigorously preserved; and, with the instructions already issued and a few minor matters to which I attended later, they comprise an absolutely comprehensive practical guide to every branch of the technique of spiritual attainment. The methods of every country, creed and clime, stripped of their dogma and prejudice, are here presented scientifically and simply. Besides these, there may be found certain methods prescribed in *The Book of the Law* or invented by myself. I will give a short synopsis of these nineteen Instructions.

LIBER I. The Book of the Magus.

This is an inspired writing. It describes the conditions of that exalted Grade. I had at this time no idea that I should ever attain to it; in fact, I thought it utterly beyond possibility. This book was given to me that I might avoid mistakes when the time came for me to become a Magus. It is impossible to give any idea of the terror and sublimity of this book, while the accuracy of its predictions and of its descriptions of the state of being, at that time wholly beyond my imagination to conceive, make it a most astonishing document.

LIBER X. This book is called 'The Gate of Light'. It explains how those who have attained initiation, taking pity upon the darkness and minuteness of the earth, send forth a messenger to men. The message follows. It is an appeal to those who, being developed beyond the average of their fellows, see fit to take up the Great Work. This Work is then described in general terms with a few hints of its conditions.

LIBER XI is a paraphrase of the instructions given in *The Book of the Law* for invoking Nuit.

LIBER XVI, called 'The Tower; or the House of God', describes a series of meditation practices, the general method being to destroy every thought that tends to arise in the mind by an act of will. The thought must be nipped in the bud before it reaches consciousness. Further, the causes which tend to produce any such thought must be discovered and annihilated. Finally, this process must be extended to include the original cause behind those causes.

LIBER LXIV gives instruction in a method of summoning suitable persons to undertake the Great Work. It includes a powerful invocation of the God of Truth, Wisdom and Magick.

LIBER LXVI. The Book of the Ruby Star describes an extremely powerful ritual of practical Magick; how to arouse the Magical Force within the operator and how to use it to create whatever may be required.

LIBER XC. The Book of the Hermetic Fish-Hook summons mankind to undertake the Great Work. It describes the conditions of initiation and its results in language of great poetic power.

LIBER CLVI. The Wall of Abiegnus (the Sacred Mountain of the Rosicrucians) gives the formula of Attainment by devotion to our Lady Babalon. It instructs the aspirant how to dissolve his personality in the Universal Life.

LIBER CLXXV. Astarte, The Book of the Beryl Stone, gives the complete formula of Bhakti-Yoga; how one may unite oneself to any particular deity by devotion. Both magical and mystical methods are fully described.

LIBER CC. The Book of the Sun. Here are given the four Adorations to the sun, to be said daily at dawn, noon, sunset and midnight. The object of this practice is firstly to remind the aspirant at regular intervals of the Great Work; secondly, to bring him into conscious personal relation with the centre of our system; and thirdly, for advanced students, to make actual magical contact with the spiritual energy of the sun and thus to draw actual force from him.

LIBER CCVI. The Book of Breathing describes various practices of controlling the breath, how to ensure success, what results to strive for, and how to use them for the Great Work.

LIBER CCXXXI is a technical treatise on the Tarot. The sequence of the 22 Trumps is explained as a formula of initiation.

LIBER CCCLXX, The Book of Creation or of the Goat of the Spirit, analyses the nature of the creative magical force in man, explains how to awaken it, how to use it and indicates the general as well as the particular objects to be gained thereby.

LIBER CD analyses the Hebrew alphabet into seven triads, each of which forms a Trinity of sympathetic ideas relating respectively to the Three Orders comprised in the A.'. A.'.. It is really an attempt to find a Periodic Law in the system.

LIBER CDLXXIV. The Book of the Mouth of the Abyss or of Knowledge. A course of study in philosophy is prescribed as a preliminary. The aspirant having assimilated all existing systems, he is instructed how to analyse the nature of the reason itself and thus how to cross the Abyss on the Intellectual Plane. Having cleansed and renewed his mental faculties in this way, he resumes his aspiration to the Knowledge and Conversation of His Holy Guardian Angel, with whose reappearance he perfects his Magical Powers so that he is ready to undertake the Work of annihilating the universe, which, being done, he becomes a full Master of the Temple.

LIBER DLV. This is a paraphrase of the instructions given in *The Book of the Law* for attaining Hadit.

LIBER DCCCXXXI, The Book of Vesta. This book describes three main methods of reducing the multiplicity of thoughts to one. (The magical method is to banish ceremonially the 32 parts of the universe in turn. One mystical method is to deny in consciousness that any part of the body or mind is real. Another is to stimulate the senses in turn with such concentration as to put it out of gear.)

LIBER DCCCLXVIII. This is an analysis of the 22 letters. To each is attributed a magical or mystical practice of progressive difficulty until attainment is complete.

LIBER CMXIII. The Book of the Memory of the Path. Here are given two methods of acquiring the Magical Memory so as to enable the aspirant to calculate his True Orbit in eternity. The first method is to learn to think backwards till he acquires the power of recalling the events of his life in reverse chronological order. The idea is to get back beyond one's birth to one's previous death, and so on for many lives. It should then be easy to understand the general object of one's existence. The second (easier and surer) method is to consider every event in one's past, determine the influence which each has had upon one's life, and by synthesizing these forces, calculate their resultant; that is determine one's general direction so as to be able to concentrate one's energies on fulfilling the function for which one is fit. Character, conduct and circumstances are to be considered as terms of a complex dynamic equation. This method is of extreme value to all. It should be applied even to the education of children so as not to force them into unnatural developments.

These nineteen books were published in numbers six and seven of *The Equinox*.[9] During this summer, I also prepared the extremely important account of the circumstances in which the stele was discovered and *The Book of the Law* written, for number seven. In this manner I published a facsimile of the manuscript of that Book and my Comment thereon. This latter is shamefully meagre and incomplete. The truth is, that despite everything, I still felt an indescribable repugnance. I knew well how unworthy the Comment was as it stood, yet I could not force myself to work on it, partly, no doubt, because I felt, as indeed I feel now, that nothing I can write can possibly be worthy of or adequate to the text; but partly also, from an instinctive fear and dislike of the subject.

And so passed away this superb summer. The autumn had a new experience in store for me. The current of my life was once more to be suddenly turned; and as usual, this critical change came about as the result of a series of casual chances. I was caught in a web, some of whose strands had been woven as early as 1902. I must deal with this new development in a new chapter.

70

That fertile passage through Paris on my return from Chogo Ri, which had already borne so much fruit in my life, had still some seed—which now came to harvest. I have mentioned Nina Olivier, whom I loved so well and sang so passionately. In my sunlight she had blossomed into *La Dame de Montparno*, the Queen of the Quarter. But I have not mentioned an obscure prig whom I will call Monet-Knott, whom I had met through my fiancée, the 'Star' to Nina's 'Garter'.[1] This brainless and conceited youth had become accompanist to the greatest dancer of her generation. Let me call her Lavinia King.[2] She, first and never equalled, had understood and demonstrated the art of dancing as a complete language of the affections of the mind and heart. Knott and Nina, as already recorded, had contracted a liaison. I met Knott for the second time when I was introduced to Fenella Lovell and wrote 'The Ghouls', as previously related. I saw a fair amount of him in the next few weeks; so that, running across him in London on October 11th, he took me after supper to the Savoy to meet Miss King.*

A boisterous party was in progress. The dancer's lifelong friend, whom I will call by the name she afterwards adopted, Soror Virakam,[3] was celebrating her birthday. This lady, a magnificent specimen of mingled Irish and Italian blood, possessed a most powerful personality and a terrific magnetism which instantly attracted my own. I forgot everything. I sat on the floor like a Chinese god, exchanging electricity with her.

After some weeks' preliminary skirmishing, we joined battle along the whole front; that is to say, I crossed to Paris, where she had a flat, and carried her off to Switzerland to spend the winter skating. Arrived at Interlaken, we found that Mürren was not open, so we went on to St Moritz, breaking the journey at Zurich. This town is so hideous and depressing that we felt that our only chance of living through the night was to get superbly drunk, which we did . . .

(Let me emphasize that this wild adventure had not the

---

* This incident and its sequel are described in *The Net*, chapter one. [Later Crowley changed the title of *The Net* to *Moonchild*.—Editors.]

remotest connection with Magick. Virakam was utterly igno-
rant of the subject. She had hardly so much as a smattering of
Christian Science. She had never attended a séance or played
Planchette.)

. . . *Lassati sed non satiati* by midnight, I expected to sleep;
but was aroused by Virakam being apparently seized with a
violent attack of hysteria, in which she poured forth a frantic
torrent of senseless hallucination. I was irritated and tried to
calm her. But she insisted that her experience was real; that
she bore an important message to me from some invisible
individual. Such nonsense increased my irritation. But—after
about an hour of it—my jaw fell with astonishment. I became
suddenly aware of a coherence in her ravings, and further
that they were couched in my own language of symbols. My
attention being thus awakened, I listened to what she was
saying. A few minutes convinced me that she was actually in
communication with some intelligence who had a message for
me.

Let me briefly explain the grounds for this belief. I have
already set forth, in connection with the Cairo working, some
of the safeguards which I habitually employ. Virakam's vision
contained elements perfectly familiar to me. This was clear
proof that the man in her vision, whom she called Ab-ul-Diz,
was acquainted with my system of hieroglyphics, literal and
numerical, and also with some incidents in my magical career.
Virakam herself certainly knew nothing of any of these. Ab-ul-
Diz told us to call him a week later, when he would give further
information. We arrived at St Moritz and engaged a suite in
the Palace Hotel.

My first surprise was to find that I had brought with me
exactly those Magical Weapons which were suitable for the
work proposed and no others. But a yet more startling circumstance was to come. For the purposes of the Cairo working,
Ouarda and I had bought two abbai; one, scarlet, for me; one,
blue, for her. I had brought mine to St Moritz; the other was
of course in the possession of Ouarda. Imagine my amazement
when Virakam produced from her trunk a blue abbai so like
Ouarda's that the only differences were minute details of the
gold embroidery! The suggestion was that the Secret Chiefs,
having chosen Ouarda as their messenger, could not use anyone else until she had become irrevocably disqualified by insanity. Not till now could her place be taken by another; and
that Virakam should possess a duplicate of her Magical Robe

seemed a strong argument that she had been consecrated by them to take the place of her unhappy predecessor.

She was very unsatisfactory as a clairvoyant; she resented these precautions. She was a quick-tempered and impulsive woman, always eager to act with reckless enthusiasm. My cold scepticism no doubt prevented her from doing her best. Ab-ul-Diz himself constantly demanded that I should show 'faith' and warned me that I was wrecking my chances by my attitude. I prevailed upon him, however, to give adequate proof of his existence and his claim to speak with authority. The main purport of his message was to instruct me to write a book on my system of mysticism and Magick, to be called *Book Four*, and told me that by means of this book, I should prevail against public neglect. I saw no objection to writing such a book; on quite rational grounds, it was a proper course of action. I therefore agreed to do so. But Ab-ul-Diz was determined to dictate the conditions in which the book should be written; and this was a difficult matter. He wanted us to travel to an appropriate place. On this point I was not wholly satisfied with the result of my cross-examination. I know now that I was much to blame throughout. I was not honest either with him, myself or Virakam. I allowed material considerations to influence me, and I clung—oh triple food!—to my sentimental obligations towards Laylah.[4]

We finally decided to do what he asked, though part of my objection was founded on his refusal to give us absolutely definite instructions. However, we crossed the passes in a sleigh to Chiavenna, whence we took the train to Milan. In this city we had a final conversation with Ab-ul-Diz. I had exhausted his patience, as he mine, and he told us that he would not visit us any more. He gave us his final instructions. We were to go to Rome and beyond Rome, though he refused to name the exact spot. We were to take a villa and there write *Book Four*.[5] I asked him how we might recognize the right villa. I forget what answer he gave through her, but for the first time he flashed a message directly into my own consciousness. 'You will recognize it beyond the possibility of doubt or error,' he told me. With this, a picture came into my mind of a hillside on which were a house and garden marked by two tall Persian nuts.

The next day we went on to Rome. Owing to my own Ananias-like attempt to 'keep back part of the price', my relations with Virakam had become strained. We reached Naples after two or three quarrelsome days in Rome and began house-hunting. I imagined that we should find dozens of suitable places to choose from, but we spent day after day scouring the city and suburbs in an automobile, without finding a single place to let that corresponded in the smallest degree with our ideas.

Virakam's brat—a most god-forsaken lout—was to join us for the Christmas holidays, and on the day he was due to arrive we motored out as a forlorn hope to Posilippo before meeting him at the station at four o'clock or thereabouts. But the previous night Virakam had a dream in which she saw the desired villa with absolute clearness. (I had been careful to say nothing to her about the Persian nuts, so as to have a weapon against her in case she insisted that such and such a place was the one intended.)

After a fruitless search we turned our automobile towards Naples, along the crest of Posilippo. At one point there is a small side lane scarcely negotiable by motor, and indeed hardly perceptible, as it branches from the main road so as to form an acute-angled 'Y' with the foot towards Naples. But Virakam sprang excitedly to her feet and told the chauffeur to drive down it. I was astonished, she being hysterically anxious to meet the train, and our time being already almost too short. But she swore passionately that the villa was down that lane. The road became constantly rougher and narrower. After some time, it came out on the open slope; a low stone parapet on the left protecting it. Again she sprang to her feet. 'There', she cried, pointing with her finger, 'is the villa I saw in my dream!' I looked. No villa was visible. I said so. She had to agree; yet stuck to her point that she saw it. I subsequently returned to that spot and found that a short section of wall, perhaps fifteen feet of narrow edge of masonry, is just perceptible through a gap in the vegetation.

We drove on; we came to a tiny piazza, on one side of which was a church. 'That is the square and the church', she exclaimed, 'that I saw in my dream!'

We drove on. The lane became narrower, rougher and steeper. Little more than a hundred yards ahead it was completely 'up', blocked with heaps of broken stone. The chauffeur protested that he would be able neither to turn the car nor to back it up to the square. Virakam, in a violent rage, insisted on proceeding. I shrugged my shoulders. I had got accustomed to these typhoons.

We drove on a few yards. Then the chauffeur made up his

mind to revolt and stopped the car. On the left was a wide
open gate through which we could see a gang of workmen
engaged in pretending to repair a ramshackle villa. Virakam
called the foreman and asked in broken Italian if the place was
to let. He told her no; it was under repair. With crazy confidence she dragged him within and forced him to show her
over the house. I sat in resigned disgust, not deigning to follow. Then my eyes suddenly saw down the garden, two trees
close together. I stooped. Their tops appeared. They were
Persian nuts! The stupid coincidence angered me, and yet some
irresistible instinct compelled me to take out my notebook and
pencil and jot down the name written over the gate—Villa
Caldarazzo. Idly, I added up the letters $6 + 10 + 30 + 30 +$
1 and $20 + 1 + 30 + 4 + 1 + 200 + 1 + 7 + 7 + 70$.
Their sum struck me like a bullet in my brain. It was 418,
the number of the Magical Formula of the Aeon, a numerical
hieroglyph of the Great Work! Ab-ul-Diz had made no mistake. My recognition of the right place was not to depend on a
mere matter of trees, which might be found almost anywhere.
Recognition beyond all possibility of doubt was what he promised. He had been as good as his word.

I was entirely overwhelmed. I jumped out of the car and
ran up to the house. I found Virakam in the main room. The
instant I entered I understood that it was entirely suited for a
Temple. The walls were decorated with crude frescoes which
somehow suggested the exact atmosphere proper to the Work.
The very shape of the room seemed somehow significant.
Further, it seemed as if it were filled with a peculiar emana-
tion. This impression must not be dismissed as sheer fancy.
Few men but are sufficiently sensitive to distinguish the
spiritual aura of certain buildings. It is impossible not to feel
reverence in certain cathedrals and temples. The most ordinary
dwelling-houses often possess an atmosphere of their own;
some depress, some cheer; some disgust, others strike chill to
the heart.

Virakam of course was entirely certain that this was the villa
for us. Against this was the positive statement of the people
in charge that it was not to be let. We refused to accept this
assertion. We took the name and address of the owner, dug
him out, and found him willing to give us immediate possession
at a small rent. We went in on the following day and settled
down almost at once to consecrate the Temple and begin the
book.

The idea was as follows. I was to dictate; Virakam to transcribe, and if at any point there appeared the slightest obscurity —obscurity from the point of view of the entirely ignorant and not particularly intelligent reader; in a word, the average lower-class man in the street—I was to recast my thoughts in plainer language. By this means we hoped to write a book well within the compass of the understanding of even the simplest-minded seeker after spiritual enlightenment.

Part One of *Book Four* expounds the principles and practice of mysticism in simple scientific terms stripped of all sectarian accretion, superstitious enthusiasms or other extraneous matter. It proved completely successful in this sense.

Part Two deals with the principles and practice of Magick. I explained the real meaning and *modus operandi* of all the apparatus and technique of Magick. Here, however, I partially failed. I was stupid enough to assume that my readers were already acquainted with the chief classics of Magick. I consequently described each Weapon, explained it and gave instructions for its use, without making it clear why it should be necessary at all. Part Two is therefore an wholly admirable treatise only for one who has already mastered the groundwork and gained some experience of the practice of the art.

The number 4 being the formula of the book, it was of course to consist of four parts. I carried out this idea by expressing the nature of the Tetrad, not only by the name and plan of the book, but by issuing it in the shape of a square 4 inches by 4, and pricing each part as a function of 4. Part One was published at 4 groats, Part Two at 4 tanners, Part Three was to cost 4 'Lloyd George groats' (at this time the demagogue was offering the workman ninepence for fourpence, by means of an insurance swindle intended to enslave him more completely than ever). Part Four, 4 shillings. Part Three was to deal with the practice of Magick, and Part Four, of *The Book of the Law* with its history and the Comment; the volume, in fact, indicated in the Book itself, chapter III, verse 39.

The programme was cut short. The secret contest between the will of Virakam and my own broke into open hostility. A serious quarrel led to her dashing off to Paris. She repented almost before she arrived and telegraphed me to rejoin her, which I did, and we went together to London. There, however, an intrigue resulted in her hastily marrying a Turkish adventurer who proceeded to beat her and, a little later, to desert her. Her hysteria became chronic and uncontrollable; she took to furious bouts of drinking which culminated in *delirium tremens*.

The partial failure of our partnership was to some extent, without doubt, my own fault. I was not whole-hearted and I refused to live by faith rather than by sight. I cannot reproach myself for this; for that, I have no excuse. I may nevertheless express a doubt as to whether full success was in any case possible. Her own masterless passions could hardly have allowed her to pass unscathed through the ordeals which are always imposed upon those who undertake tasks of this importance.

The upshot has been that, although I dictated Part Three to Laylah in the spring of 1912, I felt that it was not sufficiently perfect to be published. From time to time I revised it; but it remained unsatisfactory until in 1921 I took it in hand seriously, practically rewrote it and expanded it into a hand volume, a really complete treatise on every branch of Magick. Part Four is still incomplete. I feel that I cannot publish the Comment on *The Book of the Law*[6] until I am absolutely satisfied with it, and there is still much work to be done.

My midwinter wandering was so wholly taken up with Virakam that there was no adventure of interest to recount, with one exception. In Naples we had a sitting with the famous Eusapia Palladino.

Her claim to extraordinary powers rests entirely on the famous report of Messrs Feilding, Baggalay and Carrington. Feilding I knew personally very well. I had cross-examined him repeatedly about her without shaking his testimony. I met Baggalay once or twice and his evidence corroborated Feilding's. When I came to know Carrington later, I found myself unable to attach serious credit to anything he said, and it certainly seemed suspicious that he should have acted as impresario to Eusapia shortly afterwards and exploited her in the United States.

Besides this, I had analysed carefully the printed reports of the sittings. I could find no loophole; until one day my precious memory came to the rescue. It told me what is not by any means apparent on a straightforward reading, that in one of the séances, I think number six, no phenomena occurred in the cabinet. Somewhere else in the book, quite disconnectedly, we find that during this séance there was no table in the cabinet. 'Aha!' said I, 'so when the trumpets and tambourines and so on are really out of her reach (never mind whether her arms are under control or not!) she cannot sound them.' It may seem arbitrary and unjust; but to me that one fact knocked away the props from the whole structure.

I had had sittings with many celebrated mediums and never seen any phenomena which impressed me in the least as being caused by occult forces. (It is to be remembered that I have seen so many phenomena of absolutely indubitable authenticity in the course of my magical work that I am predisposed to expect such things to happen.)

In sitting with Eusapia, my main objects were first to get an idea of the atmosphere, so as to visualize more clearly the events recorded in the famous report, and second to criticize my own evidence. The question had suggested itself: 'Feilding and the rest are clever, wary, experienced and critical, but even so, can I be sure that when they describe what occurs they are dependable witnesses?' As luck would have it, my single séance threw a glaring light on this point.

Eusapia was sitting at the end of a table with her back to the cabinet. Virakam was on her right, I on her left. It was my business to make sure that she did not kick and to keep hold of her left wrist. After a short time the fun began in the customary manner by the curtain of the cabinet bulging and finally falling across Eusapia's left arm and my right. I could thus see into the cabinet, that is, into the corner of the room, by turning my head. Now, Eusapia was supposed to have a third arm, an astral arm, with which she could do her deadly deeds. My attention was attracted to the cabinet by seeing a shadowy arm moving about in it. My intellectual faculties were completely alert. I reasoned as follows: 'The arm which I see is a left arm, not a right arm. It cannot therefore be Eusapia's left arm, because I am holding her left wrist with my right hand.' Almost before I had completed this syllogism, the arm disappeared from the cabinet; at the same moment I felt Eusapia replace her left wrist in my hand, which had not informed me that she had removed it.

It is a small premise on which to found an universal proposition and yet I do so without serious hesitation. I dare not for a moment compare myself with such expert investigators as Feilding and the rest. Still, I have some experience. I am not entirely an ass and I certainly know a great deal about psychology for one thing, and the unreliability of sensory impressions for another. *Ex pede Herculem.* If I, such as I am, cannot be relied upon to say whether I am or am not holding a woman's wrist, is it not possible that even experts, admittedly excited by the rapidity with which one startling phenomenon succeeds another, may deceive themselves as to the conditions of the control? It seems to me extremely significant that Feilding has never obtained a cabinet phenomenon with any medium when he has interposed netting between the man and the curtain.

Feilding invited me to some of the séances of the then famous medium Caracini, who had been turning Rome upside down by turning tables upside down, teaching grand pianos the turkey-trot and materializing mutton chops. I was inclined at first to believe that there was some slight element of genuineness in the man for the simple reason that he failed to bring off anything at all in my presence. The trumpery elementals that amuse themselves at the expense of the spiritist type of imbecile keep very clear of Magicians. (Readers of Eliphas Lévi will remember that D. D. Home was panic-stricken at the approach of the adept.) After two hours of watchful waiting Feilding suggested trying for cabinet phenomena. The cabinet was, as usual, a corner of the room with a cloth pinned across, behind this being a table furnished with trumpets, tambourines and similar baitful bogies. At the suggestion Caracini sprang from his seat and extended his hands towards the upper part of the curtain. I required no further information. There was nothing suspicious in his act but the psychology was final. There was an association in his mind between cabinet phenomena and physical manipulation.

I take this opportunity of pointing out that no cabinet phenomena of any sort have ever taken place when netting has been placed between the curtain and the medium. We can hardly conceive of any type of force capable of blowing trumpets, impressing wax, etc., which would be intercepted by netting, except that normal to humanity.

May I further remark that, in our generation, no professional medium has ever produced evidential phenomena of any kind with the exception of Eusapia Palladino, Mrs Piper, Eva C (if she can be classed as professional) and Bert Reece. I have dealt already with Eusapia. I never met Mrs Piper, but her record somehow fails to impress me as remarkable. Eva C is still *sub judice* and I will now deal with Bert Reece, after permitting myself the single observation that spiritists who talk about the cumulative value of their evidence have only four doubtful integers to add to an interminable string of zeros.

I met Bert Reece in London just before the war of 1914. His claim to fame was based on two items. First, if you put your hand on his head you could sometimes feel a throbbing, which of course proves beyond all possibility of a doubt the immortality of the soul. In this calculation I have adopted the official American standard of proof. Second, he was able to read and answer questions which had been previously written on slips of paper in his absence (presumed), folded up and distributed in various pockets. Having answered the first question a paper was handed to him; he then answered the second and so on.

This *modus operandi* suggests that he relies for success on some variation of the trick known as 'the one after', though I personally believe that he changes his methods as much as he can. It seems perfectly obvious in any case that a trick of some sort is being worked.

The real point of interest is that Hereward Carrington, who boasts that he has explained every single 'sealed letter reading' that has come under his notice, admits failure to explain this case, and he has assured me personally that he is completely baffled and inclined to believe that some occult power is at work.

Bert Reece is an Americanized German or Polish Jew from Posen. He was, I suppose, at this time about sixty years old. He commanded enormous fees for consultations. Many of the biggest business men in the States acted habitually on his advice. My own interest was limited to the curiosity aroused by Carrington's statement.

I went to see him at the Savoy Hotel in London. His personality is delightful and he received me with charming courtesy. He then asked me to write five questions on five slips of paper as usual, fold them, and put them in separate pockets. I said that I could not possibly think of troubling him to that extent. I should be perfectly convinced if he would read a word of three letters already in my pocket. (I had put the word TIN inside the back of my watch.) He of course refused the test and I knew where I was. However to humour him, and incidentally to observe his method, I did as he asked. Some of my questions were such that he was unlikely to know the answer. Others concerned the Cabbala. In one case I did not know the answer myself; but if he was really in touch with a high intelligence he could find out and I could check his correctness by the method elsewhere explained.

He read my questions correctly, but failed to answer any of them. Before answering the first time he made a number of suspicious movements that inclined me to think that he manages to pick one's pocket of the first slip after which, of course, the 'one after' method proceeds merrily.

I called on him in New York early in 1915 with the idea of trying him out by offering him a share of the proceeds of persuading one of my friends to invest in a certain financial scheme. (Needless to say, my friend was a party to the plan.) Reece agreed without hesitation. I simply told him to answer the questions in such a way as to persuade the inquirer of certain facts. As luck would have it the test was even more conclusive than I had arranged for. In one of the questions a certain man's name occurred. According to my arrangement with Reece, he should have answered that this man was not to be trusted. The name bears a distinct resemblance to my own. He jumped to the conclusion that I was meant and praised the man up to the skies.

There was still one more sitting. He was to do his utmost to persuade his consultant to adopt a certain course of action. He tried every trick for the best part of an hour, without producing the slightest result. The atmosphere was one of cold disgust, mixed with a certain contemptuous pity. At the same time, one could not but understand that, given the original *sine qua non,* he could lead his client by the nose into the most absurd actions. This *prima materia* of the work need not be the pure gold of confidence. It is quite sufficient if the client is morally and mentally unstable from fear, credulity, anxiety, desire or even natural uncertainty—this last being, of course, an evident condition of any serious consultation whatever. Give him something to work on and little by little one is bound to fall into his line of thought, after which it is child's play to turn every incident to advantage. The client will come away from the consultation convinced of the supernatural powers of the charlatan.

From the beginning of my investigation of so-called psychical research. I felt sure from mere consideration of the conditions of the problem that the adhesion of so many prominent men of science to spiritism must be explained by psychological facts. This saved me a great deal of time. The first key that I tried fitted the lock.

I noted immediately that the scientific men concerned were in some cases, though not in all, indisputably trustworthy as observers. They were capable of detecting fraud and of devising methods to exclude it. I was faced with the alternative of accepting the hypothesis of spiritism, which revolts my scientific spirit and is repudiated, by my instinct as an initiate, for a foul blasphemy and profanation, or I must find some reason for supposing that a number of men reputed trustworthy observers are for some reason rendered suddenly incompetent.

I have said a number of prominent men of science, but in point of fact very few of them have any sort of claim to rank in the first flight. However, such as they are, it is certainly curious that their first leaning towards spiritism becomes manifest on their reaching an age when the sexual power begins to decline.

I submit the following explanation of the psychological process of conversion in these cases.

1. The failure of the sexual energy turns their attention to death.

2. The inexpugnable fear of death demands the resort to some spiritual soporific.

3. Their scientific training makes it impossible for them to take refuge in any superstitious religion.

3a. They probably lack the pagan courage to accept the situation philosophically, their moral integrity having been injured in childhood by their Christian upbringing.

4. They seek consolation in some theory of immortality which promises to verify its theses by scientific evidence such as they are accustomed to accept.

5. They approach their first séances with a subconscious will-to-believe of great intensity.

6. They are sufficiently aware of this attitude to make a point of exaggerating their scepticism to themselves; that is, they affirm their scepticism with an emphasis the more passionate in proportion as they hope, at the bottom of their hearts, to find sufficient evidence to shake it.

7. They satisfy their consciences by making a great display of their acuteness in detecting fraud, actual or possible, and thereby excuse themselves for adding, as if by afterthought, 'obviously there are a few minor points whose explanation is not immediately obvious.'

8. They concentrate their attention on these unexplained points until they fill the entire point of view.

9. What with overstrained attention, Freudian forgetfulness and the illusions of desire, they quiet their consciences sufficiently to assert the genuineness of some few of the phenomena, preferably those which are, so to speak, the thin end of the wedge and are explicable on hypotheses not fundamentally repugnant to the main body of scientific truth.

10. The critical attitude of their colleagues excites the usual

reaction and rouses them to defend vigorously propositions originally put forward tentatively under every reserve.

11. Feeling their sand castle crumbling with each wave of the purifying salt water of criticism, they shovel fresh sand to the support of the threatened edifice. In their haste and eagerness they abandon all pretence of examining the quality of the material and no longer distinguish between the qualities of evidence.

12. It is now quite easy for mediums to persuade them that they are chosen captains of a crusade. Even when they continue their original methods of testing the genuineness of phenomena, the mediums have become familiar with their methods and found out how to circumvent them. In the words of Browning: 'So off we push.'

So much for the so-called scientific contingent. Browning's 'Mr Sludge, "The Medium" ' [7] is to me the deepest and completest psychological study ever written. I only wish it could be matched by a parallel exposure of the half-hidden perversities and trickeries of the scientific mind.

71

The spring of 1912 found me once more hovering between London and Paris. I wrote a few first-rate lyrics, a few more or less important essays, such as 'Energized Enthusiasm',[1] but on the whole, the virtue had gone out of me as far as big conceptions and elaborate executions were concerned. The campaign of 1911 had exhausted my heavy ammunition for the time being.

None the less, I could point to one solid achievement on the large scale, as I must consider it, although it is composed of more or less disconnected elements. I refer to *The Book of Lies*. In this there are ninety-three chapters: we count as a chapter the two pages filled respectively with a note of interrogation and a mark of exclamation. The other chapters contain sometimes a single word, more frequently from half a dozen to twenty phrases, occasionally anything up to a dozen paragraphs. The subject of each chapter is determined more or less definitely by the Cabbalistic import of its number. Thus, Chapter 25[2] gives a revised ritual of the Pentagram; 72 is a rondel with the refrain 'Shemhamphorash',[3] the Divine name of 72 letters; 77 Laylah,[4] whose name adds to that number; and 80, the number of the letter Pé, referred to Mars, a panegyric upon war.

Sometimes the text is serious and straightforward, sometimes its obscure oracles demand deep knowledge of the Cabbala for interpretation; others contain obscure allusions, play upon words, secrets expressed in cryptogram, double or triple meanings which must be combined in order to appreciate the full flavour; others again are subtly ironical or cynical. At first sight the book is a jumble of nonsense intended to insult the reader. It requires infinite study, sympathy, intuition and initiation. Given these, I do not hesitate to claim that in none other of my writings have I given so profound and comprehensive an exposition of my philosophy on every plane. I deal with the inmost impulses of the soul and through the whole course of consciousness down to the reactions of the most superficial states of mind.

I consider this book so important as a compendium of the contents of my consciousness that I beg leave to illustrate the above points.

'Mind is a disease of semen' asserts a theory of the relations between the conscious and subconscious, whose main thesis is that the true ego lurks silent in the quintessence of physical form, whereas the conscious self is no more than the murmur of its moods whenever its supremacy is challenged by environment. In Chapter 37, thought is compared to the darkness of a lunar and spiritual ecstasy to that of a solar eclipse. Both shadows are rare accidents in a universe of light. Again 'In the Wind of the mind arises the turbulence called I. It breaks; down shower the barren thoughts. All life is choked.' Elsewhere, deep spiritual wisdom is evoked by tea at Rumpelmayer's, dinner at Lapérouse, breakfast at the Smoking Dog, a walk in the forest, or the dealings of the Master with his disciples.

Let me further brag that even uninstructed souls have found enlightenment and ecstasy in these mysterious mutterings.

One brilliant boy wrote in *Poetry and Drama* as follows:

Creation and destruction of gods has been for centuries mankind's favourite religious mania and philosophical exercise. *The Book of Lies* is a witty, instructive and wholly admirable collection of paradoxes, in themselves contradictory, summing up and illustrating various experiments in god-making. Frater Perdurabo, however, has not written a philosophical or mystical treatise; on the contrary, his book leaves one with a feeling of intense exhilaration and clearheadedness. The book cannot be judged by the mere reading of excerpts; nor can it be read straight through. Indeed, if one is really desirous to appreciate its subtleties, this should not be attempted before twelve p.m. To be carried about and discussed at leisure, to annoy, repel, stimulate, puzzle and interest, are evidently some of its functions. Stupendously idiotic and amazingly clever, it is at the same time the quintessence of paradox and simplicity itself; yet when all this is said one is still far from the core, for just when one thinks to have discovered it, one finds that many obvious beauties of thought and expression have been overlooked, others misinterpreted. Sometimes one is even doubtful if the author himself could translate into definite terms the exact meaning of his aphorisms and paradoxes without detracting from the value of the book as an artistic expression of his personality. This is, however, an individual appreciation. *The Book of Lies* will therefore be interpreted differently by each reader and judged accordingly.

The best short story, as some think, that I have ever written belongs to 1912, 'The Testament of Magdalen Blair'.[5] The idea was based on a suggestion of Allan Bennett's made in 1899, and fallow in my mind ever since. It was this. Since thoughts are the accompaniments of modifications of the cerebral tissue, what thoughts must be concomitants of its putrefaction? It is certainly as ghastly an idea as any man could wish for on a fine summer morning. I thought I would use it to make people's flesh creep. My difficulty was how to acquaint other people with the thoughts of a dead man. So I made him a man of science and provided him with a wife, a student at Newnham, endowed with extraordinary sensibility which she develops into thought reading. She and her husband make a series of experiments and thus develop her faculty to perfection. He gets Bright's disease and dies, while she records what he thinks during delirium, coma and finally death.

I managed to make the story sound fairly plausible and let myself go magnificently in the matter of horror. I read it aloud to a house party on Christmas Eve; in the morning they all looked as if they had not recovered from a long and dangerous illness. I found myself extremely disliked!

Encouraged by this, I decided to offer the story to the *English Review;* but (for various reasons) sent it in as from another hand. I got a friend of mine to enclose it with a letter to say that it was the work of her daughter at Cambridge. (The story ends, by the way, with the widow, unable to endure the horror of knowing what was in store for her and the rest of humanity, urging everybody to blow out their brains with dynamite as the most practical method of minimizing the agony. She is then put in an asylum, where she demonstrates the genuineness of her claim to report accurately what people are thinking but fails to impress the English doctor though implored by the most eminent German professor in that department of science to allow her to work with him.) The editor wrote to my friend that he would like to publish the story, but required proof of its literal truth.

I cannot comment upon such incidents. I have never been able to understand the psychology of such crass stupidity as I have found almost universal among editors and publishers. I can understand any man considering any piece of literature worthless, or thinking it a supreme masterpiece. Hume's remarks on the 'unhappy barbarism' of Shakespeare, and Shelley's delusion that Leigh Hunt was a poet, are perfectly intelligible to me; but I am completely baffled by such mental operations as here indicated. Another instance will be found in connection with my story 'The Stratagem' on a subsequent page.

A third symptom of the disease of the same individual is brought out in my poem, 'To A New Born Child'.[6] The editor protested that it was rather rough luck on a kid to predict such misfortunes for it. In other words, he had not the remotest idea what the poem was about. Considering that this particular editor is quite justly reputed to be far and away the best man in England in the matter of appreciating first-class work, it is perfectly incomprehensible to me that he should be such an arrant blockhead.

Most of my time in 1912 was taken up by the O.T.O.[7] The Order was a great success and ceremonies of initiation were of almost daily occurrence. I was also very busy helping Laylah [8] in her career. The problem was not easy. I soon discovered that it was not in her to undergo the dreary remorseless drudgery demanded by ambition to the classical concert platform. Striking too as her success had been in the Rites of Eleusis, it soon became clear that its source was the impulse of my personality. I could invoke the gods into her; I could not teach her to invoke them herself.

The truth of the matter was that her art was a secondary consideration with her. Secretly, she herself was probably unconscious of it. She was obsessed by the fear of poverty, the Oedipus-complex wish for a 'secure future', snobbish ambition to improve her social standing. As soon as she passed the age of thirty and came into contact with the atmosphere of America, the spiritual and even the romantic sides of her character wasted away. She rushed desperately from one prospect of prosperity to another, only to find herself despised and duped by the men she was trying to deceive. At last she dropped to the depth of despair and in her drowning struggles lost her last link with life and love. She became a traitor and a thief; and bolted with her spoils to hide herself, like Fafnir, from the very eye of heaven.

I failed to divine the essential hopelessness of helping her. I idealized her; I robed her in the royal vestures of romance. The power and passion of her playing inspired me. Her beauty, physical and moral, bewitched me. I failed to realize to what extent these qualities depend upon circumstances; but it was clear by the beginning of 1912 that she could never get much higher than leading the Ladies' Band in *The Waltz Dream* as she had been doing. The best hope was to find something equally within her powers which would yet give her the opportunity to make an individual impression. I therefore suggested that she should combine fiddling with dancing. My idea was, of course, to find a new art-form. But of this she was not capable. She failed to understand my idea.

I acquiesced. I turned my thoughts to making a popular success for her. We collected six assistant fiddlers, strung together a jumble of jingles and set them to a riot of motion; dressed the septette in coloured rags, called them 'The Ragged Ragtime Girls' and took London by storm. It was a sickening business.

Laylah had spent some weeks in New York with *Two Little Brides*. I had given her introductions to various correspondents of mine in the city; people interested in my work. One of these demands attention, both for her own sake as one of the most remarkable characters I have ever known and for the influence of her intervention on my affairs.

Her name was Vittoria Cremers. She claimed to be the bastard of a wealthy English Jew and to have married a knavish Austrian baron. She was an intimate friend of Mabel Collins, authoress of *The Blossom and the Fruit*, the novel which has left so deep a mark upon my early ideas about Magick. In 1912 she was in her fifties. Her face was stern and square, with terribly intense eyes from which glared an expression of indescribable pain and hopeless horror. Her hair was bobbed and dirty white, her dress severely masculine save the single concession of a short straight skirt. Her figure was sturdy and her gait determined though awkward. Laylah found her in a miserable room on 176th Street or thereabouts. Pitifully poor, she had not been able to buy *Liber 777* and had therefore worked week after week copying in the Astor Library. She impressed Laylah as an earnest seeker and a practical business woman. She professed the utmost devotion to me and proposed to come to England and put the work of the Order on a sound basis. I thought the idea was excellent, paid her passage to England and established her as manageress.

Technically, I digress; but I cannot refrain from telling her favourite story. She boasted of her virginity and of the intimacy of her relations with Mabel Collins, with whom she lived a long time. Mabel had however divided her favours with a very strange man whose career had been extraordinary. He had been an officer in a cavalry regiment, a doctor, and I know not how many other things in his time. He was now in desperate poverty and depended entirely on Mabel Collins for his daily bread. This man claimed to be an advanced Magician, boasting of many mysterious powers and even occasionally demonstrating the same.

At this time London was agog with the exploits of Jack the Ripper. One theory of the motive of the murderer was that he was performing an Operation to obtain the Supreme Black Magical Power. The seven women had to be killed so that their seven bodies formed a 'Calvary cross of seven points' with its head to the west. The theory was that after killing the third or the fourth, I forget which, the murderer acquired the power of invisibility, and this was confirmed by the fact that in one case a policeman heard the shrieks of the dying woman and reached her before life was extinct, yet she lay in a *cul-de-sac*, with no possible exit save to the street; and the policeman saw no signs of the assassin, though he was patrolling outside, expressly on the lookout.

Miss Collins's friend took great interest in these murders. He discussed them with her and Cremers on several occasions. He gave them imitations of how the murderer might have accomplished his task without arousing the suspicion of his victims until the last moment. Cremers objected that his escape must have been a risky matter, because of his habit of devouring certain portions of the ladies before leaving them. What about the blood on his collar and shirt? The lecturer demonstrated that any gentleman in evening dress had merely to turn up the collar of a light overcoat to conceal any traces of his supper.

Time passed! Mabel tired of her friend, but did not dare to get rid of him because he had a packet of compromising letters written by her. Cremers offered to steal these from him. In the man's bedroom was a tin uniform case which he kept under the bed to which he attached it by cords. Neither of the women had ever seen this open and Cremers suspected that he kept these letters in it. She got him out of the way for a day by a forged telegram, entered the room, untied the cords and drew the box from under the bed. To her surprise it was very light, as if empty. She proceeded nevertheless to pick the lock and open it. There were no letters; there was nothing in the box, but seven white evening dress ties, all stiff and black with clotted blood!

Her other favourite story is more to the point. At the critical moment of her mission, Madame Blavatsky had been most foully betrayed by Mabel Collins with the help, according to the stratagems and at the instigation of Cremers, who not only justified, but boasted of her conduct.

It may be matter for surprise that I was not warned of the woman's character by this confession. But I have one invariable rule in dealing with those that come to me for training and that is: to pay no attention whatever to their relations with myself, but to advise them according to the principles of the A∴A∴, as if we lived in different planets. For instance, if a man tells me he is a thief, I refuse on principle to lock up my spoons; I use the information solely as a key to his character, and tell him that in robbing others he is really robbing himself by violating the principle which protects him from theft. I trusted Cremers absolutely, though I knew this—and even that she had, at one time, been the paid spy of some blackmailing vigilance society in America, which, under cover of moral indignation, forged false evidence against convenient candidates, implicating them in the white slave traffic, extracting hush money, or prosecuting when the victim was not worth despoiling or refused to pay up, and sometimes by way of 'making an example', in order to frighten the next batch whose blood they proposed to suck.

I left a book of signed cheques in her charge; I allowed her access to my private papers. I gave no sign that I saw how she was corrupting the loyalty of Laylah and making mischief all round. Presently, at the end of 1913, she got influenza. I went to visit her unexpectedly; there, on the table by her bed, was a memorandum showing unmistakably that she had embezzled large sums of money by fraudulent manipulation of the aforesaid cheques. I failed to conceal from her that I had seen and understood, but I continued to act towards her with unvarying kindness and continued to trust her absolutely. It was too much for her! She had hated me from the first, as she had hated Blavatsky, and vowed to ruin me as she had ruined my great predecessor; and now, when she had robbed me and betrayed me at every turn, I had not turned a hair. The consciousness that her hate was impotent was too much for her to endure. She developed an attack of meningitis and was violently insane for six weeks, at the end of which time she melted away to hide her shame in Wales, where she supposed sensibly enough that she would find sympathetic society in thieves and traitors after her own heart. I understand in fact that she is still there.

During the whole period up to the outbreak of the war, my work gradually increased and consolidated. I must mention the visit of my representative in South Africa, Frater Semper Paratus.[9] This brother possessed the most remarkable magical faculties, within a certain limited scope. It was natural for him to bring into action those forces which impinge directly upon the material world. For instance, his ability to perform divination by means of geomancy (which presumes the action of intelligences of a gross type) has no parallel in my experience. Let me illustrate what I mean.

By profession Frater Semper Paratus was a chartered accountant. He would be called in to audit the finances of some firm. He would find himself confronted by an overwhelming mass of documents. 'It means three weeks' work,' he would say to himself, 'to discover the location of the error.' Instead of exploring the mass of material at random, he would set up a series of geomantic figures and, after less than an hour's work, would take up the volume geomantically indicated and put his finger at once upon the origin of the confusion.

On another occasion, he bethought himself that, living as he did in Johannesburg, surrounded by gold and diamonds, he might as well use geomancy to discover a deposit for his own benefit. Indifferent as to whether he found gold or diamonds, he thought to include both by framing his question to cover 'mineral wealth'. He was directed to ride out from the city by a given compass bearing. He did so. He found no indication of what he sought. He had given up hope and determined to return when he saw a range of low hills before him. He decided to push on and see if anything was visible from its summit. No, the plain stretched away without promise, a marshy flat with pools of stagnant water dotted about it. At this moment of complete disappointment, he noticed that his pony was thirsty. He therefore rode down to the nearest pool to let him drink. The animal refused the water, so he dismounted to find out the reason. The taste told him at once that he had discovered an immensely rich deposit of alkali. His geomancy had not misled him; he had found mineral wealth. He proceeded to exploit his discovery and would have become a millionaire in short order had he not met with the opposition of Brunner, Mond & Co.

On the other hand, his clairvoyance was hopelessly bad, so that he could not pass the examination for the Grade of Zelator of A∴A∴ though in other points entitled to a much higher degree. One of his practical objects in visiting England was to ask me personally to get him over the stile.

I did so. At the very first trial I enabled him to use his astral eyesight. Our joint work developed and we resolved to make a series of investigations of 'The Watch Towers of the Elements', beginning with that of Fire. The question arose: 'Why does the instruction tell us to rise vertically in the astral body for a great distance before penetrating the symbol under examination?' I said, 'It seems to me a mere superstition connected with the idea that heaven is above and hell beneath one.' To clear up this point, we decided to enter the Watch Tower directly, without rising. Our visions, occupying three successive days, showed no abnormal features. But—and here one cannot help feeling that Semper Paratus's faculty of making connection with forces in close contact with the material plane is involved—no less than five fires broke out in the studio during that period. On the third night, Semper Paratus decided to walk home to the house of the friends with whom he was staying in Hampstead. It was late at night when he approached; but his attention was at once attracted by smoke issuing from the house. He gave the alarm and the fire was quickly got under. The mysterious and significant point about the incident is that the fire had got started in the one place in a house where there is no rational explanation for an outbreak—in the coal cellar!

One further illustration of the peculiar qualities of this Brother. I had advised him to evoke the forces of Fire and Air on return to South Africa, they being naturally plentiful in that part of the world. He began with the fiery part of Fire, which includes lightning. When he began his ceremony there was no indication of electrical disturbance; but in a few minutes a storm gathered and his temple was struck.

Another Brother similarly evoking the forces of Water, the cistern of his house burst during the ceremony and flooded it.

Similar incidents constantly occur to those Magicians whose forces tend to manifest in concrete expression. But such men are rare. In my own case, though many similar phenomena have occurred, as already recorded, I regard them as due to defects of insulation. They warn me to take pains to perfect my circle.

The art of producing phenomena at will is a totally different question. The simplest, most rational, and most direct method had been known to me since the summer of 1911; but for some reason, I had never practised it systematically or recorded my results methodically. I believe this to have been due to an instinctive reluctance in respect of the nature of the method. It was not until January 1st, 1914 that I made it my principal engine.

72

I think it proper to devote an entire chapter to the subject of my relations with freemasonry. I have mentioned that I had obtained the 33° in Mexico City.[1] It did not add much of importance to my knowledge of the mysteries; but I had heard that freemasonry was a universal brotherhood and expected to be welcomed all over the world by all brethren.

I was brought up with a considerable shock within the next few months, when, chancing to discuss the subject with some broken-down gambler or sporting-house tout—I forget exactly —I found that he would not 'recognize' me! There was some trivial difference in one of the grips or some other totally meaningless formality. A measureless contempt for the whole mummery curled my lip. I squared the matter (as already related) by having myself initiated in Lodge Number 343 'Anglo-Saxon' in Paris. What that led to I have recounted elsewhere and now quote:

> I happened to know that the chaplain of the British Embassy in Z— was Past Grand Organist of a certain English province. He proposed me, found a seconder, and I was duly initiated, passed and raised. I was warmly welcomed by numerous English and American visitors to our Lodge; for Z— is a very great city.
> I returned to England some time later, after 'passing the chair' in my Lodge, and wishing to join the Royal Arch, called on its venerable secretary.
> I presented my credentials. 'O Thou Great Architect of the Universe,' the old man sobbed out in rage, 'why dost Thou not wither this impudent impostor with Thy fire from heaven? Sir, begone! You are not a Mason at all! As all the world knows, the people in Z— are atheists and live with other men's wives.'

I thought this a little hard on my Reverend Father in God, my proposer; and I noted that, of course, every single English or American visitor to our Lodge in Z— stood in peril of instant and irrevocable expulsion on detection. So I said nothing, but walked to another room in Freemasons' Hall over his head, and took my seat as a Past Master in one of the oldest and most eminent Lodges in London!

Kindly note, furthermore, that when each of those wicked visitors returned to their Lodges after their crime, they automatically excommunicated the whole thereof; and as visiting is very common, it may well be doubted whether, on their own showing, there is a single 'just, lawful and regular mason' left alive on the earth!

By the end of 1910, thanks to my relations with the Grand Hierophant 97° [2] of the Rite of Memphis (a post held after his death by Dr Gerard Encausse ['Papus'], Theodor Reuss ['Merlin'], and myself), I was now a sort of universal inspector-general of the various rites, charged with the secret mission of reporting on the possibility of reconstructing the entire edifice, which was universally recognized by all its more intelligent members as threatened with the gravest danger.

I must briefly explain the circumstances.

(a) There is a great multiplicity of rites.

(b) There is a great multiplicity of jurisdictions.

(c) Even where rite and jurisdiction are identical, there are certain national jealousies and other causes of divergence.

(d) The progress of feminism has threatened the Craft. (The meaning of the 3° having been totally lost, orthodox freemasons are unable to explain why women cannot become Master Masons. They cannot. I, the fiercest of feminists, say so.) Co-Masonry, under Mrs Besant, whose hysterical vanity compels her to claim any high-sounding title that she happens to hear, *Le Droit Humain* in France, and similar movements almost everywhere, were bringing masonry into contempt by their sheer silliness. They were so obviously exactly as good as real freemasons.

(e) The history of freemasonry has become more obscure as the light of research has fallen on the subject. The meaning of masonry has either been completely forgotten or has never existed at all, except insofar as any particular rite might be a cloak for political or even worse intrigue.

(f) It has become impossible for people living in modern conditions to devote adequate time even to learning the merest formalities.

(g) The complete lack of understanding which is now practically universal has made men inquire why in God's name they should cherish such pretentious pedantries?

A few anecdotes will illustrate the situation for the average non-mason.

1. A certain rite in England derives its authority from a document which is as notoriously a forgery as Pigott [3] ever penned. The heads of this gang wished to break, in the most shameless and rascally manner, an agreement made some years previously with John Yarker. Yarker pointed out that their only real authority was derived from their agreement with him, since he, working under a genuine charter, had 'heled' their breach with antiquity by recognizing them. They replied that they relied on the forged document. He said that he would cut away the ground from under their feet by publishing the proofs that their charter was worthless. Then they said that they knew as well as he did that the document was forged; but they didn't care, because they had induced the Prince of Wales to join them!

2. Several of the main rites of English masonry are not recognized by each other, and some of these are not even tolerated (that is, if a member of A joins B, or even discusses freemasonry with a member of B, he becomes liable to immediate expulsion); yet a certain royal duke was actually the head of two incompatible rites.

3. There is no uniformity with regard to toleration. Thus A and B sometimes recognize each other, but, while A recognizes C, B does not, so that a member of B and a member of C might find themselves meeting in a Lodge of A, and thereby automatically excommunicate each other.

4. English Craft masons do not permit religious, political or commercial motives to enter into freemasonry, yet they are in official relationship with certain masonic bodies whose sole *raison d'être* is anti-clericalism, political intrigue or mutual trade benefit.

5. The Scottish Rite, the degrees of Knight Templar, Knight of Malta and others in England are definitely Christian, e.g. the point of one degree is the identification of prophet, priest and king, three in one, the Trinity of the Royal Arch, with Christ; and in the Rose Croix degree, Christ is recognized as the 'corner stone' of earlier symbolism. But in America, the Christian elements have been removed so that wealthy Jews may reach the summit of masonry.

6. I once attended a Lodge whose Master was one of the two local bankers. He used his influence to get business for his bank. The other banker promptly obtained a charter from some 'clandestine' body and started an opposition. In this district, the clandestine Lodges greatly outnumbered the orthodox.

7. I have visited Craft Lodges and Royal Arch Chapters in Fraternal Accord in England, where the 'raising' and 'exaltation' were carried out in shirt sleeves, while cigars were smoked and the legs conveniently disposed on other chairs, and only employed to kick the candidate as he went round.

8. At one ceremony in America, the officers being 33° masons, recognized by the orthodox Scottish Rite in England, there were two candidates, both Jews. They were hoodwinked and introduced into opposite ends of a tube through which they were instructed to make their way. In the middle of the tube was a live sow.

9. In Detroit, a member of the 32° was threatened by certain 33°s with expulsion unless he complied with their views as to his domestic life. The matter was one with which they had no right to meddle on any conceivable theory of human relations.

10. In some parts of America, financial and social pressure is put upon people to *compel* them to take the 32°! It is common to boycott men in trade or business for refusing to give unfair advantages to their fellow masons.

11. A 33° mason, of many years' standing, holding high office in the Supreme Grand Council, who had joined in order to obtain the traditional secret knowledge, told me that he had never learnt anything from any of the degrees. The only peculiarity in this case is that he should have expected anything of the sort—or wanted it!

12. With hardly an exception, the 'secrets' of freemasonry are strictly arbitrary. Let me explain what I mean. If I am given the combination of a safe, I expect to be able to open it by the use of the word. If I can do so, it proves that that is the correct word. The secrets of freemasonry disclose no mysteries; they do not do what they profess to do; they are meaningless conventions.

13. With the rarest exceptions, freemasons make no attempt to keep their obligations so far as the moral principles inculcated are concerned. For instance, the Master Mason is sworn to respect the chastity of the wife, sister and daughter of his Brother. Those who do so probably respect the chastity of any woman irrespective of her male connections.

14. Freemasons, generally, but especially in England and America, resent any attempt to take masonry seriously. I may quote an essay by a Past Grand Master. It appeared in the *English Review* for August 1922. It sets forth the initiated view. The question is: Why does a man become a mason?

We ought to cross off the pettier human motives first, love of vanity, of mystery, of display, of make-believe; but the average man in England becomes a mason for as serious a reason as he becomes a Church member or a theosophist; and the average man is usually most abominably disillusioned.

He may join the Craft with some idea of fellowship, because it is a tradition in his family to do so, or because he hopes to find in the Secret of the Mysteries something which he does not find in any of the exoteric forms of religion.

How is it the same Order satisfies—more or less—aspirations so diverse?

We are brought at last face to face with the fundamental problem of the masonic historian—the origin of the whole business.

Without any hesitation at all, one may confess that on this critical question nothing is certainly known. It is true, indeed, that the Craft Lodges in England were originally Hanoverian clubs, as the Scottish Lodges were Jacobite clubs, and the Egyptian Lodges of Cagliostro revolutionary clubs.

But that no more explains the origin of freemasonry than the fact 'many Spaniards are Roman Catholics' explains why the priest says and does certain things rather than others in the Mass.

Now here is the tremendous question: we can admit all Mr Yarker's contentions, and more, as to the connection of masonic and quasi-masonic rites with the old customs of initiating people into the trade guilds; but why should such a matter be hedged about with so severe a wardenship, and why should the Central Sacrament partake of so awful and so unearthly a character?

As freemasonry has been 'exposed' every few minutes for the last century or so, and as any layman can walk into a masonic shop and buy the complete Rituals for a few pence, the only omissions being of no importance to our present point, it would be imbecile to pretend that the nature of the ceremonies of Craft masonry is in any sense a 'mystery'.

There is, therefore, no reason for refraining from the plain statement that, to anyone who understands the rudiments of symbolism, the Master's degree is identical with the Mass. This is in fact the real reason for the papal anathema; for freemasonry asserts that every man is himself the living, slain and re-arisen Christ in his own person.

It is true that not one mason in ten thousand in England is aware of this fact; but he has only to remember his 'raising' to realize the fundamental truth of the statement.

Well may Catholic and freemason alike stand appalled at the stupendous blasphemy which is implied, as they ignorantly think, not knowing themselves of the stuff and substance of the

Supreme Self, each for himself alike no less than Very God of Very God!

But suppose that the sublimity of this conception is accepted, the identity admitted; what sudden overwhelming billow from the past blasts their beatitude? What but the words with which Freud concludes *Totem and Taboo:* In the beginning was the deed!

For the 'sacrifice of the Innocent' celebrated alike in the Lodge and in cathedral is this identical murder of the Master of the Fellow-Craftsmen, that is of the Father by his Sons, when the ape system of the 'Father-horde' was replaced by the tribal system which developed into the 'military clan'!

These statements are undeniable, yet it may be doubted whether there are five hundred freemasons of all the rites put together who would assent to them, or even refrain from objecting to them as bitterly as the average man in Victorian times disliked being told of his kinship with the other primates, and as his children and grandchildren are annoyed when science demonstrates that their religions are survivals of savage superstitions and their dreams determined by bestial instincts.

15. The W.M.⁴ of an exclusive English Lodge told me that he had learnt his part by saying it over to his wife in bed, justifying himself for this apparent breach of his obligation by remarking, with a laugh, that the secrets were lost and that therefore he could not betray them however much he wanted to.

Faced with these, and similar difficulties, I gladly accepted the task laid upon me by the most intelligent freemasons of the world, united as they were by their sincerity, understanding and good will, though divided by sectarian squabbles about jurisdiction.

My first object was to answer the question, 'What is freemasonry?' I collated the rituals and their secrets, much as I had done the religions of the world, with their magical and mystical bases. As in that case, I decided to neglect what it too often actually was. It would be absurd to judge Protestantism by the political acts of Henry VIII. In the same way, I could not judge masonry by the fact that it had denounced the Concordat. I proposed to define freemasonry as a system of communicating truth—religious, philosophical, magical and mystical; and indicating the proper means of developing human faculty by means of a peculiar language whose alphabet is the symbolism of ritual. Universal brotherhood and the greater moral principles, independent of personal, racial, climatic and other prejudices, naturally formed a background which would assure individual security and social stability for each and all.

The question then arose, 'What truths should be communicated and by what means promulgated?' My first object was to eliminate from the hundreds of rituals at my disposal all exoteric elements. Many degrees contain statements (usually inaccurate) of matters well known to modern schoolboys, though they may have been important when the rituals were written. I may mention one degree in which the candidate is portentously informed that there are other religions in the world besides Christianity and that there is some truth in all of them. Their tenets are explained in many cases with egregious error. The description of Buddha as a god is typical. I saw no point in over-loading the system with superfluous information.

Another essential point was to reduce the unwieldy mass of material to a compact and coherent system. I thought that everything worth preserving could and should be presented in not more than a dozen ceremonies, and that it should be brought well within the capacity of any officer to learn by heart his part during the leisure time at his disposal, in a month at most.

The eighteenth-century Rosicrucians, so-called in Austria, had already endeavoured to unite various branches of Continental freemasonry and its superstructures; in the nineteenth century, principally owing to the energy and ability of a wealthy iron master named Karl Kellner, a reconstruction and consolidation of traditional truth had been attempted. A body was formed under the name O.T.O. (Order Templi Orientis) which purported to achieve this result. It purported to communicate the secrets, not only of freemasonry (with its Rites of 3°, 7°, 33°, 90°, 97°, etc.,) but of the Gnostic Catholic Church, the Martinists, the Sat Bhai, the Rosicrucians, the Knights of the Holy Ghost and so on, in nine degrees, with a tenth of an honorary character to distinguish the 'Supreme and Holy King' of the Order in each country where it was established. Chief of these kings is the O.H.O. (Outer Head of the Order, or Frater Superior), who is an absolute autocrat. This position was at this time occupied by Theodor Reuss, the Supreme and Holy King of Germany, who resigned the office in 1922 in my favour.

The O.H.O. put the rituals of this Order at my disposal. I found them of the utmost value as to the central secret, but otherwise very inferior. They were dramatically worthless, but the prose was unequal, they lacked philosophical unity, their information was incomplete and unsystematic. Their general idea was, however, of the right kind; and I was able to take them as a model.

The main objects of the instruction were two. It was firstly necessary to explain the universe and the relations of human life therewith. Secondly, to instruct every man how best to adapt his life to the cosmos and to develop his faculties to the utmost advantage. I accordingly constructed a series of rituals, Minerval, Man, Magician, Master-Magician, Perfect Magician and Perfect Initiate, which should illustrate the course of human life in its largest philosophical aspect. I begin by showing the object of the pure soul, 'One, individual and eternal', in determining to formulate itself consciously, or, as I may say, to understand itself.

It chooses to enter into relations with the solar system. It incarnates. I explain the significance of birth and the conditions established by the process. I next show how it may best carry out its object in the eucharist of life. It partakes, so to speak, of its own godhead in every action, but especially through the typical sacrament of marriage, understood as the voluntary union of itself with each element of its environment. I then proceed to the climax of its career in death and show how this sacrament both consecrates (or, rather, sets its seal upon) the previous procedure and gives a meaning thereto, just as the auditing of an account enables the merchant to see his year's transactions in perspective.

In the next ceremony I show how the individual, released by death from the obsession of personality, resumes relations with the truth of the universe. Reality bursts upon him in a blaze of adorable light; he is able to appreciate its splendour as he could not previously do, since his incarnation has enabled him to establish particular relations between the elements of eternity.

Finally, the cycle is closed by the reabsorption of all individuality into infinity. It ends in absolute annihilation which, as has been shown elsewhere in this book, may in reality be regarded either as an exact equivalent for all other terms soever, or (by postulating the category of time) as forming the starting point for new adventure of the same kind.

It will be clear from the above that the philosophical perfection of this system of initiation leaves nothing to be desired. We may write Q.E.D. The practical problem remains. We have already decided to incarnate, and our birth certificates are with our bankers. We do not have to worry about these matters, and we cannot alter them if we would; death, and what follows death, are equally certain, and equally able to take care of themselves. Our sole preoccupation is how best to make use of our lives.

Now the O.T.O. is in possession of one supreme secret. The whole of its system at the time when I became an initiate of the Sanctuary of the Gnosis (IX°) was directed towards communicating to its members, by progressively plain hints, this all-important instruction. I personally believe that if this secret, which is a scientific secret, were perfectly understood, as it is not even by me after more than twelve years' almost constant study and experiment, there would be nothing which the human imagination can conceive that could not be realized in practice.

By this I mean such things as this: that if it were desired to have an element of atomic weight six times that of uranium that element could be produced. If it were desired to devise an instrument by which the furthest stars or the electrons could be brought within the range of every one of our senses, that instrument could be invented. Or that, if we wished to develop senses through which we could appreciate all those qualities of matter which at present we observe indirectly by means of apparatus, the necessary nervous structure would appear. I makes these remarks with absolute confidence, for even the insignificant approaches that I have been able to make towards the sanctuaries of this secret have shown me that the relations between phenomena are infinitely more complex than the wildest philosophers have ever imagined, and that the old proverb 'Where there's a will there's a way' needs no caveat.

I cannot forebear to quote from Professor A. S. Eddington, Plumian Professor of Astronomy and Experimental Philosophy at Cambridge:

> Here is a paradox beyond even the imagination of Dean Swift. Gulliver regarded the Lilliputians as a race of dwarfs; and the Lilliputians regarded Gulliver as a giant. That is natural. If the Lilliputians had appeared giants to Gulliver, and Gulliver had appeared a dwarf to the Lilliputians—but no! that is too absurd for fiction, and is an idea only to be found in the sober pages of science.

The injunctions of the sages, from Pythagoras, Zoroaster and Lao Tzu, to the Cabbalistic Jew who wrote the Ritual of the Royal Arch, and the sentimental snob who composed those of the Craft degrees, are either directed to indicating the best conditions for applying this secret, or are mere waste of words. Realizing this, it was comparatively simple for me to edit masonic ethics and esotericism. I had simply to refer everything to this single sublime standard. I therefore answered the question 'How should a young man mend his way?' in a series of rituals in which the candidate is instructed in the value of discretion, loyalty, independence, truthfulness, courage, self-control, indifference to circumstance, impartiality, scepticism, and other virtues, and at the same time assisted him to discover for himself the nature of this secret, the proper object of its employment and the best means for insuring success in its use. The first of these degrees is the V°, in which the secret is presented in a pageant; while he is also instructed in the essential elements of the history of the world, considered from the standpoint of his present state of evolution and in his proper relation to society in general with reference to the same.

The degree of Knight Hermetic Philosopher follows, in which his intellectual and moral attitude is further defined. In the VI°, his position having been thus made precise, he is shown how to consecrate himself to the particular Great Work which he came to earth in order to perform. In the VII°, which is tripartite, he is first taught the principle of equilibrium as extended to all possible moral ideas; secondly, to all possible intellectual ideas; and lastly, he is shown how, basing all his actions on this impregnable rock of justice, he may so direct his life as to undertake his Great Work with the fullest responsibility and in absolute freedom from all possibility of interferences.

In the VIII°, the secret is once more manifested to him, more clearly than before; and he is instructed in how to train himself to use it by certain preliminary practices involving acquaintance with some of those subtler energies which have hitherto, for the most part, eluded the observation and control of profane science.

In the IX°, which is never conferred upon anyone who has not already divined from previous indications the nature of the secret, it is explained to him fully. The conclusions of previous experiments are placed at his service. The idea is that each new initiate should continue the work of his predecessor, so that eventually the inexhaustible resources of the secret may be within the reach of the youngest initiate; for at present, we are compelled to admit that the superstitious reverence which has encompassed it in past ages, and the complexity of the conditions which modify its use, place us in much the same position as the electricians of a generation ago in respect of their science. We are assured of the immensity of the force at our disposal; we perceive the extent of the empire which it offers us, but we do not thoroughly understand even our successes and are uncertain how to proceed in order to generate the energy most efficiently or to apply it most accurately to our purposes.

The X°, as in the old system, is merely honorary, but recent researches into the mysteries of the IX° have compelled me to add an XI°,[5] to illustrate a scientific idea which has been evolved by the results of recent experiments.

In the reconstituted O.T.O. there are therefore six degrees in which is conveyed a comprehensive conception of the cosmos and our relation therewith, and a similar number to deal with our duty to ourselves and our fellows, the development of our own faculties of every order, and the general advancement and advantage of mankind.

Wherever freemasonry and allied systems contribute to these themes, their information has been incorporated in such a way as not to infringe the privileges, puerile as they often seem, which have been associated hitherto with initiation. Where they merely perpetuate trivialities, superstitions and prejudices, they have been neglected.

I claim for my system that it satisfies all possible requirements of true freemasonry. It offers a rational basis for universal brotherhood and for universal religion. It puts forward a scientific statement which is a summary of all that is at present known about the universe by means of a simple, yet sublime symbolism, artistically arranged. It also enables each man to discover for himself his personal destiny, indicates the moral and intellectual qualities which he requires in order to fulfil it freely, and finally puts in his hands an unimaginably powerful weapon which he may use to develop in himself every faculty which he may need in his work.

My original draft of these rituals has required modification in numerous details as research made clearer, deeper and wider the truth which they comprehended; and also, as experience showed, the possibilities of misunderstanding on the one hand, and of improved presentation on the other. Great practical progress was made until the work was suspended by the outbreak of the war in 1914.

One of my original difficulties was to restore the existing

rituals to their perfection. There were innumerable corruptions due to ignorance of Hebrew and the like on the part of the unworthy successors of the founders. To take a gross example.

The word *Jeheshua,* spelt in Hebrew in the 18° of the Scottish Rite, was habitually spelt with a Resh instead of a Vau. So brutal a blunder is conclusive proof that the modern Sovereign Princes of Rose Croix attach no meaning whatever to the name of Jesus—which they profess to adore more intelligently than the mob because it represents the descent of the Holy Spirit into the midst of that tremendous name of God which only occurs in their ritual because of its power to annihilate the universe if pronounced correctly.*

The intelligence of the average mason may be gauged by the following quotation from the R.A.M. degree. The twentieth century!—and such stuff is solemnly offered as instruction to grown men!

Some have doubted whether the Ark was capable of containing two of every sort of creature, with provisions necessary for their support for a whole year; for so long and more did Noah stop in that Ark. But on a careful inquiry it has been found that only about one hundred different sorts of beasts, and not two hundred birds, are known, the greater part of them are of no bulk, and many exceedingly small, and it has been said all the creatures in the Ark would not take up the room of five hundred horses. After four thousand years human ingenuity cannot now contrive any proportions better adapted than that of the Ark for the purpose it was intended for. A Dutch merchant, two hundred years ago, built a ship answering in its respective dimensions to those of the Ark; its length being one hundred and twenty feet, breadth twenty feet, depth twelve feet; while building, this vessel was laughed at, but afterwards it was found that it held one third more and sailed better than any other merchant vessel of the time.

Thus we have a collateral proof no way inconsiderable that the Spirit of God, from whom cometh all understanding, directed Noah in that manner.

Again, the central secret of a Master Mason is in a Word which is lost. This fact has induced various and ingenious persons to invent ceremonies in which it is found (in some more

---

* The ignorance of masons is quite boundless. In the Red Cross of Rome and Constantine Degree, for example, we read, 'Lord God of Sabbath'. No one knows the difference between ShBTh and TzBATh! [i.e. Sabaoth (TzBATh), Lord God of Hosts, not Sabbath (ShBTh), Lord God of Sabbath.—Editors.]

or less remarkable manner) amid the acclamations of the assembled populace, and proclaimed in pomp to the admiring multitude. The only drawback is that these Words do not work. It apparently never occurred to these ingenuous artisans to test it. It is useless to label a brick 'This is the keystone of the Royal Arch', unless the arch stands when it is put in place.

Much of freemasonry is connected with the Hebrew Cabbala. My knowledge of this science enabled me to analyse the Secret Words of the various degrees. I soon found myself able to correct many of the corruptions which had crept in, and there was no doubt that my conclusions were not mere conjectures, since they made coherent good sense out of disconnected nonsense. (I am naturally unable to publish any of these discoveries; but I am always ready to communicate them to inquiring Brothers. When I have done so, my arguments have been found cogent and convincing.)

I supposed myself to have reached the summit of success when I restored the Secret Word of the Royal Arch. In this case, tradition had preserved the Word almost intact. It required only a trifling change to reveal it in all its radiant royalty. And yet my success only left me with a sense of deeper annoyance at my complete failure to deal with the abject anticlimax of the III° with its lamentable excuses for having made a fool of the candidate, its pretentious promises and its pitiful performance.

As I lay one night sleepless, in meditation, bitter and eager, upon this mystery I was suddenly stabbed to the soul by a suggestion so simple, yet so stupendous, that I was struck into shuddering silence for I know not how long before I could bring myself to switch on the electric light and snatch my notebook. At the first trial the solution sprang like sunlight in my spirit. I remained all that night in an ecstasy of awe and adoration. I had discovered the lost Word!

The obvious line of criticism is this: How can you be sure that the Word which you have discovered is really the lost Word after all?

This may be made clear by an illustration. On the apron of the 18° I find IHShRH in Hebrew characters. I find that this word means nothing; the context suggests that it may be an error for IHShVH, Yeheshuah or Jesus; but how do I know that this word and not another has power to make man triumphant over matter, to harmonize and sanctify the blind forces of the universe? Thus: I know that IHVH represents the four elements; that 4 is a number symbolizing limitation. It is the square of 2, the only number which cannot be formed harmoniously into a 'Magic Square'. (Two represents the Dyad, the original Error.) I know also that the letter Shin represents a triune essence,[6] the fire of the Spirit, and in particular Ruach Elohim, the Spirit of the Gods, because these two words have the numerical value of 300, which is also that of Shin itself.

I thus interpret the word Yeheshuah as the descent of the Holy Spirit into the balanced forces of matter, and the name Yeheshuah is therefore that of a man made divine by the descent of the Holy Spirit into his heart, exactly as the name George means a farmer. This exegetical method is not a modern invention. When Jehovah selected a family to be the father of Israel, he changed the name ABRM (243) Father of Elevation into ABRHM (248) Father of a multitude; and by way of compensation changed SRI (510) Nobility to SRH (505), Princess. There are several other similar stories in the Bible. A change of name is considered to indicate a change of nature. Further, each name is not arbitrary; it is a definite description of the nature of the object to which it is attached. By a similar process, I am certain of my results in the matter of the Lost Word, for the Found Word fulfils the conditions of the situation; and furthermore, throws light on the obscure symbolism of the entire ritual.

I am thus in a position to do for the contending sects of freemasonry what the Alexandrians did for those of paganism. Unfortunately, the men who asked me to undertake this task are either dead or too old to take active measures and so far there is no one to replace them. Worse, the general coarsening of manners which always follows a great war has embittered the rival jurisdictions and deprived freemasonry altogether of those elements of high-minded enthusiasms with regard to the great problems of society which still stirred even its most degenerate sections half a century ago, when Hargrave Jennings, Godfrey Higgins, Gerald Massey, Kenneth MacKenzie, John Yarker, Theodor Reuss, Wynn Westcott and others were still seeking truth in its traditions and endeavouring to erect a temple of Concord in which men of all creeds and races might worship in amity.

I attempted to make the appeal of the new system universal by combining it with a practical system of fraternal intercourse and mutual benefit. I formulated a scheme of insurance against all the accidents of life; the details are given in the Official Instructions and Essays published in *The Equinox*, vol. III, no. 1; and to set the example I transferred the whole of my property to trustees for the Order. The general idea is this; that every man should enjoy his possessions and the full fruits of his labours exactly as he does under his original individualistic system, but the pooling of such possessions by economy of administration, etc., leaves a surplus which can be used for the general purposes of the Order. I wished to introduce the benefits of co-operation without interfering with the individual absoluteness of the elements of the combination.

The plan promised excellently. The working expenses of the Order were almost negligibly small. We were therefore able to allow members to borrow in case of necessity up to the total amount of their fees and subscriptions; to give them a month's holiday for less than a week would have cost an outsider; to save them all medical, legal and similar expenses; to solve the problem of rent, and so on. We offered all the fabled advantages of socialism without in any way interfering with individual dignity and independence.

I can hardly be blamed for the catastrophe which has temporarily suspended the work. During the war the Grand Treasurer became insane. His character changed completely. He developed a form of persecution mania, in which his oldest and best friends seemed to him to be conspiring against him. Abetted by a dishonest solicitor, he alienated the whole of the property of the Order with extraordinary thoroughness. He actually destroyed a great part of the library; he falsified the figures; and after opposing all sorts of delays to the demand for his account, he actually made away with my very underclothing. My only remaining resources were some twenty thousand pounds' worth of books which he could not touch without paying the sum of three hundred and fifty pounds or so, which was due to the people with whom they were stored. I paid this amount in 1921 and the warehousemen then refused to hand over the books or to pay me the balance owing to me on their own statement. They trusted to be able to steal them, having heard that I was unable to find the money necessary to sue them.

I thus found myself after the war entirely penniless and without clothes, except for some of my Highland costumes which had been sent for repair to a tailor just before the outbreak of hostilities and had remained safely in storage. I do not regret these events, except that I grieve over the calamity to my Brother. I believe it to have been part of the plan of the gods that I should be compelled to face the world entirely without other than moral resources. Such is certainly a supreme test of the essential strength of any economic proposal.

The system has justified itself astonishingly even in these unheard-of difficulties; I have been able to establish a branch of the Order with entire leisure to work at high pressure at its own objects, without internal friction or economic collapse, although the income is derived exclusively from casual windfalls. If we were able to carry out the full principles of the system, we should already be so prosperous as to be able to devote ourselves exclusively to extending the advantages of the scheme to the world at large.

With regard to the original purposes of the Order, there can be no doubt that the reduction of the cumbersome mass of masonic and similar matters to a simple intelligible and workable system enables people to enjoy the full advantages of initiations which, in the old days, were too multiple to be conferred even on those who devoted a disproportionate amount of their lives to the subject. The central secret of free-masonry which was lost, and is found, is in daily use by initiates of our Order. Scientific facts are accumulating rapidly; and it is certain that within a short time we shall be able to dispose of a force more powerful than electricity and capable of more extended application, with the same certainty. Our qualitative results are unquestionable. Quantitative methods, the lack of which has for so many centuries prevented the systematic application of our knowledge, will soon be supplied.

I may say that the secret of the O.T.O., besides what has been mentioned above, has proved to all intents and purposes the simplification and concentration of the whole of my magical knowledge. All my old methods have been unified in this new method. It does not exactly replace them, but it interprets them. It has also enabled me to construct a uniform type of engine for accomplishing anything that I will.

My association with freemasonry was therefore destined to be more fertile than almost any other study, and that in a way despite itself. A word should be pertinent with regard to the question of secrecy. It has become difficult for me to take this matter very seriously. Knowing what the secret actually is, I cannot attach much importance to artificial mysteries. It is true that some of the so-called secrets are significant, but as a rule they are so only to those who already know what the secret is. Again, though the secret itself is of such tremendous import, and though it is so simple that I could disclose it and the principal rules for turning it to the best advantage in a short paragraph, I might do so without doing much harm. For it cannot be used indiscriminately.

Much fun has been made of the alchemists for insisting that the Great Work, an ostensibly chemical process, can only be performed by adepts who fear and love God, and who practise chastity and numerous other virtues. But there is more common sense in such statements than meets the eye. A drunken debauchee cannot perform delicate manipulations in chemistry or physics; and the force with which the secret is concerned, while as material as the Becquerel emanations, is subtler than any yet known. To play great golf or great billiards, to observe delicate reactions, or to conduct recondite mathematical researches, demands more than physical superiorities. Even the theological requirements of alchemy had meaning in those days. An Elizabethan who was not 'at peace with God' was likely to be agitated and thereby unfitted for work demanding freedom from emotional distraction. I have found in practice that the secret of the O.T.O. cannot be used unworthily.

It is interesting in this connection to recall how it came into my possession. It had occurred to me to write a book, *The Book of Lies*, which is also falsely called *Breaks*, the wanderings or falsifications of the one thought of *Frater Perdurabo* which thought is itself untrue.

Each of its ninety-three chapters was to expound some profound magical dogma in an epigrammatic and sometimes humorous form. The Cabbalistic value of the number of each chapter was to determine its subject. I wrote one or more daily at lunch or dinner by the aid of the god Dionysus. One of these chapters bothered me. I could not write it. I invoked Dionysus with peculiar fervour, but still without success. I went off in desperation to 'change my luck', by doing something entirely contrary to my inclinations. In the midst of my disgust, the spirit came upon me and I scribbled the chapter down by the light of a farthing dip. When I read it over, I was as discontented as before, but I stuck it into the book in a sort of anger at myself as a deliberate act of spite towards my readers.

Shortly after publication, the O.H.O.[7] came to me. (At that time I did not realize that there was anything in the O.T.O. beyond a convenient compendium of the more important truths of freemasonry.) He said that since I was acquainted with the supreme secret of the Order, I must be allowed the IX° and obligated in regard to it. I protested that I knew no such secret. He said, 'But you have printed it in the plainest language.' I said that I could not have done so because I did not know it. He went to the bookshelves and, taking out a copy of *The Book of Lies,* pointed to a passage in the despised chapter. It instantly flashed upon me. The entire symbolism, not only of free masonry but of many other traditions, blazed upon my spiritual vision. From that moment the O.T.O. assumed its proper importance in my mind. I understood that I held in my hands the key to the future progress of humanity. I applied myself at once to learn all that he could teach me, finding to my extreme surprise that this was little enough. He fully understood the importance of the matter and he was a man of considerable scientific attainment in many respects; yet he had never made a systematic study of the subject and had not even applied his knowledge to his purposes, except in rare emergencies. As soon as I was assured by experience that the new force was in fact capable of accomplishing the theoretically predictable results, I devoted practically the whole of my spare time to a course of experiments.

I may conclude this chapter with the general remark that I believe that my proposals for reconstituting freemasonry on the lines above laid down should prove critically important. Civilization is crumbling under our eyes and I believe that the best chance of saving what little is worth saving, and rebuilding the Temple of the Holy Ghost on plans, and with material and workmanship, which shall be free from the errors of the former, lies with the O.T.O.

73

In the early part of 1913, my work had apparently settled down to a regular routine. Everything went very well but nothing startling occurred. On March 3rd, the 'Ragged Ragtime Girls' [1] opened at the Old Tivoli. It was an immediate success and relieved my mind of all preoccupations with worldly affairs. Most of my time was devoted to developing the work of the O.T.O. In May I took a short holiday in France and the Channel Islands. Only one incident is worthy of record. I had gone down to my beloved Forest of Fontainebleau for a walk. One morning, climbing the Rocher d'Avon, I saw a serpent cross my path. A little higher the same thing happened. This time I was impelled to kill the reptile, which I did.

I took it into my head that the Masters had sent this as a warning that treachery was at work in London. I returned and found that Cremers was intriguing against me; and that, in particular, she had corrupted the heart of Leila Waddell. The O.H.O.,[2] moreover, had found out that the Grand Hierophant of the Ancient and Primitive Rite of Masonry, John Yarker, had died some months earlier and that his death had been concealed from his colleagues by the machinations of a sort of man named Wedgwood, in the interest of Annie Besant who wanted to obtain control of the Rite. The outrage was baroque, it being the first condition of membership that the candidate should be a freemason in good standing under the jurisdiction of the Grand Lodge of England. However, the conspirators had illegally convened a secret council at Manchester to elect a successor to Yarker. I was deputed to attend and convey the protests of the various Grand Masters on the continent. I did so. I challenged the legality of the council. I showed that Wedgwood was not a freemason at all. I exposed the whole intrigue. At the conclusion of my speech (printed in *The Equinox,* vol. I, no. x) the meeting was adjourned *sine die.* A council was then legally convened; and a man designated by Yarker himself as his successor in one of his last letters to me was elected Grand Master for Britain, with myself as his principal officer. Yarker's office as Grand Hierophant was filled by Dr Encausse (Papus), the Grand Master of France.

Having accomplished these duties, I was free to accompany the 'Ragged Ragtime Girls' to Moscow, where they were engaged for the summer, at the Aquarium. They were badly in need of protection. Leila Waddell was the only one with a head on her shoulders. Of the other six, three were dipsomaniacs, four nymphomaniacs, two hysterically prudish, and all ineradicably convinced that outside England everyone was a robber, ravisher and assassin. They all carried revolvers, which they did not know how to use; though prepared to do so on the first person who spoke to them.

At the Russian frontier, we plunged from civilization and order, headlong into confusion and anarchy. No one on the train could speak a word even of German. We were thrown out at Warsaw into a desolation which could hardly have been exceeded had we dropped on the moon. At last we found a loafer who spoke a little German, but no man knew or cared about the trains to Moscow. We ultimately drove to another station. A train was due to leave, but they would not find us accommodation. We drove once more across the incoherent city and this time found room in a train which hoped to go to Moscow at the average rate of some ten miles an hour. The compartment contained shelves covered with loose dirty straw on which the passengers indiscriminately drank, gambled, quarrelled and made love. There was no discipline, no order, no convenience. At first I blamed myself, my ignorance of the language and so on, for the muddle in Warsaw; but the British consul told me that he had himself been held up there by railway mismanagement on one occasion for forty-eight hours. When we reached Moscow there was no one at the station who could take charge of our party. We found an hotel for ourselves, and rooms for the girls, more by good luck than design. About one in the morning they sent for Leila to rescue them. She found them standing on rickety tables, screaming with fear. They had been attacked by bed-bugs. Luckily I had warned Leila that in Russia the bug is as inseparable from the bed as the snail from his shell.

In a day or two things calmed down. Then there came suddenly upon me a period of stupendous spiritual impulse—even more concentrated than that of 1911. In a café, I met a young Hungarian girl named Anny Ringler; tall, tense, lean as a starving leopardess, with wild insatiable eyes and a long straight thin mouth, a scarlet scar which seemed to ache with the anguish of hunger for some satisfaction beyond earth's power to supply.

We came together with irresistible magnetism. We could not converse in human language. I had forgotten nearly all my Russian; and her German was confined to a few broken cries. But we had no need of speech. The love between us was ineffably intense. It still inflames my inmost spirit. She had passed beyond the region where pleasure had meaning for her. She could only feel through pain, and my own means of making her happy was to inflict physical cruelties as she directed. This kind of relation was altogether new to me; and it was perhaps because of this, intensified as it was by the environment of the self-torturing soul of Russia, that I became inspired to create for the next six weeks.

How stupid it is, by the way, that one is obliged to use words in senses inappropriate to, and sometimes incompatible with, the meaning which one wishes to convey! Thus the idea of cruelty is bound up with that of the unwillingness of the patient, so that in the case of masochism the use of the word is ridiculous. We fail to see straight on such points whenever they concern emotional complexes like love. Love, that is, as the wrong-headed Anglo-Saxon defines it. We do not call it cruel to offer a man a cigar, though a small boy may suffer intensely from smoking one. An enormous amount of erroneous thinking springs from the mental laziness which allows us to acquiesce in a standardized relation between two things which is, in fact, dependent upon occasional conditions.

This constantly leads to the grossest injustice and stupidity. Words like 'miscreant', 'atheist' and similar terms of abuse in matters which excite the emotions of the vulgar, are constantly applied as labels to people whom they nowise fit. For instance, Huxley was branded as a materialist, Thomas Paine as an atheist, when they were nothing of the sort. It was particularly annoying during the war to observe the indiscriminate plastering of people with such mud as 'pro-German', 'pacifist', 'Bolshevist', etc., without the slightest reference to their actual opinions. The proof of the pudding is in the eating; my relations with Anny must be judged by their fruits; happiness, inspiration, spirituality and romantic idealism.

I saw Anny almost every day for an hour or so. The rest of my time I spent (for the most part) in the gardens of the Hermitage or the Aquarium, writing for dear life. In Moscow, in the summer months, day fades into night, night brightens into day with imperceptible subtlety. There is a spiritual clarity in the air itself which is indescribable. From time to time the bells reinforce the silence with an unearthly music which never jars or tires. The hours stream by so intoxicatingly that the idea of time itself disappears from consciousness.

In all that I wrote in those six weeks, I doubt if there is a single word of Anny. She was the soul of my expression, and so beyond the possibility of speech; but she lifted me to heights of ecstasy that I had never before consciously attained and revealed to me secrets deeper than I had ever deemed. I wrote things that I knew not and made no mistake. My work was infinitely varied, yet uniformly distinguished. I expressed the soul of Moscow in a poem 'The City of God', published some months afterwards in the *English Review*. It is a 'hashish dream come true'. Every object of sense, from the desolation of the steppes and the sheer architecture of the city, to the art, attitude and amusements of the people, stings one to the soul, each an essential element of a supreme sacrament. At the same time, the reality of all these things, using the word in its grossest sense, consummates the marriage of the original antinomies which exist in one's mind between the ideal and the actual.

A prose pendant to this poem is my essay 'The Heart of Holy Russia', which many Russians competent to judge have assured me struck surer to the soul of Russia than anything of Dostoyevsky. Their witness fills me with more satisfaction as to the worth of my work than anything else has ever done.

Another poem, 'Morphia', has no ostensible reference to Russia, but the insight into the psychology of the 'addict' was indubitably conferred by my illumination. I had no experience, even at second hand, of the effects of the drug; yet I was assured by a distinguished man of letters who had himself suffered from its malice, that I have expressed to the utmost the terrific truth. He could hardly believe at first that I had written it without actual knowledge.

During this period the full interpretation of the central mystery of freemasonry became clear in consciousness, and I expressed it in dramatic form in 'The Ship'.[3] The lyrical climax is in some respects my supreme achievement in invocation; in fact, the chorus beginning:

Thou who art I beyond all I am . . .

seemed to me worthy to be introduced as the anthem into the Ritual of the Gnostic Catholic Church which, later in the year, I prepared for the use of the O.T.O., the central ceremony of its public and private celebration, corresponding to the Mass of the Roman Catholic Church.

While dealing with this subject I may as well outline its scope completely. Human nature demands (in the case of most people) the satisfaction of the religious instinct, and, to very many, this may best be done by ceremonial means. I wished therefore to construct a ritual through which people might enter into ecstasy as they have always done under the influence of appropriate ritual. In recent years, there has been an increasing failure to attain this object, because the established cults shock their intellectual convictions and outrage their common sense. Thus their minds criticize their enthusiasm; they are unable to consummate the union of their individual souls with the universal soul as a bridegroom would be to consummate his marriage if his love were constantly reminded that its assumptions were intellectually absurd.

I resolved that my Ritual should celebrate the sublimity of the operation of universal forces without introducing disputable metaphysical theories. I would neither make nor imply any statement about nature which would not be endorsed by the most materialistic man of science. On the surface this may sound difficult; but in practice I found it perfectly simple to combine the most rigidly rational conceptions of phenomena with the most exalted and enthusiastic celebration of their sublimity. (This Ritual has been published in *The International*, New York, March 1918, and in *The Equinox*, vol. III, no. 1.)

Numerous other poems, essays and short stories were written during this summer. In particular there is a sort of novel, *The Lost Continent*,[4] purporting to give an account of the civilization of Atlantis. I sometimes feel that this lacks artistic unity. At times it is a fantastic rhapsody describing my ideals of Utopian society; but some passages are a satire on the conditions of our existing civilization, while others convey hints of certain profound magical secrets, or anticipations of discoveries in science.

From my brief description of the conditions of travel in Russia, the intelligent should be able to deduce what I thought of the immediate political future of the country. I returned to England with the settled conviction that in the event of a serious war (the scrap with Japan was really an affair of outposts, like our own Boer War) the ataxic giant would collapse within a few months. England's traditional fear of Slav aggression seemed to me ridiculous; and France's faith in her ally, pathetic. The event has more than justified my vision. I have no detailed knowledge of politics; but, just as my essay, 'The Heart of Holy Russia', told the inmost truth without even superficial knowledge of the facts which were its symptoms, so I possess an immediate intuition of the state of a country without cognizance of the statistics. I am thus in the position of Cassandra, foreseeing and foretelling fate, while utterly unable to compel conviction.

I cannot leave the subject of Russia without rescuing from oblivion some of the significant stories which I had from the excellent British consul, Mr Groves. The most deliciously fantastic is that of what I may call the phantom battleship. This vessel cost well over two million sterling. She was to be the last word in naval construction. She was launched at Odessa in the presence of a great gathering of notables, and the scene lavishly photographed and described in the newspapers. Alas! upon her maiden cruise she was *spurlos versenkt*. The fact of the matter was that she had never existed! Her cost had gone straight into the pockets of the various officials, the photographs were simply faked, and the descriptions imaginary.

Here is another ray of searchlight on Russian rottenness. A crisis had arisen between England and France. A strong Chauvinist element was urging the government to hurl a flat defiance at St James's. The Minister of Marine was asked to report on the readiness of the French navy. He replied in terms of absolute confidence; but within an hour of his doing so, one of his officers came to him in agitation and begged him to make a personal inspection of the arsenal at Toulon. He rushed south on an express engine and found that the fortress was absolutely denuded of munitions. They had been quietly sold off by a gang of dishonest officials and the reports systematically falsified.

On this discovery, he advised the President to agree with England quickly while he was in the way with her, which was done. The Russian ambassador got wind of this affair; it suddenly struck him that Sebastopol might be in the same street as Toulon; he hurried to St Petersburg and put the matter personally before the Tsar. Investigation proved his fears well-founded. The Tsar was roused to bite. Every officer above a certain rank was left in a room with a revolver. They had the choice between suicide and shameful execution. Naturally, they all chose the former and the whole affair was hushed up by reporting their decease from sickness, accident and so on during the next few weeks.

At Vladivostok corruption was so universal and open that on pay day an agent of the contractor sat at the next desk to the naval paymaster and handed each man his share of the profits of the organized system of swindling the government.

One last luminous anecdote. The representative of a Birmingham munition factory called on our consul about some permit or other, and told him the following story. The Russian naval agent in England had accepted the tender of his firm for supplying an immense number of shells. 'About the price, now,' he said to the managing director, 'of course we pay you a hundred and fifty thousand pounds' (or whatever it was) 'but understand that so much of this must go to Admiral A., so much to Councillor B., so much to the Grand Duke C.'— a long list followed. 'My dear sir,' cried the Englishman, aghast, 'surely I have made it plain that our price is bed rock. We shan't take a penny of profit. We only put in so low a tender because trade is so bad and we don't want to shut down.' The Russian spread his hands mournfully. 'Why, hang it,' exclaimed the manufacturer. 'If we were to allow you all those rake-offs, we should have to make the shells of tinfoil and load them with sawdust.' The Russian brightened instantly. 'But exactly,' said he; 'how I admire you practical English! I knew you would find a way out.' And that was how they settled the business, and those were the shells with which Rodjiestvenski was sent round the world to meet the navy of Japan.

Our own red tape was responsible for a really Gilbertian stupidity in consular matters. It had been decided to raise Moscow from a consulate to a consulate-general. Mr Groves had been for many years in Moscow and spoke practically no Polish. Our consul at Warsaw had been in that city also for many years and spoke practically no Russian. But he was senior in the service to Groves by a year or so. It was therefore impossible to continue Groves at Moscow over the head of the man in Warsaw, and they were therefore ordered to change their position, each being ejected from the city whose language he spoke, and whose affairs he had by heart, into one where the conditions were utterly unfamiliar and the language unintelligible.

From early boyhood my imagination had been excited by accounts of the Great Fair at Nijni Novgorod. Finding 'the time and the place and the loved one all together', at the cost of a slight effort, I decided to trot off and see 'The Fun of the Fair', by which title I called the poem in which I describe my excursion. The way in which I wrote it is, I imagine, unique in literature. I wrote down in heroic couplets every incident of the adventure exactly as it occurred and when it occurred. The only variation is that occasionally I permit myself to exaggerate the facts (as in enumerating the races of men whom I met) when the spirit of humour takes charge.

This poem should have appeared in the *English Review* in the autumn of 1914. It was pushed out to make way for my 'Appeal to the American Republic', reprinted from boyhood's happy days, with such politically necessary revisions as 'the traitor Prussian' instead of 'the traitor Russian'. It has thus never yet seen the light.[5]

74

As I was sitting at lunch one day in the Hermitage beginning a lyrical ritual intended for the use of an individual in his private work, I found myself, in the middle of a sentence, at a loss for the next word. I have already explained how swiftly and spontaneously my spirit soars from stanza to stanza without need of previous reflection or subsequent revision. In all these weeks my pen had swung like a skater over the paper. Now suddenly it stopped; an eagle in full flight stricken by a shaft. That sentence has never been completed. The inspiration was withdrawn from me. My light had gone out like an arc-light when the cable is cut. It was long before I wrote again.

Three days later the contract at the Aquarium was due to expire; and those days proved to me how perfectly my existence depended on inspiration. The city, from a crashing chorus of magical music, a pageant of passionate pleasure, became a cold chaos of inanity. The bells no longer sang; the sun and moon were stagnant, soulless spectres in a senseless sky—like a ghost on the gusts of the gale. I went from miraculous Moscow into a world of inarticulate impressions. St. Petersburg failed to rekindle the wonder and worship which it had awakened in me of old. The Nevski Prospekt seemed narrower, meaner; a mere street. St Isaacs no longer enthralled me. I was able to compare the Neva with the Nile, the Ganges, the Rangoon River, and even the Rhine, as coldly and critically as Baedeker. My spirit needed infinite repose after its incomparable effort, and this repose was granted to it by the voyage to Stockholm.

There are ways amid the Western Isles of Scotland, through the Norwegian fjords, and sometimes upon tropic seas, which speak to the soul in a language unknown to any other scenes. There is a solemnity and a serenity in their continual silence which seem not of this world. But the summer voyage across the Baltic, amid the archipelago, is sovereign above any of these. There is no single ripple on the sea, no stirring in the air; the night is indistinguishable from the day, for neither suffers interruption; the steamer skims the surface of the sea as swift and silent as a swallow. One cannot even hear the engines, so utterly does their rhythm interpenetrate the totality of experience. There is a sense of floating in fairyland. One forgets the land whence one has come; one has no vision of the coast to which one is speeding. It seems impossible that the journey even began, still less, that its end is appointed.

One seems to flit between innumerable islands, some crowned with foliage, some mere bare grey knolls, scarce peeping from the waveless mirror of water. There is a sense of infinite intricacy of intention as the steamer insinuates itself into one curving channel after another, or comes out suddenly from a labyrinth of lyrical islands into a shoreless silence. One's mind is utterly cut off, not only from terrestrial thoughts, but from all definite ideas soever. It is impossible to accept what we commonly call actuality as having any real existence. One neither sleeps nor wakes from the moment when Kronstadt fades to a pale purple phantom of the past till Stockholm springs from the sea, as if the Lethean languor of a dreamless death, a mere deliciously indefinite serenity, were being gently awakened to understand that its unguessed goal was at last in sight. The negative ecstasy of perfect release from the pressure of existence developed into its positive equivalent when the soul, soothed and made strong, by its swoon into stainless silence, was ready to spring, sublimely self-sufficient, to the summit of its starry stature, to grasp and grapple with the manifested majesty of the Most High . . .

In vain have I striven to compel language to convey the meaning of that miraculous voyage. It stands aloof, so pure and perfect in itself that naught can blur its beauty. It remains in my memory uncontaminated by the sordid stupidity of Stockholm, the tedium of the discomfortable dreariness of the return to London.

I found my work precisely where I had left it. The tenth and last number of *The Equinox* was published in due course. There was a certain pride in having triumphed over such opposition, in having 'carried on' despite neglect, misunderstanding and treachery; in having achieved so many formidable tasks. There was also infinite satisfaction in so many signal successes. I could not doubt that I had made the Path of Initiation plain. It was beyond doubt that any man of ordinary energy, integrity and intelligence might now attain in a very few months what, until now, had meant years of desperate devotion. I had destroyed the superstition that spiritual success depended on dogma. I was thus able, to some extent, to go fearlessly into the presence of the Secret Chiefs who had chosen me to carry out their plans for the welfare of mankind, and say with upright head that I had not wholly proved unworthy of their trust. Yet withal, there was a certain sadness such as, I suppose, every man feels when he comes to the end of a definite stage in his career. Nevertheless, I knew that those who had thus far used me would not now throw me aside; that higher and holier service would be found for me.

During the autumn and until the solstice I went on with my regular work as usual, but with a subconscious awareness that my future lay in other fields; something was sure to happen to change the whole current of my life. Subtly enough, this change came about by diverting me from the public action to which I had so long been bound by the sheer necessity of producing *The Equinox* on definite dates. I began to pay more attention to my own personal progress.

It must here be explained that my innate diffidence forbade me to aspire to the Grade of Magus in any full sense. Such beings appear only in every two thousand years or so. I knew too well my own limitations. It is true that I had been used as a Magus in the Cairo working; that is, I had been chosen to utter the Word of a New Aeon. But I did not regard this as being *my* Word. I felt myself ridiculously unworthy of the position assigned to me in *The Book of the Law* itself. When therefore I proposed to devote myself to my own initiation, I meant no more than this: that I would try to perfect myself in the understanding and powers proper to a Master of the Temple. At the end of 1913, I found myself in Paris with a Zelator of the Order, Frater L. T.[1] I had been working on the theory of the magical method of the O.T.O.; and we decided to test my conclusions by a series of invocations.

We began work on the first day of the year and continued without interruption for six weeks. We invoked the gods Mercury and Jupiter; and obtained many astonishing results of many kinds, ranging from spiritual illumination to physical phenomena. It is impossible to transcribe the entire record, and to give excerpts would only convey a most imperfect and misleading idea of the result. As an example of actual intellectual illumination, however, I may quote the very impressive identification of the Christ of the gospels with Mercury. This came as a complete surprise, we having till then considered him as an entirely solar symbol connected especially with Dionysus, Mithras and Osiris.

In the beginning was the Word, the Logos, who is Mercury, and is therefore to be identified with Christ. Both are messengers; their birth mysteries are similar; the pranks of their childhood are similar. In the Vision of the Universal Mercury, Hermes is seen descending upon the sea, which refers to Maria. The Crucifixion represents the caduceus; the two thieves, the two serpents; the cliff in the Vision of the Universal Mercury is Golgotha; Maria is simply Maria with the solar R in her womb.

The controversy about Christ between the synoptics and John was really a contention between the priests of Bacchus, Sol and Osiris, also, perhaps, of Adonis and Attis, on the one hand, and those of Hermes on the other, at that period when initiation all over the world found it necessary, owing to the growth of the Roman Empire, and the opening up of means of communication, to replace conflicting polytheisms by a synthetic faith. (This is absolutely new to me, this conception of Christ as Mercury.) Some difficulty about the . . . (This sentence is now quite unintelligible.)

To continue the identification, compare Christ's descent into hell with the function of Hermes as guide of the dead. Also Hermes leading up Eurydice, and Christ raising up Jairus's daughter. Christ is said to have risen on the third day, because it takes three days for the planet Mercury to become visible after separating from the orb of the sun. (It may be noted here that Mercury and Venus are the planets between us and the sun, as if the Mother and the Son were mediators between us and the Father.)

Note Christ as the Healer, and also his own expression, 'The Son of Man cometh as a thief in the night'; and also this scripture (Matt. XXIV, 27), 'For as the lightning cometh out of the east and shineth even unto the west, so shall also the coming of the Son of Man be.'

Note also Christ's relations with the money changers, his frequent parables, and the fact that his first disciple was a publican.

Note also Mercury as the deliverer of Prometheus.

One half of the fish symbol is also common to Christ as Mercury; fish are sacred to Mercury (owing presumably to their quality of movement). (This I did not know before.) Many of Christ's disciples were fishermen and he was always doing miracles in connexion with fish.

Note also Christ as the mediator: 'No man cometh unto the Father but by Me', and Mercury as Chokmah through whom alone we can approach Kether.

The caduceus contains a complete symbol of the Gnosis; the winged sun or phallus represents the joy of life on all planes from the lowest to the highest. The Serpents, besides being active and passive, Horus and Osiris, and all their other well-known attributions are those qualities of Eagle and Lion respectively, of which we know but do not speak. It is the symbol which unites the Microcosm and the Macrocosm, the symbol of the Magical Operation which accomplishes this. The caduceus is the universal solvent. It is quite easy to turn quicksilver into gold on the physical plane, and this will soon be done. New life will flow through the world in consequence. The god now lays his caduceus upon my lips for silence; bidding me only remember that on the following night he is to come in another form.

The temple was then closed.

Our occasional failures produced results as striking and instructive as our successes. For instance, having made an error in invoking Mercury, and thus having created a current of force contrary to his nature, we observed that events of a Mercurial character, no matter how normal, failed to occur. For one thing, all communications with the outer world were completely cut off for some time. It had been arranged that I should receive a daily report from London from my secretary. None arrived for five days; and that although nothing had gone wrong in London. No explanation was ever forthcoming. This is one of the many incidents tending to similar conclusions, all explicable only on the theory that the natural energy, which is normally present and is necessary to the occurrence of certain types of event, had somehow been inhibited.

The Jupiterian phenomena were especially remarkable. We performed in all sixteen operations to invoke this force. It seemed at first as if our work actually increased the normal inertia. Jupiterian phenomena which we had every right to expect simply failed to happen. Even in the matter of banqueting, which we were supposed to do lavishly in his honour, the opposition became overwhelming. Hungry as we might be, we seemed unable to force ourselves to eat even a light meal. Quite suddenly the invisible barrier broke down and Jupiterian phenomena of the most unexpected kind simply rained on us. To mention one incident only; a Brother who had always been desperately poor suddenly came into a fortune and insisted on contributing five hundred pounds to the use of the Order.

I must mention one incident of the Paris working as being of general interest, outside technical Magick. During the operation I had a bad attack of influenza, which settled down to very severe bronchitis. I was visited one evening by an old friend of mine and her young man, who very kindly and sensibly suggested that I should find relief if I smoked a few

pipes of opium. They accordingly brought the apparatus from
their apartment and we began. (Opium, by the way, is sacred
to Jupiter, and to Chesed,[2] Mercy, as being sovereign against
pain, and also as enabling the soul to free itself from its gross
integument and realize its majesty.) My bronchitis vanished;
I went off to sleep; my guests retiring without waking me. In
my sleep I dreamt; and when I woke the dream remained
absolutely perfect in my consciousness, down to the minutest
details. It was a story, a subtle exposure of English stupidity,
set in a frame of the craziest and most fantastically gorgeous
workmanship. Ill as I was, I jumped out of bed and wrote down
the story offhand. I called it 'The Stratagem'. No doubt it was
inspired by Jupiter, for it was the first short story that I had
ever written which was accepted at once. More: I was told—
nothing in my life ever made me prouder—that Joseph Conrad said it was the best short story he had read in ten years.

We ourselves became identified with Jupiter, but in different
aspects. Frater L. T. was for some months following the personification of generosity, though himself with the most meagre
resources. All sorts of strangers planted themselves on him
and he entertained them. In my own case, I became that type
of Jupiter which we connect with the idea of prosperity,
authority and amativeness. I received numerous occult dignities; I seemed to have plenty of money without quite knowing
how it happened; and I found myself exercising an almost
uncanny attraction upon every woman that came into my
circle of acquaintance.

To me, however, as a student of nature, the one important
result of this work was the proof of the efficacy of the magical
method employed. Henceforth, I made it my principal study,
kept a detailed record of my researches, and began to discover
the rational explanation of its operation and the conditions
of success.

More important yet, in the deepest sense, was a feature of
the result which I failed to observe at the time, and even for
some years after. In veiled language are hints, unmistakable
as soon as detected, that I was even then, by means of the
working itself, being prepared for the initiation thereto. The
actual ceremony (using the word in its widest and deepest
sense) extended over some years and is in fact the sole key to
the events of that period. An outline therefore must consequently form a separate chapter, for without the light thereby
thrown upon the facts of my career, they must appear incoherent, inconsequential and unintelligible. I was destined to

undergo a series of experiences which apparently contradict the whole tendency of the past. My actions seem incompatible with my character; my environment seems incomprehensibly unnatural; in short, the effect of the narrative is to suggest that by some jugglery the life of a totally different individual has intruded upon my own.

Now, years afterwards, it still seems to me as if for the whole period of the initiation I had been transported into an unfamiliar world; their history is a magical history in the most comically complete sense. Its events are neither real nor rational—save only in relation to the condition of an experiment, exactly as a candidate in freemasonry sees, hears, speaks and acts with his normal senses, yet in a way which has no relation to his previous experience. The stolid old gentleman in evening dress is really King Solomon. He hears a rigmarole both false and meaningless in itself, which he must understand as conveying something entirely other than it apparently implies. His words are put into his mouth, and produce an effect neither expected, desired, nor understood. He performs a series of gestures neither comprehensible in themselves, nor even (so far as he can see) calculated to assist his purpose. And even when, at the end, he finds that he has complied with the prescribed conditions and achieved his object, he is unable to bring what has taken place into rational relation with his ordinary life. The situation is only the more bewildering that from first to last each incident in itself is perfectly commonplace.

Such is my own point of view with regard to my adventures in America. They are all perfectly probable in themselves, perfectly intelligible regarded as details of a ritual; but they contradict every probability of human life as commonly understood. The chain of my career snaps suddenly; yet it continues as if it had never been broken from the moment that my initiation is over. The effect is to persuade me that this period of my life is in the nature of a dream. I meet strange monsters; one phantom succeeds another without a shadow of coherence. Even those incidents which help me to recognize that I am the central figure of the dream complete my conviction of its unreality.

75

It is one of the regular jokes in India that people on the strength of the season in Calcutta write a book about the peninsula, but even the tourist of genius, like Charles Dickens, is far more presumptuous when he tackles the United States. India indeed is huge and varied beyond hope of human comprehension, but America, though its population is only a third of that of Hindustan, is composed of elements infinitely more varied, besides which India does at least stand still and allow one to look at it, whereas the United States undergoes a revolutionary change continually. I passed through the country in 1900. In 1906 I found it unrecognizable. My third visit in 1914 gave me another surprise, and during the following five years when I was actually resident the panorama shifted with kaleidoscopic swiftness.

I have now learnt enough to realize that any attempt at description must inevitably be futile and that any opinion cannot but be presumptuous and misleading. Yet the subject is by far the most important in every respect which I have ever had to consider and I cannot possibly offer my autohagiography to the impatient public without doing my best to set down what I think.

Intellectual generalizations must be discarded as insulting to my own intelligence as much as to the reader's. There is only one possible procedure; to state boldly a number of striking facts which came under my direct observation, leaving their significance and importance to fight for their own ends, but also to call upon the only testimony of equally assured liability, my spiritual intuition.

I admit frankly that the whole of my intellectual opinion and practically all my personal prejudice combine to condemn the United States wholesale with absolute contempt and loathing and this attitude will undoubtedly manifest itself whenever the subject crops up in the course of these reminiscences, for my normal conscious self is generally speaking as the writer of these pages. Against this my subconscious intuition, whose judgment is to be trusted absolutely, is altogether opposed. I propose therefore to set forth first of all that which the Holy Spirit within me moves to utter, and afterwards to record the observed facts which influence my human consciousness to be so antagonistic to almost every feature of life and thought as I found it.

I definitely appeal to my American readers to stand apart from their natural gratification at the first and their natural indignation at the second of these sections of my work, and to understand that my spiritual apprehension of truth represents my real self, while my intellectual perceptions are necessarily coloured by my nationality, caste, education and personal predilection. I am not trying to shirk the responsibility for the harsh judgments which I promulgate. I should prefer to keep silent. I speak only in the hope that Americans may learn how shocking much of their morals and manners is to the educated European, and I insist upon the intensity of my utmost love for them and faith in their future, so that they may discriminate between my criticisms and those of such people as Mrs Asquith who are unable to go deeper than the facts and cherish an unalloyed animosity.

Let me then begin by an analysis of my inmost spiritual sympathy for the people of the United States. First of all, let me explain about Europe. The war of 1914, and its sequel of revolution and economic catastrophe, is in my eyes the culmination of its many centuries of corruption by Christianity. The initial lesion was due to the decay of the Roman republican virtue. The immediate effect of the rise of Christianity was the break-up of social order, the supersession of philosophy and scholarship by fanaticism and the gradual engulfment of enlightenment in the Dark Ages. A partial resurrection was brought about by the Renaissance and from that moment began the long struggle between science and freedom on the one hand and dogmatism and tyranny on the other. During the nineteenth century, the triumph of the former seemed assured and almost complete. The forces of obscurantism and reaction were driven into dark corners but their natural cunning developed by centuries of experience inspired them to a final effort to regain their lost prestige and power. They adopted a new policy. They ceased to oppose openly the advance of science and the associated ethical and political principles which science indicated. They clipped the claws of the Lion of Enlightenment by establishing an unspoken convention to the effect that it was bad form to insist upon applying the new ideas to practical politics. The Church of England was to retain its official status in spite of its spiritual death. Dissent and agnosticism ought to be tolerated indeed but ignored. The system of social snobbery was to continue concurrently with the boast of the triumph of democratic principles. In every subject which might give rise to controversy there was a tacit agreement not to tell the truth. The people who persecuted Byron, Shelley, Darwin, Bradlaugh and Foote smiled amiably at the much more outspoken blasphemies of Bernard Shaw. The hollowness of Christianity and feudalism became shameless. No one dared to defend his convictions, if indeed he possessed them. There was a universal conspiracy to shirk facing the facts of life, with the result that the most complete moral darkness shrouded the causes and conduct of the war. We maintained our stupid shame with desperate determinations. A sham peace succeeded the sham war and the only realities were the revolutions which reduced civilization to chaos. Such reactions as that of Fascismo are manifestly phantasmagoric and I cannot but conclude that at least for a long period anarchy will triumph in Europe. I turn therefore to America from an expiring solar system to a nebulous mass which I expect to develop into an organized galaxy.

The elements of the United States are heterogeneous in a manner unprecedented in history. Every race, language and creed of Europe is represented. There is, moreover, an established contingent of Africans, a new infiltration of Asiastics, of whom the Jews are a critically important factor in the social and economic problems of the day, while even the Far East, despite fanatical opposition, is seeking to obtain a foothold. That so many inimical elements should consent to even a semblance of fraternity indicates some common spiritual impulse sufficiently strong to dominate lesser prejudices. I find this unity in the aspiration to escape from the restrictions of crystallized conventions. Germans who resented military service, Jews who found the pressure of persecution and ostracism unendurable, Armenians obsessed by the fear of massacre, Italians to whom the pettiness, poverty and priestcraft of their country were paralysing, Irish insulted and injured by English oppression, all alike bring me to America as a paradise of elbow room, liberty and prosperity.

One aspect of this aspiration has a more general bearing. All Americans are eager for power, in one form or another. They therefore pursue with passionate ardour every path which promises knowledge as well as those which lead directly to mastery of environment. So powerful and so irrepressible is this enthusiasm that the most grotesque disillusionments fail to disgust them and no charlatanism so crude, no pretence so puerile, no humbug so outrageous as to deter them from running after the next new religion. Their dauntless innocence persuades me that just as soon as they have acquired the critical faculty, they will progress spiritually more swiftly and sanely than has ever been known.

At present two hindrances hamstring them. Firstly, the desperate death struggles of dogmatism, and secondly the practically universal ignorance of the elements of spiritual science. They insist on impossible ideals and hoax themselves about their holiness to an extreme that English hypocrisy at its zenith never approximates and their credulity is so crass that the followers of Joanna Southcott, the Agapemonites and the peculiar people seem by comparison philosophers and sages. Yet all this extravagance is but as the froth upon the crest of an irresistible breaker. Even the puritan cruelty, the social savagery, the extravagant racial ribaldry and the monomaniac stampede to acquire dollars testify more to the energy and enthusiasm of the people than to its casual concomitants of ignorance, delusion and fatuity which impress the ordinary observer. They are shrewd; none shrewder, lacking only the data to direct that shrewdness. They will soon discover how to distinguish between genuine teachers and quacks, as also the fact that the power of money is limited and can buy no food either for spirit or soul. They will then pursue the path of evolution on sane and scientific lines eschewing unsound methods and unsatisfactory aims.

My instinct has always assured me of this and stimulated my eagerness to educate and initiate everyone I met. I felt that fundamentally we were brothers, and I believe that this intense sympathy was just what deepened my disgust and darkened my despair at the impossibility of reaching them. Morally, socially, intellectually, the gulf was not to be bridged. There was no common ground of comprehension. When I insisted on scientific methods, I met with fear lest the foundations of their faiths should be shaken and every one of them come to some crazy creed, pompous, pretentious and puerile. When I tried to show them that conventional canons of conduct were children of circumstance, belief in whose absolute ethical value merely masked the face of truth and prevented them from perceiving nature, they were simply shocked. They had never inquired why any given virtue should be valid. The same of course applied to the question of creed. Even those who wandered from teacher to teacher were fanatically convinced that their momentary cult was perfect at every point. I could not persuade them that their admitted fickleness was evidence that their present creed reflected a mere mood.

My real fear for America is that when it finds a few axioms on which a working majority can agree, a few dogmas to which it can rally, there will be an immediate effort to crush out all incompatible ideas, and even to atrophy its own possibilities of further development by extirpating any growth of genius within its own ranks, exactly as was done by Rome. In this event the tyranny would be infinitely worse than anything in the history of Christianity, for the worst of the moral defects of Americans is cold-blooded cruelty—their struggle against nature and the corrupting influences of such vices as drunkenness and sexual immorality has led them to value the harder virtues at the expense of the more human.

The latter indeed are regarded as vices even by those who cherish them in secret. Thus, in spite of the extraordinary diversity of creeds, cults, codes, fads and ideals, there lies the instinct to compel conformity. The whole history of the country has hammered into their heads the evident truth that unity is strength. Their very motto affirms it—*E Pluribus Unum*. Their history itself bears witness to this. What was the Civil War but a murderous struggle against secession? Prussian methods were used to dragoon the pacifist majority into fighting Germany, and prohibition was put over by every unscrupulous trick against the will of the people. Today, we see the Ku Klux Klan attempting to impose, by secret society methods of anonymous menace backed by boycott, arson and assassination, the ideals of a clique; and nearly as noxious are the arrogant aims and brutal tactics of Catholics and freemasons.

In their own way capital and labour are influenced by the same idea, that of imposing a rigid and uniform rule on the entire community regardless of local conditions or any other considerations which might make for diversity. I need hardly point out that this principle is in flat contradiction with the Declaration of Independence in the constitution. I am afraid that the root of the evil lies in the psychological fact that men proclaim the principles of freedom only when they are suffering from oppression. No sooner do they become free and prosperous than they begin to perceive the duties of discipline.

It is already shockingly manifest that the moral correspondences of this tendency are in operation. As Fabre D'Olivet points out in his examination of *The Golden Verses of Pythagoras,* initiation, that is progress, requires that at every point the candidate should be confronted with the free choice between actions dependent upon the three principal virtues, courage, temperance and prudence. The aim of American statecraft is on the contrary to atrophy these virtues by making them unnecessary, and indeed limiting full choice to unimportant matters. A third spiritual danger arises from the dogmatic idealism which determines social and economic conditions. So multiform is the prevailing error that the only course is to oppose to it the true doctrine as follows:

The growth of a nation depends on its ability to draw the greatest nourishment from the greatest area of soil as against the pressure of rival plants. This depends, *ceteris paribus,* on numbers. Now numbers depend on the willingness and ability of women to make child-bearing and rearing the main business of life, and of the men to protect them and support them at their task. The surplus wealth may, nevertheless, be invested in another way, calculated to increase efficiency and potential; that is, in the support of a class which is not directly wealth producing as such, the class of the learned. This class must be abundantly supplied with leisure and the apparatus for research and freed from all anxiety or similar distractions. It should in fact be treated as a guild or spiritual fraternity. The existence of any other class which does not pull its own weight in the boat is evidence of plethora.

The above principles are extremely simple and self-evident, but in America they have been pushed out of sight by doctrinal propositions based on *a priori* considerations of things as they ought to be in the mind of the dogmatist.

I still hope that experience will eliminate these errors, and in that hope I address myself first of all to the American republic.

Having thus affirmed the instinctive attitude to the American people, let me turn to the other extreme and record a number of observations which seem specially significant, the deductions from which appear unmitigatingly damning, but the antinomy with my spiritual standpoint is to be overcome by interpreting these flagrant and atrocious faults as symptomatic only of infantile and adolescent aberration, with the exception of a very few individuals indeed, and those, almost invariably, either of pedigree stock or educated by experience of Europe.

An adult American is a *rara avis.* The actual conditions which confront the developing intelligence are so incoherent and unintelligible that the unity of background which Europeans inherit and imagine to be the common property of mankind is absent.

Let me illustrate my meaning. In Europe we take for granted such first principles as the limits of the possibility of development of any given type of energy. We assume, for instance, that the efficiency of the aeroplane depends upon the ratio of power to weight in the first place, the increase of the former being limited by the theoretical potential of the sources of energy at our disposal. We also reflect that increase of size, power and velocity involves the overcoming of obstacles which become more formidable in geometrical progression. Again, at certain points in the advance, entirely new considerations begin to apply, such as the resistance of our material to the pressure of air, and the physiological potentiality of the airman. To us this nexus seems an integral element of necessity.

The average American argues in complete ignorance of any such restriction. To him, to double the power is to double the pace and so on. His whole experience inflamed by his native enthusiasm reminds him that during the last century innumerable inventions, which the greatest authorities declared to be theoretically impossible, are now in daily use.

Consider the discovery of radium; how it revealed the existence of a form of energy enormously greater in quality than anything previously known. More, we can now calculate that atomic energy—could we only grasp it—would stand to radium as radium to steam, or more so. He is therefore perfectly right in refusing to discredit, on common sense grounds, the report that a cannon has been constructed to carry a shell across the Atlantic, or a flying machine to go to the moon; an instrument capable of detecting any conceivable fact about a man from a drop of his blood; of penetrating the past or foretelling the future. There is, in fact, no theoretical limit to human attainment, for the simple reason that nature is known to contain all conceivable and inconceivable forms of energy and perceptive potentiality. Concentrated on this conviction, he constantly makes himself ridiculous, through ignorance of the details of the patient progress of science. Like other varieties of faith it lays its votaries open to the most fantastic follies.

I have shown elsewhere the psychological considerations which make Americans accept this liability to error as an evil less than that of hypocritical scepticism. The condition is, of course, somewhat similar to that produced by the administration of cocaine and the analogy is confirmed by the fact that American nerves are ragged and raw. The realities of life wreck their victim. In case of a general collapse of civilization under economic stress, such as seems actually imminent at present, it is to be feared that the shock to their spiritual self-sufficiency will find them unable to resist reactions. America, resenting the arrogance of Europe, refuses angrily to admit the extent of her indebtedness, but in the case of European anarchy, the main source of energy would be withdrawn. Few Americans realize that the moral, economic and selfish attitude towards sex means ultimate disaster. The emancipation of women, her ambition to compete with men in commercial and intellectual pursuits is, at bottom, a refusal to bear children, and this evidently implies the excessive increase of a parasitic class which the community will be unable to support.

It is notorious that the birth-rate is maintained by the immigrants. After very few years of life in the States sterility sets in. This, again, is a symptom of the insensate idealism of American psychology. Perceiving that progress depends on transcending animality, and refusing to realize the theoretical limitation of any such aspiration, they plunge into perdition. It is as if a man, admiring the beauty and perfume of the water-lily and loathing the miry darkness of the bed of the lake, were to sever the blossom from its root. This fatuity is shown directly by their attitude towards sex and indirectly by the attempt to suppress everything that suggests self-indulgence. The policy is disastrous.

We should found society upon a caste of 'men of earth', sons of the soil, sturdy, sensual, stubborn and stupid, unemasculated by ethical or intellectual education, but guided in their evolution by the intelligent governing classes towards an ideal of pure animal perfection. In such a substratum variation will produce sporadic individuals of a higher type. History affords innumerable examples of the lofty intelligence and the noblest characters shooting up from the grossest stock. Keats, Burns, Sixtus the Fifth, Lincoln, Boehme, Faraday, Joseph Smith, Whitman, Renan, Arkwright, Watts, Carlyle, Rodin and innumerable other men of the highest genius came of peasant parentage. Few indeed of the first class have been born of intellectually developed families.

The conditions of genius are not accurately known. But we may divide the class into two great groups; those in whom the development is a system of degeneration, and those who, though sometimes exhibiting the most exquisite fruition, fail to attain full development and achieve the work of which they should be capable through their frailty. The men whose achievement is uniform are always constitutionally robust; despite all difficulties they attain a great age and produce continuously. Rodin, Browning, Carlyle, Pasteur, Lister, Kelvin, Gladstone, Whitman were all grand old men. (That Carlyle was an invalid merely emphasizes this essential figure.)

To insure the supply, we need only plant a prosperous and prolific peasantry, watch the children for indications of genius, and pick out any promising specimens for special training on the lines which their tendencies indicate. The worst thing they can do is what is done in America, to disenchant the man of earth with his destiny; to fill him with the facts and fancies that enthral etiolated and degenerated idealists and unfit him for his evident purpose, that of supplying society with supermen. It is not only impossible to try to make a silk purse out of a sow's ear. It is an idealistic imbecility. The demand for silk purses is extremely limited, whereas sows' ears always come in handy.

America is seething with anarchy on every plane, because of the constantly changing economic conditions, the conflict between creeds, castes, codes, cultures and races. Society has never had a chance to settle down. The expansion westward, the discovery of gold, coal, iron and oil, the slavery question, the secession question, the silver question, the immigration question, the labour question, the constant flux caused by the development of technical science, the religious and moral instability, the conflict between federal centralization and state sovereignty, the congestion of cities, the exploitation of the farmer by the financier, the shifting of the economic centre of gravity, these and a thousand other conditions arising from the unprecedented development of the country combine to make it impossible even to imagine stability in any plane of life. There is thus a radical distinction between Europe and her daughter. We know more or less what to expect in any set of circumstances. Heterogeneous as we are there is a common ground of thought and action. We are even able to draw reasonable conclusions about Asia and Africa. London and Tokyo are sufficiently alike in essentials to make our relations intelligible, but in spite of the community of language, customs, commercial conventions, and so on, between London and New York, the difference between us is really more radical.

There are many incalculable factors in any formula which connects the United States with Europe.

Let me give a few obvious illustrations. Almost all Europeans suppose skyscrapers to be monstrosities of vanity. They are in fact necessary consequences of the conditions of New York City, as fogs were of the climate and situation of London and the physical properties of the available fuel. New York expanded as it had on account of, first, the vastness of its harbour, and, second, its situation on the Hudson, and as the most convenient outlet for the produce of the hinterland.

Manhattan Island, being so long and narrow, presented peculiar problems of transportation. To this is due the system of elevated and underground railways. The width of the water which separates it from Long Island, New York State and New Jersey limited its expansion in those directions. Even with bridges and subways, transport was tedious and congested. The evident consequence was that the value of land in Manhattan became prohibitive. The final determinant is the fact that the island consists of a scant deposit of soil on a foundation of granite capable of supporting any possible strain. It was accordingly an architectural possibility and an economic advantage to increase the height of the buildings, and this height was, in its turn, limited by economic considerations.

The early architects went gaily ahead. They saw no reason to suppose that they need ever stop, but presently actuarial calculation showed that thirty-six storeys represented the maximum of economic efficiency. Beyond that height the disproportionate increase in the cost of building and the difficulty of renting the loftier suites, on account of the fear of fire, made the higher buildings unprofitable. It is of peculiar interest, by the way, to observe that the artists were so impregnated with the Buddhist ideal of impermanence that in even the costliest buildings they calculated the life of the plumbing as at no more than twenty years; that is, they expected, from one cause or another, that the building would be superseded within that period.

The actual situation, by the way, is critical. There are, roughly speaking, two and a half of the seven and a half million people of Great New York put to grave inconvenience by the congestion and all alike are embarrassed by the ratio of rent to income. In Europe we reckon that rent should not absorb more than one tenth or at most one eighth of one's earning. In New York, this proportion is rarely less than one fourth and sometimes more than one third. Again, despite all

efforts to establish a satisfactory system of transport, conditions
are appalling. In the rush hours, the people are crushed like
corn in a mill. One sees clusters of citizens hanging to the steps
of a trolley car like a swarm of bees. The surface traffic is
practically paralysed. I have known it to take fifty minutes for
a motor bus to get from 34th to 58th Street, walkable easily in
less than twenty minutes. Except the few plutocrats with automobiles of their own, or residences within reasonable distance
of their places of business, the average citizen has anything
from fifty minutes to two hours to travel in this packed and
pestilential conveyance twice daily. The waste of energy, the
nervous strain, the physical fatigue and the annoyance all tell
on his health and spirits. No wonder if indigestion and neuras-
thenia make him an old man at thirty-five.

But the worst is yet to come. Every year the congestion increases. The percentage of time and strength and money wasted
and unnatural effort becomes more oppressive and exhaustive.
Every desperate device imaginable is being tried, but the problem grows faster than the palliatives and one really wonders
what will happen when things reach a deadlock, when nobody
can pay his rent or get to his business; when, in short, it becomes impossible to carry on, what will follow the crash. Any
diminution in the population would mean that rates and taxes
would have to be further increased and so drive more and
more away from the city. The logical issue seems to be deser-
tion and decay; this obviously involving the collapse of the
machinery of export, and so the ruin of the producer in the
interior.

In the past, if my suspicions be sound, cities like Nineveh
perished in some such way. Their prosperity led them to live
beyond their means. They made up the deficit by constantly
bleeding the provinces, thus eventually killing the goose that
laid the golden eggs. To me, the present prosperity of the
United States, like that of England under Queen Victoria, is
due to the coincidence of various favourable but temporary
conditions. In England, the invention of the spinning jenny,
the steam engine and similar automatic ways of producing
wealth, the opening up of new markets, the expansion of
commerce and colonial success made us rich factitiously. Similar processes are still at work in the States.

The vast wealth in almost every commodity became easy
to exploit through the introduction of scientific methods and
labour-saving machinery. The supply of cheap labour from
exhausted Europe, and the removal of all restrictions to ex-

pansion by the extent of elbow room and the overcoming of natural obstacles; all these conditions have made America the commercial mistress of the planet.

She has not even been disturbed and hampered by any serious internal or external struggle since 1865. The Spanish War was a holiday and the A.E.F. little more than an organized extension of the normal tide of tourists. She has never had to fight for her life; she has never had a serious sickness, but now this curve is approaching if it has not already attained its summit. The colonization is complete. People are beginning to jostle each other. Europe can no longer pay for her produce. The absence of moral unity is creating class conflict. The problems of politics are too vast and varied for even genius to grasp; the apparatus of order, both moral and physical, is showing signs of an imminent breakdown. The interests of the five principal sections of the country become more obviously incompatible. Any serious setback might cause disaster in a dozen different directions.

They talk of the melting pot. The metaphor is not bad. For the last sixty years they have pitched into it indiscriminately everything that came along. They protest passionately that the product must be that perfect gold, the 'one hundred per cent. American', which may be defined as the wish phantasms of a Sunday School superintendent, a romantic flapper, an unscrupulous usurer, and a maudlin medium, worked up into a single delirious nightmare. More likely the interaction of all these formidable forces will result in an explosion. My faith in the future of the States is fixed on some rational reconstruction after revolution. The present attempt to amalgamate this fortuitous hotch-potch, neither calculating probabilities nor observing actualities, but asserting an amiable postulate as if it were axiomatic, is born of an illusion invented by despair of acting with intelligence; and when the moment of awakening arrives the disillusionment may shock them at first into insanity. Nothing less is likely to show them that human nature is a stubborn reality which no amount of humouring, befooling and bullying will alter.

These preliminary speculations set forth, I will now try to justify the diagnosis by exhibiting the salient symptom. For convenience I have classed my observations under a few principal heads. I shall show how America differs from Europe in its attitude towards law and order. I shall give examples of the unfathomable ignorance which prevails even among the most highly educated people, not merely of well established facts of what in Europe is called common knowledge, but of the most elementary principles of nature, that is to say of facts which quite illiterate Europeans would know instinctively without having to learn them. I shall give examples of the impotence of their extravagant idealism to preserve them from outraging European convention of honour and good manners. Lastly, I shall illustrate the callousness and cruelty which characterize the people as a result of their fanatical faith in absolute standards of rectitude and definition of duty to one's neighbour as espionage and tyranny.

I will ask the reader to analyse each incident in order to discover the simple and radical motive which underlies the overt action. I hope thus to make it clear that even the most absurd and atrocious abominations are, so to speak, accidents caused by the impact of facts with which the American is unfitted to deal, owing to his childlike ignorance, inexperience and lack of all sense of proportion; so that to every crisis he can bring only the intense impulsive energy of instinct.

In 1912 I took it into my head to write three essays on American art and literature, past, present and future. I only completed the first, which is published in the *English Review*. It aroused a hurricane across the Atlantic and, hard as it is to believe, the echoes have not yet died away.

Within the last twelve months it was violently attacked by one of America's best poets, Robert Haven Schauffler. I make a point of mentioning the fact. He accused me of prejudice and unfairness, ignorant of course that my essay was but one of three and that my plan had been to express the friendliest faith in the future. As it stands, my judgment is no doubt severe, but I see little to modify.

Poe and Whitman are still in my opinion the only first-rate writers until very recent years. I still find Longfellow, Bryant, Whittier, Emerson, Bret Harte, Mark Twain and the rest devoid of any title soever to rank among the sons of genius. I might admit that they possessed great talents, but that is foreign to the question. I had been prevented from writing the other two essays partly because the editor, following his invariable rule, broke his pledged word to me, and partly because my heart was broken by the perusal of the books which I had asked Leila Waddell to bring back from America to furnish me with material. They left me without a glimmer of hope. The trashiest piffle of England was Swinburne and Stevenson by comparison. The morality of American authors was too ghastly to contemplate. The artistic unity of the entire output consisted in its commonplace coarseness, behind which was the fixed determination to go for the dollars. There was neither ambition nor conscience anywhere. My already zero opinion dropped below the liquid air mark.

My first personal acquaintance with the actual conditions of the present time did not improve matters noticeably. My first glimmer of hope was supplied by the 'candle and the flame' of George Sylvester Viereck. Here at least was a man with a mind of his own, a worthy aspiration and an excellent technique, even though the actual achievement was nothing to leave home for. His prose was better. The *Confessions of a Barbarian* which purport to describe Europe are excellent. Europe is the stalking horse from behind which he shoots his wit. Every shot tells, and all are aimed at America. No better study of the United States has ever been written.

Through Viereck I met his friend Alexander Harvey who professed to admire my work and offered me the opportunity to reciprocate. At first I failed. I had somehow got the fine idea that he lacked virility and seriousness, and that his work was a shadow show. I had not understood my author. Only after reading *Shelley's Elopement* and his book on Howells [1] did I attain full insight into his mind and manner. But, having done so, a great light dawned upon me. I had to acknowledge him as a master. In the series of essays on which I am working at present I have consecrated one to him. I need only observe here that Alexander Harvey, more subtle and ethereal than Poe himself, possesses a delicacy and a sense of humour as exquisite, elfish, elusive as any man that ever wrote. His irony is incomparably keen. That I should have missed the point taught me a much needed lesson.

To pick up a book, persuaded that no good thing can come out of Nazareth, makes appreciation impossible.

Harvey introduced me to Edwin Markham, whose *The Man with the Hoe, and other poems* is assuredly first-rate of its kind. His work is uneven and it would be absurd to assert that he is of outstanding excellence. He lacks the stature of the sacred legion, but at least he proved to me the existence of what I had till then doubted; a poet true to himself and fearless of opinion; capable of high aims, conscientious in pursuing them and courageous in proclaiming them. I looked about me from that moment for a second poet, but here indefatigable research proved fruitless. Self-styled poets and

poetesses are as common in America as common bacilli in a
choleraic colon. They swim and squeal and squabble and stink
unbelievably.

The principal poetess present was E. W. Wilcox, looking
exactly like a shaved sow plastered with brilliant unguents
in a Greek dress and with a wreath on her wig. It was to
vomit! In Europe, outside negligible cliques in Soho, buzzing
round people like Ezra Pound and even smaller patches of
pretence in Paris, poets have some sense of dignity. They do
try to write, and talk as little as possible about it. In America
poetry is a branch of the patent medicine business. The medicine does not matter; what does is the label, the puff and the
faked testimonial.

A very few manage somehow or other to turn out occasional
stanzas, with some kind of idea in them fluently and even
powerfully, but with the exception of Markham and Schauffler
there is practically nobody at all who even understands what
poetry means. The one aim is self advertisement.

In the matter of prose, the situation is altogether different.
As remarked elsewhere, the first urgent need of the country
is a critic whose words carry weight, who knows good from
bad, and could not be bullied or bribed. These were found in
William Marion Ready, Michael Monahan and H. L. Mencken.
The two former were not fully efficient. They were too refined
to take off their shirts and plunge head foremost into the
rough and tumble, but Mencken understood the psychology
of the cattle he was out to kill, and he poleaxed them properly.
Having thus secured the services of a fighting editor the rest of
the staff felt free to do their work as they wanted it done and
the result has been the startling sudden appearance of a regular
army of authors and even dramatists who really matter. Conditions being as they are all red revolutionists are necessarily
savage satirists; they dare not waste time in wooing beauty till
the war is won. We find, therefore, Theodore Dreiser, Sinclair
Lewis (as opposed to his hysterical, though well-intentioned,
namesake Upton) and others of their school, who seem to
regard themselves as a committee appointed to report on the
ravages of respectability. Novel after novel describes unflinchingly the realities of life in America in its various departments.

Upton Sinclair and his school fail by overdoing it. Their
sentimental indignation is just as false as the shop on the other
side of the street. Howells and Chambers and all those pullulating boosters of the red-blooded, clean living, hundred per
cent. Gibson young man and his female rival them in inverte-

brate idealism. But the new school of realism makes a point of being just. The characters live; they are not mere excuses for piling up epithets. Yet beneath the feet of the actors is the stage and behind them a background. That stage is rotten. The foundation is equally social injustice and moral falsity. The background is equally bad. The scene is set for an obscene farce. The work of this school is at last beginning to tell. A constantly increasing percentage of Americans are beginning to understand that the vague horror which haunted them is the miasma of manufactured immorality. They see that the deliberate attempt to standardize social conditions, to trample originality under foot, to ostracize genius, to discipline life in every detail is turning the land of the free into a convict settlement and modelling civilization upon that of the ant.

Alexander Harvey stands outside this body of warriors. His spirit is less in touch with the brutalities of daily life. His race is unblemished and he began his career in diplomacy. He was thus able to develop his fine and intricate passion for pure beauty without being constantly jostled by the hurrying fiends of commerce. He is able to treat American society as a joke. His characters are, for the most part, raised above the hubbub of hustle. America wounds him only in his spiritual nerves. The most hideous of the demons which haunts him is what he calls the native American of Anglo-Saxon origin and his ivory is aimed at the less obvious atrocities of his environment.

One other figure stands apart, olympic and titanic in one. As I have tried to show in my essay (*The Reviewer*, July 1923) James Branch Cabell is a world genius of commanding stature. He comes of famous stock and occupies an excellent social position, being secluded on his own property in Virginia. The turmoil of Main Street and the animal noises of the jungle are borne to him as echoes from afar. The realities of modern America consequently occupy only one salient of his battle front, which extends from the seat of Jove himself to deepest Tartarus. All periods of history contribute to his pages and his characters include personifications of eternal principles, legendary demons and monsters of every type; eponymous heroes of fables and romance, and the everyday individuals of the modern world. Between these infinitely diverse orders of being, he makes no difference. All are equally real and mingle freely with each other. His epic includes Mother Cerida, one of the seven powers of destiny, her function being to cancel everything out. Helen of Troy, Merlin, the tyrant Dionysus and President Roosevelt fall each one in the proper place. His thesis covers the whole field of philosophy, but its ultimate conclusion—to date—seems to be almost identical with that of Main Street: that all aspiration is futile, attainment impossible in the nature of things.

Like James Thomson, however, as I have demonstrated in my essay on him, he has so extended the scope of his argument as to leave no possible escape by withdrawal to some loftier plane. Nevertheless, his intellectual acquiescence in the ineluctable futility of life, his gentle blood and his godlike genius compel him to make an irrational exception of this law in some quite inexplicable manner, and heroism wins through. Even as things stand, I regard Cabell as by far the greatest genius of his genus that has yet appeared on this planet. Before him nobody ever conceived so all-embracing a theme. Yet I am still unsatisfied! I demand that he shall be developed towards the solution of his problem, and perceive that the contradictory thesis is equally true: that the most trivial, vain and fatuous events, if rightly understood, are sublime; that the slough of despond is but an optical illusion created by the shadow of the snow-pure summits of success.

I have been accused of exaggerated enthusiasm for Cabell. The more stupid and mean-minded have even explained my ardour by my appreciation of the compliment which Mr Cabell paid me by using my Gnostic Mass as the material for Chapter XXII of his *Jurgen*. The suggestion is utter rubbish; though, at the same time, I admit cordially that no other form of appreciation of my work would have pleased me half so well.

I regard his epic of such supreme importance to mankind as an exposition of the nature of the universe that I have not only sent him a copy of *The Book of the Law* in the hope that he may find in it the way out of his Buddhistic demonstration that 'everything is sorrow' but followed it up by letter after letter urging him to use it, for his work cannot attain perfection until it culminates in a positive conclusion.

For many years he toiled at his task almost neglected. It is hardly nice to reflect that he only became famous when the smut-smeller society succeeded in suppressing *Jurgen* as obscene. I must admit, none the less, that when *Beyond Life* was sent me for review (the first I had heard of him) while perceiving straight away its excellence, I had no idea of its importance. I let the matter rest there. Then *Jurgen* reached me and I saw at once not only that the book was a supreme masterpiece, but extended my understanding of its stable companion. I proceeded to grab as many of his books as I could.

Each volume opened a new world to my vision. It was now clear why he had not impressed even the best critics as he deserved. Nobody had seen that each volume, apparently self-sufficient, was in reality one chapter, a single vast epic. The more I read and re-read, the more fully I realized the extent of his empire.

I have gone into this at some length in order to firstly stress the importance of the work, and to prevent any reader supposing that any one book will give an adequate idea of his genius.

76

Since December 1914, I have thought, time and again, how best to make public my political actions in America and the motives which determined my policy. I should have settled any other question off-hand, but I am already sensitive about my loyalty to England. I hasten to explain that by loyalty I mean neither admiration, approval or anything amiable of any kind. I reserve the right to speak as severely as Milton, Wordsworth, Byron, Shelley and Swinburne. All this does not touch the point. I am English, and that in a very special sense, as being the prophet and poet appointed by the gods to serve her. We do not accuse Isaiah of being unpatriotic because he thunders against Israel. Isaiah's motive is mine. There does not exist an essence which constitutes England, uncorrupted and incorruptible by any possible phenomenal facts. I feel myself to be an integral element of this England; what I do I do for her sake. I may have to scrub her face with yellow soap, open an abscess, or extirpate a cancer. Working as I do in a world of spiritual causes altogether beyond the comprehension of common people I am liable to be misunderstood.

The essence of my adventure in America may be put in a nutshell. From August to October 1914 I had tried every means to get the government to use me—without success.

In America chance showed me a way, for which I was peculiarly fitted, by which I might conceivably play as important a part in the war as any man living. The price of success was moral courage up to the theatrical limit. I must beggar myself of funds, friends and honour for the time being. I doubt whether I considered this clearly beforehand; I might have funked if I had. I do not want to claim undue credit for courage. I did what I did because it lay in my way to do it. My first step was the natural reaction to the opportunity. But this at least I do claim, that when I found how loathsome my work was, what humiliations and privations it involved, I set my teeth and stuck to the job.

Now then, as to the form of my report. From time to time I sketched various statements intended for various readers.

I have chosen the one which I wrote in a moment of heartbreak, when, after my work had been crowned with success, I found that my two oldest friends understood me so little that they thought it their duty to urge me to justify my conduct to the world by bringing an action against the most scurrilous blackmailing weekly in London. I was the angrier because at the moment I was practically penniless, and because I hoped by submitting in silence a little longer to calumny, to make myself again useful to England in a similar capacity if certain eventualities, which I then thought not impossible, should materialize.

Outraged in my most sensitive spot, I went to the Cadron Bleu at Fontainebleau, lunched, and began my reply to Horatio Bottomley. I found myself too indignant to write, so I went back to the house in the rue de Neuve which I had hired and got the Ape of Thoth to take down the tornado from dictation. When she wilted, her stable companion, Sister Cypris,[1] took her place; and so on by turns till I was appeased, some twenty-four hours later.

One circumstance conspired with another to hold up the publication, but some two years later, intending to go to England, I revised it, with the idea of publishing it immediately on my arrival as a challenge to my critics. Fate once more interfered. Bottomley's long lease was about to expire. The constable he had outrun was on his heels. The blackmailer, attempting to resist being blackmailed, was beginning to see one of the magical virtues of silence. I couldn't publish an attack on a man in the witness-box which was evidently temporary accommodation on the way to the dock. So I held my peace and wrote to Bottomley to tell him that I bore no malice and hoped he would clear himself. I hope it comforted him in penal servitude to remember that one, at least, of the men whom he had wantonly wronged wished him well. I wish him well no less today, but alas that he cannot be hurt by the hard things I happen to say. Any alteration of my pamphlet would destroy the whole spirit of the spasm, the venomous virulence of my vituperation is the essay. I showed the manuscript to poor Tommy Earp who might have been a poet if he had not been a plutocrat. He said that 'The Last Straw' was the limit in its line and my judgment jumps with his. Any considered statement, any documented plea, would lack the note of intensity and genuineness which my careless spontaneity and impulsive indignation taught me. I shall therefore print the scorpion as I wrote it. Its devil must excuse its indecorum. The savage contempt of Swift composed an indictment of human nature far exceeding the utmost ordered combination, and my 'smashing blows' at my own best friends, at Bottomley, obscure officials in particular, and bureaucratic blockishness, may, I hope, by their very lack of philosophical proportion or aimed animosity, demonstrate into what blind rage my normally imperturbable spirit is whirled when any man whom I consider worth wasting a word on suggests that my loyalty to England could be brought in doubt by any aggregation of protoplasm whose intellectual level is above that of a Woodrow Wilson himself.

THE LAST STRAW

It is a shameful fact that in July 1914 there was an Englishman so dirtily degenerate—I quote the Patriot Bottomley—that he was engaged in solitary climbs among the High Alps, daring native and foreigner, professional and amateur, to follow him. He did not do this to annoy anybody; he had too often already exposed the cowardice of the moneyed 'Herren' of the English Alpine Club; but he wanted to encourage the younger generation to climb alone, and to keep himself in good training for his third expedition to the Himalayan Mountains, which he intended to make in 1915.

The dirty degenerate, whom I shall hereafter designate by the first personal pronoun, had the idea that the war was a serious matter. He thought that he had ideas and virility, and that his country needed him.

The event indicates his fatuity. Descending the Jungfrau by the Rothsthal with a bruised toenail, for which it is not altogether fair to blame Messrs Dowie and Marshall, Bootmakers, West Strand, London, W.C., who are the best yet, and may be a pound or two on the wrong side of the ledger, which this advertisement should square, our degenerate, I mean I, went to Berne and asked the British Minister how to get home. The B.M. (which does not mean Blasted Mutt) did not know: he said it was impossible—there might be a train in six weeks. Would Mr Crowley write his name in a book to reserve a seat in that phantasmagoric train? Mr Crowley wrote it; the B.M. might be hard up one day and get a meal—or an annuity—by selling my autograph.

But he didn't wait for the train. The 'British Committee'—headed by two gentlemen who sounded like a vaudeville combination, Mr Whitehead and Mr Waggett—asked Mr Crowley what he would do. Mr Crowley would go to London: if there was a train, good; if not, he could walk and swim.

Luck—no, common sense!—favoured him; while twenty thousand English, and thirty thousand American, millionaires were stuck in dirty Switzerland for months, because they hadn't the sense to take a train to Paris, unable to cash their drafts, and living on the charity of calculating thieves—I refer to the Swiss hoteliers—he walked down to the station and took the train to Paris, as aforesaid.

I spent a week in Paris. I was amazed at the sang-froid of the people. They turned from peace to war as simply as a man turns over in his sleep. I arrived in London—I found that Bernard Shaw had told the truth. Twenty years of cheap newspapers had turned the British from the most stolid to the most hysterical nation in Europe. According to them the German was a monster like a bogey in a nightmare, and it was useless to struggle against him. At the same time, he was a coward who did not dare to advance unless behind a screen of Belgian nuns. He had no discipline, no morale, nothing but a talent for rape, torture, petty theft. His first line troops had been annihilated to a man by *les braves Belges*, whom we had hitherto only considered as persons who cut off the hands and feet of the innocent natives of the Congo basin.

I was more than ever convinced that I was needed by my country, which is England, and to hell with everybody. In my excitement, I had the hallucination that England needed men. I found, on the contrary, that the guiding stars of England needed 'business as usual'.

I was interrupted in my futile attempts to fight for my country as I had been interrupted in my attempts to climb the Alps, this time by an attack of phlebitis. I lay six weeks in bed, warned that the slightest movement might result in sudden death, and advised that in all probability I should never be able to climb a mountain again. The period of my illness covered September and most of October 1914.

At that time any man who suggested the advisability of conscription was regarded as a traitor. Conscription was the very thing we were fighting. Austin Harrison said that we were fighting for our golf and our weekends, Raymond Radclyffe said with, as it seemed to me, somewhat more plausibility that if we beat the Germans, it showed that the amateur was better than the professional.

From my sick bed I dictated an article called 'Thorough' in allusion to the plan of the Earl of Strafford in the time of

Charles the First. I said, 'Commandeer every man and every munition in the country.' I said, 'This is not a continental quarrel—this is life and death for England. We don't want debates in the House of Commons, or even in Earlswood asylum. We want a dictator.' No editor would publish it.

Everyone wanted 'business as usual', while Europe was overrun by madmen, fired by commercial ambitions, as it had been a hundred years before, fired by the military ambition of a man greater than Bloody Bill. Napoleon, at least, stood for humanity and for civilization. He gave France a code of laws better than any since that which Manu gave to India. Wilhelm offered nothing but the *Kultur* of the pig-iron-brained Herr Professor, and the conception of woman as the *Kuh* of *Küche, Kirche und Kinder*. That was what we were fighting— not for our golf and for our weekends. There has been no golf since the introduction of Haskell ball—and if our weekends are to mean nothing but 'adultery with home comforts' (in the great phrase of Frank Harris) I think Sunday a regrettable superstition.

I grew tired of the heroic defence of Liège. I looked at the map and I couldn't reconcile it with the folds of our ragged line of absent-minded beggars. I didn't like the way in which the journalists excused our 'contemptible little army' for running away because of the treachery of French generals who were always being shot at sunrise, and always subsequently writing to the papers to say how much they liked the war. My phlebitis affected merely my left leg and the fact that I was a sharp-shooter and an old artilleryman didn't interest the War Office. I couldn't use my leg—could I use my brains?

I was at dinner with an old friend, the Honourable A.B.,[2] the brother of the Earl of C. He mentioned that he was in the censor's office. I said, 'What about me? I have some little reputation as a man of letters—as a critic—I am an expert in cipher—I read and write French as well as I write English (and the world knows how well that is)—I have a fair acquaintance with a dozen other languages, including Hindustani —my leg will keep me out of war as effectively as Mr Woodrow Wilson will keep America—is there nothing I can do to serve my country as it appears that you are serving her?'

He said, 'I'm afraid you can't do anything—you see I started in the Navy—I had a year or two on a training ship before I became a barrister—I have a locus standi. You didn't even take honours at Cambridge, as the Patriot Bottomley will one day suppose you to have done—you did not even take the ordinary degree. You wear a short blue gown and an extremely battered mortarboard. You have an extraordinary personality —a reputation for having committed every crime from murder, barratry and arson to quaternio terminorum. You have the subtlest mind, the deepest knowledge of psychology and the most unusual way of brushing your hair in England. I cannot hold out any hopes that any way can be found whereby you might serve your country.'

He drank eight cups of coffee; he swallowed fifteen glasses of 1811 brandy. But he could not make me a naval lieutenant who had forgotten the difference between a powder monkey and a taffrail.

'You cannot serve your country.'

I said, 'Lord Kitchener has asked for a hundred thousand volunteers. Damn this leg, but couldn't I write or talk?'

He said, 'Lord Kitchener is only bluffing. We don't want men; Liège is holding out.' (This was about a month after it fell.) 'A million and a half Russians of the steam-roller brand passed through England last night in a first-class carriage on their way to Flanders. They travelled from St Petersburg to Archangel by a railway which has a single line and whose rolling stock consists of three engines, one tied up with really serviceable iron wire, and the others with pieces of excellently efficient string—and four trucks which aren't so bad, I honestly believe. And why they disembarked all those men in Scotland and sent them through England in a first-class carriage with the blinds drawn, instead of sending them direct to Dunkirk, I don't know.'

My leg and my Sunday School record alike conspiring to keep me out of the trenches, and my deplorable lack of stupidity disqualifying me for the Intelligence Department, I accepted an invitation to go to New York. It looked as though there might be fifteen or twenty million dollars in it, and I had a feeling that my country, the richest in the world, would shortly be going, cap in hand, to the savages for cowries. I went to America by the *Lusitania,* on October 24th, 1914, expecting to stay a fortnight and return with the sinews of war. It did not take me forty-eight hours to discover that my egg was addled.

I had taken with me the equivalent of about fifty pounds in American coinage. As luck would have it, one of the first people I met in New York, Mr D,[3] whom I knew as a collector of rare books, paintings and sculptures, including some of my own *introuvable* publications, showed an interest in the purchase of some of my unique editions and manuscripts. I arranged to stay in New York until these could be sent over for his approval. (As a matter of fact, I had understood him as offering to purchase them all outright. Money was at this time of considerable moment to me. In the upshot, he purchased between seven and eight hundred dollars' worth of my goods, instead of between three and four thousand dollars' worth, as I had expected; and this disappointment left me in great straits financially, as I had at that time no immediately available resources in England.)

The Patriot Bottomley is in error, I pray that he may pardon me if I indicate it. It is his kindness to me which seeks to flatter me unduly when he says that I took honours from Cambridge. Posterity will understand, on the contrary, that Cambridge has taken fresh honours from me. Nay, Patriot though thou be, Horatio, it is human to err. Homer and Jupiter have been known to nod. The Patriot Bottomley makes a worthy third to these. But I did not even take the poll degree at Cambridge. I am an undergraduate of Trinity College. But I am a life member of that college; so much so, that when the Junior Dean attempted to prevent me from exercising my right to walk into its courts, I confronted him at the door of the chapel and called him a coward and a liar to his face. To rebuke the authorities of one's college is a distasteful duty; one too often imposed upon the modern undergraduate. But there is in me Roman virtue and I never shrink from a moral obligation.

I found myself, then, in New York, awaiting the arrival of my books and manuscripts, an event, unfortunately as I then thought, long delayed. So I bethought me whether I could not, irrationally, immorally, unphilosophically, with a game leg but with all my heart and brain, serve England.

I was furious at the stupidity of the British propaganda. It was worse in America than it had been in England. At its best, it was exaggeration and sheer falsehood, so transparent that Woodrow Wilson himself, to say nothing of a legion of Italian bootblacks, saw through it.

As for the German propaganda, it was hardly noticeable. Was it that they did not understand the importance of America in the Wilhelmstrasse? Was it that they had the good sense to rely upon the stupidity of the English apologists to defeat their intentions?

I had a considerable opinion of the intelligence of Germans, dating from the time in my boyhood when Helmholtz was the great name in physics, Haeckel in biology, Mommsen in history, Goethe in poetry, Bach, Beethoven and Wagner in music; the time when one might say that the whole of organic chemistry had been developed in Germany. I had further to remember that the German social system was considered by nearly all thinking Englishmen as a sublime model. German thought and action had been made immortal by Carlyle. German social economy had been slavishly adopted by Lloyd George in the Insurance Act. Great lawyers like Lord Haldane and talented errand boys like H. G. Wells mingled their voices (of course, in the latter case, with a somewhat cockney accent) to extol the greatness of Germany and to hold her up as a pattern to all good Englishmen. I reflected that Bismarck was not exactly a fool in politics, that von Moltke had been hardly an amateur in the art of war. I had read von Bernhardi with admiration, both for his intellectual ability and his moral simplicity. I did not argue whether or no he came from Italian stock. Nietzsche was to me almost an avatar of Thoth, the god of wisdom; and, whether or no he was a Polish Jew, Germany had possessed sufficient intelligence to profit by the thwackings that he gave her. Yes, I was almost convinced that the German directorate had decided to allow British hypocrisy and stupidity to win their battles for them by making themselves absurd and obscene in the eyes of all sensible people.

One day, I think early in 1915, I was seated on the top of what the American purist calls a stage, and we a bus. This vehicle was proceeding (or attempting to proceed) up Fifth Avenue, which is a sort of ditch lined with diamonds and over-rouged stenographers, all at a price totally disproportionate to the value of the article. I was not interested in these objects of merchandise; I was occupied by my own vanity. Somebody in England had sent me press cuttings which described me as the greatest poet, philosopher, blackguard, mountaineer, magician, degenerate and saint of all time; and I was thinking that, as in the case of the Queen of Sheba, when she visited King Solomon, the half had not been told.

I was aroused from this mood of mingled gratification and disappointment by a tap on the shoulder. A voice asked me to excuse its intrusion. Its owner explained that, seeing me reading cuttings with the superscription of a London firm, he assumed me to be at least English-speaking, in a city where Yiddish was the language of romance. If so, was I in favour of a square deal for Germany and Austria? I replied that I was. I have often thought how much nicer Germans and Austrians would be if they were cut up into little squares and made into soup.

I did not reveal to my interlocutor this interpretation of my reply, for at my initiation I was taught to be cautious. He, with the frank bonhomie of the Irishman, told me that his name was O'Brien, that he had to get off at 37th Street, but that if I could accept his card, he would be pleased to hold further conversation with me at his office. Like Jurgen in the masterpiece of James Branch Cabell, I am willing to taste any drink once, and I may incidentally remind my admirers that, if the drink should be Courvoisier over fifty years old, I will go on till something breaks and do good work all the time. So I went to see Mr O'Brien.

Mr O'Brien was not in. I think I never saw him again. But I discovered that his office was the office of a paper called *The Fatherland*, appearing weekly. To my surprise, the inmates seemed to know all about me; and, in the absence of Mr O'Brien, they produced the most extraordinary little amniote—half rat, half rabbit, if I am any zoologist at all—whose name is Joseph Bernard Rethy. I looked at this specimen of the handiwork of the Creator with somewhat mixed feelings, gradually sagging towards a pessimistic atheism, especially when I learned that, like anyone in New York who can string together a dozen words without sound or sense, he was a shining light of the Poetry Society. (But he is quite a nice boy.)

I must admit that I did not know how to talk to him. With all the quickness of his Jewish apprehension, he decided that I was meat for his master, for whom he sent by means of the complicated manual gestures which form the true language of Jews, and, *pace* Professor Garner, of the other anthropoids. To my surprise, this master of his recognized me and came forward with extended hands, bulging eyes and the kind of mouth which seems to have been an unfortunate afterthought. The name of this person was George Sylvester Viereck.

I have a decided admiration of sorts for this individual. He has the extraordinary faculty of awakening an instructive repulsion in most people similar to that which many feel with regard to a toad. He is mean and cowardly to an extent psychologically almost unfathomable; but his cowardice is so protected by cunning that he is able to execute a desperate purpose. I may arouse a storm of execration for saying so, but I believe him to be fundamentally one of the bravest of brave men. He runs away all the time, but he never forgets to 'fight another day'. At one time he boasted that he was the grandson of the first German Emperor by an actress, Adele Viereck. The statement wounded America in its two worst places. It asserted superiority and defied propriety. Viereck has tried to live down his boast; but I believe that, in his heart of hearts, he fortifies himself in any crisis by saying secretly, 'I am not of dregs like Americans.' His manners are pleasant, too much so to be a gentleman's. He is homosexual at heart—though I believe not so in practice—and conscious of this inferiority, which makes him timid. This is accentuated by a nervous temperament. He has a remarkable gift for epigrammatic phrases, a strong sense of rhythm and a great critical ability, which is masked by his opportunism. His *Confessions of a Barbarian* is probably the cleverest book ever written by an American about Europe. Some of his poems are so simple and direct that, if they miss sublimity, which may or may not be the case, the blame is to be laid to the disastrous Jewish trait of conscious cleverness which came so near to shipwreck the greatness of Heine.

He recalled himself to my recollection by saying that he had met me in the office of Mr Austin Harrison, the editor of the *English Review*. It has been a lifelong rule of mine to take no notice of my contemporaries. My companions are the great men of antiquity and my children those of posterity. I did not remember him; but as it has been another lifelong rule of mine to be polite, even to poets, I feigned the recognition and enthusiasm which I judged appropriate.

Viereck is a man of considerable talent for conversation. He knows the world well. He is not deceived by the humbug of public men and the prostitute antics of the press. He is able to see both sides of any question. His point of view possesses the sanity which comes from the second rater's perception of the necessity of compromise. I was able to talk to him as I could have done with an Englishman of similar education.

But his intelligence was not sufficiently subtle to comprehend the moral paradox in myself. I praised Germany—I sympathized with Germany—I justified Germany—and he erroneously deduced, as the average Englishman might have done, that I was pro-German. He did not understand the attitude which I held. I can hardly blame him, for it would puzzle myself if I allowed myself to worry about it. I may or may not be a burglar; but even if I am, I am going to drill a hole through the householder who interrupts me in the exercise of my profession. This is my position. But Viereck could not guess it. I might be a high-souled cosmopolitan, like Romain Rolland; I might be an Irish fanatic, like Roger Casement; I might be a sordid traitor, like Mata Hari. But he could not understand my being sincere in thinking like Bernard Shaw would think if he could think, and equally so in acting like Sir Edward Grey would act if he could act.

During the conversation, it dawned upon my dull mind that here were the headquarters of the German propaganda. Viereck was a man of suave insinuating manners and address, a man of considerable political experience and immense intellectual capacity, fortified by the cunning of one who has studied long in the hard merciless school which the world throws open to homosexuals. Poor fool, his innocence had betrayed him into indiscretion! The homosexual is comically innocent, and cannot understand the loathing with which the average man regards what to him is a natural impulse. More, it is not merely moral righteousness, but moral exaltation above what he considers the animal instinct of the normal man. So he had plucked violets from the grave of Oscar Wilde and framed them with an autograph copy of one of the sonnets written by Lord Alfred Douglas to the shade of that most distinguished of His Ludship's 'Messieurs'. Is it imaginable that anyone should suppose that he can advertise himself and his sexual peculiarities on so crude a poster without obtaining the kind of publicity that will hurt him most with men of cruder sexual prejudices? But Viereck had learned his lesson. He had learned to deny everything. Even to me, knowing my reputation, totally undeserved as it happens to be, for similar abnormalities, he would admit nothing. This is a most remarkable circumstance, for the persecution attached to this passion has created a freemasonry among its devotees which makes them frank to the point of indiscretion when they think they recognize sympathy in an acquaintance. Bitter must have been Viereck's initiation that it should have taught him to be so extravagantly cautious; but it fitted him to handle the German propaganda.

I claim this credit, that from the first I recognized him as a master of craft, an opposite well worthy of every trick of fence. I am still unable to agree with Captain (now Commodore) Gaunt (Director of the British Intelligence for some time, including this time, in New York) in classing him 'as one of the lesser jackals around von Papen', as he wrote me during our correspondence on the subject. I claim further credit for perceiving the limitations of Viereck. Brilliant though he was, he was not old enough, solid enough or unselfish and high-minded enough to be trustworthy enough to handle a propaganda involving the destiny of a people.

I looked for what the Americans call the 'man higher up'. I did not look in the direction of honest, well-meaning, sentimental von Bernstorff with all his capacity for routine, his noble credulity, his quite genuine desire to arrange everything amicably, and his hackneyed training in the diplomatic service with its hamstrings of etiquette and its chessboard punctilio. I did not look towards von Papen, with his stultifying conviction that he was so much cleverer than anybody else; still less towards Boy-Ed, who was a breezy naval ass with the instincts, ineradicable in the Turk, of a gentleman. Von Mack was a capable person of professional mind, adequate to gather and present statistics, and obsessed with the universal lust of the German university man to prove everything five times over after everybody else has ceased to take the smallest interest in the question. There were lots of small fry, good for subordinate positions. But was there not someone authentically anointed for the work, someone who had made a special study for years of the psychology of Americans, who had written books about them? Was there no man of master mind, ripe experience, balanced wisdom?

I found such a candidate for the secret director of the German propaganda in Professor Hugo Münsterberg. As it happened, the professor was an old enemy of mine. We had quarrelled about philosophy and physics. His mind was intensely positive, brutally matter-of-fact, but capable of appreciating subtlety, and far more open to new facts and theories than most of his opponents supposed. His arrogance was, to a great extent, the Freudian protection against his own uncertainty. He knew psychology, he knew men; he understood business; and in his capacity of instructor at Harvard, he had acquired the habit of forming and directing minds. So much I knew, and I pictured my duel with him in romantic terms of Sherlock Holmes and Moriarty.

But the facts were less enthralling. The professor had the great German gift of Being Always Right. My task was simplified; I had merely to keep on telling him how very right he was. He soon ceased to gauge the temper of the community correctly, began to lay down the law instead of arguing with moderation and good sense, was hardened in arrogance by opposition, and became as violent and stupid on his side as our own chosen propagandists were on ours. My meat!

But I am overrunning myself. My immediate problem was to confirm Viereck in his conviction that I was pro-German. There was a very serious snag in the *English Review* for November 1914. There was a poem of mine called 'An Appeal to the American Republic' inviting an Anglo-American alliance. This poem having been written in 1898, I had had to alter 'the traitor Russian' to 'the traitor Prussian', to suit the political kaleidoscope. Fortunately I had no difficulty in persuading Viereck that this action was in the nature of camouflage, designed to exploit the stupidity of the British public in general and Austin Harrison in particular. His knowing Mr Austin Harrison made this easier.

But personally I was so terribly English! My accent betrayed me as his did Peter. My clothes were obviously Savile Row. I had not even taken the precaution to be sufficiently un-English to pay for them. I clutched at the straw of my name. From the myths of antiquity looms a phantom Crowley somewhere near Kilkenny where the cats come from, and though my particular Crowleys have been mercifully well-behaved in England since the bishop of that name who published his naughty epigrams in the time of Queen Elizabeth, there are lots of Crowleys in America who come direct from Ireland.

I found Viereck very sympathetic about Irish independence and I billed myself as the only and original Sinn Feiner. My trouble was that I knew nothing about the Irish question and possessed nothing but the hazy idea common to most Englishmen, including those who have studied Ireland most profoundly, that it was a devil of a mess and a devil of a nuisance. However, Viereck wanted to believe; and he believed, like a Catholic who is afraid to sleep in the dark.

Having thus established myself as an Irish rebel and a pro-German, I went away and considered what I could do about it. I read *The Fatherland;* I found the German case presented with learning, with logic and with moderation. The motifs were scholarship, statistics and statesmanlike sobriety. It seemed to me that, in the peculiar temper of the United States, whose people, however ignorant and dishonest individually, are always, as a whole, curiously anxious to know the truth and to do justice, this propaganda was infernally dangerous to British interests. I talked to my friends about it. All they could say was that Viereck was personally despicable. Some, like Captain Gaunt, affected to ignore the importance of *The Fatherland*. Others, even more hopeless from my point of view, seemed to think that they could suppress *The Fatherland*

by continuing their lifelong policy of omitting to invite Viereck
to dinner parties which would have bored him and given him
indigestion.

I decided on a course of action, which seemed to me the
only one possible in a situation which I regarded as immensely serious. I would write for *The Fatherland*. By doing
so, I should cut myself off temporarily from all my friends,
from all sources of income, I should apparently dishonour a
name which I considered it my destiny to make immortal, and
I should have to associate on terms of friendship with people
whose very physical appearance came near to reproducing in
me the possibly beneficial results of crossing the Channel with
a choppy sea.

But the German propaganda was being done as well as the
British propaganda ill. With a little moral ascendancy over
Viereck, I could spoil his game completely by doing as much
mischief to Germany as the Patriot Bottomley and the other
hoarse-throated fishwives of Fleet Street were doing to England. I met with more success than I had hoped.

Münsterberg was not Argus. I think moreover that folly is
contagious. He could hardly keep his young men in hand,
especially when apparent victory turned their heads. I found
some of them incredibly silly. I had always known Paul Carus
for an ass since he published *The Gospel of Buddha*, but I had
no idea that he was such an ass! In *The Open Court* he published a fancy portrait from my pen of Bloody Bill as Parsifal!
Poor old earnest Christian Endeavour Wilhelm, with his megalomania and his theatricalism and his fat-witted Lutheran
Gott and his withered hand and his moving-picture-star galaxy
of uniforms as the up-to-date Messiah! What a model for
'King Arthur come again', to give the heathen *Schrecklichkeit!*

I must have been beautifully drunk to write that. I don't
remember anything about it—but I must have been much
more than drunk when I sent it to Paul Carus. I suppose I
had become acclimatized to the idea that all serious and eminent people are perfectly brainless. He swallowed it, hook, line
and sinker; and a poor little bookseller in London who had
been agent for the paper for years, and had never read a line
of it, got three months in prison! The truth is that the British
lost all sense of humour when the war broke out. I wonder
how many millions in blood and treasure it cost us to 'jowk'
with such 'deeficulty'!

I worked up Viereck gradually from relatively reasonable
attacks on England to extravagances which achieved my ob-

ject of revolting every comparatively sane human being on earth. I proved that the *Lusitania* was a man-of-war. I dug up all the atrocities of King Leopold of Belgium, from mutilated niggers in the Congo to Cléo de Mérode and Anna Robinson. I translated atrocity, not merely into military necessity, but into moral uplift. I put haloes on the statue of von Hindenburg with his wooden head and his nightgown of tintacks. But (on the whole) I took few chances of letting the Germans perceive the tongue in my cheek.

One day, however, I got genuinely drunk, not with alcohol but with indignation. It was the day of the murder of Edith Cavell. I sat down and wrote an article—a stained glass window representing von Bissing as Jesus Christ, 'that great-hearted, simple-minded, trusting German'. He extends his hand to her; and says, with tears in his eyes, 'Miss Cavell, I trust you!' Then she acts the part of Judas; and I conclude with a display of fireworks, in which she is welcomed to hell by Lucrezia Borgia and the Marchioness de Brinvilliers and several other vampires, whose names I have forgotten, having others closer to hand.

It makes me weep for Germany when I think that Viereck published such hideous and transparent irony without turning a hair! Americans do not understand irony at all. But Viereck should have done so, considering the Jewish hetaera and the wily old robber baron in his ancestry. But are any tears salt enough to weep for England when I think that none of my countrymen could read my bitterness and anger between the lines of that comic travesty of blasphemy?

I must explain here that I had more than one string to my bow. It was really a minor part of my programme to wreck the German propaganda on the proof of reductio ad absurdum. I had hoped to gain the full confidence of the conspirators whom I had identified and deal with them as somebody whose name I forget dealt with Cataline; and Lord Mount Eagle or whoever it was, with Guy Faux. But nobody in British Intelligence had sufficient of that quality to notice me.

I have always been unduly optimistic about England. I know such a lot of people who are far from being fools. But war seems to deaden perception. Men who are in ordinary times quite acute become ready to assume that anyone who is waving a Union Jack and singing 'Britannia Rules the Waves' must be an Admiral of the Fleet. Everybody assumed that the irritating balderdash I wrote for *The Fatherland* must be the stark treason that the Germans were stupid enough to think it was.

A person in my position is liable to see Sherlock Holmes in the most beef-witted policeman. I did not feel that I was advancing in the confidence of the Germans. I got no secrets worth reporting to London, and I was not at all sure whether the cut of my clothes had not outweighed the eloquence of my conversation. I thought I would do something more public. I wrote a long parody on the Declaration of Independence and applied it to Ireland.

I invited a young lady violinist who has some Irish blood in her, behind the more evident stigmata of the ornithorhyncus and the wombat. Adding to our number about four other debauched persons on the verge of delirium tremens, we went out in a motor boat before dawn on the third of July to the rejected statue of Commerce for the Suez Canal, which Americans fondly suppose to be Liberty Enlightening The World.

There I read my Declaration of Independence. I threw an old envelope into the bay, pretending that it was my British passport. We hoisted the Irish flag. The violinist played the 'Wearing of the Green'. The crews of the interned German ships cheered us all the way up the Hudson, probably because they estimated the degree of our intoxication with scientific precision. Finally, we went to Jack's for breakfast, and home to sleep it off. The *New York Times* gave us three columns and Viereck was distinctly friendly.

Over in England there was consternation. I cannot think what had happened to their sense of humour. To pretend to take it seriously was natural enough in New York, where everybody is afraid of the Irish, not knowing what they may do next. But London was having bombs dropped on it. There was, however, one person in England who knew me—also a joke when he saw it: the Honourable A.B., my old friend aforesaid. Owing to the confusion inevitably attached to the mud with which we always begin muddling through, this gentleman had been inadvertently assigned to the Intelligence Department.

When he saw the report in the *New York Times,* he wrote to me about it. I knew he would not talk. I knew he would not blunder. I wrote back explaining my position, which he immediately understood and approved. But intelligence such as his is a rare accident in an Intelligence Department. He could not authorize me to go ahead without appealing to his superiors. He put the case before them. They were quite unable to understand that I was merely in a position to get into the full confidence of the Germans if I had the right sort of assistance. They idiotically assumed that I already possessed a knowledge of the enemy's secrets and they sent me a test question on a matter of no importance—did I know who, if anybody, was passing under the name of so-and-so? I was not going to risk my precarious position asking questions. The official English idea of a secret agent seemed to be that he should act like a newspaper reporter. The result was that the negotiations came to very little, though I turned in reports from time to time.

There was a Temporary Gentleman named H . . . d in the British Military Mission with whom I had such dealings as is possible with the half-witted. He thought that he detected hostility in my attitude towards him, whereas it was merely the University Manner. It was this poor thing whom our secret service sent to interview me. I told him that I could find out exactly what the Germans were doing in America. I also told him that I had the absolute confidence, years old, of a man high in the German secret service—that I could go to Germany in the character of an Irish patriot and report on the conditions of the country. (There was desperate need of accurate information as to Germany's resources at this period.) He said, with the air of one detected in the act of adultery by sixteen separate sleuths, to say nothing of being doomed by the Black Hand, 'But how do I know that you won't go straight to Viereck and tell him I have been to see you?'!!! I am loath to record accents of human speech so eloquent of mental undevelopment. I said to him, 'What harm would that do? How would that save Bloody Bill from his predestined doom?' He did not know the answer to that. But then, he did not know the answer to anything else.

I must now return to the main subject of this report. Partially baffled by the failure of the British to apply common sense to my proposals, I was compelled to go on playing a lone hand. It was necessary to persuade the Germans that arrogance and violence were sound policy, that bad faith was the cleverest diplomacy, that insult was the true means of winning friendship, and direct injury the proper conjuration to call up gratitude. It could not have succeeded had they not been hardened by temporary success, duped by the rigidity of their own logic, and rendered arrogant by the conviction of their own uprightness.

But it succeeded. Von Bernstorff's superficiality could not estimate America. He was too much a gentleman. He knew indeed the unhappy truth that Wilson had been elected because he had kept America out of the war. I drummed it into both his donkey ears. But he was deceived by the humbug of 'the world kept safe for democracy'. The people ruled—the people had voted against war. One can almost envy him his simple creed. Such a man might trust his wife and live happy ever afterwards.

He did not see that 'the people' in America are slaves who count for nothing in the minds of their masters. But America had lent fabulous sums to the Allies, and would get nothing if Germany won the war but the kicks which so much pusillanimity and selfishness deserved. He did not see that America wanted a pretext for calling the conduct of Germany intolerable. The scabby old camel, almost ready to start for its trip through dryness, was looking wistfully for the last straw.

For some time I had been contemplating the military situation in its largest sense. I had been thinking of water, air and earth as units. I had been at some pains to study the question of the necessary limitations of the three arms of war. I knew the history of Napoleon gazing glumly across the Channel, after his triumphant snatch at Europe. I had written a paper in *The Fatherland* called 'The Future of the Submarine'. I pointed out that hardly anyone had believed in the naval value of these craft until three British cruisers were sunk in fifteen minutes. I pointed out that this demonstration would convince treasuries. Every nation would mobilize all the brains and all the gold and all the influence to find a means of opening the wound. I prophesied a development of the submarine as astounding as that of railways and automobiles—which dated from the hour when they were proved practicable and useful.

On January 3rd, 1917, I returned to the charge with an article which was ostensibly a criticism of Count von Reventlow's *Vampire*, but in reality my own sermon on that text. The Patriot Bottomley has quoted one of my best passages, that in which I proposed to reduce England to the status of a German colony. (The Germans printed it without a smile!) I was very proud of that article. It proved that all island races were primarily fishermen, who lived by snatching fish and must therefore become pirates. The argument is quite in the style of a real German professor. I advocated the 'Unrestricted Submarine Campaign'. I secretly calculated, rightly as the gods would have it, that so outrageous a violation of all law would be the last straw, and force America to throw off the burden of neutrality.

My German friends were loud in their congratulations. It was confidently whispered among the *cognoscenti* that von Bernstorff's judgment swayed at its impact. He withdrew his objections to that brutality, that insane savagery, that brought America into the war.

But there's a tick in every sleeping-bag. My countrymen stayed right with me to the finish! In what high glee did I not keep my secret rendezvous with a friend from a certain British consulate, waving my article, and crying, 'The damned fools have printed it—and it's going to turn the trick!' He read it; his face fell; he turned disgustedly and growled, 'I didn't know you were a German.'

The secret service people, while considering my application for employment, asked a friend of mine to explain my attitude. 'We don't understand him,' they wailed piteously; 'we don't understand him at all.' 'Cheer up,' said my friend; 'you're not the first people to fail to understand Mr. Aleister Crowley!'

It is rather irrelevant; but it is certainly very amusing and very characteristic, the following incident of my campaign. I had asked the Honourable A.B. to help me consolidate my position with the Germans by heating the branding irons of infamy for me in the fire of publicity. I therefore attributed it to his ingenuity when I heard that the police had raided the office of an acquaintance of mine in Regent Street. They didn't know what I was after, took my articles at their face value, and thought to annoy, perhaps to intimidate me by the raid.

The person they arrested was a motherly old fool who had been prophesying with tea leaves for about twenty years at the same old stand, with the full knowledge of the police. The ordinary course in prosecuting a fortune-teller is for a polite young man to hand, with deference and apologies to his prospective victim, a summons to appear before a magistrate. But the charge against this woman was factitious. They wanted to get at me, at me barely more than three thousand miles away, and confidently supposed to be sitting in a luxurious suite at the Ritz-Carlton, quaffing beaker after beaker of champagne to the health of the Kaiser, as I conspired with the fanatical brewers of Milwaukee.

One would really have thought that modern education would have taught the police that the best zoologists agree unanimously that it is hard to please a tortoise by stroking its shell. And a comparatively brief course of logic might easily have enriched this theorem (by a syllogism containing the minor premise that tortoises are not so sympathetic and altruistic as, shall we say, policemen) with a corollary that it is even harder to please a tortoise by stroking the shell of another tortoise many miles away. Of course, there is no rigid proof of this. The premises may be disputed by the sceptic.

But at least the police should have heard of Sir Henry Hawkins, a being, after all, zoologically more akin to me than any tortoise. When he was presiding at the trial of some Fenian agitators, some of their friends planted a bomb on the doorstep of the Honourable Reginald Brett. Brett suggested that these earnest folk had committed one of those errors of judgment which seem inseparable from earnestness, and that the bomb had really been intended for Sir Henry. The judge replied, 'Do they really think that they can intimidate me by putting a bomb on your doorstep?'

So, at the zero hour, reckless of peril, a devoted band of detectives, with revolvers drawn, went over the top, cheering wildly, to the third floor of 93 Regent Street,[4] broke down the door, which I think was unlocked, and found a dozen mild old people trying to browse on the lush grass of my poetry.

The police did not even calculate on the possibility of my revenge. They imprudently entrusted the conduct of the raid to Inspector Currie, though they might have known that I was perfectly capable of some stupid joke about his being hot stuff. The Crown solicitor, too, who conducted the prosecution, was so named that I might have said, Their artillery is composed of an old rusty Muskett. But I matched my fortitude by my magnanimity and forbore.

However, I made the best of it. When I had done laughing, I made a wonderful scene of indignation in the office of *The Fatherland*, which helped me quite a little on my weary way. But I must admit that I was downhearted. How could we hope to win the war if London had got as hysterical as that? I looked at the Germans and took courage.

In the upshot, at last I got enough money to settle my

affairs in New York, where I had been dodging starvation for five years. That legend of my growing fat on German gold! I lost no time in coming home to England. But I was not at ease. I was fed up with human beings. I resolved to disappear into the desert and give myself wholly to the religious life. I knew that my personal friends in England would understand what I had done in America: they would perhaps be proud of me. So far, so good.

But I supposed, from the conversation of some genuinely intelligent Englishmen in high official positions who were travelling with me across the Atlantic, that England had recovered sang froid and settled down to reconstruction and the enjoyment of the fruits of victory. I wrongly judged that authority would administer a stern rebuke to any maniacs who aimed at the perpetuation of bad feeling. Indeed, I saw little in London to remind me that there had ever been a war.

Was there one man who thought that it might still pay to work upon the baser passions of the mob? It seemed so: it was Christmas; there was a man who made a two-page splash about abolishing the wicked German Santa Claus!* No! I was again in error. I must have misinterpreted the motives. The man was that great soul, the Patriot Bottomley!

Such a man would doubtless be as difficult to understand as others had found me. He must have had some noble reason for his apparently vile and baseless attacks on bishops, judges and ministers of the Crown, to say nothing of firms like Waring and Gillow. I could not concur in the prevalent opinion that he was as much a blackmailer as De Wend Fenton. I could appreciate the eloquence and knowledge of law which, to the amused amazement of London, had thrice saved him from penal servitude at the hands of a British jury. I could not foresee that I should live to be horrified by the insults of that Shallow, Sir Charles Biron, 'I cannot believe Mr Bottomley on his oath.' †

I did not think that anybody took his *John Bull* more seriously than we used to do the 'Ally Sloper's Half-Holiday' which it has—not too advantageously—replaced in the affections of the people. I must confess that I was rather disgusted when my own solicitors sent me half a page of ravings about myself and asked the explanation of my crimes. They must

* *John Bull,* Christmas number, 1919.
† I wrote this in January 1922, when Mr Bottomley was prosecuting Mr Bigland for criminal libel, and the magistrate made this remark.

have known that there was hardly one statement which was true in fact. The article was full of careless blunders about matters within their knowledge.

But that was not what worried me. I kept on saying to myself, 'Why only half a page?' The Headmaster of Eton had had a whole page about his advocating Platonic pleasures for boys. My own father-in-law, a charming old gentleman with not even a national reputation, and not an enemy in the world but a worthless curate he had discharged, had had a whole page (inspired by the aforesaid curate) about the way in which he swindled his servant-girls out of their savings. I knew that if the great Patriot seemed to be not giving me my duty, it was from shortage of paper or writer's cramp, not from lack of kindness of heart.

I had indeed ample evidence of what wealth of magnanimity was buttoned beneath that patriotic waistcoat. A well-known journalist,[5] who has never written a book on the Musical Glasses, a biography of either Lord Henry Somerset, Canon Aitken or F. E. Smith, any novel about Fenian dynamiters, or any short story about Portuguese matadors, had written various articles for the Patriot Bottomley; and he had not been paid. Now it came to pass in the fulness of time that the Patriot felt it his painful public duty to make weekly attacks upon the firm of Waring and Gillow. A few days before these attacks ceased, which they did very suddenly, the journalist chanced to pass the offices of *John Bull* in a taxi and saw Mr Sam Waring—the principal director of Waring and Gillow—descending the steps. Quick as thought, he paid off the chauffeur, bounced upstairs into the private office of the great Patriot and said firmly, though gently, 'I've come for my three hundred pounds.'

'How did you know?' was the Patriot's only question.

'Never mind. I know.'

And Horatio handed over three hundred pounds in notes. This was indeed kindness of heart.

I could not doubt that if he seemed to be neglecting my publicity, it was inadvertence. However, the Patriot Bottomley doubtless felt that he had wronged me for he made amends by publishing another article to refresh public enthusiasm about my crimes, a month later. I have not seen it, but I hope he pitched it strong.

My conscience was clear. I had been loyal to England. I had suffered for her sake as much as any man; I had 'fought the good fight, despising the shame', starvation and solitude of soul and body: I was content.

But, as in a Greek tragedy, just when I thought myself most safe, the last straw was gently but firmly placed on my back by two of my oldest friends. The first of these is named George Cecil Jones. I had known him intimately since the autumn of 1898. We had been co-workers in the most arduous task known to mankind: that which Bergson—so far as his ignorance allows—described as 'creating oneself a God'. But he had weakened in late years. He had married. Life to his optimistic eyes looked like a green field with a watering trough. Death in his mind became inseparably connected with the idea of mutton chops.

When De Wend Fenton was trying to blackmail me in 1910, he found to his chagrin that I would not even meet him at dinner, so that he might propose a 'friendly arrangement' over the coffee and cigars, by which I should pay cash for credit, sovereigns for silence. Balked by my contempt, he cast about him for some less wary bird. If he could only get one of my friends to sue him for libel, he would be able to wriggle out of it somehow. Then, think of all the free publicity! Even if he lost the case, it didn't matter, for his paper was bankrupt anyhow. So he put in a paragraph so dexterously penned that anyone with a mind less clear than that of the solicitor who read it over, *ad hoc,* might have taken it to mean that Mr Jones was a sodomite.

Mr Jones ought to have known better than to waste his time reading papers of this class. He ought to have known much better than to take any notice of such rubbish. He ought to have known very much better than to air his grievance in a court of law. His youngest baby ought to have known better than to employ a personal friend with no experience of such cases to act as his solicitor. And one would have thought that even such a solicitor would have known better than to brief a barrister of the kind that 'will see the whole job through for a ten pound note'.

When the case came to trial, the defendants pleaded that they had not suggested that Mr Jones was a sodomite. They had not, and never had had, any intention of suggesting that Mr Jones was a sodomite. Mr Jones explained elaborately and excitedly that he was not a sodomite. The judge, summing up, said that, doubtful as the case might be on some points, one thing at least stood out sun-clear, that Mr Jones was not a sodomite. It was also evident that the expressions which had offended the plaintiff were inoffensive; that nobody had ever suggested that Mr Jones was a sodomite.

The jury then retired. They were dazed by suppressed sexual excitement. Their imaginations projected fascinating yet fearful phantasms. When this psychological delirium became articulate, each man was terrified lest he should let slip some phrase which might arouse suspicion of sympathy with sexual irregularities against the speaker. Instinct clamoured that a victim must be found on which to concentrate the frenzy of the crowd. Thus, obfuscated by panic, they stammered out confused and incoherent comments on the case.

They thought that there was something curious about the evidence. All parties *breathed together* that Mr Jones was not a sodomite. The Latin for *breathe together* is conspire. That's what it was—a conspiracy! So they brought in the verdict that the article was a libel and that it was justified!!!—such verdict evidently implying that the defendants had perjured themselves, that the judge was a fool, and that Mr Jones was a sodomite after all!

I supinely thought that the farce was over, that the climax was perfect, that there could never be anything funnier than that. But the Lord keeps unsuspected bounties for them that love him, and my chalice overflowed when this very Mr Jones wrote me, in the tone of a dictator, that I ought to go to law to clear my character from the aspersions cast upon it by the Patriot Bottomley! If not, let me communicate no more with mine truly, G. Cecil Jones!

But in this jest of Mr Jones' pompous imbecility, there was something sad. He had induced my old friend Eckenstein to sign that silly letter. Eckenstein is a great man and my dearest friend. But he is an old man and (I fear me) a dying one.* His judgment cannot be what it used to be; but if his memory has not failed him, I will remind him of certain events in our long friendship.

I met him at Wastdale Head during Easter week of 1898. We soon became climbing companions, a relation which endured so long as he was physically able to climb. We were together in the English, Welsh and Scottish mountains; in the Alps, in Mexico; and ultimately in the Himalayas. Between

---

* This paper was first drafted in March 1920 E.V. I revised it finally in January 1922 E.V. In the interval Eckenstein had died. I prefer to leave the passages which relate to him as they stand. His death adds grief to my thoughts of him; nothing can add to the love I have always had for him, or the honour in which I have always held him.

us, we hold all but one or two of the world's records for various feats of mountaineering, both amateur and professional.

In 1898, I was barely more than a boy, pitiably innocent and ridiculously ambitious. (In a sense, I am so still!)

My other climbing friends, with hardly an exception, came to me and warned me to 'have nothing to do with that scoundrel Eckenstein'. 'Who is he anyhow? A dirty East End Jew.' (I quote Mr Morley Roberts, the cobbler of trashy novelettes, who said this to me at Zermatt.) Furthermore, Eckenstein had done something in India *so bad that nobody could even guess what it was!* But that Unspeakable Infamy was the real reason of his quitting the Conway expedition in 1892, and it was generally supposed that the murder of several natives, in cold blood, was one of the less unmentionable ingredients.

That was rather a hard test of comradeship, I think. But I knew my Eckenstein and I disdained to make investigations. I went on climbing with him as if the pompous humbugs of the English Alpine Club had never spoken. By paying guides to haul one over rocks like luggage, one can get a reputation —in England—as a hardy mountaineer. The envious snarls of such craven impostors did not disturb me.

Yet there was something in it, too! There was enough for Eckenstein to be arrested in India by a 'superior person' whose Christian names were George Nathaniel. I never knew the truth of the business; and Eckenstein always protested that he did not know it himself. It didn't matter much then; it doesn't matter at all now. But I want to recall to Eckenstein that I stood pat! I did not ask him to vindicate himself. I do not empanel a jury of jackals to try a lion.

I do not believe that Eckenstein was in full possession of his senses when he signed that silly letter.

POSTSCRIPTUM: New Year, 1922; two years less two months since I wrote this paper. I 'got it off my chest'; next day I had relapsed into my normal indifference to human imbecility. I never so much as troubled to revise it until yesterday. Then I rescued it from its dusty pigeon-hole simply because I heard from my representative in London that my supposed pro-Germanism was a bar to the recognition of my work in England.

I care nothing for public opinion. I care nothing for fame or success. I am perfectly happy in my retirement. The full leisure to work, the freedom from all interruption, the absence of temptations to distraction: Cefalu realizes my idea of heaven.

But I am pledged to give my life to the establishment of the law of Thelema: 'Do what thou wilt shall be the whole of the Law.' So, if the operations on behalf of that Law are being tampered by the insensate belief that I ever was, am, or ever could be, disloyal to my country, which I love with an unreasoning passion, altogether beyond the interference of my intellectual opinions, I am willing to make this public statement as to what I did in the war, and why I did it.

My attitude is unaltered by time. I still think the English pot as black as the German kettle, and I am still willing to die in defence of the pot. Mine is the loyalty of Bill Sikes's dog; you can't make me believe that my master is an injured innocent; and the fact that he starves and beats me doesn't alter the fact that I am his dog, and I love him.

Let the publication of this paper make clear my integrity! Let the British public come to honour me for my stubborn endurance of the shameful martyrdom, still cruel and still dear.

77

I propose to summarize briefly my adventures in America. This chapter should form a framework into which may be fitted the special accounts of my activity. My worst encounter was with the *New York World* which had distinguished itself by printing Harry Kemp's rubbish about my magical exploits. The editor, a genial Irishman—remarkable precisely for being half educated neither more nor less correct to eight places of decimals—observing that Kemp's statements involved numerous physical impossibilities took him to a notary and made him swear to their truth. I have told elsewhere how it came to be written. Hearing of my arrival Kemp hurried to implore me not to give him away. I contemptuously agreed to save his face. Of course, I could not admit the truth of such asinine balderdash, so said that by magical power I had caused him to see what was not, as indeed in a certain sense I had done.

Cosegrave sent a sob sister to interview me on my arrival. She pestered me with a string of foolish questions, such as 'What is your opinion of America?' I was insulted. What did she take me for that I should pronounce judgment on a continent after twenty-four hours? I replied, nevertheless, 'I regard America as the hope of the planet—the white hope.' About this time Jack Johnson was *hors concours*. White hope had become a slang phrase for a challenger without a chance. Of course she did not see the joke. I became so weary of the woman's stupidity that she was bound to make a hopeless hash of what I had said. I told her to try something easier. Reporting a dog-fight would have been about her mark. She went off in a huff, a sagging, shapeless suet pudding. He then sent Henry Hall, who had married a French wife and learnt courtesy. He had read a good deal of good stuff and possessed natural intelligence. I found him charming. He confirmed my diagnosis of W. T. Stead, whom he interviewed. In walking down the street, Stead broke off every minute or two to indulge in a lustful description of some passing flapper and slobber how he would like to flagellate her. Hall wrote a clever and accurate article about the evocation of Bartzabel.

I dined at Cosegrave's house one night. He had asked Evangeline Adams to meet me as being a famous astrologer. The meeting led to a lengthy association. She wanted me to write a book on astrology for her. The plan failed through her persistent efforts to cheat me out of the profits, and her obstinate ignorance of the elementary facts of nature combined with an unconquerable antagonism to the principles of applying common sense to the science.

I learned a good deal, nevertheless. The work kept me concentrated on the subject. At this time, it was my invariable practice to judge from the personal appearance of every stranger I met the sign rising at his birth. Having made up my mind, I would ask him to tell me either the hour or the day of his birth. I could then calculate the missing day as thus: Suppose I judge my man to have Libra in the ascendant and he tells me his birthday is October 1st. When the sun is in 5° or 6° Libra, I can tell him he was born at sunrise, within a limit of error of about two hours. Alternatively, should he say, 'I was born at midnight', I can give his birthday to within a fortnight or so of Christmas. I tabulated my results over a considerable period and found that I was right in a little over two cases in three. Where I was wrong, I found that either the sign I had chosen for his ascendant was that occupied by his sun, which in some people determines the personal appearance more effectively than the ascendant, or else, in erecting his horoscope I found the rising sign occupied by planets whose nature modified the sign so that it could be mistaken for the one I had picked out.

(For instance, a person with Aries rising with the moon and Jupiter conjoined on the cusp. The aggressive martial characteristics of the sign would be toned down by their impelling influence. I might, therefore, state his ascendant as Sagittarius or even Pisces.)

There were, of course, a few cases in which I came a complete cropper, but the cause of this was almost always an instinctive personal antipathy to the individual which confused my judgment. By the most severe standards I may claim fairly to have been correct in not less than eighty per cent. of the cases and considering the chance of getting right at random, I consider it demonstrated beyond dispute that a real relation exists between the personal appearance and the sign rising at birth.

Lest any reader should seek to emulate these efforts and meet with disappointment, let me warn him of two common factors of failure:

1. People of unfamiliar races manifest the astrological appearance of their ethnological branch and this masks that due to their nativity. Experience enables one to penetrate the superficial indication.

2. The skill required to judge this matter develops with surprising speed as soon as a certain point has been reached. It is best to proceed systematically by asking onself, first of all, to what element the examinee belongs. It is then simple to discriminate between the three possible signs. One might mistake Taurus and Scorpio, Gemini and Sagittarius, but the three signs of any given element are always distinguishable as easily as a child, an adult and an old man.

Some signs are almost unmistakable from the first. But others are so weak in character that their influence is rarely found unmodified by planetary considerations. One must further remark that each sign governs two main types—the active and the passive. Thus Aries: the high brows, long face, aquiline nose, tall thin muscular figure, shows the fiery and martial qualities of the sign. But there is an evil and averse counterpart corresponding to the ovine nature. We have the gross, hooked, pendulous proboscis; the thick, flabby, moist lips; the patient stupid eyes, and timid, hunted gait of the bad type of Jew.

Thanks to the resolute refusal of even the educated astrologer to adopt scientific methods of study, their contemptuous indifference to the attitude of the recognized sciences towards them, and their adhesion to tradition, in the right interpretation of which they seek authority, rather than in the indications of critically analysed experience, the general ignorance of the subject is as great as ever.

I propose to demonstrate once for all the truth of the proposition, that the aspect of the heavens at the time of birth is connected with the observed characteristics of the native by collecting a large number of photographs, full face and profile for each subject, and classifying them according to the horoscope. I will thus have twelve sets, one for each sign ascending, twelve showing the possible positions of the sun. I should also examine the assertion that people with Mars rising have some scar or other abnormality on the face, by collecting the photographs of such people. Again, Saturn in the ascendant is said to give a melancholy cast to the countenance.

Should it, then, appear that one hundred Aries men showed a marked and characteristic difference from one hundred Taurus men, and so on through the zodiac, physicists would be hard put to it to deny some nexus. The *apparatus criticus* should, of course, be very perfect. Complications of the ascendant by the presence of planets must be considered separately. Their failure to manifest the characteristic appearance of the sign ought not to be considered fatal to the theory.

Where the history of the subject is available it would furnish material for much further research. We would discover, for instance, whether the presence of Saturn in the seventh house invariably concurred with matrimonial misfortune, or in the tenth with rapid rise of fortunes followed by a sudden crash as in the case of Napoleon, Oscar Wilde, Woodrow Wilson, Lord Northcliffe and several private cases in my own collection. The labour required for this research would be enormous, but the bulk of it would be done by ordinary clerks. And as for the preliminary difficulty of collecting material, any great newspaper could carry out the scheme easily enough. It would of course be necessary to publish an explanation of the proposal with a questionnaire covering the principal points, and asking for good photographs to be sent with the filled up form.

One final remark. I found myself able, as my experience increased, to divine not only the rising sign and the position of the sun, but both points together. Accordingly, on several occasions, I succeeded in telling a man I had never seen before both the house and the day of his birth. I could also judge, now and then, such matters as the angular distance between Sol and Luna, or the aspects and the zodiacal position of other planets.

The psychological reactions to these demonstrations were most interesting. Some people were quite unaffected by the most brilliant successes. Some were scared half out of their wits, such as they had. Others again fell prostrate in awed admiration and jumped from the facts to the fancy that I must be a Mahatma able to juggle with the stars in their courses if the wind took me. Only a small percentage showed intelligent interest. I made a great impression on Frank Crowninshield, editor of *Vanity Fair*. I was in form that night and told everyone exactly right. He realized it could not be guessing. The chances against me ran into billions.

I hung about New York all winter trying to get a foothold. My effort to countermine German intrigue was my worst handicap, in the case of the best people. But as to my literary career, I was a snowflake in hell. Nobody knew my name, bar the educated *rari nantes in gurgito vasto*.[1] Nobody would look at my work, either in periodical form or volume.

I shall tell later of my grotesque failure to make good as a Master of Magick. The people I met knew nothing and thought they knew everything, and whatever scraps of information they had, they had all wrong.

I took a week off in March to go to Philadelphia, where the great Billy Sunday was conducting a revival. The immense notoriety of the man, and the incompatibility of the accounts which my queries elicited, determined me, like the man in the gospel, to hear and see for myself. I ran the fox to earth in a vast wooden tabernacle; I forget what won by a narrow margin on points; and when he came to New York where they had built a barn bigger than the Albert Hall for the purpose, he could not even get an audience. Beelzebub had the best of every round. Shrewd to the last, he retired from the ring and left Lucifer with the laurels. He had had a great time and had made his pile. I suppose, at this hour, he is sitting under his own vine and fig tree, meditating with cynical enjoyment the Shakespearean aphorism, 'Lord, what fools these mortals be!' and on Sundays that sublime saying of the Saviour—who had saved him if he had never saved anyone else—'Ye are of more value than many sparrows.'

All this time, I had been getting into deeper water financially. I had intended, when I left England, to conclude my special business in New York within a fortnight, to make a little splash in any case, and to get home in a month at the outside. What kept me, was that in the first week I sold over one hundred pounds' worth of first editions to a prominent collector.[2] He then expressed a wish to possess a complete set of my works and also two or three hundred manuscripts. This should have meant at least five thousand dollars. It sounded good to me; since the war nobody in England remembered the existence of such a thing as poetry. So I cabled for the stuff and hung around, with the result that my political opportunity came along. When the books arrived from England, the collector changed his mind and only bought a small proportion of the consignment. This left me flat, and besides, I was getting into my stride in countermining Münsterberg. So I stagnated in New York, getting lower in the water every day.

I was nearly down and out, when I got an introduction to the editor of *Vanity Fair,* a perfectly charming man, who reminded me not a little of Austin Harrison. He was, however, extremely intelligent and understood his business thoroughly. In a couple of years he had pulled the paper up from nothing to one quarter of a million. He treated me, through some inexplicable misunderstanding, as a human being and asked me to write for him.

I began with an account of a baseball game as seen by a professor from the University of Peking. This was followed up by a series of Hokku. This is a Japanese verse form. It contains three lines totalling seventeen syllables. I modified this by introducing regular meter, the first line dactyl-spondee, the second line spondee-dactyl-spondee, and the third dactyl-spondee. A Hokku must contain a very definite finely chiselled idea or rather, chain of ideas. Such is the strict rule, but one is allowed a certain degree of latitude.

The first line announces the subject of the meditation; the second the moral reflection suggested thereby, and the third some epigrammatic commentary. For instance:

BUDDHISM

I am a petal
Darkling, lost on the river
Being—illusion.

We analyse this as follows: In saying 'I am' one implies that one is only a detached derelict in the darkness of ignorance, whose essential quality is the illusion of existence.

I wrote a double Hokku on the Hokku itself. Here it is:

THE HOKKU

Catch me, caress me,
Crush me! Gather a dewdrop—
Star to a system!

God in an atom!
Comets revel around it—
That is a Hokku.

I became a frequent contributor to *Vanity Fair*. I can never be sufficiently grateful to Frank Crowninshield for his kindness and patience. My association with him is the one uniformly pleasant experience of dealing with editors that I can quote. He always took pains to make the most of his material. If a contribution did not suit him, he did not reject it without a word of explanation. He talked it over, and suggested modifications. I thus found out how to suit his taste without injuring my self-respect. Most editors drive away their best contributors by treating them like street beggars and leave them bewildered at the rejection. Others, again, haggle over the terms and as often as not delay or evade payment. They then wonder why they fail to hit the public taste. It soon goes around that getting a cheque from so-and-so is like fishing for sharks with a trout rod. The editor is tacitly boycotted.

This and my work with Evangeline Adams kept me going through the summer. I had a glorious time, what with love and sea bathing. I wrote a good deal of poetry; in particular 'The Golden Rose', and a set of lyrics, mostly sonnets to Hilarion,[3] who appears later, in 'The Urn', as 'The Cat Officer'. This woman possessed a unique atmosphere. I can only describe it as 'sweetness long drawn out'. This translated itself in terms of rhythm. I quote a typical sonnet:

IN THE RED ROOM OF ROSE CROIX

The bleeding gate of God unveils its rose;
The cavernous West swallows the dragon Sun:
Earth's darkness broods on dissolution,
A mother-vulture, nested on Repose.
Ah then, what grace within our girdle glows,
To garb thy glee-gilt heart, Hilarion,
An Alpenbluehn on our star-crested snows.

O scarlet flower, smear honey on the thigh
Of this shy bee, that sucks thy sweetness dry,
O bower of sunset, bring me to thy sleep
Wherein move dreams stained purple with perfumes,
Whose birds of Paradise, on Punic plumes,
Declare dooms undecipherably deep.

Compare this with any previous sonnet of mine and notice the lusciousness of the lines.

I also wrote a one-act play *The Saviour*. The main idea of this had been in my mind for a long while as a presentation of irony. The council of a city in the extremity of despair invoke a long-expected saviour. He appears to their rapturous relief but turns out to be the enemy they feared in his most frightful form. I elaborated this theme by introducing episodes where they are given a chance to escape. They throw this away for the sake of the saviour. The poignancy is further increased by various vicissitudes. The council is guided by a fool whom they ignore, being the only character with a grain of common sense, and by a prophet whose insane purpose is to deliver the city to destruction. By his inspired advice, the council are lured into one disastrous folly after another, and when the catastrophe occurs the prophet throws off the mask and gloats over the ruin he has wrought.

This play was accepted by Morris Brown but as bad luck would have it, war conditions obliged him to close his theatre before it could be produced. I published it in *The International* in March 1918, but only after a struggle with my lawyer, who was seriously alarmed lest Washington should think the cap fitted and suppress the number. The play being written three years earlier, and there being not the slightest allusion to or analogy with current events, his protest showed how dire a reign of terror had been established by the megalomaniac in the White House and his brutal and thick-headed bravo, Burleson.

On October 6th, I left New York for a trip round the coast. I wanted to see the San Francisco exhibition, and I wanted to get first-hand facts about the attitude of the people, outside the Wall Street machine, to the war. With this I combined a honeymoon with Hilarion; though the sky was cloudy and windy, she popped in and out all the time, having decided to spice the romance and adventure by taking her husband in tow.

My first stop was Detroit, where Parke Davis were charming and showed me over their wonderful chemical works. They had installed countless and ingenious devices for conducting the process involved in manufacture by machinery. Many of these produced effects of exquisite beauty of a land till then dreamed of in my philosophy. A great mass of pills in a highly polished and rapidly revolving receiver was infinitely fascinating to watch. The spheres tumbled over each other with a rhythmical rise and fall in a rhythm which sang to the soul.

They were kind enough to interest themselves in my researches in Anhalonium Lewinii [4] and made me some special preparations on the lines indicated by my experience which proved greatly superior to previous preparations.

In Chicago, I met Paul Carus, who received me royally and showed me the city. The man had always interested me as being widely learned, yet understanding so little. After meeting him, I decided that I liked him for it. He was a big-hearted, simple-minded creature, with a certain childlike vision, by the light of which he judged the external world, a little like the White Knight in *Alice!*

I confess to dislike Chicago. It resembles New York more than its citizens would like to admit, but lacks altogether the cosmopolitan and man-of-the-world atmosphere of Gotham. It gives the impression of being a pure machine. Its artistic and cultured side shares the deadness of the rest. It compares with New York rather as Manchester with London.

I called on Narnet Munroe, described in the charge sheet as a poetess. She edits a periodical called *Poetry*. I am still not sure if she knew my name and my work, but she showed no interest whatever! She was loaded to the gunwale with a cargo of conceit. She was the standard of perfection by which Milton and Keats might be measured in terms of their inferiority to her. Incidentally these two were bracketed zero. The first article of her faith was that rhythm and rime were incompatible with poetry. Her creed contained many similar dogmas, all fixed with bigoted intolerance. I got away from this dessicated spinster and her dreary drone with alacrity.

I proceeded westward.

> As I came through the desert, thus it was.
> As I came through the desert . . .

Chicago is the forlorn outpost of civilized man. Every mile beyond marks a lower rung on the ladder of evolution. St Paul and Minneapolis are merely magnified markets always open. There is no life of any kind outside business. I suppose the poor damned souls are sweating all they know to get out somehow, somewhere.

West of the twin cities, even towns become rarer and each is more transient and inhuman than the last. The vastness of nature and the stupendous strength of her elemental forces have cried in vain. They move no man to wonder or admiration. He goes about his ant-like work with hurrying intentness, incapable of seeing or hearing anything not directly bearing on the problems that preoccupy him. Nobody reads, nobody thinks. When anyone does, they make short work of him. Not until one crosses the Rockies is there a semblance of resurrection. The coast, in touch with the Pacific archipelago and Asia, has caught a little of their culture.

I was warmly welcomed in Vancouver by my 'Son',[5] who had established a large and increasing Lodge of O.T.O. They had made with their own hands admirably effective furniture and ornaments, and they had been splendidly drilled in the Rituals. I regretted the necessity of going on so soon.

I travelled by sea via Victoria to Seattle. My principal observation is that the inhabitants of the Pacific coast have almost everything in common; original racial differences seem to matter little; I suppose because the great distance from the base makes them feel that they have burnt their boats. It would be quite impossible to distinguish a British Columbian from a Californian, while, on the other hand, the people of the coast differ very widely from anyone east of the Rockies. The point is important. The common psychology and common interests of the coast tend to unite them as against the transmontane tribes. The divergence of economic aims widens yearly. It seems certain that a time will come when the antagonisms of their neighbours will reach a climax. Few English, even those who have travelled in the States, have any real grasp of the geography. West of St Paul only Denver and Salt Lake City boast of over a hundred thousand inhabitants in all that weary wilderness. One thinks of Chicago as the capital of the Middle West, as if it were half way across. In fact the distance of the two coasts is something like four to one. The political link which joins the coast with the Middle West is very much too long to be natural; it would have snapped long ago, but for the idealistic fancies about unity. They will have to yield to the persistent hammering of fact. Secession is certain, sooner or later, but the conditions are so peculiar that to forecast its form would be an insolence to fate.

The Middle West is predominantly Teutonic and Scandinavian. I found little overt sympathy with Germany for all that. Still less, any impulse to show active sympathy. But as for going into the fight on our side, the suggestion outraged elementary common sense. One prominent Kansas paper had a long editorial, angrily refusing sympathy with the ideas of 'those fools down east' and expressing the hope that an air-raid on New York would teach them a much needed lesson. It was argued with the utmost vehemence that the Middle West was independent of the east. They refused to admit for a moment that their prosperity as producers could be imperilled by the calamities of their transport agents and customers.

On the coast, this hard, cold-blooded selfishness was tempered by the climate. I met much superficial sympathy with both sides. But there was a universal agreement to refuse to judge the rights and wrongs of the war. It was Europe's business and nobody else's. It would be a crime, a blunder and stark treason to the constitution for America to take a hand.

Since my last visit San Francisco had been rebuilt. The old charm had vanished completely. It had become a regular fellow. The earthquake had swallowed up romance, and the fire burnt up the soul of the city to ashes. The phoenix had perished and from the cinders had arisen a turkey buzzard.

I hurried south, stopping off at Santa Cruz, to see the famous big trees. I snatched a meal in the town and walked out in the gloaming. My sweetheart was waiting for me in the dusk just beyond the town limits. 'How glad I am you have come,' she whispered. 'Let us walk together to the grove. You shall sleep on my bosom all night, beneath the shadow of the giant sentinel whose spear points salute the stars.' My sweetheart wove herself about me, an intoxicating ambience. Drunk with delight I strode through the silence. It must have been sheer luck that I found the grove, for one cannot see it from a distance, at least on a dark night. But I walked straight to the clump and threw myself down dog-tired and happy beyond all whooping. I gazed awhile through the tangle of branches up to the stars. They closed. I slept.

At dawn, I woke refreshed, had breakfast in a cabin hard by and wandered back to the railway. I had had a perfect holiday from the Spirit of America! The fresh morning air became articulate and whispered a sound in my ear. Here it is:

AT BIG TREES, SANTA CRUZ

Night fell. I travelled through the cloven chasm
  To where the redwood's cloistered giant grove
  Sprung gothic and priapic; wonder wove
God's glory, gathered in the Titan spasm
Nature's parturient anguish. Murk phantasm
  Moving I seemed! I found the treasure trove
  Of fire, and consecrated all to love,
Smiting my soul within the protoplasm.

Within that temple of the midnight sun
I cried all night upon Hilarion!
  All night I willed, I loved, I wrought the spell
That Merlin muttered low in Broceliaunde,
Till over Santa Cruz the day star dawned.
  God should have heard me, had I cried from Hell!

I wandered on to Los Angeles, and, having been warned against the cinema crowd of cocaine-crazed, sexual lunatics, and the swarming maggots of near-occultists, I came through undamaged. I found a range of hills north of the city and had a marvellous day speeding from crest to crest. I was so exhilarated that walking would not serve my turn. I had to run! As I ran, this sonnet shaped itself in my spirit:

I ran upon the ridges of the hill
    That from the North-guard watch Los Angeles.
    Now I lift up my priestly hands to bless
The Sun, from whose emblazoned cup God spills
The wine to comfort all earth's infinite ills;
    The cordial of man's heart, whose dour distress
    Heals only in immaculate silence
According as he knows, and loves, and wills.

Ay! Thought is grown a geyser-gush of flame
Since those two hours this morning when you came,
    When, like a comet swirling to its sun,
    You strangled me in your Astarte's tress,
    And wove me into serpent silences
    Upon your body's loom, Hilarion!

My outward journey ended at San Diego. Near the city is Point Loma where lived Katherine Tingley, who with William Q. Judge seceded from the Theosophical Society when Annie Besant snatched the reins. I knew nothing of the woman, but her refusal to accept the unscrupulous usurpation was in her favour, and a casual glance at her official organ had impressed me not unfavourably. I decided to see her and discuss the possibility of an alliance. To my amazement she refused to receive me when I called at the settlement. From the moment I entered the grounds I was aware of the most nauseating atmosphere that I had ever met magically. The suggestion was of a putrefying and entirely bloodless flesh, as if a cannibal had sucked out its life to the last drop and flung it away. Her disciples corresponded. They moved about limp and listless, corpse-pallid, with the eyes of dead fishes. I got out of the cesspool without wasting time, but even so I had to pay for my imprudence.

San Diego possessed one most attractive feature. It is within a short motor ride of the frontier of Mexico. One comes to a town, Tia Juana, which thrives on refugees from righteousness. It is composed exclusively of brothels, drinking saloons and gambling hells. I don't care for this sort of thing, but it was at least much better than anything north of the border.

Going east, I stopped off to see the Grand Canyon. It is superb, of course, the best thing in the whole country; but, at that, it is not in the same class as Himalayan scenery. The sunset effects are certainly splendid, but to me the many interests lie in the geological problem.

The canyon is a zigzag slit cut out deep through a practically

level plateau. The upper part of the gap seems to show that
side streams fed the main river at some time, and this explanation is usually offered. My objection is that the level is squarely
cut away. One looks down over the edge to a perpendicular
depth of some hundreds of feet before the sheer rock eases off
to slopes. The flatness of the plateau makes it impossible that
it could ever have been crossed by streams and I could hardly
believe that tributaries so numerous and so short, springing
from nowhere in particular, could have gouged out the gorges.
I prefer to suspect that the original event was an earthquake,
which opened a long crack, and that the river took advantage
of this natural channel.

I went down the Colorado River by Angle Trail. I wanted
to make sure I had not lost my old speed and surefootedness.
The previous record from the edge of the cliff to the river was
some minutes over two hours. I did it in one hour twenty minutes to a second! I paid the price; the nails of my big toes were
so badly bruised that they came off completely. I rested by the
river's edge and wrote this sonnet:

> I lie beneath the cliff of the canyon.
>   Down the long trail I flitted like a swallow,
>   Daring the very elements to follow,
> Nor paused to mark the crags I leapt upon.
> Now, lying in the sun, my soul's a swan,
>   Soars through the boundless blue to greet Apollo:
>   I call my love by name. Remote and hollow
> The rocks re-echo me: 'Hilarion!'
>
> How pure and beautiful the body is
> Lapped in fatigue's caressing ecstasies!
>   For then the soul is free to leap above it,
> To soar, to dive, to seek and find his mate
> In the dominion of the uncreate,
>   And lastly—to return to it, and love it!

This was my last adventure. I returned to New York by
short stages and resumed the anchorless tossing. The one new
feature was my affair with Stuart X.

The next act was the appearance of Ananda K. Koomaraswamy, the Eurasian critic of religion and art, with his wife,
Ratan Devi, a musician from Yorkshire, who had fallen in
love with him and filched him from his first wife. He soon got
sick of her and took refuge in India, but finding it a continual
nuisance to have to send her supplies, wrote her to join him.
It had been suggested, with the secret hope that the climate

would rid him of his incubus. She made the journey in charge of his best friend, a wealthy Punjabi, whom she promptly seduced.

After a series of violent scenes in Bombay, the half-breed accepted the situation and all three travelled together for some time in the hills. Ratan Devi possessed a strange seductive beauty and charm, but above all an ear so accurate and a voice so perfectly trained, that she was able to sing Indian music, which is characterized by half and quarter tones imperceptible to most European ears. His idea was to bring her out to New York. He introduced himself to me, knowing my reputation on Asiatic religions and Magick. I invited them to dine and to pass the evening at my apartment, so that she might sing to the tamboura her repertoire of Kashmiri and other Indian songs. I was charmed and promised to do all I could to make her a success. I introduced them to several influential people and wrote a prose poem about her singing for *Vanity Fair*.

She and I lost no time about falling in love. This suited her husband perfectly. The high cost of living was bad enough without having to pay for one's wife's dinner. All he asked was that I should introduce him to a girl who would be his mistress while costing him nothing. I was only too happy to oblige as I happened to know a girl with a fancy for weird adventures.

He was anxious to rid himself of even theoretical responsibilities and therefore proposed a divorce. I agreed with a yawn. Details never interest me. Meanwhile, she had made her debut and scored a superb success. This had never occurred to her husband, who, being unable to appreciate her supreme art, hardly took her singing seriously. In fact, her success was largely due to my assistance. I taught her how to let her genius loose at the critical moment. However, to her husband, only one thing mattered at all. There might be money in her. Right about face! He wriggled out of the divorce on various puerile pretexts and then pulled out the pathetic stuff, and pleaded with her to come back to him. She was the only woman he had ever loved, etc., *ad nauseam*.

These manoeuvres were conducted at the top of their voices. It was a series of scolding matches and epileptic fits. I had a gorgeous time! What annoyed them both more than anything was my utter indifference to the whole affair. My position was that if she chose to live with me, she could. When she wanted to get out there was the door wide open. But I wouldn't lift a finger for any purpose whatever.

The situation was complicated by her becoming pregnant. This changed my attitude. I still refused to interfere with her will, but now I was prepared to make any sacrifice necessary to insure her welfare and that of our child.

She was making quite a lot of money by now so he pestered her day and night, whenever he could spare a moment from the German prostitute with whom he was now living, having been thrown out by my eccentric friend. He had queer ideas, had the eminent mongrel. The cost of a double room being slightly less than that of two single, he effected a prudent economy by putting this girl in the same bed with his wife when he was out of town.

During this time I was often away in Washington, thus missing a good deal of the fun. In June, I came back proposing to spend the summer in a cottage by Lake Pasquaney. Ratan Devi was one of those women whose chief pleasure is to show her power over men. She tried it on me, but a bath brick would have done quite as well. Convinced after many desperate efforts that I would not run after her or even walk her way, she began to understand true love, to recognize me as her master and quit playing the fool. She did not divine that my Gibraltar firmness was calculated policy. I really loved her and knew that the only hope of making her love me was to kill the vanity which prevented her from being true to herself, and giving her whole heart.

Before I left for New Hampshire, we had a farewell meeting. She was now too far advanced in gestation to appear in public, so her husband had persuaded her to go to England for the confinement, and also to make various necessary arrangements with regard to the future. He had now cunningly pretended to give way about the divorce, admitting my right to my child and its mother. His real motive was very different. She was a particularly bad sailor. During a previous pregnancy, she had been obliged to break the journey to save her life. She was in fact on the brink of death when they carried her ashore and she lay for weeks so ill that a breath of wind might have blown her away. It was, at least, not a bad bet that the Atlantic voyage would end in the same or an even more fortunate way.

I still refused to put pressure upon her. I said, 'Here's my address. You're welcome whenever you like to come, and I love you and will serve you with every ounce of my strength.'

I went off. In a few days she joined me. The peace and beauty and solitude renewed the rapture of our love. I had given my word to do nothing to hold her and after a few days she decided to go to England; her children needed her. It was her peculiar perversity to be at one time the artist absolute; at another the mother and no more, and the trouble was that whenever common sense wanted her to be the one, she invariably assumed the personality of the other. So now, just because I represented art, music and love, her troll tugged at her to be maternal.

Off she went. The Eurasian's calculations were not far wrong. The voyage caused a miscarriage and she lay between life and death for over six weeks. Needless to say, the moment the mischief was done, she repented bitterly. When she returned to America, I was in New Orleans. She implored me to come back to her. She wrote once, and often twice, every day, each averaging a dozen pages. There were also telegrams. I replied with immovable firmness. 'You insisted on going away, with the result of killing our baby. I love you and I'll take you back, but on this condition; that you make a clean break with the past.'

Her unhappy temperament kept her at war with herself. She wanted to have her cake and eat it as well. She wouldn't burn her bridges. I maintained firm correctness and it all came to nothing. My heart is still not wholly healed, but I relieved myself of part of my pain by using the whole story, exact in every detail, as the background of my Simon Iff yarn 'Not good enough' (*The International*, January 1918). I made one change. Koomaraswamy, Haranzada Swami; Haranzada being the Hindustani word for 'bastard'. The publication of this tale came as a slight shock to the self-complacency of the scoundrel.

I must not omit one characteristic incident. He happened to be momentarily hard up and conceived the really brilliant idea of concocting a fable that his German girl was a new Sappho. He made her copy out a number of poems from my *Collected Works* and sent her round to Putnam's to persuade them to publish the really remarkable work of this romantic young American beauty rose. The girl told his wife in bed one night, they having found a bond of common sympathy in their contempt and loathing for 'The Worm' as we had familiarly called him. She told me at once, and I have every reason to believe that the letter I wrote to Putnam's is treasured in the archives of the firm as the last word in savage contempt.

So ended my adventures with these fascinating freaks. I must now run back to New Orleans.

78

New Orleans and San Antonio are said to be the only two towns in the United States which possess souls of their own. That of New Orleans was already being driven out under my eyes, and I dare say that by this time the work of destruction is complete. Probably San Antonio has shared its fate. The most depressing feature in the country is the uniformity of the towns. However singular the geographical situation and its topographical peculiarities, the possibilities of beauty have been nullified by the determination of the people to do everything just right, according to the measure in fashion. Wherever one is, sooner or later, one gets tired of one's surroundings. In Europe, the cure is easy. One toddles along to the next place sure of finding some novelty. In America, however far one goes, the same hideous homogeneity disappoints one. The relief conferred by the old quarter of New Orleans threw me instantly into an ecstasy of creative energy. I wrote day and night continuously—poems, essays and short stories. My principal invention was the detective 'Simon Iff' whose method of discovering the solution of a problem was calculation of the mental and moral energies of the people concerned.

I wrote a series of six stories about his exploits and followed it by *The Butterfly Net* or *The Net*, a novel in which he is a secondary character. In this novel I have given an elaborate description of modern magical theories and practices. Most of the characters are real people whom I have known and many of the incidents taken from experience.

During this time, I was also granted what mystics describe as 'The Beatific Vision' which is the most characteristic of those attributed to Tiphereth,[1] the archetypal idea of beauty and harmony. In this vision one retains one's normal consciousness, but every impression of daily life is as enchanting and exquisite as an ode of Keats. The incidents of life become a harmonious unity; one is lost in a rosy dream of romantic happiness. One may compare it to the effect produced by wine on some people. There is, however, no unreality in the vision. One is not blinded to the facts of existence. It is simply that the normal incoherence and discrepancy between them has been harmonized.

While on this subject, let me mention that Tiphereth corresponds to the grade of initiation on the Threshold of the Order of R.R. et A.C., and to the Knowledge and Conversation of the Holy Guardian Angel. It therefore marks a critically important stage in initiation. Only one other is equally cardinal: the grade of Master of the Temple, which is the Threshold of the Order of the A∴A∴. I have called the vision corresponding to this the 'Vision of Wonder' which permeates one's daily life in a similar way. The difference is that penetrating beyond sensory perceptions, one is aware of the mechanism of events, of the subtle chain of causes which connect them. One perceives in detail how each impression necessarily succeeds its forerunner. The effect is that one is lost in wonder at the ingenuity of the universe, to use a very inadequate word, as being the only one available. One feels the intense awed admiration which the greatest masterpieces of Kant, Beethoven, Shakespeare, Rembrandt, Riemann, Kelvin, and such as they inspired, with this difference: that all impressions are equally puissant to produce it.

My best essay was 'The Green Goddess' written in the old Absinthe House itself, and adorning its main theme the philosophical reflections suggested by absinthe with descriptions of the inn, its guests, and the city.

From New Orleans I went to stay with my cousin Lawrence Bishop on his orange and grapefruit plantation in Florida. I shall describe elsewhere the spiritual abyss in which these lost souls were plunged. I cannot think of Florida, but in my ears rings the exceeding bitter cry of poor little sixteen-year-old Alma, 'I've found it doesn't pay to tell the truth.'

This visit opened up an expanse and depth of heartache which I had thought impossible. Cousin Lawrence saw how ill I was. The family fed on offal which I would not have thrown to a decent pig. He had stayed with us in England and realized that I could not be expected to eat such garbage, so he asked me kindly what I would like to eat so as to build up my strength. I said, 'Don't bother about that. All I need is plenty of fruit and milk.' It seems too rotten to be true but his wife made a point of cutting me off from milk as much as she dared, and went to the utmost pains to hide the supply, so as to cheat me out of the glass of milk I was supposed to have before going to bed. (I always stayed up late working.)

The mean malice of this hag is too dreadful to contemplate,

yet all things serve the poet's turn. She gave me the idea of one of my best *Simon Iff in America* stories, 'Suffer the Little Children'.[2]

Let us hurry back to New York. I arrived there in the spring still sick of some malady which produced depression and weakness and took the spirit out of me without showing any obvious symptoms. I found once more that I was a stranger. I had nothing definite to do, no plausible plans. I wandered wearily through the weeks utterly powerless to concentrate on anything, to interest myself in anything: I simply suffered. Things got worse and worse. My resources came to an end.

One of my old disciples, Leon Engars Kennedy, a portrait painter, had arrived from Europe. We renewed our friendship. Indeed he needed my help badly enough. His moral tone, never high, had been almost destroyed by the war. The trouble with him was that he had never grown up; he was still childishly irresponsible and unable to take care of himself. He was in receipt of an ample allowance from his family, but it was always gone before it arrived, and he dragged on from month to month borrowing a dollar here and a dollar there from everyone he met.

I remember a scene almost too humiliating to tell. The janitor of his studio was a crippled lad, with a large family— a half-starved creature with the pathetic eyes of a wounded fawn. It was horrible to hear Kennedy, the adopted son of a multi-millionaire, pleading almost on his knees with eloquent appeals for pity, mingled with the cunning arguments of a confidence man, for a loan of two dollars. I am glad to think that I helped the boy both spiritually and practically. I badgered him into working regularly at his art, arranged an exhibition for him, interested a number of influential people in him, persuaded others to help him out, wrote him up in *The International*, and otherwise pulled him through. I failed, however, to keep him out of the clutches of a very beautiful red-headed Irish typist, hysterical from sexual suppression. She finally persuaded him to marry her, and I am afraid his last chance of a career is among the dusty documents in the files of the marriage bureau at City Hall. At least, I have heard no more of him since his return to Holland.

He, in his turn, showed me great kindness. When it came to the point where I could not pay for a bed, he let me sleep on the sofa in his studio. This was a garret in an old half-decayed house on Fifth Avenue, lacking even a water supply. But to me it was a paradise. Its poverty and discomfort were transformed into luxury by the thought of Kennedy's kindness. I slept here for quite a long time. My health picked up gradually and, as the result of a Magical Operation on May 27th, became suddenly perfect. I was thus able, on May 28th and 30th, to perform two important Magical Operations completed by a third a few days later, with the object of giving effect to my will to establish the Law of Thelema. The result was that I secured control of *The International* and became contributing editor (implying practically sole responsibility for the contents) in August.

This magazine was originally the organ of pure literature, the only one in the United States of any authority. Unfortunately, the editor—and to all intents and purposes the proprietor—was Mr George Sylvester Viereck. At the outbreak of the war, he transformed the character of *The International*, introduced pro-German propaganda and thus ruined its reputation. It was now on the black list in Canada and refused admission by the postal authorities of the colony. Its best friends had withdrawn their support; its circulation had dwindled almost to nothing, and it staggered on mechanically from month to month without heart or hope. In eight months I pulled it up so successfully that it became saleable. It was bought by Professor Keasbey, who issued one number so dreary, unintelligible and futile that it died on the spot.

Keasbey had been professor of institutional history in the University of Austin, Texas. He was a charming and cultured man, but full of cranky notions about socialism, which he held with arrogant obstinacy. His literary style, on which he prided himself, as would have been ridiculous in Ruskin or Walter Pater, was turgid, convoluted, incoherent, over-loaded, redundant and beyond the wit of the most earnest and expert reader to comprehend. He was not far behind William Howell Williams, elsewhere mentioned, in his power to baffle inquiries. Frank Harris agreed on this point, no less than all the other people to whom I put it. He told me with amazement that he had been badgered into printing a half-page article of Keasbey's in *Pearson's*, of which he was then treasurer, able, therefore, to put pressure on the editor. This number came under the censure of Burleon. He had gone to Washington to justify himself. Burleon had shown him the copy which had been submitted to the censors. Keasbey's article was marked as objectionable by all three pencils. Harris exploded. 'You can't understand it,' he raged. 'I can't understand it. I don't believe there's any man alive who could make head or tail of a single sentence. How can it do any harm?'

Keasbey's socialistic opinions had cost him his chair at Austin. He had read and admired some of my work, and sought me out in my cottage by Lake Pasquaney. We spent three delightful days without even stopping talking, bar odd snatches of sleep. In conversation, he was delightful, breezy and instructive. Our acquaintance had ripened into something like friendship. He behaved very strangely in this matter of *The International*. He professed the warmest friendship for me, spent some time almost every day in my office chatting; we lunched and dined together quite often, but he never breathed one word of his intention to buy *The International*, and when the transaction became public, he went one better. He asked me to continue my contributions and even suggested that I should work jointly with him, yet all the time, his idea was to oust me altogether. He refused to print a single line from my pen, and that, although he was in despair about filling the number. He must too have known that the success of the paper was entirely due to my personality; he knew that I had written nearly everything myself, and that the only other important elements had been given to me by their authors purely as a token of their personal admiration and friendship for me. I suppose he was utterly blinded by his conceit, which he possessed to a degree to which I can recall no parallel. However that may be, the result was that the May number was a monument of incomprehensible, worthless and unreadable rubbish, and that he found himself in his brand new and portentous offices, monarch of all he surveyed, with his overlaid infant a corpse at his feet. The episode is excellently mirthful.

I shall describe in its due place the course of my friendship with Maitland Ambrose Payne. One day he told me of a Singalese joint on 8th Avenue where they made real curry. I began to frequent it and thus met the lady who appears, in 'The Urn', as the 'Dog-headed Hermes or Anubis'. She was a Pennsylvania Dutch girl, the only member of her family not actually insane. We joined forces and took a furnished apartment in a corner house on Central Park West near its northern limit at 110th Street. From the bow window of the drawing-room trees only were to be seen. They rested and rejoiced my spirit. I could forget New York, although within half an hour from my office.

My salary was twenty dollars a week; two dollars more than

that of my typist. Life had taught me to enjoy outrages of this kind. It gave me pleasure to contrast my own generosity with the meanness of the rich and to take pride in my ability to accept smilingly such insults and privations. During this autumn as fully detailed in another place, the passion to express myself through art was born in me. The months passed in a pageant of delight.

My liaison with the Dog came suddenly to an end. Exactly as in the case of my wife, the half-suppressed strain of madness in her blood came to the surface. She took to orgies of solitary drunkenness. This was nothing new; in fact, when I met her they were of almost daily occurrence. I succeeded in pulling her together for a time, but she relapsed. When I found this out, I told her the story of my wife and put my foot down. I gave her to understand that if it happened again I was through. She knew me for a man of my word and quit, but a few days later it was as bad as ever. I gave her one more chance, but of course in vain.

Early in October, I broke up the menage and transferred my headquarters to a studio in West 9th Street, which I shared with a friend of the Dog's, hereafter described as the Camel.

Her name was Roddie Minor, a married woman living apart from her husband, a near artist of German extraction. She was physically a magnificent animal, with a man's brain well stocked with general knowledge and a special comprehension of chemistry and pharmacy. She was at this time employed in the pathological laboratory of a famous doctor, but afterwards became managing chemist to a prominent firm of perfumery manufacturers.

I have said that she had a man's brain, but despite every effort, there was still one dark corner in which her femininity had taken refuge and defied her to expel it. From time to time the garrison made a desperate sortie. At such moments her womanhood avenged itself savagely on her ambition. She was more frantically feminine than any avowed woman could possibly be. She was ruthlessly irrational. Such attacks were fortunately as short as they were severe, but unfortunately too often did irreparable damage.

In the upshot, this characteristic led to our separation. I treated her as an equal in all respects, and for some months everything went as smoothly as if she had been really a man. But that beleaguered section of her brain sent out spies under cover of night, and whispered to the besiegers sinister suggestions, to shake their confidence in themselves. The idea was born and grew that she was essentially my inferior. She began to feel my personality as an obsession. She began to dread being dominated, though perfectly well aware that I wished nothing less, that her freedom was necessary to my enjoyment of my own. But she failed to rid herself of this hallucination, and when I decided to make a Great Magical Retirement on the Hudson, in a canoe, in the summer of 1918, we agreed to part. There was no quarrel. Our friendship and even our intimacy continued. My last night in New York before leaving for Europe was spent in her arms.

Such weekends as she could manage were passed in my camp on Oesopus Island. Her first visit was rather an adventure. She had brought up supplies of canned stuff from New York to Staatsburg, where I met her with the canoe. She had understood from my letter that the island was close to this town, and had foolishly failed to consult a map. She was tired with her week's work and the long journey; the train was late, night was falling, the wind was getting up, and the rain beginning to skirmish. The canoe was loaded down within an inch of the gunwale. The wind blew dead in our teeth. The river began to roughen and the rain to come down more steadily. Our progress was tediously slow and the journey not without peril. At one point the stream is bayed out so that for something like a mile one is right out of reach of land. The slightest accident would have been critical. We hardly dared paddle with our full strength. We took something like five hours to reach the island using our utmost effort. It was after eleven o'clock when we beached the canoe. By this time the poor girl was drenched to the skin, completely exhausted and almost starving. Her femininity took advantage of the weariness of the besieging army to sally forth from the main gate. She wanted to curse God and die, and, presumably to get into training, cursed me. I could not comfort her. She threw herself on my couch and collapsed. I covered her with rugs and watched by her side all night. Refreshed by sleep, she was herself again when the sun struck the rocky ridge which walled the lilied creek which my camp overlooked. The sky had cleared, the rain dried off the rocks. We brought the provisions across from the southern inlet and made breakfast. We patted our bellies, contemplated life and behold it was very good.

79

My summer was uneventful. Such adventures as I had were pleasant variations from routine. I must tell one tale from its interest to amateurs of coincidence and philosophers whose favourite subject of meditation is 'What a small world we live in!'

To ascend the Hudson in a sailing canoe is not so simple as it sounds. No great effort is required to come to grief. It had taken me all I knew to get round a certain rectangular bend against a gusty wind of uncertain temper. The river was white with foam, and what with cross currents and sudden squalls I had wondered more than once how matters would turn out. In case of capsizing it might have been no joke to scramble up the perpendicular cliffs which hemmed in the stream in many places. Once or twice, while trying to use my sail, I had just shaved upsetting. The bend once past, the breeze had steadied, and I was able to lounge luxuriously in the stern and watch the shores stream past. The only question was where to sleep. The hours passed and no sign of human habitation. In the end I submitted to fate and spent the night in the open on a stony slope.

The next day, after lunching gloriously on a convenient islet, I came to Newborough Bay, where the river widens out to something like three times its average. There is a town on either bank connected by a steam ferry. I was merrily sailing along, when a squall struck the canoe without warning. I found myself rushing recklessly through the water, with the spray shooting from beneath my bows high into space. I was then aware that I was being driven helpless between the two steamers. My sail refused to come down. At infinite risk, I crawled forward and unshipped the mast, thus managing to pull up before reaching the point of danger.

I looked south. The weather threatened to worsen. It might be nasty. I was more than a mile from the shore. My best chance was to reach safety before the storm came to its full powers. I therefore put the tackle in order, reshipped the mast, and half-hoisted the sail, ready to lower again if things got bad.

I flew upstream at a terrific pace for over an hour. The threatened tempest passed clear to the south. It was now dark and once again I bethought me of a bivouac. Exhausted by my struggle, I paddled wearily, the wind having dropped entirely, past a wharf. Having no money to waste on a bed—my two dollars, twenty-five of original capital not having noticeably increased—I shook my head and shouted a genial refusal to a stripling who hailed me from the quay and suggested my sleeping in the village. But an older man came forward and offered to let me doss it in a boathouse. I was really all in and decided to accept.

He hailed some boatmen who carried my canoe on shore, while I walked with the kind old captain to the boat club. We had settled on where I was to sleep, when in came a man, obviously a gentleman and obviously English. He made the same observation about me, though what with my inch of beard, deep sunburn and general air of ruffianism, I presented an aspect rarely to be found in the Royal Enclosure at Ascot. He insisted on taking me to his house for supper and putting me up for the night. I gratefully accepted. Five minutes later we had found out that he had at one time been a master in King Henry VIII's School in Coventry, and had known my Aunt Annie and her family who honoured that town with their residence since their childhood. The next morning after breakfast I resumed my journey. He took me in his launch with the canoe in tow as far as Poughkeepsie where we parted.

I promised to write and tell him where my permanent camp was, in the hope that he would allow me to share his hospitality by bringing his family to lunch. The sequel has one more amusing coincidence. There was, of course, no way by which he could warn me of his visit. One morning there came to me a quite irrational wish. I found myself thinking, 'How I wish I had prawns for lunch!' The thought recurred despite indignant attempts to banish it. An hour or so later, I heard my name shouted. I jumped up and found no trace of the shouter. I knew the voice must come from a boat, and ran up and down the island furiously. Still nothing in sight. It must have been half an hour before we found each other, though looking everywhere, and the island being quite small. Whitehead had brought his wife and her sister with various luxuries to mitigate the austerity of the fare traditionally proper to hermits, and one of these was—prawns!

On August 19th, I was obliged to go to New York for two days on O.T.O. business. The result was amusing. I called on

my old friend Tony Sarg, the artist, and gave him an enthusiastic description of my holiday. 'There is only one fly,' I
said, 'in the apothecary's ointment. Like Adam in Eden, I lack
an Eve.' He laughed. 'Don't worry! I know a girl game for any
adventure. She has wonderful hair—orange-red curls, calculated to produce delirium tremens at a moment's notice. Here's
her name and address.' At that moment a small crowd called
and for the next hour we rocked with laughter at the astounding imitation which Tony gave of me wooing a woman. I
left a note for the girl—Madeline was her name—at her
hotel, asking her to drop in to lunch any day she felt like it. I
didn't expect her to come and once more I was wrong.

I went back to Oesopus the following day, supplied with
several large cans of red paint. On both the east and west
shores of the island are wide steep cliffs of smooth rock, obviously provided by Providence for my convenience in proclaiming the Law. I devoted a couple of days to painting 'Do what
thou wilt' on both banks for the benefit of passing steamers.
The little paint left over was dedicated to Madeleine. I barked
a tree in front of my tent for the 'name of the beloved, and
again on a convenient rock hard by. No sooner was this done
than a man came off from the mainland in a boat with a telegram from Madeleine to meet her at Hyde Park Station, a
few miles below the island. I went down. As I paced the platform I noticed a tall, distinguished, military-looking man, who
seemed to be eyeing me strangely. He finally made up his mind
to speak. 'Are you Mr Crowley?' he said. In my surprise I
nearly forgot to say, 'Do what thou wilt shall be the whole of
the Law.' We then got into conversation.

It appeared that he was in charge of the 'Intelligence' of
Dachers County, New York; whereupon I confided to him
that the Department of Justice had instructed me to keep my
eyes open for any suspicious incidents. He requested me to
report anything of the sort also to him, to which, of course, I
gladly agreed. He then confided that my own behaviour had
turned the county upside down. The mysterious stranger, the
fact of my having no companion, had aroused suspicion, as
also my habit of sitting for hours in an apparently uncomfortable attitude and absolutely motionless. Reports had been
made to him. He had set inquiries on foot. The mystery only
grew deeper. Nobody seemed to know anything definite. He
had had all Staatsburg 'on the grill'. He had found it impossible
to identify me, until at last one of the girls in the post office,
evidently in a class by herself in the matter of intelligence,

supplied a clue. She knew me by the scarlet tassels of my golf stockings. He had had me watched, and of course found nothing wrong, but on asking New York City if they could supplement the information, he learned to his intense amazement that I was myself working for the Department of Justice. He told me of various sinister rumours about spies. 'Hang it,' said I, 'what could a spy possibly do in a section like this?' 'Well,' said he, 'there are rumours of flashes of light on the west shore at night which suggest signalling. It might mean serious mischief. We are sending the troops to New York by night train. A spy might easily estimate our numbers, send the news east by a chain of flashed signals, and have it wirelessed to Berlin!'

I promised to keep watch, and then the train came in. There was no difficulty in recognizing Madeleine in that background of barbarism. She stood out like a strawberry among a heap of hips and haws; a short sturdy figure trimly tailored, with a round smiling face, and an ivory complexion framed in that pyrotechnic display of hair. Sarg's eloquence had failed to do her justice. She had brought a huge trunk. My face dropped. What would the canoe say? We managed to get it aboard and started upstream, reaching camp without incident bar a narrow squeak of being swamped by the wash of a passing steamboat. We had a great lunch with the burgundy and absinthe and old brandy, which I had brought back from New York.

But some people are never satisfied. She apparently expected to find a young palace with livery lackeys by the dozen, so she explained that she had merely dropped in for lunch, as per invitation, on her way to visit her brother, the incumbent of the parish of Staatsburg. She gave so many details so ingenuously that I might have believed her if I had not happened to know that the amenities of Staatsburg did not include any such person as she described. I politely professed to credit her and promised to take her ashore in time to reach him by dinner. To pass the afternoon we went for a paddle round the island. Near the northern point I noticed that my feet were wet. I knew that the canoe leaked slightly and forgot it. A hundred yards or so further on I found my ankles immersed. It was evident within the next minute that the leak was serious. We were opposite the cliffs, landing was impossible. The water gained. Nothing remained but to bale and paddle for dear life and reach the south inlet before sinking. She thought the opportunity unequalled for a display of hysterics. But I spoke so sharply and sternly that she postponed the performance and began to bale. We just did it and only just, thanks to the help of two boys who had come to camp close to the landing place a couple of days earlier.

They rushed in waist deep and pulled us in. By that time the water-logged wreck hardly answered the paddle. We dragged the canoe up the beach. The water poured from the stern through a gap six inches across.

We sat and smoked and swapped stories, while Madeleine had her hysterics. When she tired of being not noticed, I took her back to the tent and made tea. 'And that', I remarked, 'is good night to the visit to the vicarage. If we can mend that bundle of firewood at all, which I doubt, we can't even begin till we've got materials from Staatsburg, which means tomorrow morning!' 'But I must get to my brother's!' she persisted petulantly.

I gave a short, but instructive lecture on the physical geography of islands, especially insisting on the definition as a piece of land wholly surrounded by water. She began to howl like a hyena. (I knew, of course, that she had not the slightest intention of going, had Neptune himself arrived to conduct her.) 'But I must go!' she wailed, and then put up a big bluff about her virtue and her reputation. I said I would ask the boys to row her ashore in their boat. They of course agreed, but when I came back with the good news, she had bethought herself of the privilege of her sex, and declared that here she was and here she would stay. Again I acquiesced.

She spent some time trying to think up some excuse for a fresh fuss, but the best she could do was to say that she must have a bath. 'Make your mind easy,' said I, and quoted statistics about the area of the Hudson river. It took her quite a long time to convince herself that I was really one of those inhuman monsters who cannot be dislodged from the fortress of patient smiling politeness and imperturbable good temper. But after dinner she gave it up with a sigh.

'Oh well,' she thought, 'if I can't have my holiest joy of keeping a man on the jump, I suppose I may as well make shift with the next best thing, my famous imitation of a grand passion.' She suited the action to the thought, and swooned into my embrace.

Having mended the canoe as well as I could—it was old and rotten beyond permanent repair—I took her to Central Park on Tuesday.

Meanwhile, her stay had been otherwise exciting. I spent my nights watching for signals on the west shore, and sure enough, from time to time the dark mass of the woods was lit up, now here, now there, by shafts of momentary brilliance at irregular intervals. I noted the exact time of each and compared them. They showed a periodic function. Further analysis convinced me of the cause. Whenever a train passed, the light from the funnel became visible whenever the trees thinned out. I explored the woods, and found the gaps corresponded to these calculations. That ghost was laid. I could see only a narrow section of the river close to the shore. At 10.07 on the second night this section was traversed by a rowing boat manned by two men and a shapeless heap in the stern, which might have been a third or a cargo—it was too dark to make sure. They rowed in dead silence with muffled oars. They were clearly about some secret business.

The next morning, looking for something under my pillows, I found my revolver was missing. I did not like it. The evening before, both the boys and I thought we saw a strange man on the island just after dark. We gave chase and thought we saw him slipping through the trees, but failed to report him.

I decided to call on my friend the colonel and report. He was very pleased with my solution of the mystery of the alleged signals, and agreed that the incident of the boat looked bad. On his part, he had a new yarn. An old boatman, as steady and sober as one could wish, swore to having seen an object of the size and shape of a football surmounting a stick about two feet out of the water, and moving against the current at a regular rate. The word 'submarine' was whispered by the pallid lips of patriots. Every day the new type of submarine chaser might be seen steaming downstream, to be fitted with its armament, five or six a day. No one knew the limits of German genius. The *Deutschland* had crossed safely with her supplies of 606, America's most urgent need.[1] It was perfectly possible that they had built a new type of submarine capable of raising hell in the Hudson.

When I got back to the island, one of the boys brought me my gun. Madeleine, expecting me to bring back a squad of secret service men, had owned up that she had found it in my pillows, got scared and thrown it into the brushwood.

The climax of the joke came after my return to New York. The secret service, unaware of my relation with the colonel, got wind of the rumours about the mysterious hermit and sent two men to investigate. They found the island desolate and no more illuminating clues to crime than the words 'Madeleine' and 'Do what thou wilt' on the rocks.

PART SIX

At the Abbey of Thelema

The Mark of the Beast within the seven-pointed star of Babalon. The Sun in the arms of the Moon, symbolizing Babalon and the Beast conjoined. The Sun is the creative force in the universe (macrocosm) and the Phallus in man (microcosm). (Babalon, so spelt, is the cabbalistically restored form of the name which appears in the Apocalypse as Babylon. Crowley's authority for this orthography is *The Book of the Law*. Babalon is numerically equivalent to 156, which is also that of Zion, the Holy Mountain, and of the City of the Pyramids. See John Dee's Enochian system in which each angelic tablet consists of 156 pyramids.)

80

I was back in New York on September 9th and started at
once to make arrangements to publish volume III of *The
Equinox*. (I should explain that volume II consists of ten
numbers of silence to balance those of speech.) I found a
studio at 1 University Place, at the corner of Washington
Square. Having only one room I thought I would camouflage
the bed and had a large screen with three sections made for
me. I covered the canvases with a triptych, my first attempt at
painting in oil. The design was symbolic of the three principles,
Sun, Moon and Agni (fire), of the Hindus. The bed being still
visible from some parts of the room, I got a second screen of
the same pattern, which brought me to fame. For some days
it stood patiently pleading to be painted, but I could not think
of a subject.

Early in January, I received a visit from the lady hereafter
called the Ape of Thoth [1] and her elder sister.[2] The chain
of circumstances antecedent is strangely tenuous.

I had brought a letter of introduction, from England, to
Hereward Carrington from my friend the Hon. Everard Feilding. Through Carrington, it came about that I was asked to
lecture under the auspices of a particularly transparent charlatan named Christiansen, who worked the sealed letter swindle
with a crudity that paid a very poor compliment to his audience. Among my hearers was only one bearing even a remote
resemblance to the human species, an old lady painted to resemble the cover of a popular magazine. I went to talk to her
after the lecture and found she was an intimate friend of dear
Hereward's. I saw no more of her except by accident for a
few minutes' chat on two or three occasions.

One evening in the spring of 1918, I was surprised by her
calling with her youngest sister. I could not ask them into the
studio, being engaged in an important conference with an
antique, but sprightly German lady who boasted of having
introduced cabarets into America, and had abandoned worldly
pleasures for spiritual joys. She had been entangled in the toils
of one of the charlatans who worked the Rosicrucian racket,

merrily disdainful of criticism based on his elementary blunders in Latin and his total ignorance of the history of the Order which he claimed to rule. The old lady was simple-minded, sincere and earnest. I did not grudge the labour of trying to get her to use common sense, but as almost invariable in America, and heartbreakingly common even in Europe, the task was beyond my powers.

Just as extreme hunger makes a man shovel down anything that looks like food, so the ache of the soul for truth makes it swallow whatever promises. The poor old woman was so pathetically eager to find a Master, that she would not banish the phantasm. I proved in a dozen different ways that the man was a foul liar. That was easy enough. His claims were grotesquely absurd. For instance, he said that I don't know how many knights of England and France—the most improbable people—were Rosicrucians. He said the Order was founded by one of the early Egyptian kings and professed to have documentary evidence of an unbroken hierarchy of initiates since then. He called the Order Rosae Crucis and translated it Rosy Cross. He said that in Toulouse the Order possessed a vast temple with fabulous magnificent appointments, an assertion disprovable merely by consulting Baedeker. He said that Rockefeller had given him nine hundred thousand dollars and at the same time sent round the hat with an eloquent plea for the smallest contributions. He professed to be a learned Egyptologist and classical scholar on terms of intimacy with the most exalted personages. Yet, as in the case of Peter, his speech betrayed him. He was a good chap at heart, a genuine lover of truth, by no means altogether ignorant of Magick, and a great fool to put up all this bluff instead of relying on his really good qualities. But her faith in him was built on the rock of her wish that his nonsense was true, and because he stood between her and blank despair.

To return, I went out to excuse myself to my visitors. The 'little sister' reminded me of Solomon's friend, for she had no breasts. She was tall and strangely thin, with luminous eyes, a wedge-like face, a poignant sadness and a sublime simplicity. She radiated an indefinable sweetness. Without wasting time on words, I began to kiss her. It was sheer instinct. She shared it and equalled my ardour. We continued with occasional interruptions, such as politeness required, to answer her sister in the rare intervals when she got out of breath.

They went away after a while and I saw them no more

until this equally unexpected call in January. They wanted my advice about finding an apartment in the village (a geographically vague section in this part of New York is called 'Greenwich Village'). She wished to be near the New York University, having begun a course of lectures on law, being sick of her job as a teacher in Public School No. 40, the Bronx, which meant telling lies to an amorphous mob of adolescent Hebrew huskies, the only consolation being the certainty that no one would notice the nonsense she was obliged, by the city, to grind out.

While we talked, I took off her clothes and asked her to come and pose for me when she felt inclined. I proposed, half in joke, to solve her problem by taking her as a lodger. They drifted out and I never expected to hear any more of the matter. But on the eleventh of January she suddenly blew in. (She swears I telephoned to ask her and perhaps I did. I have my moments of imbecile impulse. I undressed her again, but this time not with impunity.)

To appease conscience I proceeded to make a sketch, a rough rude scrawl. I had never drawn from the nude before. The essential simplicity of the human body beneath its baffling complexities was the Sphinx itself. I threw down my pencil in disgust and despair. But after she had gone I could not sleep. I lay in the dark and found my thoughts drawn by invisible gossamer to the drawing. I picked it up and was suddenly aware that looked at with the figure vertical instead of horizontal, it meant something. I was seized with a spasm of creative energy and all night long I splashed the central canvas with paint. When she took the pose I had asked her, 'What shall I call the picture; what shall I paint you as?' She had said, 'Paint me as a dead soul.' My screen is called Dead Souls.

She stood central, her head the keystone of the arch of monsters. Her face is ghastly green. Her fleshless body lustreless, white with grey-blue shadows beneath the ribs. On the left-hand panel is a kneeling Negress, bestially gross, her gaze fixed adoringly on the Queen of Dead Souls. Perched on her shoulder, a parrot of brilliant plumage, many hued, surveys the scene with insolent indifference. On the opposite canvas is a kneeling woman huddled as if in agony, a cascade of lustreless hair tumbling to her hips.

Along the entire base are rows of misshapen heads; all anguish, all perversity, all banishment from the world of reasonable things is portrayed in almost endless variety. The screen is grotesque, yet is undeniably a work of genius. It possesses a unity. The dead souls have composed a living soul. Everyone who saw it went away horror-struck or in the spirit of Shimei. But they all talked of nothing else. Bob Chandler came again and again to gaze and gloat. He brought everyone he knew to look at it. And even artists famous for their classical refinement had to admit its grisly power. In short, the dead souls conquered the city and their Queen their creator. She came like Balchis to Solomon, bringing gifts, an endless caravan of fascinations. Innumerable elephants groaning under their treasury of virtues, while in her own slim-fingered hands, she brought her heart. Before her coming the concubines covered their faces and fled. We found almost at once a splendid studio on the south side of Washington Square, a long and lofty room with three wide windows, looking out across the tree tops to the opening of Fifth Avenue.

From this point of vantage the ensuing months appeared tolerable. I was occupied in defeating the dishonest intrigues of the people in Detroit who had sent emissaries to approach me in the winter. I was persuaded to put the publication of *The Equinox*, vol. III, no. 1 into the hands of those latter, and they immediately began to try to evade fulfilling the terms of the contract. I spent the summer in a tent beyond Montauk at the extremity of Long Island. The Magical Retirement made it clear that the current was exhausted. I had finished my work in America and began to prepare my escape.

In the autumn I accepted an invitation to visit my friends William and Kate Seabrook on their farm in Georgia to which they had retired. He had held an important position on the Hearst papers, and his sanity and decency had revolted against so despicably disgusting a job. He knew he was a genius and the effect of knowing me was to make him ashamed of himself. Alas, not long after my influence was removed, he became a backslider. He made sporadic attempts to escape from his environment, but the caress of this world and the deceitfulness of riches choke the artist's word and it becomes untruthful.

I passed a delightful six weeks in the south. Political and social conditions were of great interest. The standardized surface has overspread the south, but it has not completely smothered the old violence of passion and prejudice. The hatred of the Yankee and his fear of the Negro are as great as ever. In the latter case it has increased. The recent revival and the nation-wide spread of the Ku-Klux-Klan is one of the most sinister symptoms of recent years.

From Atlanta I went to Detroit and then took in the Mammoth Caves of Kentucky. I need not describe them. I content myself with the remark that they make a third wonder of the world worth seeing, from Niagara to the Grand Canyon. Except for the Yellowstone Park, which I have not yet seen, nothing else in America is worth seeing first or last for the matter of that.

A final inspection of the bughouse in Detroit left me free to get back to Europe. I reached London a few days before Christmas 1919.

81

In *The Vision and the Voice,* the attainment of the grade of Master of the Temple was symbolized by the adept pouring every drop of his blood, that is his whole individual life, into the Cup of the Scarlet Woman, who represents Universal Impersonal Life. There remains therefore (to pursue the imagery) of the adept 'nothing but a little pile of dust'. In a subsequent vision the Grade of Magus is foreshadowed; and the figure is that this dust is burnt into 'a white ash', which ash is preserved in an Urn. It is difficult to convey the appropriateness of this symbolism, but the general idea is that the earthly or receptive part of the Master is destroyed. That which remains has passed through fire; and is therefore, in a sense, of the nature of fire. The Urn is engraved with a word or symbol expressive of the nature of the being whose ash is therein. The Magus is thus, of course, not a person in any ordinary sense; he represents a certain nature or idea. To put it otherwise, we may say, the Magus is a word. He is the Logos of the Aeon which he brings to pass.*

The above is obscure. I perceive and deplore the fact. The idea may be more intelligible, examined in the light of history. Gautama Buddha was a Magus. His word was Anatta; that is, the whole of his system, which revolutionized the thought of Asia, may be considered as based upon and consecrated in that one word, which is his denial of the existence of the Atman or 'soul' of Hindu philosophy.

Later, Mohammed also partially overturned an age by uttering his word, Allah. But to us, practically, the most important case of the kind is that connected with such 'gods' as Dionysus, Osiris, Baldur, Marsyas, Adonis, Jesus, and other deifications of the unknown Magus concerned. The old pagan worship of the Mother-idea was superseded by the word IAO or its equivalents, which asserted the formula of the Dying God, and made the Male, dying to himself in the act of love, the engineer of the continued life of the race. This revolution

---

* Cf. Rabelais: the final secret is in the bottle inscribed TRINC.

cut at the root of all previous custom. Matriarchy vanished; self-sacrifice became the cardinal virtue, and so through infinite ramifications.

This idea of accomplishing the Great Work by a voluntary death was bound up with the belief that the sun died, and was reborn with the hours and the seasons. Astronomy having exploded this fiction, mankind was ready to gain a further comprehension of its own parallel case.

My own word, Thelema, supplies a new and scientifically sound basis for ethics. Self-sacrifice is a romantic folly; death does not end life; it is a temporary phase of life as night and winter are of terrestrial activity. Many other conceptions are implied in this word, Thelema. In particular, each individual is conceived as the centre of his own universe, his essential nature determining his relations with similar beings and his proper course of action. It is obvious that these ideas are revolutionary. Yet to oppose them is to blaspheme science. Already, in a thousand ways, the principles involved have replaced those of the Dying God. Little remains but to accept Thelema consciously as a statement of law, so that any given problem may be solved by applying it to each case.

The man Crowley had been chosen to enunciate this Law, that is, to exercise the essential function of a Magus. But he had yet to understand it, a task which involved the crossing of the Abyss, already described; and further, to identify his will with the Law, so that his personality might act as the focus of its energy. Before he could be that pure will whose name is that word, he had to be purged by fire of all competing volitions; and this was done by those who had chosen him during this part of his life, which I am about to record.

He had indeed got rid of his sense of the personal self, yet his force was discharging itself dispersedly through all sorts of channels appropriate to the various elements in his nature. It was necessary to constrain every particle of his energy to move in one sole direction. (The physical analogy of a gas whose electrons are polarized and one not so organized is not so bad.)

It must now be explained how he was able to understand what was happening to him in this initiation—his life from 1914 to 1919. The Grade of Magus is traditionally connected with the idea of the number 2; male creative energy, wisdom and the expression of a single idea in terms of duality. It transmits the idea of the divine unity to its feminine counterpart, the understanding, somewhat as a man transmits the essence of his racial character to his wife so that he perceives his inmost nature, itself unintelligible to him directly, by observing the flowering of that essence in his son. The Hebrew title of the idea embodying these characteristics is Chokmah, whose numerical value is 73. This fact appears arbitrary and irrelevant; but it forms part of the symbolic language in which the praeterhuman intelligences who control the initiate communicate with him. Thus, my adventures in America seemed a series of stupidities for a long time. Nothing I did produced the expected results. I found myself suddenly switched from one episode to another so irrationally that I began to feel that I had somehow got into a world where causality did not obtain. The mystery only became clear when analysis disclosed that the events which threw me about in this manner occurred at almost exact intervals of 73 days, or of some multiple or sub-multiple thereof. I understand from this that 73 terrestrial days made up a single day of initiation. As soon as I had grasped this singular fact, I was able to interpret each such period by considering how its events influenced my spiritual development. In this I succeeded so well that towards the end I became able to predict the sort of thing that would happen to me beforehand, which helped me to meet circumstances intelligently and make the fullest and most appropriate use of them.

One further point with regard to this initiation must be mentioned, though it sounds so fantastic even to myself that I can scarcely smother a smile. In the ancient ceremonies of the Egyptians the candidate was confronted or guided on his journey by priests wearing the masks of various animals, the traditional character of each serving to indicate the function of its wearer. Quaint as it sounds, I found myself discovering an almost stupefying physical resemblance to divers symbolic animals in those individuals whose influence on me, during their appointed period, was paramount.

From these and other indications I have been able to construct an intellectual image of the initiation; and if these preliminary remarks be thoroughly understood, it should be easy to follow the course of my progress to the Grade of Magus.

The first period of my sojourn in the United States was consecrated to my preparation for more active instruction by isolation and darkness. I had arrived with a not inconsiderable reputation, both as a man of letters and as a Magician. I had numerous connections with prominent people in both camps and was furnished with excellent introductions. I was positively stupefied to discover, by the most baffling experiences, that by none of these means could I make my way into public life. I lectured with apparent success; yet literally nothing came of it. I was welcomed by editors and publishers, written up and entertained with surprising enthusiasm; yet I failed to sell a single poem, story, essay or even article (except in the special case of political writing in one paper of no credit) and no one would hear of publishing a book. Occasionally, a man promised great things; but the arrangements always fell through suddenly and unreasonably. I had a host of friends in the city, yet days and weeks would pass without my seeing a soul except in the most casual way.

I was even unable to practise my personal Magick. An inscrutable paralysis had me by the spine. After many days I said to myself that I must break up these conditions forcibly; I would a-wooing go whether my mother would let me or no. I set my teeth and began my ritual. But I was now confronted by a new obstacle. I could not do the proposed operations, urgently necessary as they were. I found myself forced to a daily invocation of Mercury (the god corresponding to the Grade of Magus) with whom I did not consciously want to have any dealings. For three times three-and-seventy days I remained thus blind and impotent, oppressed and overwhelmed by the sense of my utter failure and futility, although on the surface all the conditions were in my favour, and there was not anywhere one single visible obstacle. I met dozens of interesting and important people; yet on none of these did my personality seem to produce the slightest effect, while (equally) none had any message for me. The surprise of the situation can only be understood if it be remembered that during my whole life I had never failed to attract eager attention wherever I went, to bring off whatever I planned, and to feel myself in every way a centre of electric energy.

My paralysis extended to every relation of life. I had never known what it was to lack human love; and now, not only did I fail to find a single friend, but when Laylah came from England to join me, I recognized instantly that she was a stranger.

The three Chokmah days (let me so call these periods of 73 days) ended on June 9th, 1915. On the tenth the oppression and obscurity were over. I was asked to dinner by a journalistic friend. He had bidden two women to meet me; one prominent as a poetess; the other, as a actress. I will call one the Cat, the other the Snake; Pasht and Apophis. The

Cat was ideally beautiful beyond my dearest dream and her speech was starry with spirituality. The Snake glittered with the loveliness of lust; but she was worn and weary with the disappointment of insatiable desire. Her intellect was brilliant but cynical. She had lost faith in the universe. Her speech was like a sword, to shear away the subtlest sophistries by which we so pitifully persuade ourselves that the perfection which we seek is possible.

A magnetic current was instantly established between the three of us. In the Cat, I saw my ideal incarnate, and even during that first dinner we gave ourselves to each other by that language of limbs whose eloquence escapes the curiosity of fellow guests. It was the more emphatic because we were both aware that the Snake had set herself to encompass me with the coils of her evil intelligence.

The sequel was as strangely significant of the symbolic character of the ordeal as its beginning. I took tea with the Cat at her club the next afternoon. We lost no time. She told me—a string of lies—of her loveless marriage with an old satyr who had snatched her almost from the cradle. She was about to divorce him; and having loved me at first sight, not sensually, but as my spiritual sister, we could be married quite soon. We sealed the sacrament with a kiss; and there was no reason why, in the ordinary course of events, we should not have proceeded to an immediate liaison. But the gods wished to test me. I really believed in her spirituality. I really loved her with a love more exalted than aught in all my experience. Yet in my soul I knew, against all reason, that she was a fraud; her aspirations affectations; her purity a pose; a false, heartless, brainless, perverse imitation of my ideal. I fought down the intuition; I swore with all the passionate power of the poet that she was what she seemed. I staked my happiness on her truth and made oath to be utterly worthy of her love.

They tested me by sending her out of the city for nearly a month. I endured the torture of absence, of doubt, of despair, with all the might of my manhood. To confirm myself ceremonially in this course of combat, I saw her rival occasionally, so as to affirm my absolute devotion to my ideal. To repulse the demons of realism, I set my foot upon the neck of the Snake that strove to shake my faith in the existence of perfection.

On July 8th, the Cat returned to New York. Love had conquered. We consecrated ourselves that same night to its service. But though the Cat had given herself thus simply and straightforwardly, she enjoyed the exercise of her power over me by tormenting me with doubts of her truth. She pretended to be disgusted by the sexual side of love and in a thousand ways kept me on pins and needles. Not many days elapsed before she suddenly left the city without leaving word for me. She had driven me to such desperation that I nearly lost control of myself when I heard that she had gone.

Summoning my veteran chief of staff, General Gynoniastix, I was readily convinced that this was a case for employing the strategy familiar to all men who have made up their minds to preserve their independence even at the cost of a broken heart. I telephoned straightaway to the Snake and asked her to lunch, after which we went round to my apartment. I was not moved by love; I simply wanted to torture the woman I hated as the woman I loved was torturing me. I made no advances; I was brutally rude; and to clinch the matter, I inflicted physical pain.

I had unusually pointed canine teeth. I fix a fold of flesh between the two points; and then, beating time with one hand, suddenly snap, thus leaving two neat indentations on the flesh concerned. I have often done this as a demonstration; often as a jest or a psychological experiment, sometimes as an intimation of affection, but never till then as a callous and cruel insult. Probably I misjudged my own motives. Somehow or other the genuineness and integrity of this lost soul began to appeal to me. I began to contrast her hard bitter cynical disbelief with the soft honied superficial assurance of her rival: before I knew what I was doing, our duel had developed into a death struggle in which my hate and hopelessness strove to swamp themselves in a surge of amorous frenzy.

The spasm swept me away. I no longer remember how we went out and dined, or how we got down to her house. Every nerve in my soul was screaming with implacable pain. Through it all I stuck to my guns; I never forgot that I loved the other woman and all that she stood for. But when at last exhaustion ended the orgy, twelve hours or more of indescribably insane intoxication, I sank into a sleep deeper than death—and woke at dawn to find myself inscrutably purged of iniquity. I knew myself *innocent* in a sense more sublime than any imagination can conceive, and from this state I came mysteriously into a trance of a kind which I had never experienced. Its occurrence marks a definite stage in my spiritual career.

It is so important to the understanding of my life that it must be quoted verbatim from the record which I made immediately on my returning to my apartment—where I received an additional proof that I had come successfully through the ordeal in the shape of a telegram from Pasht explaining why she had left the city, and how she had been prevented from letting me know. (Another string of lies!)

> Result: This is one of the greatest experiences of my life. Curious that the 1906 success also came through a magical thanksgiving under stress of passion. I went off to sleep almost at once. In the morning I woke early, before seven, in an absolutely renewed physical condition. I had the clean fresh feeling of healthy boyhood, and was alert and active as a kitten —post talem mortem! Mentally, I woke into *Pure Love*. This was symbolized as a cube* of blue-white light like a diamond of the best quality. It was lucid, translucent, self-luminous and yet not radiating forth. I suppose because there was nothing else in the cosmos. This verb love is intransitive; the love has no object. My gross mind vanished; when, later on, memory pictures of Hilarion† arose, they were rejected automatically. All the desire—quality, the clinging, the fear, were no more; it was Pure Love without object or attachment. I cannot describe the quality of the emancipation given by this most wonderful experience. Aum.

It may not at first sight be apparent why this rather silly and common-place intrigue should merit the attention which I paid it. The reason is this: just as the Master of the Temple is sworn to interpret every phenomenon as a particular dealing of God with his soul, so is the Magus to make his every act an expression of his magical formula. Being in course of initiation at the time, I did not realize what was going on. It is only on reflection that I have come to understand that my relations with these two women constituted an ordeal; a test of my fitness for the Grade. It is written 'as below, so above'; and my reaction to these women furnished a sure indication of how I should act in the greatest circumstances. For having succeeded in completely harmonizing the various energies of

---

* I say 'a cube'; yet its most salient property was that it was without boundaries. Experience of similar trances is necessary for the understanding of this statement, which is a perfectly proper expression of a perfectly observed fact, despite its intellectual self-contradiction.
† This was the 'mystic name' chosen for herself by the Cat. She had a smattering of theosophy and remembered this as being the name of some 'Mahatma'.

my being, there was no longer any danger that I should regulate my actions by conflicting standards. When therefore I rejected the Snake and chose the Cat, I was affirming magically that I would insist upon realizing my ideal (most people idealize the real—which they dare not face) even though I knew it not to exist and was broken-hearted by the continual mockery of the deception.

The word of a Magus is always a falsehood. For it is a creative word; there would be no object in uttering it if it merely stated an existing fact in nature. The task of a Magus is to make his word, the expression of his will, come true. It is the most formidable labour that the mind can conceive.

Having made this decision, my next task was to cause my word to become flesh. The morning of the fifth Chokmah day was devoted to the begetting of a son. I wanted to fulfil the love which I had found. As before, I understood nothing of this; I simply wanted to have a child by the Cat, and performed a series of Magical Operations with this object. I did not know that I was attempting a physical impossibility.

(I must digress to explain that every cause must produce its proper effect; so that, in this case, the son whom I willed to beget came to birth on a plane other than the material.) I must have been very blind indeed not to recognize my true situation, if for no other reason than the following. The celebration of the autumnal equinox coincided with an Operation with the object above stated. It was the last of this series of Operations, though I had no reason whatever for stopping, and only discovered the fact, much to my surprise, long after. Now, the word of this equinox was 'Nebulae',[1] which evidently points to the conditions which result in the birth of a star. What I had really done was therefore to beget a Magical Son. So, precisely nine months afterwards, that is, at the summer solstice of 1916, Frater O.I.V.[2] (the motto of C. Stansfeld Jones as a probationer) entirely without my knowledge became a Babe of the Abyss.

I failed completely to understand the telegrams in which he announced the fact. His action was unprecedented in the whole history of Magick. It was utterly beyond my imagination to conceive of such an occurrence. He, on the other hand, while ignorant of my Operation in the autumn, understood perfectly at the time what he was doing; that he was being born as 'The Child' predicted in *The Book of the Law*. This interpretation does not rest upon any arbitrary ideas, either on his part or mine. *The Book of the Law* speaks of this

'Child' as 'One', as if with absolute vagueness. But the motto which Frater O.I.V. had taken on becoming a neophyte was 'Achad' which is the Hebrew word for 'One'. It is further predicted that this 'Child' shall discover the Key of the interpretation of the Book itself, and this I had been unable to do. (The Book asserts that I should not succeed in this, astounding as it may seem, as I had 93 well in my mind, as 31 [93 ÷ 3] as the value of AL and LA, whose importance in the Book I understood perfectly. The text literally teems with hints; yet I never thought of 31 as the Key. Such blindness is a miracle more surprising than any amount of perspicacity.) And in actual fact he did so discover that Key, two and a half years later.

Those unacquainted with our methods may ask for the basis of the assurance that the key in question really fitted the lock. The answer is that the moment it was communicated to me, I applied it to a number of obscure passages in the Book, and found that it elucidated them completely. Incidentally, I received another very striking proof of the genuineness of the discovery. Every six months, at the equinoxes, it becomes my duty to obtain a word from the gods, whose symbolic meaning indicates the events of importance to the Order which will occur in the course of the ensuing equinox.

(For instance, in the autumn of 1918, the word was 'Eleven'. Apart from its special technical meanings, there was this: that the Armistice was signed at 11 o'clock on the 11th day of the 11th month of the year.) Now, the word of the equinox in which this Key was discovered was SAC. I was greatly puzzled to interpret this word and it did not become clear in the light of the events of the period as it usually does. Only now, when I am writing this account, some four years later, has it suddenly flashed upon me that the numerical value of the word is identical with that of the Key!* There

---

* SAC=Shin, Aleph, Cheth, 300+1+8=309.

(Tarot Trumps corresponding to these letters.) XX+XI+0=31. The compound letter (Greek ΣT) in special reference to this combination of Tarot Trumps is the third of the words of value 31 (AL and LA) which complete 93. A volume might be (and has been) written on the fitness of this whole symbolism.
SAC=Tzaddi, Aleph, Kaph, 90+1+20=111=ALP=Aleph. 1=AChD= 'One'. (Frater O.I.V. and the predicted discoverer of the Key.) Both spellings are valid to reveal the word and its discoverer! Such intricacy of device is one of the most evident proofs of the praeterhuman intelligence of the author of *The Book of the Law*.

are numerous other confirmations; but the above ought to suffice for the most sceptical that the author of *The Book of the Law* possessed an accurate knowledge of future events.

The next important stage in my initiation was the formal proclamation of my attainment. As the Master of the Temple I wore a seal ring; the lapis lazuli, engraved with my cipher, was covered by a platinum lid studded with pyramids to represent the City in which the Masters of the Temple abide. On October 12th, in the train from Chicago to Vancouver, while engaged in my annual Sammasati meditation upon my Path since the previous birthday, I was suddenly impelled to tear off this lid. A little later I left the train; and on reaching the hotel found that the lapis lazuli had dropped out of its setting. In the morning I sought and found it on the platform of the station, broken into seven pieces. I picked them up and put them away with the utmost care in my travelling safe, intending to distribute them on my death to my nearest representatives. Just over a year later, looking through my belongings, the packet was missing. (I have noticed that every time I receive an important initiation, some cherished article mysteriously disappears. It may be a pipe, a pen or what not: but it is always an object which is impregnated with my personality by constant use or special veneration. I cannot remember a single occasion when this has not happened. The theory is that the elementals or familiar spirits in attendance on the Magician exact, so to speak, a tip on all important occasions of rejoicing.) My idea in tearing off the lid was to proclaim ceremonially that I would come out of the darkness of the City of the Pyramids. (The exact period between these two initiations was predicted during the former; of course, in symbolic language, whose meaning appeared only on fulfilment.)

By thus accepting the Grade of Magus I had incurred certain responsibilities. Previously, I had taken the attitude that, while *The Book of the Law* had been given to the world through me, and though I was ineluctably bound thereby, I could stand aloof to some extent. I could consider myself as a Magician pledged to the Law, accepting it and working by its formula: but not identified with its promulgation to the exclusion of all other aims.

My formal attainment of the Grade involved my identifying myself with the word Thelema. My personality must be completely merged in it. On realizing this I realized also how carefully I had avoided compromising myself in this respect. I had never openly proclaimed the Law in the first person, as one might say, either in speech or writing.

Accordingly, when (on arrival at San Francisco) I found myself invited to address a semi-public gathering, I began my speech with the words, 'Do what thou wilt shall be the whole of the Law', and proceeded as best I could to explain their import.

Again, on the last day of the year, whose midnight I habitually devote to a meditation on the past, culminating in a formulation of my future career, I was moved to write what was shortly afterwards published first as a pamphlet in England,[3] secondly as an article in *The International*, New York, thirdly in *The Equinox*, vol. III, no. 1, and fourthly as a pamphlet in Australia by Frater Ahah.* In this I summarized shortly the events which had led to my attainment of the Grade, and explained that I was thereby committed to an irrevocable and absolute identification of myself with my office as the Logos of the Aeon of Horus. For the future my whole essence must be conterminous with that of the word, and my dynamical formula with that of its utterance.

I continued by setting forth the import and purport of that word. I announced that since 'Every man and every woman is a star', each of us is defined and determined by a set of co-ordinates, has a true will proper and necessary, the dynamic expression of that nature. The conclusion from these premises is that the sole and whole duty of each of us is, having discovered the purpose for which he or she is fitted, to devote every energy to its accomplishment.

It need hardly be said that the theory of ethics thus outlined involves the consideration of many difficult and important problems. I did not understand at that time the extent of the implication and have devoted immense labour in recent years to the solution of the theorems which are corollary to the

---

* G. H. Frater AHAH 6°=5□ R.R. et A. C. is the humblest and simplest of the Brethren of the Order. He has worked with his hands since he was nine years old and he understands and loves the Law and its Logos as a child does its mother and father. He has my respect and affection as no other of my Brethren: for he represents to me mankind incarnate at its weakest (and therefore strongest) and noblest (and therefore most 'common'). He is, in a word, that 'Man' of whom I am, being 666 (the number of a man) and whom I love and serve. An illuminating incident: he cannot spell, but under inspiration writes as none has ever done save one—John Bunyan! [Frater Ahah was the Australian, Frank Bennett.—Editors.]

fundamental proposition. It must suffice for the present to record the writing of this message. The act was the ceremonial gesture significant of my attainment: as one may say, the King's speech at the opening of the Parliament of the New Aeon.

82

The sixth Chokmah day was devoted to a terrible ordeal. I had by this time been enlightened as to the falseness of the Cat; it therefore became my duty to slay her. I had created truth by means of an untrustworthy material and must therefore no longer cling to the image of the ideal. I must destroy it, well knowing that it would never again be possible for me to delude myself with poetical puppets. I must face reality for good and all.

The desolation in my heart was unspeakably dreadful and the seventh Chokmah day found me in the same solitude and silence as the first three; with this difference: that a minister was appointed to comfort and console me. Exactly as before, every single relation that I had established snapped suddenly. I had plenty of friends; but none of them meant anything. However, my consolation was supreme. On the one hand, the despairing cynicism of the wise realist Snake, on the other, the heartless vanity of the foolish idealistic Cat, had left me hopeless for humanity.

In this extremity, I met a very rare animal. A woman! She was a regular street-walker. She had been familiar with hardships, callousness, obsession, shame and poverty from her cradle; but she possessed every noble quality to the full. Hers was the true pride, generosity, purity and passion to which the Cat so basely pretended; and hers also the clear-insighted intelligence, the wide experience and deep insight of the Snake. Yet she had faced and conquered her foes, instead of acquiescing in despair.

I am not one of those sentimental slop-mongers who are always finding angels in the mud. On the whole, my experience of outcast women had not provoked any excess of sympathy. I thought that in most cases their own defects were responsible for their misfortunes. Indeed, I failed to realize consciously the sublimity of this girl until long afterwards. But today, I see clearly enough the nature of her mission; which ended as strangely as it began, at the close of the Chokmah day. She disappeared into the *Ewigkeit* without a word and all my efforts to trace her were fruitless.

This day of repose and reward had prepared me for my next ordeal. At the beginning of the eighth day appeared a Monkey and an Owl. Once again I was confronted with the necessity of choosing between two ideas. The Monkey had all the insensate passion, volubility and vanity of the less developed primates. She was a great artist and a great lover; yet in each of these functions she displayed the utmost inanity of conceit. The Owl, on the other hand, was incapable of sublimity and at the same time free from affectation. She was as pleasant and sensible as the Monkey was excruciating and absurd.

The nature of my ordeal was twofold. In the first crisis, it was put up to me to do the right thing without permitting any interference from personal inclination or consideration of the ultimate consequences of my line of action. The test was applied at a conference of the parties chiefly concerned. The Monkey's husband wanted me to take her off his hands. A divorce was to be arranged and a marriage to follow. Asked to give my views, I began, 'I have no personal feeling in the matter.' The words were a bombshell. Both husband and wife realized, to their amazed horror, that they had neither of them any means of influencing my conduct. I found myself completely master of the situation. It is only necessary to destroy in oneself the roots of those motives which determine a man's course, in order to enjoy the omnipotence and immunity of a god.

The second point of the ordeal concerned the choice between the women. The Owl offered all the delights of carefree ease and placid pleasure; but there was nothing to be gained. The Monkey represented a life of turmoil and anxiety, with few magnificent moments amid the hours of fretfulness; but progress was possible. It was as if the Secret Chiefs had asked me, 'Are you content to enjoy the fruit of your attainment and live at peace with the world, surrounded by affection, respect and comfort, or will you devote yourself to mastering and fertilizing mankind, despite the prospect of continual disquietude and almost certain disappointment?' I chose the Monkey. I was perfectly willing to make the best of the Owl, in my spare time, so to speak; but I accepted the responsibility attached to her rival without reservation.

A single day was sufficient for this part of the initiation. At the dawn of the ninth day all had been arranged. The Monkey went to England to wind up certain of her affairs and the Owl had no string on me. I was thus able to undertake a Great Magical Retirement in June. For this purpose I went to live in a cottage on the shores of Lake Pasquaney in New Hampshire. My initiation now took on a more strictly magical character. I was able to enter into direct communication with the realities of existence instead of conducting them by means of symbolic gestures.

My very first experience was the announcement of the birth of my 'son', as above mentioned. I did not understand the matter in that light but in this: that by means of my system of training, a man had crossed the Abyss and become a Master of the Temple in a much shorter period than had ever been known. My own case had been extraordinary. Eleven years had sufficed me to accomplish a task which in human experience had never required much less than triple the time. Moreover, the conditions had been almost uniquely favourable for me. I possessed all the qualities, all the resources requisite.

In the case of O.I.V. the period was shorter still, and by much; while for him the conditions had been wholly adverse. He was obliged to earn his living in a distasteful and exhausting manner. His domestic circumstances were atrocious. He had not the means of travel or even of scholastic research. I could only conclude that his success was almost wholly due to the excellence of the system which I had given to the world. In short, it was the justification of my whole life, the unique and supreme reward of my immeasurable toils.

Fortified and rejoiced by this good news, I began at once to devote myself to research in the strict sense of the word.

And then the fun began! I found myself unable to do anything of the sort. I am not quite sure how the circumstances responsible for this fit in with my general situation, but they are well worthy of record for their own sake.

I have mentioned elsewhere that in the bosom of the Sanctuary of the Gnosis of the O.T.O. is cherished a magical formula, extremely simple and practical, for attaining any desired object. It is, however, peculiarly appropriate to the principal operations of alchemy, most of all the preparation of the Elixir of Life and the Universal Medicine. At first I used this method casually. It was only when various unexpectedly and even astoundingly successful operations compelled my attention, that I devoted myself systematically and scientifically to the serious study and practice of it. For some two and a half years I had conducted a careful and strenuous research into the conditions of success. Experience had shown me that sometimes this was complete, but at others partial or even negligible, while not infrequently the work would result in failure, perhaps almost amounting to disaster.

Just before leaving New York I had prepared by this method an elixir whose virtue should be to restore youth, and of this I had taken seven doses. Nothing particular happened at first; and it never occurred to me that it might be imprudent to continue.

I was mistaken. Hardly had I reached my hermitage before I was suddenly seized with an attack of youth in its acutest form. All mental activity became distasteful. I turned into a mere vehicle of physical energy. I could hardly bring myself to read a book even of the lightest kind. I could not satisfy my instincts by paddling the canoe which I had imported. I spent about an hour every day in housework and cooking; the remaining fifteen hours of waking life were filled by passionately swinging an axe without interruption. I could hardly stop to smoke a pipe.

There was no self-delusion about this, as I might have persuaded myself to believe in the absence of external evidence. But this was furnished by an irrefutable monument. I wanted to build a wharf for my canoe. With this object I cut down a tree and trimmed a twenty-two foot log. Its circumference at the smaller end was too great for my arms to meet round it. My only instrument for moving this was a wooden pole. The tree had fallen about a hundred yards from the bank; and though it was downhill all the way to the lake, the ground was very uneven and the path so narrow that it was impossible to roll the log at all. Nevertheless, I moved it singlehanded into the lake, where I fixed it by driving piles. Passers-by spread the story of the hermit with superhuman strength, and people came from all parts to gaze upon the miracle. I should mention that normally my physical strength is far below the average, especially for work of this kind. It is quite an effort for me to shift a sixty pound load for even a few feet.

So much for the sufficiently remarkable truth. Of course imagination improved on the story. I received an indignant letter from New York from the lady who had lent me the cottage, reproaching me for having built a dam right across the lake, to the detriment of navigation!

This spasm of energy continued without abatement for some three weeks, after which I gradually recovered the balance of my normal faculties. The effect of my operations was now to increase the energy of each of them, but in reasonable proportion. I was now ready to begin my proposed magical research.

In order to erect the temple of the New Aeon, it appeared necessary to make a thorough clearance of the rubbish of its ruined predecessors. I therefore planned and executed a Magical Operation to banish the 'Dying God'. I had written in 'The Wizard Way': [1]

> He had crucified a toad
> In the Basilisk abode

and now I did so. The theory of the Operation was to identify the toad with the 'Dying God' and slay it. At the same time I caused the elemental spirit of the slain reptile to serve me.

The result was immediately apparent. A girl of the village, three miles away, asked me to employ her as my secretary. I had had no intention of doing any literary work; but as soon as I set eyes on her I recognized that she had been sent for a purpose, for she exactly resembled the aforesaid toad. I therefore engaged her to come out every morning and take dictation. I had with me a copy of Bernard Shaw's *Androcles and the Lion* and bethought myself that I would criticize the preface. The almost unparalleled knowledge of the text of the Bible which I had acquired in early childhood was shocked by Shaw's outrageously arbitrary selection of the texts that sustained his argument. His ignorance of Asiatic life and thought had led him into the most grotesque misapprehensions. I set out to criticize his essay, section by section; but the work grew under my hand, and in three weeks or so, I had produced a formidable treatise of some forty-five thousand words. I had intended to confine myself to destructive criticism of my author; but as I went on, my analysis of the text of the gospels revealed the mystery of their composition. It became clear that both those who believe in the historicity of 'Jesus' and their opponents were at fault. I could not doubt that actual incidents and genuine sayings in the life of a real man formed part of the structure. The truth was that scraps of several such men, distinct from and incompatible with each other, had been pitch-forked together and labelled with a single name. It was exactly the case of the students who stuck together various parts of various insects and asked their professor, 'What kind of a bug is this?' 'Gentlemen,' he replied, 'this is a humbug.'

In writing this book, I was much assisted by Frazer's *Golden*

Bough and, to a less extent, by Jung's *Psychology of the Unconscious*. But my main assets were my intimate knowledge of
the text of the gospels, of the conditions of life and thought in
the East, of the details of magical and mystical work, and of
the literary conventions which old writers employed to convey
their ideas.

I may mention the absurdity of Shaw finding difficulty in
the fact that the visit of the three 'Kings' is not mentioned in
profane history. Shaw did not realize that a 'King' may be the
equivalent of a very minor chieftain in the Highlands.

Again the injunctions to abandon family ties and worldly
cares involve no social theories. They are addressed only to
would-be disciples, and have been so given—from the dawn of
history to the present day—by every Eastern teacher that ever
balanced himself upon one thumb, used a hip bath instead of
a soup plate, or rode the Wheel of Samsara in preference to a
bicycle.

Once more, the irrational incidents of the life of Christ become entirely normal when understood as the rubric of a
ritual of initiation.

I claim that my book establishes the outline of an entirely
final theory of the construction of Christianity. The subject is
far too vast and complex to be adequately discussed in this
autohagiography. But I have no hesitation in referring the student to my essay for the solution of any and every difficulty
which he may have found in the consideration of this matter.[2]

Having completed this treatise, I discovered myself to be
inspired to write a number of short stories based on *The
Golden Bough*. They are 'The Hearth', 'The God of Ibreez',
'The Burning of Melcarth', 'The Old Man of the Peepul Tree',
'The Mass of St Secaire', 'The King of the Wood', 'The Oracle
of Cocytus' and 'The Stone of Cybele'.

Now with regard to my magical work strictly speaking, its
character was presumably determined by my Grade. The
Magus corresponds to the Sephira Chokmah, whose manifestation in the universe is Masloth, the Sphere of the Fixed Stars.
It was accordingly proper that I should receive a revelation of
the universe in this aspect. I began my meditation with no
special objective in view. Almost immediately (instead of after
a long-continued effort, as had been the case generaly speaking
in the past) I obtained a Samadhi of which my conscious
memory brought back the account 'Nothingness with twinkles',
adding subsequently 'but what twinkles!' This Samadhi developed in the course of time, as I repeated it, into such impor-

tance that I feel almost justified in calling it the radix of my whole philosophical outlook. I have described it, giving historical details, in my Comment on *The Book of the Law*, ch. I, v. 59. It seems convenient to quote this in this place, as throwing light upon the progress of my inmost apprehension of the universe from this time forward.

THE 'STAR-SPONGE' VISION

There is a vision of a peculiar character which has been of cardinal importance in my interior life, and to which constant reference is made in my magical diaries. So far as I know, there is no extant description of this vision anywhere, and I was surprised on looking through my records to find that I had given no clear account of it myself.

The vision developed gradually. It was repeated on so many occasions that I am unable to say at what period it may be called complete.

I was on a retirement in a cottage overlooking Lake Pasquaney in New Hampshire. I lost consciousness of everything but a universal space in which were innumerable bright points, and I realized this as a physical representation of the universe, in what I may call its essential structure. I exclaimed, 'Nothingness with twinkles!' I concentrated upon this vision, with the result that the void space which had been the principal element of it diminished in importance; space appeared to be ablaze, yet the radiant points were not confused, and I thereupon completed my sentence with the exclamation, 'but what twinkles!'

The next stage of this vision led to an identification of the blazing points with the stars of the firmament, with ideas, souls, etc. I perceived also that each star was connected by a ray of light with each other star. In the world of ideas each thought possessed a necessary relation with each other thought; each such relation is of course a thought in itself; each such ray is itself a star. It is here that logical difficulty first presents itself. The seer has a direct perception of infinite series. Logically, therefore, it would appear as if the entire space must be filled up with a homogeneous blaze of light. This however is not the case. The space is completely full and yet the monads which fill it are perfectly distinct. The ordinary reader might well exclaim that such statements exhibit symptoms of mental confusion.

A further development of the vision brought to the consciousness that the structure of the universe was highly organized, that certain stars were of greater magnitude and brilliancy than the rest.

While at Montauk, I had my sleeping bag to dry in the sun. When I went to take it in, I remarked, laughingly, 'Your bed-time, Master Bab,' as if it were a small boy and I its nurse. This was entirely frivolous; but the thought flashed into my mind that after all the bag was in one sense a part of myself. The two ideas came together with a snap, and I understood the machinery of a man's delusion that he is a teapot.

From this I came to another discovery: I perceived why platitudes were stupid. The reason was that they represented the summing up of trains of thought, each of which was superb in every detail at one time. A platitude was like a wife after a few years; she has lost none of her charms, and yet one prefers some perfectly worthless woman.

It would be quite impracticable to go fully into the subject of this vision of the Star-Sponge. It must suffice to reiterate that it has been the basis of most of my work for the last five years, and to remind the reader that the essential form of it is 'Nothingness with twinkles'.[3]

83

It is a remarkable fact that physical phenomena of an appropriate character frequently accompany a spiritual event. I fail to see any special significance, from a magical point of view, in the experience now to be related; but it is highly interesting in itself, and there is unquestionably a striking correlation between it and the vision just described.

One morning I had started before dawn for the upper reaches of the lake. The day was breathlessly intense, the calm was somehow positive rather than negative, and seemed to conceal some huge menace. It was as if the heart of the world had stopped. I felt an indescribable awe, overwhelming in its solemnity. The act of paddling seemed almost a blasphemy. However, I made a fire on a rocky islet and cooked and ate my lunch, returning to the cottage in a curiously exhausted state. It was one of those days when the electrical conditions seem to abstract every particle of energy from one's nerves. The condition is familiar enough to me, and I understood that it foretold an approaching thunderstorm; in fact, an hour later, as I sprawled lazily on the verandah, I saw the imminence of the tempest. I realized that, wharf or no wharf, my canoe could not possibly live through what was coming. I dashed down to the water's edge at the exact moment when the first drop of rain fell, and although the distance was barely a hundred and fifty yards in all, and I picked up the canoe and tucked it under my arm like an umbrella, I was soaked and dripping before I got back to shelter. At this moment, a dog-cart, occupied by a man, a woman and a child, was hastily backed up away from the road, and they asked leave to take refuge till the rain stopped. I showed them into the main room, staying outside myself to watch the wonder of the storm. Daylight had disappeared with the utmost suddenness. A pall of purple black drove down the valley at a height of scarce a hundred feet above the water, and this pall was veined with a network of incessant lightning. Beneath it the air seemed praeternaturally clear. It was the most spectacular performance I had ever seen. Ahead of the storm, the vast blue sky stood speckless above the unrippled sheen of the lake. Then the advance guard of the tempest, the hail and the rain splashed down in giant drops like bullets. Then came the berry purple of the cloud, and under it the wind lashed the lake into tempestuous froth so fiercely that no water remained visible.

The storm struck deadly chill: and, having been reminded recently of the lurking malaria in my blood, I decided to put on dry clothes.

I must give a brief description of the construction of the cottage. It was of wood, built round a chimney stack and fire-place of brick. The main room faced the lake; and on the other side of the stack were a bedroom which I did not use and the kitchen. The main room, where I slept, being occupied by my guests, I had to take my dry clothes into the bedroom. This room had two small windows. I forget whether they were both closed; but if open, the slit was not more than two or three inches wide. There was a door, also closed, leading into the kitchen. The other door which led to the main room may possibly have been a little ajar. To put on my stockings, I sat down on a chair close to the brickwork of the chimney stack. As I bent down, I noticed, with what I can only describe as calm amazement, that a dazzling globe of electric fire, apparently between six and twelve inches in diameter, was stationary about six inches below and to the right of my right knee. As I looked at it, it exploded with a sharp report quite impossible to confuse with the continuous turmoil of the lightning, thunder and hail, or that of the lashed water and smashed wood which was creating a pandemonium outside the cottage. I felt a very slight shock in the middle of my right hand, which was closer to the globe than any other part of my body. I must emphasize that I was not in the slightest degree alarmed or otherwise mentally disturbed. It will be remembered that I had been struck by lightning on the Pillar Mountain many years earlier. I have always felt extreme oppression while an electrical storm is gathering and a corresponding exhilaration the moment it breaks. I have a powerful instinctive feeling that I am myself a wholly electrical phenomenon, and the wilder the storm, the more completely do I feel myself in my element. I am impelled to physical enthusiasm expressed in delightedly triumphant magical gestures and outbursts of ecstatically re-ligious incantations. I am thrilled to the marrow by the mere full title of the Tarot Card called the Knight of Wands, 'The Lord of the Flame and the Lightning, the King of the Spirits of Fire!' I want to shout aloud the superb Enochian invoca-

tion of that force. Something of that exaltation may be divined
from the rhythm and swing of the lyric into which I have introduced this title:

> By the Brood of the Bysses[1] of Brightening, whose
>   God was my sire;
> By the Lord of the Flame and the Lightning, the King
>   of the Spirits of Fire . . .

This spiritually sublime intensity does not in any way interfere with my intellectual activity. On the contrary, I become
more alert than in almost any other conditions. It is as if the
illumination of the flash interpenetrated my spirit, as if my
mental faculties entered into enjoyment of their ideal nourishment and stimulation thereby.

I was consequently in the best possible condition to observe.
My perfectly impersonal interest, and of course my scientific
training, stood me in excellent stead. My time sense was markedly altered, much as I have described in the account of the
attack on me in Calcutta. I was thus able to observe the events
of what was probably not more than five seconds as if it had
been as many minutes.

I thought the phenomenon of sufficient interest to record;
and wrote a brief description to the *New York Times*. The
result was surprising. I found myself inundated with letters
of inquiry from so many electrical students that I had at last
to have an account multigraphed to send out.

I had supposed that globular electricity was a well-known
and undoubted, if rare, phenomenon, and was amazed to
learn that until then it had never been seen by any reliable
and competent observer. I had quite an elaborate correspondence with Professor Elihu Thompson, one of the greatest
living authorities on electricity, about it. It appeared that
previous accounts were the statements of common sailors.
They left considerable room for doubting the existence of
globular electricity at all. This doubt was strengthened by the
extreme difficulty of framing any satisfactory hypothesis to
explain the occurrence. My observation turned out, therefore,
to be (in its way) a matter of primary importance. I ventured
to suggest an explanation of my own; but Professor Thompson
felt that, while it covered the facts of the case and even those
of previous observations, it involved a conception of electricity
which was not easy to reconcile with the implications of certain
other phenomena.

In the course of our correspondence, Professor Thompson communicated several extremely subtle and stimulating ideas as to the nature of matter, electricity and indeed of nature in general. They perhaps helped me to envisage consciously, for the first time, a strictly formal identification of the results of rational intellection with those of immediate intuition. I had felt, not without severe qualms, that the data of Neschamah might be in irreconcilable antagonism with those of Ruach. I was not in any way shaken in my opinion that the crown of Ruach (Daäth, Knowledge) had no true place on the Tree of Life, that it was essentially illusory and self-contradictory. It had been my constant preoccupation to find a means of expression for the truth of spiritual illumination in terms of rational comprehension, and moreover to justify the former without denying the validity of the latter. Professor Thompson's remarks filled me with hope. It must be remembered that at the period when I studied science most exclusively, the reaction against mysticism was in full swing. The persecution of Darwin was like an unhealed scar; its contemplation bred resentment against the very root of any religious interpretation of the universe. I had been forced into the awkward position of having to be ready to go to the stake with Maudsley, Ray Lankester and Haeckel, as against superstitious religion, and yet to attack their conclusions with the utmost vehemence in the interests of the impregnable spiritual position which I had built on the rock of my own actual experience. At last it had become conceivable that this antinomy might be overcome, and that in the best way, in the way indicated by the symbolism of the Cabbala itself; that is to say, the eyes of science were opening gradually to the perception that the results of observation and experiment demanded an interpretation as repugnant to common sense (as understood by the man in the street and the Rationalist Press Association) as the utmost conceptions of Pythagoras, Paracelsus and that Great Order itself of which I was an initiate. My subsequent researches have been almost exclusively determined by considerations of this kind. While I have done my utmost to advance directly towards truth by the regular traditional magical and mystical methods which *The Book of the Law* had perfected, I have constantly sought *pari passu* to correlate my results with those of modern intellectual progress; indeed, to demonstrate that the deepest thinkers are unwittingly approaching the apprehension of initiated ideas, and are in fact, despite themselves, being compelled to extend their definition of the Ruach to include conceptions proper to Neschamah, that they are, in other words, becoming initiates in our sense of the word without suspecting that they are committing high treason against the majesty of materialism.

The remaining Chokmah days of the initiation proper seemed to be devoted principally to showing the candidate the material on which he is to work. I hope it will not sound too strange if I say that up to this time of my life I had been to a certain extent living in a fool's paradise. In one way or another, either by actual shelter, by the protection of social and financial resources, by my own poetic rose-coloured spectacles, or by the singularly happy choice that I had made of the people among whom I dwell, I had not seen in all its naked nastiness the world of mankind. I had seen a good deal of cruelty, stupidity and callousness; I realized how ignoble were the lives of the average man and woman, but there had been practically always a reasonable amount of compensation. It is necessary to live in the United States and know the people well to get a really clear view of hell with the lid off. I had already been some time in the country, but the truth about New York had been camouflaged. I, being who I was, had come into contact with the very cream of the city, and on my travels about the Union, I had seen little more than the superficial life of the people as it appears to the wanderer whose tent is a pullman car, a swagger hotel, or the abode of some friend who by that very fact is not truly representative of his community. I was soon to be brought into intimate relations with a society so primitive that it had no means of knowing who I was or recognizing the class I represented; to experience what the French rather neatly call le-struggle-for-lifeisme; and that with the absolute moral certainty of being completely beaten from the very nature of things. In a country where the most weak and ignorant, the least intelligent and resourceful, find it easy enough on the whole to earn a fairly decent living, and where the slightest capacity of almost any sort makes it a safe bet that ten years will put its possessor on Easy Street, I was to find myself a candidate for complete destitution. For many months I was, for the first time in my life, constantly preoccupied with the problem of keeping myself alive, and did so only by the operation of periodical windfalls. Again and again my coracle sank under me and each time those responsible for the conduct of my initiation handed out something to go on with from some totally unexpected source, in order to keep me on that psychological razor-edge whence one can always see the abyss as one can no longer do when one is in it. In this way, I saw all classes and all races, but no longer from the privileged standpoint, with the result that I was able to understand thoroughly what they were like to themselves and to each other. The horror and loathsomeness of those conditions left a permanent mark upon my character. It went far to destroy my capacity for lyrical expression, or perhaps rather to make impossible the point of view necessary to that kind of creative impulse. Love itself was to appear in a totally new form. I had never before understood its roots in the moral weakness and physical incompetence of our breed of monkeys. I had been familiar enough with its romantic and spiritual implication, with the social and economic complications which degrade its ideal, and even with the brutalities and blasphemies which lust and greed impose upon it. I had never understood it as the expression of the bitter need of desperation which is after all its true nature so far as all but a very few individuals *rari nantes in gurgito vasto* are concerned.

It would be impossible for me even to attempt the merest outline of the abomination of desolation upon which the Chiefs forced me to gaze during these long dreary dreadful days. It was not that I saw only the vilest and basest elements in society; on the contrary, I was deeply impressed by the essential virtue which forms part of every human being, and the poison upon the barb of my experience was the fact that ignorance, unskilfulness, moral weakness and the like made the helplessness and hopelessness of virtue utterly complete. Everywhere I saw unspeakably loathsome and inhuman vices triumphing with scarce a show of resistance; commerce in its uncleanliest forms had harnessed morality, religion and even science to its Jaganath car. Every decent instinct, whether of the individual or of the community, was the prey of this ghoul. In another chapter I shall give instances of the kind of thing which was not wholly dominant but practically universal. I have said enough to convey a general idea of the nature of the ordeal through which I was passed at this period. I need only record a few of the actual magical results.

The misery which I underwent at this time had done much to cloud my memory. I do not clearly remember, for example, my reasons for going to New Orleans almost immediately after returning from Lake Pasquaney. It was my last glimpse of beauty for a long while. The old French-Spanish quarter of the city is the only decent inhabited district that I discovered in America. From the architecture to the manners of the people, their clothes, their customs and their cookery, all was delightful. It was like being back in Europe again with the added charm of a certain wildness and romance; it was a civilization *sui generis,* with its own peculiar adornment in the way of history. It enabled me to realize the spirit of the Middle Ages as even the most remote and time-honoured towns of Europe rarely do. I took a room conveniently close to the Old Absinthe House, where one could get real absinthe prepared in fountains whose marble was worn by ninety years' continual dripping. The result was that I was seized by another of my spasms of literary creation, and this time, the definite sexual stimulus which I had imagined as partly responsible for such attacks was, if not absent, at least related to an atmosphere rather than to an individual.

It lasted, if I remember rightly, some seventeen days. I completely lost track of the properties of time and place. I walked over to the Absinthe House in my shirt sleeves on one occasion without being in the slightest degree aware of the fact. My best work was an essay 'The Green Goddess', descriptive of the Old Absinthe House itself in particular, and the atmosphere of the quarter in general. It may be regarded as the only rival to 'The Heart of Holy Russia' for literary excellence and psychological insight. I wrote also *The Scrutinies of Simon Iff,* a series of six more or less detective stories; two or three less important essays; some short stories, of which I may mention 'Every Precaution' for its local colour; and all but the last two or three chapters of my first serious attempt at a long novel, *The Net.* I also began from the very depths of my spiritual misery a very strange book of an entirely new kind; so much so that I describe it as 'A Novelissim'. Its title is *Not the Life and Adventure of Sir Roger Bloxam.* It remains unfinished to this day; in fact it is hardly theoretically possible to finish it, strictly speaking. I have indeed serious qualms as to whether I have not overstepped the limits of truth in saying that I began it. To be safe, I should be content to say I wrote a good deal of it.

The lyrical faculty remained almost entirely dormant, no doubt owing to the fact that in a quarter where almost every woman attracted me intensely, I was quite unable to fix my affection on any single specimen. Perhaps also it was inhibited by the iron which was entering my soul inch by inch and being twisted in my heart by the pitiless love of the Secret Chiefs of the Order. It was this, without doubt, which threw a monkey-wrench into my creative machinery and its destructive energy may be measured by the frightful circumstance which must next be recorded.

The city of New Orleans is divided into two main sections by a broad thoroughfare. On one side is the Spanish quarter, on the outskirts of which was a large and picturesque red light section; one of the most interesting places of its kind that I have ever seen. In fact, if we except Cairo, it would have been hard to beat. Across the main street was the modern commercial Americanized section where hardly a brick but screamed an obscene blasphemy against everything that might delight a poet, arouse enthusiasm in a lover, or abstain from revolting the instincts of a gentleman. Before I had been long in the city, it had become obvious that this cancer was eating away the breast of the beautiful city, and the conviction was stamped into my soul by a very definite hoof-mark of the mule morality.

A millionaire with a very large interest in the racecourse at Havana bethought him that it would be good business to do away with the competition of New Orleans in that form of sport. He therefore proceeded to organize what is called a 'clean-up' of the city. He bribed prominent pulpits to awake the consciences of sincere puritans, squared the politicians and the newspapers, brought blackmail to bear on any honest people that seemed likely to stand in his way, and in every other respect fulfilled the conditions requisite for plundering the city and persecuting the poor, in the name of righteousness according to the most approved methods. His most spectacular success was to shut up the red light district, so far as the poorest classes were concerned. The effect of these proceedings was brought home to me by an incident which, happening in the United States, appeared to me vastly comic. I had been to the library in Lee Circle to get a book and descending the steps was accosted by a woman with a request for charity. I recognized her as one of the denizens of the wooden shanties of the red light district. My sympathy was aroused by the shameful cruelty to which she had been subjected by the hypocritical and dishonest manoeuvres of the millionaire and his myrmidons. Her case was peculiarly pathetic as she was suffering from an active and contagious form of disease. The most elementary common sense and decency would have come to her rescue long before, in the interest of her clients, no less than her own. I asked her what she was going to do now that her office had been closed. To my surprise, she was perfectly cheerful. The relief which she sought was only temporary, for she had got a good position as a nursemaid in a family of three young children for the following week!

Such was one of the innumerable similar symptoms of the foul disease which is ravaging the United States, and has already destroyed almost every vestige of the political, religious and individual liberty which was the very essence of the original American idea. My spirit sank under the contemplation of the irremediable calamity which threatens to engulf the whole of humanity since it is now an accepted principle of business to endeavour to make tyranny international, to suppress all customs of historical interest, and indeed everything which lends variety or distraction to human society in the interest of making a market for standardized products. The moral excuse for these activities is miserably thin, for the element which it is most important to suppress is originality as such, even when the question concerns the very idea of craftsmanship in itself. The idea at the back of puritanism is the reduction of the mass of humanity to a degree of slavery which has never previously been so much as contemplated by the most malignant tyrants in history; for it aims at completing the helplessness of the workman by minimizing his capacity. He must no more be permitted to exercise the creative craftsmanship involved in making a pair of boots; he must be rendered unable to do more than repeat mechanically, year in, year out, one meaningless item in the manufacture, so that when the pinch comes it shall be impossible for anyone to have boots at all except through the complex industrial conspiracy of the trusts. This idea, consciously or subconsciously, lies underneath all attempts to extend 'civilization'. The progress of this pestilence is only too visible all over the world. Standardized hotels and standardized merchandise have invaded the remotest districts, and these would be economically impossible unless supported by the forcible suppression of local competition. When, therefore, we find the newspapers indignant at Mohammedan morality, we may suspect the real trouble is that American hatters see no hope of disposing of their surplus stock as long as the wicked Oriental sticks to his turban or tarbush. The exquisite, dignified and comfortable clothes of remote people, from Sicily to Japan, must give way to the vile shoddy products of foreign factories, and the motive is supplied by a worldwide campaign on behalf of social snobbery. The people are persuaded that they ought to try to look like a sporting duke or a bank president. Such plans obviously depend on the destruction of everything that makes for originality, self-respect, the love of beauty or the reverence for history.

It took me a long while before I could formulate consciously this idea, so protean are its disguises and so subtly sinister its stratagems. But I have always possessed the instinct, I have always reacted automatically against this principle whenever I found it. It should be obvious that 'Do what thou wilt' cuts diametrically athwart this modern civilization to destroy the distinctions which constitute the sole hope of humanity to make real progress by the selection and variation which are the means of evolution. It may be said that my own work is in the nature of missionary enterprise; and that this is, in fact, the very thing to which I object, since its idea is to persuade people to abandon their established beliefs and customs. This criticism is invalid. I do, as a matter of fact, object to missionary enterprise as such, whether it take the form of imposing the cult of Osiris on the worshippers of Adonis, of persuading the Chinese to eat with knives and forks, or of making Eastern women obscenely ridiculous by changing their superb and suitable robes for frocks which pretend to have been made in Paris. But my message differs fundamentally from all previously promulgated precisely at this point. My predecessors have invariably said, 'My belief is right and yours is wrong; my customs are worthy, yours are ignoble; my dress is decent, yours is not; think as I think, talk as I talk, do as I do, or you will be wretched, poor, sick, disgraced and damned; besides which, I shall cut your head off, burn you alive, starve you, imprison you, ostracize you and otherwise make you sorry you did not agree to be a good boy.' The essence of every missionary message has been to assimilate the taught to the teacher; and it has always been accompanied by bribes and threats. My message is exactly opposed to any of this. I say to each man and woman, 'You are unique and sovereign, the centre of an universe. However right I may be in thinking as I do, you may be equally right in thinking otherwise. You can only accomplish your object in life by complete disregard of the opinions of other people. You must not even take the outward signs of success as indications that the course of action which has produced them would serve your turn. For one thing, my coronet might not suit your complexion but give you a headache; for another, the measures which I took to obtain that coronet might not succeed in your case.'

My mission is, in short, to bring everyone to the realization and enjoyment of his own kingship, and my apparent interference with him amounts to no more than advice to him not to suffer interference. It may appear from this as if I were opposed to joint action directed to the attainment of a common purpose. But, of course, this is not the case. The advantages, not merely of co-operation but of disciplined union are the same as they were with previous theories of life. Yet there is a certain practical difference which, by the way, is curiously illustrated by the parallel of military discipline. In primitive warfare, the nexus between comrades is practically limited to an agreement to forget their individual quarrels in face of the common enemy. The training of a soldier thus amounted to encouraging his personal prowess. It was gradually seen that some sort of plan for combined action made for victory, so that one leader or chieftain should be detailed to carry out a definite duty. It soon became clear that isolated action was dangerous to the whole army; and the consequent tendency was developed to the point at which the Prussian drill sergeant was invaluable. The aim was to reduce the soldier to a brainless bulk of brawn, to be manipulated as mechanically as a chessman, exercising his inherent energies without the slightest wish or power to think or act for himself. (This stage corresponds to that which we are rapidly approaching in industry.) Now at least we have reached a further stage. The complexity of a battle and its mere extent in space have made it impossible for a single man to handle his troops as was done by Marlborough and Napoleon, and therefore it has become once more necessary for the subordinate officer, and even, to some extent, the private soldier, to understand his responsibility, to exercise initiative within limits, and also to train himself to be able to carry out a variety of operations demanding very varied knowledge and skill, instead of, as before, being confined to a highly specialized task demanding blind obedience and the suppression of all intelligence. The Charge of the Light Brigade has in fact become impossible. We are moving intelligently enough back in the direction of Sir Launcelot and Crillon. The necessities of warfare are the more truly instructive in that the military type of mind is so contemptible. The commander-in-chief is always hopelessly incompetent either to conceive or to perceive correctly the very elements of his business. The progress of military science is imposed upon stupidly by the facts, and it affords us, therefore, the best possible illustration of the blind workings of evolution. That is why industry, whose chiefs are just one degree less brainless than the

Kitcheners and Frenches, is actually behind war in its biological adaptation to environment. Industrial crises are not so immediately fatal as those of tactics. Necessity has not so free a hand with the birch rod; and so, conditions alter more slowly, and their significance is less easy to interpret.

84

Considerations of this kind were constantly present to my mind at this period. Before my eyes was the sickening spectacle of humanity sinking ever deeper into the sticky slime of slavery. The tragedy of New Orleans illustrated one phase of the calamity. While as to the individual, his position might be gauged by the case of my own cousin in Florida, who quite seriously believed that God had sunk the *Titanic* to rebuke the presumption of the builders, of the pitifully comic worship of the weakly megalomaniac at the White House, and of the moral and mental level of such people as I met in the masonic lodges whose gambols I have described in a previous chapter.

Hope died in my heart. There was not one glimmer of light on the horizon anywhere. It seemed to me an obscene mockery to be called a Magus. I must have been afflicted by 'lust of result'; at least it came to this, that I felt that I could not go on with my work. On every side the wizened witches of religion and morality were shrill in celebration of their obscene sabbath. I felt that I had not only failed, but that it was little short of lunacy to imagine that I could ever make the slightest impression upon the monstrous mass of misery which was soaking through the very spine of mankind. My faith failed me; I made a gesture of despair; I committed spiritual suicide, I closed my Magical Record and refused to write. 'If the Masters want me to do their Work,' said I, 'let them come forward and call me.'

This action is the only one of my life of which I am really ashamed. I should not have surrendered while there was breath in my body. Well, perhaps it was not altogether a surrender; but it was at least a desperate appeal of anguish.

The penalty of my momentary lapse was frightful. Its effects are still observable today. The subject is really too painful to discuss at length. I need say no more than this: that my lack of confidence in the Secret Chiefs recoiled on myself. (In Magick, of course, the punishment always fits the crime.) At the same time, the Secret Chiefs themselves had made no mistake. They knew perfectly well what was my breaking strain and they deliberately pushed me beyond my limit for several excellent reasons. They wanted me to know the extent of my capacity to endure; and thereby, of course, to increase that capacity in the future by showing me that even when I thought I had broken the chain it held by invisible links as firmly as ever and was, in fact, unbreakable; for it is an essential element of my being to be pledged to the performance of the Great Work. They also taught me by this means the consequences of any such error; and this has been very useful to me in dealing with those who may be in danger of making a similar blunder. The penalty itself was also the means of arranging events in such a way as to be of service to me in subsequent initiation.

I don't know whether I thought the world would come to an end, because I chose to turn nasty—but I was certainly very much annoyed to find that, as in the case of the great Lord Cardinal, when he had finished cursing 'nobody seemed one penny the worse'. The Secret Chiefs were to all appearance entirely unconcerned at what I had done. Like my own Blind Prophet, I had pulled down the pillars on which I supposed the temple to be supported, but he at least succeeded in crushing himself, and I had not even done that!

What happened was in fact extremely curious. Stevenson observes that when a Magi is cashiered, he does not fall to be a rural dean or words to that effect. I found myself, like Othello, with my occupation gone. I might not be able to perform the task of a Magus, but there was certainly nothing else for me to do. I had no remorse, not so much as a qualm of conscience. The Secret Chiefs kept silent. And I found that after a fortnight or so I simply could not stand it any longer. I felt more than a little like a naughty dog, but there was simply nothing to be done but to crawl back with my tail between my legs, and I remember with somewhat shamefaced amusement, that I had a sort of hope that I had escaped notice.

The situation had not in any way changed; when I reopened my Magical Record I did so entirely without hope of any kind; in fact, perhaps the best way to express the situation is that my misdemeanour had served to purge me of the 'lust of result'. But as for having escaped notice, if I had really harboured any delusions on that point, my mind was completely disillusioned in the first eleven seconds.

I said to myself that the obvious first step was to invoke Mercury. I instantly found myself, with a little internal laugh

simmering in my solar plexus, saying, 'But I am Mercury.'
The suppressed chuckle was cut short suddenly by that feeling
akin to alarm which a man often feels when he is sitting up
late at night enjoying a book, and is suddenly reminded, perhaps by some slight noise, of some serious matter; an unexpected visitor, can it be, outside his door? For I was aware
that there was something more in what I was saying to myself
than its plain implication, and it came to me by some inscrutable instinct to couch the idea otherwise. *'Mercurius sum,'* I
murmured, and now the unheard voice, not so loud as a whisper yet more compelling than a burst of thunder, told me
without the use of language, 'No, that isn't it, say it in Greek.'
"Ἑρμῆς εἰμί,' I affirmed solemnly, and knew immediately that
I had done what was required of me, yet wondering almost
contemptuously what was the object of the translation, and
then, far more rapidly than I could have discovered by conscious calculation, I knew that "Ἑρμῆς εἰμί' had the numerical
value of 418, the Magical Formula of the Aeon.[1] At the very
first moment of resuming communication with my soul, the
Secret Chiefs had given me an indubitable token of their existence, of their vigilant guardianship, by communicating their
password, so to speak, in this cipher. My spirit leapt with joy
to be reassured once more by this superbly simple means, this
exquisitely neat and convincing language; yet stark shame
savaged me. How could even such a mule of a mind as mine
have been so obstinate to resist such perfect control? How
could I ever have been such a coward as to lose my courage
even for a moment, seeing that year after year the Secret
Chiefs had never failed me? I had never despised myself so
deeply. Bu the very sharpness of my scorn had also its use. It
guaranteed me for ever against a repetition of any such collapse. I did not ask for any further token; I did not even form
resolutions, or so much as ask for instruction. I simply became
alive to the fact that I was a Magus, with every implication
possible, and that I should infallibly perform whatever tasks
might be given me. I even began to understand that the actual
absence of any task was evidence that my present conditions
were essential to the Great Work; that my apparent impotence was part of the plan of the Secret Chiefs. I had been
childishly petulant in wanting to bathe in 'Abana and Phar-
phar rivers of Damascus', and thinking myself insulted by
being told that the petty trickle of Jordan, a stream that did
not even lead to the ocean, would suffice to cleanse my limbs
of leprosy. Somehow or other, the ghastly situation in which I

found myself, the stagnation of my career and the paralysis of my powers were essential to my proper progress. I ceased to fret about the future, as to protest against the present. I took everything as it came almost without comment, confident that at the right moment I should find myself in the right position to do what was right.

Having witnessed the bedevilment of New Orleans, I was sent to Titusville, Florida, to complete my contemplation of the unspeakable degradation of humanity which is constantly being wrought by Christianity and commerce. I saw my cousin Lawrence, as decent a lad as one could wish to see, spiritually stunted and corrupted in every way by savage superstition; his wife, hardly turned thirty, a wrinkled hag of sixty, with no idea of life beyond the gnawing fear of the hereafter and the horrible pleasures of venting her spite on her neighbours and thwarting and persecuting her children; his son, deprived of every boyish amusement, driven to secret indulgence in the most wretched vices, and his sisters (one of them with a voice which would have made her a queen in any civilized capital) thwarted in every innocent aspiration, and their eyes wide open to the frightful knowledge that they could never be anything but drudges sold into the worse slavery of marriage at eighteen, and ruined old women, dead to every possibility, at twenty-five. Their constant cry was 'I don't want to grow up to be like Mother!' Their least actions were spied on, their every attempt to fit themselves by education to get out of the ghastly swamp where they sweated away their youth in conditions which made the fever and famine themselves, with which they were familiar, more bearable than the malignant tyranny of the people to whom the very crocodiles might have served as a reproach and an inspiration.

From this hell of ignorance and family life I was removed to a very different place of punishment. I was to have a view of New York as it must appear to the average stranger, to all such of its inhabitants (these must constitute a very considerable percentage) who have not established business and social connections. It is striking evidence of the ability of the Secret Chiefs to arrange the conditions of an initiation that such an experience was possible for me; for, by this time, I was pretty well-known in the city in very varied sets, and as it happened, I had under my hand as good a means of making myself not only prosperous but popular, as any man could possibly wish for.

During my retirement by Lake Pasquaney I had, according

to my custom when in solitude and in need of relaxation, passed the time by dealing myself hands in such games as skat, piquet and bridge. I was led to invent a new game, a variation of auction bridge, which we subsequently called 'pirate bridge'. This appeared to me such an improvement on the ordinary game that I thought I would introduce it to the public. I convinced the editor of *Vanity Fair* of its merits and suggested that R. F. Foster should be called in to put the rules into definite shape.

It gave me a very curious feeling, by the way, to be in such relations with a man who, twenty years before, had been the inaccessible godhead of the universe of card games to my undergraduate enthusiasm! As a matter of fact, he misunderstood one of my rules; and I think the game was spoilt in consequence. However, even as it was, *Vanity Fair* was devoting a long article every month to the subject, and I had only to wander into the appropriate circles to make myself the darling of the community. But the Secret Chiefs had it in mind that so far from doing anything of the sort, I should spend months of absolutely sickening solitude, direst poverty and impotence to take any action whatever, so that I might realize how the world feels to the very vast majority of the inhabitants of its civilized sections, to people without resources, prospects, friends or exploitable abilities. I was also to be prepared to take up a public career for the first time in my life; my previous manifestations having been of a semi-private or amateur kind.

This period was inexpressibly distressing; apart from other unpleasantnesses, my health broke down in a quite inexplicable way. There was no satisfactory diagnosis; the symptoms were confined to a spiritual and physical malaise which deprived me alike of ambition and energy. (I have good reason to suspect that this was partly due to the reaction from my experiment in reviving youth.) And there were other trials. At one time I was so poor that I had to lie on the sofa of a friend in the garret which he called his studio to have anywhere to sleep, and I really don't quite remember what I did about eating. I suppose I must have earned a few dollars now and again in one way or another.

The Chokmah day beginning in June saw the break-up of these conditions. A new officer appeared. The initiation had now entered upon an entirely different phase. The function of the officers was no longer to administer ordeals (I had passed the tests); they were sent as guides to lead me on a journey through the Desert to the appointed 'House of the Juggler' in which a Magus symbolically lives.

The first part of the initiation had occupied thirteen Chokmah days counting from November 3rd, 1914 to June 9th, 1917. I was able to recognize my guide. During the past days I had done much work in analysing and interpreting the mysterious events which had characterized my sojourn in America. From this time on my progress was far less unintelligible than had hitherto been the case. I was therefore not surprised when an officer appeared at about the expected date, and her physical appearance told me at once where I had got to in my journey; for the god whose place is on the Threshold of the Temple, whose function is to guard the portal of the sanctuary and introduce approved candidates to the assembled deities, is Anubis. This god is always represented with the head of a jackal. (This has sometimes been interpreted as a dog; whence the dog-headed Hermes in the mythology which the Greeks borrowed from Egypt.)

Now this guide exactly resembled a dog; not only physically but morally.[2] She had all the canine qualities, the best and the worst, in perfection, and she certainly served to start me on my new journey. The impending section of my initiation was easy to understand. In the former I had been prevented from establishing any regular relations as a teacher or prophet with humanity. I had been prepared in solitude to become such. I was now, little by little, to enter upon my life as the Prophet of the Law of Thelema.

In July I was made the editor of *The International,* a monthly which had the distinction of being the only publication in the United States with a genuine claim to represent the best literary tradition. The editor had made the fatal mistake of prostituting its columns to political propaganda. The paper was, therefore, on the rocks. Its literary merits had been entirely forgotten in the salient fact of its pro-German tendencies. I explain elsewhere how I came to be connected with anti-English sentiments, and part of my plan in taking over the paper was to restore it to political propriety, unknown by its backers, and also to keep close watch upon their activities, on behalf of the Department of Justice. But my main object was, of course, to obtain a medium for the proclamation of the Law.

For all practical purposes, I was in complete control of the policy of the paper; but as far as pushing it was concerned I was obliged to rely on the broken reed of merit, for it was conducted financially with short-sighted meanness. I had no idea that cheese-paring could be reduced to such a fine art. My own salary was twenty dollars per week, which was, at that time, little more than the wage of an unskilled stenographer, and it was a Titan task to extract as much as ten dollars or the price of a lunch for a long article or story by a well-known writer. They expected me to get a cover design by a first-rate artist for five dollars and would try to cheat him or her out of it at that. I was horribly ashamed of having to cadge contributions in this way, but very proud to remember that many brilliant people seemed only too glad to give their work. They felt it an honour to support a magazine with such high standards as I introduced. One little fact illustrates the position with lurid light. Having got my article free, the least I could do was to have half a dozen copies of the number in which it appeared sent to the authors. The proprietor would countermand such instructions behind my back, not because of the cost of the paper, for there were always ample 'returns', but to save the postage.

The upshot of all this was that I wrote the bulk of the paper myself, camouflaging the fact by the use of pseudonyms. After eight months I had so improved the reputation of the paper that it had become a valuable property, and it was accordingly sold to a man who was so stupid as not to know that its sole asset was myself, and so fat-headed that he thought he could run it himself. He would not even accept a contribution from me, though I offered him one out of pure kindness. He pretended to be a great friend of mine and I had not realized the dirtiness of the intrigues against me. Well, he had his way and got out just one number. As soon as people found my name absent they would not buy it. Its sudden destruction was the greatest compliment I had ever received.

During the three Chokmah days of my control of the paper I devoted every energy to proclaiming the Law of Thelema in its pages both directly and indirectly.

My first important step in this direction, the thin end of the wedge, was an article 'The Revival of Magick' which ran serially, ending in November. The last paragraph, a mere coxcombical flourish, though written with the quite serious idea of indicating to some person of adequate intelligence, the direction in which to seek for a Master, proved an element in an incident of the utmost complexity. I propose to recount this in great detail, because it gives an idea of the extraordinary strength and subtlety of the proof that I am in communication with some intelligence possessing knowledge and power altogether superior to anything that we can reasonably ascribe to any human being.

This paragraph runs as follows:

Herein is wisdom; let him that hath understanding count the number of The Beast; for it is the number of a man; and his number is six hundred and three score and six.

I must now return to the feature of my initiation; for the other conditions of the incident in question are connected therewith.

After only one Chokmah day [3] I was obliged to get rid of my faithful Anubis. She had been a fine friend, but her manners were such that I could not really have her about the camp. Besides this, such a journey as I was now about to undertake required an animal of greater strength and size than the dog. To take me to the oasis I required a camel; and at the beginning of the next Chokmah day I found an admirable Mehari at the door of my tent. It is to be noticed that in this part of the initiation I was in no perplexity. I understood the proper function of the officer in charge of my progress and wasted no time in discussing right relations.

In January 1918, I published a revised version of the 'Message of the Master Therion' and also of the 'Law of Liberty',[4] pamphlet in which I uttered a panegyric upon the Law as the key to freedom and delight. (To get rid of the subject I had better mention here the other magical essays which appeared in *The International:* 'Cocaine', 'The Ouija Board', 'Concerning Death', 'Pax', 'Hominibus Bonae Voluntatis', 'Geomancy', 'Absinthe', 'De Thaumaturgia', 'Ecclesiae Gnosticae Canon Missae'. Of these, *Liber XV,* its scope and purpose, I have already described at length.) The point which I wish to bring out is that despite the constraint imposed upon me by the requirements of public taste, I succeeded in proclaiming the Law to a wide audience of selected readers, explaining its main principles and general import in straightforward language, and also in putting over a large amount of what was on the surface quite ordinary literature, but implying the Law of Thelema as the basis of right thought and conduct. In this way I managed to insinuate my message perhaps more effectively than could possibly have been done by any amount of visible argument and persuasion. *The Scrutinies of Simon Iff* are perfectly good detective stories, yet they not only show a master of the Law as competent to solve the subtlest problems by considerations based upon the Law, but the way in which crime and unhappiness of all sorts may be traced to a breach of the Law. I show that failure to comply with it involves an internal conflict. (Note that the fundamental principle of psychoanalysis is that neurosis is caused by failure to harmonize the elements of character.) The essence of the Law is the establishment of right relations between any two things which come into contact; the essence of such relations being 'love under will'. The only way to keep out of trouble is to understand and therefore to love every impression of which one becomes conscious.

Even in my political articles I make the Law of Thelema the sole basis of my articles. I apply it, in short, to every circumstance of life, securing in this way a completely coherent point of view. Most men and practically all Anglo-Saxons have an elaborate system of mental watertight compartments. One of the most important elements of the panic fear of truth in every form, the distrust of any man who seems likely to investigate things seriously, is due to the consciousness that even a superficial analysis will reveal a state of spiritual civil war whose issue it is impossible to foresee. They all pretend to be Christians, yet the injunction 'Love your enemies', which by the way is really the first corollary of the Law of Thelema, is universally regarded as infinitely objectionable. I am myself in all kinds of a mess simply because I insist upon putting this into practice. I refuse to consider my enemies as irreconcilable: I take the utmost pains to understand and love them. By this means I invariably succeed sooner or later in destroying them, that is, of incorporating them into my own idea of myself. (I am liable to express this operation by saying that having slain my foe in ambush, I devour his heart and liver raw in order to fortify myself with his courage, energy and other fine qualities, and then I become very sad when I am currently quoted as a cannibal. Picturesque metaphor is not always appreciated.) I cannot make the public understand that to treat a man as an enemy in the ordinary sense of the word, to damage him in every possible way, and otherwise to disintegrate him, is simply to cut off one's nose to spite one's face. There is nothing in the universe which is not indissolubly one with every other thing; and the greatest man is he who makes no difference between any one thing and any other thing. He becomes the 'chief of all' as stated in *The Book of the Law*.

85

We may now return to the subject of the initiation itself. Besides my work of proclaiming the Law to the profane and expounding it to the aspirant, I was set the task of analysing it in such a way as to illuminate the most advanced. During most of the winter I gave most of my spare time to the creation of literature which corresponded nobly with this threefold labour. I wrote the twelve stories *Simon Iff in America*. These were a continuation of the previous *The Scrutinies of Simon Iff*, but constructed for the most part on mere mechanical principles. I may even compare them to chess problems. The general method was to think of a situation as inexplicable as possible, then to stop up all chinks with putty, and having satisfied myself that no explanation was possible, to make a further effort and find one. I find it hard to consider this sort of thing as serious literature, and yet so ineradicable is the artistic instinct in me that the Old Adam peeps out sufficiently often to remove these stories from the category of *jeux d'esprit*. In particular, the story 'Suffer the Little Children', whose setting is in Florida as I knew it, flames so fiercely with the passion excited in me by the conditions which I found there, a passion which I cannot fairly describe as pity, scorn, disgust, indignation, or even any combination of these, that I believe this tale may stand like the broken statue of Osymandias, in the eyes of a new civilization, as a witness of the tyranny and abomination which Christians have taught us to associate with the name of Christ. It is at least an extremely accurate study of life in Florida; the accuracy is guaranteed by the acuteness of the suffering of the observer. One does not see children vivisected before one's eyes without receiving an impression, and the emotion which in ordinary cases might obfuscate and mislead the looker-on was in my case transformed into an ideal stimulant of clear-sightedness. I felt intensely that I had to have all my wits about me in order to expose the atrocity of the abominations which I was compelled to witness. The brilliance of the story is striking evidence of the fierceness of my reaction against the conditions of the backwoods life of the United States. One of the chief reasons for the inexpressible intensity of my feeling is doubtless that the nameless tortures which I saw inflicted a mere matter of routine upon women and children as such broke open the sepulchre in which I had long since buried my own sufferings at the hands of Evangelicalism and released these fetid, noxious and malignant spectres once more to prey upon my mind.

So much for the profane. For the aspirant I wrote the book called *De Lege Libellum,* otherwise called *The Sandal,* in which I analysed the Law as the source of light, life, love and liberty, and pronounced a panegyric upon it in each of these respects successively. For sustained sublimity of prose this book perhaps ranks next to those in which my pen was definitely and authentically inspired. (The criterion of such inspiration, by the way, is that in the case of an inspired book such as *Liber VII* [1] or *Liber LXV* [2] I do not dare to 'change as much as the style of a letter'.[3] I show, in fact, precisely that reverence for the author which should always be observed by the mere editor, and in this case, having not only the manuscript but my memory to assist me in case of any question arising as to the text in consequence of what my earliest tutor would doubtless have considered imperfections of caligraphy, there is fortunately no reason for anxiety as to the critical perfection of the text.)

The above remarks may appear strange as a preliminary to the statement that I regarded and still regard this book *The Sandal* as essentially an exercise in technique undertaken in order to fit myself to write *Liber Aleph, The Book of Wisdom or Folly,* which is beyond question a consummate masterpiece in its particular sphere in literature. It has always been my custom to practise with a rapier very thoroughly before fighting a duel. If occasionally these friendly bouts have resulted in a few deaths—the more the merrier!

Liber Aleph, The Book of Wisdom or Folly was intended to express the heart of my doctrine in the most deep and delicate dimensions. (Before using the word dimensions many considerations occurred to me. It is startling; that quality itself is not repugnant to its use in such a connection. Its use was followed by a discussion between myself and my cynocephalus,[4] who was herself struck by the singularity of the word, so much so, that I had to warn her not to spell it with two d's, and my explanations, though unsatisfactory, decided me to insert this note in the text of my autohagiography.)*

Liber Aleph is the most tense and intense book that I have ever composed. The thought is so concentrated and, if I may use the word, nervous, that both to write then, and to read now, involved and involves an almost intolerable strain. I remember how I used to sit at my desk night after night—it was the bitterest winter that had been known in New York for many years—but even if the central heating had been the flames of hell itself, I doubt whether I should have been warm. Night after night I sat, all through, rigid as a corpse, and icier; the whole of my life concentrated in two spots; the small section of my brain which was occupied in the work, and my right wrist and fingers. I remember with absolute clearness that my consciousness appeared to start from a perfectly dead forearm.

The book is written in prose, yet there is a formal circumscription more imminent than anything which would have been possible in poetry. I limited myself by making a point of dealing thoroughly with a given subject in a single page. It was an acute agony, similar to that of Asana, to write, and the effort removed me so far from normal human consciousness that there was something indicibly ghastly in its unnaturalness when I got into bed in full daylight in the hope of acquiring a particle of warmth from the complacent Camel.

I may now deal thoroughly with the complex and astounding incident which I promised to describe above. The Camel was a doctor of pharmacy, employed in pathological analysis, and later in manufacturing perfumery. She had never had any interest in Magick or any similar study, and I had not attempted to rouse it. One weekend she was lying on a mattress on the floor smoking opium, the apparatus having been lent us by a famous chiropractor who had bought it during a trip to Cuba, out of curiosity. I was sitting at my desk, working. To

---

* The content of the above passage, properly analysed, should serve as an immensely valuable indication of the methods employed by my mind. Note in particular my reliance on obscure allusion. The remark about spelling expects the reader to be instantly reminded of the story of the 'Something . . . Marquis of Queensberry' who, receiving the sympathetic condolences of a friend on having been mixed up with the trial of Oscar Wilde, replied that he regretted only one thing about the whole case; which was that on the libellous card, handed by him to the porter of the club, to be given to Oscar Wilde, he had spelt the word 'sodomite' with two 'd's'. [In point of fact, he wrote *somdomite*.—Editors.]

my surprised annoyance, the Camel suddenly began to have visions. I shut off my hearing in the way I have learnt to do; but after some five minutes babbling she pierced my defences by some remark concerning an egg under a palm tree. This aroused me instantly, for the last instruction given to myself and Soror Virakam [5] was to go to the desert and look for just that thing. I saw then a kind of continuity between those visions and these. It was as if the intelligence communicating were taking up the story at the point at which it had been dropped. Of course, it might have been a mere coincidence. But that point could be easily settled by cross-examination. I began to ask questions. The Camel said that someone, whom she called 'The Wizard', wished to communicate with me. I am not a spiritualist who accepts any message as of divine origin. I insist on knowing with whom I am talking, and on his showing such qualities of mind that the communication will benefit me.

Now, as it happened, I had a test question to my hand. I had taken the name Baphomet as my motto in the O.T.O. For six years and more I had tried to discover the proper way to spell this name. I knew that it must have eight letters, and also that the numerical and literal correspondences must be such as to express the meaning of the name in such a way as to confirm what scholarship had found out about it, and to clear up those problems which archaeologists had so far failed to solve. Here, then, was an ideal test of the integrity and capacity of the Camel's Wizard. I flung the question in his face. 'If you possess the superior knowledge which you claim, you can tell me how to spell Baphomet!' The Camel knew nothing of the Hebrew and little of the Greek. She had no idea that a conventional system existed by which one could check the accuracy of any given orthography. Her Wizard answered my question without hesitation. 'Wrong,' said I, 'there must be eight letters.' 'True,' he answered, 'there is an R at the end.' The answer struck me in the midriff. One theory of the name is that it represents the words βαφὴ μήτεος, the baptism of wisdom; another, that it is a corruption of a title meaning 'Father Mithras'. Needless to say, the suffix R supported the latter theory. I added up the word as spelt by the Wizard.[6] It totalled 729. This number had never appeared in my Cabbalistic working and therefore meant nothing to me. It however justified itself as being the cube of nine. The word κηφας, the mystic title given by Christ to Peter as the cornerstone of the Church, has this same value.[7] So far, the Wizard had shown great qualities!

He had cleared up the etymological problem and shown why the Templars should have given the name Baphomet to their so-called idol. Baphomet was Father Mithras, the cubical stone which was the corner of the Temple.

I therefore felt justified in concluding that the Wizard really possessed sufficient intelligence to make it worth my while to listen to him. I hastily recorded the dialogue to that point. My next question inquired his name. He replied 'Amalantrah'. I added this up. This time the result was conclusive. Its value is 729. Already he had shown me that I, in my office as Baphomet, was the rock on which the New Temple should be built, and he now identified himself with me through his own name being of equivalent value. There was however so far no link between the Order to which he belonged and the Great Order; 729 is not a significant number in the Cabbala of Thelema. But when I asked him to assign a mystic name to the Camel, he replied 'Ahitha' which adds to 555, an obvious correlative with my own number in the Great Order, 666. It defined, so to speak, the function of the Camel in that Order.

Striking as were these results, I maintained my sceptical method and proceeded to apply test after test. The Wizard never made the slightest mistake. Taking his answers as a whole, he made it mathematically probable to a degree approximating certainty as closely as the most exact physical equations that he spoke with conscious knowledge.

We began a series of interviews with him. There was what I may call a permanent background to the vision. He lived in a place as definite as an address in New York, and in this place were a number of symbolic images representing myself and several other adepts associated with me in my work. The character of the vision served as a guide to my relations with these people. More especially there were three women, symbolized as three scorpions of the symbolic desert which I was crossing in my mystic journey. It is not yet clear whether I dealt with these women as I should have done. One was Eva Tanguay, the supreme artist, whom I hymned in the April *International;* one, a married woman, a Russian aristocrat in exile, and one, a maiden, to whom the Wizard gave the mystic name of Wesrun.[8] This name can be spelt in two ways: one adding to 333, the number of Choronzon, Dispersion, Impotence and Death; the other to 888, the number of Redemption. It seemed that it was my task to save her as Parzifal saved Kundry. But as I say, I am not clear whether I did not fail completely in my dealings with all three women. I doubt whether I trusted the Wizard as I should have done. It may be that I made 'a great miss', the result of which has been to ruin my work temporarily.

Besides this regular visit to the place where the Wizard lives, it was my custom to ask his aid in the solution of any problems which occurred in the course of my regular working. On the night of February 24th, I happened to want to know whether I could use my name in the Great Order, TO ΜΕΓΑ ΘΗΡΙΟΝ, in conjunction with Hebrew letters. The Wizard replied, 'Yes.' I asked, 'Shall I use the whole name or ΘΗΡΙΟΝ alone?' He answered, 'ΘΗΡΙΟΝ alone.' I then spent some hours in trying to transliterate ΘΗΡΙΟΝ into Hebrew in such a way as to give a number which would mean something in my general Cabbalistic scheme. I failed completely! This is very remarkable in itself, I having had twenty years' experience of the art, and the possible spellings being very numerous. Ingenuity can nearly always find a more or less satisfactory orthography for any given combination of letters. However, I was completely baffled. I gave it up as a bad job, cursing Amalantrah heartily for having made me waste my time.

On Monday morning I went to the office of *The International*. It was a 'workless Monday', Dr Garwood having ordered that no office buildings should be heated on Monday for five weeks, on account of the coal famine. I stayed only a few minutes to look over my mail. On Tuesday I returned to the office, and found on my desk a letter addressed to Viereck and transferred by him to me to be answered. This letter had therefore arrived the day before and had been written in Bridgeport, Connecticut, on Saturday evening at the identical hour at which Amalantrah had told me that I could use a Hebrew spelling of ΘΗΡΙΟΝ in my work. The writer of the letter was one Samuel A. Jacob, a designer of Syrise and similar founts of type. He was an entire stranger to anyone in the office, as to myself. His letter concluded, 'Please inform your readers that I, Shmuel bar Aiwaz bie Yackou de Sherabad, have counted the number of The Beast; and it is the number of a man: Th = 400 R = 200 I = 10 V = 6 N = 50,' giving the spelling ThRIVN = 666. At the exact time, therefore, when the Wizard had told me that this could be done, a stranger in a distant town was actually writing the solution which baffled me. Observe that the preparation of this was the problem in my article 'The Revival of Magick' published three months earlier!

This incident in itself is sufficiently startling. On the theory that Amalantrah is what he claims to be it is quite natural and simple. Any other theory, such as coincidence, or telepathy outrages reason. But this was not all.

Besides his Americanized signature 'Samuel A. Jacob', he gave his true name: 'SHMUEL Bar AIWAZ bie YACKOU de SHERABAD'. I could hardly believe my eyes. Till that moment I had had no idea that Aiwass was anything but an artificial name, like Ahitha. I had tried to find a spelling for it, having never seen it written except in the English in *The Book of the Law,* but only heard it. I had decided on AIVAS = 78, the number of Mezla, the influence from the highest unity, and therefore suitable enough as the title of a messenger from Him. I wrote to Mr Jacob for the Hebrew spelling, which he gave as OIVZ, whose value is 93. The import of this discovery was terrific; 93 is the value of ΘΕΛΗΜΑ, the Word of the Law proclaimed by Aiwass, and of ΑΓΑΠΗ, Love, part of the interpretation of ΘΕΛΗΜΑ. It was also that of the Lost Word of freemasonry, which I had re-discovered, thus linking up the mysteries of the O.T.O. with those of the A∴A∴. 93 is also the number of the Secret Word of the Neophyte of A∴A∴, a word indicating symbolically the whole course of existence. It is in fact a completion of the ideas contained in the Sacred Word of the Hindus, AUM. It was to be discovered later that the Secret Key of *The Book of the Law* is the number 31, ⅓ of 93. There are three words, each of the value of 31 which represent perfectly the whole mystery of existence. That Aiwaz should have, so to speak, signed himself with His Law, was irrefutable proof of his existence.

I must add one cumulative proof which came to light only in 1923. *The Book of the Law* claims to express its ideas not by its literary meaning alone but by the actual letters of the manuscript. It had annoyed me—after the above demonstration—that in the manuscript the name was spelt AIWASS, which does not add to 93. But this year, reflecting that *The Book of the Law* is connected more with the Greek Cabbala than with the Hebrew, I transliterated AIWASS into Greek off-hand. Its value is 418! and this is the number of the Magical Formula of the Aeon. It represents the practice of the Book as 93 does the theory. It is now evident with what inconceivable ingenuity AIWAZ has arranged his expression. He is not content to give one spelling of his name, however potent; he gives two which taken together are not merely twice as significant as either alone, but more so, in a degree which is beyond me to calculate.

This incident with its many ramifications is perhaps the most remarkable thing that has ever happened to anybody. I was not only shown the knowledge and ingenuity required to choose a name for himself which will sum up my life and thought both in the past and in the future as also to include explanations of historical mysteries; but he seems able to arrange for people that I never hear of to exercise an intimate influence on my life at the exact moment when the effect will give the demonstration its highest possible dramatic value. Suppose, for instance, that Jacob had sent me his solution within a month of the publication of the problem. It would have been no more than an interesting contribution to the Cabbala. It is necessary to obtain a comprehensive idea of the facts of the relationship between him and myself as a whole in order to grasp the subtlety and strength of his plan and its execution.

Any man who studies the circumstances with intelligence will be forced to the hypothesis as to the nature of AIWAZ which I myself entertain. It is true that this hypothesis involves difficulties of its own; it implies a magical theory of the universe altogether incompatible with materialism. One might call it an Arabian Nights theory. But one must dismiss one's prejudice from the start. This theory, however antecedently absurd, is constantly bearing fruit of new facts and new discoveries. This after all is what science requires. I have already given a number of other instances where fresh facts confirm the old. For myself in particular the ultimate fact is that I have been able to govern my life quite satisfactorily year after year on the basis of this theory. My life, interpreted by it, is intelligible, and when guided by it, successful. Whenever I do anything reasonable I come a cropper, and if I were to attempt to explain the events of my career in any other way, I should be confronted by a piled chaos of utterly unintelligible absurdities.

The sale of *The International* left me stranded. War hysteria had reached its height. The British would not employ me, failing to understand or to trust. The Department of Justice, though warmly appreciative of my work, did not offer to pay me for it, nor did I ask them to do so. My stupid kingliness still stood in my way. I should have felt dishonoured by accepting payment for my patriotic service. All sources of income dried up completely. I therefore borrowed a canoe, tent and camp outfit from a friend and started up the Hudson on a Great Magical Retirement with two dollars and twenty-five cents as my total capital, no prospect of obtaining more when that was exhausted, and full confidence that the Secret Chiefs would supply my physical needs. It was my business to do their work and theirs to look after their servant.

This Magical Retirement proved of critical importance. A week's paddling put me in perfect physical and mental condition. I found an ideal solitude on Oesopus Island. The Camel spent the first weekend with me, bringing me a supply of canned provisions. I began at once to work on a new translation, with Commentary, of the *Tao Teh King*. This book, one of the oldest in existence, is surely one of the wisest. But all previous translations, however scholarly, had completely failed to convey the meaning of Lao Tzu. An uninitiated translator is bound to meet constantly with apparently nonsensical passages. One must know what the author is likely to mean by any given phrase, and this can only be done by a man who has intimate experience of the spiritual states and magical principles set forth. Otherwise, the translator is in the position of a scholar ignorant of football who should try to translate some slangy description of a cup tie. He will think that 'wing' has something to do with a bird and be puzzled as to how it got into the game; a 'hot shot' will set him thinking of the siege of Gibraltar, and the result of his labours will be a farrago of nonsense. Alternatively, realizing the general character of the text, he will wrench every passage to suit his own ideas on the subject. No one has understood what Lao Tzu meant by either Tao or Teh. I, possessing the keys to the Universal Cabbala, and also experience of the spiritual states which Lao Tzu is discussing, was able to produce a lucid and coherent version of the classic. Those who have seen my manuscript after bitter disappointment with previous translations, have instantly recognized the sublimity and wisdom of the Chinese Master.

86

I found that my long abstinence from magical practices had injured my powers. I resumed elementary drill and soon got back to my old form. For one thing, my protection against mosquitoes had worn off. I spent a night motionless, offering my body to them and concentrating on the thought that they were equally divine with myself, I forced myself to love them, so that in union with them the apparent differences between us might vanish in ecstasy. I compelled my body to accept, to welcome and even to long for their bites, as being acts of love whereby I nourished their lives. In the morning, though badly bitten all over, there was no inflammation whatever; and from that time on they never bit me at all.

I soon recovered the powers of Pratyahara [1] and Dharana.[2] My mind became still; the impact of impressions ceased to obsess me, I became free of the illusion of the reality of material things. All events became equally indifferent, exquisite phrases in an eternal symphony. (Imagine listening to Beethoven with the prepossession that C is a good note and F a bad one; yet this is exactly the standpoint from which all uninitiates contemplate the universe. Obviously, they miss the music.)

I soon began to acquire the Magical Memory, to recall my past incarnations. I refuse to assert any theory of what this really means. All memory is a re-awakening of ancient impressions. What I was really doing was penetrating to the deeper layers of my unconscious self. When, therefore, I remember my life as Cagliostro or Pope Alexander the Sixth, I am quite willing to interpret the experience as a dreamlike imagination, a dramatization of certain deeper elements in my character. I may, however, argue on the other side, that my present life is, almost equally, an artistic representation of my nature. There are also some fairly strong arguments for the actuality of such memories. Events in the past sometimes throw light on the present. For instance, when I came to remember what had happened to me in Rome, Naples and Paris, I understood certain obscure instinctive feelings about those cities which had always been unintelligible,* and were in direct conflict with my conscious ideas about them. I will summarize as follows:

Shortly before the time of Mohammed, I was present at a Council of Masters. The critical question was the policy to be adopted in order to help humanity. A small minority, including myself, was hot for positive action; definite movements were to be made; in particular, the mysteries were to be revealed. The majority, especially the Asiatic Masters, refused even to discuss the proposal. They contemptuously abstained from voting, as if to say, 'Let the youngsters learn their lesson.' My party therefore carried the day and various Masters were appointed to undertake different adventures. Mohammed, Luther, Adam Weishaupt,[3] the man we knew as Christian Rosencreutz, and many servants of science, were thus chosen. Some of these movements have succeeded more or less; some have failed entirely. In my present incarnation I have met several such Masters, who, having failed, are now building up again their shattered forces. My own task was to bring oriental wisdom to Europe and to restore paganism in a purer form. I was involved in the catastrophe which overtook the Order of the Temple, and as Alexander the Sixth, failed in my task of crowning the Renaissance, through not being wholly purified in my personal character. (An appropriately trivial spiritual error may externalize as the most appalling crimes.)

Before this Council, there is a long gap of complete amnesia. I merely remember that I was Ko Hsuen, a disciple of Lao Tzu, the author of the *King Khang King*, the classic of Purity; which, by the way, I translated into English verse during this Retirement. All I know is that somehow or other I made a 'great miss', forfeited my Mastership, and had to climb the ladder again from the bottom. It is the shame and agony of this which have prevented me from facing the memory—so far.

Almost every day I found myself in some new trance, each of course perfect in its own way, and each of a depth and sublimity which makes description impossible to attempt; yet

---

* Revising this chapter, in Tunis, my Ape reminded me of how much of these past lives was spent in Sicily and North Africa; and that, when my present life came to an end (of a sort; all the forces which had till then acted upon me having been worked out) I drifted quite aimlessly to that part of the world, as if my unconsciousness, its labours accomplished, had automatically turned its face towards home!

all the time it seemed to me that each trance was no more than the letter of a word, as if some truth were being revealed which could only be expressed piecemeal. The crown of these trances was an angelic vision such as I had never before enjoyed. The communication was perfect on all planes of being; and this completeness conferred a sense of reality altogether beyond previous experience. It was the difference between meeting a friend face to face, and trying to reconstruct his personality from letters, photographs, gramophone records, memories and cherished flowers.

It may be that this vision was granted me in order to fortify me for the climax of my Retirement. On September 5th, my record contains the following entry.

I feel that I am more likely to be able to convey some hint of the colossal character of this revelation if I simply quote the broken staggering words in which I wrote it down at the time. As will be seen, I did not dare to write what it actually was, but I remember at this moment how I had to invoke the deep-seated habit of years to get courage to drag myself to my diary. I felt like a soldier wounded to death, scrawling in his own blood the horrifyingly disastrous information which he has lost his life in seeking.

5.00 p.m. The meditation of this afternoon resulted in an initiation so stupendous that I dare not hint at its Word. It is the supreme secret of a Magus, and it is so awful that I tremble even now—two hours later and more—2.20 p.m. was the time—as I write concerning it. In a single instant I had the Key to the whole of the Chinese wisdom. In the light —momentary glimpse as it was—of this truth, all systems of religion and philosophy became absolutely puerile. Even the Law appears no more than a curious incident. I remain absolutely bewildered, blinded, knowing what blasting image lies in this shrine. It baffles me to understand how my brother Magi, knowing this, ever went on.

I had only one foreshadowing of this Vision of Jupiter— for so I may call it!—and that was a Samadhi which momentarily interrupted my concentration of Sammasati. This can only be described vaguely by saying that I obtained a reconciliation of two contraries of which 'There is a discrimination between good and evil' is one.

This experience has shaken me utterly; it has been a terrible struggle to force myself to this record. The secret comes along the Path of Aleph to Chokmah.[4] I could write it plainly in a few words of one syllable, and most people would not even notice it.* But it has might to hurl every Master of the Temple into the Abyss, and to fling every adept of the Rose Cross down to the Qliphoth. No wonder One said that the *Book T* [5] was in ashes in the Urn of a Magus! I can't see at all how it will affect me at present. Even the Way of the Tao looks idiotic—but then of course that's what it is! So I suppose that's it, all right. And its freedom, in an utterly fascinating and appalling sense, is beyond my fiercest conception.

An experience of this intensity demands a period of repose, no less than a boat race or any other form of intense effort. The adepts have always insisted on due preparation for any initiation. As *The Book of the Law* says, 'Wisdom says: be strong! Then canst thou bear more joy.' I accordingly broke up my camp after a few days' holiday from magical work, and returned to New York.

The next period is strangely confused. It was as if I were left in the Desert [6] with no idea of direction and surrounded by a series of mirages. Innumerable people came into my life and passed out again, without leaving any trace.

The fact was that none of the people appointed by Amalantrah to various tasks were willing to undertake them. It may well be that this was due to a lack of real faith on my part. The communications from the Wizard had become confused and even contradictory. I had failed to understand his plan and to acquiesce unreservedly in it. This weakness of mine naturally reacted on the other people concerned.

Only one clear duty lay before me. The five years of silence which were to follow the publication of number 10 of *The Equinox* were at an end. I therefore devoted myself to planning another ten numbers, beginning at the spring equinox of 1919. I had an immense amount of material ready for publication. The one critical omission was the Comment on *The Book of the Law,* which I had constantly shirked rewriting. I pulled myself together and went down to Atlantic City for the purpose of getting this done. My idea was to write it inspirationally; which is correct. The only drawback was that the inspiration was forced and feeble. I know now that the writing of this Comment must be a definite miracle, parallel with that of the production of the Book itself.

I stumbled on through the Desert somehow. Even today I

---

* I find that I wrote it down plainly seventeen years ago! But I had no conception of its terror—one must be a Magus to get that!

hardly understand the object of the ordeals of this journey. At the beginning of the next Chokmah day I found myself on the edge of the oasis which I was to make my home. I had identified myself with the god of my Grade of Magus, Tahuti, the Lord of the Word, and I was invested accordingly with the attributes proper to him. The last of the officers in my initiation was the Ape of Thoth. This creature translates into action his thought or, in other words, is the instrument through which his idea assumes sensible form. This Ape became my permanent companion. At this moment, she is beside me in a bathing house at Marsa Plage near Tunis, writing these words.

Tahuti being the Lord of Speech, I published number 1 of volume III of *The Equinox* on March 21st, 1919. I arranged for it to contain something like a complete programme of my proposed Operation to initiate, emancipate and relieve mankind.

The first item is a 'Hymn to Pan',[7] which I believe to be the most powerful enchantment ever written. Next, after explaining the general idea of my work, I issued a curriculum, classifying the books whose study should give a complete intellectual knowledge of all subjects which bear on the Great Work.

The book of *The Sandal* presents a lyrical interpretation of the Law of Thelema. This is followed by the first instalment of 'The Magical Record of my Son', Frater O.I.V.V.I.O.,[8] to show how in actual practice a fairly normal man came to attain to be a Master of the Temple. Every pertinent detail of his career from the start is clearly set forth.

The latter half of the volume is devoted to explaining the principles of the O.T.O. showing how men and women may work in groups publicly, and giving outlines of a social system free from the disastrous defects of our present civilization. I republished the Ritual of the Gnostic Mass in this section. The supplement consists of Blavatsky's *Voice of the Silence* with a very full commentary. My purpose was to bring back Theosophists to the true principles of their founder; principles which have been shamefully abandoned by her successors— to the utter ruin of the society, either as a nursery for adepts or as a civilizing influence in barbaric Christiandom.

During this winter, I was approached by a powerful body of high grade freemasons in Detroit. They knew only too well that their Order was at the best tomfoolery; and, for the rest, anything all the way down to fraud and blackmail. They desired the light which they knew me to possess. I offered to reorganize freemasonry, to replace the pomposities and banalities of their ragbag of rituals by a simple, lucid and coherent system.

I soon saw that any effort would be waste of time. Even their compact group was torn by bitter jealousies. Their leader, for all his fine talk, had only one real desire—to communicate with his dead wife, a silly smirking society waxwork, a pink-tea princess! Their second string was a doctor, who spent sleepless nights sweating with shame and sentimentality in an agony of anxiety as to whether it was his duty to get divorced in order to marry a white-haired spinster, half-crazy with the pain of cancer, with whom he had no sexual relation at all, but an overwhelming obsession that she was his sister-soul, his mystic mate, his psychic partner and his Ouija Wife. A third, illiterate and bigoted, was a mere spat of ignorant argument that the signs of the zodiac had somehow got mixed up, apparently owing to some confusion about the precedence of the twelve apostles! The only member of the group who had even a smattering of education, as we understand it in Europe, was more than half insane on the subject of sex. He had got it into his head that a secret method of managing such matters existed, the possessor of which could perform all sorts of miracles, from curing consumption to making a million dollars. He spent his life hunting for books on sexual Magick; and, knowing that I was in possession of the secret he sought, spent a whole night shivering in the corridor with his ear to the keyhole of my bedroom, in the hope of hearing something that would give him a hint. He even tried to use his own mistress to spy on me: when she came from my room, he started to browbeat and bully her into giving the minutest details of her adventure!

The best of the crowd was a young doctor who had sufficient sense to see how stupid the rest were, to disdain the bluff of the advertising adepts, and to realize that genuine magicians were necessarily gentlemen and scholars. He felt himself utterly lost in the darkness of Detroit, but despaired of mending the matter by setting forth to seek the Graal without guidance. He was so fixed in doubt and distrust that even the truth, soiled by his suspicion, could not quell the whispers of the demons of denial. They persistently persuaded his shaking soul that the weeds of falsehood grew so rank that never a seed of truth might find a space to shoot. Thus, doubting the whole world, he had learnt to doubt himself. His will was sodden with scepticism. He could never make up his mind to do anything definite. The man had many great qualities, but the dollar-snatching charlatans that pullulate in America had driven him to drift and potter. He did not even understand that he might have saved his soul by devoting himself to the shallowest quack in Chicago, daring death and damnation for the hollowest humbug that ever wrote himself Rosicrucian without knowing how to spell it. Pluck would have pulled him through in the long run; as Blake said, 'If the fool would persist in his folly he would become wise.'

It did not take me long to see that the real object of this gang was to exploit me. They wanted something for nothing; instead I was the only man to profit—I gained the knowledge of the astonishing variety of dirty tricks that men could play under the mask of friendship and respect.

But I was immune to the virus. I possessed not only something, but everything, and was only too eager to give it for nothing. I naturally became an object of the deepest suspicion. Unable to comprehend honour, unselfishness and generosity, my frank loyalty and royal largesse baffled their brains. They felt sure that it concealed some super-subtle scheme for swindling them or getting them into my power. They thought they knew that the more noble an action appeared, the deeper the deceit and the dirtier the design beneath it. I adhered to simple straightforward sense. I told the truth without a thought of what might happen in consequence. It was inconceivable to them that I, knowing so much, should yet be innocent. They knew me poor. It was strange indeed that I never tried to make money, or even accepted it when offered! The result of all this was that I, doing my utmost to enlighten them, deepened their darkness. I simplified and emphasized the truth; they merely floundered further into falsehood.

I tried my hardest to manifest myself, to explain my point of view, my mental methods, my morals, manners, motives and magical objectives. I merely became the more mysterious. They could never guess how I would act in any circumstances. My purpose being single, it was incomprehensible to their complex confusion of cravings. My 'yes' appalled them—it was such a sinister way of saying 'no'; and when I said 'no' they sweated and swooned with fear of what I might mean by so satanic a way of saying 'yes'. I kept on smiling; I became silent; they saw me as the Sphinx. They began to quarrel among themselves; scandal, divorce suits, bankruptcies and every sort of nastiness followed. My 'son', who had lived in Detroit for some months trying to teach them the elements of sense and decency, left them to stew in the stinking soup they had cooked, and went off to Chicago. Both he and I learnt a priceless lesson in our dealings with these demoniacs. We have that to thank for the steady, quiet, natural success of his campaign in Chicago.

One cannot deal with Americans on the principles which seem inevitable in Europe. One often sees a placard in offices, 'Come in without knocking. Go out the same way.' They would rather not hear unpleasant truths. What! Shoot a sleeping sentinel? Nope; rush the chloroform in case he wakes! They have learnt the psychological fact that confidence is a real asset. A man works best when he feels he is sure to succeed. A fear of failure palsies every faculty. The vogue of Christian Science, and countless cults for drawing in dollars by wishing one had them, persuading oneself that somehow or other they will arrive, scoring every success, forgetting every failure, shutting one's eyes to unpleasant facts, and interpreting every bit of good luck as a triumph beyond the power of trumpets to tell—a token of the intense interest taken by the Almighty in His favourite child—this course of conduct, though its more reasonable practitioners are ready to admit that it is rant and rubbish, is pursued as part of a calculated policy. They are ready to fool themselves in order to take advantage of the stimulating effect of optimism.

The other side of the medal is this: when any man points to any fact that shakes this opium serenity, checks this cocaine self-assurance, that man takes a chance of a free ride out of town on a rail. The spirit of criticism is detested and dreaded. It is easy to understand why this is. The States have been won from the wilderness by a system which demanded courage and clear sight from the pioneers; but once the trail was blazed, the rest of the work was done on a basis of credit which a European banker would consider utterly reckless gambling. Everyone, from the farmer and merchant to the manufacturer and financier, entered into a tacit agreement to bet that any given enterprise would succeed. As the natural resources were there, while luck decreed that the commonwealth should not have to face any overwhelming obstacle, the gamblers have won. It is obvious that any man in an outpost besieged by nature (such as is every new settlement outside New England, the Atlantic coast and the old settlements in the south) was really a traitor if he said, however truthfully, anything which might daunt the spirit of his comrades. Those men won out through sheer ignorance of the chances against them, stolid stupidity which blinded them to their desperate plight and bestial insensibility to the actual hardships which they had to endure. It was criminal to insist on the existence of evils for which there was no remedy.

This spirit has persisted, though its utility is past. It has become a fixed feature of the religion of the country. It was the deadliest delusion that I had to meet. Spiritual attainment, magical development, any line of work soever whose material is subtler than the sensible world, demands (as the first condition of success) the most severe spirit of scepticism, the most scientific system of research. For immediately one becomes aware of impressions and ideas which are not subject to the criticism of sensory perception, they are inevitably influenced by the individual characteristics of the observer and the distortion is difficult to detect because, until one is very advanced indeed, one is not aware of the aberration caused by the error of the instrument. Even in the world of sense, similar troubles occur. To a man who is colour-blind, the red light is 'really' green—beyond his power to make any correction, because the source of his error is in the instrument of sight itself. He might well say, 'But if, as you tell me, this green lamp is red, how do I know that it is a lamp, not a tiger? I have only my eyes to depend on.'

I found it impossible to persuade even the most intelligent people who came to me to take the first step—that of clearing the ground of their minds of every preconceived idea. They yearned for me to fill them up to the neck with any ridiculous rubbish that flattered their vanity, fed their folly, doped their dread of death and damnation, and inflated their idle fancies, intoxicated their inane ideals. I simply hammered away with cold common sense. I drenched them with douches of doubt. I pricked their bladders of bluff; I tapped their dropsical sentimentality and applied a clyster of candour to the constipation of their respectability. By this simple expedient I drove them all away. I made myself enemies everywhere. The crowd of charlatans were particularly annoyed. They were eager to hail me as their master and even to give me the lion's share of the swag. It hurt them horribly when they found I would not play the game, or even take the trouble to hail them to my barn door. Every people has the prophets it deserves; the credulous cowardly ice-cream-soda idealist is best left with the illiterate Illuminati, rascally Rosicrucians, magpie mediums, parrot psychics, and cockroach clairvoyants with whom they feel at home. One cannot initiate imbeciles.

My adventures in Detroit came as the climax which confirmed the conclusions I had already formed from casual conversations and correspondence with a fairly large and varied selection of would-be disciples. Only in rare individuals could I detect a trace of genuine aspiration, of the ambition to attain, either for their own sake or for that of others, in any allowable sense. They wanted more social success. Nobody seemed to have the faintest idea of what is really meant by knowledge and power. Some seemed anxious to help the progress of humanity; but here again, the wish was partly a puff-ball of pride, partly a maudlin sentiment such as one finds in servants' hall novelettes.

The ignorance of all, without exception, was simply without limit. It was rare to find a man who knew so much as the names of the most famous classics. Their ignorance was not even accessible to instruction. It was armour-plated, and adorned with a bigoted belief in the most blatant balderdash. I met the heads of four flourishing cults who claimed to be Rosicrucians. Not one of them had so much as heard of *The Fama Fraternitatis* [9] or *The Chymical Marriage*.[10] The most famous astrologer in the States, who makes fifty thousand dollars a year, did not know that the solar system was essentially a disk. She thought the planets were stuck at random in the sky like so many plums in a suet pudding. In thirty years of daily use of the Ephemeris, she had never observed that Neptune takes fifteen years or so to pass through a sign of the zodiac, and told her clients that Neptune being in such and such a sign at their birth, they must possess various curious powers. When I pointed out that this applied to everyone born in three lustres, she was at first bewildered, then incredulous; and, proof being produced, angry and insulting.

These were the highest class of merchants of Magick. The majority of writers on the subject bleat on from blunder to blunder. I met no single man in the United States in five years who had any idea what Yoga actually is, much less of the metaphysical theories on which it is based. Its objects and methods were either understood so vaguely as to be a mere variation on Sunday School sob stuff, or distorted by dreams of the dollar or the dread of disease; their information being based on some book purporting to be the secret instruction of a particularly prominent yogi, but in fact the illiterate rubbish of an unsuccessful horse doctor from Idaho who could hardly find India on the map—even if you offered him a dollar to do it.

This illiterature is distributed indiscriminately; a vast venomous vomit! There being no background of education, no standard of criticism, the reader has no means of distinguishing between the best and the worst. He has no means of forming a groundwork on which his mind might build. It is impossible for the European to understand the helplessness of these people. We have definite principles in our minds by which, consciously or unconsciously, we judge with fair correctness of things which may be in a sense entirely strange to us.

For instance, suppose that I am unable to read a single word of Russian. I am nevertheless able to get a fair general idea of the probable character of the contents of any book by applying what I may call Sherlock Holmes methods. Obviously, I might be deceived. Gogol's masterpiece might be badly printed on rotten paper and defaced with vile illustrations in order to fool me. A series of such traps would teach me to distrust my judgment.

Now, this is just the position in which the American finds himself. He has been sold so many pups that he flinches when he hears 'the watchdog's honest bark'. He has been told, till his ears are nigh bursting, every sort of falsehood, even a truth being exaggerated until its original nature hardly matters, on every conceivable subject.

From earliest infancy, every American citizen is trained in 'make-believe'. That is why *Huckleberry Finn* is the one masterpiece of character drawing that America has produced. The American is at heart acutely ashamed of his defects. His ideal of perfection is intensely dear to him, and I am the last person to blame him for refusing to admit that its attainment is impossible. But his nerves are constantly raw from realizing in his inmost heart that he is, after all, lacking in all sorts of ways.

In one way or another practically every American is devoured by this demon of discontent, which is by no means the species which we call divine. The yearning of the poet to surpass all other singers, his rage at the resistance of the language to his rapture, have their root in his absolute trust in and worship of himself.

I cried, like Elijah: This is no country for the poet Aleister Crowley, or the adept, To Mega Therion, whose hope to help his fellow men has this one anchor: Truth shall make you free!

87

However, now that we have been sufficiently surprised and shocked to satisfy our feeling of what is due to ourselves, we may as well realize that what in Europe is crudely called falsehood is in America a virtue without which the structure of society would collapse. Roughly speaking, they are the same size as we are; but their environment is so much more huge and hostile that it would crush them out of existence unless they persuaded themselves that they were very much bigger than we are. Our total ignorance of American conditions, our failure to understand that what we regard as fundamental truths and virtues, may be to them mere prejudices, is creating a chasm between the continents into which civilization itself is only too likely to fall.

I was simply too young, ignorant and bigoted to make any impression on the United States. The real work which I accomplished in my five years was the unconscious preparation for my real mission, which is not a matter of flags and trumpets, but of silent growth in darkness. This preparation was now practically complete. With the appearance of the cynocephalus [1] my journey through the Desert had reached its last stage. I went on struggling for some months to get things done, not understanding that I was attempting what was not impossible but undesirable. But at least my impotence was only too evident; and I returned to Europe in December. Even at the time, I felt more or less clearly that I had come to a definite turning-place in my career. It is still difficult to interpret the next period, if only because, for one thing, it is incomplete, and for another, too close to see in proper perspective. But so far as I understand it at all, it seems as if my work were to construct a model of a new civilization to replace that which we see before our eyes reeling towards catastrophe.

For the next three years, then, I was to build, as it were, an ark of refuge, in which that which was worth saving from the Aeon of the Dying God might be in safety while the floods covered the face of the earth; and it is really not for me but for history to record and interpret the events of my life following my return to England at the end of 1919. I will only say that my main idea had been to found a community on the principles of *The Book of the Law,* to form an archetype of a new society. The main ethical principle is that each human being has his own definite object in life. He has every right to fulfil this purpose, and none to do anything else. It is the business of the community to help each of its members to achieve this aim; in consequence all rules should be made, and all questions of policy decided, by the application of this principle to the circumstances. We have thus made a clean sweep of all the rough and ready codes of convention which have characterized past civilizations. Such codes, besides doing injustice to the individual, fail by being based on arbitrary assumptions which are not only false, but insult and damage the moral sense. Their authority rested on definitions of right and wrong which were untenable. As soon as Nietzsche and others demonstrated that fact, they lost their validity. The result has been that the new generation, demanding a reason for acting with ordinary decency, and refusing to be put off with fables and sophistries, has drifted into anarchy. Nothing can save the world but the universal acceptance of the Law of Thelema as the sole and sufficient basis of conduct. Its truth is self-evident. It is as susceptible of the strictest mathematical demonstration as any other theorem in biology. It admits that each member of the human race is unique, sovereign and responsible only to himself. In this way it is the logical climax of the idea of democracy. Yet at the same time it is the climax of aristocracy by asserting each individual equally to be the centre of the universe. When, therefore, it comes to the question of the relations between groups, those truths whose utterance has smashed all theories of government lose their destructive qualities. The Law of Thelema does not require the individual to behave himself because God set the squire and the parson to boss him. In obeying the law of his country he is fighting for his own hand. Modern social unrest is largely due to misunderstanding of the Law of Thelema. The workman has learnt to covet motor cars and portfolios, which he was not born to have. When he gets them, he becomes still more unhappy—a fish out of water—and ruins the community into the bargain. Under the Law of Thelema, all false ideals and incongruous ambitions will be driven away as delusions. The first principle of moral education will be the biological truth that the health and happiness of a cell depends upon the fulfilment of those functions which are natural to it. Intellectual education, which is not education at all, is the basis of our present critical position. It has, so to speak, insisted on each cell becoming conscious. The result has been to make society hyper-aesthetic. Those elements which were satisfying themselves and supporting the total organism have been forced to suffer; they have been rendered conscious of their apparent inferiority to other elements. So, what between artificial anguish and false ambition for impossible attainments, they have become intensely painful to themselves and unable to perform their proper function; to their own ruin and that of the state.

The Book of the Law was given to mankind chiefly in order to provide it with an impeccable principle of practical politics. I regard this as more important for the moment than its function as a guide in its evolution towards conscious godhead. It is only while writing this chapter that I have come to understand the real purport of the Book, and it is evident that the Secret Chiefs have prevented me from putting in the clutch, as I may say, from releasing the enormous energy of the New Aeon, until on the one hand, I had become capable of directing that energy wisely, and on the other, until civilization had reached the crisis in which my interference would save the race from crashing into chaos.

For three years I have laboured to construct an Abbey of Thelema in Sicily on the principles of the Law, so that I might have experience of the problems of government. Those years have taught me how to deal with all classes of people of all ages and races. It had been practically proved to me that the intelligent application of the Law of Thelema solves all social problems, and that its violation is immediately and automatically avenged. I am now getting ready to write the Comment on *The Book of the Law* as it bade me do. I had stupidly supposed this Comment to be a scholarly exposition of the Book, an elucidation of its obscurities and a demonstration of its praeterhuman origin. I understand at last that this idea is nonsense. The Comment must be an interpretation of the Book intelligible to the simplest minds, and as practical as the Ten Commandments. For the time is at hand when the bankruptcy of all theories of religion, all systems of government, will become obvious to all. Already we see the corruption of tsarism collapsing in the chaos of communism. We see that communism is utterly unable to put its principles into practice, being in fact a desperate despotism which is bound to break down even more completely than the system which it replaced, because of the internal conflict between its principles and its performances. We see the paralysis of parliamentary government. In Italy, for instance, those very classes who naturally respect the law and the constitution have acquiesced in the usurpation of power by the chief of a gang of banditti, simply on his promise to put an end to the insecurity of exercising power because uninspired by any principle of action sufficiently rigid to contend with circumstances.

It is evident to all serious thinkers that the only hope of saving mankind from a catastrophe so complete that the very name of civilization will perish is in the appearance of a new religion.

The Law of Thelema fulfils the necessary conditions. It is not limited by ethnological, social, religious or linguistic barriers. Its metaphysical basis is strictly scientific. Its principle is single, simple and self-evident. It does not deny human nature or demand impossible virtues. It offers to every individual the fullest satisfaction of his true aspirations; and it supplies a justification for all types of political systems beyond the criticisms which have undermined all previous theories of government. There is no need for the fraud of divine right or the cant of democracy. The right of the ruler to rule depends solely upon the scientific proof of his fitness to do so, and this proof is capable of confirmation by the evidence of the experience that his measures really result in enabling each individual in his jurisdiction to fulfil his own peculiar function as freely as possible.

In many respects, no doubt, the Law of Thelema is revolutionary. It insists on the absolute sovereignty of the individual within the limits of his proper function. And this principle will be resented by all those who like to interfere with other people's business. The battle will rage most fiercely around the question of sex. Hardly any one is willing to allow others their freedom on this point. Sometimes it is a personal matter; false vanity makes men try to enslave those whom they desire. They cannot understand 'there is no bond that can unite the divided but love', and they outrage others in every way in order to obtain the outward show of affection. It is the most hideous error conceivable, yet nearly all men make it, and nine tenths of the misery caused by wrong sexual relations is due to this determination to enslave the soul of another. It seems impossible to make men see what to me is obvious; that the only love worth having or indeed worthy of the name is the spontaneous sympathy of a free soul. Social conventions which trammel love are either extensions of this stupid selfishness, or expressions of the almost universal shame which results from false ideas on the subject. Mankind must learn that the sexual instinct is in its true nature ennobling. The shocking evils which we all deplore are principally due to the perversions produced by suppressions. The feeling that it is shameful and the sense of sin cause concealment, which is ignoble, and internal conflict which creates distortion, neurosis, and ends in explosion. We deliberately produce an abscess, and wonder why it is full of pus, why it hurts, why it bursts in stench and corruption. When other physical appetites are treated in this way, we find the same phenomenon. Persuade a man that hunger is wicked, prevent him satisfying it by eating whatever food suits him best, and he soon becomes a crazy and dangerous brute. Murder, robbery, sedition and many meaner crimes come of the suppression of the bodily need of nourishment.

The Book of the Law solves the sexual problem completely. Each individual has an absolute right to satisfy his sexual instinct as is physiologically proper for him. The one injunction is to treat all such acts as sacraments. One should not eat as the brutes, but in order to enable one to do one's will. The same applies to sex. We must use every faculty to further the one object of our existence.

The sexual instinct thus freed from its bonds will no more be liable to assume monstrous shapes. Perversion will become as rare as the freaks in a dime museum.

I have insisted on this because my experience in the Abbey of Thelema demonstrated the possibility of emancipating humanity from this obsession. At first and in the case of newcomers, the familiar troubles threatened our harmony. But by sticking to the Law, by training ourselves to treat our sexual life as a strictly personal matter, we abolished jealousy, intrigue and all the other evils usually connected with it. We eliminated quarrels, spitefulness, back-biting and the rest.

So far so good. But the gods had a surprise in store for me. I had rather expected that by releasing and encouraging the instinct it would loom larger in our lives. The exact contrary was the case. In healthy people this instinct is not particularly predominant. The importance of the subject, its omnipresence, is due to the constant irritation set up by its suppression. We are always thinking of it, like an Anglo-Indian of his liver. In the abbey we removed the sources of irritation, with the result that it slipped back into its proper physiological proportion, into serenity and silence. We almost forgot its existence. It began to surprise us when the sexual symbols which we had exhibited in the abbey, so that familiarity might breed forgetfulness, excited strangers. A man who is either stimulated or shocked by an obscene photograph is just as much of an invalid as one whose mouth waters at the sight of a cookery book.

Economic relations, again, were solved by the Law. Whatever funds we had—and we experienced all conditions from absolute want of the barest necessities of life to overflowing abundance—were regarded as means to enable each of us equally to do his or her will. Whatever anyone needed in his work was provided without a moment's grudging. None of us hankered after anything unnecessary to our work. We had found out and fixed in our minds that all such possessions, however delightful as new toys, were in the long run a nuisance. Whatever is not ultimately useful is a source of distraction and anxiety. It gets in one's way. It is like having to live with someone whom one does not love. We thus got rid of that senseless envy which embitters life by filling the mind with perverse cravings for things neither good nor bad in themselves, things fruitful of pleasure and profit to the people to whom they properly belong, but a source of misery to oneself, yet desired and hugged by the foolish who have not sense enough to see that what the mass of men imagine they want on the evidence of newspapers and salesmen may bring to themselves nothing but disappointment.

We accordingly found in the abbey that happiness and peace which comes from contentment. We each had all we wanted; and nobody made himself wretched by wanting something belonging to somebody else merely because it was in itself beautiful or convenient. It should be clear to the stupidest statesman that the economic problem can be solved on these lines, and that any other principles are wasteful as well as irrational. The world is bankrupt today chiefly because well-meaning philanthropists have tried to make people happy by loading them with what they believe to be benefits because they are so to themselves.

'The mind is improved by reading.' We therefore insist on everyone learning to read, with the result that their minds have been unsettled, clouded, confused and filled with falsehood by cheap fiction, sensational nonsense and deliberately dishonest propaganda. We praise the dressmakers of Paris and the tailors of London till we persuade the poor to deny themselves comfort in order to imitate the leaders of fashion. The logical error is essentially this unfitness which violates the Law of Thelema.

In the abbey each of us respected the will of the others as absolutely as they respected his. It was nobody's business to inquire what the will of another might be. And so the total energy of each of us was perfectly free to achieve its own end, sure that no one would interfere, and that he could count on the moral support of the rest to assist him. He therefore saw that in giving his own support to the abbey he was helping himself. He did not have to be threatened with hell or urged to be altruistic. Society has always been asked to regulate its actions either on grounds which everyone knows in his heart to be absurd, or on motives which nobody really accepts. The Law of Thelema avows and justifies selfishness; it confirms the inmost conviction of each one of us that he is the centre of the cosmos. Previous prophets have invariably tried to dodge this truth as making all social systems impossible. Now, for the first time, we can build practically every variety of social structure on this fact. All laws, customs and co-operative efforts can be constructed by the application of this principle for the conditions of environment. And all such structures will be stable, being free from the flaw which has been the bane of all previous systems. The theocracies of antiquity broke down as soon as their theory was challenged by science. Divine right met with disaster immediately that its absurdity became apparent, so that humanity will never repeat the experiment; despite the fact that in many cases the absurd axiom led to the greatest prosperity. Social systems founded upon philosophy have failed even more frightfully, for the premisses of the syllogism were false. It was always implied that man as such possessed various virtues which are in reality only found in a few individuals.

In the New Aeon, each man will be a king, and his relation to the state will be determined solely by considerations of what is most to his advantage. The worker will support a strong government as his best protection from foreign aggression and seditious disturbance instead of thinking it tyrannical. Everyone, whatever his ambtion, will feel that he can rely on the whole force of the state to assist him; for all ambitions alike will be respected by all, with the single proviso that they shall not tend to restrict the equal right of the rest. No man will be ashamed of himself, and so be forced into concealment and hypocrisy, while at the same time having his idea distorted into monstrous shapes of disease by the pressure of public opinion.

Of course (in practice) many people, perhaps the majority, will not accept the Law of Thelema. We found that life in the abbey with its absolute freedom was too severe a strain on those who were accustomed to depend on others. The responsibility of being truly themselves was too much for them; but sooner or later, without any action on our part, without any quarrel or ostensible reason, they found themselves ejected into their 'previous condition of servitude'. *The Book of the Law* anticipates this: 'The slaves shall serve.' The bulk of humanity, having no true will, will find themselves powerless. It will be for us to rule them wisely. We must secure their happiness and train them for ultimate freedom by setting them tasks for which their nature fits them. In the past, the mob without will or mind have been treated without sense or scruple; a mistake socially, economically and politically, no less than from the humanitarian point of view. We must remember that each man and woman being a star, it is our duty to maintain the order of nature by seeing to it that his orbit is correctly calculated. The revolutions and catastrophes with which history is crammed are invariably due to the rulers having failed to find fitting functions for the people. The obvious result has been social discontent ending in the refusal of the cells to perform their work in the organism.

So-called education (on which countless millions are squandered with the sole result of unsettling and unfitting the vast majority of its victims for their work in the world) becomes inexpensive, efficient and profitable when the Law of Thelema dictates its principles. The very word means 'leading out' of each child the faculties which he naturally possesses. The present system deliberately discourages the development of individuality and deforms minds by forcing them to perform functions for which they were not designed. In the abbey, our plan was to watch the children to discover in what direction they wanted to develop, having given them the greatest possible variety of facts from which to choose. We helped them in every way to carry out their choice, but refrained from any efforts to persuade them to pursue any line of study, however necessary it might seem to ourselves.

Extending this principle to the world at large, my plan would be to classify children in infancy according to the subtle indications afforded by their gestures and reactions to various stimuli. Any child who showed a desire to read and write would be given every possible encouragement altogether irrespective of social and other considerations. Similar principles would apply to other activities: draughtsmanship, building, mechanics and the rest. He would be made to understand that the fulfilment of his ambitions would depend on his willing submission to discipline, the conquest of idleness and so on. But unless and until a child showed real discontent with his ignorance on any subject, we should not try to enlighten him. His lessons should be a relief; the satisfaction of a real appetite.

By this plan the resources of the state available for education would be concentrated on the development of all really promising children instead of being in the first place wasted on stuffing all alike with a smattering of knowledge and then leaving them to shift for themselves, probably in danger of moral ruin by acquiring a taste for bad fiction and shallow sedition, and in the second, of blunting the best minds by penning them with the herd.

The Abbey of Thelema has thus demonstrated practically how to cope with the three main problems of our time: sex, economics and education. We dealt with a host of minor difficulties. But the most striking phenomenon of all was that the majority of petty worries never appeared at all. It became clear that many such troubles have no real root in the facts of life, but are artificial symptoms suggested by the fundamental diseases.

My final interpretation of my five years in America may be summarized somewhat as follows. Firstly, before I was fit to take my place as the prophet of the Law of Thelema I must complete my personal initiation into the mysteries of the Grade of Magus.

Secondly, that I might understand the problems which I should later on be called upon to settle, it was necessary to bring me into intimate personal contact with the very varied conditions of mankind. Before this journey I had not even begun to understand what America meant. I ignored it, disliked it; my only idea of dealing with it was that of an ignorant nurse to smack it into propriety. It had hardly occurred to me to inquire why such poetry as that of Keats and myself was not the daily joy of Minnesota farmers. I thought it simply showed their baseness. I now understand that the bonds of brotherhood which make mankind a spiritual unity are everywhere identical, though their appearance varies so as to be unrecognizable to all but very few initiates.

I have attained to understanding, I have made my magical model of society, and I await the moment when those who have chosen me to carry out their colossal conception summon me to stand forth before the world and execute their purpose. At this point, then, I leave my memoirs. My individual life is ended forever. It was always a mere means of bringing *The Book of the Law* to mankind. No man yet lived whose personal adventures were worth wasting a word on. I feel a sort of shame at intruding myself in this way on the public. And yet this book will not be altogether an impudent inanity if it shows how every adventure may serve to bring about some achievement of eternal importance.

88

The last lap! I sweep into the straight. The last jump has been cleared. Nothing now between me and the winning post.

I made a rapid summary of my situation. The bronchitis and asthma, which were the symptoms of the emphysema exacted by the God of the Mountains as the sacrifice due from whoever would approach his altars, had become a regular feature of winter. My obvious course was to dodge it by migrating to North Africa. There was no opposing argument. England was still upside down. I perceived the futility of any campaign to establish the Law there at present.

My original plan had been to join the Ape of Thoth in Switzerland where she was staying with her sister pending my arrival. But I found myself disinclined for some obscure reason to go there. I wanted to be within easy reach of London for the time being, and accordingly wired her to join me in Paris, which she did on January 11th, the first anniversary of our liaison. With her was her two-year-old son who appears in *The Diary of a Drug Fiend* as Dionysus. We were hoping to 'put his nose out of joint' in February or March.

My object in staying near London was as follows.

When I left for New York, I had confided the administration of the O.T.O. to the Grand Treasurer, George Macnie Cowie, VIII°, Frater Fiat Pax, a Neophyte of A∴A∴. He was a man of over fifty years, the art editor of Nelson's, the publishers of Edinburgh. He was deaf and dumb. His character was unselfish and noble, his aspiration intense and sincere.

> He was a gentleman on whom I built
> An absolute trust.

During the war, he wrote voluminously to keep me informed of the affairs of the Order. I had but one complaint to make of his conduct. I asked repeatedly for his accounts as treasurer and he would not send them. As time passed his letters became increasingly rabid against Germany. Deprived of adequate verbal communication with others, he trusted the newspapers

and took their frenzy for fact. I was alarmed at his attitude
and referred him to *The Book of the Law*.

Cap. II, v. 60:   Therefore strike hard & low, and to hell with
                   them, master!
Cap. III, v. 59:   As brothers fight ye!

'Don't hate the Germans,' I urged. 'Love them. Keep cool
in order to help them in the only way possible; by smashing
them up to teach them how to behave.' He only grew worse.
I warned him at last that such virulent hatred would end in
his going mad. And my words came true. His character
changed completely; he began to intrigue against me secretly
and even to rob me, or rather the Order, outright. I cannot say
how far he was abetted by the solicitors of the Order but they,
no less than he, evaded rendering any account of the property
of the Order. I was ultimately compelled to appeal to the
police. Under this pressure he sent a balance sheet. The cat
was out of the bag. The Order had been systematically
defrauded. Let me instance only one item. A sum of five hundred pounds was entered twice. It was the most barefaced outrage in experience. The Grand Secretary General had had the
same idea. A sum of one thousand pounds had been entrusted
to her. She realized the securities and disappeared into the
unknown. As to the furniture and other assets, practically all
the more valuable items had been taken out of the warehouse
by Cowie and were not to be found. Cowie's insanity was
made the excuse for endless delays in settling these various
matters. I found myself almost penniless. My available funds
scarcely sufficed to postpone starvation for more than a few
weeks. It was quite impossible to seek legal redress against the
thieves. I was also foolish enough to hope that Cowie might
explain his actions and restore the property. (I have not yet
succeeded in extracting the account from the lawyers.)

I bethought myself of Fontainebleau and took the Ape to
Moret. We encamped at a charming inn, the Hotel de Bour-
goyne, while looking around for a house where the Ape could
receive proper care when her crisis arrived.

During the Atlantic crossing she had made friends with a
Provençal girl, born in Paris, who had spent some years in
America as nursery governess to some first-class people; in
particular a well-known ambassador. She had married and
given birth to a son. Her husband being killed in an accident,
she had gone back to her old work, but sickened and wearied.
So she had made up her mind to return to Europe.

It struck me that the Ape ought to have a woman to look after her and I suggested her writing to this girl to join us. She brought her boy down from Paris. They gave me the shock of my life. The girl was bloodless, drooping like a thirsty flower, and she dragged her brat along listlessly, he as lifeless as she. His face was ghastly white and his limbs as a damp rag. I thrilled to the marrow with pity and made up my mind then and there to begin my work of saving mankind by bringing these two back to life.

The new current of courage and confidence was irresistible. I found a charming house at 11 bis rue de Neuville, Fontainebleau. We took it from February on. My new patients, who appear in *The Diary of a Drug Fiend* as Sister Cypris and Hermes, had joined us without any definite agreement as to the future. Hermes was in shocking shape. He whined and wailed unceasingly like a puppy in pain. He clung to his mother with pitiful helplessness and she had no idea beyond spoiling him in every way. My personality and moral fortitude soon took effect on Cypris. I made her take long walks through the forest with me, the Ape being of course unable to exert herself beyond mild exercise. Cypris regained physical health and strength rapidly with the natural result that her spirits recovered their tone. She saw me as her saviour no less than Jairus's daughter must have seen Jesus and her gratitude soon turned to an ecstasy of romantic love. It carried her beyond herself. She was almost ready to kill herself in despair at the thought of my attachment to the Ape.

One superb afternoon, sunny and spring-like—it might have been May—we had lunched at the Barbison, the wine went to our heads. After our first burst of speed, we sat down in a glade upon a bank of soft green moss and, without a preface of words, fell into each other's arms. We walked home on air and the next few days passed like a pageant of purple pleasure and passion.

And then she struck a snag. She had taken it for granted that my love for her would make me forget my friendship, cancel my obligations and abrogate my affection. She was amazed and angry to find that my attitude to the Ape had not been altered in any way whatever by my liaison with her. She supposed the conventional stupidities, cruelties and crimes were laws of nature; not understanding the Law of Thelema and hankering after exclusive possession, she fell into a frenzy of mistrust and jealousy. It made things worse that I smilingly accepted her tantrums exactly as an alienist with the outbursts of a maniac. I refused to quarrel; my kindness, tenderness, affection and nonchalance were inexpugnable. She went from bad to worse during the following months, but I maintained firm correctness and at last she gave up trying to drag me down to her ignoble ideal. In the depths of her despair there grew a glimmer. She began to understand that love was not necessarily accompanied by meanness, falsehood, callousness and selfishness. Beholding beauty afar off, she staggered stumblingly up the ragged rocks towards the light, and in the end cast off the chains of selfish lust and became a free and happy woman, as she is today.

'He must teach; but he may make severe the ordeals.'[1] In her case, she had to suffer indescribable anguish to attain salvation, because her ignorance and animal appetite had usurped the throne of her soul and reigned so long unchallenged. Yet even of this came a marvel.

Her command of English was imperfect; her spelling and grammar very defective. She had read little and that little worthless. Nor had she any ambition to learn to write. I had, of course, insisted on her recording her experiences in a Magical Diary, and what was my amazement, on reading the first section, to find it an unsurpassed masterpiece! This ignorant untrained nursemaid had analysed herself so deeply and accurately, had dramatized her tragedy so powerfully, and had expressed her experiences in intense and emphatic language, eked out by metaphors derived from direct observation, that this record is more pitilessly truthful than Marie Bashkirtseff at her best; the stark savagery, the naked cruelty of her passions, is no less fierce than anything in *Wuthering Heights*. She had plumbed the bottomless pit of damnation and ravaged the heights of heaven with rage and rapture.

Some passages in this marvellous manuscript contain expressions which propriety declares unsuited for publication. She had no skill in polite euphemisms and, of course, no idea that her work would ever be read, save by me. In fact, she tried to destroy it on my asking to see it and I only secured it after physical struggle. We must, I fear, bow in the temple of Rimmon to the extent of editing such passages, which I hate to do; their brutal obscenity is an essential element in her character. Should a tiger describe his sensations while eating a man, we should lose by amending his account so as to make it as elegant as that of a city banquet. I will either publish it in a country with common sense or edit it in such a way that the intelligent reader, by the use of a little imagination, will be able to reconstruct the text.

(How ridiculous and disgusting this mealy-mouthed morality is! We print Mark Twain's schoolboy smut about Sir Walter Raleigh at the court of Queen Elizabeth—it circulates under the rose among the most prominent people in society. Why balk at a masterpiece, sublime by virtue of its naked truth, and its spiritual intensity and exaltation, in every way the greatest work ever yet achieved by a woman? I say, emphatically, on my honour that I know of nothing in the whole range of literature which compares with it for all those qualities which are the root of beauty and power, and so saying, I am mindful of my exaggerated enthusiasm about my own achievements in precisely these directions.)

89

I go back in time to Fontainebleau. The winter was superb. It rained rarely, and the sun was so strong that even in February we used to picnic in the forest and snatch an hour's sleep upon the hillside. Everything went well.

Little by little Hermes was weaned from his woes; his wail grew less continuous; he began to enjoy life as a child should. I gave him and Dionysus their first lessons in rock climbing. In two or three days they began to find the best way to tackle a crag and to use their muscles to the best advantage. The central principle of my teaching is to compel the pupil to rely on his own resources, and having thus acquired good judgment and confidence, to develop intelligent initiative. One must show them how to choose the best hand holds and foot holds, but not let them acquire the habit of looking for the teacher to tell them what to do. They must be forced to find out for themselves how to meet any possible emergency. It is important to give them from the beginning as great a variety of crags as possible; smooth slabs, rough ridges, narrow chimneys, shallow gullies, straight faces, some with ample holds, that they may select the best from the abundance; scanty holds to teach them to make the best use of what scarcely suffices; sound rocks to measure their full strength; smooth faces to teach them the value of friction, and rotten or loose cliffs to exercise their judgment as to what strain they may safely put on a hold and to check a slip when it breaks suddenly away from hand or foot.

Both boys showed great capacity for cragmanship, but their qualities were very dissimilar and gave me any amount of clues to their moral characters. The soul is one, and in whatever way it expresses itself its characteristics are invariable. Let me watch a boy climbing a cliff, or playing chess, or building sand castles, or listening to music, and I will tell you how he will act when he grows up, whether to be a statesman, a soldier, a doctor, a lawyer or an artist. Hermes would look at the cliff which I asked him to climb with cool wary wisdom. He thought out every step one by one, and when he had made up his mind he would execute his plan in every detail as he worked it out. When he had made a mistake of judgment and found himself obliged to improvise, he was bewildered and frightened. At first he used to begin to cry and look round piteously for his mother. The unexpected difficulty threw him right out of his sense of reality. He lost his head and the old instinct of infancy reappeared. He never showed excitement or eagerness to climb, and after the victory never exulted in the normal fashion of children, but he was suffused with the satisfaction of having demonstrated his ability.

Hermes had nothing in common with his companion. To him a rock was almost like a living thing. His first reaction was a passionate fear, which a few successful climbs transmuted into an equally eager enthusiasm. It suggested the sexual parallel of a boy's shrinking shyness from women turning into an almost spasmodic lust to conquer them. He would tackle a cliff without considering the details, and when he came to a point which his first impetuous assaults failed to carry, he would call upon his genius to come to the rescue, and overcome the obstacle tempestuously. On reaching the top his triumph was pure ecstasy. I found it impossible to get him to use intelligence in choosing his holds. He defied the laws of mechanics. The obviously most suitable projection did not appeal to him. He made his choice at the bidding of an irrational instinct.

It is surely plain common sense and not a mystical fancy to foretell how these two boys will act in the future. Suppose they enter public life. Hermes will never be a Mohammed, nor Dionysus a Colbert. Hermes might write like J. S. Liliel, paint like Verestchavin, rival Ernest Haeckel in biology, or play chess like Qarrasch. Dionysus would rather challenge comparison with Blake, Dandin, or Bolyai, or Capablanca. One is genius, the other talent without a mixture. And I half believe that these two young boys and no others were given to me by the gods as pure example of the two extreme types, so that I might study how best to develop each to its theoretical optimum. If indeed it must be that in the first few years of life, at any rate, all children must be trained alike, the problem may be stated as the discovery of a method applicable to all. We must not stamp down, discourage or deform genius, nor must we try to obtain from talent qualities beyond his scope.

Elsewhere I have laid down the fundamental principles of early education which my experience with these two boys has led me to formulate. My first practical difficulty was to wean them from self-distrust. I had to break up the Oedipus complex. I had to destroy the false and fatal link between mother and son. A child needs a woman to look after him, no doubt, but we found that his own mother was the worst woman possible. Whenever Cypris and Hermes were together the morals of both suffered. She became hysterical with phantom anxieties and he collapsed into an invertebrate jelly quivering with querulous agitation. I trained the four little by little to treat each other as equals. I destroyed the idea of possession. When a child needed attention, I insisted on a spirit of comradeship almost manly in tone. If a wound had to be dressed there must be no slopping over of sympathy. The child must not whimper and abdicate his dignity nor the mother disgrace the dignity of her function as healer. At first I feared that habit and convention would be hard to overcome. But I was surprised how soon all four found their feet. This self-respect and respect for others made them disclaim the abject attitude which they had supposed natural and right, with this unexpected result: that having got rid of such false ideas as that a child was the property of its mother, in the same sense as a limb to be controlled and used without consulting its inclination; and on the child's part, that it need not face reality but run to its mother for comfort in any trouble, the psychological root of quarrelling, pestering, lying and cringing was torn up and thrown on the bonfire of self-apprehension as a sovereign soul. The boys never cried, never lied, never made themselves a nuisance and never disobeyed. We respected their rights, we conformed to the rules of the Abbey as devised for our protection, and nothing ever happened to create even five minutes' discord after this understanding had been established, which I may say roughly as having taken place by the end of 1920, nine months after the foundation of the Abbey. It was really amusing to contrast the calm certainty and inevitable ease of the five founders with the awkwardness, irritability and vacillation of newcomers.

At the end of February, the Ape had passed through the valley of the shadow of birth, and our household was gladdened by the addition of a tiny girl whom we named Ann Léa in honour of the great mother goddess of summer and of the Ape herself. We wanted a pet name and while discussing various suggestions when walking home from the forest, Hermes suddenly broke in, 'I shall call her Poupée.' This was delightfully apt and was adopted on the spot by acclamation. The newcomer fulfilled the dearest wish of my heart. As a man only one gift would have seemed more excellent, and yet I dared not give myself over to gladness, for on the birth of the child I had inquired of the *Yi King* concerning her. She was symbolized by the 41st Hexagram, called Sun, which signifies diminution. My intuition, quickened by meditation upon this symbol, warned me to beware of getting grained to my love for my child, or nourishing my human hope upon her. As ever, the *Yi* made no error; despite every effort she never took firm hold of life. She grew feebler and frailer constantly, and in the second week of October bade us farewell.

Weak fool that I am! I would not accept the warning of the wisdom of the *Yi*. I set my teeth and swore that she should live. Her helplessness only inflamed my love. I clutched the broken straw of hope more desperately every day, and when at last the axe fell it was as if my own neck had been upon the block. For over a week I could not trust myself to speak. I fought my anguish in silence. The agony of my earlier bereavement came back with tenfold terror. I cannot tell why, insane as I was with grief, I escaped being tempted to revenge myself upon the gods by betraying their trust and breaking my oath of allegiance. It was indeed my most poignant pang to reflect that this was part of the price I had paid for my success in Magick. In my original oath I had pledged myself to pursue the path without withholding the minutest fraction of my earthly assets or permitting human affection to influence my actions. By this I debarred myself from using my magical power either to procure wealth or in the interests of my natural affection, and thus I was impotent to save the life of my child.

This almost mortal stroke was followed up instantly by an even more atrocious thrust, as I shall tell a little later.

In March, we began to discuss the immediate future. Various considerations decided us to send the Ape to England to stay with my aunt and see to various business details. Cypris and I and the boys were to look for a more or less permanent abode. We consulted the *Yi* with great care, asking successively whether it would be wise to settle in this place or that. The only favourable suggestion was Cefalu.

We reached there on the last day of March. I could not doubt that the gods had guided our steps for finding the hotel so sordid, dirty and disgusting, I swore I would not spend a second night there. The gods rose to the occasion. A man named Giordano Giosus came round after breakfast and said he had a villa to let. Anyone who knows Italy will appreciate the magnitude of this miracle. To get the most trifling business through demands the maximum of good luck at least a month before the first move is made.

Giosus took me up the hill and lo! a villa that might have been made to order. It fulfilled all my conditions; from possessing a well of delicious water to a vast studio opening northwards. The gods took no chances. They meant me to live there and guarded against any possible perversity on my part by planting two tall Persian nuts close to the house. They might have been the very same trees as those in the garden of the Villa Caldarazzo, which, as I have told, I had taken for a token in the days of Ab-ul-Diz. I struck a bargain on the spot, sent for the family, and the furniture with all our belongings were installed the same day. We hired a man to market, cook and clean ship; and there we were as much at home as a mummy in a pyramid, in the loveliest spot of the entire Mediterranean littoral.

A week or two later the Ape arrived, and I began to occupy myself with Magick, poetry and painting on my own account, and on theirs with a systematic training essential to establish the Law as the ethical basis of the new social order of which I intended to construct a working model from such material as the gods might supply.

My cornerstones represented considerable diversity. The Ape was German-Swiss, with long experience of America. Cypris, French; her son's father American, while the other boy was half English. More diverse still were the four personalities. To harmonize them should be most instructive.

I had begun to get them more or less into shape and found out the nature of the essential obstacles to perfect success by the end of June, when I went to Tunis to meet a new disciple.

Since 1918, I had been in correspondence with this lady, Jane Wolfe, of Pennsylvania Dutch stock, about my own age, by profession originally an actress, but now a star of the screen. In order to test her courage I had told her to meet me on the day of the summer solstice at Bou Saâda. She cabled consent and then my heart smote me. It was rather rough to ask a woman to take that uncomfortable journey to a place, which at that time of the year was frequented chiefly by the devil and the more favoured of the damned for hell on account of the heat. So I wired and wrote proposing Tunis instead. She never received this message. I stayed a fortnight in Tunis wondering where she could be. She sweated in Bou Saâda equally perplexed. In the end she decided to come to Cefalu. The Ape and I met her at Palermo and took her to the abbey—and then the fun began!

Jane Wolfe was full of fixed ideas about America, of the regular spreadeagle stuff. ('Los Angeles is the modern Athens'!! This actual phrase is hers.) The stars and stripes stood for wisdom, virtue and truth; for spirituality, good manners, progress, civilization—you know, it goes on till somebody faints. Woodrow Wilson was the reincarnation of Jesus Christ and the Hearst newspapers the standard of literary excellence.

Her aspiration was utterly pure, unselfish and all-absorbing. She disdained to count the cost or to seek reward. But alas, in her eagerness she assumed that so long as she ran, it did not much matter which way she was going. She had fallen in with a crowd of charlatans of the vulgarest sort, sheer frauds without knowledge of any one fact about Magick and only concerned to dupe. She accordingly claimed to have received messages from several 'masters on the other side'. She showed me this stuff. I have read a lot of rubbish in my life, but nothing in the same street, city, county, country or continent which would stand a moment's comparison for sheer asininity. These 'masters' did not even take the trouble to invent plausible accounts of themselves; e.g., there would be a Persian guide named Schmidt and her Chinese master who issued instructions which were on the level of, and quite indistinguishable from, Sunday School exaltation. Her pet persuasion was that she was to travel eastward for three years and after some adventure with a 'M. Joperal', an Englishman (the well-known Shropshire or the Essex branch of that typically English tribe), she would proceed to Japan where her destined soul-mate was waiting to marry her, the climax being the birth of a Messiah.

Amid this steaming midden of putrefying manure, I detected rare posies. She had got two or three symbols both intelligible and indicative of initiation.

During her first few weeks at the abbey, every day was one long battle. I hacked through her barbed wire of aggressive axioms. I forced her to confess the incongruity of her assertions. I drilled holes in her vanity and self-satisfaction. I dug her critical spirit out of its corner, and made her clean off the rust, sharpen the edge and the point, and polish the steel till it shone. When she saw it, she feared it all the more; but I forced her to grasp it and use it. At every stroke she split the skull of one of her dearest delusions and shrieked as if its destruction were her own. She dropped the sword every time my eye was off her, but I always made her pick it up and do some more damage, till at last she found out that killing false-hoods, never so smiling and so like her idea of herself, did not hurt her, but on the contrary freed her, and she also found that the harder she struck at truth the stronger it stood. So in the end, she learnt the value of the critical spirit and made it one of her regular weapons.

Besides this intellectual trouble she suffered from moral maladies of a similar sort. She had always taken for truth any assertion that sounded impressive and seemed to suit her ideas of right and wrong. She was shocked to the limit by our principles and conduct. She gazed with a dropped jaw and glassy eyes, wondering how it was that the frightful catas-trophes which were bound to result did not happen. It was a little like those crofters at Foyers waiting to see the wrath of God consume the aluminium works that scorned the sabbath. Was she dreaming? Were we really living, loving and laugh-ing, healthy and happy, when, by all rules, we ought to be shrieking with agony in the madhouse, the gaol or the lock hospital? Worse still, she missed all those familiar features to be observed in even the best of families, petty jealousies, scolding, quarrelling, bickering, tyranny and the rest. Can you beat it? Being a woman of sense, it soon struck her that there must be some reason for these strange phenomena, and we took every chance to point out how in any particular case, whose circumstances would have created trouble in other communities, the strict application of the Law of Thelema provided a solution which satisfied all parties. She observed also in her own case that for the first time in her life she was really free to do what she willed. Her only trouble came from her own attempts to interfere with us in the interests of some cold-storage convention, whenever she tried to put forward some opinion or popular principle originally invented to suit medieval conditions, and so cherished through centuries as a fetish, despite its irrelevance to reality.

Let me illustrate this by one case. In her room was a sketch of a famous group in the museum of Naples. It shocked her; blinded her eyes. She could not see what it was, that is, a sym-phony of exquisitely harmonized lines. The subject obsessed her; whereas we, being trained to seek truth and beauty in each and every impression, saw the implication of the sketch as a secondary and quite unimportant quality. More, granting the subject to suggest the expression of a passion which might or might not be sympathetic, we could at least temper our approval or aversion by reflecting that whatever we personally might feel about it, its right to existence was absolute, exactly as we acquiesce in the horse, the tiger, the eagle and the snake as equally essential to the perfection of the universe. But to her, perception was paralysed by emotion, and emotion was at the mercy of the idea which assailed it. She was incapable of reasoning about the sketch or even of resisting its influence as being unworthy to occupy her mind. What she thought evil was to her so terrible and irresistible that she surrendered herself to its loathed embrace without an effort, or even the faith in herself or in God that its empire might end.

The attitude is, of course, characteristic of that vast class of moral cowards, whose only remedy for evil is to remove the occasion; whether it is a glass of cognac, a piqué blue blouse or a dollar left lying about. They feel themselves helpless. Sin must follow temptation. Righteousness is only possible in the absence of an alternative. We of Thelema pursue a policy exactly contrary. We resist temptations through the moral strength and the enlightening experience which comes of making a series of systematic experiments with divers iniquities. A few trials soon teach us that wrongdoing does not pay. We find also that as soon as the arbitrary penalties of misconduct, which society adds to the automatic reaction, are removed, and we do all in our power to mitigate the evil effects, the sting of the serpent loses its virus. It is an old saying that one sin provokes another. This is only true when the sinner, driven into a corner by the avengers, tries to escape by some desperate deed. Thus a boy robs the till to pay for his folly in gambling away his earnings, and being found out is maddened by the thought of jail, sees red and kills his employer. We should rather sterilize sin.

The sense of shame is cowardly and servile. It is based on ignorance that one is a star. 'Conscience makes cowards of us all.' The man who respects himself will not act unworthily, but if we hammer into his head from infancy that most of his natural impulses are evil, we enslave his spirit. The most natural actions are done furtively. He lurks and lies. Brought up to believe that his right is wrong, he will do what he thinks wrong as easily as what he thinks right. In this way canned ethics breed crime.

Jane Wolfe soon found that we were immune from the effects alleged to follow various causes. Erotic pictures did not stimulate us sexually. Descriptions and illustrations of diseases neither disgusted nor frightened us. The girls did not dress against each other. The new hat of one aroused no envy in her friend. The most cutting criticism made no wound. I would say frankly and even brutally what I thought of this or that trait in one of the girls, and she would take it in the same spirit as a patient submits to the surgeon's knife, knowing first, that whatever I said was inspired by the wish to eliminate error, and secondly that beneath the most ruthless contempt there was absolute respect as due to a star. 'If he be a King, thou canst not hurt him.' [1] The instant Jane realized that she was a sovereign soul, unique and of equal splendour to every other, she was no longer hurt by criticisms of the complexes which blasphemed her simplicity and which she had been silly enough to suppose organic functions of her essence.

So passed the summer. With autumn came calamity. I have already told of my own great sorrow. The second sword stroke was that her own inconsolable grief so prostrated the Ape that our hope to retrieve our great loss dragged its anchor. The past had perished and now the future failed us. An operation was necessary to save her own life. My faculties were utterly paralysed. I stood as if petrified in the studio, while in the next room the surgeon drew forth the dead from the living. I shall never forgive myself. I can only say that my brain was benumbed. It was dead except in one part where slowly revolved a senseless wheel of pain. Thus, although I had ether in the house, and I was competent to administer it, it never came into my mind to suggest to the surgeon to use it.

What really pulled me from the pit was the courage, wisdom, understanding and divine enlightenment of the Ape herself. Over and over again, she smote into my soul that I must understand the way of the gods. They had sent our Poupée for their own ends, and she, having accomplished her visit, had gone on her way. One of the principal conclusions to be drawn from the ruin of our earthly joy was this. We must not look to the dead past, or gamble with the unformed future; we must live wholly in the present, wholly absorbed in the Great Work, 'unassuaged of purpose, delivered from the lust of result.' [2] Only so could will be pure and perfect. More grossly, we must understand that being chosen by the gods to do their work for the world, we must not waste our love on any one child. The race of man is our real offspring begotten by my word Thelema upon her vessel of fulfilment thereof, viz: Love. We must train up our child in the way which it should go, foreseeing every danger and providing a safeguard thereto.

By her heroic and inspired interpretation heartened, I set my feet upon my sorrow and used it to make firm my feet. I went on with my work. My energy came back, little by little, and I was able after a time to silence the complaint that continually called to my consciousness, but only in the spring did I fight my way to freedom. I had gone to Paris, and went down to Fontainebleau for fresh air and exercise, and also to make a little Magical Retirement. As soon as I sat down to look at myself, I was aware of the old wound. I knew there was only one way. I must open it up and cleanse it thoroughly. I went out northward. On my left, as I came to the city wall, was the hospital where just over a year before, the child was born. I strode fiercely forward with clenched teeth. But at the first breath of forest air the universal sorrow of nature flooded me and I broke out into strong sobbing. I refused to fool myself in any of the familiar ways. I faced it open-eyed. I felt its fullest force in every nerve. So having attained the courage to accept it, without resistance or resentment, I conquered it. I slew the fiend that had beset me. From that hour to this I have suffered no more. When memory brings it back the sorrow is as a shadow—the shadow cast by a drifting cloud upon the sea, powerless to darken it, gone swift and silent as it came, leaving no mask, and even adding beauty to the sunlit splendour of the sea by varying its values.

90

My precise motive in going to Paris eludes me. I seem to have acted upon general principles. My visit proved eventful. Firstly, I met a man named Sullivan,[1] 'a fellow almost damned with a fair wife' named Sylvia. They had been married some time and she had developed a pain in the old place. A friend of hers asked my advice. I gave it, not suspecting the object of her solicitude. The situation suddenly developed by Sylvia and myself starting trouble.

Sullivan came of the people. His brilliant brain had pulled him up to the position of 'mathematical and scientific reviewer' for *The Times* and the *Athenaeum,* besides casual contributions to various papers. Absorbed in his work, he had no taste in common with Sylvia bar music, and he had begun to find it rather a nuisance to have to trail her along at his heels. He asked me point-blank to take her off his hands for a time. As in the case of Ratan Devi I was glad to oblige. He could have her back when he liked by whistling for her.

The dialogue reverted after this short digression to the subject that enthralled us—*The Book of the Law*. I astounded his science by setting forth the facts of its origin, and the evidence of its contents that the author possessed the key to several problems insoluble by any intellect hitherto incarnate. We talked day and night for a fortnight. On his part, he showed me a great many mysteries in *The Book of the Law* that I had not suspected till then. I may indeed say that more than once he asked me some questions on a subject of which I was quite ignorant, and that on searching *The Book of the Law* I discovered a satisfactory reply in a text whose meaning had escaped me through my ignorance of the subject in question.

Our conversation was uninterrupted except for the tyranny of sleep and Sylvia. She became pregnant, a complication necessitating a further brief digression. It was agreed that she should return to Cefalu with me, he to join us and work out fully the mathematical theories of *The Book of the Law* as the convenience of his editor permitted. After Sylvia's confinement, we would confer more about the proper course of action. He then went off to Mentone to bid god-speed to the girl he really loved, a woman writer who was living with one of his editors so long as her lungs would let her (they lasted till 1922). Alas for gods whose wings are clipped by love and their feet hobbled by habit. We were to meet Sullivan at Marseilles, sailing for Palermo with or without him as his editor might permit. The few days of absence had wrecked him mentally and morally. We had no sooner sat down to lunch than he burst into a torrent of maniacal ejaculations.

All this was spouted by a whale answering to the name of 'I want Sylvia back'. When his breath failed, and he fell back panting like a mad dog, I remarked between mouthfuls, 'Righto! I'll have to get the cabin changed and take a few of Sylvia's things out of my trunk. I think there's nothing else, provided, of course, Sylvia wishes it.' The poor man was flabbergasted and Sylvia flew into a royal rage. My contempt for him was one thing; my indifference to her quite another. But neither ran any danger of pride. They were reduced to shamefaced stammering. My cheerful calm daunted them. Sullivan, selfish and stupid, actually proposed to hurry back that night to Paris, though Sylvia was obviously fagged out with the journey of the day before, to say nothing of her having set her heart on spending a few days enjoying the beauties of the Riviera—it was her first escape from England.

On that point only did I try to influence Sullivan. He saw that I was right and grudgingly agreed to give the poor child a few days' enjoyment. With this exception I concentrated my whole energy on impressing Sullivan with the supreme importance to science of *The Book of the Law*. I further offered to prove the efficacy of its formulae by developing him within three months into a first-rate man.

I repeated my invariable epitome, ' "Every man and every woman is a star!" You, being a man, are therefore a star. The soul of a star is what we call genius. You are a genius. This fact is obscured either by moral complexes which enmesh it, or lack of adequate machinery to express it in terms of action.' To this universal theorem must be added a rider suited to any case under consideration.

To Sullivan I explained, 'You already possess a perfected machinery. Your knowledge is enormously above the average. You reason clearly and correctly. You have a fair command of English. You lack only the link between soul and sense. You admit yourself second-rate and refuse to believe in the possibility of becoming first-rate, despite my theoretical demonstration and the testimony of my previous successes. That despair is, itself, one complex which inhibits your genius. Today you have shown me another. A mere animal appetite sharpened by a few days of starvation can wreck your intellect, sweep every decent instinct overboard and make you treat your word of honour as idle.'

He had then just enough sense to understand me; but the foul fiend tore him the more terribly at the least effort of his sanity and decency to assert itself.

I saw them off by the train, very heavy at heart. I was sorry for Sylvia buried alive in a south coast village without a soul to speak to and no resource in herself but her music. Yet after all she did not much matter. She was one of millions in a similar plight. Also even if saved, the profit was mostly personal. The case of her husband was altogether more serious. His abject surrender to the brute was a defeat involving a whole world in the disaster. I could have made him the evangelist of Thelema; with his abilities he might have been more important in history than St Paul. But he could never do any great work as long as he was liable to be obsessed by the body, any more than a motorist could break the record from Land's End to John o'Groats if he shied and ran off the road every time his eye was caught by a tree.

I found the abbey in admirable order. We had a new member, a boy named Godwin, whom I had known in America. When he first wrote me, he was in Annapolis, an attendant in the naval hospital. The boy had amazing ability, backed by exceptional energy and other moral qualities such as the Great Work, or indeed any work worth the name, requires. Out of his scanty savings he had bought a set of *The Equinox* for a hundred dollars and several other expensive items. He grudged his time as little as his cash. He learnt by heart an astounding number of our sacred books, and when later on I asked him to compile a dictionary of Sanskrit roots for my use on a certain research, he went at it with a will and made good. As against all this, he was surly, mulish and bitterly rebellious. He raved against the injustice of being punished for breaking the regulations of the navy. I vainly showed him that when he signed on as he did of his own free will, he pledged himself to conform with the regulations and that in breaking them he blasphemed himself.

Reckless in his ardour for knowledge, he injected himself with forty grains of cocaine. He had never tried it before.

All he knew was that half a grain had been known to cause death. The record of his experiment makes interesting reading. He began by trying to set a piece of glass on fire by the force of his will.

The next act was plagiarized from Samson. He hung on to a pillar while the Philistines, some half a dozen husky sailor boys, tried to pull him off. They finally managed to sit on his head and control his frantic punches and kicks. They then got surgeons on the job who pulled him through. In a couple of days he was all right again. His experiment, if intended to escape notice, failed. They hauled him before the Lord High-Muck-Amuck, who told him, with the best respects and wishes of Uncle Sam for a prosperous passage to perdition, that after a careful consideration the Navy Department had unanimously decided that they could sweep the seas clear of the White Ensign without troubling themselves to put him to the inconvenience of co-operating. Shaking the pipe-clay of Annapolis from his person, he favoured New York with a flying visit, dropped in on me, and—please could I find him a job? I did what I could, but before I found him work, he had got the Lafayette to try him as a waiter. I thought he might be of use to my 'son' [2] in Detroit and wrote asking him to find an opening. He did so and Godwin went off.

In all he said and did, one peculiarity obtruded itself—this violent reaction against any act of authority as such, however reasonable, however much to his own advantage. When he noticed the suggestion of discipline, he became blind with rage. His mental faculties were simply snowed under. Having habitually yielded to this impulse, it became a fixed form of his mind, so that even between spasms he would brood incessantly over his wrongs. I hoped the abbey would break up this complex. For a time he improved greatly, but in my absence the Ape, in whose hands I had left the sole authority, had very ably established a routine, adherence to which minimized the time necessary to the prosperity of the household, and thus allowed each mentor the theoretical maximum of leisure for his own chosen work. Godwin rebelled. On two occasions he became, if not literally insane, at least so lost to self-control as to assault her murderously. In both cases, she cowed him by sheer moral superiority as wild beasts are supposed to shrink from the eye which is fixed fearlessly upon their fury. After my return he improved. I recall only one outbreak. My experience was the same as the Ape's. I stood up to him and made him obey, and he obeyed.

The occasion is not without interest. Frater Prograbior,[3] 1° = 10▢ A∴A∴, and IX° O.T.O., was expected to arrive from New South Wales to spend some four months seeking initiation under my personal guidance. His age was fifty-three and his rank in both Orders such as to command the utmost respect from junior members. Apart from this, his age and the fact of his having come so far should have made Godwin eager to show him all possible consideration. The question arose where he should sleep. The answer was self-evident. The only possible arrangement for many reasons was for Godwin to give up his room temporarily. We gave Godwin several opportunities of making the suggestion spontaneously. The propriety was as obvious to him as to anyone else. He sulked in silence. I was sorry to have to issue an order, a thing I had not done for many months, but I had to do so. Godwin refused point-blank. I pointed out quite kindly the various considerations which applied. I might as well have talked to a turnip, better in fact, for a turnip's eye would not have got bloodshot, nor the eyes swollen with blood almost to bursting. He again refused violently. It was absurd, he being our guest with no claim whatever upon us. I had to say, 'Out of your room by six o'clock, or out of the abbey and you don't come back!' By six o'clock he was in his new quarters.

Alas for these men who cannot be taught the elements of common sense by any means soever. Not long afterwards some trivial incident touched the same spot. I thought he would be the better for a holiday from the abbey. He was working so hard that his health began to make me anxious. He interpreted my suggestion as a banishment and instead of going, as I proposed, to Palermo, and putting in a month working up the interest of the people there about us, he went off to the top of the Rock without any provisions of any kind. He had taken an oath not to come down before eight days. In subsequent clauses appeared such austerities as this: not to allow water to touch his face! It was a rotten thing to do. Cypris was very fond of him and she went through agonies watching him pace to and fro on the parched sun-blistering crags like the possessed of Godara among the tombs. I refused to interfere. He was up there by no will of mine. Whenever he chose he could come down and eat and drink, sitting and clothed and in his right mind. So Cypris filled a rucksack with food and drink and dragged herself up those sweltering slopes to the ruined stone hut, where the crazed creature had made his headquarters. He refused to speak to her, but I think she got him to drink some water. He must indeed have perished for thirst otherwise.

I wish I had a copy of his Magical Record of this Retirement. It was an incoherent scrawl of furious ravings mostly aimed against the innocent Jones (Jesus Stansfeld Christ was his favourite brickbat) in Chicago. I have no idea what excited such animosity. His magical work was chiefly to count the loose stones on the floor of his hut, and divine from their number the most erratic nonsense which seemed to him the sublime arcana of Grades so exalted that a mere Magus was in comparison one poor pip of a China orange to all Lombard Street and the City of London to boot. For a magical wand, he had picked up a piece of dry stick which he chewed incessantly under the impression that by so doing he was putting the affairs of the planet in shape during such moments as he could spare from adjusting the solar system and showing the gods how to run the universe, any recalcitrant deity being ruthlessly smacked into repentance.

Cypris begged me to intervene, urging that he was irresponsible. She said she felt sure that he would come down if I wrote to him to do so. I consented. That day after lunch, washed, his movements violent and jerky and his eyes rolling as I lay half asleep on a couch by the main door, Godwin rushed in. His appearance really alarmed me; unshaven, unwildly, I should not have mistaken him for the Prince of Wales. He flung a rucksack on the floor at my feet and roared out 'Aleister Crowley' in a harsh, angry, uneven growl. He then went off as suddenly and strangely as he had come. When I saw him next he was himself again, merely showing signs of exhaustion. He was tired and penitent like a naughty child who has found forgiveness. His final fireworks had been dramatically admirable. He had gone to the barber's to be shaved. But no sooner was he thoroughly lathered than he remembered his oath not to let water touch his face. He bolted out of the shop and stamped up the street, the foam from his face flying in all directions. He put his head down and charged through somebody's private estate, vaulted the wall at the back and spurted up the slope as if the devil were at his heels instead of merely in his heart.

This was the beginning of the end. Even after he had regained sanity in most matters, he clung to the conviction that his adventure on the Rock had initiated him to a Grade far superior to mine. I should, of course, have been only too glad if this had happened. The decaying debris of my Oedipus complex still stinks, which stink being interpreted may be rendered in English, 'How I wish I had someone to go to, a man like myself, not an angel, whose humanity would understand and sympathize with my weakness and weariness, and on whose shoulders I might shift at least a little of the responsibility which is breaking my back!'

Poor Godwin tried to smother his shame by piling pride upon it. His megalomania grew on him at a frightful pace. His conscience was crushed into a pulp and his common sense scattered to the winds. He suddenly developed an entirely new defect. I had always found him truthful. He now adopted a policy of deliberate deceitfulness with the greatest subtlety. It was perfectly imbecile. He had only to say what he wanted and I should have done whatever I could to help him, whatever it was. He, however, persuaded himself that he must keep his plans dark and the final absurdity of the whole thing was that I was aware from the beginning exactly what he intended to do. Our relations ended, bar occasional correspondence, towards the end of the year, when he left us to go to Australia avowedly to help Frater Progradior in establishing the Law. However, he only stayed a short time in Sydney and went on to San Francisco, where, free from all guidance or control, he broke out into a series of spasms of which I do not know the details, and which are of little interest as being merely casual symptoms of a state of mind which I had already studied sufficiently.

I asked myself, 'How now?' Has Thelema failed in this case? I have thought this over ruthlessly, but my final judgment is that the Law is not touched by these events. It seems to me beyond dispute that any conceivable code of conduct presumes implicitly that men always act on certain fundamental principles which they carry out, well or ill, within wide limits; those limits being exceeded, the man is not a man 'within the meaning of the act' and the Law ceases to apply to him. For instance, we feel safe in acting on the assumption that a man will not walk into a blazing house, and we make no law to punish any such action. We assume that a man always acts in what he believes to be his own best interest. The conduct of Godwin was irrational, his motive had no logical link with his actions. It is therefore impossible to imagine any formula by which to judge him.

So far, so good, but at least I failed to break up the complex which obsessed him. That is true, but I blame my inexperience and nowise the principles on which I proceed. I am not without excuse. Let me give one example to illustrate the impossibility of guiding him or even enlightening his mind. He was anxious to do certain magical work, which forms part of the task of a Grade which he had not attained. In order to devote himself to this, he proposed to neglect the work prescribed for the Grade which he actually possessed. I pointed this out, and after some show of sulks, he agreed. A day or so later, in discussing some point of magical theory, I happened to say, 'I want you to understand very thoroughly what this implies.' He retorted violently, 'I'm not an $8°=3^\square$! To understand is not a part of the work of my Grade!' To that he stuck. It was useless to argue that the understanding of an $8°=3^\square$ has a technical definition, and that a child of two years old must understand the alphabet, if it is to be any use to it. Stupidities of this type were constantly coming up.

In matters like chess, he was just as bad as he was about Magick. He begged me to teach him the game. I prescribed a system of study to be vitalized by daily practice with me over the board. For some reason which I never succeeded in grasping, he refused obstinately to follow my advice in any single point. When we played he grew steadily worse and when asked to account for this, he took up the position that nothing was to be gained by winning. He was even ass enough to quote *The Book of the Law* about lust of result. He could hardly help seeing that unless one played to win, there was no point in playing at all. Nothing moved him. He simply gave up playing. The stupidity was really disheartening. He had a fine natural ability to judge position and invent combinations. A little technical knowledge of the openings, and a systematic study of the end game which he might have acquired in a year, should have made him a first-class amateur. My worst weakness is this: I hate to see good material wasted.

So much for Godwin. In brilliant contrast stands the figure of Frater Progradior.

My success with him is enough to wipe out a dozen failures and more. He was a Lancashire man of good family which had fallen into undeserved distress. As a result he had had to work with his hands from the age of nine. He had always been eager and earnest about spiritual affairs. He had begun by joining the Theosophical Society, but after seventeen years found himself unenlightened in the slightest. He had then put in eleven years with the A∴A∴, but in the absence of personal guidance his progress had been slow. He arrived weary of life, despairing of truth.

I begin my training as a general rule by prescribing a few preliminary practices such as are universally beneficial. In the meantime I watch quietly for symptoms by which to determine the diagnosis. He was rather a hard case. I was puzzled. There was clearly something very wrong indeed, but I could not imagine what. Of course in my conscious self I am always stupid, but the Magus who uses me knows his job.

One afternoon we went off bathing with the Ape. I prattled as we walked quite pointlessly and just as we reached the edge of the cliff above the bay I made some casual remark which proved a winning shot. He stopped short and gasped; his eyes starting from his head. I am so stupid, let me report, that I failed to notice anything special. I was mildly surprised to see him dash down the path like a young goat, tear off his clothes, and sprint into the sea like an alarmed seal. He never spoke a word till after the swim and the return to the road. He then said with a pale face and in awed accents, 'Please tell me again what you said just now?' 'How the devil should I remember?' I returned courteously. He stammeringly reminded me of the subject, and of course I was able to repeat my remarks, which were nothing specially striking. He asked me to discuss the subject more fully, which I did, after which he relapsed into silence. Directly he reached the abbey, he passed into a state of trance which lasted three whole days without a break. He then came to me looking like an incarnation of pure joy and told me what had happened. Without knowledge of his need I had unwittingly given him the key to the inmost treasury of his soul. One minute facet of truth unveiled from the matrix by the wheel of my word had let in the light. In three days he had achieved the critical initiation which had baffled him for nearly thirty years. I prescribed a Magical Retirement so that he might fix in his consciousness that lightning flash as a permanent arc-lamp. This proved a success.[4]

My own joy was boundless. I was inspired to prepare a perfected ritual for the attainment of the Knowledge and Conversation of the Holy Guardian Angel, and presented him with a copy of the manuscript for use in his operation. I entitled it *Liber Samekh*.[5] It is the most powerful and exalted of all my magical instructions. I think he was helped not a little, not only by the ritual itself, but by the feeling that I had sufficient care for him—he suffered from humility—to devote myself so passionately to making his path plain.

One result of this Retirement is astounding from the point

of view of the profane. The Spirit of the Lord descended upon him and opened his eyes to a series of visions of a class far more exalted and intense and intimate than anything he had hitherto experienced. He was inspired to write these down during their actual occurrence, and here is the marvel. His education had been quite elementary. He could neither spell nor construct his sentences correctly, nor had he command of any extended vocabulary. What, then, was my amazement to perceive in his style an originality and power of the first order. It, not less than his subject, was quite dissimilar from that of John Bunyan, and yet the suggestion of identity was undeniable. It was a kinship of soul.

Parallel with this spiritual attainment, his mental and physical powers were renewed as the eagle's. His depression vanished and was replaced by calm, deep joy, overflowing and manifest to all of us. He began to take long solitary walks across the hills and did his twenty miles a day as he had not done for a quarter of a century. We felt it as an actual bereavement when the time came for him to go back to Sydney.

91

Few jewels in my collection of freaks are more precious than Cecil Maitland. From his birth, he aroused the liveliest hopes among students of entomology; for his father, a distinguished Anglican controversialist, followed Newman and Manning into apostasy. His projects for attaining the papacy were, however, thwarted by the unscrupulous action of a charming lady, who insisted upon dragging him from the very foot of the altar to a rival sacrament pedlar, who promptly conjoined them in wedlock at the regular rates. This escapade did not escape the notice of the Vatican. The Pope was surprised into the exclamation 'Tut', or its Latin equivalent. He scratched his head and muttered, 'Martin Luther!' After a moment's reflection he dispatched his chamberlain for bell, book and candle; and proceeded to the magical operation against this occasion made and provided. As in the case of the Jackdaw of Rheims, the effect of the curse was to ruffle the feathers of the audacious follower after the false god Hymen. A touch of rheumatism brought matters to a climax. He rang up Harrods and ordered a supply of sackcloth and ashes. Receiving, like Job, visits of condolence from various righteous friends he besought them to intercede with the Almighty on his behalf; and as they numbered not a few influential people, with strings on the College of Cardinals, the Pope was eventually persuaded to 'silence that dreadful bell', return the book to its shelf and snuff the comminatory candle. The Rev. Mr Maitland was restored to the bosom of the Harlot of the Seven Hills; though not to the priesthood; and on the strict condition that for the future he should regard his wife as tabu. Things thus satisfactorily settled, she brought forth a man child and called his name Cecil James Alexander, rejecting with contumacy the suggested alternative Caoutchouc. He grew in stature and in favour of God and man, so far as research has hitherto been able to determine. But he was subject to amiable delusions, one of which took the sinister shape of *Cacoethes Scribendi*. In the Great War he joined the army and became a real 'capting'. Advised of this fact, the Germans wisely refrained from entering Edinburgh. His next step was to become a dipsomaniac and lose his teeth. During this period he suffered from hydrophobia and did not wash for eighteen months. This romantic situation enflamed the virgin heart of a large, white, red-haired maggot named Mary Butts, or rather Rodker.

In a previous spasm she had rushed to the registrar the most nauseating colopter that ever came under my microscope. It was a Whitechapel Jew [1] who proclaimed himself a poet on the strength of a few ungrammatical and incoherent ramblings, strung together and chopped at irregular intervals into lines. He used to hang about studios in the hope of cadging cigarettes and drinks. He even got into mine on one occasion, owing to a defect in the draught excluder. Luckily the plumbing was perfect. One tug on the chain, a gush and a squeal, and I saw him no more. But somehow he squirmed out of the sewers and, as I said, obtained the official position, louse pediculosis, with Mary Butts. She washed him and dressed him, which naturally led to disenchantment, and Cecil reigned in his stead.

In 1922, they were paying the price of their outrage on morality. They were both in very bad health and very hard-pressed for money. One of their favourite amusements was playing at Magick. Idle and mentally muddled, they were attracted by all subjects which seemed to require no orderly thought or steady work. Nothing is easier than to pick up a few awe-inspiring terms and stir them into soup. It is the only way to impress those even more ignorant. They therefore came to me. With my invariable optimism, I picked out all the promising points and overlooked the faults, or promised myself that I could easily correct them. Their wretchedness kindled my pity and I invited them to spend their summer in the abbey at Cefalu. I really believed that a month or two of simple life, free from temptations and distractions, with the quiet discipline of our regulations, might put them on the right road.

They arrived.

The very next day I got the shock of my life. I must mention first that, some time earlier, Maitland had had some sort of job mining or planting in the East. On his journey out, his ship was standing off Colombo pending quarantine inspection. He was sitting on the rail talking to a girl. Suddenly he fell backwards and was pulled into a boat by Singhalese pedlars who had no consideration for the perfectly justifiable feelings of the local sharks, or any philosophical care for the welfare of humanity.

He told this story to excuse his aversion to water. It was, however, of vital importance to his health that he should learn to swim. We went down to the Caldara alone, took off our clothes and started round the rocks. I showed him how to proceed without the slightest need of swimming, by letting the water take most of his weight, and using his hands to hang on to the large convenient knobs of rock which abound everywhere. He showed the most abject fear, but I supposed that a few minutes would give him confidence. On the contrary his terror increased and I had infinite trouble to get him to come even a couple of hundred yards. We reached the breaking point. He found a ledge, scrambled ashore and shivered. I gave up and swam back. I dressed and smoked. No sign of Captain Webb. I climbed to the top of the cliff, where I could see the whole edge. There he was like a cat on hot bricks, with all due apologies to the feline race. He had chosen to try to find an overland route, stark naked on sharp rough rocks—and there really wasn't a way. He reached, at last, a cave, which possessed a fairly broad opening above water, so that I could throw him his sandals. He had merely to walk home on a broad flat shelf which would not have asked him to wade more than waist high. But he insisted on the most excoriating and dangerous scramble across slimy crags. An hour or so later, he finally got to his clothes. The unfortunate wretch was bleeding all over. We then walked home and he took occasion to thank me for the most unpleasant afternoon he had ever spent in his life. Even then I took the remark lightly. I could not seriously believe that he had been really in torture. It is a fixed idea in my mind that any Englishman of good blood enjoys an adventure, the rougher the better. But the spirit was not in him. Of course, I know that his father's psychology amply accounts for this abject attitude. In him the exhaustion of the stock had reached its climax. I learned later that he had already attempted suicide. He had tried to shoot himself in the heart with a revolver. One would imagine that it would have been safe to bet on his doing some damage. But no! His pistol was spiritually his twin. The bullet thought that it might hurt itself if it happened to hit a bone, so it skipped nimbly round his ribs and sought repose from the tribulations of existence in a comfortable cushion.

I soon discovered the root of his rottenness. After all, there must be a star somewhere there behind that bank of trembling fob. I worked with a will to save him. And one of the most pathetic incidents in my memory is that he came to me one morning with tears on the threshold of his eyes, and said in a quivering tenor, 'I want to live!', grasped my hand, fell on his knees and broke out sobbing. I felt that I had won the fight. The root of his weakness was that the will-to-live was absent.

From that moment he began to mend. Of course, all sorts of suppressed perversities externalized, and had to be analysed and destroyed. But I had great hopes of him when he left the abbey. Alas! it is easy to cure evil whose source is error; enlightenment restores righteousness. The misdirected energy returns to its proper course. But weakness is usually incurable; even the most hopeful cases require the discipline of years to establish habits whose inertia will protect the will from interference.

In the case of Maitland, the moment he showed the wish to become independent, the vanity of Mary Butts was wounded and her jealousy inflamed. She might have won the love of a first-rate man, but she preferred to dull the anguish of the consciousness that she was a weakling, as she admitted, by keeping in abject dependence upon her a man on whom she could look down. She accordingly did all she could to push him back into the mire of misery and self-contempt; and of course, no sooner was my influence removed, than he slipped back into the stinking slime from which I had tried to rescue him.

Less than a year later, I heard that he swallowed a bottle of poison—not even a decent poison, such as a self-respecting suicide might be expected to use. I forget the precise ingredients. I think it was some sort of disinfectant, such as is sold without restriction because legislatures had failed to imagine anyone asinine or abject enough to make it a beverage. The luck still held. I don't know whether it disinfected him, but it certainly made him as sick as a sewer. He pulled through and I am only sorry not to be able to say, in the present edition, what happened next.

I cannot be serious and yet I am honestly sad beyond expression whenever the man comes up in my mind. His character was charming as few other men I ever met. His talent for writing, though limited by his moral weakness to trivialities, possessed many admirable qualities. His expression was simple and effective, and his fascination undeniable. It is hard to have to think of him as fit only for the garbage man.

And yet if indeed it were possible to build him up sufficiently to make him of positive value, one would have to ask oneself whether the most optimistic estimate of success would not have to be weighed against the cost in patience and perseverance and found wanting.

The great value of such men as Maitland and Neuburg to me has been to strengthen my conviction that in the absence of will power, the most complete collection of virtues and talents is wholly worthless. Combine in one man the strength of Hercules, the beauty of Apollo, the grace of Antinos, the wisdom of Athena, the intelligence of Hermes, and every other gift of every other god, unless the anatomist is careful to supply a spine to support the structure, you will have a mollusc and not a man. You must have a fulcrum, not only to move the world, but to move a feather.

Besides our regular members we had a short visit from the two sisters of Cypris, Mimi—her twin—and Helen, nearly twenty years her senior.

Mimi was delighted. She yearned intensely to throw in her lot with us for life and yet she was inhibited by subconscious fear. The chains from civilization clanked on her ankles and wrists. She stayed with us for a fortnight and then went back to her work with the Red Cross in the devastated districts round Soissons. But the gods had their rod in the pickle for her.

I must explain that members of the abbey bore certain distinguishing marks. The official costume for those not entitled to the special robes of the A∴A∴ was a vestment of bright blue hanging from neck to ankle with sleeves widening from shoulder to waist so that on extending the arms horizontally from the body it suggested the letter Tau. It was lined with scarlet and provided with a hood. When desired the dress was completed by a golden girdle. In addition the male members shaved the head with the exception of a single lock in the centre of the forehead. The women wore bobbed hair dyed red or yellow with henna. In these customs were symbolized certain spiritual or magical affirmations. The aureole of the women was in honour of our father the sun, and the upstanding lock of hair worn by the men a token of worship to his viceregent in the microcosm.[2]

One afternoon the women were retouching their hair with henna, and Mimi took it into her head to tint her own tresses slightly with the same paste. The change was barely perceptible to any sane eye, but the moment she showed up at Soissons the horrible hags in authority pounced on the child, overwhelmed her with outrageous insults and cast her forth from their chaste company. It was an abominable abuse of power, no less than a foul-minded frenzy and a sadistic injustice. I wrote congratulating her on having achieved such a drastic demonstration of the truth of what we had told her about such people, and reminded her that she would always be welcome in the abbey.

But now a strange obsession assailed her. During her visit I had been even more absorbed in my work than usual and had hardly exchanged a dozen words with her. I had not urged her to undertake the Great Work.[3] On the contrary I had been specially careful to maintain an attitude of simple friendliness. Yet she found herself the prey of a mingled fear and fascination. I was constantly present in her mind. She desired passionately to live in the shadow of my personality, yet at the same time was filled with panic fear of what seemed to her a surrender of her soul. The obsession grew to insane intensity. She felt that she was not safe in France. She must escape to the ends of the earth. She would hide herself in America. The poor child never guessed that she was trying to elude herself. However, she was carried away by her fears and fled to the States, where she paid the penalty of her panic. Fate has smitten again and again, and I hope that suffering will teach her what intelligence failed to impart. I shall be very surprised if sooner or later, she does not find her true will. For her only foes are ignorance and fear. Her heart is whole and honest.

With Helen the case was very different. I had met her in Paris early in '21, taken her to lunch at Lavenue's several times, and introduced her to some of my friends. I saw in the first few minutes that her life was one long pang. She had nothing to look back upon with pleasure or any hope for the future. Her face told the tale. The skin was dry, wrinkled and jaundiced; the thin lips were compressed with constant bitterness. Her intelligence was sufficient to tell her what was wrong. She had never known freedom. She had been robbed of her soul so that her masters might have a machine they could trust not to play any trick. The steam roller of social injustice had flattened her. Every drop of her blood had been drained by sterile servitude to soulless wealth. Yet she would not accept the way of escape that we offered so freely. Her suffering was intensified by the sight of the carefree happiness which she found in the abbey. At the time of her visit, we happened to be particularly short of funds, and it enraged her to see that poverty was powerless to destroy our happiness or drag love from his throne in our hearts. Why couldn't we quarrel and scold like the people she was accustomed to? Envy gnawed at her liver and black bile oozed from the wounds. She began to hate us with insane intensity and the fiend fattened on the fact that her malice was impotent to make us unkind to her.

However, she succeeded at least in making herself impossible. She started a campaign of venomous falsehoods, which she knew to be such. The Ape and I had planned to go to England before she arrived, but by a series of accidents we were obliged to postpone the journey. However, in view of our plans we had given up the second house, so that when she began to try to corrupt the children I was obliged to interfere. I gave her the choice between retracting some of the more malignant lies, in which I had caught her out, or pursuing her career of crime in some more favourable environment within fifteen minutes. She had no defence. The witnesses were unanimous. Her denials and evasions were nailed to the counter with a single smack the instant they were out of her mouth. So out she went, and we gave a great gasp of relief. Yet still I felt sorry. Even such cold malignity as hers only confirmed me in compassion. In other circumstances she might have developed into a human being. My action surprised her completely. I had seemed so easy-going and unobservant, so uniformly considerate and kind. When that lazy big lion suddenly leapt from his lair, she suffered the shock of her life. 'I thought there might be something of the sort,' she said, startled out of prudence, 'but I didn't think it would come for a long while.' She had hoped to do irreparable damage before being found out, and now she learnt, as so many before her and since, that the big lion sleeps with one eye open. Baffled and broken, her only idea was revenge. She did an amazing thing. She went to some consul in Palermo and swore to a long list of lies. She thought she could make trouble for us, though even after racking her brains for slanders she could only think of one thing which might bring us into conflict with the law. It was an act of unspeakable vileness. Success could only mean that her sister would be utterly ruined, torn from her home and her children, and either put in prison or thrown upon the world penniless in a foreign country without resources of any kind. Having shot the poisoned arrow, she pursued the Parthian policy of putting as many thousand miles as possible between herself and her victims. Before we found out what she had done she must be safe from pursuit. It was no part of her scheme to have to confront us and be cross-examined.

Of course the whole thing fizzled out. On the one alleged breach of the law, we were raided by the Cefalu police, of course without warning. They did their duty, while, of course, well aware that they had been sent to look for a mare's nest. They behaved with charming courtesy and withdrew with many apologies for their action. We have heard from time to time of Helen. She is back on the treadmill, lonely and loveless, wearily and miserably dragging her despair through life—to call it life—down to death. Should these words come under her notice, let me assure her that we bear no ill-will, that she will always be welcome when she learns her lesson: that love is the only principle which makes life tolerable.

I gladly leave this wretched episode. The Ape and I left Cefalu for Paris early in February as usual, our abode with our friends Monsieur and Madame Bourcier, 50 rue Vavin, a few doors below the Boulevard Montparnasse near the Rotonde. I cannot let pass this occasion of expressing my affection and gratitude which these good folks have won. Their hotel has been my headquarters in Paris for over fifteen years and from the very beginning they treated me more like a son than a stranger. When people talk against the French and complain of the difficulty of getting on with them, I smile only a little at their stupidity, and all the rest at the memory of the kindness which I have received from the Bourciers.

Nor is the case unique. I confess that now and again, I have met French people without real politeness or real good feeling. I will add that the wealthy and alleged aristocratic classes are sprinkled much too thinly with individuals for whom I have any use. I find them selfish and boring. The first is the cause of the second, for the secret is that they lack faith in life; seeking self they have found an inane nullity, and being bored with themselves they naturally bore other people. But French artists, the professional classes and the much abused bourgeois are almost always delightful. What's more, you can trust them to do you a good turn when opportunity occurs. As to the peasant in the provinces, I find *La Terre* very one-sided. No doubt thrift often becomes avarice and meanness, and contact with the soil a hardening and dehumanizing influence. But if you know how to take them the right way, you will find them a pretty good sort.

I have a theory that English people find the French unsympathetic for one fundamental reason. Our neighbours and allies, from the President to the most primitive toiler, possess one quality which I have analysed at length elsewhere. They insist on refusing to fool themselves. They see no sense in pretending things are pretty when they are not. They think it stupid to dope themselves and an insult to the intelligence of others to kiss the blarney stone. The English mind is accordingly shocked. It is so fixed in the point of politeness to refuse reality.

For the first time in my life, Paris disappointed me. All the old enchantments had somehow vanished. I felt that my work lay elsewhere. London called to me. It was quite unreasonable. I had no motive for going. I had no means to go. Uneasy and undecided I got through the days as best I could.

I decided to seek a solitude favourable for concentration at Hardelot, near Boulogne, in a delightful old inn where I had stayed before. The Ape of Thoth was in London. I wired her to meet me at Boulogne. So far there was no hitch in the proceedings. She met me at the train.

92

For some time past the City of London had amused itself by wondering mildly what could have happened to a dear old friend of theirs named Bevan. He was the head of several important concerns which, in fact, felt such dependence upon his gracious and intelligent guidance that they could hardly get on without him, especially as he had absent-mindedly packed in his portmanteau all their available assets. His absence aroused such anxiety and his speedy return was so desirable, that his friends had succeeded in interesting even Scotland Yard in the matter. Sympathetic friends all over Europe joined the rescue party and the *Daily Mail* lent its aid by publishing a photograph of the missing millionaire every day, week after week, and offered a prize of twenty-five thousand francs for information calculated to reassure the bereaved ones.

Excuse the digression. Both I and the Ape of Thoth strolled across the station to the Hotel Christol é Christol, proposing to dine and sleep, and go on to Hardelot in the morning. Tired by the journey we lay down for an hour and then came down to dinner. The restaurant opens out of the hall; to reach it from the staircase one inclines to the right. I was slightly surprised to find the whole staff of the hotel, from the manager to the porter, drawn up in a line between me and both the entrance and the restaurant. They all smiled and bowed obsequiously and awkwardly, like so many marionettes.

The manager stepped forward, louted him low, and motioned me towards a passage leading to the left. I supposed that, it being out of the season, the regular restaurant was shut and meals served elsewhere. He bowed me into a sort of smoking-room and suddenly shut the door behind me. I found myself, with no little surprise, in the presence of six men, dressed in black, sprinkled about the room. Only one was seated; and he jumped up and asked me my name. I told him. He asked for my papers. By the merest chance I had left my passport, which I usually carry with me, in the bedroom. I told him I would go and get it. Two men sprang to the door. My inquisitive friend snapped out, *'Apportez-moi le bagage!'* which a couple of his satellites proceeded to do.

I was, by this time, completely bewildered, but he motioned me to a chair and sat down, asking various questions, especially about the Ape of Thoth. Had she come from London, and why, and so on, which only served to increase my wonder as to what it could all be about. From time to time he consulted a large thin sheet of paper as if to guide him in his queries. The light fell on it and all of a sudden I saw from the back that its centre was occupied by a photograph which I instantly recognized.

'Mais, Monsieur,' I said, breaking into laughter, *'vous n'imaginez pas que je suis pour quelque chose dans cette affaire de M. Bevan.'* He retorted instantly, *'Mais vous êtes M. Bevan!'* I behaved very badly. I roared with laughter. Of course he was not put off by any such crude camouflage. 'But this is absurd,' I said, 'I am perfectly well known as a poet and explorer. I don't know the difference between a joint stock company and a debenture.' By this time my baggage had been brought. I found my passport which was, of course, in perfect order, but as evidence of identity produced no more effect on his mind than the initials of a shirt; we argued the matter for nearly an hour. One of his myrmidons after another stood at my side to be scrutinized for comparative height and width. One man thought my nose good enough to arrest me; another urged that my mouth cleared me of the crime. But the chief of police was tenacious. He had in his mind his step and the Legion of Honour and the *Daily Mail's* twenty-five thousand francs. Almost in despair I pulled out Guillamod's account of the 1902 expedition and showed him my photograph with my name printed under it. 'Do you really wish', I said, 'to maintain that I am a defaulting director?'

I don't know why, but this piece of evidence convinced him that I was not his man. He changed his tone, his men filed out, he bowed and apologized. I did not mean to be cruel, as no doubt I was. I told him that no excuse was necessary. I had not enjoyed myself so much in five years. What could a man want more—official reception, and the rest? It was a bitter pill for him but it still is sweet in my mouth. One serious reflection only mars the music. Suppose I had happened to be an unknown man, unarmed with every possible proof, I might quite well have been a week or more in jail before establishing my identity.

I must not leave this subject without a few remarks on the tendency in recent years of the police to attempt to arrogate themselves a function of authority altogether beyond a theoretical limit. Even in England, in 1922, there were several cases in which magistrates had to rebuke the police for encroaching upon judicial functions. In the United States, of course, conditions are outrageous. The extreme case is that of Becker. But apart altogether from individual iniquity the police claim that they cannot control crime unless they are empowered to make an inquisition into every man's private affairs. They take every opportunity of exceeding their powers of bluffing and badgering anybody that seems to them objectionable in total absence of any evidence whatever to establish so much as a *prima facie* case against them. In England so far we have not reached the stage of regular frame-ups with deliberate perjury, but there are suspicious signs of movement in that direction.

Let me quote from my own experience. As early as 1907, I was warned by a friend, I cannot say with what truth, that the police were watching me. My conscience being clear, I replied, 'Good, I shan't be burgled.' In 1910 during 'The Rites of Eleusis' in Caxton Hall, to which we purposely invited a police representative, they had other men in plain clothing outside the building, apparently hoping that something indictable would ooze through the brickwork.

In 1913–14 again, my studio near Onslow Square was a regular rendezvous for spies. I was always seeing them in the courtyard, skulking behind trees as I went to and fro from dinner. What they had hoped to find out I cannot imagine.

In Detroit, months after my return to Europe, they repeatedly raided poor half-crazed Ryerson's house in search of some evidence of the 'Devil Worshipper's Mystic Love Cult' and of course found nothing; from which they concluded not my innocence, but that my pact with the devil contained a clause guaranteeing me against the discovery of my crimes. If any of those obstinate asses had possessed sufficient intelligence to study a single page of my writings, he would have seen at once what ridiculous rubbish were the accusations made against me by foul-minded and illiterate cheats whom I had never so much as met.

While I was in America, the London police not only disgraced themselves by the brutal raid on poor old Mrs Davies, described in 'The Last Straw', but covered themselves with shame and ridicule by sending to prison a poor little bookseller who had sold for many years *The Open Court*, a well-known philosophical magazine of the highest character.

Again they sent round a man to Frank Hollings [1] to frighten him out of selling *The Equinox*, though no complaint had ever been made about it. Even my personal friends were haunted by sinister spies who made mysterious inquiries and uttered oracular hints about the frightful things that might happen if they happened. They wrote to my lawyers, and called on them to inquire my address which they knew perfectly well, and on my complaining to them about the theft of some of my property, not only refused to take up the matter, but answered me through the local police of the place where I lived, saying that I was 'well-known' in Scotland Yard. The fact is undeniable, but the insinuation cowardly and dirty.

The latest news from the front is that the special commissary in Tunis, having asked me to call with regard to an irregularity in my *permis de séjour*, amplified his remark with the cock-and-bull story intended to persuade me that I ran the risk of assassination by ferocious Fascisti. I asked the British consul to make inquiries and as with Hamlet—the rest is silence.

What interests me is the perverse psychology in this case. What can be their object? I am not annoyed but amused. But why should they waste so much energy and public money on watching a man year after year when one would have thought that the most elementary common sense would have told them anyhow, after the first few months, that I was no more likely to infringe the law than the Archbishop of Canterbury?

I vaguely assume some connection between this puerile policy of half-hearted pin-pricks and the perennial flowering of the fantastic falsehoods about me. It suggests that I possess some quality which attracts the attention of the half-witted so that they cannot leave me alone. I have often wished to collect 'The Thousand and One Nights of Nonsense', of which I am the hero. Seabrook's serial in 1923 is absurdly incomplete.[2]

My arrest in mistake for Bevan, whom I resemble about as much and as little as I do any other featherless biped, is rather typical of the odd incidents that help to keep me young. But when people ask me to clear my character of the aspersions upon it, my mind runs back to that scene in the smoking-room. I say to myself, 'My dear man, if it took you an hour to prove to a perfectly sensible Frenchman so simple and clear a case with all the trumps in your fist, how long would it take to persuade a prejudiced ignorant public, congenitally incapable of understanding your point of view, that you are innocent of crimes, the witnesses to which are unavailable, and whose very nature translates the court into a wonderland far more weird than anything in the adventures of Alice?'

My second stay in Paris was short. Everything pointed to my trying my luck in London. One of the most amusing results of the wholesale robbery of my money and effects was that I had no single suit of clothes fit to wear in London. I had worn out what I had taken with me to America and had never had enough spare cash to replenish my wardrobe.

All the clothes I had left in London had been stolen with this exception; that in the summer of 1914 I had sent my Highland dress to Scott Eadie to be overhauled. I now recalled this fact and wrote to them to send it to Paris. I had three kilts, a dress tunic and waistcoat, a tweed coat and vest and a green military tunic.[3] *Faute de mieux*, I donned the garb of old Gaul which, if unusual, was dignified, and scraping together very nearly ten pounds, I crossed the Channel in the first week of May.

The first problem was to find rooms. I was taking tea with my old friend Gwendolen Otter and asked if anyone knew a suitable place. The vague reply was that there were plenty round the King's Road, Chelsea. I went off, weary in body and spirit. I could hardly drag one foot after the other. I had alighted at a horrible hotel in Russell Square thronged with hustling hooligans of the middle classes. My heart sank at the thought of going back there. I wanted to save the five-penny bus fare. I came to the corner of Wellington Square and was suddenly seized with a direct inspiration to try my luck. 'Try the sacred numbers, especially the Secret Key of *The Book of the Law*—31!' Fagged as I was, I obeyed. The first number connected with my work was this very '31' and in the window was a card 'Apartments to Let'. A van stood at the door, which was open. I went in. The landlady showed me a large front room on the first floor, with French windows opening upon a balcony which overlooked the spirit-soothing oasis of the square; the small green oblong with its ancient trees. It was clean and comfortable, the rent reasonable, and the people of the house sympathetic and intelligent. The bow drawn at venture had hit the ideal at the first twang of the string. The miracle was the more striking that the card had not been in the window till a few hours before; they had in fact not finished moving in.

I must flit back to Paris for a moment to mention that before starting I had asked the *Yi* for a general symbol of my visit to London. I had obtained the hexagram 'Shih Ho', whose indications I may thus summarize. General Comment: It will be advantageous to use legal constraints.

I took this to mean that my proper course to restore my stolen property was to take legal action. The special comment on each of the six lines indicates the successive events of the period covered by the question. My campaign would clearly end disastrously through the enmity of others. I resolved not to be deterred by this forecast, since the previous lines absolved me from blame. I should make no error. 'Hew to the line, let the chips fall where they may!'

In a second hexagram, asking for advice how to conduct myself, I received one emphatic warning: avoid getting mixed up with unworthy people.

I now propose to narrate the principal events of my sojourn in England and show how exactly they confirmed the *Yi King*.

My first objective was obviously to obtain possession of my published works which had been warehoused with the Chiswick Press. This press, under the auspices of Mr Charles T. Jacobi, had no rival, except Constable's, for excellence of printing. I had entrusted them with the production of the majority of my books. When I left England in 1914, I owed them some three hundred and fifty pounds; their security was the stock of the approximate value of twenty thousand pounds. In 1920, Jacobi wrote to inform me the firm was changing hands, and although he would remain as a director of the new company, it was essential that I square the account. I therefore sent them three hundred and fifty pounds. They had authority from me to sell any copies which might be asked for.

On my arrival in London the position was that after paying warehouse charges to date, they owed me a little over ten pounds. They had written several times to urge me to remove the stock, alleging lack of space in their warehouse. I called and renewed my friendly acquaintance with Jacobi who agreed to hold the books till the end of May, to give me time to arrange for their removal. He furnished me with a complete set of the books as samples. I had approached Heinemann's with a scheme to dispose of the stock. They were to publish every month for a year a small volume of selections, lyrics, religious verses, essays, stories, plays, etc., with the idea that the readers would acquire the taste and buy the original editions. Heinemann's ultimately rejected this proposal—very reluctantly, and I believe on account of the violent personal opposition of one of their staff, a man whom I had never met. I found a new warehouse in due course and called to arrange a convenient day to remove the books.

To my surprise a perfect stranger came into the outer office, a weird creature of nightmare, long, loose-jointed, shaking and tottering with palsy, with a head grotesque and ghastly, rocking upon narrow sloping shoulders that seemed to shrink from its weight. This fantastic horror announced itself as the managing director of the new company. I stated my business. To my amazement, he broke out into a spate of unmeaning insults. He refused point-blank to deliver the books on the ground that Scotland Yard would be down on him if he did. I said, 'But this is ridiculous. What has Scotland Yard to do with the matter? If you really think they are concerned, ring them up at once. Ask them!' He went off saying he would telephone, and returned in a few minutes saying that they would make inquiries and let him know in a few days.

Of course the police had no interest in the matter at all. But this goblin still refused delivery. I could only suppose him a lunatic. He did not merely insult me but Mr Jacobi, the best of printers, by far the most eminent in England, a man who had spent his life in the service of the art and who had done more for it than any single man since Caxton.

Warner, for so my lunatic called himself, spoke of Jacobi in terms that would have been harsh applied to a dishonest office boy. I wrote to Jacobi personally. He replied as I anticipated, but admitted that the control had passed from his hands. Warner flew in even a more furious rage than ever at my having written, and his having replied. I had known Jacobi since '98, and our business relationship during the twenty-five years had been unbroken and uniformly pleasant. I found my friends scarcely able to believe the story. Such conduct as Warner's was incredible. It was obvious, however, even to him that some settlement was necessary. We had a final interview. He resorted to all kinds of absurd arguments quite impertinent to the business on hand and took an attitude in flat contradiction to that adopted by the firm. At the last moment, he suddenly shifted his ground. A furtive gleam of cunning came into his eyes and he suggested that it would be all right if I took the books away without his official knowledge. It was the first sensible thing he had said. It was arranged that he should consult the directors as a matter of form, and then arrange an hour for the removal over the telephone as it might be convenient for him to be out of the way at the time. We parted on this understanding. But the next morning I got a letter that everything was off.

I reflected on the *Yi's* research: 'It will be advantageous to use legal constraints' and went round to my lawyer. He advised me that they had no case. The one technical difficulty which related to some few volumes could be obviated easily enough. Correspondence ensued, and finally he interviewed the solicitors of the firm and came to a satisfactory arrangement. Warner was away on his holiday, but the business would go through directly he returned. Not at all! He went back on everything and defied me to obtain possession. And there the matter stands, as far as I know. I have never been able to collect sufficient funds to recover my property which constitutes my principal asset. If Warner is even partially sane the motive is beyond my wit to imagine. Can he possibly hope that I shall drop the matter, and let him get away with twenty thousand pounds of stolen property?

To keep a straight story, I have admitted that at Warner's suggestion two roundabout ways were tried. I was to make a fictitious sale of the stock to another man, and he, having taken them away, could transfer them to me. When he called he was assailed in the most intemperate language and the delivery refused. The second idea was to get my tailor to obtain judgment against me for the few hundreds I owed him, to be executed by seizing the stock. But the sheriff received the same treatment as everyone else. Warner started at once to heap insults upon, and hurl defiance at, the representatives of the law. What interests me most in all this is the problem of how such a man ever does any business. In my own case, part of my original plan involved the placing of large orders with his firm. When a stranger calls to bring him gold he is thrown out. It beats me altogether.

My next important business was to re-establish my connection with editors. I called on the *English Review*. Austin Harrison welcomed me as warmly as ever, and asked me to write the centenary article on Shelley and some minor work. I signed the Shelley essay 'Prometheus'. I created a furore in literary London. They were stupefied. Who the devil could have written it? There were not three men in England anywhere near that class. It was the best boost the *English Review* had had since Frank Harris and I had left England. Mond had withdrawn his support, turning over the *Review*, lock, stock and barrel, gratis, on his attention being called to the fact that Harrison possessed a letter from Lord Roberts denouncing Mond in such terms that its publication would have probably been followed by the wrecking of Mond's house in Lowndes Square, and, as likely as not, a lynching. Sir George Lewis called at the office (Harrison boasted to me that Lewis never went outside his lair for anyone less than a royal duke) and concluded the deal on the terms stated above on Harrison's giving his word not to make public the letter. It went through. But when Harrison looked for the lethal letter he failed to find it, and believes that Mond had arranged for someone to pay an unauthorized visit to his sanctum and extract it. This hypothesis involves the assumption that Mond harboured doubts as to the value of Harrison's word of honour, which is too painful to think of.

Deprived of financial support, and of the guidance of Frank Harris and myself, he was left to plough his lonely furrow and a crooked furrow it was. The *English Review* lost interest for the educated classes whose taste it was designed to please. The circulation sagged lower every month. Its dullness became devastating. Harrison's own work is always amazing and sometimes first-rate. But other contributors fell off. They got tired of being asked to write at nominal rates, and at that to have to extract the cheque with a Big Bertha corkscrew. He paid me five pounds for my Shelley essay. Subsequent articles were even less adequately remunerated. And it was not only a task which Jove would have thrown up to get paid at all, but after prolonged humiliating haggling over the price, the ultimate cheque was more annoying than agreeable. He would argue for an hour that he had said pounds and not guineas. I put up with the pest because it amused me. I can hardly explain why I enjoy watching such contemptible wrigglings. I suppose it is the same sort of fascination as makes one stop to watch a street squabble between two prostitutes.

A further unpleasantness was that he always wanted to mutilate what I wrote by removing the strongest passages or reshaping them so that my style was spoilt entirely and diluted with his journalistic commonplaces and clichés. I made the best of a bad job. My reply to Rabbi Joel Blau, 'The Jewish Problem Re-Stated', for example, seemed to me so important that any sacrifice was worth making. I doubt my wisdom. His emendations reduced a masterpiece of reasoning and eloquence to a comparatively unremarkable pleading, and it fell almost flat.

My real plan was to put persistent pressure upon Harrison.
I thought that in time my moral superiority and intelligence
would convert him to a course by adopting which thoroughly
and enthusiastically, the stone might be rolled away from the
sepulchre, and the *English Review* regain its pre-eminence as
the only organ in England with a soul of its own. In fact, so
long as I stayed in London I made a good deal of headway.
But the moment the cat was away, the mice began to play.
I ran over to France for a fortnight in August, and when I got
back he had broken his word on every point. My return restored order, but on leaving for Sicily, it was the same story.
He had promised to publish something of mine every month
and send me not less than eight pounds every time the first
came round. He did not even send me the ten pounds he had
promised when we parted, knowing well that I counted on
him for this to stand between me and actual starvation.

I could have borne with his treatment of myself, but he
used me to injure others. In our early conversations he had
argued with perfect justice that the English market for the
English Review was hopeless, at least for a long time, and
that therefore the only chance of restoring solvency was to
push it in America. It was obvious that I could do this with
success. He agreed to my plan, and I wrote accordingly to
several of my friends, first-class writers, far better than any
in England—bar Conrad and Hardy—asking them to contribute. They one and all wrote charmingly and enthusiastically,
and sent a number of admirable stories. They further promised
to use their influence—in two cases enormous—they being
editors of periodicals whose combined circulation must be
in the millions, to introduce the *English Review* to the American public. The scheme prospered beyond my greatest expectation. H. L. Mencken himself came to see us, and he
formulated a plan of action which would have certainly succeeded and put Harrison's circulation up to thirty thousand
at the lowest estimate within a few months.

But this was not all. Hearing that my friend Otto Kahn, the
famous financier and the admirably judicious appreciator of
fine creative work, was in England, I asked him to lunch with
me to meet Harrison. His agenda was full, but he proposed to
call at the office. We talked matters over some two hours,
and laid down the outlines of a scheme, the success of which
was that a chronic invalid magazine called the *Forum* should
be bought and amalgamated with the *English Review*. We
were to publish two editions, I to be in charge of the *English*

Review in New York. The bulk of the contents was to be identical, but a proportion to cover matters of local interest in the respective countries. Otto Kahn, while not pledging himself definitely to finance the proposal, gave us to understand that he would not be unwilling to support it.

The sequel is really too stupid. We discussed the details of the scheme and wrote to Mr Kahn accordingly. But when Harrison showed me the draft of his letter I could hardly believe my eyes. He wanted six thousand pounds for the paper which everyone knew was being literally hawked about London on the chance of finding a fool to pay two thirds that amount, and besides he was to be guaranteed two thousand pounds a year for three years. And on top of all he was to have an interest in the company. I didn't tell him that Otto Kahn was not in the market to buy gold bricks and that nothing would disgust him so thoroughly as so obvious an attempt to pull his leg. I knew that moderation and—well, hang it, common honesty would determine Kahn to do his utmost for us. To him twelve thousand pounds is of course a microscopic object, but he would resent any attempt to take advantage of that fact as strongly and rightly as a diner in a Soho gargote objects to mistakes in his bill. I was furious at the abuse of my introduction, but I kept my temper, put things as pleasantly as I could, and begged Harrison to moderate his grab. His conscience convicted him. He put up the feeblest arguments I ever heard in my life about the great value of the property which he constantly declared a thankless burden and a financial loss. I knew it was hopeless, and of course Kahn wrote back briefly that he had inquired and found that the *Forum* was not for sale. We had discussed that point. It made little difference, but it saved Kahn from having to say what he thought about the try on.

Having enthusiastically accepted my plan about pushing the paper in America by publishing the work of their best men and a series of essays by myself to introduce them to English readers, a line of attack quite independent of the more wide-read big proposal, he suddenly broke away. 'What would happen to the English market?' he wailed. 'What do they care about American writers?'

'My dear man,' I replied, 'the whole point of the game is that you have told me again and again that the English market is hopeless. Whatever you do you cannot win out in England. And even if the American campaign does diminish your sale by a few hundred copies, what's that as against the splendid chance of building up a circulation in the States?' But he wouldn't see it. He dropped the whole thing.

I made one other suggestion—to try to get readers among occult students. I arranged a scheme of co-operation with the *Occult Review*. Ralph Shirley was enthusiastic and willing to help in every possible way. But Harrison never liked the scheme. His ignorance of the importance of the occult public was not merely complete, but invulnerable to all information. I gave him the figures. I proved that for one person who cared for poetry, there were at least a thousand whose only form of reading was spiritualism, theosophy, psychical research, Magick, Yoga, mysticism, Christian Science, and its congeners, occult freemasonry, etc., etc., *ad libitum*. He flatly refused to admit the facts. I begged him to try it out, if only by asking a few dozen strangers what they themselves cared to read. His very secretaries rose up against him and confirmed my statement. It was useless. His own objection to the occult was so strong, that he deliberately shut his eyes to the facts; even the vogue of Conan Doyle's senile dementia did not move him. And that is the end of that.

I have not seen the *English Review* this year. I can only suppose that it has dropped back after the spurt of last summer into its regular ditchwater dullness, if indeed it has not passed away altogether by that kind of passing away which leaves nothing whatever behind.

My third string was to publish new books. Sullivan had suggested my trying Grant Richards, firstly with a plan for marketing the existing stock, and secondly with a proposal to write my memoirs. He promised to put in a good word for me as he knew Grant Richards well and was influential as being a man of sound business and literary judgment. I therefore called and made my proposals. But after some consideration, Grant Richards could not see his way to accept my terms. I think we were both reluctant to part; and one night I was inspired to try him with a third artificial minnow. I would write a shocker on the subject which was catering to the hysteria and prurience of the sex-crazed public: the drug traffic insanity. It provided a much needed variation from the 'white slave' traffic. I proposed as a title *The Diary of a Drug Fiend* and sketched out a synopsis of its contents on a sheet of notepaper. This was mostly bluff. I had not really any clear idea of my story. I took this round to Grant Richards, who said it was not in his line. I asked him to suggest a likely firm. He said Hutchinson or Collins. Neither name meant anything to me. I gave Collins the first chance simply because he was on my way home.

Invited to interview the responsible man, I found myself wondering who he was—I had surely met him before. He shared my feeling and was the first to discover the source. Over fifteen years earlier he had been on the staff of a paper called *What's On* belonging to my old acquaintance Robert Haslam and at one time edited by poor crazy Dartnell.

The gods had certainly started a new drama. The accident of this man, J. D. Beresford his name is, being the literary advisor of Collins probably made all the difference to the fate of the book. The synopsis was accepted enthusiastically and I obtained the pledges of money and advances, as per the *Yi* forecast, to the extent of a sixty-pound advance and a contract on much better terms than a new author could have hoped.

I contracted to deliver the manuscript within a month. My idea was to rush the book through as suitable for holiday reading. I wired to Paris for the Ape, who hurried over. We sat down at once to work. She takes my dictation in long hand, and it was therefore some 'stunt' to have written the 121,000 words in 27 days, 12¾ hours. Mrs Marshall, the best typist I ever employed—she had worked for me off and on since '98 —could hardly believe her eyes as one stack of manuscript came tumbling on the top of another. It gave me a chance to boost the Law of Thelema. I was able to show how the application of the principles increases efficiency as the profane deem impossible.

Beresford was delighted with the manuscript and in high hopes of making a big hit. Unfortunately, my plan for publishing the book in August was not adopted. For various reasons they kept it hanging about till November. This annoyed me greatly. I expected its publication to arouse a tempest in the teapot around which the old women of criticism nod and talk scandal. I wanted to be on the spot when the fur began to fly, so as to give as good as I got. However, the gods have their own ideas.

I now put forward my scheme for publishing my memoirs— my autohagiography I playfully called it—before Collins. Beresford knew Sullivan well, another lucky coincidence; and when I sent him a fairly full synopsis, they accepted my proposals gladly. I took a short holiday in Paris, chiefly to give the Ape a good time at the seaside, and on my return settled down to dictation.

93

Another thread is now woven into my destiny. Before the war, one of my best men in the O.T.O. was a man named Hammond. He was an engraver of astonishing skill and had been very useful in preparing plates for the diplomas of the Order. He was enthusiastic about its principle and advanced rapidly from the IV° to which he had been affiliated from Royal Arch of old-fashioned masonry, to the very exalted rank of Grand Inquisitor Commander. I liked Hammond personally so well that I even asked him to spend a week with me in Paris and see life, which till then had meant to him only the narrow and sordid circle of lower middle class English in parts of London barely distinguishable from slums. He beheld the heavens opened. Overflowed with gratitude and adoration, he acquired the sort of affection for me that a dog has for its master.

Alas! this dog had the mange! Supposedly as the result of vaccination in childhood with an impure preparation, he suffered the tortures of psoriasis. The irritation was perpetual. He had tried every known treatment and received from none more than temporary relief. (I think it throws light on my character that ever since I met him, I have never forgotten, whenever I met anyone likely to be able to suggest some new remedy, to ask him about it.)

Hammond had executed the work entrusted to him by the Order with rapidity and excellence beyond praise. I gave him a new job of the utmost importance. I had written a short treatise on the central secret of the O.T.O. for members of the IX°,[1] and proposed to issue this embossed in the style of headings on notepaper and illustrated with numerous symbolic designs. Hammond was to cut the dies for the text, a really tremendous job. The reward was of course commensurate. It implied his initiation to the IX°, which otherwise might have cost him years of effort. But now appeared a strange defect in the man's character. After preparing nearly one third of the dies he broke off. I was out of London. Letters and telegrams sometimes elicited no reply; sometimes he wrote explaining his failure and promising immediate amendment; but I could not keep him up to the mark even when I got back; and I could not be angry with him if only because of his disease which seemed to me as the excuse for his conduct. Nor did I want to wound such affectionate enthusiasm. In his devotion, he had even called his latest son after me, Aleister Crowley. I left London, leaving him to complete the work as best he could.

I wrote several times from America, but failed to get any reply. On my return I tried to find him, but without success. It became vitally important to re-establish relations as Cowie claimed that the missing property of the Order was in his charge. I tried all sorts of plans, but without result. One day, however, as the Ape and I were taking a short cut through Soho, she insisted on inquiring at one of his old addresses. I objected to waste time on a certain failure. But she insisted and went round. Incredibly enough we found him. He was enraptured. We had tea and dinner together, and then went home with him to his house in Highbury. He had some of the missing assets and had kept them faithfully with all possible care. I was overjoyed to find that my trust had not been misplaced in at least one instance. I rewarded his loyalty by conferring upon him the IX° O.T.O. The prize should have been infinitely precious, for it put in his hands an almost certain cure for his lifelong affliction. We held numerous conferences and concerted plans for re-establishing the Order in London, the old Lodge having suspended its labours in consequence of the ridiculous raid described in 'The Last Straw'.[2] For greater convenience, it was decided that the Ape and I should rent from him the top floor of his house, which we did on my return from the Continent.

But now a new ordeal was prepared for me. Despite her quality, the Ape of Thoth began to show the effects of her long strain, anxiety and suffering. I called in a doctor who suspected the beginnings of phthisis, complicated with nervous weakness so serious that practically all her reflexes were abolished. The girl's courage is so infernally sublime that she performs miracles of camouflage to prevent me discovering her condition lest my anxiety should distract me from my work. But at last the cat was out of the bag. It was imperative that she should return to Cefalu at once and regain her health by freedom from work and anxiety, fresh air, fresh food, easy exercise and medical care. It was easy to prescribe this cure but its execution was another matter. I spent the next week chasing round London trying every expedient to collect sufficient cash for her journey and the living expenses of the next few weeks. I pawned every object of value and extracted every penny I could from everyone I knew. Finally I succeeded and off she went to Sicily. She picked up at once. A month later, she was almost herself again, though of course she needed a long period of care to replace the vital capacity which she had spent in the service of the Great Work.

I, too, was very far from well. My desperate situation, my anxiety about the welfare of those for whom I had made myself responsible, unremitting overwork and the eternal disappointments were beginning to break me down. At this moment a letter was forwarded to me from Cefalu addressed to me by Betty Dartnell. Her crazy husband had taken her and his daughter to British Columbia, I think about 1913. The new conditions had transformed her. When I saw her in Victoria in 1915, the flabby sensual debauched rake had become clean, muscular, trim, bright-eyed and self-controlled. I begged her to break entirely with her maniac who had steadily drifted into crazier courses. She was within an ace of cutting the painter, but could not quite bring herself to take an irrevocable step. I had only an hour with her. If I could have stayed a week in Victoria I might have rescued her. Soon after they drifted to Los Angeles, where Dartnell got into the movie job and took to writing scenarios. In that crowd of debauched degenerates, his own insanity was not so fatal as in more sober surroundings. He took to writing me voluminous letters raving about some cinema star or other whom 'God designs for his soul mate! And what was he to do? Was he to yield to unchaste impulse?' Page after page, he poured out the most violent megalomania. I wrote back the obvious advice; to act sensibly without imagining that the solar system would go to smash on account of his sexual explosions. At last even Los Angeles found him a nuisance.

Lydia Yonska had taken pity on him at a time when he was desperately in need of money. He had shown his gratitude by pestering her with his unwelcome attentions, even climbing into her house at night through an open window and scaring her half out of her wits with frantic protestations and threats. She found herself obliged to protect herself. Dartnell wrote me a long letter abusing her. He said that she was a vampire and had tried to seduce him, and on his refusal had begun to persecute him. She had been deputed by the devil to destroy men's souls, and God had appointed him to avenge her victims by killing her when opportunity offered.

It happened that Madame Yonska was in New York when this letter reached me. I had, in fact, met her a few days before, and painted her portrait, one of my best pictures, by the way. I thought I would warn her and showed her his scrawl. She told me of course the true facts as narrated above.

Since that time, the winter of 1918–19, I had heard no more of him directly. But Jane Wolfe had seen a good deal of them in Los Angeles. They had separated finally. (They were always doing that, but always the madman had come back and started some new scrap.)

Sheila, his child by his first wife, now in her teens, had shown the taint of his insanity by developing incurable kleptomania. Having inherited also her father's cleverness and cunning, her thefts had escaped detection for a long while, with the natural result that innocent people were always suffering from her misdeeds. Even when found out, she succeeded as often as not in putting her crimes on to others. No one would accept the responsibility of looking after her. She had returned with her parents to England. Betty and she lived in a big house in Cleveland Gardens. Dartnell had buried himself in Devonshire, turning up only when some demoniac impulse to make mischief seized him. Since 1920 Betty had written to Jane for help and advice. Her sexual obsessions had begun to turn into religious channels as so often happens to women on reaching the forties. Jane begged her to come to Cefalu and develop her spiritual and moral self beyond reach of the constant temptation of London to drown her aspiration in drink and debauchery. Betty knew in her heart that her only salvation lay in some such decision. But her almost complete lack of self-control prevented her from taking the plunge.

Such were the conditions when she wrote direct to me, begging me to take her in hand and save her from the stinking mire in which she felt herself slowly being sucked down.

I took this letter as a sign. It was surely strange that I should be in London still. The delays which had annoyed and puzzled me became comprehensible. I went round to Cleveland Gardens. Betty was out. Sheila, whom I had not seen since she was a baby, gave me tea. She fascinated and horrified me. I had never seen a girl so perfectly evil. She had no trace of heart. Such callous cynicism would have been abominable in a rake of sixty. A sinister malice lurked in her most casual remarks. Her deceitfulness was overpoweringly evident in her looks, no less than her words. Her eyes gleamed with ghastly glee. It suggested that she imagined herself as a sort of scourge to inflict obscene suffering upon anyone she might meet. I waited some time hoping Betty would return. She did not and it was arranged for me to come to tea the next day.

I found her in a curious state. She had lost most of the wholesomeness and health which she had enjoyed when I last saw her. She knew she was going downhill and in danger of stumbling and pitching over the cliffs in the dark. She clung to spiritual aspirations as her only hope and told me her experiences. They resembled Jane's for the most part, but certain incidents were indubitably evidential of genuine communication with intelligences of a very high order of initiation. Her trouble was that she lacked the means of discrimination between the most contemptible drivel and the most exalted truth.

She begged me to stay in her house till I left for Cefalu, urging that I was ill and in need of loving care. She overcame my hesitation by emphasizing her need of a strong hand to guide and help her. Finally I consented. I was well aware that she was precisely one of those wrong people against mixing with whom the *Yi* had so earnestly warned me. I went with my eyes open, saying to myself, 'Whatever mischief may come of this, it is none the less my duty to save this woman's soul. I will keep my oath, come what may!'

At first things went well beyond my highest hope. I showed her how to invoke the gods, and to banish evil and malignant entities that had hitherto deceived her by impersonating them. The very first experiment succeeded. She brought back information of great value. Its truth and the exalted nature of the being who uttered it was guaranteed by internal evidence of the strictest accuracy. Shortly after this the sun entered the sign of Libra. I chose her to assist me in obtaining the word of the autumnal equinox. She made good. The word was given by her as 'THIGHS', to which she assigned the number 542 and the meaning 'Light, Eyes, Flame and Will'.

I wrote this in Hebrew: Teth+Ayin+Shin+93, which might be pronounced Thighs. Teth is the letter of Leo, the House of the Sun, and therefore a hieroglyph of Light. Ayin means an eye. Shin is the letter of fire or flame; while 93 signifies Thelema—Will. Further 542 is a number which I had long sought to interpret as being the arithmetical mean between 418 (the Magical Formula of the New Aeon) and 666, my own cipher. I had never succeeded in finding a word to express this idea of the unification of my own nature with that of my dynamic structure. It must surely strike the most sceptical mind as remarkable that an untrained woman, wholly ignorant of Cabbalistic formulae, should obtain words, letters and numbers, so accurately interwoven, so complete an hieroglyph of an idea which defied my skill to analyse. As is my custom I sought in the Holy Books and in the *Yi King* for an interpretation of the word in terms of the events of the ensuing six months. I will mention one or two signal examples of the trustworthiness of such divination.

1. The hexagram which defined the scope of the work of the Order was 'Kieh' meaning 'Regulations'.[3] In the first three months I am described as unable to organize the affairs of the Order. But in the last three, a sudden change takes place. A way is found of establishing the proper system.

Now, until the winter solstice the chaos grew more confused than ever. A few days later a man suddenly came forward precisely fitted to undertake the organization required. I say suddenly, for he had steadfastly resisted the Secret Chiefs for years. His soul was torn by an earthquake and he broke with his past ruthlessly, devoting himself wholly to the Great Work from that hour henceforth.

The work of the abbey was described by the 51st hexagram 'Kan'. The first month indicates anxiety mingled with cheerful intercourse with friends. Till the last week in October I was worried indeed, but meeting many pleasant people and enjoying agreeable conversation with them.

Line two indicates peril which makes one abandon one's immediate business and go to an exalted place. The affairs which he dropped will be taken up again without effort on his part. This describes my last month in England, which brought about a new crisis in my affairs. I dropped them and went to the high house of Cefalu. After a time the abandoned business was resumed.

Line three. To Christmas. Startling events occur. This corresponds to the attacks on the abbey in the Sunday papers and *John Bull*.

Line four. The abbey is supinely sinking in the mud. We were unable to do anything to improve our position and our activity was hampered by illness.

Line five. All ways in peril and assailed by startling events;

there is a coming and going, which hints at the gathering storm of persecution, the constant assaults of ill-health, and the irregularity of the work, or perhaps even the death of Raoul Loveday is implied by the word going.

Line six. Startling events continue causing breathless dismay and anxious watchfulness. In this one might read the renewal of the newspaper attacks on the abbey and the discouragement and worry produced by events.

My own fortune was described by the 9th hexagram 'Hsiao Khu'.

The first line. 'Returning and pursuing his own course.' Fulfilled by my lectures and new disciples in London.

Two. 'Returning', i.e. to Cefalu.

Three. Various symbols of a check to progress and sudden opposition. As happened on publication of *The Drug Fiend*.

Four. Shows sincerity averting murderous attacks. My attitude put an end to the libels.

Five. My sincerity attracts sympathy and help. This was fulfilled by the adhesion of several new disciples.

Six. 'The rain has fallen and progress checked.' Raoul's death put a stop to my regular work.

Even the symbols for subordinate members of the Order forecast accurately their fortunes. For instance, Hammond had the 32nd hexagram, whose symbolism is that of a ram attempting more than he can do, becoming entangled with the obstacles, and finally being paralysed.

The description is marvellously accurate. He made fierce quick attempts to achieve his ends. They were baffled. He dashed himself against a wall, was enmeshed in the intrigues of my enemies, and found himself in the end neither able to go forward to victory, nor to extricate himself from the circumstances. He had committed himself to my interests irrevocably.

94

In the following month, Betty arranged two lectures on the Law of Thelema in her house and brought a number of friends to seek my assistance.

One such introduction proved pregnant with fate. A brilliant boy, just down from Oxford, where he had distinguished himself by his attainments in history, had long wished to meet me. For over two years, he had studied my magical writings with the utmost enthusiasm and intelligence. His character was extraordinary. He possessed every qualification for becoming a Magician of the first rank. I designed him from the first interview to be my magical heir. He possessed, of course, the defects of these qualities.

His daring had made him reckless, and his insight contemptuous of phenomena. He had thus been notorious at Oxford as the leader of madcap escapades, in one of which, escaping from the proctors, he had taken a leap in the dark and landed on a spike which transfixed his thigh. He lay between life and death for some months and was still weak from the effects of the loss of blood. Even worse, perceiving the splendour of his soul, he refused to be daunted by its sheath, which led him to commit the fatal folly of marrying a girl whom he had met in a sordid and filthy drinking den in Soho, called the Harlequin, which was frequented by self-styled artists and their female parasites. One of these went by the name of Betty May. Born in a slum in the East End, she had become an artist's model of the most vicious kind. She had been married and divorced, remarried and widowed by the war. In her childhood an accident had damaged her brain permanently so that its functions were discontinuous, and she had not mended matters by taking to cocaine at the age of about twenty. After some years of addiction, she found herself using a quarter of an ounce or more daily. She suddenly took fright and cured herself by switching over, first to injections of morphia, and then to plain alcohol. She made no secret of this, and I admired her immensely for her frankness about it and her superb courage in curing herself. She was a charming child, tender and simple of soul.

Yet with all that, Raoul should not have married her. It meant the sterilization of the genius of success in life. Already the evil effects were manifest. His university career was closed. The friends who might have helped him refused to succour a man who had deliberately cut himself off from decency. The mere fact of marriage, had his wife been a duke's daughter, disqualified him for most of the positions which otherwise might have been open. His parents were poor, self-made and at that only on the fringe of the middle classes. They could not help out. He had struggled along by getting odd articles into various papers. He and Betty lived in one filthy room in Fitzroy Street, a foul, frowsty, verminous den, stinking of the miasma of that great class who scrape through the years by dint of furtive cunning in dubious avocations. They were living from hand to mouth, with disaster eternally looming ahead, and the whisper of hope more faint and feeble as each effort ended in failure.

Again, I thought I saw the design of the gods. This was the man I had needed for the last ten years, a man with every gift that a Magus might need, and already prepared for initiation by practically complete knowledge, not only of the elements but of the essence of Magick.

I wasted no time. I urged him to join me and work with me until his initiation was complete. My proposal not only fulfilled the holiest hope of his soul, but solved his material problem. In the abbey he would be able to make himself a career as a writer as he could not hope to do in the loathsome surroundings of slum life in London. His health, too, demanded urgently a complete change. He had already been ill at frequent intervals. During October the foulness of Fitzroy Street fastened its foetid fangs on his throat. Both he and Betty escaped death by a hairbreadth. It decided him to accept my offer which I had renewed in a long letter written from Rome. I was equally anxious to rescue him from the verminous vagabonds, squalid and obscene, who constituted the court of Queen Betty. He had taken me to the Harlequin one night. In a corner was his wife, three parts drunk, on the knees of a dirty-faced loafer, pawed by a swarm of lewd hogs, breathless with lust. She gave herself greedily to their gross and bestial fingerings and was singing in an exquisite voice, which might have put her among princes, an interminable smutty song, with a ribald chorus in which they all joined, hoarse and harsh from drink and disease. The beauty and charm of the girl, the pure music of her notes, emphasized the contrast with the incarnated filth that swarmed over her. I expected an explosion. In Raoul's place, I should have fallen like a thunderbolt on the swine and driven them into the street, taken my wife straight home, washed her and thrashed her, and told her that if it happened again I was through. But he, poor innocent lad, took it all as a matter of course.

I am not a prude, as I hope this book may prove. But passion is one thing and dirt another. In my letter from Rome, I wrote the naked truth—that an Oxford man should look after his wife and that if he mixed with such creatures infection was inevitable. I think my straight speaking opened his eyes. He collected the necessary cash and came to the abbey. Betty had done her best to hold him in London. Her only idea of life was this wallowing in the hog trough nuzzled by the snouts of the swine of Soho.

The success of Betty Dartnell in her spiritual work increased her enthusiasm at first, and I was still so young in experience that it surprised me one day, when she came into my room full of rubbishy rigmarole purporting to come from some angel. 'Have you learnt nothing in all this time?' said I. It was all no good. The verbose pomposity and extravagant promises of the false meant more to her than the calm wisdom of the true. Having fallen on one plane the others were sympathetically affected. Next day she was hopelessly drunk, broke her evening appointment to work with me and went to the Harlequin. She brought home half a dozen drunken wastrels and their female friends with a supply of whisky. They drank themselves into a stupour and slept all over the house like so many swine. The debauch produced the usual reaction. Betty Dartnell repented and promised never to do it again. But she would not do the one thing that would have saved her, cut that crowd once and for all. She found excuses for them. She persuaded herself that it was her duty to rescue them, which, of course, only meant that subconsciously she craved the oblivion of the mire.

Needless to say, I did not repeat the warning. I concentrated on my work, ready to welcome her back to comradeship whenever she chose. But she began to see me as a skeleton at the banquet. I was an avatar of her conscience. She accordingly did what people who are determined to follow the primrose path always do with conscience. She avoided me when she could and insulted me when she couldn't, with the ultimate aim of eliminating me entirely. In this, of course, Sheila abetted her eagerly.

It had been understood that Betty Dartnell was to come with me to Cefalù as soon as the necessary arrangements could be made. The proposal was advantageous to her in every way. Spiritual progress, moral reconstruction, physical welfare and economic freedom. She was to come provisionally for three months and then consider further plans. In these circumstances, I felt free to borrow twenty pounds from her. For this I gave her my note due at the end of October on the understanding that, should I be unable through any misfortune to repay her, it should be regarded as an advance on her dues to the abbey. Only a few days later came her relapse and from that time she did all in her power to prevent my bringing off any of my business deals. It was, therefore, entirely her own fault that I could not meet the note on the date it fell due. I explained the position and she had a generous movement of real regret that her moral collapse had injured me as well as herself. She promised amendment and said that she would come to Cefalù as soon as possible, the twenty pounds being put to her credit. Yet the next day she was again attacked by hysteria. Sheila took advantage of her half-crazed condition to get her to spend the entire weekend with some friends in the country while she got rid of me.

I had observed this unhappy child with great care, in the hope of finding some remedy for her paranoia. I felt little hope. The mischief was rooted in her essence. She stole right and left both from me and others in the house. It was never possible to prove guilt. The evidence amounted merely to this: that she was known to be a thief and only she had the opportunity in most of the cases. The insane element was manifest; she stole for stealing's sake. She stole things that she could not have sold for sixpence. I suspect that part of her complex was that she enjoyed the annoyance caused by the theft.

Betty once out of the way, Sheila told me a string of the most stupid lies I ever heard, each absurd and incompatible with known facts in itself, and in contradiction with the rest of her remarks. She then proceeded to lock up all the rooms and hide all the keys on ridiculous pretexts so that I could not get at various articles to pack them. I decided, of course, to go elsewhere at the earliest opportunity and had only stayed at first to satisfy myself that I had done all I possibly could to save Betty from the frightful abyss for which she was head-ing, and after she had gone, in order to study the psychology of poor Sheila. I saw Betty twice more before leaving London. She had begun to realize what a fool she had been and promised on her honour to join us a month later. We parted in perfect amity, but my influence being removed Sheila's plans for destroying her stepmother, body and soul, proceeded gaily. She made her drunk and got in a man from one of the Sunday papers for an interview. Betty was worked up to indignation against me. She twisted all my sayings and doings into evil, and those which involved her co-operation were garbled. Most of her statements were barefaced falsehoods and the rest falsifications of fact. When this filth was published she saw for a moment how vilely she had been induced to act, and wrote to me expressing the bitterest remorse; but at the same time pleading that they had reported her falsely. I begged her to make amends in the only possible way; by coming forward publicly and testifying under oath to the falsehood of the allegations. Alas, poor Betty! It has been the curse of her life that she cannot act decisively.

Sheila had still one more chance to steal from me and she took it. She knew where I had sent my property to be warehoused, and guessing that I had left in London such things as were useless in Sicily, rang up the warehouseman, announced herself as Mrs Crowley, and told them to send to her the goods they were holding to my order.

It does not say much for the regulations of the firm that this transparent trick succeeded. They had strict instructions to hold the goods to my order or Hammond's, and it was certainly a shock to find that they would part with property entrusted to their safekeeping on the unsupported statement of an unknown person that she was my wife.

I must now retrace my steps to the summer. Austin Harrison has a house in Seaford where he lives with his wife, a charming lady whom he had successfully removed from the protection of her previous husband. He worked the scheme with extraordinary ability. A man of his prominence in London might expect the fullest details in every newspaper of a divorce case in which he was co-respondent. But he managed the matter so craftily that only a few of his intimate friends even got wind of the game.

When in London, he had his rooms in the house of a man named Robinson Smith, a retired concert agent with a wife apparently selected in order to prevent him imagining that life is nothing but music. I met him at Seaford one day after playing golf with Harrison. Nothing much transpired, but later in London, he suddenly appeared in the character of a brother adept. His attainments were considerable, though his knowledge was unsystematic and his judgment correspondingly unbalanced. But his genius and his enthusiasm warmed the cockles of my heart. His idea of helping humanity was through social simplification and economic readjustment, with corresponding rectifications in other directions. He allowed his inspiration too much liberty. It being late in life when he devoted himself exclusively to the Great Work, he had not learned that Pegasus should be ridden on the curb when riding out with friends who bestrode spavined hacks. Harrison constantly hinted he was insane. This he was not. But I thought that his friend and his wife were conspiring to put him into an asylum; in fact I was definitely warned by the Secret Chiefs of his danger, and wrote in veiled language, in view of his mail being tampered with, to put him on his guard.

To his kindness I owed it that I was able to leave London at all. He paid me a month in advance for his proposed visit to Cefalu at Christmas.

At his house in Gordon Square occurred a most amusing incident, the climax of a whole series. It started thus. H. L. Mencken had written me to expect his visit on a certain date. We had corresponded a good deal while I was in America. But he lived in Baltimore and I managed to miss meeting him. On the day expected I saw in a paper a notice that he had arrived, and went at once to the office of the *English Review* expecting him to call. No word had arrived so we thought we would hunt him up, and assuming he would be staying at the Savoy, telephoned. 'Mr Mencken is at lunch. Please hold on!' Presently he came to the 'phone.

I welcomed him warmly after telling him who I was and made the usual kind inquiries. Yes, he had had a pleasant voyage. Thank you, his health was excellent. Well, of course he was very busy. He couldn't possibly dine that night, but wouldn't we call at the hotel about it? We would and we did. He would be disengaged in five minutes. Would we please wait?

It was the day of Northcliff's funeral and Harrison got into communication with some friend who had been among the mourners. While thus engaged, Mencken appeared. I greeted him with enthusiasm though not a little surprised at his appearance. I did not expect to see such a giant, so robust and hearty, so rubicund. It was not my idea at all of what the keenest critic in the United States should look like. However, we strolled off to the smoking-room. Harrison would join us in a few minutes. The conversation became fluent and friendly. He ordered the best brandy and the biggest cigars. But, somehow I could not help feeling that his reaction to my remarks was peculiar. Could I possibly have offended him somehow? Impossible; he was friendliness itself! Then why did he fail to catch fire at my suggestions, or even appreciate the cordial compliments with which I interspersed my remarks.

He, on his side, seemed embarrassed. But we had talked quite ten minutes before he said, 'You will excuse me, I'm sure; but I don't understand what you mean by that last observation.' This was absurd. It was some perfectly simple straightforward comment on his last book. I began to suspect him of pulling my leg in some supersubtle system invented since my return to Europe. 'Are you sure?' he said . . . and then stopped. 'I am not sure of anything,' I retorted, 'that's just where a critic of your ability comes in to guide our wanderings.' He apologetically answered that nothing was further from his mind than to criticize anything I said. He agreed entirely; but what he wanted to know was—well, to put it plainly, who I was, and why I had asked to see him? 'But you're Mencken!' I gasped. 'I certainly am,' he admitted. 'Well,' said I, 'I'm Aleister Crowley.' He bowed deeply. 'I don't doubt it for a second, but as I have not had the pleasure of hearing your name till now—' I saw a great light. 'Heaven help me for a fool,' I cried. 'You can't be my Mencken at all!' Explanations took place. He was a business man from South Africa. At this moment Harrison strolled up and we all enjoyed the joke over more brandy and still bigger cigars.

When the real Mencken turned up, the tale of the conversation wagged out the message—Jane Burr. This lady had recently arrived in London and created a silly-season scandal by walking about in knickerbockers. On this frail foundation, she had erected a superstructure of sexual ethics which bored the educated, excited the suppressed, and scandalized the orthodox. That night she was to be the lioness at a reception at Robinson Smith's. I said, 'What rot this sensation stunt business is. I'll bring a girl who wears knickerbockers for their convenience in playing Thelema and climbing rocks in Sicily. This Miss Burr will look like a model of Madame Tussaud's beside the original.'

I did not know that Jane Burr was to be escorted by Mencken himself, and he told her what I had said. The Ape in her flowered black suit and stockings, wearing the silver and scarlet Star of the Temple, arrived with me and Harrison. Some took her to be Jane Burr, but all were spontaneous in admiration. Her success was due to her having the secret of wearing clothes, oblivious of their existence. She had been acclaimed the Queen of the Evening when Jane Burr arrived. She had realized that she stood no chance against the real thing, put her principles in cold storage and donned her best evening dress. She did her best to oust her rival, but the failure was grotesque. And the worst of the whole thing was that the affair got into the papers. Her recantation had ruined her chance of being taken seriously.

The incidents of my London campaign have constrained me to a somewhat zigzag course. But I think this completes the account. I need add only a brief epitome of my successes.

Besides *The Diary of a Drug Fiend* and my autohagiography I had contracted with Collins for the publication of *Simon Iff*. By this they pledged themselves to pay me an advance equivalent to the subscription sales of *The Drug Fiend*. They promised to let me have this before November 9th. I had also sold to Ralph Shirley the rights of my translation of Eliphas Lévi's *La Clef des Grands Mystères* in volume form, and he had paid me the advance due. The position was that on leaving London I had about twenty pounds on hand after paying my fare and allowing for bare subsistence on the pledged word of Collins, Hammond and Austin Harrison.

All three failed me! If I have survived, it is that the gods have some further use for me. My own efforts break down every time, and that in circumstances such that the improbability of their doing so is enormous. The one miracle matches the other. If I were even tempted to doubt that my career is planned in every detail by my spiritual superiors with the precision of a chess player whose pieces are powerless to move except at his command, incidents of this surprising kind would bring me back with a jerk to a sense of reality.

95

I broke the journey at Rome. All through northern Italy we had been held up by bandits of Fascisti, who had occupied the railway stations. It was the day of the coup d'état. For some time I had interested myself in Fascismo which I regarded with entire sympathy even excluding its illegitimacy on the ground that constitutional authority had become to all intents and purposes a dead letter. I was delighted with the common sense of its programme and was especially pleased by its attitude towards the Church. It was proposed to use forcible means to prevent the Vatican employing the influence of the priests to attain political ends. I was also convinced of the importance of the movement and of its almost immediate success. I did my utmost to persuade Austin Harrison of the soundness of my judgment. He pooh-poohed the whole thing and only after interminable argument did I persuade him to let me write an article on the situation. He ultimately agreed, and I hunted all round London for a representative of Fascismo from whom I could obtain documentary material for my article.

(The sequel is characteristic of Austin Harrison. He printed an article written not by me but by one of the men I had discovered, and he never paid me a penny for my work, which had kept me busy most of the time for a week.)

The Fascisti patrolling the railway were delightful. They had all the picturesqueness of opera brigands. They were armed with a most miscellaneous assortment of weapons. They had the irregular discipline of banditti, which of course they, in fact, were.

My English friends had anticipated the success of the movement to follow naturally upon the forthcoming election. Mussolini would not accept power, they told me, even if it were offered. He had too much sense. I was consequently amazed to hear of the coup d'état. Rome was wild with enthusiasm. The Fascisti swarmed all over the city. I thought their behaviour admirable. They policed the towns and suppressed any attempted breach of the peace with the utmost efficiency; but for all that my first doubts disturbed my pleasure in the victory. I thought Mussolini was acting rashly in overthrowing the constitutions. Not only was a reaction certain to follow, as always when success is not the final flowering of regular growth, but I foresaw that Mussolini would be obliged to play politics just as fatally as his predecessors in order to survive the first few crises of his government.

My apprehension has proved only too true. Almost at once, he had to sell his soul to the Vatican in whom a real statesman would have recognized his most dangerous foe. Like the devil, Rome takes care that its part, however fair it seems on the surface, really involves the giving of nothing and the gain of all. During the winter I heard nothing from the outer world, but when I went to Naples in April I found that my worst anticipations had been exceeded. The price of power had proved exorbitant. Mussolini was bankrupt. He had been compelled to purchase papal support by attempting to re-establish the darkest hour of the Dark Ages. Superstition and priestcraft were the real masters. It could not endure. A country cannot wipe out the evolution of a thousand years without becoming an opéra bouffe absurdity. I began immediately to write epigrams against Mussolini, and every fresh act of farcical folly and blustering braggadocio furnished me with fresh facts for the fires of my wrath. My own personal experience of this farcical despotism, though characteristically ridiculous, did not increase my indignation or contempt. There was no lack of much better material.

I spent three days in Rome, observing the course of events. Everything passed off quietly, so I wandered on to Cefalu. My troubles began almost at once owing to the three men I had trusted breaking their word as above narrated. In all other ways, things were in fine shape. I settled down to dictate these memoirs with my usual energy. The Ape and Jane took turns to take down my story and to type it out. On November 26th further help arrived. With great kindness Robinson Smith had lent Raoul enough money to take the journey. Both he and Betty were still suffering from the remains of septic sore throats and general cachexy, but within a month they both recovered their health.

At first Betty moped. She craved the excitement of being mauled about in boozing dens by tipsy vagabonds. But the clean living and atmosphere of love and happiness gradually weaned her from this artificial appetite. She became a gay and careless child finding pleasure in every detail of everyday life. She went about singing. On increasingly rare occasions she would suddenly relapse into her old self and feel wretched for a few hours. I expected this, of course, and watched for the first symptoms. It was easy enough to comfort her. Unfortunately, she was not a wholly sane individual. The lesion in her brain gave rise to symptoms difficult to control. The complete disassociation of her consciousness may be illustrated by such incidents as the following.

One of her fixed ideas was that she was a miracle of modesty. She used to confide in one or another of us that she had never allowed anyone, not even her husband, to see her naked. This seemed strange in view of her career as a model, and one day she brought out a fat package of photographs of herself in the nude. But this was in no sense a confession that she had been telling us lies. She maintained quite sincerely with the photographs under her eyes that no one had ever seen her naked. This incident is typical of her. Almost in the same breath, she would say that she had never known happiness till she came to the abbey, and that she had been uniformly wretched since her arrival. She would boast of her superiority to sex, and continue by complaining that her husband absorbed in his work was starving her. She would proceed to claim great credit for being faithful to him, but we found out that she was carrying on any number of intrigues with the young bloods of Cefalu.

Raoul, on his part, amply justified my faith in his future. A few weeks' work enabled him to fill the gaps in his knowledge of Magick and to unify its elements. He showed an understanding of the subject which was almost enough to satisfy the requirements of the Grade $8° = 3°$. I admitted him as a probationer in the Order on the day of the solstice, and he took the name A V D.[1] I advised him to repress any ambitions to pass quickly to higher Grades, and to concentrate on thoroughness. With admirable good sense, he agreed. As evidence of his amazing genius for Magick, let me mention that I showed him a thesis which had been sent me by a member of the Order in support of his application for admission to the Grade $7° = 4°$, the highest of the Second Order, implying complete knowledge of all matters magical, and command of all powers. Frater A V D wrote a criticism of this thesis to which I could find only some three or four suggestions to add, and in which I could find no error of any kind. There are not alive a dozen men today who could do as well.

In practical Magick, he showed promise of the same order,

though, of course, not having previously attempted any work of the kind, he had much to learn. Nevertheless, he progressed with astonishing rapidity. Within a fortnight, he was able to perform the Banishing Ritual of the Pentagram sufficiently well to produce unmistakable modulations of the Astral Light.[2] He acquired the faculty of visions in astonishing perfection from the very first. The usual preliminary practice on unimportant explorations was unnecessary. In January I gave him a talisman symbolizing the alchemical mystery of V. I. T. R. I. O. L.[3] He travelled straight through to the corresponding plane of the Astral, and entered into relation at once with an intelligence who gave his name Neral, who demonstrated his authenticity and authority in the approved manner by means of letters and numbers, but also by straightforward statements which had no meaning for Raoul but which I recognized as correct expositions.

96

To turn to other matters. At the end of November I received a telegram from Hammond which I took as a sort of joke. He said:

> English press states you are guilty of sending girls on streets in Palermo or Naples and that you served prison sentence in America for procuration tone (?) *ans* (answer) *per imperative pire* (wire immediately).
>
> (Signed) HAMMOND.

I replied 'Allegations utterly absurd.' My only annoyance was having to pay for the telegram. Presently copies of the Sunday papers for November 28th arrived. I read them with tireless amusement. I had read in my time a great deal of utter balderdash, but nothing quite so comprehensively ridiculous. It gave me the greatest joy to notice that practically every single detail was false. There was, for instance, a description of the abbey, without a single failure to misstate the facts. If a thing was white, they called it red, if square, circular, if stone, brick; and so for everything.

I saw no reason for taking any action. I was content to enjoy the absurdity and profit by the publicity. Unfortunately the sense of humour is rare in England. My friends wanted me to prosecute the paper for criminal libel, which was all very well, except that I had not enough money to get to Naples, much less London, to say nothing of the costs of an action against a corporation backed by millions and the influence of its coroneted proprietor. Five thousand pounds would not have given me a dog's chance. Incidentally, there was internal evidence in the article that they had not taken the risk of printing it without making sure that I was not in a position to prosecute.

In earlier chapters, I have given my views with regard to libel actions in general; I should refuse to fight in any circumstances for the simple reason that I cannot waste my time on anything of the kind. I must maintain my concentration upon creative work. There is a further objection, mixing oneself up with people of alien mentalities.[1]

The only misfortune in the matter was that my publishers reflected that doing as they did a large business in bibles and similar pious publications they could not profit by the publicity as their clear duty was to do. They professed all sympathy with my position, but insisted on some sort of vindication before proceeding to carry out their contracts. I find their attitude inexcusable. They live in a country which boasts of sportsmanship and fair play as their copyright, but refuse to apply their principles, to say nothing of elementary justice, to cases which involve the suspicion of sexual irregularity. The accusation is sufficient. Even a successful public defence does not clear the character of the person attacked. It is notorious that most exculpations of this sort are the result of compromise or the payment of blackmail and it is universally assumed that everyone is guilty of the offences of which they know themselves at least potentially capable and whose commission is a function of opportunity and moral courage. The sense of sin assures the English that all men alike are inevitably transgressors.

What struck us as the best joke in the whole article was the description of the abbey as a focus of all possible vices. We were all drug fiends devoting ourselves uninterruptedly to indulgence in all conceivable sexual abominations. Our morality compared favourably with that of the strictest puritan. The only irregularity that had ever occurred at any time was intercourse between unmarried people, which is, after all, universal in good society, and in our case was untainted by any objectionable features apart from the question of formality. I fail to understand why it should be considered excusable to seduce a woman and leave her to shift for herself, while if one receives her as a permanent friend and cares for her well-being long after the liaison had lapsed one should be considered a scoundrel. The idea seems to be that it is immoral to prevent love resulting in every kind of ill-will and misfortune. O fools and blind, not content with inventing a sin, you insist on the fears and pains which haunt the nightmares of superstitious slaves.

By this particular period, our conduct was so moral by the strictest standards that it would not be matched by any community of equal numbers in the world. We were all working so hard, to say nothing of having so little to eat, that we had neither time nor need to think of sex at all. The one exception was Betty and her actions did not affect the abbey. She had to go outside for sympathy in such affairs.

Two events of far-reaching influence upon the course of events occurred about the New Year. I received a long cable from my old friend Bill Seabrook asking me for photographs and other material to assist him in composing a serial on the subject of myself, opinions and adventures. He hoped to syndicate this widely throughout America by means of simultaneous publication in a large number of Sunday papers. The plan prospered. He was naturally hampered by having to consider his public. The most trivial and common-place incident must be cooked up with all possible spice of sensationalism. When the facts fail they must be filled up with fiction, and where they obstructed his wild career, they must be distorted into fantastic form. He did his work well on the whole. He was as fair as his circumstances permitted and in my judgment the ultimate effect of his hotel polish mixed fact and fable will be to familiarize the American public with my name and interest them in my career sufficiently to induce the few intelligent individuals who have read it to inquire independently into the facts of the case. The strong point of my position is that there is nothing in my life of which I need be ashamed. Inquiry must inevitably result in clearing my character, and any person whose attitude is worth a moment's consideration should experience a reaction of indignation and disgust. The stench of the cesspool of calumny will offend his nostrils and he will insist on restoring equilibrium by long reviving inhalations of the perfume of my personality.

The other event was that a seed which had long slept in darkness suddenly shot up into the light. My proposal that Sullivan should devote his mathematical abilities to demonstrating the sublimity of the origin of *The Book of the Law* having failed, I bethought me of Norman Mudd. Since the skirmish at Cambridge, he had sunk below the horizon, having emigrated to the most barbarous and benighted realms of perdition; he had in fact become lecturer in applied mathematics at Grey University College, Bloemfontein. All these years, his conscience had never ceased to accuse him in respect of his conduct at Cambridge. He thought of it as the 'great betrayal'.

For my part, I find every excuse for him. He was hardly more than a boy, without resources, friends or influence. Against him were arrayed the entrenched forces of authority. Their power was arbitrary and extended for all practical purposes to life and death! Stripped of his scholarship and expelled from the university at the most critical moment of his career, he would have found himself almost as desperately situated as a tramp with a bad record thrown out of work on to the Embankment. Yet so conscious of their guilt were his oppressors that they feared to face the consequences of any such action and they therefore assailed him in various underhand ways; even trying to induce his father to put pressure upon him by appealing to his filial instincts and begging him not to destroy the hope of his family.

I cannot blame him for pretending to yield and proceeding as before to defy them by his actions. None the less, the Lords of Initiation exacted the penalty of surrender. Shame dogged him by day and haunted him by night; in 1919, he could not stand it any longer and went to England to find me. Having heard I was in America, no one knew exactly where, he crossed the Atlantic and ultimately discovered Frater Achad who admitted him as a probationer of the Order with the motto *Omnia Pro Veritate*. It seems strange that he missed finding me. Once again I perceived the design of the gods. The time was not ripe.

He wrote me a letter which I answered at once, but I failed to elicit further communication. However, when Sullivan broke down at the first ordeal, I said to myself, 'Why, of course, Norman Mudd is the man for the job.' I wrote immediately, asking him to work with me on the demonstration indicated above. He did not answer. Thinking my letter might have failed to reach him, I wrote again sometime later with similar fortune. About Christmas 1922, his problem reached a crisis. His obstinate resistance collapsed. He opened and read my letters, which he had put aside till then, being instinctively aware that if he read them he would be unable to withstand the call of his own soul to be true to himself and take the consequence. His way became suddenly clear. He was on this earth with one object and one object only; he must devote his energies exclusively to the welfare of mankind; in other words, to establishing the Law of Thelema. He cabled and wrote, putting himself entirely at my disposal. I accepted and told him to come straight to Cefalu and work with me. He did so, arriving on April 20th, and has since that time been exclusively occupied in collaboration in the Great Work.

These encouragements were balanced by fresh tribulations. The enemies of mankind, seeing that despite everything my work was nearing manifest success, redoubled their malice. Both Raoul and I began to have attacks of rather inexplicable illness which increased in frequency and severity, until we were both almost continuously ill. My trouble was a strange fever—Mediterranean fever, I finally concluded. The temperature never reached any great height, but quinine had no effect. The local doctor diagnosed it as an infection of the liver and spleen, but confessed that he had no idea of what could have caused it. I grew steadily worse and at one time, for a few days, my condition caused some alarm. Not until early in April was I well enough to walk. But on the thirteenth I felt fit enough to go to Naples with the idea of convalescing in favourable circumstances, and buying a few things which the imminent arrival of Frater O.P.V. made requisite.

Raoul was less unlucky. How could the gods help loving him, who in so many ways partook of their pure nature. At first he suffered mostly from a recurrence of malaria of many years' standing. The attacks were hard to throw off, owing to his accident at Oxford already described. Various complications ensued. We called in the doctor at the first sign of any symptoms with which we were not familiar and able to deal. For some time he got neither better nor worse, but then, without warning, developed acute infectious enteritis. The doctor, summoned in all haste, did what he could, but his answer told me at a glance that he expected a fatal issue. I wrote out a telegram informing his parents so that they might come if they thought fit. Betty offered to take it to the office, but instead of returning, collapsed hysterically in the street before sending it off. It was a common trick of hers to excite sympathy, attract notice or annoy her husband if he happened to say or do anything which she disliked. In her absence, Raoul developed paralysis of the heart and died at once without fear or pain. It was as if a man, tired of staying indoors, had gone out for a walk. At the first appearance of symptoms which alarmed me as to the immediate issue, I dressed myself, ill as I was, and hurried to bring the doctor. Alostrael,[2] being already ready to go out, had gone on ahead. But even in those few minutes matters had gone so far that I felt sure he was already dead. It was all so quiet that certainty on the point was hardly possible. When we returned with the doctor and Betty, all doubt was at an end.

The usual arrangements were made and on the following day I conducted the burial service according to the ritual of the Order; improvised and simple as the ceremony was, its dignity and sublimity were not unworthy of our brother. My duty done, I surrendered to my own bodily assailants. I had probably done myself harm, both by going into Cefalù and by presiding at the obsequies. Till then I had been able to get out of bed and crawl about for an hour or two every day. It was many weeks before I managed to leave my bed even to walk on somebody's shoulder to another mattress and drink in the early spring sunlight.

Except for Betty, whose ideas of nursing were restricted to an alternation of lamentation, savage abuse of a patient, petulant complaints about his selfishness in not looking after her instead of her looking after him, and attempts to obtain restitutions of conjugal rights, Raoul had been tended with all possible care. In fact, during the absence of Betty, owing to circumstances to be described shortly, he picked up surprisingly and I feel pretty sure that if she had not come back he would be alive today.[3] The Ape and Jane Wolfe are the best nurses I ever struck. They do everything just right. I never had to ask for anything I wanted, they had foreseen the need and supplied it in advance. They never showed the faintest sign of fatigue and anxiety, which they must have felt. The doctor spared no pains to study my complaint, but he confessed frankly that it puzzled him. It was common enough, he said, in Sicily; one could not say what caused the mischief or what its nature really was, and there was certainly no definite cure. All one could do was to treat the symptoms empirically. So I think he should not receive more than ten to fifteen per cent. of the blame attached to my survival; the balance must be borne as best they can by my nurses, and in the background, Sister Cypris, invisible, but indefatigable in seeing that nothing went wrong.

I must now explain the incident which led to Betty's temporary absence from the abbey from the Sunday evening before the Friday of her husband's death, till the following day. It is an absolute rule of the abbey not to attack people behind their backs. Betty had taken a frantic dislike to Sister Cypris and pestered us with complaints, not of anything definite that she did, but on general grounds. I happened to hear an outburst of this sort and put my foot down at once. I told Betty that we all agreed with her on many points, but it was none of our business. 'If you must abuse anyone, do it to their faces as you see us all do every day, and no ill feeling comes of it.'

Betty said, 'But she's breaking the rules of the abbey.'

I replied, 'Quite true, we've been getting slack. We'll start right now to be stricter.'

Now one of the most important rules is that no newspaper is allowed, unless it bears directly on some point of the work. The reason, of course, is that having a library of first-class books we should not spoil our appetites by eating between meals, especially the dirt of the streets. It chanced that the very next day a bundle of rubbish was sent to Raoul. Here was the very chance to be strict. Betty was reminded that newspapers were forbidden; she flew into a fury—she would leave the abbey instantly unless allowed to read them. I agreed. She was free to stay or to go but while she was there the rules were the rules, and she was the only person who had objected to them being relaxed. She flew into a fury even more furious. Heedless of Raoul's pitiful appeals to control herself, she was actually smashing things. The noise brought me in; she flung a glass at my head and attacked me like a maniac. I tried to soothe her and abate her violence. Poor Raoul, weak as he was, got up and held her and begged her to be quiet. At last she calmed down, but the room was a wreck. It was imperative to move Raoul to proper surroundings and prevent his being disturbed and neglected by the tantrums of the termagant. We carried him into my own room and made him comfortable. Betty continued to conduct the concert in the absence of an audience, so she finally announced her intention to go. Both Raoul and Alostrael begged her to be sensible, but off she went to the hotel where she was at once consoled by a series of admirers. She wrote a string of lies to the British consul in Palermo, but the next morning came up to the abbey on receipt of a note from Raoul, saying that he hoped she would return and behave decently, but if not, to send for her effects and go back to London for good. I offered to pay her fare if necessary. She came back on condition of promising amendment, writing to the consul to ignore her letter as mere hysteria and admitting the entire falsehood of its contents. This letter was countersigned by Raoul. She also signed a statement of the whole episode drawn up by us and signed. She justified our faith in her better nature and gave us no further trouble as long as she remained with us.

After Raoul's death, she came to me for comfort and I am glad to think that I helped her through the worst. It was arranged for her to return to England. Raoul's parents cabled and wrote, asking us to take various steps, and pledging themselves to repayment. It is hard to believe that any human beings should act as they did; repudiating all liabilities. They wouldn't pay to have their son decently buried—not they.

Every day Betty seemed to grow fonder of us all. We told her, of course, that she was welcome to stay if she chose, and it seems hard to design a reason for her decision to leave. But on her arrival in England trouble began. The reporters of the gutter press got after her, made her drunk and prompted her to give them a sensation story which was one long series of falsehoods. The rabble resumed their chorus of calumny. They completely lost touch with reason. Each fresh article was crazier than the last. I was accused of the most fantastic crimes up to cannibalism. Their principal liar was poor Dartnell, but he was ably assisted by some Dutch interpreter whose name I had never heard. He pretended to know me well. In one article, he let himself go about my cynical audacity in returning to London. He had seen me in Holborn, a decrepit derelict, hardly able to walk. This was fine! My only difficulty in believing everything he said was that at the time of my visit to London I was lying ill at Cefalu.

In due course, Frater O.P.V. arrived at the abbey and on his heels two Oxford men: Pinney and Bosanquet. We put them up for three nights. They were flabbergasted to find us perfectly normal decent people. They were keen rock climbers. I was too ill to join them, but I dragged myself to the foot of the crags and showed them the two problems which I had not cared to attempt without a trustworthy companion. These were the outside way up the Cavern Pitch in Deep Gill and the Deep Gill pillar. They succeeded in climbing both, to my great joy. The morning after their arrival, I was summoned to the police, who showed me an order from the Minister of the Interior expelling me from Italy. No reason was given, no accusation made. The policy of backstairs intrigue and foul strokes, whenever they felt sure that I could not defend myself or hit back, was still the order of the day. The Commissary of Police was staggered by the smiling calm with which I received this stab in the back. I did not even protest or ask for the reason of the outrage. I courteously requested a week's grace to arrange my affairs, which he, with equal politeness, granted. He tried one dirty police trick. These people seemed unable to help themselves. He tried to persuade me that the order included the whole community.

The injustice and tyranny of this order excited the utmost sympathy and indignation in our guests, who promised to do all they could to secure fair treatment. My behaviour in this ordeal aroused their admiration. It became abundantly manifest that my conscience was clear. Such calm courage, not only on my part, but on that of the others, who were really much more deeply injured than I was myself, showed that we possessed the secret of sailing triumphantly above the clouds of circumstances in the pure air of freedom in the sunlight of happiness.

I left O.P.V. in full charge of the business of the abbey. Despite my world fortitude, I was near a physical breakdown, and at Palermo seemed so ill that the Ape decided to accompany me to Tunis. We reached our City of Refuge on May 2nd and I knew that the spirit of liberty still lived and laughed under the banner of France.

During the first weeks of my illness, I had hung on grimly to the preparation of these memoirs, but the weak flesh had overcome the willing spirit from the time of Raoul's death to the end of March. We now tackled it with renewed energy and, for the sake of fresh air and quiet, left the city for La Marsa, where we stayed at Au Souffle du Zephir working day and night, so far as my health permitted, for nearly two months, when O.P.V. joined me, while Alostrael returned to Cefalu for a rest. I had once more worked her beyond her strength.

We were joined shortly afterwards by Eddie Saayman, an old pupil of Frater O.P.V.'s in Bloemfontein, and now a mathematical scholar at New College, Oxford, one of the most brilliant students in the university. He became interested in the mathematical theorems of *The Book of the Law,* which he thought, no less than myself and O.P.V., capable of revolutionizing mathematical ideas and marking a new epoch in that science. We agreed that to demonstrate this would prove that the author of *The Book of the Law* was an intelligence beyond any hitherto known. He therefore decided to write a thesis on this subject for a fellowship of his college.

Early in August, I returned to the city for a little Magical Retirement of about a fortnight, at the conclusion of which Alostrael rejoined us in Tunis where I dictate these actual words.

I must now give a short summary of my personal spiritual work during the three years of my residence in Cefalu. The hopelessness of getting anything published operated to discourage me from producing formally perfect work. I wrote a considerable number of poems and short stories, but found myself horribly hampered by the overwhelming abundance of creative ideas. I need a staff of at least a dozen colleagues and secretaries to keep up with my work, and all the time there is the subconscious worry about the possibility of carrying on.

Since 1909, it has become constantly more difficult to keep afloat. The gods have taught me to trust them absolutely to provide me with everything I really need for my work, as opposed to my own ideas on the subject. Yet despite this long experience of being saved from smash at the critical moment, almost always through some channel which I had no reason to expect, I have not succeeded in entirely dismissing doubt from my mind on these constantly recurring occasions when there were no funds in hand and no rational expectation of receiving any. That is, of course, when the current of creative energy is checked so that my mind, temporarily exhausted, becomes the prey of apprehension. Yet even so I find myself better able, as every year passes, to set my heel on the serpent of worry. Only in moments of complete mental and spiritual collapse from the overstrain of prolonged effort does my faith falter for a few hours. Perhaps the gods intend to insist on my acquiring the power to triumph, even at such moments, over adversity. The serpent's fangs will fix themselves in my heel if it share the vulnerability of the heel of Achilles. It is not enough to dip the Magus in the Styx, he must be thrown in left to sink or swim.

In one way or another, for all that, I achieved an enormous amount of work in the three years. But my most important labours have been definitely magical.

I practically re-wrote the third part of *Book Four*.[4] I showed the manuscripts to Soror Rhodon (Mary Butts) and asked her to criticize it thoroughly. I am extremely grateful to her for her help, especially in indicating a large number of subjects which I had not discussed. At her suggestion, I wrote essay upon essay to cover every phase of the subject. The result has been the expansion of the manuscript into a vast volume, a complete treatise upon the theory and practice of Magick, without any omissions. I further added appendices, the first giving an account of the system of initiation of the A.˙. A.˙. . Next comes a curriculum of the classics of Magick and mysticism. Thirdly, I illustrate the text of the treatise by giving actual examples of ritual. Fourthly, I propose to reprint the more important books of instruction of the A.˙. A.˙. from *The Equinox;* and finally, I crown the work by *Liber Samekh,* the operation of the Sacred Magick of the Attainment of the Knowledge and Conversation of the Holy Guardian Angel, as proved effective in my own experience, and confirmed by that of Frater Progradior for whose benefit I set it forth in writing.

More important still, I applied the formula of *The Book of the Law* to the solution of the classical antinomies of philosophy. I resolved such triads as being, not-being and becoming into a unity. I identified free will with destiny. I proved that action was impotent and non-action omnipotent. As I went on, new problems constantly presented themselves, and each one in its turn yielded to the Law of Thelema. I wrote all these theorems in my Magical Record. I was greatly assisted in all this work by the constant study of the work of Einstein, Whitehead, Russell, Eddington and Henri Poincaré, whom Sullivan had recommended to me. They seemed to be on the very brink of discovering those truths which *The Book of the Law* concealed and revealed. Their passages directed my attention to *The Book of the Law*. Obscure passages in the text became clear when interpreted as solving the problem of modern higher mathematics.

From this huge mass of work I extracted the quintessence and transferred it to my New Comment upon *The Book of the Law*. This is now an extensive work, and I have not yet succeeded in making a systematic study of the technical Cabbalistic proofs of those based on the facts of experience which demonstrate that Aiwass is an intelligence of an order altogether superior to that of man. The proof of his existence is therefore the proof of the postulate of all religion, that such beings actually exist, and that communication with them is a practical possibility. Thus, apart from the stupendous value of *The Book of the Law* itself, it opens up a path of progress to mankind which should eventually enable the race to strike off the fetters of mortality and transcend the limitations of its entanglement with earth.

I continued my researches in many other lines of Magick, from the preparation of a new edition of *Liber 777* with an elaborate explanation of each column and a further analysis of the *Yi King*, to such matters as the critical observation of success in the Operation of the IX° O.T.O.

I have written a very full comment on *The Book of the Heart Girt with a Serpent*, which as I proceeded manifested innumerable mysteries of transcendent importance which I had till then never suspected to inform the text.

I also began an examination of *The Golden Verses of Pythagoras*. I was struck by the fact that it was incumbent on disciples to commit them to memory and repeat them daily. From this I deduced that the somewhat shallow meaning of their injunctions concealed the heart of the initiated doctrine. This speculation was confirmed by research. For instance, the phrase 'Honour the gods' which 'needs no ghost come from the grave to tell us' is proper, conceals a magical injunction of the first importance. 'Tima' honour etymologically means 'estimate' or 'calculate'. The instruction thus is to make a scientific investigation of the formulae of the various gods, i.e., to discover the laws which express their energies, exactly as in physics to honour gravitation is senseless, but we may increase our control of nature by inquiry into its nature and action. The more I studied these verses, the more tremendous seemed their import and should I succeed in completing my translation and commentary, the long lost secret of Pythagoras should be brought to light and Greek philosophy assume an aspect hitherto hidden which must revolutionize our ideas of the ancient wisdom.

The true significance of the Atus of Tahuti, or Tarot Trumps, also awaits full understanding. I have satisfied myself that these twenty-two cards compose a complete system of hieroglyphs representing the total energies of the universe. In the case of some cards, I have succeeded in restoring the original form and giving a complete account of their meaning. Others, however, I understand imperfectly, and of some few I have at present obtained no more than a general idea.[5]

It is heartbreaking to have to write on this matter, 'So much to do, so little done.' I am overwhelmed by the multiplicity of urgent work. I need the co-operation of a whole cohort of specialists and my helplessness lies heavy on my heart, yet the word which I uttered at my first initiation, 'Perdurabo', still echoes in eternity. What may befall I know not, and I have almost ceased to care. It is enough that I should press towards the mark of my high calling, secure in the magical virtue of my oath, 'I shall endure unto the End.'

EDITORS' NOTES

PART ONE

Prelude

1. Crowley's invariable salutation; it echoes Rabelais's *Fay ce que voudras*, but it carries a serious implication. See *The Book of the Law*.
2. The constructive side of the thelemic doctrine. Each individual, like a star in orbit, has his own path or true will.
3. Era Vulgari: Crowley's term for Anno Domini, the Christian era which, according to him, came to an end in 1904.
4. Crowley is here referring to articles which appeared in the press during 1922–3, following the publication of his novel, *The Diary of a Drug Fiend* (Collins, 1922).
5. Frater Aud or Raoul Loveday.

1.
1. Shakespeare was born in 1564.
2. The allusion is to the discovery of America.
3. At the age of fifteen he was circumcised.

2.
1. The thelemic funeral of his young disciple, Raoul Loveday, who died at Crowley's abbey of Do What Thou Wilt at Cefalu, Sicily, during 1923. See chapter 96. See also *The Great Beast*, chapter XXI, by John Symonds.
2. See chapters 54 and 55.
3. The heart of Crowley is Magick, not magic, six letters instead of five, to affirm the identity of man (the pentagram) with God (the hexagram). Through Magick the human consciousness is made divine; hence Crowley the Magus is equivalent to a Logos, an embodied Word, like Christ, Mohammed, Buddha.

3.
1. The *Book of Changes*, commonly known, through Wilhelm's and Baynes's translations, as *I Ching*. Crowley used Legge's earlier translation which appeared in the series *The Sacred Books of the East*, edited by F. Max Müller.
2. Cambridge University Chess Club.
3. Now (1968) Sir Gerald Kelly, former President of the Royal Academy.

4. 1. See *The World's Tragedy*, 1910, by Aleister Crowley.
   2. 'Epilogue', *Dramatis Personae*, 1864.
   3. *The Second Mrs Tanqueray* by Arthur W. Pinero.

5. 1. Sir Henry Enfield Roscoe. 'Little Roscoe' was probably his *Lessons in Elementary Chemistry*, 1866; the sixth edition was published in 1892.

10. 1. Published by Crowley's 'Society for the Propagation of Religious Truth' in three volumes, 1905–7. *The Works of Aleister Crowley* is printed on the title page, and *The Collected Works of Aleister Crowley* on the cover.

11. 1. *Mountaineering*, 1892, by Clinton Thomas Dent (Badminton Library).

13. 1. Orpheus, 1905.

14. 1. By A. E. Waite.

18. 1. Brother Omnia Pro Veritate or Norman Mudd. Eleven years later, in 1934, after having been rejected by Crowley, he committed suicide. See chapter 96. See also *The Great Beast* by John Symonds.
   2. Gerald Rae Fraser.

19. 1. The triangle of dots indicates that the order is a secret sodality connected with the Ancient Mysteries. The triangle is the sign of Horus and represents fire, light or spirit. 'Salutation on All Points of the Triangle' is a formula used by freemasons.

22. 1. Crowley is here using Dr John Dee's Enochian system of Keys or Calls for invoking the Angelic forces. A brief abstract of this system is given in *The Equinox*, vol. I, nos. VII and VIII.
   2. The all-conquering solar energy, Râ, triumphant over the dragon of darkness, Apophis.
   3. 'S Rhiogail Mo Dhream' ('Royal is my Race', the cry of the MacGregors) and 'Vestigia Nulla Retrorsum', the magical mottoes of MacGregor Mathers and his wife, Mina.
   4. W. Wynn Westcott, one of the founders of the Golden Dawn.
   5. 'Greatly Honoured Sister': Anna Sprengel.
   6. Deo Duce Comite Ferro, i.e. MacGregor Mathers.
   7. E. J. Dingwall has given an account of Mme Horos and her companion Theo Horos in his *Some Human Oddities*, Home and Van Thal, 1947. Theo Horos was accused of raping a certain Daisy Adams during a 'magical' ceremony.

He denied this, said he was impotent. Crowley's copy of Dr Dingwall's book has this marginal comment on Horos's alleged impotence (in Crowley's writing): 'No. He used to wander naked round the house, always with a superb erection.'

PART TWO

23. 1. Liberty, Power, Duty; or Light, Proportion, Density; or Law, Principle, Right (*Droit*).

  2. According to Hebrew Cabbala,

$$
\begin{array}{lll}
\text{L (Lamed)} & = & 30 \\
\text{P (Peh)} & = & 80 \\
\text{D (Daleth)} & = & 4 \\
\hline
& & 114
\end{array}
$$

  114 is a key number in Rosicrucianism.

  3. Yetzirah is one of the four worlds of the Cabbala. In the context it denotes the Rosicrucian formula of redemption. See *Magick*, p. 319.

  4. The expression 'Atus of Tahuti' or Houses of Thoth refers to the Tarot Trumps—in this case to those of *Equilibrium*, *The Blasted Tower*, and *The Empress*.

  5. *Magick*, p. 427.

  6. 33° is the highest degree of the Ancient and Accepted Scottish Rite of Freemasonry.

  7. The Dove, symbol of the Holy Ghost.

25. 1. Volo Noscere or George Cecil Jones.

  2. The true word of power, according to Crowley's Cabbalistic Working, is ABRAHADABRA.

  3. i.e. by Hebrew Cabbala.

  4. Dr Tom George Longstaff. He died in June 1964. See Introduction.

26. 1. *Orpheus, a lyrical legend*, 1905.

  2. The Hebrew god-name for 'Lord of the Earth', i.e. the element, not the planet, a technical name for the Holy Guardian Angel.

  3. MacGregor Mathers.

  4. Mrs Mina Mathers.

  5. Sister Fidelis in the Golden Dawn was Elaine Simpson.

  6. Sister Fidelis.

  7. It was published as *Alice: An Adultery*, 1903.

  8. The name of the author of *How to be Happy though Married*, 1885, is Edward John Hardy.

27. 1. Another name for the Great White Brotherhood.

  2. Perdurabo's, i.e. Crowley's.

  3. i.e. The hunger of the individual for continuous personal existence.

    4. Crowley published an account of these yogic states in *Book Four*, Part I, 1913.

28. 1. Yogic control of the vital airs; it usually refers to the breath.

    2. Crowley must have been nodding when he wrote this sentence.

29. 1. Crowley is alluding to Madame Blavatsky and her astral bell; it was the signal that her Hidden Master was present. The phrase 'Hidden Master' is an unfortunate one in view of the accusations of fraud which were made against her by the Society for Psychical Research; she meant, of course, an Invisible Master.

    2. One purifies or cleanses the Nadi by raising the force of Kundalini up the subtle centre in the spine: in other words, through yogic exercise. There are, according to some traditions, 72,000 Nadi or occult centres in the ramifications of man's subtle anatomy. The three main Nadi are Ida (the Moon), Pingala (the Sun) and Sushumna (the Fire at the base of the spine, otherwise called Kundalini, the Magic Fire). On the stirring of Kundalini, interior sounds which resemble the tinkling of a bell, the drone of a bee, the sound of a flute and the clash of cymbals are experienced.

    3. An aspect of the goddess Kali.

    4. The Cosmic root-vibration AUM or OM, pronounced ONG.

    5. Madame Blavatsky's comment on the tooth when she saw it during 1880 was, 'Of course it's his tooth. One he had when he was born as a tiger!'

    6. 'Move, therefore, and show yourselves! Open the mysteries of your Creation! Be friendly unto me, for I am the servant of the same your God: the true worshipper of the Highest.' Part of an Enochian Call from the system of Dr Dee.

30. 1. The companion of Madame Blavatsky and co-founder of the Theosophical Society.

    2. They are actually in such bad English as to be almost unintelligible.

    3. The title of MacGregor Mathers's book is *The Kabbalah Unveiled*. Crowley preferred *Qabalah* because it is the nearest to קבל.

    4. The lingam of Shiva is symbolic of that adamantine Consciousness which underlies all phenomena; hence its representation as rigid.

32. 1. The real Christ according to Crowley is the Christ of the Gnostics.

33. 1. Hoor-Paar-Kraat, the Egyptian god; Harpocrates is the Greek form.

39. 1. This cypher Crowley used on several occasions with reference to things having gone wrong. Its exact meaning, we do not know.

42. 1. Perdurabo, 'I will endure to the end', Crowley's motto when he entered the Golden Dawn.
    2. MacGregor Mathers.
    3. Mathers's wife, Mina.

43. 1. *The Book of the Law*.
    2. Ibid.

44. 1. *The Blossom and the Fruit* by Mabel Collins, an account of the Mystical Path.

45. 1. Taken from the tenth chapter of *The Book of the Sacred Magic of Abra-Melin the Mage*.
    2. The name of the spirit of the planet Mercury, i.e. the densest vibration of the mercurial current which is closest and most easily accessible to human consciousness. The scale (of the mercurial current) descends thus: God, Archangel, Angel, Intelligence, Spirit, Man.

46. 1. A Buddhist meditation on the illusoriness of sense impressions.

47. 1. The Third Eye, between the eyebrows.
    2. The 13th Key of the Tarot is called Death. Its full title is: the Child of the Great Transformers; the Lord of the Gate of Death.

48. 1. 'Oh! All is sorrow.'

PART THREE

49. 1. This was Crowley's intention; it was not fulfilled. However, he saw the appearance of *The Book of the Law*, and all relevant material, including a facsimile of the actual script, in a separate and magnificently produced publication, *The Equinox of the Gods*, in 1937.
    2. Crowley's wife, Rose.
    3. Each element—earth, fire, air, water—has its own particular elementals or inhabitants. The sylphs inhabit the airy realms.
    4. Samadhi: the goal of Yoga, union with the Lord, very

rarely achieved and only by advanced adepts on the Spiritual Path.

5. The Boulak Museum is no longer in existence; its antiquities are now in the National Museum, Cairo.

6. The G∴D∴ (Golden Dawn) was the First or Outer Order of a universal brotherhood known as the Great White Brotherhood. Mathers who, with others, founded the Golden Dawn, was also a member of a Rosicrucian order known as the Order of the Red Rose and the Golden Cross (Rosae Rubeae et Aureae Crucis); this constituted the Second Order of the Great White Brotherhood. The Third Order of the Great White Brotherhood was the Silver Star, the Astrum Argenteum or the A∴A∴. Crowley began his magical career as a neophyte of the G∴D∴ and worked his way up to the Third or Inner Order of the A∴A∴.

7. Gnana-Yoga, union through knowledge. A typical Gnana-yogi of a high order was Shri Ramana Maharshi (1879–1950) of Tiruvannamalai, S. India.

8. Aiwass, the intelligence who communicated *The Book of the Law*, did not tell Crowley how his name was spelt. In Greek it is Aiwass and in Greek Cabbala the name has a numerical value of four hundred and eighteen, the number of the Great Work; in Hebrew it is Aiwaz, adding up to ninety-three, the key number of *The Book of the Law*. Crowley used Aiwass or Aiwaz, depending upon the nature of the work he was doing at the time, that is, whether his experiments were of a mystical (Aiwaz) or of a magical nature (Aiwass).

9. Elementals of the Hindu cosmology: *Nats*, tree spirits; *Pisachas*, seductive female water spirits; *Devas*, Shining Ones or gods.

10. Crowley's account of the Grade of Magus. See *The Equinox*, vol. I, no. VII, and *Magick*, p. 423. His attainment of this exalted grade, equivalent to that of Buddha or Christ, is described in chapter 81 of the present work.

11. The 'Dying God' is Christ; this means that *Thelema* transcends Christianity.

12. *Zanoni* by E. G. E. Lytton Bulwer-Lytton.

50.
1. 'Now is the time for drinking; now is the time for a dance of freedom.' (Horace, *Odes*.)

2. 'A harmless thunderbolt'.

3. *The Book of the Law*.

4. Crowley had particularly in mind James Branch Cabell's *Jurgen*, chapter XXII of which is based upon his 'Gnostic Mass', first published in *The Equinox*, vol. III, no. I (Detroit).

5. Written in 1890. First published in Belgium under the title

of *D'aucunes*, seized by the police and burnt; very few copies survived. (See *Les dernier jours de Paul Verlaine* by F. A. Cazals and Gustave Le Rouge, 1911.)

6. Written in 1891, first published by A. Messein in 1904. (See G. Legman, *The Horn Book*, 1964, p. 44.)

7. Author of *Memoirs of a Woman of Pleasure*, commonly known as *Fanny Hill*, 1749, the best-written English pornographic novel. Cleland was brought before the members of the Privy Council for this scurrilous work; he won their sympathy, and when they heard of his poverty, they agreed to pay him a pension of one hundred pounds a year (not four thousand) but on the condition that he wrote no more such books.

8. J. Jacot Guillarmod.

9. *Sepher Toldoth Jeschu* (or *Toledot Yeshu*), the Book of the Life of Jesus, a collection of medieval Jewish legends.

51. 1. E. J. Garwood, *Catalogue of a Collection of Photographs . . . taken during the tour of Kanchinjinga*, etc., 1900.

52. 1. Guillarmod called Crowley a careless and unscrupulous individual—*un individu négligent et sans conscience*. (*Au Kangchinjunga*, 1914.) See *The Great Beast*, chapter VII.

53. 1. Kali, hence the nature and title of the poem. The goat is one of the animals sacred to her.
2. pretty damn quick.

54. 1. By Octave Mirbeau, published by E. Fasquelle, Paris, 1898. An English translation by Alvah C. Bessie under the title of *Torture Garden* appeared in New York in 1931. Not to be confused with *La Maison des supplices* by Aimé Van Rod, published in Paris by Roberts et Dardaillon, 1909.

55. 1. The name of the Sun God (Râ) at night.

56. 1. Published in *The Winged Beetle*, 1910.
2. *The Equinox*, vol. I, no. II.
3. *The International*, New York, 1917.
4. Ibid., 1918.

57. 1. The Abyss: a technical term to denote the gulf existing between individual and cosmic consciousness. At this stage, aspirants to the Higher Wisdom experience the disintegration of ordinary consciousness with accompanying anguish.

PART FOUR

58. 1. *The Equinox*, vol. I, no. III.
2. According to the Cabbala, *Neschamah* is the higher intelligence, of which intuition, God's greatest gift to man, is

one aspect; *Ruach* is the reasoning faculty; *Nephesch* is the animal soul of man, his senses and emotions.

3. 'Visit the interior parts of the earth: by rectification thou shalt find the hidden stone.' The *lapis* or alchemical stone is the True Self, which can only be found by rectifying one's attitude, by seeking inwards.

4. Augoeides, αὐγοειδής, from αὖγος, the morning light, the dawn. Crowley borrowed this word from Περὶ Μυστρίων, *De Mysteriis,* of Iamblichus, who was the greatest of the anti-Christian philosophers. The letter A∴ signifies in this, and similar contexts, the ritual invocation of the Holy Guardian Angel.

5. 'Aha!'

6. A Buddhist term signifying a meditational practice in which one recollects one's actions and thoughts for the day.

7. 'Liber Thisharb', also called 'Liber Viae Memoriae' (Path of Memory), is described in the list of A∴A∴ publications as a method for attaining the magical memory, or memory of past lives. See *Magick,* p. 228. It was originally published in *The Equinox,* vol I, no. VII, under the number 913, which is the number of *Berashith* (meaning 'In the beginning . . .', the first word in the Bible). *Thisharb* is *Berashith* written backwards; hence the nature of the instruction which is to learn how to remember in reverse, arriving eventually at the beginning or source of all.

8. The Egyptian life-giving *crux ansata,* in the form of a loop or girdle, which later became stylized as the sign of Venus.

9. i.e. The Record of the Magical Retirement of G[reatly] H[onoured] Frater O. M. [Aleister Crowley]. Published in *The Equinox,* vol. I, no. I.

10. See *Magick,* p. 265. 'Liber Samekh' is described as 'a complete explanation of the barbarous names of evocation' used in the Preliminary Invocation of the *Goetia.* It is subtitled CONGRESSUS CUM DAEMONE and was the ritual employed by the Master Therion (Crowley) for the attainment of 'the knowledge and conversation of' his Holy Guardian Angel.

11. Ar Thiao Rheibert A-Thele-ber-set: the barbarous names used in the ritual invocation of the element of Air. See *Magick,* p. 267.

12. Sister Fidelis, i.e. Elaine Simpson.

13. Aiwaz.

14. *The Book of the Law.*

15. The Scarlet Woman: a technical term complementary to that of the Beast for the office held by any directly inspired female medium of the gods.

16. Great Retirement.

17. Brahmacharya, in this context, chastity in the physical sense.

18. Open Temple with Augoeides Invocation.
19. Invocation of Ra Hoor Khuit. The text of this invocation
    was probably the one composed by Crowley in Cairo in
    1904, just before Aiwaz communicated *The Book of the
    Law;* it is published in *The Equinox,* vol. I, no. VII.
20. The name is missing.
21. The invoking and banishing rituals of the Pentagram are
    given in *Magick,* pp. 379–82. Here Fidelis is using the
    banishing ritual.
22. Great Work.
23. Guardian Angel.

59. 1. Augoeides invocation.
2. Perdurabo.
3. Hua is one of the many titles of Kether; the name is
   numerically equivalent to 12, and therefore identifies
   Kether with the Zodiac, the twelve-fold home of the stars.
4. The Path of the High Priestess, path number 13 on the
   Tree of Life. It joins Kether and Tiphareth, and is attributed to the Moon.
5. Scire, Audere, Velle, Tacere: to know, dare, will and to
   keep silent—the four powers of the Sphinx. They are
   attributed to the four elements, Air, Water, Fire, Earth.
   The harmonious exercise of these powers formulates the
   fifth element, that of spirit, in the being of the Adept.
6. *Igni Natura Renovatur Integra,* Nature is completely renewed by fire.
7. The TARO is the Book of the Hidden Wisdom; TORA
   is the Law; TROA is the Gate; ATOR, the Lady of the
   Path of Daleth, or Love; ROTA is the Wheel. These five
   mutations of the word TARO are all ultimately equivalent.
8. Literally the vision (*darshana*) of the God Shiva. It is the
   highest of the Hindu Trances and the equivalent of
   Nirvikalpa-samadhi and Neroda-samapatti.
9. A Sanskrit term meaning vision (*darshana*) of the Self
   (*Atma*).
10. Crowley's dictionary of Cabbalistic correspondences, which
    he describes thus: 'A complete Dictionary of the Cor-
    respondences of all magical elements, making it the only
    standard comprehensive book of reference ever published.
    It is to the language of Occultism what Webster or Murray
    is to the English Language.' Published in 1909, pages
    $x + 50$. It was republished in an emended edition, with a
    comment by Crowley, some years after his death.
11. The Operation out of which came *The Book of the Law*
    in Cairo during 1904.

60. 1. *The Equinox,* vol. I, no. I. The exclamation mark (the
    soldier) implies affirmation; the question mark (the hunch-
    back), doubt.

2. *The Equinox*, vol. I, no. II. It was published under the name of Oliver Haddo, the hero of Somerset Maugham's novel, *The Magician*.

61. 1. A mixture of resin, wine, galangal root, juniper berries, root of aromatic rush, asphaltum, mastic, myrrh, grapes and honey. See The Ebers papyrus.

2. 'Oil of Abra-Melin' is mentioned in *The Book of the Law*. It consists of cinnamon, myrrh, galangal and olive oil.

3. 'Nothing that concerns a man is indifferent to me.' (Terence)

4. During the performance of the Pentagram Ritual, the consciousness of the magician follows the projection of the sacred word at the climax of the operation.

5. *The Equinox,* vol. I, no. IX. Crowley's first published account, during 1913, of the magical use of wine, music and sex, and their influence on certain centres of consciousness.

6. 'La Gitana.'

7. Kathleen Bruce.

62. 1. Crowley is referring to his 'Berashith, An Essay in Ontology'. See *The Works of Aleister Crowley*, vol. II, 1906.

2. See *Magick*, p. 375. Magic is the art of illusion, of the conjuring up of something from nothing. Hence the title of this work, *Liber O* or nought, the Void.

3. *The Equinox*, vol. I, no. IV. Also published in *Magick*, p. 427.

63. 1. By Alexander Dumas, H. G. Wells and Mabel Collins respectively.

2. By Knorr von Rosenroth (translated and introduced by S. L. MacGregor Mathers), Franz Hartmann and Eliphas Lévi respectively.

3. *The Equinox*, vol. I, no. III.

4. Ibid., vol. I, no. IX.

5. Ibid., vol. I, no. II.

6. 'Mr. Todd: A Morality.' First published in *The Winged Beetle*, 1910, and republished in *The Equinox*, vol. I, no. IV.

7. *The Winged Beetle*, 1910.

8. Euphemia Lambe.

65. 1. *The Equinox*, vol. I, no. I.

2. Ibid, vol. I, no. II.

3. *The Winged Beetle*.

4. Ibid.

5. There are ten numbers to each 'volume' of *The Equinox*; each number weighs about three and a half pounds.

6. *Yi King* or *I Ching*.
7. Hexagram 22. Pi—Grace. 'Grace has success in small matters. It is favourable to undertake something.'
8. Hexagram 36. Ming I—Darkening of the Light. 'In adversity it furthers one to be persevering.'
9. Hexagram II. T'ai—Peace. 'The small departs, the great approaches. Good fortune. Success.'
10. Crowley claimed to be a reincarnation of the Priest Ankh-f-n-Khonsu of the XXVIth Dynasty.
11. Hexagram 36. The upper trigram represents the female element, the lower, the sun.
12. Society for Psychical Research.
13. *The Equinox*, vol. I, no. I.
14. Ibid.
15. Ibid., vol. I, no. III.
16. Vishvarupa-darshana, the vision of the splendour of the universe.
17. In this context, a meditational trance.
18. The sacred Fire.
19. Vision of the Self.
20. The Vision of Shiva, the highest of the Hindu trances, the the equivalent of Nirvikalpasamadhi.

66. 1. Thomas Windram.
2. The art of seeing ethereal forms with the help of a bright object; for example, crystal-gazing, or darb-el-mendel, gazing into a glittering pool of ink.
3. *The Equinox*, vol. I, no. v.
4. An exalted Grade in the Hierarchy of the Great White Brotherhood. In some cases a Master of the Temple is a Secret Chief.
5. Lao Tzu, Siddartha, Krishna, Tahuti, Moses, Dionysus and Mohammed. See *The Book of Lies*, 1913.
6. The opening words of the First Key or Call, which invokes the whole Tablet of Spirit, are *Ol sonuf vaoresaji* (I reign over ye). These three words Crowley took as his motto in the Golden Dawn when he attained the Grade of Adeptus Major. Crowley's chanting of the whole Key in the Enochian language was recorded; the record is extant.
7. $A(1)B(2)R(200)A(1)H(5)A(1)D(4)A(1)B(2)R(200)$ $A(1) = 418$. And in Hebrew script Makhashanah = Makashanh which is $M(40)A(1)K(20)A(1)Sh(300)A(1)$ $N(50)H(5) = 418$.
8. Arms raised above head at an angle of sixty degrees, the head thrown back.
9. The name of the 14th Aethyr.
10. 'My God, my God, why hast Thou forsaken me?'
11. *New Mad Tom of Bedlam or the Man in the Moon drinks Claret, with Powder-Beef, Turnip and Carret*, circa 1670.

67. 1. This essay is extant in typescript.
2. *The Equinox*, vol. I, no. v.
3. Ibid., vol. I, no. IV.
4. Ibid.
5. Ibid.
6. George Cecil Jones (Frater Volo Noscere), not to be confused with Charles Stansfeld Jones (Frater Achad), Crowley's magical son. The editor of *The Looking Glass* was De Wend Fenton. According to P. R. Stephensen, author of *The Legend of Aleister Crowley*, 1930, De Wend Fenton had been convicted of sending indecent articles through the post.
7. *The Equinox*, vol. I, no. VI.
8. Several examples of such vulgar words are to be found in *Ambrosii Magi Hortus Rosarum*, 1902, published in *The Works of Aleister Crowley*, vol. II, 1906, and in one of two editions of *Amphora*, 1909.
9. 'Well known for his bleary eyes and shaven head.'

68. 1. Bhang or hashish.
2. *The Equinox*, vol. I, no. VI.
3. Ibid., vol. I, no. v.
4. Ibid.
5. Ibid., vol. I, no. VI.
6. Ibid.
7. Ibid.
8. Ibid., vol. I, no. VII.

PART FIVE

69. 1. *The Equinox*, vol. I, no. VII.
2. Ibid., vol. III, no. I.
3. Ibid., vol. I, no. VII.
4. Ibid., vol. I, no. VIII.
5. Ibid. Republished in *The Stratagem*, 1930.
6. Ibid., vol. I, no. VII.
7. Ibid.
8. For these Greek and Hebrew forms, see *Magick*, p. 260.
9. Some of these books are reprinted in *Magick*. They vary in length from one to twenty pages.

70. 1. *The Star and the Garter* by Aleister Crowley, 1904.
2. She was, in fact, Isadora Duncan.
3. The magical name of Mary d'Este Sturges.
4. The Arabic for night. Here it refers to Leila Waddell.
5. Three parts of this work were eventually published; the third part is *Magick*. The fourth part was to contain *The Book of the Law* and the full comment.
6. *The Comment* is extant in typescript.
7. See *Dramatis Personae*, 1864.

71. 1. *The Equinox,* vol. I, no. IX.
2. This chapter is also published in *Magick*, entitled 'Liber XXV, The Star Ruby'.
3. Also called the Divided name. It is formed of three times 72 letters. This yields 72 names, each of three letters, read from above downwards. To each name was added either AL or AH, thus forming the names of the 72 Angels of the Ladder of Jacob which led to heaven. See *The Kabbalah Unveiled,* p. 171, by S. L. MacGregor Mathers, Kegan Paul, 1938.
4. $L(30) \ A(1) \ Y(10) \ L(30) \ A(1) \ H(5) = 77.$
5. See *The Stratagem,* the Mandrake Press, 1930.
6. *Olla,* published by the O.T.O., 1946, where it appears under the title of 'Figure Genethliacal (To any Unborn Child)'.
7. *Ordo Templi Orientis* or Order of the Oriental Templars or Order of the Temple of the Orient.
8. Leila Waddell's name in the A∴A∴. Its value is 77, the number of Oz, a goat, symbolic of the magical current of creativity. Cf. note 4.
9. Thomas Windram.

72. 1. During 1900.
2. John Yarker.
3. John Hugh Smyth-Pigott, the Agapemonite.
4. Worshipful Master.
5. The IX° constituted the highest degree of the original O.T.O.; the X° was merely a nominal office held by the Outer Head of the Order (Crowley). The IX° involved the use of sexual magic. Crowley added the XI° for homosexual workings (i.e. IX° invested). Cf. 'The Paris Working', a series of magical rites performed by Crowley and Victor Neuburg ('Lampada Tradam'); for details, see *The Magic of Aleister Crowley,* 1958, by John Symonds.
6. The Hebrew letter Shin is represented by three tongues of flame.
7. Theodor Reuss.

73. 1. Crowley gives no details of his unexpected departure into show business. In point of fact it arose out of the Rites of Eleusis.
2. Outer Head of the Order.
3. *The Equinox,* vol. I, no. x.
4. It is unpublished.
5. Published by the O.T.O., 1942.

74. 1. Lampada Tradam or Victor Neuburg.
2. Title of the fourth Sephira of the Tree of Life.

75. 1. Alexander Harvey, editor, essayist and short-story writer, born Brussels 1868, died 1949. *Shelley's Elopement* was published in New York in 1918, and *William Dean Howells* in New York in 1917.

76. 1. Ninette Shumway, née Fraux.
2. 'Lord Anthony Bowling', a character in *Moonchild*, drawn from the Hon. Everard Feilding, younger brother of the Earl of Denbigh.
3. i.e. John Quinn.
4. The headquarters of the O.T.O. at that time.
5. Probably Frank Harris. See Ch. 65 n 13.

77. 1. 'A few swimmers in the vasty deep.' (Virgil)
2. John Quinn.
3. Jane Foster.
4. The vision-producing drug peyotl, analysed by the German chemist, Louis Lewin. Crowley had been taking it for some years.
5. Frater Achad or Charles Stansfeld Jones, the magical child begotten on Hilarion by the Master Therion (Crowley) as prophesied in *The Book of the Law*. The magical circumstances surrounding the begetting of this 'child' are described in *Liber Aleph*, Thelema Publishing Company, California, 1962.

78. 1. The central sephira of the Cabbalistic Tree of Life which consists of eleven spheres arranged upon three columns.
2. Unpublished.

79. 1. '606' (Salvarsan), a compound of arsenic which was used in the treatment of syphilis, so-called because it was the six hundred and sixth substance which the discoverer, Paul Ehrlich (1854–1915), had tested. He was awarded the Nobel Prize in 1908.

PART SIX

80. 1. Leah Hirsig.
2. Marion Dockerill.

81. 1. The Word of the Equinox was usually obtained from one of the Holy Books of Thelema. Crowley would open either *The Book of the Law*, or *The Book of the Heart Girt with the Serpent*, or *The Book of the Lapis Lazuli*, and the word on which his magic ring fell was taken as oracular. Sometimes, as in the present instance, the word flashed into his specially prepared consciousness during the rite of sexual magic.

2. Omnibus in Vnus. Also known as Frater Achad. A partial account of his attainment of the Grade of Master of the Temple is given in *The Equinox*, vol. III, no. I.

3. It is entitled *The Message of the Master Therion*, circa 1917.

82.

1. *The Equinox*, vol. I, no. I.

2. *The Gospel according to St Bernard Shaw*, Thelema Publishing Company, California, 1953.

3. A complete description of this vision with a comment was published in *The Equinox*, vol. III, no. IV, otherwise known as *Eight Lectures on Yoga*, 1939.

83.

1. i.e. Abysses.

84.

1. E P M H C E I M I = 5 + 100 + 40 + 8 + 200 + 5 + 10 + 40 + 10 = 418 (Hermes eimi Mercurius sum. By Greek Cabbala).

2. Ann Catherine Miller, sometimes referred to as Anubis, the jackal- or dog-headed god.

3. One Chokmah day = 73 ordinary days; Chokmah (Hebrew) adds up to this number.

4. *The Equinox*, vol. III, no. I.

85.

1. *The Book of the Lapis Lazuli*, one of the 'Holy Books', which was printed for private circulation among adepts.

2. *The Book of the Heart Girt with the Serpent,* 'an account of the relations of the Aspirant with his Holy Guardian Angel'. This is published in *The Equinox*, vol. III, no. I.

3. *The Book of the Law*.

4. i.e. Leah Hirsig, the Ape of Thoth, to whom Crowley dictated these memoirs.

5. Mary d'Este Sturges. See chapter 70.

6. Baphomet, correctly spelt according to the Wizard, is BAFVMIThR, which by Hebrew Cabbala equals 729, taking Vau as Ayin (70 instead of 6); this is legitimate Cabbala.

7. $K = 20, \eta = 8, \varphi = 500, \alpha = 1, s = 200 = 729$.

8. Dorothy Troxel.

86.

1. 'Gathering towards', or checking the outgoing tendency of the mind, thus freeing it from the thraldom of the senses.

2. 'When the mind is limited or confined to a certain place (or object), this is called Dharana.' (Sankaracharya)

3. Adam Weishaupt (born 1748), founder of the Illuminati. He is included in the list of saints and gnostics sung in Crowley's Gnostic Mass. 'Two Fragments of a Ritual', written by Crowley but based on material said to have been found among Weishaupt's papers, is published in *The Equi-*

    nox, vol. I, no. x. The Ritual shows a close similarity to the sexual magic of the O.T.O.

4. The Path of Aleph is the eleventh Path on the Tree of Life. It joins Kether and Chokmah, the first and second emanations of the Boundless Light.
5. *The Book Tarot* (i.e. *The Book of Thoth*).
6. Metaphor for a period of spiritual aridity.
7. Also published in *Magick* and in *Olla*.
8. *Omnibus in Vnus Vnus in Omnibus*, the extended motto of Charles Stansfeld Jones which he assumed on attaining a more advanced grade in the Order.
9. *The Manifesto of the Rosicrucian Fraternity* by Johann Valentin Andreae, published in Germany in 1614.
10. By Christian Rosencreutz (pseudonym of Johann Valentin Andreae), translated by E. Foxcroft, London, 1690.

87. 1. Leah Hirsig.

88. 1. *The Book of the Law.*

89. 1. Ibid.
    2. Ibid.

90. 1. John William Navin Sullivan (1886–1937), mathematician, author of *The History of Mathematics in Europe from the fall of Greek Science to the rise of the conception of mathematical rigour*, 1925; *Beethoven, his spiritual development*, 1927; *The Bases of Modern Science*, 1928.
    2. Charles Stansfeld Jones, Crowley's magical child.
    3. Frank Bennett.
    4. We know from Frank Bennett's diary what Crowley said to him on this occasion. 'Progradior, I want to explain to you fully, and in a few words, what initiation means, and what is meant when we talk of the Real Self, and what the Real Self is.' And there and then Crowley told him that it was all a matter of getting the subconscious mind to work; and when this subconscious mind was allowed full sway, without interference from the conscious mind, then illumination could be said to have begun; for the subconscious mind was our Holy Guardian Angel. Crowley illustrated the point thus: everything is experienced in the subconscious mind, and it (the subconscious) is constantly urging its will on consciousness, and when the inner desires are restricted or suppressed, evil of all kinds is the result. Crowley then went on to say that sex is mankind's most deeply rooted problem; it starts very early in life and causes the most harm; it is carried with us throughout our lives and torments most people with the tortures of hell. Sex is centred in the subconscious mind and no amount of

suppression can keep it down, for it always works its way up again, and in all kinds of ways, such as in dreams and in sickness, and if unsatisfied, will turn one mad or to 'some hellish abortion'. See *The Magic of Aleister Crowley*, chapter 9, 'The Redemption of Frank Bennett', John Symonds, 1958.

5. '. . . being the Ritual employed by the Beast 666 for the Attainment of the Knowledge and Conversation of His Holy Guardian Angel . . . Prepared An XVII [1921] Sun in Virgo at the Abbey of Thelema in Cephalaedium [Cefalu] by the Beast 666 in Service to FRATER PROGRADIOR.'

91. 1. John Rodker, poet, translator, publisher.
2. i.e. the phallus.
3. i.e. the realization and enactment of her true will.

92. 1. A bookseller who dealt in occult books at 7 Great Turnstile, Holborn, W.C. He advertised frequently in *The Equinox*.
2. See chapter 96.
3. See plate 16.

93. 1. The IX° involves a peculiar use of the sexual energies; it is the central secret of the O.T.O.
2. See chapter 76.
3. See *I Ching*, the 60th hexagram.

95. 1. Aud, the Magic Light; its number is eleven, the general number of Magick.
2. The Astral Light is the universal menstruum, sometimes called the Ether. It is a plastic medium of such high sensitivity that it registers the slightest stress, and thus responds to the subtle vibration of thought itself. When thought-waves are concentrated and magically directed the Astral Light may be moulded or coagulated into the form of an image. In this way, elementals are generated and the phenomena of thought-transference and telepathy made possible.
3. See note 3, chapter 58, p. 1028.

96. 1. Nevertheless, he brought in 1934, rather unnecessarily, an action for libel against Nina Hamnett and Constable & Co. because of the light-hearted remarks about him in her autobiography, *Laughing Torso*. He lost the case, was unable to pay the costs and was made bankrupt.
2. Leah Hirsig's magical name which she adopted for her role of Scarlet Woman as described in *The Book of the Law*. The name was Cabbalistically expressed as 31=666=

31 to contain the key number of the Book (31) and of the Beast.

3. Betty May has given her own, rather different, account of these events in her autobiography, *Tiger Woman*, Duckworth, 1929.

4. i.e. *Magick*, Paris, 1929.

5. Crowley published this work in 1944; it is entitled *The Book of Thoth*. Only two hundred copies were printed.

INDEX

Page footnotes are indicated by fn, and end notes by n.

ABOUT THE EDITORS

JOHN SYMONDS met Aleister Crowley in 1945 and worked with him during the last two years of Crowley's life. He is Crowley's literary executor and the author of Crowley's biography, *The Great Beast;* he is also the biographer of Madame Blavatsky, a founder of modern occultism.

KENNETH GRANT studied Magick under Aleister Crowley and was initiated into the two major secret societies (A.'.A.'. and O.T.O.) of which Crowley was the head. After Crowley's death in 1947, he took over the British Branch of the Ordo Templi Orientis and is now the head of the Order. He is a contributor to the occult encyclopedia *Man, Myth and Magic.*

PSYCHIC WORLD

Here are some of the leading books that delve into the world of the occult—that shed light on the powers of prophecy, of reincarnation and of foretelling the future.

☐ **THE SEARCH FOR THE GIRL WITH THE BLUE EYES** by Jess Stearn. The story of a young woman's reincarnation. (N4591—95¢)

☐ **PSYCHIC PEOPLE** by Eleanor Touhey Smith. The revealing account of 19 men and women with strange and supernatural powers. (N4471—95¢)

☐ **CROISET, THE CLAIRVOYANT** by Jack Harrison Pollack. The exploits of a Dutchman with the power to see the past, present, and future. (N4756—95¢)

☐ **EDGAR CAYCE: THE SLEEPING PROPHET** by Jess Stearn. The bestselling study of the late mystic's prophecies and astounding readings. (N3654—95¢)

☐ **A GIFT OF PROPHECY** by Ruth Montgomery. The phenomenal account of Jeane Dixon's uncanny ability to foresee the future. (N4223—95¢)

☐ **A SEARCH FOR THE TRUTH** by Ruth Montgomery. The author of the bestseller, A GIFT OF PROPHECY, tells of her own brushes with the occult. (N3725—95¢)

☐ **YOGA, YOUTH AND REINCARNATION** by Jess Stearn describes the skeptical author's experience with the ancient art of yoga. (Q6508—$1.25)